Eleanor Bailie

The Pianist's Repertoire

CHOPIN

A graded practical guide

with a foreword by Peter Katin

KAHN & AVERILL
LONDON

First published in 1998 by
Kahn & Averill
9 Harrington Road, London SW7 3ES

British Library Cataloguing in Publication Data

A catalogue record for this book is available from the British Library

ISBN 1 871082 67 6

Music examples produced by Halstan & Co. Ltd.
Printed in Great Britain by
Halstan & Co. Ltd., Amersham, Bucks.

To Jimmie and Marjorie

CONTENTS

FOREWORD

It is my very great pleasure to write this Foreword. I haven't often come across a musician who can not only talk and write about Chopin with such confidence and enthusiasm, but also share one's own feelings about the music within a framework of instructiveness. Mind you, to do all these things at once is quite an achievement when it comes to considering any composer, but Chopin has always seemed to me unique in posing the special problem of how to stay away from the two extremes of sentimental outpouring on the one hand and the unfeeling kind of intellectualism on the other. Eleanor Bailie tells us what it is all about in the first page of her survey of the *Preludes*, when she quotes an unintentionally funny description by Hans von Bülow of the ninth one, but goes on to say 'Perhaps we should not laugh too loudly: in these more prosaic times and in the quest for correctness and authenticity we are often in danger of letting imagination fly out of the window'. This observation gives the key to Eleanor Bailie's own approach, a very disciplined yet refreshingly natural way of dealing with the necessary regard for structure and detail, and ceaseless care for the very many technical problems present in Chopin's works, balanced simply and convincingly by sheer love of the music. This kind of talent is rare indeed, and it isn't only the student, but teachers and performers too, who will be grateful for the fact that so much of that talent has happily come together in the course of producing this book.

PETER KATIN
London, 1997

ACKNOWLEDGEMENTS

In the first book in this series I expressed my gratitude to Jimmie McKay Martin and Marjorie Roberts, without whose generous help this project would never have seen the light of day. Although they have now both died, they have in many ways helped me almost as much with this present volume through the legacy of their musical wisdom, their standards and opinions. To them both in retrospect my heartfelt thanks.

I am above all grateful to two people. Firstly, to Professor Jean-Jacques Eigeldinger, author of *Chopin, Pianist and Teacher* and of many important studies on the music of Chopin, for his kindness in reading much of this manuscript, and for his many helpful comments. In view not only of his profound knowledge, but also of his especially sympathetic understanding of the musical personality of Chopin, his help and encouragement have been particularly valuable to me. I warmly appreciate his generosity in allowing me access to his researches into the music of Chopin, and in particular to his work on the scores belonging to Jane Stirling. Attention is drawn throughout this volume in footnotes to many of the significant annotations to these scores.

Secondly, I thank Peter Katin, both for the time he has generously given to reading and discussing large parts of this manuscript, and also for the example of his performance. With a long-established reputation as an interpreter of Chopin, he seems over recent years to have acquired a special affinity with the essentially intimate spirit of this music. On this account I have particularly valued his comments and his encouragement.

I also thank Adam Harasowski, author of *The Skein of Legends around Chopin*, for his meticulous reading of all my introductory material to this book, and for his helpful suggestions and corrections.

I am grateful to Dr John Rink for pointing me in a number of worthwhile directions; to the Polish Cultural Institute in London for organising valuable financial and practical help; for permission to use the library at the Chopin Society in Warsaw; to Professor Kazimierz Gierzod of the Akademia Muzyczna in Warsaw for his illuminating demonstrations; to Dr Irena Poniatowska of the Institute of Musicology, Warsaw, for kindly arranging tapes of Polish folk music for me; to Dr Janusz Zathey of the Academia Muzyczna in Kracow for his kindness and interest; to Derek Melville for allowing me to use his Pleyel piano; and also to David Winston for permission to try the Broadwood piano being restored by him that was used by Chopin during his visit to England; to Angela Lear for helpful information; to Roy Howat for advice on aspects of Chopin's ornamentation; to George and Cynthia Isserlis for their help and counsel at many junctures; to Anne Perks for ordering and typing my notes with patience and often intuition; and finally to Jane Palmer, for her editorial help, her unfailing good humour, and her special ability to be decisive yet flexible.

ELEANOR BAILIE
London, 1997

PREFACE

The solo repertoire for the piano is vast, far outstripping that for any other single instrument, or indeed for most other instruments put together. Many of us, players and teachers alike, stupified by this embarrassment of riches, find ourselves cruising along the same tracks, sticking to what we know, or to what we think the public knows and likes. To the large and growing body of amateur players, the choice is particularly bewildering. How, confronted with the huge output of, say, Beethoven, is the aspiring pianist to know which works lie within his capabilities, and which are most likely to appeal to him? To the enthusiastic adult amateur, in many ways often the most rewarding and receptive of students, I hope this series will be of particular help. I also hope it will be helpful to teachers in selecting material for their pupils, to professional players in choosing programmes, and to students at schools of music, universities and teacher training colleges; also to the compilers of examination and competition syllabuses, and to those planning courses for study, public or personal.

The objective of the series is threefold:
  a) To provide reference books-cum-guides to help players and teachers find their way around the repertoire of the major composers for the keyboard, and to help in the choice of music to suit their playing tastes and teaching requirements.
  b) To give suggestions and guidelines for study and performance.
  c) To draw attention to the most rewarding (and particularly to some neglected) areas of the repertoire.

Each book consists of three sections:
  i) An introduction to the keyboard music of the composer, giving an outline of the distinguishing features of his style.
  ii) A graded list of the keyboard works of the composer. This list aims to contain all the works that are published in generally available editions.
  iii) Detailed commentaries on the study and performance of every work, or part or movement of a work up to a post-Grade 8 standard (called Grade 8+).

The Lists of Works

In the present volume the music is listed in order of difficulty in the following categories:
  Grades 4-5
  Grade 6
  Grade 7
  Grade 8
  Grade 8+
  Very advanced

The grading is based on the standards set by the various examining bodies, and is intended only as a general indication, and not as a **definition** of technical or musical difficulty. In grading the pieces the criterion has not necessarily been the suitability of each piece for **performance**, but rather its potential for worthwhile and satisfying study at the stage in question. No one likes the idea of grading music (and obviously some of my grading standards will be questioned, as indeed are frequently the selections in recognized examination syllabuses); there is, however, no other way of giving an indication of the degree of difficulty of each piece.

In the case of Chopin there is little music for the real novice and none at all for players of less than a Grade 4 standard. It seemed preferable to group the simplest pieces, no more than ten or so, together in Grades 4-5. Their 'difficulties' will be differently perceived according not only to individual technical strengths or weaknesses, but also according to the musical understanding, or perhaps to the hand size of the player. For the same reasons players are begged to regard all the grading as flexible.

The Mazurkas are a special case. Here my grading may be found somewhat conservative, and a piece may look 'too easy' for its graded listing. This is done deliberately, for it is safe to say that with their niceties of rhythm and articulation and so on, the Mazurkas are almost always more complex than they may at first appear.

The Symbols * and O

In this series the intention is to mark thus * those pieces or movements that are especially recommended. In the case of Chopin, however, this seems something of an absurdity, since **most** of his works are so widely known. I have therefore used the * to draw attention to those pieces or works which are not included in many of the widely used editions, and have only rarely or recently been published at all, some of which would be of interest particularly to less experienced players. These include several early Mazurkas and Polonaises now published in the Henle Edition, and some pieces published in the volume entitled 'Minor Works' in the Paderewski Edition (see below, under 'Editions').

The 'O' indicates **either** that a piece contains a number of wide stretches or octave passages, and is therefore unsuitable for players with small hands; **or** that in a musical sense it seems more suited to the older player. This applies more often in the earlier Grades, when although a piece is relatively simple technically, its content and sentiments may be somewhat esoteric. But these are, of course, generalized indications, for a talented child can be wonderfully intuitive musically. From about Grade 6 it is assumed that an octave can be stretched. And, of course, octaves can often be omitted by those with small hands, except where the octaves are particularly important to the texture of the music.

The Introduction to the Music of each Composer

This aims to give some general pointers towards an understanding of the individual qualities of the composer. Rather than giving a potted biography, I have tried instead to show how his personality, and the circumstances of his life and times, have helped to shape and characterize his style.

In the present volume this section is comparatively extended and detailed. This is inevitable in view of Chopin's pre-eminence in the history of the piano, both as composer and player, and also of the special and highly individual characteristics of his style.

The Commentaries on the Music

In this series, music for players in the 'Very Advanced' category is not (with occasional exceptions) discussed in detail. Players capable of tackling the Beethoven *Hammerklavier* or the *Finale* of the Chopin Sonata in B minor are out on their own! And in any event we have to stop somewhere, or the project would become unmanageable in every sense.

I had intended to finish the detailed commentaries at Grade 8, but found so many works lying tantalizingly just beyond a conventional Grade 8 standard that I decided to add a Grade 8+, rather open-ended, but in general stopping short of music in the 'Very Advanced' or 'Virtuoso' categories. In the case of Chopin a large proportion of the works fall into the 'Very Advanced' category. Most of these are briefly discussed in general, rather than specific practical terms. But I should like to urge here that these 'big' works, the Ballades, Scherzos, Sonatas and so on should not be placed in a special box reserved for concert performers only. I am not suggesting that anyone should get up and perform such works unless they really **can.** But it is not a sin at least to examine the music at the keyboard, as has often been urged below. The 'sub-virtuoso' player can gain immeasurably in understanding, both of Chopin and of the keyboard in general, by, at his own pace, picking out and **listening** to the marvellous resonances and harmonic effects of, for example, the F minor Fantaisie, or the Barcarolle. The Studies are a special case, where the capable player of around a Grade 8 standard can learn so much from pondering and trying out the technical and athletic, as well as the musical tests that Chopin has so magnificently presented. The Studies are therefore discussed in a rather different way to the rest of the music, since in the main they propose a single technical-musical idea. (This also applies to many of the Preludes.)

It is stressed that the detailed commentaries are intended to deal only with the **practical** (in the sense of strictly non-musicological) aspects of the performance of each work or movement. There is as little technical jargon as possible, though a knowledge of general musical terms and of the basic principles of form is assumed; but matters of form and structure are touched upon only when directly applicable to the performance of the music. I have tried to give an impression of the fundamental character of each piece, and to discuss its technical and musical demands as they arise. **Except where I am simply drawing attention to the indications of the composer, the suggestions for dynamics, articulation, tempo and general interpretation are entirely personal, and players are begged to treat them as such.** I realize, and indeed welcome the thought, that these suggestions will often be disagreed with – again they will at least provide a starting-point for players' own ideas. And, for help in getting one's own ideas moving, there is nothing like being given a proposition with which we can have the pleasure of disagreeing!

I have tried to anticipate the kind of pitfalls into which, as every teacher knows, the inexperienced pianist will almost invariably fall. In discussing the music in the earlier Grades, details are pointed out which, it is assumed, can be taken as read by more advanced players. Inevitably, certain exhortations recur many times in the commentaries: 'be sure to **listen** to the LH'; 'show the implied emphasis on the tied upbeat', and such-like. But, since no one is going to sit down in an armchair and read the book right through, this was felt to be less irksome than to be continually referred to Prelude, or Waltz No. –, bar –, page –.

My overriding objective, in every instance, is to try to help the player make the music **live.** This is the area, the most important of all, where so many students fail; anxious to have every note in place, to get the 'style' right, hamstrung by the fear of 'overdoing' things, they opt for safety, with the resultant painful dullness of timid dynamics and neutral tone-colour. The careful learning of notes, and all the conscientious groundwork are to no avail unless we can then transcend the dots on the page. In the last resort, a performance, either in private or on the concert platform is never just good or bad. It either comes to life or it doesn't. If we play ever so well, with every detail thought out, every note correct, and merely produce a neat, business-like account of Chopin, we fail. If, on the other hand, despite the odd note flying off in the wrong direction, and the occasional passage sounding too loud, too soft, too slow or too fast, we bring him to life in all his delectable complexity, his brilliance and poetry, his unique blend of fervour and restraint, then we have succeeded.

Lithograph c1844 by Hermann Raunheim

*'Chopin is the greatest of them all,
for through the piano alone he discovered everything.'*
Debussy

INTRODUCTION

A Profile

Chopin is an enigma. As we swoon to our first Nocturne, fumble through our first Waltz, or fire to the patriotic fervour of a Polonaise, we may find this a surprising, even irrelevant piece of news. But such is the case. On the one hand he is one of the most popular composers of all time. On the other, he is the most sphinx-like and complex. Everything about him is a contradiction. He worked to all intents and purposes within the single medium of the piano, a mere tributary, however important, to the overall stream of symphonic, vocal, and chamber works of most of the great composers. Yet his influence was so immense as to extend to our own times. He was, as Gerald Abraham says: 'the forerunner of Liszt and Wagner, and hence of the modern atonalists, the first composer seriously to undermine the solid system of diatonic tonalism created by the Viennese Classical masters...' (p.viii).

He was an outsider in terms of his musical traditions and education, yet from the time of his arrival in Paris when he was twenty-one, Chopin won almost immediate acceptance and esteem, if not always complete understanding, on the international musical scene. While his music has been hummed, danced to, 'Palm Courted', and variously appropriated by the pop industry, his more recondite works, such as the Polonaise-Fantaisie Op.61, the late Nocturnes Op.55 No.2 and Op.62 No.1, the Impromptu in F sharp Op.36, or the Cello and Piano Sonata Op.65, have puzzled musical minds almost to this day.

He was a devoted and unaffected patriot, yet he left Poland at the age of twenty, and never returned. He was a master purveyor of emotion, and an architect of dramatic and rhythmic tension of the most potent kind. His music can rouse a rabble, sear the spirit, or tease the sensibilities with the finest and most ambivalent shades of musical thought. Yet in life he guarded his feelings behind a polished, almost impenetrable reserve and a ready wit that could turn to icy sarcasm when he chose. That powerful undercurrents coursed beneath his reserve cannot be doubted. The pride and splendour of the Polonaises, the grandeur of the Ballades, the wild momentum of the Finale of the B minor Sonata Op.58, the 'Revolutionary' Study, or the Preludes in B flat minor or F minor can only have sprung from emotions of the most intense nature, and a highly developed and concentrated imagination. Again, in his later work there emerges an element of musing abstraction that verges on the mystical in such pieces as the late Nocturnes already mentioned, the Polonaise-Fantaisie and the 'single' Prelude in C sharp minor, Op.45. An occasional hint of this inner world is revealed in his letters: 'At this moment I am not with myself, but only as usual in some strange outer space. Granted it is only those imaginary spaces; but I am not ashamed of that.' (*Chopin's Letters*, p.285).

As a player he came from no school, and formed no school, yet his reputation as a performer amounted almost to a mystique – it was not so much a question of the 'school of Chopin', said Liszt, as the 'church of Chopin'. It is estimated that during the last ten years of his life in Paris he was heard by no more than '600 or so persons, mostly aristocratic music lovers'(Walker, p.14), and throughout his entire adult career he gave no more than a handful or two of public performances. Yet he became a legend in his own lifetime, casting a spell that will endure as long as pianos are played.

In many ways he has become the victim of his own popularity. Cast by paperback and celluloid 'faction' as the archetypal Romantic, he has, in a personal sense, been cocooned in a fog of sentimental claptrap, while musically he has been exploited by generations of flamboyant virtuosos intent on peddling their own version of the Chopin 'tradition'. Early impressions die hard, and there can be few of us who have not imagined him pale, languorous, preferably poor and solitary, coughing gracefully into that essential romantic prop, the delicately bloodstained handkerchief, with the looming figure of the voluptuous, cheroot-smoking, pantaloon-clad George Sand breathing down his neck.

The truth is very different. Of all the great composers, Chopin's childhood must have been the happiest and most propitious. His father, Nicolas Chopin, was of solid French country stock. In 1787, for unknown reasons, he left France, settled in Poland, and found employment as tutor to various families of the minor nobility. Eventually he married a relative of the Skarbek family, and Frederick was born at the Skarbek estate Zelazowa Wola in 1810. Soon afterwards the Chopin family moved to Warsaw; and Nicolas became a teacher in the prestigious Lyceum (where Frederick himself became a pupil), establishing a niche for himself in the cultural and social life of the capital.

It was a loving and cultivated home, and although the family's means were modest, Chopin had the opportunity through his father's connections to mix in a wide social circle, thus acquiring that ease and grace of manner that were to serve him so well in the future. While his remarkable gifts were soon apparent, and from an early age he was received and petted by Princes and Countesses, he was blessed by the counteractive influence of this solid family background, and by the wisdom of his father, who fostered and encouraged, but never exploited his talents.

His professional life was remarkably successful and, until his illness took its final hold, comfortable and prosperous. It comes as a surprise to many people to discover that far from wilting day and night over his piano, Chopin was high-spirited and outgoing, the life and soul of any party, and someone who loved to improvise and clown to amuse his friends. He was apparently peculiarly supple, could contort his face in wonderfully funny expressions, and 'like a clown, throw his legs over his shoulders' (Eigeldinger, p.101). A charming description is given by a childhood friend: 'When we visited the Chopins, all we had in mind was playing games. That Frederick was already considered the best pianist in Warsaw didn't mean nearly as much to us as that he was ready for jokes and fun... running, clowning, imitating people we knew – he did that best – sketching... Sometimes he would sit at the piano, but because we were too young to take music seriously, he would play tricks or play dance tunes... I remember he was the gayest.' (Marek and Gordon-Smith, p.12).

Chopin was, and remained, a sharp caricaturist and a clever mimic. Kleczyński records that even in later life 'in his circle of intimate friends, he sometimes exaggerated his joviality to an almost puerile extent; [however], in the presence of strangers he became transfigured. At the touch of an alien hand he was like a sensitive plant that closes up its corolla.' (Kleczyński, p.20). Even when he visited England, and later Scotland, in the year before his death, in a sorry state of health and in depressed spirits, Chopin's letters make amusing reading, particularly in his accounts of the habits of the Scottish gentry; social territory more alien to this elegant adopted Parisian can scarcely be imagined.

It is often said that as a player Chopin was self taught. This is true to the extent that his first, and virtually his only teacher, Adalbert Zywny, was primarily a violinist, and therefore from an early stage had no option but to allow his pupil to go his own way. But for a child of such prodigious and individual gifts, perhaps Zywny was the most fortunate possible choice of teacher. He was a native of Bohemia, a lovable eccentric whom Chopin adored, and a musician of informed enthusiasms who, from the first, opened his pupil's ears to Bach and to the Viennese classics. To what extent a more formal training would have schooled Chopin into a more conventional mould we cannot know. But there can be no doubt that his personal 'discovery' of the keyboard, of his own technique and his own pianistic effects without fear or favour from schools, professors, or pre-formed theories, contributed in large measure to the original that Chopin became, both as composer and player.

Later, his teacher in composition, Jozef Elsner, was equally enlightened, giving Chopin a thorough grounding in theory and counterpoint while at the same time recognising and respecting the special nature of his gifts. One of Chopin's most endearing characteristics was his lifelong loyal and respectful regard for his teachers. Amid all the euphoria of his first success on (what was for him) the great international stage of Vienna, he stoutly proclaimed that 'under Zywny and Elsner the greatest donkey could have learned.' (*Chopin's Letters*, p.57).

An artist is, it has been truly said 'an apportioned being, letting the world around him crack while his symphony is written, his canvas painted.' (Marek and Gordon-Smith, p.43). Chopin was assuredly of this ilk. He seemed to have an unerring instinct for what was right for him, to the extent perhaps, in our current jargon, of 'choosing' his background, his parents, his teachers. From an early age he accepted both his own value and his own limitations, and concentrated his efforts in the medium he understood. Resisting the efforts of the celebrated virtuoso Kalkbrenner to capture him as a long-term pupil, he wrote to Elsner 'nothing will interfere with my perhaps overbold but at least not ignoble desire to create a new world for myself.' (*Chopin's Letters*, p.161). And he pursued this 'new world' of harmonic exploration, adventures in sound and technical daring, with single-minded certainty, and concentration of purpose – impervious to trends, fads, or outside influences that were not relevant to his own direction. His musical personality and style of playing were fundamentally formed before he left Poland. Through the next sixteen years he refined, expanded and deepened his range without altering this essential direction. In many ways confident in his own power and achievements at the age of twenty, he sensed the right moment to leave Poland and, deeply though he loved his family and homeland, he was ready and eager for experience and for recognition in the wider European scene. It seems inevitable, with Chopin's background, style, and predilections, that his future would lie in Paris – he took to it like the proverbial duck to water, and Paris took to him. There was already a distinguished resident enclave of exiled Poles, and through them Chopin was launched into the highest echelons of society.

Little more than a year after his arrival, he was able to write 'I have gained the entrée to the first circles; I have my place among ambassadors, princes, ministers... All this is absolutely indispensable for me today, for on it "bon ton" depends'... My carriage and white gloves cost more than I earn; without them I should not be "de bon ton".' (Hedley, p.53). There is no doubt that Chopin valued this exclusive world, and was far too canny to bite the hands which fed him – throughout his life "bon ton" was of the greatest importance to him. In later years, during his summer spells at George Sand's country home, Nohant, he ceaselessly bombarded his old friend Julian Fontana with requests to select 'elegant' clothing, and even apartments, appoint valets, and to attend to financial matters great and small. In terms of money too, he knew his value, and was not willing to be short-changed on his manuscripts. He was able to command good fees as a teacher – his aristocratic pupils would discreetly place the money on his mantelpiece before leaving.

While never a robust man, Chopin was for the greater part of his life less sickly than is generally supposed, and bore up remarkably well through his busy professional and social life. He was slight in stature, but by all accounts exceptionally neatly built, and as every pianist will instinctively understand, blessed with muscular coordinations of an altogether extraordinary kind. His appearance was pleasing but apparently not remarkable; his most notable characteristic, about which he liked to joke, being an overprominent nose. But there can be no doubt that he was a man of rare charm and distinction of personality. He entranced Countesses and Princes, and was esteemed, even revered, by a wide circle of artists, musicians and writers. Liszt found him to have the bearing of 'a prince'. Berlioz described him as 'something you have never seen and someone you will never forget'. Delacroix wrote that he was 'the truest artist I have ever met, one of the very few whom one can admire and value'. At the same time he could be bigoted, obsessive, and small-minded; while not wholly a snob, he was crudely anti-Semetic. Beneath the urbane exterior, temper often seethed and occasionally erupted. He was prey to wild changes of mood. As Arthur Hedley has said: 'He could be cool, calculating and cynical, and then a moment later enthusiastic, cheerful and, at times, boisterously vulgar' (p.38). His language among his intimates could be anything but refined, particularly when directed against his publishers, favourite targets for his vituperation.

He was cultivated without being overtly intellectual. From the momentous social and political changes that were sweeping Europe, and particularly France, he remained aloof. 'Gifted with the lightning lucidity of momentary insight, he had no patience with reasoned explanations, still less with manifestos.' (Eigeldinger, p.4). He was ill at ease with many aspects of the Romantic movement that heaved around him – fastidious in his tastes, there was no place for excess in either his musical or personal life. He thus stood at the opposite end of the romantic spectrum from the flamboyance and grandiloquence of his near-twin, Liszt. If his language was romantic, his voice was classical. His daily companions were Bach and Mozart, his respect for Beethoven was guarded, and he had little regard and seldom a generous word for the music of most of his contemporaries – in contrast, it may be said, to the open-hearted admiration accorded to **him** by Liszt himself, Schumann, Mendelssohn and many others.

Relationships with women in the physical sense cannot be said to have played a large part in Chopin's life, although he enjoyed the devoted friendship of a wide circle of women. Apart from youthful infatuations, the inconclusive suggestion of an affair with the beautiful Delfina Potocka, and the dashing of somewhat tenuous hopes of marriage with Maria Wodzińska (the daughter of a Polish family of substantial means, for whom he wrote the Waltz in A flat, Op. posth. 69 No.1), George Sand was the central, indeed, only female reality in his adult life. That this meeting of opposites should have spawned a whole industry of speculative fiction is hardly surprising – he, as Jim Samson says, 'anxious to preserve proprieties, refined in manner, aloof, [she] flaunting her unorthodox lifestyle and advanced views; he living only and narrowly for music, she embracing the whole world of ideas, however insecurely.' (p.20). It was, however, hardly the torrid affair of popular imagination – indeed, in the accepted sense it appears that they were lovers only for a matter of months. Nevertheless, their lives remained closely intertwined over a period of eight years; and while she has often been painted as a destructive, even malevolent *éminence grise*, the fact remains that she provided Chopin with a settled, and in the main congenial ambience in which much of his greatest work was achieved. Once the dust of the famous Majorcan adventure had settled, they fell into a routine of winters in Paris, and summers at her country home at Nohant. And while Chopin was, on his own admission, no countryman, these long rural interludes away from the bustle of his Parisian social life can only have benefited his constitution and equilibrium. It is also the case that following the break with George Sand his health and creative spirit fell into a rapid decline, and he died only three years later. Tensions had multiplied over the years, and their incompatibilities of nature and style told in the long run. Her family relationships were tempestuous and complex, and the final rift was set in train by, literally, a family punch-up of farcical dimensions (from which, however, Chopin himself was absent). The tantalising puzzle of their relationship will always remain, the gulf between their natures typified by their manner of dealing all that had passed between them – she with high-coloured loquacity, he with total silence.

Another complex aspect of Chopin's character is the nature of his patriotism. The Poles are an extraordinary people, who, with their tragic history and chivalric image, exert a peculiar and undeniable fascination, as great in Chopin's time as it is today. Chopin is a figure who remains inescapably 'different' – subtly so in his personality, and self-evidently so in his music, both as composer and performer. That charm of person which captivated so many undoubtedly carried a hint of the exotic: that factor, similarly inherent in his music that is sensed, if not defined, by the most innocent musical ear. The extent to which his music is permeated by Polish folk elements has been much debated, and perhaps exaggerated by some commentators and underestimated by others. But we all know instinctively that this factor is part and parcel of his musical character, and in a far more profound sense that in the cosmetic injection of the odd ethnic touch, Lydian fourth, augmented second, or syncopated second beat 'stamp'.

As already said, Chopin 'knew' he had to leave Poland for the wider world, yet it is also true to say he left a large part of his heart behind. As late as 1845 he wrote to his family 'I am a real blind Mazovian' (that area of Poland surrounding Warsaw). The fresh, open-hearted affection he retained towards his family shines through his letters, and he maintained intimate friendships with old school friends as well as with his family throughout his life. Indeed, it was with his Polish friends that he was happiest, and came nearest to dropping his habitual reserve. In his self-imposed exile, Poland became for him a 'spiritualised conception which existed in his imagination and continually nourished his emotions.' (Walker, p.10). It is significant that he took the opposite course to Grieg who, half a century later, tested the waters of the central European mainstream, and turned tail for home to explore his own musical roots *in situ* in a much more overt and political manner. Had Chopin done the same, or even revisited Poland just once, he might well have broken the fine thread of that 'spiritualised conception' that he pursued with such fervour in the Polonaises, and with such concentrated intimacy in the Mazurkas.

On the subject of his music Chopin was like a clam. Such references as occur in letters are laconically dismissive, or else merely refer to the price he expected for a manuscript. The Finale of the B flat minor 'Funeral March' Sonata, for example (as cryptic and extraordinary a concept as ever touched a keyboard), he famously refers to as 'the LH and RH gossip in unison after the March.' (Eigeldinger, p.4); the F sharp Impromptu 'perhaps is poor; I don't know yet, it's too new. But I hope it's good... because by my reckoning it ought to bring me at least 800 francs.' (*Chopin's Letters*, p.218).

We are confronted with a nature that can never be fully understood, least of all perhaps by his contemporaries. Nevertheless the gleanings from the memories of these contemporaries and the rather more lusty, forthright, even earthy attitude to life revealed in his letters, create a picture that lodges vividly in our imaginations – a picture of a man who was very much of the world, yet who stood apart from it; so elegant and refined as to verge on dandyism, but capable of projecting emotive and imaginative concepts of the most potent kind; a romantic who was at the same time both a classicist and a modernist; the darling of the salons who, however unwittingly, sparked a revolution in music; in Alan Walker's memorable phrase 'one of the displaced persons of musical history – a twentieth-century composer forced by a freak of nature to wander through the nineteenth' (p.247).

Chopin's Period and his Influence
The years 1809-11 produced a remarkable clutch of musical talent. The three front runners in romantic piano music, Chopin, Schumann and Liszt, were born within months of each other. Yet it is extraordinary to reflect that Haydn, the last of the retained court musicians, had only died in 1809, which was also the year of Mendelssohn's birth. Beethoven (still only forty) had well and truly stormed the barricades of the eighteenth century, defying all conventions of structure and style. By the time of his death, when Chopin was seventeen, his late piano works had strayed into distant areas of abstraction and isolation, leaving the way open in any, or every direction. Nevertheless, Beethoven's sources lay in the mainstream, with the figures of Mozart and Haydn clearly discernible behind him. Chopin, as has already been said, was a virtual outsider in terms of his origins and musical education, yet it was he, above all others, who brought the piano of age, setting his indelible stamp upon it, and thereby initiating pianism as we understand it today. He immediately captured the public imagination, and is unquestionably the most consistently popular composer in the history of the piano. This is not to say that he has

always been fully understood. Scholars of the nineteenth century, and even those nearer to our own times, have been mystified by his later works, and have felt that he strayed into chaos of form and tonality, and into areas of 'dangerous' and unhealthy introspection. Conversely the very popularity of his 'easier' music together with his omission to produce symphonies, masses, or operas, has tended to militate against his acceptance in certain influential spheres of critical opinion. His pre-eminence in terms of the keyboard has, of course, never been questioned, and with it, the remarkable expansion in technique, pianistic and expressive effects which he initiated. But even among professional musicians there has been a tendency to dismiss him as a miniaturist, a salon composer, even if one of significance.

Of latter years, however, in the light of developments in twentieth-century music, there appears to have been a major reassessment of Chopin: of his significance in general as opposed to merely in keyboard terms. While the opinion that he was the greatest harmonist since Bach, which I have heard seriously propounded, may be somewhat partisan, there is no doubt that he introduced harmonic concepts that were revolutionary to an extent that could not be fully assessed until the dust had to some degree settled, following the progressive disintegration of the tonal system through the first half of the twentieth century. The modal features, sharpened fourths, augmented seconds and so on, referred to above (and used by other Polish composers merely to titillate aristocratic ears with a tinge of 'ethnic' piquancy) were woven into Chopin's harmonic textures in, for example, the Mazurkas in an integral sense, creating effects which can startle the ear even today. He would loosen the confines of tonality with chains of dominant sevenths that anticipate Debussy, or with open-ended series of diminished sevenths (Gerald Abraham, pp.9-10, suggests that his predilection for the diminished seventh harmony derives from its aptness in harmonising the Polish sharpened fourth); and he leaves the ear adrift in protracted atonal sequences, such as the opening of the C sharp minor Scherzo, the A minor Prelude, or the Finale of the B flat minor Sonata, which were half a century or more ahead of their time. Links with Wagner have been noted by many scholars, and to understand this we have only to listen to the opening sequences of the Polonaise-Fantaisie or, slowly and listening to every note, go through the astonishing codas of the Mazurkas Op.50 No.3 or Op.56 No.3. Again, as has often been remarked, in Chopin's supposedly last piece, the Mazurka in F minor Op.posth.68 No.4, the progression of bb.14-15 is pure Tristan. As Arthur Hedley said, 'From our point of vantage in the twentieth century we can see what Elsner could not in 1831 – that for Chopin there could be no looking back to 1800; that for him, although he did not realise it, music began to look forward to 1900 and beyond. Others, like Schumann and Berlioz, might raise a louder uproar, but it was Chopin who, for all his reserve and indifference, was the real revolutionary: it was he who placed the first explosive charge against that long-revered edifice of classical diatonic harmony which now lies in utter ruin and disintegration. Strange that a poet's reverie should forbode the end of an epoch.' (p.138). For detailed discussion of Chopin's influence, see *Frédéric Chopin. Profiles of the Man and his Music,* ed. Alan Walker, pp.258-76 (the chapter by Paul Badura-Skoda); *The Music of Chopin* by Jim Samson (in particular the Epilogue); *The Cambridge Companion to Chopin,* ed. Jim Samson (pp.246-83, Chopin's influence on the *fin de siècle* and beyond, by Roy Howat).

General Aspects of Chopin's Style

In Chopin, to a unique extent, the composer is inseparable from the performer – indeed, the one could not have existed without the other, in terms both of style and content. The way in which, virtually on his own, without rules or schools, he 'discovered' the keyboard, has been touched on above. This is not to say, of course, that he was isolated from earlier or current influences.

The lavishly ornamented style of Hummel, the bravura of Weber, for example, were part and parcel of the keyboard language with which Chopin grew up, and formed the natural framework of his own early musical language (see Jim Samson, *The Music of Chopin*, in particular Chapter 2 'Apprenticeship', and Chapter 3 '*Stile Brillante*'). It is well known too that he was influenced by John Field, one of the few composers among his near contemporaries for whom he expressed genuine admiration, and from whom it is assumed that he adopted the title and the style of the Nocturnes – that of the singing right hand and flowing left hand accompaniment. We also know that he frequently played Field's pieces, and in later years used them as teaching pieces. But even at an early age, in the Polonaise in G sharp minor, Chopin displays a sophisticated command and understanding of keyboard effects. We know that he had already found his own way of 'throwing off' in performance such refined and delicately wrought flights of virtuosity as he presents in this piece, with apparently effortless grace – here indeed executant had romped well ahead of composer. But by the time he left Poland at the age of twenty, he had in all essentials found his own voice; and his style, in terms of the **use** of the keyboard and of his manner of playing, were formed. His maturity, and mastery of his medium are incontrovertibly demonstrated in the Op.10 Studies, which were in train during this period – works which were to revolutionise as much the whole concept of the resonant and expressive horizons of the keyboard as the athletic potential of the player.

Bach and Mozart

But central to Chopin's style and development is his devotion to Bach, and above all to Mozart. Numerous instances are recorded of his declared veneration for Bach's '48', which were his daily companions. He told his pupil von Lenz that before his public concerts (admittedly rare events) 'for a fortnight I shut myself up and play Bach. That's my preparation. I don't play my own compositions' (Eigeldinger, pp.135-6). And as Eigeldinger says, the influence of Bach 'asserts itself continually in the independence of the melodic lines weaving through his polyphony, culminating in the imitative passages, canons and fugatos of his last works; the Sonata Op.65 [for cello and piano] is its high point.' (p.135). Such polyphony is especially striking when embodied in the Polish context – particularly in the Mazurkas, where there are numerous instances of the most intricate part-writing – at its most concentrated and hauntingly expressive in the principal and recurring motifs of the already mentioned Op.50 No.3 and Op.56 No.3. Indeed it could be said that such complex textures are inherent in Chopin's conception of these dance forms.

Again in the large works (the Ballade in F minor, the Fantaisie Op.49, the Barcarolle), the building up, and subsequent defusing of intensely concentrated and complex harmonic voice textures are integral to the architecture of Chopin's highly organised 'evolving' structures. In the late Nocturnes too, notably Op.55 No.2 and Op.62 No.1, the textures are interwoven in three- or four-voiced writing of the most subtle expressive effect.

Chopin idolised Mozart, and this knowledge must, I believe, be at the forefront of our minds in our search for an appreciation of Chopin's style. Every pianist understands the inherent vocality of Mozart's melody, and as Jim Samson points out in his chapter 'Bel Canto' (p.81 onwards) the connecting link from Mozart to the often elaborately ornamented melodic style of Chopin is palpably clear. Also the clarity of his accompanying figures, whether of a relatively simple, easy-flowing kind, or of intricately woven complexity is part and parcel of Mozart's legacy to Chopin. But accompaniment is an inadequate term for most of Chopin's left hand or inner figures, save in the most obvious cases such as the Waltzes (though even there the frequent emergence of left hand lines or inner fragments elevate such dance-based pieces into a class of their own). Complementary counterpoint is a better description of his left hand or inner-voice patterns. Even in such seemingly obvious cases of melody and accompaniment as the Nocturne in D flat, Op.27 No.2, or the central section of the Fantaisie-Impromptu Op.posth.66, the undulations of the left hand complement the melody of the right hand in a partnership that goes far beyond mere rhythmic and harmonic back-up. 'How far we are from the old conventional Alberti bass prattling away within the space of a fifth or so.' (Hedley, p.147). Arthur Hedley here is discussing the wild left hand of the Prelude No.24 in D minor, but this observation applies equally in the gentler context of the above two examples, the D flat Nocturne and the Fantaisie-Impromptu. And even in the early E minor Nocturne (published posthumously as Op.72 No.1) the arpeggiated accompaniment acquires a special significance, with the fifth and eleventh note of each bar forming, as Lennox Berkeley says, 'an appoggiatura to the harmony' (Walker, p.172). But this clarity is always apparent: in the complex rhythmic and melodic patterns of the Prelude No.1 in C major, or the stark dissonances of the Prelude No.2 in A minor as much as in the simple charm of the Waltzes, the Prelude No.7 in A major, or the Impromptu in A flat, Op.29. To help us in our attempt to get to the heart of Chopin's style we do well to appoint Mozart as our lodestar, as did Chopin himself. If we have the **idea** of Mozart in the back of our minds – the vocal eloquence of his melody, the clarity of his textures, the precision without rigidity of his rhythm (see below under '*Rubato*'), we acquire a built-in guard against the excesses with which Chopin's music has so often been encumbered, distorted and debased.

The Italian Influence

As with Mozart, the vocal quality of Chopin's melody is paramount. His other passion along with Bach and Mozart (and of course his 'spiritualised conception' of the music of his homeland) was for the Italian, *bel canto* style of singing. Chopin's love of fine singing dates back to his early years in Warsaw, when he had the opportunity to hear much Italian opera, and throughout his life he stressed the importance of the singing line and of the need to phrase and to declaim like a singer. The much-vaunted specific influence of Bellini upon Chopin is evidently exaggerated, since it has been demonstrated that the Italianate characteristics of Chopin's style were apparent long before he had even heard of Bellini, although a warm friendship grew up between them later (see Hedley, p.58). Chopin commanded his pupils to take singing lessons: 'You must sing if you wish to play', he said (Eigeldinger, p.45). And again, 'We use sounds to make music just as we use words to make a language' he wrote in his 'Sketch for a Method' (Eigeldinger p.195). The exhortation to 'think vocally' has, of course, been repeated by all teachers worth their salt going back to C.P.E. Bach in his *Essay on the True Art of Playing Keyboard Instruments*, and beyond. Students who succeed in flattening the curves of a phrase to a robotic monotone are time and again amazed and consumed with embarrassment when asked if they have tried singing, or adding words to it. When they can be persuaded to do so they are then equally amazed, but delighted at the ease with which they can translate the sung and verbal shape to the keyboard. But as any teacher knows, this simple idea is the hardest to inculcate, and even with relatively advanced students this scenario has to be re-enacted week after week. The keyboard music of some composers, such as Haydn or Beethoven, impels us to 'think' predominantly orchestrally; that is, we 'hear' and seek to invoke orchestral timbres. Chopin – save in the Mazurkas, with their effects of bagpipe drones, shrill flutes and fiddles and so on – did **not** think orchestrally. His timbres are (almost) exclusively pianistic, while at the same time being imbued with this sense of the **sung** melodic line. (The exceptions are his occasionally cello-like left hand melodies in, for example, the Study in C sharp minor, Op.25, or the Prelude No.6 in B minor – the cello being virtually the only other instrument for which he wrote. The principle however remains the same, for few instruments have a more singing quality than the cello).

Chopin delighted in effects of *coloratura* – the vocal style of ornamentation, the arabesques and roulades which he translated freely to the keyboard – in a more lavish and 'obvious' sense in his early works, and in an increasingly integrated manner as he matured. In his later works, as Gerald Abraham says, he confronts us with 'the paradox of "ornamentation" that constitutes the very substance of the thing ornamented.' (p.70). This is not to say, of course, that Chopin merely **copied** the effects of *bel canto*. To quote Gerald Abraham again, 'Chopin had an instinct amounting to genius for inventing melodies that would be actually ineffective if sung, or played on an instrument capable of sustaining tone but which, picked out in percussive points of sound each beginning to die as soon as born, are enchanting and give an illusion of singing that is often lovelier than singing itself.' (p.64). It is therefore the **idea** rather than the imitation of the sung line that we need to embrace as we shape Chopin's phrases, whether in a single *cantabile* line, or interwoven as in duet or in triple-voiced melodies. It is in the Nocturnes that Chopin's singing melody flowers most obviously and characteristically whether in tranquil or turbulent mood, although just to think of Chopin is to think of melody. In the Preludes, the Studies, the Scherzos, the Ballades, his melody is everywhere, not only in the obvious treble *cantabile* sense, but embedded in chords, in wild arpeggios, in flying cadenzas or in bass lines (for further discussion see under 'Phrasing').

Poland

As has already been said, the degree to which Chopin's music is motivated by Polish folk elements remains, as it doubtless always will, a subject for debate. This is part of the conundrum which Chopin presents – part of the mystique that surrounded him both during his life and today – which again is part of the mystique created by Poles wherever they go. His mother was Polish, and he was raised in Poland – we could therefore say that he was three-quarters Polish. On the other hand, he was also more than half French. Besides the fact that his father was a Frenchman, French was also the cultural language of the educated Pole. (I am told that between the wars, in the 1930s, Warsaw was still like a 'little Paris'.) Chopin and Paris thus recognised each other from the first meeting, and, seen in perspective, it seems uncannily neat and at the same time inevitable that he should have spent almost exactly half of his life in Poland and the other half in Paris. This has every bearing on his music. Early sensations, sounds and atmosphere are, as we all know, embedded in our consciousness throughout our lives. From the age of twenty he was for ever cut off from these early associations, which in his case were particularly happy. As we have seen, he loved Poland deeply, and all things Polish, while at the same time French elegance and sophistication of language, both personal and musical, were equally important to him. As he grew older and his reserve deepened, he increasingly poeticised his Polish associations in his national music, the Polonaises and particularly the Mazurkas.

Chopin was certainly conscious of this element in his musical make-up. In 1831 he wrote to his friend Titus Woyciechowski 'You know how I have wanted to feel and understand our national music, and how far I have succeeded in doing so.' (*Selected Correspondence*, p.108). And in 1847 he describes the indulgent nostalgia of an evening 'playing and singing to myself the songs of the Vistula' (*Selected Correspondence*, p.279). Again, in the year before he died he wrote of the Swedish singer Jenny Lind, whose voice and artistry delighted him: '[She] sang Swedish things for me till midnight. They have a very special spirit, just as our music has. We have something Slavonic, they something Scandinavian, and they are completely different, but we're closer to each other than an Italian is to a Spaniard.' (Zamoyski, p.311). He deplored the exploitation of folk music in a cheap, superficial manner, 'decked out with false noses, rouged cheeks,' and spoiling the serious attempt to 'unravel and reveal the truth.' (*Selected Correspondence*, p.277).

Every authority on Chopin agrees that it was in the Mazurkas that he expressed his most intimate and personal musical thoughts, and it is for this reason that, as I have pleaded below, the Mazurkas are central to any serious study of Chopin. He is Polish to the extent that only a Pole could have written this music – and a measure of the 'Polish-ness' of the Mazurkas is the widespread diffidence which most pianists feel in approaching them. That certain rhythmic and harmonic elements apparent in the Polonaises and Mazurkas extend into other areas of his work cannot be gainsaid, though except in the more obvious instance of the Waltzes, such elements are more sensed than definable. It is more a question of a cast of thought which we recognise as a certain factor of wayward melancholy or sometimes of impassioned sadness, or of equally impassioned exultance. Arthur Hedley talks of the 'Slavonic element which colours practically all Chopin's thoughts, whether in Ballade, Scherzo or Sonata, and which neither "Italianism" or anything else could totally obliterate' (a view with which other scholars do not all agree) (p.165). But as Hedley goes on to say, this 'did not prevent him from speaking first as a poet and only secondly as a patriot. The whole world has understood the poet's super-national message, addressed to the heart and imagination of mankind at large'.

Chopin and his Contemporaries

It is perhaps helpful briefly to consider Chopin in relation to his close contemporaries, Schumann and Liszt, for it is these three who to this day provide the staple fare of the Romantic recital repertoire. So far in this discussion of Chopin's style, the dreaded word 'Romantic' has, so far as possible, been avoided – dreaded not only because Chopin's reputation has been bedevilled by the romanticising zeal of biographers and novelists from the very moment that he died, but also because the Romantic umbrella, with its all-enveloping connotations of behaviour and expression embraces his contained figure so uneasily. We have only to picture him literally standing under an umbrella along with Berlioz, Liszt, Schumann and Wagner to spot the odd man out. The true romantic (musician, as well as writer or painter) was vociferous, blazoning his views and his aspirations, for art and for mankind. Schumann was quick to throw himself into the fray; he not only founded his own influential musical journal, the Neue Zeitschrift für Musik, and formed an imaginary band of artists, the Davidsbund, dedicated to the antagonising and vanquishing of the 'Philistines', but he also adopted the guise of two fanciful characters, Florestan and Eusebius, to represent the different sides of his own nature. Romantic gestures such as these were unthinkable to the prudent Chopin, who anyway (despite Schumann's generous championship of Chopin himself, both directly and in the Neue Zeitschrift) had little time for Schumann's music. Schumann's world, that of the German romantic movement, of quixotic literary fancies, rustic dreams, cryptic programmes, idealised depictions of merry peasants, lonely birds, wayside flowers and chattering brooks, was a world far further removed from Chopin's than the mere distance between the Rhine and the Seine.

As for Liszt, the ambivalent friendship and ostensible similarities between him and Chopin only serve to underline the gulf that separated them. And with unconscious irony, each, in one word, staked out the territory of the other: Chopin spoke of the 'empire' of Liszt – Liszt of the 'church' of Chopin. As a pianist Chopin wholeheartedly admired the strength and all-encompassing splendour of Liszt's playing: 'I should like to rob him of his way to play my own Studies', he wrote early in their friendship (Eigeldinger, p.124). But as time went on Chopin grew increasingly irritated by what appeared to him as Liszt's grandiosity, his wilful frittering of his talents, and his inability to refrain from interfering, rearranging and adding embellishments to other people's music – worst of all, to Chopin's own. 'He does have to put his stamp on everything; well, he may, he plays for **thousands** of people, and I rarely play for **one**' (Eigeldinger, p.124). Chopin was doubtless too discreet and too proud to express overt jealousy, but the tinge of pique is clear. 'As a creator he is an ass', wrote Chopin (Beckett, p.87). But this opinion might have been revised had Chopin lived longer. For Liszt the serious composer emerged later, after he had retired from the concert platform, and as in the case of

Chopin, his significance has only become fully apparent in the light of later developments in music. As for their natures, they were worlds asunder – Chopin, as we have seen, refined, charming and elegantly witty, with his emotions discreetly pinioned, his behaviour governed by the rules of good taste – Liszt with the éclat of his very public 'private' life and amorous adventures, inseparable from the consummate stage-management of his professional life, always retaining the whiff of the *parvenu*, 'half gypsy, half-Franciscan, half-saint, half-charlatan, a mixture of priest and circus rider' (Beckett, p.1). The wonder is that they remained on good terms for as long as they did. Amid these manifestations of Romantic expression typified by Schumann and Liszt, Chopin remained silent, observing the scene but carrying on along the individual path of his own 'new world'. It is, as George Marek says, Chopin's classical bent that 'saves him from being wholly the child of his time... To understand Chopin we must understand this classic-romantic amalgam... Although very much a part of the Romantic movement, he rose above it, distilling the best of its sentiment but shedding its excesses, tempering emotion with elegance, and often with irony' (Marek and Gordon-Smith, pp.61-2).

Chopin's Playing

It does no harm to repeat that in Chopin composer and player are uniquely interdependent, so central is this factor in the evolution of his very personal style. He was, as Berlioz said, 'an artist apart, bearing no point of resemblance to any other musician I know' (Eigeldinger, p.272) – a view borne out by numerous contemporary accounts of his playing, which almost unanimously emphasise his 'different', 'new' and 'individual' style. The nature of this difference and newness was, and is, more difficult to pin down.

One of the principal factors mentioned (and criticised) so frequently by his contemporaries was the relatively small tone that he produced. This is often ascribed to his physical frailty, and certainly near the end of his life he had become too weak to do justice to his more powerful works. But though no Liszt in terms of physical and musical vitality, neither was he, as we have seen, for most of his life a bloodless weakling. He had the stamina to burn the candle at both ends, socialising half the night and teaching all day – and besides, brute force is not needed to produce a large volume of sound, as many a diminutive lady executant can show us. He must have played as he did because he **wanted** to – that is, less loudly than many of the 'piano-pounders', as he called them, of his day. On the other hand, there are also accounts – from knowledgeable witnesses – which tell a different story. Georges Mathias, a long-time pupil of Chopin, and one who as a teacher and player was a genuine upholder of the Chopin tradition, records: 'Chopin as a pianist? First of all, those who have heard Chopin may well say that nothing remotely resembling his playing has ever been heard since. His playing was like his music; and what virtuosity! what power! yes, what power! though it would only last for a few bars; and the exaltation, the inspiration! the whole man vibrated! The piano became so intensely animated that it gave one shivers. I repeat that the instrument which one heard Chopin playing never existed except beneath Chopin's fingers: he played as he composed...' (Eigeldinger, p.277). And Mikuli, another of his professional pupils, wrote, 'the tone which he could **draw** from the instrument, especially in *cantabile*, was always immense... He gave a noble, manly energy to appropriate passages with overpowering effect – energy without roughness, just as, on the other hand, he could captivate the listener through the delicacy of his soulful rendering – delicacy without affectation'. (Eigeldinger, p.275).

Again, Emile Gaillard, another pupil, wrote 'Thumping is not playing... Chopin never flattened his piano, and yet, under his fingers, everything came out wonderfully.' (Eigeldinger, p.276).

Each of these accounts throws important light on this question of loudness. Firstly, Mathias talks of his 'power', but says that this power only lasted for a few bars. It is self-evident that Chopin intended powerful climaxes (see even the **triple** *fortissimo* indicated in the Nocturne in C sharp minor, Op.27 No.1 (bb.49 and 81); Studies in C sharp minor, Op.10 No.4 (bb.70-1) and Op.25 No.11 (b.93); and Prelude in D minor Op.28 No.24 (b.73) among numerous occurrences). But it is the relentless 'blanket' *fortissimo* to which we are too often subjected by many a lion of the keyboard that is so inimical to the very thought of Chopin. Thus in so many instances below I have pleaded for differentiation between *mezzoforte, forte* and *fortissimo,* particularly in such predominantly but not **uniformly** loud pieces as the Polonaises in A major Op.40 No.1 and in A flat major Op.53. It is also vital to observe *descrescendos* as well as *crescendos* within a long passage of **overall** rising dynamics. The long *agitato* sequence from b.49 of the Nocturne in C minor Op.48 No.1, for example, starts *pianissimo* and then gradually rises, through a cumulative series of hairpin *crescendoing* and *decrescendoing* **surges,** towards a magisterial *fortissimo* at bb.72-4. What one more often hears is, at best, a *mezzopiano* start at b.49, rising quickly towards a relentlessly battering *fortissimo* by around b.65, thereby undermining the grandeur of this climactic passage, bb.72-4.

Secondly, Mikuli emphasises that Chopin '**drew**' this immense tone from the instrument. This ability to draw tone from the piano has nothing to do with physical strength in the sense of hitting power, but everything to do with the **natural** immaculate muscular balance, coordination and responses which we know that Chopin possessed.

Thirdly, Emile Gaillard: 'Thumping is not playing...' A hard hand and wrist can certainly produce a whacking loud 'solid-block' sound – an anathema to Chopin. 'What was that?', he would exclaim irritably, should a pupil make a harsh or crude sound. 'Was that a dog barking?' (Eigeldinger, p.60). A supple, finely tuned, not necessarily large hand – Chopin's hand – can produce a tone that **seems** as loud because its suppleness enables the individual 'voice' of each finger to resonate within the overall sound, whether in large chords or many-voiced textural strands.

However, among the various descriptions that have come down to us, there appears to be a consensus that Chopin played in a quieter **general** dynamic level than was, or is, usual. This no doubt was linked with his intense dislike of playing in large public concerts – he was undoubtedly at his best in more intimate gatherings, and above all in his own teaching room. Within this level, however, we repeatedly read that he found a matchless variety of dynamic shadings.

It was his poetic shading and colouring of sound that accounted for much of the individual character of his playing. Among many descriptions of his elusive and personal quality of sound, perhaps Marmontel (a professional pianist and teacher, and connoisseur of Chopin's playing) provides the most telling: 'But where Chopin was entirely himself was in his marvellous way of leading and modulating the sound, in his expressive, wistful way of colouring it. He had a completely individual manner of touching the keyboard, a supple, mellow touch, creating sound effects of a misty fluidity whose secret he alone knew... If we draw a parallel between Chopin's sound effects and certain techniques of painting, we could say that this great virtuoso modulated sound as much as skilled painters treat light and atmosphere. To envelop melodic phrases and ingenious arabesques in a half-tint which has something of both dream and reality: this is the pinnacle of art; and this was Chopin's art.' (Eigeldinger, pp.274-5).

Most magical of all was his *pianissimo*. Berlioz spoke of Chopin playing with 'the utmost degree of softness, *piano* to the extreme, the hammers merely brushing the strings, so much so that one is tempted to go close to the instrument and put one's ear to it, as if to a concert of sylphs or elves.' (Eigeldinger, p.272). This exquisite softness combined with his 'sound effects of a misty fluidity' described by Marmontel, certainly had a great deal to do with his combined use of the sustaining and soft pedals (see below under 'Pedalling').

Within this 'misty fluidity' however, there was always a perfect lucidity (observed time and time again) – a 'rightness' of line and direction that could not be questioned. Chopin's pupil von Lenz wrote of an 'infinite perfection in the continuity of structure' (Eigeldinger, p.278).

Another aspect of Chopin's playing that was so individual was his rhythm. Mikuli recorded that 'in keeping time Chopin was inexorable, and some readers will be surprised to learn that the metronome never left his piano' (Eigeldinger, p.276) – and there are other reports in the same vein. It is clear that he adhered to the Mozartean principle that the left hand should keep time – i.e. that it should create a steady rhythmic foundation for the melodic and ornamental line of the right hand. That highly developed sense of rhythm inherent in every great musician was clearly in his case of an exceptionally fine-grained and elusive kind. Undoubtedly he had certain idiosyncracies of rhythm (see the Introduction to the Mazurkas), and the ability common to supremely rhythmic people to 'lean about within the bars' – in the words of Arthur Hedley – without destroying the overall sense of the continuing pulse. Mikuli continues: 'Even in his much maligned *tempo rubato*, the hand responsible for the accompaniment would keep strict time while the other hand, singing the melody, would free the essence of the musical thought from all rhythmic fetters, either by lingering hesitantly or by eagerly anticipating the movement with a certain impatient vehemence akin to passionate speech.' (Eigeldinger, p.276). And Berlioz said, 'his playing is shot through with a thousand nuances of movement, of which he alone holds the secret, impossible to convey by instructions.' (Eigeldinger, p.272). Unfortunately the attempt to emulate these 'thousand nuances of movement' has led generations of pianists into blatent rhythmic licence, with 'superimposed' as opposed to 'integral' rubato effects that would send Chopin into paroxysms of horror. Mercifully the more objective light thrown on Chopin by modern scholarship has done much to suggest a more disciplined and 'classical' approach to his music, and excessive rhythmic distortion is heard less among the younger generation of pianists (for further discussion, see under 'Rhythm', '*Rubato*' and ' 'Free' runs').

Chopin was a master extemporiser – it is said, as in the case of Bach, that his finished compositions were 'merely reflections and echoes of his improvisations' (Eigeldinger, p.282). His improvisations on Polish themes, or in the **spirit** of Polish themes, induced transports of emotion in his compatriots – an indication of how he returned again and again to his idealised vision of Poland. There are also many accounts of the improvisational **quality** of his playing, which accords with the also frequent testimony that he never played a piece in the same way twice. His rhythmic finesse (and at the same time freedom) is something which we can only attempt to understand by ever greater knowledge of his music (see also below under '*Rubato*').

Chopin's virtuosity was of the most exalted kind, in that it was experienced by his listeners as an element of the poetry of his sound rather than as an accomplishment in itself. He played octaves, thirds, sixths, scales and embellishments with consummate ease, and his method of getting around the keyboard was another facet of his individual style. He had, as we have seen, found his technique on his own, in contrast to the other great pianists of his day, Liszt included, who had all passed through the hands of such legendary pedagogues as Clementi, Czerny or Kalkbrenner. Chopin's hands were not large, but despite their delicate appearance, they were, like the hands of all pianists, strong. It is said that when he was angry he could break pencils as if they were straws (Marek and Gordon-Smith, p.86). Most important of all, they were of an exceptional suppleness. The most telling description of this is recorded by Niecks, who was told by Heller that 'it was a wonderful sight to see one of those small hands expand and cover a third of the keyboard. It was like the opening of the mouth of a serpent which is going to swallow a rabbit whole.' (Vol.2, p.96). And as Niecks also says 'the startlingly wide-spread chords, arpeggios, etc. which constantly occur in his compositions and which until he introduced them had been undreamt of and are still far from being common, seemed to offer him no difficulty, for

14

he executed them not only without any visible effort, but even with a pleasing ease and freedom.' His virtuosity was equal to Liszt's, but of an entirely different and less overtly dazzling kind. 'The Hungarian is a demon; the Pole is an angel', said Balzac (Eigeldinger, p.285).

Overall, of course, it was the uniquely poetic quality of his playing which so captivated his listeners, and raised him amongst his admirers to a position of almost haloed eminence. We cannot all be poets, and this is the area, most elusive of all, where neither teachers, performers, nor scholars can in the last resort help us. We can only absorb and try to understand the comments of those that heard him as best we may. The impressions quoted below are taken from J.-J. Eigeldinger's *Chopin: Pianist and Teacher.*

Ferdinand Hiller: 'What in the hands of others was elegant embellishment, in his hands became a colourful wreath of flowers; what in others was technical dexterity seemed in his playing like the flight of a swallow. All thought of isolating any one quality – novelty, grace, perfection, soul – fell away; it was simply Chopin.' (p.270).

Hallé: 'I sat entranced, filled with wonderment, and if the room had suddenly been peopled with fairies, I should not have been astonished. The marvellous charm, poetry and orginality, the perfect freedom and absolute lucidity of Chopin's playing... cannot be described. It was perfection in every sense.' (p.271).

Schumann: 'It was already an unforgettable picture to see him sitting at the piano like a clairvoyant lost in his dreams; to see how his vision communicated itself through his playing' (p.269).

Liszt: 'Such a poetic temperament as Chopin's never existed, nor have I ever heard such delicacy and refinement of playing.' (p.274).

Balzac: 'This beautiful genius [Chopin] is less a musician than a soul manifesting and communicating itself through all manner of music, even through simple chords.' (p.285).

Baron de Trémont (public figure and patron of the arts): 'What one hears is no piano; it is a succession of fresh, touching thoughts, often melancholy, sometimes tinged with terror; and to convey them the instrument undergoes a thousand transformations under his fingers, through a finesse of touch, from what one can only compare to spiders' webs up to effects of the most imposing strength.' (p.286).

Léon Escudier (musical scholar and publisher): 'He wishes to speak to the heart, not the eyes... Chopin makes poetry predominate... all these sounds, all these nuances – which follow each other, intermingle, separate and reunite to arrive at the same goal, melody – one might as well believe one is hearing small fairy voices sighing under silver bells, or a rain of pearls falling on crystal tables.' (pp.293-4).

Above all Chopin's playing enshrined and embodied the concept of simplicity.

Kleczyński: '(His) style is based upon simplicity, it admits of no affectation... This is an absolute condition for the execution of all Chopin's works.' (p.54).

And in Chopin's own words; 'Simplicity is everything. After having exhausted all the difficulties, after having played immense quantities of notes, and more notes, then simplicity emerges with all its charm, like art's final seal.' (p.54).

The Instruments

It is important always to bear in mind the kind of instrument for which Chopin wrote, and upon which he played. We have to remember that in Chopin's day, the piano was still a **relatively** young instrument, in a continual state of evolution. The effects of technique and sound that he introduced, and which still astonish us today, must have been amazing and totally bewitching to the audiences and musicians of his time. But these effects were achieved on an instrument with a far lighter tone and touch than our present-day giants. The French Pleyel was Chopin's favourite piano, an instrument 'with a light touch on which one can nuance with more ease than on a fleshy-sounding instrument' (Eigeldinger, p.25) as Lenz was to say, some twenty years after Chopin's death. And Liszt commented on the 'silvery and slightly veiled sonority, and lightness of touch of the Pleyel' (Eigeldinger, p.25). The Pleyel of Chopin's day has a unique quality; allowing the sense of 'making' the note oneself, almost as if with direct action of the finger upon the string. This obliges the player to listen with peculiar and demanding intensity to ensure the desired sound to be created by each finger – a process described in the reported statement of Chopin himself: 'If I am not feeling on top form, if my fingers are less than completely supple or agile, if I am not feeling strong enough to mould the keyboard to my will, to control the action of keys and hammers as I wish it, then I prefer an Erard with its limpidly bright, ready-made tone. But if I feel alert, ready to make my fingers work without fatigue, then I prefer a Pleyel. The enunciation of my inmost thought and feeling is more direct, more personal. My fingers feel in more immediate contact with the hammers, which then translate precisely and faithfully the feeling I want to produce, the effect I want to obtain.' (Eigeldinger, p.91). This has everything to do with the interpretation of Chopin's music, in terms not so much of volume, but of quality of sound: classical clarity in loudness as opposed to the deep-piled Brahmsian resonance characteristic of the modern concert grand. And we have to work, and to listen extra diligently to find the fine *pianissimo* which is native to the early instrument. The resonance of the sustaining pedal was also far less 'blanketing', and this needs to be taken into account in the interpretation of Chopin's pedal indications (see under 'Pedalling' below).

It is not easy to track down an early Pleyel piano, but the serious student should at least take the opportunity of trying the pianos of Chopin's period such as are to be found in the various public collections. One of the most striking effects is the way that the notes stand out, each with its own 'ping', even within a complex and **pedalled** texture – in contrast to the overall 'boom' in which the notes tend to be enveloped on the modern piano. In addition, the different registers are much more clearly defined, each with its own 'orchestral' timbre, as opposed to the much smoother, more streamlined merging of the registers in our pianos. This is by no means a decrial of the all-embracing capabilities of that marvel of engineering, a fine modern piano. It is merely to suggest that by becoming **aware** of the effects which Chopin could and did make, we correspondingly become aware of the need to tame and coax, to some extent, our instruments in order to arrive, not at a carbon copy, but at a recreation of the **idea** of the Chopin sound.

Chopin's Teaching

Chopin was an inspired teacher. We might suppose that he would have found teaching a chore, if a necessary one (for the constant procession of pupils to his door provided the main source of his considerable income). On the contrary, he took his teaching with the utmost seriousness, and gave his pupils (at any rate the more talented ones) meticulous attention and care. It is true that he established no royal line of pupils, partly perhaps because his teaching was of too quiet and personal a kind, and partly also because most of his pupils were titled ladies rather than aspiring professionals. But many of these were talented and accomplished pianists. Indeed his great friend the Princess Marcelina Czartoryska was considered to be the truest heir of Chopin in the style and accomplishment of her playing. Among the 'chosen' pupils, the gifted amateur as well as his few professional pupils, he inspired a devotion that bordered on reverence, not to say awe. His customary courtesy could turn to biting sarcasm, and many a young lady is reported to have left his room in tears. In later life, as Adam Zamoyski says, he 'could become very irritable and then he would pace the room, breaking pencils or nervously tugging at his hair. He was even known to fling scores across the room, and once broke a chair in his irritation.' (Zamoyski, p.140).

Chopin's approach was entirely his own, and many, many years ahead of his time. With him, suppleness was all. The art of touch, the **use** of the hand, arm and shoulder and the whole body, in relation to the production of sound came **before** gymnastics, in contrast to the orthodox piano schools, where you perfected your manual gymnastics first. For him virtuosity would grow naturally, provided that the body was used correctly, in other words maintaining the optimum **natural** balance and muscular coordination vis-à-vis the keyboard. It is fascinating to find that his principles of integrated physical movement pre-date by some fifty years those of the Alexander Principle (the 'Use of the Self') which, over the last twenty years has become an accepted part of the general curriculum in many schools of music and drama, sports training programmes, and so on.

As has already been said, the idea of programming, or of inspiration drawn from romantic or fanciful scenes is quite alien to Chopin's style. Nevertheless, like most teachers he evidently used imagery in his teaching – and in a specific and highly graphic manner. He told his pupil von Lenz that the 4-bar introduction to the Waltz in D flat major Op.64 No.1 should 'unroll like a ball of yarn' (Eigeldinger, p.87). And in the central section of the Nocturne in F sharp minor Op.48 No.2, he told another pupil, Adolph Gutmann, 'A tyrant commands, and the other asks for mercy' (Eigeldinger, p.81).

Near the end of his life Chopin began work on a piano Method, of which, to our loss, he completed only a few fragments. Nevertheless some of his basic principles of use of the hand and arms, the production of sound, and so on, are touched upon in clear and practical terms. These fragments are reproduced in full in J.-J. Eigeldinger's *Chopin, Pianist and Teacher*. Once more readers are recommended to this book for many glimpses of Chopin as a teacher.

Summing Up: Some Thoughts for Pianists

The interpreter of Chopin's music is faced with problems of a special kind. Firstly, as we have seen, the complexities and contradictions within his musical and personal nature preclude any kind of convenient pigeon-holing of his style. Thus the attempt to find helpful similarities, or alternatively, contrasts with the works of other composers can throw light on only half of the story. We **think,** however clumsily or inadequately, that we know how Mozart should sound, or Haydn, Beethoven or Debussy. The Chopin character is something altogether more elusive. Not only is there the 'outsider' factor referred to above, there is also the particular single-mindedness of his musical thought – a facet of the intense reserve of his nature – the way in which in both a personal and musical sense he was very much part of the world while remaining aloof from it.

Secondly, although it was the last thing he sought, this reticent figure generated a peculiar mystique, becoming in his lifetime what we would now call a cult figure. From the moment of his death the bandwagon started to roll, and on it has rolled ever since. It became a standing joke in Paris that there was hardly a Countess who had **not** been at his deathbed. Fiction took over and romanticised and sentimentalised the events of his rather uneventful life out of all recognition. Inevitably the hyperbole spilled over into the professional musical world, and indeed has been eagerly fastened upon and exploited by succeeding generations of pianists. Links with Chopin, however tenuous, spelled money and acclaim, and spurious Chopin pupils sprang up in every corner of the globe, generating a new wave, and again a new wave of 'authentic' Chopin traditions.

The late nineteenth century and early years of the twentieth were the heydays of the virtuoso pianist. With the introduction of the iron frame, pianos were able to produce a more powerful, thicker resonance, and styles of playing grew more flamboyant and pugilistic. Even musicians of serious intent indulged in romantic programming, an idea quite alien to the contained world of Chopin's music. Von Bulow's imagination reached dizzy heights in his programmes for Chopin's Preludes (see the Introduction to the Preludes); and for the Barcarolle the famous pianist Carl Tausig pictured a 'two-voiced, two-souled' love scene in a gondola, pinning down the precise moment of the 'kiss and embrace' to the modulation to C sharp major at b.77-8! (Niecks, Vol.2 p.266). Egocentric performers happily appropriated Chopin – most famous of all were the antics of the long-lived Pachmann, nicknamed Chopinzee, who capered about in bogus dressing-gown, gloves and so on supposedly 'owned' by Chopin, and regaled his delighted audiences with anecdotes as he played. Players have been bamboozled to a unique extent by phoney and conflicting interpretative 'traditions'. The worst specific distortions have been in the areas of dynamics and above all of rhythm: dynamics that are too heavy and **thick**-textured, forgetting the essential clarity and refinement of Chopin's texture and line which I have attempted to describe above; and rhythmic licence, often of the most grotesque kind, as opposed to the contained rhythmic flexibility practised by Chopin himself (see under 'Rhythm' and 'Rubato').

We are fortunate today in that modern scholarship and editing has stripped away much of the nonsense and the excesses with which Chopin's music has been encumbered. On the other hand, from the kind of performances often heard nowadays, neat, business-like and dull, we might well wonder if, with the craving for authenticity added to the exigencies and standards of the recording market, we are not in danger of throwing the baby out with the bath water.

How, then, is the innocent grass-roots pianist to set about 'finding' Chopin for himself? We have to be guided, I believe, not just some of the time but virtually **all** of the time by the two main ideas discussed above: that of the sung or declaimed line, and that of the 'classic-romantic amalgam'. And above all, by the **idea** of Chopin himself as best we can picture him. For as Arthur Hedley has said, 'Chopin's own playing was the counterpart of his personality. Every characteristic which may be distinguished in the man came out in the pianist – the same precision; the horror of excess, and all that is sloppy and uncontrolled; the same good manners and high-tone of breeding, combined with poetic warmth and a romantic fervour of expression.' (Walker, p.16). With the picture of this poet-aristocrat in our mind's eye and ear there is one searching test-question we can apply to each of our would-be interpretations: 'Could Chopin have liked it this way?'

More Specific Aspects of Style

Fingering

Since this is not a technical treatise it is only possible to discuss Chopin's fingering in general terms. In the piano schools of Chopin's day fingering was prescribed according to strictly formulated rules. Chopin knew nothing of all this. His style of fingering evolved in tandem with the growth of his own playing skill. Contortion of any kind was anathema to him, and his fingering followed two main principles: a) the natural conformation of the hand in relation to the keyboard; and b) the appreciation of the natural **characteristics** of each finger in terms of strength, flexibility, and expressive potential. He saw that the conventional objective, that of **equalisation** of the fingers (as it was then taught, and often still is today) was an impossibility. He sought instead to develop optimum suppleness, and then to dispose the fingering of a phrase in such a way as to 'fit' the expressive shape of the music. Accepting, for example, the comparative weakness of the fourth finger – 'the Siamese twin of the third', as he called it (Eigeldinger, p.33), he used it accordingly, as and when a gentle nuance was required, as the second note of a slurred couplet or slurred phrase ending, for example. There are, he said, in his sketch for a piano Method 'as many sounds as fingers!'. Similarly he capitalises on the singing capacities of the third finger (due to its stable position in the 'middle' of the hand) and frequently uses it on successive notes (see below regarding the opening of the Nocturne in C

18

minor Op.48 No.1, and also under '*Legato* and *Cantabile*').

J.-J. Eigeldinger points out that Hummel, in his piano *Méthode*, paved the way for much of Chopin's ostensibly innovative fingering. It was undoubtedly Chopin, however, who legitimised such ideas as the free use of the thumb on black notes; crossing the longer finger over the shorter, e.g. the third over the fourth, or the third over the fifth as in the Study Op.10 No.2, b.1

or the leaping upwards over the fifth finger to the thumb, or downwards over the thumb to

the fifth finger as in the Study Op.25 No.11, b.9

the use of the same finger on one note **or** on successive notes in the interests of dynamic or tone equality or expressive emphasis, and so on.

I say 'legitimised', but the fact is that although Chopin's principles of fingering were seen to work by his contemporaries, they still, it seems, one hundred and fifty years later, have not penetrated some of the more dimly lit corridors of the teaching profession. One still encounters students who blench at the idea of using thumbs on black notes, or who have been taught religiously to fiddle about with complicated finger-changes on repeated notes – whereas '(for repeated notes in a moderate tempo) Chopin could not tolerate the alternation of fingers... He preferred the repeated note to be played with the fingertip, very carefully and without changing fingers.' (Eigeldinger, p.48).

In every instance his objective is the achievement of the most natural possible distribution of the fingers over the notes, and the **regaining** of that natural position ready for the next sequence. Thus in the second example above the hand shifts down from the first 'set' of

four notes   to regain the same 'natural' position over the second 'set'.

etc.   A similar instance occurs in the decorative run in the Impromptu in

A flat Op.29 (b.81).

In many instances his fingerings for the left hand, in cases of wide leaps, are designed to preserve maximum equilibrium of the hand, as well as subtly favouring the harmonic resonance.

In the Nocturne in B major Op.32 No.1, in b.37 for example   

allows the hand to retain a more compact position than the more obvious but more 'splayed-out'

In addition the 5-5 fingering subtly 'points' the harmonic importance of the bass note as it is reiterated an octave higher. Here it may be noted that in octave sequences those with small hands can often create the best effect (and with the greatest facility) by the consistent use of the fifth finger. The resulting equilibrium of the hand predisposes a more consistent line (particularly in passages of *cantabile* intent – see for example the Nocturne in F sharp Op.15 No.2, bb.25 onwards), than by squirming around between the fifth, fourth and even third fingers. Chopin's hand had, as we have seen, special qualities of suppleness, and also, as the casts of his hand show (photographed in many books) a very individual conformation. Thus it is possible that while his fingerings may not always suit our own hand, they invariably, however, 'confirm' and complement the shape of a run, an arpeggiated pattern or left hand figure in relation to the natural cast of the hand. Whether or not, therefore, we actually adopt them in every instance, they invariably warrant the closest attention and appreciation, both from a 'manual' and a musical point of view.

Often the aptness of a particular fingering becomes apparent only after careful study of the relevant passage. This is particularly illuminating in certain melodic phrases, where he will often use the same finger on consecutive notes, usually the third finger, thumb, or fifth finger, in order to favour a particular expressive, 'speaking' nuance. In the beginning of the C minor Nocturne Op.48 No.1, for example, he uses the third finger on the three opening

detached crotchets.  To an experienced pianist this immediately suggests a quiet declamatory kind of articulation, with the clear intimation that something important is afoot, as indubitably and splendidly it is. (There are several other fingerings of particular expressive significance in the opening section of this Nocturne.) In the Nocturne in E flat, Op.9 No.2, there are again several instances of successive use of the fifth finger. In b.4, for example, Chopin obliges us to punctuate the phrase as he intends by using

the fifth finger successively on the high D and C,

something we would not 'bother' to do, like as not, if we used the more obvious fingering

etc. (see also under 'Articulation'). Again in bb.27-8 of this Nocturne,

Chopin underlines his intended *dolcissimo* 'speaking' articulation of the little downward run by again using the fifth finger successively.

He also used the thumb on successive notes to create special eloquence in occasional melodic fragments, as, for example, in the left hand in the Study in C sharp minor Op.25 No.7, bb.4-5. Then there is a revealing instance of successive use of the thumb in the Study in F minor (*Trois Nouvelles Études*), in bb.40-41, 42-3 and 46-7, to give an added upbeat importance to the last two crotchets of the bar as they move on towards the subsequent first beat in an implied slightly *marcato* effect (see also the commentary on this piece). Most remarkable of all is the instance near the end of the Nouvelle Étude in D flat major, where by his audacious use of the thumb, Chopin shows us exactly how to bound downwards through bb.69-71.

In the interests of achieving a *legato* line, and also of his insistence on the maintenance of the equilibrium of the hand (i.e. avoiding any kind of contortion, thus enabling the hand to function in a **natural** position) Chopin advocated the use of finger substitution. This means the technique of silently changing fingers (for example 1-3 or 5-1) on the key while it is depressed, a technique used by organists to maintain a *legato* line. Indeed, it was said that 'he changed fingers upon a key as often as an organ-player' (Eigeldinger, p.48). Among many examples of this are in the Nocturne in F sharp Op.15 No.2, the change 3-1 on the

quaver on the first beat of b.17;  and in the

Nocturne in F Op.15 No.1, the change 1-3 on the left hand G sharp on the first beat of b.8

 (see also the commentary on this piece). In other instances

he will 'engineer' the use of a certain finger on a certain note because of his realisation of the different expressive potential of each finger. A good example of this occurs in the left hand melody at the opening of the Waltz in A minor Op.34 No.2. Here in his pupil Jane Stirling's score this fingering is marked:

This not only enables the hand to remain in its natural more 'closed' position as opposed to the more 'splayed-out' position on the sixth in bb.2 and 4 in the fingering given in many editors, [musical notation] it also, by repeatedly using the thumb on the minim on each first beat, suggests the kind of quiet but expressive **weight** that Chopin seeks to obtain on these long notes.

In every instance then, we realise, and realise increasingly the more we study the music, that his fingerings are governed by the two factors mentioned above: the 'convenience' of the hand, and the expressive tendency of each finger.

We are fortunate in that Chopin has indicated fingerings in numerous instances. As might be expected, his fingerings are particularly thorough in the Studies. Many of the original fingerings that have been traced, including those marked by Chopin in copies belonging to his various pupils, are given in the Henle and (more fully) in the Vienna Urtext and Paderewski Editions.

For further discussion and many examples of Chopin's fingering, see J.-J. Eigeldinger's *Chopin, Pianist and Teacher*.

Rhythm
Chopin's highly developed and especially sensitive rhythmic sense has been discussed above (under 'Chopin's Playing'). The only way that we can attempt to 'get inside' his rhythmic character is to ensure that we find and **physically** feel the individual, fundamental rhythmic pulse of every piece or movement that we play. In order to find the pulse that 'feels' right (and this will inevitably differ from person to person), walk, dance, wave your arms, conduct, do anything that has a **physical** rhythm. All the 'mental' counting in the world will not help unless at the same time the rhythm is **felt** (in the solar plexus), as Ralph Kirkpatrick has so rightly said. If we do not feel the beat we find ourselves fighting the music, uphill, all the way. When we do feel the beat, we find that we are 'going with' the music, and that the majority of apparent stumbling blocks simply melt away. Furthermore, it is essential to feel the rhythm **before** we start. It is no good launching in blindly, and then fumbling for the beat in the middle of the first bar. This 'pre-engagement' with the rhythm manifests itself in the instant of stillness with which the practised performer (gymnast, athlete, dancer or musician) gathers himself with a total, almost tangible physical concentration ready to launch into movement.

This is particularly vital in the dance pieces: the Waltzes, Mazurkas, Polonaises and any other pieces that have a dance-like character. Also the alternating patterns of 'plain' quavers or semiquavers, triplets and dotted rhythm that often occur in these dance pieces need to be clearly defined, and this in turn depends on a secure sense of the prevailing crotchet pulse. But in every piece that we play it is essential to 'understand' in a physical sense the fundamental rhythmic **unit** upon which the rhythm is based, which may be a minim, a crotchet or dotted crotchet, or sometimes a quaver. It is only when the fundamental pulse is **carried** securely in the system that we can properly 'fit in' the smaller units of rhythm, the demisemiquavers, triplets, and so on. When in the commentaries I talk of having the rhythm 'in the system' I therefore mean this sense of actually **feeling** the pulse **physically**, not merely **counting** the beats (see also under 'Left Hand', '*Rubato*', 'Ornamentation' and ' 'Free' Runs', and the specific rhythmic idioms under Mazurkas, Polonaises and Waltzes).

Rests, Ties, Pauses and *Rallentandos*
Following on from the above, it is equally vital, in some senses even more so, to **feel** the beat through rests. Most players, it has been said truly, are afraid of silence! But failure to give proper value to rests is just as damaging to rhythmic equilibrium as failure to time the written notes.

Once again this is particularly important in the dance pieces. For example, in Waltz No.1 in E flat Op.18, b.84 (second-time bar at the end of the first D flat section) it is essential to **feel** the crotchet rest on the second beat so that you can 'pounce' onto the fierce *fortissimo* upbeat chord to the next section with a powerful but perfectly controlled

onward thrust.      Failure to **feel**

this rest will mean that this upbeat chord will not be properly timed, and you will 'fall into' the next first beat. Again, in the more tranquil example of the Waltz in A minor Op.34 No.2, it is essential to **feel** the crotchet rest on the second beat of b.16, ready to lead on

with a poised RH upbeat into b.17.

Fortunate are those who are taught from an early age to count rests **physically** (e.g. with a slight intake or exhalation of breath on the beats) rather than merely mentally.

Similarly the beat needs to be **felt** through tied and held notes. For example, in the Nocturne in G minor Op.15 No.3, rhythmic nonsense is made of the strange declamatory passage from b.121 unless the beat is securely **felt** through the held second beat of bb.121, 123, etc. (and similarly through the rests on the third beat of bb.122 and 124).

Again, in the Nocturne in F minor Op.55 No.1 the *Più mosso* section from b.48 falls to pieces unless the crotchet pulse is **felt** through the held minim chords in bb.49, 51, etc.

In the Prelude in D flat Op.28 No.15, bb.81-2, the first beat of b.82 has to be **felt** through the held B flat, otherwise not only does this note lose half its sorrowful impact, but the downward falling fragment through bb.82 and 83 will not be properly 'phased'.

 Again, in the great Mazurka

No.32 in C sharp minor Op.50 No.3, the first beat of b.1 must be **felt** through the tied upbeat, so that the opening statement of this all-pervading motif is immaculately presented.

Players often wonder how long they should wait on a pause. There can be no clear answer. In my experience students, 'afraid of silence', almost never wait long enough. On the other hand, too long a wait of course destroys suspense and leaves a vacuum. The solution which I find never fails because it is **natural**, not calculated (and which I have seen an eminent conductor try to inculcate into a batch of sceptical students) is to suspend the breathing as you pause. Then, when the urge to take a breath becomes irresistible, you are naturally impelled onwards.

There are numerous instances of pauses, or *tenutos* (indicated or implied) in the Mazurkas. In No.16 in A flat major Op.24 No.3, for example, on the spread chord on the second beat of b.6. Here it is as if the dancers have sprung into a momentarily **held** position as they poise themselves to lead on from the upbeat to b.7. Then there is a sense of a slightly longer 'hold' as you leap up to the pause on the higher chord in b.10, ready to lead on with the falling *dolce* triplet upbeat to b.11.

Then in b.36 of this piece, the pause is of a different type, when the bell-like sound of the repeated C's has to have time almost to 'disappear'. Nevertheless, we need to retain the **sense** of the beat as we listen to the fading sound, so that we are ready to move on in tempo from the upbeat to b.37.

We know that Chopin deplored exaggerated lingerings and *rallentandos*. Thus any indicated slowing down during the course of a piece should never be overdone, and never to the extent of losing the *sense* of the pulse (see also under '*Rubato*'). Similarly near the end of a piece, it is a mistake to slow down too soon and too much. Particularly in a slow piece, an ending that is too drawn out becomes tedious. And in a fast piece a far more exciting effect is usually achieved by forging on through the ending with unabated impetus, as for example in the Study in C minor Op.10 No.12 (the Revolutionary),

or the Prelude No.22 in G minor.

Chopin's *Rubato*

Tempo rubato is a ticklish subject at the best of times – the pity is that instead of being understood as a naturally arising slight rhythmic elasticity, it has been placed in a separate box – ground for endless discussion among professionals, and the cause of a kind of bewildered embarrassment among 'ordinary' players. In the case of Chopin, the whole matter has got out of proportion. We know that Chopin was a stickler for rhythmic exactitude, but we also have numerous and often poetic accounts of his own *tempo rubato*, which have been interpreted by generations of pianists as a licence for a rhythmic free-for-all – the most sentimentalising and vulgarising of all the falsifications to which the spirit of his music has been subjected. Players are thus left floundering in a mire of learned controversy.

In broad terms, Chopin's conception of *rubato* followed the baroque principle, which also applied to the tradition of the Italian *bel canto* with which his style of melody and ornamentation is permeated. This principle is that the degree of freedom allowed to the melodic line is subject to the **fundamental pulse** of the music. In keyboard terms this means that the melodic line (usually taken by the right hand) is subject to the fundamental pulse of the accompanying figure (usually maintained in the left hand). (Sometimes the process is reversed. In the Prelude No.6 in B minor, for example, or the main theme of the Waltz in A minor Op.34 No.2, the melody is in the left hand, while the right hand maintains the main pulse.) Mozart expressed this in the famous quotation from a letter to his father: 'What these people cannot grasp is that in *tempo rubato* in an *adagio* the left hand should go on playing in strict time...' This was Chopin's principle. In performance, of course, the left hand cannot always maintain a **rigid** 'strict time'. It is impossible, for example, in the case of the Nocturne in F sharp major Op.15 No.2 to think of the left hand maintaining an absolutely immoveable quaver pulse beneath the lavish arabesques and expressive details of the right hand. The essential, however, as Arthur Hedley says, is that the 'give and take... which *rubato* implies is always subject to the discipline of the **presiding measure**' (p.124). Thus, although the rhythm may bend, stretch or contract with a degree of **elasticity**, the rhythmic **sense** of that presiding measure (be it minim, crotchet or quaver) is always felt. (See also under 'Ornamentation' and ' 'Free' Runs'.) This can be illustrated by an analogy with the natural rhythms of the heart or the breath. If we begin to run, the heart gradually beats at a faster rate, and the breathing also increases its rate. But the heartbeat and breath quicken in an organised, graded acceleration, not in a series of random jerks. Similarly when we slow down again, the heart and the breathing also slow down, again in an organised, not random pattern of deceleration. Thus if we make an *accellerando* or a *rallentando* in music, it must proceed within the **sense** of the overall pulse, and never lose sight of that pulse. Chopin himself expressed the idea admirably to his pupils, 'The left hand is the conductor (or choirmaster)... Do with the right hand what you want and can.' (Eigeldinger, pp.50 and 120. There are several versions of this favourite exhortation recorded by different witnesses – in slightly varying words but expressing the same idea.) No conductor implements a rigid beat, save in certain works or passages which are dependent on the cumulative effect of a powerful beat such as a vigorous march or relentless dance movement. The idea of the left hand as conductor therefore clearly conveys the idea of a degree of rhythmic elasticity within the overall prevailing rhythmic discipline. Music must proceed in a continuing rhythmic **direction** from the first note to the very end of the final sound (not merely to the striking of the final note). When it fails to do this, and is sidetracked into wayward meanderings and distortions that bear no relation to the overall pulse, the rhythmic cohesion and logic that is essential to all great music is destroyed. Essential to this whole idea is that following any fluctuation of the melody, there should be a return to and resumption of the normal beat, or as the composer Saint-Saëns so tellingly put it, a falling back of the melody 'upon its axis' (Eigeldinger, p.49).

This principle of keeping the left hand rhythm steady is extremely hard to inculcate in those who are not endowed with a natural sense of rhythm. Taking, for example, the runs in the Nocturnes in F sharp major Op.15 No.2 (bb.11 and 51) and in D flat major Op.27 No.2 (bb.51-2) (see examples under ' 'Free' Runs') it is essential to learn the left hand thoroughly first, and in **strict** time. Then when the notes of the right hand have similarly been learnt, the hands should be practised together **very** slowly, again with the left hand keeping **strict** time – **concentrating** the attention on the left hand, so that the right hand is **obliged** to fit in with the left hand. Students left to themselves (unless exceptionally well endowed rhythmically) will invariably do the opposite, and concentrate on the right hand. Panic will then set in, the left hand will flounder, and the right hand will give up the ghost, precipitating a general collapse. Such runs are extreme cases, but the principle remains the same. While the left hand may make **allowances** for the agogics and curves of the right hand, it must never do so at the expense of the overall rhythmic impulse. In any event, it is an invaluable discipline to practise a *cantabile* and expressively ornamented piece slowly in strict time, and then to feel and gauge any *rubato* effects in the light of the **sense** of that stable pulse. It will be seen from the foregoing that the question of *rubato* is bound up with the idea of ornamentation and of melody itself. See also therefore under 'Ornamentation', and ' 'Free' Runs'.

The rhythmic idioms of the music in the national spirit (in particular the Mazurkas) suggest certain displacements of the regular beat, a slight holding back or moving on which is implicit in what J.-J. Eigeldinger calls the 'mobile rhythm' of the music. However, as he goes on to say, 'This type of national *rubato*... is by no means incompatible with that derived from Italian Baroque: the best Polish folk musicians, in monodic chants, employ the compensatory system (lengthening or shortening one note value to the detriment or gain of the next) while stamping a strict triple meter with the foot.' (p.121). One could say that the principle is the same, except that here the rhythmic elasticity is subject to the actual sense of **physical** dance movement. But likewise physical movement, whether walking, running or dancing is by its nature rhythmic, and therefore once again the **sense** of the rhythmic movement must always rest in the consciousness.

The actual increase or decrease of speed over whole sections is a different matter. In several of the Waltzes, for example, a new section will be marked *più mosso* or *più lento* (see the Waltz in C sharp minor Op.64 No.2, bb.33 and 65). Or equally (both in the Waltzes and in the Mazurkas) a slight change of tempo may be implicit in the varying character of succeeding sections. In such instances such changes, whether stated or implied, must be distinct and immediate, ensuring that the sense of the dance movement is instantly re-established in the new tempo, either faster or slower.

This can be no more than a brief discussion of the characteristics of Chopin's *rubato*. Typically, Arthur Hedley manages to say a great deal on the matter in the space of a paragraph (pp.124-5). And it is discussed in some detail by J.-J. Eigeldinger in his *Chopin, Pianist and Teacher*. In the light of the quotations from this book given below, we may reflect on the strange paradox of Chopin's own highly disciplined approach to rhythmic flexibility, and the licence with which exponents of his music have felt entitled to pull his music around. 'Chopin required adherence to the strictest rhythm, hated all lingering and dragging, misplaced *rubato* as well as exaggerated *ritardandos*.' (p.49).

'Chopin... often required simultaneously that the left hand, playing the accompaniment, should maintain strict time, while the melodic line should enjoy freedom of expression with fluctuations of speed.' (p.49).

'What characterised Chopin's playing was his *rubato*, in which the totality of the rhythm was constantly respected.' (p.50).

'Look at these trees,' [Liszt] said, 'the wind plays in the leaves, stirs up life among them, the tree remains the same. That is the Chopinesque *rubato*.' (p.51).

Ornamentation and 'Free' Runs
Note concerning the use of the term acciaccatura:
I use this term as it appears to be understood by most pianists today, i.e. as a **short** appoggiatura. This is, of course, a loose (and according to Grove, incorrectly anglicised) version of its original definition as a 'non-harmonic tone sounded simultaneously with a harmonic tone' (*Harvard Dictionary of Music*). However, it is a useful term to indicate an appoggiatura that is 'shorter than

long'. Its interpretation may range from a very short, almost simultaneous execution (as in the Waltz in E flat Op.18 bb.85-6 etc. and bb.133-48) to the more lingering but still relatively short implication in, for example, Nocturnes Op.27 No.2 (on the first beat of b.8), or in Op.55 No.1 (b.4).

Ornamentation: Chopin's manner of ornamentation in all its beauty and eloquence would in itself provide material for an entire book. Once again only general principles can be discussed here, but many specific instances are treated in the commentaries below. With Chopin, ornamentation is no mere accessory – it is the very stuff of his melody (see under 'Italian Influence'). In performance we have to be continually aware of this – the way that ornamentation **grows from** the melodic line, and at the same time expands and is in itself a 'flowering' of that line. Unfortunately this is also an area that has become a minefield for players and teachers alike for, as George A. Kiorpes has said 'virtually every tenet of a tradition which had been widely accepted a mere generation ago has been challenged (*Piano Quarterly* No.113, 1981). In the points discussed below I aim to suggest guidelines and **possibilities** rather than formulated 'rules'.

The 'regular' figures of ornamentation, trills, appoggiaturas, grace note figures, arpeggiations, and so on, will normally begin **on** the beat. This is clearly indicated by Chopin in the scores of various pupils. In the Nocturne in G minor Op.37 No.1, for example, various grace note or appoggiatura figures in bb.1, 5, 6, etc. are connected to the left hand note or chord

by a diagonal line   and

In all similar instances, as, for example, in the Scherzo in B minor Op.20, bb.322, 324, 325, etc. such grace note figures will begin on the beat. This inevitably involves a slight delaying of the melody note, creating a subtle *rubato* effect in the melodic line. The 'extra' acciaccatura as in b.5 of Op.37 No.1 (and which occurs elsewhere in Chopin's work) is more problematic.

If this is also placed on the beat, this second beat may seem somewhat

overcrowded, and many players allow this note to 'speak' in slight anticipation of the beat (but in the sense of belonging to the whole ornament rather than to the previous beat). However, when this acciaccatura **is** placed on the beat it causes a slight momentary extra drawing out of the pulse, and further delaying of the melody note, which could be said to heighten the significance of the opening motif as it is restated in *forte*. In practice the exact placing of such an ornament by a skilled player is hardly remarked as it passes through the listening ear within the overall context. There is a similar instance in the Impromptu in A flat Op.29, bb.58 and 74. Here the score belonging to Camille O'Meara-Dubois has again been marked. But according to J.-J. Eigeldinger the ornament

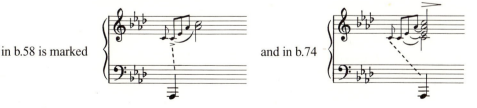

in b.58 is marked   and in b.74

28

And who with impunity would care to pronounce a cast-iron 'rule', taking into account the different placing of the emphasis in these two bars, as shown here! (For further comment on possible anticipation or non-anticipation of ornaments see under Waltz in F minor Op.70 No.2).

J.-J. Eigeldinger also notes the expressive significance of 'the auxiliary note which emphasises an interval by repeating the first note just before the second note sounds', citing bb.18-19 of the Nocturne in C minor Op.48 No.1 (in which the acciaccatura is connected thus to the bass note

in the score belonging to Camille O'Meara-Dubois),

Op.9 No.2 bb.8 and 22, and many other examples (Eigeldinger, pp.114-15).

Similarly the grace note prefix to the trill is marked thus in the Nocturne in A flat, Op.32

No.2, b.8: Such a prefix, starting below the main note, occurs

frequently (see also, for example, amongst many others, the Nocturne in F minor Op.55 No.2, b.14, and the Nocturne in F sharp Op.15 No.2, b.56, etc.). This notation does **not** mean that the trill is 'hiccoughed', i.e. that the B flat is repeated – the trill will read:

Such **prefixed** trills beginning on the lower note

also occur frequently in the left hand, as, for example, at the end of the Study in A flat Op.25 No.1, the Preludes in E, bb.3 and 4, and in F, bb.2, 6, etc.

'Plain' trills without prefixes are rather rare in Chopin, and the question of whether these should begin on the upper or main note must depend upon the taste and experience of performers within each context, and once again no definitive rules can be prescribed. J. Petrie Dunn (see note at the end of this section) takes the view that trills for which Chopin has given 'no direction... should begin with the principal note, albeit there are some which, without detriment to the melodic line, **might** begin with the auxiliary note.' (p.23). On the other hand, contemporary accounts suggest that Chopin considered that trills **should** begin on the upper note (Eigeldinger, pp.58-9). Often Chopin will make his intention clear, as for example in the Waltz in A minor Op.34 No.2, b.5. Here, since the main note is preceded by the upbeat F, the left

hand trill will begin on the main note E.

Then in the Study in C sharp minor Op.25 No.7 upper appoggiaturas are added by Chopin to the left hand trills in bb.7, 37 and 51 in the copy belonging to his pupil

Mme Dubois, indicating that the trill should run:

On the other hand it might be assumed that the mighty unison trills in the Polonaise in A major Op.40 No.1, b.57, etc. will begin on the main note to create their maximum impact. And in the Ballade in A flat major Op.47, there is the case of the right hand trills which in bb.26 and 28 have prefixes, while those in bb.29-32 do not. The context of the two 'sets' of trills is different: those in bb.26 and 28 fall on the first beat of the bar, and have the duration of a dotted crotchet; those in bb.29-32 occur on the 'upbeat' to the second main beat of the bar, and have only the duration of a quaver. It is presumed that these four shorter trills begin on the main note as written (see Jan Ekier's Introduction to the Vienna Urtext Edition).

Then there is the special case of chains of trills as in the Impromptu in A flat Op.29, bb.62-3 and the elaborate span in the Nocturne in B major Op.62 No.1, bb.67-71. Here, as in most other instances of such chains, Chopin makes his intentions clear. In the Impromptu the first trill begins with the prefix falling **on** the beat, and then the second and third trills begin on the main note.

In the Nocturne the chain begins with the appoggiatura, i.e. on the main note, and proceeds downwards with each trill beginning on its main note

(see also the commentaries on these works).

In the case of a long trill in one hand during which the other hand is carrying on the main melody or rhythmic impulse, inexperienced players so often focus their whole attention on the **trill** in frantic anxiety to 'get in' as many notes as possible. Invariably the 'other hand' (i.e. the 'main' hand) then falters or starts to scramble, and the 'trill hand', attempting to take over, strangles itself and sets into rigor mortis, bringing about a general and ignominious collapse. We have to do exactly the opposite. The essential is that the main 'business', melodic, rhythmic, or both, proceeds **undisturbed,** enhanced but not swamped or undermined by the trill. A simple example occurs in the Waltz in A flat, Op.64 No.3, bb.59-60 and 63-4.

Here we need to concentrate our attention on the left hand as it carries on with its own melodic/harmonic phrases beneath the trills, allowing the right hand trill to run easily, not frantically, towards the quaver on the first beat of b.61. Never mind if our trill is not in the Horowitz class providing that the overall musical momentum, 'led' by the left hand, is carried along convincingly and with poise. The principle for practising is similar to that for ''Free' Runs' (see under this heading).

The sign ⌇ occurs frequently, sometimes called the 'compact trill'. This is normally, though not always played on the beat thus: or . There are numerous examples

in the Mazurkas, Op.17 No.4 for instance, b.19 played

and b.47 played [musical notation] In instances of short note-values this sign is

often interchangeable with *tr*, as in the Fantaisie Impromptu Op.66, b.43, etc. played

[musical notation] As in classical music this ornament may be shortened

to [musical notation] in fast passages when the 'getting in' of the usual three notes would cause a hiccough in the overall fluency (see commentary on the Waltz Op.64 No.1 regarding this ornament in b.10).

Arpeggiated figures will usually, but again not always, begin on the beat, and here once again, particularly in the case of wide-apart arpeggios in the left hand, there can be no rule of thumb. Often considerations of pedalling in order to 'catch' bass notes will decide the issue. (This applies particularly to those with small hands.) Arpeggiated figures in the right hand

such as [musical notation] will be played [musical notation] again usually

upon the beat.

Chopin was especially particular about the execution of the turn [musical notation] or

[musical notation] and the long or short appoggiatura [musical notation] or [musical notation] , for which, as Mikuli reports,

'he recommended the great Italian singers as models'. J.-J. Eigeldinger points out (p.133) that although the sign ∾ is occasionally used, Chopin usually preferred to write out turns in full in order to indicate his intended nuance, as for example in the Nocturne in E flat Op.9 No.2, b.10,

[musical notation] or in the Nocturne in C sharp minor Op.27 No.1, b.22.

[musical notation]

The long or short appoggiatura (or acciaccatura) has to be treated according to context, and interpretation in most instances is discussed in the commentaries on the works. Again, these will **usually** be placed on the beat. However, in the Scherzo in B minor Op.20, for example, Chopin ensures an anticipation by placing the acciaccatura figures at bb.177-8 and repeatedly from bb.293-304 **before** the bar line (see also Mazurkas Op.7 No.2 bb.11-12 and Op.7 No.3 bb.36-7). May he not similarly, therefore, sometimes intend an anticipation when such a figure occurs **within** the bar? As a last word I repeat that hard and fast rules can never be formulated for ornamentation of such a rich and diverse kind as that created by Chopin. The fact that we know it was his habit to introduce extemporary ornaments when he played only reinforces this truth (see Eigeldinger pp.74, 122-3, 150-2, etc.).

The essential in all instances of trills, grace notes, turns and longer ornamental figures, is to **think** of them vocally – to imagine how a fine singer would execute them – realising that they are there to embellish the melodic line, growing from and expanding through the melodic line, and **not** as 'stuck-on' excrescences, nor as an exhibition of how many notes can be 'got in'.

Note: A special study: *Ornamentation in the works of Frederick Chopin* by John Petrie Dunn (Novello 1921, Da Capo 1971) is now difficult to obtain, but may be found in some libraries. In the light of later scholarship this authority's realisations of ornaments may be queried in some instances, but he makes many pertinent observations on the mainsprings of Chopin's style of ornamentation. There are also valuable chapters on ornamentation by Thomas Fritz and George Kiorpes in the journal *Piano Quarterly*, No.113, a special edition devoted to Chopin (obtainable from PO Box 815, Wilmington, Vermont 05363 USA).

'Free' Runs: By 'free' runs I mean those runs, arpeggiated figures, arabesques and roulades which are not marked out in clear rhythmic groups, and are often in odd number of notes so that they do not 'fit' the overall rhythm of the piece. This type of ornamentation, almost a trade-mark of Chopin, strikes terror in the heart of the relatively inexperienced player, who might take a glance, for example, at bb.2-3 of the Nocturne in B flat minor Op.9 No.1

or bb.11 and 51 of the Nocturne in F sharp major Op.15 No.2

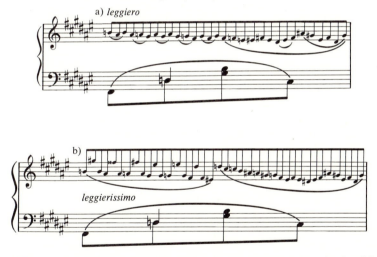

and pass on. This is a great shame, for players thereby miss out on a lot of splendid repertoire with which in all other respects they could cope well enough. The terrors are to a large extent more imaginary than real. Panic induces scurrying, with a consequent collapse of rhythm and all idea of shape as the player scrabbles frantically for dry land on the next 'normal' beat, or alternatively goes into a spasm and dries up in mid-span. The first essential is to mark out the 'little notes' in groups to 'fit' in a provisional pattern with the left hand (see detailed examples of this under the commentary on the Nocturne in B flat minor Op.9 No.1. We know that Chopin worked like this with pupils – see also the final run in Op.48 No.2). The next essential is to make perfectly sure of the left hand, practising in a perfectly steady rhythm. Then learn the right hand, practising it in the rhythmic groups already marked out, and **imagining** the left hand proceeding steadily beneath. When both hands are thoroughly learnt, and you begin to put them together, go very **slowly** at first, concentrating on keeping the left hand steady, and feeling that the right hand 'little notes' are fitting in with the left hand, and **not** the other way about. As you are able gradually to increase the tempo, continue to keep the left hand **steady,** feeling that the rhythm of the left hand is 'guiding' the right hand.

As you increase the tempo towards the overall pulse of the piece as a whole, the left hand may give a little here or move on a little there, to accommodate the number of notes in the right hand, or to allow the right hand to negotiate a 'vocal' curve, or to 'point' a chromatic nuance. But the immutable principle is that the left hand is the 'guardian' of the rhythm. It may 'bend', i.e. get a little slower or faster, but it will do so in a measured, rhythmic, not random manner (see also under '*Rubato*'). In the case of the long run in the Nocturne in D flat Op.27 No.1, bb.51-2 for example, the left hand may have to 'give' considerably, to accommodate the curves of the right hand but it must always maintain the **sense** of the **6/8** pulse (see the commentary on this piece).

In the case of a solo, cadenza-like figure as at b.32 of the Nocturne in E flat Op.9 No.2, we are similarly guided by the melodic shape of the 4-note figure, and the inherent rhythm of these semiquaver groups as we 'move on' and then *rallentando* (see the commentary below). It cannot be too strongly emphasised that elaborate ornamentation, such as these 'free' runs and arabesques, are not occasions for demonstrations of virtuosity and speed *per se*. They are there to adorn the music, to make a beautiful effect of sound, or a 'speaking' nuance in the melody. While we cannot all have the fingers of a Horowitz, we can still create a beautiful effect if we can 'get inside' the essential vocal shape and nuance of Chopin's ornamentation. This said, however, we need to beware of exaggerated and portentous lingering through ornamentation, something quite foreign to Chopin's style. An important point in this connection is Chopin's preference for the idea of accelerating rather than making a *rallentando* through the end of a run. A simple example of this occurs in b.16 of the Nocturne in E flat Op.9 No.2, where the implied triplet within an implied **5**-note group of demisemiquavers suggests a slight acceleration towards 'home', i.e. the dotted crotchet E flat on the third main beat of the bar.

Similarly as we cascade lightly down the arpeggio at the end of the long run in b.52 of the Nocturne in D flat Op.27 No.2, we need to feel the sense of moving on to reach the B flat on the first beat of b.53, rather than delaying the arrival on this 'home' by an artificial *rallentando*. Kleczyński describes this idea graphically: 'Again, these ornamental passages should not be slackened, but rather accelerated towards the end: a *rallentando* would invest them with too much importance, would make them appear to be special and independent ideas, whereas they are only fragments of the phrase, and, as such, should form part of the thought, and disappear in it like a little brook which loses itself in a great river; or they may be regarded as parentheses which, quickly pronounced, produce a greater effect than they would if they were retarded.' (Eigeldinger, p.53. See the appendix to this book (section A) for Kleczyński's fuller exposition of this idea). Kleczyński then goes on to cite the above example from the Nocturne in E flat. Perhaps this does not always apply, but it is an idea we should bear in mind lest we distort the overall rhythm by overdelaying the **resumption** of the normal pulse.

Often there are detailed indications for articulation during the course of a run. In the run quoted above, for example, in b.16 of the Nocturne in E flat, we have to allow time for the *portato*

 demisemiquavers to 'speak', and to 'point' quietly the emphasised C flat before

moving on through the last five notes.

Articulation

The detailed articulation which Chopin constantly indicates is another aspect of the expressive 'speaking' intent of his melody. 'The wrist: respiration in the voice', he said (Eigeldinger, p.45) meaning that the lifting of the hand (by means of the **supple** wrist for which he continually begged) creates an effect of punctuation, like the breathing of a singer. An example of this has already been quoted under 'fingering' in b.4 of the Nocturne in E flat,

Op.9, No.2, b.4  when the lifting of the hand

(i.e. by means of the flexible wrist) necessitated by the fingering (5-5) 'points' the intended punctuating of the phrase, with a further slightly punctuating 'lift' down to the lower C.

The indications for articulation are particularly detailed in this

Nocturne and repay the closest study: the offbeat emphasised slurred effect in b.6 indicating a gentle falling and lifting of the hand;

details of slurs, 'speaking' semi-staccato effects through b.8;

the 'speaking' (*parlando* – see below) of the repeated E flats in b.10;

the details of b.16 already mentioned under ''Free' Runs'

and so on. But how often does the average student notice these things – and how often do we hear this relatively simple piece delivered as by a person reciting in a flat monotone?

The observation of details of articulation is equally relevant to expressive and musical sense whether or not they are pedalled. This is particularly important in the case of short rests. In the Nocturne in D flat Op.27 No.2, bb.12-13

the gentle **lifting** of the hand through the rests gives the figures marked b) a certain lightness and vitality as opposed to the smoother effect of the figure marked a). It is a question of a subtle nuance which is a **natural** result of the 'lift' and 'fall' of the hand. Hence my frequent plea to **lift** the hand from a detached note, and through a rest. This is particularly important and occurs

particularly frequently in the Mazurkas in the figures ⌐♩♪♩ as opposed to ⌐♩♩ .

The **lifting** of the hand from the quaver and through the rest gives that feeling of 'spring' and vitality, and the 'fall' of the hand onto the semiquaver gives the semiquaver a natural kind of onward, 'upbeat' movement. This is a nuance that is inherent to the rhythm of this figure, which in turn is characteristic of the special rhythmic impulse of the Mazurka movement (see also the Introduction to the Mazurkas).

Another important detail of articulation is the ♩ ♩ ♩ ♩ style of articulation

referred to in the example of the repeated E flats above, indicating a semi-staccato, or just-detached style of articulation. This occurs frequently in Chopin, and denotes a 'speaking' style of articulation, particularly in the instance of repeated notes, as in this above example, or again in the Nocturnes in B flat minor Op.9 No.1, bb.1, 4, etc. and C sharp minor Op.27 No.1, bb.3,

7, etc. This style of articulation is often referred to as *parlando* (i.e. speaking). However, since at different periods there has often been confusion between *parlando*, *portato*, *portando* and *portamento* (the latter meaning a smooth 'carrying' of the voice or instrumental sound from one pitch to another in a 'slide' or *glissando* effect), I have avoided the use of *parlando* in the commentaries below, and referred to the 'speaking' quality of such notes or figures (see below for definitions of these terms, under 'Some Explanations and Amplifications').

Phrasing

The affinity of Chopin's melody with the sung line, and in particular with the Italian style of singing, has been discussed above. It follows from this that the style of his phrasing, both in its details and overall sweep, is based upon the **idea** of the sung and declaimed line, which again is intimately bound up with the style of articulation and punctuation. Part and parcel of the sung line is, of course, the declamation of words, and the idea of the vocal **and** spoken line was central to Chopin's concept of melody and phrasing. It is only if we can really understand this, not merely as a theory to be read about and stored at the back of the mind, but as a physical reality, that we can hope to **understand** both the details and the overall 'direction' of his phrasing.

The punctuation of the sung line is achieved by the use and control of the breath, and the sense of the sung words. Similarly so is the punctuation of Chopin's phrases governed by the **idea** of the use of the human breath, and the **idea** of the spoken word. This is implemented on the piano by the allowing of the lift and fall of the wrist ('the wrist [equals] respiration in the voice', see also under 'Articulation'). This is well illustrated in the opening bars of the Nocturne in F sharp Op.15 No.2:

The wrist falls lightly to begin the opening upbeat figure; and then gently **lifts** the hand from each of the repeated C sharps in b.1. The wrist and hand **fall** again on the tied quaver C sharp on the first beat of b.2, then the wrist rises through the little demisemiquaver arabesque and **lifts** the hand again from the high quaver C sharp on the second beat of b.2, ready to **fall** again on the upbeat to b.3, and so on. There will then be a more pronounced 'lift' from the detached quaver D sharp on the first beat of b.6, with a more accentuating 'fall' on the high tied quaver F sharp (the high point of the phrase) after which the phrase unwinds as it moves towards the middle of b.8, ready to 'start again' on the upbeat to b.9. There is an immense amount of detail within this 8-bar phrase, which we observe in terms of subtle punctuation, rather than fragmentation within the overall melodic flow **towards** and **'back from'** the high

F sharp in b.6. This is an essential point – the details are a part of the **overall** flow of the phrase, and the phrases are part of the **overall** flow of the piece, in the same way as the ornamental details of a fine building contribute to, rather than distract from the overall ensemble. See Kleczyński's exposition of the 'Chopinesque' punctuation of the opening bars of the Waltz in A flat Op.69 No.1 (quoted in the Appendix to this book). This is also quoted by J.-J. Eigeldinger in *Chopin, Pianist and Teacher*, pp.42-4). There is no contradiction between Chopin's insistence on punctuation, while at the same time avoiding fragmentation. As with the sung line, or spoken sentence, the punctuation occurs **within** the overall line, phrase or sentence.

The other sense in which the phrase adheres to the vocal idea is in the shaping of the curves of a melody. A singer always shapes the phrase 'towards' and 'around' the highest note. This is not a theory, it is a matter of how the voice naturally behaves. It is not so much, and not necessarily a question of a *crescendo* towards the highest note, but the sense of rising towards such a note, 'rounding the curve' with the sense of a slight expansion of the line, ready to return downwards again. This principle is well illustrated in the Nocturne in F sharp minor Op.48 No.2.

Here the line of the introductory 2-bar fragment rises towards its little peak, the A on the third beat of b.2, and then turns downwards to 'settle' momentarily on the tonic F sharp on the first beat of b.3. Then the line 'lifts' to its highest point, the F sharp on the second beat of b.3, and descends in an overall line towards the second quaver of b.5, but with little 'returns' upwards to the quaver E on the first beat of b.4, the C sharp on the third beat, and the ornamented upbeat to b.5. The whole sequence, slightly varied, begins again with the 'lift' up to the F sharp on the second beat of b.5. Then the curves gradually extend higher towards the G sharp on the third beat of b.8, the B on the third beat of b.10, and the C sharp in b.11, and so on. The impetus of the whole of this vocalise-like melody (bb.3-27) moves on towards the climax on the high F sharp on the third beat of b.18, with a gradual winding down from b.19 towards bb.27-8. This is a principle that applies equally in long or in short breathed phrases, in virtuosic arpeggiated passages, chord sequences, and so on. In the Waltz in E flat Op.18, bb.21-8, for example, we 'go to' the F on the first beat of b.22, 'turn the corner' around the A flat on the third beat of b.24, rise to the summit of this 8-bar section on the high F on the first beat of b.27, and descend through b.28 ready to 'start again' in b.29.

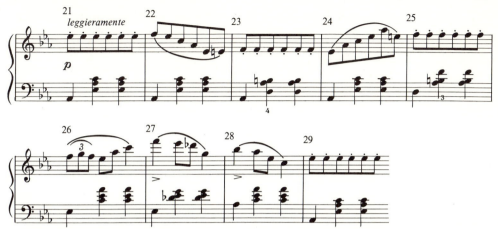

In the Study in A minor Op.25 No.11, the *Allegro con brio* **starts** from the high point of the treble F on the first beat of b.5, curves down through a series of undulations to the lowest point on the fourth beat of b.8, curves up towards and down from the high E in bb.9 and 10, then up to and down from the high A in b.11, and shoots up to 'poise' on the high E in b.12 ready to cascade down from the high F in b.13.

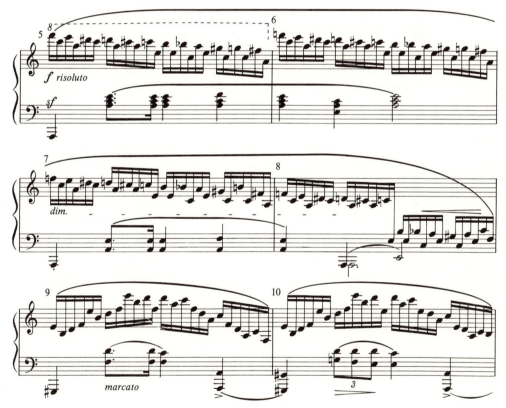

(b.11 continued overleaf)

The shaping of these phrase curves is just as essential in such a virtuosic passage as in the melody of a Nocturne. It is the sense of moving towards and 'rounding' the curves in the sense of 'turning a corner' through and around the topmost note, and similarly the lowest note, in the same way that we 'arrive' and turn a corner at the maximum point of both inhalation and exhalation.

Once again the ideas of Chopin himself define his conception of phrasing. The following quotations are taken from J.-J. Eigeldinger's *Chopin, Pianist and Teacher* (p.42).

Kleczyński: 'All the theory of the style which Chopin taught to his pupils rested on the analogy between music and language, on the necessity for separating the various phrases, on the necessity for pointing and for modifying the power of the voice and its rapidity of articulation'.

Mikuli: 'Chopin insisted above all on the importance of correct phrasing. Wrong phrasing would provoke the apt analogy that it seemed to him as if someone were reciting a laboriously memorised speech in an unfamiliar language, not merely failing to observe the right quantity of syllables, but perhaps even making full stops in the middle of words. Similarly, by his illiterate phrasing the pseudo-musician reveals that music is not his mother tongue but something foreign and unintelligible to him: and so, like that orator, he must relinquish all hope of his speech having any effect on the listener.'

Mikuli/Koczalski: 'Under his fingers each musical phrase sounded like song, and with such clarity that each note took the meaning of a syllable, each bar that of a word, each phrase that of a thought. It was a declamation without pathos; but both simple and noble.'

Legato and *Cantabile*

Following on from the above it goes without saying that Chopin's own playing was characterised by an exceptionally fine *legato*, *cantabile* line. 'Under Chopin's hands,' wrote Mikuli, 'the piano needed to envy neither the violin for its bow nor wind instruments for their living breath. The tones melted into one another as wonderfully as in the most beautiful singing.' (Eigeldinger, p.46). It is a remarkable fact that there are plenty of even relatively advanced pianists who cannot play three or four notes together in a true *legato*. Admittedly the skill of releasing one note at the precise moment that the next is put down is quite a complicated one in terms of muscular coordination. Further, to be able to vary this coordination at will – either overlapping the notes slightly to create a 'closer' *legato*, or to vary the extent of separation between the notes in an infinite array of degrees from barely detached to sharpest *staccato* – is an important factor in the equipment of the virtuoso. A large part of the skill of *legato* playing depends upon the ability to listen. On the piano the sound of a note begins to die from the moment it is struck, as opposed to a sung, blown, or bowed note, whose sound can not only be maintained, but increased or diminished through its duration. It therefore follows, as Chopin said, that a long note is always a relatively **strong** note, in order that it shall make sufficient tone to last through its full duration. And there is always the sense of the previous notes 'going to' a longer note. A good example of this occurs at the beginning of the Nocturne in C sharp minor Op.27 No.1, when the first phrase 'goes to' the longer, stronger tied minim F sharp on the third beat of b.4. Then, at the beginning of b.6, the C sharp 'goes up to' the longer, stronger G sharp on the second beat:

We then have to listen particularly acutely to the sound of a **long** note through its full duration. We can then judge how much sound is left, which in turn enables us to gauge how much tone to give the next note, so that the sounds blend as smoothly as possible to create the most convincing and/or expressive simulation of a sung *legato*. This process of continuously evaluating the sound becomes second nature to the ear-to-finger response system – the responses have to be immediate, particularly in faster sequences of *legato* notes. To Chopin a true *legato* line was a prerequisite of good playing, and he was insistent that his pupils studied assiduously to acquire this skill. He referred to a faulty *legato* as 'a pigeon hunt' (Eigeldinger, p.32). In order to achieve a certain kind of 'speaking' *legato*, or to make a subtle nuance of punctuation, he would also play consecutive notes with the same finger. It is possible to do this, as he did, with a barely perceptible break in the continuity of the line while at the same time suggesting a 'speaking' quality of sound (see also under 'Fingering' and 'Articulation'). There are numerous examples of this kind of articulation – one of the most interesting is in the

Nocturne in G minor Op.37 No.1, b.6　　　　when the

relevant notes are actually accented. This almost *legato* effect is achieved by raising each note as little and as late as possible, i.e. only 'just in time' to play the next. The same technique is often required in repeated chords (see under Prelude No.4 in E minor).

Pedalling

Friederike Müller (later Mme Streicher, one of Chopin's finest pupils) records that 'In the use of the pedal [Chopin] had... attained the greatest mastery, was uncommonly strict regarding the misuse of it, and said repeatedly to the pupil: "The correct employment of it remains a study for life".' (Niecks, Vol 2, Appendix 3, p.337). How true this is, but how little time is usually given to this study. Even today many a relatively advanced pianist only regards the sustaining pedal as a 'joiner-up', at worst a useful device for saving the trouble of playing *legato*, and is astonished by the idea of considering the pedal as a 'paintbrush' for the colouring and characterisation of sound. It is in this sense of the colouring of sonority, of creating haloes of sound with the pedal (a favourite term of Poulenc) and effects of 'distancing' sound, and so on, that Chopin was such an innovator. We all know what Debussy achieved with the pedals, and understand that the realisation of his unique sound effects depends on highly skilled and imaginative use of the pedals. He was a devoted disciple of Chopin, and we do well to reflect, as various authorities have pointed out, that it was Chopin who first, and literally, lifted the dampers from the strings. The climate of Debussy's music has little to do with that of Chopin's, yet in this, as in other ways, it was Chopin who passed on the torch.

In many of his works Chopin has left detailed pedal indications. In many others, however, he has not. The editor of the Paderewski Edition suggests that 'those passages in which Chopin has not marked the pedalling are generally explained by the fact that the pedalling required is very simple [i.e. would be suggested by obvious changes of harmony]; **or** on the contrary that it is so subtle as to be too complicated, if not impossible to indicate.' Through numerous accounts we know that Chopin's pedalling was one of the most individual and entrancing characteristics of his playing. Liszt commented on his 'incomparably artistic use of the pedals' (Eigeldinger, p.273). Marmontel said that 'while making constant use of the pedal, he obtained ravishing harmonies, melodic whispers that charmed and astonished', and again, 'Chopin used the pedals with marvellous discretion. He often coupled them to obtain a soft and veiled sonority, but more often still he would use them separately for brilliant passages, for sustained harmonies, for deep bass notes and for loud ringing chords.' (Eigeldinger, pp.274 and 58).

Two important points have to be made. First, that the pianos of Chopin's day had a much clearer lighter sound, and a thinner overall resonance. This is particularly apparent when the sustaining pedal is used (when the dampers are raised): the strings vibrate less resonantly, and the resonance clears more quickly. On the other hand, when the sustaining pedal is **not** being used, a *staccato* will sound less sharp because the damping mechanism is less efficient. On the modern piano some of Chopin's pedal indications would create a heavy blurring, inimical to the clarity of his style, and we thus need to raise the pedal earlier, change it more frequently, or use effects of half-pedalling (see below). It has obviously been impossible to discuss the pedalling of each piece in detail. But in many of the more conspicuous cases, for example the coda of the Nocturne in D flat Op.27 No.2, bb.66-72, I have suggested judicious half-pedalling as opposed to the overall pedal indicated in Henle. Again, through the runs in the Nocturne in F sharp Op.15 No.2 (bb.11 and 51) we would either 'flutter' the pedal lightly or half change it lightly, or alternatively 'halo' the whole run in an overall but only very lightly **touched** pedal, in combination with the soft pedal. A particular problem arises in the case of the Waltzes and the Mazurkas, when on the modern piano the 'through-bar' pedalling indicated by Chopin would dull the essential spring of the dance movement (see the Introduction to each of these sections). None of the above is to suggest that we should **ever** disregard Chopin's indications. Invariably they throw light on his **intended effects,** effects which we may nowadays only achieve by the subtle tempering of our modern instruments.

Secondly, the attempt to realise Chopin's pedal effects on the modern piano depends on a proper understanding of the technique of half-pedalling. This means that instead of being raised to its full extent during a pedal change, the pedal is only **partially** raised. Then when it is re-depressed a proportion of the previous sound is retained in the 'new' pedal, so that a slight blurring or 'hazing' of the sound is created. This slight hazing was obviously the effect that Chopin wanted in the examples given above, and for which he indicated an overall pedal, suitable to his lighter piano. In fact the term half-pedalling is an inexact one, but I use it since it is the term in general use for the **idea** of partial depression of the pedal. Astonishingly it appears that even today many reasonably advanced students, and even many teachers, are unaware of the effects obtained by this partial depression and partial lifting of the pedal. The principle is as follows: when the pedal is fully depressed the dampers are lifted from the strings to the fullest possible extent, and the overall reverberation of the strings is at its fullest. When the pedal is depressed to half of its full extent, the dampers are only raised to half of **their** full extent, and consequently the overall reverberation is correspondingly reduced. For an experienced artist the possibilities are infinite – by varying the degree of pressure, i.e. by depressing the pedal to three-quarters, a quarter, or seven-eighths of its full extent, and similarly by raising it to varying proportions of its full extent, the degree of reverberation can be constantly varied, and the sound coloured and characterised at will. The merest touch of the pedal will give the sound a light glow, and can thus subtly highlight a single note or ornament. At the other extreme the fully depressed pedal will expand the sound of an arpeggio (as, for example, in the mighty arpeggios of the Study in C minor Op.25 No.12), or of a single *forte* note or chord. For example near the end of the Scherzo in B minor Op.20, one would give each of four staccato crotchet chords a short stroke of pedal (depressing and lifting the pedal in synchronisation with the hands) to give a 'boost' to the *fortissimo* resonance of these chords.

The 'fluttering' of the pedal referred to above (sometimes called *vibrato* pedalling) is self-explanatory – light, very quick touches of the pedal which can be used in quick passages for the subtle colouring and highlighting of certain 'points' of line or harmony (see the commentaries on the Studies in C minor Op.10 No.12 (Revolutionary) and F minor Op.25 No.2 for the application of this technique in very different contexts). Pedalling of this kind is dependent on the finest degree of aural and muscular coordination, such as we know Chopin possessed to a high degree. It is a question of instant communication and response between ear, fingers and feet, and the ability to adjust instantly to the qualities or failings of different pianos or acoustics – a 'study for life' indeed.

Where does this leave the averagely endowed player or the striving student? Chopin urged his pupils to 'use the pedal with the greatest economy' (Eigeldinger, p.57). He insisted, as thousand upon thousands of teachers have insisted since, that we should practise the music **without** the pedal. Firstly, because without the pedal we hear our mistakes and shortcomings, not merely of notes but of tone production, phrasing, etc. more clearly. Secondly, because we then hear and aurally 'understand' the pure unadorned sound of the music. Thus the purer the sound we absorb in the first place, the more discerning the ear becomes in 'directing' the colouring, or characterisation (rather than the distortion) of that sound by skilful use of the pedals. Chopin's exhortation to be economical with the pedal may seem to conflict with his own free but finely judged effects of pedalling. Perhaps, though, we can again find a guiding principle in the 'classic-romantic amalgam'. As J.-J. Eigeldinger suggests, 'It seems that Chopin's warning stems from his classical instincts, and from an anxiety that the multiple iridescence of his own playing should not be exaggerated.' (p.129).

Some students jam the sustaining pedal down to create an all-enveloping blanket of sound. Others, on the other hand, are often peculiarly puritanical in their approach to pedalling. In the opening of the Nocturnes in C minor Op.48 No.1 or in F minor Op.55 No.1, some will persistently change the pedal on each crotchet beat instead of holding the sound of the bass octave or note through each half-bar as indicated by Chopin. Or they will change the pedal in the **middle** of each bar in, for example, the Study in C minor Op.25 No.12, or the Study in F minor (Trois Nouvelles Etudes), thereby losing the resonance of the bass note through each whole bar. Instances of particular pedal effects required by Chopin occur between bb.1-2 in the Study in A flat Op.25 No.1, and the Ballade in F major Op.38. In the Study he deliberately 'mists' the melody line by changing the opening pedal only on the second beat of b.2. In the Ballade he sustains the opening pedal through to the second main beat of the second complete bar, thus allowing the tonic harmony to **merge** in, rather than announce itself, beneath the quietly advancing unisons. And J.-J. Eigeldinger notes an interesting peculiarity in Chopin's pedal indications, particularly in the Preludes and Nocturnes: often the final pedal is not cancelled – presumably to allow individual licence in the gauging of the duration of the last chord or note.

Similarly, the capacities of the soft pedal are widely underestimated. Students are often reluctant to use it, suggesting quaintly that they feel it is 'cheating'. As with the sustaining pedal, we should practise at first without it, encouraging the fingers to create the finest possible shades of *pianissimo* sound by means of touch alone. But the soft pedal does not merely soften the sound, it also creates a thinner quality of sound. It can thus invoke effects of distance or ethereal wraithes of 'disappearing' sound, and in combination with the sustaining pedal, the most subtle and fine-drawn variations and shadings of sound colour. Chopin gives no indications for the use of the soft pedal (save for a pencilled hint in the copy of the Nocturne in F sharp Op.15 No.2 belonging to Jane Stirling, bb.12, 18 and 58 – see commentary on this piece), but we know that he made free use of both pedals, and it would be unthinkable to play his veiled *pianissimo* or *leggierissimo* passages such as the ornamental runs in the same Nocturne in F sharp bb.11 and 51, or the coda of the Nocturne in D flat Op.27 No.2 without the use of both the sustaining **and** soft pedals. On the other hand Marmontel records that 'he would use the soft pedal alone for those light murmurings which seem to create a transparent vapour round the arabesques that embellish the melody, and envelope it like fine lace.' (Eigeldinger, p.58).

Readers are recommended once more to J.-J. Eigeldinger's book (pp.57-8 and 128-30); also to Joseph Banowetz's book *The Pianist's Guide to Pedalling* (Indiana University Press 1985), in which Chopin's pedalling is discussed in some detail.

Note: The old style of pedalling indication is cumbersome, 𝒫𝑒𝑑.   ✲   and does not allow exact definition of the moment of raising and depressing the pedal.
Thus

means

or better still

in the more accurate modern type of indication.

The means of achieving *legato* pedalling is not always precisely understood. To give a simple example: in the Prelude in C minor Op.28, the pedal is often changed too 'early', i.e. it is lifted just **before** each chord is struck and redepressed precisely **as** the chord is struck. In other words hands and feet lift and fall simultaneously thus producing the worst of all worlds:

not only will there be a break in the sound  but there

is also the risk of some 'hangover' from the previous harmony. To achieve the overall smooth sound with, at the same time, perfect clarity of harmony, the pedal needs to be raised at the moment that the new sound is **heard**, and re-depressed a further instant later, once that new

sound is clearly established: 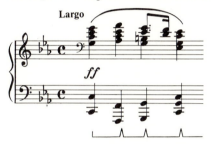 It is, it cannot be too

strongly emphasised, the responsibility of the **ear** to ascertain that the new sound is thus clearly established with no hangover from the previous harmony.

Another good example occurs in the Nocturne in F minor Op.55 No.1. Here, if the pedal is raised too early and redepressed simultaneously with each bass note, there will be the

'jiggy' effect of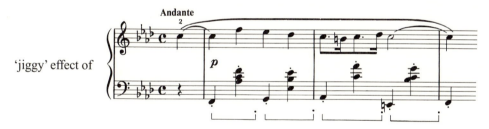

In addition, each bass note has to be held for an instant so that the foot has time to redepress the pedal to catch its sound. If the hand is whipped off the bass note in too sharp a *staccato* the foot will not have time to catch the essential quiet resonance of that bass note.

As Kendall Taylor says in his *Principles of Piano Technique and Interpretation* (Novello 1981) the 'advanced player who knows what he is doing' may well on occasion slightly delay the changing of the pedal, to create a deliberate overlap of sound for an ultra 'close' *legato*, or for some special expressive or atmospheric effect.

Tempo

Many of Chopin's earlier pieces have metronome marks, for example the Mazurkas up to Op.24, the Studies, the Nocturnes up to Op.27. We cannot however imagine that Chopin, of all people, set a fixed, one and only tempo for a work. Some of the metronome tempos given for the Studies are very fast, and doubtless Chopin himself could and did play them at such speeds. There are two points to bear in mind, however. Firstly that the pianos of his day had a shallower, lighter touch, and it was therefore easier to play faster than on a present day piano with its 'deeper' action. Secondly, that the sound was lighter, thinner and more clear-toned so that the sound remained clearer at faster speeds than may be possible on the modern piano with its more powerful booming resonance.

But this is not the whole story. As Thomas Higgins demonstrates ('Tempo and Character in Chopin', *The Musical Quarterly* No.59, USA 1973) it is evident that in quieter, more expressive pieces Chopin **also** tended towards faster tempos than we might expect today. For example, three pieces marked *lento ma non troppo*, the Study Op.10 No.3, and the Mazurkas Op.17 Nos 2 and 4 have metronome marks of ♪ = 100, ♩ = 144, and ♩ = 152 respectively – distinctly brisk, we may feel, for our idea of the character of each of these pieces. Then the Mazurka Op.7 No.2 has a metronome mark of ♩ = 160 – not so much faster than those for Op.17 Nos 2 and 4. But to increase our confusion it is marked *VIVO* ma non troppo, although it is of somewhat melancholy cast, like the two *lento ma non troppo* pieces in Op.17. The key here is evidently the modifying *ma non troppo*; as Thomas Higgins suggests, the difference between *vivo* (or *vivace*) *ma non troppo*, and *lento ma non troppo* was apparently only a slight one in Chopin's mind. In support of this idea is the example of the Mazurka Op.24 No.1 which has a straight *lento* with a metronome mark of ♩=108, more in line with our expectations of *lento* and also of the nature of the piece. But where does this leave us players, anxiously trying to realise Chopin's intentions? The possibility of faster speeds on the early instruments in, for example, the Studies, has been mentioned above. As a rider to this, is it not likely that Chopin, with his apparently unique refinement of touch, was able to convey nuances of expressive sound at faster speeds than we – our sensibilities blunted by the capacities of the nine-foot concert grand, the resonances of the vast public concert arena – can imagine, let alone realise today? We can but do our best, by **respecting** Chopin's metronome marks while at the same time realising that they may in certain circumstances need to be **tempered**. Time and time again students arrive with a new piece which they have barely begun to get to grips with, and say 'How fast does it go?' (or worse 'How fast do you want it?'!). This is, needless to say, an irrelevant question until the piece is thoroughly 'understood' in terms not only of notes, but of shape, rhythm, and expressive intent. It cannot be too strongly emphasised once these elements **are** fully absorbed, that it is always better to achieve a controlled, rhythmic and **shaped** performance than an over-ambitious and therefore scrambled one. In the matter of tempo in a 'fast' piece, we achieve what we can as best we can, as Chopin himself, as a busy teacher, coping with pupils of widely varying abilities must, however ruefully, have had to accept. This said, it is of course ridiculous to get up and try to **perform** a virtuosic piece without adequate technical equipment (although, as said below, the domestic pianist has nothing to lose and much to gain from the private **study** of Chopin's more virtuosic works). When Chopin has left no metronome marks, **all my suggestions for tempos are personal,** and are only intended as an approximate mean. Similarly personal are any suggestions for modification of Chopin's metronome marks.

Some Explanations and Amplifications

'Hairpins'
This is a nice descriptive term used by all musicians, but seldom found in musical dictionaries. It means the ⤐ ⤏ signs conveying smaller nuances of *crescendo* or *decrescendo* as opposed to a longer overall swelling or diminishing of sound.

'Pointing'
This is another term used by musicians, and certainly **not** found in musical dictionaries! It

means the marking of a fine nuance of line, harmony or rhythm by a subtle emphasis, or perhaps a slight lingering on a certain note or chord. In the Prelude No.4 in E minor for example, I have said 'Quietly "point" the interrupted cadence at bb.20-21 with a tiny swell as indicated'. Or in the Prelude No.6 in B minor I have said ' "Point" the emphasised RH upbeat to b.23 as if with a tiny push', meaning in both instances a subtle drawing attention to (as opposed to an actual accent on) this chord or cadence.

Breath Points

I use this term to indicate those naturally occurring points of punctuation in a phrase at which a singer might take a breath – part and parcel of the idea of shaping a melody as if it is being sung (see under 'Articulation', 'Phrasing', and '*Legato*'). Hence, in the commentaries I may say 'take a breath', or refer to a breathing point at various junctures in a phrase.

Portamento, Portato (or *Portando*) and *Parlando*

There has often been confusion between these terms, even among professional musicians and commentators. To clear the ground of at least one of these terms, as mentioned above, I have avoided the use of *parlando* (meaning speech-like) and have instead referred to the 'speaking' quality of such and such a figure or phrase, or suggested that certain notes be played in a 'speaking' manner. This intended 'speaking' quality is usually indicated in the music (and

frequently occurs in Chopin – see also under 'Articulation') by the notation ♩ ♩ ♩ ♩ .

In string playing this type of bowing is called *portato* (or sometimes *portando*), meaning 'carried'. To clear the ground yet further, I have used these terms, *portato* or *portando*, as little as possible, i.e. only in the occasional context when an analogy with this type of bowing seems particularly appropriate.

    Portamento means the 'carrying' of the voice in a different sense, from one pitch to another in a *glissando* effect, i.e. in a 'sliding' slur, so that the voice glides over the notes without actually articulating them. Sometimes I have suggested imagining the *portamento*-like effect of a rising or falling slurred figure or of a tiny cascade of falling grace notes.

Letting the Hand 'Come with You', and the 'Open' and 'Closed' Position of the Hand

Frequently in discussing the practising of technical passages I stress the importance of allowing the hand to 'come with you'. This is well illustrated in the Study in C Op.10 No.1. When the hand is in repose in its natural 'closed' position (lying loosely on a table-top or hanging by our side) the fingers rest in an easy curve, almost touching each other. When the hand is laterally extended in a fully 'open' position, the fingers are stretched as widely apart as possible. When the hand is in its natural 'closed' position, the fingers work with optimum ease and freedom. When the hand is fully extended it is under considerable tension, and the fingers can hardly move at all. Whenever possible, therefore, we want to maintain the hand in the natural 'closed' position, and when it has to stretch to reach a distant note, we want it to return to this natural 'closed' position as instantly as possible. Following a stretch, it is a common fault to 'leave' the hand in the open splayed-out position, with the result that the fingers cannot work freely, and that tension is maintained instead of being able to relax for an instant ready for the next stretch. Tension is then allowed to build up and the hand soon seizes up. In the following extract from the Study in C, once the right hand thumb has struck the C and the hand begins to move towards the E on the second beat of the bar, the inexperienced or tense player will tend to leave the thumb hanging over the C (i.e. leaving the hand in the 'open' position) instead of letting the body of the hand 'come with itself' as it moves up the keyboard towards the E. On reaching the

E the hand has to be completely and loosely 'closed' so that the thumb can play the C, ready for the whole hand to move up towards the next E, and so on. Then the process is reversed on the way 'downhill' through b.2.

Similarly in the Study in A minor Op.10 No.2 the instant that the thumb and forefinger have struck the third beneath the upper chromatic line on the first beat of b.1, this inner part of the hand needs to move upwards 'along with' the outer fingers so that the hand is maintaining a relaxed 'closed' natural position, and the thumb and forefinger are ready to strike the inner fourth on the second beat, and so on.

What tends to happen is that the thumb and forefinger 'hang on' over the semiquaver third on the first beat so that the hand remains in an 'open' extended position – the outer fingers then cannot work properly and tension immediately starts to build up. This principle applies in numerous instances, see also for example the Study in E flat Op.10 No.11.

'Directioning' the Hand

This is another term I use in discussing the technical problems of wide leaps, as, for example, when you have to leap off a bass note to a chord some distance 'up' the keyboard, and back

again  . The arm and hand need to leap from the bass

note with a little spring or 'kick' which 'directions' the hand in an economical arc **up** the keyboard towards the upper chord. Having played this upper chord the arm and hand is then 'directioned' downward towards the next bass note, and so on. What so often happens is that the hand leaps off the bass note in a vague 'up-in-the-air', undirected movement instead of 'using' the time and space in the most economical way by 'directioning' the hand towards its objective. When there is a continuing series of such leaps, as in the left hand of the Study in A minor Op.25 No.4, for example, a neat pendulum-like movement needs to be established with the hand continually being 'directioned' upwards and downwards between each bass

note and chord

See also the study in F Op.25 No.3 for a similar application of this principle.

'Lifting the Hand From' or 'Lifting Up To'

In the commentaries there are frequent exhortations a) to 'lift' the hand from a note or chord; b) to feel the 'lift' **up to** a note. In case this causes confusion, lift the hand from (or lift the hand after) a note means bring the hand **off** the keyboard, in order to 'show' a rest; or to implement

the intended articulation of a figure, such as, for example ♩ 𝄾 ♩ ♩ or ♩ 𝅗𝅥 (see above under 'Articulation').

'Feel the "lift" up to', or 'imagine a vocal "lift" up to' means feel the rise in the melodic line up to a higher note. A good example of this occurs in the Nocturne in F sharp minor Op.48 No.2, bb.3 and 5. Here I say: 'imagine a vocal "lift"' as you rise lightly to the F sharp on the

second beat of b.3 [music example] . Then again in b.5 'lift' lightly up

to the F sharp on the second beat [music example] . This suggests

the manner in which a singer shapes a *cantabile* melodic line, with the sense of a 'lift' of the voice up to, and down from the highest note in a phrase (see above under 'Phrasing'). In keyboard terms this means feeling the 'lift' of the line in this vocal sense, up to such a higher note, within an overall *legato* (unless specific articulation is indicated.)

The sense of such a 'lift' is often implied through an upbeat: see for example the upbeat

to the Prelude in E minor [music example] or to the Mazurka Op.17

No.1 [music example] *fz*

Allowing the Hand to Come 'Well In'

The relatively inexperienced player is inclined to play 'off the edge of the keyboard', getting as far away from the black notes as possible. This means that frantic inward lurches have to be made to 'reach' the black notes. This is disastrous for the equilibrium both of the hand and the nerves. It will be observed that when we play the chord of F sharp, the hand has to be 'well in' towards the back of the keyboard in order for the thumb and fifth finger to be placed securely on the F sharps. In this position the hand is so 'well in' that, providing the fingers are lying loosely (i.e. not stiffly 'curled under') the longest finger, the third, will be virtually touching the lid of the piano. This shows how far 'in' towards the back of the keyboard the hand has to be when we have to reach a black note with the thumb or fifth finger. Hence, in a passage in which the hand has to be 'ready' for the black notes, I often say 'Keep the hand well in', meaning well **onto** the keyboard, not hanging off the edge of the keys.

A simple example occurs in the opening of the Prelude No.20 in C minor. If we play the first right hand chord with the thumb and fifth finger on the outer edge of the two G's we then have a long way to 'move in' in order to reach the A flat chord on the second beat. If instead we play the first chord with the hand 'well in' towards the black notes, we have only to shift the hand a

very little inwards and up towards the right to reach the A flat chord.

Judging Climaxes

The deadening effect of relentlessly maintained *fortissimo* has been touched upon under 'Chopin's Playing'. Often, however, we encounter a different problem – that of failing, either through diffidence or misperception, to 'go through' to the climax of a *crescendo*, and/or to a harmonic or expressive **objective** which may well be the climax of the whole piece. I thus suggest that in various instances many players do not 'follow through' a *crescendo* or onward impetus to the point Chopin appears to indicate. Examples of this occur in the Study in A flat Op.25 No.1 through the *crescendo* from b.32 towards b.36, in the Study in G flat Op.25 No.9, the *fortissimo appassionata* from b.33 to b.37, and in the Nocturne in C minor Op.48 No.1, the continuing *crescendo* from b.72 through to the grand final arrival on the unison tonic on the first beat of b.74. These, however, are personal opinions which it is apparent that many eminent performers do not share!

'Going to'

In case the frequent exhortations 'let the quavers "go to" the minim on the first beat', or 'feel that the semiquavers are "going to" a singing dotted crotchet', etc. are not quite understood, they merely mean: feel the onward-moving impulse from the 'weaker' (usually shorter) notes, towards the 'stronger' (usually longer) one. This feeling of onward (but not hurried) movement towards stronger stressed notes is vital to the shaping of the phrases, and to the overall onward impetus of the music.

The Left Hand

In the commentaries it will be noticed that I continually stress the importance (ad nauseam, as it may seem) of the left hand. Its importance and true role is, I believe, in general greatly underestimated. In the vast majority of instances (although the roles are, of course, sometimes reversed), the left hand (LH) gives the fundamental rhythmic and harmonic foundation to the music. Various composers at various times have pointed this out, and Chopin himself said it best: 'the LH is the conductor, it must not waver or lose ground; do with the RH what you will and can'. This applies as much to the music of the Classical period as to that of Chopin's own day. And Ralph Kirkpatrick, the great harpsichordist and teacher, describing his method of studying, for example, a Bach Prelude, said that he would 'nearly always start with the bass line'. When the rhythm is going awry, and the motion of the piece is faltering, it is amazing, when a student is asked to pay attention to the LH, how naturally things will often right themselves.

I am not talking here of those instances when the LH carries the obvious melodic line, as, for example, in the opening of the Waltz in A minor Op.34 No.2, or in the coda of this piece from b.169; or the Prelude No.6 in B minor. (In these instances it is the RH which is the 'conductor'.) It is often when the LH is ostensibly providing 'merely' an accompaniment (as for instance in the Waltzes or in many Nocturnes, particularly, for example, in Op.15 No.2 or Op.27 No.2) that its role is especially important as 'guardian' of the rhythm, as the ever present guide to the RH, and as chief motivator **and** controller of the overall rhythmic impulse of the piece or movement (see more detailed discussion of this matter under '*Rubato*' and ' 'Free' Runs'.

Upbeats

Explanations of this term, not always familiar to or entirely understood by players who have never had experience of ensemble playing, are not always easy to find in musical dictionaries. It means the beat before, or leading to, the main accent. The Prelude No.7 in A major gives a simple example

The opening crotchet E is the upbeat to the first beat of b.1; the RH third on the third beat of b.2 is the upbeat to the first beat of b.3, and so on. An upbeat can consist of more than one note. There may be a dotted rhythm figure as, for example, in the opening upbeat to the Prelude No.4

in E minor  *etc.* or a longer group as, for example, in the ornamented

opening upbeat group to the Waltz in G flat major Op.posth.70 No.1

In the case of the Nocturne in B flat minor Op.9 No.1 the opening solo quaver group, half a bar's worth, has very much an upbeat sense, drawing us on into the beginning of the movement proper from the first beat of b.1.

In Chopin's music upbeats assume particular importance. The upbeat not only announces and leads us into the rhythm of the piece as a whole – it similarly announces and prepares the way into the prevailing mood of the piece or of a new section. In the examples quoted above, the opening dotted rhythm upbeat figure to the Prelude in E minor has a 'laden' expressive significance, preparing us for the sorrowful mien of the piece as a whole; while the airy treble upbeat group to the G flat Waltz careers us straight into the spirit of this dizzy waltz movement. Where a piece begins on the upbeat it is all the more essential to have the beat and mood 'in the system' before starting (see under 'Rhythm'), and to **feel** the silent first beat (or beats) of the opening bar so that the opening upbeat can be perfectly timed and poised to give a clear sense of 'leading in'. Similarly during the course of a piece, upbeats must always give the sense of 'leading on', into the next bar, phrase or section.

Often when upbeats are slurred or tied, a degree of emphasis, a feeling of 'leaning' is

50

implied (see also under 'Slurred and Tied Notes'). In the large majority of instances, in order to convey the 'onward' feeling, I use the term 'upbeat' rather than 'last beat'. So I will refer to the 'upbeat' to b.2, for example, rather than to the 'last beat of b.1'. Similarly, although it may be a loose use of the term, I may, in a movement in **4/4** time for example, refer to the 'upbeat to the third beat of the bar'.

Dotted Rhythm

The timing of dotted rhythms is a cause of endless frustration. In Chopin's music dotted rhythm figures are often of special expressive significance, and are also a particular feature of his Mazurka rhythms. The recurring dotted rhythm figure in the Prelude No.15 in D flat, for example, has a most expressive 'fall'; similarly the opening dotted rhythm figure of the Mazurka in A in Op.17 No.4 has an equally expressive 'rise'. In these instances there may be a hint of lingering on the dotted quaver with the semiquaver also having a special 'speaking' quality. In a grand march-like dotted rhythm, on the other hand, as in the Prelude No.20 in C minor,

the dotted rhythm has to be timed with absolute precision. The usual problem is that the dotted quaver is not given its full duration, so that the semiquaver 'arrives' too soon and is then 'allowed' too long a value. The rhythm then becomes sloppily tripletised, and loses its clear-cut martial quality, usually in addition giving the feeling of continually 'falling onwards' into the next beat. If the player counts in **quavers**, and really **feels** each quaver pulse, they can then usually place the semiquaver mid-way **between** one quaver pulse and the next. The other fault is that of 'double dotting', or making the dotted quaver too long and cutting the semiquaver short. In the C minor Prelude this effect would be too clipped, even 'jiggy' and the overall rhythm would lose its 'backbone' and grandeur.

For inexperienced (and sometimes **not** so inexperienced players) who have trouble in 'getting' dotted rhythms, it is a good plan to practise simple exercises i.e. 'five finger exercises', scale figures, or simple broken-chord figures in a dotted rhythm throwing the main weight onto the **dotted** notes, and keeping the semiquavers relatively light. Almost immediately, although the first few beats may be fairly well timed, the 'short' note, the semiquaver (or the demisemiquaver), tends to get gradually longer and heavier so that the overall beat is progressively undermined. The problem is that the player finds it difficult to **wait** for long enough on the **dotted** note, consequently the short note arrives too soon and it is therefore too long – it becomes 'tripletised', or in extreme cases even 'quaverised'! It is essential to feel the dotted note as the **main** beat, and to feel that the short note, the semiquaver or demisemiquaver is 'going to' the main beat in the sense of an **upbeat**. Hence in the commentaries I frequently suggest feeling the short notes as the upbeat to the dotted note.

If all else fails, walking around the room in dotted rhythm, pretending that the left leg is lame so that all the weight is thrown onto the right leg, can sometimes do the trick!

Note: The ♪ ♪ ♪ figure which occurs so frequently in Chopin's music is, of course, in effect an 'articulated' dotted rhythm. Since there is no generally accepted term for this figure, it is also, for the sake of simplicity, referred to in the commentaries as a 'dotted rhythm'.

Chords
We usually think of a chord as a combination of three or more notes. In the commentaries, for the sake of simplicity, I refer to all combinations of notes (thirds, fifths, etc.) as well as to triads and larger combinations, as chords.

Beat and Pulse
These terms are more or less interchangeable. The one may seem more appropriate than the other for reasons that can be sensed but not always defined! The connotations of 'beat' are more outward, defined, mathematical, than those of pulse, more inward, living, even metaphysical. On the other hand I might say, in a **4/4** bar for example: 'Come in clearly on the sixth **quaver pulse** of the bar', to differentiate between the quaver 'pulse' and the main crotchet 'beat'. Unless the term 'beat' is qualified ('quaver beat', 'crotchet beat', etc.), it always refers to the **main** beats of the bar, e.g. the **crotchet** beat in a **2/4, 3/4**, or **4/4** time and the **dotted crotchet** in a **6/8** time.

Pedal Points
This is a term not always clearly understood, and not to be confused with references to the sustaining, or soft pedal of the piano. It is particularly prone to cause confusion when it is referred to just as a 'pedal'. It derives from the foot pedal notes on the organ, which can be held beneath a series of progressions, often of considerable length, played on the manuals. On the piano it takes the form of a note (frequently the dominant or tonic) held, or consistently repeated, in the lower part, beneath the progressions or varying activities (often sequential) of the upper parts. If the held or consistently repeated note occurs in one of the upper parts it becomes an 'inverted pedal'.

There are many instances of long pedal point effects in Chopin. In the Nocturne in D flat Op.27 No.2, for example, the entire coda (sixteen bars) proceeds over a tonic pedal point (b.62 to the end). Again in the Prelude No.21 in B flat there is a dominant pedal point through the *crescendo* from bb.33-9.

The pedal point occurs widely in folk music, when it is usually referred to as a drone or bourdon. These effects are inherent to the harmonic and textural character of the Mazurkas, and occur to some extent in almost every number. There are clear examples in No.5 (Op.7 No.1) the reiterated LH fifth through the *sotto voce* section (bb.45-51) or in No.11 (Op.17 No.2) in the bass (bb.38-51). Often they occur less obviously, embedded in the harmonic texture, as the long tied note through the opening motif of No.35 in C minor (Op.56 No.3) – the long G from the opening upbeat through to b.4 and then the long D from bb.5-7, and so on. This Mazurka also has a tonic pedal-point through most of its magnificent coda (bb.189-220).

'Finish Off'
Failure to 'finish off' a phrase or figure properly is the cause of the frequent tendency to 'fall

52

onwards' onto a subsequent beat or phrase, or over a rest. This applies particularly in the Waltzes and Mazurkas when the RH may finish a phrase or section on a crotchet, minim, or dotted minim or slurred figure while the LH carries on to 'finish' its own line, for example

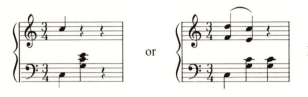

or   Hence my frequent exhortation to

'finish off' the LH clearly before leading off into the next bar. For example, in the Waltz in A minor Op.34 No.2, b.36, the LH must 'finish off' neatly on the second beat ready for the RH to lead on with a clear emphasised upbeat to b.37 to 'prepare' the new mood of this

next section.   Or in the Mazurka No.1 in F

sharp minor (Op.6 No.1) b.16, I stress the importance of 'finishing off' the *pianissimo* triplet figure neatly to a precise crotchet on the second beat, ready to 'kick off' with the upbeat to the

subsequent *fortissimo* section   This may apply

equally in the RH. For example in the Prelude No.6 in B minor, the RH needs to 'finish off' its phrase cleanly and graciously through the second beat of b.8, ready for the LH to lead on

with the upbeat quavers to b.9.

Slurs and Tied or Syncopated Notes

Slurs are immensely important to the rhythmic and expressive character of the music. For some strange reason students who will happily 'show' them on a stringed instrument or in a vocal part, will ignore them when playing the piano. Consequently I frequently draw attention to them – I feel that the right effect is better conveyed by the suggestion of 'leaning on' rather than 'accenting' a slurred note. Slurs are an important part of Chopin's expressive language, and true to his devotion to the singer's art, need to be felt and implemented in a 'vocal' manner.

Tied notes (or chords) always require a degree of emphasis, gentle and melodic, or strong, even forceful according to context, in order that their sound shall carry over the subsequent beat or beats. A number of the Mazurkas have tied upbeats, and these need a specially significant 'onward leaning' emphasis ready to launch off into the rhythm from the subsequent first beat. Syncopated notes require a similar emphasis in order that they shall 'make their point' and that they shall also sound on over the subsequent 'normal' beat. Hence, I frequently say: ' "feel" or "show" the implied emphasis on such-and-such a tied or syncopated note'.

Practising in Rhythms

I frequently suggest practising a rapid semiquaver passage in various rhythms. This is a standard method of practising, and one constantly advocated by Cortot in his Study Editions of Chopin's works. The causing of the longer, stronger beats to fall on different

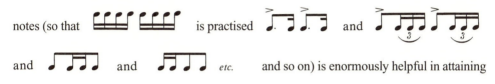

notes (so that ⬚⬚⬚⬚ ⬚⬚⬚⬚ is practised ♩.♪♩.♪ and ♩♫♩♫ and

and ♩♫♩ and ♫♩♩ *etc.* and so on) is enormously helpful in attaining

eventual fluency, evenness and control.

Dynamic and Agogic Accents

The term 'agogic' has gained increasing currency over recent years. An agogic accent means an emphasis created by a slight **lengthening** rather than dynamic emphasis on a note or chord.

The realisation of Chopin's indications for accentuation (*sf,* or *fz,* > and ⬐) is a complex matter, particularly in view of their varying interpretations by different editors. The *sforzato* sign *sf* (or *fz*) clearly means a dynamic accent, of varying intensity according to the context. If the prevailing dynamic is *piano,* the *sforzato* will be required to 'make its point' in relation to, and in proportion with, that prevailing *piano.* In a prevailing *forte,* the *sforzato* will require a correspondingly stronger emphasis in order to stand out from that prevailing *forte.*

In his Preface to those volumes of the Vienna Urtext which he has edited, Jan Ekier points to a clear difference between the indications > and ⬐). He says that 'for Chopin, the short accent (>) denotes a louder dynamic, whereas the longer accent (⬐) implies an expressive stress'. This will be implemented respectively as a shorter, sharper accent, or a longer, more expressive and slightly lingering agogic 'lean'. Numerous instances of both types occur within the same piece. In the Nocturne in F sharp major Op.15 No.2, for example, the longer accent occurs on the dotted semiquaver on the opening upbeat, the quaver on the first beat of b.2, and so on, suggesting this kind of expressive, very slightly lingering 'lean'.

Then on the high tied quaver F sharp in b.14 we have the short accent suggesting a firmer, more

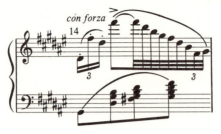

emphatic emphasis.

Again we have a short accent

on the inner LH minim on the first beat of b.33,

and in b.36

there is a particularly illuminating instance: a **short** accent in the RH on the treble minim G sharp and the inner LH B on the first beat, and then a staggered, softer 'lean' effect on the inner LH

C natural and then the inner RH C natural.

These differences of nuance go unremarked in many editions, but are admittedly difficult to interpret in print since the autographs display a variety of lengths and accents between > and ➣.

Also, in the context of the Mazurkas, J.-J. Eigeldinger states that 'this dynamic accent (*sf* or *fz*) should be distinguished from the agogic accent which lengthens the note, indicated by ➣' (p.148). This, again, we would interpret as a slightly lingering 'lean'. He goes on to quote cases in which Chopin uses both a *sforzato* and a > on the same beat or note – Op.6 No.1 (bb.42, 44, etc.); No.2 (b.40); and No.4 (bb.4, 8, etc.), implying here, he suggests, both a dynamic **and** an agogic emphasis. He goes on to cite a particularly telling example of varying types of accentuation within a short passage in Op.24 No.1, bb.17-21.

Here there will be an agogic 'lean' on the first triplet note on the second beat of b.17 with a sense of 'moving on' over the third beat, and similarly as this figure repeats through the first two beats of b.18, creating a momentary **2/4** pattern. (Most editions do not differentiate between the longer or shorter agogic 'lean' here, or elsewhere (> or ➣)). This slight 'hold' on the first note of the triplet accords with the idea of the idiomatic slight 'distortion' of the rhythm mentioned in the introduction to the Mazurkas. These are, need it be said, subtleties of emphasis upon which no hard and fast rules can be propounded (particularly as regards the > or ⋗ emphases) and have to be interpreted according to context, and in the light of the experience that we hope to acquire in the continuing study of Chopin's music.

The  **Question ...**

Jan Ekier, editor of several volumes of the Vienna Urtext Edition, has raised a hornets' nest by his statement that in Chopin's music the occurrence of a triplet and dotted rhythm within the same beat should be understood 'in the eighteenth-century sense'; i.e. that the dotted note

should be treated also as a triplet, so that   becomes   Thus in his editions

he indicates that, for example, in the Nocturne in F Op.15 No.1, in b.3 the melody should sound

And similarly in the Nocturne in C sharp Op.27 No.1, b.5 etc.

should sound   *etc.*   Players must consult their own gurus and

their own intuitions on this matter. Suffice it to say that in a slowish, expressive context as in the above examples, I have never heard this interpretation except in Professor Ekier's own recordings on the Polish label Muza. In nine cases out of ten in a slowish context I prefer the conventional reading – the more expressive and/or piquant nuance of the dotted rhythm 'against' the triplet. But this is a personal view – the controversy will doubtless roll on. (In a faster context however – as for example in the Polonaise-Fantaisie in the long passage from

b.254 – the Baroque/Classical practice, i.e.   =   , will indeed usually apply.)

Editions

Chopin, so meticulous in so many ways, was apparently surprisingly haphazard in the matter of shepherding his manuscripts through the actual process of publication. Also, since most of his works were published in simultaneous 'first' editions in France, Germany and England, and since he also made alterations in the scores of various pupils, there are inevitably many discrepancies. Editors thus have almost insoluble problems in attempting to settle upon his 'final' versions. Needless to say, over the generations every known publisher has leapt on to the bandwagon, and legions of irresponsible editors have added to the problems. Until recently the Peters, Schirmer and Augener Editions were perhaps the most widely used, all of which were to some degree 'edited'.

Special mention must also be made of the Cortot *Editions de Travail* which have been extensively quoted below, particularly in connection with the Studies. Unfortunately Cortot has not differentiated between his own and Chopin's indications in the music. But he was an eminent, if sometimes erratic interpreter of Chopin, and his practice plans and exercises are thorough, and often illuminating. Cortot was born in 1877. If some of his verbal interpretations of the music may today provoke a smile, his imaginative flights, which stop short of actual programming, often have something to say to our more prosaic age.

In the 1930s a valuable edition edited by the French scholar Edouard Ganche was published by Oxford University Press. This was based on the scores belonging to Jane Stirling, as well as various manuscript sources, and is usually known as the 'Oxford Edition'.

Of recent years three reliable editions have emerged, or are in the process of completion. First came the Complete Works published by the Frederyk Chopin Institute (Polish Music Publications), based on autographs and original editions. This is an excellent and inexpensive edition, only marred by the fact that certain modifications made by the editors, particularly in the matter of phrase slurs, are not always specified. It must also be mentioned that the paper has been of poor quality, and there is a tendency for the bindings to split. (Recent copies, however, seem much improved in these respects.) The titular editor is Paderewski, 'assisted' by L. Bronarski and J. Turczyński. This is the preferred edition of many players. It is by far the most user-friendly of the relatively modern editions, with copious critical commentaries, and some advice on performance in a helpful short section entitled 'The Character of the Present Edition'. This widely available edition is published in no less than eight languages, and is usually known as, and referred to below as the Paderewski Edition.

The Henle Urtext Edition has recently been virtually completed, save for some of the unfamiliar pieces published in the Paderewski Edition's Volume of 'Minor Works'. This, like all Henle editions, is beautifully and spaciously printed. I keenly wish, however, as I urged in my previous volume on Haydn, that these publishers would descend from their ivory tower, accept that the 'grass-roots' pianist is not a scholar, and supply more information and guidance on matters of performance.

The Vienna Urtext Edition is equally scholarly, and a great deal less aloof, particularly in those volumes edited by Jan Ekier, who gives excellent introductions to the Nocturnes, Scherzos, Ballades and Impromptus. A wider range of sources is taken into account than by Henle, resulting in a generally more comprehensive coverage of annotations (including fingerings) made by Chopin in the scores of various pupils. The Editorial Notes are given in English as well as in German.

In our present climate, with its continuing quest for authenticity, I have felt obliged, in compiling the commentaries below, to use one of these two 'Urtext' Editions. (It must always be remembered that Urtext – meaning 'original text' – is always, with the best will in the world, an inexact term, above all in relation to Chopin for the reasons given above.) Since the

Vienna Urtext is unfortunately as yet incomplete, the choice inevitably fell upon Henle. However, in view of the reservations already expressed, players may prefer to opt for the Paderewski Edition, or where possible, to the Vienna Urtext, in which the Preludes, Ballades, Studies, Nocturnes, Impromptus and Scherzos have appeared to date (1997).

In Poland a new National Edition is in the course of production under the editorship of Jan Ekier (Polskie Wydawnictwo Muzyczne). At present (1991) the Ballades, Scherzos, Études, Impromptus, Concerto in F minor, and a volume of Minor Works has been issued.

Bar Numberings

Bar numberings, tempo and dynamic indications, etc. are all taken from the Henle Urtext Edition unless otherwise stated (see under 'Editions'). For those with editions without bar numbers, there are two important points concerning the calculation of the numbers.

i)   Bar 1 is always the first **whole** bar. Therefore, if a piece or movement is divided into 16-bar sections, and starts on an upbeat or half-bar, that upbeat or half-bar will be 'added up' with the part bar at the end of the section to make bar 16, and the first **whole** bar of the new section will be bar 17. In the Mazurka in A minor Op.7 No.2, for example, the opening upbeat is 'added on' to the end of the last bar of the first section to make a complete bar 16 and the first complete bar of the second section is bar 17.

ii) In cases where there are first- and second-time bars, only one of them is 'counted', in effect the second-time bar. See the Mazurka in G minor Op.24 No.1: when the first section is played for the first time, the first-time bar is bar 32, and when the section is repeated, the **second-time** bar becomes bar 32 and the first bar of the next section is bar 33.

Note: This has been the general practice in most editions and applies in the Henle Edition. However, in the Paderewski Edition, and in some new editions, notably some of those recently published by the Associated Board, the policy is to count **both** the first- and second-time bars. In those few cases where Chopin gives first- and second-time bars, for example in a few of the Waltzes and the Mazurkas, this would cause discrepancies in the bar numberings.

Suggestions for Further Reading

The literature on Chopin is vast, running into not hundreds but thousands of volumes. Most of these are mainly biographical, and many, as has been said above, give an inaccurate and romanticised picture. For a brief general account, that devoted Chopin scholar Arthur Hedley's *Chopin* in the Master Musician Series (Dent) can seldom have been bettered. He presents a clear and objective yet acutely perceptive view both of the man and the musician. This volume, however, has now been superseded in the Master Musicians Series in an expanded new book by Jim Samson incorporating the latest research and thinking, in an authoritative new account of Chopin's life and music (Oxford University Press 1966). George Marek and Maria Gordon-Smith, in their *Chopin* (Weidenfeld and Nicolson) succeed admirably in freeing Chopin from his 'poor, frail and tubercular image appearing like a wraith in the overheated salons of oversentimental countesses', as also does Adam Zamoyski's *Chopin* (Collins). Jeremy Siepmann's new book, *Chopin, the Reluctant Romantic* (Gollancz 1995) is unmissable, both for its cogent presentation of Chopin in the context of his time and his relationships, and for the author's refreshingly personal, persuasive and thought-provoking views of the music. The title of Adam Harasowski's *The Skein of Legends around Chopin* (MacLellan 1967) speaks for itself. For those with a particular interest in the subject the author builds a detailed and fascinating case-book on the circumstances and persons responsible for the Chopin mythology.

(This author's further work 'Frederic Chopin, His Life and Music' is unfortunately not yet published.) Frederick Nieck's two-volume work *The Life of Chopin* (Novello, 1888) gives the view of a scholar much closer to Chopin's own time, and as such is of immense interest today, as well as providing many direct links with those who knew Chopin or had heard him play.

Chopin's letters make delightful reading. He is seldom dull, often funny and touching as well as biting, even catty, and sometimes refreshingly earthy. Unfortunately there is no complete Edition of the existing letters in English. However, there is a selection of letters edited by Arthur Hedley (Heinemann, 1962) and another collected by Henryk Opieński (this latter said to be inaccurate in details and dates).

Jan Kleczyński's *Chopin; an interpretation of his works* (Felix Mackar, Paris 1880) throws valuable light on Chopin, both as player and teacher. Kleczyński was not a pupil of Chopin, but worked with three of his most faithful students, Marcelina Czartoryska, Camille O'Meara Dubois and Georges Mathias, all of whom contributed warm appreciations of Kleczyński's exposition of the Chopin tradition. A particularly important section of this book, concerning the 'main precepts of punctuation and musical reading and delivery' is given in the Appendix below.

Until comparatively recently there have been surprisingly few books in English dealing principally with the music. Herbert Weinstock in his *Chopin, the Man and his Music* (Alfred A. Knopf, 1959) does discuss the music in general terms (detailed under Opus Numbers). While his observations on the music are often of value, he has also been quoted below in several instances to demonstrate how much the appreciation of Chopin has grown, even since the date of his book. Gerald Abraham's *Chopin's Musical Style* (OUP, 1939) and *Chopin, Profiles of the Man and his Music,* edited by Alan Walker (Barrie and Jenkin, 1966), were apparently until recently the only books in English devoted to the music. In the latter a distinguished array of musicians contribute individual sections on different aspects of Chopin's work and style. Now we have Jim Samson's *The Music of Chopin* (Routledge and Kegan Paul, 1985) which has been extensively quoted below. Although some aspects of Schenkerian analytical thought will perhaps be lost on many 'ordinary' musicians, his insights into Chopin are unfailingly penetrating. In another interesting but little-known work, *Chopin the Composer*, (Schirmer, 1913), Edgar Stillman Kelley discusses the influences of folk music on Chopin. In this individual and doubtless controversial study he details widespread modal and even Eastern characteristics in, in particular, the Mazurkas.

Recently translated into English is a 'bible' for pianists, J.-J. Eigeldinger's *Chopin, Pianist and Teacher, as seen by his pupils* (Cambridge, 1986). This is a veritable Aladdin's cave of insight into Chopin's style, both from the recorded impressions of contemporary musicians as well as from his pupils, and also for Professor Eigeldinger's own interpretations and expansions upon the reminiscences. He brings us as near as we are ever likely to approach the complex and unique musical personality of Chopin.

And further major additions to the literature have appeared within the last few years. *Chopin Studies*, edited by Jim Samson (Cambridge 1988) and *Chopin Studies 2*, edited by John Rink and Jim Samson (Cambridge 1994) are important collections of analytical essays by leading scholars, representing the most recent research into all aspects of Chopin's music.

The Cambridge Companion to Chopin (Cambridge 1992) equally important but more geared to the general reader, and again edited by Jim Samson is a further collection of extended essays by leading authorities covering the growth of Chopin's style, and with profiles of the various genres and discussions of historical reception.

A GRADED LIST OF CHOPIN'S WORKS FOR SOLO PIANO

All works are published in the Henle Edition **unless otherwise stated** (see General Introduction under 'Editions'). They are also numbered below as in the Henle Edition. **Numberings may differ in other editions**. For further details about publication of little-known works see individual commentaries.

Bar numberings and indications for tempo, dynamics, and phrasing, referred to below, are also based on the Henle Edition unless otherwise stated, and **may differ from those in other editions** (see General Introduction under 'Editions').

* = Works which have only recently (or rarely) been published (see Preface).

O = More suitable for older players (see Preface).

Grades 4-5

PRELUDES
    No.4 in E minor (Op.28)
O No.7 in A major (Op.28)
O No.20 in C minor (Op.28)

MAZURKAS
    No.9 in C major (Op.7 No.5)
    No.48 in F major (Op.posth.68 No.3)
O No.49 in F minor (Op.posth.68 No.4)

WALTZES
   *No.17 in A minor
   *No.18 in E flat major

MISCELLANEOUS WORKS
   *Cantabile in B flat major (published in Paderewski Edition
        Vol.XVIII – Minor Works)
O*Feuille d'Album (published in Paderewski Edition Vol.XVIII –
      Minor Works)

Grade 6

PRELUDES
    No.6 in B minor (Op.28)
O No.9 in E major (Op.28)

MAZURKAS

    No.5 in B flat major (Op.7 No.1)
    No.6 in A minor (Op.7 No.2)
    No.11 in E minor (Op.17 No.2)
    No.14 in G minor (Op.24 No.1)
    No.15 in C major (Op.24 No.2)
    No.16 in A flat major (Op.24 No.3)
O   No.18 in C minor (Op.30 No.1)
    No.19 in B minor (Op.30 No.2)
O   No.22 in G sharp minor (Op.33 No.1)
O   No.24 in C major (Op.33 No.3)
O   No.40 in F minor (Op.63 No.2)
    No.43 in G minor (Op.posth.67 No.2)
    No.44 in C major (Op.posth.67 No.3)
    No.45 in A minor (Op.posth.67 No.4)
    No.47 in A minor (Op.posth.68 No.2)
  *No.50 in G major (No.53 in Paderewski – two versions)
  *No.51 in B flat major (No.52 in Paderewski – two versions)
  *Appendix – No.1 in A flat major (early version of Op.7 No.4)
  *Appendix – No.2 in D major (No.54 in Paderewski)
  *Appendix – No.3 in A major (early version of Op.7 No.2)

WALTZES

    No.3 in A minor (Op.34 No.2)
    No.10 in B minor (Op.posth.69 No.2 – two versions)
    No.12 in F minor (Op.posth.70 No.2 – two versions)
  *No.14 in A flat major (No.16 in Paderewski)
  *No.15 in E major (also No.15 in Paderewski)

POLONAISES

  *No.11 in G minor
  *No.12 in B flat major

NOCTURNES

  *No.21 in C minor (Also published in Vienna Urtext Edition,
     and in Paderewski Edition Vol.XVIII – Minor Works)

MISCELLANEOUS WORKS

  *Contradanse (published in Paderewski Edition Vol.XVIII
     – Minor Works)
O *Largo in E flat major (published in Paderewski Edition Vol.XVIII
     – Minor Works)

Grade 7

PRELUDES

O No.2 in A minor (Op.28)
   No.13 in F sharp major (Op 28)
   No.14 in E flat minor (Op.28)
   No.15 in D flat major (Op.28)
   No.21 in B flat major (Op.28)
 *Prelude in A flat major

MAZURKAS

   No.2 in C sharp minor (Op.6 No.2 – two versions)
   No.3 in E major (Op.6 No.3)
O No.4 in E flat minor (Op.6 No.4)
   No.7 in F minor (Op.7 No.3)
   No.8 in A flat major (Op.7 No.4)
   No.12 in A flat major (Op.17 No.3)
   No.13 in A minor (Op.17 No.4)
   No.26 in E minor (Op.41 No.1. Often listed as Op.41 No.2 – see
      commentary)
   No.28 in A flat major (Op.41 No.3. Often listed as Op.41 No.4 – see
      commentary)
   No.31 in A flat major (Op.50 No.2)
   No.41 in C sharp minor (Op.63 No.3)
   No.52 in A minor (No.43 in Paderewski)
 *No.55 in B flat major (No.56 in Paderewski)
 *No.57 in A flat major (No.58 in Paderewski)

WALTZES

   No.6 in D flat major (Op.64 No.1)
   No.7 in C sharp minor (Op.64 No.2)
   No.8 in A flat major (Op.64 No.3)
   No.9 in A flat major (Op.posth.69 No.1 – two versions)
   No.13 in D flat major (Op.posth.70 No.3)

POLONAISES

 *No.13 in A flat major

NOCTURNES

   No.2 in E flat major (Op.9 No.2)
O No.6 in G minor (Op.15 No.3)
   No.11 in G minor (Op.37 No.1)
   No.15 in F minor (Op.55 No.1)

No.19 in E minor (Op.posth.72 No.1)

*No.20 in C sharp minor (*Lento con gran espressione* – two versions) (Also published in Vienna Urtext Edition, and in Paderewski Edition Vol.XVIII – Minor Works)

TROIS NOUVELLES ETUDES
No.2 in A flat major

SONATAS
No.1 in C minor (Op.4) (Not published by Henle, but available in many other editions, including Paderewski)
    Third movement – *Larghetto*
No.2 in B flat minor (Op.35)
  O Third movement – *Marche Funèbre*
No.3 in B minor (Op.58)
  O Third movement – *Largo*

VARIATIONS
*Variation in E major on the March from Bellini's *I Puritani*, from the 'Hexameron' (Published in the Paderewski Edition Vol.XIII)

MISCELLANEOUS WORKS
*Funeral March in C minor (Op.posth.72 No.2. Published in the Paderewski Edition Vol.XVIII – Minor Works)
Three Écossaises (Op.posth.72 No.3)
    No.2 in G major
*Fugue in A minor (Published in the Paderewski Edition Vol.XVIII – Minor Works)

Grade 8

PRELUDES
No.1 in C major (Op.28)
No.3 in G major (Op.28)
No.17 in A flat major (Op.28)
Prelude in C sharp minor (Op.45)

MAZURKAS
No.1 in F sharp minor (Op.6 No.1 – two versions)
No.10 in B flat major (Op.17 No.1)
No.17 in B flat minor (Op.24 No.4)
No.20 in D flat major (Op.30 No.3)
No.25 in B minor (Op.33 No.4)
No.30 in G major (Op.50 No.1)
No.34 in C major (Op.56 No.2)

No.36 in A minor (Op.59 No.1)
No.37 in A flat major (Op.59 No.2)
No.38 in F sharp minor (Op.59 No.3)
No.39 in B major (Op.63 No.1)
No.42 in G major (Op.posth.67 No.1)
No.46 in C major (Op.posth.68 No.1)
O No.53 in A minor (No.42 in Paderewski)
  *No 54 in D major (No.55 in Paderewski)
  *No.56 in C major (No.57 in Paderewski)

WALTZES

No.1 in E flat major (Op.18)
No.4 in F major (Op.34 No.3)
No.16 in E minor (No.14 in most editions)
  *No.19 in E flat major (No.17 in Paderewski)

POLONAISES

No.1 in C sharp minor (Op.26 No.1)
No.4 in C minor (Op.40 No.2)
No.10 in F minor (Op.posth.71 No.3 – two versions)

NOCTURNES

No.1 in B flat minor (Op.9 No.1)
No.5 in F sharp major (Op.15 No.2)
No.8 in D flat major (Op.27 No.2)
No.9 in B major (Op.32 No.1)
No.10 in A flat major (Op.32 No.2)
No.14 in F sharp minor (Op.48 No.2)

STUDIES
Opus 10
No.6 in E flat minor
Opus 25
No.2 in F minor

TROIS NOUVELLES ETUDES

No.1 in F minor

SONATAS

No.1 in C minor (Op.4.) (Not published by Henle, but available
    in many other editions, including Paderewski)
    Second movement – *Menuetto*

MISCELLANEOUS WORKS

Andante Spianato (Prelude to Grande Polonaise Brillante (Op.22) (Not published by
Henle, but available in many other editions, including Paderewski)
Three Écossaises (Op.posth.72 No.3)
No.1 in D major
No.3 in D flat major

Grade 8+

PRELUDES

No.8 in F sharp minor (Op.28)
No.10 in C sharp minor (Op.28)
No.11 in B major (Op.28)
No.22 in G minor (Op.28)
No.23 in F major (Op.28)

MAZURKAS

No.21 in C sharp minor (Op.30 No.4)
No.23 in D major (Op.33 No.2)
No.27 in B major (Op.41 No.2. Often listed as Op.41 No.3 – see
commentary.)
No.29 in C sharp minor (Op.41 No.4. Often listed as Op.41 No.1 – see
commentary.)
No.32 in C sharp minor (Op.50 No.3)
No.33 in B major (Op.56 No.1)
No.35 in C minor (Op.56 No.3)

WALTZES

No.2 in A flat major (Op.34 No.1)
No.5 in A flat major (Op.42)
No.11 in G flat major (Op.posth.70 No.1 – two versions)

POLONAISES

O   No.2 in E flat minor (Op.26 No.2)
O   No.3 in A major (Op.40 No.1)
No.8 in D minor (Op.posth.71 No.1)
No.9 in B flat major (Op.posth.71 No.2)
*No.15 in B flat minor

NOCTURNES

No.4 in F major (Op.15 No.1)
No.7 in C sharp minor (Op.27 No.1)
No.12 in G major (Op.37 No.2)

No.13 in C minor (Op.48 No.1. See commentary regarding grading.)
No.16 in E flat major (Op.55 No.2)
No.17 in B major (Op.62 No.1)
No.18 in E major (Op.62 No.2)

STUDIES
Opus 10
No.3 in E major
No.9 in F minor
No.12 in C minor
Opus 25
No.1 in A flat major
No.7 in C sharp minor
No.9 in G flat major

TROIS NOUVELLES ETUDES
No.3 in D flat major

IMPROMPTUS
No.1 in A flat major (Op.29)
Fantaisie-Impromptu (Op.posth.66)

VARIATIONS
Variations on a German National Air
*Souvenir de Paganini (Published in Paderewski Edition Vol.XIII)

Very Advanced

PRELUDES
No.5 in D major (Op.28)
No.12 in G sharp minor (Op.28)
No.16 in B flat minor (Op.28)
No.18 in F minor (Op.28)
No.19 in E flat major (Op.28)
No.24 in D minor (Op.28)

POLONAISES
No.5 in F sharp minor (Op.44)
No.6 in A flat major (Op.53)
No.7 Polonaise-Fantaisie (Op.61. See commentary regarding grading.)
*No.14 in G sharp minor
*No.16 in G flat major

NOCTURNES
No.3 in B major (Op.9 No.3)

STUDIES
(See Introduction to Studies regarding grading)
Opus 10
No.1 in C major
No.2 in A minor
No.4 in C sharp minor
No.5 in G flat major
No.7 in C major
No.8 in F major
No.10 in A flat major
No.11 in E flat major
Opus 25
No.3 in F major
No.4 in A minor
No.5 in E minor
No.6 in G sharp minor
No.8 in D flat major
No.10 in B minor
No.11 in A minor
No.12 in C minor

SCHERZOS
No.1 in B minor (Op.20. See commentary regarding grading.)
No.2 in B flat minor (Op.31. See commentary regarding grading.)
No.3 in C sharp minor (Op.39)
No.4 in E major (Op.54)

BALLADES
No.1 in G minor (Op.23)
No.2 in F major (Op.38)
No.3 in A flat major (Op.47)
No.4 in F minor (Op.52)

SONATAS
No.1 in C minor (Op.4) (Not published by Henle, but available
   in many other editions including Paderewski)
   First movement – *Allegro Maestoso*
   Fourth movement – *Finale – Presto*
No.2 in B flat minor (Op.35)
   First movement – *Grave – Doppio Movimento*
   Second movement – *Scherzo*
   Fourth movement – *Finale – Presto*

No.3 in B minor (Op.58)

    First movement – *Allegro Maestoso*

    Second movement – *Scherzo – Molto Vivace*

    Fourth movement – *Finale – Presto, non Tanto*

IMPROMPTUS

No.2 in F sharp major (Op.36. See commentary regarding grading.)

No.3 in G flat major (Op.51. See commentary regarding grading.)

RONDOS

No.1 in C minor (Op.1. Published in the Paderewski Edition Vol.XII)

No 2 in F major Rondeau à la Mazur (Op.5. Published in the Paderewski Edition Vol.XII)

No.3 in E flat major (Op.16. Published in the Paderewski Edition Vol.XII)

No.4 in C major (Op.Posth.73. Published in the Paderewski Edition Vol.XII)

    (Solo version and 2-piano version)

VARIATIONS

Variations Brillantes (Op.12)

MISCELLANEOUS PIECES

Bolero (Op.19)

Tarantella (Op.43)

Allegro de Concert (Op.46)

Fantaisie (Op.49)

Berceuse (Op.57)

Barcarolle (Op.60)

Author's Notes

1. The American equivalents for the British time-values used throughout this book are as follows:

semibreve	whole-note
minim	half-note
crotchet	quarter-note
quaver	eighth-note
semiquaver	sixteenth-note
demisemiquaver	thirty-second-note
hemidemisemiquaver	sixty-fourth-note

2. The following abbreviations have been used throughout:

LH	left hand
RH	right hand
b.	bar
bb.	bars

3. The figure in brackets following the title of each piece indicates the approximate suggested Grade.

4. Bar numberings and indications for tempo, dynamics, and phrasing, referred to below, are based on the Henle Edition unless otherwise stated, and **may differ from those in other editions** (see General Introduction under 'Editions').

5. Regarding the discussion of works in the 'Very Advanced' category, readers are referred to the Preface, under 'The Commentaries on the Music'.

THE PRELUDES
Op. 28

Introduction:

Were the Preludes suddenly to appear from an unnamed, undated source, however would musical historians place them? Such starkly epigrammatic ejaculations of fury and violence, beside moments of thistledown lightness of spirit, of incorporeality, grandeur or grinding despair, are startling enough, even shocking today. And reaching far into the future in harmonic and technical terms, as many of them do, one would love to know how they were received by the habitués of the Paris Salons. As J.-J. Eigeldinger says, 'this volume gazes at us like a sphinx proposing a riddle, and one that has remained more or less unsolved.' 'Ignoring the legacy of his immediate predecessors, deaf to the contemporary world, the Chopin of the Preludes anchored himself in Bach so as to see himself more clearly – and, despite himself, into the future. This work is a two-faced Janus, not only within his own output, but in the development of keyboard music from Bach to the present day.' (*Chopin Studies,* pp.167 and 185).

Like the Studies, as Arthur Hedley has remarked (p.145), each of the Preludes, with few exceptions, is concerned with a single musical (and/or technical) idea. But within this gamut of 'single ideas' the Preludes touch every shade of musical colour and feeling, and their technical demands range from exquisite simplicity to the highest flights of virtuosity. Nos 5, 16, 18 and 19 need particular agility and flexibility, technical small change to Chopin, no doubt, whose hands were remarkable in these respects. Nos 12 and 24 are also very taxing to the stamina of the RH and LH respectively. These all assume technical accomplishment of a high order. Since many of the Preludes are so short, we also need the special ability, which really amounts to **courage**, to seize and instantly transmit a mood and atmosphere.

Again, like the two volumes of Studies, but unlike the other genre pieces, the Waltzes, Nocturnes and so on, the Preludes were published as a single collection. By romantic tradition they will remain for ever identified, if not almost synonymous with the time of the 'honeymoon' with George Sand in Majorca, in the autumn and winter of 1838-9. Disappointingly though, for it would suit our imaginations to see these kaleidoscopic mood pictures as a record of that time of trial both of body and spirit, almost all of the pieces had apparently been written or sketched at various times over the previous few years. Niecks sees them as 'pickings from the composer's portfolios of pieces, sketches and memoranda, written at various times ['eagle's wings' as Schumann said], and kept to be utilised when occasion might offer.' (Vol.2, p.44). Recent evidence suggests however, that at least some (numbers 4, 5, 7(?), 9, 10, 14, 16, and 18) were actually written in Majorca (and not Nos 6 or 15, both contenders, *vide* George Sand, for the title of 'Raindrop').* The whole set was then polished and fine-tuned in Chopin's usual meticulous manner, and sent off for publication from Majorca in January 1839.

It is amusing to read of Von Bülow's interpretations of the Preludes and, rather nearer to our own times, those of Alfred Cortot. Von Bülow entitles No.4 'Suffocation'. No.9 is 'Vision', No.10 'The Night Moth', and the programme he supplies to each piece must make Chopin cringe in his grave – his 'interpretation' of No.9 is a graphic example:

> Here Chopin has the conviction that he has lost his power of expression. With the determination to discover whether his brain can still originate ideas, he strikes his head with a hammer (here the sixteenths and thirty-seconds are to be carried out in exact time, indicating a double stroke of the hammer). In the third and fourth measures one can hear the blood trickle (trills in the left hand).

*See under Prelude No.6

He is desperate at finding no inspiration (fifth measure); he strikes again with the hammer and with greater force (thirty-second notes twice in succession during the crescendo). In the key of A flat he finds his powers again. Appeased, he seeks his former key and closes contentedly. (Schönberg, p.129.)

Perhaps, however, we should not laugh too loudly: in these more prosaic times and in the quest for correctness and authenticity we are often in danger of letting imagination fly out of the window.

Today the Preludes are, of course, often or even usually played as a complete cycle, making a fine showcase for performers to demonstrate their agility and stamina both of technique and spirit. Chopin himself played no more than three or four in one programme. This, however, does not necessarily mean that he would not have played more, or all of them together, today. In those days the pot-pourri reigned supreme in the concert room: in these more earnest times we take our music in more serious slabs. Essentially interrelated as the Preludes feel, particularly in the climactic finality of the last in D minor, I find them uncomfortable material for the concert platform. Sometimes passing too quickly to grasp each piece – so intensely drawn, so detailed, so brilliantly coloured or minutely shaded – Chopin at his most cryptic presents us with too much on one plate. We need to stop, listen, ponder, go back – in short, the Preludes are happier territory for the domestic pianist and indeed the compact-disc owner.

Note: As said above, many of the Preludes are concerned with a single musical or technical idea. In such instances a large proportion of the discussion is inevitably centred upon this one 'idea', and the text is therefore not divided into bar-numbered sections as is the case elsewhere in this book. As with the Studies players are recommended to explore the practice plans given in the Cortot Edition.

Prelude No. 1 in C major (8)

This is an immense piece in the space of a mere 34 bars. The agitation it conveys, so intense and erupting so powerfully, has subsided almost before the listener knows what has passed. It is a splendid 'learning' piece, in terms of the rhythmic coordination, pedalling, and the projection of dynamics and mood. Performances by different pianists vary widely, and to convey the essential *agitato*, a very fast tempo is not necessary. What **is** necessary is the exact implementation of the 'breathless' RH offbeat rhythmic pattern, with the implied syncopated emphasis on the dotted RH quavers taken with the RH thumb. At the same time the bass notes must be given due importance or you will give the impression that the RH dotted quaver falls on the first beat of the bar. To this end it is a good plan to practise playing the piece with the first two notes of each bar only, taken with a firm LH

fifth finger and RH thumb respectively. *etc.* Do this in

strict time so that you can imagine and absorb the rhythmic **feeling** of the **written** two groups of triplet semiquavers. Then add the upper melody notes (i.e. the quaver G and semiquaver A in

b.1) and practise **this** combination in strict time.

Then practise the complete LH and complete RH figures carefully, separately. Feel that the LH 'falls' onto the first bass semiquaver, and play each semiquaver triplet in a strong, smooth, **slurred** effect, lifting the hand after the third note so that it 'falls' again with a natural emphasis on the subsequent first beat, and so on. The LH thus performs in a series of self-generating 'arcs' as the hand 'falls' and 'lifts' through each bar.

Turning to the RH, allow the thumb to 'fall' onto the first dotted quaver, holding it as long as possible before releasing it to play the last semiquaver of the bar. Providing that the weight is allowed to rest on this thumb, and the remainder of the hand is really free it will then be found relatively easy to play the remaining RH notes, 'showing' the line of the treble melody notes (G and A) without undue effort. Then **lift** the hand at the end of the bar, **feeling** the semiquaver rest, ready to let the thumb 'fall' again onto the subsequent dotted quaver, and so on, creating a similarly overall self-generating movement to that of the LH. Then when you put hands together be sure to preserve the triplet rhythm and the shape of the LH and RH figures intact. Feel in

each bar that the overall figure 'grows' from each bass note.

The balance needs to be finely tuned so that, as already said, the bass note is clearly established as the first beat of the bar, and the inner melodic line taken with the RH thumb is clearly defined and 'expanded' into the treble notes G and A. These treble notes, repeating the inner 'thumb line' notes at the higher octave in a stretto effect, complete the brilliantly calculated *agitato* impulse of the whole figure. It is well to memorise bb.1 and 2 and to practise them over and over, very slowly at first, until you feel at ease with the pattern. Then when you add the pedal, be sure always to catch the bass note within the pedal, coordinating the raising and re-depressing of the pedal at the beginning of each bar so that you both catch the bass note **and** show the RH semiquaver rest. It is effective to make a moderate *crescendo* towards b.7, then to *decrescendo* with a little 'give' in the tempo through b.8, ready to 'start afresh' at b.9. Then as you start the big *crescendo* from b.13, be sure that you do not make the common mistake of getting too loud too soon (nor of letting the stretto, from b.17, get out of hand). Note the telling change in the RH rhythm at b.18. This suggests a steeper *crescendo* from this point, with the added 'bite' on each first beat provided by an implied stronger 'lean' on the RH thumb. If you implement this stronger lean on the thumb on the first beat, the cross-rhythm effect will fall into place quite naturally. Opinions vary as to where the climax should come. Most editions show it at the highest point of the upward curve (b.21) with a downward *diminuendo* and 'give' in the tempo through bb.22-4. My own feeling, and this is purely personal, is that the implied *forte*, or *fortissimo* should 'go on' to b.23, which again for one bar only has the RH cross-rhythm effect over the six-four LH harmony. This necessitates a steeper *diminuendo* and a more dramatic 'give' through the dominant harmony in b.24. In any event, arrive at your dynamic 'peak' at b.21, either making a longer *diminuendo* through bb.22-4, or carrying on the full tone and making a shorter *diminuendo* through b.24 itself. Then 'point' the pending return to the tonic at b.25 through the six-four and dominant harmonies in bb.23-4, allowing a 'give' through b.24 ready to 're-start' in *piano* at b.25. Do not go flaccid here, for the *agitato* feeling still hovers. Quietly but clearly 'point' the rhythmic difference between bb.25-6 and 27-8, and then bb.29-32, feeling the implied 'lean' on the upper tied C's from the second beat of b.29, as you gradually tail the sound away through these bars. Relatively inexperienced players find this RH figure difficult to negotiate. As you 'lean' on the tied treble C, treat the inner triplet as if it is

slurred 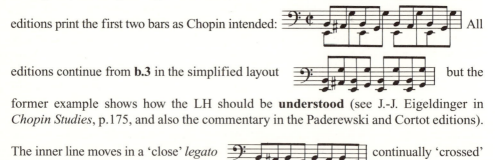 bringing the third **off** at the end of the bar while still holding the

treble C. Shape the whole figure in an overall slur as indicated

retaining the treble C with the fifth finger until its sound is 'caught' within each new pedal, so that this tonic treble note sounds continuously through these bars. The LH must remain very steady here, performing just a light but very even 'flick' of triplet semiquavers. *Diminuendo* to a whisper at b.32, and then shape the notes of the final spread chord with quiet and carefully spaced resonance up to the treble E.

The overall dynamics need to be finely judged. Many inexperienced players make the mistake of starting far too loudly, thus leaving no room for the long *crescendo*. Note that Chopin specifies a *mezzo forte* opening and a *crescendo* from b.13 towards b.21, but does **not** then specify a *forte* or *fortissimo*. Inevitably, therefore, players arrive at b.21 in varying degrees of *forte*. The important thing is to shape the dynamics, within your chosen dynamic range, towards this peak, then gradually subside towards the final bar.

Prelude No. 2 in A minor (7) (O)

This stark and unrelievedly lugubrious piece, startling enough in its effect today, must have been incomprehensible and even horrifying to the listeners of Chopin's day. The louring LH, with its grinding dissonances, needs careful examination and practice. Not all editions print the first two bars as Chopin intended: All editions continue from **b.3** in the simplified layout but the former example shows how the LH should be **understood** (see J.-J. Eigeldinger in *Chopin Studies*, p.175, and also the commentary in the Paderewski and Cortot editions).

The inner line moves in a 'close' *legato* continually 'crossed' by the outer line, which creates both the harmonic foundation and at the same time a pendulum-like rhythmic *ostinato* Even large hands cannot stretch the wide intervals of this outer line from b.4 onwards, and these outer quavers are played in an even, quiet, 'dragging' *portando* effect as they cross back and forth

over the inner line:  (see General Introduction under

'Articulation'). At the same time listen acutely to the intervals created by the two voices: the bare fifths alternating with the diminished sevenths and octaves through bb.1-3. Then listen to the effect as the fifths change to sixths in b.4, to the grating offbeat major and minor sevenths in b.5, and the alternating minor and major thirds through bb.6-7, and so on.

Set a steady crotchet pulse. Laden though the LH quavers are, they need to convey a continuing sense of movement – a doleful but inevitable progress at a suggested tempo of around ♩ = 63-69, but with a clear overall sense of two-in-the-bar.* Have your tempo 'well in the system' so that you bring in the LH quietly but dead in time. It is best to think of these first two bars not so much as an introduction, but as an emergance perhaps, of a column of shadowy figures, **already** embarked on their journey, and from among whom a doleful voice will declaim the 5-bar song motif, played three times with variants and extending into a coda. 'Superimpose' this melodic motif, as it were, without 'disturbing' the onward walk of the LH quavers. Play out the melody with a quiet and resonant deliberation, always ensuring that the long notes have sufficient tone to sing through their full duration. Feel the sense of the sub-phrases (bb.3-4 and 5-7) within the overall phrase-line (bb.3-7). Feel also the sense in which the first figure through b.3 is 'going towards' the long D in b.4, with the long D 'leaning on' towards b.5, and the figures of b.5 'going on' towards and through the march-like dotted rhythm figure towards the long tied B from the

second main beat of b.6.

Feel each RH quaver (e.g. the last quaver of b.3) as the ongoing upbeat towards the subsequent long note, and similarly the quavers in b.5 as the 'upbeat' to the dotted crotchet on the third beat and the crotchet on the first beat of b.6 respectively. Without breaking the sense of continuity, make it clear that you are 'closing' the first overall phrase at the end of b.7, ready to 'start anew' in the higher register at b.8, perhaps in a rather fuller tone. Then *crescendo* a little as indicated towards a penetrating long tied F sharp on the second main beat of b.11, over the grinding LH augmented fourth and major seventh intervals. This is the dynamic climax of the piece, albeit a subdued one. Maintain your dynamic 'plateau' almost through to the end of b.12, beginning the **gradual** long *diminuendo* as you 'point' the change to the less harsh LH contours from b.13, and then bringing in the RH in a correspondingly lower-tiered dynamic in b.14. Inexperienced players tend to hurry through the solo fragments (bb.17-18 and 20-1). These, on the contrary, need to convey even greater heaviness of spirit as the overall sound gradually subsides towards the last *sostenuto* chords. 'Bring in' the LH quavers again in b.18 in an even, *slentando* drift, and 'leave off' simultaneously in both hands on the second main beat of b.19. **Listen** to the silence through the second half of the bar before resignedly continuing in the RH from the

*This piece is often played somewhat slower than this, but in setting a tempo the two-in-the-bar movement must be kept in mind. (See Introduction under 'Tempo').

first beat of b.20. 'Point' the tied quaver upbeat to b.21 a little, again **listening** to its resonance beneath the repeated B's through the first half of b.21. Then feel that the solo line 'merges' into the quiet *sostenuto* chords, and allow an extra instant to spread the dominant seventh chord on the second beat of b.23 before sinking to the final quietly spread tonic, allowing this final chord to reverberate almost into silence.

The grace note in bb.5, 10 etc. may be played like a rather lingering acciaccatura on the

beat. 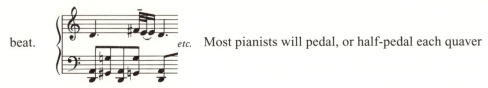 *etc.* Most pianists will pedal, or half-pedal each quaver

couplet, in other words changing the pedal on each crotchet beat, save at bb.18-19 (see Chopin's original pedal mark).

Note: Those with very small hands **can** try this piece, taking the upper LH notes (i.e. the offbeat G's through bb.1-5 and so on) with the RH thumb. But in the interests of the equilibrium of both the RH melody and the LH quavers this is not recommended.

Prelude No. 3 in G major (8)

This is an inspired antidote to the dolours of No.2. The LH is, of course, relentlessly exposed, as if riding a monorail big dipper. But in pianistic terms this is not merely a study for the LH. It is as much a study in coordination. Any fleet-fingered prodigy can run the course of semiquavers with fair success. The artistry comes in the dovetailing of the RH fragments which have to 'catch' the LH as it flies by – a feat of fine-tuned coordination.

First practise the LH alone, taking the tonic-based pattern of bb.1-6 and mastering this before moving on. Practise at first in different rhythms [rhythm notation] , [rhythm notation] , *etc.*

and particularly dotted rhythms [rhythm notation] and [rhythm notation] etc. Absorb the shape

of the pattern thoroughly: the first small curve up to the B on the second crotchet beat, the main overall curve and 'lift' up to the eighth semiquaver E, and the further 'subsiding' curve 'back' up to the fifteenth semiquaver B. Be conscious (without labouring the point) of the fourth crotchet beat, and in particular the last two notes of each bar as the **upbeat** to the subsequent bar, to avoid the possible tendency to be continually 'falling into' this subsequent bar. Practise very slowly at first, insisting on immaculate evenness, and 'thinking' in crotchets. Then as you gradually notch up the speed, 'change gear' to an overall two-in-the-bar pulse. Always be conscious of the need to **lighten** the sound, using the kind of finger articulation that is so clean that it sounds almost detached, until you begin to achieve that special aerated fleetness of sound that is at the same time not 'wispy', like the scurrying feet of squirrels who know where they are going, and not the movement of a wafting cobweb.

Then practise the RH alone in strict time, again feeling the overall two-in-the-bar. 'Point' the dotted crotchet D with neat, quiet firmness on the first beat of b.3. Then be sure to **lift** the hand on the quaver rest so that it 'falls' again with neat precision on the dotted crotchet third on the second main beat (see General Introduction under 'Articulation').

Then lifting the hand again on the semiquaver rest, slur the semiquaver third neatly, in the sense of a clear upbeat, towards the dotted minim third on the first beat of b.4, taking care to let this sing through its full value. Lift the hand again, and slightly raising the dynamic level, slur the semiquaver sixth towards the semibreve sixth in b.5, feeling an **overall** slurred effect through to the minim sixth on the first beat of b.6 as indicated. At speed these semiquaver upbeats will be like quick slurred 'flicks' towards the subsequent first beats. Shape each melodic fragment carefully 'within itself' while at the same time showing the sense of the overall line from b.3 through to b.12. When you put hands together, at first very slowly, listen acutely to ensure that the hands are perfectly synchronised, particularly in respect of the semiquaver upbeat figures. Notch up the tempo only very gradually, according to your abilities. Feel (rather as in No.2, despite the very different climate) that the LH is not so much providing a two-bar introduction, as setting a wheel in motion onto which the RH will land, as with a little spring, on the first beat of b.3. Then feel that the RH is 'riding' the ceaseless switchbacking arcs of the LH. Create a rather more concentrated sound on the 'clustered' RH chord on the first beat of bb.7 and 9, and then allow an extra instant to 'reach up' to the spread chord and down to the bass D on the first beat of bb.8 and 10. Place the RH F sharp on the first beat of these bars, to coincide with the bass D,

then lifting lightly and easily up to the high minim A

(the same applies at b.18). Avoid panic here by 'pointing' the upbeat semiquaver down towards this F sharp with the above mentioned neat slurred flick, rather than in an undirected 'splat' towards the overall spread of the subsequent chord. Give the slurred semiquaver figure in b.11 a jaunty 'flick' down to the dotted crotchet third on the second main beat, and then allow the tiniest 'give' as you 'flick' the upbeat second down to 'start again' on the first beat of b.12.

From b.16 be conscious of the long-breathed melody line through to the end of b.26, in contrast to the 'busier' feeling of the melodic fragments through bb.3-15. Also feel the new, more expressive, but at the same time rather more purposeful sense of the melody line as you progress through bb.16-17 in the dominant seventh harmony towards a definite 'arrival' on C major at b.18, allowing a little extra time through to end of b.17 to prepare for this generously spread RH C major chord on the first beat of b.18. Then let the melody line move with quiet and close smoothness over the continually switchbacking LH towards a quiet home tonic at b.26. Be sure to take the RH **off** through b.27 as it prepares to join in a delicious unison flurry from b.28, evaporating through b.31 as on a puff of breeze up towards tiny pinpoints of sound on the high crotchet B's. End with quiet and steady, evenly spread chords. This unison passage is exceedingly treacherous, and slow rhythmic practice will be required by **any** pianist, as outlined for the LH above.

Use only light touches of pedal, perhaps at the beginning of each bar from b.3 onwards, to define the harmony (particularly when the chords are spread, bb.8, 10 and 18), and raise the pedal again approximately on the third semiquaver or second crotchet beat of each bar. Bring your speed up from very slow to one at which you feel comfortable and in control, and no further. This piece sounds magical in the hands of a virtuoso, scudding past on the lightest west wind. Never mind if you have to set your sights a little lower – it can still sound delightful at quite a few notches below the usual performing tempo, providing that the spirit is there, the texture beautifully clear, and the lines perfectly shaped and coordinated.

Prelude No. 4 in E minor (4-5)

This much loved Prelude is as profoundly melancholy as anything Chopin wrote, but in a gentler and more resigned way than the starkly desolate No.2. It is an excellent piece for players of about a Grade 5 standard (or perhaps earlier for older players), providing a valuable exercise in the sustaining of an expressive melody line over constantly changing LH harmonies, and in acquiring the skill of playing continuous chords with an almost *legato* effect.

Set a steady crotchet pulse within an overall two-in-the-bar feeling, at a tempo which moves but still allows time to listen to the chromatic inflections in either hand. This can vary widely from player to player, but a mean of between ♩= 58-66 is suggested. At much more than this the subtle harmonic shifts begin to lose their significance. At much slower (and the inexperienced player inevitably tends to drag rather than hurry this piece), these harmonic shifts lose their shadowy quality and become too solid; and the melody line, preoccupied as it is through bb.1-8 with only semitonal, then whole tone stepwise

movements *etc.* is prone to set into rigor mortis within

a few bars. However, although novice players often **cannot** reach this 'moving' tempo, they should not be discouraged from attempting this piece. Young players particularly love sorrowful music and will gain a great deal of keyboard lore, as well as enjoyment, even if they can only reach a fairly stolid plod.

Practise the LH alone at first, listening acutely to the harmonic inflections of all the voices. It is a good plan first of all to define these shifts aurally by holding the tonic chord through b.1, then tying the upper tonic into b.2 as you shift the lower notes downwards,

and so on. *etc.* When you practise the chords as

written, 'establish' the tonic harmony soberly through b.1, then **listen** as the two lower voices descend on the first beat of b.2, while the upper tonic remains through the first half of b.2, descending by a semitone on the second main beat, and so on. Place each chord firmly though quietly, feeling each not just as a vague block of sound, but as three melodic voices within the whole chord. Release each chord as little and as late as possible, raising the hand only just enough to enable you to play the next chord clearly (with the fingers remaining in contact with the keys), so that the sound of these LH chords is as continuous as possible, feeling that the hand is 'rooted' in the keyboard. Cortot creates a good image when he talks of 'imprinting' the notes in the keyboard (see his comments on the Study in F minor Op.10 No.9, Cortot edition). Or one can imagine 'imprinting' the fingers in sand, for example. Inexperienced players find this technique quite difficult, and will invariably tackle these chords in a tense, juddering *staccato*. This is not only quite alien to the 'laden' character of the chords in this piece (whether in *piano* or in *forte*) but also makes it impossible to 'catch' the relevant chord in the sustaining pedal each time it is changed.

Lead off in the RH with a carefully timed upbeat figure, feeling at the same time its onward 'lean' and upward 'lift' towards the first beat of b.1. (Again, inexperienced players are often reluctant to give this figure its full value and import.) Feel that this upbeat figure is 'going to' a quiet but penetratingly singing long B on the first beat of b.1, and then feel that the upbeat crotchet C is slurred within the overall phrase line, i.e. that it has a slight implied emphasis as it 'goes to' the next long B on the first beat of b.2, and so on. I can never find a better way of suggesting the 'speaking' quality of this repeated figure than by imagining, and indeed **saying** or **singing** a sorrowfully sighed **Oh** Dear . . . **Oh** Dear . . .

 This gives the sense of a **very** slight drawing out of each

crotchet, which at the same time gives an onward upbeat 'lean' towards the long note on the subsequent first beat.

bb.1–7   When you put hands together have the LH 'ready' to meet the RH on the first beat of b.1, and let the LH establish the quiet, rhythmic two-in-the-bar movement securely through this first bar. Subtly vary the nuance of the 'Oh Dear' as you **listen** to the downward creeping shifts of the LH through bb.1-4, and then from the upbeat to b.5 feel an even greater dolefulness as you slide down to the just-lower register through bb.5-8.

bb.7–13   Give an even more sorrowful lean on the RH upbeat figure to b.8, and then feel the implied emphasis on the tied crotchet upbeat to b.9. **Listen** to the sound of this G sharp singing over the bar line, and then take a little extra time to shape the quaver fragment expressively through b.9, showing the little 'vocal' curve up to and down from the D on the second main beat of the bar. Let the grace note in b.11 'speak', treating it like a slightly lingering acciaccatura as in Prelude No. 2 b.5 etc. Arrive on a definite yet expectant dominant seventh chord on the first beat of b.12, bringing the LH **off** as you curve the RH solo quavers onward through b.12. Inexperienced players invariably scuttle with embarrassment through this bar as if to get through it and return to the real 'meat' in b.13 as soon as possible. In fact this linking solo is supremely expressive. As you lead on from the first beat, feel the appoggiatura-like 'lean' on the emphasised quaver C on the second crotchet beat, and the upward curve and 'lift' towards the high quaver D on the fourth crotchet beat. Then feel the 'onward' movement of the triplet upbeat leading into b.13. It is a good plan (as shown in some editions) to change fingers (3-2) on

the F sharp preceding the high D.   Not only does this stop

the player from hurrying, but it 'points' the curve up to the D. Feel a degree of recitative-like freedom through b.12, and then re-establish the quiet regular movement from b.13.

bb.13–25   Feel a rising sense of urgency from the first beat of b.16, but beware of letting the stretto get out of hand. Feel that you are *crescendo*-ing **through** the notes of the RH turn as you 'lift' up towards a strong crotchet G on the

second main beat of b.16,   supported by increasingly

resonant descending LH chords. Deliver a strong bass octave B on the first beat of b.17 and, as the RH lifts eloquently up to the high C on the second crotchet beat and presses on in a gradual *diminuendo*, support this melody line with resonant and carefully balanced LH chords, particularly 'pointing' the telling chord on the second main beat of b.17. It is vital that the sound of the bass octave B is held within the pedal through the first half of b.17 as

Chopin has indicated. The pedalling will thus read

(Small hands can omit the top A of the repeated chords, and then take the top F sharp of the subsequent chord with the RH.) The cross-rhythm in b.18 is an awkward moment for novice players. Do feel that the RH triplet is fitting in with the continuingly even LH quaver pulse, and **not** the other way about. Let the momentum subside through b.18, towards a return to the original movement in b.19, but in a more reposeful, resigned mood. Quietly 'point' the interrupted cadence at bb.20-1 with a tiny swell as indicated, and show the 'lift' of the upper LH line up to the B flat on the second main beat of b.21. Then let the sound gradually die to a whisper, **listening** to the descending upper LH line towards the minim chord on the first beat of b.23. **Listen** to this scarcely breathed chord, and **listen** to the silence through the minim rest. Then play the final chords in measured, quiet as possible *pianissimo*, allowing the final tonic chord to fade almost to silence through the pause. (Some editions wrongly spread these chords.) Small hands can leave out the lower RH E-D sharp-E.

This piece gives an excellent lesson in pedalling. The pedal will normally be changed whenever there is a change of harmony **or** melody, i.e. on the fourth crotchet beat of b.1, the first beat of b.2, the second **main** beat and fourth crotchet beat of b.2, and so on. More experienced players may choose to change or half change the pedal more often, e.g. on the second main beat of b.1, to define subtly the two-in-the-bar movement, or even more often, depending on the resonance of piano or acoustics. Then the pedal may be changed on each crotchet beat through b.9, and could be used lightly to enhance the eloquence of the solo quavers through b.12, and so on. Chopin's only indications are in b.17, already discussed, and through the **second** crotchet beat of b.18 (taking in the cross-rhythm effect).

Prelude No. 5 in D major (VA)

This is a difficult piece – one of those, as said in the Introduction to the Preludes, that is best left to the virtuoso player. In musical terms the tracery of LH and RH semiquavers, threaded with intermittent melodic fragments, is highly complex, and the technical demands are equally daunting. In a physical sense, a high degree of lateral flexibility in the wrist is required. There is no opportunity to establish a pattern since the semiquavers pursue each other in a tangle of ceaselessly varying intervals (see, for example, the LH through bb.8-9: semitone, diminished fifth, major sixth, major second, minor seventh, major second, tenth, and so on). And scarcely for more than a moment do the hands 'share' the same intervals, as they switchback wildly between fragmentary similar or contrary motion. Amid this organised chaos of semiquavers, when one adds the placing of the delicately stepping 'doubled' offbeat melodic fragments from the middle of bb.1, 17 and

33, we have a test of coordination and poise indeed, ideally invoking, as Cortot poetically suggests, 'the delicate rustling of leaves in the breeze – elated twitterings in the shadows of the branches'.

Prelude No. 6 in B minor (6)

This is another much loved piece, and an excellent study in the shaping of a LH melody beneath *sotto voce*, ostinato RH quavers. It is thought possible, as mentioned in the Introduction to the Preludes, that this (or No.15 in D flat) was the piece described by George Sand in full romantic flood in the famous quotation from her *Histoire de ma Vie*. 'His composition of this evening was indeed full of the drops of rain which resounded on the sonorous tiles of the monastery, but they were transformed in his imagination and his music into tears falling from heaven on his heart.' (Niecks, Vol.2, p.43).* Chopin may indeed have played these pieces on one of many such evenings when the rain dripped dolorously upon (or through) the roof, but it appears that both this and No.15 were composed sometime before the Majorcan adventure. The overall mood is of sighing melancholy – rather less laden than in No.4 in E minor, since here the phrases through the first half are predominantly upward curving.

Set a steady crotchet pulse, at a suggested mean of around $\bullet$ = 46-50. Interpretations of the *lento assai* differ widely, but if the tempo is too slow the LH melody will 'stick' in mid-arpeggio in bb.1, 3, 5, etc. If too fast, the arpeggios will sound gabbled, instead of allowing each semiquaver to make itself felt in an expressive sense. Practise the LH alone, shaping the line in smooth curves as indicated by the phrasing, i.e. a smooth arc through bb.1-2, another through bb.3-4, and then a longer line through bb.5-8, and so on. Imagine just how a cellist would shape the opening arpeggio in a light swell up to a quietly singing crotchet D on the second beat, and then articulate the dotted rhythm figure expressively towards the dotted crotchet B on the first beat of b.2, letting the sound 'fall away' a little as the line dips through the remainder of b.2 ready to 'start again' in b.3. Take this wider spanned arpeggio up to a slightly higher dynamic level on the F sharp on the second beat, dipping downwards again through the end of b.4. Then take the third and still wider spanned arpeggio up to a yet more resonant (though by no means loud) crotchet G on the second beat of b.5 and, keeping up this fairly full warm tone, shape the line with all possible eloquence through to the second beat of b.8. 'Finish off' the phrase on a quietly resonant crotchet F sharp, and then make it clear that you are 'starting again' with the upbeat quavers to b.9.

Then practise the RH alone. The very particular indications here are often referred to as a 'bebung' effect. This term refers to a vibrato effect obtained on the clavichord by means of alternating heavier and lighter pressure on the keys. Here it indicates a 'lean' on the stressed first quaver of each couplet, followed by a light, barely audible sounding of the second quaver. This produces a quiet, 'treading' effect, a gentle ostinato running through the piece. Practise this carefully, just using the pattern of b.1 until you can create a perfectly even, 'stronger lighter/stronger lighter' effect over quiet but firm inner crotchets, that can run on automatic pilot. Then learn the first eight bars **listening** to the harmonic inflections, as you carry on this effect through to the second beat of b.6. Then from the upbeat to b.7 allow the treble melody line to emerge. 'Go to' a warmly singing dotted crotchet E on the first beat of b.7 and, ensuring that this note sings **over** the second beat, place the inner

*See Niecks's substantial quotation from *'Histoire de ma Vie'* on pp.42-3 of his Vol.2.

chords relatively quietly so that the melody line sounds

and **not**, as inexperienced players invariably do,

This musical shaping of bb.7-8 has to be carefully studied and listened to. Feel the little swell through b.8 as you prepare to 'finish off' the line cleanly, as if with a slurred effect.

When you put hands together study the balance between the hands assiduously. Feel that the RH is setting and maintaining the overall steady sense of the crotchet pulse (a reversal here of Chopin's maxim 'the left hand is the Conductor' (see General Introduction under 'The Left Hand'). This RH will give a little here, move on a little there, but basically the LH is conforming to the RH pulse and **not** the other way about. Maintain the shapes of the LH line as already studied, supported and enhanced but never swamped by the RH treble quavers and inner chords. Thus the RH will slightly swell and recede in complement to the LH curves. Then from the upbeat to b.7 let the treble line open out in duet with the LH melody through to b.8, 'finishing off' the RH carefully as described, over the LH dominant crotchet on the second beat. Then be sure to **lift** the RH as the LH leads off quietly but definitely with the upbeat quavers, ready to resume the previous balance from b.9. Feel a slight heightening of expressive intensity from b.11, with a sense of moving on in *crescendo* through b.13 towards an arrival, as if with a question, on the minim E on the first beat of b.14. Then draw back through the end of the bar ready to answer in the LH, 'leaning' a little on the dotted crotchet on the first beat of bb.15 and 16, and playing the LH line with a sense of weary but composed resignation. Curve down from b.16 in a smooth phrase towards a quietly resonant F sharp minim on the second beat of b.17, 'going on through' to 'point' the interrupted cadence into b.18. Then make it clear that you are beginning a new phrase on the upbeat to b.19, playing this restatement of bb.15-17 perhaps in a quieter tone.* Take an extra instant to 'point' the arrival on a quiet bass tonic on the first beat of b.22. Then 'point' the emphasised RH upbeat to b.23 as if with a tiny 'push', and then gradually phase out the melody line from b.23, arriving on a whispered tonic tied dotted minim in b.25. Do **feel** (something the novice player can almost never manage) the crotchet rest on the second beat of this bar so that the RH quavers 'die' in whispered hesitancy.

Most pianists pedal this piece quite lightly, i.e. changing the pedal on each crotchet beat so that, for example, the crotchet on the second beat of bb.1, 3, 5, etc. can sing, unencumbered by the resonance of the previous rising arpeggio. This also ensures the subtle definition of the RH quaver couplets. Then through the concentrated harmonic progressions of bb.7-8 the pedal needs to be changed on each **quaver** beat. From bb.15-22 the pedal changes with the harmonic shift on each crotchet beat.

*The score belonging to Jane Stirling shows a pencilled *pianissimo* in b.20, and a triple *pianissimo* in b.21.

Prelude No. 7 in A major (4-5) (O)

It is difficult – disconcertingly so – to peel away the layers of sickly-sweet string sound that surround this piece and to hear it in its pristine simplicity. Some commentators find it Mazurka-like. But were it to appear suddenly from some unnamed source, I cannot believe anyone would ascribe it to Chopin. In its direct, fresh and waltz-like charm it could sit happily among the Ländler or Waltzes of Schubert.

Set an easy moving, waltz-like rhythm at a tempo of around ♩ = 88-100, and practise the LH first. Give a quietly resonant bass note on the first beat of b.1, and then feel you are 'going on through' the repeated crotchet octaves towards the minim on the first beat of the subsequent bar. Play each 2-bar fragment thus, in perfect time, always with the feeling of 'going on through' to the minim, and placing that minim with a sense of arrival. Practise the RH with a similar gentle rhythmic impulse. When you put hands together be sure to have the quiet dance-like pulse 'well in the system' so that you lead in with a clear, perfectly timed RH upbeat crotchet, giving this at the same time the sense of an onward upward 'lean' towards the first beat of b.1. Feel a little 'lean' again on the dotted quaver on this first beat to match the quiet resonance of the bass note. Make sure the dotted rhythm is precisely timed – the semiquavers neither too long nor too short – and move on with quiet, smooth-stepping precision to arrive with slight extra definition on the minim chord on the first beat of b.2. Be sure to give this chord its full value, then come **off** in both hands ready to move on with a slight onward leading 'lean' on the upbeat third to b.3, and so on. While each 2-bar fragment needs to be shaped as a little entity in itself, feel at the same time the sense of proceeding overall in **4-bar** phrases. Each 2-bar fragment has a subtly different character. Listen to the difference between the lower, more concentrated sound of the chords through bb.1-2, and the higher, more open sound of the chords in bb.3-4. Then feel the more unctuous tone of the sixths from the upbeat to b.5, filled out by the added held resonance of the inner lower RH tied D. Make it clear that you are finishing off the first 8-bar period with the minim chord in b.8, and 'starting again' with a little extra emphasis on the tied upbeat to b.9. Then draw out slightly in a little *crescendo* as you approach the wide-spanned chord on the first beat of b.12. Those with small hands will have to decide between breaking the chord, or leaving out the lower RH A sharp and also perhaps the lower C sharp and probably the LH upper F sharp. (If broken it sounds best thus (omitting the lower RH C sharp if

necessary):  rather than in the more sentimental arpeggiated

effect given in many editions.)* Allow a little pause for this chord to make its quiet impact. Then end quietly in an almost matter-of-fact manner allowing just a little give through the end of the penultimate bar towards the final quiet chord. Place the tied RH appoggiatura A **on** the second beat of this penultimate bar, and be sure to **hold** this tied tonic through to the last chord.

Chopin's pedalling is somewhat heavy on a modern piano, and most players change on each crotchet beat through bb.1, 3, etc. Then, holding the pedal through the minim chord in bb.2, 4, etc. be sure to raise it so that each crotchet upbeat sounds as a **solo** over the LH rest.

*In the score belonging to Jane Stirling the two upper LH notes E and F sharp are erased and the LH and RH are connected with a vertical line indicating that the chord is to be played as a 'block' and not spread.

The fingering needs to be carefully worked out for optimum smoothness of line between each dotted rhythm figure and the chord on each second beat. The fingering for the first fragment is simple.  For the second there are several possibilities.

Prelude No. 8 in F sharp minor (8+)

This is one of the most glorious of all Chopin's short pieces. Robert Collett records that Baudelaire, 'paraphrasing' Delacroix, described it as resembling 'a brilliant bird flying over the horrors of an abyss' – a graphic thought, although since this is such magnificently affirmative music, I should prefer the bird to be soaring over a splendid canyon rather than a horrifying abyss. It is a virtuosic piece, but nevertheless one that is worth an attempt by the competent domestic player. It must both shimmer and surge, the 'little' notes flying clearly and freely over the inner melody taken with the RH thumb, with the LH triplet figuration in cross-rhythm with the RH through the first half of each beat. This cross-rhythm effect is not as difficult to achieve as it might appear on the page, but the tumultuous onward movement from first note to last requires considerable technical stamina and endurance of spirit. First practise the LH carefully alone, feeling the implied little lean on the first semiquaver of each triplet/quaver figure, treating the whole figure

in an overall slurred effect down to the lower quaver as indicated.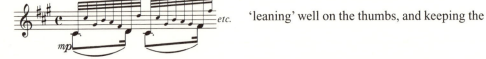

There are various ways of practising the RH. Divide each group of eight notes into overall chords, thus: 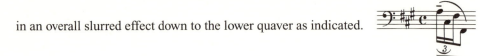 *etc.* This is helpful from the point of view of learning the harmonies and absorbing the general shape. Then practise thus:

 *etc.* 'leaning' well on the thumbs, and keeping the

'little notes' very light. Practise also in dotted rhythm  and

 . When you start to put 'hands together' practise the thumb melody

alone with the LH.

Do this in strict time so that the

LH bass quavers fall precisely on the second quaver pulse, and then ensure that the RH semiquaver is given its proper value and not treated as a vague triplet. Always think of this semiquaver as the **upbeat** to the subsequent dotted quaver. Then practise 'stopping' each figure on the fifth demisemiquaver (i.e. on the second quaver pulse) to coincide with the lower LH quaver, again taking care to give full value again to the **second** half of

each group.

etc.

It is then a good plan to memorise and practise

bb.1-2 over and over (as with Prelude No.1). Practise very slowly at first, listening acutely to the inflections of the RH against the LH harmony, and gradually increasing the speed until you feel at ease with the cross-rhythm effect, always bringing out the inner melody by 'leaning' to a greater or lesser degree on the RH thumb so that the remainder of the hand is relaxed and able to play the 'little' notes freely. Be careful not to fall into the frequent pitfall of 'hanging on' with the fifth finger to the second note of each group (i.e. the upper RH C sharp on the first and second beats of b.1) thus causing the hand to 'jam' so that it is almost impossible to play the remaining notes clearly. The balance between the thumb-line melody, the LH and the upper demisemiquavers has to be finely gauged. While the thumb-line obviously needs to predominate, it must not do so to the extent that the LH and the demisemiquavers are relegated to the roles of mere accompaniments. The melody needs to be underpinned by a supportive LH resonance, while the marvellously inflected RH demisemiquavers 'fill out' and enhance the melody, rather than merely accompanying, or at the other extreme, swamping it.

Learn the whole piece in short sections, i.e. up to the end of b.4, then through to b.8, and so on. Feel the implied little surge up to the fourth beat of b.1, then dropping the tone a little through the end of the bar, ready to 'start again' in b.2. Then from the end of b.2 slightly expand the tone into b.3, gradually subsiding a little through b.4 with a little give at the end of the bar ready to begin the next 4-bar period from b.5. Expand the tone a little more into b.7, and allow a little 'give' into b.9 as you prepare to begin the gradual long *crescendo* towards b.13 and on towards b.15, taking care not to get too loud too soon. At b.13 feel the new 'instrumentation' of the melody line as it moves into the lower register. Arrive in a fine full tone at bb.15-16, but leaving room for the climb to the climactic bb.22-3. Many players anticipate the *subito piano* at b.17 with the lovely effect of a wafting 'lift' to a **quiet** B flat on the fourth beat of b.16. Making a *poco ritenuto* as indicated at the end of b.18, begin fairly quietly at b.19 as in a **suppressed** *agitato*, gradually opening the valves and pressing on as you climb through bb.20-1. Unleash your most radiant sound at b.22 (taking particular care here to support the high RH with a full-toned LH), and descend with a splendid 'peal' through b.23. Grade the *diminuendo* very carefully from b.24, or you will have nothing left by the time you reach b.29. The effect of the descending LH line beneath the RH dominant pedal point effect through bb.25-6 is exquisite, as are the skimming inflections through bb.27-30. The $\diagdown$ sign through bb.25-6 indicates an expressive 'lean' on each dotted quaver C sharp (see General Introduction under 'Dynamic and Agogic Accents'). Allow an extra instant to make a lovely light 'lift' to the F sharp on the fourth beat of bb.28 and 30, and again to 'point' the move to the D sharp on the first beat of b.30. Phase away the sound without too much of a *ritenuto* through the end of b.32, making just a little dynamic rise to the minim chord on the first beat of b.33. Play these last chords with quiet serenity, 'pointing' the E sharp a little as you incorporate it in the measured

upward spread of the final chord  or in some opinions and

perhaps more expressively.

The tempo must to some extent depend on the capacity of the player, but this is a piece which needs to move, ideally at around ♩ = 72-84. At much faster than this the music loses its grandeur and begins to scurry, and the ear cannot take in the richness of the demisemiquaver inflections. Much slower and the 'works' of the cross-rhythm effect begin to show, instead of merging in their splendid effect of rhythmic cross-fertilisation.

Prelude No. 9 in E major (6) (O)

This is like a ceremonial march of splendid pomp and majesty. It makes a fine study in dynamics, in learning to grade a long *crescendo*, and how to project an immense sound without banging. It is in effect a duet between the equally important treble and bass lines, filled out by a resonant inner triplet line. It could well be tackled by older players before Grade 6. Here we are in the thick of the triplet/dotted rhythm controversy (see General Introduction

under 'The [figure] Question'). The matter is further obfuscated by the differently printed

notation in the Vienna Urtext Edition and in Henle, the two authoritative Urtext modern editions. The Vienna Urtext prints this figure in accordance with the original editions, as

was usual until this controversy surfaced, i.e.  as in b.1.

However, in his 'directions for performance' Jörg Demus draws attention to the facsimile of the manuscript (the frontispiece to this Urtext volume where Chopin clearly aligns the semiquaver with the third triplet quaver) 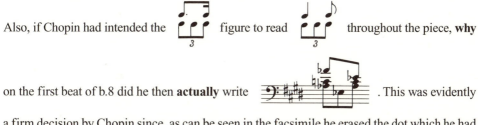 saying that the semiquaver

'should certainly be understood as part of the triplet'; Henle, however print this figure as in the **second** example (i.e. in accordance with the **manuscript**) although the commentary, detailed as it is on the subject, does not come down conclusively on either side. Then the Paderewski edition prints it as in the **first** example, and their commentary suggests on balance that it should be played exactly as shown, i.e. with the semiquaver coming after the third triplet (noting that this notation was evidently passed by Chopin himself in those first editions). And writing in

1926 Cortot states categorically that 'the difference between the rhythms and must be observed with the utmost exactness, both when opposing each other in the two hands, and when, as in the last five bars they unite in their second aspect, and thus add a heroic accent to the majestic character of the prelude' (Cortot edition). The innocent grass-roots player is thus left totally at sea. In practice most players, particularly those of the older generation, adhere more-or-less to the Cortot instructions, although he himself on his re-issued recording hedged his bets and threw in triplets, semiquavers and demisemiquavers with his typical confident abandon. Pianists must decide for themselves. I have no doubt that the observance of the dotted rhythms throughout creates an infinitely grander effect, and this for me must decide the issue.

Also, if Chopin had intended the figure to read throughout the piece, **why**

on the first beat of b.8 did he then **actually** write . This was evidently

a firm decision by Chopin since, as can be seen in the facsimile he erased the dot which he had at first placed after the high A flat on the first beat. This appears as an inspired touch which **highlights** the impact of this, the climactic moment of the piece – the point towards which the overall *crescendo* mounts. (Even here however there is some uncertainty – some players

interpret this figure as above, others prefer the perhaps stronger effect of

On the question of the double dotted figures, i.e. in the LH from the opening, and in both hands from b.9, there seems to be no doubt, and authorities appear to be agreed that they should be played as written.

At first, study the treble and the bass lines separately. Practise the RH using the fifth finger all the time, endeavouring to keep the line as *legato* as possible, i.e. holding each note as long as possible and only raising it (as **little** as possible) just in time to play the next note. Then practise the treble and bass lines together **without** the inner triplets. If you are following the Cortot course, enunciate both the single and double dotted rhythm with meticulous accuracy, always thinking of each semiquaver or demisemiquaver as the **upbeat** to the subsequent beat (see General Introduction under 'Dotted Rhythm'). The obvious technical/musical problem here is the bringing out of the RH melody line played with the 'weak' fifth finger over the inner triplets played with the 'stronger' fingers. So practise the RH bringing out the melody line as resonantly as possible while playing the inner triplets in a light *staccato*, to get accustomed to the necessary 'leaning' on the weaker part of the hand while leaving the remainder of the hand

feeling light and free.  When you put hands together set

a rock-steady, slow, march-like pulse, with a crotchet 'tread' of around ♩ = 40-2. Enter in a full, resonant tone, but not too loud in order to 'leave room' for the *crescendo* to the *fortissimo* at bb.8 and 12. Listen acutely to the balance of sound so that the treble and bass lines sing out confidently, 'filled out' but never swamped by the inner triplets. Shape the first phrase in a steady resolute line through to the third beat of b.2, then making it clear that you are beginning a new phrase on the upbeat to b.3. Begin the LH trills in bb.3 and 4 on the grace note

on the beat (see General Introduction under 'Ornaments')

and, taking care to keep the RH triplets rock-steady, feel the sense of an upbeat 'push' through the trill as you *crescendo* towards the first beat of b.4. Inexperienced players who find they

cannot fit in so many notes, can try   (Those following the

Vienna Urtext advice will, of course continue to align the treble semiquaver with the third triplet quaver.) At the end of b.4 allow a little extra time to articulate the grace note suffix through the end of the bar as you poise yourself to 'start again' from b.5. Play these grace notes in a just-

detached style, as indicated, fitting them in thus:

Feel through these trills that the LH is conforming to the steady RH quavers and **not** the other way about. The tendency is for the trills to take over, sabotaging the steady RH rhythm and causing a chaotic scrabble and a consequent 'falling into' the subsequent first beat.

'Point' the arrival on the dominant of C major on the third beat of b.5, and then grade the *crescendo* carefully as you proceed majestically in an inexorable tread through bb.6-7, to reach a huge resonance on the first beat of b.8. There is no need to bang. If you balance the sound carefully, using natural weight, giving resonant support with the bass octaves, and with optimum help from the pedal, you can achieve an immense volume without forcing. Allow an extra instant to maximise the climactic arrival on the first beat of b.8, and then make a dramatic *diminuendo* through the second half of the bar. Allow a little give through the last beat of b.8 to prepare for the *piano* on the first beat of b.9, and then once more grade the *crescendo* carefully, listening to the modulatory inflections, and beginning a slight *ritenuto* through the second half of b.11 as indicated, to arrive in *fortissimo* again on the first beat of the last bar. Do not allow the sound to peter out through this last bar as the inexperienced player is inclined to do, but carry the volume of sound through as you continue the magisterial 'drawing out' towards an almost defiant, partly tied, final chord.

Prelude No. 10 in C sharp minor (8+)

Here a sudden fancy flies in, circles, and vanishes on the lightest breeze. It **sounds** highly virtuosic, and indeed the most precise and sensitive coordination is needed, but the constant RH patterns lie easily for a small hand and are not too hard to learn and memorise. Practise the RH semiquaver figure at first **without** the upper note, so that the inner line descends from b.1 with

the fingering:  *etc.* Then add the upper

notes, C sharp, G sharp, etc. with a **short** light stroke of the fifth finger. If these notes are allowed to 'hang on' they will not only give a heavy effect to the whole pattern, but also impede the downward progress of the hand. Keep the hand fairly 'well in' towards the back of the keyboard, so that the black and the white notes can be covered with minimum disturbance to the equilibrium of the hand. Feel a tiny 'push' on the fourths or fifths, i.e. on the first

semiquaver of each 5-note group   with a natural

lightening of the sound through the remaining notes as indicated by the ▭. The impetus given by this little 'push' facilitates the quick, neat 'twirling' of the remaining notes of the triplet, thereby enabling the 5-note effect to happen quite easily without having to labour the point. Then practise the LH alone. Note that the opening spread chord is a **crotchet**. Give this a quiet but clear definition, therefore, and then, strictly in time, give the spread **quaver** chords a lighter, more insouciant 'flick'.

When you put hands together realise that the LH is very much the 'conductor' here. (See General Introduction under 'The Left Hand'.) Practise slowly at first, and have your pulse 'well in the system' so that you enter with a perfectly placed upbeat sextuplet, using this to poise yourself ready to fly off from b.1. Have the LH ready too, so that it precisely defines the first beat of b.1, and thereby sets the rhythm off with a secure start. Practise through to the first beat of b.3, over and over, gradually increasing the speed to reach a stable **3/4** pulse at a tempo at which you can fit the RH comfortably in with the LH chords, and no faster, always feeling that the flying RH is fitting in with the perfectly timed LH chords, and **not** the other way around. Let the RH 'go to' a resonant, though not loud, emphasised tied dotted minim G sharp on the first beat of b.3, and then phrase the chords beautifully smoothly, poising yourself for a fractional extra instant on the emphasised third beat of b.4 ready to leap up for the next downward flight. **Listen** to the resonance of the held G sharp through bb.3-4. This, with the light broken octave figures in the LH, creates a 'double' dominant pedal point effect here. Note the dancing effect of the bass through b.4 (see General Introduction under 'Articulation'). Feel each of these chord passages (bb.3-4, 7-8, etc.) as quiet multivoiced conversational interludes intervening between each bout of evanescent twittering chatter.

Place the grace note prefix **on** the third beat in b.7. (see General Introduction under 'Ornaments'), and poising yourself again on the emphasised upbeat to b.9, 'point' the change to F sharp minor in a new, perhaps more whispering tone. Take an extra instant to 'point' the emphasised octave A on the third beat of b.16 – like a sudden warning call. Linger a little on this note, allowing the sound to fade slightly. Then, having changed fingers on the lower tied A as indicated in order to hold this note through b.17, end quietly and a little soberly, but without too much of a *ritenuto*.

Chopin's pedalling indications here need to be treated with some caution on the modern piano. Most players confine themselves to a shortish pedal on the first beat of b.1, say to last just **through** this first beat, and then a **very** short 'flick' of pedal on each quaver chord through bb.1-2, with a more warmly resonant effect through bb.3-4, changing the pedal on each beat.

Prelude No. 11 in B major (8+)

This is another delectable miniature, the LH and RH interacting like the comfortable lighthearted chatter between familiar friends. Practise hands separately, following the easily undulating curves of either hand. Lead in with a quiet but warm-toned introductory treble dotted minim F sharp, and poise yourself to run down easily in gentle *diminuendo* towards the 'proper' start on the first beat of b.3. Articulate the RH in a smooth but clear burbling style through bb.3-4, feeling the light 'lift' up to the D sharp at the end of each bar. Then feel the implied gentle cross-rhythm effect through b.5 (and again through bb.9-10). Listen to the intervals through b.6 as the RH curves up towards and back from the sixth on the third quaver of the bar. The RH here is saved from being too awkward for a small hand by the naturally occurring 'give' in the tempo as you go up to and down from this highest point of the phrase, easing through the second half of the bar ready to 'start again' from b.7.

The undulation of the LH has a light, smoothly 'bobbing' quality through bb.3-4. Then curve up through b.5 towards the D sharp on the first beat of b.6, easing down again through the remainder of the bar towards b.7. When you put hands together, listen to the individual curves of each hand through bb.3-4, and then take care to keep the LH steady through b.5 beneath the momentary cross-rhythm effect in the RH. Then listen to the 'staggered' effect as the LH reaches the peak of its curve on the first beat of b.6, and the RH on the third **quaver** pulse. Then easing through this bar as described to 'start again' in b.7, make a more positive *crescendo* from b.9. Listen to the lower LH line descending towards the first beat

of b.11  and then 'open out' the tone through bb.11-12.

Support the RH with a quietly resonant bass E on the first beat of b.13, and 'point' the sustained

treble melodic fragment through bb.13-14 over the

continuing inner quaver line, taking a little extra time to curve the LH quavers in an expressive arc through b.14 as you poise yourself to set off again in b.15. Listen to the LH line again through b.18 moving in tenths with the treble (like a deep-fetched sigh, says Weinstock (p.221)), and subtly 'point' the LH rest in b.19. Ease up to a warm-toned treble dotted minim F sharp on the first beat of b.21, playing the grace note on the beat with the LH fifth like a

slurred acciaccatura (and catching this note in the pedal).

Give this high F sharp its full value, if not more, before letting the quavers run down towards b.23 (this time with a more wistful air than through b.2). Then play on through bb.23-5 as if closing the conversation with a tinge of regret, ending with quiet finality through the last two bars.

The charming intimacy of the piece is dispelled if the tempo is too fast. Most players settle at around ♩. = 116-20, allowing a considerable degree of give and take to highlight the details of nuance. But it can still sound delightful at several notches below this if the detail is sketched with affection and grace. Once again, as in No.10, Chopin's pedalling needs to be lightened on the modern piano, e.g. pedalling just the first half of bb.3 and 4 etc. and changing the pedal several times through bb.5-6.

Prelude No. 12 in G sharp minor (VA)

This is a fearsome piece, both in its technical demands, and in its vicious hectoring spirit. Nevertheless, as in the case of some of the most virtuosic of the Studies, it is one from which the competent sub-virtuoso player can profit, at least from the study of just a few bars. The LH propels the RH along with an unflagging pattern through the first twenty bars. Thereafter there is the hint of a momentary respite in a partly tied upbeat chord (to bb.22, 25 and 26) and a short sustained fragment, bb.39-40. Similarly in the RH through bb.21-2, 24-5, etc. there is a momentary give in the prevailing pattern of hectoring treble quavers over inner crotchets. The LH needs to be firmly 'planted' on the emphasised crotchet chord on the first beat of b.1, which is **not** *staccato*, and then, springing off this chord, 'direction' the hand downward (see General Introduction under 'Some Explanations and Amplifications') to 'grasp' the *staccato* octaves G sharp and D sharp with a strong 'pluck' on each, 'directioning' the hand upwards again to the crotchet chord on the first beat of b.2, and so on. Then through bb.5-8 the chords are continuously *staccato*.

The treble quavers have to be treated as slurred couplets. Nevertheless Chopin did **not** indicate slurs, implying thereby perhaps that the **second** note of each couplet should not be too light, i.e. that the two notes should have a more equal volume than might be normally suggested by a pattern of slurs. Practise the quavers alone, using the **eventual**

fingering  performing the normal 'down-

up' movement of the hand as for a slurred couplet, i.e. raising the hand slightly from each **second** quaver so that it 'falls' with slight natural emphasis on the subsequent quaver. But in this instance give a little 'kick' to each second, virtually *staccato*, quaver as you **lift** it, so that it by no means sounds flaccid but, as already said, sounds almost as strong as each **first** quaver.

Next, practise thus:  *etc.* Then

practise as written, **holding** each inner crotchet note or chord, to come **off** concurrently with the

virtually *staccato* treble quaver *etc.* so that both thumb and

third finger 'fall' with natural emphasis on the subsequent crotchet beat. This slurred 'down-up' movement provides that essential recurring split second of relaxation without which the hand would seize up within a few bars. And the little 'kick' on the second quaver described above provides a tiny 'rebound' which helps to 'send the hand on' towards the next beat in an onward movement that becomes to a large extent self-generating.

When you put hands together, very slowly at first, feel the goading character of the *crescendo* through bb.2-4 (starting **not** too loud in b.1). Then bb.5-7 have a more open quality as the RH 'peaks' its curve through b.5, and the LH leaps back and forth with a springing, pendulum-like *staccato*. Then, 'pointing' the treble quaver rest on the first beat of b.8, allow the sense of a little 'give' through b.8 ready to snap off again from b.9. Take this longer curve up to a higher dynamic level as you rise towards the middle of b.15, and again with a **slight** easing through the end of b.17. Then there is the sense of pressing on menacingly from b.18, ready to land as if with a vicious pounce on the *fortissimo* chord on the first beat of bb.21 and 22. The RH has a slight respite here as you 'lean' on the sustained treble dotted minims, but without any slackening of impetus, nor any sacrifice of the biting quality of the inner thirds. 'Point' the implied emphasis on the partly tied LH upbeat to bb.22, 25 and 26 as if with an onward 'push'. There is a slight lowering of the tension from b.24 down towards the end of b.28. Then following the turn into C major at b.29, there is a powerful upward thrust towards the end of b.30, and another from b.31, carrying on with furious propulsion towards the climactic hammer blows through bb.37-8. From the second beat of b.39 there has to be a pronounced retraction, **using** the sustained lower LH dominant D sharp to help in this reining back, ready to set off again from b.41. 'Point' the bass octave line as it jabs viciously downwards on the second beat of bb.49-52. Following the strong 'landing' on the subdominant seventh chord on the first beat of b.53, there is a gradual subsidence, but not in the sense of supervening serenity – the angry mutterings persist to the last, coming to an abrupt final stop with stabbing dominant-tonic unisons. Tempo has to be governed by practicalities, but every student of this piece should listen to the Cortot recording. At a tempo of around $\downarrow$. = 88 (and with his customary shower of wrong notes!) he generates a white-hot tension that is unlikely to be surpassed.

Prelude No. 13 in F sharp major (7)

This is a poem of a kind of veiled tenderness that is too intimate, perhaps, for the glare of the concert hall. Arthur Hedley tells of a 'hard-bitten' music critic who felt that 'it was the music of a vanished age, heard as in a shell that has been cast up on the shore of time.' (p.147). The slow breathed melody of the outer sections is carried along on quiet quaver waves, one of Chopin's most beautiful 'accompanying counterpoints'. This is one of the more complex of the Preludes in that it is concerned with more than one idea (see the Introduction to the Preludes).

Tempo varies widely among pianists. The essential is to find a motion at which the LH quavers can flow unhurriedly, but at which the RH melody can also maintain a forward impulse. This can be interpreted very differently according to individual metabolism. Some eminent performers go as slow as ♩ = 90-100 (which is too slow to find the ♩. on the metronome). My own feeling is for rather more movement, nearer to ♩. = 40, which allows for a considerable slowing into the *più lento.*

bb. 1–20
Practise the LH first, shaping each group of quavers in expressively rounded arcs. Feel that you are 'going on through' the first three main beats towards the dominant bass and wider-spanned curve through the second beat of b.2, then feel a tiny 'give' through the end of this bar, ready to 'start again' in b.3. It is helpful to realise that the salient notes in each group invariably fall on the crotchet pulse.

 This is not to suggest **accents** on these notes, of

course, but the consciousness of this fact helps both to shape the curve clearly and to maintain the even forward flow. Notice also that almost invariably the highest note of the curve (i.e. the A sharp through b.1) falls on the third crotchet pulse of each group, so that this 'peak' of each little curve provides an 'upbeat' lead towards the next main beat.

For less experienced players it is a good plan to practise the RH thus

Play the long melody notes in a fairly full singing tone, and the inner chords in a soft light *staccato* to get the sense of 'leaning' on the outer, 'weaker' finger so that the melody line sings out gently over the inner harmonies. Then practise the RH as written **in time**. Bring in the first chord in a softly singing tone, and **hold** the sustained chords, releasing them as late as possible, and raising the hand just sufficiently to be able to play the next chord clearly (see under Prelude No.4 for this technique of playing repeated chords in a simulated *legato*). Feel, as in the LH, that you are 'going on through' the first three chords to rise to the fifth on the second beat of b.2 as the 'objective' of the 2-bar phrase. Then again feel a little 'give' as the line falls ready to 'start again' in b.3. When you put hands together try to create a softly dreaming tone, and practise this 2-bar phrase over and over in a continuous movement so that you absorb that sense of the quiet melodic chords gently 'waved' along by the LH quavers. You will then be set fair to carry on through the first section, always retaining the consciousness of the six-crotchet pulse moving within the overall 2-in-the-bar rhythm. Feel the implied sense of a slight swell as you rise to the second beat of b.2, and then let the tone 'fall' a little with a slight 'give' through the end of the bar as described, ready to continue into b.3 in the same smooth tone as before. Let the RH upbeat third to b.4 'speak' as you prepare to shape the cross-rhythm 'turn' in thirds with a little 'lift' up towards an expressive 'lean' on the appoggiatura-like chord on the second beat of b.4. Be sure to keep the movement of the LH quavers perfectly steady here, feeling that the five-quaver group is fitting in

with this steady LH, and **not** the other way about.

Listen to the held resonance of the inner RH C sharp (often given as a dotted minim rather than a semibreve), and be sure to **lift** the preceding upper third (without a bump) to show the quaver rest on the sixth crotchet pulse, ready to lead on with the quaver upbeat to b.5 (see General Introduction under 'Articulation'). Then make a smooth swell up towards the chord on the first beat of b.6, listening also to the shape of the wider, higher-reaching LH curve. Then listen again to the LH 'going on' through the second beat of this bar before tailing the phrase away graciously towards the second beat of b.7, and take a little extra time as you listen to the LH 'curling' back towards the first beat of b.9. Interpret the arpeggiated chord on the first beat

of b.7 thus:  Listen to the wider LH intervals through

the second half of b.8, allowing a little 'give' as you prepare to lead off quietly again

from b.9, placing the appoggiatura thus on the first beat:

Feel an increased sense of yearning as the triplet chords 'grow' from the tied chord on the second beat of b.11 in an expressive swell towards the second beat of b.12. Feel the semiquaver at the end of bb.13, 14, etc. in the sense of an expressive upbeat to the subsequent chord. Listen to the inflections of the LH as you go towards a slight 'lean' on the chord on the second beat of b.16; and then let the line subside towards the tonic on the first beat of b.18, 'coming back' as if with a little afterthought on the second beat, and then subsiding again towards the first beat of b.20. Let the LH ease a little through b.20 beneath the sound of the tonic chord, noting the upbeat effect of

the slurred C sharp and then the E

as you lead into the slower tempo at b.21.

There is more of a sense here of the six-crotchet pulse (as opposed to the more

bb.21–28 apparent overall feeling of 𝅗𝅥. 𝅗𝅥. through bb.1–20), and if you allow this

alteration in rhythmic nuance to 'happen', the tempo will slow naturally to the motion that feels right. There is also the sense of a quiet deliberation in the emerging inner LH line which helps to set the tempo.

Practise hands separately once more. In the LH listen to the expressive melodic fragments in the inner line through b.21, and the lower line through b.22, and so on, feeling the light 'lift' of the inner line towards the D sharp on the fifth quaver pulse of b.21 and in the lower line towards the D sharp on the fourth quaver and the F sharp on the tenth quaver of b.22. Once again practise the smooth, 'close' touch as described under Prelude No.4. Then practise the treble line alone. 'Bring in' the high F sharp in a soft yet carrying tone on the first beat of b.21, and let the line 'fall' as if in a *portamento* towards the A sharp on the second beat. Then feel the sense of 'going on' towards a slight 'lean' on the tied minim B sharp on the first beat of b.22, and go on to ease through the turn with a little 'lift' moving towards the long C sharp as a singer would. Then feel the sense in which the phrase carries 'on and over' into the sequential phrase in b.23.

Next practise the treble line in combination with the inner RH repeated notes. At first exaggerate the effect of 'leaning' on the melody notes in a rather strong tone, and playing the inner repeated notes in an extra light but very even tone. Then practise the treble line in combination with the **inner LH** line through b.21, carrying on into the **lower** LH line through b.22, and so on. Study the effect of the voices in all the possible different combinations, **listening** to their interrelating effects. When you finally assemble all the voices together, practise through from b.20, and introduce the treble line in a quiet clear tone that 'drifts' over the softly intermingling inner voices. The inner RH line and the repeated quavers in the LH (lower line through b.21, inner line through b.22) provide a softly murmuring *ostinato* amidst the predominant line of the treble song and the alternating voices of the LH counterpoint – the whole moving in a dream-like haze. Feel the cumulative little syncopated 'leans' on the tied treble G sharp on the second and fifth crotchets of b.25 and the tied dotted minim in b.26, and then, following the little 'lift' to the C sharp near the end of b.26, gradually phase away the chords towards the chord on the second main beat of b.28. If you **sing** the treble melody of this section, you will immediately understand how to shape its expressive nuances within the sense of the overall line of bb.21-8.

bb.28–38   As you arrive on this chord on the second beat of b.28, linger for an extra instant on the tonic octave in the LH, and then make it clear that you are leading on from the quaver E sharp (as indicated by the slur) in a slight *rallentando* as you prepare to return to Tempo I in b.29. Take this LH down to a quietly resonant bass F sharp as you 'bring in' the RH on the augmented fourth in such a way as to 'return into' the original thought, rather than giving the sense of making a break to 'start afresh'.

The negotiation of the 'separate' high notes (bb.33-6) which, as Cortot says, 'come and rest upon the melody like fleeting signs of hope' (see Cortot edition), induces understandable panic in the inexperienced player, who will usually both fluff the chords **and** overshoot the high notes, lurching through bb.33-6 in an increasing confusion of 'grab and miss'. The chord is always placed **on** the beat followed by an unhurried, slur-like 'lift' to the high note. At first it is best

to think of placing the high note on the second quaver thus:

aspiring later, perhaps, to the more subtle effect of

(Those with small hands will need to treat the chord on the second beat of b.30 and the first beat of b.31 similarly.) The shape of the chord-phrases here is essentially the same as that from bb.13-20. Endeavour therefore to recreate the smooth poise of those bars through the chords and LH quavers while letting the high notes 'rest' celestially upon the overall sound. Allow a tiny 'give' through the end of b.35 as you prepare to arrive on a quiet tonic on the first beat of b.36. Tail the LH quavers gently away beneath this held tonic sound towards a *pianissimo* bass F sharp on the first beat of b.37, then re-pedalling as indicated so that you 'show' the RH quaver rest, ready to shape the inner line and last upper fragment as if in a lingering afterthought towards the final tonic.

    Chopin's pedal markings are only spasmodic, i.e. through the second half of bb.2, 4, etc; in some bars of the middle section; and through the sequence of broken chords and high notes through bb.33-5. (But this does not mean that he intended no pedal elsewhere – see General Introduction.) Overall pedalling is a very individual matter in this piece. Some players will prefer a light skim of pedal over each half-bar through bb.1-19, others will change or half-change the pedal on each crotchet beat (or on each third and sixth crotchet beat) to define better the inflections of the LH. Chopin's 'entire' half-bar pedalling (i.e. in bb.2, 4, and 6) may be found somewhat heavy on the modern piano, and similarly through the middle section. A sensitive half-change on the second main beat of bb.33 and 35, in combination with the *una corda* will enable the treble and bass sound to 'hang' through the bar without creating too thick an effect.

Prelude No. 14 in E flat minor (7)

The obvious similarities between this Prelude and the Finale of Op.35, the Funeral March Sonata, are at first sight confusing in view of the opposing indications: *Allegro* and *pesante* here as compared to *Presto, sotto voce e legato* for the Op.35 movement. However, closer study demonstrates that they are, in fact, very different animals. Or to put it another way, they show that a similar musical idea, differently handled, can take on an entirely different character. The spectral frissons of the later movement, bound up as they are in the concept of the whole Sonata, are far removed from these stark, earthbound unisons. Iron has indeed entered the soul here, or to quote Cortot's different and graphic analogy, 'the feeling of a moving mass of liquid which should be evoked by the compact tone of the heavy waves of triplets.' (Cortot edition). In fact we can understand this by a glance at the printed page. In Op.35 the triplets flit across the bars in wisp-like

diagonal surges:  in contrast to the much

more 'lumbering' up-and-down pattern here

indeed, the idea of heaving primeval liquid, or worse, is a telling one.

    To absorb the sense of the harmonic basis it is a good plan at first to practise

in chords  and then, as Cortot suggests

Then practise hands separately as written, slowly at first,

thinking in clearly defined triplet groups, i.e. crotchet beats. Then as you gradually increase speed, let the sense of the overall two-in-the-bar take over. Proceed similarly hands together, and practise

also in different rhythms  etc.

Even when practising slowly **and** when practising in varying rhythms, observe Chopin's detailed 'hairpin' indications so that you indelibly absorb the sense of the dynamic surges and thrusts, and thereby the architecture of the piece, i.e. the overall build-up towards the *fortissimo* at b.11, carried through to the end of b.14, and the shorter period of subsidence therefrom. Do not start too loud, and feel the small surge towards the middle of the third beat through bb.1 and 2 (i.e. to the third of the C flats) retracting a little through the fourth beat. Then feel the longer surge through bb.3-4 to carry you on into bb.5-6 in the higher register in a rather higher dynamic. Then, surging and retracting as indicated through bb.7-10, feel an enormous thrust through the end of b.10 into a roaring *fortissimo* in b.11, carrying on this tone in a final thrust up towards the end of b.14. Then hurtle precipitately downwards through b.15, 'pointing' the hidden offbeat line like 'braking' downhill footholds,

and finally suggest these last little

surges like dying mutterings within the

overall *diminuendo*. Take a tiny extra instant to prepare to leap down to sepulchral quiet final crotchets, coming **off** precisely on the second beat.

Interpretations of this piece vary widely, and different inner touches can be 'pointed' to show significant chromatic inflections here, or to create a deliberate rhythmic jerk there, e.g. on the first C naturals and on the B double flats in b.3; the B double flats, A flats, D naturals and C flats through b.6; and so on, as well as through the downward line through b.15 already mentioned. The touch needs to be heavy in the sense of thick, incorporating a degree of overlap, varied in extent according to whether you incline to the 'heavy liquid' effect or to a more metallic clangour. This may, as Cortot enjoins, include partial holding of some harmonic notes

to create a chordal effect. *etc.* **Touches** of pedal can be used

to implement certain points, such as the peak of each little surge in bb.1 and 2, the arrival in *fortissimo* in b.11, and so on. Tempos again can vary widely – a mean of around $\frac{1}{2}$ = 66-76 is suggested, but with wide margins on either side. (The field is thrown wide open by the startling replacement of the *Allegro* with a pencilled *Largo* in the copy belonging to Jane Stirling. This, however, is thought by J.-J. Eigeldinger (p.125) to be an instruction for practising.) A 'thicker' overall sound will imply a rather slower tempo, a more articulated effect a rather faster one. If you merely try to play the notes of this piece, you will produce only an exercise in unison triplets. The essential is to conceive the effect **you** want – your **own** effect, using your **own** visual imagery – and 'go for it'.

Prelude No. 15 in D flat major (7)

This is the piece that is stuck forever with the 'Raindrop' title (see under No.6). It is a favourite student piece, with useful lessons in the balancing and building of resonances. These resonances are considerably complex, and although not technically difficult, it is a piece that requires close study in a musical sense.

bb.1–8
It is important to understand that the principal motif (bb.1-4) is not merely a melody and accompaniment, but a combination of several interrelating layers of sound. Play the RH melody of these first four bars, and then see how the inner LH line moves with the treble in similar, though not identical duet, over the almost continuous presence of the lower bass quavers.

Practise the RH alone in a quietly singing tone at a tempo of about ♩ = 72. Make an expressive little 'lean' on the opening dotted quaver, and then listen to the fall of this recurring figure towards the minim A flat on the second beat. **Listen** to this note singing through its full value, and then move in an overall very gentle swell up towards the minim G flat on the second beat of b.3. Feel this note as the peak of the little curve and swell, then let the line subside gently towards the third beat of b.4.

Now practise the LH holding down the A flat continuously through bb.1-4 thus

Shape the melodic upper voices in a warm singing tone over the held dominant resonance, with the upper, i.e. the thumb line quietly predominating with a smooth horn-like sound. Then practise singing out the melodic notes again, but playing the repeated A flat in

a quiet soft *staccato*.

Endeavour to keep the dual lines of the melodic notes as smooth as possible (see under Preludes Nos.4 and 13), 'leaning' a little on these notes, and feeling that the weight of the hand is concentrated on this inner 'strong' part of the hand, the thumb and second finger, while the outer, weaker part of the hand, the fifth finger, remains light and free.

Next play the LH as written, still 'leaning' on the melody notes, and now playing the repeated quavers as smoothly as possible so that they move in a quiet, even murmur of almost continuous sound, and delicately 'pointing' the rise up to and down from the B flat on the second beat of b.3. Always use this LH fingering  here and in b.5, etc. and also in bb.9, 10, etc. – this use of the fifth finger brings the hand 'into position' ready to play the melody notes. (See General Introduction under 'Fingering'). As you play this LH, actually **sing** the RH line, or if you cannot cope with this, at least **imagine** its smooth line moving expressively above. **Listen** to the sustained inner dotted minim C through b.3 as the thumb-line 'edges' upwards to the B flat, and again through the first half of b.4 as it returns downwards. Note also the 'doubled' A flat on the second quaver pulse of b.3 which gives the sense of a little upward 'push' towards this little 'peak', the minim B flat. Now play the RH line **with** the two LH melody voices but **without** the lower quavers, and then play the RH just with the lower quavers. When you finally assemble all the voices as written, play bb.1-4 over and over until you are thoroughly familiar with the movement at a tempo around the 60-72 suggested above. This is a piece that can easily become sticky. On the other hand, at too fast a tempo the finer nuances of its shadowy, melancholy character are lost. Listen, listen, listen to the different strands – continually monitoring the balance to ensure that the treble melody gently predominates, closely 'backed up' by the LH melodic voices, the whole cushioned and quietly propelled along by the almost continuous even murmur of the lower quavers to create an overall sound that is softly clear, smooth and dream-like. Make sure that you are **poised** with the pulse 'well in the system' so that the hands are perfectly synchronised from the first beat. Allow just a fraction of extra time **through** the first beat as you lift the LH from the D flat to the A flat, at the same time listening to the expressive 'fall' in the RH so that once again the hands are perfectly synchronised as they 'meet' on the minims on the second beat, and then feel that you are moving on just a fraction on the **third** beat, from which point you securely establish your even pulse. Quietly 'point' the little step in the lower line up to the B flat on the third beat of b.2 beneath the held upper voices, and then feel the very gentle curve as described up towards and down from the second beat of b.3. Then as you 'return' to the tonic chord on the third beat of b.4, feel at the same time a sense of carrying on through the upbeat 7-note 'turn', to 'start again' from b.5. The inexperienced player invariably panics at the sight of this upbeat turn, and goes into spasm in a frantic scrabble for home in b.5 (and similarly at bb.23-4). The essential is to keep the LH quavers **steady**, though allowing a little 'give' through the very end of the bar as the RH 'rounds the corner' into b.5. Practise at first **without** the preceding grace note E flat. It is simplest to think of the RH in groups of three and four

quavers to 'fit in' with the LH thus:

(More experienced players may well 'merge' the notes more loosely.) Practise this through to the first beat of b.5 until you can negotiate the turn quite fluently. Always think of it in the sense of an **upbeat** 'easing' you into b.5. When you add the grace note, let it just precede the beat in a 'speaking' manner. The fingering shown above is **not** usually given, but I find that it allows the smoothest 'bridge' into b.5. There is plenty of time to change fingers on the dotted quaver

98

and, furthermore, the act of doing so predisposes the very slight expressive *tenuto* that is implied on this note.

bb.8–27 Arrive on the crotchet D flat on the third beat of b.8 in such a way as to make it clear that the overall first period (bb.1-8) is closing here. Then feel that you are taking a breath, ready to move on towards A flat minor in a new, rather more resolute tone from the upbeat to b.9. Feel the sense of an ongoing 'lean' on the repeated minim E flat on the second beat of b.9, which reinforces this sense of moving into a different phase. Most hands had best take the upper LH F with the RH

etc. (This is another awkward corner which

frequently causes a further onward collapse into the subsequent bar.) The grace note figure

in b.11 and b.15 etc. sounds more eloquent shaped thus:

rather than as a triplet:

Shape the RH line in a smooth expressive curve through to the first beat of b.12, then making it clear that you are starting the new phrase from the second beat, allowing the tone to expand somewhat here, and then subsiding gradually again from b.17, ready to ease back through b.19 to the opening motif in b.20. From b.9 the LH is less overtly melodic. Nevertheless it needs to be listened to and balanced just as carefully as through bb.1-8, its harmonic inflections always 'filling out' and buoying along the RH melody. Listen particularly to the quietly 'tolling' effect of the upper LH thirds through bb.18 and 19, 'pointing' also the lower 'doubled' G flat which applies a touch of 'brake' as you prepare to ease into b.20. (Remember the 5-5 fingering at the beginning of b.9, and on the third beat of b.10, etc. – see above.) Shape the 7-note turn similarly to the one in b.4, but perhaps a little more lingeringly if, as you may feel inclined, you choose to play from b.24 in a quieter, still more dream-like manner. (The suggested

fingering  is again a personal one.)

A significant phrase mark is pencilled here in the copy belonging to Jane Stirling as shown above (and equally applicable at bb.4-5) showing the intended 'on and over' sense of the ornamental turn 'into' the sound of the minim A flat in b.24. 'Tail the sound away' to a whisper towards the first beat of b.27, and then feel the sense of moving on very slightly as the repeated A flats lead on from the second quaver pulse of the bar.

bb.28–59 Have the LH ready to enter with a sepulchral but definite bass fifth as you 'slide' enharmonically into C sharp minor on the first beat of b.28. Here we can indeed imagine the 'visions of deceased monks and funeral chants' with which George Sand tells us Chopin was beset (Harasowski, unpublished MS). **Listen** to the LH intervals, and the alternate movement of the lower and upper line (i.e. through bb.28, 29, 30, etc.) as you move in an ominous-toned slight *crescendo* towards the long tied fifth on the first beat of b.31. Let the murmuring repeated G sharp complement the dynamic rise of the LH, and **listen** again to the bare sound of the held fifth through b.31 before letting the overall sound subside a little through bb.32-3. Then let the sound rise again towards a **stronger** LH fifth in b.35. (Take the LH E on the upbeat to b.35 with the RH.) Let the sound build **gradually** through the RH octaves through b.35, ready for the LH to enter again in a continuing *crescendo* from b.36. **Use** the resonance of the 'reinforcing' inner RH crotchets from b.36 to help build up the sound

 *etc.* and arrive on a powerful chord on the first beat

of b.39, ready to unleash full power at b.40. Be sure to catch the bass grace note G sharp within

the sustaining pedal at b.39.  This can be done by 'holding over'

the last RH octave G sharp from b.38 while you play the bass note and change the pedal, or if this proves too daunting a feat of coordination, by holding the pedal through **from** the last beat of b.38 right through b.39 as suggested in some editions. In any event, be sure to give that bass note a splendidly resonant sound to 'boost' the *crescendo* as you progress towards the *fortissimo* at b.40. The balance of sound needs to be carefully gauged all through this section, and particularly through the *fortissimo* bars. Realise that the immense volume of sound that you want here is achieved by a commanding bass line filled out by resonant **inner** RH harmonies and quaver octaves and **not** by whacking sledgehammer blows on the quaver octaves. Carry the *fortissimo* through to an immense chord on the first beat of b.43, 'pointing' the splendid resonance of the augmented chord on the third beat of b.42 like a mighty upbeat to this 'final' chord. Then from the second beat through the remainder of b.43 'flicker' the pedal a little to clear the sound, ready to 'start again' in *pianissimo* from b.44.

bb.59–75 Arrive on a similar and if possible even more immense chord on the first beat of b.59. Clear the sound again, and then 'point' the telling B sharp octave on the first beat of b.60. Shape the lines of both hands with equal care from here as you move on in an implied *crescendo* towards the interrupted cadence (bb.62-3), **listening** to the marvellous effect of the sevenths gathering and resolving through bb.61-3 'within' the line of the RH octaves. Listen again to the tolling effect of the RH repeated quaver couplets through b.63 'between' the held resonance of the octave semibreve C sharp. Allow a tiny 'give' through this bar as you prepare to move into the more quiescent phase (bb.64-7). Quietly bring out the inner RH thirds over the continuing dominant repeated quavers, and quietly tolling LH dominant-tonic progressions. As you come to rest on the dominant chord on the first beat of b.67, feel at the same time that the inner quavers are leading on again towards b.68. Listening to the resolving sevenths again through b.70, feel that the last chord is giving an upbeat 'push' to maximise the impact of the astonishing *forte* dominant seventh of F sharp minor on the first beat of b.71. I believe it is a mistake to *diminuendo* immediately following this chord, as many players do. The 'hairpin' indications and the musical sense imply that the subsidence of tone should be only very gradual through bb.72-5, with then a fairly steep *diminuendo* through the second half of b.75. Players with small hands have some problems in the RH through bb.62-75. When in doubt leave out the **lowest** RH note. On the fourth beat of b.64, the third beat of b.65, the fourth beat of b.72, etc. the omission of the quaver G sharp will hardly be detected with the pedalled sound. Similarly the lowest note of some of the chords through b.62 etc. (particularly the first) may have to be omitted.

bb. 75–89 Arrive with a sense of finality in b.75, and 'finish off' the RH chords as in a slurred effect. Then be sure to clear the sound of the treble chord as you *diminuendo* through the second half of the bar, allowing time to ease back towards b.76. (The '*senza ritenuto*' given in some editions is not Chopin's.*) You may like to bring back the opening motif in a yet quieter and more dream-like tone. Allow a little longer through the end of b.79 than at bb.4 and 23, particularly through the very last quaver beat as you tail away the little run to a delicate wisp, and continue the *smorzando* effect as you let the line drift into ethereal nothingness at b.81. (Most players divide this run in b.79 in the obvious way, i.e. into two groups of five notes to fit in with the LH quavers, see General Introduction under 'Free Runs'). Then 'bring in' the emphasised tied treble crotchet B flat as if in a sorrowful cry. Pedal this note to maximise its solo resonance, and **listen** to it through its full tied duration (which novice players never do!). Then shape the solo crotchets in two eloquent 'falls' through bb.82 and 83 towards a quiet reposeful chord on the first beat of b.84. Listen acutely once more to the composite resonance here as you shape the inner RH line with 'speaking' expressiveness through to the end. In particular listen to the eloquent 'lift' to the high B flat on the third beat of b.86 as the inner line crosses the held third, returning to a quietly emphasised dominant seventh harmony on the first beat of b.87. Then let the repeated quavers 'die' towards a just-breathed final chord.

Prelude No. 16 in B flat minor (VA)

This hyper-charged piece is one of the most difficult of the Preludes – it is, need it be said, strictly for the virtuoso. Even so, there are few players who can ride the vertiginous rapids of bb.18-25 in anything but a state of controlled panic. Chopin, we may be sure, would have managed it, not as loud as some modern lions of the keyboard, but with a spate of controlled nervous energy and technical brilliance to compensate for volumes of Steinway *fortissimo*.

The electrifying sequence of opening chords screw up the tension as if preparing to set in motion seething forces of demonic machinery. The LH goads the manic careering of the RH with a pounding figure on each main beat. But it is the calculated LH vacuum on the second and fourth crotchet beats which on the one hand gives the rhythm its demonic quality, but which at the same time makes the overall rhythm so hard to control. And the problem is compounded when the LH augments into slicing octaves from b.18. The upward unison streak from b.42 is a final test. Rapid unison passages are always a challenge, this one particularly, with its wide climbing intervals. It is a stupendous piece. As Robert Collett says, 'It is incomprehensible that anyone who has heard music like this can still think of Chopin as primarily a composer of drawing-room music.' (Walker, p.141).

---

*However, another phrase mark is pencilled in Jane Stirling's copy from the last crotchet beat of b.75 to the first of b.76, indicating an 'up and over' movement into this final reprise, and by implication, little if any *rallentando*. A skilled player is able to 'give' a little while still conveying the sense of onward movement.

Prelude No. 17 in A flat major (8)

This is one of the loveliest of the Preludes, and one of the least complex from an interpretative point of view. This does not mean it is easy to play – indeed, such an expanse of continuous melody borne by the 'weak' fingers of the RH, presupposes a fine degree of control and aural sensibility. Nevertheless, it is not too difficult in technical terms for a competent player at around Grade 8.

Many eminent virtuosi take this piece at a tremendous speed, interpreting it as an impassioned outburst, instead of the spontaneous, predominantly easeful song that Chopin seems to intend. The *Allegretto* gives us the clue, and the mood seems sunlit with afternoon rays and an overlay of nostalgia. A tempo of around ♩. = 60-72 is suggested. The technical problems are twofold and perennial: a) that of 'bringing out' the melody principally with the fifth or fourth finger of the RH over inner notes or chords played with the stronger thumb and/or second finger; and b) that of playing repeated chords in the smoothest possible simulated *legato* style. Nothing is more agonising than early attempts to accompany the melody in juddering *staccato* chords: it is therefore best to tackle the chord problem first.

It is as well to practise the introductory chords first (bb.1-2). (See under Prelude No.4 for the technique of playing chords in this simulated *legato*.) Start playing the RH single note preferably with the third finger and, keeping as close to the keys as possible, try to produce as *legato* a sound as you can. Then add the LH chords, very slowly at first, and gradually increasing speed, trying to create a smooth, soft but vibrant hum of sound, imagining the kind of sound you will want for the chords throughout the piece beneath the treble melody. As you practise these two bars **think** in 2-bar periods, making a little swell and retracting as indicated through bb.1-2. Finally add the pedal, and with its aid (but still playing 'close' to the keys) try to achieve your 'finished' sound. Carry on now in the LH. The fear here is that of missing the bass note at the beginning of each bar or half bar. At first

practise thus:  *etc.* staying as long as possible on each

chord, and then making a quick leap down to a **firm** bass quaver. Do this **precisely in time**, so that you **feel** the second held beat of each bar, making a neat leap-down-and-return to the next chord exactly on the second quaver of the bar, and so on. Never mind if the bass notes misfire at first. If you practise bb.3-10 over and over, your aim will soon improve. Now practise the LH as written. It is extremely important that you **feel** the second beat of each bar, not so much as an accent, but being **conscious** of it within the pattern of repeated chords so that there is a continual sense of the 2-bar pulse. At all costs avoid the unfortunate effect of a hiccough in the rhythm **as** you leap downwards each time. Do exactly the opposite: leap down to play each bass note in time, and then allow the barest hint of a *tenuto* **on** the bass note, and then feel the sense of 'making up' the time as you 'go towards' the second main beat. This very slight *tenuto* effect serves two interrelated purposes: a) it establishes and 'sets' the harmony of the bar or half bar; and b) it allows time to change the pedal and 'catch' the bass note so that its resonance lasts **through** the bar or half bar. Try this at this juncture to establish the coordination of foot and hand (changing the pedal as indicated, on the first beat of each bar, and again on the **second** main beat of bb.6, 8 and 9), and then your pedalling pattern will be set fair for the entire piece. Of course, the *tenuto* effect on the bass notes is only a hinted nuance – if the effect is exaggerated it is as irritating as that of the continual hesitation **before** the bass note. In every instance the bass note has to stand out a little, to be a little stronger than the accompanying chords. (But this overall balance of bass notes, chords and melody has to be adjusted and considered when all the voices are assembled.)

Now practise the RH from b.3. Try at first letting the treble line sing out in a perfect *legato* while holding down the lower note *[music example]* *etc.* Then play the treble similarly, but playing the repeated inner D flats in a light, soft, detached or *staccato* style.

[music example] *etc.* Feel that you are 'leaning' on the smooth melody notes with the outer, 'weaker' part of the hand, so that the melody predominates, while leaving the inner, 'stronger' part of the hand light and free to play the inner notes lightly and quietly. Practise bb.3-4 over and over thus, concentrating on differentiating between the melodic and accompanying strands. Then still 'leaning' on the melody notes, play the inner notes in the smooth, 'close' manner already practised for the chords through bb.1-2, but still keeping the inner notes relatively light. It is vital that this technique is thoroughly studied and understood in a physical and aural sense, since it has to be applied throughout the piece, and continually adjusted according to the varying density of the accompanying chords. Through b.13, and from b.19 onwards, for example, the treble has to sing out over as many as five or six notes in the combined LH and RH accompanying chords. This is taxing work for the melody fingers, and unless the inner part of the hand remains free to play relatively lightly, as described above, the hand will seize up before the first page is through.

When you finally put hands together, learn from bb.1-10 thoroughly before going on. Practise very slowly at first. Bring in the introductory chords in a quiet, even hum as described, allowing a tiny 'give' as you 'retract' the little swell through the end of b.2, ready to lead off in a quiet, sweet tone from b.3. Make it clear that the melody begins **on** the single quaver D flat, and then feel a light 'lift' and vocal curve up to and down from the high D flat on the second beat, with the feeling of 'going towards' a warm-toned 'lean' on the dotted crotchet B flat on the first beat of b.4. Then feel that you are 'going on' to a further implied 'lean' on the tied dotted crotchet A flat on the second beat, so that this note leads 'on and over' into b.5 and through a more 'open' vocal curve through b.5, leading towards the emphasised dotted crotchet on the first beat of b.6, and so on. Thus, instead of the phrases being chopped up into 2-bar 'boxes' (bb.3-4, 5-6, etc.) the tied crotchet on the second beat of b.4 (and similarly on the second beat of bb.6 and 8) carries the melody 'on and over' into the subsequent bars, and we therefore have a long vocalise-like span of melody right through bb.3-10. Practise this span at first without the pedal, creating the smoothest possible melody line and 'hum' of accompanying chords, being sure to hold the tied notes **over** the first beat of bb.5, 7, etc. Then when you add the pedal (as described when practising the LH), be sure that you **continue** to hold these tied notes so that in each instance the melody note is 'caught' along with the bass note when you change the pedal on the first beat of bb.5, 7, etc. Take care also to show the inner quaver rest on the first beat of b.4, the first and second beats of b.6, etc: in other words do not allow the inner note or chord from the preceding bar to 'hang over' into the new harmony of the subsequent bar. Do practise this opening period, (bb.3-10) until it is perfectly fluent, since the principles studied here apply to the whole piece, through all the dynamic and harmonic fluctuations. Allow a certain amount of rhythmic give and take, letting yourself 'go with' the natural rise and fall of the line within the easy overall two-in-the-bar pulse (see General

Introduction under 'Rubato'). Listen to the momentary contrary motion movement of the treble and inner LH line through the first half of b.9, and then allow a little 'give' through the end of the bar as you prepare to arrive on the dominant on the first beat of b.10. Then feel a sense of moving on through b.10, **holding** the treble B flat right through into b.11, ready to set off again from the second quaver of b.11 in a fuller tone (launched by a resonant dominant bass on the first beat of the bar).

'Point' the little dotted rhythm variant through the end of b.17 in the sense of an upbeat to the long A flat in b.18. Then take an extra instant to 'point' the enharmonic change of this treble note as you shift to the dominant seventh of A major on the first beat of b.19. **Listen** to the inflections of the accompanying chords as you begin a gradual *crescendo* towards b.24. Ensure that you 'lift' to a warmly resonant dotted minim C sharp in b.20, and a stronger E in b.22, 'pointing' the upward chromatic movement of the LH through these bars as you 'terrace' upwards towards the high G sharp on the first beat of b.24. Then *diminuendo* slightly through bb.24-5, taking a little extra time to point the rich harmonic inflections here, and then swelling a little again towards b.27. Feel a slight onward 'push' through the inner chords of this bar, and then forge on rather more purposefully through the reiterated fragments (bb.28-9 and b.30) towards a ringing tied E natural through bb.31-2. Then feel another, and stronger onward 'push' as you *crescendo* through bb.32-3, drawing out a little through b.34 as you shape the LH octaves in a bold sweep down to a powerful bass octave on the first beat of b.35, to launch you into a ringing *fortissimo* version of the opening motif. There is no need to bang here: resonant bass octaves caught within the pedal will 'open' up the strings to produce a resonant peal of sound without forcing. Arrive on a full-toned chord on the first beat of b.42, and then 'retreat' again ready to lead on in a *subito piano* from b.43. There is a new, more suppliant, yet eager tone from here as the music rises towards b.51. Interpret the spread chord and grace notes in

bb.43 and 47 thus:  and then take a little extra time

to listen to the inner LH descending line through bb.44 and 48. Create a pealing treble line as you *diminuendo* through bb.51-3. Then feel a surge as the hands move outwards in contrary motion through b.54 beneath the singing tied treble F sharp, ready to sing out from b.55 in a ringing tone. Then there is a sense of a *diminuendo* from b.58, with a hushing of the repeated chords through bb.63-4 towards the *pianissimo* from b.65. It appears that Chopin intended the eleven tonic bass notes to be struck with the same resonance through bb.65-84 'because the idea of the Prelude is based on the idea of an old clock in the castle which strikes the eleventh hour.' Chopin's pupil Camille O'Meara-Dubois told Paderewski that 'he always *struck* that note in the same way and with the same strength because of the meaning he attached to it . . . (in spite of playing everything else *diminuendo*)'. (Eigeldinger, p.83. See also p.157.) Play from b.65 in an overall *sotto voce* using the *una corda* and striking these bass notes in a *sforzato* that is resonant yet soft-toned, using the sustaining pedal exactly as indicated. This creates an atmospheric, slightly muffled effect startlingly similar to the striking clock effect at the end of Schumann's *Papillons*. Leave room to disperse the sound yet more distantly from b.84 within the continuing resonance of the bass chimes. Then after the last chime in b.88, draw back a little as you make a little swell towards the middle of b.89, letting the final melodic fragment 'speak' expressively as it 'falls' towards the final chord.

Prelude No. 18 in F minor (VA)

We have all experienced the fearsome spectacle of an habitually reserved person in the grip of an ungovernable burst of fury. So it seems to be in this Prelude where the customary containment of the urbane Chopin erupts, as Weinstock says, in 'enraged outbursts that skirt incoherence.' (p.223). It is like an explosive recitative – the wild flights of invective punctuated by stabbing chords. Apart from the advanced degree of keyboard athleticism and coordination required to negotiate the careering volleys of unison semiquavers, the feat of holding the piece together is one which few players manage. There has to be some sense of the crotchet pulse: rushing on here, reining back there, but always underlying the overall eruptive force of the tirade. There is an overall gradual increase of dynamics and tension, bursting the banks with the wildly leaping sequence through b.16 towards the huge sound of b.17, with the downward streak of demisemiquavers carrying on the volume of sound through the thundering double trill and jolting *staccato* triplets towards swingeing final chords.

Prelude No. 19 in E flat major (VA)

This seraphic but highly exacting piece, strategically placed between the strident raspings of No.18 and the dolours of No.20, has the happy spirit of many of the Studies, as well as that pursuit of a single technical pattern common to most of Ops.10 and 25. Played in a fleet, accurate, 'soft-pearled' tone, it seems, and is, one of Chopin's most exquisite notions. But like many of even the most virtuosic of the Studies, it is well worth the while of the less advanced player at least to explore the technical idea by studying even a few bars.

The fact that the leaps are 'staggered', i.e. the LH leaps up to the **second** note of each triplet group, and the RH to the first, makes the pattern easier in one sense, in another more difficult. As will be seen, the harmony is tonic based through bb.1-2. It is a good plan first to memorise these two bars so that you can concentrate upon the mastery of the **physical** movement required

throughout the piece. Think of the LH pattern thus:

so that you make the 'effort' of each upward leap, and then feel an easy slurred effect down to each subsequent bass note. As you leap off the bass note, 'direction' the hand upwards, as if with a tiny 'kick', keeping the hand 'close' over the keys, in other words making a **shallow** arc as you leap and 'fall' onto the thumb, rather than raising the hand too much in a wasteful high arc. As you 'slur' downwards, feel the third finger on the B flat as a pivot 'helping' the hand down towards each bass note. Practise the first figure (the first two beats of b.1) over and over until this movement becomes fluent, and then carry on towards the first beat of b.3, aiming higher with the thumb through each beat.

When you practise the RH, think of the pattern thus:

so that you imagine a slur over the first triplet, then leap off the third note to 'land' on the first note of the next slurred triplet, and so on.* This generates the natural desirable effect of slightly

*There is doubt as to whether the third RH quaver in b.1 should be E flat, or G (as in b.8), and editions vary.

emphasising the first note of each group, which creates the implied upper melody line throughout the piece. (This is not to suggest that the 'other' notes are mere accompaniment – the inner notes create a continued shimmer of implied complementary melodic and harmonic strands.) Be sure to release the thumb immediately so that the instant this thumb leaves its note it is ready to shift up towards its next position. In effect, in order to maintain the equilibrium of the hand, the melody note has to be **held** for an extra instant as you ascend through the

wide leaping climbs (bb.1-2, 9-10, etc.) in effect thus:

Then as the RH pattern proceeds in 'closer' position from b.3, the slurred effect becomes less obvious, and similarly in the LH from b.4. When you put the hands together the LH and RH patterns will coalesce quite happily. Feel the light, airy swell up to, and down from the third beat of b.2, and the first beat of bb.6 and 8, and then feel a little give through the end of b.8, thinking of the third triplet group as an upbeat as you prepare to leap off again from b.9. From the upbeat to b.17 the music takes a more serious harmonic turn. The discordant implications of bb.29-32 are reminiscent of the upward sweep through bb.40-2 of the Study in E minor Op.25 No.5. But here perhaps players cannot stomach such a strident intrusion into the idyll, for almost all pianists *diminuendo* down to a wisp at b.32 instead of rising in a *crescendo* as Chopin indicates. There is a ravishing thread of treble chromatic vacillation from b.49 and through the glorious chromatic cross-rhythm effect descending through bb.65-8 – this is not the only occasion when Chopin looks forward to Rachmaninov. In truth there are few pianists who can play the piece with the flawless ease for which it begs. With Chopin himself technique and poetry were inseparable. The recording by Maurizio Pollini comes close to this – a poem in sound indeed.

Prelude No. 20 in C minor (4-5) (O)

There can be no pianist who has not played this piece, and to many of us, as soon as we could reach an octave, it seemed the summit of ambition. We cannot recall a time when we did not know it, and the pop world has discovered it at least once. It remains, and always will, one of the greatest short pieces ever written for the piano. It is in addition a magnificent study in sustained sonority, the prime occasion for helping a pupil to play *fortissimo* without banging, by using natural arm, shoulder, and indeed body weight, and by optimum use of the sustaining pedal. It is at its most effective when played absolutely 'straight' with the leaden tread of a Funeral March, on three distinct dynamic levels, *fortissimo, piano* and *pianissimo*. The essential requirement is a rock-steady, slow crotchet pulse at a suggested ♩ = 40. For inexperienced players who find it hard to 'hold' the slow beat, it is a good plan to count in quavers – this also helps to ensure correct timing of the semiquavers. These must be exact: neither too short nor too long. If they are too long, in other words sloppily 'tripletised', the martial exactness of the rhythm will be undermined. If they are too short, in other words too 'snapped', the weighty strength of the rhythm will be weakened (see General Introduction under 'Dotted Rhythms'). It is essential to realise that this piece is not just a series of crotchet chord-blocks. The treble melody line must sing out, 'filled out' and enhanced but not swamped by the harmonies. To this end, practise the treble melody line **with the fifth finger**, holding each note as long as possible, and raising it only just in time to move on to the next (see under Prelude

No.4). Then practise thus ♪ *etc.* 'leaning on the melody

notes and playing the inner chords in a relatively light, detached style.

When you put hands together, always feel that the RH is leaning slightly outwards towards the fifth finger so that this melody line sings out. At the same time ensure that the other fingers of the RH are working to produce a full-blooded, rounded sound supported by a splendidly resonant bass octave line. With your beat 'well in the system', lead off in a full-toned but not forced *fortissimo,* leaving room for a telling *crescendo* through bb.3-4. Notice how the music proceeds in two 1-bar periods (in which the RH chord pattern is similar, the bass identical) and then show the longer overall phrase through bb.3-4. At the same time feel the sense of these phrase periods within the overall phrase (bb.1-4). Do be sure to carry the *crescendo* right through to a climactic 'arrival' on the dominant chord on the last beat of b.4. Inexperienced players tend to wilt towards the end of b.4, lacking the courage either to 'push' the *crescendo* through to the end, or to implement the dramatic *subito piano* at b.5. So, arriving on the dominant chord in a half-hearted *mezzo-forte,* and sidling into b.5 in a vague *mezzo-piano,* they completely nullify the intended dramatic effect of the dynamic 'clamp-down'.

Allow an extra instant for this 'finality' of this dominant chord to register, and then **feeling** the change not merely mentally but in a physical sense, lead off into b.5 in a smooth *piano* tone without altering the basic beat by a hair's breadth. Do not make the mistake of playing **too** quietly, bearing in mind the third 'level', the *pianissimo* from b.9. Maintain a glassily smooth treble line, 'pointing' the treble sound a little on the first beat of b.5 in order to establish the new line. At the same time **listen** acutely to every inner harmonic inflection of the RH, and in particular to the creeping chromatic descent of the LH octave line through bb.5-6. Allow a tiny extra instant again at the end of b.8 ready to lead off again from b.9 with the aid of the *una corda,* to create a distant, fine-drawn thread of sound, as hushed as is humanly possible. Try here the

beautiful effect of subtly 'pointing' the inner RH fragment.

This piece is also a good study in basic pedalling, demonstrating how to change the pedal at the optimum moment, just after each chord is struck, to achieve perfect clarity and at the same time to boost the volume of resonance. Do, however, practise at first without the pedal, **holding** each chord for the value of a quaver before lifting the hand to 'prepare' for the next chord. When you do add the pedal, continue to **hold** each chord for a quaver value rather than lifting the hands in an almost *staccato* effect as inexperienced players are inclined to do, and flapping them around in anxiety to 'get on' to the next chord.

There is another way of timing the pedalling which gives a good effect: lifting the pedal **after** each chord is struck, and only depressing it again just before you lift the hands. This has the effect of giving a tangible boost to the sonority.

Some players ignore the *ritenuto* through bb.8 and 12, and also the *crescendo* from the end of b.11. Most of us inevitably think of this as a Funeral March – and marching feet do not *ritenuto,* they recede into the distance. I do therefore feel that this is a better effect: 'distancing' the sound almost to nothing at the end of b.12, and ending with a quietly echoing, yet clearly placed final tonic chord.

On the E flat/E natural problem at the end of b.3, players must consult their own ears. Recent generations of pianists have been raised with the idea that it is poor form to play E flat (in other words, a C minor chord). It raises a wry laugh to find that the E flat has been generally 'reinstated'. Chopin evidently forgot to indicate the 'return' to the E flat here, and it is actually pencilled into the copy belonging to Jane Stirling. (See the Critical Notes in Henle, the Vienna Urtext and Paderewski Editions).

Prelude No. 21 in B flat major (7)

This is an extraordinary idea – a sustained, nocturne-like treble melody with a ceaseless undertow of LH quavers opening out through each bar in swathes of constantly fluctuating intervals, predominantly in contrary motion (bb.1, 3, 4, etc.). Like No.17 this piece, in my view, is often taken far too fast, with the result that the LH proceeds in gusts rather than in smoothly shaped curves, giving no time to listen to the marvellous succession of continually varying intervals.

Practise the LH slowly alone. Start with a nicely resonant bass note and then, making a controlled upward leap, make it clear that the swathe of quavers starts on the **second** quaver pulse. Listen acutely to the widening intervals as you shape the quavers towards the B flat on the first beat of b.2, then leap up to start the second swathe similarly from the second quaver pulse, and so on. Practise this LH until you feel familiar with the quiet self-generating momentum of the quavers towards each bass note. Be conscious all the time of the crotchet pulse within the overall movement (though without obvious accents) so that although the curves are flexibly shaped, they remain fundamentally rhythmic. Gradually increase speed until you arrive at a suggested pulse of around ♩ = 76-88. Note the swell **towards** the first beat of bb.2-5 when the inner line is turning **upwards** through each bar, and in contrast the tailing away when the line is **falling** through bb.5-6. Take the upper E flat at the end of b.4 with the RH, taking great care when you put hands together not to make an untoward bump with the RH thumb.

Then study the RH alone in a smooth singing tone, shaping each 4-bar phrase as a singer would, and with the utmost expressiveness. The crotchet appoggiatura in b.2 is usually treated

as a rather 'long' semiquaver   Give the ornament in b.6 time to 'speak',

starting it **immediately** after the LH quaver sixth G flat/E flat.

When you put hands together take care to preserve the shape of the LH curves, feeling that these LH quavers are buoying the melody along in 'cushioning' waves. Bring in the RH in a warmly singing *mezzo-piano* tone, balancing this clear pure sound carefully with the LH so that the LH enhances and 'fills out', but never swamps, the treble sound. Be sure to catch each bass note in the pedal as indicated. Then you could lightly pedal each crotchet beat through each bar or, alternatively, more experienced players may prefer to use varying effects of half-pedalling through these second and third beats. Feel the impulse through bb.1-2 towards the long D through b.3, and then imagine a *portamento*-like slur down to the minim G on the first beat of b.4. (Make it clear that you are beginning an answering phrase from b.5, but at the same time feel the sense of the overall line from bb.1-8.) Similarly feel the impulse through bb.5-6 towards a 'lean' on the tied minim G on the first beat of b.7, then allow a slight 'give' through the end of this bar as the line falls expressively to the D on the first beat of b.8. As the LH quavers 'draw the music on' through b.8, feel you are 'taking a breath' ready to bring in the treble line in a higher dynamic and with a rather more expansive feeling, on the high B flat on the first beat of b.9. Allow a little extra time for the grace note turn to 'speak' through the first beat of b.12,

feeling the 'lift' up to E flat. (Shape this turn approximately thus:

Take care to 'finish off' the phrase towards clear dominant quavers on the first beat of b.13, then allow an extra instant to leap up in both hands to descend from the high quaver sixths in a warm-toned peal of unison intervals towards the first beat of b.16. Note Chopin's pedalling indications, retaining the pedal from the third beat of b.12 through to the second beat of b.13, and thus creating an overall dominant seventh resonance through the beginning of the downward sequence. On the modern piano, however, many players change the pedal on the **first** beat of b.13, holding this clear dominant sound rather longer into the bar. In any event, be sure to hold the bass sound within the pedal at least through to the second beat, and then change the pedal on each crotchet as before.* Note the 'hairpins' carefully, feeling a slight swell **into** b.13, and then, swinging up to 'land' on a fairly full-toned sixth, draw out a little through the first three or four quavers of the bar, and then moving on a little as you

descend.   Be sure to show the RH quaver

rest on the first beat of b.15, ready to begin another little sequence as you 'tail away' towards b.16. Listen to the LH quavers carrying on through b.16 in a continuing *diminuendo,* allowing a tiny 'give' through the end of the bar as you prepare to place a resonant bass quaver G flat, and bringing in the RH in a weighty resonance on the first beat of b.17. The arrival of this *subito forte* is a magnificent effect, whose impact would be ruined by a nervous anticipatory *crescendo* through b.16. Play out the RH in a fine ringing tone over the carefully balanced sound of the rolling LH double-stopped quavers with a definite sense of moving on. Aim to create a cathedral-like resonance abetted by Chopin's pedal indications (being sure to 'catch' the bass note from the first beat of b.17). Some players however may half-pedal through bb.17-18, and 19-24 according to taste and circumstance. Finger the LH as indicated in most editions:

allowing this LH quaver pattern to roll on in splendid

reverberation. Allow an extra instant at the end of b.24 to clear the sound, and then enter without a flicker of 'expression' in an immediate far away *pianissimo* echo, changing the sustaining pedal, adding the *una corda,* to create a haze of pedalled or half-pedalled sound right through to b.31. Then gradually clear the 'haze' as you make a slight swell through b.32, ready to bring

*In some editions b.12 is only pedalled through the first beat, as through bb.1-11, and with no further indication until the long pedal through bb.17-18.

in the RH with a bell-like emphasised treble F on the first beat of b.33. Having 'moved on' from b.17, draw back a little through b.32 ready to resume the opening movement from b.33. From this point there has to be the sense of a slight *tenuto* on each treble crotchet and bass quaver. Thus, lingering for an instant on the first beat of b.33, shape the quavers in both hands with a sense of moving on towards a slight *tenuto* on the next bell-like crotchet and quaver, then 'starting again' with the next set of quavers, and so on. This *tenuto* and slight moving on must be very slight, avoiding the gusting stop and start effect so often heard. From b.33 there is a new, more *agitato* feeling, with the implication of a slight *accellerando* as you gradually *crescendo* in heightening intensity, but without getting too hectic, and above all maintaining the shape of the quaver curves and the sense of the crotchet pulse over the bass pedal point through to b.39. Show the slurred effect of the treble fragments, with an extra 'lean' on the emphasised

crotchet on the first beat of bb.33, 35, etc.  Draw out a little

through b.38 as the *crescendo* makes a final 'push' ready to deliver a resounding dominant bass octave on the first beat of b.39. Hold the sound in the pedal as indicated, and swing strongly upwards to ring out the reiterated treble figures with powerful emphasis. Then keeping up the volume of sound as you begin the splendidly pealing descent, listen to the magnificent succession of intervals as you **gradually** *diminuendo* from the end of b.41. Note the emphasised upbeat crotchet as you prepare to arrive on a quiet tonic on the first beat of b.45. **Listen** to the curve of the LH solo quavers through bb.45, 47, etc. and then shape the double quavers as indicated through bb.46 and 48. Listen to the inner RH fragment through bb.50-1 and 52-3 as you prepare to come to rest on the long tonic chord through bb.53-5. Then shape the LH quavers in a bold upward sweep towards a resonant crotchet D on the first beat of b.57. End with clear strong chords, showing the falling inner fragment C to B flat. For students this piece is a splendid adventure in the creation and management of varying resonances.

Prelude No. 22 in G minor (8+)

This furious tirade in LH octaves is 'filled with the smoke of revolt and conflict', as Huneker says (p.129). In a technical sense it is not as daunting an assignment as it may sound, given proper management of the dynamics and rhythm; and it makes a magnificent technical and rhythmic study, even if you cannot rise to a virtuosic tempo. The LH obviously takes the decisive lead throughout, with the RH offbeat figure in a punctuating, onward goading role. Practise the LH alone first slowly. **Feel** the first beat so that you enter in precise time, not too loud, and feel the impulse of the opening figure towards a strong tied dotted crotchet on the first beat of b.1. Again **feel** the held second beat, and then let the offbeat quaver octaves 'go towards' a strong first beat of b.2, and so on. Always feel the two octaves at the end of each bar as the **upbeat** figure towards the long octave on the subsequent first beat, as implied by

Chopin's phrase indications.

Allow an extra instant at the end of b.4 to make a clean leap, as if with an upward 'heave' towards an extra powerful tied octave C sharp on the first beat of b.5. Then from this high point feel a **very** slight diminution of volume and tension, though not of impetus, as you progress through bb.5-8 ready to 'start again' from the second beat of b.8. Practise this LH through bb.1-8 over and over until it is perfectly fluent at a moderate tempo. Be sure to **hold** each tied crotchet through to the second main beat of each bar until the instant that you have to release it in order to play the next two octaves, so that the overall effect is smooth, despite the fierceness of the octaves. Then practise the RH alone, feeling the implied lean ($\underset{}{\longrightarrow}$) on each partly tied, partly slurred chord, while articulating the lower quavers clearly down to the crotchet on each second beat. Practise this RH in **strict** time, **imagining** the movement of the LH octaves beneath until, once more, bb.1-8 are perfectly fluent. (Feel, as described for the LH, that you surmount the 'peak' of the overall phrase at b.5.) Then when you put hands together, very slowly at first, ensure that the emphases remain intact in either hand. The coordination between the hands seems as though it should be very awkward. In fact it will be found that providing the rhythm and alternating emphases remain intact, the RH provides a vital punctuation, which in one sense gives a kind of rhythmic anchor for the LH, and in another an onward propelling syncopating 'push'. Draw out a little through the second half of b.8, ready to launch off again from b.9. Be sure to **lift** the LH to show the semiquaver rest here and to 'point' the semiquaver upbeat (see General Introduction under 'Articulation') – this also helps to poise the return to b.9. Be sure most particularly not to start too loud. So many players bash in with a blustering *fortissimo,* leaving no room for the fierce *crescendo* into b.17. In any event, *agitato* implies fevered anxiety, not the arrival of a roaring bull. Convey a discernible heightening of tension as you lead off in the higher register from b.9, *crescendo*-ing gradually towards the more brittle, still higher texture from b.13. Feel the change of rhythmic emphasis here as the LH 'goes towards' the emphasised crotchet on the second beat of bb.13 and 14, goaded on by the 'strettoed' slurred figures in the RH (but taking particular care that the RH does not get beyond itself here and capsize the LH rhythm!). Take care also to **lift** the hand from these slurred RH figures to show the RH rest on each main beat, allowing each LH crotchet octave to sound 'solo' for an instant. Then let the overall *crescendo* begin to 'bite' as the LH descends in a determined curve from b.15. Let the RH break off in a

a defiant effect as the LH makes a forceful onward downward push

towards a stentorian *fortissimo* octave D flat on the first beat of b.17. Then leaping up deftly, take care not to **start** the run of repeated octaves too loudly, feeling instead an onward rushing (but controlled) *crescendo* like a salvo of gunshots through to the C on the first beat of b.18, with a **slight** relaxation of the tone as you 'gather yourself' through the descent, ready for the next onslaught from b.19, and so on. Through these eight bars of continuous octaves also be sure that you feel the presence of the two **main** beats of each bar within the overall impulse towards each first beat. If you hammer **each** octave with equal and relentless vigour, the hand will 'jam', and you will grind to a halt within a few beats (see the Study in octaves, Op.25 No.10). From b.22 let the descending line 'go down to' a powerful octave B flat on the first beat of b.23. Then place the crotchet octave on each main beat in such a way as to create a vigorous kind of swing through bb.23-4 as you gather yourself for the next series of salvoes from b.25.

At b.30 feel you are 'taking the bit between your teeth' into a controlled hurtle through bb.31-3. Land on an extra resonant octave on the first beat of b.34, and then feel that you are applying a powerful 'brake' through this bar (articulating the LH upbeat effect as at bb.8-9), ready to *accellerando* in a final burst of fury towards a huge crotchet chord and bass octave on the first beat of b.39. Give this chord a **short** stroke of sustaining pedal to add resonance, and end with mighty but firmly controlled chords.

Chopin's pedal indications are only intermittent (see bb.17, 19, 23-4, etc.). Be sparing with the pedal elsewhere, using a stroke through the first beat of bb.1-7, 9-12, etc. and perhaps a short stroke on the second beat of bb.13 and 14. Less experienced players are begged to maintain a relentlessly controlled rhythm as they practise. Notch up the speed very gradually, never exceeding a tempo at which you can keep this control. This is one of those pieces in which a taut rhythmic tension, electric articulation and fire in the vitals are far more effective than mere brute force and a supersonic metronome mark.

Prelude No. 23 in F major (8+)

This is yet another number which is often ruined by too fast a tempo, reducing the delicious airborne dialogue between the hands to an earthbound scamper. It is at its loveliest at a tempo of around ♩ = 112, though gracefully handled it can still sound enchanting at several notches below this.

The LH takes the lead, and it is well to study first the thrice-stated pattern (bb.1-4, etc.), so that when you work at the RH you fully understand the **LH** nuances to which the RH is contributing its delicate counterpoint. Practise **in time**, at first without the trill in b.2. Spread the opening chord with a gracious harp-like touch, and imagine the RH semiquavers running above as you **listen** to the chord. Then shape b.2 as if in an overall suave vocal curve, feeling a 'lift' up towards a 'lean' on the A on the third beat, and curving smoothly down to the quaver F on the first beat of b.3. Articulate the repeated figures through b.3 in a more perky, blithe, yet smooth style, again shaping the curve up towards and down from the quaver A on the second and fourth beats. Then 'lift' the line upwards as if on a breeze, to 'finish off' on a neat quaver A on the fourth beat of b.4. This little upward flight is awkward. Various fingerings are suggested by different editors, and must be worked out according to the individual hand. My own preferred fingering is

 which works neatly provided that as you arrive on the

quaver C you quickly slide the fourth finger in towards the 'back' of the keyboard so that the thumb falls nicely on the subsequent semiquaver B flat. When you add the trill, place the prefix

on the beat

feeling the 'lift' up to the A as already described. Take care to retain the minim C from the end of the trill through the second half of b.2. I like the fingering given in Henle (see example a) above), making a deft finger-change immediately you arrive on the C. This subtly helps to 'point' the 'lift' up towards a light 'lean' with the thumb on the crotchet A.

The RH semiquaver pattern lies nicely under the hand, provided that it is fingered according to the natural 'fall' of the hand.

Practise the 'central' 8-note pattern over and over, i.e. from the seventh semiquaver F

etc. until it is quite fluent. The essential is a perfectly flexible

wrist. Cultivate a neat downward 'flick' over the thumb, scrupulously avoiding 'bumping' the thumb as you descend towards the C, with a further neat 'flick' over the thumb as you 'lift' to the high F, and so on. Again different fingerings are given for the RH through b.3, and these must again be carefully tailored to fit the hand. My own preference, reading from the middle

of b.2 is: etc. Once more practise the

central 8-note pattern over and over (i.e. as before from the seventh semiquaver – the diminished fifth). Then carry the semiquavers lightly up through b.4 to 'round the corner' at the end of the bar, ready to 'start again' in b.5.

As you play the RH, absorb the physical shape of its curves: the dip down to each C on the second and fourth beats, and the light 'lift' up to the high F's through b.1 and the first half of b.2. Then from the end of b.2 the curves are 'closer', a little more concentrated (with the addition of the diminished fifth), before the line flies upwards through b.4 towards the higher register in b.5. When you put hands together again omit the trill at first, and practise slowly and soberly until you feel at ease with the quite complex coordination between the hands. It will be seen that the RH second finger has to be lifted nippily from the fourth and twelfth semiquavers of b.3, and again the fourth semiquaver of b.4, so that the LH can take the A again on the subsequent main beat. When you add the trill, do not worry about how many notes should be 'got in'. This trill is an effect, a little flutter, **not** an exhibition of finger technique. The important thing is to start the 'flutter' with the B natural, placed neatly 'against' the RH C, and then to arrive with perfect rhythmic poise on the A exactly on the third beat, 'pointing' the A with a little 'lean' as described. Practise bb.1-4 over and over, gradually increasing speed, and as you do so, continually refining the sound. The RH has to be articulated in the most delicate *pianissimo,* skimming yet clear, with the LH giving an airily 'harped' tonic harmony through b.1, and a smiling-toned melodic fragment through b.2. Then b.3 has a more bustling articulation as the hands bob about through their alternating curves, with b.4 'tailing' upwards with a more wispy feeling. Weinstock calls this piece a 'marvel of swinging delicacy' (p.224), and indeed, I always think (at risk of aping von Bülow) of tiny birds swinging insouciantly on high branches through bb.1-2, drawing closer to exchange snatches of busy chat through b.3, and dispersing upwards through b.4 to resume their swinging from b.5.

Allow a tiny 'give' as you 'round the corner' at the end of b.4, ready to swing off again in the higher register in the dominant from b.5. 'Space' the LH triplets in a harp-like upward trail through the first half of b.8, and then allow another tiny 'give' as you dip through the 'corner' carrying you up into the yet higher register back in the tonic from b.9. Point the delicate chime of the emphasised LH E flat in b.12, and excel and amaze yourself through these bars (bb.12-16) with the exquisite shimmers of sound that you can evoke. Point the delicately harmonic effect of the LH dotted minims through b.15, giving the high F a little extra ring so that it 'connects' with the slurred fragment in b.16.

 Then let the RH ascend almost out of earshot to the

tiniest tinkle through bb.17-18 (there is more than a tinge of humour here), and gradually trail the sound away yet further as you descend to b.20. The way the sound veers upwards through b.21 again, catching the chime of the enigmatic LH E flat, is a touch of the purest genius. Disperse the sound as the hands diverge outwards from this E flat towards the tiniest filaments of sound on the far apart tonics, **holding** this overall sound within the pedal from the beginning of b.21 as indicated.

The pedal indications through the principal pattern (bb.1-4, 5-8, etc.) may be found somewhat heavy on the modern piano. The pedal could be half, as opposed to fully depressed through b.1, or half-changed at the half-bar (see General Introduction under 'Pedalling'). Then the pedal could be more frequently changed through b.2, and just lightly skimmed or touched through bb.3-4. From b.12 the pedal needs to be lightly hazed through the whole of each bar, reverting to a more frequent change from b.18, but holding the sound from the penultimate bar as already said.

Prelude No. 24 in D minor (VA)

The climactic impact of this piece owes something, no doubt, to its placing. On the other hand, by the fact of its monumental character, it provides the only possible ending to this extraordinary series of adventures. This is music that you cannot argue with. It has been called rhapsodic – but this is rhapsodising on a magisterial scale, power-driven by an inexorable rhythmic force. This character, both in terms of the huge resonance of the relentless mono-pattern in the LH, and its impassioned declamation in the RH, is ruined by too fast a tempo. When it is played too fast, the LH cannot pound, toll and drive as it must, and instead of an *Allegro appassionato,* we get a frenetic *Presto con fuoco.* Jorge Bolet in his recording takes it barely as fast as ♩ = 66, and, hardly deviating by a fraction of a second from first note to last, builds up a resonance and a head of steam of awe-inspiring proportions.

It goes without saying that enormous demands are made upon the technique and stamina of the player. The pattern of the LH is similar to that of the Study in F minor, Op.10 No.9, but here, since the extensions are wider in span and more unremittingly forceful, the LH is both more difficult and more tiring. And the huge-spanning RH runs are for steel-clad fingers, with at the same time fine-tuned overall coordination. Most players, having ridden the switchback down and up through bb.35-7, prepare to take a more placatory line from the second main beat of b.37, well in advance of the short-lived *piano* from b.46. In any event, the ear needs room, at least in terms of a dynamic easing (whether or not by means also of a lessened impetus) to be able to listen to the rhapsodising modulations from bb.37-51. From b.50 the RH bites into octaves, streaking down in white-hot thirds through bb.55-6, and then from b.57 expands the principal motif into a passage of almost uncontained passion. This is one of the most powerful passages in all Chopin's work – and the ending one of the most extraordinary. Maintaining the white heat to the end, he slams the book shut with the cryptic three bass D's like thudding blocks of granite.

Prelude in C sharp minor, Op. 45 (8)

This remarkable piece, written and published in 1841, has nothing to do with the 24 Preludes Op.28 published in 1839. Within these two years Chopin's life had emerged on to a kind of plateau. He had settled into his semi-partnership with George Sand, with its routine of winters in Paris and summers in Nohant, and had completed, or worked on, a number of important works: the Sonata in B flat minor Op.35, the Scherzo in C sharp minor Op.39, the splendid Mazurka in C sharp minor from Op.41, the Polonaise in F sharp minor Op.44, and the F minor Fantaisie Op.49, among others. Chopin was moving into that phase marked by Gerald Abraham as 'his last and greatest' (p.96). This is significant in this context since this piece is entirely given up to those strange strayings which were to grow more abstracted and visionary through the following years. It is here, and increasingly in the Nocturnes, Op.55 No.2 and Op.62 No.1, the Polonaise-Fantaisie and so on, that, as Arthur Hedley says, 'he stretches his hand out to the future' (p.148). In a letter of 1841, amid his customary list of fiddling directives to the long-suffering Fontana, Chopin comments that this piece is 'well modulated [one of his rare references to the quality of his work]. I have no hesitation in sending it' he goes on, naming his intended price from the publishers 'which must not be reduced by a penny' (Hedley, *Letters*, p.207).

This Prelude is built on musing, richly inflected waves of ascending quavers, which in every instance expand into melodic fragments of varying extent. Interestingly, when we look at the **page,** the manner in which these melodic fragments emerge from and 'double' with the quaver figuration could be Schumann's. But in the character of the sound and in the futuristic wanderings, there is nothing of Schumann. While this piece is not difficult in purely technical terms, it does assume a degree of **understanding** of the keyboard. And from what has already been said, it is clearly not a piece for the novice, musically speaking, however smartly he or she may be able to run around the keys. It is no use searching for demarcating points of form, or patterns of phrasing. The resonances are subtle and transient, passing in shifting layers and registers. The player has to have the musical experience and **aural** understanding to allow the strands to interweave as they continuously condense and disperse, evolving in apparently improvisatory fashion.

So interrelating are all these strands that this is a difficult piece to practise in a conventional way hands separately. It is essential though to master the predominating quaver pattern (see bb.5-6, 7-8, 9-10, etc.). To this end the following arpeggio figure can be practised in all the keys:

The introductory bar of 'terraced' chords of the sixth looks forward to the magnificent opening of the Barcarolle Op.60. Although this introduction needs to be played with a sense of freedom, the underlying tempo must **relate** to the overall tempo of the piece as a whole. The last thing one wants to do is to try to 'pin down' the tempo for a piece such as this. The essential is that there is a continual sense of onward 2-in-the-bar movement, otherwise the music will meander to a standstill. There is inevitably a wide degree of give and take – an **expansion** of the rhythm as each arpeggio 'grows' into its RH melodic fragment, with the subsequent LH arpeggio moving on to regain the 'mean'. Thus the basic tempo will be established as the arpeggio ascends through b.5, with a little drawing out from the second half of b.6, and the mean regained as the next arpeggio ascends through b.7, and so on. (The need for, and the extent of this elasticity can readily be established by making the unnerving experiment of trying to play bb.5-13 or so with the metronome!) A basic tempo of between $\downarrow$ = 56-66 is suggested, although there may still be considerable margins on either side of this. With your overall tempo in mind, bring in the introductory phrase on the second crotchet beat of b.1 in a warm *sostenuto* tone, and let the chords 'run on' a little, then drawing out slightly through the end of b.3 towards the sustained cadential resonances through bb.4-5. As you go towards, and make an expressive 'lean' on the treble dotted minim on the first beat of b.4, listen acutely to the inner and lower resonances, particularly to the inner LH crotchet A resolving to the dotted minim G sharp on the second crotchet beat. Then, synchronising events with care as the bass descends to the low tonic to begin the first ascending arpeggio figure while the RH D sharp resolves in an appoggiatura effect to the offbeat quaver C sharp, introduce the LH arpeggio in a quietly moving dreaming *piano*. Shape the quavers expressively, feeling the sense of the wide span as you 'lift' from the bass C sharp up towards the fourth quaver E, and then the stepped movement back to the C sharp on the sixth quaver, ready for the next upward 'lift'. Then feel that the quavers through the first half of b.6 are 'growing into' the RH minim octave on the second main beat, which in turn is 'growing', with a slight swell through the continuing inner quavers towards a 'lean' on a singing chord on the first beat of b.7. As you reach this 'objective' in the RH, have the LH ready to start the next upward climb quietly, but with a sense of inevitability, **listening** meanwhile to the resolution of the inner RH dotted minim to the C sharp on the last quaver of the bar. Then as the LH climbs into b.8, have the RH ready to 'take over' again on the second beat, 'pointing' the doubled E a little on the fourth beat as you 'go towards' an expressively spread chord on the first beat of b.9, resolving to a clear B major chord and so on. (Place the acciaccatura on the

beat, in such a way that it has time to 'speak'.)

etc.

Practise these five bars (bb.5-9) over and over, at first without the pedal, until they are quite fluent, and the sense of natural elasticity well absorbed. Chopin's pedal indications are not, as will be seen, comprehensive. On the modern piano one could continue his overall pedalled effect through b.5 **into** the first half of b.6, but perhaps lightening the effect by a half-pedal change on the first beat of b.6. Then change to a new pedal through the second beat of b.6, with another overall but 'lightened' pedal through b.7 and the first half of b.8, and so on. Having mastered the rhythm, shapes and pedal effects of these bars, you are now set fair to cope with the piece as a whole. As the RH 'finishes off' in b.9, you could begin the next LH ascent in a rather quieter, more 'enquiring' tone. Then swelling a little again into b.13, play the RH chord sequence with restrained ardour, moving on and swelling a little towards a fuller-toned RH line through bb.15-16. Take care that the LH buoys along the RH through b.14 with onward moving offbeat slurred figures, with the quaver sweeps 'opening out' through bb.15-16 to support the sustained RH. 'Point' the indicated 'lean' on the RH upbeat fifth to b.17 with the sense of a slight *tenuto*. You could then arrive on the G major chord in a *subito piano,* giving this chord a quiet singing *tenuto* as indicated as you move towards the gentle quiescence of bb.18-19, ready to rise to the higher register from b.20 in a more yearning tone. Open out the tone more freely as you move into b.27, and then 'point' the interrupted cadence (bb.30-1) ready to pour onwards rhapsodically from the second main beat of b.31.

Listen to the Mahlerian quality of the upturning phrase-ending through the first half of b.35, then carrying on into b.36 as if in a lingering echo effect. A little later the eloquent musings have, astonishingly, a tinge of the quiet, sunfilled afternoon quality characteristic of Vaughan Williams, particularly in the chromatic rise through the second half of bb.38 and 46, carrying over into

the falling fourth figure in bb.39 and 47.

Then from the second half of b.50 the music returns to the passage of bb.27-35, now transposed a semitone downwards. Tail away the sound once more through the Mahlerian resolution in b.59, and then shape the LH quaver line up towards the high A at the end of the bar and downwards in a long, expressively 'curling' *diminuendo* through bb.60-3. Then as you begin the ascent from b.63, 'point' the indicated 'lean' on the tied offbeat quavers through bb.63-5, feeling these as onward urging 'upbeats' to the chromatically ascending RH minim on each second beat. Draw out the resonances of the marvellous cadence through bb.66-7 – who can fail to hear Rachmaninov here, and indeed, through this whole passage from bb.60-7. Take time to 'finish off' the RH through the first half of b.67 as the opening motif prepares to return quietly in the home key. Let the RH break off as if in mid-thought on the poignant quaver octave F double sharp at the end of b.76 as the LH drifts on into b.77. Then 'taking hold' again through b.78, draw out towards a resonant pause on the dominant seventh of D major through b.79. The cadenza is very much easier to learn than its daunting appearance on the page suggests, once it is realised that the descending sequence through its first half is based on a series of dominant sevenths, and the ascending sequence through its **second** half on a series of

diminished sevenths. Practise the descending series first,

then  then practise the ascending pattern:

and

Begin the cadenza in a feathery *pianissimo,* starting not too fast, then gathering a little speed, but taking a little extra time to 'round the corner' as you end the descent and prepare to rise again. Then tail the sound away on a breath, up through the last eight quavers. Once you have worked all this out, aim for a shimmering abstraction of sound – this is not an occasion for display, and need not be too fast – think of a mysterious, multi-tinged, vaporous mist collecting, passing and disappearing into thin air again. Take the last six quavers in one pedal, and let the sound 'hang' for an instant. Then bring in the six-four chord in a resolute tone, and, **holding** the bass resonance within the pedal, shape the solo quavers in an expressive downward curve towards a resonant G sharp in b.83. Be sure to give this its full value, and **listen** to the reverberation of the long drawn out cadence. Arrive with an air of finality on the tonic in b.85, and then lead on quietly with the ascending quavers, to play the remaining sequences as if in a quiet, nostalgic afterthought. Feel an expressive 'lean' on the appoggiatura-like chord on the first beat of b.89, synchronising its resolution to the C sharp carefully with the LH quaver at the end of the bar. Then trail the last ascending quavers up towards a pinpoint of sound on the last high C sharp, and end with quiet, measured chords.

Prelude in A flat major (7)*

This short piece is published by Henle at the end of their volume of Preludes, and also in the Paderewski edition, and in the *Oxford Keyboard Classics* selection of Chopin pieces edited by John Vallier (Oxford University Press). It dates from 1834, and was published for the first time in 1918. It is a charming, joyous concoction in Chopin's lightest style, consisting of almost continuous running semiquavers in both hands.

Do not be daunted by the *Presto*. A seasoned performer might take it at about ♩ = 116-20, but lightness and grace are more important than a breakneck speed, and it can sound well at considerably less than this. In setting a tempo, take account of bb.9-10 and 11-12. A neat-fingered player who could rattle through bb.1-8 quite easily does not want to have to slam on the brakes at b.9, although there is a natural sense of expansion at the beginning of b.11, and again at b.15, moving back into tempo as each of these sequences descends.

Practise carefully hands separately. Try the LH at first thus:

 Feel the third finger as a pivot allowing the wrist

to make an easy lateral movement as you go down to the A flat, and up as if with a little 'push' towards the D flat on each second beat. Then when you practise the pattern as written, continue to feel the third finger as a light pivot. Then practise the RH alone, feeling the little curve and 'lift' up to and down from the E flat at the end of b.1 and b.2, and then feeling the airy expansion of the third curve, up to and down from the F near the beginning of b.4, as you prepare to 'start again' in b.5. Practise both

hands also in different rhythms.

118

When you put hands together feel the sense in which the little curves are 'staggered' in each bar, where the LH 'goes up to' the D flat on the second beat, and the RH curves up to the last **semiquaver** of each bar. This creates a pretty effect as these tiny implied 'surges' alternate.

Put hands together very slowly at first, and practise bb.1-4 over and over in a continuous movement, gradually increasing speed until you are quite fluent at a comfortable tempo, allowing a tiny 'give' through the end of b.4, ready to 'start again' in b.1. From the end of b.8 prepare to launch into a rather fuller, more 'harmonic' (though still light) tone from b.9, pointing the curve of the implied offbeat treble melodic fragment G, A flat, F in bb.9-10. Then play out the descending treble fragment insouciantly through bb.10-12 (though allowing an instant to 'point' the tied RH upbeat quaver C, as you prepare to set off again in b.13). Support the RH with a lively LH through these bars, giving the bass note a clear resonance on each main beat. *Crescendo* confidently through b.14, drawing out very slightly as you 'round the corner' into b.15, and then 'peal out' the RH, as you descend jubilantly through bb.15-16. Imagine that the RH couplets here are slurred, buoying the RH along with vigorous swathes of LH semiquavers. Slow a little as you *diminuendo* towards the end of b.16, taking an extra instance to 'point' the emphasised RH F flat and LH upbeat D flat as you poise yourself to set off again from b.17.

Point the emphasised RH semiquavers with a light chiming effect through bb.17-19. Then as you embark on the long *crescendo* from b.21, 'lean' a little and with increasing emphasis on the accented semiquaver on the second beat of bb.22-4. The LH semiquavers from the middle of b.22 can be a problem for a small hand (although a flexible young hand can often cope remarkably well with such widely spaced intervals). It is essential to cultivate a supple lateral hinge-like movement of the wrist, and practice in this rhythm

will help. *etc.* When you play the LH as

written, 'point' the thumb notes a little from bb.22-4, and then 'lean' more definitely on the doubled bass notes with the fifth finger from bb.25-8, once more using the 'middle' note (the second and fourth notes of each group) as a light 'pivot'. Control the *crescendo* carefully, avoiding getting too loud too soon, and surge into a jubilant *fortissimo* at b.29. Then as you begin the descent from the end of b.30, allow a fraction of extra time to listen to the chromatic inflections of both hands. Linger a little through b.32, 'pointing' the tied offbeat D flat as you prepare to shape the treble cadential fragment neatly towards a clear A flat on the first beat of b.33.

With the return of the principal motif here in the higher register, you could move off with the semiquavers from the second quaver pulse in a tinkling *pianissimo,* delicately 'pointing' the emphasised semiquaver F flat on the second beat of bb.35 and 36. Tail away the sound to a mere whisper in b.40, letting the sound disperse downwards and upwards, as it were, to the tiniest flick on the final quavers.

On the modern piano the pedalling needs to be very light – just a light touch perhaps on the first and second beats (or just the first beat) of bb.1-8. There could be a touch on the first and second beats of bb.9-10, with a rather fuller pedal through each beat through bb.11-12 and 15-16. Then from b.37, using the *una corda,* hold the sound within the pedal as you *accellerando* to the end.

THE MAZURKAS

Introduction:

The Polonaise, as interpreted and developed by Chopin, derives from the processional dances of the nobility (see below in the Introduction to the Polonaises). In the Mazurkas, on the other hand, with their modal tinges, bagpipe drones, their characteristic dotted rhythms, triplets and ornaments, Chopin draws on his memories of the folk songs and dances he knew and loved in his boyhood. And, true to their roots, Chopin's realisation of these two types of dances is entirely different, both in style and in dimensions. The Mazurkas, as Niecks said, are 'social poems, poems of private life, in distinction from the Polonaises, which are political poems' (Vol.2, p.232). The Mazurkas are essentially miniatures (albeit in several instances very substantial ones) of inexhaustible variety of design, mood, rhythm and style, as against the essentially large-scale, heroic 'set' plan of the Polonaises. The wonder is that in the almost sixty Mazurkas Chopin never came near to repeating himself; on the contrary, his interpretation of this rich dance form never ceased to evolve – you feel he could have written sixty more.

Like the Polonaise, the Mazurka had become 'Salonised' in the early nineteenth century, and Chopin was therefore equally familiar with both the genuine and the stylised versions of these dances, and indeed must have composed or improvised numerous pieces in this idiom from the earliest age (see the very early No.50 in G, and No.51 in B flat). Aristrocrats through the centuries have amused themselves by playing at rusticity, and doubtless were delighted by the 'quaint' harmonic seasoning and bucolic rhythmic jolts. But only so far. Speaking of the Mazurkas, Arthur Hedley says: 'the moment Chopin crossed the line of the piquantly familiar he found himself alone; the Polish note in his music . . . was accepted only up to a point. Thus the B flat Mazurka, Op.7 No.1, quickly made its way in France, Germany and England, while the A minor, Op.17 No.4, considered 'primitive' in character, called forth only comments like 'bleak and cheerless', 'jarring notes', 'weird character'.' (p.165). Today we find this one of the easier numbers, indeed, it is one of the most popular. The early numbers are, on the whole, of a relatively overt, dance-like, character. From Op.41 onwards, however, the writing grows increasingly abstract and complex, incorporating passages of rich polyphony and imitative writing. We can only imagine what Chopin's contemporaries would have made (or rather, *not* have made) of the more esoteric later numbers, some of 'symphonic' stature (Hedley, p.164), in which the dance element is all but lost amid these strands of complex part-writing and intricately expressive nuances (see Ops. 41 No.4, 50 No.3, 56 No.3, etc.). But if such intense, 'primitive' music was not what Paris expected from the elegant Chopin, there are still, even today many music lovers who find the Mazurkas crude and 'folksy'. And even today many of these later numbers are little played in public. Indeed, in a sense, such inward-looking, aurally complex works are not 'performance' pieces. But, to quote Arthur Hedley again, they 'contain beauties which Chopin reserved for these intimate tone-poems alone. Every kind of light and shade, of gaiety and gloom, eloquence and passion, is to be found in them'. (p.168). Encompassing Chopin's expressive range as they thus do, the Mazurkas read like a diary of his musical thought, his rhythmic, harmonic and textural processes from his earliest years up to and including the last notes he wrote. It follows that they are central to any serious study of Chopin, and to the very idea of Chopin in both a musical and a personal sense, providing the context to which all his work relates. Without the Mazurkas the rest of his output would remain like the wings of a razed great building, splendid in themselves, but lacking their central context. A matter of special interest to players is the perception by J.-J. Eigeldinger of a planned sequence of key and pattern within each Opus of the Mazurkas (as also with the Nocturnes). He suggests, therefore that there is a good case for the performance of each Opus as a complete set.

Most of the early numbers are constructed on an ABA plan, or on extended forms of this, ABACA and so on. But later the forms grow increasingly diverse, often with important codas which, in some of the larger numbers (Ops. 50 No.3 and 56 Nos. 1 and 3 for example) assume the dimensions of actual developments. Phrases generally, but by no means always proceed in 8-bar periods (4+4). But, because the melodies tend to be built up in short motifs, or 'cells' (a frequent characteristic of folk music), there may be any number of sub-diversions, regular or otherwise, within these 8-bar periods. These short motifs (of two bars, one bar or even two beats) may be repeated, used sequentially, may evolve over bar-lines, temporarily disrupting the regular meter, or be compressed into a temporary 2/4 rhythm. In other instances phrases will overlap, or the phrasing will be deliberately ambiguous – part and parcel of the teasing subtleties and refinements of Chopin's treatment of the folk idiom.

Many players are made frankly nervous by the Polish-ness of the Mazurkas. Louis Kentner for one, records that he tended to avoid them, feeling that 'understanding in this case means not a function of the reason but one of the blood' (p.145). It goes without saying that no one can fully 'understand' the mind of a great composer, least of all of the enigmatic Chopin. I believe, though, that to know and love the Mazurkas is to begin, at least, to have a **glimmer** of that understanding. However justified our diffidence may be, therefore, we positively must throw it aside sufficiently at least to plunge in and get to know them. So often a relatively advanced student at around grades 7-8 will be cast upon the waters with a set Mazurka to study, perhaps for an exam, relying only upon the odd injunction to 'accent the second beats' or 'stamp' the *sforzatos*. In such an instance it is a good plan to seek out some of the simpler numbers (e.g. Ops. 7 Nos. 2 and 4, and 24 Nos. 1 and 2, and many more) so as to become familiar with the varieties of style and spirit, the rhythmic idioms and so on. Rhythm is, of course, the major stumbling block, perhaps more imagined than real. As in the case of the Polonaises, it is the Polish dancers themselves who provide the best lesson in Mazurka rhythm, and every player should by hook or by crook try to seek out a local or professional troupe. It is not so much the understanding of the routines, which are often complex, but the appreciation of the way that the dancers carry themselves, the kind of steps they take, and the spirit in which the various numbers are performed, which is so crucial to the feel of the rhythm, and which will enable points of emphasis, articulation, tempo changes, etc, to click into place in a **physical** sense, rather than merely as dots on the paper.

It is not generally understood that the mazurka is a generic type encompassing various dances all in triple time, principally the kujawiak, the mazur and the oberek. The kujawiak has a slowish, smooth step, tending to expressive minor melodies. The mazur is faster and more energetic with more intricate rhythms and varying emphases. The oberek is a brilliant, whirling affair with the men twirling and lifting the women, accompanied by virile leaps and stamps and shouts. These different types are all incorporated in Chopin's Mazurkas, and often characteristics of the mazur and kujawiak will alternate within a single piece – accounting for the changes in style and implied variance of tempo between different sections of the same piece. Such folk dances were freely combined or intermixed with songs, so that the melodies of many of the slower dances would have been sung as well. However, even if he had not said it, it would be obvious from the complexity of nuance and so on that Chopin's Mazurkas (apart, perhaps, from the juvenile numbers) were not intended for dancing (he did in fact say this in connection with Op.6). Nevertheless the **sense** of the physical rhythm is always there, and if we relate the rhythms, **as we play** to this sense of the physical movement, we cannot go too badly awry. Never has Ralph Kirkpatrick's great maxim been more appropriate: 'If you can't feel the rhythm, **dance** it!'. In instances of emphases, *tenutos*, pauses, etc. if we imagine and **feel** the momentary 'holding' of a movement, the spanning of a leap, the preparation for and implementation of a stamp, we shall convey the sense of the rhythm in the only valid way, in terms of physical movement.

In dance music for the keyboard, the left hand is normally the guardian of the rhythm (see also the General Introduction under 'The Left Hand'). It is important to realise that a mazurka rhythm is **not** a waltz-rhythm, although it may now and then tend to grow waltz-**like**. A glance at Op. 6 Nos 1 and 3 will show this. While in No.1 the LH pattern in the first two bars might be taken for a waltz-rhythm, different emphases appear with the tied upbeat to b.4, the sustained inner and lower minims through bb.5-8, the leaping, stamping emphases from b.17, and so on. In Op.6 No.3 emphatic cross-rhythm effects immediately emerge through bb.1-8, with thereafter **evenly** 'spaced' repeated chords through bb.11-14. Thus we do not have at all the **oom**-pah-pah, the 'strong-weak-weak' rhythm of the waltz, but something much more strongly and evenly balanced with, into the bargain, accents on second or third beats wherever there may be an extra strong step. Often, for example, the dancers perform a kind of churning running step, kicking their heels behind them, or a strong step-**hop-hop**, so that the **hop-hop** on the second or third beat is as strong or stronger than the step on the first beat. And often phrases or sections end with an emphasised second or third beat, as if with a little jump, pounce, or sometimes a powerful stamp (see for example, Op.30 No.3, bb.9-10, 11-12, etc, when each 2-bar phrase ends on an emphasised minim on the second beat; or Op.24 No.2, bb.5-6, 7-8, etc, when each 2-bar phrase ends on an emphasised third beat).

Throughout the Mazurkas Chopin has been extremely specific with his indications for accents, articulation, and so on. J.-J. Eigeldinger draws a clear distinction between the different types of accent in the Mazurkas: the *sforzato* (*sf* or *fz*) indicating a firm dynamic accent, and > or ⟩ indicating a short, or longer, more agogic accent. He also quotes instances in which Chopin uses a *sforzato* and a > on the same beat or note (see Introduction under Dynamic and Agogic Accents). In addition there are numerous **implied** emphases and nuances which have to be taken into account, and which influence the rhythm, e.g. 'leans' on tied notes, slurred notes or chords, etc. Particularly in the LH or inner voices these implied emphases or extra resonances influence the melodic line. Looking at Op.6 No.1 again there is, as already said, an implied slight emphasis on the tied LH and inner RH upbeat to b.4, and then the slight extra resonance of the minims alternating between the inner and lower LH lines through bb.5-8 exercises a slight 'braking' hold as the RH line descends through these bars. Often LH chords

are marked ⟨notation⟩ see, for example, Op.7 No.2, where these offbeat chords are played

in an 'equal' style, as if lightly pressed into the keyboard to support the RH with an even, spaced rhythmic step. Then again there will often be a downward or upward slur on the second beats (see Op.33 No.1, bb.5-6, 9-10, etc, where there is an implied lean on the slurred second beat). When there is a rest in the LH on a third beat it is usually particularly important to place the LH chord or note with a certain definition on the **second** beat (see Op.63 No.3, bb.16-18, etc, where a rhythmically placed chord on each second beat 'sends' the RH on towards the next bar). Again, time after time the RH will come to rest on a minim on the first beat at the end of a phrase or section while the LH finishes downward or upward on the second beat (see Op.7 No.2 bb.8 and 16, and Op.17 No.2, bb.4, 12, etc.). In these instances we have to take care to place the LH on this second beat, not as a vague after-thought, but with clear definition. Similarly with the LH third beat, when the RH ends on a second beat (e.g. Op.30 No.2, bb.2, 4, etc.). The LH in every instance has to support, propel, guide and sustain the RH both rhythmically and in terms of supporting resonance. Above all it must always move with the sense of a **step** – a smooth step, a delicate feminine step, a springing step, a leaping step, or a stamp, whatever it may be. Rests must, need it be said, be felt as surely as played beats. Failure to feel rests will throw out the next entry, be it on first, second or third beat – we have only to imagine what effect a premature or late entry caused by an inaccurately felt rest or rests would have on a set of dancers.

Frequently in the comments below I beg the player to have the pulse 'well in the system' before starting. This is discussed in the General Introduction under 'Rhythm', but is especially important in the instance of dance rhythms as individual as here. In this connection, as again is constantly urged below, upbeats are particularly significant, either at the beginning of the piece, or when announcing a new section in a different mood or tempo, in the sense that the dancers poise themselves **on** the upbeat ready to 'go' on the first beat proper (see again the General Introduction under 'Upbeats'). In this connection it may be mentioned that there is a widespread misapprehension about semiquaver upbeats. It is widely taught, as I certainly was, always to 'snap' the semiquavers. In Op.7 No.1, to take a typical example, the semiquaver in bb.1, 2 and 3 will usually be 'snapped' like a smart anticipatory acciaccatura before each second beat. This, however, is not idiomatically correct. We should, rather, think of this note as the 'upbeat' to this second beat, thus giving it more weight. If we imagine a hopping step being taken on this note, we shall give it its proper weight and importance.

Occasionally, but not often, variations of tempo are indicated, e.g. in Op.24 No.4 where we have *accelerando* and *ritenuto* (bb.35 and 36), *più agitato* and *stretto* (bb.45-6), etc. But in numerous instances fluctuations of tempo are implied by the differing figures of the sections, and I have suggested these changes as they occur. Since Chopin's playing particularly in the Mazurkas was capable of such minute subtlety of nuance, and since we are told he never played these pieces (or any others) alike twice, he was doubtless reluctant to define such rhythmic variations in a way which would 'fix' their interpretation. The question of *rubato* is discussed in the General Introduction. While it is particularly relevant to the Mazurkas, it is on the other hand governed here by the sense of the dance movement discussed above. There are certain rhythmic peculiarities which also apply here. An experienced player will subtly alter a triplet rhythm (see Op.6 No.1, bb.1, 3, etc, and Op.30 No.2, bb.1, 3, 5, etc.), lingering slightly on the first triplet of the group so that the rhythm of

the triplet sounds more like ♪ ♪♪ Again, in Op.6 No.1, b.13, and similar instances, we

may hear an extra hold on the quaver on the first beat so that the effect is more like ♩. ♪♪

But these are slight nuances which should not be overdone, and which occur merely as a tiny fillip within the **sense** of the regular beat.

There can be no doubt that it was in the Mazurkas that Chopin's own amalgam of rhythmic nuance and agogic emphasis was heard at its most exquisite and most teasing. (One of his funniest party tricks was, we are told, his adoption of a poker-faced style as he churned out a mazurka in strict metronomic beat!) Amusing incidents are recorded of Hallé, who insisted that Chopin appeared to be playing a Mazurka in **4/4** time, and Meyerbeer, who in similar circumstances was certain he was playing in **2/4**. With Hallé he laughed the idea off, explaining that it was 'the natural character of the dance which created the oddity'. Lenz, however, describes how Chopin lost his temper when Meyerbeer pressed his point in connection with Op.33 No.3. This famous story, too long to quote here, is recorded in many studies of Chopin.

Articulation is again discussed in the General Introduction, and is crucially important in the Mazurkas. The conscious 'lifting' of the hand from a detached quaver in the frequent

♪ ᶼ ♩ ♩ figure is essential to the 'spring' of a quick movement, see for example

Op.30 No.3, bb.9-20, where this springing effect is contrasted with the gliding smooth variation through bb.21-2. Then in a more contemplative number, such as Op.24 No.1, it is the points of articulation which indicate the expressive intention of the melody: the 'lift' from the quaver on the first beat of b.1, the 'speaking' separate crotchets on the second and third beats, the smooth line through b.2, the 'lift' from the first beat of b.3, the emphasis on the upbeat to b.4, and the short, slurred 'fall' to the dotted crotchet in b.4, and so on.

Pedalling is a difficult matter. Often Chopin's pedal marks are quite specific, but on a modern piano would create far too thick an effect. Opus 24 No.1 is an example where Chopin often gives a pedal mark right through a bar (bb.1, 2, 5, 6, 9, 10, etc.) where today we would feel inclined to change the pedal more frequently. We might, in this relatively leisurely context, lightly pedal **each** beat of b.1, hold the pedal through the first and second beats of b.2, changing it on the third, and giving a separate pedal each to the second and third beats of b.3, and so on. On the other hand, there are many instances when a bass note or octave needs to be held within the pedal. For example, in Op.7 No.1, the bass octave on the first beat of b.3 needs to be held in the pedal to add resonance to the *sforzato* chord and trill through the second beat. And in Op.17 No.1 the sound of the bass octaves (see bb.1, 4, etc.) needs to be retained in the pedal at least through two or three beats if not through the entire indicated duration. These are matters, as ever, for the ear of experience (see also the General Introduction under 'Pedalling').

Opinion is divided as to the extent of folkloric influences upon Chopin, and it is often said that the folk mystique is overstated. One thing though is certain, these influences, however great or peripheral in a general sense, are seen at their most concentrated in the Mazurkas. In a rhythmic sense, triplets, dotted rhythms, cross-rhythms abound, intermixing and interacting upon each other in marvellous vitality. Their harmonies are 'different', so different as already said as to horrify most of Chopin's contemporaries and to startle us still today. These different sounds, the modal colourings, particularly with the Lydian fourth, the augmented seconds, the biting sevenths, can only have their roots in one culture, that of Poland (see also the General Introduction under 'His period and influence' and 'Poland'). Not that they are copied. As Arthur Hedley says 'Chopin's multicoloured progressions, which fascinate the modern listener, would have made the Polish peasant stare. They are his personal commentary on the national theme' (Hedley, p.168). Part and parcel of this 'commentary' are the instrumental implications: drone sounds in fifths or in pedal point tonic or dominant are ubiquitous (see for example Op.6 No.2, bb.1-8; Op.6 No.4, bb.1-8; Op.7 No.1, bb.45-51, Op.30 No.1, bb.30-35, Op.56 No.2, bb.1-28, etc. – see also the General Introduction, under 'Pedal Points'). In addition, as suggested above, we can hear sung melodies, or raucous fiddle sounds, the shrill piping of high flutes, and so on. Thinking of the testimonies of his contemporaries, that Chopin never played in the same way twice, we can find every time we return to even the most familiar Mazurka that there is always a new nuance, a new sound, a new way of 'pointing' a rhythm. Players are particularly recommended to J.-J. Eideldinger's *Chopin – Pianist and Teacher*, whose collection of reminiscences and personal observations on the subject of the Mazurkas is invaluable.

As in the case of the Waltzes, repeats, where they occur, are not a mere formality. They are essential to the overall balance, and should always be played, taking the opportunity for small variations of dynamics or rhythmic nuance.

Notes: Since the Mazurkas are so numerous, it would be far too space-consuming to comment on each one in detail. Most of the fifty-odd numbers are therefore discussed in mainly general terms, while I have selected three for detailed discussion: Op.6 No.1 because it is as representative a number as one can find, incorporating numerous typical, and strongly contrasting features; Op.17 No.4 as an example of the slower, more expressive type; and Op.56 No.3 as one of the most striking of the larger-scale pieces, and perhaps the most abstracted of all the Mazurkas – the furthest point to which Chopin stretched in his poeticising and personalising of the dance idea.

Chopin gave metronome marks for the first seventeen Mazurkas (Ops 6, 7, 17 and 24). I have occasionally suggested modifications of these given tempos, and have also given suggested approximate tempos for the later numbers. It is again stressed here (as in the General Introduction) that these suggestions are purely personal, and are intended only as guide-lines. As ever, the inner consciousness of the sense of the dance movement will avoid the likely danger of wallowing through the more expressive pieces (or at the other extreme, of uncontrolled scampering in the faster numbers).

Most earlier editions published fifty-one Mazurkas, including Ops 67 and 68 (published posthumously by Chopin's friend Fontana) and the two important mature numbers in A minor (Nos 52 and 53 in Henle, 50 and 51 in **most** other editions) usually identified as 'Notre Temps' and 'Emile Gaillard'. The Henle and the Paderewski Editions both publish six additional numbers. The Paderewski Edition gives two versions of three of these, and also gives three versions of Op.67 No. 4. The Henle Edition has an appendix giving early versions of Op.7 Nos 2 and 4 and of their No.54 in D major. From No.42 onwards the Mazurkas are differently numbered in the Paderewski Edition. They place the two numbers in A minor (see above) as Nos 42 and 43, **before** the posthumous sets Ops 67 and 68. Thus Op.67 No.1, No.42 in Henle, is No.44 in Paderewski. The miscellaneous Mazurkas from Henle's No.50 onwards are also differently numbered in Paderewski (see individual commentaries for details).

Mazurka No. 1 in F sharp minor
Op. 6 No. 1 (8)

Chopin leaps into the first of his published Mazurkas with a fully fledged example of the genre, incorporating a wide variety of characteristic features – triplets, dotted rhythms, offbeat *sforzandos*, sudden changes of mood and so on. It is one of three numbers which are discussed in especial detail (see Note above).

Two versions of this piece are given in Henle, Nos 1 and 1a. The notes below refer to No.1, which corresponds in most details to the versions given in the majority of other editions.

bb. 1–17 Feel a steady, almost deliberate **3/4** before starting. Chopin's tempo of ♩ = 132 or thereabouts will accommodate the changes of mood throughout the piece with only minor fluctuations. If, however, like many players, you play the first section in a rather slower tempo there will need to be some increase at b.17 (see comments from that point). Practise the LH thoroughly alone through the first section. Feel a clear *1, 2, 3* through bb.1-2 (see above in the Introduction to the Mazurkas) and *crescendo* as indicated from the middle of b.2, feeling the implied emphasis on the tied upbeat to b.4, and the sense of 'opening out' through the further little *crescendo* in b.4 towards the third beat. Then from b.5 listen acutely to the overlapping resonances created by the alternating chromatic descent of the upper thirds and the lower line. Shape the lines as smoothly as possible, changing fingers 5-4 in the lower line when necessary, and poise yourself with a slight 'hold' on the third beat of b.8 ready to 'start again' in b.9. Mark the implied emphasis on the tied (inner) upbeat to bb.13, 14 and 15 with a little 'push' and **listen** to the held minims as the lines divide in b.15. Then make a final little 'push' on the upbeat to b.16, 'holding' this octave slightly to allow a momentary clearing of the sound before you finish off the section with a *subito piano*, but perfectly clear inner triplet over the sustained lower minim F sharp.

Then practise the RH alone, marking every expressive and rhythmic inflection and every detail of articulation meticulously. Again feel the steady **3/4 before** starting, and then 'plant' the opening tied upbeat with a quiet but definite 'lean' (see the Introduction to the Mazurkas). Take care to give this note its full value and more, and as you listen to its quiet resonance, **imagine** the precise entry of the bass note on the first beat of b.1, so that you move smoothly and rhythmically on into the remainder of the triplet. Then make the little swell towards the dotted quaver G sharp, again with the sense of a tiny 'hold' on this note so that the upbeat semiquaver to b.2 is by no means anticipated, but rather, if anything, fractionally delayed – thus ensuring that the staccato quaver on the first beat of b.2 will be perfectly poised rather than being 'fallen into'. Then be sure to **lift** the hand from the *staccato* quaver so that it 'falls' naturally onto the slurred 'upbeat' to the second beat (see General Introduction under 'Articulation'). Then **lift** the hand again so that it again falls, with a clear emphasis this time, onto the crotchet third on the upbeat to b.3. Take care once more to give this third its full value or a fraction more so that the triplet on the first beat of b.3 is again rhythmically timed as you move into b.3 in a stronger dynamic. (In many editions the upper melody note, as well as the inner F sharp is **tied** over into b.3, as in the case of the opening.) Listen also to the descending line of the inner RH voice, which brings a natural reinforcement to the volume, and feel the strong onward impulse towards the emphasised C sharp on the third beat of b.4. 'Hold' this note for an extra instant as you poise yourself to move into b.5, and then feel the sense in which the music unwinds in *decrescendo* through bb.5-8, ready to 'start again' on the upbeat to b.9. In bb.5-7 **lift** the hand from the quaver on the second beat so that it 'falls' naturally onto the slurred semiquaver to 'go to' the emphasised tied upbeat to the subsequent bar. Then in b.8 show in contrast the smooth bridge-over effect of the quaver couplet on the second beat towards the tied upbeat to b.9. From bb.13-15 feel the indicated quiet 'lean' on the quaver E on the first beat, and the delicate fall of the treble line from this note. Listen also to the effect of the changing intervals (7th, augmented 4th and 6th, etc.) in the RH through these bars, and allow an extra instant to 'point' the shift to the inner minim F sharp on the first beat of b.15. Allow another instant to 'point' the upbeat chord to b.16, and then finish off the phrase with a neat clear *pianissimo* triplet and crotchet over the sustained inner minim.

Having studied each hand thoroughly, it is a good plan to play the LH while **singing** the RH, implementing all the details of rhythm and emphasis. You will then soon understand the sense in which the LH propels and guides the overall rhythm although 'giving' a little here and moving on a little there. Then, to ensure that this 'giving' and moving on remain within bounds, (i.e. that you retain the sense of the overall pulse), practise the RH while **imagining** the *1 2 3* in the LH. (Alternatively, play the RH through once or twice with the metronome.) An experienced player will, as Chopin did himself on the evidence of contemporary accounts, subtly distort the rhythmic details, such as lingering fractionally 'too long' on the first triplet quaver of bb.1, 3, etc, so that the two remaining quavers sound more like semiquavers. Similarly, a 'hold' on the upper quaver on the first beat of b.13 etc, produces the suggestion of a 'dotted' effect, with the subsequent semiquavers then sounding almost like demisemiquavers. But these are subtle idiomatic effects occurring within the overall 3-in-the-bar pulse (see also the Introduction to the Mazurkas).

When you put hands together make sure that all the details absorbed hands separately are incorporated. Take particular care to 'launch in' in a poised manner. As already said, 'plant' the RH upbeat very surely giving it a generous value, while at the same time feeling its onward leading 'lean', as if the dancers are poising themselves for action (see the Introduction to the Mazurkas). Then place the bass note on the first beat of b.1 with quiet definition, judged carefully in relation to the sound of the tied upbeat. It is essential that this bass note gives a clear 'kick-off' to the steady rhythm of the opening bars. Ensure that the LH and RH complement each other as they 'go towards' an emphasised third beat (implied or stated) of each of bb.1-4. Then carefully shape the gradual fall of the lines in both hands from bb.5-8, with an 'easing' into b.9 indicated by the *rubato*. (Chopin seldom, and only in relatively early works, specifies a *rubato*. Here he is catering for this 'easing back' into the principal motif.) Through bb.13-15 feel the quiet insistence of the repeated one-bar figure with the implied emphasis on (and 'fall' from) the seventh on the first beat, balanced by the implied little 'push' on the tied LH inner upbeat. 'Point' the inflection to the inner F sharp on the first beat of b.15 as you slow slightly towards the *pianissimo* ending, taking care to synchronise the treble and inner LH triplets immaculately as they fall towards carefully placed crotchets on the second beat of b.16, over the quietly sustained lower minims. Throughout this section there is, as will now be seen, a continual slight impetus towards, and emphasis and/or 'hold' (in varying degrees) upon, the third beat of each bar i.e: the little swell up towards the dotted quaver on the third beat of b.1; the stated emphasis on the third beat of b.2; the implied emphasis on the inner and lower tied upbeats to b.4; and then a stronger emphasis on the third beat of b.4 – the objective of bb.1-4, and the point from which the music unwinds (still with an emphasis on each third beat), ready to 'start again' from the upbeat to b.9.

bb.17–40   As said above, some players take the opening section rather slower than Chopin's ♩ = 132. In this case the second section from b.17 will need to move on. If, on the other hand, the first section was played at about the given tempo, there will be little actual increase of speed here, although, on account of the overt masculine spring into *subito fortissimo*, following the previous *ritenuto*, there will inevitably be a **sense** of whipping up the tempo. In any event, having 'finished off' the previous section cleanly, make a fractional break, just enough to prepare to give a real 'bite' to the crotchet upbeat to b.17. Be sure once more to give this note its full value as you poise yourself for a powerful 'stamp' on the detached octaves on the first beat of b.17. Holding the sound within the pedal as indicated, allow both hands to spring off the octaves so that they 'fall' emphatically onto the quavers on the second beat. Take care to retain the lower dominant drone (in C sharp) through its full value as you pursue the treble and inner LH figures vigorously. Practise this **slowly** so that you can savour and **believe** the marvellous jarring of the intervals between the treble and inner quavers – the perfect fourth, the fifth and major sixth, then **minor** instead of major sixth, and so on. Make a little swell as indicated so that you can feel the onward propulsion towards and through the energetically 'bounced' *staccato* crotchet on the second and third beats of b.18, making a powerful spring outwards off the third beat towards another great 'stamp' on the first beat of b.19. This time, 'go towards' a resonant *sforzato* chord on the second beat of b.20, (with the hint of a 'hold' through this second beat) then taking care to place the LH crotchet purposefully on the third beat so that this note and the RH quaver are played as deliberate, staggered upbeats to b.21. 'Space' the five crotchets with a sense of freedom as you *rallentando* through b.24. Some players follow the overall 'five' effect – others make a triplet effect through the first three notes, and then treat the last two notes as if they were the 'normal', though progressively slowing second and third beats of the bar. The essentials are that the whole effect sounds free yet rhythmic, and that you poise yourself in an upbeat sense at the end of the bar to return to Tempo 1 immediately on the first beat of b.25.

bb.40–72   Having 'finished off' neatly once more in b.40, again make a fractional break ready to spring up to a strongly 'planted' RH upbeat to b.41. Take care again to give this its full value, and have the feeling that you are rebounding off this fifth to launch into the *scherzando* from b.41. The effect of these heavy upbeats to bb.41, 43, etc, is essential to the rhythmic sense of this section. Play the RH chords in a sharp, jangling manner (the chords will inevitably be detached) with the acciaccatura so 'crushed' that it is struck *almost* simultaneously with the chord. Practise this at first with the lower notes only:

making a biting 'flick' from second finger

to thumb, endeavouring to maintain this 'flick' effect when you practise with the complete fifths, sixths, etc. (Note that in performance this recurring acciaccatura/F sharp creates an inner drone effect through bb.41-3 and 45-7, etc.)

This passage is far from easy, particularly for those with small hands, who may have to omit the **lower** F sharp on the third beat of bb.42 etc. (In this case play the acciaccatura with the thumb, and support the RH with a particularly resonant LH F sharp.) Make a calculated leap up to the high C sharp on the first beat of b.44 and down again to a powerful C sharp on the second beat as if in a wide arc, and similarly with a yet wider arc in b.48. Practise this with a confident deliberate aim, **risking** wrong notes at first (it is remarkable how quickly the ratio of bull's-eyes shoots up!) The poise of this section depends greatly on the supporting articulation and emphases in the LH. 'Bring up' the LH with rhythmically spaced *staccato* quavers towards a **firm** minim third on the second beat of bb.41, 43, etc, and then underpin the RH with an emphatic inner crotchet on the third beat of these bars and with clearly articulated sixths in bb.42 and 44. Take care that the LH ascending quavers in b.41, etc. are energetically detached, and that the quaver sixths in b.42 are steadily, even deliberately played – this averts the tendency of the **RH** quaver chords to 'run into each other'. **Listen** to the held resonance of the LH inner F sharp through the first and second beats of bb.42 and 44, using this note as an anchor for the hand as you play the sixths – and similarly with the held C sharp through bb.46 and 48. Leap off the LH crotchet sixth on the second beat of b.42 ready to support the RH *sforzato* with a resounding F sharp on the upbeat to bb.43 and 47. Also 'brake' yourself after the RH *sforzato* on the second beat of bb.44 and 48 with a deliberately 'planted' LH crotchet on the third beat as you poise yourself to 'start again' in bb.45 and 49. Chopin's pedal indications demonstrate that he requires an overall clanging effect through bb.41, 43, etc. (although many pianists favour a sharper effect with more frequent pedal changes). Nevertheless the correct articulation of *staccatos*, slurs, etc. **within** the pedal is, as always, vital to the rhythmic poise of such passages (see General Introduction under 'Articulation'). The emphasis on each RH chord through b.56 indicates a very deliberate slowing through that bar, ready to launch into the reprise from b.57. Needless to say an experienced player will find various subtly different ways to inflect the opening section on its return at bb.25 and 57 – note the more vigorous dynamic from b.25; then you could for example return again in *forte* at b.57, and then play the final statement from b.65 in a near *pianissimo*, with a more lingering effect from b.69.

Mazurka No. 2 in C sharp minor
Op. 6 No. 2 (7)

Two versions of this piece are given in Henle, Nos 2 and 2a. The notes below refer to No.2, which corresponds in most details to the versions given in the majority of other editions.

This is another splendidly varied number, this time with a characteristic introductory drone sequence. Chopin's metronome mark creates some confusion: ♩ = 63 as given in Henle is obviously impossibly slow, while the interpretation of this mark in most editions as ♩. = 63 may seem on the fast side. Against this, at a fairly fast tempo, the opening *sotto voce* section with its long-breathed drone effect creates a haunting, slightly furtive, fleetingly gliding effect that was perhaps what Chopin intended (with the sense of a slight 'braking' at b.9). On the other hand, Henryk Sztompka in his recording (Muza) starts slowly – though nowhere near as slow as ♩ = 63 – gradually speeding up through bb.1-8 to settle at about ♩ = 116 from b.9, but incorporating a heavy *rubato*. (The second version of the piece in Henle, gives a non-specific *tempo giusto*.) The essential is to arrive at a broadly compatible overall pulse, since, with the possible exception of the introductory bars 1-8, this is not a piece in which the character of the different sections seems to imply a **marked** change of tempo (see however the remarks concerning the *gajo* section).

bb.1–16   Play bb.1-8 very smoothly so that the outer drones enclose the snaking inner line with as continuous a sound as possible. Mark the quiet emphasis on the treble and LH drone minims on the second beat of bb.1-4. Be sure to give the inner, dotted crotchet on the second beat of b.2 its full value, **feeling** the held third beat so that the upbeat quaver to b.3 is properly timed. Similarly in b.4, be sure to give the minim chord its full value, and feel you are taking a tiny 'breath' at the end of the bar before leading on again from b.5 (marking the quietly but insistently emphasised treble crotchets through bb.5-7). Be sure to play the *staccato* RH quavers through the third beat of b.7 in such a way that they are understood as the **upbeat** to b.8, and then draw out the triplet quavers a little towards a quiet but definite 'bare' chord on the second beat of b.8. Again take a tiny 'breath', ready to lead on with a strong slurred upbeat to b.9, being sure to give this upbeat crotchet its full value or a little more while at the same time feeling its strong upward pull towards the first beat of b.9 (see Introduction to Mazurkas). Place the LH detached crotchet on the first beat of b.9 in such a way that you seem to leap off from here with a lively 'spring'. Be sure also to **lift** the RH from the quaver G sharp on the first beat of b.9 so that it 'falls' naturally onto the semiquaver, 'going to' an implied emphasis on the dotted crotchet on the second beat (see General Introduction under 'Articulation'). Support the RH with a 'dancing' LH, feeling the overall onward impetus towards the emphasised dotted crotchet on the second beat of b.12 (implementing on the way the emphasis on the upbeat to b.12). Take particular care to place the LH chord firmly on this second beat of b.12 to support the RH emphasis, and to 'point' the fact that there is a rest on the third beat. Be sure also to give the RH dotted crotchet its full value before making a clear onward lead with the 'solo' RH quaver upbeat to b.13. Make a tiny break after the second chord of b.14, ready to lead on with a vigorous *forte* emphasised, ornamented upbeat to b.15, and end the section with a masculine 'stamp' on the RH minim on the first beat of b.16, followed up with a vigorous LH spread chord on the second beat.

bb.16–32   Take another quick breath here before leading off again, this time with a lighter 'spring' with the upbeat to b.17. Feel the impetus through b.18 up towards a slight 'lean' on the crotchet on the third beat, and then another 'lean' on the first beat of b.19. Note the RH articulation closely here; the slurred 'flick' up to the *staccato* crotchet on the second beat of b.19, the slurred upbeat lead towards another 'lean' on the first beat of b.20, and so on. Listen also to the resonance of the held LH inner A sharp on the first beat of bb.19 and 20 over the descending lower LH thirds, matching the RH emphasis with a 'lean' on these LH first beats and coming **off** the *staccato* octave G sharp beneath the RH upbeat to b.20 and b.21. Slur the upbeat quaver up to the dotted quaver on the first beat of b.24, and then draw out the dotted rhythm broken octaves a little through b.24 as you prepare to lead off again from the slurred semiquaver upbeat to b.26.

bb.32–72   Ending the previous section with another vigorous 'stamp' on the first and second beats of b.32, some players race into the *gajo* (gay) section from the upbeat to b.33 – indeed the Associated Board Edition states that it 'should' go faster. My own feeling is that it should be played with joyous insouciance, with no more than a slight sense of moving on. On the other hand the more hectic, headlong spirit engendered by a faster speed is indeed often inherent in Mazurka movements – the tempo here must therefore be a matter of personal choice. In any event, lead on showing the upward 'lift' from a smooth upbeat crotchet to the C sharp on the first beat of b.33. Feel the smooth impulse towards, and implied slight emphasis upon the dotted crotchet on the second beat of b.33, and then down towards the emphasised minim on the second beat of b.34, supporting the RH with a 'dancing' LH (see Introduction to Mazurkas). Ensure that the RH emphasised tied minim on the second beat of b.36 sounds **over** the first beat of b.37, dropping the tone here to a furtive *piano* over the continually dancing LH. 'Go to' a powerful *sforzato* RH octave on the second beat of b.40, and propel yourself into the *forte,* higher restatement of the *gajo* theme with vigorous detached LH crotchets on the second and third beats. Draw out a little through b.48, 'holding' the chord on the second beat momentarily, ready to 'slide' back into the *sotto voce* through the slurred upbeat to b.49. Note the *rubato* at b.65, allowing time to articulate the detached, even-rhythmed version of the opening motif through bb.65-6, and also to allow the subtly nuanced triplet to speak in b.67. Then switch smartly back to *forte* in b.69 to end with an extra spurt of bravado. Hold the pedal right through the final bar as indicated, noting the pause over the RH tonic dotted minim and the LH rest.

Mazurka No. 3 in E major
Op. 6 No. 3 (7)

This is a piece of galvanising vigour and propulsion. To play it faster than Chopin's ♩. = 60 (as many pianists will insist on doing) is to emasculate its rhythmic 'spring', reducing it to mere scampering.

bb.1–32
Set a secure crotchet pulse therefore within the overall ♩. = 60, and play the introductory LH drone fifths in a quiet, but taut-rhythmed *staccato*, 'pointing' the displaced accents vigorously. Give an extra upbeat 'point' to the last accented fifth to poise the rhythm for the entry of the RH. Articulate each RH scale figure in a neat procession down to the accented E in bb.6 and 8. Some pianists play the grace notes **on** the beat here, in accordance with Chopin's habitual practice (see General Introduction under 'Ornaments') with a smart 'snapped' effect, while others let them anticipate the beat – and this must be a matter of choice. Rubinstein, in his RCA recording, gives these little scale figures a rhythmic bounce that is quite intoxicating, even hilarious! Poise yourself with a firmly 'planted' RH fifth on the upbeat to b.9, ready to launch into the *forte* on the first beat of b.9. Leap into this passage with a vigorous upward rhythmic swing, implementing all accents emphatically (on the upbeat to bb.10 and 11, and on the second beat of b.12, etc.). Be sure to **lift** the RH from the quaver chord on the first beat of bb.9, 10, etc, so that it 'falls' naturally onto the slurred semiquaver chord, feeling each of these semiquaver chords as the 'upbeat' to the crotchet on the second beat of the bar (and similarly to the accented minim on the second beat of b.12 and bb.14 and 15 – see General Introduction under 'Articulation').*
Feel the overall impetus from b.9 towards the strong minim on the second beat of b.12. Then from b.13 see how this impetus towards the rhythmic objective – the accented minim – is shortened in a 2-bar phrase (bb.13-14) and then further telescoped towards the second beat of b.15 and finally and especially, towards the 'early' syncopated treble minim in b.16. Support the RH with a springingly rhythmic LH through bb.9-10, and then keep the LH

---

*Again, be sure to LIFT the RH from the quaver third on the second beat of bb.11 and 13, so that the hand 'rebounds', to run dashingly up through the slurred thirds to a ringing staccato third on the first beat of bb.12 and 14.

semi-detached repeated chords going implacably through bb.11-14. Maintain a vigorous *forte* through to the end of b.16, with a fractional break here to clear the sound before you jump back into *piano* at b.17.

bb.32–40 Let the tautly rhythmic LH drones propel you on through b.32 into the new section at b.33. Blazon out the chords in b.33 in a ringing *fortissimo* with a powerful 'crack' on the chord on the second beat, coming off smartly with hands **and** pedal on the third beat, so that you **feel** the crotchet rest. I like to carry on with a vigorous swing through b.34, then drop the tone as indicated, to play the intervening bars (bb.35-7) in a clear but subdued *piano* as if gathering forces for the next 'burst' at b.37. I notice however that many pianists anticipate the marking here, dropping to *piano* at b.34, and again at b.38. In any event take care to 'point' the upbeat chord to b.37 a little, as you poise yourself for the renewed *fortissimo*.

bb.40–90 Poise yourself again on the emphasised upbeat to b.41 ready to lead on into the next section in a new tone. Try playing from here in a 'tinkly' *piano* in the RH, listening to the drone effect of the inner RH offbeat held B's over quietly insistent (and also partly 'droned') LH chords. Then open out the tone through b.46, 'braking' for an instant on the tied upbeat crotchets to b.47, ready to play this unison linking passage with improvisatory freedom. Feel the sense of pressing on through b.48 with just a tiny easing through the last beat, ready to launch into b.49. This passage has a splendidly braggardly momentum (*risvegliato* means literally 're-awakening'). Play the RH in a broad tone, feeling the impetus towards and implied emphasis upon the RH dotted crotchet E on the second beat of b.50. Support the RH with steady yet 'ongoing' LH chords, noting the phrase grouping of these chords, and feeling in particular the indicated onward 'push' of the upbeat chords to bb.51 and 55 beneath the treble RH dotted crotchets. Give the RH phrase ending in b.56 a jaunty 'lift' up to the high A on the second beat as the LH goes on down to the low A, ready for the RH to lead on with the quaver upbeat to b.57. Give this *piano* echo of the *risvegliato* passage a gentler, more feminine feeling, listening to the smooth movement of the LH chords as they edge expressively downwards this time in a smooth overall phrase. 'Lifting' cleanly up to the RH A again on the second beat of b.64, **use** the LH fifth on the third beat of the bar in an upbeat sense, to 'click' you back into the mood of the *vivace* downward bounce in b.65. Poise yourself momentarily on the third beat of b.86 for the *subito piano* in b.87, and play the final bars with quiet whimsicality.

Mazurka No. 4 in E flat minor
Op. 6 No. 4 (7) (O)

This is one of the shortest of the Mazurkas. But with its web of inner moving parts and tied and held notes and its fairly swift tempo, it is certainly not one of the easiest, particularly for those with small hands. In any event these held resonances are quite complex and require the acute attention of an experienced ear. Most players in fact seem to adopt a slightly slower tempo that the ♩. = 76. But if possible not too much slower. At Chopin's tempo these held resonances through bb.1-8 within the 2-bar phrasing (punctuated by the frequent offbeat accents), suggest a fleet, almost skimming one-in-the-bar movement. The further we fall below around ♩. = 69, the more we tend towards a **trudging 3/4** step. And this, given his indication *presto ma non troppo* ♩. = 76, Chopin cannnot have wanted. Given such a short piece, with hardly a startling change of pattern in bb.9-16, there seems little justification for the pronounced slowing down of this middle section favoured by some players.

bb. 1–8   Practise the upper line carefully alone so that you absorb its shape and emphases thoroughly. Note the continuing insistent 'lean' on the tied upbeat to each 2-bar phrase (implied on the opening upbeat and indicated thereafter). Then practise the inner voices separately so that you fully understand aurally what is going on in each. When you put the parts together practise **slowly** at first so that the ear **learns** the sound of the intervals created by the relation of the moving voices over the subtly permeating continuous lower drone through bb.1-8 (and similarly through bb.17-24). Always have the pulse well 'in the system' before starting, and place the unaccompanied opening tied upbeat with quiet intent, taking care to give this its full value, while at the same time feeling its strong onward lean (see the Introduction to the Mazurkas). Be sure to let this note sing over the bar line so that the treble line 'lifts' smoothly up to the quaver E flat in b.1. Place the inner and bass crotchets definitely but quietly beneath this held upbeat so that the treble melody sounds clearly

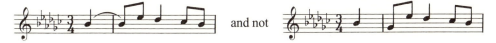

Show the increased 'bite' on the tied upbeat to b.5 without necessarily heightening the overall dynamic level. The piece is at its most effective when played in a rather subdued, breathless *piano*, like a smoothly scudding dream sequence, with just a little clearing and opening out of the tone in the middle section. Pay particular attention to the part-movement in b.8, though without breaking the impetus as you 'bite' into the upbeat to b.9.

bb.9–24   Listen to the inner RH held chords or notes beneath the clear ornamented upper line from b.9, as well as to the alternating movement of the LH inner and lower lines. Feel the little 'lift' from the upbeat quavers up to the E flat on the first beat of b.10, and from the upbeat trill to bb.11 and 12 up to the quaver on the subsequent first beat. Then be sure to **lift** the fifth finger from the quaver on the first beat of bb.14 and 16 to point the effect of the rest and semiquaver in contrast with the smooth quavers in bb.10 and 12 (see General Introduction under 'Articulation'.) Poise yourself to lead into the reprise with a little 'hold' on the *sforzato* upbeat to b.17 (rather than making a pronounced *rallentando* through b.16).

Mazurka No. 5 in B flat major
Op. 7 No. 1 (6)

This must be the best-known of all the Mazurkas – there can be few of us who did not cut some exciting early teeth in the discovery of its masculine pulse, abrupt dynamic changes, delicious sounding discords, and exotic drone effects. And an excellent piece it is for young players – short, clear-cut, and embodying many characteristic Mazurka features in relatively simple form.

bb. 1–24   Lead off in a virile style, as near to the ♩. = 50 as possible (although a slightly slower tempo will suffice provided that the rhythm is vital and springing).

Establish a clear steady pulse in the LH, feeling a strong impulse towards a powerful spread *sforzato* chord on the second beat of b.3. Articulate the RH in a sharply defined manner, 'matching' the impetus of the LH as you rise towards the high spot on the second beat of b.3. (Take care to **lift** the hand from the quaver on each first beat so that it 'falls' naturally onto the subsequent semiquaver – see General Introduction under 'Articulation'). Make a vigorous short trill on this second beat allowing the sense of a slight rhythmic 'hold' here, though

without losing the rhythmic impetus.  or

 (Be sure to support the RH trill by **holding** the

LH spread chord **through** the whole of the second beat, rather than letting it go vaguely as soon as it is played.) Then switch to *piano,* maximising the *scherzando* dancing effect of the RH through bb.4, 5 and 6, as it **lifts** from the quaver on each first beat, and 'falls' with a neat slurred flick to the minim on each second beat (especially 'pointing' the piquant effect of the discordant Lydian E natural in b.6). Take care again to show the exact effect of the articulation through bb.7-8 and 11, and again in b.12, poising yourself for an instant on the second beat of b.12 ready to 'start again' from b.13.

bb.24–44 End the first section with a clear chord on the second beat of b.24, poising yourself once more for an instant on this chord as you prepare to move into a smoother, more gliding movement from the upbeat to b.25. Then press on from b.29 as indicated, drawing out again through the beginning of b.32. Inexperienced players are often worried by the 'join' here, although Chopin's indications are very precise. Draw out through the *poco rallentando* towards the second beat of b.32 and allow a slight 'hold' on this emphasised dotted quaver note. Then think of the slurred semiquaver G as the 'upbeat' to the

triplet on the third beat, so that you feel these four notes

as an overall upbeat figure to b.33 as you whip up the speed towards tempo 1, ready to leap off into b.33.

bb.44–64 'Point' the single LH crotchet B flat on the upbeat to b.45, and then switch to a muted *pianissimo*. Maintain a quiet, drum-like beat in the LH drone fifths (playing these in an evenly spaced, just-detached style as indicated) as you articulate the RH in a thinly piping *sotto voce*, 'loosening' the rhythm of the RH a little from b.49, as indicated by Chopin's *rubato* and gradually slowing towards the quietly emphasised and momentarily held second beat of b.52 as you poise yourself to 'kick' back into tempo 1. Note Chopin's long pedal through bb.45-51, indicating his intention that this passage should have some degree of 'veiling'. On a modern piano a fully depressed pedal through these bars would create a unacceptably heavy blurring. In fact, few pianists take any notice of this marking, but in her recording (Calig) the Polish pianist Maria Szmyd-Dormus (among others) creates an attractive lightly veiled effect (see General Introduction under 'Pedalling').

Mazurka No. 6 in A minor
Op. 7 No. 2 (6)

Note: For those using the Paderewski Edition, there will be a discrepancy in bar-numbering from b.33, since in this edition both first **and** second-time bars are counted (i.e. for b.33 read b.34 and so on – see General Introduction under 'Bar Numberings').

This is one of the simplest of the Mazurkas, and another excellent piece for novice players. Since its mood is predominantly contemplative, it makes a good companion to the previous energetic number. I have never heard it played anywhere near as fast as Chopin's ♩= 160, and it certainly feels rushed at that tempo. However, in view of Chopin's *vivo ma non troppo*, we should not play it so slowly that it wilts to a standstill. It is particularly important therefore that the underlying sense of the dance rhythm is maintained in the offbeat LH just-detached chords through bb.1-3, etc, and offbeat slurred figures through bb.4-6, etc. (see the Introduction to the Mazurkas). Try a tempo of around ♩.= 120-132, allowing for a certain amount of give and take (see bb.7, 13, etc.). (See, however, discussion in the General Introduction under 'Tempo'.)

bb.1–16   Lead off in an expressive *cantabile* tone, making sure that the opening upbeat is given its full value (see Introduction to Mazurkas). At the same time feel the sense in which this upbeat crotchet gives a clear onward 'lean' towards the indicated further 'lean' on the dotted quaver on the first beat of b.1. Then feel the smooth onward impulse towards the emphasised minim on the first beat of b.2 (and similarly the impulse through b.3 towards the minim on the first beat of b.4). Support the RH with evenly 'spaced' LH just-detached chords on the second and third beats of each bar, playing each pair of chords with equal quiet definition and equal value (**not** as if the first is more important than the second).

Inexperienced players often have trouble with a 'composite value' beat as through the first

beat of b.3. Practise at first thus: keeping the quavers

very even within a strict crotchet pulse. Then when you add the triplet, play it with a neat 'twirl', ensuring that it 'fits' into the space of the first quaver without disrupting the equilibrium of the second quaver (and thereby of the whole bar). Take extra care to keep the LH chords steady in this bar so that the RH can 'depend' upon the continuing even rhythm of these offbeat crotchet chords. Show the slurred effect in the LH crotchet figures, upwards in b.4 and downwards in bb.5 and 6, feeling the onward impetus from b.5 as you *crescendo* towards the accented minim on the second beat of b.6. (Be sure to **lift** the RH cleanly from the crotchet B on the first beat of b.6, ready to 'plant' the E squarely on the second beat.) Then, taking the bit between your teeth, press on towards a vigorous 'stamp' on the first beat of b.8 (carrying the LH 'on down' to a strongly placed crotchet on the second beat). Clear the sound with a momentary break after this bass note before leading on with a *cantabile* upbeat to b.9. Draw out in a yearning but not too languid manner towards the second beat of b.14, and **feel** the silent pause through and beyond the rest before ending the section with neat precision.*

bb.16–40   Making a tiny break after the bass note on the second beat of b.16, resume the *cantabile* tone from the upbeat to b.17, but feeling the increasing intensity of the music as you move in *crescendo* towards the high B flat in b.21. 'Lean' expressively on this minim, and similarly on the minims on the first beat of bb.22 and 23

*In Jane Stirling's score Chopin wrote a delicate variant for b.11:

In the score belonging to Camille O'Meara Dubois there is a similar ornamentation for B.27, and also an indication for a glissando-like chromatic run from the A flat to the B natural in b.23.

(feeling an expressive *portamento*-like 'fall' to the crotchet on each third beat) as you *decrescendo* towards b.24, **listening** acutely throughout this section to the subtle chromatic inflections of the LH chords. Linger a little on the dotted crotchet on the first beat of b.24, and allow a little 'give' as you ease back into the reprise, feeling the three RH quavers as an overall upbeat to b.25. In b.32 (the second-time bar) quietly 'point' the inner inflection to the major beneath the treble dotted minim A. Then play the RH with quiet, but dance-like precision from b.33, underpinned by steady LH crotchets. Be sure to **lift** the RH from the treble quaver on the first beat of b.33, and from the sixth on the second beat of bb.35 and 39 (see General Introduction under 'Articulation'). **Listen** to the varying intervals of the RH chords (so often fourths) through this section, and 'space' the triplet quaver chords whimsically through the first beat of bb.37-41. **Lift** the LH between each group of three slurred crotchets so that you show the special 'circling' effect of these offbeat groups.

bb.41–56   Strike off from b.41 in a more martial manner. Practise the contrary motion leaps in b.44 like this:

If you do this **boldly**, risking wrong notes at first, aim will rapidly improve. Make sure in performance that the *sforzato* octaves are given **equal** force on the second **and** third beats, imagining an energetic 'stamp' on each. Then draw out pronouncedly towards the second beat of b.47, and again through b.48. You could place the appoggiatura on the

second beat in b.48, lingering a little thus:

as you poise yourself to move back into the *dolce* motif. At the end of the repeat allow a little break at the end of the second-time bar, ready to lead back into the opening section with a poised RH upbeat.*

---

*Von Lenz gives an amusing account of working with Liszt on this piece. 'He made me aware of important little variants, and was very strict with me, particularly concerning the deceptively simple-looking bass in the major section . . . What pains he took with me there! "Only an ass could believe this is easy," he said. "It's these *legato* slurs that identify a virtuoso! Play it like **this** to Chopin and he'll notice it; it will please him. This is how you should read these slurs in the bass! [i.e. bb.33-40, see above]. If you play it to him like **this**, then he'll give you lessons."' (Eigeldinger, p.74).

Mazurka No. 7 in F minor
Op. 7 No. 3 (7)

This is one of the most masterly of the early Mazurkas, bursting with life and variety within a taut and economical structure.

bb.1–24   The *sotto voce* introduction immediately grips the imagination. Let the two voices 'speak' in sepulchral but clear low tones. Feel that the lower LH fragment through b.1 is 'going to' the dotted minim F on the first beat of b.2, and that the upper line through b.2 is 'going to' the dotted minim C on the first beat of b.3, and so on, thereby establishing a secure pulse near to the ♩. = 54 marking. Let the mysterious lower *staccato* quavers *decrescendo*, slowing a little through b.8 like tiny disappearing steps, as you gather yourself to launch into the *con anima* at b.9. This principal motif is sometimes played in an almost questioning style with considerable *rubato*. Others prefer a tauter, more pent-up feeling, as if powerful forces are straining at the leash, starting *piano* and gathering power towards b.15; and then playing the restatement from b.17 in a more lingering, contemplative manner as suggested by the *rubato* indication. If you favour the former interpretation, the LH spread chords will obviously have a looser, more relaxed beat – if the latter, they will have a tauter, more martial 'thrum'. In either event be sure to **lift** the RH after the quaver on the first beat of bb.9, 11, etc, so that it 'falls' onto the semiquaver, feeling this semiquaver as the 'upbeat' to the **second** beat of the bar as you shape this 5-note fragment in an overall slur (see General Introduction under 'Articulation'). An experienced player may then subtly 'distort' the rhythm of the triplet figure on the first beat of b.10 etc. so that this triplet sounds more like:

(see the Introduction to the Mazurkas). Then raise the hand cleanly

again from the crotchet on the second beat of b.10 so that it falls emphatically, as if 'planted' onto the accented slurred upbeat to b.11. 'Lean' well on the accented C on the upbeat to b.15, ready to implement the haughty *con forza* through b.15. 'Go through to' a sonorous dotted C on the first beat of b.16, then 'give' a little, lingering slightly on the third beat, as you gather yourself to 'start again' with the upbeat to b.17.

bb.24–40   End this first section with powerful alternating unisons in b.24 taking care to let the LH tied minim sing over the bar line and allowing the overall unison sounds to linger for an instant across the bar line, before you switch to a hurrying (but controlled), neatly articulated *piano* at b.25. Ease into a melting *dolce* at b.29, making a fractional 'hold' on the dotted quaver on the first beat here. Then allow a little extra time to point the chromatic movement of the lower LH line through b.32, then poising yourself for an instant on the LH upbeat chord, ready to hurry off again in b.33. 'Hold' the chord momentarily on the second beat of b.40 as you prepare to launch into the new section from a powerful upbeat.

bb.41–72   Blazon out the chords with brilliant urgency feeling a vigorous impetus towards the *tenuto* spread chord on the second beat of b.42. Allow an extra instant to place this chord as if with a powerful 'pounce', and **hold** it for another extra instant as you prepare to maximise the echo effect in bb.43-4. Play these bars in perfect time, but on a 'tight rein' as if straining to burst out again in b.45. Again momentarily 'hold' the chord on the second beat of b.56, ready to lead smoothly into b.57 with the LH upbeat quavers. Let the LH melody sing out quietly but buoyantly and expressively from here beneath carefully balanced and very steady RH chords. Make a little 'push' as indicated up towards the long tied minim on the second beat of bb.60 and 68. Then 'hold' the emphasised RH upbeat chord fractionally to balance this LH note as you poise yourself to move on again in bb.61 (and 69).*

bb.72–105   Draw out a very little through the end of b.72 ready to switch to a hushed *pianissimo* at b.73, and listen acutely to the marvellous inflections as the RH chords edge us back to F minor over the long tied bass notes. The returning introductory bars sound even more mysterious from here beneath the strange distant tolling of the upper dotted minim chords. At b.97 Chopin gives notice of his progressive *smorzando* effect through the final bars. Play these RH quavers through bb.97-8 in an eloquent, slightly hesitant semi-*staccato*, and gradually fade the sound towards the *pianissimo* ending. However much you may slow the tempo, do it in a carefully graded manner so that the sense of the overall pulse is always present. Then point the telling inner B flat on the third beat of b.104 before 'dispersing' the tonic sound up to the high F.

Mazurka No. 8 in A flat major
Op. 7 No. 4 (7)

This is a deliciously hectic, flighty affair.

bb.1–8   Set a tempo as near as possible to the ♩. = 76, though less experienced players will find the acciaccaturas and dotted rhythms in bb.7 and 22-3 difficult to articulate at this tempo. It is better to take a slightly slower tempo than to risk smudging these details – a vital, springing rhythm is more important than sheer speed. In any event, bb.9-16 need a very slightly slower tempo or the 'pointing' of the *scherzando* effect will be steam-rollered. Be clear that it is the **LH chords** which control this piece. Provided that they are immaculately rhythmic, implementing all emphases and phrasing indications, the RH will to a remarkable extent look after itself. Practise the LH through bb.1-3 in a taut but smooth rhythm, marking the accented second beat of b.1 and the first beat of b.2 as if with a little 'push' on each, and with the feeling of pressing on towards the quaver chord on the first beat of b.3. Bounce **off** this chord and then play the subsequent five chords in a *subito piano* as smoothly as possible. When you put hands together have the LH rhythm thoroughly 'in the system' before starting. Enter with a 'keen' RH quaver upbeat, then feel that the LH is 'taking on' and establishing the rhythm from the first beat of b.1. Articulate the RH with all possible vitality and wit, but with the feeling of allowing it to fit in with the rhythm of the LH chords. Feel a little 'push' in the RH as indicated, towards the slurred upbeat to b.3 so that the RH, like the LH, 'bounces' off the *sforzato* quaver on the first beat of b.3. 'Hold' the rest for an extra instant, to

*These LH fingerings are marked in Jane Stirling's copy, from b.57.

allow the hands to 'fall', with the RH 'flicking' the semiquaver neatly towards the quaver on the second beat in perfect synchronisation with the LH chord. Allow a momentary 'hold' on the emphasised upbeat to b.5, as if crouching, ready to dash off again.

bb.8–24   Take a quick breath on the semiquaver rest at b.8 so that the upbeat semiquaver can 'flick' cleanly to the slurred crotchet C on the first beat of b.9. 'Bounce' off the high C again in a new, insouciant, but more pliant *scherzando* style to 'flick' the semiquaver towards a clearly accented tied crotchet A flat on the upbeat to b.10, and so on, 'pointing' all the details (in particular the persistent little jerk on each slurred RH upbeat) over smoothly moving LH chords. 'Go to' a firm accented tied crotchet on the upbeat to b.16, then drawing out a little and **listening** to the startling LH inflections as you *crescendo* back into b.17.

bb.24–44   The third section from b.25 is the most difficult, and again most pianists anyway take a rather slower tempo here. 'End' cleanly on the quietly emphasised crotchet chord on the third beat of b.24. Make a tiny break ready to switch to a quiet *dolcissimo* in b.25, keeping the treble line as smooth as possible (with the aid of the pedal) over quiet, even inner RH crotchets and LH chords. Listen to the inner inflections of these chords over the persistent quiet D flat drone, showing the little emphasis and implied tiny *tenuto* on each third beat. Slow gradually from b.29, letting the upper quavers 'speak' in a light, distant *staccato* in contrast to the previous smoothly phrased effect.* Allow an instant at the end of b.32 to clear the D flat sound, and then play the slower, *sotto voce* figure nostalgically, like distant calls, allowing time for the sound to fade through the pause at b.36. Then 'pounce' on the accented upbeat to b.37, ready to race off briefly again. Break off as if in mid-air at b.43, and 'hang' momentarily through the pause before ending in a busy clatter.

Mazurka No. 9 in C major
Op. 7 No. 5 (4-5)

As Weinstock says, this 'wisp of a Mazurka . . . breaks off without a true ending, leaving in the vibrating air a question almost as enigmatic and unanswerable as that asked by Schumann's 'Prophet Bird' (Weinstock p.187). And indeed the apparent intention of this miniscule piece to echo the hectic flight of the previous Mazurka only enhances the piquancy of this mid-air vanishing act.

bb.1–12   As in the previous number, it is essential that the LH raps out a rock steady rhythm, and that the RH fits in with this, and **not** the other way around. Needless to say (at the given tempo) it is not so easy as it looks, but when the spirit is truly caught, this piece can be marvellously funny, like a circle of wooden dolls jumping around to the churning, jerking rhythm. Have your ♩. = 60 beat (or less, according to abilities) thoroughly 'in the system' before you start, enter with a good 'clonk' on the first LH octave, and maintain a clockwork beat as you gradually reduce the sound through bb.2-4. Enter with the RH in an immaculately articulated *mezza voce* marking the emphasis on the RH G on the second beat of bb.5 and 6, and the slurred accentuation on the LH upbeat chords. **Lift** the hand from the RH accented G's so that it 'falls' onto the dotted rhythm upbeat figure, making a natural slight emphasis. Then make a little 'push' from the upbeat to b.7 up towards the *sforzato* crotchet on the first beat of b.7, and similarly up to the high dotted quaver on the third beat of b.8. Allow an instant to clear the sound at the end of b.8 ready to 'start again' in b.9.

*Those with small hands could try (although this is not easy) taking the inner LH E flats in b.26 etc. with the RH thumb.

138

Allow another instant at the end of b.12 ready to mark the sharp 'drop' from
bb.13–20   b.12 to the *sotto voce* at b.13. Point the startling F sharp on the first beat of b.19,
and hurtle back through b.20 to return to b.5, either dropping back to a *subito mezza voce*, or, perhaps playing the repeat in a more raucous tone. With his *Dal segno senza fine* Chopin jokily leaves this piece open-ended. Some players break off at the end of the repeat, i.e. at the end of b.20. Or, perhaps more amusingly we could (like Rubinstein in his recording) return to b.1 with a nice bump on the first octave, and then fade the sound of the octaves into thin air with barely a hint of a *rallentando*. A sequence of dotted rhythms as through bb.7-8 and 15-16 is often difficult for novice players. Always feel the semiquaver as the **upbeat** to the subsequent dotted quaver so that there is a continuous ongoing feeling towards each crotchet beat (see General Introduction under 'Dotted Rhythms').*

Mazurka No. 10 in B flat major
Op. 17 No. 1 (8)

This, as its indication *'vivo e risoluto'* announces, has a grand, chivalric stride. Chopin's ♩ = 160 seems on the fast side, and most players settle at a tempo around ♩ = 144. A vigorous rhythmic swing is the essential here – not the search for a 'correct' metronome mark.

It is important that this rhythmic swing is convincingly launched in the first bar.
bb.1–8   Lean in, therefore, from a strong crotchet upbeat, feeling an energetic 'lift'
towards a powerful *sforzato* third on the first beat of b.1. Blazon out the RH thirds through b.1, and the sixths thereafter, with a trumpeting ring, supported by a springingly rhythmic LH. Take particular care through b.1 to place the LH chord resolutely on the second beat beneath the RH dotted crotchet third, and then to place the chord on the third beat with a good upbeat 'push'. Be sure to **lift** the RH from the chord on the first beat of bb.2 and 4 so that it 'falls' naturally onto the semiquaver, feeling this as the 'upbeat' to the second beat of the bar (see General Introduction under 'Articulation'). Place the LH chord particularly surely on the second beat of bb.3 and 7 as if to 'point' the fact that there is a rest on the third beat. Point the emphasised upbeat to b.7, and then ensure in b.7 that the treble dotted crotchet sings out over

the second beat so that the treble line is clearly  and not

The grace note figures (bb.1, 5, etc.) are best placed on the

beat with a keen 'kick'. These are not easy. It is essential to **lift** the hand from the previous quaver (or crotchet) third sufficiently to ensure a clear attack on the grace note third. Be sure to 'finish off' emphatically in b.8, i.e. to give the chords on the second and third beats an **equal**

*A nice comment on the *senza fine* question comes from T.A. Zielinski: 'Chopin, His Life and Creative Work; PWM Publishers, Cracow 1993'. 'The C major Mazurka, being exceptionally short, is actually based on a four-bar phrase (repeated with a somewhat altered ending, then transposed to G major). The utterly ostentatious simplicity of the structure and harmony bears all the signs of a lively movement that [echoes] the unusual joyfulness of the melody itself, provided moreover with a repetition mark and with the words '*senza fine*' – endlessly, over and over again! This is simply a hint to the peasant musicians practice, who play to dance one melody for an unlimited number of times. The ending, unavoidable for a pianist, or a humorous break perhaps of the music with the last bar of the notation (in G major) that leads to the first one, comes to the point of the magnificent humour of the whole miniature'.

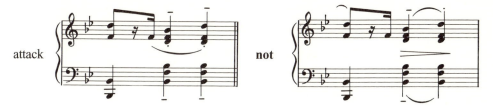

attack   not

| | Launch into b.9 in a yet grander manner with powerful dominant unisons, and |
| bb.9–40 | then spring up (and similarly in bb.11 and 13) to 'plant' the dotted crotchet chord |

Launch into b.9 in a yet grander manner with powerful dominant unisons, and then spring up (and similarly in bb.11 and 13) to 'plant' the dotted crotchet chord on the second beat with vigorous emphasis. Play each of these 2-bar fragments (bb.9-10, 11-12 and 13-14) with equal conviction. Then relax the momentum a little as you **listen** to the modulating sequential figures descending through bb.15-16 ready to move into b.17 (the varied version of bb.1-8). Play these bars in a still full-throated, but more ruminative, nostalgic manner, listening to the minor inflection at bb.18, 21, etc. End the section with a strong 'stamp' on the unison octaves on the third beat of b.24 and again b.40, allowing an extra instant at the end of b.40 to clear the sound ready to drop to a *subito piano* at b.41.

bb.41–60   This section in E flat has a musette-like tonic pedal point, with a light, piping-toned folk-like tune. Play the LH introductory figures (bb.41-4) with neat, dance-like precision, and with a slight sense of moving on (noting the overall pedal effect – see General Introduction under 'Pedalling' and also Introduction to Mazurkas). Enter with the RH in a quiet but clear tone. Note the details of articulation and emphasis precisely: the little **lift** from the quaver G on the first beat of b.45; the little 'push' up to the dotted crotchet G on the second beat of b.45; the **lift** from the crotchet A flat on the second beat of b.46; the implied little emphasis and 'hold' on the high C on the upbeat to b.47, imagining a *portamento* effect as you slur this note down to the *staccato* on the subsequent first beat and so on. A considerable degree of rhythmic give and take is implied throughout this section. Note the further emphasis on the high detached crotchet F on the third beat of b.50, and then 'twiddle'

the line of ornaments *etc.* neatly down through bb.51 and 52.*

Tail the sound away in a *smorzando* effect up to a whispered high F on the third beat of b.58 allowing time for this sound to 'hang' through the pause. Then some pianists play the little 'tail' in bb.59-60 more or less in time, ready to launch straight back onto the upbeat to b.1, while others make a pronounced *rallentando* through these two bars, allowing a clear little break at the end of b.60. This perhaps allows the upbeat to b.1 to lead off with a more convincing 'grasp'.

Mazurka No. 11 in E minor
Op. 17 No. 2 (6)

This is another excellent piece for players around Grade 6 (or even perhaps Grade 5 for older players). It has a striking linking passage, with a creeping chromatic chord sequence from b.39 through which Chopin impels the music back into the reprise from b.53. The principal motif (bb.1-4) is of a rather mournful cast (see the falling shape of each fragment – from the opening

---

*In Jane Stirling's copy a pencil stroke indicates a clear break in the melody line after the second crotchet of b.46, and again between the second and third beat of b.48. There is then a phrase mark from the upbeat to b.49 through to the second beat of b.50. A break is again marked before the upbeat to b.51, with a further phrase mark from this upbeat through to the quaver on the first beat of b.53.

upbeat through b.1, and from b.2 through b.3), and the general atmosphere somewhat brooding, even sullen. Nevertheless, there is a feeling of underlying energy, borne out by Chopin's *lento* which, at ♩ = 144 is definitely *non troppo* (though in fact most players adopt a slightly slower tempo – see, however the General Introduction, under 'Tempo').

bb.1–24

'Lean' in from a full toned and full valued crotchet upbeat, and shape the RH with a purposeful kind of expressiveness down through b.1, and then with a strong 'lift' up to the emphasised minim on the first beat of b.2. Feel the overall impulse from the opening upbeat towards this strong minim, and similarly on towards the emphasised ornamented fourth on the first beat of b.4. At the same time feel the strong onward 'push' of the preceding upbeat crotchet towards each of these strong minims. Support the RH with resonant bass notes and LH chords through bb.1-2 (see Introduction to Mazurkas). Listen to the inner LH thirds descending through b.3 above the lower dotted minim. Then be sure to place the LH fifth firmly on the second beat of b.4 ready for the RH to lead on with a strong upbeat crotchet. Feel the vigorous onward impetus towards the emphasised third beat of b.5 (the B on the first beat of b.5 is struck, not tied), and on again as the RH rises towards the emphasised third beat of b.6. Then feel a sense of slight 'unwinding' as you descend with a whimsical 'skip' through bb.7-8 ready for the next upward 'push' from b.9. In bb.5 and 6 and again through bb.7 and 8 be sure to **lift** the hand from each *staccato* quaver so that it 'falls' naturally onto the subsequent semiquaver, feeling each semiquaver (whether slurred or not) as the 'upbeat' to the subsequent quaver (see General Introduction under 'Articulation'). In b.10 'scoop up' confidently to the high detached quaver from a strong semiquaver on the first beat with an upward *portamento*-like 'throw' effect. Support the descending high quavers with a firm LH sixth on the second beat of this bar, and then 'open out' the tone through b.11 towards a strong acciaccatura third and minim on the first beat of b.12. 'Finish off' here with a firm LH chord on the second beat ready to lead on into the restatement with the upbeat to b.13. Linger a little over the light triplet tracery through b.23.

bb.24–68

Arrive on a quiet but definite minim chord on the second beat of b.24, giving this a *tenuto* effect as you listen to the tied treble E carrying you over into the *dolce* C major section. Play this with an easy-moving simplicity, and with a slight sense of moving on, listening to the drone effects through bb.25-8, etc., and 'leaning', with a hint of a *tenuto* on the emphasised upbeat to bb.27, 29, 30, etc. Then underpin the treble dotted rhythms from b.29 with quietly resonant lower voices. 'Point' the crotchet chord on the upbeat to b.32 with a quiet emphasis, and then 'space out' the repeated crotchet E's through b.32 in a 'speaking' manner as you poise yourself to move on again from b.33. From b.39 Chopin makes the transition back to the reprise at b.53 through a remarkable series of snaking chromatic shifts over a continuing bass drone. Feel the little 'push' on the emphasised tied A flat on the second beat of b.39 (and similarly in bb.43, 45, etc.) as the inner parts move in smooth little surges towards, and receding from, the first beat of bb.40, 44 and 46. 'Hold' the last beat of b.47 fractionally as you prepare to drop to a *subito pianissimo* in b.48. Then open out the tone as, on a taut rhythmic rein you drive on in *stretto* towards the reprise. Drop to *piano* again at b.63, and then 'scoop up', this time to a whispered top E at b.66. From this topmost point of sound, take time to 'curl' the triplets delicately downwards towards the final chord.

Mazurka No. 12 in A flat major
Op. 17 No. 3 (7)

This is a bewitching piece. With its shadowy chromatic wanderings the mood of the recurring main section bb.1-16 is ambiguous – 'enclosed' and hesitant, yet whimsical. Then at b.57

Chopin takes a wayward sidestep into a delicious series of upward flying scales. **Note:** For those using the Paderewski Edition there will be a discrepancy in bar-numbering from b.41, since in this edition both first **and** second-time bars are counted (i.e. for b.41 read b.42 and so on – see General Introduction under 'Bar Numberings').

bb.1–16   Given Chopin's tempo of ♩ = 144 (although some pianists take it a little slower) there is inevitably a good deal of rhythmic give and take through the first section.

But this must be accomplished with infinite subtlety and discretion or the music will lose shape and cohesion. Make a quiet but clear 'lean' on the opening upbeat so that it sings well over the bar line and then, bringing the LH in, again quietly but definitely on the first beat of b.1, establish your basic tempo clearly through bb.1-4. In the LH there is a subtle sense of 'going to' the chord on each second beat, and in the RH the merest suggestion of a *tenuto* on the third beat of bb.1 and 3. Then linger a little through b.4 as you **listen** to the lower LH fragment making a fractional break at the end of the bar, as if taking a breath, ready to 'start again' from b.5. Note the little emphases, more like tiny 'holds' on the tied upbeat to b.6 and the doubled second beat of b.6; then a little sense of pressing on to the doubled second beat of b.7 and the first beat of b.8, as this truncated fragment is reiterated in a momentary **2/4** effect. Then feel a slight drawing back through the remainder of b.8 as you poise yourself once more to start again in b.9. Take a little time to let the triplet ornamentation 'speak' through b.11 (and similarly the LH again through b.12), and again to show the different articulation in b.13 (see General Introduction under 'Articulation'); and then move on through b.14, 'twirling' the demisemiquaver ornament lightly, **lifting** the hand from the quaver on the second beat, and allowing a slight *tenuto* effect on the third beat. End this section in neat time as the harmonies emerge from their chromatic preoccupations to finish in a clear tonic. Listen acutely through this whole section (bb.1-16) to the chromatic inflections of the LH.

bb.16–40   Make a tiny break after the second beat of b.16 ready to switch to a more virile, positive tone as you lead into b.17 from a strong slurred RH upbeat. 'Move on', feeling the impetus towards the accented third beat of bb.17-22 and with a keen sense of pressing on through bb.21-2. Support the RH with vigorous detached LH chords on the second and third beats. Those with small hands will need to spread these, of course, but make sure that this is done not with a lax 'scoop', but with a smart 'rip', with a **short** separate pedal to each chord. Break momentarily after the accented chord on the third beat of b.22 to clear the sound, and then play this haunting slower fragment like a distant warning call, listening again to the inflections of the LH, and lingering a little on the **third** beat of b.24 before moving back into Tempo 1. 'Hold' the second beat of b.40 momentarily (second-time bar) as you prepare to poise the emphasised LH C flat on the third beat which, beneath the sound of the tied A flat-G sharp, pivots us beautifully into E major.

bb.41–80   Play from b.41 buoyantly, almost with a swagger. Then, making a sudden *diminuendo* from b.46, 'disperse' the sound through a diminishing wisp of *smorzando* quavers. 'Hold' the tempo a little through the end of b.49 as you poise yourself to launch off again from b.50. 'Plant' the RH upbeat to b.57 with quiet definition, going almost straight onto it from the neat ending of the previous section. Then, supporting the RH with the neatest and most immaculately controlled LH chords (listening to the inflections of the inner notes) fly up the scales in a flurry of immaculately clear *staccato* triplets. The more quietly these are played, the more effective these scales will sound, making a *diminuendo* each time you ascend towards tiny pin-points of sound on the top notes. (Point the little dotted rhythm 'kink' in the middle of the second and fourth scales, and give the high minim D sharp on the second beat of b.60 a tiny extra ring.) 'Give' a little as you end the last scale, ready to lead back into the E major section with a good 'lean' on the accented upbeat to b.65. Arrive on a resonant minim RH

E on the second beat of b.80 (second-time bar) and **listen** to the reverberations of this E, through the pause, and again as it is 'taken over' by the LH, as you poise yourself to return to the opening.

Mazurka No. 13 in A minor
Op. 17 No. 4 (7)

This is one of the best-loved of the Mazurkas, and with good reason. Its harmonies explore the finest shades of quiet melancholy, and the little runs and arabesques in the RH create exquisite frissons of chromatic sound. Von Lenz records that 'Even in Chopin's presence we called it "the mourner's face" – he was quite happy about this name.' (Eigeldinger, p.74).

This is one of the three numbers which are discussed in special detail (see Notes at end of the Introduction to Mazurkas).

bb.1–12 On a practical level Chopin's metronome mark presents a problem. But if the ♩ = 152 seems impossibly fast, we do, on the other hand, need to beware of going too slowly. If the music begins to plod, the harmonic inflections lose their shadowy effect and begin to sound too 'set' or two-dimensional, or on the other hand will droop to the point of expiry. Most pianists settle for a basic tempo of about ♩ = 112-120, but with a considerable degree of rhythmic give and take (see however, discussion in General Introduction, under 'Tempo'). It is important that the introductory bars are finely judged, for they set the scene for the entire first section. Feel your basic pulse **before** starting, and enter as quietly as possible, but ensuring that all the notes of each chord can be heard, as you delicately point the hinted inner melodic line. Establish the sense of a **3/4**, albeit with a little freedom, by feeling the gentle impulse towards the first beat of b.2, then hastening a very little towards the first beat of b.3 and then drawing out slightly towards the tied chord on the second beat of b.4. Feel that the RH triplet on the first beat of b.4 'grows out of', and 'returns to' the LH chords. Then **listen** to the quiet reverberation of the tied chord as you prepare to enter with the RH. Phrase the melody with the utmost expressiveness in a quiet, fine-drawn (rather than rich) tone, supported by quiet, evenly pulsing LH chords (listening acutely to the inflections of these chords). Keep quite an even tempo – there is plenty of room for *rubato* later. Allow just a **hint** of a lingering on the dotted quaver on the third beat of b.7, then feel the slurred semiquaver as the upbeat to the *tenuto* minim in b.8. 'Lean' expressively on the crotchet on the first beat of bb.9 and 10, slurring each of these, as if in a light *portamento*, down to a quietly singing minim on the second beat. Also make a tiny 'leaned' emphasis on the semiquaver on the first beat of bb.11 and 12, conveying the melancholic fall of each of these slurred figures.

bb.13–35 'Drift' into the triplets in the ornamented restatement at b.13. Inexperienced players invariably panic at the very sight of the run in b.15. This question of the management of 'free' runs arises frequently in Chopin, and is discussed in the General Introduction under 'Free' Runs'. Here and in b.31 the runs are relatively plain sailing since the RH notes fit in equal groups of five notes to each LH crotchet. Keep the LH steady at all costs, feeling that the RH is being guided by this steady LH and **not** the other way round. Curl the RH upwards through b.15 in a finely shaded thread of sound, allowing a very slight expansion through the third beat as the RH turns the corner through the high B, and falls delicately towards a softly singing *tenuto* dotted minim E on the first beat of b.16; and then quietly pick up the pulse in the LH through b.16. Then take particular care to place the

LH chord with quiet definition on the first beat of b.17 beneath the RH rest. Feel a sense of moving on from here so that the 6-note ornament on the first beat of b.18 is 'twirled' clearly, and neatly and quickly, with the feeling of 'going on towards' and 'through' the clear minim D natural towards b.19. You could play b.19 with perhaps rather more 'masculine' energy (although conversely others play this bar lightly and delicately). In any event be sure to **lift** the hand from the high *staccato* quaver C on the first beat (see General Introduction under 'Articulation'), and again from the quaver on the second beat, ready to 'lean' the slurred upbeat G sharp on towards a clear dotted minim A on the first beat of b.20. Then draw back a little through b.20 listening to the rising LH chords, as you prepare to 'start again' from b.21. Take a little extra time to point the varied detailing in bb.23 and 29. Space the semi-*staccato* triplets in b.23 so that they 'speak', making a little *diminuendo* up towards the detached quaver G and allowing an extra fraction of time as you 'lift' over the rest. Again allow a little extra time to 'space' the repeated note ornament in b.29 so that once more it 'speaks' rather than jamming. (This figure becomes much easier if you divide it mentally into two groups of three notes.) The run through b.31 is more difficult than at b.15. This time allow a little expansion through the **second** beat, allowing for the barest suggestion of a *tenuto* as the RH 'lifts' to the high B, ready to oscillate delicately down through the broken fourths, and then with the sense of running on a little through the third beat towards 'home' once more on the first beat of b.32.

bb.36–60   'Finish off' the slurred LH chord cleanly on the second beat of b.36, and then, allowing a tiny break, adopt a new, more positive tone as you 'plant' the emphasised crotchet on the upbeat to b.37. Slur this note up to the *staccato* quaver on the first beat of b.38, and move on from here feeling the rather more urgent, still quiet, but slightly hectoring tone of this passage, over the dominant pedal point. Show all the eloquent little details of RH slurs, *staccatos*, rests and emphases faithfully. 'Flick' the slurred RH semiquaver strongly down to the emphasised crotchet on the third beat of bb.38, 40 and 42, 'pointing' the clash of the D sharp against the bass E on the third beat of b.40. (The expanded version of this figure in b.42 is not difficult to manage if you use the second finger on the semiquaver E as a 'pivot' as you make a quick lateral downward movement of the wrist.) Support the RH through this section with quite resonant slurred LH figures, not forgetting to place the 'separate' crotchets clearly on each third beat. Draw back markedly through b.43, and further again through b.44, listening to the mournful downward sliding effect of the triplet figures. Then **listen** again to the quiet resonance of the RH third held over the LH chord on the first beat of b.45, as you prepare to set off once more into the principal motif.

bb.60–77   Quietly 'point' the inner inflection to the major third on the second beat of b.60. Then move on in a quiet *dolce* tone, keeping the treble line glidingly smooth (with the help of the pedal) over quiet and very evenly 'spaced' LH drone fifths, and a carefully balanced inner RH line. Be sure to let the dotted minim E sing out over the inner RH fragment through bb.62 and 64. This little figure is none too easy to manage – there is a tendency to hold onto the **F sharp** instead of the minim E. Most players play the grace notes **before** the beat, and this is certainly easier. Feel the onward impulse up towards and back from the first beat of b.67 as you *crescendo*, then *decrescendo*, through bb.65-8, ensuring that the treble line sings above the dense lower chords. Slur the upper quaver couplet cleanly on the first beat of b.68, also **lifting** from the inner and LH quavers as indicated so that you then place the emphasised chord clearly on the second beat. Bb.74-6 are far from easy to manage. Practise the RH carefully alone, 'bringing out' the treble line with a ringing emphasis on the accented dotted crotchet on each second beat, and playing all the **inner** chords at first in a light *staccato* so that you grow accustomed to 'leaning' on the melody notes played with 'weak' fingers. Then, when you play the passage as written,

ensure that the treble line rings out:  *etc.*

and **not**: *etc.* Some players, particularly

those with smaller hands, may find they get a better sound on these second beats with the fifth finger, but that is of course a matter for the individual hand. Feel that you are 'pressing on' through bb.74-5, and then draw back again a little after the second beat of b.76 as you poise yourself to return to the *dolce* tone at b.77.

bb.77–109 *Crescendo* steeply through bb.89-90, towards a powerful quaver chord on the first beat of b.91. Then **lift** the hands so that they 'fall' onto the semiquavers E with the feeling of 'going on' to the acciaccatura and dotted crotchets F natural (see General Introduction under 'Articulation'). Feel these unison figures through bb.91-2 like cries of desperation, 'leaning' with heightened insistence on the F naturals, and **holding** the last one until the sound has faded a little before falling to an eloquent tied RH upbeat to b.93. Some players hold the pedal from the chord on the first beat of b.91 through to the dotted crotchets on the second beat, and some release it to 'show' the semiquaver rest – this must be a matter for experiment and choice. And do not forget the **sense** of the crotchet beat here, going faster through b.91 and slowing through the end of b.92, but nevertheless always present, underlying your progress through these two bars, however much freedom you may or may not take. Shape the triplet tracery with expressive delicacy through b.103, and then listen to the movement of the inner RH fragment through the first two beats of b.107.

bb.109–32 The extended coda from the upbeat to b.109 has a *scherzando*-like, yet at the same time plaintive character. 'Lean' expressively on the emphasised tied crotchet upbeat to b.109. Then placing the bass A quietly and precisely on the first beat of b.109, **lift** the RH from the tied-over quaver to perform a sad little downward slurred skip to the second beat. **Lift** the hand again ready to slur the crotchet D sharp with a slight 'lean' up to the emphasised augmented fourth on the first beat of b.110, and then **lift** the hand from the tied-over D sharp on the first beat of b.111 and so on. **Listen** to the augmented fourth or diminished fifth intervals through bb.110, 112, etc, always ensuring that the tied treble note sounds over the subsequent bar line so that the line is carried over towards the next little downward skip through bb.111, 113, 117, etc, over the quietly resonant lower LH dotted minims and relatively lighter inner chords. Try playing from b.108 in chords (one chord per bar, 'spread' where necessary) so that you fully understand aurally the marvellous sequence of intervals over this sustained lower pedal

point through to b.124. *etc.*

Observe all rests and slurs, and imagine that the acciaccaturas in bb.117 and 121 are lightly slurred down to the emphasised upbeats to the subsequent bars, making a progressive *diminuendo* from this point. From b.124 do not grow so slow that you lose all sense of the **3/4** pulse. Play the rising, and then descending RH minor crotchet-minim third (bb.125-6 and 127-8) like valedictory calls, giving the A in b.128 a little extra tone to sound through bb.129-30. Let the LH chords drift into the distance at the end of b.131, and then play the RH triplet in an eloquent whisper, holding the final LH chord until it fades into virtual silence.

In a piece such as this there are, need it be said, a thousand possible interpretative inflections. The expressive details of the recurring A minor 8-bar motif will vary from performance to performance, and of course, **within** each performance also. No one, for example, will play bb.9-12 and 97-100 in exactly the same way, nor bb.23 and 95. It is, however, important to maintain an overall sense of an onward moving crotchet pulse, whenever and in whatever sense it may temporarily 'give' or move on.

Mazurka No. 14 in G minor
Op. 24 No. 1 (6)

This is one of the least complex of the Mazurkas in both a technical and rhythmic sense, and its clear-cut sections are nicely varied. Since there are also attractive harmonic touches in the inner parts (bb.7, 23-4, 36-8, 48, etc.) which are again not too complex aurally, it is an excellent piece for relatively inexperienced players. (There are a few wide stretches for the LH, but these can relatively comfortably be taken by the RH thumb).

Note: For those using the Paderewski Edition there will be a discrepancy in bar-numbering from b.33, since in this edition both first **and** second-time bars are counted (i.e. for b.33 read b.34 and so on – see General Introduction under 'Bar Numberings').

bb.1–16   As in Op.17 No.2 there is a sense of underlying vitality beneath the apparently mournful character of the main motif which, despite Chopin's comparatively slow metronome mark, suggests that it should not be played too languorously. (See General Introduction under 'Tempo'.) Lead off from a fairly full-toned emphasised tied upbeat crotchet, taking care to give this its full value, or a little more. Then take care to place the LH bass note beneath this tied note on the first beat of b.1 in such a way that the rhythm gets off to a good start (see Introduction to the Mazurkas). **Lift** the hand from the quaver on the first beat of bb.1, 3, etc. so that it 'falls' onto the semiquaver, feeling this note as the 'upbeat' to the second beat (see General Introduction under 'Articulation'). Feel the onward impulse through b.1 towards the emphasised minim on the first beat of b.2, and then on again up towards the first beat of b.4. Some players *crescendo* through to this this first beat – others 'melt' the end of b.3 up towards a quiet first beat of b.4. In any event, listen to the complementary inner LH upward steps as you rise through b.3, making a good onward lean on the RH upbeat crotchet F sharp as indicated, and then slurring the quaver G on the first beat of b.4 expressively down to the dotted crotchet D. Ensure that this figure is properly timed (i.e. not 'clipped' like a semiquaver) and

played with a 'lean' on the quaver: and not   . Feel

also the slurred onward 'lean' of the inner RH dotted minim B flat, using this B flat as a bridge to carry you on and over into b.5 to carry on the phrase as if in a continuing overall sweep on towards the acciaccatura and minim on the first beat of b.8 (listening again to the downward movement of the inner LH fragment in b.7 beneath the 'speaking' detached RH crotchets). This particularly interesting fingering between bb.4-5 appears in Jane

Stirling's score.  *etc.* The sliding of the thumb off

146

the inner B flat to the quaver A on the first beat of b.5 underlines the intended onward leaning pull of this inner B flat towards the detached quaver. Poise yourself for an extra instant on the emphasised upbeat to b.9, ready to set off again into the restatement.

bb.16–32   Arriving on a full-toned acciaccatura and dotted minim D on the first beat of b.16, feel the sense in which this note, while ending the previous phrase, also gives an onward 'lean' (though without hurrying) towards the *sforzato* quaver on the first beat of b.17. Feel that you **spring** off this note, and similarly leap up from the LH bass crotchet ready to move the tempo on a little from the second beat. Feel a soft little 'lean' on the first note of each triplet as indicated, before 'twirling' the remainder of the triplet towards the *staccato* crotchet F; and then leap up from the second beat of b.18 to make a more pronounced 'lean' on the high upbeat to b.19, then moving on through b.19 to arrive on a clear RH minim and spread LH chord on the second beat of b.20. Be sure to give this minim its full value (**feeling** the third beat of the bar) while at the same time feeling once more the sense of 'leaning onwards', ready to spring off again from the *sforzato* first beat of b.21. The 'leaning' emphasis on the first note of each of the triplet 'twirls' in bb.17 and 18, and again on the upbeat to b.19 and the second beat of b.19 creates a momentary **2/4**

cross-rhythm effect  *etc.* (see reference to this

passage in General Introduction, under 'Dynamic and Agogic Accents'). Take a little extra time to listen to the descending inner LH line from the upbeat to b.23, and to point the chromatic inflection of the RH and lower LH on the second beat of b.32 (first-time bar). 'Hold' the RH dotted crotchet on this second beat for an instant too (in both the first- and second-time bars) so that the subsequent quaver is clearly shown as the upbeat as you either return to b.1 or continue into b.33.

bb.33–64   Toss off bb.33-6 with carefree spirit, as you move into the *con anima*. 'Brake' a little on the emphasised chord on the upbeat to b.37. Then, pressing on again through bb.37-9, **listen** to the movement of the LH inner line and to the insistent LH sevenths through b.39, drawing back again in b.40 as you poise yourself to set off into the restatement from b.41. Note all details of hairpin *crescendos* and *decrescendos*, slurs, etc, meticulously through bb.33-47. **Lift** the hand from the quaver third on the first beat of bb.33-6 (and similarly from the sixth on the first beat of b.38) so that you can slur the semiquaver third with a neat little fall towards the dotted crotchet third on each second beat (see General Introduction under 'Articulation'). Take time again to listen to the inner chromatic movement as you *ritenuto* through b.48, easing back into the reprise in b.49 beneath the emphasised held treble G. Point the little extra touch in b.57. Then, drawing back finally in b.62, play the solo fragment expressively, and end with a light *pianissimo* outward 'flick' to the unison G's on the second beat of the last bar.*

*In the score belonging to Chopin's pupil Camille O'Meara/Dubois a delicate variant is marked in b.59, which, as J.-J. Eigeldinger says 'felicitously answers the ornamented version in b.57.'

   A similar variant appears in Jane Stirling's score.

Mazurka No. 15 in C major
Op. 24 No. 2 (6)

This is a delectably airy affair. *Allegro non troppo* Chopin says, adding a spanking fast ♩ = 192! There is no doubt, however, that the nearer to this tempo you can play it the more scintillating it will sound. (This tempo mark refers to the autograph. Other editions give a sober 108, or again sometimes 138.)

bb.1–12   Enter in a real *sotto voce*, playing the tonic-dominant chords with fleetly 'gliding' smoothness. Poise yourself momentarily at the end of b.4, then launch into b.5 playing the high RH line as if on a trilling pipe. Give these bars (5-12) a continuously 'whirling' character, poising yourself as if with a little pounce on the emphasised crotchet upbeat between each 2-bar phrase. Most pianists cheerfully ignore Chopin's direction for the LH chords (*il basso sempre legato*) and play these brightly detached. It is much more difficult to keep the LH smooth against this whirling RH, but at least try it – playing the chords as smoothly as possible, keeping the hand close to the keys, and only raising the hand from each chord as little as is necessary in order to play the next one clearly. In any event the RH needs to be cushioned by the fast but **steady** LH crotchet pulse. And providing the LH chords are perfectly even, the alternating values of RH plain quavers and triplets will 'look after themselves'. Do, however, take particular care to 'space' the detached quavers sportively through the first beat of bb.6, 8, etc.

bb.13–56   From another 'pounced' upbeat, march into b.13 with a more masculine step, implementing the details of articulation spiritedly, and making a nicely rhythmic 'jerk' on each third beat of bb.13 and 14, and the second **and** third beat of b.15. Poise yourself again with a 'pounce' on the upbeat to b.17 and yet again on the upbeat to b.21, allowing an instant longer here to clear the sound for the *dolce* in the subsequent bar. Fly upwards from here in a deliciously soft but clear, airy tone over a more waltz-like LH (see the Introduction to the Mazurkas). Linger a little as you reach the high crotchet A on the first beat of b.26, 'picking out' the detached quavers delicately as you descend. Then draw back as indicated on the upbeat to b.28, 'pointing' the effect of the Lydian B natural. Play from b.29 with more freedom, allowing an extra instant as you curve the quavers up to the highest note of b.30 and b.34 as a singer would, but without losing the sense of the underlying dance-rhythm. Draw back again from the upbeat to b.36 as you prepare to dash off again from b.37. Point the offbeat lurches from b.54 as you 'pretend' to go into a momentary **2/4** and pressing on until you draw back as indicated in b.56. Go suddenly *pianissimo* on the second beat of b.56 and then poise yourself again on the upbeat to b.57, ready to 'slide' into D flat major.

bb.57–120   Return to tempo in b.57 while at the same time playing the repeated chords in a spaced manner, as if 'braking', and then 'letting go' in the waltz-like rhythm of bb.58-60. Again here imagine a little pounce on the emphasised upbeat to b.58, as you prepare to fly off lightly into b.58. Make a light 'lean' on the RH upbeat to b.59, and then a more pronounced slurred 'lean' on the high upbeat to b.61 as you poise yourself to swoop down to carry on into b.61. Brake again through b.61, this time in a sturdy *forte*, and similarly give these fragments maximum dynamic and rhythmic contrast as they alternate through to b.69. 'Take over' clearly with the LH as the melody is transferred to the lower register at b.70, taking care to keep the RH chords going evenly and in careful balance. Linger for an extra instant to point the momentary poignancy of the LH minim F slurred to the C flat in bb.73-4, etc. Then draw back once more through bb.87-8 as you prepare to ease back towards the reprise. Allow a tiny break at the end of b.88 as you poise yourself to race off again in b.89. Drop to a *subito sotto voce* again at b.105, and then break off into thin air after the first beat of b.108 and again in b.112. Then play the little slurred figures in time, but with questioning hesitancy, only

148

gradually slowing from perhaps b.17. **Feel** the silences, and gradually fade the sound as if the harmonies are 'sliding' out of earshot towards the final quiet chord.

Mazurka No. 16 in A flat major
Op. 24 No. 3 (6)

This is another good number for novice players. It has a cheerful, almost 'jogging' motion, and needs to be played fairly briskly, near to the given ♩ = 126, and with as much tonal variety as possible lest the multiple recurrences of the principal motif grow tedious.

Note: For those using the Paderewski Edition there will be a discrepancy in bar-numbering from b.49, since in this edition both first **and** second-time bars are counted (i.e. for b.49 read b.50 and so on – see General Introduction under 'Bar Numberings').

bb.1–9   Note the consistent rhythmic impetus through each 2-bar phrase: bb.1-2, 3-4, 5-6, etc. There is an impulse towards an implied lean on the dotted crotchet on the second beat of b.2; then through b.3 towards the indicated lean on the second beat of b.4; and then through b.5 towards a yet stronger lean on the *sforzato* second beat of b.6, and so on. Notice also the importance within this pattern of the upbeat leading onwards after each of these 'leans' into bb.3, 5 and 7. Lead in from a firm toned emphasised upbeat crotchet, with a little 'lean' on both this upbeat and on the dotted quaver on the first beat of b.1 as indicated. Then feel the onward impulse towards, and 'lift' up to, the dotted crotchet on the second beat of b.2, lingering for an extra instant on this note. (Take care that the upbeat quavers to bb.2 and 3 are given their full value and not 'clipped' to sound like semiquavers.) Support the RH with a lively LH through bb.1-2 (see above in the Introduction to the Mazurkas). Then listen to the LH inner fragment in b.3 'between' the sustained minim seventh, moving in sixths with the RH fragment. Take a little extra time to **listen** again to the slurred chromatic movement of the lower LH crotchets in b.4. Then, as you move on into b.5 be sure to **lift** the RH from the quaver on the first beat of b.5 so that it 'falls' naturally onto the semiquaver, feeling this as the 'upbeat' to the second beat of the bar (see General Introduction under 'Articulation'). Take care to place the LH chord clearly on the second beat (as if to emphasise the fact that there is no chord on the third beat) as you 'twirl' the triplet neatly, feeling the onward movement towards the second beat of b.6. **Lift** the hand again from the quaver on the first beat of b.6, then slur the semiquaver neatly up to a nicely ringing high A flat over a resonantly spread LH chord. Do not wait so long on this pause as to break the feeling of movement – within the pause effect here there is also the sense of an onward 'lean' on this chord, ready to lead on in tempo with a clear upbeat to b.7 (note the 'telescoping' of the pattern of bb.1-6 in this second phrase).*

bb.10–55   At b.10 rise to a fuller-toned chord, letting this vibrate for a little longer than at b.6 (see discussion of these pauses, and again at b.36 in the General Introduction under 'Rests and Pauses'). Then let the upbeat triplet and quavers 'uncurl' gracefully downwards through b.11. 'Hold' the crotchet for an instant on the second beat of b.12 before leading on into the restatement with the upbeat quavers to b.13. Make a tiny break after the second beat of b.24. Then moving the tempo on a little, glide into b.25, playing the RH in a 'close' *legato* and noting the slurred effects in the LH chords. Listen acutely to the

---

*A striking fingering is marked in Jane Stirling's copy for the RH in bb.5-6, presumably indicating a sense

of deliberation in the articulation of this melodic fragment.

creeping chromatic inflections, and draw out a little toward the long held C major harmony at b.32. Hold the sound within the pedal as indicated, playing the repeated treble C's above with a quiet bell-like tone. Let this sound fade through the pause before moving on from the upbeat to b.37. At the end of the repeat carry the quaver curve smoothly over from b.47 into the second-time bar and, playing the quaver curves like soft little 'waves', gradually 'disperse' the sound through the little coda. Allow an extra instant to lift from the detached quaver on the first beat of bb.48 (second-time bar) and 50 up towards the high C on the second beat, and then feel the sense of 'returning' up to these C's as you shape the quaver curves delicately through the remaining bars. Support the RH with a neat, *pianissimo* waltz-like LH, and slow a little towards the final note, holding the sound in a light haze of pedal as indicated.

Mazurka No. 17 in B flat minor
Op. 24 No. 4 (8)

This is one of the most splendid of all the Mazurkas. As Jim Samson says, 'Some hint of [its] structural weight is already offered by the tone of the 4-bar introduction' (p.114). Whereafter one masterly-coloured idea succeeds another, 'chivalric and romantic' (Hedley, p.168) and ending through an exquisitely inflected coda over a long tonic pedal point.

Note: For those using the Paderewski Edition there will be a discrepancy in bar-numbering from b.53, since in this edition both first **and** second-time bars are counted (i.e. for b.53 read b.54 and so on – see General Introduction under 'Bar Numberings').

bb.1–20   Lead in from an onward-leaning tied crotchet upbeat, and, entering on the first beat of b.1 with a clear-toned treble minim at the octave, listen acutely to the diminishing intervals as the voices move inwards by alternately creeping semitones. As the dance-movement proper begins at b.5 on a dominant harmony, go on **listening** to the inner RH line continuing upwards to reach the tonic only on the second beat of b.6. It is important to realise aurally that the upper melody from b.5 is **not** [musical example] *etc.*

but that the RH continues in two separate lines: [musical example] *etc.* and

[musical example] And that this two-voice effect continues

through the whole of this first section. But show the different effect from b.13 where the treble **does** become [musical example] *etc.* and similarly in bb.15 and

17. Support the RH with a carefully balanced and 'dancing' LH (see Introduction to Mazurkas). *Crescendo* gradually from b.5, amplifying the sound with a resonant lower dotted minim on the first beat of b.10, and then blazon out the octaves from the upbeat to b.11 over a powerful LH, and resonant inner RH emphasised minim. Take a little extra time to 'plant' the *fortissimo* tied RH upbeat to b.11, and draw out a little through bb.11-12, pointing the strong upbeat to b.12, and then dropping the tone after the first beat of b.12 as you ease towards b.13. Rise with even greater ardour towards the high dotted quaver octave on the first beat of b.19, allowing an extra

instant after the second beat as you drop, both in register and dynamics, to the upbeat to b.20. Then poise yourself quietly through b.20 ready to set off in a new *dolce* yet dance-like tone from b.21.

Listen to the long tied B flat singing over the bar line into b.21, and then be sure *bb.21–52* to **lift** the RH from the quaver on the first beat of each of bb.21-3 so that the hand 'falls' naturally onto the semiquaver second or third (see General Introduction under 'Articulation'). Always feel the semiquaver as the 'upbeat' to the second beat of the bar, and then feel that you are 'going to' the high emphasised crotchet on each third beat (in an overall slurred effect, and with, in each instance, a nice 'lift' towards this note). Feel the onward impulse from b.21 as this line of emphasised treble crotchets climbs towards the first beat of b.24. Show the slurred effect as you 'lift' from the RH acciaccatura chord up to this tied B flat, allowing a slight *tenuto* here. Then, with a feeling of moving on, 'flick' the slurred semiquavers and then the demisemiquavers down to the dotted quavers on each crotchet beat in a light *scherzando* manner, **listening** to the deliciously inflected discordant effects, and drawing out a little through b.28 ready to set off again at b.29. Note the more specific indications from here – the *forte* at b.32, then the *diminuendo, accelerando* through b.35, and *ritenuto* through b.36 as you prepare to 'settle back' into b.37. Then drop to the upbeat to b.44 in such a way as to prepare to lead 'on and over' through b.44 into the varied restatement. Listen acutely to the varied touches, in particular to the inflections of the inner RH line from b.45 as you implement the *stretto*, in heightening *agitato* towards b.51, then drawing back as before.

Drop to a clear *piano* on the tied upbeat to b.53 and play the unison interlude in *bb.52–114* a veiled smooth *sotto voce* as if from a far distance. This is an exquisite moment of stillness amid the passion and kaleidoscopic movement of the whole. It is evidently one of the rare examples of Chopin's use of a genuine folk melody (Samson, p.113). Lenz records that 'Chopin taught us that the third section [bb.53-60] is a mixed choir; the opening unison is answered by the chords. Nobody ever managed to satisfy him with these unisons, which have to be played very lightly; the chords were an easier matter. But these unisons! "They're the women's voices in the choir" he would say, and they were never played delicately enough, never simply enough. One was barely allowed to breathe over the keyboard, let alone touch it!' (Eigeldinger, p.75). **Listen** to the held minim B flat singing over from b.56 as you glide into the smooth quiet chords from b.57. When this section is repeated, the previously tied crotchet F on the first beat of b.53 is, of course, played. After the second beat of b.60 (second-time bar) make a tiny break and then 'plant' the tied RH upbeat to b.61 resonantly as you prepare to swing into b.61 with purposeful vitality. Experienced players may subtly 'distort' the rhythm of the triplets in bb.61, 65, etc. (see Introduction to Mazurkas). Be sure once more to **lift** the hand from the quaver on the first beat of bb.62, 64, etc. so that it 'falls' with firm emphasis on the minim on the second beat (see General Introduction under 'Articulation'). Observe all details of articulation and nuance as you implement the *forte* and *piano* echo effects through to b.90, contrasting these dynamic levels with maximum 'keenness'. Take a little extra time as you show the **different** *semi-staccato*, then *legato* effect through bb.73-4, and finally draw back a little through the *sotto voce* (bb.89-90). Then from b.91 whip up the tempo and dynamic level, controlling the whole with powerfully placed LH bass notes and chords, and with a climactically 'big' LH bass octave and spread chord in b.95. Allow the hint of a *tenuto* on this second beat, and then make a steep dynamic descent incorporating the *accelerando* and *ritenuto* through bb.97 and 98 as you prepare to launch into the reprise at b.99.

Arrive on a clear B flat on the first beat of b.114, drawing out this bar a little as *bb.114–46* you prepare to move into the coda. Every pianist will seek out the expressive refinements of this passage in their own ways, moving on a little here, drawing back a little there, but always maintaining the **sense** of the **3/4** pulse while listening to every tiny inflection over the continuing tonic pedal point. There is perhaps a feeling of moving on a little from b.115, easing fractionally again towards the poignant little fall to the G flat on the second beat of b.118, then once more moving on a little from b.119, and so on. 'Phase' the sound and the momentum down in a dream-like *diminuendo* and *rallantando*, **feeling** all the tiny emphases, and pausing hesitantly at the end of b.138. Then let the long tied F's (on the second beat of b.139 and the first beat of b.142) sound like the chimes of a distant bell over the continuing, but slowing, quiet movement of the LH. Play the final sad fragment like a valedictory call.

Note: From this point there are no original metronome marks.

Mazurka No. 18 in C minor
Op. 30 No. 1 (6) (O)

I cannot agree with Weinstock that this is 'one of the least grateful of the Mazurkas to listen to or to play' (pp.226-7). To listen to, perhaps, in that it lacks immediacy. But behind its rather austere exterior there is much of interest for the player. It is not as easy to play as it may appear on the page, and is perhaps more suitable for older players at about Grade 6. (In addition the acciaccaturas and octaves in b.3 etc. require a fair stretch.)

bb.1–16   It is in the shaping of the treble line over the inner RH notes, and in the rhythmic propelling of the syncopated melody from b.17 that a fair degree of musical sophistication is required. The curve of the recurring motif bb.1-2, 5-6, etc. 'peaks' in a momentary solo through the first beat of bb.2, 6, etc. and this curve has to be carefully and smoothly shaped. If the fingering outlined in Henle and in the Associated Board

edition      is impossible

to negotiate smoothly, the inner RH F on the third beat of b.1 can be taken with the

LH, with the treble fingered   

(or a large hand could play the minim on the second beat of b.2 with the second finger as in Paderewski). Set an easy moving tempo around $\quarternote = 126\text{-}32$, and lead in with a quiet but definite 'lean' on the tied upbeat to b.1, making sure that this note is given its full value (see above in the Introduction to the Mazurkas and also General Introduction under 'Upbeats'). Then shape the first phrase in a quiet, smooth 'vocal' curve up to and down from a 'speaking' acciaccatura and E flat on the first beat of b.2 over carefully balanced and placed LH chords and inner RH crotchets, taking care that these do not 'hang on' over the rest on the first beat of the subsequent bar. (Give these chords a quiet **equal** weight 𝄞 rather than 𝄞

(see Introduction to Mazurkas). Then curve up to the **second** beat of b.3 as if with a little emphasis on this beat, also listening to the movement of the inner LH and the ninth effect caused by acciaccatura and inner RH F. Allow a tiny break at the end of b.4 as you prepare to enter with the more vigorous *forte* rejoinder at b.5. Arrive on a singing dotted tied minim on the first beat of b.8, and then listen to the onward movement of the inner RH thirds and the LH crotchets towards the restatement from b.9. Ease carefully from the treble tied G (still sounding on the first beat of b.9) back into the quaver melody line in b.9.

bb.16–24 Arriving again on a quietly resonant minim G on the first beat of b.16, draw back a little as you prepare to 'plant' the emphasised partly tied chord on the upbeat to b.17 ready to swing into the *con anima*. **Listen** to the intervals of this upbeat chord, and then move the melody line on in a broad singing tone over a resonant lower LH A flat and rhythmically placed inner chords. Take special care to ensure that the RH syncopated A flat sings over the inner C in b.17 so that the upper melody is clearly

𝄞 *etc.* and **not** 𝄞 *etc.* (and similarly in b.19,

etc.). Implement the accents on the syncopated minim in bb.17, 19, etc. with a confident emphasis, and then feel the 'lift' up to a singing dotted crotchet on the second beat of bb.18 and 20. Support the RH with a strongly rhythmic LH (see Introduction to Mazurkas). Feel the overall onward impetus towards the dotted crotchet G on the second beat of b.20, and then draw back a little as you listen to the upward chromatic inflection of the LH fragment from the upbeat to b.21. Then play from b.21 with hymn-like simplicity, taking care to give the minim chord on the second beat of b.22 its full value.

bb.24–53 Carry the melody line down to a quiet but definite crotchet G on the second beat of b.24, and then make a tiny break ready to move on again from the emphasised upbeat to b.25. Rise to a clearly ringing minim E flat on the second beat of b.28, and then, while feeling a sense of moving on from b.29, at the same time listen acutely to the inflections of the LH chords beneath the reiterated RH dotted rhythm motif. Tail the RH away from b.33 over the quiet sustained LH dominant seventh chord towards a quiet but singing high solo minim A flat on the first beat of b.36 as you prepare to ease into the reprise. Draw out gradually from b.50 as you expressively 'point' the high A flat on the first beat, and take time to listen to the beautiful LH inflection to the subdominant on the second beat of the penultimate bar. End with a whispered unison figure beneath the quietly singing held treble C.

Mazurka No. 19 in B minor
Op. 30 No. 2 (6)

This is a particularly attractive number – more straightforward and therefore more apt for novice players than the preceding one.

bb.1–16 Thinking of a lively dancing rhythm, set a fairly quick tempo, if possible around ♩ = 138-152, and lead off from a quiet but clear crotchet upbeat, taking care to give this its full value (see Introduction to Mazurkas). Feel the onward impulse towards a singing minim octave on the second beat of b.2, feeling that you are 'leaning' onwards through this minim towards the *forte* rejoinder in b.3, and then 'going on through' to the emphasised quavers and crotchet in b.4. The music thus proceeds from bb.1-16 in 2-bar subphrases within overall 4-bar phrases, always with this 'on and over' lean on the minim octave in bb.2, 6, 10 and 14. Feel a nice 'lift' up to the high quaver G through the first beat of b.2, and feel the LH upbeat chord beneath the minim octave 'drawing you on' into b.3. 'Space out' the emphasised RH quavers and crotchet purposefully in b.4, and then take a 'breath' at the end of the bar, allowing an instant to clear the sound as you prepare to drop to piano at b.5, and so on. 'Twirl' the triplet figures insouciantly (experienced players may 'distort' these figures a little (see the Introduction to the Mazurkas), and support the RH with a lively dancing LH (see again the Introduction to Mazurkas). 'Point' the different details as you proceed through bb.9-16: the acciaccatura in bb.9, 13, etc, and the varied rhythm in bb.10, 12, etc. Be sure to **lift** the hand after the quaver in b.10 so that the hand 'falls' onto the slurred semiquaver octave, feeling this as the 'upbeat' to the second beat (see General Introduction under 'Articulation'). Also note the more resonant LH through the 'rejoinder' bb.7-8 and 15-16 (as compared with bb.3-4 and 11-12).

bb.16–64   Make a little break after the second beat of b.16 and then 'plant' the emphasised RH crotchet firmly on the upbeat to b.17 as if with a little pounce. Then set off quietly from b.17 in a **gradual** *crescendo*. Feel a sense of moving on, at the same time listening acutely to the chromatic inflections of the inner and lower voices as you climb upwards. Draw out through the end of b.23 towards ringing unisons on the first beat of b.24, then 'brake' sharply ready to 'pounce' again with quiet emphasis on the upbeat to b.25. 'Leaning' again on the upbeat to b.33, toss off the next section with a light heart, supporting the RH with a lightly springing waltz-like LH. The grace notes may airily anticipate the first beat

of bb.33, 36, etc. (and take care that the quaver rhythm ♩♩ ♩ is not sabotaged).

Delicately point the falling third figure in a knowing manner in bb.34, 36, etc. 'Give' a little, as indicated at b.38. Here in b.39 the 'extra' acciaccatura sounds effective placed on the beat

causing a slight 'expansion' through

this first beat. Then again make a little break after the second beat of b.48 ready to begin the climb once more from the upbeat to b.49. Draw out just a little as you reach the peak of the *crescendo* in b.63, and end with ringing unisons, and a firmly placed crotchet chord on the second beat of the final bar.

Mazurka No. 20 in D flat major
Op. 30 No. 3 (8)

This is a magisterially dramatic piece. Lenz records: ' "It seems like a Polonaise for a coronation festivity," said someone to Chopin. "Something like that," was his reply' (Eigeldinger, p.75) [typically laconic, one might add]. At the same time there is more than a hint of sabre-rattling in the ominous echo effects and jolting turns of mood.

bb. 1–24   The introductory bars set a tone of caged vitality. Visualise a tempo that will give a powerful momentum to the principal section (bb.9-24 and then b.79 to the end), without diminishing its ruggedness by a sense of hurrying (a suggested ♩ = 132-44). With this in mind, play the A flat calls in a strict rhythm (which might be a little faster than your eventual *risoluto* tempo) and with a penetrating ring. Then play from b.5 with a feeling of whipping up the momentum and then (according to the extent of your 'whipping up') with a slight sense of 'braking' through the end of b.8 as you prepare to launch into b.9. Kick off with a powerful bass octave on the first beat, and underpin the RH throughout this section with a carefully balanced, springing and onward propelling LH. Practise this LH pattern alone until its physical shape is thoroughly 'in the system'. **Lift** the hand with an upward-directed spring from the *staccato* quaver on each first beat so that it 'falls' onto the high semiquaver, feeling this as the 'upbeat' to the crotchet on the second beat (see General Introduction under 'Articulation'), and then use the second finger on the second beat as a pivot to 'slur you down' to the crotchet on the third beat and on down to the subsequent *staccato* quaver. Feel the movement as a series of 'arcs' so that you achieve the continual 'ongoing' rhythmic swing that is essential to the cohesion of this whole section. Match the *staccato* and slurred articulation of the LH in b.9 with ringing-toned RH thirds. Then in b.10 feel the slurred 'lift' of the RH up to the high minim third on the second beat, proceeding with similar articulation as you turn downwards through bb.11-12. Feel the impulse through b.9 towards an implied very slight *tenuto* on the minim third through the second and third beats of b.10, and similarly through b.11 towards the second beat of b.12 and so on. (This **sense** of a slight *tenuto* is particularly pointed in bb.15 and 16, when Chopin has emphasised the minim third.) Then make a tiny break at the end of b.12 to clear the sound as you poise yourself to play bb.13-14 in an echoing *pianissimo*, faithfully observing the same articulation, while pointing the threatening minor inflections. Then maximise the violent contrasts through bb.15-16 before setting off upwards again, this time in a higher register from b.17. Play bb.21-4 with gliding, dream-like smoothness, (only broken by the little 'lift' in b.23).

bb. 25–95   Make a tiny break at the end of b.24 ready either to return to b.9, or to surge into the *con anima* in a broad, buoyant tone, once again making a powerfully contrasting echo effect at b.29. Then point the LH diminished seventh chord on the first beat of b.33 and the 'delayed' entry of the RH melody note. 'Point' the mysterious chord on the second beat of b.40. Imagine that this partly tied LH minim chord is slurred down to the chord on the first beat of b.41, allowing a little extra time for the grace note arabesque. Every player will of course find their own ways of playing this bar. But it is helpful at first to think of the trill occupying a 'lengthened' second beat of the bar, with the arabesque occupying the **delayed** and also lengthened third beat. Alternatively and rather more easily, you could think of the first two grace notes, A natural and B flat as the **suffix** to the trill with the remaining

notes occupying the third beat.

In either event feel the 'lift' up to the high G, allowing the hint of a vocal *tenuto* here, and then letting the little arpeggio fall gracefully towards the E natural on the first beat of b.41. Drop to a furtive *sotto voce* in b.41, and then gradually build the dynamics, creating an increasingly impassioned but tautly controlled rhythmic tension towards b.56. Deliver a ringing (partly tied) minim chord on the first beat of b.56, feeling a slight *tenuto* through the first and second beats of this bar. Place the LH chord with a slight sense of 'braking' on the second beat, so that you can make it clear that you are leading on with the tied RH upbeat sixth into the more pliant *piano* in b.57. This passage in sixths from b.57 has almost a ballroom graciousness, tinged with nostalgia, and growing increasingly ardent again from b.61. Break off in full flood on a resonant chord on the second beat of b.71, and play the RH solo fragment in sixths with hovering anxiety. The lower LH detached crotchets through bb.73-4 are like distant ominous drumbeats beneath the long held inner F. Be sure to play these with **equal** quiet emphasis, and in immaculate rhythm, **feeling** the rest on each third beat. Let the RH sixths disappear to a whisper through bb.75-6, and then feel the resurging momentum as the bass detached crotchets make a carefully judged *crescendo* towards the reprise from b.79. Ease through the penultimate bar as you poise yourself to 'point' the sudden final inflection to the full-toned major chord.

Mazurka No. 21 in C sharp minor
Op. 30 No. 4 (8+)

From the Op.17 Mazurkas onwards, Jim Samson points to a pattern in which the final piece of each Opus is cast in a more ambitious and extended mould (p.114). And this example, by any standard one of the greatest, certainly belongs, like Ops 41 No.4, 50 No.3, and 56 No.3, to that select band which Arthur Hedley has described as 'symphonic', or attaining the stature of 'tone-poems' (pp.164-9).

bb.1–31 The introductory bars set the tone of brooding foreboding. The tempo needs to be very carefully judged. The spread LH chords from b.5 are grander, more deliberate than the similar ones in Op.7 No.3 in F minor, and most players adopt a tempo of around ♩ = 120-30. **Listen** to the quiet reverberation of the held RH augmented fourth as you play the opening LH figure like a distant, ominous summons, 'joined' by the inner RH voice a tenth higher as the upper third eases into the dominant seventh harmony in b.3. 'Give' a little through the end of b.4 ready to set off from b.5 in a furtive, 'stalking' *sotto voce*. Play the LH spread chords with a soft, but rock-steady, drum-like 'thrum', and articulate the RH precisely as indicated. **Lift** the hand from the detached quaver on each first beat so that it 'falls' onto the slurred triplet third (see General Introduction under 'Articulation'). 'Twirl' the treble triplet in a slurred effect towards the detached quaver third on the second beat of bb.5, 7, etc, **lifting** the hand again so that it 'falls' with natural emphasis on the accented crotchet third on the upbeat to bb.6, 8, etc. Then as you let the hand fall again onto the semiquaver 'upbeat' to the second beat of b.6, show the overall slurred effect through to the first beat of b.7, and so on. Increase the volume of sound gradually, but not too overpoweringly, towards the spread chord on the second beat of b.11. 'Hold' the RH crotchet third momentarily here before letting the line of thirds fall from the third beat towards the syncopated emphasised crotchet third in b.12. Poise yourself here as you pause, ready to set off again from the quaver upbeat to b.13. 'Open out' the dynamics more fully this time as you rise towards b.17, and on towards bb.19-20, allowing time in b.19 to 'space' the 5-quaver run of thirds up to the high point of the curve, and lingering momentarily on this emphasised third B/D sharp. Then let the upbeat thirds fall expressively, ready to resume the tempo briefly through b.20. Feel through the whole of bb.5-20 that the 'thrumming' LH is propelling the music along, 'giving way' through bb.11-12 to the RH recitative, to resume immediately in tempo in b.13. Then 'give way' only momentarily through b.19, as already said, to resume the tempo briskly in b.20. 'Hold' the emphasised third beat of b.20 for an instant, ready to drop to *piano*, to play from b.21 in a whimsical, more 'dancing' style. Spring airily up to the LH spread chord and high RH quaver on the second beat of bb.23 and 25, then allowing a generous 'give' as you ease up towards the high D natural on the second beat of b.27. Linger a little on the emphasised A on the first beat of each of these bars, thinking

of this A almost as a quaver on the first beat of b.23

then lingering a little less in b.25

and less still in b.27.

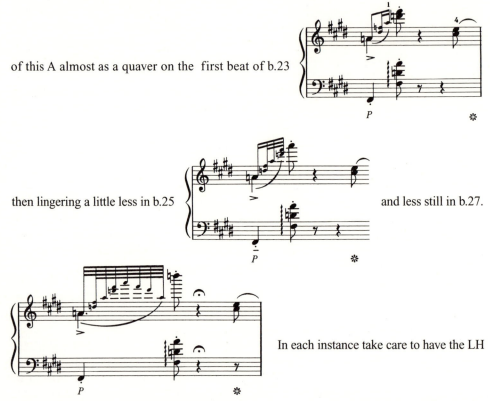

In each instance take care to have the LH

ready to synchronise the spread chord with the high RH quaver on each second beat. Let the sound of each of these arabesques hang in the air, held within the pedal as indicated, and move on (as if slightly uneasy) from the upbeat to each intervening bar (bb.24 and 26). In b.27 let the sound hang for longer through the pause before moving on into bb.28-30, still with this sense of unease. 'Brake' at b.31 and play the unison G sharps like clear but distant bells.

bb.32–64   Taking care to give the last G sharp on the second beat of b.32 its full value and a little more, 'lean' into b.33 again in a dance-like fashion. Practise the LH carefully so that the semiquaver is neatly slurred towards the crotchet chord on each second beat, then give a softly 'leaning' emphasis to the slurred crotchet upbeat to each subsequent bar. Articulate the reiterated RH motif animatedly over this 'dancing' LH. Draw back through the trill at bb.39-40, keeping the LH going rhythmically though momentarily slower, and then ease gracefully back into tempo at b.41. *Diminuendo* to a whisper through b.48 as you poise yourself to set off again in b.49.

bb.64–139   'Point' the G natural on the second beat of b.64, 'holding' this note for an extra instant as you ease on into the *con anima*. Feel that the LH is propelling the music onwards with a controlled but powerful momentum as you ascend towards bb.73-4. 'Lean' expressively on the treble dotted crotchet on the first beat of b.65, feeling the impetus towards a further 'lean' on the first beat of b.66, and so on. Ensure that each dotted crotchet sings out over the second beat of the bar so that in b.65, for example, the melody line is clearly 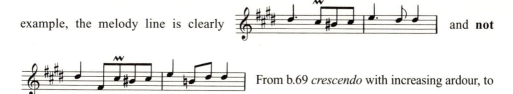 and **not**

 From b.69 *crescendo* with increasing ardour, to

unleash the dynamics at b.73 in an impassioned *fortissimo* (though leaving a little volume in reserve for the second 'summit' at bb.89-90). You could either maintain the volume, or *diminuendo* a little towards the tied minim chord on the second beat of b.76. In either event, 'hold' this chord a little to clear the sound as you prepare to return to a momentary dancing *piano* at b.77. Build the sound again from b.85 to an even greater volume at b.89. **Listen** to the emphasised tied upbeat chord held over into b.95, and then 'disperse' the sound as the reiterated *legato* figure leads back towards the ominous figure of the introduction. Notice this time how the principal motif enters with a *sforzato* 'push' on the first beat of b.101. From b.124 Chopin

extends the figure ![music] towards a remarkable chain

of sevenths: as Paul Hamburger says 'he dissolves the tragic heroism of this Mazurka . . . into the atonal anonymity of the unconscious' (Walker, p.80). This is one of Chopin's much-quoted forward-looking passages stretching towards Debussy's future use of chains of sevenths (see Paul Hamburger again). Hurrying a little from b.126-7 as you prepare to 'slide' down the incline, draw out a little again as you approach b.133, and play bb.133-6 in a hushed, 'backward-glancing' *pianissimo*. Then let the final solo phrase fall in a fine thread of sound towards the last quiet chord.

Mazurka No. 22 in G sharp minor
Op. 33 No. 1 (6) (O)

After the stirring events of Op.30 Nos 3 and 4, this is a comparatively unassuming number. It is by no means insignificant though, and, since in technical and rhythmic terms it is one of the simplest of the Mazurkas, it is an excellent piece for the relatively inexperienced player. (However, since there are a number of held notes involving fairly full stretches, it is not really suitable for those with small hands.)*

bb.1–12　　Despite the *mesto* indication, do not adopt too slow a tempo or you will be in danger of grinding to a halt. There has anyway been considerable confusion over Chopin's tempo and expressive indication. An original, apparently erroneous *presto* was altered, also perhaps erroneously, to *mesto*. The pencilled alteration to *lento* found in the copies belonging to Chopin's sister and to Jane Stirling may be taken as authentic. Try a tempo at around ♩ = 108-116 with a certain amount of give and take. Lead in from a fairly full-toned emphasised crotchet upbeat, and be sure to give this its full value (see Introduction to Mazurkas). Then feel the 'lift' up to the chord on the second beat, 'joining in' confidently with the LH slurred upbeat to b.2 as the hands 'close in' towards the unison tonic minims on the

---

*The musical sense of the irregular phrasing through the opening section is also perhaps too complex for the young mind.

first beat of b.2. Be sure that the RH G sharp sings out over the detached inner third on the

second beat so that the melody is clearly  and **not**

 *etc.* Then, taking a breath, let the RH solo

fragment 'take off' from the upbeat to b.3, and rise songfully towards the high semiquaver G sharp in b.4. Be sure to **lift** the hand from this detached semiquaver so that it 'falls' with natural emphasis onto the singing minim D sharp (see General Introduction under 'Articulation'). Then placing the tied chord carefully on the third beat of b.4 (in a clear upbeat sense, and in such a way that it does not swamp the melodic D sharp), play bb.5-6 in neat time, showing the slurred effect of the LH octaves through the third and fourth beats (see Introduction to Mazurkas). As you take a 'breath' at the end of b.6 and 'start again' from b.7, feel the sense in which these two bars (bb.7-8) end the first overall phrase (bb.1-8) and at the same time begin its telescoped restatement. 'Overlapping' again through bb.11-12 as at bb.7-8, point the minor harmony on the third beat of b.12, feeling a smooth 'on and over' upbeat lean in both hands towards bb.13-14 within the overall shape of the phrase. The Paderewski Edition gives a more descriptive phrasing here

as opposed to the overall six-bar phrase (bb.11-16) given in Henle.

bb.12–48   Conveying a feeling of moving on from the upbeat to b.13, **listen** to the parallel movement of the treble and inner LH lines over the drone-like inner RH and lower LH dotted minim sevenths. Then draw out a little through b.16 as you 'open out' the tone, taking a little extra time to listen to the imitative inner LH figure through the end of the bar, and giving a little extra emphasis to the tied LH upbeat C sharp to b.17. Move on again as you play the reiterated fragment through bb.17-20, imagining a different 'instrumentation' in the alternating upper and lower register. Allow a tiny 'give' and break at the end of b.20 as you poise yourself to launch into b.21 with a buoyant rhythmic swing. Rise towards a full-toned emphasised crotchet on the third beat of b.22, and then play bb.23-4 in a broad-toned *appassionato*, supporting the RH with a 'dancing' LH (see Introduction to Mazurkas). Take a fraction of extra time to clear the sound at the end of b.24 ready to drop to *piano*, and glide into bb.25-8 with floating smoothness, tailing away the sound towards b.28 as indicated. Make a tiny break again after the second beat of b.28, ready to set off again in a broad *forte* from the upbeat to b.29. **Listen** to the sound of the chord (held within the pedal) through the pause in b.36 before leading into the reprise from a clear upbeat to b.37.

Mazurka No. 23 in D major
Op. 33 No. 2 (8+)

This hugely popular piece, while one of the simplest of the Mazurkas in a structural sense, is far from easy to play. Indeed, to ride the course of this ceaseless 'whirligig' of 'frantic gaiety'

(Walker, p.81) is something of an endurance test. And it is not just a case of Chopin churning out a series of meaningless repetitions, as suggested by Weinstock (p.235). Like a tarantella it depends for its effect on cumulative repetitions of its frenetic movement, which need, to quote Paul Hamburger again, 'hammering in'. It can (as it often is on the concert platform) be taken as fast as is possible, short of losing clarity of rhythmic coherence. On the other hand, at a more measured tempo, around ♩. = 60 but with a ceaselessly bounding rhythmic spring it can be just as effective. In any event there is no point in playing it (before an audience, at any rate) unless you can make the listeners want to leap up and shout!

Note: For those using the Paderewski Edition there will be a discrepancy in bar-numberings from b.73, since in this edition both first and second-time bars are counted (i.e. for b.73 read b.74, and so on. See General Introduction under 'Bar Numberings'.)

bb.1–48   It will immediately be apparent that the fingering of the RH presents considerable problems, particularly for smaller hands. There is really little

alternative to the obvious treble fingering for b.1:   But then

the ornament placed on the first beat of b.2 could be fingered

(or these fingerings could be alternated). And at b.5 where there is **not** a tied upbeat, the hand

could 'have a change' with the rather easier   ('slipping' the fifth

finger from F sharp to the G). The maintenance of this ceaselessly 'churning' RH line with the 'weak' fingers is extremely taxing for the hand. Practise **slowly**, playing the inner RH crotchets with the thumbs in a **light** *staccato* at first to get used to leaning the weight towards the outer side of the hand.

'Lean' in from a vigorously emphasised RH crotchet upbeat and then place the inner F sharp on the first beat in such a way that the upper line clearly sounds

and **not**   At the same

time give a good 'kick-off' with the LH detached crotchet D, and support the RH throughout with a springingly rhythmic waltz-like LH (see Introduction to Mazurkas) while at the same time feeling the upbeat emphasis on each third beat (bb.1-8, etc.). (This is, as Weinstock has observed, of all the Mazurkas the closest to being a waltz.) Feel the overall impulse of each 'set' of 'churning' figures (bb.1-3, 5-7, etc.) towards the 'objective', i.e. the dotted minim on the first beat of b.4, and then b.8, and so on. At the same time be conscious of the subphrasing within each 'set' so that you avoid 'falling onwards' from b.2 into b.3 by very slightly 'pointing' the first beat of b.3, and again taking a tiny instant to point this 'objective', the emphasised minim on the first beat of b.4. (These phrasing subdivisions are not observed in all editions. Schirmer for example, gives **one** phrase slur over bb.1-3.) Again, be conscious of 'pointing' the emphasised third beat of b.4, imagining a tiny intake of breath at the end of the bar, ready to carry on into b.5. Then feel that you are applying a momentary 'brake' on the tied upbeat to b.9 to clear the sound for the *subito pianissimo* in b.9. Play the *forte* (bb.1-8) in a joyous clatter, and the *pianissimo* from b.9 in an immaculately clear 'echo'. Launch with renewed vigour into the dominant at b.17, imagining a different instrumentation in this lower register. Then break out with yet greater brilliance at b.33.

bb.48–135   'Brake' again through b.48 ready to launch into the B flat section in a more measured and courtly (though not necessarily much slower) manner. Then declaim the RH chords from b.53 in a proud, clarion *forte*, allowing time to **listen** to the persistent dotted rhythm fragments in the LH through bb.54-6. Draw back through the end of b.56 ready to move into b.57 in a more serious vein, taking time to point the chromatic inflections in the upper and inner RH parts. Rise to a ringing *sforzato* crotchet octave (supported by an equally strong bass note) on the upbeat to b.61, 'holding' this for an extra instant ready to unleash full power at b.61.

Pursue the reiterated triplet figures from b.65 with clangourous insistence. Think of the RH third triplet quaver, the tied diminished fifth, as the 'upbeat' to the second beat of each bar. Then play the inner RH crotchet D and the LH diminished fifth with carefully balanced, ringing emphasis. Consciously show the rhythmic difference between bb.65 and 66, etc: 'point' the emphasised **crotchet** upbeat to b.66 with, again, ringing emphasis, and in b.66 allow a slightly stronger emphasis on the **second** beat, then carefully pointing the LH crotchet upbeat and deliberately timed RH **quaver** upbeat. Poise yourself at the end of b.72 (second-time bar) ready to hurtle off again at b.73. Poise yourself once more as you set off into the coda at b.121, gradually increasing the speed a little. Play the upper dotted minims like a clear quiet bell as you articulate the inner couplets with immaculate quiet precision over carefully controlled LH chords. Avoid too much of a *rallentando* as you fade the sound from b.129. Then, from b.133, holding the tonic fifths within the pedal as indicated, 'disperse' the high quaver run to a wisp, reaching a tiny pinpoint of suspended sound on the high D.

Aleksander Michalowski, a pupil of Mikuli, graphically describes a performance of this piece by Princess Czartoryska, one of the finest exponents of Chopin's music, suggesting a special interpretation from b.73. 'I was struck by the way she interpreted its main theme. At first she played it in a brash, forthright way, with no subtlety of nuance. It was only towards the end of the piece, at the theme's second appearance [b.73 to the end] that she played it with a soft, caressing touch, utterly subtle and refined. When I asked her about this contrasting treatment, she replied that Chopin had taught it to her that way; in this piece he wanted to present the contrast between the 'tavern' and the 'salon'. That was why he wanted the same melody played so differently; at the beginning it was to evoke the popular atmosphere of the tavern, and towards the end, the refinement of the salons . . .' (Eigeldinger, p.75).

Mazurka No. 24 in C major
Op. 33 No. 3 (6) (O)

This is more difficult than it appears at first glance owing to some chord shifts which are awkward to finger – in particular at bb.5-6. In other respects however, it is, like Op.33 No.1, a good piece for (rather older) novice players.

bb.1–16   For the relatively untrained hand there is the problem of shaping the upper melody line, played with the 'weaker' fingers, to sing out smoothly over the inner notes played with the 'stronger' ones – a simpler version of the taxing RH work in the preceding number. Again, it is a good plan to practise singing out the melody line with these 'weak' fingers while playing the inner notes in a light *staccato* to get accustomed to 'leaning' the weight on the outer part of the hand. Practise the LH alone too, absorbing the easy swing of the **3/4** movement – which is propelled along by the continuing gentle emphasis on the inner minim drone on each second beat. When there is a good balance between the voices, this inner drone effect is like a kind of integral 'sail' which bears the phrases along.

Set an easy crotchet pulse that is unhurried, yet 'moves' at a suggested tempo of around ♩ = 112-20. There is a particular danger of 'sticking' here, arising from the rather static nature of the melodic line. Lead in from a quiet but firm RH crotchet upbeat, taking care to give this note its full value, or a little more, with at the same time a good onward 'lean' (see Introduction to Mazurkas). Then listen acutely to the balance, so that the melody sings out over the inner RH chords, balanced and cushioned but not swamped by this inner LH 'sail', and by the lower rocking minims and crotchets. As you end the first sentence at the end of b.4, feel that the same 'conversation' is carrying on into bb.5-8, but in a different tone of voice. At b.8 **lift** the RH from the treble quaver C sharp on the first beat so that it 'falls' onto the semiquaver, thinking of this slurred semiquaver as the rising 'upbeat' to the emphasised chord on the second beat (see General Introduction under 'Articulation'). Then, giving the treble note of this RH minim chord a slight *tenuto* effect, point the LH G on the third beat (feeling it as the upbeat to b.9) as you prepare to move into the restatement. In b.16 'lift' up to the high C on the second beat with an insouciant 'flick' of the acciaccatura.

bb.16–48 Make a little break after the second beat of b.16 before 'planting' the tied *forte* crotchet firmly on the upbeat to b.17 as you prepare to swing into the middle section with the feeling of moving on. Shape the melodic phrases in broad sweeps. Feel the impulse towards the emphasised minim on the first beat of b.20 and then show the 'on and over' lean of the tied upbeat into b.21. Allow a slight 'vocal' *tenuto* on the dotted crotchet F on the second beat of b.21, and then relish the added richness as the inner line in sixths joins in from b.23. Buoy the RH along throughout this section with a vigorously onward-sweeping LH. Draw out a little through b.32 as you prepare to move into the reprise, allowing time for a gracious spread chord effect on the first beat of b.33 (playing this, as also the grace note figure in bb.10, 14, 32, etc. **on** the beat).

b.33   b.10   b.32   *etc.*

Mazurka No. 25 in B minor
Op. 33 No. 4 (8)

Although this is one of the 'big' Mazurkas (and one of the longest), its material is more *galant*, lighter both in texture and dramatic import than, for example, Op.30 No.4, Op.50 No.3, or Op.56 No.3. There have been various suggestions that it has some kind of narrative significance, which in this instance has some foundation, according to Lenz. 'This piece is a Ballade in all but name. Chopin himself taught it as such, stressing the narrative character of this highly developed piece, with its ravishing trio (B major: bb.129 ff.). At the end a bell tolls a heavy bass carillon G-C-G-C, and the sudden arrival of the final chords sweeps away the cohort of ghosts, Chopin would say.' (Eigeldinger, p.75). It is undeniably repetitive, the first motif of its opening section occurring no less than ten times. (The welcome cut, from bb.87-110, made in several teaching copies, and unaccountably ignored by most editors, may be regarded as authentic – see Eigeldinger, p.150.) Nevertheless, its material is finely contrasted, and it makes a good concert piece – better, perhaps, for public showing than some of the more concentrated inward-looking numbers which are so absorbing to the domestic pianist. Most editions, but not Henle, give a *mesto* indication.

bb.1–47   Set a rather stately yet 'moving' **3/4** at a suggested ♩. = 46-50, and lead in with a quiet but definite, emphasised tied crotchet upbeat. Take care to give this note its full value while at the same time feeling its onward 'lean'. Play the melody of the opening bars in a quiet but cleanly articulated style. Feel the impulse of the first, and similarly the second 2-bar phrase towards the dotted minim on the first beat of bb.2 and 4, and 'flick' the acciaccatura neatly down onto each dotted minim as if it is slurred (playing it **on** the beat). Support the RH with a carefully balanced and springing LH (see Introduction to Mazurkas), taking particular care to place the first LH crotchet clearly on the first beat of b.1 beneath the tied crotchet upbeat in such a way as to give a good kick-off to the rhythm. Take the RH line clearly 'up to' the crotchet C sharp in b.6 with an implied little syncopating emphasis on this note, 'followed on' by the LH, slurred cleanly to the sixth on the second beat. Then 'plant' the tied emphasised crotchet firmly on the upbeat to b.7 and play this low registered solo fragment in a full bassoon-like tone, again 'going up to' the C sharp, this time placing it squarely on the second beat of b.8. Some players then drop the tone to a *sotto voce* here. Others, to point the contrast with the *sotto voce* at b.17 continue in the full tone of the previous solo fragment. In any event play the upper and inner voices in an even, 'equal' tone **listening** acutely to their smooth movement over the lower LH drones. These recurring figures (see bb.33-7, 73-6, etc.) have a mysterious, 'waiting' sense, as if gathering for the next dance movement. Feel a sense of moving on at bb.9-10, and of drawing out slightly again as you point the major inflections in bb.11-12. 'Finish off' to clear unison F sharps on the second beat of b.12, and then make a tiny break in the RH as you poise yourself to set off again from the emphasised tied upbeat to b.13. Following on from the quiet but definite low RH upbeat to b.17, drop the tone further and feel a sense of moving on from b.17, playing the low RH line in a clear, but furtive *sotto voce* beneath glidingly smooth, but quietly insistent LH **treble** chords. *Diminuendo* yet further and draw out a little as you play the hollow-sounding unison dotted minims in a clear *pianissimo* through bb.23-4. Make another tiny break before breaking out once more into the opening motif.

bb.48–126   Feel through bb.47-8 that you are 'leading on' ready to burst in in a rumbustious *forte* at b.49. 'Kick off' with a strong bass note and keep control of the rhythm with the help of strongly and rhythmically placed emphasised LH chords on the second and third beat of bb.49, 51, etc. and a strong inner minim chord on the second beat of bb.50, 52, etc. This LH minim chord acts as a focal rhythmic point, a kind of 'anchor' for each 2-bar segment. Articulate the RH with the utmost vigour over this springing LH rhythm. Feel the overall slurred effect over the second and third beats of b.49 up to the *staccato* quaver on the first beat of b.50. Articulate this *staccato* quaver with a strong 'ring', springing **off** this note so that the hand 'falls' onto the slurred dotted rhythm figure (see General Introduction under 'Articulation'). Imagine that the crotchet on the third beat of b.50 is also slurred so that you 'go up to' the *sforzato* crotchet on the first beat of b.51 from a strongly placed thumb, with as powerful a strike of the fifth finger as you can muster. Let this powerful fifth finger strike 'bounce' the hand off the key so that it again 'falls' onto the chord on the second beat, and so on. Help this fifth finger *sforzato* (and your confidence!) with a powerful bass B flat. Take care also to give the crotchets on the third beat of b.50 their full value so that you have time to poise yourself to place the bass note and prepare the RH fifth finger strike (avoiding the danger of 'falling into' b.51). Then poise yourself even more deliberately on the third beat of b.54 to prepare for the wide outward leap to the unison octaves on the first beat of b.55. This section needs to achieve a **stable** rhythmic swing. Practise the LH thoroughly therefore, for it is the LH which both propels and controls the rhythm. Point the tied emphasised RH crotchet F flat on the upbeat to b.61, **listening** to the clash with the LH E flat, and then *diminuendo* steeply, listening acutely to the shifting intervals as you 'move inwards' through bb.61-2. Then draw out through bb.63-4 as you ease back towards the reprise. (See above regarding the possible cut from bb.87-110.)

bb.126–160   Ease again through bb.127-8 and then move on as you launch into the B major section. Play the melody in a light-toned yet expressive style. While creating a sense of overall continuity through bb.129-36, feel at the same time the sense of 'going to' the 'objective' of each 2-bar fragment: the *sforzato* dotted crotchet on the second beat of b.130 (giving this note and chord a warm-toned 'lean', not a bump); the emphasised minim on the first beat of b.132; the 'peak' of the little curve up to the quaver F sharp on the first beat of b.134, and the dotted minim on the first beat of b.136 and so on. Support the RH with a 'dancing' LH, taking care to place the chord particularly carefully on the second beat of those bars that have a rest on the third beat: bb.130, 134, etc. (see Introduction to Mazurkas). And in each of these bars (130, 134, etc.) feel the onward leading significance of the RH upbeat to the subsequent bar, taking care to define the crotchet or quaver value unequivocally. Allow a little give through the end of b.136 as you poise yourself to move into the varied restatement from b.137. It is effective to play bb.137-8 with gossamer lightness while shaping the curve like a singer, up to and down from the high D sharp on the third beat of b.137.*

bb.160–224   Most players make a *crescendo* and onward thrust, through b.160 into b.161. Whether or not you do this, poise yourself once more at the end of b.160 ready to set off from b.161 with athletic vigour. Like the B flat section, this needs a tremendous rhythmic swing. Again practise carefully hands separately, implementing all slurs, *staccatos* and emphases. Feel in particular the indicated emphasis on the upbeat to bb.162, 163, etc. These strong upbeats serve to propel and at the same time control this vigorous rhythmic swing. Some players make a *diminuendo* towards the 'break-off' at b.175, while others carry on in *forte* and break off at full tilt. In either case, arrive on **definite** crotchet thirds, whether quiet or forceful, on the third beat. Then make a clean break, and start this extended linking passage in a muted clear *pianissimo*, consciously shaping the dips and rises of the line through bb.177-80. Then 'lean' lightly with the thumb on the 'doubled' dotted minim on the first beat of bb.181-3, playing the lower dotted rhythm line in neat time.† Point the G natural on the first beat of b.187, as if with a tiny 'hold', and then from b.189 feel a sense of 'leading on' towards the final reprise. Keep moving as you progressively fade the sound from b.212, and play the single minims (bb.217-22) like far distant calls. Then play the final fragment in a ringing *forte*, ending with vigorous 'stamping' chords.

Mazurka No. 26 in E minor
Op. 41 No. 1 (7)

Note: The present order of the four Mazurkas of Op.41 differs from that in most editions. Usually the C sharp minor Mazurka is placed as No.1 with this one in E minor as No.2.

---

*A *rallentando* is marked through the end of b.144 in the copy belonging to Jane Stirling, giving time to 'gather' the end of the phrase, ready to move into the reprise in b.145.

†These minims have a pencilled accent in Jane Stirling's copy.

However, the E minor was composed in 1838 in Majorca, the year before the remaining three in the set, and Henle place it accordingly as No.1, with the C sharp minor Mazurka as No.4.

Interpretations of this piece, one of the most splendid of the shorter Mazurkas, differ widely (as, it must be said, do critical opinions on its merits). I feel that it has a processional quality with its steady crotchet pulse moving in a continuous tread to impressive cumulative effect, until it bursts forth in full splendour at b.57. The only dynamic indications are the opening *piano*, the *forte* at bb.17 (and 41) and thereafter periodic *crescendo* marks up to b.56, and then a final *rallentando* through the last two bars. Since these *crescendos* are never 'cancelled' by a *decrescendo*, nor by any suggestion of a 'give' in the tempo, my feeling is that Chopin must have intended this cumulative effect of a relentless tread always increasing in volume towards b.57. Others, however, take a different view, and play the first section in a contemplative and pliantly expressive style, moving on more urgently at b.17 and unleashing the dynamics from about b.52. Others again continue the contemplative mood and play the section from b.17 in a plaintive and still pliant manner.

The construction is extremely compact with no clear cut sections and no 'linking' passages – indeed, there is a strong sense of onward movement from the end of the first section into the middle section at b.17, and again on to the second part of that middle section at b.33, and so on.

bb.1–16 Set a secure **3/4** that is measured but at the same time 'moves', at a suggested ♩ = 96-100 (there is an inherent danger of 'sticking' in this piece). Ensure that the melodic line sings out over the chords in an even tone, while also **listening** to the movement of the harmonies. Feel the impulse of each 2-bar phrase towards the first beat of its **second** bar (i.e. feel that you are 'going through' b.1 towards the chord on the first beat of b.2, and so on). At the same time show the way in which the melody line carries through to a clear crotchet on the third beat of b.2, and similarly b.4, and so on, as the melodic line 'settles' onto the overall subdominant, or tonic harmony.

Give the sense of taking a little 'breath' between each 2-bar phrase though without breaking the sound nor the sense of continuity. Feel the 'lift' up to and down from the high quaver E on the first beat of b.6, and then play the unison fragment (bb.7-8) with a mysterious, hollow, open sound. Take a more substantial 'breath' after the second beat of b.8 before leading off again from a clear upbeat to b.9, perhaps in a stronger (or lesser!) dynamic.

bb.16–68 Strike off into b.17 in a new, more vibrant tone, making sure that the melodic minim here (and at bb.19, 20, etc.) sings out over the second beat so that the melody line is clearly ♩ *etc.* and **not** ♩ *etc.* Feel a sense of moving on, propelled (but also controlled) by the implied emphasis on the partly tied upbeats to each bar, and by the insistent rhythm of the reiterated treble D sharps from b.18 through to the first beat of b.21. Keep the crotchet pulse on a tight rein all through this passage, **within** the overall onward movement. Take particular care not to hurry through b.21. Keeping the LH perfectly steady, feel that the quaver thirds are making an onward thrust 'back into' the reiterated D sharp motif (and similarly in b.25). There is a sense of lightening of the texture from b.33. Keep the rhythm under control here with a steady but more dance-like LH, **listening** to the melodic resonance of the lower LH line from the upbeat to b.37, and to all held and tied resonances through bb.37-41. Feel also the implied slight 'lean' and *tenuto* effect on the treble dotted crotchet on the second beat of bb.33, 37 and 39. Resume the strong forward movement from b.41, gradually accumulating the volume until you 'open' into full *fortissimo* from b.57. 'Point' this unleashing of the dynamics with a slightly 'held' emphasised upbeat chord to b.57, and thereafter, allowing the inner unison melody to sing out, give all the resonant weight you can muster (without banging!). Gradually diminish the sound from b.63 but maintain the insistent tread as you articulate the dotted rhythm like a disappearing march motif. Then, finally slowing through the penultimate bar, play the unison figure in a whisper, **listening** to the sound of the final dotted minim E's as you place the lower minim chord.

Mazurka No. 27 in B major
Op. 41 No. 2 (8+)

(See note at beginning of Op.41)

This is another piece which, unaccountably, has had a bad press. Weinstock says it could well have been called 'Miscarriage of a Polish Mazurka' and finds it 'ponderous and lacking in appeal to a deadening degree' (p.249). I can only assume that he played it or heard it played at a 'ponderous' tempo. When played *animato* at a fleet tempo, as it must be, it has the intoxicating whirl of the fast oberek, with a middle section of dazzling rhythmic pomp. Once again Lenz gives us an impression of Chopin's interpretation: 'Chopin used to say that this piece opens with a chorus of guitars, and that it is particularly difficult to render because of the tangle of groups of dancers changing direction at every moment. The first four bars and their repetitions (bb.9-12, etc.) are to be played in the style of a guitar prelude, progressively quickening the tempo. The Mazurka proper only starts at the fifth bar. These were Chopin's instructions' (Eigeldinger, p.76). Here one minute and gone the next, it is no good attempting to play this Mazurka unless you can throw it off with complete technical and rhythmic command.

bb.1–38   Aim to achieve a tempo of at least ♩. = 60, and faster if possible. There is no opening dynamic marking (and few thereafter).* You could therefore start in a fairly loud dynamic but with a sharp, clear, not thick tone. Or (and preferably, in my view) in a subdued and furtive (though clear) *piano*, as if 'crouching' ready to streak off at b.5. In any event, establish a taut rhythm, feeling that the slurred quaver thirds are insistently 'going to' the accented minim chords on each second beat, and taking care to give each of these its full value. Give an extra little 'push' on the tied chord on the second beat of b.4, then 'lash out' with a strong LH fifth finger to the *sforzato* lower *staccato* B on the first beat of b.5. Make sure that this is done in perfect time so that you give a good kick-off to the shaft of upward unison quavers. Practise these until they are immaculately 'together' (no easy assignment) and you can play them like greased lightning, shooting up in *crescendo* to the detached quavers on the first beat of b.7. Be sure to **lift** the RH here (as well as the LH) so that it 'falls' naturally onto the semiquaver A sharp (see General Introduction under 'Articulation'). 'Flick' the semiquaver towards the 'twirled' triplet, supporting the RH with an immaculately articulated LH as you return to 'crouch' again from b.9. Keep your jauntily articulated RH under control as you

*Many editions give an opening *piano*.

descend sequentially through bb.15-21 with the help of an immaculately rhythmic 'dancing' LH. Pursue each 'rework' of all these figures with equal (or greater!) verve and animation.

bb.38–78   Taking an instant to poise yourself at the end of b.38, 'plant' the RH dotted minim on the first beat of b.39 in a ringing tone, 'braking' sharply in the LH, and playing this section with braggardly pomp. Support the RH with a 'measured' but springingly rhythmic LH (see Introduction to Mazurkas). Note the accents on the upbeats to bb.42, 46, etc, interpreting these not only as emphases but as poising 'holds'. From b.45 shake out the triplet RH octave figures with a clangourous ring, gradually increasing the volume, but always holding a reserve, until at b.54 you unleash a burst of unison sound, blazoning out the unison octaves with a huge 'ring' (not bang!) within the maximum **held** pedalled sound. 'Hold' the octave on the third beat momentarily as you poise yourself to hurtle off again at b.55. From b.71 'disperse' the sound like the disappearing tail of a comet, and 'crouch' down again, ending in mid-air without a hint of a *rallentando*.

Mazurka No. 28 in A flat major
Op. 41 No. 3 (7)

(See note at beginning of Op.41)

Op.41 is a splendidly balanced set. This, a nice foil to the other three numbers, is a waltz-like piece, charmingly simple but with 'knowing' beneath its apparent naivety.

bb.1–16   Set an easy-moving jogging *allegretto* at around ♩ = 132-138 (the motion here, if not the actual tempo, is rather reminiscent of the waltz in A flat Op.64 No.3).

Lead in from a quiet but definite crotchet upbeat, taking care to give this its full value while also feeling the onward leading 'lean' into b.1 (see the Introduction to the Mazurkas). Then, as you shape the quavers in neat curves, feel the overall impulse of each 2-bar phrase (bb.1-2, 3-4, etc.) towards the emphasised crotchet on the third beat of bb.2, 4, etc.). Within these 2-bar phrases be conscious of the chatty subdivision, though without labouring the point: there is a rather suave quaver curve through b.1 to the first quaver of b.2, and similarly

through bb.3 and 5, etc. Then the little  figure in b.2,

recurring in slightly varied form in bb.4, 6, etc. is like a pert little 'I told you **so**' rejoinder. Take care to give each of these emphasised crotchets on the third beat of bb.2, 4, etc. its full value while at the same time feeling its onward 'lean' towards the next 2-bar phrase, so that there is a continuing onward 'jog'. Be sure to **lift** the RH from the quaver on the first beat of b.6 so that it 'falls' naturally onto the subsequent semiquaver (see General Introduction under 'Articulation'). Then listen to the natural filling out of the texture with the 'double-stopping' through b.7, and then allow just a little easing through b.8, with at the same time a sense of 'rounding in' ready to set off again at b.9. Support the RH throughout the section with a quietly rhythmic LH (see Introduction to the Mazurkas).

bb.16–32

Point the upbeat to b.17 with a little extra emphasis, and the hint of a 'hold' as you prepare to move into the more sustained D flat section. Study the part-writing of both hands thoroughly here, so that each line is clearly understood aurally. Move easily into b.17, letting the minim F on the first beat sing out quietly so that you

make it clear that the upper melody line is ♪♪♪♪ *etc.* and **not**

♪♪♪♪ and play this section in a smooth ruminative

manner, without letting the tempo drag. Listen carefully again to the upper line through b.23, and then take a little extra time through b.24 as the treble makes its little curve towards the minim C, and the lower LH line plays its expressive little fragment, leading on to 'start again' from b.25.

bb.32–74

At b.32 feel the 'on and over' impulse on the dotted crotchet C on the second beat, towards the upbeat to b.33, and play the reiterated figure from here with a feeling of gently heightening, onward-pressing intensity, as the treble and inner RH lines move alternately, propelled onwards by the implied emphasis on the tied LH upbeat chords to each bar. Listen acutely here to the quite complex resonances created by the RH voices, alternately moving or sustained, over these reiterated, or tied LH chords. Draw back a little as you inflect to the major at b.40. Then leading off again with a clear bass crotchet C on the first beat of b.41, play the charmingly inflected fragmented version of the principal motif in a thoughtful, perhaps rather slower tempo, delicately pointing the piquant quaver B flat in b.43.* Drop to the *sotto voce* at b.45, and listen as intently to the inner LH line as to the treble, over the quiet lower drone. Allow a little extra time to listen to the beautiful intervals of the treble and inner LH voices moving partly in sixths through b.47, and then move into the RH solo in a whispered, hesitant *pianissimo*, gradually increasing the tempo as if turning a wheel as you return towards the reprise at b.53. Do not spoil Chopin's charming 'mid-thought' ending by making a pronounced *rallentando*, but, with just a hint of hesitation on the last quaver B flat, place the final chord with a tiny melodic ring, allowing the sound to fade into near silence through the pause.

Note: In many editions including Paderewski, the reprise is repeated from bb.53-60.

Mazurka No. 29 in C sharp minor
Op. 41 No. 4 (8+)

(See note at beginning of Op.41)

This is another of the four or so large-scale Mazurkas of special stature and significance (see under Op.30 No.4) though it is less complex in form and texture than Ops.50 No.3 and 56 No.3. But this one has an especially magisterial quality while retaining a potent spirit of the dance.

bb.1–32

The *Maestoso* indication tells us precisely how to set the opening. Play the quiet but intensely evocative solo introduction like a 'call', but with a measured 'tread' (around a suggested ♩ = 120), which, as you 'join in' with the LH in b.4, moves straight on into a restatement from b.5 through to b.8 to 'expand' on into b.9. This LH here has a steady, 'onward-walking', rather than dance-like character. With the *crescendo* into b.8 there is a heightening of intensity which some pianists interpret with a definite but carefully

*This is B natural in many editions.

controlled 'moving on'. Others maintain the reined-in tread and then 'whip up' the tempo through the solo quavers (bb.15-16). In any event, there is this irresistible sense of 'whipping up' through bb.15-16 carrying you into the whirling, stamping passage ahead at about ♩ = 160 or more. Point the dotted crotchet on the first beat of b.17, as a 'launching-pad', at the same time giving yourself a good kick-off with a strong bass note. Control the natural acceleration with a powerfully rhythmic but 'dancing' LH (see Introduction to the Mazurkas) as the quavers hurtle towards b.20. 'Brake' sharply here, being sure to **lift** the RH from the quaver on the first beat so that it falls naturally onto the slurred semiquaver (see General Introduction under 'Articulation'), and then play bb.21-4 in a rather more measured manner. Then 'poising' the 3-quaver upbeat group to b.25, hurtle off with an even greater 'whirl' through the triplet quavers (bb.26-7).

bb.32–64   Drop the tone and let the tempo 'give' through b.32 ready to ease into b.33 in a completely different, quiet, almost pensive tone. (Be sure that the minim B sings over the inner RH E sharp on the second beat of b.33 so that the upper melody is

clearly *etc.* and **not** *etc.*

There is still, however, a sense of suppressed rhythmic tension in the implied emphasis on the tied LH upbeat chords to bb.34 and 36, and this shows more overtly as this 4-bar motif is varied and 'notched up' a tone from b.37. Suddenly though, from b.41, Chopin 'disperses' the melody line over a dominant seventh chord which 'points' towards the move into F sharp major at b.49. From b.41 let the treble and inner LH line float above and 'among' the lower LH chords, within the pedal sound as indicated, with the unison motif 'falling away' from b.46, in *diminuendo* towards b.49. Feel the sense in which the RH dotted quaver on the first beat of b.49 both ends the previous descending sequence and begins the new section. This is made clearer in the

Paderewski Edition. Move into this section

with a quiet yet proud rhythmic swing, 'pointing' the emphasis on the partly tied upbeat to bb.50, 51 and 52. Support the RH with a quietly resonant and very steady LH, **listening** particularly to the lower LH line descending by steps to b.52 and rising again to b.54, and listening also to all held and tied resonances in either hand. Keep a steady pulse as the dotted rhythm ascends through bb.53-5 (and 61-5) with the help of a secure LH. Move into b.57 in a stronger dynamic, making a broader *crescendo* from b.61.

bb.64–105   You could either *crescendo* through to the end of b.64 to make a *subito pianissimo* at b.65, or alternatively, **ease** and *diminuendo* through b.64. If you take the former course, and *crescendo* through to the end of b.64, allow an extra instant to clear the sound at the end of b.64 ready for the *subito pianissimo*. In any event, this 'tipping over' into A major is an exquisite moment, and the change to F sharp minor at bb.68-9 scarcely less so. Play from b.65 in a dreamy *pianissimo* in a relaxed tempo, letting the inner line alternate in easy curves between the hands within the continuing sound of the held, soft outer chords. Take a little time to listen as the LH line dips down to the B sharp on the upbeat to b.73, to 'end' on the tonic on the first beat of b.73, as at the same time you **lift** the RH from the quaver chord on this first beat to ease into the even, accompanied version of the opening figure. Then as you get under way from b.74, feel a gentle, gradual but insistent sense of moving on, **gradually** 'whipping up' again towards b.89. The ornamented variant from b.97 is extremely difficult, and there can be few pianists who do not take the inner RH G sharp with the LH where possible, or omit it judiciously when they must! To avoid the tendency for the treble line to be drowned by the inner G sharp, practise 'bringing out' the treble line with exaggerated strength while playing such G sharps as you can with the RH thumb in an exaggerated *pianissimo*, adjusting to a proper balance as you gain fluency. Draw out b.102 somewhat as you 'peal out' the emphasised RH thirds with all the fervour you can muster. Then ease through b.104 to start the long climb from b.105 in *piano*.

bb.105–139   Keep this taxing dotted rhythm passage under control with the help of an implacably rhythmic though springing LH. However much you can, or may wish to, accelerate, this increase must be tautly controlled, and the continuing implementation of the emphasis on each upbeat chord is the key to maintaining this control (see also though, General Introduction under 'Dotted Rhythm'). Be sure too to **lift** the RH through each occurring semiquaver rest, so that it 'falls' naturally onto each subsequent semiquaver imagining that this semiquaver is 'slurred' to the next quaver (or dotted quaver). This 'up-down' movement of the RH, which creates a vigorous skipping effect within the overall slurred effect of each bar, is not only vital to the sense of the passage (see General Introduction under 'Articulation'), it also makes it incomparably easier. Draw out a little as you *crescendo* finally through b.118 ready to 'brake' as you unleash full dynamic throttle at b.119. Play this passage with all possible pomp and splendour in a magisterially measured rhythm (and **not** as an exhibition of firework octave technique). Carry the grand tone through to the last emphasised chord on the third beat of b.126. Then making a little break to clear the sound, drop the tone and play the upper line from b.127 in a clear but subdued *piano*, still in measured rhythm, over the quiet, steadily-moving lower drone effect. Drop to a murmur as you move to the lower register and gradually fade the sound through the last bars to a final barely whispered chord.

Mazurka No. 30 in G major
Op. 50 No. 1 (8)

This seemingly open-aspected number takes us down various byways in charming and unexpected nooks and crannies. With its complex interplay of contrasting motifs and strands, and numerous changes of mood and colour, this is a difficult piece in an interpretative, if not technical sense. Von Lenz records that Chopin considered this piece difficult to play, and that he 'set great store by the transition from b.40 into the modulatory passage from b.41' (Eigeldinger, p.76).

bb.1–16   Set a fairly lively tempo, around the ♩. = 50-55 mark, and play the opening motif in a vigorous, cheerfully animated style. Deliver the opening detached unison quavers with a lively 'kick', and 'bounce' off these so that the hands 'fall' onto the chord on the second beat with an implied natural emphasis, the impetus of which 'sends on' the treble and inner LH quavers towards the first beat of b.2, and on again towards the emphasised minim chord on the second beat of b.2. There is thus an overall impetus from the second beat of b.1 through to the second beat of b.2 (taking care to lift the treble quaver from the quaver on the first beat of b.2 on the way – see General Introduction under 'Articulation'). Be sure to give this minim chord its full value through the second and third beats of b.2 while at the same time feeling its onward 'lean' towards b.3, again **lifting** the RH from the quaver chord on the first beat. Feel a similar rhythmic impulse through b.3 towards the emphasised chord on the second beat of b.4, although the general effect here is smoother and more sustained as compared with the 'skipped' effect in b.2. Feel that you are 'leaning onwards' again on the minim chord through the second and third beats of b.4 so that you 'bounce' off the unison quavers again on the first beat of b.5, and so on. While implementing these forward impulses, lifts, 'leans', and so on, **listen** to the drone-like effect created by the various held, minim and tied resonances – these provide a kind of sonic 'anchor' amid the activity of the treble and inner voices. Point the partly tied chord on the second beat of b.8 with a slightly greater emphasis, and with the suggestion of a tiny extra 'hold' as you prepare to 'start again' at b.9. Rise to a little peak on the RH seventh and LH tenth on the first beat of b.12, again with the suggestion of a *tenuto*, and then 'unwind' in a neat but relaxed rhythm from b.13.

bb.16–72   Poise yourself for an instant on the upbeat to b.17 ready to strike into b.17 in a momentarily stronger tone, landing as if with a 'pounce' on the emphasised tied minim chord on the second beat. Drop the tone again at b.18, then play the upper line as if in a veiled half-light over the lower tied drones, listening to the smoothly gliding treble and inner LH line in parallel tenths from the upbeat to b.19. Poise yourself momentarily at the end of b.24 ready to bounce back into the opening motif from the unison quavers on the first beat of b.25. Poise yourself again at the end of b.40, allowing a tiny break, ready to begin in a new mood at b.41 as the LH takes the melody line in a warm ruminative tone. Shape this LH melody in expressive wide-sweeping curves, balancing the RH inner chords carefully beneath quietly singing treble line in longer notes, and **listening** to all upper and inner tied and held resonances. Feel the increasingly yearning intensity of the LH line as it rises towards b.47. Allow a little extra time to listen to the expressive dueting treble fragment through bb.47-8, pointing the *tenuto* tied minim A on the second beat of b.48 as the LH line begins to descend, 'unwinding' again in a relaxed manner. Then 'take hold' again with the dominant seventh chord on the first beat of b.53, as you prepare to rise towards the spread chord on the

second beat of b.55, most comfortably executed thus:

Allow the sense of a generous *tenuto* here, and then make an easy *diminuendo* through bb.55-6. Feel the emphasised third beat of b.56 as the onward-leading upbeat into the reprise from b.57.

bb.73–104   Strike a new, almost threatening note with the three unison crotchets at b.73. Space these in a 'summoning' 'equal' tone, and then move on through bb.74-6 playing the unison lines quietly but purposefully within the pervasive sound of the inner and lower drones. Then play from b.77 in an 'open' toned, more dance-like manner. Feel a little 'hold' on the chord on the second beat of b.78 and a longer one as you ease up to the spread octave on the second beat of b.80. Then let the broken chord fall graciously, ready to renew and increase the resolute tone from b.81, now filled out with octaves. Then at b.86 Chopin suddenly veers into an improvisatory sweep of augmented fourths and diminished fifths within an overall diminished seventh harmony. Listen to the aural impact of this succession of intervals, pedalling as indicated and taking time to make a broad curve up to and down from the chord on the third beat of b.86, poising yourself through b.88 ready to move into the coda. **Listen** to the *tenuto* tied upper G as the LH begins its quiet, easily undulating melody based on the opening motif, balancing the sound of the quiet inner chords carefully. Shape the curves up to and down from the high E at the end of bb.91, 95, etc. as a singer or a cellist would. Give the RH triplet at the end of bb.92, 96, etc. the feeling of a quiet but definite onward-leading upbeat. Keep the tempo moving, though with relaxed flexibility, gradually fading the sound from b.97. Quietly point the subdominant minor chords on the upbeat to, and the first beat of b.103, and then 'glide' the penultimate chord up towards a quiet final high chord.

Mazurka No. 31 in A flat major
Op. 50 No. 2 (7)

The clear-cut sections of this piece are comparatively straightforward both in texture and rhythm. Apart from the wide span of the chords between bb.68 and 74 (most of which can be adapted), it therefore makes a good piece for the relatively inexperienced player. On the other hand it is **not** one of the most interesting numbers – as Weinstock says 'clearly a stately dance of countesses and uniformed officers' (p.263).

bb.1–28   Set an easy-going *Allegretto* with a relaxed but dance-like swing at around ♩. = 50. Play the introductory bars in a smooth *mezzo voce* as if the dancers are gathering, ready to move off at b.9. Show the quiet emphasis on the minim chord on the second beat of each bar above the continuing quietly persistent lower LH figure and inner LH drone. Be sure to **feel** the held third beat of each bar, and then feel the lower quaver D natural is giving a continual little upbeat 'push' towards the chord on the subsequent first

beat. Allow a little extra time to spread the chord in b.4 gracefully

In Paderewski this chord is not spread, and may equally be interpreted

Make a little swell as indicated through b.6, drawing back again through b.7 and poising yourself through the tied chord on the second beat of b.7, **feeling** the held beats, ready to lead off with the upbeat to b.9. Give a clear though quiet lead in with the B natural, being sure to give it its full value while at the same time feeling its onward 'lean'. Shape the RH melody in gracious curves supported by a carefully balanced and rhythmically 'dancing' LH (see Introduction to the Mazurkas). Feel the gentle impulse towards the dotted crotchet on the second beat of b.9, quietly 'pointing' the LH chord on this second beat (most players spread this chord, or you could take the A flat with the RH). Be sure to give this dotted crotchet its full value, allowing a slight *tenuto* effect, though without any feeling of 'stopping'. Then with the merest suggestion of similarly 'pointing' the dotted crotchet on the second beat of b.10, feel a sense of moving on towards the end of the phrase on the second beat of b.12. Be sure to **lift** the RH after the quaver on the first beat of b.12 so that it 'falls' naturally on to the semiquaver (see General Introduction under 'Articulation') with the feeling of 'going to' the crotchet A flat, in perfect co-ordination with the LH crotchet sixth. Make a tiny break before leading on into the rejoinder in F minor with the RH upbeat to b.13, perhaps in a rather fuller tone. Listen to the resonance of the 'doubled' held F on the first beat of b.16 as you articulate the RH as indicated, feeling the 'lift' up to the high F and E flat. 'Hold' this dotted crotchet E flat for an extra instant as you place the inner RH E flat and LH partly tied sixth on the third beat, showing clearly that the

treble melody is  and **not**

and also making it clear that the quaver D flat is the **upbeat** to the restatement from b.17. Point the little curve up to the 'extra' appoggiatura-like quaver G on the third beat of b.17 and all the little varied touches of ornamentation. Allow a little vocal 'hold' on the A flat through the second and third beats of b.26, and then let the RH quavers 'curl' graciously down towards the A flat on the second beat of b.28.

bb.28–59   'Finishing off' the previous section on the tonic chord on the second beat of b.28, feel the sense in which the LH crotchet B flat gives a clear upbeat lead into b.29. Play from b.29 in a stronger, more purposeful manner with a slight sense of moving on. **Lift** the RH from the chord on the first beat of b.29 so that it 'falls' with natural emphasis on the dotted crotchet C on the second beat – and similarly the LH so that it in turn emphasises the tied crotchet upbeat to b.30. Through this little section there is the continual sense of an impulse towards the crotchet on each second beat, enhanced by the 'lean' on the slurred LH figures through bb.30-2. Then feel a slight *tenuto* on the dotted crotchet on the second beat of b.33, and an increasingly emphatic 'lean' on the minim on the second beat of bb.36-7. There is a sense of pressing on here – feel the implied emphasis also on the tied LH upbeat chord to b.37. Relax the tempo again through bb.38-9, ready to lead back into the reprise from the upbeat to b.40. Take a little time to play the LH chord (definitely spread this time) gracefully on the second beat of b.40.

bb.59–103   Once again feel the onward upbeat lead of the crotchet G flat on the third beat of b.59 into b.60. Play this middle section in a spirited, more masculine style, starting in a subdued 'military' rhythm and then opening out through the repeat towards the second section from b.68. Define the dotted rhythms cleanly, again being sure to **lift** the hands from the quaver chords on each first beat (see General Introduction under 'Articulation'), and 'planting' the crotchet chord firmly, if quietly, on each emphasised upbeat. Take care to give these upbeat chords their full value while at the same time feeling their slurred effect and onward 'lean', like a little 'push', and **listen** to the LH augmented interval on the upbeat to bb.62, 63, etc. Play the RH spread effect on the first

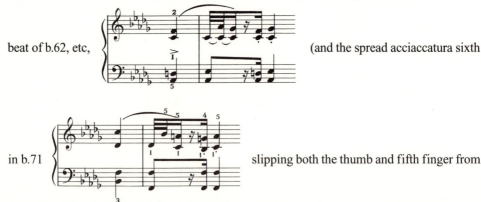

beat of b.62, etc,   (and the spread acciaccatura sixth

in b.71   slipping both the thumb and fifth finger from

the black notes onto the white). As you repeat bb.60-67 make a *crescendo* up towards b.67 ready to set off from b.68 in a fuller tone. Give an extra 'lean' on the upbeat to b.76, like a 'push' towards a powerful *sforzato* chord and bass note. Carry the *forte* on to the end of b.83 and then make a little break to clear the sound as you poise yourself to lead into the reprise in the elegant movement of the opening.

Mazurka No. 32 in C sharp minor
Op. 50 No. 3 (8+)

This is certainly one of the greatest of all the Mazurkas. Attention is drawn in the General Introduction to the frequent occurrence in Chopin's music of passages of beautifully 'turned' part-writing. Here, as in Op.56 No.3, he exploits his mastery of counterpoint in passages of concentrated and expressive intricacy. As Jim Samson says, 'At times indeed we need to remind ourselves that this is a dance piece' (p.117).

bb.1–16   The opening solo phrase has a haunting, call-like quality. It makes four appearances within the first eight bars through which it is worked in canon. This four-entry pattern recurs three times: from the upbeat to bb.33, 93 and 125, and this motif is then reiterated four times in the same voice near the end of the coda. Since fragments and hints of the shape and rhythm of this motif also recur constantly, it exerts a preoccupying and powerfully cohesive influence on the piece. Study its shape carefully therefore, set a measured *moderato* pulse and bring in the RH with a quiet but definite emphasis on the opening upbeat. Be sure to give this note its full value as you **feel** the held first beat of b.1. Then feel the impulse on towards the dotted crotchet on the second beat of b.2, and then the slow fall towards D sharp in b.4. Take care to place the inner RH B sharp carefully on the third beat of b.2 (so that the upper line sounds clearly

and **not** as in turn you bring in the LH on the emphasised

upbeat to b.3. Practise the parts separately and then in different combinations, as you would the voices of a fugue, listening acutely to the resonances both here and at every recurrence of these patterns. Play this motif in a simple quiet tone (it is quite evocative enough – indeed, far more so – without being overloaded with emotion), letting the resonance accumulate naturally with the entry of each voice, again as in the opening of a fugue. Take care to 'finish off' the last LH entry to the B sharp on the first beat of b.9, (taken with the RH) making it clear that the new phrase starts with the **second** RH quaver C sharp. Move on as the quavers *crescendo* upwards and play this little passage (bb.10-12) in an easy 'whirling' style. Then draw out gradually towards the double bar, feeling the 'lift' up to, and implied quiet emphasis on the RH dotted crotchet on the second beat of bb.13-15, and holding the overall dominant seventh harmony within the pedal as indicated as you disperse the sound in *diminuendo*, like distant calls.

bb.17–40   Take a good 'breath' through the rest on the upbeat to b.17, and launch into A major with a powerful bass octave, leaping up and letting the hands 'fall' with another powerful emphasis on the dotted crotchet chord on the second beat. Play this passage with all possible masculine spirit and verve, implementing all accents, details of articulation, etc. Be sure to **lift** the hands again from the quavers on the first beat of b.18 etc. so that they 'fall' onto the semiquaver chord, feeling this as the 'upbeat' to the second chord on the bar (see General Introduction under 'Articulation'). Feel in particular the powerful slurred 'lean' on the upbeat chord to bb.19, 21, etc. feeling a slight 'braking hold' on these chords, ready to make a *portamento*-like plunge down to the bass octave and RH quaver or crotchet on the subsequent first beat. It will be seen that the pattern here moves in 2-bar 'bouts' (bb.17-18, 19-20) motivated by a powerful 'thrust' on the bass octave on the first beat of b.17, with a slightly lighter effect in b.18, and moving towards another powerful thrust on the first beat of b.19, and so on. Poise yourself for an instant on the emphasised third beat of b.24 to clear the sound, ready to make a *subito piano* at b.25. Shape the LH quaver figures in smoothly rising swathes beneath the expressive RH fragments. 'Finish off' the first LH figure melodiously in perfect co-ordination with the re-entry of the RH on the upbeat to b.27. Shape the LH in a longer curve from b.29, rising towards an implied emphasis and slight 'hold' on the high tied upbeat to b.31, and then leading on into the reappearance of the opening motif on the upbeat to b.33. Take particular care with the entry of the inner RH voice in b.35 – this time this motif is treated fugally, and the texture here is more complex than in the opening and therefore needs to be even more carefully studied.

bb.41–93   'Disperse' the sound again through bb.41-4, but this time with a sense of moving on and leading into the new section at b.45. Shape the long phrases from b.45 with happy grace, supporting the light toned RH with a lightly dancing LH (see Introduction to Mazurkas). Allow just a little 'give' through the end of b.52 as you prepare to 'start again' at b.53. Point the descent of the bass-line to the G sharp at b.57, marking the more serious tenor of these four bars over the G sharp pedal point. Then lead into the *sostenuto* at b.61 with the feeling of a slight 'braking', and then expanding in a more important and fuller tone. Show the 'lift' up to the dotted crotchet G sharp on the second beat of b.63, and take a little time to point the LH details through bb.64-5. Feel a sense of moving on from b.69, and then through b.75 a little drawing out towards, and vocal 'hold' upon, the dotted crotchet G sharp on the first beat of b.76, before moving on again from b.77. 'Brake' again as you prepare to plunge into G sharp major at b.89, drawing out towards the pause on a full-toned tied G sharp in b.92. **Listen** as this sound reverberates within the pedal (see the long pedal from b.89) and move on into the opening motif when, and only when your ear tells you that the moment is right for the sound of the held G sharp and the 'new' G sharp to meet and merge onwards in b.93.

bb.93–192   Following a complete restatement of bb.1-41, from b.93, the music develops into a coda of astonishing size and range. As you end this restatement listen again as the two RH lines 'finish' on the first beat of b.133, before leading on with the inner quaver line. In the ensuing development of the quaver motif (of bb.9-12) practise the RH carefully to ensure that the treble fragments sing out clearly over the reiterrated inner quaver patterns, underpinned by a scrupulously rhythmic LH. Think of the high D sharp in b.135 and b.137 as the 'delayed' conclusion of these melodic fragments: (A) B sharp, C sharp, D sharp.

Paderewski makes this clear: Listen to the

descent of the inner RH quavers through b.140 towards the syncopated crotchet B sharp on the second quaver of b.141, which both ends the previous phrase and begins the next. (Again the phrasing in Paderewski clarifies this passage). Feel the impulse of each of the melodic fragments bb.141-3 and 145-7 towards, and back from the dotted crotchet on the second beat of b.142 and 145, and then play the little intervening dotted rhythm figures from the second beat of b.143 and 147 in precise, almost military rhythm, as if marking time. Listen acutely through these bars (141-8) to the inner, often held, or tied LH resonances over the lower pedal point notes. Then through b.149 and then b.151 go towards strong *sforzato* crotchets on the first beat of the subsequent bars, rebounding into the quiet dotted rhythm in both instances. Deliver a powerful bass G sharp on the first beat of b.153, and then shape the parallel quaver figures in close harmony through to the tonic chord on the first beat of b.157. A remarkable modulatory passage follows based on the figures of the opening motif. Build the dynamics gradually towards the first beat of b.165, always listening acutely to the relating resonances between the hands, and feeling the strong impulse towards the dotted crotchet on each second beat as you climb from b.160-65. Then drop the tone as indicated, ready to climb again with greater power and intensity towards b.173. Blazon out the impassioned reiterated treble figure from here in all the fervour and radiance of tone you can muster, supported by strongly resonant LH and inner RH chords. Carry the *forte* through to the chord on the first beat of b.177, and then let the solo line fall expressively towards b.181. Gradually decrease the sound as the opening motif is reiterated over the tonic pedal point, listening just as carefully to the subtly varying RH counterpoint. Phase the sound of the last solo call to a whispered C sharp on the second beat of b.191. Then taking a breath, rap out the final unisons like gunshots.

Mazurka No. 33 in B major
Op. 56 No. 1 (8+)

Extended though this little-played piece is, it is on a very different scale to its mighty neighbours Ops.50 No.3 and 56 No.3 – its length is mainly achieved through repetition. It has a somewhat enclosed, inward-looking character, which, nevertheless, grows upon the mind's ear, and the *poco piu mosso* section from bb.45 and 103 have that abstracted straying quality characteristic of late Chopin works. Three statements of the principal section are separated by two identical episodes, the first in E flat, the second in G. Then the lengthy coda lifts the piece onto a different plane. Here, as so often, this darling of the Paris Salons blazes a trail towards the future with a stream of masterly, evolving sonorities that can astonish the ear even today.*

bb.1–44   Rhythmically the principal sections (i.e. bb.1-44, 81-102, and the long final section from b.143 including the coda) are preoccupied with the figure ♩. ♪ ♩   ♩

Set a tempo that moves sufficiently to avoid any tendency to stick, and play bb.1-6 in a simple, quiet tone. Keeping an even tempo, shape the sequential LH 2-bar phrases in quietly expressive curves beneath the neatly timed treble dotted rhythm figures and quiet inner dotted minims. As Jim Samson says, 'the phrase structure is carefully ambivalent' (p.118) (not to say initially confusing to the player!). Following the two opening 2-bar RH phrases the next bar (b.5) 'ushers in' the climbing RH figure starting from the tied quaver upbeat to b.6. This rises, through three bars, then doubles back to usher itself in again through b.9. Meanwhile the LH line ends its third 2-bar phrase in b.6, then arcs from b.7 through to b.10 over a quiet bass drone fifth thus covering the join between the RH phrases, bb.8-9. If you quietly 'point' the tied RH quaver upbeat to b.6 and shape the treble curve up towards the minim on the second beat of b.8, and similarly follow the LH line through to b.10, allowing yourself to 'go with' the music, all this will fall into place quite happily. Note Chopin's *dolcissimo*, and phrase the upward curve in a beautifully soft, smooth tone, expanding a little towards a singing minim D natural, and allowing a slight *tenuto* here as you place the inner RH crotchet D quietly, ready to 'start again' from b.9. (This rising motif has something of the melodic ring of Grieg.) *Crescendo* from b.11 into *forte* at b.13, 're-taking' the upward climb from b.14 towards b.16. Right through from b.6 (where there is a sense of moving on through to b.22) there is an implied slight emphasis on each second beat, with a continual sense of 'going to' these beats. Note the **definite** emphasis on the inner LH minims on the second beat of bb.14 and 15 which provide a kind of anchor as you climb and *crescendo* here. Play out from b.16 in a joyous tone; and then take care to poise the cadence rhythmically at bb.19-20, i.e. be sure to give full value to the dotted crotchet dominant seventh chord on the second beat of b.19 so that you 'finish off' poisedly on the tonic quaver chord on the first beat of b.20. Here again the phrasing overlaps. **Lift** the hands to show the rest after this tonic chord

*In the Paderewski Edition the first twenty-two bars section is repeated, with a first and second-time bar, creating a twenty-one bar discrepancy, i.e. for b.45 read b.24.

and, dropping the tone, play bb.20-22 like a little tail-end, or linking fragment. Arrive on a quiet but firm E major chord on the second beat of b.22 as if with a little 'crouch' ready to lead off again from b.23. Be sure to **lift** the hands from the quavers on the first beat of bb.14-21 so that they 'fall' naturally onto the subsequent semiquavers, feeling these semiquavers in each case as the 'upbeats' to the second beat (see General Introduction under 'Articulation').

bb.44–164 Allow time through b.44 to 'ease' towards the E flat section, poising yourself for an instant on the upbeat to b.45. Move the tempo on and play this section in a light tone that is airy but at the same time has a slightly veiled, far-off quality – even here, beneath the apparently easy waltz-like movement, there is a curiously subdued, still, slightly enclosed feeling. Support the RH with lightly placed, but very rhythmic LH slurred figures as you curve up to and down from the highest note of each 4-bar 'arc' (the high E flat on the third beat of bb.46, 50, etc.). Allow a little 'give' as you listen to the LH through b.48 and again through b.52 as you prepare to 'start again' in A flat at b.53, while at the same time feeling the continuing run of the quavers like the turning of a wheel. Let the quavers run on from b.74 in an only gradually decreasing flow, delicately pointing the F flat on the first beat of b.77, and then the doubled C in b.78 descending to C flat in b.79, allowing time to ease through bb.79 and 80 back into your Tempo 1 at b.81.

bb.164–204 Arriving for the third and last time at the equivalent point of bb.20-22 (i.e. at bb.162-3), draw out a little through b.164 as you prepare to launch into the coda.

Dropping to *piano* through b.165 (as indicated in most editions, though not in Henle), give the curves of RH sixths a soft golden glow over a quietly resonant LH, listening to the tonic pedal point effect from bb.165-70. The sonorities of this passage are almost Brahmsian. Shape the RH sixths from b.172 in short slurred sweeps as indicated, propelled along by actively articulated LH dotted rhythm figures, swelling as you climb through b.176 towards the first beat of b.177. (This passage, from b.172-177 has a dance-like, capricious even ironic quality). Then from b.177 feel that you are pressing on towards b.181. From this point Chopin develops the prevalent ♪♩ ♩ |♪ 𝄾 ♪♩ ♩ |♪ *etc.* figure in a remarkable series of downward progressions in 4-bar sections. Having arrived on the dominant chord on the first beat of b.181, make it clear that you are 'starting anew' as you lead on from the semiquaver chord, feeling this as the 'upbeat' to the tonic chord on the second beat, and indeed as the 'upbeat' to this whole 'final stretch'. Play out in a radiant tone, always observing the rhythmic articulation of the chords while shaping the overall phrase through to the first beat of b.185. Then 'begin again' as the sequence is repeated a minor third lower, listening to the changes in harmonisation. From b.189 when this whole passage is repeated in combination with a glowing quaver counterpoint, practise **slowly** so that you can **listen** to the stream of changing sonorities created by this running counterpoint. And listen even more acutely from b.193 when the counterpoint grows yet more elaborate, and the ear is almost saturated by the array of audacious intervals passing between the hands. At b.198 when Chopin returns from this splendid detour to the patterns of bb.172-7 you could either maintain a *forte* to the end or make a gradual *diminuendo* towards the penultimate bar and end in a *subito forte*. In either event, maintain the 'moving' tempo rather than making an exaggerated *rallentando*. Hold the tonic sound within the pedal through bb.201-4, and show the indicated 'lean' on the upbeat to bb.200, 202 and 203, with the slurred effect towards the subsequent detached first beats. End precisely in time with a strong-toned final dotted rhythm figure and minim chord.

In the absence of any dynamic markings save for the *piano* in b.165 (see above), occasional hairpins and a *forte* in the last bar, and with its shifting textural layers, chains of transient tonalities and ambivalent shadings of mood, this magnificently equivocal coda section is open to any number of interpretations, and is far from easy to handle. The suggestions above that it should be interpreted in the main in a radiant paean of sound, are, of course purely personal, based on the textural and harmonic richness of the whole, and upon passages of similarly rich tonal resonance in other late works of Chopin.

Mazurka No. 34 in C major
Op. 56 No. 2 (8)

When this is played by a master of rhythm and sonority, the urge to leap up and dance is well-nigh irresistible! In its 'roughness', the starkness of its bare fifths, and the jolting movement of the treble line, it has something of Grieg's uncompromising late pieces, the Slätter Op.72.

bb. 1–28 Simple as it may look on the page, successful performances of this piece predispose a vivid aural imagination and understanding of sonorities, the courage to make and enjoy a 'crude' sound, and the ability to maintain a taut, virtually unchanging beat from first note to last. Set a lively crotchet pulse within an overall beat of around ♩. = 54-6. Much faster than this and the vigour of the 'stamps' in bb.32, 36, etc. will be steam-rollered; much slower, and the piece will begin to drag. Kick off with a sonorous tied dotted minim, being sure to have your beat well in the system **before** you start so that you can establish it securely through these four introductory bars as you 'beat out' the stark sound of the bass fifths. Then, 'planting' the LH and inner RH dotted minims with special emphasis on the first beat of b.5, play out the RH figures in a raucous, jerking manner that is nevertheless under rigorous rhythmic control and not **too** loud. At the same time feel the overall shape of each 4-bar phrase (the overall arc from the middle C on the first beat of b.5 up to the high C on the first beat of b.7, and down again to the middle C on the first beat of b.9) and **listen** to the pungent sonority of the intervals, particularly the fourths and diminished fifths, and the recurring Lydian sharpened fourth. Listen also to the all-pervading sound of the bass drones which, maintaining the implacable beat, propel the music along, with the crotchet fifths giving an onward-pushing, hectoring effect in each alternate bar. With no more than a hint of a momentary 'give' at the end of b.12 to clear the sound, drop the tone to an echoing *piano* at b.13, and play from here with a smoother overlay to the continuing jerking movement. Play the spread chords with a quiet but vigorous 'thrum-thrum', and 'snap' the ornaments as smartly and clearly as possible – not so easy since they fall on sixths! (**Lift** the hand after the second chord of bb.7, 11, 14, 18, etc, so that it 'falls' naturally on the upbeat chord. The impetus of this 'fall' will facilitate the execution of the ornament – **on** the beat –

and implement the implied stress on this upbeat chord. This stress is more

strongly implied by the partial tie on the upbeat to bb.15, 19, etc.)

bb. 28–52 Poising yourself for an extra instant on a quietly but firmly 'planted' LH upbeat to b.29, move on into the new A minor section in the same tempo, and shape the LH melodic line in an ingratiatingly suave curve, balanced by neatly placed and rhythmic offbeat RH chords. Then, emphasising the slurred upbeat chord to b.32, 'open out' towards two leaping 'stamps' on the second and third beats of b.32. Allow a fraction of extra time here, as if 'braking' slightly, to allow time to give each 'stamp' a powerful rebounding 'spring', before resuming the suave curve in the LH. Allow an instant for a quick 'breath' at the end of b.36 to clear the sound ready to return to b.29. At the end of the repeat make a more defined break. Then place the LH octave neatly on the first beat of b.37 and play the treble melody in a dainty *dolce*, over neat supporting crotchet chords (taking care to balance these carefully, particularly in respect of the inner RH crotchets). Feel the implied slight impulse towards the dotted crotchet on the second beat of bb.38 and 40, at the same time feeling the 'on and over lean' of this note towards the next phrase. Take particular care to ensure that this dotted crotchet sings over the quietly placed inner crotchet on the third beat, then think of the treble quaver as a clear onward leading upbeat into the subsequent bar. Then, opening out the tone again with a sudden 'push' through b.42, let the LH lead with a powerful stride from b.43 towards and through the RH 'stamps' in b.44. Through the restatement of the *dolce* motif (bb.45-9) note the **tied** LH fifth and RH inner crotchets on the upbeat to bb.46-9, feeling the implied emphasis on these as if with a little 'push'.

bb.52–84 Collect yourself again at the end of b.52 and, making a lightning switch of mood and dynamics, play from b.53 in a muted *piano*, making a smooth overall curve through bb.53-6, and again through bb.57-60 etc. In b.54 etc. listen acutely to the effect of the upper note of the LH drone fifth merging into the canonic imitation of the RH, and savour the Lydian sharpened F, first in the RH, then LH in bb.54 and 55, etc. (which reverts to the natural in b.56) and the delectable piquant intervals that arise through bb.54, 55, etc. At b.68, the only moment when a real 'give' is indicated, **listen** to the LH descending to settle again on the drone fifth on the first beat of b.69, beneath the sound of the long held RH second, whose upper note G sings over to b.70 as you ease into the reprise. Play this in an even quieter tone than from b.13, and perhaps with a smoother overall feeling. I suggest, however, that you maintain the tempo as you gradually phase out the sound rather than making a progressive *rallentando*. Then with a brisk 'snap' of the acciaccatura fourth 'hold' the first chord of the last bar within the pedal as indicated, and 'shoot' the final spread chord upwards with a vigorous 'punch'.

Mazurka No. 35 in C minor
Op. 56 No. 3 (8+)

This is perhaps the most splendid of all the Mazurkas. Like Op.50 No.3 it has a preoccupying motif which is worked contrapuntally with masterly effect. But here Chopin wanders even further into his 'strange spaces' – into harmonic regions completely baffling to his generation. Even Weinstock writing in 1949 seems to have 'missed' this piece, like others of similarly inspired abstraction (the Prelude in C sharp minor Op.45, the two Nocturnes Op.55 No.2 and Op.62 No.1, for example). He says of this Mazurka that 'its improvisatory air and inconsequential manner suggest Chopin expending on rather inferior ideas more science and effort than would have been necessary if the ideas in themselves had been more vivid' (p.272). But as Arthur Hedley, a more percipient authority on Chopin though writing at about the same time, says 'It is to be hoped that few modern musicians will speak of these later Mazurkas as being "less spontaneous", "composed more with the head, not the heart, nor yet the heels" (James Huneker) or "lacking in those 'beautés Sauvages' which charmed us in the earlier ones" (Hedley, p.165). None of Chopin's music is charged with such intense emotion as these 'scholarly and reflective works'. Here again, as Jim Samson says in connection with Op.50 No.3, we 'have to remind ourselves that this is a dance piece'. And talking of the present piece he says 'the sheer fecundity of new, albeit related material, is unprecedented in the Mazurkas' (Samson, p.119). It follows that musically, in the sense of 'holding it together', it is the most demanding of them all to play.

Note: This is one of the three numbers which are discussed in special detail – see the Notes at the end of the Introduction to the Mazurkas.

bb.1–46   Set a measured *moderato* pulse which moves, yet allows time for Chopin's harmonic pageantry to reach the inner ear. As in Op.50 No.3, the opening motif broods over, and thus unifies the whole work. Study its contours and expressive implications thoroughly, therefore. Lead in with a fairly full-toned slurred upbeat, rising to a 'carrying' though not overloud G on the first beat of b.1. This tied note (like the call of a summoning horn) resonates through to b.4 (see similarly the D held through bb.5-7, and the G from the upbeat to b.8 through to b.12, etc.). Then while making the entry of the lower line, and the immediately following entry of the upper lines perfectly clear, feel at the same time that they 'grow', in succession, out of this dominant note. Play on from b.1 and through the reiterated figures through bb.2 and 3 in a smooth overall shape as indicated, completing the phrase at the end of b.3 in such a way that the G is left resonating on through the first beat of b.4. Then (without making a break in the line) make it clear that you are 'starting again' as you enter with the upward scale of four quavers, feeling this as an upbeat group to the long held D, and so on. Practise bb.1-4 thoroughly, absorbing the overall shape of the phrase, studying the movement of the voices and feeling the sense of a little hastening as the voices move into b.2, then of an almost imperceptible drawing back through the end of b.3 towards the lonely sound of the single held G. Always be aware of the subtly pervasive effect of this held inner G between

the movement of the outer lines. The haunting rhythmic figure ♪.♪♪ ♩ is like a leitmotif

running through the piece. **Listen** to the different instrumental sound of this opening motif as it enters in a lower and again lower register in bb.5 and 9, 'pointing' en route the emphasised chord at b.8, making an overall slurred effect through b.8 towards the dominant

chord at b.9.   Also point the previous LH tied crotchet upbeat

G to b.8 (which here has longer to last), taking care again to leave it to sound over the bar line at b.12 before moving on in the extended version of the upbeat quaver scale to b.5. Listen to the intervals of the contrary motion quavers as you *crescendo* towards resonant unison minims on the second beat of b.14, noting the major-minor inflection F sharp-F natural at bb.13-14. Allowing an instant to clear the sound at the end of b.14, play on from b.15 in a clear toned, yet mysterious *piano* echo effect over the long held pedal point D. Be sure to **lift** the RH and inner LH quavers from the first beat of bb.15 and 16 so that the hands 'fall' onto the subsequent semiquavers (see General Introduction under 'Articulation'), feeling these semiquavers as an 'upbeat' to the slightly emphasised minims on the second beat of the bar (and taking care to give these minims their full value). Then, tying over the lower RH minim D into b.17 (which creates an additional quiet inner resonance above the long lower held D), play the unison figures in a fine-toned distant *piano* with a sense of moving on through bb.17-20. Then drawing back through bb.21-2, 'distance' the sound still further, and ever more mysteriously towards b.23, allowing a tiny extra instant to poise the extraordinary shift to G major at b.23. The alighting of the hovering figures of bb.21-2 upon this chord is a glimpse into a 'strange space' indeed. Give this G major chord the quiet sonority of a faraway bell, continuing the sense of the *rallentando* so that the sound has time to register fully upon the ear before moving on in tempo at b.24, into the restatement of bb.1-23.

bb.46–87   Rise from the upbeat D's to quiet but definite unison D's at b.47 as if 'pointing' the approaching, more vigorously dance-like passage, as opposed to the glance beyond the grave at b.23. *Crescendo* in purposeful rhythm through b.48, to lead off from b.49 with a full-toned RH minim D, and *crescendo* upwards in spirited rhythm towards the end of b.52 (taking care to **feel** the held third beat of b.50 – it is easy to 'mis-feel' this dotted crotchet and quaver as two crotchets!). Then take an instant for a quick breath ready to 'start again' at b.53, making a yet stronger *crescendo* towards the second beat of b.56. Take an extra instant again to point the upbeat crotchets to b.57 and then drop the tone and play this short section in a smooth dream-like *dolce*. Place the LH delicately on the first and second beats of b.57 in such a way that the melody line can 'drift' on from the held upbeat B flat-A sharp. Then place the lower LH tied minim with quiet resonance on the second beat of b.58, ready for the inner line to join in in sweet-toned sixths from the upbeat to b.59. Feel the gentle impulse towards the lightly emphasised first beat of b.60, and then poise yourself on the dotted crotchet chord on the second beat of the bar ready to 'drift' upwards again into the next phrase. Take particular care how you place the quiet bass F sharp on the second beat of bb.57, 61 and 65 since this 'sets off' the little upward run, ensuring that the upward 'drift' makes rhythmic sense. Poise yourself once more on the upbeat to b.67 for the further astonishing (and much criticised) shift to B flat major. Note the *forte* here, and the just-detached articulation of the upward scale – Chopin's way, perhaps, of 'pointing' this lateral 'key-slide'. Then 'round in' from the emphasised upbeat chord to b.69 to play from this bar purposefully, as if to clinch the matter of the key change. Enter, still purposefully, with the inner LH line on the second beat of b.71, and make a broad curve up to the inner quaver B flat on the first beat of b.72, ready to 'follow' the RH descending quavers of b.70. But all save the recurring opening theme is transient in this most episodic of the Mazurkas – and this resolute 'new beginning' is soon stopped in its tracks. Point the emphasised third beat of b.72, ready to drop the tone to *piano* at b.73. Play from here in a quietly rhythmic, ongoing manner, articulating the lower LH line meticulously clearly, almost jauntily (then darkening the tone a little as you point the minor inflections in b.77). Take care with the join between bb.73 and 74 – the partly tied upbeat resonances need an attentive ear. Then, as well as the indicated emphasis on the upbeat chord to b.76, there is an implied slight emphasis on each upbeat chord to bb.74-7 – it is this which contributes to the momentarily jaunty air. Take an instant at the end of b.76 to prepare for the minor shift. Then feel the onward impulse towards, and slight *tenuto* effect on, the chord on the second beat of b.78 ready to move on from the upbeat to b.79 in a resolute *crescendo* towards b.81, taking an extra instant to poise the spread tenth on the upbeat chord to b.81. Then drive on from b.81 playing the amplified version of bb.73-80 with a triumphal ring.

bb.87–172   Diminishing the tone slightly from the end of b.87 as indicated, arrive on a clear B flat chord on the first beat of b.88. Making a tiny break, plunge into the new *forte* melody with conviction, descending to the quaver C flat as if with a powerful downward swoop. This further extraordinary shift takes us through A flat minor on the way to B flat minor at b.95. Play the four solo quavers in resolute *sostenuto* as you swing into b.89 with a slight sense of 'braking'. Shape the RH in a grand broad-toned sweep, propelled along by resonant and rhythmic LH spread chords played with a vigorous 'thrum-thrum'. Feel the sense in which the phrase goes on 'through' the resonant E flat in b.92, into an 'ongoing tag' through to b.95. Having reached the temporary 'home key' in the minor at b.95, Chopin extends and varies the previous phrase with stunning effect. Play from b.96 in a smooth echoing *piano*. Linger through the 'extra tag' in b.103 with a hint of a vocal 'hold' on the high quaver E flat on the third beat. Then, letting the line fall from the end of b.103 as if in a *portamento*, play the dotted minims C and F with quiet emphasis and with a sense of leading on to 'connect' this 'tag' into the subsequent phrase.* Taking an extra instant to clear the sound at the end of b.105, 'float in' the high G flat in a beautiful *piano* on the first beat of b.106 and let this 4-bar phrase fall with a feeling of delicate nostalgia (moved along by the slurred LH figures) towards b.109, returning with the upbeat to b.110 to play its restatement in an even quieter tone. Move through bb.114-16 with a sense of dying down, even if with a slight hastening on the way. Then easing into b.117, listen to the chromatic inflections as the solo line

181

'curls' easily through bb.117-20. Feel a sense of leading on from b.119, then easing fractionally through the end of b.120 as you prepare to lead off from b.121 with the restatement of the passage from b.73. At b.134 there is another extraordinary interruption. Marking the emphasised chords from the upbeat to b.133, 'go to' a resonant quaver chord on the first beat of b.134, holding this briefly within the pedal as indicated. Then, in sharply defined rhythm, **listen** to the upward shifting harmonies as you press on in anguished *crescendo* towards the diminished seventh chord on the second beat of b.136. Giving this no more than a momentary extra 'hold' while making the mental enharmonic change to A flat in the LH, lead on from the LH upbeat to a powerfully resonant LH high G as you merge into the opening motif. (The treble B is tied in most editions from b.136 to the first beat of b.137, though Henle appear to take a different view.)

bb.172–188   As in most of the other large-scale Mazurkas, there is a powerful and extended coda, and this, in character with the piece as a whole, is perhaps the freest and most outward-reaching of them all. From b.172, instead of leading on towards D minor as from bb.12 and 36, Chopin cuts short the upward sweep of the quavers to land on the chord of F minor at b.173, from which he sidesteps through bb.174-5 towards the home dominant at b.176. Point the arresting effect of this F minor chord on the first beat of b.173 and continue with a sense of pursuing a new train of thought (albeit incorporating the

inescapable ♩. ♩♩ ♩ motif) only to be cut short at b.176. Then 'starting again' in

b.177 feel that the LH is 'leading' from here through to b.182, as if finding the way to carry through the idea of bb.174-6. Listen acutely at the same time to the rich harmonic progressions of the RH with its inner fragment of melodic counterpoint in bb.179-80. Through b.180 Chopin appears to be 'opening out' into E flat major. But then in b.183 the treble takes over the dotted rhythm figure which then alternates between the hands through an extraordinary series of downward chromatic progressions which lands back on the dominant of C at b.188. Study this passage **slowly**, listening equally to the movement of all the voices and to the relationship between them. Play the passage musingly, without hurry, so that the ear (of both player and listener) can take in the harmonic processes, but at the same time maintaining the underlying rhythmic impulse towards bb.188-9.

bb.188–220   Arriving on the dominant harmony at b.188, Chopin embarks from b.189 on a long and potently expressive passage over a tonic pedal point. Curve the LH up through b.188 and down to the first beat of b.189 in a broad sweep as you set off into this culminating passage with full-toned *sforzato* unisons. Dropping at once to *piano* as

*The complex phrasing of this passage is open to different interpretations. From b.96, however, this phrasing is made clearer in the Paderewski Edition.

But this passage needs to be carefully studied and **sung** in order to arrive at a convincing, not merely theoretical interpretation of its impulses and punctuations.

indicated, play from here with the utmost expressiveness, but again without losing the onward momentum (there are references here to the *piano* passage, bb.57-66). Feel the impulse towards, and slight lingering upon the dotted crotchet A flat on the second beat of b.190, with a slight 'moving on' through bb.191-2. (Allow a similar degree of freedom through the melodic quaver passage, bb.193-4, 197-8, etc, and then quietly 'gather up' the rhythm through the intervening bars, 195-6, 199-200, etc.). 'Arc' up to the high quaver G from the first beat of b.193 as a singer would, and, as you let the line fall expressively through bb.193-4, point the implied little emphasis on the tied quaver upbeat to bb.194 and 195, then making another little 'push' on the partly tied upbeat to b.196. 'Point' also the little varied touches as this 8-bar passage is restated from b.197, taking the line 'into the air' as you rise to the high quaver on the first beat of bb.199 and 203.

Feel an onward momentum as the texture thickens again from b.205, listening acutely at the same time to the movement of the voices, and in particular to the 're-entries' of each rising 4-quaver figure in the LH. Feel the heightened intensity as the three emphasised treble crotchets press on through b.209 towards the minim of the first beat of b.210. Arriving again on a clear tonic major at b.213, gradually 'disperse' the sound towards b.217, though maintaining the rhythmic movement in the lower LH line beneath the sustained upper chords. Then 'pointing' the inner RH inflections (bb.217-18, 219-20), attenuate the *diminuendo*, fading the chords away like distant drum beats, towards the last chords played with quiet finality.

Mazurka No. 36 in A minor
Op. 59 No. 1 (8)

Although on a more modest scale than the 'symphonic' Mazurkas referred to by Arthur Hedley (Ops.41 No.4, 50 No.3, 56 No.3, etc.) the three pieces of Op.59 eloquently demonstrate typical aspects of the concentrated harmonic processes characteristic of Chopin's mature musical thought. This piece starts plainly enough, giving little hint of the complex improvisatory musings of the middle section (bb.37-78). This is a real 'musician's' piece (in the sense that we talk of a 'plantsman's' garden as opposed to a show garden).

bb.1–6   Set a steady **3/4** at around $\downarrow$ = 138 (this piece has an easy, almost 'jogging' movement) and play the opening solo motif in a simple clear-toned style. Then as the LH joins in, swell a little through bb.3-4 ready to play the higher version of the opening phrase in a rather fuller tone from b.5. Feel the impulse of each of these 2-bar phrases towards the minim on the second beat of bb.2, 4 and 6, while at the same time conveying the sense in which these held second beats 'lean' onwards towards the next 2-bar phrase (thereby avoiding the sense of 'stopping' on these minims with the resultant effect creating a series of 2-bar 'boxes'). The rhythmic placing of the LH chord or note on the third beat of bb.2, 4, 6, etc. also provides an upbeat 'lead' into the subsequent bar. Take particular care to place the LH chord rhythmically on the third beat of **b.2** and then join in with a confident LH on the second beat of b.3 so that the rhythm becomes securely established.

bb.6–37   Make a *crescendo* through bb.7-8 as indicated, feeling the onward impetus towards the second beat of b.8 while at the same time conveying the 'on and over lean' of this *tenuto* trilled minim into the second half of this overall phrase, so that you then feel the further onward impetus towards the minim on the second beat of b.10. Then feel a sense of unwinding towards the second beat of b.12. (Some editions repeat bb.1-12.) There is, however, no sense of 'stopping' here, as you 'lean' onwards into b.13. But there is a sense of greater flexibility from this point as the quaver line curves decoratively through bb.13-18. Continue nevertheless to feel this sense of the impulse towards (and onward lean of) the tied minim on the second beat of b.14, and similarly the dotted crotchet on the second beat of b.16. Be sure to **lift** the RH from the quaver on the first beat of bb.10 and 12 so that it 'falls' naturally onto the semiquaver, 'going to' the minim on the second beat (see General Introduction under 'Articulation'). Support the RH with an always rhythmic LH, feeling its more overtly dance-like rhythm from b.9 (see the Introduction to the Mazurkas). Absorb these rhythmic niceties discussed above thoroughly, for they set the motion of the piece as a whole. Feel a sense of moving on slightly from b.17, as the curving quavers lead on towards the dotted rhythm passage at b.19. Continue this sense of moving on into and from b.19, though keeping this slight *accelerando* under control by means of a consistently rhythmic LH (delivering a resonant bass note on the first beat of bb.20 and 22, and feeling the emphasis, like a 'push' on the tied LH upbeat to bb.23 and 24. Even relatively experienced players have problems with protracted sequences of dotted rhythm such as this. Always think of the semiquavers as the 'upbeat' to the subsequent dotted quaver so that there is a continual onward impetus towards the main beats of each bar (see General Introduction under 'Dotted Rhythm').

As you bring the LH **off** after the second beat of b.24, 'brake' a little, as you poise yourself for the entry of the opening motif in the LH in b.25. As you shape this LH entry expressively down through b.25 towards the minim E on the second beat of b.26, maintain the continuing line of the RH through the flattened intervals through b.25, to 'finish off its own phrase' in unison with the LH on this minim E. Then 'take over' clearly with the RH in b.27 as it reclaims the melody line in an embroidered version of bb.3-6, reverting to the 'straight' restatement from b.31. 'Brake' again from the end of b.36 ready to 'point' the shift to the major at b.37.

bb.37–56   Dropping the tone, play from here in a subdued but clear and rhythmic *sotto voce* with a sense of again 'moving on' (this is one of Chopin's occasional ventures – here very brief – in a *religioso* style). Then *crescendoing* from b.39, Chopin expands into one of his most splendid improvisatory passages. **Listen** with aural antennae fully extended to the chromatically shifting sonorities as the dynamics swell and recede in natural waves of sound, while at the same time maintaining the underlying rhythmic movement. As you rise and swell through b.41 feel the 'expanding' onward impetus towards the high dotted crotchet A on the second beat of b.42 (with a slight vocal 'hold' on this note), and then the gradual unwinding through bb.43-8, ready to climb again from b.49, where the progressions of bb.41-4 are varied with a subtlety that is entrancing to the gourmet ear. Throughout this passage (bb.41-53) listen as carefully to the lower voices as to the treble (having studied the movement of each separately), paying particular aural attention to the inner and lower tied held resonances through bb.44-50. Then from b.53 Chopin moves on in a more *scherzando* manner. Feel the 'lift' up to the high quaver C sharp on the second beat of b.55, letting this note hang in the air for an instant, and then run down the semi-chromatic scale almost in a slither, controlled by a neat LH in b.56.

bb.56–79   From b.57 Chopin introduces a whimsical 4-bar phrase in E minor which he proceeds to vary through three restatements. 'Ease' through the very end of the chromatic downward run through b.56 and move into b.57 in a quiet tone playing the RH in a neat dancing rhythm while the LH quavers 'carry on' the downward run through bb.57-8. Then in the *scherzando* manner of bb.55-6, 'lift' to the quaver G natural on the second beat of b.59, and run down the scale as before, reverting to your neat dancing rhythm through bb.61-2 and so on. Listen to the varied inflections of the downward run through bb.63-4 and 67-8, allowing each 'lift', and run to 'expand' a little more than the last. At b.70 Chopin inflects to the inner D sharp with a sense of impending 'arrival' in B major. Clinch this pending arrival by moving purposefully through bb.71-2 and again through bb.73-4.* Then swell the tone through

---

*Feel that the LH through bb.72 and 74 (now performing the diatonic version of the descending chromatic scale in the RH through bb.56, 64 etc.) is subject to the rhythmic control of the *crescendoing* RH chords.

the B major flourishes from b.74, pressing on into the augmented extension at b.76, which points onwards towards the G sharp minor version of the principal motif from b.79. **Hold** this augmented harmony within the pedal as indicated as you rise to a ringing high quaver sixth on the third beat of b.76. Then dropping the tone as indicated at b.77, stretch your ears as you shape the astonishing inflections of the upward curving quavers, homing in towards G sharp minor at b.79.

bb.79–130 From b.91 Chopin neatly cuts back into his 'normal' reprise. Then at b.113, instead of turning into A major as at b.37, he diverts into the coda, another improvisatory passage. Point the interrupted cadence with a quietly resonant LH D sharp dotted minim on the first beat of b.114, and long RH A on the second beat, letting the sound hover within the pedal (bb.115-17) as indicated. Shape the RH fragment up to the high spread tenth in b.118 a little hesitantly the first time, and more positively through bb.121-2. Then lead on with the LH from b.123 'following' closely with the RH with a sense of moving on towards the emphasised dominant unison tied minims on the second beat of b.124. From here you could either feel a sense of pressing on towards the second beat of b.127, then swelling through the penultimate bar and 'easing' from the high F natural on the third beat towards the final chord – or alternatively you could gradually *diminuendo* and ease right through from the second beat of b.124. In either event feel the swell (greater or smaller!) towards the third beat of the penultimate bar, allowing a little vocal 'hold' on this F natural, and then 'finishing off' neatly towards the final chord. (Note in this penultimate bar the 'Franckian' sound of the rising ninth effect on the first beat.)

Mazurka No. 37 in A flat major
Op. 59 No. 2 (8)

Set against the improvisatory convolutions of Op.59 No.1, this piece is more consistently 'metric', in a sense more formal. It is, however, hardly less interesting, incorporating, as Jim Samson says 'one of the most tortuous of Chopin's sliding chains of chromatic harmonies' (bb.81-8) (p.119).

bb.1–23 Set an easy-moving **3/4,** and enter with a quiet but definite bass A flat so that the steady movement is established from the outset. Enter (again quietly but confidently) in the RH feeling the slight implied emphasis on the dotted crotchet which reinforces the 'setting' of the tempo. This piece has something of the 'jogging' motion of Op.59 No.1, with perhaps just a little more movement. Play the RH melody in a simple style in a clear *dolce* tone. Feel the 'lift' up to the A flat on the third beat of b.4, and then as the LH leads on with another onward directing bass note, take a 'breath' before entering again with another slight emphasis on the dotted crotchet on the second beat of b.5. Support the RH throughout the first section with a carefully balanced, 'dancing' LH (see the Introduction to the Mazurkas). Place the third beat of b.8 with a clear emphasis and with a slight *tenuto* effect, while at the same time feeling the onward 'lean' of this note towards the next phrase. 'Finish off' neatly with the RH quaver E flat on the first beat of b.9, allowing an instant for another quick 'breath' through the quaver rest, ready to enter again on the second beat. Feel the lift again up to the high C on the third beat of b.12, then allowing an instant to 'point' the bass G on the first beat of b.13. From b.15 there is a sense of moving on as a more urgent reiterated 2-bar fragment takes over. The shape of these fragments creates a series of naturally occurring emphases on the second beat of bb.15, 17 and 19. Feel also the onward-urging effect of the slurred RH upbeat to bb.17 and 19. Then from the upbeat to b.20 expand a little as you prepare to 'lift' up to the high crotchet C on the second beat of b.20. Allow a slight vocal 'hold' on this note and then let the solo quavers descend with some freedom, but at the same time with a sense of driving on into the more masculine restatement from b.23.

bb.23–60   Amplify the sound here in full-toned RH sixths and 'springing' bass octaves, swelling towards a radiant, or perhaps even rumbustious-toned *fortissimo* from b.31. **Listen** to the upper line at b.29, ensuring that it sounds

as   [musical notation] *etc.*   and **not** as   [musical notation] *etc.*

(and similarly at b.31). Take time to 'lift' to the high RH third as you spread the powerful-toned chord on the third beat of b.34, taking a quick 'breath' before you continue slightly less loudly from b.35 (though with a resonant onward leading bass octave on the first beat of this bar, and also on the first beat of bb.36 and 37). Allow a slight 'hold' to accommodate the LH spread chord and RH acciaccatura on the third beat of b.35, and again to poise yourself on the third beat of b.36. Note also, and implement, the implied emphasis on the second beat of b.37, the third beat of b.38, etc, and in bb.38 and 40 allow time to leap up to the high third as if in an 'arc' (not a lurch) from the sixth on the first beat. While observing all these rhythmic emphases, do be careful not to let the overall momentum flag too drastically, although there is an implied sense of gradually 'subsiding' from b.37 towards b.43. 'Lift' up to and slightly 'hold' the high C once more on the second beat of b.42, and this time taper the quavers through bb.43-4, easing a little through the end of b.44, ready to enter with the new melody from b.45 in a more wistful, slightly veiled tone. Shape the line in a smooth overall arc, up to b.47, and down again to the emphasised minim on the first beat of b.49 over a quietly supportive LH, feeling the implied emphasis on the tied upbeat seconds to bb.46 and 47. **Listen** to the RH intervals in bb.46, 50, etc, and to the subtle variants as this phrase is repeated from bb.49, 53 and 57. Then, the last time, from b.57 feel the onward upward pull towards a ringing high C on the first beat of b.60.

bb.60–89   From the first beat of b.60 (being sure to **lift** the hands here so that they 'fall' naturally on to the RH semiquaver and LH crotchet sixth (see General Introduction under 'Articulation') play the reiterated 2-bar figure (alternating major and minor) with increasing passion. Ensure the RH comes **off** at the beginning of bb.62, 64 and 66, as if to make a quick intake of breath over the onward impelling bass *sforzato* crotchets. Feel the emphasis on the upbeat chord to bb.61 and 63, and reinforce the LH sound in b.64 with the enlarged chord on the second beat. Then allow time to hear the remarkable intervals created by the LH detail in bb.65 and 67 (listen to this **slowly**). Draw out a little through b.68 again listening acutely to the inner RH and lower LH inflections as you prepare to launch into the opening melody with the LH from the second beat of b.69. Ensure that the LH sings out here beneath carefully balanced and placed relatively *piano* RH chords, noting the 'dancing' articulation of these RH accompanying chords. Then from the upbeat to b.75, the RH joins in duet with the LH ready to blazon into *fortissimo* again at b.77. This transition into an apparently 'straight' reprise is soon cut short, however, at b.81. Arrest this reprise with a commanding chord on the second beat of b.81 allowing a slight *tenuto,* and then pursue the 'tortuous chain' in a smooth yet perfectly clear 'slide', always feeling the implied poising 'lean' on each upbeat chord, i.e. on the upbeat to b.83 and b.84 and so on through to the upbeat to b.89. Feel the mounting harmonic tension as you climb with increasing resonance towards the highest chord at the end of b.84, gradually subsiding again from b.85. Take plenty of time as you end this passage in b.88, and bring the RH **off** through the semiquaver rest as you prepare to 'home in' to the tonic through the spread dominant seventh chord on the upbeat to b.89. Practise this whole passage snail-slow so that you can fully absorb the shifting sonorities of this aural feast.

bb.89–110 Chopin leads into the coda with 2-bar fragments based on the opening motif, over a 7-bar tonic pedal point. Play from b.89 in a quietly musing yet 'ongoing' manner, listening to every nuance of melody and harmony, 'pointing' the inflection to the minor at b.95 and drawing out a little from b.97. Point the downward chromatic step of the LH on the first beat of b.99, and take a little more time to listen to the further 'flattening' through b.100. 'Hold' the tied dominant seventh chord for an extra instant on the upbeat to b.101, and then move *a tempo* into easy-running quavers. Shape these quavers in smoothly undulating curves in a slight 'billowing' up towards b.104, and then let the line fall as if sliding downwards. **Listen** once more to the intervals as you 'join in' with the LH in b.106. Then let the tonic arpeggio fly up as if on a breeze to the high crotchets on the first beat of b.109, holding the sound in the pedal as indicated. End with quietly defined tonic chords.

Mazurka No. 38 in F sharp minor
Op. 59 No. 3 (8)

This is the last of the really large-scale Mazurkas, described by Paul Hamburger as 'a fantastic piece of large melodic gestures and sprung rhythms' (Walker, p.84). While in a sense more of a 'performance' piece than, for example, Ops 50 No. 3, 56 No. 3 and 59 No. 1, it also has several passages rich in harmonic subtleties: bb.65-81 and 97-104, etc, and above all the long coda beginning at b.115. As is the case in many of the greatest of the mature Mazurkas, it is not until such passages have been studied closely and **slowly** that (to those of us with average ear at least!) their full splendour is revealed.

bb.1–16 The piece is dominated by the opening F sharp minor motif rising in a wide arc towards a brief 'plateau' at b.3, and descending again from the upbeat to b.4, to another brief 'plateau' at b.8, to 'start again' from b.9. Many editions give an opening *forte*. Whether or not you start in *forte*, (and most players do start in a fairly full tone), this opening motif has a powerful rhythmic momentum. Set an 'active' **3/4** therefore at a suggested ♩. = 56, not so fast as to dilute the proud and chivalric quality of the overall arc, not yet so 'measured' as to emasculate the 'spring' referred to by Paul Hamburger. The upward-directed stride of the upbeat immediately commands the attention. Lead in with an emphatic 'lean' therefore, up towards a ringing dotted crotchet F sharp on the first beat of b.1, over a resolutely placed bass F sharp, to give a good kick-off to the rhythm. Play the LH as if with purposeful 'leaps' through b.1 (taking particular care to place the chord rhythmically on the **second** beat beneath the RH dotted crotchet), so as to establish the tempo securely, and thereafter ensure that the LH always underpins the RH with a dance-like 'spring'. Feel that this buoyant LH is 'carrying' the RH up through the second half of b.1, to 'twirl' the triplet figure confidently through to the crotchet on the second beat of b.2. Then, implementing the phrasing of each 1-bar fragment **lift** the hand from this crotchet on the second beat of b.2 so that it 'falls' to create a natural implied emphasis and onward 'lean' on the upbeat to b.3, and similarly as you begin the descent on the upbeat to bb.4-7 (see General Introduction under 'Articulation'). Then mark the emphasis on the second beat of b.7, feeling the onward impulse towards the emphasised first beat of b.8. Give this note a slight *tenuto* effect, allowing a further fraction of extra time to **listen** to the 2-part movement of the RH as it 'gathers itself' to set off again from b.9 (feeling these three quavers through the second half of the bar as the overall upbeat to b.9). Point the different harmonic progress from b.12 taking us towards A major at b.16.

bb.16–44   Allow a little 'give' here as you end this second overall 8-bar phrase on the second beat of b.16 and, easing into b.17, play this passage in a quieter more thoughtful tone, over a gentler LH 'dance' step. Note the original RH fingering

in b.21  typical of Chopin's appreciation of the natural disposition

of the fingers. You could bring back the opening motif from the upbeat to b.25 this time in a quieter tone. Then the addition of an inner RH note on the upbeat to bb.28, 29, etc, together with some inner LH detail creates the aural illusion of 'filling out' the texture with a continuous

inner counterpoint

Take a little time to point the syncopated treble crotchet on the fourth quaver pulse of b.31 and the tied upbeat to b.32 as you listen to the emergence of a true inner fragment as you prepare to 'round in' towards b.33. Then, from b.37 listen to the resonance of the lower dotted minims through the reiterated 2-bar fragment with a sense at first of moving on, and then from the upbeat to b.41, of drawing out towards the chord on the second beat of b.42. Make a slight *tenuto* on the RH dotted crotchet D here, holding the harmony of the whole bar within the pedal as indicated and continuing the *ritenuto* through to the dotted crotchet on the second beat of b.43. Then make a little swell as indicated as you ease, in a graceful rise through b.44 towards the F sharp major section.

bb.45–55   Resume the tempo from b.45 in a gentle light-toned *dolce*. Here the melody line, mainly in thirds, has a whimsical, almost *scherzando* character over a steady LH moving entirely in crotchets. Feel that the LH is supporting and carrying the RH, and listen particularly to the smooth rising swathes of LH crotchets through bb.45-6, 49-50, etc. Study the articulation of the RH carefully. 'Lean' on the tied crotchet third on the first beat of b.45, and then, showing the overall slurred effect down towards the third beat, be sure to **lift** the hand from this quaver C sharp so that it 'falls' with natural implied emphasis on the tied semiquaver upbeat to b.46 (see General Introduction under 'Articulation'.) Then similarly **lift** the hand from the quaver on the second beat of b.46 so that it 'falls' onto the semiquaver third 'going to' the emphasised crotchet fourth on the upbeat to b.47, and so on, accomplishing all this within the even movement of the rising LH crotchets. Lean again slightly on the first beat of b.47 and then swell the tone a little as indicated, noting the slurred effect on the second quaver of b.48, and then 'twirling' the treble triplet neatly as you lead on towards another 'lean' on the first beat of b.49, and so on. Following the LH rest on the first beat of b.47, 'enter' clearly with the LH on the second beat, to support the RH swell into b.48. Practise **slowly** over a rock-steady LH until these somewhat complex details of articulation and rhythmic emphases are thoroughly absorbed, and as you increase the tempo, continue to rely on the rhythmic guidance of the stable LH crotchet line. As you *crescendo* upwards from b.51 feel the onward impetus towards the emphasised chord on the third beat of b.52 (and similarly from bb.53-4), and then allow a little time to ease back into b.55. Take care to let each little swell (e.g. through bb.47-8, 53-4, etc.) return to 'base' through bb.49-50, 55-6, etc, thus avoiding a build-up of sound, and ensuring that the overall tone remains light, perhaps even a little veiled.

188

bb.55–96   As the figures from bb.51-4 recur from b.61, make a greater *crescendo* to b.64 with the sense this time of leading on into b.65 (using the LH lower upbeat quavers C sharp and B to give this emphatic 'on and over lead'). Start this magnificent descending passage from b.65 (described by Paul Hamburger as 'a torrent of descending modulation' (Walker, p.84)) in a full, resonant tone, grading the dynamics as indicated towards b.71 so that you diminish a little through each 2-bar section, 'starting again' at a progressively lower dynamic at b.67 and again at b.69. **Listen** to the inflections of the RH, always feeling that the RH is being 'propelled' along by the rising LH crotchets with an implied upbeat emphasis (**stated** in bb.68 and 70) on the chord on each third beat. Poise yourself on this emphasised upbeat to b.71 ready to give a strong 'push' on the *sforzato* chord on the subsequent first beat. Then, allowing an extra instant to clear the sound, drop the tone immediately ready to move on from the second beat in a smooth-running *legato* and with an anticipatory feeling as if gathering yourself to launch into the next torrent from b.75. Make another 'poising hold' on the emphasised upbeat chord to b.75, allowing another extra instant to make a confident outward leap towards a ringing treble and bass on the first beat of b.75.

Make the little swell through bb.85-6 ready to 'point' the minor inflection on the first beat of b.87, then drawing back the tone towards b.89. Play from here musingly **listening** to the intervals of the quietly sustained RH chords (diminished 5th, perfect 5th, augmented 4th, etc.), while maintaining the overall sense of the rhythmic movement as you shape the LH 2-bar phrases in expressive curves beneath these quietly resonant RH tied chords. Resist the temptation to take the detached crotchet on the third beat of bb.90, 92, etc. with the RH. The natural 'spacing' which occurs when the pattern is 'completed' with the LH conveys that sense of the overall continuing curve which is easily lost if you take the lazy way out.

bb.96–114   Take time through b.96 to ease into the tonic $\overset{6}{4}$ harmony at b.97, holding this chord for an extra instant before drifting upwards in a smooth solo swell into the passage described by Jim Samson as the 'glorious canonic bridge to the reprise' (p.119). Enter cleanly with the LH on the first beat of b.99, and shape each voice in a wide overall curve as indicated, **listening** to the passing intervals between the hands. Point the emphasised RH upbeat to bb.102 and 103 and then draw out a little through b.103, again **listening** to the syncopated treble emphases as the inner line descends chromatically, ready to 'round in' exultantly through b.104 towards the *forte* reprise from b.105. Note the upbeat emphasis to bb.107-9 (implied at bb.3-6 etc, and **indicated** here). Draw out once more towards the chord on the second beat of b.114, ready to move into the coda, one of Chopin's most rhapsodic and inspired.

bb.115–154   Move into b.115 quietly, with a sense of pressing on towards b.119. Listen acutely to the shifting resonances of the RH, propelled along and controlled by the **steadily** onward moving LH crotchets. Feel the impetus towards, and implied emphasis upon the dotted crotchet on the second beat of each of bb.115, 116, etc. taking care that each of these dotted crotchets sings out over the third beat (so that the melody line in b.115, for example, is clearly [musical example] *etc.* and **not** [musical example] *etc.* Play out b.119 in a radiant tone, 'holding' the dotted crotchet G sharp on the second beat for an extra instant, and then gradually diminish the sound as the RH line 'subsides' and the LH enters on the second beat of b.121, preparatory to introducing its melody line proper on the first beat of b.122. Again feel the impetus towards, and emphasis upon the dotted crotchets on the second beat of bb.123, 124, etc. as in the RH in bb.114, 115, etc., as you shape this LH line in a long curve up to b.127, punctuated by carefully shaped and expressive RH fragments. Play the LH line from b.127 (reaching its 'peak' on the dotted crotchet on the second beat) with all the ardour you can muster, followed by the RH in b.128. Maximise the splendour of the resonances of this passage (who can fail to think of Schumann here) feeling the emphasis on the second beat of b.129 and on the partly tied upbeat to b.131 (taking care to give this its full value). Draw out from b.132, **listening** to the movement of the inner and lower LH lines beneath the held dotted minim G naturals, taking time again to listen to the quiet held resonances through b.133 as you prepare to resolve to the tonic major on the first beat of b.134. Then, taking a tiny break and playing the RH tied C sharp with quiet emphasis, move on quietly and smoothly from the inner quaver upbeat to b.135. Feel a little 'hold', like a momentary crouch, on the emphasised third beat of b.138 as you poise yourself to 'start again' from b.139, hastening a little from b.143 as you *diminuendo* towards a sudden jolt on the *sforzato* third beat of b.146. Then allowing a tiny break, but not enough to lose the momentum, launch into b.147 with the air of moving towards a grand conclusion. Give a good 'kick-off' with a strong bass crotchet C sharp and then let the magisterial melody move in implacable rhythm, as if in ceremonial splendour over the carefully balanced and placed inner and LH crotchet chords. Feel the compelling grandeur of this march-like tread as you implement the implied emphasis upon the dotted crotchets on the second beat of each bar, and feel also that the LH octave is giving a strong 'upbeat' lead towards the first beat of bb.148, 149 etc. Feel an extra emphasis and slight 'hold' upon the tied minim D sharp on the second beat of b.150, feeling the sense in which this note leads you 'on and over' into the second phrase of this final passage. Invoke all the resonance you can without banging as you *crescendo* from b.151, drawing out a little towards the final chords.

(Many pianists make an entirely different but equally telling effect here, playing this final passage as if in a nostalgic, valedictory afterthought.)

Note: With Op.59 we finally leave behind the largest and the more complex of the Mazurkas. But there is still much of interest (particularly for technically less advanced players) among the remaining numbers of Ops 63, 67 and 68, as well as the outstanding 'single' Mazurka in A minor dedicated to Emile Gaillard.

Mazurka No. 39 in B major
Op. 63 No. 1 (8)

With its proudly chivalric bearing and rhythmic punch this number presents as 'typical' a Mazurka opening as one could hope to find.

bb.1–32   Set a measured **3/4** that allows the principal motif to 'leap' in, rather than to scurry, at a suggested ♩. = 48-52. Give a good kick-off with a resounding quaver *sforzato* chord, and then shape the RH line up towards the first beat of b.3 in a boldly rising curve. **Lift** the hands from the opening *sforzato* chord so that the RH 'falls' onto the quaver F sharp on the second beat (see General Introduction under 'Articulation') to shape the quavers in a vigorous overall slur up towards the quaver third on the first beat of b.2. Then **lift** the hand again so that it 'falls' onto the semiquaver, 'going to' the crotchet third on the second beat, to *crescendo* again towards a ringing spread subdominant chord on the first beat of b.3, again shaping this figure in an overall 3-beat slur. Support the RH with a purposeful LH from the second beat of b.2, shaping the three chords similarly in a 3-beat slurred curve as indicated, in contrary motion to the RH. Continue with similar rhythmic momentum from the second beat of b.3. The ornamentation in bb.5, 7, etc, is far from easy to enunciate clearly. It is always necessary to raise the hand slightly from the preceding quaver to allow a clear 'attack'

on the ornament, placed **on** the beat. Draw out a little as

you *crescendo* through b.8 ready to launch into b.9. In this varied restatement of bb.1-8 exploit the brass-like potential of the higher registration, 'pointing' the numerous differences in notation, articulation and nuance. In particular note the longer 6-beat slur from the second beat of b.9 through to the first beat of b.11. Feeling an implied emphasis on the tied treble minim on the second beat of b.16, 'draw back' a little, ready to 'point' the *subito piano* at the end of the bar,* and then play from b.17 in a smooth-running *legato* with a sense of moving on. Support the RH with even-moving LH chords, listening to the lower drone effect through bb.17-20. Feel the impetus towards and slight emphasis and *tenuto* effect upon the treble dotted crotchet on the second beat of bb.18, 20, etc. Listen to the chromatic inflections as you *diminuendo* through b.23, and then feel the quiet emphasis and *tenuto* on the tied treble minim E flat, giving the ear time to hear the enharmonic change to D sharp. Then place the LH bass E and chord quietly but clearly on the first and second beat of b.25 ready to shape the solo quavers with a certain freedom downwards to lead into the light-toned curving melodic fragment beginning from b.27. Let the RH quavers billow delicately up 'through' the high G sharp towards the first beat of b.29, and then unwinding through bb. 30 and 31, to ease through b.32 towards the A major section.

bb.33–52   This little melody has a kind of artful naivety. Play it in a simple style, feeling the light impetus towards and slight emphasis upon the treble minim on the second beat of each alternate bar. Give these minims their precise value, but at the same time feel the onward 'lean' of each towards the subsequent bar so that there is a continual sense of onward momentum, prompted by each 'dancing' *staccato* upbeat chord. Take care to place these inner *staccato* crotchets in such a way that the melody line in bb.33-4, for example,

sounds clearly *etc.* and **not** *etc.*

Make a *subito forte* at b.40, and move on, implementing the strong emphasis on each upbeat chord. Then allow a tiny break to clear the sound at the end of b.42, ready to revert to the *piano* movement at b.43. Feel from here that you are moving in continuing 'arcs' up towards and down from each 1-bar fragment (rather than jumping from one 'box' to another) while at the same time feeling the different instrumentation of the lower and higher register.

bb.52–102   Allow a little break again at the end of b.52 to clear the sound, and then play from b.53 in a hushed *piano*, almost furtively, as if looking over the shoulder as you play the minim chord on the second beat of bb.53 and 54, and then moving on through b.55 towards the second beat of b.56. Feel that the lower LH is 'leading' through this passage beneath the quiet RH chords and within the pervading quiet sound of the inner drone. Take care in bb.59 and 63 that the cross-rhythm effect of the treble triplet figure does not disrupt the even curve of the lower LH quavers. *Diminuendo* gradually to a whisper at bb.65-6 and then let the LH solo quavers 'round in' confidently through bb.67-8 towards the reprise. As the reprise 'branches off' into the coda from b.83 (compare with b.15) feel that you are pressing on with increasing intensity towards b.87, and on again towards the first beat of b.89. Deliver a powerful bass octave here, holding this sound with the pedal as indicated, and then feel a sense

*(placed at the beginning of b.17 in many editions)

of gradual unwinding from this point, as you progressively diminish the sound and the rhythmic tension (though without allowing the tempo to flag). Point the doubled inner RH minims on each second beat from b.87, and also the descending line of the doubled inner crotchets from b.91 as the treble quavers curve easily over the sustained LH chord (also showing the gradual descent of the **inner** LH voice from b.92. 'Ease' into b.95, and then play the *pianissimo* treble like a far distant, or half-remembered echo over the quiet lower drone, feeling the quiet emphasis on the tied inner and lower upbeat to bb.96-9. *Diminuendo* to a whisper at bb.99-101, and end with ringing *subito forte* chords smack in time.

Mazurka No. 40 in F minor
Op. 63 No. 2 (6) (O)

The melody of this piece makes no bones about its heavily laden spirit, entering as it does with a downward fall from a sorrowful minor dominant 9th. Technically and rhythmically simple, short and poignantly expressive, it is an excellent piece for more mature novice players. Although those with small hands can, of course, spread the LH chords in bb.19, 33-6, etc. some of the RH 2-voiced patterns between bb.23 and 36 are awkward for a young hand.

bb.1–16   Comparing this piece with the *lento* of Op. 24 No. 1 at ♩= 108, we might set a similar tempo here, or perhaps with just a little more movement at around ♩= 112-116 (see General Introduction under 'Tempo'). This is a piece that suggests a certain amount of give and take – and if you prefer a rather slower tempo than this, as some players do, take care that you do not let the music wilt to a standstill, and in particular that you **regain** the tempo after the occasional expressive 'give'. With your intended pulse well 'in the system', move off from a quite resonant bass dominant crotchet, and 'bring in' the RH melody with a telling minim D flat, which will arrest the attention with its poignant quality – giving this note sufficient tone to last through its full duration, and still leave room for the line to fall expressively through to b.3 without disappearing. Be sure that you place the LH chord rhythmically on the third beat of b.1 and the first beat of b.2 so that you immediately establish your rhythmic movement beneath the held melody note. This is an excellent instance of the value of **singing** the phrase. If you play the LH in a steady rhythm and **sing** the melody, you will soon see how, as you 'fall' from the opening D flat, there is an onward impulse as the phrase turns upwards, towards the dotted crotchet C on the second beat of b.3, and then on again towards the tied minim F on the second beat of b.4. Feel the vocal 'lift' up to and implied emphasis on this dotted crotchet C and similarly as you swell up to the F. Then feel a sense of slightly pressing on to another eloquent emphasis on the repeated tied minim on the second beat of b.5, then letting the line fall again from this note, 'curling' down through b.7 towards the minim on the second beat of b.8. Show the curve of this overall 8-bar phrase, with the tied F in b.4 giving the sense of an 'on and over lean' from the first half of the phrase to the second. Support the RH with a continually rhythmic LH, taking particular care with the placing of the chord on the second beat of those bars (bb.6, 13, 14 etc.) when there is a rest on the third beat (see the Introduction to the Mazurkas). Chopin's fingering at bb.7-8 is a notable example of his predilection for using the same finger on successive notes as a means of enhancing the

eloquence of a melodic line ![musical notation] (see General Introduction

under 'Fingering'). As you finish the RH phrase on the minim on the second beat of b.8, listen to the LH sixth on the third beat giving an upbeat onward lead into b.9 as you prepare to lead into the varied restatement with an eloquent slurred upward 'scoop' from the RH acciaccatura to the D flat. Listen acutely to the subtle chromatic curls of the RH through bb.13-15 towards the second beat of b.16.

bb.16–56 As the RH 'resolves' on to the tonic on the second beat of b.16, prepare to lead on clearly with the LH upbeat chord to b.17. Move on a little here as you shape the RH melody in broad overall curves. Lead off with a full toned RH minim E flat, feeling the impetus towards the third beat of b.18, feeling the 'lift' towards this emphasised octave, and at the same time its onward upbeat 'lean' towards the subsequent 2-bar phrase, and similarly through bb.19-20. Support the RH with evenly placed LH chords on the second and third beats of these bars. Take care that the minim **sings** over the second beat of bb.17, 19, etc. (so that in b.17 for example the melody line is

clearly [musical notation] *etc.* and **not** [musical notation] *etc.*

Allow a little extra time to point the imitative lower LH detail in b.22, and to place the partly tied RH sixth with an implied emphasis on the upbeat to b.23. Then 'lean' a little on the treble minim on the first beat of bb.23 and 24. This reiterated treble falling fourth through bb.23 and 24 is like a horn call over the quiet inner line and LH drone fifths. Then, as you move on into b.25 (the elaborated restatement of bb.17-24), 'point' all the little variants: the inner LH fragment through b.25, the tied inner RH upbeat to b.26, and the different harmonisation in b.30, etc. Be sure to **lift** the RH after the sixth on the second beat of b.28 so that it 'falls' naturally onto the semiquaver octave, feeling this as the 'upbeat' to the third beat, and drawing out fractionally as you *crescendo* towards the third beat. (See General Introduction under 'Articulation'.) Poise yourself for an instant on this full-toned third beat as you prepare to 'start again' in b.29. From b.33 a linking passage leads back towards the reprise, in which Chopin develops the 4-quaver figure from bb.24 and 32 sequentially. You could either play each 1-bar phrase with increasing momentum, poising yourself on the emphasised upbeat to b.37 ready to lead in a broad *crescendo* back to the beginning of the reprise at b.41, or you could make a *diminuendo* and slight *rallentando* through these four bars, and then 'take over' with a strong onward melodic lead from b.37. In either case let the treble fragment sing out through each of bb.33-6 over the inner RH figures. It is not easy for relatively inexperienced players to articulate the upper repeated note dotted rhythm figure in bb.34 and 36 without disrupting

these inner quavers. Practise at first [musical notation]

Then when you add the semiquaver keep it relatively light, thinking of it as the 'upbeat' to the crotchet on the second beat (see General Introduction under 'Dotted Rhythm'). Shape the melody line from b.37 in a broad, grand tone supported by increasingly resonant LH and

inner chords, giving these pairs of chords an **equal** emphasis [musical notation] not [musical notation]

Then feel a strong onward 'push' on the upbeat chord to b.41, ready to launch with a grand sweep into the reprise. Having reached b.41 in *crescendo* you could play the first half of the reprise in a more resolute tone than the opening, perhaps dropping the tone from b.49 and then making a little *rallentando* through b.55, approaching the final chord on the second beat of the last bar with quiet resignation.

Mazurka No. 41 in C sharp minor
Op. 63 No. 3 (7)

This is one of the most charming of all the Mazurkas, with a ravishing canonic passage in the Coda. In this late piece, as Arthur Hedley says, 'the music is stripped of every superfluity. All the composer's feeling is concentrated into a page or two of deceptively simple-looking music' (Walker, p.8).

bb.1–16 Set an easy-moving tempo at around $\downarrow$ = 126 – the movement of the principal section here is one of the most waltz-like among the Mazurkas. Have your pulse well 'in the system' before you start so that as you lead in smoothly with the upbeat quavers, you immediately establish the steady dance-like rhythmic movement. Then **lift** the RH a little from the crotchet G sharp so that it 'falls' with an implied slight natural emphasis on the dotted crotchet on the second beat. It is as if the first fragment forms a little introduction with the melody proper starting on the second beat. Note this effect carefully, for this slightly emphasised 'entry' on the second beat of bb.3 and 5 etc. is essential to the rhythmic motivation of the melody line. Then through the longer phrase from the second beat of b.5 the melody is still characterised by the movement towards the dotted crotchet or crotchet on the second beat of each bar. 'Meet' the RH with a neat LH crotchet C sharp on the first beat of b.1, and then support the melody with a lightly 'dancing' LH beneath the gracefully shaped RH fragments (see the Introduction to the Mazurkas). Feel that the RH is 'taking a breath' after the second beat of b.2, entering in a slightly stronger dynamic on the second beat of b.3, and again on the second beat of b.5, helped by a little extra 'pointing' of the LH crotchet on the first beat of these bars. Feel the gentle onward impulse up to this point taking a little extra time to place the low LH E on the first beat of b.5, as you prepare to open out the tone expressively through bb.5-6. Then feel the sense of slightly unwinding as the line descends, easing a little through the end of b.8 ready to 'start again' at b.9. When you have studied all these little refinements and emphases, endeavour to phrase 'over the rests' as a singer would, so that you create a feeling of an overall phrase-curve up towards the little peak at bb.5-6 and down again through bb.7-8, rather than a series of stops and starts. Feel the 'lift' up to the high B on the second beat of b.13, and play this high line with increased expressiveness.

bb.17–32 Introducing the new motif at b.17, feel the implied 'lean' on the first beat of b.17 in contrast to the prevalent second beat emphasis through the previous melody. Most editions begin a new phrase on the first beat of b.17 as opposed to Henle's 'on and over' effect to the first beat of b.18. Take particular care with the placing of the LH chord on the second beat of those bars which have a rest on the third beat (bb.16-18, 20-21, etc. See again the Introduction to the Mazurkas.) Feel a slight sense of moving on from the second beat of b.18, 'pointing' the repeated note figure neatly through b.19 and then ease slightly as you 'turn the corner' through the high quaver at the end of b.20 ready to 'lean' again on the first beat of b.21. Play the *subito forte* phrase from bb.23-4 with a touch of bravado, taking time to **listen** to the wide-curving intervals of the RH quavers, and to the LH detail through b.24 before moving on from b.25, after allowing an extra instant to spread the LH chord graciously on the second beat. Expanding the rising RH quavers slightly through b.28, move on a little as you 'curl' the RH quavers down from the second beat of b.29.

bb.32–49 Hold the second beat of b.32 for an extra instant as you prepare to lead into the next section (in D flat)* from the LH upbeat quavers. Play from here in a smooth hushed *sotto voce* almost like the *Religioso* passage in the Nocturne in G minor,

---

*The key-signature of four flats, apparently given in the first German edition, is retained in Henle.

194

Op.15 No.3, but maintaining the underlying sense of the dance movement. Phrase bb.33-41 in a long overall line, **listening** to all held and tied resonances, and to the quiet drone effect of the intermittent inner pedal point A flat. Take an extra instant to curve, with a light 'lift' rather than a lurch, up to and down from the semiquaver D flat in b.39. Then increase the momentum from b.41 as the D flat motif is notched up a fourth, to the key of G flat, over a lower D flat pedal point. Press on as you *crescendo* resolutely from b.46, and then draw out through the first beat of b.48 towards an expressive 'lean' on the *tenuto* dominant seventh harmony on the second beat of b.48, ready to ease into the varied reprise from the second beat of b.49.

bb.49–76 'Point' the expressive detail of the quaver upbeat figure to bb.51, 53, etc. Then expand from b.60 (**listening** to and 'using' the resonance of the descending bass-line) towards the high RH C sharp on the third beat of b.62, holding the harmony within the pedal from the previous upbeat as indicated. Listen to this sound through the pause, and then 'gather up' the tempo neatly through bb.63-4, ready to lead on from b.65 in a softly musing ethereal *piano*. Take time to listen to the imitative inner fragment in b.66, and then, 'bringing in' the inner RH line quietly but clearly on the second beat of b.67 (spreading the ninth as indicated), shape the lines smoothly and expressively in canon over a rhythmic but flexible LH. Do not adopt what appears to be the easy way out by taking these notes of the inner RH line with the **LH** when they 'cross' with the inner LH notes (e.g. on the second beat of b.69 and the second and third beats of b.70). Great composers know exactly what they are doing (Chopin above all) when they cause convolutions of this sort – he **wants** the sense of 'time taken' to span the wide spread interval on the second beat of b.69, and to show the 'distance apart' of the upper D sharp and the inner detail in b.70. To play this canonic passage beautifully is, however, far from easy, and entails careful practice and **listening,** even from the most experienced player. Take extra time then to span the still wider interval on the second beat of b.71, and then drawn out expansively and improvisationally from b.72 towards the high C sharp in b.74. Pedal as indicated but then re-pedal on the third beat of b.73 so that you can hold the sound of the bass octave A natural through b.74 to include the high C sharp as you take time to 'disperse' the sound upwards. Then taking a breath through the pause, throw off the final fragment in a vigorous *subito forte,* ending with two masculine 'stamps' on the first and second beats of the final bar.

Note: Ops 67 and 68 contain Mazurkas from various periods of Chopin's life, collected and edited by his friend Fontana (who appointed himself as a posthumous amanuensis) and published five years after the composer's death. It is presumed that the metronome marks are Fontana's.

Mazurka No. 42 in G major
Op. Posth. 67 No. 1 (8)

Written around 1835 this piece has the extrovert exuberance of some of the early numbers. A player lacking an inborn rhythmic sense will make nothing of it, for this is one of the most overtly dance-like of all the Mazurkas – Weinstock suggests that it is a 'pure *pièce d'occasion*' (p.294). Perhaps so – but performed by a master of rhythm it can make the listener want to leap up and join in.

bb.1–13 Set a tempo not more than a few notches below the $\downarrow$ = 160 – it is no good attempting this piece unless it can 'spring' – at much below about $\downarrow$ = 144 it will begin to plod. Establish your basic rhythm securely through the four introductory bars, articulating the RH thirds with all possible verve over the steady LH drone fifths. Mark the strong emphasis on each third beat with a suggestion of a very slight 'hold', or 'touch of the brakes' on these chords while at the same time feeling the sense in which they give an upbeat push, like an anticipatory 'crouch', to the rhythm. Be sure to **lift** the RH from the quaver third on the first beat of bb.2-4 so that it 'falls' naturally onto the ornamented semiquaver, feeling this semiquaver as the 'upbeat' to the second beat of the bar (see General Introduction under 'Articulation').

Play the ornament with a quick 'twirl' thus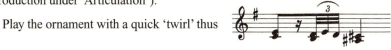

Crescendo through bb.3-4 allowing an extra strong 'pounce' on the third beat of b.4, ready to give a good kick-off with a vigorous crack on the accented crotchets on the first beat of b.5. Collect yourself instantly as you leap up with the LH to drop the tone, and then articulate the RH quaver thirds in a cracklingly clear *piano*, feeling the onward impulse as you *crescendo* towards the *sforzato* chord on the third beat of b.6. Spring off the chord on the **second** beat of b.6 so that you can land on this third beat, again with the sense of a pounce, even more pronounced this time, imagining that this chord is vigorously slurred down towards another 'kick-off' on the unison D's on the first beat of b.7. Then shape the swell towards and back from the first and second beats of b.8, with an implied slight *tenuto* through the dotted crotchet third as you poise yourself to kick off again from the first beat of b.9; and so on. Allow an extra 'hold' on the spread chord on the third beat of b.10, and poise yourself through the second and third beats of b.12 to lead on into b.13 in a broad-toned *forte*. (Whether the grace notes are placed on or before the beat in bb.5, 6, etc. may be a matter of expediency – these figures are in any event difficult for a relatively inexperienced player. In b.5 they could perhaps **anticipate** the beat, and then be played **on** the first beat of b.6. **Lift** the RH slightly at the end of b.5 to facilitate a clean attack on the ornament.)

bb.13–66

Ensure that the dotted crotchet A sings over the second beat of b.13 (so that the melody line is clearly [music] *etc.* and **not**

[music] *etc.* and support the RH with a resonant bass note and

a strong fifth on the second beat. Make it clear that the third beat of bb.14, 18, etc. is the upbeat to the next 2-bar phrase rather than the 'end' of the previous one. 'Lift' cleanly to the high quaver B on the first beat of b.16, and skip airily down the scale here, and at b.20, etc, being sure to **lift** the hand from each quaver, and then feeling each slurred semiquaver as the 'upbeat' to each quaver (see again General Introduction under 'Articulation'). Lead straight on into b.29, into a powerful *subito forte*, holding the unison G's in the pedal as indicated and leaping athletically upwards to make a great 'stamp' on the *sforzato* minor chord on the second beat. After each of these *fortissimo* bursts (bb.29, 33, etc.) allow an instant to clear the sound and then, dropping the tone instantly, 'point' the changes of detail through the intervening bars: the waggish *scherzando* from bb.30-2, the glidingly smooth *pianissimo* through bb.34-6, and through bb.38-40 the more jagged *marcato* with the **different** articulation. Through each of these 3-bar episodes support the RH with a 'dancing' LH, imagining the movement of dancers making a little jump or 'pounce' on each of the emphasised upbeat chords. Then draw out as indicated through b.44 ready to launch into the reprise. End with a huge 'stamp' on the second beat of the final bar at extreme ends of the keyboard.

Mazurka No. 43 in G minor
Op. Posth. 67 No. 2 (6)

See note before Op. Posth. 67. No. 1

Written in 1848-9, this is one of the simplest of the Mazurkas. With its clear-cut sections, clean texture and straightforward rhythm, it is another excellent piece for novice players.

bb.1–16   The metronome mark indicates a fairly spirited tempo, but it seldom seems to be played as fast as this. (See note before Op. 67 No. 1.) Nevertheless we should not play it too wiltingly, so set a tempo which 'moves' sufficiently to convey the dance-rhythm, but which also allows the *cantabile* melody to curve expressively. Less experienced players could try a tempo of about ♩= 116-26 – see however General Introduction, under 'Tempo'. With the pulse well 'in the system', lead in with a smoothly slurred crotchet upbeat. Be sure to give this note its full value while at the same time feeling its onward upward 'lean' (imagining a *portamento*-like upward slur. See the Introduction to the Mazurkas.). Feel that the LH is 'meeting' the RH with a quiet but definite bass note on the first beat of b.1, and then place the chords quietly and rhythmically beneath the RH crotchets on the second and third beats of b.1 so that you immediately establish the dance rhythm (see again the Introduction to Mazurkas). Play the RH in a clear lightly singing tone, feeling the impetus towards the dotted crotchet on the first beat of b.2, and then on and upwards towards the first beat of b.4 (feeling the three quavers in b.2 as an overall upbeat group, expanding a little as you rise into b.3). Feel the rest on the second beat of b.4 as if taking a breath, before leading on with the upbeat repeated quavers, to curve down through b.5 towards the second beat of b.6. Make a tiny break here, and then 'plant' the *sforzato* chord on the third beat, making a fractional 'hold' while also feeling the onward upbeat 'lean' of this partly tied chord, so that you 'move on' into b.7, and similarly into b.8. Poising yourself on the upbeat to b.9 you could then either drop the tone to revert to the opening *piano*, or carry on from b.9 in a fuller tone. In either event 'expand' the RH quavers through b.14, and curve expressively downwards to end the section quietly on the second beat of b.16. (Take a little extra time in b.14 to 'lift' up, rather than lurching, to the high quaver B flat as a singer would, supporting the RH with a carefully placed LH chord on the third beat.)

bb.16–56   Be sure to 'finish off' the LH quietly but rhythmically in b.16, and then leap into b.17 with a vigorous RH *sforzato* acciaccatura and dotted minim, 'moving on' the tempo a little with springingly rhythmic LH chords. Take care to keep a steady *1 2 3* through b.18, making a little 'lean' on the first triplet quaver in both hands as indicated by the 'hairpin', and then 'spacing' out the second and third crotchet beats ready to make another *sforzato* effect on the first beat of b.19.* Allow a tiny break after the chord on the second beat of b.20, so that you feel the RH quavers on the third beat of b.20 as the upbeat to b.21; and then, dropping the tone to a hushed *pianissimo* at b.21, descend through the chain of sevenths with gliding smoothness (but without letting the rhythm flag), ready to leap athletically into b.25 with another big *sforzato*. Expand a little through b.31, listening to the inflections of the LH, then space out the *staccato* crotchets through b.32 with a little 'pinging' sound, held within the pedal as indicated. Begin the RH solo passage in an eloquent *sotto voce*, feeling a little vocal

*Lean the acciaccatura confidently ON the first beat of bb.17 and 19 thus:

and similarly at bb.25 and 27.

'lift' up to the A on the third beat of bb.33 and 35. Then curve up more strongly to the C on the third beat of b.37, and 'open out' the tone, with a feeling of pressing on towards the reprise, leading off this time in a fuller tone. At b.54 make a more pronounced 'vocal' curve up to the high B flat, lingering a little on this note and then drawing out just a little towards the final chord.

Mazurka No. 44 in C major
Op. Posth. 67 No. 3 (6)

See note before Op. Posth. 67. No. 1

This is another good piece for less experienced players. Here, the tempo and indeed the mood are similar to that of the previous piece (although this was written much earlier, in 1835), and we need to be equally careful not to let it wilt. (See this preceding number for comments on tempo.)

bb.1–32   Lead in from a warmly slurred crotchet upbeat towards a little emphasising 'lean' on the dotted crotchet on the first beat of b.1. Then, feeling the three quavers as an upbeat group to b.2, shape the melody in gentle curves towards another 'lean' on the first beat of b.3. The first four bars move over a tonic pedal point. Support the RH therefore with quietly resonant lower dotted minims on the first beat of bb.1-4, and quiet, rhythmically placed inner chords on the second and third beats (see the Introduction to the Mazurkas). Take particular care to place the LH rhythmically through b.1 so that you establish the rhythmic, quietly dancing movement securely. Be sure to **lift** the RH from the quaver on the first beat of b.4 so that it 'falls' naturally onto the slurred semiquaver, feeling this semiquaver as the 'upbeat' to the crotchet D on the second beat (see General Introduction under 'Articulation'). In b.5 place the LH chord with a little extra definition on the second beat, thus 'pointing' the fact that there is a rest on the third beat, as the RH upbeat quavers lead on into b.6. In b.6 articulate the RH as in b.4, but letting the semiquaver 'go to' a definite melodic emphasis on the tied minim E, and then 'expand' a little as the quaver line rises through b.7 towards another 'lean' on the minim A on the first beat of b.8. Feel the overall continuity of the melodic span through the first eight bars, with an 'on and over lean' through the tied minim E on the second beat of b.6, 'sending on' the line towards this little peak on the first beat of b.8. Make a little 'hold' on this slurred A before finishing off the phrase gracefully, bringing up the LH sixths to meet the RH on the third beat. Then make a tiny break before moving on into the restatement in full-throated sixths. Rise to make another 'on and over lean', as if with a sudden surge of spirit on an emphatic tied sixth on the second beat of b.14, expanding the tone to a full resonance as you draw out a little through b.15 with the hint of a vocal 'hold' as you **lift** from the sixth on the third beat. Then follow the phrase through with the sense of coming to a momentary 'stop' on the second beat of b.16, and then allow an extra instant to clear the sound before leading on into the restatement in a poised *piano* with the

upbeat to b.17. In b.4 and again in bb.10, 12, etc. interpret the ornament thus:

or (see General Introduction under 'Ornamentation').

bb.32–56   End with a similar 'stop' on the second beat of b.32, taking care to give the minim chord its full value, and then allowing a tiny break as you prepare to strike off into b.33 with echoingly resonant unison D's. **Hold** these D's resolutely, again taking care to allow them their full value, and then play the upper and inner lines in a muted *pianissimo*, making a tiny swell towards, and a little 'push' upon the accented chord on the third beat of b.34. Make a tiny 'hold' on this chord, while at the same time feeling its upbeat 'lean' towards the next unison *sforzatos* (note original – though possibly Fontana's – fingering in bb.34 and 36).

(Small hands will have to let go of the held RH D on the third beat of b.34.) Draw out through b.40, **listening** to the inner RH F natural, which, as the dominant seventh of C, draws us back towards the reprise. Feel the acciaccatura as a leisurely 'upbeat within the upbeat' to b.41.

Mazurka No. 45 in A minor
Op. Posth. 67 No. 4 (6)

See note before Op. Posth. 67. No. 1

With rather more substance than the two preceding numbers, this is again an excellent piece at Grade 6 or so. It was written towards the end of Chopin's life in 1846, or according to some authorities, 1848. The Paderewski Edition gives three versions. The first corresponds in essentials to that given in Henle and most other editions (i.e. the Fontana version – see note above before commentaries on this Op. 67 set). (Paderewski's second and third versions are based on Edouard Ganche's Oxford Edition, and an autograph belonging to Brahms.)
Note: For those using the Paderewski Edition there will be a discrepancy in bar-numbering from b.33, since in this edition both first **and** second-time bars are counted (i.e. for b.33 read b.34 and so on – see General Introduction under 'Bar Numberings').
   Those with small hands can leave out the upper LH note through bb.1-3 etc. and then take this upper note with the RH through bb.4 and 5, and elsewhere where practicable.

bb.1–16   The rhythmic impulse here is stronger and more overtly dance-like than that of the two preceding numbers. Since the pulse seems to want to move a little faster, and the construction is more compact, with a more direct continuity between the sections, there is less danger of wilting: a tempo of approx ♩ = 138-44 is suggested (i.e. near to the **given** metronome mark of Op. 67 Nos. 2 and 3 – see note above again). With the pulse well 'in the system', lead in with a full-toned tied crotchet upbeat. Be sure to give the note its full value, or even more, while at the same time feeling its strong onward 'lean' (see the Introduction to the Mazurkas). Then take care to place the bass crotchet clearly on the first beat of b.1 beneath this tied note, and then to place the LH rhythmically on the second and third beats in such a way that your dancing rhythmic impulse is immediately established. Play the melody in a purposeful manner, feeling the impetus of the first 2-bar phrase towards another 'lean' on the dotted crotchet on the first beat of b.3, and so on, towards b.5. Arrive with a more emphatic 'lean' on the first beat of b.5, 'followed up' by a purposeful LH chord on the second beat, and then play the solo quavers with some freedom but at the same time with a strong onward 'pull' towards b.7, and on through towards the end of the overall 8-bar phrase on the first beat of b.8. Take care to place the LH crotchet sixth clearly on the second beat here as the RH takes a 'breath' ready to lead off again from a strong RH upbeat to b.9. Support the RH with a rhythmic and dance-like LH through this first section (see the Introduction to the Mazurkas). Take particular care to 'enter' precisely with the chords on the second beat of bb.2, 4, etc. when there is a crotchet rest on the first beat, and to place the LH chords firmly on the second beat of bb.5 and 8 where there is a rest on the **third** beat. At b.7 feel that the LH is 'joining in' again to propel the phrase towards its end at b.8. From b.14 show the more impetuous 'run-on' of the quavers towards b.16.

bb.16–80   At b.16 allow a tiny 'hold' on the upbeat to b.17 as you prepare to drop the tone on the first beat of b.17. Play this section in a light *dolce* tone with a more yielding melody line, although without letting the overall rhythmic impulse flag. **Lift** the RH after the crotchet on the second beat of b.18, and then feel the onward 'lean' and the *portamento*-like slur of the upbeat crotchet down to the first beat of b.19. Make a light *crescendo* up to the end of b.20, feeling a slight vocal 'hold' on the high A's, on the upbeat to, and on the first beat of b.21; then 'unwind' through bb.22-4 ready to start again from b.25. Rise to a more drawn out 'hold' on the high tied upbeat to b.29, and then feel a sense of moving on as the quavers 'uncurl' down towards b.32. 'Point' the LH chord on the upbeat to b.33 (second-time bar) ready to ease into the major on the first beat of b.33. Play this section in a smooth-toned, perhaps more thoughtful manner, with the 'thought' growing momentarily more ardent from b.37, but easing again through b.40, ready to 'start again' from b.41. 'Point' the quietly descending inner crotchets through bb.41-3, taking an extra instant to spread the RH ninth on the third beat of b.42. But take care that these inner crotchets are carefully balanced so that the melody line through b.41 is clearly [musical notation] *etc.* and **not**

[musical notation] *etc.* also that the expressive treble variant through b.42 is not sabotaged by a heavy thumb on the inner F sharps. Then, letting the RH quavers 'run on' a little through bb.44-5, tail away the sound gracefully through b.46 up to the high semiquaver on the third beat, letting the overall harmony 'hang' within the pedal as you pause, as if in mid-air. Then 'gather up' the rhythm again quietly through bb.47-8 ready either to return to b.33 or to lead on into the reprise. Conclude without an exaggerated *rallentando*, but allowing just a little 'give' as you end the 'thought' neatly on the second beat of the final bar.

Mazurka No. 46 in C major
Op. Posth. 68 No. 1 (8)

See note before Op. Posth. 67. No. 1

Of this piece written in 1829-30 Weinstock says 'if it is really by Chopin – and I should prefer to learn that it is not – this is conceivably the poorest piece of music legitimately to bear his name' (p.295). And this time most of us will agree – all is clatter and glitter, but without the joyous 'spring' of, for example, Op.67 No.1 in G.

Note: For those using the Paderewski Edition there will be a discrepancy in bar-numbering from b.33, since in this edition both first **and** second-time bars are counted (i.e. for b.33 read b.34 and so on – see General Introduction under 'Bar Numberings').

bb.1–20   Set a lively pulse as near as possible to the ♩ = 168, and play bb.1-4 with all possible rhythmic verve. Rap out the chords with gun-shot 'cracks' feeling the 'push' towards the *sforzato* crotchets on each third beat. Make a slight 'hold' on these chords while at the same time feeling their onward upbeat 'lean'. Finish the phrase with a sharp 'rap' on the second beat of b.4, and then make a tiny break to clear the sound. Drop the tone as you lead into b.5 from the upbeat quavers and play from here in a more pliant, perhaps consciously naive manner. Support the cleanly articulated RH with a 'dancing' LH (see the Introduction to the Mazurkas) and place the wide chord (spread if necessary) with a little extra emphasis on the second beat of b.6, as if to point the fact that there is a rest on the third beat. Mark the emphasis and implied slight 'hold' on the second beat of bb.5, 7-9, etc. and allow a little 'give' through the end of b.8 as you prepare to 'start again' from b.9. Then allow a little extra time for the RH quavers to make the curve up to and down from the high quaver C at the end of b.10. End the phrase with a clear chord on the second beat of b.12 (letting the inner quaver G coincide with the **third** quaver of the triplet through the first beat), again making a tiny break as you poise yourself to 'start again' from the upbeat to b.13.

bb.20–72   Poise yourself on the second beat of b.20 as you prepare to launch into b.21 with all the gusto you can muster. Take an extra instant after the second beat of bb.21-3 ready to place the *sforzato* chord on each third beat with a great, leaping 'stamp', and then, collecting yourself after the second beat of b.24, drop the tone again with a fractional 'hold' on the upbeat to b.25. Make a clear break after the second beat of b.32 (second-time bar) before leading on with a clear slurred quaver upbeat to b.33. Be sure to **lift** the hand from the high quaver on the first beat of b.33 so that it 'falls' with a natural implied emphasis on the dotted crotchet sixth on the second beat (see General Introduction under 'Articulation'), and again play this section more pliantly, perhaps in a lightly 'tinkling' manner. Feel the continual impulse towards and implied emphasis upon the second beat of bb.34-8, making a little break after the second beat of b.36, ready to lead off again with the slurred upbeat to b.37. Then feel the sense of moving on through b.39, with a slight 'drawing back' through the end of b.40, ready to 'start again' from b.41. Make a pronounced and emphatic 'hold', as if with a 'pounce', on the treble dotted crotchet and chord on the second beat of b.46. Then *crescendo* recklessly through b.47 towards another huge 'stamp' on the *sforzato* chord on the second beat of b.48, collecting yourself to take a quick 'breath' through the rest before setting off into the reprise.

Mazurka No. 47 in A minor
Op. 68 Posth. No. 2 (6)

See note before Op. Posth. 67. No. 1

Written as early as 1828, well before Chopin left Warsaw for good to settle in Paris, this is one of the most charming of the Mazurkas, with its finely balanced rhythmic emphases and predominating Lydian implication (the persistently sharpened fourth in bb.1, 5, 17, 18 etc.). *Note:* For those using the Paderewski Edition there will be a discrepancy in bar-numberings from b.29, since in this edition both first **and** second-time bars are counted (i.e. for b.29 read b.30 and so on – see General Introduction under 'Bar Numberings').

bb.1–16   The rhythm here, at the given ♩ = 116 has an entrancing poise, as if the dancers are moving in a subtle state of suspension, scarcely touching the ground. Hardly any faster and it will begin to scurry – very little slower and the feet will be firmly earthbound. In this instance, above all **dance** it! (See the Introduction to the Mazurkas.) In addition to its special charm, this is an excellent little study in dotted rhythms, which are often such a problem for novice players. The essential is always to feel each semiquaver as the **upbeat** to the subsequent **main** beat, rather than as the tail-end to its own beat (see General Introduction under 'Dotted Rhythms'). With your gentle dancing movement well 'in the system', **count** and **feel** the first two beats so that you enter with a perfectly poised upbeat group, making an overall slurred effect up towards the dotted quaver on the first beat of b.1. Have the LH ready to enter with a quietly resonant bass A, using the LH to launch the gentle rhythmic pulse with a secure *1 2 3* through b.1 beneath the whimsical melody of the RH. There is a slight emphasis (stated or implied) on the third beat of each bar. Be sure to give these third beats their full value, and at the same time feel the sense in which they give an onward upbeat 'lean' (see the Introduction to the Mazurkas, and also General Introduction under 'Upbeats'). To establish this continuing very slight but essential rhythmic nuance, 'point' the indicated emphasis particularly in the first bar of each 4-bar phrase (i.e. on the upbeat to bb.2, 6, 10, etc.). Give each RH upbeat trill seven notes (or five if this is too difficult) with a tiny emphasis on the first note (to 'point' the D sharp in b.1, etc.):

Be sure to **lift** the RH from each *staccato* quaver through b.4 (so that it falls onto each slurred semiquaver with a feeling of 'going to' the subsequent *staccato* quaver with an overall 'skipping' effect), as you make a little *crescendo* through b.4 towards another 'lift' from the *staccato* quaver on the first beat of b.5 (see General Introduction under 'Articulation'). Support the RH with a light, very rhythmic and gently dance-like LH, conscious of the light tonic and dominant drone effect persisting through the whole of the first section. 'Flick' the *acciaccatura* neatly up to the crotchet of the first beat of b.8 with a light, insouciant slurred 'lift'. Then take care to place the LH sixth neatly on the second beat as the RH 'takes a breath' ready to lead on with the upbeat group to b.9.

bb.16–64   Make a little break on the second beat of b.16 ready to lead on, perhaps with a sense of slightly 'moving on', and in a rather brighter tone into C major at b.17. Place the grace note ornament **on** the beat on the first

beat of b.20      and feel as if you are 'braking' slightly on this beat

ready to make a little *ritenuto*, 'pointing' the slurred LH chords on the second and third beats, as you poise yourself to return to A minor at b.21. Take a 'breath' again in the RH at b.28, ready to lead into the return to b.17 or on into A major at b.29. Move on noticeably but not exaggeratedly here, and articulate the RH chords in a bright, fuller horn-like tone over the lower 'drones'. Point the implied slight 'lean' on the slurred third on the second beat of bb.29 and 30 as you *crescendo* towards b.31, and then play out the treble and inner LH thirds in a ringing tone through b.31, 'going to' a strong implied 'leaning' emphasis on the second beat. Be sure to **feel** the held third beat here so that you give this dotted crotchet its full value, and then also poise yourself on the upbeat quaver third so that you do not 'fall into' b.32, and also to allow an instant to clear the sound for the *pianissimo* echo in b.32. The grace note ornament is best placed **on** the first beat of b.32.

These fragments (bb.31 and 32) could either sound martial (immediate, then distant), or yearning, as the player may feel them. In any event, linger a little again on the second beat of the 'echo', and on the upbeat to b.33 ready to resume the forward movement in b.33. Place the

acciaccatura sixth again on the beat in b.35 — this not

only sounds more convincing, it is also much easier to synchronise with the inner LH semiquaver and minim. Draw out the echo a little through b.36, lingering momentarily on the second beat, and then move on from b.37 with gliding smoothness. 'Point' the inner LH and RH detail through bb.39, 41 and 43, drawing out gradually from b.42, ready to resume Tempo 1 quietly from b.45. End without an exaggerated *rallentando* – but with just a little 'give' through the penultimate bar.

Mazurka No. 48 in F major
Op. Posth. 68 No. 3 (4-5)

See note before Op. Posth. 67. No. 1

The most interesting part of this rather plain number written in 1829-30 is the short section in B flat, one of the rare instances in which Chopin apparently makes use of a genuine folk-tune (Jim Samson (p.113) cites another in Op.24 No.4). This is not a particularly appealing piece for young players, though unfortunately by virtue of its relative simplicity it turns up rather too often in albums and examination syllabuses.

bb.1–16   Set a brisk tempo at around the ♩ = 132, and play out the chords of each 2-bar phrase in a bright-toned and confident *forte*. Have the pulse well 'in the system' before you start so that your clear rhythm is immediately established. Feel a decisive *1 2 3* through each bar, making sure that you **feel** the held third beat of bb.2, 4, etc. just as securely as if it was being **played.** At the same time feel a strong onward 'lean' through these held third beats so that there is a sense of onward movement from each 2-bar period to the next, **listening** to the held resonance of the minims, particularly of the lower dotted minim through these bars.

Articulate the dotted rhythms with military precision, being sure to give the dotted quaver its full value on each first beat (see General Introduction under 'Dotted Rhythms'). Make a little break at the end of b.8 to clear the sound, and then drop the tone and play from b.9 in an echo effect, but maintaining the crispness of articulation and the onward impetus of bb.1-8.

bb.16–60   Point the emphasised upbeat to b.16, and draw out just a little through b.16, poising yourself on the held third beat ready to blazon out the unison A's with a clarion ring in b.17. 'Point' the slurred thirds on the second beat of b.18, poising yourself again on the third beat, ready to blazon out the unisons once more in b.19. Raise the hands slightly after the dotted quaver thirds on the first beat of b.20 so that they 'fall' naturally onto the slurred semiquaver thirds 'going to' the resonant minim fifths on the second beat, (see General Introduction under 'Articulation') then making another tiny break to clear the sound for the *piano* echo from b.21. Draw out a little towards the pause on the A major chord on the second beat of b.24 (interpreting the *sforzato* as a strong 'lean' rather than a bang) ready to lead on into the reprise. Make a rather more definite break at the end of b.32, and then leap up with the LH to launch into the LH fifths in a new, considerably brisker (and strongly rhythmic) 'step'. Feel a clear *1 2 3* beat through bb.33-4, switching to a smart, temporary 1 2̰ 1 2̰ 1 2̰ through bb.35-6, and then switching back to the 'normal' triple rhythm at b.37 as you bring in the high-pitched RH tune. Imagine the sound of a quiet but shrill, thin-toned pipe as you play this tune in immaculate time over the rock-steady, quiet LH drones, feeling the impulse towards the accented crotchet on the third beat of b.38, then similarly bb.40 and 42.* Note the overall pedal from bb.33-44 evoking the sound of continuous bagpipe drones (though on the modern piano this may need tempering with a half-pedal effect and/or the occasional change of pedal, according to the individual piano, and the quietness with which the passage is played – see General Introduction under 'Pedalling'). Draw back through b.44 ready to lead off into the *forte* reprise from b.45.

Mazurka No. 49 in F minor
Op. Posth. 68 No. 4 (4-5) (O)

See note before Op. Posth. 67. No. 1

According to his friend Fontana, this was Chopin's last composition. Inevitably the 'last words' of a great composer have special significance for us (assuming, that is, that these are indeed Chopin's last words! Some doubts have now been voiced, notably by Jeffrey Kallberg in 'Chopin's Last Style', *Journal of the American Music Association*, 1985). In this instance the poignancy of these few quiet bars is heightened by our knowledge of the sad circumstances of Chopin's last months as he gradually grew weaker and more dispirited. It is additionally affecting, and indeed tantalising to find that even at this point (when Fontana tells us that he was too weak to try the piece on the piano) he was still, in these strange chromatic musings, 'stretching out towards the future'. The sketch which Chopin left was assembled by his friend, the cellist Auguste Franchomme, and edited by Julian Fontana along with the rest of Op.68. This generally known version however, omits a section in F major, which was almost impossible to decipher. Various attempts have been made to complete the Mazurka, and the most easily available version is the one realised in the 1950s by Arthur Hedly and John Vallier, which appears in John Vallier's selection of Chopin's works in the *Oxford Keyboard Classics* series (Oxford University Press). (Other realisations have been made by Jan Ekier, Polish Musical Editions, 1965; by Wojciech Nowik, Annales Chopin VIII, 1969; and by Ronald Smith, Hansen House, New York.) Owing to the difficulties in deciphering the original sketch,† and the consequent uncertainties of assessing Chopin's intentions, there are inevitably many differences of detail in various editions. See Commentary in Paderewski, and John Vallier's edition mentioned above. See also Jeffrey Kallberg in 'Chopin Studies', pp.11-14.

	Despite (or perhaps because of) the putative emotive significance of this piece,
bb.1–12	we should not overload it with exaggerated *rubato* and over-expressive gestures.
	Its refined chromatic inflections speak for themselves, and the more simply we

*Savour also the piquancy of the Lydian inflection through this section, the persistent E natural.
†(i.e. even for the main body of the piece)

play it the more effective it is. The metronome mark of ♩ = 126 (whether or not it is Chopin's), gives a tempo that moves, yet allows time for the ear to take in the chromatic effects. With the tempo 'in the system', 'lean' quietly and expressively on the opening tied crotchet being sure to give this its full value, and judging carefully here as in bb.3, 5, etc. the amount of tone that remains so that the quavers 'move on' from the tied note in a smooth yet 'speaking' manner. Enter with a carefully placed LH chord on the second beat of b.1, and play the two chords in

perfect time and with an 'equal' gentle emphasis: 𝅘𝅥 𝅘𝅥 as if with a quiet 'padding' step,

so that you immediately establish your basic rhythm. Take the greatest care to balance the sound of these chords in each bar so that they quietly support and complement, but never swamp, the melody. Feel the gentle 'lift' of the RH line up to the crotchet on the third beat of b.2 while at the same time feeling the sense in which this note gives a 'connecting' upbeat lead towards the 'lean' on the tied crotchet on the subsequent first beat, and so on through bb.3-6. (See Paul Hamburger on the question of the implied tiny agogic delay on these high upbeat notes (Walker, pp.77-8).) 'Lean' again on the first beat of b.7, and then feel the gentle overall onward upbeat 'pull' of the RH quavers towards the first beat of b.9. In this varied restatement shape the curve up to and down from the high fourth quaver of bb.10 and 12 as a singer would, while at the same time listening to the chromatic inflections of the quietly 'padding' LH chords.

bb.13–24
Through bb.13-14 Chopin diverts the music towards a passage of abstracted curving quavers from b.15. Listen even more acutely to the subtle downward movement of the LH chords through bb.13-14 (the rising eleventh in the RH above the dominant harmony of A major at the end of b.14 is, as has often been remarked, pure Wagner). Shape the quaver line from b.15 in easy-moving curves – there is a sense of moving on a little here. Support the RH with a carefully placed LH. Place the chord particularly carefully on the second beat of bb.15, 17, etc. where there is a rest on the third beat. Also **feel** the LH rest on the second beat of b.19, making it clear, perhaps by a drop in the tone, that the RH is beginning a new phrase here (a reworking, a third below, of bb.15-18) on the second beat. Ease a little through b.23 as you prepare to move into the new section at b.24.

bb.24–41
Adopt a more positive tone here with a definite sense of moving on, supporting the RH with a more overtly rhythmic dance-like LH (see Introduction to Mazurkas).
From b.31 Chopin embarks on one of his remarkable chains of modulating sevenths extending downwards to 'rejoin' the reprise at b.40. You could either *crescendo* from b.29 and lead off from b.31 in a purposeful, resonant tone, gradually diminishing as you proceed downwards, or you could 'ease' upwards through bb.29-30 and descend in a quiet, more musing manner. In either event, notice how the RH voices divide on the upbeat to b.31 as you rise to a singing tied dotted minim G in the treble (either full-toned or quiet). Listen to the sound of this sustained high G as the inner quaver voice 'curls' towards the repeated inner C's in b.32, and then shape the movement of the 4-quaver figure expressively as it alternates between the treble and inner RH voice, to be 'joined' by the inner LH line on the second beat of b.33. Study the voices separately and in different combinations so that you fully understand the movement of each in an aural sense. Show the curve of each 4-quaver figure up to its highest note, i.e. the B natural on the third beat of b.32, with the 'fall' down to the D natural on the first beat of b.33. Then feel the melodic emphasis on the treble tied minim on the second beat of b.33 as the inner voice makes its little curve up to the E natural and down to the B flat in duet with the inner LH and so on. Feel the implied emphasis again on the treble minim D flat on the second beat of b.37, imagining that this note is slurred down to the crotchet A natural on the first beat of b.38, and similarly with the subsequent minim C, at the same time listening just as carefully to the progressions and partly tied resonances of the inner and lower voices. Then, emphasising the minim B natural again on the second beat of b.39, ease a little as you prepare to move into the reprise at b.40, and on back

to b.3. The usual version ends quietly, almost in 'mid-thought' on the second beat of b.23.

The completed new section in F major, mentioned above, begins from the third beat of this bar at the end of the reprise.) The 2-bar chord passages are rather in the style of the *Religioso* section of the Nocturne in G minor, Op.15 No.3 (though much more chromatically complex) and alternate with lighter textured 2-bar sections of a more dance-like character. After thirty-one bars we return to a final statement of the opening section.

Mazurka No. 50 in G major (6)*

Mazurka No. 51 in B flat major (6)*

Note: These two pieces are not published in most editions. But the Paderewski Edition gives two versions of each, (the G major numbered 53, and the B flat major 52) differing in some details from Henle. The **second** version of each piece is also written out in full, whereas in the first version, as in Henle, most of the sections are repeated. The bar numberings below refer to the Henle Edition (the discrepancies in bar numbers arising between the different versions are too complicated to tabulate!)

These two pieces were written when Chopin was sixteen.* Perhaps they were really intended for dancing, and it is tempting to imagine Chopin in his merry younger days like a Warsawian Schubert improvising for the amusement of his friends. Indeed Maurice Brown records that both pieces 'were said to be improvised by Chopin during dancing entertainments at the home of Dr Samuel Lindw, the Rector of the Warsaw Lyceum, and written down by friends of the composer. The Mazurka in G was known to them as the 'Kulawy' Mazurka because of the style of the dance (Kulawy = lame)' (p.17). Since both pieces are so overtly and innocently dance-like (and the player is therefore less inhibited by the striving for 'artistic' excellence!) they make useful short practice or demonstration pieces in Mazurka rhythms and movement. In both, the Lydian fourth occurs prominently – see No.50, bb.4 and 32, and No.51, bb.2 and 16.

No. 50 in G major

According to the Paderewski Edition this is a type of oberek (see the Introduction to the Mazurkas) 'in which the man kneels to his partner, hence its nickname, the "lame" Mazurka'. However, within the 'whirlygig' momentum of this piece there is a quaint jerkiness which could also account for the 'lame' title.

Set a brisk rhythm at about ♩. = 50-60, and articulate the RH in a bright, vigorous
bb.1–24   tone, underpinned by energetic LH bass octaves and chords played in a lively
'pumping' manner, strongly rhythmic without being heavy. Count a firm *1 2 3,* so that you enter with a precisely timed and **definite** quaver upbeat, 'going to' a clear repeated quaver on the first beat of b.1 (see the Introduction to the Mazurkas). Be sure to **lift** the RH from this quaver on the first beat (and from the similar detached quaver on the second beat of bb.2 and 3, the first beat of bb.4 and 5, etc.) so that it 'falls' naturally onto the semiquaver, feeling this semiquaver as the 'upbeat' to the quaver on the subsequent main beat (see General Introduction under 'Articulation'). It is this continual alternating jerk between the dotted rhythm and 'plain' quavers that creates the apparent 'lame' effect (but see above). Then feel the onward movement of the RH line up to the vigorously trilled crotchet on the first beat of b.2, and on again up through the peak of the curve on the accented crotchet E on the first beat of

*(and thought to have been published shortly afterwards)

b.3, towards a firm RH crotchet and chord on the third beat of b.4. Also feel the implied little emphasis on the RH dotted quaver (the Lydian fourth) and partly tied LH chord on the second beat of b.4, which gives a slight 'braking hold', and at the same time an onward 'lean' as you 'go into' the chord on the third beat. (Give a smart 5-note trill on the first beat of b.2, etc.).

Make a tiny break at the end of this 4-bar phrase

ready to 'start again' from b.5. End the section with a clear-cut triplet 'going up to' a ringing crotchet G on the second beat of b.8 over a firmly 'planted' LH chord. Take a quick 'breath' before either launching back to b.1, or leading on from a clear quaver upbeat to b.9. Feel the strong impetus up towards the trilled crotchet and firm LH chord on the first beat of b.10, noting en route another 'lame' effect through b.9 (and again b.11 etc.). Again be sure to **lift** the RH from the quavers on the second and third beats of b.10 so that it 'skips' exuberantly towards b.11 (making a jaunty downward slur from the upbeat semiquaver to the first beat of b.11) with a further impetus up to b.12, and so on. Let the RH arrive on a strong crotchet on the third beat of b.24, and be sure to give this its full value while at the same time feeling its onward upbeat 'lean' taking you back to b.1 (see footnote in the Henle edition). The LH through bb.9–16 has a less 'pumping', more 'springing' action.

bb.25–40 Taking a quick 'breath' again at the end of b.8, lead into the Trio with a clear, onward-leading RH quaver G. This section has a tremendous rhythmic bounce.

Play the LH in a 'dancing' rhythm, imagining a 'bounce' on every beat as you articulate the RH like a high-pitched pipe, 'spacing' the *staccato* crotchets through the second and third beats of bb.25, 29, etc. with a springing 'bounce'. Feel the impulse towards the dotted crotchet on the second beat of b.26, with the sense of a 'lean', like an onward 'push' on this note towards the dotted crotchet on the first beat of b.27. Then letting the line 'fall' towards the first beat of b.28, feel you are 'gathering' yourself as you run up through b.28 to 'start again' in b.29. Point the Lydian fourth again as you dip down to the second beat of b.32. Take care to 'finish off' smartly on the second beat of b.40, snatching a quick 'breath' on the quaver rest ready to jump off again with the upbeat to b.1.

No. 51 in B flat major

This suggests a similar tempo to No.50, or perhaps very slightly slower.

bb.1–12 Have your tempo well 'in the system' so that you give a good lead in with the three RH quavers (thinking of these as an overall upbeat group) towards a clear quaver on the first beat of b.1 (see the Introduction to the Mazurkas). Be sure to 'lift' the RH from the quaver on the first beat so that it 'falls' naturally onto the semiquaver, feeling this semiquaver as the 'upbeat' to the crotchet on the second beat (and similarly in bb.2 and 3) (see General Introduction under 'Articulation'). Point the upbeat to b.2 a little, then feeling the overall impetus up towards a clear crotchet G on the third beat of b.2; and, while giving this G its full value, feel its upbeat 'lean' towards the first beat of b.3 (acting as an 'on and over' link between the first and second part of the overall 4-bar phrase). Then feel the implied emphasis on the dotted crotchet on the third beat of b.3, going on to end the phrase on a firm crotchet on the third beat of b.4. Through these four bars there is thus the sense of an emphasis on the third beat of bb.1 and 2, then on the second beat of b.3, and, again on the third beat of b.4. Make a tiny break at the end of b.4, ready either to return to b.1, or to carry on into b.5. Leading into this new section, feel the upward impulse towards the dotted crotchet on the second beat of b.6. Let the RH skip bouncily through b.7, and then feel the implied emphasis and momentarily 'hold' like a little 'pounce', on the trilled upbeat to b.9 as you poise yourself to lead off again from the subsequent first beat. Support the RH through bb.1-12 with a springy 'dancing' LH (see the Introduction to the Mazurkas). Feel the insouciant 'lift' up to the high B flat on the second beat of b.12, with another implied emphasis and slight 'hold' on the subsequent upbeat as you prepare either to return to b.5, or to lead on to the third section.

bb.13–28   Play the high treble line from b.13 in a clear, thin tone like a high-pitched pipe, as in the Trio of No.50. Feel the implied little expressive 'lean' on the dotted crotchet on the second beat of b.13, and then 'point' the accented dotted quavers as you articulate the descending dotted rhythm figure precisely in b.14. Note the different shape of the LH here, implying a slight extra upbeat emphasis on the single crotchet on the third beat of each bar. At the end of the section (second-time bar) draw out the repeated-note upbeat group a little (as if with mock sentimentality) as you 'go towards' a light 'lean' on the dotted crotchet on the first beat of b.21, moving here into the lower register in a fuller, more unctuous tone. Linger fractionally on this dotted crotchet, and then move on a little as you descend through bb.21-2, then making a little swell as indicated towards the first beat of b.24. Then ease a little through the end of b.24 ready to 'scoop' suavely up from the acciaccatura up the interval of a ninth to 'lean' again on the first beat of b.25. Poise yourself momentarily on the third beat of b.28 (first- or second-time bar), making a little upbeat 'lean' ready either to return to b.21, or go back to b.1.

Mazurka No. 52 in A minor (7)

No.43 in the Paderewski edition.

This is something of a curiosity – a piece that Chopin was commissioned to write in 1840 for an album of pieces by contemporary composers, to be called *Notre Temps*. Other contributors included Mendelssohn and Czerny. It is somehow incongruous to think of the fastidious-minded Chopin contributing to a hotch-potch publication of this kind, and the result is something quite unlike anything else he wrote. Somewhat repetitive, it is rather in the style of Schubert, but lacking Schubert's capacity to touch a string of primary harmonies with poetry. However, it is a pleasant piece, the more so if cuts are made (e.g. perhaps omitting bb.25-32, 67-74 and 81-8).

bb.1–16   Set a tempo that moves sufficiently to avoid the tendency of the somewhat four-square rhythm to 'stick'. Think of an easy walking stride, about ♩ = 104-12. Lead in with a clear upbeat chord, taking care to give this its full value, while at the same time feeling its clear onward 'lean' (see the Introduction to the Mazurkas). Take care to time b.1 perfectly rhythmically so that a steady tempo is established, feeling the gentle impulse towards and implied slight 'lean' upon the dotted crotchet on the second beat of b.1, and then being sure to 'feel' the held third beat so that the quaver upbeat to b.2 is perfectly timed. (The motion here recalls that of the Schubert Impromptu in A flat Op.142, with its implied slight emphasis on the second beat of bb.1 and 2.) Then feel the impetus on towards a quietly singing minim chord on the second beat of b.2. Be sure again to give this minim chord its full value, so that you do not 'fall into' b.3. At the same time feel its 'on and over lean' into bb.3 and 4, so that you thus create an overall phrase curve through bb.1-4, rather than two separate 2-bar boxes. As you finish the phrase on the RH minim chord on the second beat of b.4 show the onward upbeat movement of the LH quavers towards the first beat of b.4. Play this higher registered phrase in a different tone, perhaps fuller and clearer, or, alternatively, more subdued. Arriving on a clear crotchet chord on the second beat of b.8, feel the dotted rhythm figure on the third beat of b.8 as the upbeat to

the restatement at b.9. Place the ornament in b.3 etc. thus:

bb.16–112   'Finishing off' the previous phrase clearly on the second beat of b.16, show the LH crotchet C clearly as the upbeat to b.17. Let the treble and LH lines sing out in duet from here, 'filled out' by the inner RH voices, but with the sense that the LH line is leading, as you shape the downward scale in a smooth overall curve with a feeling of slightly moving on towards the first beat of b.20. At the same time be very conscious of the steady rhythm of the RH chords, again feeling an implied 'lean' on the minim chord on the second beat of bb.17, 18, 21, 22, etc. Take care to keep the LH quavers steady through the third beat of bb.17, 21, etc. as you 'point' the RH semiquaver rhythmically on the upbeat to the subsequent bar. Ease a little through b.32 ready to 'point' the turn to the major on the upbeat to b.33 as you lead into the new section. Make sure that the RH and the inner LH minim B's sing out over the second beat of b.33 so that the treble melody sounds clearly

etc. , and **not** *etc.*. This is a quaint tune with an ongoing, rather jaunty motion, as if Chopin were trying to write a popular tune. This jauntiness grows as the line 'breaks' after the first quaver of b.38, and then runs on down into b.41, into a differently harmonised version of bb.33-40. From b.37 feel the onward movement towards b.38, rising to the quavers on the first beat of b.38 with an insouciant 'flick'. Be sure to **lift** the hands from the quavers on the first beat of b.38 so that they 'fall' naturally to the semiquavers, feeling these as the 'upbeat' to the second beat (see General Introduction under 'Articulation'). As well as implementing the intended articulation, this makes the sense of the phrasing clear. From the upbeat to b.46 allow an extra instant to make a vocal 'lift' (not a snatch) up to the C sharp on the first beat of b.46, 'hovering' for another instant through the rest before leading on from the semiquaver 'upbeat' chord to the second beat – and then moving on through bb.47 and 48 ready to lead on from b.49 in the lower register in a more purposeful tone. Here, as in the outer sections, try to vary the tone and character of each restatement as much as possible, though without losing the sense of easy, onward movement. This major section is not altogether easy to poise, and for a relatively inexperienced player the layout of the LH makes some of the dotted rhythm figures difficult to manage. In bb.34, 37, etc. always feel the LH semiquaver as the 'upbeat' to the crotchet on the second beat of the bar, imagining that the LH semiquaver is

slurred up to a slightly emphasised crotchet a ninth above:

The little 'double' ornament in b.50 is awkward too, and is best allowed to anticipate the

second beat   Listen to the LH line from bb.57-60. At b.61

we seem to be leading off anew, but then the music tails away through a reiterated, horn-like figure through bb.62-4. Ease a little through b.64, ready to 'start again' at b.65. Ease again through b.80 as you prepare to make the rather awkward join back to the reprise. Finally, make a gradual gentle *rallentando* from bb.109-10 towards a quiet ending.

Mazurka No. 53 in A minor (8) (O)

(dedicated to Chopin's friend Emile Gaillard. No. 42 in Paderewski Edition)

Like the preceding A minor number and written at about the same time, this is an oddity among the Mazurkas. Rather than the 'flavour of the soil' (Huncker, p.195) of the earlier Mazurkas, or the reflective concentration of many of the later numbers, this has the charm and immediacy of the polished salon floor. And the central passage of flying octaves requires a fleet and accomplished octave technique. This octave passage from b.41 needs a fairly fast tempo. While there can well be some sense of 'moving on' into this passage, it does, on the other hand, need to 'grow' from the first section, rather than suddenly dashing off at a new tempo. The general tempo therefore needs to be in the region of λ. = 52-60, with a certain amount of give and take, but an overall sense of one-in-the-bar.

bb.1–39   The LH melody line through bb.1-8 is not as easy as it looks from the point of view of rhythmic control. Practise it over and over **in time** until it is absolutely fluent. **Feel** the rest on the first beat of b.1 so that you enter perfectly rhythmically. Be sure to give the crotchet on the third beat of b.2 its full value, then make a tiny break so that you start the second subphrase with a clear crotchet on the first beat of

b.3. You could either finger bb.3-4:   as in most

editions; or: which gives a clearer 'attack' on

the first beat of b.3. When you put hands together, have the pulse 'well in the system', and lead off from a quiet though firm RH upbeat crotchet, taking care to give this its full value while at the same time feeling its onward-leading 'lean' towards a quietly resonant dotted minim third on the first beat of b.1 (see the Introduction to the Mazurkas). Enter confidently with the LH on the second beat and play out the LH melody in a clear, quiet yet energetic, ongoing tone through to the first beat of b.4, beneath the steady RH chords. Play these RH chords with quiet resonance, as if 'pressing' them into the keyboard (so that they balance and support the LH in both a harmonic and rhythmic sense), and with an extra 'press' on the dominant seventh chord in b.3. Then, coming **off** in the RH at the end of b.3, and also in the LH **after** the crotchet F sharp on the first beat of b.4, play the LH crotchets and RH chords in a clean, spaced-out, just detached style, 'going to' a strong dotted minim chord on the first beat of b.5. There is the sense of slightly 'braking' on this first beat as you change fingers, 3-5, on the LH A. At the same time feel that the headstrong LH line is snatching a quick 'breath' through the crotchet rest ready to dash off again from the second beat, again to be 'controlled' by the steady RH chords. 'Braking' again through b.8, let the RH 'take over' and play out from b.9 in a exuberantly resonant tone, underpinned by a strong and rhythmic LH. Practise the RH carefully and **slowly** here, singing out the treble line, while at the same time listening to the resonant ring of the implied emphasis with the 'held' thumb on the doubled inner second beat of bb.9, 11, etc. and on the syncopating doubled second **quaver** beat of bb.10, 12, etc. Feel a slight emphasising 'hold' on the upbeat chord to b.11 so that you can place the *sforzato* chord with extra emphasis on the first beat of b.11, and similarly on the upbeat to, and first beat of b.13. Once you have studied all these details of rhythm and emphases, sit back and allow the bounding rhythmic swing to 'take over' through the whole of the first section. Since this is a repetitive piece, endeavour to vary the appearances of each phrase. Think of a different instrumental colour in the higher, relative major entry from b.17, for example, and perhaps a quieter tone from b.33.

bb.39–110   From b.39 you could either *crescendo* through b.40, drawing out a little and starting at b.41 in a *subito piano*, or you could make a considerable *rallentando* and *diminuendo* through bb.39-40 so that you 'drift in' with the octaves at b.41. As already said, the octaves need to 'fly' here. While there is a continuous onward impetus towards the central crotchet in each bar, this crotchet must at the same time provide an 'on and over' rhythmic pivot (avoiding the disastrous tendency to chop the line into a series of little boxes by 'stopping' on each crotchet octave). 'Float' the octave line in from b.41, and shape the RH in long curves, gathering a little momentum as you dip towards b.43, and rise again towards bb.45-6. Feel the little 'lift' up to the crotchet on the second beat of bb.45 and 46, with just the suggestion of a vocal 'hold' on these A's, and then ease just a little through b.48, ready to 'start again' at b.49. Soar upwards from b.52 with the hint of a *tenuto* as you reach the summit on the first beat of b.55, easing again through b.56 ready to set off in the higher register from b.57, playing from here in a gossamer-light *piano*. Ease with a light lift up to the high D on the second beat of b.69 (the highest point of this whole section) in the most seductive possible tone, imagining how a singer would 'melt' into this note. Then as you descend by stages, 'return' delicately up to the B on the second beat of b.71, and to the G sharp on the second beat of b.73, with again the **suggestion** of a 'hold' on these notes. 'Joining in' with the LH on the upbeat to b.74, let the unison line fall gracefully towards b.76, ready to ease into the reprise.

Encompassing the continuous octaves in the RH and the wide-leaping LH, this passage (bb.41-73) needs considerable technical and rhythmic assurance. The LH needs to be studied just as carefully as the RH. Point the quiet resonance of the occasional minim (bb.41, 45-7, etc.) and, counter-balancing the RH crotchet on each **second** beat, feel the rhythmic 'upbeat' importance of the LH crotchet on each **third** beat, which acts both as a gentle rhythmic propellent, and also a slight 'brake'. Point these upbeats particularly when they are low in the bass, as on the upbeat to bb.43 and 44, etc. and when they are tied as on the upbeat to bb.49 and 58. 'Point' also, and listen to, the resonance of the tied minim on the second beat of bb.45 and 46. Above all this LH must 'dance' in continual support and complement to the running RH octaves (see the Introduction to the Mazurkas).

bb.110–131   From b.110 the music 'unwinds' through a simple coda, with the reiterating RH motif continually 'turning' over a rocking dominant-tonic LH. Then feel the tiny 'push' on the subdominant seventh on the upbeat to bb.115 and 119-21. Hold this chord fractionally on the upbeat to b.121 as you prepare to 'float' the RH into the long trill. Let the trill run easily and lightly as you phrase the LH thirds smoothly from the second beat of b.121. Then listen to the different sound of the sixths in the lower register from the second beat of b.125, thinking of the sound of the softest possible horns. Let the sound disappear up towards the final high A over a softly spread tonic chord. Skilfully managed, the effect of these final eleven bars with the sound dissolving towards the upper ether is exquisite. Think of the final upwardly 'flicked' grace notes as a group of two, and three notes, the last grace note A slurred lightly up to

a barely touched high A thus:

Note: Like Nos 50 and 51, the following four numbers are also given in the Paderewski edition, but are **not** published in most other editions.

No.54 in D major (1832) (No.55 in Paderewski)
No.55 in B flat major (1832) (No.56 in Paderewski)
No.56 in C major (1833) (No.57 in Paderewski)
No.57 in A flat major (1834) (No.58 in Paderewski)

In the appendix to the Henle edition:
No.1 in A flat major (1824 – early version of Op.7 No.4)
No.2 in D major (1829 – early version of No.54) (No.54 in Paderewski)
No.3 in A major (1829 – early version of Op.7 No.2)

Mazurka No. 54 in D major (8)*

This not very endearing number, written in 1832, is a revised and enlarged version of the Mazurka in D major given in the appendix to the Henle Edition. It has an un-Chopinesque brashness and clatter, as if intended for a celebratory dance for a special occasion – and this is the best way to approach it.

bb.1–20   Set a brisk tempo at about ♩ = 132-44, and, launching in from a clear quaver upbeat, articulate the chords in a clarion tone with the sense of 'going to' the emphasised chord on the second beat of b.2, and similarly feel the impetus through b.3 towards the chord on the second beat of b.4. These four bars are in the nature of an introduction. Come **off** at the end of b.4, and then leap into b.5 with all possible verve. Spring **off** the *fortissimo* chord on the first beat of b.5 so that the hands can 'fall' to make a natural emphasis on the second beat, and then articulate the RH spiritedly over lively but steadily pulsating LH chords, showing the emphasis on the third beat of b.6, the second beat of b.7, and so on. You could drop the tone somewhat from b.9, and then shape the quaver curve gracefully through b.11, to finish off the phrase cleanly on the second beat of b.12. Then feel the RH dotted rhythm figure as the upbeat to the restatement from b.13.

bb.20–44   Make a clean break after the second beat of b.20, and again feel the third beat as the upbeat to b.21 as you prepare to blazon out the *fortissimo* octaves with a rhythmic 'stamp' in b.21. Then clear the sound to lead on from the upbeat to b.22 in perhaps a rather tinkly, dance-like *piano*, crescendoing through b.24 ready to blazon forth again in b.25, and so on. Take an extra instant to 'space out' the RH upbeat quavers to b.36, and then draw out the descending treble semi-*staccato* quavers, ready to leap off again from b.37.

bb.45–68   Lead off into the Trio from a quiet quaver upbeat, and play the treble melody in thirds in a pretty, *dolce* tone over an evenly dancing LH. Then adopt a richer tone as you augment into sixths on the second beat of b.48, gradually *diminuendoing* through bb.50-52, and poising yourself on the third beat of b.52 to set off in thirds again from b.53 with a more mellow sound in this lower register. *Crescendo* a little to 'plant' the crotchet chord cleanly on the second beat of b.56. Then as you leap off from the *fortissimo* chord from the first beat of b.57, you could make a little *accelerando* as you run up the scale from b.58, collecting yourself again on the second beat of b.60, ready to lead off into the final reprise.

Mazurka No. 55 in B flat major (7)*

This is a jolly number with a 'bounce' rather like that of the Trio section of No.50. It was written in 1832, in the album of a Mme. Wolowska, and was not published until 1909.
Note: For those using the Paderewski Edition there will be a discrepancy in bar-numberings from b.13, since in this edition both first **and** second-time bars are counted (i.e. for b.13 read b.14 and so on – see General Introduction under 'Bar Numberings').

bb.1–12   The tempo needs to be fast enough to sustain this 'bounce' – at around ♩ = 160-76. 'Rap out' the introductory unisons in a strong rhythm, implementing the strong accents on the second beat of b.2 and the first beat of b.3 and then feeling the onward 'push' from the upbeat to b.3 towards a 'stamping' *sforzato* on the first beat of b.5. Imagine the recoil from a vigorous stamp as you 'bounce' on into b.6, with a slight 'braking' through the 'spaced out' crotchets on the second and third beats of b.6 towards another 'stamp' on the first beat of b.7. Then feel the implied 'lean' on the slurred upbeat to bb.9 and 11, and arrive with another vigorous *sforzato* 'stamp' on the spread chord on the second beat of b.12. Make a tiny break here before leading either back to b.1 or on to b.13 with a clear RH upbeat. Support the RH through bb.5-12 with a vigorously springing LH (see the Introduction to the Mazurkas).

bb.12–32   When leading on to b.13 drop the tone on the quaver upbeat and then play the RH *staccato* line with pin-point sharpness and clarity, imagining little running steps. (Practise thus through b.13 holding the A with the thumb as you 'pick out' the *staccato* treble notes, noting the piquant effect of the Lydian fourth:

This passage is not so hard as it looks providing that the RH is supported by rock-steady (but always light and sharp) LH crotchet chords. Poise yourself with a slight 'hold' on the upbeat chord to b.17 ready either to return to b.13, or to launch off into the reprise. Make another clear break after the spread chord on the second beat of b.24. Then, in the second-time bar 'plant' the accented B flat firmly on the upbeat to b.25, imagining that this is **slurred** up to the high quaver E flat on the first beat of b.25. Play bb.25-8 with a pretty, high-pitched tinkly sound. Be sure to **lift** the RH from the high quaver on the first beat of b.25 so that it 'falls' naturally onto the slurred semiquaver, thinking of this semiquaver as the 'upbeat' to the crotchet on the second beat (and similarly in bb.26 and 27 – see General Introduction under 'Articulation'). Bb.29-32 are the most difficult. It is vital that the LH remains perfectly secure and rhythmic. Practise it alone therefore (being very sure to place the **thumb** on the upbeat to bb.30-32 so that the hand is in place to go down to the bass E flat, ready for the high leap up to the chord on the second beat. Play the RH with a tinny tinkle above this wide-leaping LH, and then poise yourself with a clearly 'planted' third beat of b.32, ready to launch back into the reprise from b.5.

Mazurka No. 56 in C major (8)*

This was written in 1833. All is festive and chivalric glitter. The Lydian sharpened fourth is in evidence in the opening bars, and in the third section in F from b.41, and other ethnic features are the rasping drone effects through bb.1-6, and the springing rhythm from b.17.

bb.1–8   Set a tempo of about ♩ = 144-60, and launch in with an energetic RH supported by rock-steady but lively, 'pumping' LH chords. While ensuring that the treble line rings out above the inner RH line and the LH chords, be conscious at the same time of the pervasive tonic drone running through bb.1-6. Feel the impetus towards and emphasis upon the minim on the second beat of bb.2 and 4, landing on each of these as if with a pounce, while at the same time feeling the sense in which the LH chord on the third beat of these bars draws you on into b.3 and b.5. Then from b.5 feel you are 'going to' the dotted crotchet G on the first beat of b.6, and similarly on from here towards the minim on the first beat of b.8. In b.6 ensure that the treble dotted crotchet sings out over the second

beat of the bar (so that the treble line is clearly *etc.* and **not**

etc. and similarly in bb.8, 10, etc.), while at the same time

'pointing' the inner and lower detail – the tied inner G on the second beat and the lower LH slurred crotchets.

bb.8–56   Poise yourself through the upbeat to b.9 ready to drop the tone to *piano dolce* and play from here in a more yielding, dancing style, again feeling the impulse towards and implied emphasis upon the dotted crotchet on the second beat of bb.10, 12, etc. Take an extra instant to 'lift' (rather than lurch) up to the high quaver A in b.15. Then, finishing off this section neatly to the minim chord on the second beat of b.16, make a tiny break at the end of this bar ready either to return to b.1, or to launch into b.17 in a grandiose *forte*. Be sure to lift the RH from the quaver chord on the first beat of b.18 (and again in b.31) so that it 'falls' naturally onto the semiquaver, thinking of this semiquaver chord as the 'upbeat' to the chord on the second beat (see General Introduction under 'Articulation'). Arrive with a ringing emphasis on the chord on the second beat of b.20, feeling a slight *tenuto* effect here as you poise yourself to lead on from the upbeat to b.21. Support the RH through bb.17-24 with a virile, springing LH. Poising yourself again on the upbeat to b.25, you could drop the tone, and play from b.25 (the varied restatement of bb.17-24) in a lighter 'echoing' tone. Take time to 'ease' through the triplet crotchet figure through the second and third beats of b.32, thinking of this as an overall upbeat group to b.33. Making another little break at the end of b.40, lead off into the *gaio* section in a ringing tone, feeling the upward impetus of the RH scale up to the dotted crotchet on the second beat of b.42, and similarly on towards the second beat of bb.44, 46, etc. Underpin the high RH with a strongly rhythmic LH. The repeated LH chords through b.41 could either be played with an energetic spread 'thrum', or you could take the inner E with the RH. Then from b.42 'bounce' from a vigorous LH chord on each first beat, down to and up from the bass crotchets on the second and third beats. Reiterate the bb.42-3 figure with bumpkin jollity through bb.44-5 and 46-7, and then taking the 'tag' bar (b.48) in your stride as you prepare to leap up to play the still higher restatement with a shrill, piping sound. End the section with a vigorous 'stamp' on the second beat of b.56, ready to set off into the reprise in b.57.

Mazurka No. 57 in A flat major (7)*

This was written in 1834 and discovered in the private album of a distinguished Polish pianist Maria Szymanowska. It has pre-echoes of the Waltz in D flat, Op.64 No.1 in the four introductory bars, and from b.21 a hint of the long modulating chain of resolving dominant sevenths from b.17 of the Mazurka in B minor, Op.30 No.2. It is a particularly charming piece, and is particularly good for the relative novice player – not complicated rhythmically, but with a neat little exercise in *staccato* playing from bb.13-17.

A tempo of about ♩= 132-8 suits the cheerful, jogging motion of the piece as a

bb.1–13   whole. With this in mind, play the introductory RH flourish with a certain freedom, but geared towards the overall tempo from b.5. 'Lean' on the opening dotted crotchet, giving this its full value and a little more, and then 'drift' the quaver line in, feeling the three quavers as an overall upbeat to b.2, as if the quavers are growing out of the E flat. Then, picking up the rhythm from this first beat of b.2, hurry on a little, letting the quavers oscillate smoothly through b.2-3. Draw back a little through b.4, pointing the inflection to the D flat as you poise yourself to set off in your steady jog from b.5. Shape the RH line in neat 2-bar phrases, feeling the impulse towards an implied slight emphasis on the crotchet chord on the third beat of bb.6 and 8. Take care to give this crotchet its full value while at the same time feeling its onward little upbeat 'push' towards the next 2-bar phrase. Make a tiny break at the end of each of these bars so that, while maintaining the feeling of continuity, you at the same time clearly 'start again' on the first beat of bb.7 and 9. 'Go to' the emphasised second beat of b.10, as if with a little pounce, then making another little break so that you show the RH quavers clearly as the upbeat to b.11, and then easing the tempo a little through b.11 as you move towards the accented second beat of b.12. Be sure to **lift** the RH from the *staccato* A natural on the first beat of b.12 so that it 'falls' with natural emphasis onto the accented B flat (see General Introduction under 'Articulation'). 'Hold' this second beat fractionally as you prepare to lead into the varied restatement from b.13. Support the RH through this whole section (bb.5-20) with very steady chords played with **even,** quiet

emphasis 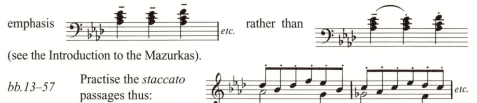 rather than

(see the Introduction to the Mazurkas).

bb.13–57   Practise the *staccato* passages thus:

'leaning' lightly on the thumbs while you articulate the treble *staccato* quavers neatly and clearly. Then when you play it as written, keep the inner line very light so that the *staccato* quavers stand out with pin-point clarity, controlled by perfectly rhythmic LH chords. Draw out a little towards the quietly emphasised chord on the second beat of b.18, and then play the little phrase from the upbeat to b.19 as an expressive little afterthought. 'Finish off' neatly on the second beat of b.20, and then, allowing a tiny break again, make it clear that the emphasised third beat is the upbeat to the next bar, whether or not you are returning to b.5, or going on to b.21.*

*There are doubts as to Chopin's intended lay-out of this piece, since he gave a repeat sign with dots on **BOTH** sides after the SECOND beat of b.20. There is then a double bar **WITHOUT** repeat dots at the end of b.28, followed by the direction '*dal segno al fine, e poi*'. While there is a '*segno*' sign at the beginning of b.5, there is no '*fine*'. Taking into account the resulting uncertainties, both Henle and Paderewski have adopted the same lay-out. (See the detailed commentary in the Paderewski Edition, which also prints a facsimile of the autograph, and see also Jeffrey Kallberg in 'Chopin Studies' pp.10-11). Regarding the return from b.20 to b.5, there should possibly be a rest on the third beat of b.20 (in a first-time bar) or alternatively, a single treble C on the third beat, tied back to the first beat of b.5 might make a more satisfactory 'join' (see again the commentary in Paderewski).

Play from b.21 in a smooth, even style, while at the same time showing that each 1-bar fragment begins on the upbeat to bb.22, 23, and so on, listening also to the complementary

inner figure between the sustained LH seventh on the first beat of

bb.21, 23 and 25. Make a little break ready to 'lift' up to the high upbeat to b.27, and then phrase the chromatic quavers down smoothly, drawing out a little through b.28 ready to lead into the reprise from b.29. 'End' neatly on the second beat of b.44, and then feel the LH is leading on into the coda, with a sense of moving on from b.45 as you prepare to shape the RH fragments graciously, 'leaning' a little on the upbeat quavers as indicated, and 'pointing' the F natural-F flat inflections. Making a little *diminuendo* from b.51, let the RH quavers grow again from the E flat on the first beat of b.52 in a little shimmer, 'pointing' the D flat in b.56 before the line disappears up to the quiet final A flat.

Appendix

The Henle Edition gives early versions of three Mazurkas in an Appendix.

No.1, in A flat major (6), is a very early version of Op.7 No.4. It makes a useful alternative for players at an earlier stage as, predictably, it is less intricate in details.

No.2 in D major (6) (1829) is a shorter and less grandiose version of No.54 in Henle. It differs in many details, and appears as a separate item in the Paderewski Edition (No.54). The stamping chords (corresponding to b.21 etc. of No.54) are differently used, and 'telescoped' so that they recur at 3-bar, then 2-bar intervals, and then in consecutive bars. This gives a useful lesson in coping with irregular rhythmic patterns. Then at the end of the Trio a 4-bar chromatic passage skips downhill in dotted rhythms to run straight on into the reprise.

No.3 in A major (6) is an early version of Op.7 No.2, furnished with an 8-bar introduction. Otherwise the outlines are similar. It is marginally easier to play, but lacking in the rhythmic niceties, details of articulation, and expressive indications of the final version. The indication *naiwnie* in b.53 means simple, plain.

THE WALTZES

Introduction:

While we may wonder how the Preludes fared in the salons of Paris, the Waltzes, like Chopin himself, were an instant success. By turns brilliant, soulful, gallant or languorous, but always within the limits of artistic good taste, they must have seemed the perfect musical expression of this elegant, exquisitely mannered newcomer, with his distinguished reserve and faintly exotic air. As appealing to audiences today as they were then, they are a treasure house for young players who have not yet heard them played to death. And they need not be sneered at, as they sometimes are, because they bear the scent of the salon; nor, as a group, because they are less original or less harmonically daring than the Mazurkas, the Preludes, or some of the Nocturnes – we cannot subsist on a diet of intense personal statements alone. Besides, as Arthur Hedley has said, 'it would be idle to deny that Chopin enjoyed and valued [and indeed, contributed to] the elegance, refinement, good manners and remoteness from vulgarity which reigned in the best Salons' (p.149).

Jim Samson concisely traces the development of the waltz, from its origins in the ländler, through its ballroom vogue, to its place in the salons frequented by Chopin (pp.120-2). Chopin's Waltzes were intended for the salon and not for the dance floor. As Schumann nicely said, Op.42 could not be danced to unless half the ladies were Countesses! And James Huneker, writing in 1900, found in the Waltzes 'a high-bred reserve despite their intoxication, and never a hint of the brawling peasants of Beethoven, Grieg, Brahms, Tchaikovsky and the rest' (p.135). Nevertheless the rhythm and the spirit of the dance are always there. As in the case of the minuet, it is often necessary to remind students of this – they **think** they remember that it is a dance, but forget to feel the **physical** rhythm of the movement. When a waltz is lumbering heftily along, the reminder of the **1**-2-3, the main forward step, and the relatively lighter sideways steps will often restore the life and spirit of the piece miraculously – and it is the LH which sets, carries and maintains this rhythm.

The typical LH waltz pattern is ![musical notation] , in which we have a strong bass note, and two lighter 'pom poms' on the second and third beats. While **feeling** this strong first beat, we have to be careful not to hurry the 'pom poms' – in other words, to ensure that they are spaced in a rhythmic and dancing style. It is also helpful to think of the chord on the third beat of each bar as the **upbeat** to the subsequent bar, rather than as the 'tail end' of its own bar. This helps to ensure that the third beat is properly poised, thereby avoiding the tendency to 'fall into' the next bar. There are a number of typical variants to this pattern, whose rhythmic implications need to be felt and 'pointed':

a) ![musical notation] see Op.64 No.1, bb.24-6. This implies a slightly more definite placing of the chord on the second beat in order to 'point' and control the rest on the third beat.

b) 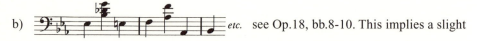 *etc.* see Op.18, bb.8-10. This implies a slight 'pointing' of the bass notes, marking the progression of each upbeat crotchet to the subsequent crotchet on the first beat, and often suggesting an extra 'lean' on the upbeat crotchet.

c) see Op.18, bb.69-74, which indicates a clean leap from the

bass note so that the hand falls with a slight natural emphasis on the slurred chord on the second beat. This 'lean' on the second beat is sometimes reinforced by lower minims, see, for example,

Op.34, No.1 bb.33-9:

d) see Op.64 No.1, bb.29-31, indicating a sustaining

L.H.

melodic 'lean' on each bass note.

It cannot be too strongly emphasised that the LH rhythm is vital. A waltz cannot be performed on the piano unless the LH is perfectly fluent, and is therefore able to carry the RH on a continuing rhythmic impulse. As always, and particularly in the waltz, the LH is 'the conductor'. It is the **LH**, with occasional exceptions (e.g. Op.34 No.2), which carries the dance rhythm; and in instances of *rubato*, it is the LH that directs the fluctuations, retaining the **physical** sense of the rhythm as the music slows down or accelerates.

Tempo is a matter in which the only rule can be that the music must always convey the appropriate sense of physical movement. For the eight numbers published during Chopin's lifetime there are no metronome marks. But his directions *vivo, lento, moderato*, and so on, are sufficient guide provided that we interpret them in the light of this sense of movement. On the dance floor there are fast waltzes and slow. Thus while Op.18 (*vivo*) will be fast and springing, Op.34 No.2 (*lento*) will be slower with a more gliding movement – but not so slow that the glide degenerates into a grind. (The metronome marks for the posthumous Ops 69 and 70 are presumed to be Fontana's (see below).)

Several numbers (Ops 18, 34 Nos 1 and 3, 42, 64 No.1 and the posthumous Nos 15 and 16) have opening flourishes which may be played with some degree of rhythmic freedom. Nevertheless these introductory bars need to **relate** to the overall tempo in the sense of creating a build-up towards the arrival of the main theme. Thus in Op.18, for example, the introductory fanfare of B flats creates a rhythmic impetus towards the launching of the main motif and tempo at b.5. And in Op.34 No.1 there is a much more grandiose build-up towards the swinging in of the main theme at b.17.

In each waltz it is as if we pass through a series of rooms – the flavour, and often the tempo of the waltz changing in each. The vitality and charm of the whole depends on the instant seizing and transmitting of each mood, whether or not the changes are defined, as they may or may not be, by a double bar, a change of key, or an indication of *con anima, più mosso, più lento, tranquillo*, and so on. In this connection it is essential to ensure that each section is clearly 'finished off', so that the tone-colour and mood of the subsequent section can be convincingly implemented from its first beat or upbeat, as the case may be (see General Introduction under 'Finishing Off'). And in this sense upbeats are particularly important since, when a new section starts with one, it is from this upbeat, either a single note or a composite upbeat figure, that the new mood is launched (see also General Introduction under 'Upbeats'). Here and there, particularly among the faster numbers, the sap of the mazurka or the polonaise rises – the dotted rhythm or triplet figure, the snapped ornament, or the dashing syncopated emphasis. Players are begged to observe all dynamics and rhythmic indications, details of slurs, *staccatos*, rests and accents. Chopin is very precise with his indications in these Waltzes, and they are all vital (in particular the accents, which are often syncopated) to the spirit of the music.

Pedalling needs special consideration. Often the 'through-bar' pedalling indicated by Chopin sounds too thick, heavy-footed, and thus un-dance-like on the modern piano. See, for example, Op.64 Nos 1 and 2, where most players will give a touch of pedal on each first beat, coming **off** on the second beat (or sometimes the third). This gives a little extra resonance to the 'strong' first beat, and allows a nice lightness and spring to the remaining beats. On the other hand, in Op.34 No.1 for example, through the rhapsodic build-up towards the coda an overall pedalled resonance is required to retain the dominant seventh harmony through bb.237-8, 239-40, etc. And the opening of Op.18 is a special case which will be discussed below. (For further discussion see General Introduction under 'Pedalling'.)

Repeats, where they occur, are not a mere formality. They are essential to the overall balance, and should always be played, taking the opportunity for subtle variations of dynamic or rhythmic nuance.

Only eight of the Waltzes were published during Chopin's lifetime. Most editions, until recent years, published fourteen numbers, including the posthumous Ops 69 and 70, and the popular Waltz in E minor (without opus number). The Henle Edition now publishes nineteen Waltzes. Four of the posthumous numbers (Op.69 Nos 1 and 2 and Op.70 Nos 1 and 2) are given in two versions: those taken from autographs, and those published after Chopin's death by his friend Fontana. The Paderewski Edition similarly gives two versions of Ops 69 Nos 1 and 2, and of Op.70 No.2. Since the majority of publishers have hitherto adopted the Fontana versions, these inevitably are the readings that are generally known to players and listeners. I have therefore used these as the basis for the notes below. But players will find comparisons of the different versions fascinating. As well as major differences in structure, there are subtle variations of nuance, inner fragments, rhythmic details and so on. Weinstock also compares several versions of Op.69 No.1 (pp.296-9), and Peter Katin in his 1977 (Decca) and more recent (Music and Arts) recordings of the Waltzes plays autograph versions of Op.69 No.1 and Op.70 No.2. Of the remaining Waltzes published by Henle, Nos 14 (A flat major), 15 (E major), 17 (A minor) and 18 (E flat major), are short and comparatively simple – welcome material for novice players. The last, No.19 also in E flat major, is apparently of doubtful authenticity. The Paderewski Edition publishes seventeen numbers: the 'usual' fourteen, and also those in E major, A flat major and E flat major (numbers 15, 14 and 19 respectively in Henle); as well as two versions of Op.69 Nos 1 and 2, and Op.70 No.2 as mentioned above.

Note

Since the Waltzes naturally conform to the same rhythmic impulse, however diverse in character and mood, I have decided to discuss **one** number in detail, and most of the others in more general terms. For this detailed discussion I have chosen Op.18, not just because it is one of the best known, but also because it is the most representative in the sense that it is the most multiform, embodying the greatest variety of 'typical' features. In it, as Jim Samson says 'Chopin crystallised the essential tone of the later waltzes' (p.121).

Waltz No. 1 in E flat major
Valse Brillante, Op. 18 (8)

This is one of the most famous and the most hacked around of all the Waltzes – and not surprisingly, since it is music of exuberant vitality: alternately brilliant, rumbustious, coquettish or glittering. Of them all it comes closest to real dance music. 'All is bedecked, gala... as close to Johann Strauss Jr as Chopin was ever to approach' (Weinstock, p.204). Of the three 'big' Waltzes (this one, Op.34 No.1, and Op.42), all of which are of about the same length, it is by far the richest in material, and the least repetitive and, by definition there is more to learn! As said above, it is vital to observe all accents, slurs, *staccatos*, etc. and Chopin's indications are particularly detailed in this waltz.

For those using the Paderewski edition there will be a cumulative discrepancy in bar numberings from bb.20, 84 and 164 since in this edition first- and second-time bars are counted (i.e. for b.21 read b.22 and so on – see General Introduction under 'Bar Numberings').

bb.1–19 Set a lively tempo. A mark between ♩. = 76-90 is suggested. Blazon the rhythm through the opening fanfare of repeated B flats, implementing the accents with a keen rhythmic bite. Some players play the repeated notes with the same finger (preferably the third) to give the maximum trumpeting effect. Others may prefer to change

fingers [musical notation with fingering 1, 3 2 1, 3 2 1, etc.] or [musical notation with fingering 1, 4 3 2, 4 3 2, etc.] . The

syncopated accents through bb.3-4 create a gathering *stretto* effect as you prepare to leap off into b.5 with a virile spring. Implement the detailing of the RH confidently from b.5. Lead off with a vigorous detached crotchet, springing off this note so that the hand falls naturally onto the quaver D, to make an upward 'push' towards and through the third on the third beat towards the next vigorous detached crotchet on the first beat of b.6, and so on. Players often find this difficult to

implement, and fall into the more obvious pattern of [musical notation]

whereas Chopin clearly indicates this 'up and over' slurred 'push' from the second beat of b.5

to the first beat of b.6, and so on [musical notation] *etc.* .This nice

effect is ignored – or fudged – by many concert artists, although spiritedly realised by Peter Katin in the recording mentioned above. Feel the overall impetus from b.5 towards the *sforzato* minim chord on the first beat of b.8, underpinned by a vigorously rhythmic 'spring' in the LH (see above in the Introduction to the Waltzes). Feel the sense of a slight *tenuto* on this *sforzato* chord; and then also 'point' the LH upbeat E natural as if with a touch on the brake, as you poise yourself to switch to a *subito piano* to descend more delicately from b.9, as if retreating to gather yourself for the next onward leap from b.13. Note the bar by bar slurs from b.9, as opposed to the 'up and over' effect through bb.5-7. 'Lean' lightly, therefore, as indicated on the first beat of bb.9-12, **lifting** the RH a little at the end of each bar ready to make the next 'lean' on the subsequent first beat. Articulate the treble line in a light, clear *piano*, at the same time

'pointing' the inner 'thumb-line' [musical notation]

matching the RH here with a more delicately 'dancing' LH.

Use the sustained lower LH dotted minim E flat in b.12 to poise yourself, ready to leap off again from b.13. Arrive once more on a ringing *sforzato* chord on the first beat of b.16 and, this time, 'point' the 'braking' emphasis on the RH **and** the LH upbeats to b.17. Then from b.17 shape this ornamented RH version of bb.9-12 in graceful slurred curves as indicated, 'pointing' the line of the emphasised minims, and coming **off** on the crotchet sixth on each third beat. 'Finish off' cleanly on the tonic chord on the first beat of b.20 (first-time bar) and then allow an extra instant as you prepare to give an onward, upbeat 'push' through the *staccato* repeated quavers, ready to set off again from b.5. There is, as we see, a great deal of detail to be absorbed through this first section.

bb.20–68   Arrive again on a clear tonic chord on the first beat of b.20 (second-time bar) and then allow a little extra time through the repeated RH quavers as the LH slurred figure 'eases' through the dominant seventh ready to set off in A flat, *a tempo* and *leggieramente.* This section has a dashing insouciance, a true gaiety which, need it be said, has to be governed by an immaculate rhythm. The RH repeated note figures (bb.21, 23, etc.) will be less likely to 'jam' if you feel you are fitting the quavers in with a **steady LH**, rather than thinking of them as a string of notes on their own, and as often happens, going into a spasm as you try to 'get them in' as fast as possible. Again some pianists will prefer to change fingers (3 2 1 3 2 1), others to use a single finger, usually the third. Feel that you are 'going on through' the repeated E flats **towards** the first beat of b.22, and then shape the quavers down through b.22 in a smooth curve ready to 'go on through' the repeated F's in b.23, towards the first beat of b.24, and so on. Make an airy swell as you 'lift' up towards a light, bell-like emphasis on the high crotchet F on the first beat of b.27, descending through bb.27 and 28 as with a light-footed, smooth skip, ready to set off again from b.29. Arrive decisively on the unison A flats on the first beat of b.36, ready to 'kick off' into b.37 from a vigorous upbeat trill, feeling the overall slurred effect through b.36 towards the 'springing' first beat of b.37. Pedalling problems loom particularly large in this Waltz (see above in the Introduction to the Waltzes, and also in the General Introduction under 'Pedalling'). On the modern piano most players will prefer a much lighter use of the sustaining pedal than is indicated by Chopin in these two first sections. For example, the *staccato* first beat of bb.5-7 is usually **not** pedalled, or given only the quickest, lightest touch. Then the pedal might be lightly applied on the third beat of these bars (enhancing the onward 'push' of these upbeat chords) coming **off** on the next first beat, and with a definite pedal through the first two beats of b.8. Then from bb.10-12 there might be a longer pedal through each bar. There could be just the lightest touch of pedal on the first beat of bb.21 and 23, with a rather longer pedal through bb.22 and 24, thus 'pointing' the *staccato-legato* contrast. While he certainly intended loudness when indicated, the one thing Chopin cannot have wanted is a thick, heavy effect. But no hard and fast rules can be given, and players must consult their own taste and judgement.

bb.68–84   Be sure to finish off the slurred LH figure cleanly beneath the treble minim A flat in b.68, and then allow a tiny break before leading on from a smooth 'onward- leaning' crotchet upbeat in a new, more sentimental yet urbane tone. Shape the RH fragments in thirds caressingly, lingering a little on the emphasised minim on the first beat of bb.69, 71, etc. and then playing the repeated note figure in bb.70, 72, 74, etc. in a neat, quiet 'rat-tat-TAT' rhythm. Always feel a nice 'lean' on each emphasised crotchet upbeat (to bb.71, 73, 75, etc.) ready to make a clear 'lift' up to the third or sixth on the subsequent first beat. Make a more pronounced *portamento*-like 'lean' on the slurred upbeat to b.81, coming **off** on the first beat of b.81, and then, from the second beat, think in an overall phrase line as indicated, as you descend towards the *sforzato* chord on the first beat of b.84. 'Point' the doubled B flat on the second beat of b.81 a little, and go on to make a good 'lean' on the tied emphasised third on the upbeat to bb.82 and 83. Be sure to **hold** each of the tied treble dotted crotchets so that it sings out over the second beat of bb.82 and 83, ensuring that the treble and inner RH lines are clearly defined through these bars. Keep this section together with a neatly placed LH, 'leaning' lightly on the slurred sixth on each second beat (see the Introduction to the Waltzes).

bb.84–116 Arriving on the *sforzato* chord on the first beat of b.84 (first-time bar) allow an extra instant to clear the sound, and then play the ♪♪ ♩ as a softer,

onward-leading upbeat back towards b.69. At the second-time bar **feel** the crotchet rest fully through the second beat, ready to launch with a swashbuckling leap into the *fortissimo* chords. Feel the hint of a *tenuto* on the emphasised upbeat chord, and then 'space' the crotchet beats with an ostentatious, braggardly swing, snapping the acciaccaturas smartly against the RH sixths. Then allow an instant to clear the sound at the end of b.86 before entering freshly with the placating *piano* figure in b.87. Rise with a breezy 'lift' to the high emphasised crotchet C on the third beat of b.87, descending with a neat skip through b.88 (taking care to 'point' the lower LH detail here) and coming *off* at the end of the bar ready to pounce into the virile chords again. On the upbeat to b.99 'lean' on the slurred LH chord for an extra instant to poise yourself for the sudden *dolcissimo* in b.99. Then curve the solo quavers expressively up through bb.99-100, drawing out as indicated, and lingering soulfully on the dotted quaver B flat ready to 'lean' into the smooth thirds again from b.101.

bb.117–32 Arrive on a clear crotchet chord on the first beat of b.116 and, allowing an instant's break, think of the ♪ ♪ ♩ as an upbeat figure to b.117. 'Plant' the

emphasised crotchet with a vigorous 'lean' and launch into the *con anima* at b.117 with a swig of healthy vulgarity, underpinning the RH with a rumbustiously dancing 'OOM-pah-pah' bass. Be sure to **lift** the hand from the detached RH third on the first beat of b.117 so that it falls with the right degree of emphasis on the slurred upbeat to b.118 (see General Introduction under 'Articulation'). 'Twirl' the grace note figure energetically **on** the first

beat of b.118   **lifting** the hand again on the second beat, and so on.

'Go up to' a ringing dotted minim sixth on the first beat of b.120, **holding** this so that you make a slurred effect towards the detached sixth on the first beat of b.121, and allowing time to show the chromatic movement in the lower LH (D natural to E flat). Then feel a slightly exaggerated 'lean' on the slurred sixth upbeat to each of bb.122-5, perhaps playing these bars in a lighter, more playful tone. 'Lean' well on the bass dotted minim on the first beat of b.124, and on the slurred RH upbeat to b.125 ready to zoom up into the higher register in a trumpeting tone.*

bb.132–64 Arrive on a clear D flat chord at the end of this section (first-time bar), and feel a full crotchet rest through the second beat of the bar, ready to launch back to b.117 from a vigorously 'planted' upbeat crotchet. At the second-time bar allow a little 'give' as you prepare to slide into the next section from the slurred upbeat to b.133. Then as you move through b.133, prepare to whip up the tempo so that from b.135 you 'move' for all you are worth, **but** keeping the implied *accelerando* under control with a securely rhythmic LH. Learn the RH first without the acciaccaturas, and then, when these are added snap them smartly against the crotchets so that they are sounded almost but not quite together. It is suggested that through the chromatic descents (i.e. from the second beat of b.135 and through bb.145-8) the acciaccatura figures are consistently fingered 3 2 3 2, etc. Similarly it is best throughout this section to keep the fingering as simple, in other words as consistent, as possible, whenever even very short sequences of similar intervals occur, e.g. from the second

---

*Alternatively many pianists play the higher restatement in a delicate *piano*.

beat of b.140 to the first beat of b.141. This is a passage which is exceedingly troublesome to the relatively inexperienced player. Since it is also the one in which adoption of a practical fingering is more than half the battle, a **suggested** overall fingering is given below:

Draw out grandly through bb.147-8 ready to swing off into the *con anima* passage again with a powerful 'kick-off' on the *sforzato* chord on the first beat of b.149.

bb.164–189 'Rein in' sharply through the rest on the second beat of b.164 (second-time bar) ready to lead with enticing upbeat quavers into the deliciously 'schmaltzy' section from b.165. 'Curl' the quavers ingratiatingly towards a warm-toned minim on the first beat of b.166. Finish the second little phrase neatly on the quaver G flat on the second beat of b.168, making it clear that you are starting the next on the fourth quaver pulse of the bar. Curve up in a vocal manner to the high B flat in b.169, coming **off** lightly as indicated, and then leading on with the upbeat quavers towards a warmly emphasised minim on the first beat of b.170. Then notice the phrasing details in b.172, 'finishing off' neatly on the quaver G flat on the first beat ready to lead up into the varied restatement from the second quaver C natural. There is a considerable degree of rhythmic give and take through this section. Support the RH, therefore, with a neat but **flexible** LH rhythm, 'pointing' the quiet resonance of the bass dotted minims in the alternate bars. Linger prettily as you 'lift' again in a vocal manner to the high C flat in b.177, taking a little extra time to articulate these triplets as indicated. Be sure to 'finish off' the LH neatly on the second beat of b.180 before leading off into the fanfare in perfect time from the upbeat to b.181. **Listen** to the chromatic inflections of the descending LH emphasised, slurred figures from the upbeat to b.182, and then from the second beat of b.183 rap out the unison octaves with a clarion ring. Come clean **off** on the second beat of b.185, and drop the tone dramatically on the upbeat to b.186. Then forge through bb.187-8 with a mighty 'whoosh', ready to leap off into the reprise from b.189.

bb.189–307 From b.189 note that the RH detailing is different to that of bb.5-7. Then implement the added *sforzato* 'punch' of the unison octaves on the first beat of bb.197-9, and again from b.229, arriving on a powerful chord on the first beat of b.232. Allow an extra instant for this chord to make its impact, and then come **off** as if with a 'kick', **feeling** the first beats of bb.233-4 as you 'cliff hang' through the rests. It is then effective to play the *piano* 'answer' in a hesitant, rather lingering manner, again **feeling** the full bar's rest through b.238. Then start the LH introduction to the coda in a light, distant, 'pounding' manner, with the sound gradually coming nearer and nearer till you blaze off in full flood from b.259.

Articulate the RH repeated quavers through b.243 like distant gunshots, and **use** the 'lean' on the upbeat to bb.244 and 245 as you make a tiny implied *crescendo* up to the end of b.244. Then pick out the acciaccatura figures like sharp pinpoints, making a *decrescendo* ready to 'start again' from b.247, and making a cumulatively larger *crescendo* here up through b.248 and again through b.252. Let the final run of acciaccatura figures glitter, almost screech, as they zoom down from b.255, drawing out a little in a terrific *crescendo* through b.258, ready to leap off with a shout in b.259. Balance the *sforzato* unisons on the first beats through bb.259-61 with a powerful 'push' towards the third beats as indicated, supporting the RH with a vigorously 'pumping' LH. Then from b.263 shape the inner RH line strongly between the chiming held octaves, and carrying this line on beneath the cleanly slurred upper fragments through bb.265-6. It is usual from here to make a gradual overall *diminuendo* towards the *piano* at b.273. The repeated note figures here (at b.273 etc.) are awkward for **any** pianist. Various fingerings are given in different editions. Most editors seem to favour 5 4 3 2 3 4 |5, or 5 4 3 2 1 3|5. I prefer to avoid the fourth finger at all costs, and find that 5 3 2 1 2 3|5, or even 5 3 2 3 2 3|5 works better. But this must of course be a matter for the individual hand. Articulate bb.273-6 in a subdued 'damping down' manner, brightening momentarily as the repeated note figure edges up to C natural at b.277, then 'subduing' again at b.279. Then make a huge *crescendo* from b.281 (balancing the rising RH with a resonant and resolute LH) as you climb steeply to an energetic *fortissimo* at b.283 ready to let the quavers tumble down in a brilliant cascade controlled by vigorous LH chords. Be sure to give the pairs of LH chords in bb.284 and 285

equal emphasis so that they sound and not

Arriving on immense *sforzato* unisons on the first beat of b.287, 'brake' for an instant as you bring the RH **off** ready to start the upward scale in a controlled *piano*. Feel that you are 'going to' the quaver C on the first beat of b.289 as with a little 'push', ready for the LH to join in perfect synchronisation on the second beat. This 'joining in' of the LH is crucial to the controlling of this passage. Let it enter quietly, in such a way that it is clearly 'going to' a well-defined chord on the first beat of b.290. You are then 'set' to accelerate in a **controlled** manner with the RH fitting in with the quickening 1-2-3, **1**-2-3 of the LH chords, and **not** the other way about! Carry the *crescendo* up to b.293 as indicated, and then, still accelerating, gradually dissolve the sound in a carefully judged *diminuendo* and *smorzando* towards a mere whisper at bb.302-3. Play the little quaver runs from b.295 like little streaks of diminishing sound, ending in a tiny 'ping' as you come **off** each high *staccato* crotchet over immaculately placed short LH chords. End on a minute pinpoint of sound at b.303, and finish with blazing tonic chords, taking care to allow an extra instant for a safe landing on the final bass unisons.

Waltz No. 2 in A flat major

Grande Valse Brillante, Op. 34 No. 1 (8+)

This is the grandest and most chivalric of all the waltzes – as long as Op.18, but less multiform, more concentrated in structure, and more powerful overall. To carry it off in its full brilliance you require considerable stamina and a technique bordering on the virtuoso. For those using the Paderewski edition there will be a discrepancy in bar numberings from b.48, since in this edition first- and second-time bars are counted (i.e. for b.48 read b.49 – see General Introduction under 'Bar Numberings').

224

Project the introductory fanfare (bb.1-16), with pomp and brilliance. Trumpet
bb. 1–48   the solo quaver flourish with all possible rhythmic élan, shooting down in an
overall sweep to a powerful *sforzato* crotchet on the first beat of b.3. Then play
out the detached chords, *crescendo*-ing as if with a powerful 'push' right through to the
second beat of b.4, avoiding any tendency to slur the two chords in b.4. Make a greater
crescendo through bb.7-8, and then drop the tone a little through b.9, ready to make a
cumulative *crescendo* up from the end of b.10, towards b.13. There is plenty of time to leap
upwards from the end of bb.10, 11 and 12, provided that you consciously 'space' these third
beats, feeling each crotchet as an upbeat 'springboard' for the upward leap towards ringing
quavers on each subsequent first beat. Cascade glitteringly downwards from a ringing high
treble F on the first beat of b.13, over a resonant LH *sforzato* chord. Draw out a little through
b.16 as you prepare to launch into a broad-toned RH melody in sixths from b.17, born along
by a swinging LH waltz rhythm. Finish off the RH phrase cleanly on the second beat of b.32,
ready to 'point' the ornamented emphasised RH crotchet A flat clearly on the upbeat to b.33.
Then sweep the RH quaver curves smoothly but brilliantly up to and down from the high F
at the end of bb.33, 35, etc. over a neatly placed LH, showing the line of the slurred inner LH
crotchets over the lower minim thirds through bb.33-47. From b.41 show the different
detailing – the clear break at the top of the RH curve at the end of bb.41, 43 and 45 (see
General Introduction under 'Articulation'), followed by the accented ornamented crotchet on
the first beat of bb.42, 44, etc.

Finish the section on a ringing RH octave A flat on the first beat of b.48 and a
bb. 48–80   cleanly placed LH sixth on the second beat, and then leap downward confidently
to 'plant' the accented RH upbeat crotchet E flat with a firm 'lean' if returning
to b.17. If going on from the second-time bar, make an even stronger 'lean' on the tied upbeat
A flat, with a very slight *tenuto* effect as you poise yourself to plunge rumbustiously into the
next section, feeling, again in each instance, the 'braking', yet onward impelling 'punch' of
these hefty tied upbeats to bb.53 and 57, and to a lesser degree on those to bb.50 and 54.
These 'braking' but at the same time 'launching' upbeats are an important feature of this
piece, and need to be given their due weight in every instance, particularly when they lead
into a new section. *Crescendo* proudly upwards towards b.60, drawing out the repeated RH
chords momentarily, in a slight *rubato* effect through b.60 before letting fly in a jubilant
descent from b.61 towards b.64. Keep the rhythm under control here with the help of resonant
and firmly placed LH bass octaves and chords, being sure to 'lift' the RH through the
semiquaver and quaver rests in these bars, and also to differentiate clearly between RH
quaver and **semiquaver** chords. In some editions the RH runs (bb.67-8 and 71-2) are started
on the **second** beat of bb.67 and 71, and divided into groups of three, three, four and three
notes to fit in with the LH chords. They sound better, freer and more brilliant if started rather
later, i.e. nearer, or on, the third beat of bb.67 and 71. This, however, is a case of 'the art of
the possible' – the important thing is to arrive in one piece on the top crotchet (F and G
respectively) precisely on the third beat of bb.68 and 72. In any event, from the tied upbeat
to b.65 execute the 'play' on the repeated A flats with a tremendous swagger, and then shoot
up the run to a ringing high F with all possible brilliance, feeling that the RH run is fitting in
with the steady waltz rhythm of the LH and **not** the other way about (see General
Introduction, under ''Free' Runs'). Then, as you spring off the high third beat of b.68 and
b.72 allow an extra instant to collect yourself as you make a controlled downward leap, not a
lurch, ready to 'start again' in bb.69 and 73. Do ensure that all RH dotted rhythms in this
section are sharply defined, in other words that the semiquavers are given their precise value,
and not allowed to degenerate into a triplet effect. On the other hand, they need a certain
weight, and must not be too 'snapped'.

bb.80–176 Allow an instant to 'clear' the LH before entering with the emphasised RH upbeat to b.81, immediately initiating the much gentler tone of this section. Take time to show the inner LH fragment (bb.83-4) over the sustained lower tied D flat. *Crescendo* through the second half of b.91 towards the chord on the first beat of b.92, and then draw out the RH chords a little, as at b.60, moving on again from b.93. Show the inner RH fragment at bb.94-5, savouring the G flat-G natural clash on the third beat of the bar. From the tied upbeat to b.113 feel the sudden change of mood. The anguished treble thirds a seventh and ninth above the held F, and the fiercely *crescendo*-ing reiterated chords clashing over a resonant bass octave F (bb.121-2) with the low-voiced answering fragments (from the tied upbeat to bb.117 and 125) momentarily evoke the intensity of the Mazurka or the Polonaise. Show the smooth sliding effect of the RH sixths (bb.127-8) as you prepare to ease into the restatement of the gentler motif from the upbeat to b.129.

bb.177–305 From b.177 we have a reprise of bb.17-80. Rise to a yet grander summit at b.236. Then shape each LH 'arc' of dominant seventh chords expansively through bb.237-8, 239-40, etc. (holding the sound of the bass octave within the pedal through each 2-bar span as indicated) as the RH chords descend tumultuously through bb.237-8 and 241-2 towards a ringing dotted minim chord on the first beat of bb.239 and 243. 'Lean' on each of these dotted minim chords, making a strongly slurred *portamento*-like effect down towards the first beat of bb.240 and 244 (changing fingers 1-2 on the tied F). 'Go to' a powerful *sforzato* chord on the first beat of b.245, and allow an instant to clear the sound as you poise yourself to enter in a *subito piano* on the second beat. A *più mosso* is implied from this point as you lead into the coda. Shape the curving RH quavers smoothly, almost in a *sotto voce*, with a kind of furtive brilliance over quietly rhythmic LH chords, with a feeling of suppressed but intense, and mounting excitement. Be sure that the LH chords control such *accelerando* as you choose (or are able!) to make, so that the RH does not run out of control. Show the LH minim F flat slurred down to the B flat in b.258, and the slightly syncopating and 'braking' effect of the slurred LH upbeats to bb.263, 265, etc. *Crescendo* towards b.274, using the resonance of the lower pedal point E flats through bb.269-73, and letting the inner LH sixths in b.272 'go to' a powerful diminished seventh chord in b.273 over the held lower E flat. Support the brilliant RH cross- rhythm effect as you cascade down through bb.274-6, with resonant, ringing LH sixths. Draw out b.276 a little as you prepare to resume a more sedate movement from b.277. Here it is as Arthur Hedley says, 'as though a door suddenly closes, and the listener begins to move away from the bustling scene; only fragments of the dance are heard, and finally nothing but the tapping of the waltz rhythm' (p.150). Articulate the repeated RH chords neatly in bb.281-4 over an immaculately rhythmic, 'dancing' LH, as you make a gradual *diminuendo* towards b.293. Draw out the end of b.292 a little as you prepare to strike a quiet but resonant bass A flat with the RH on the first beat of b.293. Keep the LH chords perfectly rhythmic again as you articulate the RH fragments with perfect clarity in a progressively diminishing *piano* (taking an extra instant to 'point' the lower LH inflection to F flat on the third beat of bb.297 and 299), then 'dispersing' the sound as if on a puff of breeze as you rise to the high C on the first beat of b.303. End with a rousing chord and long unison octaves.

Waltz No. 3 in A minor
Grande Valse Brillante, Op. 34 No. 2 (6)

Far removed from the glitter of Nos 1, 2 and 4, this gently melancholy number hardly qualifies as a Grande Valse Brillante. Ernest Hutcheson considers it to be the most beautiful of all the Waltzes (p.215) and Niecks records that Chopin told Heller that it was his own favourite (Vol.2, p.249). It makes an excellent study, too, in the shaping of an expressive LH melody line.

bb.1–16   For all that it is quiet and comparatively slow, never forget that the underlying feeling of the waltz rhythm must always be present, conveying a continual sense of smoothly swaying onward movement. A tempo of around ♩ = 112-20 is suggested.

Practise the LH alone first. Enter in a soft but carrying, rather dreamlike tone. Make a quiet, warm-toned 'lean' on the inner minim on the first beat of b.1, and then feel each quaver couplet as the onward moving upbeat to the subsequent minim as you shape the inner line smoothly and eloquently through to the first beat of b.5 over the held lower A. The characteristic LH fingering marked in the copy belonging to Chopin's pupil, Jane Stirling is eminently practical, (particularly for small hands) and at the same time 'points' the implicit expressive sense of the melody. (See General Introduction under 'Fingering'). Linger for an instant on the E on the first beat of b.5, and then let the trill 'grow' from this E so that it sounds melodic and leisurely, rather than trying to cram in as many notes as possible. Inexperienced

players can shape the trill thus at first

Feel that the upbeat quavers D sharp and E are rising in a little *crescendo* as you 'lift' towards a warm-toned C on the first beat of b.6, with a further expressive little swell through b.7 towards the high E on the first beat of b.8. When you play the first eight bars right through, show the overall long curve of this inner LH melody from b.1 up to this E in b.8. Make a *portamento*-like slur down from this singing minim E, and feel the lower crotchet E on the third beat as the upbeat as you poise yourself to 'start again' from b.9. (The addition to the Stirling fingering shown above – i.e. the finger substitution 3-5 at the end of b.5 – is comfortable, and favours the sense of the 'lift' up to the minim C on the first beat of b.6).

Then practise the RH, feeling the implied slight 'lean' on each second beat as you slur each treble crotchet figure over the quiet inner repeated notes. When you put hands together continue to show the little 'lean' in the RH on the second beat of each bar over the held LH minims. Listen acutely to the balance between the hands, ensuring that these RH chords support and enhance, but never swamp the LH melody, and be sure to **lift** the RH at the end of each bar so as not to let the sound 'hang over' into the subsequent bar. Henle do not print, and even fail to

mention the piquant addition to the RH harmony in b.8　　　　　　an 'intended

correction' by Chopin, which is given in the Paderewski Editions, Peters and many others (see Eigeldinger pp.86 and 157). Allow an extra instant to savour these RH harmonies while preparing to move on from the upbeat to b.9 as described above.

bb.16–52   Allow a little give in the tempo as you prepare to end the second overall phrase on the first beat of b.16, and then **feel** the full crotchet rest before entering with the rather more sturdy new melody, now in the RH, on the upbeat to b.17, with a slight feeling of moving on. Take care to support the RH with a perfectly steady LH through bb.17-20 as you shape the RH fragments in a new, more spirited manner here, being sure to bring the RH **off** cleanly at the end of bb.17 and 19, rather than letting it 'hang over' into bb.18 and 20, as inexperienced players invariably will. Feel the 'lift' up to a singing dotted crotchet A on the first beat of b.21, and then let the RH line 'uncurl' smoothly downwards towards b.24. Take a little extra time to show the subtle detail in b.24. The RH-LH appoggiatura effect (A-G sharp) is 'staggered' – the RH carrying on into the seven-note solo quaver figure (an overall upbeat effect into b.25) while the LH inner tied crotchet A resolves to the G sharp 'between' the sustained minim seventh. Phrasing details vary here. Henle begin the new RH phrase **on** the second quaver G sharp while many other editions carry the previous phrase over to the G sharp, 'starting again' on the quaver B on the second main beat. While more experienced players will find their own ways of grouping the irregular quavers through bb.24 and 25, it helps the less advanced to mark out a definite grouping at first, though of course without obvious accents.* The following

grouping is suggested:

(Note Chopin's fingering – 1 1 – in b.25.) From the end of b.28 'go up' from the upbeat crotchet to a resonant dotted minim A on the first beat of b.29, and go on to 'lean' well on the chiming treble dotted minims on the first beats of bb.30-6, while listening to the smooth movement of the inner melodic line. There is a definite feeling of onward movement here towards b.33, and thereafter a feeling of 'unwinding' again towards b.36.

'Finish off' the LH neatly on the second beat of b.36 beneath the RH rest, allowing a fractional break ready to lead on from the emphasised RH upbeat into the next section with a more *animato*, dance-like feeling. Feel the onward, contrary-motion impulse through each quaver figure in *both* hands towards a strong crotchet beat on the first beat of bb.38, 40, etc, showing the **suggestion** of slight emphasis on the RH upbeat quavers spanning the bar lines, tied either to the inner or upper crotchets of the subsequent bars. Feel also the implied 'lean' on the RH upbeat crotchet third slurred down to the ornamented first beat of bb.39, 43, etc. as also the indicated 'lean' on the RH upbeat to b.45.

bb.52–84   'Draw out' a little through the end of b.52 as you prepare to move into the *sostenuto* section with a full-toned, expressive RH melody line, balanced with a resonant lower LH line from b.55. Tail the quaver line away up through bb.65-6, and then shape the curves lingeringly and prettily as you descend through bb.66-8, delicately 'pointing' the doubled F sharp on the second beat of b.67. Take care to 'finish off' with a neat LH chord on the second beat of b.68, ready to lead into the minor section with the RH upbeat C natural in a quieter, more melancholy colour.

From b.85 there is an entire replay of bb.17-84, with a return of the opening melody at b.153, leading into an eloquent coda from b.169. Make it clear that you are 'finishing off' this little reprise at the end of b.168, and that you are 'restarting' with the LH melody in b.169 as if with a quietly nostalgic afterthought. This passage has the gentle, even glow of late afternoon sunlight. Make a *portamento*-like 'lift' from the acciaccatura G up to a quietly resonant crotchet A, and then shape the LH line with the utmost expressiveness beneath even RH offbeat chords, imagining how a cellist would shape the continuous curves. The marking of the treble notes of the RH chords may be misunderstood. These are **not** tied, and these chords should be played in

an even and **equal,** just detached (*portato*) style   (see General Introduction under

'*Portamente, Portato*, etc.'). Feel the gradual overall rise towards a slightly *tenuto* crotchet F on the first beat of b.173, with a gentle 'uncurling' down towards the first beat of b.177. Then in a rapt, scarcely breathed *pianissimo*, curve up towards a caressing G sharp on the first beat of bb.178 (and 182) and, as you 'unwind' through bb.178-80, 'return' to the D sharp on the first beat of bb.179 and 180 with a tiny 'push' as indicated.

---

*But be sure to **feel** the third beat of b.24, so that the 'free' quavers do not scrabble nervously through the end of the bar (even allowing these to linger a little), and then ensuring that the LH resumes a perfectly steady beat in b.25. (See General Introduction under 'Free Runs').

From the second beat of b.178 show also the expressive line of the RH as the treble voice emerges in an exquisite duet. Feel the implied gentle 'lean' on the tied treble upbeat to bb.179 and 180, and also the 'lean' on the slurred crotchet F sharp on the first beat of b.181, keeping the inner RH chords very quiet and even. Linger through b.187 as the LH finally rises towards the high minim E in b.188. Feel a slight *tenuto* on this note before allowing it to 'fall' naturally to form the RH tied upbeat to b.189 as you ease into the last quiet statement of the main theme.

Waltz No. 4 in F major
Grande Valse Brillante, Op. 34 No. 3 (8)

Of all the Waltzes published during Chopin's lifetime, this is the most tinsel – all glitter and clatter, save for some piquant chromatic touches near the end.

bb.1–48   Declaim the introductory chords with a bright clarion sound, establishing as smart a tempo as will be consistent with clarity through the prevalent quaver pattern of the piece as a whole, and feeling a cumulative onward thrust towards the *sforzato* chord on the first beat of b.9. It is best to take the LH E's with the RH rather than to break the LH chords, as most hands would have to do, but perhaps to spread this final *sforzato* chord. Then, allowing an instant to clear the sound, immediately drop the tone to *piano* as indicated, letting the 'buzzing' chromatic quavers climb in a smooth but clear *crescendo*. Have the LH ready to 'join in' at b.17 to establish an immaculately rhythmic **3/4**, assisted by the sustained lower F's on the first beat of bb.17-20, while the RH chortles along above, in an implied cross-rhythm **2/4** effect. Keep the LH inner chords on the second and third beats of these bars very light. Then, as the RH spins into the high treble, show the slurred effect of the LH sixths on the second beat of bb.25-8. 'Go up to' and 'down to' perfectly coordinated unison crotchet F's on the first beat of b.32, making a nice 'ping' in the treble, and then **feel** the full crotchet rest through the second beat as you collect yourself to 'start again' from a poised crotchet upbeat to b.33.

bb.48–127   Be even more careful to let the sound clear through the crotchet rest in b.48 before launching into the new section from a firmly 'planted' *forte* tied crotchet upbeat to b.49. Apply the brakes a little to the tempo here, as you shape the short melodic fragments in a broad tone (showing the crotchet rests clearly on the first beat of bb.50, 52 and 54, over a bouncy, shamelessly 'OOM-pah-pah' LH. *Crescendo*-ing from b.62 through to clear unison crotchet B flats on the first beat of b.64, 'brake' for an instant ready to 'start again' from the second beat of the bar. Rise to emphatic *sforzato* unisons on the first beat of b.80, with a strong 'follow up' with the LH chord on the second beat, and then swing into b.81, leaning with a full tone on the treble E flat and slurring it down to the F in b.82 as if in a sliding *portamento*. Hold the rhythm back a little through bb.81-2, 85-6, etc. and 'let it go' through bb.83-4, 87-8, etc. as if alternately applying and letting off the brakes. Snap the acciaccaturas smartly, in a 'pecking' style against the *staccato* crotchets through bb. 83-4 etc. Take an extra instant to show the implied slight emphasis on the LH minim chord on the second beat of b.92, and also to show the inner LH detailing in bb.93 and 95 beneath the RH trill, and the inner LH **and** the RH fragments in bb.94 and 96 (place the first of the grace notes, D, **on** the beat in b.93 – see General Introduction under 'Ornamentation'). Take a further instant through the end of b.112 to clear the sound for the *subito piano* shift to the dominant of D flat major in b.113 (the prettiest moment in this Waltz!) and then another moment to 'point' the B double flat on the upbeat to b.121.

Draw out the rhythm a little as you *crescendo* through bb.127-8 ready to whirl

bb.127–73 off again from b.129. Then draw out bb.143-4 a little to show the strange chromatic 'curlings' of the RH, and again at bb.151-2 when the chromatic RH clashes astonishingly with the LH. Take a little time too to 'point' the melodic fragment in the lower LH line through bb.147-8. Let the RH 'go to' a quiet but resonant tied B natural on the first beat of b.155, and then **listen** to the LH inflections through bb.155-7. Break off cleanly at the end of b.157, throw in the wisp of RH quavers in perfect time, and have courage to **wait** through bb.159-60, **feeling** the first beat of these two bars before bursting into the final *fortissimo* gallop. Support the RH treble F with an immense bass octave on the first beat of bb.161 and 165, holding this sound within the pedal as indicated and 'go up to' and 'down to' ringing wide-apart F's on the first beat of b.169, ready to 'throw' the final chords with a clear and perfectly timed 'swing'.

Waltz No. 5 in A flat major
Op. 42 (8+)

The opening motif of this number, from b.9, is one of the most entrancing of all Waltz ideas. As Jim Samson says: 'It is not the glitter of the ballroom, but the intimacy of its shadowy corners which is evoked here' (p.125). The various sections of the Waltz are connected by a recurring refrain of flying quavers (bb.41-56, 73-88, etc.). This is a piece which requires considerable dexterity, refinement of touch, and a fine degree of rhythmic control. Von Lenz described how the Waltz theme, 'springing from the 8-bar trill, should evoke a musical clock, according to Chopin himself. In his own performance it embodied his *rubato* style to the fullest; he would play it as a continued *stretto prestissimo* with the bass maintaining a steady beat. A garland of flowers winding amidst the dancing couples.' (Eigeldinger, p.87).

However, when this piece is played **too** fast, as it often is, it loses its delectable

bb.1–40 airiness and becomes merely a scramble. On the other hand, if too slow, the cross-rhythm effects start to grind. An overall tempo of between ♩. = 84-96 is suggested, although the introductory bars are usually played a little slower. Have this overall tempo in mind, though, so that these opening bars move in a 'leading in' manner towards b.9. Most players will find the 2 4 2 4 fingering the best for a long trill such as this, particularly in this position, with a lower black and upper white note. Do not just grit your teeth and embark on this trill as if going into a physical spasm, as relatively inexperienced players invariably do. Imagine that the trill (beginning on the main note) is materialising 'on a breeze', keeping a relaxed hand, and **feel** the waltz rhythm running through it, rather than seeing it merely as a daunting mileage of tight-packed 'little black notes'. Do not try to cram in too many notes, but aim rather for an easy relaxed fluency, letting the imagined first beat of each bar give a little onward 'push' to the notes. 'Join in' with warm-toned, horn-like LH sixths on the upbeat to b.6. Allow a little 'give' as you finish off the trill thinking of the suffix (D natural E flat) as an upbeat, as you poise yourself to 'unfurl' into b.9. Practise this section carefully hands separately, so that the RH 'triplet' rhythm and the LH 'normal' waltz rhythm are thoroughly absorbed into the system. You will then find when you put hands together, and allow each hand to flow in its own rhythm, that the cross-rhythm will look after itself. To facilitate the actual learning of the RH notes it is helpful at first to omit the chromatic passing notes and play

the RH in sixths thus: *etc.* Then, realising that the passing note is always a semitone, practise thus: [musical notation] *etc.* It is also

a good plan to practise in the following rhythm to get the feeling of the light 'lean' on each

'doubled' crotchet: [musical notation] *etc.* When you practise the RH as

written, feel the **suggestion** of the tiniest syncopating 'lean' on the upmost note of each little curve in the treble melody: i.e. on the second 'doubled' crotchet of bb.9, 11, 14, 15, 16, and so on. If you sing the melody you will immediately understand this. Let the melody 'swim' lightly in long continuous lines like a vocalise over the quiet chromatic movement of the inner quavers. When you put hands together practise at first very slowly, gradually increasing speed until you can let the whole effect run lightly and easily without 'working at' the cross-rhythm. It is extremely important to the rhythmic effect that the bass notes on the first beats are **definite** (though light) and perfectly rhythmic, and that the LH chords on the second and third beats are kept **very** light. Perfectly played, there is the delicious sensation of the music **almost** running away – it is, of course, perfectly controlled by this rhythmic LH. Feel a light 'lift' up towards the C on the first beat of b.23, allowing a suggestion of a *tenuto* on this note, as you prepare to end the phrase gracefully on the first beat of b.24, ready to run airily up the arpeggio without any break, towards the restatement in the higher register from b.25. Beware the pedal markings – a fully depressed pedal gives too heavy an effect on the modern piano. As always the player's ear can be the only ultimate guide – but try just a light touch of pedal on the first beat of each bar, and then add a wisp of pedal as and where you want to 'point' a particular melodic or harmonic effect.

bb.40–88   'Finish off' the LH with a neat chord on the second beat of b.40. Then allow a tiny break, ready to 'lean' a little on the ornamented RH upbeat before flying into b.41, shaping the quaver curves with gossamer lightness and transparent clarity, over a continuing beautifully light, dancing LH. Take a fraction of extra time to show the LH inflections in bb.46-8, and draw out a little through b.56 as you prepare to move into b.57, perhaps at a very slightly slower tempo. Most hands will not, of course, be able to stretch the wide RH interval in b.58 etc. – 'lean' well on the dotted minim G on the first beat of bb.58 and 59 with the second finger, using this finger as a pivot, keeping it well in towards the back of the keyboard. Then play a **short** D flat with the thumb on the second beat and, still 'leaning' on the second finger 'pivot', play the upper third, taken with the fifth and

fourth fingers, with a clean 'flick'. [musical notation] *etc.* Some players pedal

as in [musical notation] to give a smooth overall effect,

others as in [musical notation] to create a more jaunty skipping,

flicked effect. (The other alternative, of taking the D flats with the LH thumb, does **not** give quite the same overall slurred effect.) This passage has a cheerful, rather folksy quality. Play the triplet upbeats to bb.58, 62, etc. with a nice 'twirl', and make sure that the hands are perfectly synchronised – the RH conforming to the lightly 'churning' rhythm of the LH. Show the slightly syncopating 'lean' on the tied treble upbeat to b.65, and the resolution of this tied F to the E flat on the second beat of b.65.

bb.88–164

Draw out b.88 a little again ready to launch into the wilder, more Mazurka-like passage from b.89. Give the RH a horn-like quality through bb.89-91. Then through the answering, dance-like figure, be sure to differentiate clearly between the slurred **quaver** 'upbeat' to the third beat of b.91 and the shorter **semiquaver** upbeat to b.92, and similarly in b.92. Articulate these RH figures with the utmost vitality, being sure to come **off** through all quaver and semiquaver rests (see General Introduction under 'Articulation'), and underpinning the RH with a springy and perfectly rhythmic LH. Take care to place the **LH** chord accurately and firmly on the second beat of bb.95 and 96, 103 and 104, to give a clear rhythmic springboard for the emphatic RH chords. Think of these semiquaver and crotchet chords as overall strong upbeat figures to the subsequent bars. Blazon out the high chords through bb.103-4, and then allow a tiny break at the end of b.104 to clear the sound ready to fly off again from b.105. Draw out yet again through b.120 ready to move into the *sostenuto* melody from b.121. Lead off here in a broad tone, and then think of the rests in b.124 as a breath point, ready to shape the lush full-throated melody line in a long overall span right through to b.135. Support the RH with a resonant LH, **listening** to the rich harmonic inflections. Then, carrying the melody line 'on and over' into b.136 luxuriate in the added richness supplied by the inner melodic voice. Build the tension in an implied *accelerando* as you *crescendo* from b.158, breaking off again at the end of b.164 to clear the sound as at b.104.

bb.164–289

Break off quietly without a bump, as if in mid-thought at the end of b.209, before the still, mysterious unisons (bb.210-12). From b.213 the refrain motif builds up in sequence towards a tremendous *fortissimo* cascade from b.222. Support the brilliant RH with a powerful bass octave on the first beat of b.221 with a strong diminished seventh chord on the first beat of b.222, and with sharply articulated slurred quaver couplets on the first beat of bb.223-7. Following the declamatory chords (bb.237-9) you might either take the long scale in a *crescendo* up towards a ringing first beat of b.244, or alternatively, and perhaps more effectively, tail it off in a graceful *diminuendo*. From b.249 underpin the RH with increasingly powerful bass octaves on the first beat of each bar as you *crescendo* towards mighty *sforzato* unisons on the first beat of b.261. From b.277 keep the RH cross-rhythm effect under control with the help of a rhythmic **3/4** in the LH as you *accelerando* with a tremendous 'buzz' towards b.283. Poise yourself for an instant on the high RH third on the first beat of b.283 before hurtling down in a brilliant streak to the bass crotchet A flat on the first beat of b.285. Keep the rhythmic and dynamic tension up to the end, letting the unison quavers push towards powerful crotchet A flats in a fierce final parting shot.

Chopin has been sparing with dynamics through this piece, allowing scope for a variety of treatments of the recurring sections. The principal motif could be played more strongly on its second appearance from b.181, for example; the refrain passage could have greater or less brilliance at its various appearances; the motif from bb.89 and 229 be more, or less rumbustious, and so on.

Waltz No. 6 in D flat major
Op. 64 No. 1 (7)

Despite the hacking this piece endures year in, year out, its charm survives. It is an excellent piece for a nimble-fingered young student. It lies nicely for a small hand, and I have heard really musical children playing it splendidly, at about a Grade 7 standard. The first thing is to forget its ridiculous nickname – 'Minute' Waltz (not to mention apocryphal stories about little dogs chasing their tails!). Providing that the phrases are gracefully turned and that rhythm and articulation are lively, it can sound just as charming at a considerably lesser speed than the $\lessmlsim$ = 88 or so that may be usual on the concert platform.

For those using the Paderewski edition there will be a discrepancy in bar numberings from b.36, since in this edition first- and second-time bars are counted (i.e. for b.37 and b.38 – see General Introduction under 'Bar Numberings').

bb.1–36 'Lean' a little, but lightly, on the emphasised opening crotchet, and, with your eventual tempo in mind, ease into the introductory quavers accelerating through bb.2-5 like a spinning-wheel gathering speed. You might either allow a little 'give' through b.4 before entering with the LH, or alternatively, run into b.5 with a 'whoosh'. Von Lenz records that 'Chopin would compress the first four bars almost into two bars. It should unroll like a ball of yarn, he said; the real tempo came in with the bass in the fifth bar' (Eigeldinger, pp.87 and 158).* In either event have the LH **ready** to 'join in' neatly on the first beat of b.5 to establish your planned tempo. Keep the LH 'OOM-pah-pah' beautifully light and dancing as the RH spins up to the topmost note of the curve – the dotted crotchet B flat on the first beat of b.9 – feeling a tiny 'lean' on this note and again on the B flat in b.11, and then allowing the hint of a 'give' as you descend through b.12 before starting the next spin up towards b.17. Cultivate a skimming kind of touch in the RH that is at the same sure-footed and perfectly defined. Beware of the pedal markings. Here, as in the opening of Op.42, the pedal right through the bar sounds much too heavy on the modern piano, and a light touch on the first beat of each bar, or even on the first beat of each alternate bar (bb.5, 7, etc.) with a slightly longer pedal through bb.9, 11, etc. will be better. The ⌁ in b.10 is awkward at high speed and has to be interpreted approximately or if all fails (see General Introduction under 'Ornamentation'). The similar ornament in b.12 lies more easily and can be executed as a quick triplet twirl:

Think in 2-bar sections through bb.5-20 so that you feel the **principal** beats on the bass notes of each alternate bar (bb.5, 7, 9, 11, etc.) – this is an enormous help to speed and fluency. Allow another little 'give' through the end of b.20 showing the chromatic movement of the RH, and the upward step of the LH from the upbeat A flat to the A natural as you ease towards the first beat of b.21. Spin along again, 'twirling' the triplet figures chirpily on the first beat of bb.21 and 23 as you shape the curve up towards and down from the high D flat at the end of b.24. (Think of this note as the upbeat to b.25 rather than as the last note of b.24, lingering almost imperceptibly ready to run down insouciantly through bb.25-7.) Then take care to 'round the corner' neatly as you turn upwards again from the middle of b.27. Note the LH rests on the third beat of bb.24-6 and 28 – students nearly always miss them and continue to play two 'pah-pah' chords (see the Introduction to the Waltzes). Then show the sustained lower LH line

*In the copy belonging to Chopin's pupil Camille O'Meara/Dubois there is a pencilled '4 mesures' and 'tr', possibly suggesting that Chopin allowed a 4-bar trill leading into b.1. (See Eigeldinger p.158).

ascending smoothly from bb.29-32. You might make a more obvious 'operatic' hold on the high F at the end of b.32 ready to shoot dashingly down from b.33. Draw out bb.35-6 a little as you prepare either to go back to b.21, or to move into the next section.

bb.36–124   'Finish off' the LH neatly on the sixth on the second beat of b.36, allow a tiny break, and if going back to b.21, 'lean' with a slight *tenuto* on the crotchet upbeat F. This upbeat F may be tied or not – editions vary. (I feel the tied effect, implying a more pronounced 'lean', gives a better 'onward' feeling.) If going on, 'lean' similarly on the upbeat A flat which is also often tied, again with good effect, and then shape the *sostenuto* melody in a warm-toned, ingratiating *cantabile* in a rather slower tempo over a supportingly resonant and rhythmic LH. Always think of the RH crotchet on the third beat of each bar as the **upbeat** to the subsequent bars so that there is a continual onward impetus – otherwise this melody can become sticky. Swell luxuriantly up towards the high minim F on the first beat of b.40, keeping the tone up as you phrase 'on and over' into b.41. Then let the RH cross-rhythm crotchets alternate in a relaxed fashion with the 'normal' LH beats as you ease through b.44 ready to 'start again' at b.45. Realise that it is the LH, although it is 'giving' a little, that is carrying the rhythm, and feel that these four RH crotchets are fitting in with the LH and **not** the other way about (see General Introduction

under 'The Left Hand').

Notice how the phrases overlap as you end the first overall phrase of this *sostenuto* section on the first beat of b.45 with the minim A flat, which at the same time leads on again into the next phrase. Curve up again towards b.48. Feel here the continuing impulse on through this F and through b.49 towards the A flat on the first beat of b.50, and then allow the broken sevenths to 'unwind', 'giving' a little through b.52 before resuming the tempo from b.53. Play the A flat acciaccaturas neatly on each first beat from b.54, in an easy, nicely slurred, not too 'snapped' style. From the end of b.67 let the solo crotchets *crescendo* freely onwards up towards the end of b.68 as indicated. Then let the hand fall onto the A flat in b.69, lingering a little on this first note of the trill. Feel the pulse of the Waltz rhythm running through the trill (see the notes on the introductory trill of Op.42), as you swell into the spinning quavers in a progressive *crescendo*, forging into the *forte* at b.77, this time with no ambivalence, in a great onward 'whoosh'. Then drop the tone for an echo effect from b.85. At b.120 allow an extra instant to leap confidently up to the final ultra high F. You can either make a *crescendo* up to a **ringing** F, or as many pianists do, a graceful *diminuendo* up to a smilingly placed **soft** F. In either event make a really exaggerated 'vocal' *tenuto* this time before rushing down the scale as fast as possible. Most players (and many editions) divide the scale into triplets, allowing three notes to each beat as you *accelerando* through bb.121 and 122. This lands you on the A natural on the first beat of the penultimate bar. The remaining 'allowance' of two RH notes per beat here helps you to apply the brakes sharply, with the effect of a natural *ritenuto* as you *crescendo* into the final bar.

End with ringing unisons, playing the LH chord on the second beat with a showy 'throw' beneath the held RH D flat (rather than giving a tame slurred effect in the LH).

Waltz No. 7 in C sharp minor
Op. 64 No. 2 (7)

Almost as much mauled both on and off the concert platform as the previous D flat Waltz, this piece still responds magically to a beautiful performance. It is music of subtle shading and sensitive harmonic and expressive nuance.

bb.1–8   Take Chopin's *tempo giusto* in the sense of 'suitably appropriate time' – one which will allow time for the delicate detail at bb.3-4 etc. to sound clear and graceful. Most players will settle at a basic tempo of around ♩. = 50-2, but with a good deal of give and take, and a distinct feeling of moving on from bb.33, 97 and 161. With your tempo well 'in the system', lead off with a fairly full-toned tied crotchet upbeat. Allow this note its full value, or even a little more, while at the same time feeling its onward leading 'lean' as you prepare to 'lift' towards a warm-toned dotted minim E, 'leaning' also on this, over the held G sharp, with an overall slurred effect over to the sixth in b.2. This leaning, slurred effect is essential: see also the *decrescendo*, reinforcing Chopin's intended effect each time this motif occurs (bb.5-6, 17-18, etc.). 'Bring in' the bass C sharp in careful synchronisation with the RH E, immediately establishing a neatly dancing waltz rhythm in the LH, ensuring that this continues perfectly rhythmically through bb.3 and 4 to give a quiet but secure foundation for the RH offbeat figures. Practise the RH carefully alone through bb.3-4 in precise time, and then **slowly** put hands together making sure that the hands are perfectly coordinated, feeling that the RH is fitting in with the LH and **not** the other way about. Place the bass note very precisely on each first beat beneath the RH quaver rest, to provide a little 'launching-pad' for the neat entry of the offbeat RH quaver second. Take care to give this quaver second its precise value, in contrast to the offbeat **semiquaver** before the third beat, and then let the acciaccatura 'speak' delicately on the second beat rather than merely squashing it in. Be sure to **lift** the RH to show the semiquaver rest (see General Introduction under 'Articulation'), and then feel the semiquaver second as the 'upbeat' to the third beat of the bar. There is an overall impulse through each bar towards the crotchet sixth on the third beat (see Chopin's hairpin *crescendo*), with this sixth thus forming a slightly stressed upbeat to the next bar, and in particular giving an onward upbeat movement towards the next 'leaned-on' sixth on the first beat of b.5. Various elaborate fingerings are given by different editors – I find that the simplest works the best, given that we have lost our inhibitions about using thumbs on black notes, a prohibition which Chopin threw out of the window 150 years ago.

These laborious instructions are prompted by the experience of hearing innumerable 'dog's dinners', and heavy ones at that, made of these two bars. Having mastered the rhythmic and technical details, then make these bars as light and dancing as possible in contrast to the warmly sustained quality of bb.1-2, 5-6, etc.

bb.9–32   'Go to' and 'lean' again on the chord on the first beat of b.9, this time with a little more emphasis. Make a smooth slur from the treble minim A to the tied G sharp, being sure also to give this G sharp sufficient tone to sing over the first beat of b.10, and placing the inner dotted minim E relatively quietly on the first beat in order that

the tune shall sound:  and **not,** as it so

frequently does:  Now (watching these same

points as carefully through bb.11-12) feel an overall onward movement as you *crescendo* lightly towards the top of the RH curve in b.13, supporting the RH with a carefully balanced bass note and chord on the first and second beats of bb.13-15. *Diminuendo* gracefully through bb.15-16, drawing out these bars a little as you poise yourself to ease back into the restatement from b.17. The quaver spans (bb.12-16 etc.) inevitably fall into a slurred couplet effect, creating a light

'tripping' movement.

Balance the RH sound carefully from b.27 so that the resolution of the major seventh to the C sharp is clear and melodious, and take particular care that this tied treble C sharp sings clearly over into b.28 (and similarly from b.29 into b.30), changing fingers (4-5 as indicated) to ensure perfect smoothness of the treble line over sensitively balanced inner dotted minims a seventh below. Show the chromatic rise of the lower LH fragment (bb.29-30) and allow a little 'give' as you draw this section to a graceful close through bb.31-2.

Pedalling requires careful consideration. While bb.1-2 need a 'warm' and longer pedal, bb.3 and 4 on the modern piano need to be very lightly pedalled – perhaps just a **light** touch on **each beat** so that the RH detailing is perfectly clear. Then there has to be a careful pedal change on the first beat of bb.10 and 12 in order to catch the new harmony beneath the RH tied note. Then pedal precisely as indicated through bb.13-15.

bb.32–64　　'Finish off' the LH neatly and quietly with the sixth on the second beat of b.32, beneath the RH rest, and then give full value to the upbeat crotchet G sharp as it prepares to lead on in a smooth 'up and over' 'lift' into the first bar of the *più mosso.* Show the overall slurred effect of each of the RH quaver curves from b.33 which, with the continuing *diminuendo* marks, show exactly the way that these bars should be shaped, like little falling waves. It is amazing, despite Chopin's specific indications, how often the quavers descend with a determined 'clonk' onto the thumbs! Articulate the quavers with immaculate evenness and airy grace, with a continuous onward circling movement as you 'lift' towards the first beat of each bar, over a light and perfectly rhythmic, dancing LH. Steady yourself with a slight *tenuto* on the emphasised RH quaver G sharp over the low bass G sharp on the first beat of b.39, and then make a prettily shaped *crescendo* as you rise through bb.39-40 ready to 'start again' from b.41. Place the LH bass F sharp carefully on the first beat of b.45, and similarly the chord on the third beat, and then let the sound tail away up to the high C sharp like a fairy flying to the top of a tree and not, as one so often hears, like a carthorse lumbering up a hill. 'Finish off' the LH carefully in b.48, as in b.32, and waft into the restatement in an exquisite *pianissimo*, noting the long smooth overall phrase shapes here. Some pianists **do** create a light inner offbeat melodic effect with the thumb-line here,

with pretty effect:

bb.64–192 Yet again be sure to 'finish off' the LH neatly in b.64, then allow an instant's break before launching into the *più lento* with a warm-toned RH upbeat crotchet F. Practise the LH carefully alone from b.65 **in time** showing the implied emphasis on each tied chord or note and listening acutely to the inner resonances that these create: the tied upbeat A natural held over into b.67, the long tied lower B flat, held over from the upbeat to b.68, which becomes the **inner** note, held over the lower LH fragment D flat, D natural, E flat, and so on. The stretch down to the lower D flat while holding the A natural from b.66 is hard for a small hand, and a neat finger change on the A natural (3-2) may be necessary. Similarly at bb.70-1 with the B natural. As a last resort the inner F's (bb.66-8) and the inner G flats (bb.70-2) could be taken with the RH. But this must be done with the greatest aural sensitivity – none too easy for the relatively inexperienced player to manage without sabotaging the continuity of the melody line. Practise the RH alone also, similarly feeling all the tied and syncopated emphases, and building the dynamics a little higher as you start the new phrase on the G flat on the first beat of b.70, and again on the tied upbeat to b.74, rising to the highest point on the tied upbeat (D flat) to b.76. Shape this melody line as a singer would, feeling the rests (bb.69, 73, etc.) as 'breath' points. When you put hands together, balance the resonances of the LH sensitively to enhance the yearnings and sighings of the RH melody in this intensely expressive passage. (NB: details of ties, long notes, etc. vary in different editions.) Support the high RH repeated 'speaking' D flats from the upbeat to b.76 with carefully balanced LH resonances to avoid shrillness. Let the melody line 'unwind' from b.77 (taking care to balance the LH chords carefully once more) ready to 'start again' from the upbeat to b.82. Take time to shape the elaborated RH expressively through bb.84-5 (most pianists group the quavers approximately thus in b.84 to fit in with the

three beats of the bar).  Support the

high D flats resonantly again from the upbeat to b.92 being aware of the implied cross-rhythm effect through the LH chords. Throughout this *più lento* section do not become so carried away with the beauty of your playing that you lose the underlying sense of the waltz rhythm! Shape the solo line expansively down from b.93, allowing a generous *rallentando* as you ease through b.96 ready to re-enter the *più mosso* movement.

Take care how you negotiate the 'join' here. 'Finish off' the previous section to a neat quaver G sharp, and LH crotchet B sharp on the first beat of b.97, and then allow a little extra time through this bar as the RH 'lifts' lightly up, to start the new phrase on the high A as

indicated  and then establishing the

più mosso proper from b.98. (In many editions this phrasing is not made clear.) Note the little

variant at bb.159-60 (not shown in all Editions).

From b.189 let the final run disappear on a breath up to the tiniest pinpoint of sound on the final high C sharp.

Waltz No. 8 in A flat major
Op. 64 No. 3 (7)

Perhaps the overall patterns are too uniform, and the little variants and modulations too subtle to create instant éclat; but whatever the reason, this enchanting number has escaped the remorseless public hammering suffered by Nos 1 and 2 of Op. 64.

bb.1–49   It opens plainly enough with the motion (*moderato*) and the feeling more of a comfortable light jog than of a salon waltz. Enter in an easy *piano* or *mezzo piano* tone at around ♩. = 58-66 and then shape the overall curve of the phrase from b.1 through to the end of b.6, feeling the onward impulse of the implied slight 'lean' on the tied upbeat to bb.2, 3 and 4, 'climbing' to a slightly higher dynamic on each, over a steady, rhythmically 'dancing' LH. Feel an extra 'lift' up to the high C on the upbeat to b.4 with the **hint** of a *tenuto* here – a poising on this little peak ready to begin the 'layered' unwinding from b.4. The LH, in support of the RH tied upbeats needs a particularly even distribution of the beats through the bar, less of the usual waltz 'OOM-pah-pah'. In skilled hands this quaint, rather un-Chopinesque motion is as smile-provoking as anything he wrote.* Take just a little time through bb.7-8 to show the chromatic inflections, observing the *descrescendo*-ing 'hairpin' through b.7, and the little *crescendo*-ing 'push' through b.8, as Chopin veers off unexpectedly soon towards F minor, to resume the jog a shade more determinedly from b.9. Then take a fraction of extra time as you 'lift' from the quaver B flat on the first beat of b.13, shaping the curve up to the high E flat in a vocal manner, and with lesser curves 'back' up to the C and the A flat respectively in b.14, over a smoothly phrased arc of LH E flat chords. Then ease a little through the end of b.16 as you poise yourself to set off again from b.17. Expand a little through b.32, slurring the LH smoothly up from the minim E flat to the chord on the second beat before setting off yet again from b.33, this time in a more serious minor tone. Don't omit to 'point' the tied E natural a little on the upbeat to b.40, and then *crescendo* through b.40 ready to launch off yet more determinedly in *forte* from b.41.

bb.49–72   From the second beat of b.49 the music takes on a new, more dreamy colour. Starting quietly from the second beat of b.49, allow the long phrase to open out in two long, smooth curves (bb.50-3 and 54-6) within the **overall** phrase (bb.50-8). Feel a growing intensity as you *crescendo* from b.57, shaping the LH smoothly, and 'pointing' the melodic inflections of the inner LH beneath the RH trill through bb.59-60.

etc.

Show the LH rest on the first beat of

b.61 ready to bring in the new LH phrase 'keenly' on the second beat of the bar. Balance the RH trill through bb.63-4 with increasingly resonant LH chords ('pointing' the inner LH line again), allowing a generous *ritenuto* through the end of b.64, ready for a triumphant 'landing' in C minor in b.65, prepared for by an 'important' bass upbeat crotchet B natural. Start the trills on the principal note, i.e. C in b.59, and D natural in b.63. Try to let these trills run easily without worrying about how many notes you must 'get in', letting the LH lead through these bars, and **not** the other way around (see General Introduction under 'Ornaments'). Shape the marvellous

---

*This feeling of quaintness is also due to the phrase-patterns: the way in which the tune, proceeding in an overall curve through bb.1-6, 'turns back on itself' through b.7, and then changes direction, pushing on through b.8 towards the new key in b.9.

passage of RH melody from b.65 with the utmost eloquence over resonantly supporting LH bass notes and chords. Feel the overall broad curve of the line from the minim F on the first beat of b.65 down to b.68 retaking the line with increased passion on the high quavers of the upbeat to b.69. Drop the tone through bb.71-2 ready to ease quietly into the C major section.

bb.72–109   Sound a quiet but penetrating RH tied minim G on the second beat of b.72, and **listen** to its resonance right through to b.77 over very subdued but steady inner chords. The low *sotto voce* LH here is like a distant horn-call – be sure that it is perfectly rhythmic and precisely coordinated with the RH chords. Show the implied quiet emphasis on the minim on the second beat of b.74 and on the tied upbeat to b.76 and particularly b.77, as the LH prepares to open out into the long, smooth melody line from b.77. Move through this LH line with the utmost expressiveness, imagining how a cellist would shape the curves, 'lifting' up to the long tied E on the first beat of b.78, and then up to the tied minim on the second beat of b.80, of b.84, and so on. Balance the LH with carefully attuned RH chords, enhancing but never swamping the LH line, and listening particularly to the inner RH inflections through b.79. Then from b.82 let the treble melodic fragment sing out in glorious duet with the LH, while still **listening** to the inflections of the inner chords, tied notes, etc. Be sure to let the minim E sing over the second beat of b.82 so that the treble

melody is clearly [musical notation] and **not** [musical notation] and similarly

at b.89. (Editions vary as to whether the C on the first beat of b.83 is a minim or a crotchet, but in any event the third on the second beat is an accompanying chord, and the melody line is

therefore [musical notation] and **not** [musical notation]. Through the new

phrase beginning on the second beat of b.88 allow time to listen to the beautiful chromatically inflected LH curves beneath the treble melody. There is an awkward corner at bb.91-2 from the point of view of phrasing. 'Finish off' the treble phrase gracefully to the crotchet G at the end of b.91, and then bring the RH **off** to allow the LH to finish its own phrase on a clear crotchet C on the first beat of b.92. Then play the slurred RH chords as an accompanying fragment, ready for the LH melody to enter again on the first beat of b.93.

Support the LH line from b.93 again with sensitively balanced RH chords, feeling the gentle implied emphasis on the tied upbeat chords to bb.94, 98, etc, and making sure that each of these sings over the bar line and over the first beat of the subsequent bar. Allow a generous *ritenuto* through bb.107-8 as you listen to the breath-catching modulatory progressions back towards the reprise from b.109. Do not miss the subtle effect of the upbeat inner E flat tied over to the upper third of the acciaccatura that leads off into the reprise. In this foregoing middle section (bb.73-108) the dance element disappears altogether as Arthur Hedley has said (p.151). There has to be a considerable degree of rhythmic give and take to allow time to listen to the music's harmonic and expressive refinements, and this section should, I believe, be taken at a rather slower and more flexible tempo than the main body of the piece (a view apparently not shared by many performers, who whisk through it at the same tempo).

bb.110–71   Suddenly, with no warning, Chopin veers into E major at b.133, passing quickly through F sharp major to rejoin A flat major from the dominant seventh at b.140.

Take time to follow the full-throated improvisatory harmonic exploration from b.142, landing finally in the tonic at b.149 to set off into the coda, which runs in a prolonged *accelerando* over protractedly alternating tonic-dominant harmonies. Control the RH with steadily accelerating but **rhythmic** LH chords, taking care that you do not get too fast too soon. Show the implied emphasis on the LH tied upbeat chord to bb.157, 158, etc. as the treble quavers fly about. From b.161, begin to hush the sound down towards a *pianissimo*, and then make a brilliant *crescendo* from b.165, soaring up towards the end of b.168 before plunging down to a resonant final bass A flat.

Waltz No. 9 in A flat major
Op. posth. 69 No. 1 (7)

This was written in 1835 for Maria Wodzinska, an eligible young lady with whom Chopin was romantically entangled, and with whom he had hopes of marriage. These notes refer to the version published posthumously by Fontana in 1855. See the Introduction to the Waltzes. In the autograph version given by Henle however (and another in the Paderewski Edition) there are various interesting differences of detail and the piece has a shorter, and very much simpler appearance on the page – which in itself makes it seem more accessible to inexperienced players. This is a popular student piece. But the writing is quite complex compared, for example, to Op.64 Nos 1 or 3, and there are numerous pitfalls for the rash player who belts in with the idea that it is 'easy'. For those using the Paderewski edition there will be a discrepancy in bar numberings from b.64, since in this edition first- and second-time bars are counted (i.e. for b.65 read b.66 – see General Introduction under 'Bar Numberings').

bb.1–32   At first sight one might imagine that the langourous melody and the indeterminate tonality of the opening six bars predispose a great deal of rhythmic give and take. In fact the opposite is the case – because of the alternating RH 'plain' quaver and triplet figuration, the RH **needs** the security of a stable foundation in the LH. The metronome mark of ♩ = 138 (presumably Fontana's) may be found a little fast. On the other hand, if the tempo drops much below ♩ = 120 or so, the melancholy, hesitant phrases are liable to droop to a standstill. Practise the LH alone, listening to the smooth sustained lower dotted minim line beneath neat, even, and relatively light inner fourths on the second and third beats, being sure that you do not allow the chord on the third beat of each bar to 'hang on' into the next bar. Even this is none too easy for the relatively inexperienced player. It is a good plan at first to practise playing the dotted line in a rather strong tone, 'leaning' on each long note, and playing the inner chords in a light *staccato*.

Finger the lower line as indicated (or alternatively you could slip the fifth finger smoothly from the D flat in b.4 onto the D natural in b.5).

When you practise the RH alone, **imagine** the gentle rhythmic impulse of this steady LH proceeding beneath. Then, when you put hands together let the LH once more be the 'conductor' (see General Introduction, under 'Left Hand') and you will find that the RH fits in and can sound beautifully expressive without the need to tamper with the LH rhythm. It is helpful at first to play the RH melody line with the LH dotted minim line, without the inner chords, so that you feel the sense in which the steady lower line 'guides' the RH. Lead in with quiet, but warm-toned slurred upbeat quavers, and shape the little curve up through the quaver F on the third beat of b.1 with the feeling of 'going to' the slurred minim on the first beat of b.2. Making a warm-toned 'lean' on this minim, slur it off smoothly to the crotchet C, and then be sure to show the crotchet rest on the first beat of b.3, as if taking a breath, before starting the second phrase on the second beat of b.3. Continue to listen to the LH dotted minim line, always feeling the sense in which this holds the music together in both a rhythmic and harmonic sense. Take particular care to listen to the LH E flat on the first beat of b.3 beneath the RH rest, so that you 'bring in' the RH on the offbeat with perfect poise. Feel an onward impulse from b.5, and then deliver a resonant bass crotchet E flat on the first beat of b.7 to give a good springboard for the upward leap of the RH.

Imagine that the RH acciaccatura is slurred, feeling that you are making an easy, smooth **curve,** not a lurch, as you leap up to a full-toned high G on the second beat of the bar, drawing out the curve a little as a singer would. Then, letting the line fall towards a quiet 'lean' on the B natural on the first beat of b.8, notice how the phrases overlap as the first 8-bar phrase ends and the next begins on the tied upbeat to b.9. Feel the implied 'lean' also on this tied upbeat as you prepare to move into the elaborated version of bb.1-8. (See the Appendix to this book for Kleczynski's detailed exposition of the opening bars of this piece.) Shape the quaver curve gracefully up to and down from the B flat on the second beat of b.9, and again up to the G flat on the third beat of b.11, lingering a little as you 'lift' from this G flat to 'point' the semiquaver rest (see General Introduction, under 'Articulation'). Then let the offbeat semiquaver upbeat delicately 'go to' the acciaccatura and minim C on the first beat of b.12. For all that you are allowing this delicate lingering effect in b.11 and all the other 'breaths', curves, little 'gives' and so on, do feel the sense of overall continuity of the RH line from the opening upbeat right through to b.16, remembering also, as already said, that the RH is always subject to the basic rhythmic impulse of the LH. Make a little *ritenuto* as indicated through b.15, and then be sure to 'finish off' the LH neatly on the second beat of b.16 before resuming the tempo on the upbeat to b.17. (If you have access to the autograph versions (see above), you may choose to amaze your listeners by incorporating the very taking F flat on the upbeat

to b.15  .) At b.27 most pianists make a *diminuendo*

to *pianissimo* in the run up to the G flat, which is far prettier than the *crescendo* given in most editions – allowing a slight drawing out through the end of the bar, and a rather longer lingering 'lift' over the top G flat than at b.11. The 'ready-made' grouping of notes given in many

editions  is helpful for less experienced

players (see General Introduction under ''Free Runs').

bb.32–64   'Finish off' the LH cleanly again in b.32 before leading into the more Mazurka-like *con anima* section from more determined upbeat quavers. Practise the LH alone again, establishing a decisive and lively rhythm. Be sure to sustain the dotted minim chords through each bar, feeling the persistent inner rhythmic figures as a 'separate' drone-like ostinato, with an onward upbeat emphasis on the crotchet on each third beat. In the RH 'twirl' the triplet figures cheerfully, and then make a clean 'lift' up to the high B flat, feeling this broken octave figure as an ongoing **upbeat** ('matching' the LH emphasised crotchet upbeat) to a decisive dotted crotchet C on the first beat of bb.34, 36, etc. Then define the RH dotted rhythm cleanly as you descend towards a firm crotchet B flat on the third beat of these bars. Be sure also that you define the difference between the triplets and the 'plain' quavers clearly in bb.33, 35, etc. Then when you put hands together practise **slowly** in very precise rhythm, taking particular care to ensure that the RH is perfectly coordinated with the inner LH 'ostinato'. Allow a little 'give' through the end of b.40 before setting off again at b.41. This time articulate the semiquaver smartly against the emphasised LH crotchet on the upbeat to bb.42, 44, etc, 'going up' to a slurred, syncopated onward 'lean' on the dotted quaver. Then **lift** the hand from the 'detached' quaver on the first beat of bb.42, 44, etc, ready for a neat downward skip through the remainder of the bar (in clear contrast to the smoother effect through bb.34, 36, etc.). Allow a graceful *ritenuto* through the end of b.48 as the chromatic upbeat quavers lead into the more full-throated reprise from b.49. (Another engaging variant in the autograph versions is the inner LH fragment in bb.17 and 21 corresponding to bb.33 and 37 in Fontana and also in the Paderewski autograph version.)

bb.64–128   'Lean' with a warm, soft tone on the slurred treble upbeat third to b.65, slurring this smoothly down to the minim third on the first beat of b.65, and giving this enough tone to sing over the *tenuto* inner RH minim and emphasised 'doubled' LH G on the second beat. Then execute the little RH triplet figure in perfect time, and make a little swell as indicated as you go on to 'lean' again on the slurred treble upbeat to b.67, giving this section a gentle-toned lilting swing. Allow a little 'give' through bb.71-2, and then linger prettily for an instant on the emphasised upbeat to b.73 as you poise yourself to 'start again' at b.73. Make a tiny break following the minim chord in b.80 before leading on quietly, but with a more purposeful feeling, from the upbeat to b.81. Articulate the repeated chords from b.81 with neat precision. Imagine making a little 'pounce' on the emphasised chord on each second beat, with this pounce growing increasingly vigorous as you make a determined, carefully gauged *crescendo* towards the *sforzato* quaver chord on the second beat of b.88. Most pianists make a gradual and **controlled** *accelerando* as they *crescendo* here, 'going through' to arrive on the *sforzato* chord with a decisive 'stamp'. **Listen** to the ringing sound of this chord as you pause. Then as you come **off,** allow the silence to 'hang' for an instant through the quaver rest and second pause as indicated, to clear the sound before entering again with the *dolce* upbeat to b.89. Arrive on a quiet tonic minim chord on the first beat of b.112, and then allow a tiny break ready to lead into the final reprise with poised upbeat quavers. The 12-note arabesque, consisting of a 'turn' and a diminished seventh arpeggio, obviously divides conveniently into two 6-note groups, although a grouping of five and seven notes perhaps makes a more artistic effect. Since we are nearly at the end, allow a little extra time for the sound of the high G flat to 'hang' within the pedal before leading on to close in a simple quiet manner. Pedalling needs to be sensitively managed through the first section, taking account of the harmonic or/and melodic movement on the third beat of bb.5, 8, 10, etc. (See also Introduction to Waltzes).

Waltz No. 10 in B minor
Op. posth. 69 No. 2 (6)

This was resuscitated by Fontana from an earlier period, 1829, for publication along with the later Op.69 No.1. These notes below refer to the generally known Fontana version. See the Introduction to the Waltzes. (However, since in Fontana the rather whining melody of the first sixteen bars, repetitive within itself, is played no less than six times, there is much to be said for the more compact autograph version given in the Henle edition.) Another version based on the Oxford Edition is given in the Paderewski Edition.

There may be some confusion over bar numberings since in some editions including **both** versions in the Paderewski, repeats are given for the *con anima* section from bb.33-64, as opposed to the written out version in Henle. In these cases there will be a 31-bar discrepancy from b.65 onwards.

bb.1–32   Set an easy moving *moderato* tempo – the ♩ = 152 gives a comfortable ongoing motion – and lead in from a quiet but warm-toned emphasised RH crotchet upbeat. These recurring emphasised tied crotchet upbeats are important to the rhythmic impulse of this piece. Do ensure therefore that each of them, on the upbeat to bb.3, 5, 8, etc. is played with a quiet but clear onward 'lean'. At the same time be sure to give this opening solo upbeat its full value, or even a little more, and then take care to place the bass note carefully on the first beat of bb.1, 3, 5, etc. to give the right little springboard for the smooth downward curve of the RH quavers towards the minim A sharp on the first beat of b.2. Make a little swell as indicated up towards the crotchet D on the first beat of b.6, and then, in this fuller tone, make a smooth 'lift' from the slurred crotchet E sharp on the second beat up to the emphasised tied upbeat to b.7, feeling the general impulse on through b.7 towards the emphasised tied upbeat to b.8. Then allow a little 'give' as you descend through b.8, ready to 'start again' at b.9. 'Lean' well on the RH upbeat to b.13, and then 'open out' the curve up to the high quaver F sharp and through b.13 as a singer would. Make a *ritenuto* from the end of b.14 as indicated, listening to, and 'using' the quiet resonance of the sustained bass F sharp as you continue to slow through b.15. Then through b.16 feel that you are easing back into tempo, ready to set off again at b.17. Do keep the quiet LH dance movement nicely rhythmic so that the curving RH always has a secure foundation. Feel that the LH is guiding the small fluctuations in bb.8, 13-17, etc, and that the RH is fitting in with the LH and **not** the other way about. As already said, the emphasised tied RH upbeats are essential to the rhythmic impulse of the piece. But equally important is the secure placing of the LH crotchet on the first beat of bb.1, 3, 5, etc, supplying the necessary 'regular' rhythmic first beat beneath this emphasised tied note.

bb.32–96   'Finish off' the LH neatly on the second beat of b.32 before leading on with the three upbeat quavers into the *con anima* section with a feeling of slightly 'moving on' over a 'dancing' LH. Always feel the onward impulse of the 3-quaver figures in this section thinking of each of these as an upbeat **group** to the subsequent bar. In b.47 feel that the LH is impelling you onwards through the second beat, towards a slight 'drawing out' of these upbeat quavers as you 'lift' to the high F sharp in a 'vocal' swell, and then move on as the descending quavers overlap into the restatement of the opening melody through b.49. Be sure to bring the RH **off** on the second beat of bb.50 and 52, ready to make the insistent extra 'lean' on the *sforzato* upbeat to bb.51 and 53.

bb.96–176   At b.96 once again 'finish off' the LH neatly down to the B on the second beat, and then allow a tiny break before leading into the major section from a generous- toned upbeat to b.97. The *mezzo forte* here is not incompatible with the *dolce* – give this section a warm, mellifluous tone, therefore, feeling the impulse of the quavers through bb.97 and 99 towards an expressive 'lean' on the emphasised minim on the first beat of bb.98 and 100 respectively. The more vigorous character of bb.101-4 has something of the stamp of the mazurka, with the suggestion of an emphasis on the third beat of the bar. Slur the first beat of b.101 vigorously up to the dotted quaver on the second beat, then feeling the crotchet on the third beat as an 'ongoing' **upbeat** to b.102 (and similarly to bb.103 and 104). Then take an extra instant to 'point' the resumption of the more *dolce* tone on the upbeat to b.105. Launch into the restatement of the B major melody in double notes at b.113 with a fuller tone and a broader rhythmic swing. It is, of course, necessary to lift the hand to make the small leap to the seventh on the first beat of bb.114, 116, etc. Avoid snatching at these sevenths – there is plenty of time to let the hand land on a full-toned seventh without panic, 'covering' the small leap with the pedal. Allow a little 'give' at the end of b.120 as you prepare to introduce a new, more earnest minor tone-colour in b.121. As you *diminuendo* from b.125, be sure to **lift** the hand from the quaver on the second beat of bb.125 and 126, so that the RH dances gracefully here (see General Introduction under 'Articulation'). Then arriving on a quiet dominant chord on the first beat of b.127, place a resonant *sforzato* C sharp on the second beat, letting the LH carry you in an implied *crescendo* towards the *forte* reprise from b.129. Allow a gentle relaxation of the movement from b.174 as the melody 'falls away' towards the final tonic.

Waltz No. 11 in G flat major
Op. posth. 70 No. 1 (8+)

This supremely frothy concoction (thought to date from the early 1830s), is far from easy to control, even at a good many notches below the very fast metronome mark given in the Fontana version (which even most virtuosi do not care to match). Such a very fast tempo would, it is interesting to note, make a nonsense of the dotted rhythm effects in the autograph version also given in Henle (and the version given in the Oxford Edition which is also discussed in the Commentary of the Paderewski Edition – see the Introduction to the Waltzes). The essential is that the RH is immaculately articulated and the rhythm perfectly secure, with just the right amount of give and take in the right places, so that it **sounds** as if it is being tossed off, despite the earnest endeavours that may have gone on behind the scenes! Go no faster, therefore, than the tempo at which you can achieve this perfect clarity and rhythmic security.

bb.1–33   Practise the RH very slowly and perfectly rhythmically at first without the ornaments. Then it is a good plan to memorise the very simple LH dominant-tonic harmony (moving on to dominant-tonic in D flat from b.17), and then to play the LH while **singing** the RH (never mind how awful it sounds). You will then see that the LH waltz rhythm needs to be very precise overall, but with tiny, yet vital 'gives' from the third beat of bb.7, 15 and 23 (i.e. as you draw to the end of each phrase), poising yourself to 'start again' in bb.9, 17 and 25. Then start practising **slowly** hands together, without the ornaments. If the LH remains perfectly rhythmic and the hands are precisely coordinated, there will be a natural and clear differentation between the RH triplets and the 'plain' quavers in bb.2-4, etc. Be sure to give the upbeat quavers their full value, making it quite clear that these are 'plain' quavers and not triplets, at the same time feeling the onward 'lean' into b.1. When you add the ornaments, be sure that they do not disrupt the quaver values.

244

Whether or not to differentiate between the upbeat grace notes and the trill on the first quaver of b.1, few would claim to be sure. However, in practical terms the trill (often marked ∿) can

only consist of  . Thus these ornaments are, in effect, played in

much the same way. Again, whether or not they should come **on** the beat, or anticipate it, must be a matter of choice – or expediency. Again some performers place the opening ornament **on** the beat, and allow the next one to **anticipate** the first beat

of b.1 }   or vice versa.

Make an airy slurred 'lift' up to the high crotchet on the third beat of bb.2-4, being very sure that you do not skimp these third beats in your anxiety to get down to the subsequent first beats. There is, in fact, an implied slight emphasis on these crotchet third beats – poise yourself on each one therefore (particularly after the third and wider leap up to the third beat of b.4) so that you avoid 'falling into' the first beat of bb.3, 4 and 5. (Again here, your perfectly rhythmic LH will help prevent the danger of shortening these beats.) Then the slight natural 'give' which you have already discovered, from the second beat of b.7, will allow time for you to 'space' the wide-apart quavers through the third beat, rather than snatching wildly at them. Continue this tiny *rallentando* effect, so that the three upbeat quavers to b.9 are also very slightly 'braked', resuming the tempo briskly in b.9. Repeat this effect at bb.15-16 before launching into b.17 in a fuller, more rumbustious tone. Shape the curves breezily up to and down from the high F on the first beat of bb.18 and 22, and keep very steady through bb.19 and 20, again showing the slurred 'lift' up to the crotchet on each third beat. You will need a little more time through the end of b.23 to accommodate the yet wider span of the RH quavers. Then make a real *ritenuto* through b.32, leaning and lingering a little on the emphasised RH quaver on the third beat, and using this as a 'launching' upbeat as you prepare to move into the *meno mosso*.

bb.33–96   The metronome mark is exaggeratedly slow here in proportion to the almost impossibly fast one given for the outer sections, and most pianists take this section at around 112-20. In any event, ease into the delectably sentimental treble thirds establishing a comfortably easy swinging waltz rhythm with the LH. Make sure that the RH dotted rhythm is well-defined but at the same time really *cantabile* – this involves 'leaning' warmly on the dotted crotchets, and keeping the semiquavers short and relatively light, while at the same time conveying an onward 'upbeat' feeling towards the subsequent dotted quaver, and then towards the first beat of b.34 etc. (see General Introduction under 'Dotted Rhythms').

'Go to', and lean well upon the dotted crotchet on the first beat of bb.34, 35 and 36, and be sure to differentiate clearly between the dotted crotchet and **quaver,** and then the dotted quaver and **semiquaver** in these bars. In each instance a rhythmically placed LH chord or octave on the second beat of the bar is essential to the timing of the RH quaver. 'Finish off' the LH clearly on the second beat of b.48 before leading rather more purposefully into b.49. Move on then, with a good rhythmic swing as you *crescendo* towards a resonantly singing minim chord on the first beat of b.52, allowing a fair 'pull back' here to show the rising inner LH fragment G natural- A flat, as the RH 'slurs off' towards the *piano* at b.53. Play the broken chord on the first

beat of b.55 thus  and then draw out through b.56 again as you

lead back towards the restatement of the melody in thirds. Take plenty of time to finish off the section at bb.79-80 before springing back into the reprise *a tempo* from the upbeat group to b.81.

Waltz No. 12 in F minor
Op. posth. 70 No. 2 (6)

This rather anaemic number dates from 1841 and was evidently written as a private gift. It is a pity that the generally known Fontana version is drawn out to 124 bars – see the Introduction to the Waltzes – whereas the autograph version also given in Henle runs to only 72 (as does the similar, second version in the Paderewski edition). Apart from this advantage, this autograph version is simpler in some details and could perhaps be managed by older players, at Grade 5. However, for the reasons given above (see the Introduction to the Waltzes) I have used the Fontana version as the basis for these notes. Among the variants in

the autograph version are the more enterprising harmonies in b.52

and b.56.

bb.1–40   Set a steady, easy-moving tempo not too far below the given ♩ = 144, and lean with a warm tone on the tied crotchet upbeat to b.1, being very sure to give this note its full value before bringing in the LH with a carefully placed dotted minim on the first beat of b.1. Shape the melody line expressively, supporting the RH with a smoothly sustained lower LH line and with carefully balanced inner chords (see discussion of the similar LH at the opening of Op.69 No.1). Feel the sense of onward movement towards b.2, and then notice how the emphasised RH crotchet F on the third beat of b.2 (ending the first subphrase) is also the onward leaning upbeat to b.3 (and similarly at bb.4-5). This creates a continuing onward movement from subphrase to subphrase within the overall 8-bar span. Take care to give the RH quaver in b.2 its full value, and then feel a nice 'lift' from the upbeat F towards the high F on the first beat of b.3. The downward turning first phrase (bb.1-2) is distinctly melancholy – bb.3-4 with its more 'upward' turn could be played in a brighter, more open tone. 'Point' the different LH detailing through b.3 with the suggestion of a slight emphasis on the inner minim fourth on the second beat as the lower line prepares to descend towards the low F beneath the little RH swell towards the ornamented dotted crotchet on the first beat of b.4 (see below for comments on the interpretation of ornaments in this piece).

Then from b.5 let the RH quavers open out in unhurried and expressive curves, supported by an evenly spaced LH, drawing out slightly through b.7 before swelling a little through b.8, as if with a little onward 'push', to start the new, higher, major phrase from b.9 in a rather fuller tone. *Crescendo* towards the high point of this phrase, the dotted crotchet C on the first beat of b.13, lingering a little on this full-toned note in a 'vocal' manner, then moving on a little as the quavers descend. Allow a little 'give' through the end of b.16, and then rise prettily to a *piano* high quaver C on the second beat of b.17, in contrast to the full-toned high C on the first beat of b.13, and take a little time through bb.18 and 19 to listen to the inflections of the LH chords beneath the widely, but smoothly curving descent of the RH quavers. Take plenty of time through b.20, making it clear that the previous RH phrase ends on the E flat on the first beat, and that the three quavers, incorporating the grace note figure, form an upbeat group to b.21. Play these grace notes expressively over a gracefully spread LH upbeat chord before resuming the melody in tempo from b.21.

Be sure to 'finish off' the LH clearly with the inner chord in b.40 before leading
bb. 1–40   off into the new section with a firm toned upbeat crotchet E natural (be sure to 'clear' the LH here!). This section has a more resolute character, with a slight feeling of 'moving on' with more of a rhythmic swing. Support the RH with a broad-toned but not swamping LH. Be sure to let the RH come **off** at the end of b.42, being particularly careful to place the LH dotted minim E flat firmly beneath the RH rest on the first beat of b.43. Sweep the quavers up through b.45 in a *crescendo* towards a resonant *sforzato* minim third on the first beat of b.46 (taking care to articulate the tied lower acciaccatura cleanly) and carry the forward impulse on towards the high minim sixth on the first beat of b.48. Then make it clear that you are starting the new phrase on the upbeat to b.49. Carry on the *forte* from b.53 through to the tied upbeat to b.55, supporting the full-toned RH sixths with resonant LH chords. Then allow time as you *diminuendo* from b.55, lingering a little on the emphasised tied chord on the upbeat to b.56 to prepare the echo effect **through** b.56, and resuming the tempo from the emphasised second beat of b.57. Take particular care to place the LH C rhythmically on the first beat of bb.55 and 56 (and the D flat on the first beat of b.57) and in such a way that the sound of the tied sixth singing over the bar line is **enhanced,** not swamped! Be sure to show the RH rest on the first beat of b.69 before *crescendo*-ing steadily through bb.69-72 over the E flat pedal point. Here it is better to achieve trills of five clear notes than seven or more garbled ones.

Feel that you are 'going on' through b.72 towards the *forte* upbeat to b.73, lingering on this tied RH C over a full throated LH chord before moving into the reprise. Draw out a little through the penultimate bar towards the final tonic unisons, placing the LH crotchet sixth with neat finality.*

Less experienced players may have some problems with the interpretation of the melodic grace notes in this piece. In the autograph version given in Henle and the Paderewski Edition, the ornament in b.4 is (i.e. the grace notes are given as quavers).

It is thus similar to the figure in b.1 of the Nocturne in G minor Op.37 No.2, and

*The autograph version given in Henle and Paderewski ends on the tonic harmony in b.72 (i.e. as in Fontana's b.124).

should therefore be played on the beat  (see commentary on

this piece and also General Introduction under 'Ornamentation and 'Free' Runs'). In practice, however, many pianists allow the ornament to anticipate the beat. The essential is that the grace notes sound leisured – expressive rather than crammed in – so if you are going to anticipate the beat, start the grace note figure in plenty of time, in other words almost immediately after the preceding D flat. The same remarks apply in the case of the ornament on the first beat of bb.42 and 47. The tied acciaccatura in b.46 should be placed **on** the beat. The grace note figure over the arpeggiated LH chord in b.20 represents quite a difficult manoeuvre for an inexperienced player. It is best begun on the beat, in other words with the RH C coinciding with the LH C in

an arrangement approximating to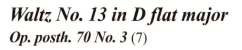

Waltz No. 13 in D flat major
Op. posth. 70 No. 3 (7)

Although it dates from a much earlier period (1829) before Chopin left Poland, this Waltz, with its two-voiced melody, has more musical substance than Op.70 No.2. He was in a state of idealised love with a young singer, Constantia Gladkowska, and writing to his great friend, Titus Woyciechowski, he described his 'ideal . . . whom I dream of . . . and who this morning inspired me to write the little Waltz I am sending you. Notice the place marked with a cross. No one but you knows of this. How I should enjoy playing it to you, dearest Titus. In the Trio the bass melody must stand out as far as the upper E flat in the fifth bar. There's no need to write about it – you will feel it.' (Hedley, *Selected Correspondance,* p.34).

 For those using the Paderewski Edition there will be a discrepancy in bar numberings from b.48 since in this edition first- and second-time bars are counted (i.e. for b.49 read b.50 – see General Introduction under 'Bar Numberings').

bb.1–16   The given tempo of ♩= 108 is on the sticky side, and most players take it nearer to the *tempo giusto* of No.12, around 132-44. Take the RH apart and work out the treble and inner lines separately.

Leading in from unhurried upbeat quavers imagine a vocal 'lift' up to a singing minim F, and shape this treble voice in a soft, smoothly singing line through to the crotchet A flat on the third beat of b.4. (In Henle the treble F on the third beat of b.1 is **played,** while in most editions it is tied – the tied version, I feel, sounds better, but is more difficult!)

Then practise the inner line using the eventual fingering

ensuring that it proceeds as smoothly as possible towards and on from the little implied emphasis on the tied upbeat to bb.2 and 3. When you put the voices together, ensure that the long treble notes sing out over the inner line, so that the upper line in b.1, for example, sounds

clearly ... *etc.* and **not** ... *etc.*

Make sure also that the inner line proceeds evenly, rather than in a series of little gusts, through bb.1-3, taking particular care to avoid a bump on the second quaver of bb.2 and 3 as the line moves on from the tied upbeat. This is not easy to manage, and those with small hands have to cope as best they can, using the thumb on the inner line through b.1 (5 1 1 1 1 rather than 5 1 2 1 1). Allow just a little give as you finish the first phrase at the end of b.4, ready to start the next phrase with another singing minim F on the first beat of b.5. Interpret the ornament on the first

beat of b.4 (as also at b.21) thus ... I find this fingering the

clearest and easiest. Allow time in b.7 to 'lift' up to the high quaver C in a vocal manner from the dotted crotchet B flat on the second beat, and then to curve down easily to end the phrase cleanly on the doubled crotchet on the first beat of b.8, ready to let the inner quavers lead on towards b.9. Support the two RH lines with a rhythmic but pliant LH.

bb.16–72   Lead on from b.16 in a rather more purposeful manner feeling an onward impulse towards the stressed dotted crotchet third on the first beat of b.17. Sing out the two RH voices from here in a warm, resonant tone over a supportingly resonant LH, with a sense of moving on a little. Feel this overall onward movement through to b.22, and then relax the movement a little as you *diminuendo* through b.23 to end the phrase cleanly in b.24. Be sure to 'finish off' the LH clearly down to the bass D flat on the second beat of b.24 before leading on again with the upbeat quavers to b.25. (Some editions give a RH quaver rest at the beginning of b.21 so that the double melody re-enters on the sixth on the second quaver pulse.) Allow a little extra time as you *diminuendo* through to b.31, to 'finish off' the LH cleanly once more down to the low D flat, ready to lead into the G flat section from a clear RH crotchet upbeat D flat. Here, notwithstanding Chopin's exhortation to let the LH 'stand out' (see above) there are again two distinct melodic lines – this time an expressive singing duet between the LH and treble. Practise the LH first, shaping the line as a cellist would, curving up towards a singing minim B flat on the first beat of b.34, and then climbing in *crescendo* towards the minim E flat on the first beat of b.36. Then feel a gradual downward unwinding towards the restatement from b.41. Turning to the RH, let the crotchet upbeat 'lift' to a singing dotted minim B flat on the first beat of b.33, and 'lean' well on this note, keeping the inner thirds relatively light, but rhythmic. Shape the melodic line in a warm singing tone through to b.36, always taking care that the melody sings out over the inner chords or single notes. Then 'lift' to a warmly singing minim E flat on the first beat of b.37, feeling that this is a 'continuing' but more ringing answer to the previous phrase, bb.33-6. When you put hands together, notice how the LH reaches the top of its curve on the minim E flat on the first beat of b.36 in 'advance' of the RH. Then let the two melodies sing out in glowing lines from b.37, taking time as you *diminuendo* through b.40 to 'finish off' the LH trill gracefully beneath the RH chords, ready to 'start again' from b.41. Then 'clear' the sound on the rest on the second beat of b.48 before 'leaning' back into b.33 from a warm-toned crotchet upbeat. Then from the second-time bar 'lean' into b.49 with a rather stressed upbeat chord. This section is the most dance-like, with rather the quality of a Schubert Ländler. Move on a little, 'leaning' on the first beat of bb.49, 51, etc, and shaping the RH lines in cheerful 2-bar phrases over a carefully balanced and rhythmic LH. Show the sense in which the RH 'goes up to' a bright and rather definite crotchet third on the third beat of b.50, and similarly 'down to' the third on the third beat of b.52. Be particularly careful once more to finish off the LH clearly in b.56 (second-time bar) before leading on again into the restatement of the G flat section. Although the indication *Fine o da Capo il Valzo* suggests that the piece can end at b.72, Chopin's intention to return to the opening Waltz movement is assumed (particularly since he referred to the middle section as a 'Trio' – see above).

Waltz No. 14 in A flat major (6)*

This little Waltz, thought to have been written in 1829-30, makes a pretty study for a young player.* Practise the LH alone until you achieve a perfectly secure and rhythmic 'OOM-pah-pah' in a lively tempo. Then, leading in from a slightly lingering quaver upbeat, shape the RH semiquavers in neat, clear curves up to the highest note on the third quaver pulse of each bar as indicated by the 'hairpins', over your neat, brightly dancing LH (learning the skill of neatly sliding the RH thumb down from black note to white on the first beat of b.2). Then shape the phrase from b.5 in a smooth overall curve, up 'through' the G on the second beat of b.6 and down again to a clear quaver E flat on the first beat of b.8. Allow a little 'give' through the end of b.7 and then take care to place the LH chord neatly on the second beat of b.8 beneath the RH quaver rest as you prepare to set off again with a clear upbeat to b.9. Curve up again with a little swell towards, and down from, the D natural on the second beat of b.14 (first-time bar), and then slur the semiquaver couplets neatly downwards over a steady LH. From the second-time bar *crescendo* grandly up towards a ringing high quaver A flat on the first beat of b.16 and finish off the LH neatly here before leading into b.17 from a clear RH upbeat C. Support the easy-running RH with warm-toned rhythmic LH chords from the upbeat to b.18, reverting to the more dancing LH from b.21. Allow a generous *ritenuto* as you ease back through b.24 (second-time bar) towards the reprise at b.25. Play the little Trio brightly and rhythmically like a little horn tune, supported by a cleanly placed and carefully rhythmic LH.

Waltz No. 15 in E major (6)*

Written in 1829, but only published in 1867 this makes a pleasing piece for a young student at Grades 5-6.

bb.1–24
Set an easy waltz rhythm, not too fast, at around $\dot{}$ = 50-4, and play the opening unison figures very rhythmically in a rousing, annunciating manner. Give a strong lead in from the slurred upbeat crotchets, and feel the renewed onward impetus conveyed by the slurred quaver upbeats to bb.2 and 3 and the onward-pressing, *stretto* effect through bb.3-4. Arrive on clear unison crotchets on the first beat of b.5 and then make a

---

*This was only published in 1902. In the version in the Paderewski Edition the main body of the piece is printed straight through, i.e. without repeats, and with a number of variants.

purposeful run up from the second beat towards resonant emphasised minim C sharps on the first beat of b.6. Be sure that these slurred minims sing out smoothly over the carefully balanced inner RH minim thirds and lower LH minims, so that the melody line is

clearly  and **not** etc. It is best, I feel, to

diminuendo through b.8, and 'ease' into b.9 – otherwise, if you keep up the *forte* through to the end of b.8 and then make a *subito piano*, the melody from b.9 (not one of Chopin's most entrancing) comes as a bit of an anticlimax after the grandiose build-up! Make a little *diminuendo* and a tiny 'give' therefore through b.8, with a tiny break at the end of the bar, ready to lead off with the main melody in b.9 in a warm, *dolce* tone. Make a little swell up towards a singing seventh on the first beat of b.10, and then go on to 'lean' again on a singing dotted minim sixth on the first beat of b.12. While shaping these 2-bar phrases neatly, over an easy-lilting, quiet waltz rhythm in the LH, do at the same time feel the shape of the overall melodic line from b.9, leading on again from b.15 in a smooth *crescendo* through b.16 to carry on into the restatement from b.17 in a rather fuller tone. Be sure to time bb.11, 13, etc. carefully so that the quaver fourths are given their proper value and not 'clipped' into semiquavers; to this end it is essential that the LH chord is accurately placed on the second beat of these bars.

bb.24–56 Be sure to 'finish off' the LH neatly down to the low crotchet E on the second beat of b.24, then making a tiny break, ready to launch into the next section with a fuller-toned RH upbeat crotchet octave. *Crescendo* warmly up towards a singing minim octave C sharp on the first beat of b.27 with a feeling of moving on with more of a rhythmic swing, and then drawing out a little as you 'point' the echoing lower LH melodic fragment from the upbeat to b.28. Then play bb.29-33 in a light, sprightly fairy-like style. Practise at first without the trills, 'leaning' on the slurred crotchet on the first beat of the bar (treating the second crotchet in each bar as well as the third, as *staccato*). Then when you add the trills be sure that you do not lose the 'leaning' effect on the first beats, giving these trills

five notes  Feel the general impulse towards

a 'lean' on the tied crotchet A sharp on the first beat of b.32, and then slur the quavers smoothly down to the crotchet G sharp on the first beat of b.33, ready to 're-take' the octave motif on the upbeat to b.34. Show the LH slurs on the second beat of bb.37-9 so that in these bars you have alternating RH-LH slurred effects. Then 'draw out' b.40 a little as you prepare to return to the more leisurely movement from b.41.

bb.56–124 Be sure once more to 'finish off' the LH clearly in b.56, again making a tiny break, before leading into b.57 from a quietly emphasised tied upbeat crotchet E.

Again feel the dance-like movement here, showing the light emphasis on the slurred LH crotchet on the second beat of each bar. Make a graceful *crescendo* up to and down from the emphasised C sharp on the first beat of b.61, and then allow a little give through bb.63-4 before starting on the next upward curve from b.65. Note all details of RH articulation in this section. Be sure to **lift** the RH from the quaver F sharp on the third beat of b.59, and then **lift** the hand in a skipping effect at the end of bb.61-4 (see General Introduction under

'Articulation'). Leap up expansively to the higher octave on the first beat of b.69 and then take a little extra time to shape the curving quavers smoothly as you descend in a *diminuendo* towards b.72. Allow a clear rest here before setting off into the reprise with the full-toned unison figure.

Waltz No. 16 in E minor (8)

This is a splendid number, short and compact with lively contrast not only between sections, but also within each section. Written in 1830, supposedly before Chopin left Poland, it has proved one of his most popular pieces, and we can only wonder why he never published it. It has on a small scale much of the exuberance, rhythmic impetus and éclat of Op.18 in E flat. Paul Hamburger analyses this piece in some detail (Walker, pp.87-9). Ideally it requires quite a turn of virtuosity, with a tempo of around ♩. = 80-84 and certainly not much less than ♩. = 72, and many a brave attempt founders within the first few bars! For those using the Paderewski edition there will be a cumulative discrepancy in bar numberings from bb.56, 72 and 96 since in this edition first- and second-time bars are counted (i.e. for b.57 read b.58 and so on – see General Introduction under 'Bar Numberings').

bb.1–24   The first pitfall is, of course, the opening flourish. Practise the LH alone first in an absolutely steady tempo, making a tremendous *crescendo* towards b.7 until you can play the spread chords confidently, in time, and **without looking** at them. Then practise the RH slowly and with immaculate articulation. The curve up to the top note in each bar to the E, G, etc. creates the **suggestion** of a cross-rhythm effect. If you 'feel' this without labouring the point, this flourish becomes much easier to play. When you put hands together feel that the RH, played with all possible brilliance, is being directed by the rhythmic impetus of the LH chords progressing vigorously towards the final and strongest chord on the first beat of b.7. Ultimately, set a tempo **relating** to that at which you are going to play the main waltz theme from b.9 (see Introduction to Waltzes), and lead into b.1 from a clear crotchet upbeat. Allow this upbeat its full value or a little more as you 'lean' into b.1, ready to launch into the flourish, making a gradual *crescendo*, and allowing a degree of controlled *accelerando* if you can manage it. 'Go up to' a ringing high quaver E on the third beat of b.7 and 'braking' a little, **lift** the hand ready to 'throw' the upbeat semiquaver vigorously down to the crotchet third on the first beat of b.8. Clear the sound through the rests as you poise yourself to set off into the *grazioso* theme in your chosen tempo. This section is disconcertingly difficult to control. Practise it slowly hands separately, precisely in time. Play the RH *staccato* figure through b.9 with a neat '**rat**-tat-a-tat', and then make an airy 'lift' up through b.10 towards the high B on the third beat. Bring the hand **off** this *staccato* crotchet, and then feel the onward impulse through b.11 towards a clear crotchet third on the first beat of b.12. Then slur each acciaccatura neatly up to the staccato crotchet on the first beat of bb.13-15, again being sure to bring the hand off so that it falls with a natural slight emphasis onto the doubled minim on each second beat.

In the LH leap with a light spring from the *staccato* crotchet on each first beat so that the hand falls with a slight emphasis onto the slurred chord on the second beat. Then when you put hands together you will find that this slight natural emphasis on each LH second beat plays a vital part in keeping the RH (and the whole section) steady. Feel the sense of onward impulse from b.9 towards b.12, and then a sense of unwinding through bb.13-16. Take care to keep the sense of your steady beat as the RH quavers descend through b.16 as you poise yourself to 'start again' from b.17.

Arrive on a neat chord on the first beat of b.24, and **feel** the rest on the second
bb.24–56 beat, ready to lead on into the *dolce e legato* section from a soft-toned but clear
crotchet upbeat B. Feel a **slightly** slower tempo here as you shape each quaver
curve (bb.25, 27, etc.) graciously towards a warmly emphasised minim on the first beat of bb.26,
28, etc. over rhythmically 'spaced' LH crotchets (showing the chromatically descending bass
line from b.25). 'Finish off' the phrase neatly at the end of b.32 as you poise yourself to leap off
into the athletic quaver passage from b.33. Many players whip up the tempo somewhat violently
here. Only move on as fast as is safe, underpinning the RH with a firmly rhythmic LH. Feel the
implied swell up to and down from the topmost note of each 2-bar RH quaver curve (bb.33-4,
35-6, etc.) and once more feel the implied (and steadying) 'lean' on the LH slurred crotchet on
each second beat as you leap energetically up from each strong bass crotchet. Allow a little 'give'
through bb.39-40 as you *diminuendo*, poising yourself to return to the *grazioso* motif at b.41.

Allow a tiny break after the second beat of b.56 (first-time bar) ready to lead
bb.56–131 back to b.25 with soft upbeat quavers. At the end of the second-time bar make a
clear break through the crotchet rest ready to set off into the major section, *dolce*
once more, but in a more sprightly vein that at b.25. Let the dotted minim sing out gently but
warmly through bb.57 and 58, and then run up prettily with a little swell towards the
emphasised slurred high minim on the first beat of b.60 over a neatly rhythmic LH, again
showing a light 'lean' on each slurred second beat. Make a little *ritenuto* through b.71 as you
prepare either to return gracefully to b.57, or to finish the section with a neat chord on the
first beat of b.72 (second-time bar). The grace note figure in b.71 (shown in many editions

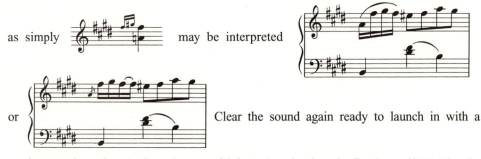

as simply   may be interpreted

or   Clear the sound again ready to launch in with a

resolute crotchet upbeat 'going to' a powerful *fortissimo* chord on the first beat of b.73. Play the
RH chords in strict time, feeling that the energetic LH rising figures are fitting in with the RH
chords and **not** the other way about. Let the LH quavers rise in a vigorous *crescendo* towards a
strong thumb stroke on the crotchet G sharp on the first beat of bb.74 and 76. (The original
fingering 5 4 2 1 5 4 1 (?) is the only practicable one here.)* Then from the upbeat to b.77 shape
the LH melody line in an expressive full-toned curve as a cellist would up to and down from the
emphasised dotted crotchet D sharp on the first beat of b.78 making a *diminuendo* and very
slight *rallentando* as you descend towards the low G sharp on the first beat of b.80. Many editions

give a spread chord on the first beat of b.81   rather than a block chord

over the tied upbeat B as in Henle. In any event, those with small hands can pedal the upbeat
crotchet and hold its sound within the pedal through into bb.81-2. From b.89 avoid running
away (as inexperienced players often do) by **listening** to the LH quavers running in neat
pianissimo curves beneath the quietly breathed RH melody.

---

*In most editions the RH minim chord in bb.74 and 76 is A sharp C sharp G sharp, rather than (and preferable to) the
B sharp D sharp G sharp in Henle. (See Commentary in Paderewski Edition).

Practise bb.107-8 carefully hands separately. Give an extra 'lean' on the slurred LH fifth on the second beat of b.107 to steady yourself, and then allow a tiny break at the end of the bar as you prepare to leap down to the vigorously spread chord on the first beat of b.108. When you put hands together coordinate this leap carefully with the RH allowing yourself an extra instant to poise yourself, so that you arrive on this repedalled chord with maximum impact. Then clear the sound before leading on from a firm treble upbeat to b.109. Most players make a progressive *accelerando* as they *crescendo* from here. Keep your *accelerando* within your own limits, however, and make it very gradual or you will run out of steam and collapse in a heap long before the end. Above all, control the *accelerando* with a firm LH, feeling the strong 'braking' emphasis on the firmly placed minim chords on each second beat beneath your brilliant RH quaver figures. As an additional 'braking' aid, think of the last two RH quavers in each bar as the upbeat to the subsequent bar. 'Go to' a powerful chord on the first beat of b.113, and then continue to feel that the vigorously ascending LH is in control (again feel the crotchet octaves as **upbeats** to the strong first beats of bb.114-17) as the RH quavers hurtle downwards. Take a fraction of extra time to steady yourself as you play the big chords on the upbeat to and on the first beat of b.117, ready for the final gallop to the end. Dash down to a **controlled** tonic on the first beat of b.119. Then allow an extra instant for the RH to leap up to the A sharp on the second beat, dropping the tone a little here so that you can 'whip up' the *crescendo* towards b.123. Rattle out the RH pattern 'egged on' by vigorous LH chords, feeling that each upbeat chord is 'going to' the tonic chord on the subsequent first beat. Then articulate the arpeggio in a brilliant curve up to the high E in b.124 to make a meteoric descent to the low octave E on the first beat of b.127, and *crescendo* through a burst of clarion chords in outward contrary motion towards a powerful final tonic.

Waltz No. 17 in A minor (4-5)*

Waltz No. 18 in E flat major (4-5)*

Both these pieces are valuable additions to the rather small selection of Chopin's pieces available to players at about Grade 5. Both could also perhaps be managed by older players at Grade 4. The E flat is a particularly charming piece with its expressive chromatic inflections and luxuriant LH melody in the second half.

No.17 in A minor*
This little waltz, thought to have been written about 1847, was published for the first time in 1955. John Vallier, who gave its first performance, also includes it in his *Oxford Keyboard Classics* selection of pieces by Chopin. It was dedicated, he says, to the Baroness Rothschild, or to her daughter, who were among Chopin's first pupils in Paris. It carries the hint of a quiet Mazurka movement in the way that each 2-bar subphrase moves towards a minim on the second beat of bb.2, 4, etc. with each of these minims conveying the sense of an 'on and over lean' into the next 2-bar period.

bb.1–15   Set an easy *allegretto* waltz movement at a suggested tempo of around $\dotted{\quarter} = 44\text{-}8$, and lead in from a warm-toned smooth RH upbeat crotchet, taking care to give this its full value while also feeling a nice onward 'lean' towards the first beat of b.1. Make a little swell as you rise towards a singing minim F on the second beat of b.2, and similarly feel the impulse of each 2-bar subphrase towards each singing minim (on the second beat of bb.4, 6, etc.). At the same time feel the sense of the overall phrase from the upbeat to b.1 through to b.8. Shape the quavers in a smooth curve through b.3 up to and down from the topmost note A, and then play the grace notes in a leisured clear style, either on or before the beat. Allow just a little 'give' through the end of b.7, ready to end the phrase on a neat crotchet C on the first beat of b.8, being sure to 'finish off' the LH cleanly on the chord on the second beat, ready to lead off again from the upbeat to b.9. Keep the LH waltz movement even and steady, imagining a smooth, rather gliding waltz step as opposed to a more springy 'OOM-pah-pah'.

bb.15–56   Allow a little 'give' again through the end of b.15 with just a hint of a vocal lingering on the high D, ready to end the section with neat definition. Then move into b.17 in a rather fuller tone, and with a sense of slightly moving on. Allow a little extra time as you make a pretty curve up to the high dotted quaver B on the third beat of b.21 – if you 'space' the LH a little between the second and third beats of the bar, there is plenty of time to fit in the five semiquavers. Poise yourself on the high B, lingering for just an instant before leading on from the upbeat semiquaver in perfect time. (While allowing this little 'give' in the LH chords in this bar, do at the same time feel that the LH is governing the rhythm, and that the RH is fitting in with the LH and not the other way about – see General Introduction under 'Rubato', and also the Introduction to the Waltzes.) It is effective to play the high registered bb 22-4 in a light, tinkling style. Feel a nice 'lift' up to the high quaver E in b.23, with a tiny 'hold' on the repeated E, ready to fall neatly to the tonic A in b.24. Return to the opening motif in b.25 in a quiet tone, and then from b.29 feel you are 'moving on' a little in an upward *crescendo.* Support the RH with firm bass notes, particularly on the first beat of bb.31 and 32 as you pass through the dominant seventh of E major en route to the dominant seventh of A major. Arrive on a resonant RH minim and LH chord on the second beat of b.32, and then let the high RH melody line open out from b.33, still 'moving on' towards b.36. Then you could play bb.37-40 in a pretty echo effect of bb.33-6. Allow a little *ritenuto* through bb.39-40, finishing off the LH neatly on the sixth on the second beat of b.40, and clearing the major sound before leading back into the reprise from the upbeat to b.41. Be sure to take the RH **off** at the end of b.50, and 'point' the bass crotchet E on the first beat of b.51 ready for the RH to re-enter confidently on the ornamented offbeat. Similarly 'point' the bass crotchet on the first beat of b.53, and then let the melody line fall expressively from the high quaver C, either in a full tone, or more quietly and in a pretty *diminuendo* towards a quiet ending.

No.18 in E flat major*

This was written in 1840 and dedicated to a pupil, Emil Gaillard. Like the little Waltz in A minor, it was not published until 1955, and is also included in John Vallier's selection of *Oxford Keyboard Classics.* The second half give novice players a good opportunity to learn to shape a LH melody line eloquently beneath carefully balanced RH chords.

bb.1–8   The movement settles at a slightly slower tempo than No.17, around $\downarrow$ = 116-20, but with a considerable amount of give and take. Lead in from a warm-toned crotchet upbeat, taking care to give this its full value while at the same time feeling an onward leading 'lean' and 'lift' towards a clear crotchet G on the first beat of b.1. Shape the *sostenuto* melody line expressively, making a little swell as you curve towards a singing minim B flat on the first beat of b.2, and then similarly shaping the second sub-phrase towards the minim G on the first beat of b.4. Because the LH has a rest on the first beat of each of these bars, it is extremely important that the RH melody note on each first beat is given its full value, and that in each bar the LH 'comes in' accurately and neatly on the second beat. Shape the wide-spanned curves of the longer phrase from b.5 smoothly and unhurriedly over a carefully balanced LH. Shape the curve up to the E flat on the third beat of b.6, and again up to the C at the end of b.7, and then through the end of b.8 feel the three quavers (B flat-E flat-F) as an upbeat group leading into the varied restatement from b.9.

bb.9–24 Linger expressively for an instant on the third beat of b.9 to 'point' the dotted rhythm. Take an extra instant again to listen to the effect of the dominant seventh harmony in the LH through b.12, 'pointing' the dotted rhythm again on the upbeat to b.13, and similarly delicately 'point' the nice RH C flat on the upbeat to b.14. Then let the RH quavers 'open out' as you rise to the high G on the third beat of b.14, allowing time to listen to the luxuriant 'double-stopped' inflections as the RH descends through b.15.

End the phrase with a clear RH sixth on the first beat of b.16, being sure to 'finish off' the LH with a clean fifth on the second beat. Then allow a tiny break ready to lead back to b.1 from a clear RH upbeat. After the repeat allow a slightly clearer break ready for the LH to 'take over', leading on into the next section with warm-toned upbeat quavers, 'going to' a singing dotted crotchet on the first beat of b.18. Shape the LH melody with the utmost expressiveness as a cellist would, supported and 'filled out' with a carefully balanced RH. Again feel the significance of the 'solo' first beats, bringing in the RH with particular care on each second beat. 'Point' the melodic upper minim B natural on the second beat of b.17 and the treble melodic fragment in b.18. Again feel the three LH quavers in b.17 as an upbeat group, 'going to' the singing dotted crotchet on the first beat of b.18, and let the next three quavers lead similarly into b.19. Incorporate the slurred acciaccaturas expressively and unhurriedly into the flowing melodic line here, balancing the LH with evenly spaced RH chords

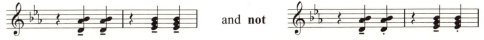

Feel the long overall span of the LH phrase from the upbeat to b.17 through to b.21, allowing a little 'give' through the end of b.20 ready to 'point' the B natural on the first beat of b.21. Then shape the wide-spanned LH upbeat quaver group smoothly up to the E flat on the first beat of b.22, and **listen** to the poignant duet between the treble and LH melodies through bb.22-4. Make a *diminuendo* and a little *ritenuto* through b.23, letting the LH make a final expressive curve up to the high G on the third beat of the bar. Holding this high G for an instant as you listen to the sound of the G against the RH augmented fourth, end with a quiet chord, showing the LH line 'going down' to the final bass E flat. (John Vallier suggests a *da capo* to *fine* at b.16, and this certainly gives a more satisfactory proportion.).

Waltz No. 19 in E flat major (8)

This number will be passed over here. It is apparently of doubtful authenticity, and these doubts are reinforced by the uncharacteristic, lumpy patterns of the RH.

THE POLONAISES

Introduction:

The origins of the polonaise dance, also called the polacca, are somewhat obscure. Early forms of various Polish dances spread through Europe in the sixteenth and seventeenth centuries, and the polonaise, with its measured **3/4** pulse and repeated rhythmic figures, was adopted by Bach and many other composers. In his yet unpublished work *Chopin – His Life and Music*, Adam Harasowski says: 'Later it became customary in Poland to start a ball or a party in a nobleman's house with a polonaise. The host would invite the highest ranking lady into the first pair, and the remaining guests would follow them in a procession around the ballroom, bowing to each other, forming foursomes, eightsomes, displaying their elegant dresses.'

In the early nineteenth century the polonaise was cultivated as an instrumental piece by popular composers of the day. The measured rhythm persisted, but the music inevitably acquired a salon gloss, laced with the kind of mock heroism owed to its stately origins. Chopin's own early Polonaises conform more or less to this salon type. The manner in which he was later to dramatise and glorify the form is graphically demonstrated by the transformation of style and content from his early pieces (Nos 8-16 below) to the mature specimens from Op.26 onwards.

Discussion on the performance of the Polonaises must begin and end with one exhortation – **think slow.** Niecks, writing in the 1880s, described the polonaise as 'not so much a dance as a figured walk, or procession, full of gravity and a certain courtly etiquette' (Niecks, Vol.2, p.240). And this is what it is – a march-like walk, with its roots in the pomp and splendour of court and nobility, and not, as with the mazurka, deriving from folk-life and the open air. A far cry is this processional idea from that scenario familiar to us all, of an audience transfixed by a piano reeling from supersonic hammer blows delivered by an implacable maestro. The formal character of this walking dance dictates a more or less uniform phrase pattern. The principal motifs, almost without exception, proceed in 8-bar periods, often built up of two 2-bar sub-phrases and one longer 4-bar phrase (see, for example, Op.26 No.1, bb.5-12, and Op.40 No.1, bb.1-8). But, given the potency of these motifs, and the manner in which they recur again and again, it is this very squareness which generates such a powerful cumulative effect. These 8-bar periods characteristically end in a feminine cadence, that is, with a slurred, dominant-tonic lean from the second to the third beat, for example in Op.40 No.1, b.8

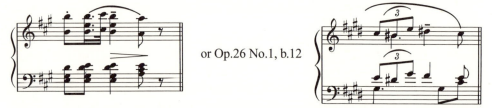

or Op.26 No.1, b.12

While in the mazurka Chopin expressed himself more intimately and also, in a musical sense, in many instances with far greater complexity, it is in the polonaise that he blazons his patriotism for all the world to see. To quote Arthur Hedley: 'A threefold motif runs through them, pride in the past, lamentation for the present, hope for the future' (p.160). This is the spirit of these works which, within the framework of the physical rhythm, must govern and direct the interpretative sights of the player.

As to the style of the polonaise 'walk', the best possible advice is to try to see it performed. The polonaise as performed today in public occurs either as a grand processional dance in its own right, or as a kind of promenade between dance numbers. Even if it is impossible to see a visiting troupe of professional Polish dancers, there are amateur groups to be found in some

British cities, and it is particularly instructive to watch these dancers rehearsing. By the very manner in which they carry themselves, they convey the rhythm in a way that no amount of theoretical learning can do. The special feature of the 'walk' is a slight dip on the third beat. Thus, walking with an erect and proud bearing, one step to the crotchet beat, the knee is bent a little through each third step, which creates an upbeat 'lean' into the subsequent first beat. Try this, imagining, or listening to, the most typical motif of all, that of the A major Polonaise, Op.40 No.1, at a tempo of ♩ = 80-90. Starting with the left leg on the first beat of b.1, the bending of this left leg on the third beat will create an upbeat 'lean' into the first beat of b.2, and then the right leg will 'lean into' b.3 and so on. This gives a special kind of 'suspension' to the walk, creating a powerful impulse towards each first beat.

Turning to the question of tempo, I have purposely not suggested approximate metronome marks as I often have elsewhere. The tempo of each number must be governed by the **sense** of this 'walk', and this only. The ♩ = 80-90 suggested above for our experimental 'walk' is a mean, around which the tempo of the various numbers will settle (see discussion of this matter in connection with the metronome marks given for the three Posthumous Polonaises Op.71). Op.26 No.1, for example, might go a fraction quicker; Op.40 No.2 a little slower. But if you 'walk' them you will find the **motion** (as opposed merely to the metronome mark) that feels right. This will, of course, differ slightly from person to person, and from day to day, but if you **feel** the rhythm you will understand it in a **physical** sense in a way that no amount of mere counting or thinking about metronome marks will do.

Conventionally the typical rhythmic pattern is ♩ ♫ ♩ ♪ ♩ (see Op.40 No.1, bb.25-30, 58, 60, etc; and Op.44, bb.9-12, etc.). But it is by no means ubiquitous in Chopin's Polonaises. It is the **quaver** pulse which is the common factor, providing a framework, either as a continuing 'background' pulse, e.g. in the RH through bb.1-18 of Op.40 No.2, or as a skeleton on which various versions of the above typical pattern may hang, e.g.

♩ ♫ ♩ ♫ ♩ or | ♩ ♫ ♩ ♫ ♫ or | ♩ ♫ ♩ ♫

and so on. Following the typical upbeat 'lean' into a strong first beat described above, there is the characteristic tendency for a **slight** lengthening of the first quaver with a compensatory slight shortening of the subsequent semiquavers ensuring a precise arrival of the second **main** beat.

Following on from this, and as a final word, it was recorded (by Bronislaw von Pozniak) that Chopin recommended that the Polonaises should be **counted** in **quavers** (Eigeldinger, p.156). Pozniak, it appears, was only a pupil of a pupil of Mikuli, who **was** a pupil of Chopin, and J.-J. Eigeldinger says that this injunction cannot be corroborated. However, it seems an unlikely suggestion to have sprung solely from the imagination of Mikuli, or anyone else, and is one which, when in doubt, we do well to heed. Hallé also records that Chopin, in sorrow rather than in anger, complained of hearing Op.53 played too fast (Eigeldinger, p.82), adding to the certainty that, as Eigeldinger says, 'Chopin wanted his Polonaises to be played at a tempo appropriate to their intrinsically majestic character' (p.156). In other words, once more **think slow**.

Most editions print ten Polonaises: the seven (including the Polonaise-Fantaisie) published during Chopin's lifetime, and the three earlier numbers which were published after his death by his friend Fontana as Op.71 Nos 1, 2 and 3. The Henle and Paderewski Editions publish six additional Polonaises (without opus numbers), including the very early G minor, Chopin's first known composition.

Polonaise No. 1 in C sharp minor
Op. 26 No. 1 (8)

Six years separate the last of the posthumously published early Polonaises and this, the first of the seven mature specimens published during Chopin's lifetime. These six years, during which he had left Poland for good to settle in Paris, encompass a world of different experiences and attitudes, and Chopin telescopes the years in one immense genetic leap, leaving the charming gestures and mock-heroics of the earlier numbers far behind. It is therefore a mistake, I believe, to treat this piece as an apprentice work (for all that its textures are sparer and its technical demands by and large less heavy than, for example, those of its companion Op.26 No.2, or of Op.40 No.1). This, though, has often been its fate, to judge from the remarks of some commentators, from the lily-livered performances it sometimes receives, and from the way it is often deemed a 'suitable' piece for young students not yet capable of coping with the rigours and physical weight of later numbers. (Niecks refers to its 'weak timidity, sweet plaintiveness and a looking for help from above') (Vol.2 p.245). On the contrary, it is clear that Chopin knows exactly where he is going and what he intends to say. Indeed, he at once proclaims the new status of the polonaise with his indication 'Allegro appassionato' (this is the only one so marked), and with his violent and jagged opening fusillade. Part of the trouble arises, perhaps, from the erroneous perception of bb.1-8: following the mighty chords of bb.3-4, players are inclined to lose courage and to play the melody from the upbeat to b.5 in an emasculated style and prettified tone. Whereas, as Jim Samson says, bb.1-4 are 'anacrusic to the main theme' (p.105): therefore bb.5-8 should **lead on** from the mighty opening bars so that this main theme, beginning on the upbeat to b.5, leads through to b.8 in a proud and chivalric style – **then** dropping the tone at the entry of the more compliant answering phrase at b.9. (For discussion of tempo see above in the introduction to the Polonaises.)

bb.1–4   Burst in with the opening unisons like cannon fire, playing the demisemiquavers fiercely **on** the beats as if with a thrust, in such a manner that they **slur** vigorously up to and down to the dotted quaver E's, as indicated by the hairpin *crescendos*. Play this sequence in rigorous rhythm, with the feeling of 'going on through' with increasingly vigorous thrusts towards the second beat of b.2. Then **lift** the hands **and** the pedal smartly on the crotchet rest to give a 'kick' to the silent upbeat to b.3. Thunder the chords of bb.3-4 (with maximum weighty, not banging, resonance), taking care to support the RH with a powerful LH. Be sure to hold the pedal through the first and second beats of b.4 so that the resonance of the LH octave C sharp is retained, as you 'finish off' with a powerful, springing 'stamp' with the partly spread chord on the second beat.

bb.4–24   Once again, lift the pedal smartly on the third beat of b.4 to allow an instant's 'breath', ready to launch into the main theme with a strong RH quaver slurred resolutely up to a ringing dotted crotchet D sharp on the first beat of b.5. Let the LH help to launch this theme with a powerful 'push' on the low bass *sforzato* quaver octave, and then support the strongly climbing RH with an immaculately timed

(see introduction to Polonaises above), noting

the 'doubled' lower notes through b.6. Feel that the RH line, having climbed to the high quaver A on the third beat of b.6, is swooping down as if in a *portamento* to the lower upbeat quaver, 'going to' a resonant tied crotchet G sharp on the first beat of b.7. Many players move on from here towards b.8 in a quieter tone. While the RH upward triplet scale obviously needs to be played more expressively, I feel, in view of what has been said above, that it is a mistake to drop the tone too much. For one thing, the echo effect from b.9 will be spoilt. In addition all the indications (the uncancelled *crescendo* from bb.5-6, the *tenuto* on the RH D sharp through b.8, and the LH quavers rising to an emphasised high G sharp) as well as the harmonic sense, point to a 'through *crescendo*' to the end of b.8. In any event, whatever the chosen dynamic, ensure that the ascending, just-detached triplet scale 'speaks' (see General introduction under 'Articulation') as it moves towards the *tenuto* dotted minim D sharp on the first beat of b.8, supported by an 'ongoing' LH quaver line. Note the slight extra resonance lent by the 'doubled' LH second quaver (D sharp) in b.7, and then take care to 'finish off' the LH curve up to the emphasised high G sharp on the third beat of b.8. Allow an instant to clear the sound at the end of b.8 as you prepare to bring in the 'echo' phrase in an expressive, nostalgic, or even rather mysterious piano. 'Spread' the RH triplet expressively through the first beat of b.9 while preserving the onward impulse in the LH (noting all LH details: the 'doubled' dominants and slurred third beat in b.9, and the lower crotchet third, diminished fifth, and third in b. 10), and only letting the movement 'give' in *ritenuto* as you 'melt' the melody line towards the *pianissimo* at b.11. Practise the LH carefully through bb.11-12, showing the gentle upward swell of the inner LH line over the quietly resonant lower F sharp. Let the treble linger fractionally on the high quaver B, and then 'point' the inward contrary-motion movement of the treble and inner LH lines in a whispering *pianissimo*, listening acutely to the subtly discordant intervals passing in cross-rhythm through b.11. Take care to finish off the phrase in sixths meticulously in b.12 over the lower dominant, noting the subtle extra resonance of the doubled RH B sharp. Then coming gently **off** from the tonic quaver chord, **feel** the quaver rest as an upbeat so that you are poised to implement the maximum shock of the return to the opening figure in b.13.

bb.25–32 Few players fully implement the inherently menacing character of bb.25-33, which is implicit in the harmonic and rhythmic layout, even if the page were shorn of Chopin's detailed indications. As it is, Chopin's explicit markings for dynamics and accentuation potently reinforce this feeling of pent-up aggression. Having taken a breath again at the end of b.24, therefore, leap down towards the low bass G sharp ready to start the new section in a completely new, furtive but threatening *sotto voce*. Practise at first **without** the upward shooting diminished seventh arpeggios so that the fundamental rhythm is

thoroughly absorbed:  Then, adding

the arpeggios, practise **slowly** in strict time so that you arrive on the quaver at the top of each arpeggio **precisely** on the second beat of bb.26, 28, etc. *Crescendo* sharply upwards so that this top quaver has a good 'ring' (the fifth finger will hope to be strong enough to make a whiplash *staccato* here), and shoot the RH down again to fall with a decisive stress on the syncopated crotchet chord, precisely synchronised with the similarly stressed LH chord. As you gradually become able to practise the passage in a faster tempo, be sure to keep strict time. Less experienced players will find it helpful to divide the arpeggios into rhythmic groups. Then as confidence grows, you can shoot upwards freely in a single 'streak'. The simplest and most effective procedure is to linger momentarily on the accented crotchet on the first beat (as if it were a semiquaver) so that the grouping will be approximately thus:

(Peters Edition gives a similar grouping to this. See also under 'Free Runs' etc, in the General Introduction.) This passage is far from easy, even for an experienced player. One of the principal difficulties, both rhythmically and 'geographically', is the way in which the hands move far apart in contrary motion but do not coincide at the outermost point (i.e. the LH goes down to the low quaver on the **second** quaver of the bar – the RH reaches the high quaver on the **third** quaver beat or second **main** beat). It cannot be too strongly emphasised that in order to negotiate this passage safely, we need to feel each **quaver** pulse securely, including (or even, particularly) the **held** third quaver pulse of bb.25, 27 and 29, and the **held** fifth quaver pulse of bb.26, 28, 30 and 31. Do, therefore, keep referring back to the skeleton version (i.e. without the arpeggios) to reinforce your sense of the quaver pulse. A fraction longer might be taken over the runs in bb.30 and 31 as if to 'point' their greater span, but in this event it is essential to pick up the tempo smartly from the subsequent emphasised syncopated chord. Indeed, this syncopated crotchet chord is the prime rhythmic **focus** throughout this passage, and it is therefore of paramount importance that it is always placed with keen and vital rhythmic precision. Manage the dynamics to maximise the dramatic effect, returning to *piano* at b.27 after the *crescendo* through b.26, and gradually increasing the overall volume towards a mighty *fortissimo* at b.32. To achieve a powerful RH D sharp at b.32 it is helpful to use the **third** finger, quickly changing to the fifth. Support this note with a huge bass octave, then

'space out' the rhythm with deliberation, drawing out a little towards the

sforzato chord on the first beat of b.33, and showing the inner RH line, 'going to' the G sharp

in b.33. Small hands can take the inner C sharp through

b.32 with the LH; and in any event to avoid 'losing' the RH D sharp when you change the pedal on the first beat of b.33, **most** hands will need to transfer the B sharp to the LH (the LH is then

best broken thus: rather than 'scooped':).

bb.33–49 Kleczynski reports that Chopin brought in the soft pedal through b.33 (Eigeldinger, p.58) to 'melt' the repeated syncopated D sharps towards b.34, and this certainly creates a beautiful effect. In any event, 'ease' these D sharps, both in the sense of dynamics and tempo, towards b.34, but without losing too much of the forward impulse (creating the effect of a continuous yet 'punctuated' sound). Then pick up the tempo clearly from b.34, letting the lower LH quaver line provide a quiet but inevitable onward movement. Phrase the treble melody with quiet, clear and expressive simplicity, showing the vocal-like curve up to and down from the crotchet A on the second beat of bb.34 and 36. From b.34 listen acutely to the balance of the treble line with the implied lower LH

melody line *etc.* as well as with

the inner LH inverted pedal point A and the quiet intermittent ostinato of the lower quaver B's. The LH writing here recalls, or perhaps anticipates that of Prelude No.15 in D flat. As in that

Prelude, shape the 7-semiquaver 'turn' in b.37 approximately thus:

Continue the 'thought' straight on down to the low A on the second beat of b.38, giving a warm but quiet resonance to this motif as it crosses the LH and descends into the lower register. Drop the lower LH quavers to *pianissimo* as indicated at the beginning of b.40, and then make a strong *crescendo* as you draw out a little towards a powerful double *sforzato* on the first beat of b.42.

As you *crescendo* from b.40 be sure to keep the lower LH quavers steady so that they draw out in an **even** and rhythmic, not random, manner towards b.42 (see General Introduction under 'Rubato'). Think of the low RH trill (starting the prefix **on** the beat) as a 'rumble' of increasing volume, with the feeling that the evenly moving LH quavers are 'leading' and **not** the other way around (see General Introduction under 'The Left Hand' and 'Ornamentation'). Space out the two LH quavers through the first beat of b.42 so that the RH has time to leap up from the double *sforzato* quaver to 'come in' vigorously with the foreshortened entry of the 'chivalric' theme on the second beat of the bar.

bb.50–65 Move into the D flat section in another new mood and sound. (Here again the writing is reminiscent of one of the Preludes – the mid-section of No.13 in F sharp.) Shape the treble melody in clear expressive curves. This melody has a quality of coolness that is at the same time sighing and nostalgic, but it must never be allowed to tip over into sentimentality. This will not happen provided that the underlying dance pulse is maintained in the lower quavers (*meno mosso*, but not exaggeratedly so), allowing a little give here and there, but maintaining a continuing sense of onward movement in the 'spaced',

slightly deliberate manner indicated by the . Practise carefully hands

separately. Show all the complementary melodic fragments or 'pointed' notes in the LH or inner RH (e.g. the ascending inner line through b.50, the G naturals and the F flats at the end of b.51 and the C flats at the end of b.53, the descending lower line from b.54 right through to b.56, etc.). In the RH ensure that the high F sings quietly over the lower quavers, 'leaning' gently on this note, and keeping the thumb very light as you shape the descending curve in cross rhythm as if with a sigh down towards the long A flat on the first beat of b.51. Ensure again that this note sings over the lower notes, then allow time for the ornamental turn to 'speak', thinking

of this in approximately two groups of three notes:  or perhaps

more subtly feeling that you are 'going to' a slightly *tenuto*

dotted quaver C on the third beat, and then 'falling' expressively to the E flat on the first beat of b.52.* Show the overall descending span of the treble line from the high F in b.50 down to the lower F on the second beat of b.53. Let the treble line 'breathe' at the end of b.53 ready to start the upward climb from b.54, with the sense of moving on towards the *forte* chord on the first beat of b.56. Balance the sound carefully so that the lower parts 'back up' but never swamp the melody, listening to the contrary motion progression of the treble and lower LH line. Lift the hands cleanly after the *forte* chord on the first beat of b.56 so that they 'fall' to create a natural emphasis on the subsequent high syncopated chord. Hold the sound of the first chord in the pedal as shown, maintaining the *forte* resonance through to the first beat of b.57, only then letting the sound fall away as you descend towards b.58. Note the detailing carefully here so that the tied treble notes *and* the tied inner G flats sing through their full value, and drawing out as indicated, ready to return to what at first appears to be a reprise at b.58. (The treble notes in b.57 are not tied in all editions, and also the phrasing varies in different editions. In Henle the overall phrase line indicates a 'carrying on' through b.57 into b.58. In others there is a break between the phrases implying a 'starting again' from b.58.) Regaining the tempo as indicated, allow a tiny lingering as you curve the ornamental demisemiquavers up to and down from the G flat near the end of b.58 – this effect is complemented by the 'pointing' of the tied last lower LH note of the bar. Having curved the phrase down to the first beat of b.59, Chopin breaks off the melody and leads on from the second beat into a concentrated modulatory passage. Listen acutely to the subtle chromatic inflections of the continually moving quaver chords creating inner melodic lines as they buoy the melody line along. Following the *crescendo* towards b.62, most players *diminuendo* a little towards the spread chord on the last quaver pulse of b.63 (the passage could be varied perhaps when repeated – or at b.95 – by keeping up the tone to this point). In any event, 'flick' this spread chord, in whatever dynamic, coming **off** to 'hold' the mid-air pause, and then give the demisemiquaver E flat a light slurred 'flick' down to the crotchet A flat on the first beat of b.64. A little extra time is needed to negotiate this figure, interpreted

approximately . Then articulate the RH

dotted rhythm figures through b.64 in a neat, dance-like, even skittish style. **Lift** the hand from the *staccato* A flat on the first beat of b.65 (see under 'Articulation' in the General

*Avoid 'bumping' the fourth inner quaver, imagining that the treble A flat is tied, as in Paderewski (see their commentary) and Peters Editions.

Introduction) and finish the section off neatly from a singing treble crotchet E flat on the second beat of the bar.

bb.66–82 This next section with its 'duet' patterns is extraordinarily similar in style to the Study in C sharp minor Op.25 (and to a lesser extent the Prelude in B minor).

Shape the treble and LH lines with the utmost expressiveness, supported by the quietly ongoing inner RH quaver chords. It is a good plan to practise the RH **holding down** the inner G flat and A natural with the thumb and forefinger as you play the treble line as smoothly and expressively as possible (see also RH practice pattern for Op.25 No.7). Shape the LH with a quiet melancholy grace (as from b.50, the continuing inner quaver movement will prevent any oversentimental pulling about of the rhythm). Ensure that the tied LH crotchet E flat on the first beat of b.66 is given sufficient tone to allow it to 'merge' smoothly into the semiquaver turn; then let this turn 'go up to', and linger fractionally upon the dotted quaver G flat, finishing off the phrase clearly but quietly with the crotchet on the second beat of b.67. Similarly shape the semiquaver arabesque up towards the dotted quaver on the third beat of b.68. Do practise this passage **slowly**, without pedal, and at first playing the treble and LH lines **without** the inner chords so that you can absorb the effect of the poignant intervals arising between the complementary voices, the treble moving mainly in smooth crotchets, the LH proceeding in shorter sentences of pleading character. From the middle of b.73 'point' the three descending treble quavers in an upbeat sense towards b.74, and from this point build up the volume gradually but persistently letting the LH sweep up on a fine *crescendo* through b.77 towards the grandly resonant passage from b.78, which leads back to the reprise at b.82 (this time in an implied magisterial *forte*). Listen acutely to the balance between the voices so that as you draw out through bb.80-1 you create a splendid resonance without banging. Mistakes easily occur here with the accidentals – make sure that they and the intervals they create are understood **aurally**, not just as signs on the page. Most players return towards the *piano* dynamic through b.89. Continuing in the 'Trio and *da capo*' pattern of the early Polonaises, the piece ends somewhat lamely at b.49 – from the performing aspect this is undoubtedly its weak feature. Draw out a little more than before from b.47 to give as convincing an air of finality as possible.

Polonaise No. 2 in E flat minor
Op. 26 No. 2 (8+) (O)

The highly coloured words of Niecks hardly exaggerate the impact of this work. He finds it 'full of conspiracy and sedition. The ill-suppressed murmurs of discontent, which may be compared to the ominous growls of a volcano, grow in loudness and intensity, till at last, with a rush and a wild shriek, there follows an explosion'. (Vol.2 p.245). Its cast is very different to that of Op.26 No.1. With its 'typical' powerful chord patterns, it is much more overtly grand (in the sense that Op.40 No.1, and Op.44 and 53 are grand), and also more homogeneous. Chopin has dispensed with the *da capo* pattern, and apart from the first twenty bars, the sections are not repeated. There is therefore a greater sense of continuity, each section leading more inevitably to the next. And the heroic posture persists throughout, 'distanced' rather than counteracted in the *pianissimo*, major, *meno mosso* section from b.69. But so skilfully is the structure integrated, as Paul Hamburger has pointed out (Walker, p.105) and so powerful the dramatic tension that there is no hint of monotony.

Technically, although this is a 'big' work in the sense that it requires sustained power and rhythmic stamina, it is, for the experience of study if not for performance, within the sights of a doughty player at Grade 8+. But for small hands the ♩♫♩ ♫ or, as frequently

in the RH ♩♫♫♫♫ ♫ rhythms in large chords are heavy work, and although many of

these can often be slightly condensed without too much damage to the texture there are, however, vital occurrences of ninths e.g. bb.33-6 and 97-8 which are difficult to edit satisfactorily.*

bb. 1–9   The construction of the first section is extraordinary. As in Op.26 No.1 there is an anacrusic opening sequence, but here, instead of 'preparing' for the theme, the chords of b.8 explode into the dominant at b.9, sweeping on to a dynamic climax at b.11, and only settling on the tonic at b.12. The tempo fluctuations of the introductory fragments create a skilfully calculated frisson – to the bemusement of the relatively inexperienced player confronted with such a series of *poco ritenutos* and *accelerandos*! Have your polonaise tempo well 'in the system' before you start (see the introduction to the Polonaises above) and play the first unison fragment in strict time in a scarcely breathed, mysterious, yet immaculately clear *pianissimo*, feeling that the four semiquavers are 'going down to' the quavers on the second beat. Come **off** precisely after the quavers on the second beat, **feeling** the silent third beat as if with a clear 'push' in the solar plexus, and then ennunciate the repeated chords (like subterranean drum-beats) in a **slight** and carefully controlled *ritenuto*. Feel that each pair of semiquavers is 'going to' each quaver so that, while

each little group ♫♪ is a fraction slower than the last, the **sense** of the crotchet pulse is

maintained.† Play the chords as quietly as is consistent with clarity, and with the kind

of 'spaced' deliberation implied by the ⌒ . . . . . indication. You may wish to abide by

Chopin's **single** pedal indication through each 'set' of repeated chords – or on the modern piano, to change or half-change the pedal on each **crotchet** beat. **Feel** the quaver rest at the end of b.2 as an upbeat so that you enter precisely on the first beat of b.3 again with the unison fragment, this time at a slightly faster tempo. Make a slight *crescendo* as you *ritenuto* again through the next chord 'set' and then notch up the dynamics proportionately from b.5 till you surge with an immense *crescendo* through b.8 towards a clarion dominant chord on the first beat of b.9.

bb.9–20   Support this RH chord with a powerful bass quaver octave, and then as you 'drive home' the LH rhythm 𝄐𝄐𝄐 sweep the RH down to a

decisively 'planted' emphasised crotchet E flat, to give a strong upbeat impetus towards the trill and upward run into b.11. This tremendous upward eruption has to be controlled by a rigorously rhythmic LH, maintaining a secure sense of the overall three beats in the bar (see General Introduction under 'Free Runs'). The faster the run can be played, i.e. starting it as near to the end of the bar as possible, the more exciting it will sound. Less experienced players who find the concept of the run as an overall upward streak too difficult, can try the interpretation in the Peters Edition: the first upward notes D and E flat are treated as the suffix to the trill, and the run proper is thought of as two groups of seven and eight notes respectively to fit within the

*This said, small-handed players will be happy to note that in the copy belonging to Jane Stirling, the bass quaver F on the first beat of b.33 is erased, presumably by, or on the authority of, Chopin himself!

†Or, interpreting the 'poco ritenuto' strictly, perhaps the series of repeated chords should be played at an overall, rather than progressively slower tempo.

last two quaver chords.

To take a less ambitious course, similarly treat the D and E flat as the suffix to the trill, but start the run on the **fourth** quaver beat dividing the notes into three groups of five:

Alternatively, less ambitious still, the run can be thought of as **starting** on the D on the **third** quaver beat and divided into **four** groups of four, four, four and five notes:

Inexperienced players in such circumstances invariably worry about the **trill**. Try to concentrate on the **LH** while letting the trill 'rumble' freely in such a way that it grows into the upward run. Note the suggested fingering, which facilitates the arrival with optimum ringing tone on the tied crotchet G flat on the first beat of b.11. Feel a very slight drawing out through the last quaver beat of b.10 in order to maximise the thrust of this immensely powerful first beat (supported by a LH six-four chord of maximum resonance), and then immediately pick up the

tempo with strongly rhythmic ♪♪♪♪♪ in the LH chords underpinning the descent

of the RH towards the *sforzato* minim on the first beat of b.12. Be sure to **lift** the hand from the semiquaver F near the end of b.11 so that the hand falls naturally to accent the slurred demisemiquaver with a vigorous slurred upbeat 'kick' towards the *sforzato* minim. It is important to feel the sense in which this forceful arrival on the tonic – the objective of the first eleven bars – has at the same time the effect of 'sending us on' into the next period from the upbeat to b.13. While giving the *sforzato* minim its full impact therefore, and also allowing an extra instant in the LH to clear the sound for the *piano* on the second quaver of b.11, be sure then to pick up the tempo smartly in the LH on the **second** main beat of the bar, to give the sense of propelling the rhythm on towards the *agitato* figure. (The 'pointing' of the doubled LH G flat and B flat helps to keep control of the pulse, while at the same time conveying the sense of 'going on.') Be sure to **lift** the RH on the quaver rest on the third beat of this bar so that you can take a quick 'breath' ready to bring in the upbeat semiquavers in an agitated *piano*. Articulate the semiquaver fragments with biting clarity (though in *piano*

until Chopin indicates his *crescendo*), 'going to' a telling accented tied crotchet C flat on the second beat of bb.13 and 14. Then *crescendo* through bb.15 and 16, creating a 'breathless' effect with the slurred treble semiquaver couplets, towards the shrill high version of bb.13-14. There is a strong feeling of 'moving on' through this passage – indeed, many players make a pronounced *accelerando* – but this must be controlled by a LH that maintains a secure sense of the **overall** crotchet pulse. Here the resolute implementation of Chopin's doubled lower LH line not only achieves this control of the rhythm, its resonance also balances the intentionally frenetic shrillness of the high RH figures. Hurtle with a powerful 'whoosh' towards a violent **stop** at the end of b.19. Then, taking a quick breath through the pause, end the section in a 'keen', not sloppy *piano*, as if the agitation has died down temporarily rather than resolved peacefully. Be sure to 'go to' a quiet but definite emphasised crotchet D natural on the second beat of b.20. Then listen to this note resolving clearly onto the tonic over the lower quavers, maintaining the sense of expectancy by making very little, if any, *ritenuto*. Then take a breath at the end of b.20, ready to play the repeat with equal, if not greater conviction.

bb.21–35   Having taken a clear breath on the quaver rest at the end of b.20, lead into the new section in the quietest possible *pianissimo*, the rhythm tautly martial, the chords like distant pinpoints of sound. Hold the sound of the first *staccato* chord with a short pedal, being sure to come **off** to take a breath on the quaver rest on the second beat of the bar, and then time the *staccato* chords with military precision. Listen carefully to ensure that these chords do not merely sound like little blocks of sound, but that the upper melodic line is always diamond clear, and also be careful to 'space out' the two quaver chords at the end of bb.22, 24, etc. (giving these an 'upbeat' feel) so that you don't 'fall into' bb.23, 25, etc. It is helpful for small hands to take the inner C flats on the repeated chords in b.22 with the LH. As in b.21, give the chords on the first beat of bb.23, 25 and 27 a touch of pedal (and also give a light, very quick touch on the quaver chord on the first beat of bb.22 and 24). Be sure to take a breath again on the second beat of bb.23 and 25, and then from the middle of b.25 start a carefully gauged but powerful *crescendo* towards b.29. Use the pedalled resonance of the LH octave minim at least through the whole of the first beat of b.26 to get the *crescendo* under way, and keep the tempo moving in inexorable rhythm. Arrive on powerful *fortissimo* unison quaver octaves on the first beat of b.29 (keeping some tone in reserve for the long further *crescendo* towards b.33), and then note the hairpin *decrescendo* (interpreted in some editions as an accent). This clearly implies an agogic lean on the

first note of the triplet whereas many players do just the

opposite and make a hairpin *crescendo* **into** the second beat. (To feel the effect, practise in plain

octaves with a pronounced 'lean' on the D sharp .) This triplet

figure needs to be played like a whiplash, coming **off** on the *staccato* quaver octave. As you progress from b.30, create maximum excitement by the very deliberation of your rhythm and your *crescendo*. Draw out fractionally through the end of b.32 to maximise the impact of the furious *sforzato* on the first beat of b.33. Beat out the implacably rhythmic

F's in the bass, causing the downward-shooting RH to fit in with the LH and **not** the

other way about.  Arrive on strong quavers

on the third beat, then **lift** the hands so as to be able to 'point' the 'push' on the *sforzato* upbeat quaver chord to b.34. Then observe Chopin's hairpins again, as if making a 'push' on the first

semiquaver of each violent figure. Arrive on a **strong**

short chord on the first beat of b.35, and then allow an extra instant to leap up to the accented chord on the second quaver pulse – the syncopated, and thereby telescoped, version of b.33.

bb. 35–68   Do not make the frequently heard mistake (a matter perhaps of failure of nerve!) of allowing both the tension and the tone to drop after b.36 – it is clear that Chopin intends to maintain both through the relentless jerking figures of bb.36-8, through the *fortissimo* of b.39 to the *sforzato* F major chord on the first beat of b.40, and on again to the resonant unison on the first beat of b.41, only then dropping to *piano* with the RH sixth on the second beat. For those who find b.39 nearly impossible to negotiate (and here many a clever fake goes undetected on the concert platform!), the best approximation to

the written effect is obtained thus: The important

thing here is not the number of notes to be 'got in' to the trill (best fingered 3 5 3 5, or 2 4 2 4 etc.), but the maintenance of the rhythmic impetus, with the sense of a strong lead into b.40 from the RH upbeat semiquavers. Arriving on powerfully resonant unisons on the first beat of b.41, **listen** to their sustained sound as you bring in the sequence of smooth RH sixths, like distant, haunting horn calls. Ensure that the tied sixth on the upbeat to bb.42 and 43 has sufficient quiet resonance to sing over the quietly placed inner and lower notes, and shape the phrases in an expressive *calando* down to the quietly slurred chords in b.44. Then from b.45 play the unison diminished seventh figures in a mysterious whisper, **feeling** the 'upbeat' rest at the end of bb.45 and 46, and poising yourself through the rests in b.48 ready to re-enter with the opening figure in b.49. There are various ways of grading the tempo of this 'bridge' back to b.49. Chopin's *calando* implies a slowing down as well as a *diminuendo* – but take care to play

the inner and lower   rhythmically though slowing through b.43. The

polonaise beat is never absent for long, and its *sotto voce* presence here is inescapably threatening. You might continue an implied *rallentando* through bb.45-8 (but do not overdo this or the music will 'stop') and then either enter at b.49 in tempo as at b.1 (the course that I prefer), or make the entry in a rather slower tempo, picking up at b.51. As another alternative some players pick up tempo from b.45 ready to lead straight into b.49.

In the central B major section, Chopin introduces a marvellously evocative 4-
bb.69–104   bar theme of which, as Paul Hamburger says, he makes 'a series of repetitions, varied by simple modulation and refined harmonisation; a static structure that is a perfect foil' to the return of the opening material (Walker, p.105). Although the indication is *meno mosso*, do not drop the tempo so much that you blunt the martial undertones that are still all-pervasive. Articulate the chords once again with pinpoint precision but with a sweeter tone than at b.21. Be sure once more to 'take a breath' on the quaver rests on the second beat of bb.69, 70 and 71. Then expand a little from the end of b.71 towards a warmly emphasised *tenuto* dominant seventh chord on the third beat of b.72, taking care to 'finish off' the phrase down to a quiet clear B major chord on the first beat of b.73 (which both ends the first 4-bar phrase, and begins the next). Some editions 'point' this sense of expanding by indicating a *legato* phrase from the middle of b.71 through to the first beat of b.73. While shaping each of these fragments (bb.69-70, 70-1, 71-3, etc.) as a little entity, phrase mentally **over** each quaver rest as a singer would, so that you create the sense of the shape of each overall 4-bar phrase. Given a player with a fine control of rhythm, this section is at its most spellbinding when kept as quiet as possible in an atmospherically distant overall *pianissimo*. Take care therefore to return to *pianissimo* after each little swell (bb.71-2, 80, etc.). Listen acutely to the little changes of detail and to the subtle harmonic 'pointing' through the recurring fragments – the inner LH E sharp on the upbeat to b.72, the lower LH G natural on the upbeat to b.76, the marvellous minor inflection on the third beat of b.82, and so on. Keep the LH tremolo in b.97 to a mere shiver – practise this bar carefully, making sure that the tremolo does not sabotage the rhythmic stability of the RH. To achieve clarity of the inner melodic line in this bar, practise it thus while **holding down**

the remaining notes of the chord. Then listen

particularly to the momentary sidestep into G sharp minor in bb.98-9. Let the repeated fragments die to a whisper in bb.101-2, 'leaning' on the emphasised chord on each second beat and **listening** to the held LH resonances beneath the 'fall' of the RH sixths. Then listen again to the marvellous 'spacing' of the resonances as the *adagio* fragment ends on the dominant of E flat minor, **listening** to the held sound through the pause as you poise yourself to return to tempo 1.

Forging up through b.171 with undiminished momentum and preparing to
bb.105–75   come to a violent 'stop' as at b.19, make it clear by the way you place the LH dominant seventh chord on the first beat of b.172 that you are about to move into an agitated *accelerando* (rather than close a section as at b.20, etc.). 'Draw' the offbeat RH semiquavers down to a resonant RH minim D natural on the second beat of b.172 and articulate the LH quavers with clear and **equal** definition (with a short pedal on

each) rather than allowing a lame semi-slurred effect down to the

dominant octave. Allow a short pause and notch up the speed, volume and agitation of this figure through b.173. Then after the next pause 'pull out' the *fortissimo* RH offbeat semiquavers like a wild cry down to a potent pedalled tied crotchet, giving this note its full value and more, as you prepare to play the final fragment in an expressive *sotto voce*. Note the dual melodic sense of the 'doubled' E flat and D natural as you 'go to' a quiet 'lean' on the emphasised crotchet on the second beat of the final bar, playing the LH quaver octaves with quietest possible finality as the D resolves to the tonic.*

Polonaise No. 3 in A major
Op. 40 No. 1 (8+) (O)

This, of course, is one of the great warhorses of the keyboard. And since, like the Funeral March and the Study in E, Op.10, it is one of those pieces with which both the music and the personality of Chopin are branded into popular imagination, it inevitably has been hounded and pounded, transcribed and vulgarised as much as, or more than, anything he wrote. But in the hands of a master architect of dynamic and rhythmic tension its power to fire the spirit remains unsurpassed. Within a strikingly simple structure it encompasses all our notions of the grandeur and chivalric prowess of the Polish nobility. Its rhythmic potency is achieved through the cumulative effect of its relatively constant symmetrical patterns and, in an interpretative sense, it is the most straightforward both of the mature Polonaises and the majority of the earlier ones.

There can be few competent pianists who do not at some time attempt to hurl themselves at this piece. And this is usually the trouble. As in the case of Op.26 No.2, the technical difficulties are not in themselves too formidable, although once more we need a well-developed hand capable of stretching a ninth, and the ability to project and control dynamics, as well as a strong rhythmic nerve. But the temptation to hurtle in like a storm-trooper, far too fast and in full throttle *fortissimo*, goes unresisted by many concert performers more intent on demonstrating their octave techniques than in conveying majestic hauteur and pomp. An actor playing a powerful and princely role will not scamper around the stage, nor will he yell unremittingly! In this, of all the Polonaises, we need to heed Chopin's reported exhortation to 'count in quavers'. (See the Introduction to the Polonaises).

Note: Many editions, including Paderewski, give repeat markings for bb.25-40, as opposed to the 'written out' repeat in Henle. This creates a 16-bar discrepancy in the bar numberings given here (i.e. for b.57 read b.41 – see General Introduction under 'Bar Numberings').

bb.1–8 Have your stately tempo well 'in the system' therefore before you start, and also your dynamic level. Although (or because) the dynamics never drop below *forte*, their layering is extremely important, so that after each *crescendo* we must retract a little (see the 'hairpins' at bb.2, 7 and 8, etc.) otherwise we shall have reached aural saturation point within a few bars. Launch in therefore in a measured tempo, in a controlled but commanding *forte*. It is a good plan to clap the crotchet pulse in a steady beat at about 80 crotchets to the minute while **singing** the melody (in a resolute tone!). Then go straight to the piano and play the first two bars over and over (going straight back from the end of b.2 to the beginning of b.1) so that you thoroughly absorb the powerful rhythmic thrust of this all-pervasive motif which dominates the outer sections of the piece. Never mind a few wrong notes at first – the important thing is to 'understand' the rhythm in a **physical** sense.

*In the score belonging to Chopin's sister the final *ppp* is altered to *fortissimo*, and in Jane Stirling's copy to a triple *fortissimo*. See Eigeldinger, p.156; and also the commentary in the Paderewski Edition.

Play the dotted rhythms in immaculate time, taking care that the semiquaver chords are neither too long nor too short (think of each of these as a deliberate **upbeat** to the subsequent beat (see General Introduction under 'Dotted Rhythms'). Then feel a sense of direction (though in no way hurrying) on towards the dotted quaver chord on the first beat

of b.2.  Throughout this work there is a particularly

strong overall impulse towards each first beat. Remembering the powerful upbeat 'lean' generated by the typical polonaise 'walk' (see the introduction to the Polonaises),

feel each ⎰ ⎱ figure as an overall upbeat 'lean' towards a **strong**

dotted quaver chord on the first beat of the subsequent bar. Be careful to 'finish off' the phrase clearly to the quaver chord on the second beat of b.2 before leaping down to

articulate the figure in perfect time. Play this figure here, and

each time it occurs, with the sense that the music is 'gathering itself' with another overall upbeat thrust towards the next bar. Note the ⟩ implying a 'lean' on the first note of the triplet figure, and then take particular care to 'space' the two detached upbeat quavers accurately, avoiding the frequent fault of letting them slurp vaguely into each other, with a resultant tendency to 'fall into' the subsequent first beat. (Players who know what they are doing will often subtly 'brake' these quavers, thus poising, and thereby maximising the urge towards the next bar, particularly as you again poise yourself to 'point' the change of direction towards the C sharp major harmony on the first beat of b.5.)

Watch the dynamics carefully. Drop the tone a little at the 'upbeat' to the third beat of b.1 so that you 'have room' to *crescendo* through to the chord on the first beat of b.2, and then draw back the level of sound a little through b.2 ready to 'start again' at b.3. Mark the spread chord on the first beat of b.4 by making a **slightly** greater *crescendo* towards it and by taking an extra instant to 'reach' the notes. Feel the sense of the two 2-bar phrases (bb.1-2 and 3-4) and then as you surge into b.5, feel the sense of the longer overall phrase (bb.5-8) so that following the chord on the first beat of b.6 you give the feeling of 'going on and over' with measured but unstoppable impetus towards the end of b.8. Underline the wide span of sound on the first beat of b.6 by making a greater *crescendo* towards it, and then (as in b.1) drop the tone a little so that the repeated C sharps can *crescendo* progressively through towards the first beat of b.7. Show the smooth sweep of the phrase through b.7, maintaining the onward impulse towards a clear, detached chord on the first beat of b.8 and a strong 'lean' on the dominant seventh chord on the second beat of b.8, resolving to a clear tonic on the third beat. Take scrupulous care at all times to ensure that your chords are not mere blocks of sound, but that the upper notes ring out sufficiently clearly to create a consistently delineated melodic line. Note Chopin's pedal indications, which ensure the retention of the bass resonance from the first beat through to the beginning of the third beat of b.1, and then from the first to the second beat of b.2, and so on, and from the first beat of b.6 right through to the first beat of b.7.

The predominant technical problem in this work is the tendency of semiquaver chord figures to jam (e.g. through the end of b.1, and particularly through the repeated chord or octave figures, as in bb.5 and 6). This happens for two reasons, a) because the sense of the basic rhythmic pulse is not securely maintained; and b) because the run of chords is started too loudly. The mere fact of beginning the run of upbeat semiquaver chords in b.1 **relatively** quietly, so that you *crescendo* **through** to the chord on the first beat of b.2 will go a long way to avoid jamming. Similarly, start the semiquaver triplet figure **relatively** quietly on the second quaver pulse of b.5 so that you go through to the quaver chord on the

second beat  and again start the run of repeated semiquaver octaves **relatively**

quietly in b.6 so that you *crescendo* **through** to the quaver octaves on the first beat of b.7. Turning to the question of rhythm – in b.1, as already described, we need to feel the 5-semiquaver run as the overall upbeat to b.2. In addition to this, if you feel the 'single' semiquaver chord as the 'upbeat' to the third beat, you will then inevitably slightly 'point' the next chord (i.e. the third beat of the bar) thereby slightly 'braking' the run, and greatly minimising the risk of jamming. It also helps if you think of **starting** the *crescendo* **on**

this third beat:

A great deal of the trouble arises from panic, and the consequent **hurrying** of these figures. If they can be persuaded to resort to the metronome, players are often amazed by the extent of their panic-induced hurrying in such instances. If, at the risk of labouring the point, we remember to count in quavers, making sure every quaver pulse is rhythmically placed within the dominating stride of the overall crotchet beat, these passages are relatively plain sailing from a technical point of view. In bb.1 and 3, in view of the rests, we need to space the quaver pulse particularly carefully. In b.5 the tendency is to 'fall' onto the triplet chords, jam them, and then 'fall' onwards onto the second main beat; again we need to feel the first three quaver beats particularly carefully. There is far more time than we may imagine to leap 'inwards' from the quaver chord on the first beat, and then to time the triplet chords so as to arrive in one piece **precisely** on the second crotchet beat. Again in b.6 we need to start the run of repeated semiquaver octaves precisely **on** the fourth quaver beat, and then feel the fifth and sixth quaver beats **within** the semiquaver octaves as we *crescendo* into b.7.

bb.8–24   Be sure to come **off** the quaver chord at the end of b.8 so that you can take a 'breath' on the quaver rest ready, either to return to b.1, or to forge ahead into the new section. Many players notch up the dynamics here with a heightened air of measured rhythmic hauteur. But take care not to bang. Conversely do not on any account allow the rhythmic impetus and pomp to flag, always bearing in mind the comments on rhythm made through the previous section. Note the slur and hairpin *decrescendo* from the first beat of b.9 towards the second beat, implying a strong 'lean' on this first chord, and again the slur implying a 'lean' on the upbeat quaver chord to b.11. Then feel the smooth onward movement of the quaver chords from the second beat of b.11 towards the second beat of b.12, followed by a powerful surge towards the massive chord on the first beat of b.13. Then from the second beat of b.15 feel the powerful onward urge towards b.16, with just a little drawing out on the upbeat of b.17 to 'point' this return to the reprise. Consciously lower the tone a little here to the controlled *forte* of the opening.

bb.25–33 Having made another clear break at the end of b.24, launch into the new theme in D major as if on a cresting breaker. Some players move the tempo on here – if you do this, make the increase so slight as to be almost imperceptible. The high hearted roll of this wide-spanned motif must never be allowed to capsize into a scamper.

As will be seen, the 'typical' ♩♫♫ ♫♫ ♫♫ motivates this whole section,

intensifying to ♩♫♫ ♫♫ ♫♫ and then ♩♫♫ ♫♫ ♫♫♫ as the music

surges towards each restatement of the principal motif (e.g. bb.31-2 leading into b.33, etc.). Ensure, therefore, that this LH rhythm is implemented with irresistible buoyancy so that it 'carries' the RH throughout. (Note the continual *staccato* marks which underline the 'separate' articulation within the pedalled sound, which Chopin clearly wants, and which will create this special kind of unsinkable buoyancy.) Note all the pedalling indications carefully so that the resonance of the bass octaves is retained through to the third beat of bb.25 and 27, until just after the fourth **quaver** beat of bb.26 and 28, and then right through b.32 to the first beat of b.33. (The quaver chords in the second half of bb.29 and 30 will benefit from a **short** separate pedal each, so that they sound just detached but not dry.) Imagine a huge man taking enormous strides as you play the main motif in a ringing and springing (not banging) *fortissimo*. Supported by the carefully balanced resonance and spring of the LH, shape the RH line in a splendid curve down from the high D to the low on the first beat of b. 26, then **lift** the hand (see General Introduction under 'Articulation') to make the proud upward turn back to the minim D on the second beat of b.26 ready to 'start again' in the lower register in the dominant in b.27, feeling the shape of this curve each time the motif occurs. Take particular care to 'space out' the quaver chords in implacable rhythm through the second and third beats of bb.26, 28, etc. beneath the RH minim, as if gathering energy for the next phrase. Allow an extra instant to 'point' the G major harmony cleanly on the first beat of b.29, and again to allow time to leap up to the upper LH octave, perhaps dropping the tone a little here. Be sure also that the RH triplet figure, articulated with whiplash clarity, is perfectly synchronised with this implacable **LH** rhythm here and **not** the other way about; and feel that the LH is 'taking command' on the second beat of bb.29 and 30 beneath the semi-tied RH chord. Then listen acutely to the contrary motion effect as the hands move apart in *crescendo* towards a strong quaver chord on the first beat of b.30, dropping the tone a little again as you 'start again' on the second quaver pulse of b.30, and so on. Grade each *crescendo* through bb.29-31 so that you increase the volume progressively, ready to make an almighty surge towards b.33.

bb.33–56 There is no need to force the sound of the triple *fortissimo* unison D's on the first beat of b.33. An immense **natural** resonance is anyway opened up by virtue of the wide-apart span of the treble and bass octaves. And this, coupled with the proper use of natural **weight** and a proper use of the pedal will create a huge sound as you launch into this amplified restatement of bb.25-28, without resort to the fruitless banging sound caused by merely **hitting** from the forearm. It is important to **balance** the sound properly to optimum effect. Almost nothing will drown a high treble sound – think how a single flute will ride a powerful orchestral sound – but it must not be left stranded. It is the bass which creates the big resonance here, and this resonance will **enhance,** not drown the treble. Allowing the tone to drop a little as indicated through b.35, 'point' the shift to the dominant seventh of B flat at b.37. Through b.37 and again b.38 feel the impulse towards the treble **crotchet** on the third beat (with a **slight** tenuto on this note) grading your overall *crescendo* carefully so as to 'peak' the climb with a powerful 'lean' on the second beat of b.40. Be sure once more to take a clear breath at the end of b.40 ready to bound off with renewed energy from b.41.

bb.57–104   Allowing time for a breath again at the end of b.56, leap downwards in such a way that you 'spear' rather than 'prod' the first note of the low trill (C sharp) on the first beat of b.57. Practise this passage at first **without** the trills. **Hold** the minims for their strict duration, **feeling** the held second and particularly third beat (as if with a strong 'push' in the solar plexus) so that the demisemiquaver upbeat figures are perfectly timed. Feel these like a 'sting in the tail' of the long notes, 'going to' a biting quaver octave (taken with the LH) on the first beat of the subsequent bar. Let the powerful spring that occurs naturally as you lift the LH from the quaver octave send the hand upwards so that it shoots up to join the RH in a strongly rhythmic ♫ ♫ ♩ ♫ ♩ with virtually no delay (see General Introduction under 'Directioning the Hand'). At bb.61 and 62 implement the intentionally more powerful effect of the upbeat figure augmented into semiquavers. Then when you add the trills, start each with powerful unisons (preferably, in my view on the main note), feeling that these unisons are growing into a double 'rumble', rigorously adhering to the crotchet pulse. Then feel that these rumbles are evolving into the stinging rising semiquavers which in turn, and still rigorously in time, 'go to' the biting quaver octave on the first beat of b.58, and so on. Once again conserve your power for the mighty *crescendo* from b.63. 'Go to' a ringing quaver chord on the first beat of b.64, and this time direct the powerful spring off this treble chord downwards to the trilled quaver B natural. Create a continuous chain of trills here with the approximate effect *etc.* as you slow towards the reprise. Then allow a little extra time for the leap up from the end of the bar, as you poise yourself to 'start again' in tempo from b.65.* At the end of b.80 make a particularly pronounced break in order to 'point' the return to A major for the final reprise.† And through the final bar take a little extra time to prepare to implement the 'punch' of the triple *fortissimo* ending.

Polonaise No. 4 in C minor
Op. 40 No. 2 (8)

The stamp of this work is very different from that of Op.40 No.1. Doubtless because it is less showy and less challenging in terms of technique and stamina it has remained comparatively neglected by concert pianists. Freer in construction and far more complex in a rhythmic and harmonic sense, it follows that it is much more difficult to hold together. But in a fine performance it is a work of disturbing dramatic power. It requires an artist capable of projecting its ominous atmosphere, its inherent rhythmic tensions, and its jarring, sometimes eerie dynamic contrasts. This said, I have studied it with students in their early teens who, gripped by this foreboding atmosphere, have played it with splendid conviction. Older players at around Grade 7 might also tackle it successfully.

Note: Many editions, including the Paderewski, repeat bb.3-18 with the indication 'second time *forte*', and this creates a 16-bar discrepancy in the bar numberings given here (i.e. for b.35 read b.19 – see General Introduction under 'Bar Numberings').

*(marked with a triple fortissimo in some editions).

†For the record, it appears that Liszt played the reprise here softly at first, 'and then loud again in the following section [from b.73]. Chopin did not particularly observe this nuance himself, but he liked it when I did so: in fact he was thoroughly satisfied'. (Eigeldinger, p.82).

bb.1–4

The opening bars of repeated minor chords set the louring mood for the entry of the principal motif, in *sotto voce*. Observing the *maestoso* indication, set a steady tempo with these quiet RH chords. (For discussion of the tempo for the Polonaises in general, see above in the Introduction to the Polonaises.) Play these chords evenly, in such a way that you clearly establish the sense of the steady three beats in a bar, though without obvious accents. Since through the outer section of the piece the RH is exclusively occupied in this type of even chord playing, it is important that you cultivate the skill of playing chords so smoothly that the sound is almost continuous, creating the illusion of a *legato* (see under Prelude No.4 in E minor). Show the slight swell towards the first beat of b.2, and then draw back a little, ready for the LH to enter in a murmurous, threatening *sotto voce*. This LH melody, which dominates the whole piece, proceeds in two 2-bar subphrases (bb.3-4 and 5-6) and a longer overall phrase (bb.7-10) within the 8-bar period (bb.3-10). Study the contours of the continually recurring 2-bar motif (bb.3-4) thoroughly. Feel the suppressed menace of the upward 'heave' from the subterranean bass octave, up to the dotted crotchet E flat on the second beat of the bar, ensuring that this figure is played perfectly rhythmically within the framework of the steady pulse of the RH chords. Observe the articulation of the LH precisely, raising the hand exactly on the second quaver pulse, and then feel the semiquaver as the 'upbeat' to the dotted crotchet on the second beat of the bar (see General Introduction under 'Articulation').

If you **sing** this 2-bar motif, you will at once understand the sense in which this dotted crotchet is the rhythmic and melodic focal point of the phrase, i.e. it is the 'objective' of the

figure, and the note from which the line then falls toward the minim

G on the second beat of b.4. Feel a quiet but definite 'lean' on this note therefore – this will also ensure that it has sufficient resonance to sound on through the third beat of the bar when the RH harmony (and consequently the pedal) changes. (Even relatively advanced players will often persistently fail to **hold** the dotted crotchet until its sound has been caught by the new pedal on the third beat, thus losing the melodic line here.) Show the slight swell towards the first beat of b.4 by marking this RH change to the dominant seventh with a tiny emphasis on the third beat of b.3, and similarly by giving the LH upbeat quaver octave a little extra definition. Play the semiquaver figure through the first beat of b.4 with just a little freedom, lingering **fractionally** on the D in a 'speaking' manner, but still within the framework of the RH chords. Then let the tone fall away a little down towards the quietly sustained low minim G on the second beat and then, in your anxiety to 'get on' with the next phrase take care not to hurry the RH chords through the third and fourth beats of b.4. These little swells, emphases and so on, are only little nuances within the overall (initial) *sotto voce*. They are nevertheless vital to the understanding of the melodic and rhythmic contours, and thus to the shaping and projection of this recurring motif in all its dynamic contexts. Therefore practise bb.3-4 over and over (going steadily on through the end of b.4 to 'start again' from b.3) until you are fully at ease with the shaping and motion of the phrase. It is important to realise that it is the **RH** chords which are maintaining the steady 'walking' pulse which 'carries' the LH melody, 'giving' a little here and there but always providing the sense of onward motion. In this instance, of course, the usual roles are reversed, and it is the RH which is the 'conductor' (see General Introduction under 'The Left Hand' and also 'Rubato').

bb.5–11

The second phrase (bb.5-6) could perhaps be played in a rather stronger dynamic, with a slight 'pointing' of the move to a higher pitch in the RH on the third beat of b.5. Let the RH chords through the second half of b.6 give the feeling of leading on (but steadily) towards the more resonant high LH octave E flat on the first beat of b.7. Make an expressive 'lean' on each of the 'solo' LH octaves on the first beat of bb.7 and 8, shaping the melodic line of each of these bars in a smooth downward sweep as indicated by the phrase marks and the 'hairpins'. 'Point' the LH octave D flat a little on the upbeat to b.9 with a sense of onward movement towards that bar. From b.7 listen acutely to the inflections of the RH harmonies, which supply not merely an accompaniment, more a chordal counterpoint. Take care that the RH does not 'hang on' over the quaver rest at the beginning of bb.7 and 8 so that you get a 'clean' LH octave on the first beat.

From the middle of b.9 a treble melodic fragment emerges, forming a link between the end of the first LH melodic period (bb.3-10) and the beginning of the next. These two bars (bb.9-10) are quite complex in both the melodic and harmonic sense, and need to be carefully studied. Take care to 'finish off' the RH quaver chords at the beginning of b.9 in a clean, slurred effect, to 'make way' for the lift of the LH up to the crotchet F on the second beat. Then as the LH moves on towards the end of its phrase in b.10, let the RH chords 're-enter' with the G major chord in the middle of b.9 in such a way that you clearly show the emerging treble line. Let this upper line sing out quietly and expressively in brief duet with the LH line as these three quaver chords move with an upbeat feeling towards the crotchet A natural on the first beat of b.10. Ensure that this A natural sings out **over** the inner second chord as the LH at the same time 'finishes off' its own phrase. Slur these two LH quavers cleanly, ensuring that the hand comes **off** as the RH expands in a *crescendo* towards a singing dotted crotchet E flat on the third beat, allowing a slight vocal 'hold' on this note as you prepare to enter again with the LH on the upbeat to b.11. Ensure once again that this high E flat sings out over the inner chord and then, synchronising the LH entry carefully with the inner RH upbeat chord, 'finish off' this treble fragment clearly down to the C on the first beat of b.11, ready for the chords to resume their more passive role from the second quaver pulse of the bar.

bb.11–34 The *crescendo* into b.11 suggests that the opening LH motif should return in a rather stronger tone, moving into the long *crescendo* from the upbeat to b.13. 'Point' this LH upbeat crotchet octave B flat, showing the slurred effect down to the quaver octave on the first beat of b.13, and then make the wide LH leap down to the E flat on the second beat of b.14 with a certain deliberation as you broaden the tone gradually towards b.15. Listen acutely to the marvellous sonorities created between the hands as the music brushes with the keys of E flat, A flat and D flat, and to the emergence of the treble line again from b.15, this time in a longer passage in duet with the LH. Take care once more to ensure that the treble crotchet sings over the inner second quaver chord through the first beat of bb.15, 16 and 17 before letting the tone fall away towards the end of b.18. Be sure again to 'finish off' the two RH chords cleanly through the first beat of b.18, as you listen to the last quiet 'heave' of the LH up to the crotchet D on the second beat. Linger fractionally on this slightly emphasised note (see the little swell), 'finishing off' the line carefully to the C, beneath the carefully placed RH chords. Be sure to 'take a little breath' at the end of the bar after this quiet ending, ready to surge in with the restatement from b.19 in a full and confident but not overloaded tone. Return to *piano* at the end of this restatement ready to maximise the shock of the *fortissimo* at b.35.

bb.35–41 In their anxiety to rush on, inexperienced players are inclined to spoil this shock effect here. Be extra careful therefore to 'finish off' and 'breathe' at the end of b.34. Play this violent chord fragment like a quick burst of gun shots, perhaps with a slight sense of moving the tempo on in this section. Leap up from the powerful low quaver chord to play the figure in perfect time in a biting *staccato,* and with the feeling of 'going on' to a piercingly resonant syncopated accented LH crotchet octave

on the fourth **quaver** pulse of the bar.  Allow this crotchet

octave to make its full impact, **feeling** the third crotchet beat of the bar as you hold it through its full value. Then place the RH upbeat quaver C so that it gives a clear onward lead into b.36, also taking care to place the **LH** octave on the first beat of b.36 in such a way that it gives the rhythm a neat 'kick-off' into this bar. (Some editions, such as Peters, give an emphasised tie on this upbeat. If you do this, make sure that the C has sufficient tone to **sing over** the carefully placed LH octave.) Play b.36 in a very rhythmic, dance-like, yet *agitato* (not skittish) style, with the feeling of 'moving on' towards the next burst of gun shots. Keep this sense of moving on under control through b.36 by careful rhythmic 'spacing' of the LH quavers. Chopin's intended RH articulation is made clear by his short slur effects:

 (Not shown in all editions. Peters, for example,

gives an overall slur from the upbeat to the end of the bar.) Be sure to set off really quietly again from b.38 so that you can make a **gradual** *crescendo* from b.39 towards b.41. There is again a sense of moving on through the *crescendo*, but ensure once more that this is kept under control with the help of the **rhythmically** placed LH quavers, whose sound is carefully balanced against the rising RH. It is essential that the **LH** controls the rhythm and **supports** the RH here – otherwise the RH will rush away, strangulating itself in hysterical shrillness as it rises. Note Chopin's pedal indications from b.35 onwards: holding the pedal through bb.35 and 37 so that the resonance of the low first quaver chord is held through the syncopated emphasised crotchet octave A flat, and raising the pedal **as** you place the RH upbeat quaver C. Chopin then pedals right through b.36 (and b.38, etc.), again so as to retain the bass octave through each of these bars. However, on the modern piano the effect of this can be too thick and heavy, and you may prefer to change the pedal on each **crotchet** beat, being sure to catch each bass note in each pedal. If the RH proves difficult to control here,

practise it thus: *etc.*

bb.41–71   Build up the dynamics within an increasingly taut rhythmic tension towards b.42. Noting the change to the smooth **long** RH phrasing from the upbeat of b.42, leap down in the LH to a powerful bass G on the first beat, and sweep the LH upward in a grand but gradually quietening curve, listening to the contrary motion movement of the hands through bb.42-3. Dynamic indications vary considerably in different editions here. While the RH seems to 'peak' through b.41, I feel that the overall volume should continue through to a grand arrival on a powerful bass dominant at b.42 (as given in some editions), with a **gradual** carefully judged *diminuendo* and relaxation of rhythmic tension from this point. This *diminuendo* is a long one, extending in effect through to b.54. Inexperienced players invariably lose volume and tension far too quickly so that there is almost nothing left by about b.47. Do observe the LH fingering given in most editions (changing 1-5 on the second quaver of b.42) which helps to reinforce the dominant resonance of the whole passage. (Note the dominant pedal point effect right through from bb.38-55.) Take care, too, to carry the curve of the LH line right up to the F sharp on the third beat of b.43. Then, placing the lower tied dominant resonantly on the first beat of b.44, show the entry of the inner LH motif clearly on the second beat. This haunting, intensely eloquent motif, is like a horn-call. Play it very rhythmically (so that the continuing downward movement of the RH is not sabotaged), feeling the impulse towards the slurred dotted minim on the first beat

of b.45.*  Bring in the next LH upward sweep in

b.46 in a lower dynamic. Then notice how the LH line is 'broken' in b.47 as you place the dominant pedal point carefully on the first beat of the bar, showing the crotchets E natural and F sharp as an **inner** melodic fragment. Listen acutely all through this passage to the inflections of the RH semiquavers above the LH melodic phrases. Still letting the sound subside progressively, shape the inner LH quaver fragment expressively from the middle of b.50 'going to' the B natural on the first beat of b.51 (and similarly in the treble from bb.51-2). If you wish to change or half change the pedal on the first beat of b.51 and cannot stretch the LH tenth, avoid losing the bass sound by taking the inner B natural with the RH thumb rather than the left (without impairing the overall even spread of the chord). Curve the RH semiquaver line smoothly down towards the first beat of b.53, bringing the tone down to a whisper and ensuring that the hands are perfectly co-ordinated as the LH upbeat fragment enters on the last semiquaver of b.52. Carrying on the horn-call analogy, this LH motif has a 'hunting' quality, giving a sense of suppressed agitation as the music gathers itself ready to launch into the reprise from b.56. To implement this *agitato* effect, ensure that these slurred LH fragments are articulated properly, rather than being allowed to slurp vaguely into each other. And while there has been an inevitable slackening of the tempo towards b.52, feel the sense of 'moving on' now, from b.53 towards b.56. Many players start the *crescendo* well before it is indicated in b.55, and the interpretation of this build-up effect must be a matter of choice. But I find that playing bb.53-4 in a suppressed, agitated *pianissimo* (and thus adhering to Chopin's apparent dynamic intentions), while at the same time whipping up the rhythmic momentum, ready to make a steep and vigorous *crescendo* downwards through b.55, creates the greater rhythmic and dynamic tension and excitement. Although Chopin did not specify a *forte* from b.56, it must be implied by the preceding *crescendo*, and the main body of this reprise is generally sung out in a full-throated manner, lowering to *piano* towards b.71 as before.

bb.72–86   Although the middle section seems to be taking us into a different world, warmly, even sweetly nostalgic, the sense of threat is never far away. There is also a wealth of harmonic detail and of melodic counterpoint, and this section needs to be studied with scrupulous attention to detail. Having taken another clear 'breath' at the end of b.71, lead into b.72 in a quietly sustained, expressive tone, shaping the curve of the treble melody smoothly in a slight swell up towards the crotchet third on the second beat of b.73

*For a different interpretation of these bars see the commentary in the Paderewski Edition, which suggests that the upsweeping LH line through bb.42-3 (bb.26-7 in this Edition since bb.1-18 are repeated) should be carried through towards a 'doubled' RH G on the second quaver beat of b.44 (28).

278

(taking care to articulate the inner semiquaver fragment clearly and eloquently on the upbeat to b.73). Then, noting the punctuating effect of the phrasing, feel an implied emphasis and fractional 'lingering' on the dotted quaver on the upbeat to b.74, sounding this 'open' fourth like a quiet warning. Practise the LH carefully alone, listening to the complementary upper melodic line of the thirds, and then when you put hands together ensure that the LH supports the RH with a very smooth and steadily onward-moving line. 'Finish off' the second phrase fragment clearly to the second beat of b.74, and then, allowing an extra fraction of a second to take a 'breath' and clear the sound, bring in the repeated chord figures on the upbeat to b.75 in a muted but immaculately clear **pianissimo**, like distant martial sounds. Ensure that, quiet as the passage is, the chords are perfectly rhythmic, feeling each pair of semiquavers like an upbeat 'going to' the quaver chord on each **crotchet** beat. Practise this passage **slowly** in

'single' chords  *etc.* so that you sort

out the complex series of accidentals with **aural** understanding, and not merely as marks on the page. Make it clear that this little passage ends with the first two quaver chords of b.77, as you prepare to 'smooth out' the RH line from the second main beat. Then curve the treble line up to the E natural on the second beat of b.78 'expanding' a little as you listen to the LH line rising in eloquent curves through this bar towards the crotchet C on the first beat of b.79. Linger a little on the chord on the second beat of b.79 as you prepare to ease through the remainder of the bar with a slurred 'upbeat' effect, ready to 'start again' in b.80. This restatement could well begin in *pianissimo*. Indeed, Kleczynski reports that Chopin played here with the soft pedal (Eigeldinger, p.58). Allow an extra instant as you shape the RH curve in a vocal manner up to, and down from the high second semiquaver third in b.81. Practise this **slowly** with both hands so that your ear absorbs the effect of the juxtaposition of B naturals and the B flat. 'Go to' a quietly, but resonantly singing RH minim E natural on the first beat of b.82, ensuring that this sings over the quietly 'pointed' inner dotted crotchet A natural, while at the same time letting the LH (noting the tied quaver A natural) give the feeling of 'moving on' towards the third beat of the bar, ready to lead on with the little martial motif. (Peters edition gives a *forte* on this third beat, underlining this sense of 'going on.') Make sure that you arrive on a 'clean' doubled tied RH E flat on the first beat of b.86, 'following on' with a confidently emphasised tied offbeat **LH** E flat. Then lean a little on the RH chord on the second beat, and co-ordinate the hands carefully to 'finish off' with a slurred effect cleanly and quietly on the third beat.

bb.86–113 Be particularly careful to take a good breath at the end of b.86, ready to burst in with the gun shot quaver chords in b.87. Create the maximum shock effect that you can muster here, articulating the chords with biting ferocity, supporting the the RH with powerful bass octaves, and making sure that the two quaver chords are given

equal emphasis 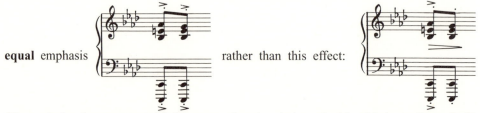 rather than this effect:

Give each chord a separate pedal, just a very short 'stroke' to coincide with the 'strike and off' of the chords, so that you maximise the resonance without diluting the abruptness. Then

feeling the second beat on the quaver rest, enter quietly but resonantly on the offbeat (particularly 'leaning' a little on the tied LH quaver C). This passage (from b.87) needs to be practised with the utmost care by **any** pianist. Play the LH line with all possible expressive eloquence, shaping the wide- spanning curves as a cellist would, and taking a fraction of extra time to 'go down to' and 'come up from' the low bass E flat in b.89. Take equal care with the RH, ensuring that the treble **and** inner lines are properly shaped (e.g. **listening** to the sustained inner minim through the first and second beats of bb.88 and 89, and taking care that the treble crotchet on the second **quaver** pulse of both of these bars is sustained over the second **main** beat, and so on). Then when you put hands together listen acutely to the glorious interplay between the hands through this passage (bb.87-90). It is essential to ensure the finest possible *legato* since, owing to the complex inflections of the continually moving LH semiquaver line, the pedal needs to be used **very** sparingly here. Let the RH 'go to' a quietly resonant tied A flat on the first beat of b.90, letting this sing over the second beat so that the melody does **not**

sound thus: Then give a little 'push' on the tied G on the fourth

quaver pulse so that the second half of the bar leads with a forward, overall upbeat movement and an implied *crescendo* towards the 'shock' chords again in b.91. (It must be remarked that many concert artists play from the middle of b.87 – and again from b.91 – in a hectic juddering manner that seems totally at variance with the character implied by Chopin's long phrase indications.) Start the climb from b.93 **quietly,** then moving on, building up the resonance in an implied *crescendo* towards b.95. The RH through bb.93-4 needs to be carefully managed and many different fingerings are suggested by various editors. I always come back to

the same fingering *etc.*

with the hand a little 'pointed' to the right, which I find strongest and most secure. But each hand must find its own preference – the essential is that your fingering favours a clear and purposeful upward movement. This passage is not easy to control. While allowing a feeling of moving on, maintain a continual sense of the crotchet pulse, feeling the fourth semiquaver of each group as the 'upbeat' to the subsequent main beat. It is easier to understand the

sense of this if you listen to the **inner** RH line: *etc.* etc.

Endeavour to keep the RH lines as smooth as possible, like a slowly rising gust of wind, guided by the steady single semiquaver line in the LH. Swell through to the second beat of b.95, and then fade the sound progressively as indicated, tailing away to a 'speaking' whisper through the carefully spaced repeated C's which, although slowing through b.97, still have the feeling of 'going on' towards the tied C on the first beat of b.98. If you give yourself time to 'gather a sigh', you will know how long to pause on the first beat of b.98. Then play the semiquaver fragment as if letting out the sigh towards b.99, immediately picking up the tempo of the gentle movement as in b.72.

bb.113–133   At the beginning of b.113 let the RH subtly 'point' the fact that here you are 'going on' instead of 'finishing off' as at b.86. Let the first two quavers, therefore, 'go to' a quietly but urgently emphasised minim B flat, ensuring that this sings well over the inner quaver fourths. At the same time let the tied accented LH quaver enter tellingly in perfect synchronisation with the second RH quaver. Grade the *crescendo* carefully through this magnificent bridge passage back towards the beginning of the reprise at b.117, letting each LH fragment enter with increased urgency on the second quaver of bb.113, 114 and 115 (ensuring also that the LH comes **off** at the end of bb.113 and 114 so that the RH has a 'clean' first beat in bb.114 and 115). Then help the *crescendo* by letting the LH 'go down to' a strong bass G on the first beat of b.116, and by feeling the onward propelling LH accents on the second and third beats of b.116. Keep control of the rhythm by ensuring that the RH quaver movement remains stable, even though giving a sense of moving on. By **listening** to everything that is going on you will avoid the danger of becoming too hectic and arriving at b.117 in too fast a tempo, thus destroying the nobility of the magnificent 'duet' (from b.117) towards which you have been building since b.113. (See Paul Hamburger's analysis of this and other such bridge passages in the Polonaises (Walker, p.96 onwards). Surge on into b.117 with the feeling of carrying on and over from b.116 in the RH, but with a sense of a final, grand 'new beginning' in the LH. Exploit the glorious resonances to the full, but **without** banging, ensuring that the contours of the LH melody so thoroughly studied at the opening are preserved. Take care too that the inner RH chords are carefully balanced with the powerfully delineated and sustained treble line so that, for example, the inner chords on the fourth and sixth quaver pulses of bb.117, 118 and 119 are placed relatively quietly ensuring the melody line sounds clearly

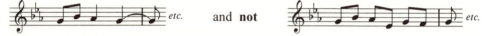

Often even relatively experienced players fail to **listen** to this reiterated melodic fragment, bashing out these inner chords indiscriminately. Ensure too that you preserve the stately yet impassioned splendour of this passage by keeping a **steady** crotchet pulse. 'Finish off' the melodic duet clearly at the end of b.120, taking the RH **off** while letting the LH 'go on' to take over powerfully on the first beat of b.121 as you rejoin the 'regular' reprise. Carry on in full splendour of tone towards a resonant chord of D flat on the first beat of b.131. (Draw out just a little through the end of b.130 in order to poise yourself to place the D flat chord with maximum impact.) Then, **feeling** the crotchet beats through the rests, play the offbeat LH quaver octave in perfect time like a strong upbeat to the immense final chords. Feel a powerful 'lean' on the dominant seventh minim chord, giving this its exact value, and listening to the upper tied G as you resolve smoothly to the tonic chord, holding the final sound to the **exact** moment you decide to release it. It cannot be too strongly emphasised that there must be **no banging** to vulgarise this superb final section. Natural **weight**, properly used, and the carefully balanced support of a resonant bass pedalled for optimum **clear** resonance, will provide all the necessary power.

Polonaise No. 5 in F sharp minor
Op. 44 (VA)

Polonaise No. 6 in A flat major
Op. 53 (VA)

As Jim Samson has said, these titanic works 'expand the framework of the genre so much that they almost lose touch with the traditional type of dance piece. They are more like tone-poems based on the dance, grander in conception and more powerful in realisation than any of the earlier essays' (p.109). It goes without saying that both are strictly for virtuoso players, and will therefore only be discussed in general terms (see Preface). And both, again it goes without saying, have been ruthlessly mauled and pounded by generations of keyboard Goliaths, more intent on demonstrating their ability to beat their shiny Steinways into submission than in exploiting the magnificence of this climactic music. As in the case of all the Polonaises, this splendid hauteur, the 'exalted anger' referred to by Weinstock is sadly devalued by the all too frequent assumption of a racing tempo. Never is the reminder to 'count in quavers' (see the introduction to the Polonaises above) more necessary. Indeed, it was the speed of a performance of Op.53 of which Chopin sadly but perhaps resignedly complained (see again the Introduction to the Polonaises). But given an artist who understands their majestic spirit and rhythmic pomp, either of these works generates electricity of sufficient voltage to galvanise a troop of dormice.

In both works the main theme is preceded by an anacrusic opening (see under Op.26 No.1). In Op.44 the beginning of this introduction is reminiscent of the ominous mutterings of Op.26 No.2. The longer (16-bar) introduction to Op.53 is one of Chopin's most highly charged and provocative pieces of writing. Over a dominant pedal point he screws up the tension in a climbing series of viciously spiked fragments alternating with seething semiquaver rumbles. The point at which this brilliantly calculated rhythmic suspense reaches breaking point and erupts, as if with an exultant shout, into the triumphal tonic theme (at b.17) is surely one of the grandest and most tumultuous moments in all piano music. It is at this point when the principal theme 'breaks' in both Op.44 and 53 that rigorous control needs to be exercised so that the essential stateliness of the dance rhythm is established. It can never be overstressed that the maximum excitement, in terms of both rhythm and dynamics, is achieved by **control**, and not by frenzied lurchings hither and thither. In two similar points in both works the pounding often becomes insupportable: bb.21-2 in Op.44, and bb.23-8 in Op.53. In both instances (although Chopin **has** accented the bass octaves in bb.25 and 27 in Op.53) we often hear an

over-accentuation of the bass octaves, creating a  effect.

Whereas if we 'count in quavers' (Eigeldinger, p.156), thinking of the offbeat quaver chord as the **upbeat** to the subsequent bass octaves, we achieve a far more exhilarating and 'ongoing' yet controlled effect.

Op.44 is, of course, an immensely long work, demanding considerable stamina. In a letter of 1841 Chopin described it as 'a kind of Fantasia in the form of a Polonaise, and I shall call it a Polonaise.' (*Selected Correspondence*, p.200). It is vital for the sake of both player and listener that there is a keen appreciation of the changing character of the various sections, especially since there are very few dynamic markings. Having reached a mighty *fortissimo* at the end of b.8, for instance, we need to take care to enter at b.9 in a controlled *forte* rather than blasting in at full throttle. Similarly at b.17, allow room for the splendid counterpoint effect to ring out without undue forcing. Seldom can a mere scale have been so radiantly harmonised as in the climb through bb.27-8 after the turn into B flat minor at b.27. Note the change of temper here as this *sostenuto* octave line arches splendidly upwards in a smooth 'bowed' phrase, with the added frisson of that suggestion of running away uphill (particularly when the line breaks into quicker note values at the expanded return of the passage at bb.53 and 286). The audacity of the famous passage from b.83 never fails to take the breath away – one can only marvel, considering the society in which Chopin moved, that he dared to risk his neck with such brazen originality. Needless to say, the rhythm has to be poised on the tautest wire, and the articulation delivered like cracks of a whip – and that does not mean unremittingly loud. Indeed, it is essential not to start too loud at b.83 as there is an implied build-up towards b.95. Then when the scale passage returns at b.103, it is effective to slide into it from the upbeat to this bar without excessive preparation so that from the moment it gets under way, its arrival seems at one and the same time both astounding and yet inevitable. Thereafter the long *decrescendo* from b.117 towards b.126 needs to be graded with the most acute ear, while maintaining the bite of the march-like rhythm till the *rallentando* eases into the 'tempo di mazurka'. Chopin's intention that this whole section should be played in a dream-like *sotto voce* is surely clear – the dynamics (**none** are marked except for this initial *sotto voce*) rising and falling a little here and there, but hardly emerging from a trance-like smoothness of line. In addition to the long RH

phrase lines, Chopin underlines his intentions by the

in the LH, implying a kind of even, suspended quality of the 'arc' of just-detached crotchets within the overall pedal. The ending is as unexpected as so much else. Launching into the coda at b.311 in a furious burst of *staccato* chords in *stretto,* Chopin pulls back sharply into a broad melodic phrase, gradually subsiding from b.320 above quietening subterranean rumbles. But peace does not supervene; the last bass fragments retain the hint of the whiplash, and the final unison *fortissimo* octaves are, as Weinstock says, 'like an uncontrollable shout of well-earned triumph'. (p.253).

Although Op.53 is shorter, more compact and less fantasia-like, it is perhaps technically even more demanding. As in Op.44, the magnificent rampaging of the principal theme needs to be rigorously controlled in terms both of rhythm and dynamics, and the contrast emphasised of the noble striding *sostenuto* interlude from b.57. And it takes a player with unassailable rhythmic assurance (and an iron nerve) to negotiate the long scales in tenths, followed (particularly at bb.47-8) by those wide-leaping chords and octaves. Those who rashly start the viciously jerking passage from the second quaver pulse of bb.49 and 53 too loudly, will leave 'no room' to *crescendo* and will so saturate the ear with general clatter as to swamp the discordant rasp of the lower parts against the treble pedal point. Again the dynamics have to be scrupulously controlled through the notorious octave passage. The quieter the entry of the *staccato* semiquavers at b.83 and of the *sotto voce* RH like muted horns at b.85, the more electric the ultimate *crescendo*. (It is astonishing that this passage – as transfixing as the similarly placed episode in Op.44 – appears to have escaped the attention of film-makers!) Once more it is a mistake to play so loudly from b.121 that the melody has to be forced rather than allowed to ring out buoyantly, continuing from b.126 in a gradual overall 'dying fall' towards b.128. The impulse needs to slacken from the upbeat to b.129 to allow time for the RH semiquaver line to breathe, though maintaining a sense of onward movement in the LH particularly in the effect of the implied slight emphasis on the syncopated crotchet octave (or ninth) in the alternate bars (bb.131, 133 and 135). Although the context is very different, the inspired, wandering inflections of the RH through this long passage recall, or rather anticipate, the writing in the coda of the Nocturne in B, Op.62 No.1. Liszt evidently admired this passage. It is recorded that (from b.138) he recommended: 'In this register of the piano, don't just play the bass notes *sforzando*, that is, reinforced, but give them a slightly lingering accentuation, like the muffled rumbling of a distant cannon. The pedal will help to obtain this effect. The idea isn't my own, I've often heard Chopin play it like that' (Eigeldinger, p.83). From b.151, the downward directed unison passage propels the music back with powerfully gathering momentum towards the final reprise.

No. 7, Polonaise-Fantaisie
Op. 61 (VA)

This is the last of Chopin's large-scale works for piano (the last large work of all being the Sonata for Cello and Piano Op.65). It is generally agreed that it represents a synthesis not only of many elements of his style and musical personality to date as it were, but also of evidence of his continual honing of his skills towards ever greater freedom, and at the same time concentration of expression. It is a profoundly significant work, both in terms of its pointers to the directions he himself might have taken, and in the sense of its visionary strayings, even towards the twentieth century.

There is no doubt that this is a 'difficult' work. Few of us, I imagine, could truthfully say that we were able to embrace it at a first, or even a second or third hearing. But as Arthur Hedley says 'It works on the hearer's imagination with a power of suggestion equalled only by the F minor Fantasie or the Fourth Ballade' (p.163).

While this is not a technical war-horse like the Polonaises Op.44 or 53 (although the rhapsodic final section requires virtuosity of a sophisticated nature), it is, by nature of the extreme freedom of its structure, difficult to hold together. As a concert work it follows that it can only succeed in the hands of an artist of the highest aspirations and accomplishment. But on the other hand there is so much to learn here about Chopin, and about the piano, and no competent pianist should miss the opportunity of, at the least, exploring this music, which is of an originality, and beauty and intensity of expression that Chopin seldom, if ever, surpassed. Both Paul Hamburger (Walker, pp.105-13) and Jim Samson (pp.200-11) analyse the structure in detail. But while one may perceive the 'bones' of the music fairly readily in a superficial sense, it takes time to absorb the remarkable sense of physical unity underlying the interweaving melodic, harmonic, rhythmic and expressive threads. The Wagnerian implications of the introductory section have been remarked on by Arthur Hedley among others (pp.163-4). Chopin's ability to invoke a mood or atmosphere with an introductory gesture of a few chords, or less, has been noted in numerous instances in this book. Here, the declamatory opening chords alone are a call from a strange land indeed. When the echoing sound of the C flat minor chord merges into the upward trail of improvisatory crotchets, our destination (either tonally or in the interpretive sense) is anyone's guess. This is a marvellous study in **listening**. The more peremptorily the *forte* chords are timed, the more effective they sound. Then we need to **listen** and wait, and then 'imprint' the aural shape of the upward curve upon the echoes of the minim chord with a kind of deliberation that is at the same time mysteriously beckoning. No pianist will play these sequences in the same way, nor will any one pianist play them twice in the same way. This is a limitless field for the varying shades of 'suspended' sound, and for experimenting with the pedals. Whether, on the modern piano, to hold each entire arc of sound within one pedal, or whether to make partial changes as you ascend, (e.g. in the first ascending arc, on the E flat above middle C, and again an octave higher) must be a matter for the individual ear, and the quality of piano and acoustic.

The multi-voiced writing from b.9 recalls that of various of the mature Mazurkas. When the polonaise rhythm proper thrusts in at b.22, it immediately withdraws its *forte* to allow the entry of the main melodic theme to enter *mezza voce* in b.24. Chopin then splendidly expands rather than develops this theme. Note the 'speaking' effect of the interruption in the melodic line (bb.34 and 35) and then from b.51 let the line flower naturally into the semiquaver passage-work in b.52. The music comes to a sudden 'stop' at b.62, with the long RH octaves sounding a strangely warning 'call' through bb.62 and 63 (show the eloquent movement of the LH and inner RH voices here beneath these bare tied octaves in the RH). Then from b.64 Chopin eases towards a long span of running semiquaver passage-work of a dance-like, almost *scherzando* character. Listen acutely here to ensure that the complementary fragments flow easily between the hands, 'pointing' the inner repeated-note fragments in polonaise rhythm (bb.68, 69, etc.). Then let the semiquavers 'grow' again from b.76 in delicious 'flying' delicacy. The dance-like sequence returns from b.80, progressing more forcefully towards b.88, and then easing back graciously through another sequence of flying semiquavers towards b.92. Here Chopin makes an entrancing fake start, trailing the RH upwards in a *diminuendo* scale before returning to the principal motif proper at b.94. The density and harmonic richness of the writing through the subsequent section of expansion (from the upbeat to b.99) recalls that of the great Nocturnes Op.55 No.2 and Op.62 No.1. This is music that needs to be studied **slowly** by **any** pianist, in order that the interrelation of the strands of part-writing is thoroughly understood in an **aural** sense. The nocturne-like section in B flat starting in *dolce* from b.116 has a clear relation to the principal theme. Once again Chopin expands the motif – this time (following on from b.125) into one of his passages of what we might call expressive virtuosity. Take care, therefore, to **listen** to every inflection of the RH semiquavers (supported by a carefully balanced LH) rather than just rattling off this passage.

Be sure to give the quiet dotted minims and chords their full value and more as you slow through bb.144-7, towards the B major section. The four introductory bars of smooth chords (bb.148-52) have a quiet *religioso* character, and the slow section itself is one of the most affecting passages in the whole of Chopin's work. Though very different in climate, it has the kind of intense, contemplative solemnity of Bach. Widely differing tempos are adopted by different players here. The essential is that the sense of onward movement is maintained, and this to a great extent depends on the LH. These LH quavers need to be phrased in eloquent and beautifully shaped arcs; and providing the slight give and take necessitated by the harmonic inflections is never allowed to undermine this sense of movement, there will be no danger of 'sticking' (and this 'rule' permits considerable latitude in the choice of **basic** tempo). Careful practice hands separately is necessary, and acute listening when the hands are put together, to ensure an expressive balance between the quietly resonant treble line, the inner quavers, and the widely curving LH. Above the 2-bar curves of the LH, note the short RH phrases (bb.153-5 and 155-7) and the longer overall phrase from the second beat of b.157 through to b.162, and so on. (This phrasing varies in different editions.) Shape the hairpins and the longer swells carefully, and 'point' the chromatic inflections as and when they occur in either or both hands (e.g. bb.158-9, 160-1, etc.). The writing, particularly from bb.160-7, with the tolling bass notes and chromatic vacillation in the inner RH, looks forward strikingly to Rachmaninov. Listen to the chromatic curling of the descending LH line, as you let the sound dissolve towards b.180 before resuming, as if resignedly, with the nocturne-like melodic motif from the upbeat to b.181. The long trill starting from a whisper at b.199 and growing in a radiant swell as it doubles, then trebles, ending in an extraordinary *sforzato* shout on the third beat of b.205, is, as Arthur Hedley says 'an unforgettable moment if the pianist is a master of his craft' (p.164). From b.222 Chopin begins the long and gradual build-up towards the triumphant final return of the principal theme at b.242, followed by the *fortissimo* version of the melody of the slow section from b.254, rising in increasing exultance towards bb.269-70, and descending in a wide-sweeping arc to an immense dominant *sforzato* unison on the first beat of b.272. This considerably taxing passage needs to be both propelled and controlled by a powerfully rhythmic LH (the LH and RH semiquavers here coincide with the third quaver of each triplet group). The music is then phased away towards distant rumbling trills from b.282. As Arthur Hedley goes on to say, 'in the last pages Chopin bids farewell to his country's heroic past. The cavalcade which he has conjured up seems to vanish across the plain, leaving him alone until a final loud chord breaks the spell.' (p.164).

Polonaises Nos. 8, 9 and 10
Op. posth. 71 (Nos. 1, 2 and 3)

While it may be true that these three pieces published by Fontana after Chopin's death, 'add nothing to Chopin's reputation' (Hutcheson, p.218), they are nevertheless of interest to students of Chopin on various counts. They demonstrate at a glance the spiritual distance that Chopin had travelled by the time he published the pieces of Op.26. While in these earlier pieces (Op.71 No.1 was written in 1827-8 and Nos.2 and 3 in 1828) Chopin is in undoubted and exuberant command of the keyboard, the dashing gestures and pianistic glitter are tailored to the tastes of the salon. By 1834/5, the date of Op.26, the heroics are for real, and the ornamentation so rigorously pruned that it exists only as an integral part of the structure, or as an essential part of his equipment in the furtherance of his expressive objectives. These three pieces also underline an important practical point about the tempo of the polonaise in general. Even if we had not seen the metronome marks, it would be found impossible to play these pieces too fast (and even assuming that the metronome marks $\bullet$ = 84 for No.1, $\bullet$ = 92 for No.2 and 80 for No.3 are Fontana's, he would have been sympathetic to the essential character of the polonaise tempo). A glance at No.1 will demonstrate this. First we remark the Allegro **maestoso** indication. Then the LH quavers through bb.5-12 are written in an obviously 'spaced' style, which immediately establishes the stately step of the Polonaise (see the Introduction to the Polonaises) and at the same time allows room for the frilly RH ornamentation. And then, turning to bb.18-24, it would be a keyboard wizard indeed who could play this difficult passage-work in anything but a scramble at a tempo much faster than around $\bullet$ = 84.

In public performance Nos.1 and 2 need to be tossed off with the kind of easy panache and glitter which can only be realised with a virtuoso technique. However, since they could be profitably studied by a capable, if not quite virtuoso player, they have been listed under Grade 8+. No.3 is rather less difficult. All three are on a *da capo* plan.

Polonaise No.8
Op. posth. 71 No. 1 in D minor (8+)

bb.1–37   Play the introductory bars with commanding clarity, perhaps rather tongue-in-cheek, so that they do not set too portentous a tone in relation to what is to follow. Give the opening unison quavers a vigorous detached 'spring' and then let the unison demisemiquavers run up in a sharp clear *crescendo* towards **strong** dotted crotchet B flats on the second beat of bb.1 and 2 so that these B flats resonate boldly over the inner and lower quavers. Then feel the implied 'lean' on the doubled tied upbeat quavers ready to 'start again' into bb.2 and 3. Notch up the dynamics as you ascend the 7-note scale in b.3, 'going to' ringing detached quaver D's, and springing off these to land on an emphatic syncopated crotchet chord on the fourth quaver pulse, taking care to **feel** the held third main beat. Then draw out the chords through b.4 in a measured *ritenuto*, so that you are ready to launch elegantly into the main theme at b.5. 'Twirl' the ornamentation of the high RH line jauntily over the carefully shaped and rhythmically 'spaced' LH quavers. 'Throw' the descending grace note figures gracefully but nonchalantly **on** the beat through b.9, and then let the RH triplet figures descend with éclat through b.11, supported by a scrupulously rhythmic LH. 'Finish off' the section with neat formality through b.12. Shoot outwards from the first beat of bb.13-16 to arrive in perfect time on a ringing treble and bass *sforzato* quaver exactly on the second beat and then play the repeated note figures with a tautly rhythmic and immaculately clear rat-a-tat tat tat. You may (if you are able to) decide to move the tempo on a little at b.13, but beware of overdoing this as you are then bound to have to draw back too obviously at b.18. As said above, this passage from b.18 is far from easy. Practise the quaver A's first in a detached springing style, so that you **spring** between the higher and lower quavers with a pendulum-like swing. Then add the semiquaver triplets, **slowly** at first, **lifting** the hand with a spring from the first slurred triplet figure, but in such a way that you 'direct' the hand downwards to 'fall' on the second triplet figure, then 'springing' and 'directing' it upwards again, and so on. Continue to think of the upper and lower quaver A's as the spring 'levers', and when you eventually achieve this pendulum-like swing again, you will find that the triplet semiquavers will to a large extent 'play themselves'. Various fingerings may be suggested:

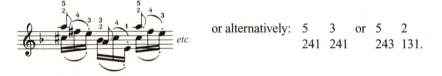

or alternatively: 5   3   or 5   2
241 241   243 131.

Take care to keep the LH quavers perfectly rhythmic and **use** this LH rhythm to help you keep steady. **Lift** the RH slightly again between each slurred triplet group through b.19, while also pointing the inner RH line, taken with the thumb and forefinger. Again in bb.22 and 23 'use' the supporting rhythm and resonance of the LH chords. Be sure to drop right down to *piano* at the beginning of b.24 so that you can make a nicely graded climb up to the *forte* on the first beat of b.26. Then play the descending triplets in a tinkly *pianissimo* over the steadily descending LH augmented fourths and diminished fifths, letting the line of the doubled RH quavers emerge naturally from b.28. Draw out in a measured *ritenuto* through b.29 so that you can lead off in a poised manner into the reprise at b.30.

bb.38–84   Be sure to 'finish off' cleanly in b.37, and allow time to take a clear breath so that you can lead off in a completely new colour from b.38. There is a feeling of moving on a little here, playing the repeating semiquaver-quaver figure in a clearly articulated but whisper-quiet *pianissimo*. These bars have a somewhat furtive 'hunting' character; note the overall pedal through bb.38-9, though this could be modified with half-pedalling on the modern piano. Then let the RH descend with a skipping, and again a tinkly

clarity through bb.40 **lifting** the hand from each quaver

(see General Introduction under 'Articulation'), and giving the sense of 'going to' the *sforzato* chord on the second beat of b.41 (give this chord a melodic 'leaning' emphasis – not a wallop). Turn into b.48 with a more masculine stride, supporting the RH with a lively ♪♪ ♪♪♪♪ ♪ rhythm in the LH in cleanly articulated arcs, and building towards a vigorous *forte* at b.52. From b.56 the RH triplet quaver figure is more 'harmonic' and *legato*, reinforced with the resonance of the upper, then lower crotchets, in contrast to the more 'skipping' effect at bb.40, 44, etc. – note also the curving LH quavers and the longer pedal spans. Once again keep the whole under the control of the carefully shaped LH quaver line, as you build up gradually towards the *forte* at b.68, driving on towards the peremptory *fortissimo* unison flourishes in the bass from b.70. Again do not make these too ponderous or portentous, and come **off** from the second beat of b.71, and again particularly of b.73 to allow a very clear break ready to enter quietly again in b.74. It is a moot point whether the grace note figures in b.68 should be placed on or before the beat. In general Chopin clearly intended such figures to fall **on** the beat (see General Introduction under 'Ornamentation'). Here, however, practicability may dictate the issue, since in this instance it is extremely difficult to manage these ornaments **on** the beat in such a way as to differentiate between these grace notes figures and the prevailing triplet effect. Allow a clear break at the end of b.83, ready to strike off again from b.1.

Polonaise No. 9
Op. posth. 71 No. 2 in B flat major (8+)

As Paul Hamburger says, this is a splendid student work (Walker, p.95). But though it is less difficult than Op.71 No.1, it still needs to be thrown off with a nice touch of virtuosity. Wit is not often apparent in Chopin's music, and we are inclined to forget that he himself was renowned for his wit and high spirits, certainly in youth. Several passages in this piece can sound genuinely funny, particularly bb.52-8, etc.

Note: For those using the Paderewski Edition there will be a discrepancy in bar numbers from b.24, since in this edition first and second time bars are counted i.e. for b.25 read b.26 and so on, (see General Introduction under 'Bar Numberings').

bb.1–51   Lead off from a strong quaver upbeat (taking care to give this its full value or even a little more, so that you 'lean' purposefully into the first beat of b.1), and play the introductory section 'with resolution' as indicated. **Lift** the hand after the first chord of bb.1-3 and 5-6, **not** *staccato* but with a **deliberate** kind of lift in order to 'plant' the emphasised chord on the second beat with an air of determination, going on to articulate the inner melodic fragment vigorously.* Make a clear break on the quaver rest on the second beat of b.8 as you prepare to lead into the principal theme, and play the three upbeat quavers with a quiet but definite sense of leading on towards the dotted crotchet D on the first beat of b.9. While this principal melodic motif is almost Nocturne-like, the sense of the steady dance rhythm at the same time needs to be established and maintained in the supporting quiet but ongoing movement of the LH quavers. While the RH ends its 4-bar phrase on the second beat of b.12, take care to 'finish off' the LH chords neatly up to the third beat of b.12. Then poise yourself on a quiet, but definite upbeat RH quaver third, ready to throw off bb.13-14 in a *scherzando* style, supported by a beautifully rhythmic dancing LH (implementing the implied emphasis on the syncopated crotchet chord on each second **quaver** pulse). As you 'finish off' the RH phrase again on the second beat of b.16, feel that the three LH repeated bass quavers are drawing you on, as you 'lean' on the emphasised RH upbeat chord to b.17, to carry you into the varied restatement, perhaps in a rather fuller tone. Take care to keep steady as you hop upwards at the beginning of b.19 with the help of a measured LH, and then poise yourself delicately on the quaver B flat ready to 'fall' gracefully towards the dotted quaver C flat on the upbeat to b.20. Underpin the skipping ornamentation in the RH in b.21 with smoothly ongoing LH semiquavers (noting the doubled lower notes), and 'rip' the LH spread chords and RH grace notes off neatly in b.23, taking care that the subsequent descending semiquaver arpeggio does not 'run away'. Be

---

*The *piano* in b.5 in Henle is not given in most editions, and is considered by the editors of the Paderewski Edition to be an error.

sure to 'finish off' cleanly in both hands on the third beat of b.24 ready to lead off with a clean quaver upbeat if returning to b.1. In the second time bar, be particularly careful again to come cleanly **off** after the third beat, ready to 'pounce' on the *sforzato* unison quaver upbeat as if with a vigorous 'stamp', ornamenting the RH quaver with an energetic

5-note trill 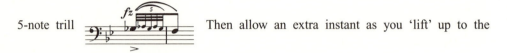 Then allow an extra instant as you 'lift' up to the

ornamented RH third and LH quaver F on the second quaver of b.25. Articulate the RH thirds cleanly, **listening** to the passing discordant effects between the hands over the dominant pedal point, in particular the telling clash on the first beat of bb.26 and 28 etc. Take an extra instant again to leap down cleanly to the emphasised upbeat to bb.27, 29 and 31, and again to leap down ready to shoot vigorously up the unison runs through bb.32-4 (letting each one 'go to' a **definite** quaver, or *tenuto* crotchet as the case may be). These flourishes through bb.32-4 might be played in a strutting manner, leading back with mock pomposity through b.35, and then 'drawing back' after the *sforzato* first beat of b.36, ready to resume the nocturne-like theme in *piano*.

As in Op.71 No.1 it is a mistake to let the virile passages sound too ponderous. *bb.52–103* The new motif in G minor from b.53 could have come in usefully one hundred years later as a theme for the arrival of the bogey-man in the silent films. Play the furtive unison dotted rhythm figures with sharp, nicely jerky definition, and make a good 'thrummmm' on the spread chord on the third beat of bb.52 and 53 etc. Support the leaping dotted rhythm in the RH through b.54 with **steady** quaver chords in the LH, and play the widely spaced RH quavers in bb.56 and 57 like the striding leaps of a male dancer in a comic ballet. Allow time again to leap up to a strong chord in both hands on the second quaver pulse of b.62, and then play the descending RH triplet passage-work in a vigorous mock-heroic style through bb.62-3, underpinned by **steady** LH quaver chords. Then support the sportive RH right through from b.64 to b.67 with a springingly rhythmic LH. The mock-heroics grow increasingly brilliant through the next section as the triplets of the previous section expand into glittering flights of demisemiquavers.

The most serious part of this piece is the passage leading from b.81 back to the reprise of the G minor motif (see Paul Hamburger's discussion of the significance of such 'bridge' passages in the Polonaises (Walker, p.98 onwards). Take the long arpeggio down through b.80 to a clear quaver A on the first beat of b.81, and make it clear that you are initiating the quiet *ostinato* quaver rhythm on the **second** quaver pulse of the bar. Listen acutely to the contrary motion movement of the treble and bass lines over the steadily ongoing inner quaver chords as you build up a gradual *crescendo* towards the first beat of b.87 – then 'giving' a little as you ease back towards the reprise at b.88. Be particularly sure to allow a good 'breath' at the end of b.103 as you poise yourself to set off sturdily again from b.1.

Polonaise No. 10
Op. posth. 71 No. 3 in F minor (8)

Of the three Polonaises in Op.71, this is the one that leans most towards the heroic mould of the later works – in spirit, that is, since in technical scope (apart from the difficult passage in bb.39-42) it is the most modest of the three. It so pleased one of the Princesses of the Radziwill family,

Chopin's friendly patrons, that he sent her a copy. Henle gives two versions, differing in various details of structure, notation, phrasing, etc. In compiling the notes below, I am following the second (Fontana) version, since this appears to be the one most generally adopted in other editions, and also because the general layout is simpler. (The first version – from the autograph – gives a *da capo* from b.50, to *fine* at b.26, then moving on to the Trio at b.51. Then there is another *da capo* at the end of b.68 (the equivalent of b.90 in the Fontana version, that is) back through the first eight bars of the Trio section).

Note: For those using the Paderewski Edition there will be a discrepancy in bar numbers from b.80, since in this edition first and second time bars are counted i.e. for b.81 read b.82 and so on (see General Introduction under 'Bar Numberings').

bb.1–22
Play the introductory bars in a quiet but well-defined and rather sombre tone. Be sure to make a clear break on the second beat of b.4 so that you can prepare to enter with a firm onward 'leaning' crotchet upbeat to the principal theme. Let the melody line sing out confidently, supported by steady but ongoing quavers in the LH. Listen to the doubled lower LH line descending through bb.6-8 in complementary line to the treble. Show that you are beginning a new, slightly more agitato phrase from the minim on the first beat of b.9. In b.13 let the scale run up confidently towards a clear dotted quaver G flat on the third beat of the bar. Feel then that the phrase is 'going on' towards the *sforzato* minim on the first beat of b.15, supported by a **resonant** LH octave. The LH figure through bb.15-22 is

not easy, *etc.* but try not to take the easy way out by playing the

upper LH quaver on the third beat with the RH – the effect will not be the same. And in any case it is an excellent exercise for the LH! Practise the lower line alone using the fingering you intend to adopt. I personally find 4 3 4 3 3 the strongest and most stable in bb.16-18, with 5 4 5 4 3 in bb.19 and 20, but this of course must be a matter for the individual hand. Then when you put the parts of the LH together, take care to define not only the lower line, but also the upper notes with a firm thumb, allowing a tiny break as you 'go up to' a firm quaver (or crotchet) sixth on the third beat. Then practise **slowly** hands together, keeping a rigorously steady crotchet beat and gradually building up speed. Ensure that the RH minim sings out through the first and second beats of bb.15 and 16, and build up the tone vigorously towards the high crotchet A flat on the second beat of b.19, letting the RH broken diminished seventh sweep down confidently through b.20 to the crotchet on the first beat of b.21. Keep the rhythm going in a martial, even if quieter, manner through bb.21-2, with just a little give at the end of b.22, ready to lead on with the *legato* motif from b.23.

bb.23–72
Launch into b.27 in a lively *mezzo forte* with a jaunty, military air, defining the polonaise rhythm cleanly beneath the tied treble minim in

bb.27, 29, etc, and articulating the treble dotted rhythm figures in a precise but breezy, ongoing manner. Then lead on into bb.35-8 in a full-throated, more *legato* tone, underpinning the RH with buoyant LH quaver chords. Bb.39 and 41 are quite awkward, and will need careful, slow, rhythmic practice, in a slurred effect, without the trills

at first: 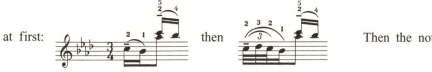 then Then the notation in b.40 is somewhat confusing. In effect it is  * When you put hands

together ensure that the LH continues to provide **steady** rhythmic support through these bars, and on through b.42 as the RH marches purposefully downwards to a strong crotchet E flat on the third beat. From b.43 keep the rhythm running steadily through the LH quaver chords as the RH sweeps up and down, as if in wide **arcs**, rather than in isolated 'plonks'. Space the ascending or descending detached RH quavers rhythmically, always with the feeling of 'going to' a strong treble or bass minim on the second beat of each bar. This passage, starting in a full *forte*, pedalled as indicated and distancing to a whisper at b.50, can make a striking effect. Take care to place the RH bass crotchet C precisely on the fourth quaver pulse of b.50, letting the LH quaver thirds ease you quietly back into the reprise of the principal theme.

bb. 72–98 Be sure to 'finish off' cleanly on the tonic quaver chord on the third beat of b.72 so that you can lead on clearly into the A flat section in a warm-toned expressive *piano*. While the feeling of this section is more lyrical, do not allow the rhythmic impulse to sag. Listen carefully to the two RH voices as the RH lines 'divide' from the second beat of b.76 and through b.77, and then run up to a rather 'schmaltzy' minim C flat on the second beat of b.78. The next bar (b.79) can all too easily collapse like a pack of cards unless you feel that the **LH** is leading, and the syncopated RH following. Practise thus at first, **playing**

the tied notes:  *etc.* The notation of this bar

in the first (autograph) version of the piece given in Henle is much easier to assimilate:

 Then shape the curving arabesques of the RH

expressively and gracefully from b.81. Practise the LH as carefully as the RH, noting all doubled notes: the LH B flat on the first beat of b.82, the RH quaver G in b.83 and E flats in b.85, and so on – all of these have a subtle rhythmic, harmonic or melodic significance. Feel a degree of rhythmic flexibility through this section expanding as you 'lift' to the high D flat on the upbeat to b.83, singing out through b.83 down towards an implied *tenuto* on the long D flat in b.84. Then let the curving RH 'go to' a slightly *tenuto* broken sixth on the third beat of b.85, and let the passage-work 'flower' from b.86 up to the beginning of b.89, retracting a little as the thirds descend, ready to finish off carefully through the rather complex part-writing through b.90. Arriving on a clear dominant 7th chord on the third beat of this bar feel the last three semiquavers as the upbeat group to the reprise from b.91. Take care to **feel** the rest at the end of b.98 as you prepare to launch back to b.1.

*or see the autograph version in Henle.

Note: A further six Polonaises (without opus numbers) are published in the Henle and Paderewski Editions.

The very early pieces, Nos 11, 12 and 13 are straightforward in style, and make useful contributions to the repertoire at Grades 6-7. The most interesting number is the remarkably assured No.14 in G sharp minor, supposedly written in 1822. The remaining two are less attractive from the point of view of the performer.

Polonaise No. 11 in G minor (6)*

It is, as has often been remarked, fitting that Chopin's first composition should have been a Polonaise, his supposedly last a Mazurka. Both Polonaise No.11 and No.12 were written when he was only eight. As Jim Samson says, 'the Polonaise reigned supreme in the drawing-rooms of early nineteenth-century Poland' (p.25), and Chopin must often have improvised pieces of this kind without troubling to write them down.

Polonaise No.11, so far as is known, is the first piece that Chopin wrote. It makes a neat rhythmic, technical and melodic study piece at about Grade 6. The first pieces of a great composer naturally appeal to our imaginations, particularly in the case of Chopin, evidently a charming little boy, whom we can readily picture in his black velvet outfit beguiling his aristocratic patrons with such pieces as this. With this association in mind, it would make an attractive addition to those albums of studies usually dominated by the names of the grim-faced worthies we all learned not to love.

Note: There are no original dynamic indications. The indications for dynamics and phrasing in the Paderewski edition are editorial, and all suggestions below are personal.

bb.1–22   It is important to have the steady polonaise rhythm well 'in the system' before starting, at a crotchet pulse of about ♩ = 88-92 (see the Introduction to the Polonaises). Play the opening chords in a confident full tone, 'leaning' well on the crotchet chord on the first beat of bb.1 and 2 with a slurred effect towards the quaver chord on the second beat (the tying of the inner D in each RH crotchet chord enhances this slurred effect). Then 'tap' out the polonaise rhythm with neat, detached chords through bb.3-4 with the feeling of 'going to' a firm chord on the third beat of b.4. Take care not to lurch down so that you 'fall into' the rising arpeggio in b.5. There is plenty of time to leap neatly down if you come **off** the previous crotchet chord on the last quaver beat of b.4, holding the chord within the pedal. This arpeggio is quite easy to manage provided that you hold fast to the sense of the quaver pulse within the overall crotchet. Enter precisely on the first beat of b.5 on the low G, crossing the LH over to 'come in' again precisely with the G above middle C on the second quaver pulse, with an overall strong upward 'direction', to arrive on a confident high tied D

precisely on the second crotchet beat.   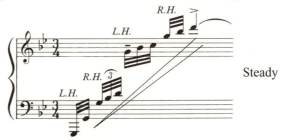   Steady

yourself beneath the high D with precisely placed LH quaver thirds, and then continue to support this high, piping melody line with carefully balanced and perfectly rhythmic LH quavers through to the end of b.8. 'Finish off' neatly in b.8, again with the feeling of 'going on 'through' the repeated quavers to a **definite** crotchet in both hands on the third beat, ready to leap down again in perfect time to the low G in b.9. Give the appoggiatura third on the second beat of b.12 a crotchet value with a clear emphasis and slurred effect towards the tonic on the

third beat.  Allow a tiny break at the end of b.12, ready

to return to b.1, or to lead off into the second section perhaps in a clearer, brighter tone. Take care to keep the LH quavers perfectly steady again through b.18 as you leap confidently down with the RH to carry on the melody in the bass, and similarly as you leap up again in b.20. You could play the bass fragment in a jolly bassoon-like tone, feeling that the repeated upbeat quavers are 'going to' a resonant tied crotchet on the first beat of b.19.

bb.23–38   You might play the broken chord figure in the Trio either in a deliberately tinkling *piano*, or alternatively in a jovial, rollicking style. In either event feel the impulse of these immaculately articulated broken-chord figures towards a definite 'lean' on the dotted quaver on the first beat of bb.24, 26, etc. (particularly 'pointing' the Lydian fourth on the first beat of b.26).

    Let the whole Trio section be as vital and brightly coloured as possible, but keeping rock-steady with the help of unfailingly rhythmic, dance-like LH quavers through bb.23-6 and 31-8, and with perfectly steady but 'keen' semiquavers through bb.27-9. You could play the 2-bar fragments in the second section (bb.31-2 and 33-4) more suavely, reverting to your tinkling or rollicking style from b.35. The turn in bb.29 and 37 could either begin on the upper or the

main note.  End cleanly on the third beat

of b.38, and then make a tiny break ready to lead off again from b.1.

Polonaise No. 12 in B flat major (6)*

This is a little more ambitious technically than No.11 on account of the busy LH broken octaves which underpin the fanfare-like proclamation of the polonaise rhythm in the RH through the introductory bars 1-4.

Note: The only original indications are the opening *forte*, the *piano* at b.5, and the slurs at bb.23-4. Additional indications for dynamics and phrasing in the Paderewski Edition are editorial, and all suggestions below are personal.

bb.1–20   As in No.11 have the steady **3/4** pulse well 'in the system' before starting, but perhaps at a notch or two faster. Trumpet the RH out in a vigorous RAT tat-tat TAT TAT TAT TAT over keenly rhythmic LH semiquaver broken octaves. Practise the LH in quaver 'block' octaves, at first alone and then (still in block octaves) with the RH. Feel that you are giving a strong upbeat lead through the last two quavers of b.1 and b.2 so that you lead down confidently to a strong first beat of b.2 and b.3. Then practise the LH thus to try to avoid the likely overweighting and consequent 'bumping'

of the thumbs: and Then, when

practising it as written, imagine that the descending broken octaves on the third beat are slurred so the fifth finger 'leads' downwards in a steady pulse rather than getting 'stuck' on

the thumbs:  *etc.* Arrive with mock pomposity on an anticipatory

dominant on the third beat of b.4. Then allow a tiny break as you leap up cleanly, ready to set off into the principal theme. Play the RH melody in a bright clear-toned *piano* over neat rhythmic LH quavers. Take another instant at the end of b.8 as you prepare to set off again in the higher register in b.9 in a shriller, more piping tone. Give the appoggiatura on the second beat of b.12 a crotchet value slurring this to a clear B flat on the third beat, over neatly

coordinated LH chords. Throughout the piece support the

RH melody line (which remains predominantly in a high treble) with very rhythmic, dance-like LH quavers within a steady overall crotchet beat. Continue into the second section in a sunny tone in the RH, over a smoother, more suave LH quaver accompaniment.

bb.21–42 You could lead off into the Trio in a clear tinkly style, or even with a bit of a jangle. **Lift** the RH from the *staccato* quaver on the first beat of bb.23 and 24, and then show the slightly syncopating effect of the offbeat slurs through these bars. Feel a slight *tenuto* on the dotted crotchet D on the second beat of b.26 as you poise yourself to set off again in b.27. Then you could lead off into the second section of the Trio at b.33 with a more robust 'kick', returning to *piano* at b.37. Alternatively you could play bb.33-6 more expressively, even rather sentimentally, and then enter *forte* at b.37. End cleanly on the third beat of b.42 and allow an instant's break as you poise yourself either to return to b.33, or to launch off again from b.1.

Polonaise No. 13 in A flat major (7)*

Chopin wrote this piece in 1821 for the birthday of his first, and to all intents and purposes, his only piano teacher, Adalbert Zywny, and as befits his age of eleven years, this is on a more ambitious scale than Nos 11 and 12. The relationship between Zywny, a genial and lovably eccentric character, and his brilliant young pupil must have been a touching and delightful one, as rewarding to the teacher as to the pupil (see 'Profile' in the General Introduction).

Note: Apart from the *ritardando* in b.25 there are no original indications. Additional indications for dynamics and phrasing in the Paderewski edition are editorial, and all suggestions below are personal.

bb.1–12 Unlike Nos 11 and 12, there are no introductory bars here, and Chopin leaps straight into his high-stepping treble theme. Have your steady pulse well 'in the system' (see the Introduction to the Polonaises) before you start, and sing out the melody in a ringing, confident tone supported by carefully balanced and rhythmic 'stepping' quavers in the LH. Take particular care to keep these LH quavers steady as you leap up from a clear ornamented RH upbeat quaver E flat to the high C on the first beat of b.3. Then shoot

294

dashingly down the scale (**but** controlled by the steady LH quaver thirds) towards a clear dotted quaver E flat on the first beat of b.4, and on down to a definite minim third on the second beat. Steady yourself here while at the same time feeling the sense in which the LH quaver thirds lead you on with an upbeat feeling towards the chain of RH trills and turns through bb.5-8. Once again 'use' the LH to keep you steady through these trills. (See the General Introduction under 'Ornamentation'.) In this instance you might start the trills on the main note rather than the upper, so that the upward minim line, B flat-D flat-E flat is clearly and smoothly established

take the opposite view, and prefer to start these trills on the upper note, to 'match' the appoggiatura effect of the upbeat semiquaver figures to bb.6, 7 and 8. Have the feeling of moving through the trills **steadily** towards the crotchet B natural on the first beat of b.8. But as you finish off the last trill take an extra instant to shape the RH upbeat semiquavers neatly down towards a graceful 'lean' on this B natural, making a slurred effect towards the minim C; and then take care to 'finish off' the LH repeated quaver chords neatly to a clear crotchet on the third beat of the bar. Then in the manner of a little interlude or afterthought to this principal theme, play the semiquaver arpeggio figures in lively but smooth curves from b.9. In order to keep steady, creating an even flow between the hands, feel the crotchet beat continuing **within** the semiquavers, though without obvious accents. 'Point' the bass note a little on the first semiquaver of each bar; and then feel the shape of the curve up to the highest note on the third beat (steadied by a carefully placed LH octave) and down again towards a carefully placed bass semiquaver on the first beat of the next bar, and so on, so that you move in a series of continuous curves rather than a series of upward and downward lurches.

The ending of this section is quite awkward to manage. Practise the 'join' carefully between bb.11 and 12. This fingering is best:

It is essential to the poise of this passage that the third beat of b.11 is clearly felt in both hands, giving the sense of a controlled and definite upbeat to b.12, and allowing time for the upward step of the thumb from the D natural to the E flat on the first beat of b.12. Allow time too to 'space' the LH quaver octave and chord through the first beat of b.12 beneath the RH semiquavers, and feel that you are 'going to' a strong RH trill and LH dominant seventh chord on the second beat. Be sure to give this second beat its full value, and then 'finish off' to a clear tonic quaver chord on the third beat. Practise **slowly** from a strong third beat of b.11 through b.12 until the hands are perfectly synchronised.

Having 'finished off' cleanly in b.12, be sure to come **off** on the quaver rest to
bb.13–38   take a 'breath' ready to lead on with the new, more thoughtful motif in the
dominant. Let the syncopated repeated treble B flats 'speak' through b.13 with the feeling of 'going on through' to the dotted quaver on the first beat of b.13, over the continuing steady pulse of the LH quavers. Allow a fraction of extra time through b.16 to ensure that the harmonies are clearly defined as you 'go to' a clear E flat chord on the third beat –

allowing an extra instant again as you leap down to carry on the RH melody in the bass. Let the RH sing out here, while at the same time listening to the counterpoint provided by the LH quavers. Listen to the horn-like momentary duet between the hands through the first two beats of b.20, ensuring that the LH fifth finger gets neatly 'out of the way' after the first quaver F, so that the RH fifth finger can then play this note cleanly on the second quaver pulse. 'Finish off' neatly on the chord on the third beat ready for the upbeat semiquavers to lead on into b.21. Feel a sense of moving on from here while at the same time holding fast to the **sense** of the crotchet pulse. Take care also to balance the LH chords carefully (still in the treble clef) over the low RH line as you *crescendo* through these bars towards a resonant quaver chord on the first beat of b.24. Then let the RH semiquavers expand upwards into the dominant seventh flourish in an improvisatory fashion, drawing out again through the end of b.25. Ease into a quietly singing minim D flat on the first beat of b.26, and then poise yourself on the upbeat D natural as if on a brink, ready to set off again from b.27.

bb.39–59   Lead off into the Trio in a new tone, playing the treble repeated semiquaver figure perhaps with a high-pitched piping sound, or with a tinkling 'churning' effect, supported once more by **steady** but springy LH quavers. Feel the implied emphasis on the syncopated RH crotchet E flat on the second quaver pulse of b.41, and then be sure to 'finish off' this phrase with a clear RH crotchet over neat LH quavers on the third beat of b.42, ready to leap up to 'start again' on the first beat of b.43. It is none too easy to keep steady through bb.45-6. Contrary to the usual exhortation to let the LH control the rhythm, it is best here to feel that the **RH** is in charge, since it is the RH that is carrying on in semiquavers, and the LH which is moving temporarily into triplets. Practise thus at first

(without the RH turn)

When you add the LH triplets practise through b.44 to b.46, concentrating rigorously on maintaining the steady crotchet pulse through b.45. Only add the turn when you feel quite at ease with the cross-rhythm. Take another clear 'breath' at the end of b.46 ready either to return to b.39, or to launch rumbustiously into b.47. (Practise the LH alone, leaping down each time to a **firm** syncopated crotchet octave B flat in strict time, until the rhythmic pattern, and your aim down to the B flat octave and up again is quite secure.) Arrive on a clear quaver chord on the first beat of b.50, allowing a slight *tenuto* here, and then run up the dominant seventh arpeggio, again in an improvisatory manner. Draw out as indicated through the last beat of the bar, and let the high A flat sing through b.51, giving this note its full value and more, while at the same time feeling that you are 'leaning onwards' ready to set off again into b.52. Be sure to make a clear break again at the end of b.59 as you poise yourself to launch back to b.1.

Polonaise No. 14 in G sharp minor (VA)*

This piece shows an impressive advance from No.13. It was previously thought to have been written as early as 1822, when Chopin was only twelve years old. Recent research however suggests 1824 as a more likely (but still remarkably early) date. However justified are the pails of cold water thrown by various critics in terms of its value in a 'serious' musical sense, Chopin shows himself perfectly at ease with the keyboard, and in sophisticated command of the virtuosic tricks of the trade at a still tender age. If nothing else, such writing gives clear evidence of his own technical virtuosity while still so young – as Jim Samson says, 'the ornate tracery . . . has something of the rhapsodic, apparently spontaneous flow of a written-out improvisation.' (p.31). Facile it may be, but it is the very facility which is remarkable.

It is the kind of piece which is not worth playing unless its roulades and darting arpeggios and arabesques can be tossed off with effortless grace, and it has therefore been listed in the Very Advanced category (see the Preface) . The tempo has to be moderate, as a glance at bb.10-12 and 28-30, etc. will show (see the Introduction to the Polonaises). This tempo needs to be clearly presented through the introductory bars 1-4. Play the quaver chord on the first beat of bb.1 and 2 in a bright clear tone, and 'rip' up the demisemiquaver arpeggio so that you arrive on a ringing treble quaver precisely on the second crotchet beat. Play the two sets of emphasised quaver chords in a just-detached, measured style, and then phrase b.3 more smoothly, drawing out a little from the middle of the bar. From b.5 it is essential that the elaborately decorated RH is 'carried' by a LH which is always rhythmic, 'giving' a little here and there to allow the RH time to breathe, but always maintaining the dance-like rhythm of the quavers within the overall **3/4** pulse. Immediately show the *dolce con grazia* character as you lead in with a nicely onward 'leaning' crotchet upbeat to b.5. Then shape the RH arpeggio with easy grace up to a singing dotted crotchet G sharp on the second beat of b.5 (in contrast to the 'ripped' effect of bb.1 and 2). From b.9 feel that the LH is both propelling and controlling the brilliant, almost Lisztian RH figuration as you move onwards towards a strong diminished seventh chord on the third beat of b.10. Show the more tranquil, expressive nature of the melody from b.13; and then from b.16 'point' the horn-call-like LH figure with pinpoint precision beneath the airy treble slurred semiquaver broken octaves. The elaborate RH figuration from b.28 lies beautifully under the hand. Here it is even more vital that the LH maintains a **guiding** pulse – flexible yet always rhythmically so – so that, for example, when it 'gives' a little to accommodate the RH sextuplet through the last quaver pulse of b.28, it resumes the rhythmic pulse immediately in b.29.

The writing from bb.36-9 is almost Beethovenian, and here the **RH** needs to take charge with vigorously rhythmic chords. Articulate the ornamented slurred semiquavers with tripping delicacy through b.40, carrying on similarly into the bass (taking care here to keep the LH treble quavers steady). Let the **LH** take charge again from b.44 as the RH sports brilliantly up and down in wide arcs. The descending chain of trills through bb.47-8 again have a Beethovenian ring.

Polonaise No. 15 in B flat minor (8+)*

This was written in 1826, just after Chopin had finished his final year at school, and his family was about to leave for Reinertz in an attempt to find a cure for his sister Emily, who was dying of tuberculosis. Following a visit to the Opera for a performance of Rossini's 'The Thieving Magpie', he wrote the piece as a farewell present for his schoolfriend, Wilhelm Kolberg, using an aria from the opera with the heading 'Au Revoir' as the basis for the Trio. This is, on the whole, more solid in texture and less difficult than No.14. The gestures here have a chivalric swagger (in the outer sections) against those of No.14, which pursue florid virtuosity for its own sake. **Note:** In the Paderewski edition the first section is repeated with a first and second-time bar. This creates a seven-bar discrepancy in bar numberings, i.e. for b.17 read b.10 (see the General Introduction under 'Bar Numberings'). There are few original indications for dynamics, phrasing, etc, and a number of editorial indications are given in the Paderewski edition. Apart from the few indications given in Henle, all suggestions below are personal.

bb.1–16   Set a very measured **3/4** (see the Introduction to the Polonaises). Ensure that the opening RH figure is properly timed and articulated to give a convincing upbeat lead, with a bit of a 'kick', towards a strong chord on the first beat of b.1. Then, underpin the vigorous RH figures with carefully balanced, very rhythmic onward-propelling but **steady** LH quavers. It is important that all tied notes are observed and given their implied slight emphasis, e.g. the tied demisemiquaver upbeat to b.1, the treble tied semiquaver upbeat to b.2, the inner RH quaver upbeat to b.3, the LH inner upbeat to b.4, and so on. Rip up the sextuplet arpeggio to arrive on a ringing high quaver F exactly on the second beat of b.4, and then allow an extra instant to leap down ready to lead on with immaculately timed chords, treating these three quaver beats as an overall upbeat towards b.5. Play the chords through bb.6-7 with 'ongoing' deliberation, marking the syncopating tied emphases purposefully. 'Finish off' cleanly on the tonic semiquaver chord on the third beat of b.8, and then make a fractional break ready to lead into the restatement with another clear RH upbeat figure.

bb.17–52   Lead on from the upbeat to b.17 in a new, clear *piano* tone over rhythmically 'spaced' leaping LH quavers. From b.19 let the LH underpin the RH dotted-rhythm figures with increasing energy as you rise in a vigorous *crescendo* towards b.21, ready to cascade showily downwards towards the low F on the first beat of b.22. (The easiest and most brilliant way to negotiate this descent is to take the succession of C's with the LH

Arriving on a resonant bass crotchet F on the first beat of b.22, allow an extra instant and then 'take up' the polonaise rhythm through the repeated RH octaves, but easing fractionally through the last beat of the bar ready to lead off into b.23 in a more melting tone. Gradually whip up the dynamics and the forward impulse again from b.27, ready to surge back towards the reprise at b.33. 'Finish off' with a tangible 'push' on the quaver chord on the third beat of b.40, as if dismissing the previous clatter, ready to bring in the low, very quiet but deliberate bass drone fifths in b.41. Then, introducing the 'aria' quietly and expressively with a quiet, carefully poised quaver upbeat to b.43, shape the melody in graceful, expressive curves as a singer would, feeling the rests in bb.44, 46 and 48 as 'breath' points. This section can well be done slightly tongue-in-cheek, imagining the conductor (the LH) 'waiting' for the singer on the dotted semiquaver upbeat to b.46, and then the burst of *tutti* in b.50, and so on.

bb.53–68   From b.53 'rip up' the arpeggios in either hand towards a ringing detached quaver on each second beat. Steady yourself with decisive, measured chords from the fourth quaver pulse of each bar 'going', in an upbeat sense, towards a strong quaver chord on the first beat of each subsequent bar. From the high F on the second beat of b.57 spill down in a brilliant trail of chromatic sound, easing out through the end of b.58 ready to take up the *bel canto* melody again, this time in *pianissimo* from b.59. It is effective to build up the sound and press forward progressively from b.66 so that you 'surge' back from b.68 into the principal theme as if with a powerful 'push'.

Polonaise No. 16 in G flat major (VA)*

It is difficult to find a reason to play this strangely strung together hotch-potch of half-worked-out, or overworked ideas, and gratuitously difficult passage-work. It was written in 1829. Weinstock talks of a 'hint' that it might be a pastiche (p.323) – whether he was referring to Niecks' view, which he quotes: 'there are here and there passages which have the Chopin ring, indeed, which seem to be almost bodily taken from some other of his works' (Vol.2, p.354), or whether to a hint from some other source is not clear. But as Niecks goes on to say 'there is also a great deal which it is impossible to imagine to have come at any time from his pen'. Perhaps it is some kind of joke – there is a hint of vaudeville in the downward slide of the tune from b.58 for example, and the bombastic sequences from b.73; we tend to forget Chopin's love of parody, and his gifts as mimic and caricaturist, so seldom do these elements appear in his music. On the other hand, there are a number of ideas which, as Arthur Hedley says, 'were put to better use many years later in Op.53' (p.161. And, I would add Ops 26 No.2 and 40 No.1.). But the clumping and uncharacteristically ungrateful passage-work from b.17 (incongruously marked *piano dolce* from b.19), the noise about nothing from bb.73-5 and bb.84-9, the overworking of the banal 'humming' figure from b.90, and the dogged upward groping for the home key from b.99 are difficult to equate with, for example, the sophistication of the earlier Polonaise in G sharp minor (No.14) supposedly written several years earlier, or with the Op.10 Studies, on which Chopin was already engaged.

THE NOCTURNES

It is from the Nocturnes that the popular view of Chopin, languid, elegant and 'soulful', is derived, as Niecks, in so many words, observed one hundred years ago (vol.2, p.261). Not only does this view linger to the present day, it still, now as then, permeates the more snobbish elements of the musical intelligentsia, predisposing many musicians and commentators to accord the Nocturnes a fairly lowly position in relation to Chopin's output as a whole. I believe, on the contrary, that they contain some of his most personal and innovative writing. Lennox Berkeley has said 'It is clear that they derive in great measure from his own very individual style of playing' (Walker, p.170) and indeed, it is here that he seemed able to develop his ideas, in many instances with fantasia-like freedom, in pieces on a larger scale than the Preludes, but not so large as to be encumbered with the structural problems with which he had to wrestle in the larger works. It is well-known that Chopin adopted the title and style of the Nocturne from John Field. Jim Samson, in his chapter 'Bel Canto', traces the origins of Chopin's ornamented melodic style in a wider context, embracing the Field connection, and thus places the matter in context (p.81 onwards).

In the Nocturnes Chopin's melodic style is at its most vocal, and by inference, most Italianate, in the sense both of line and of ornamentation. Since these characteristics apply to a greater or lesser extent to most of his work, this matter is discussed in the General Introduction. Suffice it here to say that in all melodic passages, and particularly in the long melodic spans of the Nocturnes, we must above all considerations **think** vocally, imagining in every instance how a singer would shape a phrase or run, and 'turn' an ornament. The Nocturnes are the victims of their own popularity in the sense that the character of the much-mauled few, charming and languorously flowing, has become identified with the group as a whole. But in fact they form a far from homogeneous group. For one thing, ranging as they do from the E minor Nocturne Op.72 No.1 (published posthumously, but thought to have been written between 1828 and 1830) to the two of Op.62 coming almost at the end of his creative life, they provide a significant record of the development of important aspects of Chopin's musical thought over a particularly long period. For another, they are not associated with any special rhythmic or structural pattern (like, for example, the dance-based pieces, the Waltzes, Polonaises and Mazurkas). While all, with the exception of Op.37 No.2, open with an expressive *cantabile* melody (sometimes, but by no means always, with the 'typical' LH flowing quaver or semiquaver accompaniment) they evolve with remarkable and unpredictable diversity; from the comparatively slight Op.9 No.2 or Op.32 No.2, through the extraordinary events of the dramatic Op.27 No.1 and the mighty Op.48 No.1, to the visionary wanderings of Op.55 No.2 or Op.62 No.1. The 'prototype', if there is one, derives perhaps more from Field than from Chopin himself, and even among the more 'dulcet and effeminate' numbers, to quote Niecks (vol.2, p.261), there is almost always some element of surprise and originality.

The Henle and Vienna Urtext Editions give twenty-one Nocturnes, including the three posthumously published numbers, No.19 in E minor Op.72 No.1, No.20 in C sharp minor (often titled 'Lento con gran espressione'), and No.21 in C minor. The Paderewski Edition publishes nineteen numbers in the volume of Nocturnes, and gives the posthumous C sharp minor and C minor in their volume of Minor Works.

Note: As in the case of the Mazurkas J.-J. Eigeldinger detects a pattern of key relationships within each Opus of the Nocturnes. He therefore suggests that Chopin intended each opus to be perceived and played as a 'set'.

Nocturne No. 1 in B flat minor
Op. 9 No. 1 (8)

This remarkable piece, more original than its better known companion in E flat, has often been underrated both by critics and players. In a beautiful performance the effect can be spellbinding – as if the music is passing in a thin haze, sometimes sounding more clearly, sometimes receding – the LH curving ceaselessly in consistent, smooth wave-like patterns while the treble melody moves above in a prolonged musing, decorated with delicate, chromatically inflected roulades.

bb. 1–8   You may feel that the metronome mark of ♩ = 116 is on the fast side, although some pianists take it faster still. Do not, however, adopt too slow a tempo, or the piece will lose this onward, wave-like motion and immediately begin to feel sticky (and in addition necessitate an obvious change of gear at b.19, see below). The essential is not the selection of a 'correct' metronome mark, but the maintaining of a continuous feeling of movement, while allowing for a good deal of rhythmic give and take.

Practise the LH alone, shaping each six-quaver group with perfect smoothness, while at the same time showing the shape of the undulating curve within each group. Throughout the first fourteen bars notice and **feel** how the salient notes, describing the shape of these curves (e.g. in b.1 from the low B flat, up to the D flat, on up to the high F, dipping down to the low B flat again, and so on), correspond with the crotchet pulse of the

6/4 rhythm.   Notice also how the first four

bars proceed over a tonic pedal point.

Throughout the piece shape the RH melody in a 'vocal' manner (see General Introduction under 'Italian Influence' and 'Phrasing'). Feel the opening solo RH quavers as an overall upbeat group as you lead in in a dream-like, yet confident, quiet tone. Shape the first three notes in a little curve up towards the D flat, with just a hint of a 'vocal' *tenuto* on this note, then letting the line 'fall' expressively towards the crotchet F on the first beat of b.1. Have the LH 'ready to meet' the RH on this first beat, and then feel that the LH is establishing the quiet, wave-like motion as you let the RH repeated crotchet F's 'speak' in a gentle, carefully graded swell **beyond** the fourth F on the second main beat of the bar towards the subsequent

G flat   rather than 'peaking' the *crescendo* on the

fourth F (see General Introduction under 'Articulation', for discussion of this 'speaking' style). Then let the line 'fall' again towards the quietly singing minim D flat on the first beat of b.2, slurring this D flat off expressively towards the crotchet B flat on the third crotchet beat. Absorb the 'landscape' of this melodic phrase, from the entry of the solo quavers, rising to the high D flat, and then falling in an overall curve towards the middle of b.2. If you practise this first phrase over and over through to the middle of b.2, following the expressive inflections sensitively, you will assimilate the feeling of the motion of the piece as a whole, as well as the aural sense of the balance between the RH and LH. Always feel that the LH is supporting and smoothly buoying along the melody.

The obvious problems of the piece lie in the management of the treble runs in uneven numbers of notes (see General Introduction under ''Free' Runs'). There are various ways of grouping the notes through bb.2 and 3, and each pianist will find their own preferred way – in

b.2, for example, the RH run could be grouped thus 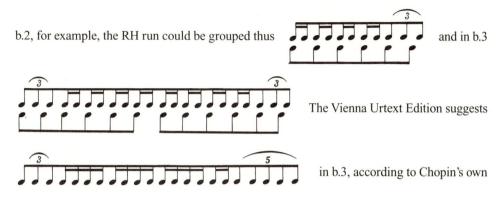 and in b.3

The Vienna Urtext Edition suggests

in b.3, according to Chopin's own

instructions in the copy belonging to a pupil (in principle approximating to the second of the above examples). Join your chosen RH grouping in pencil to coincide with the relevant LH quavers and then, when the sequence is thoroughly absorbed, the groupings can be more loosely merged to create the most eloquent and natural-sounding effect. In all instances of these 'free' runs, it is essential that the **RH** is subject to the rhythmic and musical shape of the **LH** – thus, while a degree of *rubato* may be both necessary and desirable, the LH will slacken or increase speed in a **rhythmic** and not random manner (see General Introduction under 'Rubato'). A slight 'drawing out' at the beginning of each run, and slight speeding up during its course, create a natural and free effect.

Be sure that all long notes are given sufficient singing quality to last through their full duration, i.e. let the melody line (and similarly the long run – the elaborated version of the opening motif) 'go to' a warmly slurred, singing minim D flat on the first beat of bb.2, 4, etc. Then, expanding the tone a little, let the three 'speaking' B flats 'go to' a warmly resonant, not harsh *sforzato* semibreve A flat on the first beat of b.5, supported by a carefully balanced bass note, and then clearly show the inner RH fragment entering on the second main beat of this bar. Make a delicate *smorzando* through the second half of b.7, 'easing' a little as you prepare to end the overall 8-bar section on a quietly singing dotted minim F on the first beat of b.8. As you **listen** to this F, feel that the LH quavers are 'drawing you on' ready to 'start again' from the second main beat of the bar. Through bb.1-8 feel the impulse of the first subphrase towards the singing minor D flat on the first beat of b.2, and similarly feel the overall impulse of the long run from the middle of b.2, through b.3 towards the D flat on the first beat of b.4. Then feel the span of the longer overall phrase from the middle of b.4 through to the first beat of b.8. At the same time feel the sense of the overall melodic span from the opening quavers right through to b.8. In general, as marked in most editions, the pedal should be changed on the first and second main beats of each bar, taking care to 'catch' the bass note in each instance.

bb.9–18   You could begin the varied restatement from b.9 in a quieter, even more dream-like tone. Allow a little extra time to make a pretty vocal 'lift' up to the high F near the beginning of b.11, then move on a little as the run falls in a delicate curve through to b.12 (this run, as will be seen, falls into a clear triplet pattern). *Crescendo* eloquently through the second half of b.14 (treating the last three RH quavers in a just-detached 'speaking' style) up towards a full-toned D flat on the first beat of b.14. Do not get too frenzied at the sight of the *forte appassionato* marking here, but rather leave a reserve for an increase in tone and ardour towards the summit in b.17. Build up the tone progressively as you leap higher to the first beat of b.16, and yet higher in b.17, allowing a little extra time as you reach up to an emphatic high D flat on the first beat of b.17, drawing out this whole bar a little as you 'space' the detached triplet quavers down towards a telling minim C flat on the second main beat. Even here gauge the tone carefully, aiming for a glorious fullness without banging or hardness. Then allow an extra instant again as you drop to *piano* on the upbeat to b.18, ready to 'home' towards a quiet tonic in b.18. Avoid snatching at the high notes on the first notes of bb.16 and 17 by 'scooping' up unhurriedly from the grace notes placed **on** the beat, to coincide with the bass note, imagining an upward *portamento* effect. Underpin the high registered RH through these bars with a **steady** and carefully balanced LH, **listening** to the inflections of the quavers, particularly through b.17. Note the 'reinforcing' effect of the held LH minim F in the second half of bb.15 and 16. This also helps to maintain the dominant resonance, should you feel it desirable on the modern piano to change the pedal partially on the last crotchet pulse of these bars. Returning to calm in the tonic on the first beat of b.18, shape the LH line in a careful curve up to the high F and down again, feeling that the *smorzando* quavers, while dispersing the sound of the previous passage, are at the same time leading on towards the D flat section.

bb.19–85 This is a long and repetitive section. On no account allow the movement to become sluggish, if anything moving the tempo on a very little, but in such a way that any change is barely perceptible. Kleczyński (p.32) indeed tells us that 'this *canto*' should not be played faster, implying that he quotes from a higher authority, possibly indirectly from Chopin himself. Note the new shape of the LH, creating the **suggestion** of a cross-rhythm effect – be sure, however, despite showing the shape of the curves up to and down from the fourth quaver of each group, that the feeling of the **6/4** movement is maintained. Practise shaping the RH octaves in beautiful, smoothly curving phrases, keeping the hand as close as possible to the keys with a clinging touch. Enter in a veiled *sotto voce* in b.19, and then follow all the dynamic inflections with the utmost expressiveness, feeling the accents (bb.20, 21, 24, etc.) and *sforzatos* as warm melodic 'leans' of varying intensity according to the dynamic context. This passage needs to be played with the 'open phrased' freedom of a vocalise, always buoyed along by the rolling LH quavers which, however, must be sensitively responsive to the expressive inflections of the RH melody. From the *rallentando* in b.23 take the melody down to a whisper at b.24, and then interpret the *forte* in bb.25-6 as the emergence of a momentarily more resolute thought, rather than as a sudden *forte* bump. Move on with a sense of urgency from b.35, 'peaking' the *crescendo* as the emphasised tied crotchet upbeat to b.37 'leans' onwards to the subsequent B flat, and then dying down again from b.39. Taking into account all the fluctuations of dynamics and tempo, feel the sense of a gradual overall build-up towards b.51, rising here to a glorious and impassioned fullness of tone. Let the quaver thirds 'fall' powerfully but expressively from the emphasised dotted crotchet third on the first beat of b.55, then going on to make a warm 'lean' on the appoggiatura-like chord on the first beat of b.56, and echoing this effect in *pianissimo* in b.57. Play from b.61 on a *pianissimo* breath, and interpret the *smorzando* from b.68 with the sense of preparing gradually for the reprise from b.70. 'Point' the doubled 'upbeat' (B flat) to the second main beat of b.70 as you prepare to ease back into the opening motif. In general the pedal, as before, will be changed on the first and second main beats of each bar of this middle section. But note Chopin's long held pedal effect from b.51 over the long tonic pedal point. Some judicious half-pedalling will probably be preferred by most pianists here, however, lest on the modern piano the radiant resonance of these passages tips over into mere clangour, particularly through the echo effect in b.57, and to clear the harmony on the second beat of b.58. Then beneath the held treble third from b.67, change the pedal carefully on the offbeat bass notes to correspond with

the upward phrase marks.

etc.

The run in b.73 may be grouped as follows:†

(Allow an extra instant through the second crotchet pulse for the 'lift' up to the high F as at the beginning of b.11.) In b.81 tail away the upward semiquaver arpeggio with a light airy 'lift' from the gently emphasised semiquaver C flat. It is then effective to *crescendo* through the LH quavers in the first half of b.82 with the sense of 'leaning on' towards the *fortissimo* on the second main beat. Support the full-toned high tied RH third with a resonant arpeggio in the LH rising towards a strong crotchet A natural on the first beat of b.83. Then let the RH 'double-stopped' dominant seventh intervals descend with a deliberate, but at the same time, free-sounding resonance, making a carefully graded *diminuendo* and *ritenuto* into the final *pianissimo*, but clear tonic major chords. 'Point' the inner G flat on the penultimate chord, changing the pedal discreetly on this chord and then **listen** as you space the final chord in an even 'spread' up towards the D natural.

Nocturne No. 2 in E flat major
Op. 9 No. 2 (7)

As Herbert Weinstock has said, 'Pianists who gaze upward, or close their eyes while playing should eschew the E flat Nocturne as likely to come out as syrup' (p.189). Young players love this piece, even if those of us with more jaded palates need to slough off many a mawkish 'rendering', not to mention all-pervading visions of the tu-tu. It has a quality of freshness, openness and purity of line, and needs to be played with the utmost simplicity, avoiding overloaded sentiment and exaggerated effects of *rubato*. Advanced players will be interested in the elaborate alternative ornamentation given in the Vienna Urtext Edition in their second version of the piece. Examples of selected variants are also given in the commentary in the Paderewski Edition.

The pervading 4-bar phrase (bb.1-4) recurs in varied and increasingly elaborated form (bb.5-8, 13-16, and 21-24), finally expanding into a coda from b.24. The secondary motif in the dominant (from bb.9-12 and 17-20) appears more as a conversational byway than a contrasting theme.

bb.1–8 The tempo marking of ♪ = 132 gives an easy-moving rhythmic swing. But the piece can still sound well at a few notches below this, provided that a continual feeling of movement is maintained. Practise the LH alone at first, of the first four bars, without the pedal, showing the line of the bass notes, and also the implied slight

†As in the ossia version in Henle. This preferable distribution of the RH notes appears in most other editions (see Vienna Urtext and Paderewski).

'lean' on the slurred chord within each three-quaver group. Then, when this LH can be played perfectly fluently, add the pedal, making sure that each bass note is 'caught' within the pedal. Von Lenz records that Chopin 'wanted the bass to be practised first by itself, divided between the two hands; and each of the chords following the main bass beats in the **12/8** should sound like a chorus of guitars. Once the bass part is mastered – with two hands – with a full but *piano* sonority and in strict time, maintaining an absolutely steady *allegretto* movement without the **12/8** lapsing into triplets [presumably he means avoiding an 'oom-pah-pah' effect] then the left hand can be trusted with the accompaniment played that way, and the tenor invited to sing his part in the upper voice.' (Eigeldinger, p.77; and see further illuminating discussion of this piece in this book. See also further references in the Introduction to the present volume, under 'Fingering' and 'Articulation'.). It is a good plan, then, to **sing** the melody line as you play the LH, in order to absorb the natural shape of the phrases, and to get the feel of the gentle give and take within the predominantly even **12/8** rhythm.

Lead in in the RH from a fully timed quaver upbeat, feeling at the same time the onward 'lean' and upward 'lift' of this note towards a singing tied G. Shape the first subphrase gracefully, through to the fourth beat, then making it clear that the second phrase begins on the upbeat to b.2. Feel a little *crescendo* as indicated through the turn on the lower C in b.2, then 'lifting' up to a singing high C on the second beat of the bar. Feel the dotted crotchet C on the last beat of b.3 as an onward leaning upbeat to b.4, and then let the line expand in a 'vocal' curve up through the high D on the second quaver pulse of b.4 and down towards the dotted crotchet E flat. Chopin's fingering of the quavers at the beginning of b.4 revealingly underlines the sense

of his phrasing here (see the Vienna Urtext and Paderewski Editions).

While observing all these details of phrasing etc. do at the same time feel the overall shape of the long melodic line from the opening upbeat through to the third beat of b.4. Then, from the upbeat to b.5, as you embark on the ornamented version of bb.1–4, do preserve a similar melodic shape, incorporating the ornamentation smoothly in the melodic line. (In theory the ⬳ figures will be placed **on** the beat, though in practice many pianists will allow them to anticipate the main note. The trill in b.7 (and bb.15 and 23) may begin on the main note, F, or, more subtly, on the lower auxiliary E natural, placed **on** the beat, according to a variant shown

by Chopin *etc.* see Vienna Urtext Edition, second

version of this piece.) Feel the accents in b.6 as gently syncopated 'leans' on the first note of each slurred semiquaver couplet, and allow the just-detached notes in b.8 time to 'speak' with the utmost delicacy (though within the pedal) in contrast to the slurred flow through the corresponding passage in b.4.†

bb.9–34   Lead on into b.9 from the two upbeat quavers in a new, more easeful manner, perhaps with the feeling of moving on a little. In b.10 let the three repeated quavers (E flat) 'speak' expressively, allowing a little 'give' here as indicated, and then soar in with a full-toned B flat in b.11, supported by a resonant LH. (You may feel impelled to make a little *crescendo* in the LH through the end of b.10, so as to lead with a little surge into the *forte* of b.11: see, in this connection, the end of b.18.) Make it clear that you are closing this phrase (i.e. from b.11) with the dominant chord on the third main beat of b.12, and then that you are leading on from the eighth quaver pulse of the bar, albeit through a *poco rallentando*,

†This little run is marked with a triple *pianissimo* in the copy belonging to Jane Stirling.

towards b.13.‡ Allow a separate pedal to each chord as the shifting harmonies move back in a *crescendo* through the second half of b.12 towards an expansive tonic broken chord on the first

beat of b.13 (placing the first grace note **on** the beat):  In the

alternative version an 'extra' G appears, connected with the bass note by a diagonal line

 and again in b.21 – see similar instances under Nocturne in G

minor Op.37 No.1, and see also in General Introduction, under 'Ornamentation').

Allow the LH to 'give' a little through the first half of b.16, but in a controlled and rhythmic, not random, manner (see General Introduction under '*Rubato*'), fitting in the RH demisemiquavers to the LH quavers in approximate groupings of four, four and five notes (note the subtle emphasis on the C flat). The fingering of the first four notes is Chopin's own, demonstrating that these just-detached notes should 'speak' in an unhurried

fashion  (see General Introduction under

''Free' Runs'). In b.18 space the repeated RH E flats evenly but expressively against continuingly steady LH quavers. Expand a little through the first half of b.24 to allow time to 'point' the varied detailing (compare with bb.8 and 16). Then the run can fall into approximate

groups of five notes each. Allow a fraction of

‡This intended sense of leading on anew from this chord is given added weight by the pencilled emphasis in Jane Stirling's copy.

extra time to 'point' the new minor colour as you move into the coda at the beginning of b.25, and take time again to 'lift' up to the high G on the last beat of b.27, showing the slurred *portamento* effect up from the acciaccatura, placing this acciaccatura

on the beat  and then shape

the *dolcissimo* descending phrase with the greatest delicacy (note Chopin's fingering again). Feel that the tone is building up a little through the end of b.29, and then launch into b.30 in a newly resolute tone, supporting the RH with resonant and steady LH chords as you soar up towards the high treble crotchet octave on the ninth quaver pulse of the bar. Be sure to **lift** the hand from the semiquaver E flat on the sixth quaver pulse (see General Introduction under 'Articulation'), and then, feeling the demisemiquaver F as the 'upbeat' to the slurred quaver G, 'go on up' towards this strong E flat crotchet octave. Feel a slight *tenuto* on this octave, and then press on through the *stretto* (controlled by a resonant and **rhythmic** LH) to 'go back up to' another strong, and carefully placed syncopated octave on the eighth quaver pulse of b.31. Draw out a little through the end of b.31 as you prepare the way towards a carrying dotted minim octave C flat on the first beat of b.32, 'filled out' by a rolling LH dominant seventh arpeggio rising to 'meet' the RH as this C flat 'resolves' to a resonant B flat. **Listen** through the pause to this immense sound, held within the pedal as indicated, and then play the treble cadenza in a free, improvisatory style. This figure is extraordinarily awkward to play – I personally find the fingering 3 2 **5** 1 is better than the often given 3 2 **4** 1. Also it helps if the hand is tilted somewhat towards the thumb, so that the outer side of the hand is higher, giving more freedom to the fifth finger. Despite the *a tempo* immediately after the pause, most pianists start the flourish relatively slowly, gradually building speed. The effect is more natural, as well as being easier. Still holding the sound of the arpeggio within the pedal, *accelerando* according to your abilities – it is a shimmering effect that is required, not a trial of speed. Then allow a little time as you curve upwards in a vocal manner towards the highest note D, before making a graceful *rallentando* and *smorzando* as you descend towards the peaceful rocking figure in the tonic. (You may like to lighten the pedal sound a little as you descend through the last notes of the cadenza.) Continue the *decrescendo* through the penultimate bar, and place the final *ppp* chords with delicate precision.

Nocturne No. 3 in B major
Op. 9 No. 3 (VA)

This is the one Nocturne which I suggest is best left to very advanced players (see also Hutcheson, pp.222-3). It is long, and difficult to hold together; the prolonged LH quaver figuration in the central *agitato* is extremely taxing, and the subtle effects of *rubato* and the virtuosic roulades of the outer sections require keyboard assurance of a high order. Critical opinions divide sharply on this piece. Some dismiss it as a vapid salon effusion, a view advanced, no doubt, by the kind of performance it often receives. Many players ignore, or misunderstand the *scherzando* indication, and wallow languorously through the outer sections in the received 'nocturnal' tradition. This music cannot take a slow tempo – apart from anything else, the first section (bb.1-87) will sound interminable. Perhaps it needs the galvanic hand of a Horowitz who in his re-issued recording, finds the fleet, almost scudding quality that Chopin seems to intend, both in his interpretative directions and by his tempo mark of ♩. = 66. The slightly syncopating effect of the 'doubled' LH crotchet/quaver on the second and fifth quaver pulse of each bar that accompanies the opening bars of the main theme each time it occurs, conveys in itself a subtle feeling of *agitato*. And with Horowitz the central section quivers and seethes like a vortex. Here again and even more the music must 'move', with the overall 2-in-the-bar pulse carrying on from, or even accelerating a little from the original ♩. = 66. Otherwise once again turgidity reigns, the sound becomes 'overloaded' and this frenetically agitated episode seems like a mere engorgement of the outer sections. The concluding cadenza (b.155) suddenly vaporises into the stratosphere in, as Niecks says 'a twirling line that reads plainly 'Frederick Chopin'.' (vol.2, p.263).

Nocturne No. 4 in F major
Op. 15 No. 1 (8+)

Here, as in several of the Nocturnes, Chopin explodes the calm of his quieter outer sections with turbulent central passages, and in this instance the contrast is as violent as possible. The beautifully simple, but at the same time veiled, and slightly other-worldly first section drifts into silence, to be shattered by thunderous semiquavers, *con fuoco*, a nightmare indeed. The metronome mark of ♩ = 69 gives the ideal movement. At more than a couple of notches below this the music loses this veiled quality and becomes altogether too solid.

bb.1–8   Chopin's effect here of artlessness can prove elusive, and his means, as the would-be player soon discovers, are far from simple. The three LH voices must be shaped with a smoothness and care equal to that of the long treble melody lines. Study these three voices separately:

    1) The inner line, which echoes the treble at first, and then diverges from the middle of b.3.
    2) The lower line which provides a tonic pedal point through bb.1-3, and then proceeds by downward steps from b.4 towards the low E at b.8.
    3) The inner triplet figure, which must provide a continuous even, relatively subdued, but at the same time gently insistent, murmurous accompaniment.

Then practise each of the LH parts with each of the other two parts in turn, as you would the voices of a fugue. When you put all three parts together, listen acutely to the lines of all three, and ensure that the third note of each group of inner quavers does not 'bump' nor 'hang on' over into the subsequent beat, or a careless blurring will occur when the overall harmony changes e.g. on the first beat of bb.2 and 4.

When you practise the RH alone, lead in with a fully timed 'onward' leaning upbeat, and shape the phrases with the utmost smoothness, showing the gentle swell up towards a singing dotted minim A on the first beat of b.4. Then from this 'plateau' through b.5, feel the gradual overall unwinding down towards the minim B natural on the first beat of b.8 ready to 'start again' with the *dolcissimo* upbeat group to b.9. Now practise this **RH** melody with each of the LH parts in turn. Listen particularly to the quiet clash of the RH F with the inner LH E on the second beat of b.3, and of the A on the second beat of b.5 with the LH B flat, and so on. When all the parts are finally assembled, listen as if with four ears to the smooth and expressive movement of all four parts. Show the upward chromatic movement of the inner LH line through b.4, 'drawing on' the sustained treble melody note into the next phrase. Then feel the treble line moving on towards an implied 'lean' on the dotted quaver A in b.5 before the little *decrescendo* through the end of the bar. Feel the almost deliberate placing, yet at the same time the onward 'lean' of the RH quaver E towards the third beat of b.6, in cross-rhythm with the LH triplets.

Take plenty of time as you listen to the inner LH line rising through bb.7-9 as the lower line descends towards the bass E. Chopin's fingering of the spread chord on the first beat of b.8 in the copies belonging to his sister and to Jane Stirling, nicely helps to 'point' the lift up to the

high sixth on the second beat.  Then poise yourself

through the second beat for the return to the *dolcissimo* varied version of the opening phrase from the upbeat to b.9.

bb.9–24   In bb.9 and 10 shape the *delicatissimo* triplet figures into mere wisps of sound, lifting lightly up to the quavers, and then bringing the hand **off**. Then from b.11 feel the onward lean of the treble line 'through' the long A in b.12 towards a warm-toned minim B flat on the first beat of b.13. The phrases here 'return upon' themselves, each time with an implied emphasis: first to the long G in b.16 (feel here the continuing LH movement onwards towards the subsequent bar, as at bb.12-13), then to the tied crotchet G on the second beat of b.19, to the high minim D on the second beat of b.20, and finally to the tied crotchet G on the second beat of b.21, from which point the melody gradually subsides towards b.24. Listen acutely, particularly from b.16 to the richly inflected progressions of the LH. The delicate turns in bb.14 and 18 sound more expressive if started just **before** the third quaver of the LH triplet group. The 'lift' to the high minim D on the second beat of b.20, concurrent with the LH downward leap to the telling B natural, is most eloquently expressed in a beautifully singing *pianissimo*, the emphasis created more by a tiny hesitation and 'hold' than by an accent. Then do not hurry the *dolcissimo* ornament (which can start on, or fractionally before, the third main beat in the LH), allowing time also for the LH to descend to a quietly resonant low C on

the first beat of b.21.   Fade the sound out

through bb.23-4 towards a perfectly silent pause before the shock of the *con fuoco*.

For discussion of the placing of the melodic semiquaver in the triplet context (i.e. whether in

bb.3, 5, etc. the treble semiquaver should be played with   or after   the third

LH triplet quaver) see General Introduction under 'Some Explanations and Amplifications'. Here, as elsewhere, Jan Ekier states that this figure should be played as in the first of the above examples. Suffice it here to say that I have never heard any pianist, eminent or otherwise, play these figures in this way, except for Professor Ekier himself in similar instances (e.g. his recording of Op.32 No.2, and the third movement of Op.58). In this instance, as in many others, this 'ironing out' of the line, in my view, removes the expressive touch of rhythmic piquancy, as well as subtly altering the relation of the melody to the harmonic progressions.

bb.25–74   Burst in with lashing (but contained) fury at b.25, leaving some reserve of tone for the indicated *crescendo* towards the middle of each 2-bar phrase (bb.25-6 and 27-8), and for the further upward LH *crescendo* from the bass note on the first beat of bb.26 and 28 towards a biting accented crotchet on the second beat of these bars. Players understandably often feel confused about the rhythmic pattern of this whole section. Is

Chopin continuing a) in a triplet rhythm within the **3/4** as in the first section and therefore with **three** groups of **two** semiquavers in each beat? Or b) in an 'ordinary' **3/4** i.e. with two quavers (i.e. **two** groups of **three** semiquavers) in each beat? In the absence of triplet markings denoting two groups of three semiquavers, it could be assumed that a) is the correct rhythm and this is the view taken by the editors of the Paderewski Edition: 'the semiquaver movement here is in **9/8** rhythm, i.e. the semiquavers are in three groups of two and not in sextuplets (two groups of triplets).'

However, the shape of the LH melody line through the first beat of bb.25 and 27 clearly implies (b) i.e. ♫♫♫ within the overall crotchet group, and this interpretation is perhaps reinforced by the change to a specific **6/8** rhythm at b.36 (anticipated by implication in b.35), and again in b.48. A moment's trial will prove that the attempt to play the LH in a

♫♫♫ grouping goes against the grain of the music. Most players will therefore naturally 'fall' into a ♫♫♫ grouping from b.25. The fact that accompanying RH semiquavers proceed, on the face of it in a ♫♫♫ pattern creates the **hint**

of a cross-rhythm. This slight ambivalence contributes to the tempestuous, swirling, shifting planes of sound. (These, it must be stressed, are personal thoughts. This overall rhythmic ambivalence remains, and is 'felt' in either way, or indeed in amalgam, by different players.)

Practise 'hands separately' and 'hands together' in varying rhythms:

Then practise bb.25-6, then 27-8 as written, very slowly, making sure that LH and RH are perfectly coordinated, gradually increasing speed. Feel throughout bb.25-30 that the LH is emphatically 'leading' with the RH 'bending' to the requirements of that LH, rather than as so often in early attempts, leaving the RH to stagger along on its own impetus. Never mind if you cannot quite match the ♩ = 84. The essential is that there is a great surge with the LH plunging down with a determined roar towards a powerful semiquaver F on the first beat of b.26, with, as already said, a further upward lift and surge in the LH towards the accented crotchet on the second beat of b.26. Note the leap from the staccato bass F onto the first of the slurred group of four semiquavers,* and then the

hemidemisemiquaver rest, causing the hand to **lift** ready to attack the ♪♪ (see

General Introduction under 'Articulation'.) Chopin's effective fingering for the LH in

bb.26 and 28

is given in the Vienna Urtext and Paderewski Editions but not in Henle. Make a yet fiercer surge up to the high LH C in b.28. Then as you reach a brief plateau of sound at b.29, allow the

*This phrasing detail is not given in Vienna Urtext in bb.26 and 38. See, however, bb.28 and 40 in Vienna Urtext. See this detailing also in bb.26, 28, 38 and 40 in Paderewski and many other editions.

inner LH melody line to sing out with radiant power over the lower tied D flat in a continuous *crescendo* (showing the implied emphasis on the tied LH upbeat to b.31) towards a mighty chord on the first beat of b.31. At the same time ensure that the treble line blazons out as it 'takes over' the dotted rhythm motif from the beginning of this bar. Let this upper line sing forth in resonant duet with the inner LH line, making a sharp *diminuendo* through the third beat of b.32 ready to make a really *pianissimo* echo effect from b.33. Listen also to the full, then gradually decreasing sound of the recurring D flat pedal point through from bb.29-34. *Decrescendo* again to a whisper at b.35, but then with another little surge from the middle of b.35 as you move towards the brief 'unwinding' in **6/8** through b.36. Poise yourself for an instant, and no more, at the end of b.36, ready to launch into the storm again at b.37. Referring to the problem of the placing of the semiquaver in the LH in bb.29 and 30 (and in the RH in bb.31, 33 and 35), there are three options

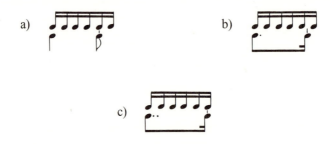

a)   b)

c)

Again Jan Ekier takes the view that the melodic semiquaver should coincide with the fifth accompanying semiquaver as in a), **except** at bb.45-7, where original editions show c). On the other hand, the Paderewski Edition supports the view that the melodic semiquaver should be in cross-rhythm to the accompaniment and should therefore consistently be placed just before the sixth accompanying semiquaver as in b). This latter counsel of perfection is far from easy to implement, and in practice it appears that most players, either from choice or expediency, opt for the sharper, more jagged effect (which I also prefer) of c). Follow the inner LH line from b.41 down to a stark B natural octave on the first beat of b.42, and on towards a powerful minim octave on the second beat, feeling the slurred semiquaver octave as an onward propelling upbeat to this strong beat; and similarly through bb.43-4. Take an instant at the end of b.44 to clear the sound for the *piano sforzato* 'lean' on the first beat of b.45, and again for the *pianissimo* on the third beat (effects which few players trouble to define sufficiently) and then gradually unwind in a carefully graded *diminuendo-rallentando* and *calando*. Make a gentle 'lean' on the emphasised A natural on the second beat of the **6/8** bar (b.48) as you poise yourself to re-enter tempo 1. Let the first RH grace note C coincide with the LH bass F as you 'scoop' up towards the melodic F on the first beat of b.49 in a graceful arpeggio. The seven semiquaver

'turn' in b.54 could be loosely grouped: 'Point' the sighing 'lean'

on the tied quaver (in cross-rhythm) in b.55, feeling this whole 'falling' 4-quaver group as the upbeat to b.56. Take time to ornament the third beat of b.56 as sweetly and expressively as possible, while still feeling its upbeat ongoing character. As always, let such figures fit in with the 'conducting' LH. Let the sound die away in a carefully graded *smorzando*, **listening** to the held pedal sound from the second beat of b.72 as you take plenty of time to arpeggiate exquisitely up to the high G, and then listening again as you wait for this note to resolve, changing the pedal to catch the bass F as Chopin indicates.†

†Those whose RH sets into rigor mortis in the attempt to master the pattern of the central section will seize upon the simplified version marked in Jane Stirling's copy.

Another 'authentic' but less radical simplification merely gives the RH a moment's 'breathing space' by omitting the **first** semiquaver chord of bb.27, 29, 39, and 41.

Nocturne No. 5 in F sharp major
Op. 15 No. 2 (8)

Deservedly one of the most popular of the Nocturnes, this is not, in technical terms, too formidable an assignment, with a middle section far less tumultuous than that of Op.15 No.1 or Op.27 No.1. Nevertheless we could spend a lifetime refining the continually varying arabesques, and experiencing the chromatic *frissons* of bb.11, 18, 20 and 51, in which the possible variations of shading are infinite. Like several of the Nocturnes (e.g. Op.32 No.1, Op.37, No.1 and Op.55 No.1) this has the motion of an easeful walk. That is not to say that the tempo, or span of the stride is the same in each case; but if you actually **walk** each of these pieces, **singing** the melody, you are bound to find the motion that is 'right'. Walk it, one stride to the quaver, which, taking the given ♩ = 40 as a mean, will therefore be around ♪ = 80. (But when you think the music through and **play** it, be sure to feel the sense of the overall **crotchet** pulse.) When this piece is played too slowly, as it often is, the motion begins to lumber, and the arabesques grow laboured. A half-light plays on this music, neither too bright nor too sombre, in a motion that is neither too fixed nor too lax. The usual maxim applies – let the LH be the conductor (see General Introduction, under 'The Left Hand'). The natural give and take occasioned not only by the arabesques and roulades of the RH, but also by the expressive flow of the melodic phrases, must be governed by the **sense** of the fundamental **2/4** pulse, which through bb.1-23 moves within almost continuous quavers.

bb. 1–8 Practise the LH carefully alone through bb.1-4, feeling the pulse of the two main beats of the bar as you rise from the bass note up to and down from the chord on the second beat of each bar in a smooth curve. Feel the second quaver of each bar, the C sharp (which acts as an inner pedal point) as an ongoing 'upbeat' to the second beat (taking the trouble to change finger 1-4 or 1-3 in bb.1-3 as indicated in many editions); it is a sense of 'sticking' on this note, rather than a sense of 'moving on' to the second beat that so often sets this piece off literally on the wrong foot into a 'plod' rather than into a light-moving step. Then **sing** the melody line while **playing** the LH through these four bars, observing all the inflections: the implied 'lean' on the upbeat figure to bb.1 and 3 and on the tied C sharps on the first beat of bb.2 and 4, the 'speaking' articulation of the repeated quaver

C sharps, ♪♪ the *decrescendoing* 'fall' of the semiquavers from the first beat of bb.1 and 3,

and the sense of taking a tiny breath before starting the second phrase on the upbeat to b.3. If you do this several times you will understand the way that the RH is governed by the fundamental rhythm proceeding in the LH, but at the same time you will find the degree to which the LH has to 'give' to accommodate the curves of the RH. As you take the breath before the upbeat to b.3, you will also gain a clear sense of the two subphrases, the second an elaborated version of the first, within the overall line of the four bars. Above all, you will absorb the sense of the **physical** motion of the piece which will enable you to bend to the expressive nuances of the first and last sections without becoming bogged down and losing direction as the ornamentation becomes increasingly ornate. (See also discussion of the shaping of this opening melody line in the General Introduction, under 'Phrasing').

When you finally put hands together, feel the gentle onward impulse from the opening upbeat through to the tied quaver on the first beat of b.2 (and similarly from the upbeat to b.3 through to the first beat of b.4); then 'tail off' the upward wisps of demisemiquavers gracefully in bb.2 and 4 rather than landing with a bump on the quaver C sharp. Move on from the upbeat to b.5 in a rather more purposeful tone as you embark on the longer overall phrase, through to the middle of b.8. In b.6 feel the 'lift' up from the detached quaver D sharp on the first beat so that the hand 'falls' naturally to make a singing syncopated emphasis on the tied F sharp (see General Introduction under 'Articulation') showing at the same time the matching slightly syncopated 'lean' on the slurred LH chord. Practise the LH carefully through bb.6-8, feeling the ongoing 'lean' on the partially tied upbeat to b.7, listening to the resonance of the lower sustained C sharp through b.7, and of the inner crotchet F sharp, and so on, while keeping the upper line, played with the thumb, as smooth as possible. In the RH always observe Chopin's *staccato* marks but feeling them as easy 'lifts', not as sharp 'points' – the 'lift' from the A sharp on the first beat of b.7 causes a natural, light 'fall' onto the dotted semiquaver B on the second quaver pulse of the bar, in a similar sense to the stronger 'lift and fall' in the previous bar. Let the little trill 'turn up' neatly towards the semiquaver A sharp and, lifting the hand again, synchronise the LH and RH demisemiquaver upbeat neatly to lead both hands towards the half close in b.8.

bb.9–16   Take a 'breath' to show that you are 'starting again' into the ornamented version of bb.1-8 in a rather fuller tone on the upbeat to b.9, giving the broken chords (with the lower RH notes, the quaver and then the semiquaver coinciding with the LH quaver) a leisurely, warm-toned 'roll'. Let the LH linger a little to allow time for the preparatory RH 'turn' on the upbeat to b.11, and then while the LH must, of course, allow time for the inflections of the RH through b.11, let it do so in a rhythmic manner, so that you retain the **sense** of the quaver motion within the 2-bar pulse, and with the overall sense that the RH is subject to the LH rhythm and **not** the other way about (see General Introduction under ''Free' Runs'). There are, naturally, many ways of grouping the RH notes and an experienced player will merge the groups in varying ways from day to day. As a guide, however, the notes fall conveniently as printed, i.e. in groups of six, nine, then in a longer overall line of fifteen with the seventh or eighth note of this group (D sharp or E sharp) approximately coinciding with the LH C sharp (or perhaps more prettily letting the LH 'wait' an instant for the RH A sharp, in which case the end of the run, i.e. the last six notes can be more gracefully 'turned'.†

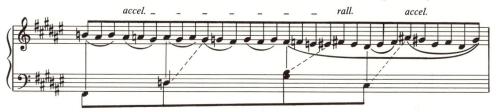

Then let the acciaccatura G sharp (coinciding with the bass note F sharp) 'speak' on the first beat of b.12, and 'flick' up lightly from the tied quaver C sharp to the detached demisemiquaver F sharp, ready to 'finish off' neatly in both hands on the second main beat.‡ The essential through bb.11 and 51 is not to allow the LH to 'panic', and to realise that these runs are not trials of speed. Chopin surely intended to create here a shimmer of finely shaded sound, not a show of finger technique. Feel a sense of moving on a little from the 'turned' upbeat to b.13, then 'turn' the upbeat to b.14 a little more purposefully as you prepare to support the RH with a resonant bass note and chords as it leaps up in full toned, 'measured' triplets towards the emphasised high tied F sharp in b.14, and swoops down again towards a clear quaver A sharp on the first beat of b.15. Lower the tone through b.15, and be sure to 'lift' from the semiquavers in both hands as you prepare to slur the demisemiquaver upbeats neatly towards the unison on the first beat of b.16.

bb.16–25   'Finish off' the LH neatly in b.16, beneath the RH crotchet F sharp and quaver rest, and then make a tiny break as if taking a breath before leading into b.17 in a new tone with a slight feeling of 'moving on'. Let the 'speaking' repeated quaver E's in b.17 'go to' a very gently emphasised and slightly *tenuto* crotchet on the first beat of b.18, before 'pearling' down in a falling wisp of sound towards the quietly sustained tied crotchet A. Time this run, and the one in b.20 (starting just after the LH chord on the second quaver pulse) so that you arrive on the A precisely on the second main beat of the bar. Feel the gently heightened intensity through b.19, and 'spread' the triplets expressively in cross-rhythm, allowing an extra instant to clear the sound for the *pianissimo* crotchet on the first beat of b.20, balancing the RH through these bars with a steady but 'ongoing' LH. *Crescendo* through b.21 and then support the warm-toned, ardent melody line with resonant bass octaves and luxuriantly spread chords, moving on towards a telling appoggiatura-like quaver B on the first

---

†J. Petrie Dunn quotes Kleczyński's grouping, shown in this example by the dotted lines. (The indications *accelerando*, *rallentando*, *accelerando* are also Kleczyński's.)

‡As noted in the General Introduction under 'Pedalling', there is a pencilled figure '2' in bb.12. 18, 20, and 58 of Jane Stirling's copy indicating the required use of the sustaining **and** *una corda* pedals (see Eigeldinger, pp.130, 152, and 206).

beat of b.24. Then as the B resolves onto the tied A sharp, feel that this note (together with the LH rising in *stringendo* towards the emphasised E sharp) and the measured, 'speaking' RH detached semiquavers form an onward leaning, overall upbeat group towards the *doppio movimento*. (The 'spacing out' of these RH semiquavers in a *crescendoing ritenuto* actually enhances the sense of this onward 'lean'.)

bb.25–33
This section is not so difficult, in a rhythmic sense, as it appears on the page. Practise the LH alone, feeling the implied emphasis and ongoing 'push' of the syncopated crotchet chord on the second quaver pulse of bb.25, 26, etc. and then spacing the slurred detached quavers carefully, feeling each G sharp as a clear ongoing upbeat to bb.26 and 27, etc.

First sort out the various melodic threads of the RH:

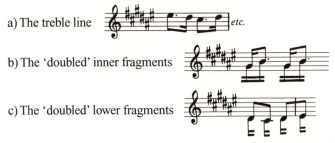

a) The treble line

b) The 'doubled' inner fragments

c) The 'doubled' lower fragments

Then when you fit all the strands together, be **aware** of the inner fragments though without 'labouring the points', so that you ultimately achieve a smooth overall five-in-a-group flow, with the treble line, phrased as glidingly as possible, gently predominating. Small hands will find it easier to keep an even upper line by using the fifth finger consistently (see General Introduction under 'Fingering'). 'Lean' a little on the upper dotted quaver on the main beat of each bar, and feel the fifth note of each group as the 'upbeat' to the next beat. When you put hands together feel once more that the RH is fitting in with the stable LH rhythm. Mathematically, the LH crotchet chord and the upbeat quaver G sharp, e.g. in bb.25 and 26, fall between the third and fourth notes of each RH five-note group. In practice if you concentrate on the LH rhythm and just let the RH flow on easily and evenly, you will find that this happens quite naturally. Feeling the onward lean from b.24 as described above, drift into the *doppio movimento* in a whispering *sotto voce*, gradually gaining speed from the previous *ritardando* and then quickly gathering momentum to 'regain', as it were, the previous tempo in an even *doppio movimento* (and no faster), rather than plumping in in an immediate 'new' tempo. Make a gentle swell towards b.27, curving back **through** b.27 towards a quietly singing long minim E on the first beat of b.28. 'Point' the inner LH and RH fragment through this bar, feeling the implied slightly syncopated 'lean' on the quaver A's in both hands on the second quaver pulse (it appears that Chopin intended these A's to coincide – see the Vienna Urtext Edition). *Crescendo* rather steeply through the second half of b.32, with the help of a strong LH chord on the second beat, towards a telling *sforzato* in both hands on the first beat of b.33.

bb.33–48
Show clearly at b.33 the change to the dotted rhythm with the first note of each RH triplet coinciding with the LH chord:

Crescendo with increasing fervour towards the climactic high octave E on the second beat of b.40, and then 'going on to' a resonant bass octave G sharp and RH C sharp on the second beat of b.41. On the way show the expressive LH and inner RH fragment at b.36, giving a 'braking lean' as indicated on the (this time) 'staggered' C in either hand, and then support the RH with increasingly resonant LH octaves and chords from b.39. Holding the bass octave G sharp from the second beat of b.41 within the long pedal as indicated show the implied emphasis on the LH tied quaver fourth on the upbeat to b.42 and the strong emphasis on the syncopated crotchet in b.42. The real *decrescendo* starts from the **second** half of this bar – the ➤ signs through b.39, and from the second half of b.40, suggest not so much a progressive *decrescendo*, but rather the intended 'lean' on each RH **main** beat, and the lightening of the tone for the remaining five notes, ready for the next 'lean'.* Let the LH rise to a telling *sforzato* quaver D natural on the second beat of b.43, and then 'lead' the RH down towards the lower register with the emphasised LH octave D on the second beat of b.45. Let the sound die away from this point in a carefully graded *rallentando* and *smorzando* towards the silent pause at b.48. Many players, I believe, make the mistake of beginning to *decrescendo* after the second beat of b.40 – whereas all the indications are that Chopin intended to maintain the full tone **through** b.41, incorporating the pedal point effect from the second beat of b.41, and then beginning the *decrescendo* proper as indicated from the end of b.42. The splendid resonances of this whole passage need to be finely judged, and the *decrescendo* from the end of b.42 carefully gauged towards a mere whisper at b.48.

bb.48–62
 If you actually take a large breath through this pause you will know by an irresistible physical urge when to lead back to Tempo 1 with a poised upbeat to b.50 (see General Introduction under 'Rests, Pauses and Rallentandos'). Practise the long run through b.51 in different rhythms until it is quite fluent. Then you will find that the first half of the run fits into groups of nine and ten notes to coincide with the first two LH quavers. Feel **three** groups of triplets to the first LH note, therefore, and three groups to the second, with an 'extra' note at the end, E sharp. Feel a slight 'hold' in the LH as the RH 'goes back up' to the D natural on the second main beat of the bar. Then allow the remaining twenty-one notes to run down freely in a clear, light-toned 'fall' from this D, lingering a little as they curl through the end of the bar, and perhaps letting the first D sharp (or one of the preceding two notes) coincide approximately with the LH C sharp. Rise to a greater resonance on the high F sharp in b.54 than at b.14, and feel the sound of this note 'carrying on' towards the higher A sharp before you descend in a beautifully smooth curve. Listen to the pedal point effect of the sustained lower C sharp as you progress through bb.55-6, the extended version of bb.7-8. Let the grace note F double sharp coincide expressively with the LH B sharp at the beginning of the trill in b.56. Then feel the onward impulse towards the chord on the second quaver pulse of b.57 as you curl expressively up to the G sharp in the RH. Let the detached demisemiquavers 'speak' as they 'fall' from this G sharp in little droplets over the inner sustained RH F sharp, and 'join in' with a quietly emphasised inner LH tied semiquaver D on the fourth quaver pulse of the bar, tailing off the sound towards carefully placed quaver unisons on the first beat of b.58. Hold these F sharps within the pedal, creating a halo of exquisitely graded sound downwards from the high D sharp (giving this note a quiet but carrying ring). Balance the RH with carefully placed LH chords, feeling the impulse of the semiquaver and demisemiquaver triplets towards the **quaver** chord on the

second beat of bb.58 and 59.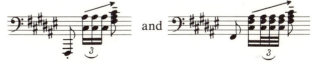

*See General Introduction under 'Dynamic and Agogic Accents'

Let the RH run easily through b.60, gathering a little speed before slowing and dying away through b.61. Linger over the last demisemiquaver group, matching it carefully with the LH dominant quaver, and playing the final minims with quiet finality, allowing plenty of time for the sound to die through the pause.

Nocturne No. 6 in G minor
Op. 15 No. 3 (7) (O)

Technically this is the easiest of the Nocturnes, unique in its almost total lack of ornamentation or pianistic effects. The pattern of quieter outer sections interrupted by a turbulent central passage is reversed, and here the first section builds to a climax through a series of arresting harmonic progressions, which yield to a chorale-like centrepiece. Then, instead of recapitulating, Chopin leads on into a repeated coda-like section. There is a story that there was a reference on the manuscript to a performance of Hamlet, in other words, that there is a hint of a programme influence. But this is discounted by Maurice Brown (p.85) . In any event, the idea of 'programming' is alien to Chopin's musical thought, and it is fruitless to seek Shakespearean clues to interpretation here. It is a curious piece, and one that is comparatively little known and seldom played. Whether or not this is because it is too 'plain' to suit our notion of what a Nocturne should be, or perhaps because it is one of those pieces that is more interesting to play than to listen to, in any event it makes a rewarding study for the domestic pianist (perhaps particularly for the older player).

bb.1–13   It is difficult to accord the indications *lento* and *languido e rubato* with the ♩. = 60.† Most pianists take it considerably slower. But when the tempo is **too** slow, as it often is, the music is prone to a stolid kind of lugubriousness at a 3-in-the-bar plod (which may indeed contribute to its comparative neglect). At a basic tempo of at least ♩. = 44-48, with a definite 1-in-the-bar feeling, the piece takes on an altogether different character – ambiguous and shadowy, almost skimming, and a great deal more alluring. (See General Introduction under 'Tempo'). In any event there needs to be a good deal of give and take: the alternating sense of moving on and drawing back. Practise the LH at first **in time**, so that you **feel** the rest on each third beat **physically**, and showing the **different** effect of the downward slur from chord to bass note whenever it occurs (bb.1-3, 6, 12-15, etc.) and the 'lift' from the unslurred bass note to upper chord in bb.4, 5, 16-17, etc. Practise bb.8-11 with particular care, changing fingers 1-3 on the tied minim F as indicated. **Listen** to the resolution of the chord on the first beat of bb.8 and 10 to the chord on the first beat of bb.9 and 11 within the sound of the inner drone-like pedal point F, also feeling the syncopated 'lean' on this F on the second beat of bb.8 and 10.

Then practise the RH alone, giving an ongoing lean on the opening upbeat (while at the same time giving this note its full value, or even a little more) and then making a strong upward curve from b.2 towards the high G and long tied F. When practising this line alone, do **hold** the F through its full three bars so that you learn how much singing sound it needs, and also so that you learn to **listen** to the amount of sound that is left, so that you can 'shade it off' towards the minim D on the first beat of b.7. When you put hands together continue to listen carefully to the upbeat, so that you 'join in' perfectly with the LH on the first beat of b.1. Allow time to poise yourself through b.1, and then feel an onward impetus, aided and also controlled by the effect of the slurred LH chords as you rise impulsively towards and 'through'

†This *languido e rubato* is erased in Jane Stirling's copy.

the high G to the long F. Be sure also to give the RH crotchet on the third beat of each bar its full value, at the same time feeling the onward upbeat 'lean' of each of these notes over the LH rest. Support the RH with a resonant bass note on the first beat of b.4 ('pointing' the 'changing of direction' of the LH at bb.4, 6 and 7) and then feel a slight drawing back as the tempo relaxes again towards the end of the 7-bar phrase. Then having 'finished off' the LH neatly on the second beat of b.7, beneath the held RH minim, lead on again from a clear emphasised upbeat to b.8. Listen acutely to the LH through bb.8-11, while at the same time feeling the continued onward 'pull' of the emphasised RH upbeats. Then let the tempo and the sound relax a little from the upbeat to b.12, noticing how the ending of this little episode overlaps with the beginning of the restatement of the first phrase from the upbeat to b.13.

bb.13–68   As you move on again from b.14, rise in a stronger, more importunate *crescendo* towards the *forte* at b.16. Feel the momentary increased urgency in the LH through bb.18-19 as the high F is held here for even longer than at bb.4-6, before the music subsides again towards the *poco ritenuto* from b.23. Take time here to listen to the chromatic upturn of the lower LH in b.24 before setting off again from the upbeat to b.25. Allow an extra instant too to take a tiny breath through the quaver rest on the second beat of b.35, as you prepare to shape the *leggierissimo* triplets (the sole fragment of decoration in the piece) expressively in bb.35 and 36, incorporating the eloquent little 'lean' on each offbeat D, and taking a little longer to show the 'speaking' acciaccatura in the second fragment. At the same time feel each of these little offbeat turns as an overall upbeat group towards the first beat of the subsequent bar. Place the long tied D carefully on the first beat of b.47, **listening** to its sound as if in suspense as the LH continues, slowing, but at the same time leading on towards the mysterious deflection to the *sotto voce* diminished seventh chord and the warning bass *sforzato* D sharp at b.51. From here allow the tempo and dynamics to fluctuate subtly and naturally, moving on here and drawing back there to give time to listen to the strange progressions. Take care to shape the RH quaver interval of a ninth with an ongoing 'vocal lift', not an upward stab through the first beat of bb.57 and 65.

bb.69–85   Lower the sound through b.68 ready to start the long climb from b.69. Support the RH with carefully balanced LH bass notes and chords as you make a **controlled** *crescendo* and *accelerando* towards b.77 over the long pedal point

C sharp. Practise at first  *etc.* to help absorb the basic

harmonic sense of the progressions. Allow a little extra time in b.75 to 'point' the powerful low-registered octave C sharp, and 'hold' b.76 a little as you prepare to give full weight to the slurred chord on the first beat of b.77, ready to descend through the marvellous sequence of diminished sevenths in a free, impassioned, but again controlled manner. This passage will not run out of hand if you really **lean** on the first chord of each slurred pair implementing the cross-rhythm effect, and **keeping up** the overall tone, to deliver the *sforzato* minim chord on the first beat of b.79 with optimum resonance. **Hold** this chord as indicated by the *ritenuto*, poising yourself for the *diminuendo* and *rallentando* towards the new section at b.89. Define the contrasting effect of the slurred chords (bb.79, 81 and 83, 'leaning' well on the minims) with the expressively articulated, almost furtive intervening reiterated fragments (bb.80, 82 and 84) as you descend in carefully graded layers of sound towards the *pianissimo* dotted minim C sharp at b.85.

bb.86–152 Show that you are starting anew as you repeat the C sharp on the first beat of b.86, as this solo phrase leads you on into the *religioso* section at b.89. Play this with the utmost simplicity in a quietly breathed, hymn-like manner, 'leaning' gently on the minim chords on the first beat of bb.89-90, 92-96, etc, as you follow the easy rise and fall of the phrases. Some players adopt a slower tempo here, although there seems no reason to do so, indeed the passage can easily drag. Pay as much attention to the LH line as to the treble melody, feeling the ongoing effect of the repeated crotchets on the second beat of bb.92-5, and of the LH crotchet phrase starting on the second beat of b.96. Show the emphasis on the accented minim G on the second beat of b.104, 'holding' this slightly as the inner and lower lines ease back towards the restatement in b.105.

Clear the sound at the end of b.120 ready to strike the unison tied *sforzato* dotted minims with a carrying ring, like a commanding horn-call. Then play the crotchet chord figure in precise time, slurring the upbeat chord smoothly and placing the repeated crotchet chords in a firm detached style, 'going on through' to the second beat of b.122 as indicated, while listening to the continuing sound of the inner tied C's. Clear the sound on the crotchet rest ready to strike the next *sforzato* unison again. Play the dotted rhythm figure precisely, 'going to' equally ringing C's on the second beat of b.125, and listen carefully to the remaining sound of the tied C's so that the line carries on convincingly from the upbeat of b.127.

etc. You could either lift the hands after the second beat of b.126 to make a clear 'restart' on these upbeat B flats, though without losing the sense of the onward line, or you could finger the RH thus after the second chord to create a smooth join: *etc.*

Continue the line thus through to b.133, listening particularly carefully to the telling effect of the tied F within the harmonic progressions at bb.129-30 and 131-2. Change fingers 1-5 as indicated on the RH D at b.133, once more listening to the tied unisons ringing out above the now *sotto voce* inner harmonies. One can only speculate as to what was in Chopin's mind as he wrote this strangely arresting, mysterious, and somewhat uncharacteristic passage.† From b.137 you could restate the passage in the same dynamic, which perhaps gives an even stranger air, or, as some pianists do, in a quieter echo-effect. Prepare for the ending, which comes upon us unawares, by feeling a clear *ritenuto* from the first beat of b.149 through the smooth, quiet final phrase which momentarily recalls the chorale-like atmosphere of the *religioso* section.

Nocturne No. 7 in C sharp minor
Op. 27 No. 1 (8+)

This is a giant among the Nocturnes, progressing from the ominous stillness of its opening, through sequences of tumultuous upheaval. Its grandeur appeals as much to the younger as to the older player, and although it is far from easy to play, I have heard it splendidly performed

† Having felt a strong foretaste of Grieg myself, it was interesting to see that J.-J. Eigeldinger also detects a Nordic tint here (p.153).

by quite young pianists (particularly boys, who can not only enjoy their power in the middle sections but, with their greater hand-span, may cope better with the wide-spread intervals of the LH accompaniment in the opening and closing sections).

bb.1–10 Nothing could be more louring than the extraordinary opening. Note the **minim** pulse of the metronome mark indicating the sense of an overall 2-in-the-bar pulse. Few players take this section up to the given ♩ = 42. On the other hand, at too slow a tempo the wave-like continuity of the LH will suffer, and the slow moving melody will grind to a halt. (See General Introduction under 'Tempo'). Set the scene with smoothly swaying sextuplets, like barely audible subterranean heavings, establishing an inexorable 2-in-the-bar swing. The smooth progress of the treble melody is dependent on the absolute fluency and rhythmic stability of these waves of sextuplets. Practise the LH assiduously alone, shaping the curve of each sextuplet up to and down from the upmost note, i.e. the third quaver in each group, through bb.1-26. Show the slight swell through b.1, drawing back again through b.2 as you prepare to place the opening melody note *sotto voce*, yet penetrating and portentous. Feel the close intensity of the upward creeping intervals as you edge upwards (giving the repeated E sharps in b.3 a separate, 'speaking' quality, and listening also as the left thumb reaches up to the high B 'against' the sound of these E sharps), towards the F sharp on the third beat of b.4, giving this tied note sufficient tone to sound over the barline. Listen to the LH inflecting to the D major harmony beneath this held F sharp on the first beat of b.5 before 'tailing off' the sound a little through the remainder of the bar. (Regarding the dotted rhythm in this bar, and bb.9, 11, etc. see under No.5 in F major – here again I have never heard this executed as the Vienna Urtext Edition suggests). There are differences of opinion as to whether the phrase carries on in one long sweep on through b.6 to begin the restatement at b.7, or begins anew on the first beat of b.6. In any event, whether or not you 'change phrases' here, do not allow the music 'stop', but feel the onward impetus towards the implied emphasis on the high minim on the second beat of b.6. Then draw out the remainder of this bar a little as the LH descends to the B, momentarily breaking the long C sharp pedal point and allowing time to reach up to the high LH D sharp as the RH tails off the phrase towards the minim E on the first beat of b.7. Notice how this E both ends the first overall phrase and begins the next. Drop to a hushed *pianissimo* at b.9, leaving the scarcely breathed B sharp hanging expectantly within the pedal from the end of b.9. The pedalling of this section calls for special comment. The long tonic pedal point needs to sound as a continuous low 'hum' through bb.1-6, etc. But when the pedal is changed on each half bar from b.3 onwards as it obviously must be, the bass note will be lost. The solution adopted by most pianists is to hold the 'upbeat' quaver C sharp with the fifth finger **through** the subsequent pedal change, releasing it as soon as the new harmony is caught within

the new pedal:  resuming 'normal'

articulation briefly in bb.6-7, and from the middle of b.11.

bb.10–28 Enter in a slightly fuller tone with the octave C sharp on the first beat of b.11 with the feeling of 'going to' the emphasised crotchet G sharp. Then in b.13 listen as the LH goes down to the low G sharp on the third beat, and to the telling clash of the emphasised D natural with the pedalled sound of the high LH B sharp. In b.17 allow an extra moment to 'point' the temporary change of pattern in the LH beneath the again emphasised RH D natural. Show the entry of the inner line clearly on the first beat of b.20, and listen to this inner line descending expressively towards the long F sharp in b.21 and on to the crotchet E on the first beat of b.22, without disturbing the continuing long overall line of the treble. Take time to space out the inner five-semiquaver 'turn' in b.22 – and don't slurp through them in a vague *legato* as inexperienced players invariably try to do: they will never 'speak' as they so expressively can unless you articulate them in a just detached style as indicated. Draw out the LH a little here, but rhythmically, feeling that the RH is fitting in with this slower, but **steady** LH sextuplet group, and **not** the other way about (see General Introduction under 'The

Left Hand', and '*Rubato*'). Fit in the five notes approximately thus: feeling

that they are 'going to' the inner dotted quaver B, and again ensuring that preoccupation with this inner 'turn' does not sabotage the continuity of the upper line. Listen to the inner line continuing downwards through b.26 as the treble line dies on the third beat. Hold the sound of the long quiet wave of D major harmony within the pedal through bb.27-8. Any distribution of the hands can be used here, provided that they enhance the atmosphere of dead-calm-before-the-storm stillness. These two versions of Chopin's own practice, are given in the Vienna Urtext Edition;

bb.28–44   Most pianists allow a significant *rallentando* towards the end of b.28, ready to 'slide' into the *più mosso*, gradually accelerating to reach their 'settled' tempo at about b.32. Less experienced players need not feel obliged to strain towards the

♩. = 54. The essential is to convey a sense of movement and of a brewing storm, leaving room for later acceleration from b.41, and b.53 onwards. Practise the LH alone, 'leaning' on the lower sustained dotted minims so that you create a continuous bass line with a consistent 1-in-the-bar momentum. This 'lean' on the lower note allows the thumb and second finger to articulate the inner triplets comparatively lightly, but rhythmically in a mounting, threatening rumble. Take the greatest care when practising hands separately **and** hands together that you do not skimp the third beat of each bar, thereby causing a continuing tendency to 'fall into' the next bar in an uncontrolled manner. When you practise the RH, 'lean' similarly on the emphasised first beats, again taking **particular** care not to skimp the value of the crotchets on the third beats, thinking of each of these as the upbeat to the emphasised chord on the subsequent first beat. Strictly speaking, when you put hands together the quaver in each bar is in cross-rhythm with the LH triplets. In the event, at speed, it usually **sounds** as if it coincides with the third quaver of the LH triplet group. If, however, you feel the note as a strong 'upbeat' to the third beat of the bar (i.e. the upbeat to the upbeat!) you will give it its proper weight, and avoid it sounding too clipped. Rise in a carefully graded *crescendo* towards the *forte* at b.37, being careful not to get too loud here – you need plenty of reserves for the long further climb. From b.37 deliver a resonant bass octave on each first beat as indicated, and show the curve of the triplets in each bar up to the high eighth quaver, and down to the next octave as if in a series of strong arcs. At this fast tempo the demisemiquaver 'upbeat' to the third beat of bb.37, 38, etc. will normally coincide with the third quaver of the LH triplet group. (However, at the climactic b.49, where it is necessary to draw out the tempo owing to the immense LH intervals – this bar anyway being marked *sostenuto* – the semiquaver chord could be placed slightly **after** the LH triplet for maximum dramatic effect.) As the tumultuous fury mounts from b.41, keep the *stretto* on a tight rein, always feeling that the continuous LH triplets are controlling the RH, and **not** the other way around. Deliver the repeated RH octaves (bb.41-2 and 43-4) like a salvo of gunshots – if you consciously **match** each salvo to the LH triplets and avoid starting too loud, so that you feel you are making a *crescendo* through to a mighty chord on the subsequent first beat, you will

avoid these repeated octaves 'jamming'.

Draw out a little through the end of b.44 ready to deliver b.45 with **almost** your full might. It is essential through bb.45-52 that you keep events under control by listening to and following the curves of the **LH**. Practise this assiduously therefore – if you consciously follow the upward line of the **thumb** through b.45 – generating a temporary cross-rhythm effect – it is much easier to maintain accuracy. Note the articulation, delivering the detached quavers with an even, pendulum-like rhythmic swing through to the first beat of b.46, and then show the different articulation of the smooth overall curves of bb.46 and 47 and the short slurred effects in b.48. When you put hands together bring the utmost passion and grandeur to this whole passage. Follow the dynamic 'dip' through b.46, ready to rise through bb.47-8 towards your maximum volume at b.49. Here follow the thumb-line with a pendulum-like swing as at b.45, but carrying a grander 'punch'. I personally find it best to use the thumb on the high C, **and** the A flat on the second beat of b.50 – it helps to 'point' the second beat and thus steady the end of the phrase. The LH fingering in this bar would therefore read 1 4 1, 1 2 1, 2 4 1. As the editor of the Vienna Urtext Edition suggests, you **could** take the high LH E flat in b.49, and the high A flat on the first beat of b.50 with the RH. I feel, however, that the natural drawing out of these *sostenuto* bars caused by the effort of the upward 'heave' of the LH to these high notes, and in particular the 'pointing' with the LH thumb of the summit of the overall LH curve through bb.49-50, maximises the climactic grandeur of these bars. In any event, take plenty of time as you draw out through b.51, taking care to shape the LH in overall curves up to a strong G on the second beat, up to the high E flat at the end of the bar, and down to a resonant A flat on the first beat of b.52, as the RH closes the period in magisterial style, arriving on a still powerful chord on the first beat of b.52.

bb.44–52

Then *decrescendo* sharply towards the *sotto voce* at b.53, to gradually *crescendo* and *accelerando* again in a breathless but controlled *agitato*. 'Lean' once more on the emphasised first beats, letting the LH triplets rumble freely, again taking care not to 'fall into' the first beats as from b.29. Note also the 'braking' effect of the syncopated emphasised second LH quaver in bb.54, 56, 58, etc. Give the RH crotchet chords a firm, but ongoing emphasis through b.63, and then through b.64 rein in the three chords as you *crescendo* steeply towards b.65. Leap off from the first chord of b.65 in an entirely new, intensely virile, dance-like *con anima* rhythm, feeling the impetus towards the strong *tenuto* chord on the first beat of b.68, again initiating a strong, but now more springy 1-in-the-bar rhythmic swing. Space out the LH detached crotchets rhythmically in bb.66, 70 and 74 beneath these resonant *tenuto* dotted minim chords. Take care to articulate the quaver chords

bb.52–84

rhythmically and clearly as you *crescendo* into b.68 and similarly into bb.72 and 76. If you **feel** the third beat of b.67 etc. within these quaver chords, and within the impetus towards the crotchet chord on the subsequent first beat, you will avoid jamming this little salvo. Take time to clear the sound at the end of b.72 ready for the sudden *pianissimo* at b.73, being sure to maintain the prevalent rhythmic vitality through this echo effect. Then be careful not to lose control as you *accelerando* impassionedly towards b.81. Space out these six chords in a magnificently full tone, **listening** acutely to the changing inflections, and with the feeling of 'going towards' a strong 'lean' on the appoggiatura-like chord on the first beat of b.83. Take time to listen as this chord resolves, and to listen to the reverberation of the dominant seventh harmony through the pause. Whether or not you play the octave *cadenza* with the LH or with both hands must be a matter of personal choice. Ensure in any event that it is shaped as indicated, showing the strong curve up to a powerful dotted crotchet E, and then playing the octaves with the feeling of a fine extemporary freedom. Curve down to the F double sharp, then back up towards the B natural, then showing the different quality of the detached octaves as they plunge down towards the emphasised minim A and down again in slurred groups towards an immensely resonant *sforzato* C sharp.†

        Hold this note within the pedal as you re-establish the still mood of the opening.

bb.84–101   Listen to the sorrowful, quietly emphasised descent of the inner line through b.93 beneath the held upper B sharp, towards the doubled emphasised C sharp on the first beat of b.94. Start anew with the new phrase in warm-toned major thirds on the second beat of the bar, feeling that here at last a shaft of sunlight has broken through. Show the slightly syncopating effect of this rocking progression from the upper thirds on the second and fourth beats to the lower thirds on the third and first beats of bb.94 and 95 with the hint of a lean on each second and fourth beat. Then show clearly from b.96 that there are two **separate** lines of sustained thirds. Listen to the warm resonance of the semibreve third through b.98, as the LH begins its *crescendo*. Listen acutely to the spacious resonance of the *adagio* bars as you make a controlled swell, spacing the LH quavers carefully. 'Lean' with a full rich tone on the RH minim chord on the first beat of the penultimate bar over a powerful bass C sharp, and space out the detached quavers deliberately within the pedal as you rise in a slow *crescendo* towards the high inner E sharp. Hear this note not only as the topmost note of the arpeggio, but also as the resolution of the inner F sharp of the previous RH chord, then listen to the quiet finality of the last tonic chords.

Nocturne No. 8 in D flat major
Op. 27 No. 2 (8)

This much played piece embodies all our ideas of how a Nocturne should be: a quietly flowing LH supporting a languorous, gracefully decorated RH melody. It is a piece that grows cloying if it is pulled around too much and allowed to grow too effusive. This is a good moment to remember Chopin's devotion to Mozart – though the pianism and the temper of their respective periods are far apart, the purity and refinement of line and texture in many ways recall the style of a Mozart slow movement. And, as in such a Mozart movement, the ornamentation needs to seem to grow and 'flower' naturally from the melodic line, rather than to be clamped on in separate boxes marked 'ornaments', as is so often the case. The metronome

---

†In Jane Stirling's copy this resonance is maximised by the addition of acciaccatura at the lower octave, thereby also completing the preceding octave cadenza (see also the Vienna Urtext Edition).

mark is extraordinarily fast. Most pianists adopt a considerably slower tempo, around ♩. = 40, or even slower, and there has to be a fair amount of give and take. On the other hand the tempo must not be too slow – the melody will begin to 'stick' unless it can rely on a continuous sense of onward movement from the LH.

bb.1–5
Once again the importance of the consistent rhythm and contours of the LH is paramount. Practise the D flat major figure (in a 'closed' position, as on the second main beat of b.1) over and over until you are quite familiar with the easy rhythmic **6/8** swing. Feel the 'lift' from a clear D flat up to the F on the second semiquaver pulse, the dip to the A flat, the rise to the F again and then the downward curve towards the D flat on the next main beat. Always feel that you are 'returning' to a definite bass note, however *piano* (noting that the music proceeds over a tonic pedal point through bb.1-6); and, within the shape of the smooth overall curve of each six-semiquaver group, never cease to feel the sense of the steady three-quaver pulse, though without obvious accents. It is essential to take time to understand the fundamental shape and motion of this LH pattern which persists from the first bar to the last through all the changes of harmony and dynamics, gently propelling, and 'cushioning' the long melodic lines of the RH.

Then practise the RH, **in time**, through bb.2-6, **imagining** the even motion of the LH below. Absorb the 'landscape' of the curves: the dip from the quietly singing opening dotted crotchet F down to the low semiquaver F (feeling this note as a 'speaking' upbeat to the tied dotted crotchet A flat on the first beat of b.3), the rise to a singing tied B flat on the first beat of b.4, the expressive descent to the quietly 'pointed' long A natural, and the tailing off of this note to the B flat in b.6. At the same time feel the continuity of the line as you shape the overall phrase as a singer would. If you actually **sing** the phrase, and every other phrase as you study the piece, you will have no difficulty in shaping the lines gracefully and expressively. If, when you put hands together, you take the time to become thoroughly familiar with these five bars, and to absorb the sense of the interdependence of the melody and accompaniment before going on, you will have a sound basis for study of the whole piece. When you play the introductory bar allow a little extra time as you 'lift' in a smooth arc from a quiet but resonant bass note on the first beat up to the high F, and then establish your basic even pulse through the second beat of the bar ready for the entry of the melody. Chopin's pedal indications are extremely detailed in this piece. It is essential that each bass note is always caught within the pedal (see bb.1, 5 and 6). On the modern piano the effect of the long pedal through bb.1-4 may be found too thick, and the pedal may be partially changed, according to the ear of the player, and the quality of the piano and acoustic. Thereafter note the pedal through the whole of each of bb.5 and 6, and then through each half bar from b.7 onwards. So many players with puritanical ears make the mistake of changing the pedal in the middle of each main beat, or even on every quaver pulse, thereby losing the essential continuous bass resonance.

bb.5–17
Having slurred off the long A natural in b.5, smoothly to the dotted crotchet B flat on the first beat of b.6, take a short breath, but phrasing over the rest as a singer would ready to re-enter clearly on the high C, (matching this carefully with the second note (G flat) of the LH group) and then *decrescendo* as indicated as the semiquavers curve expressively downwards towards a warmly slurred crotchet F on the first beat of b.7. Then *crescendo* upwards towards b.8, placing the acciaccatura **on** the first beat, and balancing the LH sound carefully with the full-toned high G flat. Allow the grace note arpeggio to 'fall' beautifully lightly, letting the first note, the E flat, sound just after (or coinciding with) the fifth LH semiquaver, D flat, as indicated in Jane Stirling's copy and accommodating the RH with just a little 'give' in the LH. (Less experienced players could begin this little arpeggio earlier, allowing the E flat to coincide with the **fourth** LH semiquaver. See General Introduction under ''Free Runs'.) Articulate the RH detached quavers in a 'speaking' manner

within the pedal as they rise towards an expressive 'lean' on the tied crotchet G natural on the first beat of b.9. Then 'tail off' the demisemiquavers smoothly but clearly towards the tied dotted crotchet F on the second main beat of the bar. Listen to the continuing sound of this F over the bar line as you bring in the second voice, and then phrase the double melody in thirds in a new, richer tone. Follow Chopin's detailed indications for dynamics and emphases as this doubled melody rises and falls from here, showing the little 'fall' from the repeated sixths in b.11, the rise towards b.12, and so on, while always feeling the overall continuity of the melodic lines, as if in an easy-flowing conversational duet. Always **lift** the hand at rests or from detached notes, e.g. in the middle of the first beat of b.11 and near the end of b.12; although the 'gap' will not show within the pedalled sound, the act of lifting the hand subtly punctuates the line, and at the same time predisposes the 'fall' which will give the required natural emphasis, slight or strong, according to context, on the subsequent note (see General Introduction under 'Articulation'). Feel the fairly strong 'ongoing' syncopated emphasis on the quaver sixth on the third quaver pulse of b.13 as you prepare to *crescendo* into b.14. Space the RH cross-rhythm figures through the second half of b.14, and through bb.15-16, etc. with a sense of freedom, feeling nevertheless that these figures are subject to the shape of the flexible but continuously moving LH.

bb.17–34   Let the hand 'fall', more strongly this time, onto the syncopated tied third in b.17, feeling the more purposeful mood as you *crescendo* towards b.18, and then shape the descending octave line in a full tone down to a strong crotchet on the first beat of b.19. Play the ornamented repetition of this phrase more fervently, but still in a smooth overall curve through bb.20-21, and clearly define the *piano* and *pianissimo* dynamics of the intervening fragments (bb.19 and 21). Then feel you are moving on as you quietly emphasise the tied dotted crotchet E flat on the second beat of b.22, listening to the smooth descent of the bass line, and to the melodic inner LH fragment in b.23. 'Re-take' the melody line with the emphasised tied D flat on the second main beat of b.24 making a slight *tenuto* as you poise yourself on this tied note at the beginning of **b.25**, ready to make a *ritenuto* into the restatement from b.26. In the copies belonging to three of his pupils Chopin deleted the *crescendo* mark through b.25 (shown in Henle), and indicated a *pianissimo* from b.26 – a happier effect (see Vienna Urtext and Paderewski Editions). Note the different articulation of the RH semiquavers in b.28 (compare with b.4) and slightly 'point' the chromatic inner offbeat movement in the LH through bb.29-30 (D flat, D natural, E flat). Let the semiquaver sextuplet fall, this time in graceful cross-rhythm from the high G flat in b.32, and then keep the LH **steady** as the demisemiquaver triplets ascend with gossamer lightness towards the dotted quaver sixth on the first beat of b.33. Cultivate a flexible lateral movement of the wrist here, feeling the sense of the slurred upward movement of each offbeat group of three demisemiquavers, so that the RH moves in a series of feather-light arcs, not spiky zig-zags. Feel in each group that the second finger (lying rather flat on its note, i.e. the E flat in the first group), is acting as a light pivot, as the wrist hinges the hand from the lowest note (i.e. the A flat) to the highest (i.e. the C), and so on through each group. This figure is far from easy to execute. So often, as the RH panics, the LH panics in sympathy, with a resulting general collapse. It is essential to start from a steady foundation (i.e. with steady LH semiquavers A flat and G flat) and then, as the RH enters, to keep the LH **steady**, while the RH nevertheless gives the sense of 'going up towards' a clear first beat of b.33. Give the treble D flat on the second beat of b.33 enough tone to sound on as the harmony shifts to A major on the first beat of b.34.

bb.34–46   Implement the more purposeful feeling again from the syncopated tied quaver sixth in b.37, and listen carefully as the RH voices 'divide' temporarily through b.38. Allow the LH to 'give' a little, but rhythmically, to accommodate the RH 5-demisemiquaver group at the end of b.39, feeling this as an upbeat group towards b.40, and feeling a general onward impulse from here towards bb.44-5. From the second beat of b.41 feel the rising sense of urgency as you press on into b.42, feeling a powerful 'lift' up to the high syncopated, tied *sforzato* crotchet G flat on the second quaver beat of bb.42 and 43. Let the RH 'fall' in improvisatory vocal manner from these high G flats over a continuously rhythmic but ongoing and resonant LH, and **use** the emphasised cross-rhythm stretto effects through b.44 as you press on again (but in a controlled manner) towards the climactic arrival on the tied F sharp on the first beat of b.45, **holding** this for an extra instant before descending luxuriantly towards b.46.

bb.46–62   Here again Chopin altered the dynamics in teaching copies, making a grand *crescendo* (as opposed to Henle's *diminuendo*) towards a *fortissimo* reprise from b.46 – even marked triple *fortissimo* in Jane Stirling's copy (see the Vienna Urtext and Paderewski Editions again). Most pianists follow this course, and continue through this final statement in a full, even impassioned tone. Arrive on a resonant toned C flat at b.49, and never fail to feel, and thus to communicate, the aural and expressive shock of this note. Again, adopting authentic corrections made by Chopin, some editions, and many players, drop to a *pianissimo* on the high C flat on the first beat of b.50, to beautiful effect, continuing in a quiet haze of sound towards a gently emphasised slurred E flat on the first beat of b.51, leading on into a **soft** trill and long run through b.52. Indeed, Chopin erased the *con forza* at the beginning of b.52, substituting a *delicatissimo* in one copy. If like most players you take this much lovelier option, ease into a short, light rather than over-brilliant trill on the D flat on the second beat of b.51, and merge into the run as late in the bar as your abilities allow. In Jane Stirling's copy the first note of the run is marked to coincide with the penultimate LH note of the bar (C flat). This, however, must be taken as a counsel of perfection. Less experienced players could begin the run after the LH A flat, thereafter grouping the upward

scale thus:  From b.52 it

will be seen that the run will continue (though without forcing any rigid 'matching') to fit in with the LH in groups of four notes. Again it is helpful to practise in different rhythms through

b.52, particularly *[rhythmic notation]* *etc.* Have the feeling of holding

back a little at the beginning of b.52, then of moving on, according to your abilities, as you make a light, airy *crescendo* up to the high F (approximately coinciding with the second F in the second LH group), allowing a slight 'vocal' hold through this note, and then falling gracefully towards a lightly emphasised B flat on the first beat of b.53. However proud you may be of your finger technique, avoid the temptation, one which many pianists cannot resist, of zooming onto the race-track here. Aim instead for shimmering droplets of sound, always held within the guiding motion of the LH. While the LH must, of course, 'give' to accommodate the curves of the RH, it must *accelerando* and *rallentando* **rhythmically,** never losing the sense of the overall onward flow (see General Introduction under ''Free Runs'). Collect yourself as you listen to the dotted quaver B flat on the first beat of b.53, thinking of the little demisemiquaver 'turn' here as the last flurry of the main run, ready to carry on into the *con anima* from the emphasised RH upbeat to b.54. At b.57 feel the onward impetus, as you 'lift' up to the full toned *sforzato* tied sixth on the third quaver pulse, 'holding' this for an extra instant, and then, letting the detached sixths cascade down, sing ardently on through b.58-9 towards a resonant chord on the first beat of b.60. Shoot with verve up to and down from a ringing high E flat feeling this arpeggio as a virtuosic ornament rather than an end in itself, so that it doesn't interrupt the fervent melodic flow towards the resonant tonic unison on the first beat of b.62. Support the RH through the whole of this passage (bb.57-61) with a full-toned and consistently carefully shaped LH.†

bb.62–77 Through the long coda the music unwinds in a halo of twilit sound over a continuously repeated tonic pedal point. Listen to the sound of the resonant tonic unisons on the first beat of b.62 within the pedal as you immediately revert to *piano* on the second semiquaver as indicated, and drawing out a little through the whole of the first beat to let the sound clear a little. Then, changing the pedal on the second beat as indicated, immediately establish the *dolcissimo* tone of the coda. Lean lightly on each emphasised treble quaver, making a smooth slur down towards each crotchet as you descend chromatically in *diminuendo* towards b.65. Let the treble A flat sing out quietly as the inner detached semiquavers ascend 'speakingly' in a slight *crescendo* towards the inner crotchet F on the first beat of b.66. Then, introducing an even quieter dynamic layer, 'lean' lightly again on each emphasised offbeat quaver, 'wisping' the [music figure] figure down in a light slurred effect so that the acciaccatura does not sound too clipped. This effect is easier to control if you actually **hold** the emphasised quaver thus: [music figure] Note the long pedal from bb.66-72 (not indicated in most editions). This is the perfect occasion to use the third pedal. In the absence of this, establish the sound of the bass D flat on the first beat of b.66, and then, with judicious half-pedalling, 'haze' the sound lightly in such a way as to preserve the sense of the prevailing tonic. From the middle of b.69 articulate the semiquavers with the utmost delicacy beneath the quietly singing A flat as the inner voice 'divides' downwards. From here shape the alternating treble and inner semiquaver fragments with a gently relaxed expressiveness, 'pointing' the inner upbeat quaver A flat as it leads into the chromatic inner 'curl' in b.72, and then let the sound fade towards the very quiet but still carrying tonic sixth at b.74. Holding this tonic sound in the long final pedal as indicated, taper the rising sixths through b.75 to a barely heard whisper – it is quite easy to fit the RH groups of seven notes to the LH if you **keep the LH steady**, playing the second RH sixth fractionally **before** the second LH note, and then alternating the RH and LH evenly as you ascend. Give the final chords a quiet, reposeful ring, and **listen** until the sound has almost faded so that you hold the spell as long as possible.

Nocturne No. 9 in B major
Op. 32 No. 1 (8)

From a technical point of view this is one of the easier numbers. But musically it is far from straightforward. If the easy-going charm of the opening melody teeters on the edge of

---

†This is amplified in teaching copies by a lower octave on the first and second main beats of b.59, and an upper octave on the first beat of b.60.

ordinariness, the music progresses with daring unpredictability, ending in a coda (from b.62) which apparently erupts from nowhere, rending the previous calm with a recitative-like outburst of extraordinary dramatic power. It follows that this is a piece which is far from easy to hold together. The secret lies in conveying the sense of a continuous onward, 'vocal' flow through the often uneven, or overlapping phrases – and with the sense of phrasing onward **over** rests, and through the little hesitant fragments (e.g. bb.27-30) as a singer would.

bb.1–13   From this point onwards the Nocturnes have no metronome marks. This piece must settle at a tempo that ensures that the almost unbroken LH quavers which support the melody have a continuous but flexible onward movement that never grows sticky. Set an easy crotchet pulse, therefore, imagining a comfortable walking stride at a suggested ♩ = 72-84. Practise the LH carefully alone. Place the opening bass quaver B with quiet resonance, and allow an extra instant to 'lift' as if in a smooth arc from this bass note up to the high F sharp. Then shape the quavers beautifully smoothly, **listening** to the intervals and to the 'hidden' melodic line descending from the high F sharp towards the C sharp on the third

beat of b.2,

Play the RH in that special **sostenuto dolce** tone that Chopin often indicates. When you put hands together, allow the LH to 'give' just a little as the RH curves up to and down from the high B in bb.2 and 4, imagining how a singer would shape these little arabesques. Show the punctuating intent of Chopin's phrase marks, while at the same time feeling the sense of the overall phrase line from bb.1-6. Advance more purposefully from b.5, feeling the overall onward impulse as you *crescendo* towards the hiatus at the end of the b.6. Listen particularly to the line of the bass notes B, A sharp, D sharp, E as you press on, and make sure that you 'go through' the second half of b.6 in a stretto (not a *ritenuto!*) although there needs to be a slight 'holding' of the last two quavers. Be sure also that you break off in a full *forte* tone, rather than tailing off in a well-bred *diminuendo* – we are **meant** to 'cut off' here in mid-stride, as if seized by a sudden arresting thought. However, in view of the fact that this figure recurs three times, do not overplay your hand this first time. Hold the sound of the C sharp minor broken chord in the pedal for an instant, and take a breath through the pause, resuming in the temporarily slower movement through b.7 as if in wistful resignation, and then pick up the tempo from b.8. **Listen** carefully to the bass notes G natural and F sharp through b.7 as you shape the RH turn with the utmost delicacy. Notice how, as this little fragment finishes on the minim of the first beat of b.8, the 'doubled' LH F sharp then gives a little onward nudge, ready to 'bring in' the new treble phrase on the high crotchet G sharp. Listen to the sound of the minim B as it 'evolves' into the inner melodic line, and sing out the two voices from here in a rather fuller tone, listening also to the inflections of the 'doubled' inner LH melody, with the lower F sharp providing a continuing pedal point, sometimes more, sometimes less prominent (i.e. sometimes 'doubled', sometimes not). Then, through the restatement of this phrase from b.10 feel the onward movement through b.11 towards the implied slight stress on the chord on the **second** beat of b.12, and then 'ease' through the second half of this bar back to the reprise.

bb.13–20   In b.13, the acciaccatura may be placed gracefully, just before, or on the beat, (see General Introduction under 'Ornamentation') in either case allowing time for the repeated D sharps to 'speak' in an unhurried manner, and then 'ease' the arpeggio up towards a warm-toned upper D sharp. Eloquent execution of this ornament naturally entails a 'give' on the first beat, picking up the tempo from the second beat. At b.16 allow the LH to 'bend' a little, but rhythmically, so that you do not lose the **sense** of the crotchet pulse. Practise this arabesque very slowly without the ornament, keeping the LH quavers at first perfectly in time and synchronising the RH demisemiquavers precisely to this LH pulse. Then as you are gradually able to increase the speed, the LH will take a little more leeway to allow time for the airy upward flight of the RH. When you are quite fluent, add the ornament, allowing it just an extra instant without jolting the overall flow. This figure is far less difficult than it may at first appear, provided that you allow the RH to be 'guided' by the LH. Tail the sound away upwards in a delicate wisp, with the high quaver F sharp 'meeting' the LH neatly on the third beat of the bar, and then let the LH resume the tempo gently through the remainder of the bar. Allow a little more time through the 'resigned' fragment this time (b.19) to 'point' the low *pianissimo* bass notes, and the lingering RH detail through the end of the bar. Then move on into the new *tranquillo* section *in tempo* from the second beat of b.20.

bb.20–36	There is the sense of moving on a little here, perhaps in a rather richer tone. Listen to the descending quaver line 'carrying on' from b.21 into b.22 beneath

the warm-toned treble crotchet motif. Feel the momentary dance-like character (languidly dance-like, admittedly!) through bb.23-4. Support the RH figures here with more purposefully ongoing LH quavers. Articulate the RH exactly as indicated here, showing the little swell up to and down from the sixth on the third beat of b.23. Be sure to 'lift' the hand from this sixth and similarly from the fourth on the first beat of b.24 (see General Introduction under 'Articulation'). Feel the onward impulse through these two bars towards a 'lean' on the RH third on the third beat of b.24, and then 'point' the LH C double sharp on the upbeat to b.25 to ease you into the D sharp minor harmony in b.25. Sing out bb.25-6 in a more luxuriant tone, listening again to the quavers descending into the inner line through b.26. 'Point' the LH once more on the G double sharp on the first beat of b.27, and shape each offbeat RH fragment expressively through bb.27-30. Feel that the semiquavers in bb.27 and 29 are 'going to' the singing minim on the third beat. Then in b.28 allow time to let the answering turn curl gracefully up to the quaver D sharp, again **lifting** the hand here. In b.30 draw out this answering turn in a whispered echo effect, this time showing the **smooth** articulation through the second beat. Linger a little on the dotted quaver C sharp before finishing off neatly to the crotchet G sharp on the third beat, ready to move on from the upbeat to b.31.† Then, as you move on into

†Readings of bb.28 and 30 vary. Most editions, including Henle and Paderewski give a 5-note, demisemiquaver turn

through the second quaver pulse.　　　　　　　　　　　The Vienna Urtext gives a different,

and preferable version　　　　　　　　　　　　　　to be read as

In copies belonging to pupils, Chopin indicated that in b.28 the RH appoggiatura B sharp is to be synchronised with the LH A sharp on the second **quaver** pulse, and that the RH A double sharp is to coincide with the LH chord on the second **crotchet** beat. These intentions are incorporated in the Vienna Urtext's interpretation. The figure in b.30 is similar except that the RH semiquaver A sharp **anticipates** the second quaver pulse.

the varied version of bb.8-11 show the ongoing effect of the 'lean' on this emphasised tied crotchet upbeat to b.31, and on the held treble dotted minim E on the second beat of bb.31 and 33, and then 'point' the RH crotchet D sharp on the second beat of b.35, as Chopin 'cuts in' to the stretto 'interrupting' figure.

bb.36–60   At b.37 Chopin suddenly veers off on a new tack. Be sure to 'finish off' to the end of b.36 in a *ritenuto*, as at b.7, as if you are going to 'finish the thought' on the first beat of b.37. (In other words do not anticipate the *forte* at b.37.) Then launch into the *subito forte* with ringing treble minims, born along by resonant, upward sweeping LH quavers. Show the inner fragment clearly entering on the slurred upbeat to b.38, feeling the general onward impetus towards the first beat of b.39, and then play bb.39-40 like a little cadenza. Arriving on a strong RH crotchet G sharp on the first beat of b.39, leap up to a ringing high dotted crotchet B on the second beat, lingering a little on this note as the five LH quavers rise freely towards a full-toned crotchet G sharp on the third beat. Then, descending in the RH in an improvisatory style, let the 'doubled' RH G sharp coincide in a full tone with the bass F sharp on the first beat of b.40. Let the G sharp 'divide' upwards into the trill, thus: and **listen** to the line of the LH thirds descending from the doubled minim G sharp over the held dominant minim. Then draw out the ornamented ending of the trill as you ease back into the restatement of the *tranquillo* section.

bb.60–66   At b.60, the elaborated version of b.39, linger proportionately longer on the high minim B, and shade the longer run freely but carefully down into the trill in b.61.

Take longer this time, too, to tail off the trill ending, allowing an extra instant at the end of b.61 as you prepare to strike a shiver of apprehension at b.62. Coincide the bass octave with the first note of the RH spread chord, and play the repeated inner LH F's dead in time, quietly but clearly, like an ominous, distant drum roll. Allow the muted sound to resonate through the pause in b.63. The timing of this highly charged coda is necessarily individual and will never, and should never, 'come out' the same way twice. If you follow the dictates of the breath, the music will evolve naturally – if you attempt to gauge it by mathematics or logic, it will not. Thus, as you hold the chord at the beginning of b.63 (see General Introduction under 'Pauses') you will, if you allow yourself, have an irresistible urge to breathe and then carry on. On the other hand we have to retain an underlying **sense** of the crotchet pulse. Thus, although the rhythm must feel very free, we need, for example, to place the chords beneath the RH minims (G natural and B) rhythmically, i.e. in a manner that relates to the crotchet pulse through the main body of the piece. Articulate the demisemiquaver fragment urgently, 'going up to' a ringing minim G natural, and **holding** this over a biting dominant seventh crotchet chord. Again you will have the urge to breathe, sooner this time, ready to articulate the next fragment up to a yet more arresting minim B and vicious *sforzato* chord. Then phrase the improvisatory unison quavers to maximum dramatic effect. Start quietly, curving up towards the third quaver E, gathering pace and volume as you curve down towards the G double sharp, and back up towards the C sharp. Linger a little, portentously, on this note, and on the dotted quaver B, feeling at the same time an onward upbeat 'lean' towards raw-toned crotchet G naturals. Then let the double grace note arpeggio roll upwards towards powerful detached quaver G's, feeling the strong impetus of this whole group (the grace notes and quavers and semiquavers) towards biting minim F sharps over vicious detached *sforzato* chords, then coming **off** in dramatic silence through the rest. You could then give the long tied C sharps a warmer tone, placing the crotchet chords more quietly as indicated. Let the tied C sharps give the impression of 'merging' into the reiterated triplets, playing these in a kind of onward 'push' towards an eloquent 'lean' on the slurred C sharps, 'leaning' onwards as it were towards a quietly ringing and telling resonance on the dotted minim D naturals. Then play the next crotchet chords evenly and quietly like receding drum beats, and **feel** the crotchet rest before ending

in a smooth full tone, timing the *Adagio* thus:

Let the sound of the final unisons fade through a long pause.†

Nocturne No. 10 in A flat major
Op. 32 No. 2 (8)

This number receives in general a rather disparaging press. Of course there is too much repetition, and the 'tune' is rather effetely pretty, as if tailored for the Salon. In addition, for those of us reared on *Les Sylphides*, it is forever enmeshed in twirling puffs of white tulle. Nevertheless, in a fresh, uncloying, but sensitive performance, it can sound truly pretty in the best sense.

bb.1–7   Play the introductory chords smoothly, mellifluously, and not too portentously in a leisurely *lento* pulse. Shape this little sequence as a complete phrase, yet in an anticipatory, introductory manner. Spread the first chord gracefully, being sure to allow it its full minim value and then **listen** to the dotted crotchet A flat singing over the inner F flat carefully placed on the fourth beat of b.1, and allow plenty of time to the upbeat quaver B flat as you prepare to spread the A flat chord generously up to a singing upper C in b.2. Listen to the warm resonance of this long chord as you poise yourself for the off. The Vienna Urtext Edition records that there is a barely legible metronome mark of ♩= 60 (66 or 80?) in one of Chopin's teaching copies. ♩= 60 seems on the ponderous side, as if attempting to impose an unwarranted gravity and self-importance. While there is naturally a good deal of give and take, ♩= 69-72 as a **basic** tempo gives the lighter, fleet-spirited onward movement that seems more apt. Establish, in any event, an easy rhythmic swing, and let the melody float in, in a light but warm and smooth *legato*, shaping the line in a gentle little swell up to and down from the E flat on the fourth beat of b.3. Phrasing details vary considerably in different editions. The Vienna Urtext Edition, for instance, starts a second phrase on the second beat of b.4, carrying on right over to the end of b.5, as opposed to Henle's extra punctuation through b.2.

Take your choice! (For the triplet versus dotted rhythm question (bb.4, 8, etc.) see under Op.15, No.1 and in the General Introduction under 'Some Explanations and Amplifications'.) Practise the LH assiduously, aiming for easy-flowing smoothness and always showing the curve up to the chord on the second quaver of each triplet group, and down to the next bass note, so that, without labouring it, you suggest the continuous, complementary offbeat inner line C, B natural, C, D flat, etc. When you put hands together always be conscious of the movement of

---

†A diagonal line appears in Jane Stirling's score emphasising the dramatic silence after repeated *sforzato* chords. The bass grace note crotchets 'within' the final tonic unisons are also marked *forte*.

the LH, 'bending' rhythmically here and there, but always 'sending' the RH along with this light, fleet, onward motion. 'Space' the RH quavers expressively in cross-rhythm with the LH triplets as you *crescendo* lightly upwards through b.5, allowing an extra instant for the turn to 'speak' as you prepare to rise towards a tiny 'vocal' hold on the high G on the fourth beat, then letting the remainder of the triplet 'fall' gracefully towards the crotchet B flat on the first beat of b.6. Take time again to 'finish off' the overall 4-bar phrase with a 'speaking' 7-semiquaver 'curl' on the second beat of b.6. Space these notes easily over the LH triplet so that the RH D flat occurs just before, or more or less with the LH A flat. Note the 'doubled' bass notes on the second, third and fourth beats, implying a little extra weight and time as you negotiate this RH 'curl' and poise yourself through the third beat to set off again on the upbeat to b.7.

bb.7–10　　Let the trill run lightly on the upbeat to b.9, letting the first grace note A flat coincide with the LH bass note D flat (see General Introduction under 'Ornamentation'). Then feel the 'lift' of the five-semiquaver turn through the first beat of b.9 up to the A flat on the second beat, allowing an extra fraction of time to let the acciaccatura C 'speak' (this note can either just anticipate, **or** coincide with the bass quaver F) and for another little 'vocal' hold on the A flat, before starting the descent from the new subphrase from the dotted quaver G. Let the hand 'lift' after the A flat to 'fall' naturally onto this G, and again at the end of the bar 'lift' from the quaver C to show the semiquaver rest, to fall naturally on to the upbeat semiquaver B flat (see General Introduction under 'Articulation').

bb.10–26　　Finish off the previous phrase neatly on the third beat of b.10, and then make it clear that you are starting afresh as you lead into the new rather more purposeful phrase from the upbeat to b.11, with added resonance given to the 'doubled' bass notes through bb.11-13. The RH semiquaver triplet in b.12 occupies a quaver value, in cross-rhythm with the LH triplets, but do not labour this effect. The acciaccatura in b.14 again can anticipate or coincide with the LH bass note A flat. The groupings of the arabesque here and at b.22 must, of course, be an individual matter. Allow the LH to 'bend' a little, particularly at b.22, but as always feel the RH is being guided by the LH, and **not** the other way around (see General Introduction under ''Free' Runs'). To begin with you could think of the groupings

in b.14 approximately thus  and in b.22

approximately thus　　　　　　　　although when the

shape of the run has become more familiar, the groupings will become more loosely merged and can, and indeed should, vary slightly from performance to performance. Feel that each run curves up to linger slightly on the highest note, the B flat in b.14, and the C in b.22, and then 'falls' lightly and gracefully to lean slightly on the emphasised crotchet A natural. In b.22 the LH will clearly have to 'bend' a little more through the end of the second beat. In both instances allow time to 'finish off' the phrase cleanly on the quaver

B flat on the fourth beat, and then be sure to **lift** the RH before leading on from the upbeat to b.15 (and b.23).

bb.26–50   Take the RH crotchet A flat cleanly off on the second beat of b.26, and allow time to listen to the melodic fragment within the LH triplets from the doubled 'upbeat' quaver (D natural) to the second beat. Then 'lean' expectantly on the emphasised tied crotchet upbeat to b.27 as you prepare to ease into the **12/8** section. There is a natural feeling of moving on here, and a gathering momentum towards b.35, and then on again towards the *forte* restatement in F sharp minor from b.39. Hold back a little, as if feeling your way into the new rhythm in b.27, and gradually increase the tempo towards a faster plateau at b.31. Practise the LH alone feeling the rhythmic pulsation of the three-quaver groups within the sense of an overall 2-in-the-bar movement, defined by the bass notes in bb.27, 28, 31, 32, etc. Within this overall 2-in-the-bar show the curve of the treble line up to and down from the F on the second beat of b.27 (with the hint of a *tenuto* on this F) and again to the D flat on the second beat of b.28. Take time to show the smooth phrase

fragment  *etc.* in b.27 and then articulate the melody notes in

an easy just-detached style through the remainder of the bar. Do take time and trouble to observe all such phrase fragments and details of articulation all through this section, so that the phrases 'speak' individually within the whole, particularly, for example, through bb.29-30 and 33-4.

♪♪♪ and ♪♪♪ sound quite different, or should do so, even within the pedalled

sound. It is a good plan to practise the RH thus 𝄞 *etc.*

Then when you play it as written, be sure that the treble melody is never swamped by too heavy a thumb – this is an excellent technical and musical exercise, considerably taxing to the fourth and fifth fingers.

Listen in b.28 to the resonance of the lower LH dotted minim C, and tied dotted crotchet F and to the upbeat melodic fragment E flat and D flat leading on into b.29. Listen also to the inner LH melodic fragment from the second quaver pulse of b.30. As you *crescendo* through the second half of b.30 feel you are notching up the tempo and dynamics as the bass notes on the third and fourth beats lead on to launch into b.31 at a rather higher level of intensity. Move on again similarly from the second half of b.34 and the first half of b.35 to 'lean' on the RH slurred octave figure on the third and fourth beats, repeating the effect with increasing fervour in b.36. Many pianists move into a nippy *accellerando* here – if you do this, keep it firmly under control, never losing the **sense** of the **12/8** pulse. In any event, feel a continual onward impulse as you *crescendo* on into b.36, and keep up a full tone as you 'lean' ardently on the slurred octaves through bb.37-8, supporting the RH with full-toned bass notes and chords in the LH. Draw out a little through the end of b.38, ready to launch into an impassioned F sharp minor version of bb.27-38, from a powerful *sforzato* on the first beat of b.39. Allow for some dynamic rise and **fall** through bb.39-50, or the clatter will become unbearable. For example, curve up in a swell through the first beat of b.39 towards the F sharp on the second beat as indicated, and then allow the dynamic level to fall a little, making another little 'push' up to, and fall from, the D sharp on the second beat of b.40, and so on. Rise to a full but not banging *fortissimo* through b.43, allowing a fleeting but impassioned *tenuto* on the high A and then dropping the tone markedly through the second half of b.46, ready for a final flight up towards the second half of b.48. Let fly in splendid freedom, maintaining a glorious flood of tone through bb.49 and 50.

bb.50–76   The 'join' at bb.50-51 is inherently awkward. Gauge the inevitable 'drawing out' through b.50 according to how much you have increased speed beforehand, and balance the LH tone carefully with the single line of the RH as you return, *appassionato*, to the opening melody. Some pianists maintain a slightly faster tempo at first, gradually subsiding to Tempo 1, others draw out b.50 sufficiently to be able to slot back into Tempo 1 straightaway at b.51. As regards dynamics, there is an inevitable gradual subsidence of volume from the *fortissimo* to return, by around b.62, to a similar level to the overall *piano* of the first section.

Do not labour the 'hidden' presence of the principal melodic motif on the first note of each five-semiquaver group through bb.71-2, but rather allow the five notes of each group to curl prettily 'among' the LH triplets, with only this first note of each group 'touching' the corresponding LH quaver. Concentrate on keeping the LH triplets **steady** here or your intended diaphanous effect will judder into an ungainly tangle.

Create a continuous chain as the trills *crescendo* through the second half of b.72 letting the grace note G coincide with the LH bass note on the third beat, and the grace note A natural with

the bass note on the fourth beat.  *etc.* Feel that

each trill 'expands' from the preceding grace note figure. Take an instant to 'point' the quiet interrupted cadence at bb.73-4, and allow the tempo to 'give' as you move towards the end of b.74. Lift the pedal to break the sound for an instant at the end of the short pause, ready to play the final chords quietly as if bowing out with a graceful gesture.

Nocturne No. 11 in G minor
Op. 37 No. 1 (7)

This is one of the easier Nocturnes, and perhaps the most suitable of them all for relatively inexperienced players. Unfortunately it is also one of the least lovable. Chopin seems merely to be 'going through the motions' here, the harmonic procedures are routine, and the mood dreary rather than engrossingly sad. It is up to the player to enliven the numerous restatements of the main motif with touches of dynamic variety. Notwithstanding the overall comparative simplicity of the piece, the execution of the numerous and varied decorative grace notes is somewhat complicated. Although Chopin clearly showed that the first note of the grace note figures in b.1 and the arpeggio figure on the third beat of b.5, and the first beat of b.6 should coincide with the bass note, the figure with the 'extra' acciaccatura in b.5 is perhaps more problematic – see below, and in the General Introduction under 'Ornamentation'.

bb.1–4   Establish an easy-moving tempo – the implications of *andante sostenuto* are greatly to be preferred to the *lento* given in many editions. (Apparently Chopin himself originally indicated *lento* and later corrected it to *andante sostenuto*.) Acceptable tempos for this piece can vary widely. I suggest a crotchet pulse of ♩ = 66-76, although the margins may well be wider. This is music which can all too easily 'stick' and the essential is that there is a continual sense of movement. As ever, if you 'walk' it you will find the motion that **feels** right. As so often, and particularly here, a secure LH movement is essential to the expressive sense of the RH. Here the RH proceeds in 'sentences' of varying length: the first from the opening upbeat through to the end of b.1, the second through b.2, and the third from bb.3-5, and so on, while the LH walks serenely on from beginning to end (there is only one rest, in b.66). Practise the LH alone, imagining this easy stride to the crotchet pulse, while at the same time feeling a sense of an overall 2-in-the-bar. This helps to avoid the plod to which this piece so often succumbs. Place the opening bass G with quiet definition, and then show the overall curve through bb.1-2 as you 'lift' smoothly to the octave D, and then feel an easy 'rocking' back and forth between the E flat and D, with a slight 'lean' on the E flat on the third beat of b.1 and the first and third beats of b.2. Quietly 'bring out' the upper LH thumbline so that when you put hands together this quietly suggested inner LH line will sound smoothly beneath the 'speaking' RH melody line. In b.3 the 2-in-the-bar feeling mentioned above becomes more obvious. Give the bass notes a quiet resonance, making a smooth 'lift' up to the chords on the second and fourth beats. Feel the sense of 'going on' towards a more resonant bass note F on the first beat of b.4. Then 'lift' as if in a wide arc up to the high third on the second beat (feeling a slight 'lean' on this beat) and 'ease' the line of thirds downwards, ready to 'start again' from b.5. The LH needs to be particularly carefully studied through bb.9-12, **listening** to the extra resonance created by the sustained pedal point effect (the lower F) through bb.9-10, and the held minim resonances through bb.11-12.

When you bring in the RH, 'lean' in with a fully timed, rather stressed tied crotchet upbeat, feeling that the first little phrase 'falls' from this note, to be 'tailed off' towards the quaver A in b.1. Play the grace note ornament unhurriedly **on** the beat (see above), and be sure to bring the RH **off** gently, not with a bump, on the fourth beat as the LH 'walks on', ready to bring in the next RH fragment on the offbeat in b.2. Feel that this little fragment is 'going to' a warmly emphasised minim F sharp on the third beat, and that the resonance and onward 'lean' on this note is carrying you on into the longer phrase (bb.3-5). Show the little swell up through b.3 as indicated towards a singing tied minim A on the first beat of b.4, and **listen** to the LH (as already practised) as it 'lifts' up from the bass F beneath this held A and eases down from the high third on the second beat, while at the same time giving the feeling of leading on, ready to 'start again' from b.5. Notice how the RH echoes the curve of the LH as it 'lifts' up to the high G, ready to ease downwards in tandem with the LH towards b.5. Then understand how the phrases overlap on the first beat of b.5, allowing an instant at the end of b.4 to 'prepare' for the new fuller tone from b.5. While shaping each of the two short fragments through bb.1 and 2, and the longer phrase through bb.3-5 as entities in themselves, do at the same time phrase 'over the rests' as a singer would, so that you create the sense of an overall line from the opening upbeat through to the first beat of b.5.

bb.5–22   Lead on from the first beat of b.5 in a warm, full tone. Shape the grace note figure in a luxuriant 'roll' up to a singing treble note on the second and third beat of b.5. As said above, such grace note figures will normally be placed on

the beat thus: But in the case

of the figure on the **second** beat of b.5 the 'extra' acciaccatura may well be placed before the beat (see discussion in General Introduction under 'Ornamentation'). In any event there is a great deal to be 'got in' here, and in order to allow the grace notes to 'speak', the LH must inevitably 'give' a little through the second and third beats of b.5, and again through the first

half of b.6. Let b.6 read   Chopin's highly

individual fingering  whether or not you use it, shows exactly how he wanted this

triplet figure to 'speak' (see the General Introduction under 'Fingering'). This time be sure to bring the RH off on the fourth beat of b.6, and then 'walk on' into b.7 more quietly, taking care not to labour this bar, as you *crescendo* gently towards the first beat of b.8. In b.8 ensure that the dotted crotchet G sings through the second beat over the quietly placed inner crotchet B flat

so that the melody does **not** sound   Then move easily into the trill,

playing the first grace note G **on** the beat. Let the trill *crescendo* lightly through towards a warm 'lean' on the crotchet B flat on the first beat of b.9, and then be sure to bring the RH **off** after the B natural so that the hand 'falls' with natural emphasis on the syncopated crotchet C. Feel the hinted sense of urgency here as the LH moves on a little, slightly emphasising the partly tied LH upbeat to b.10. Allow a little extra time, however, for the decoration in b.10 (and b.12), starting this turn soon after the first beat of the bar, rather than leaving it too late and then having to squash it in as inexperienced players invariably do. Execute these figures

approximately thus: Feel a graceful 'lift' from the

acciaccatura up to the dotted quaver G, allowing a little 'vocal' hold on this note. Then let the LH move on once more, again feeling the slight ongoing 'urge' of the partly tied upbeat to b.11, and making an onward moving *crescendo* through b.11. Let the melody line 'breathe' again through the rest on the third beat of b.11, and then feel that the melody is 'opening out' as you *crescendo* onward through b.12. Play the ornamental turn more expansively here as you prepare to 'lift' to the summit of the curve on the second beat. Then from b.13 allow the music to unwind a little, guided by a more relaxed 'walk' in the LH. Again on the second beat of b.14 the acciaccatura could anticipate the beat. Then be sure to **lift** the hand from the quaver on this second beat (see General Introduction under 'Articulation'). *Crescendo* warmly through b.16, taking care to place the inner RH offbeat dotted minim D with a firm resonance, and drawing out a little as you listen to the rising line of LH sixths beneath the 'speaking' repeated RH D's. Feel a kind of 'push' of resonance as you swell through this bar, ready to 'walk on' once more in a full tone, into the restatement from b.17.† Keep some tone in reserve, however, for the coming *fortissimo* at b.21, and when

†A significant phrase mark is pencilled into Jane Stirling's copy indicating this 'on and over' movement into b.17.

you reach this *fortissimo* balance the LH resonance carefully with the RH through bb.21-2 to avoid harshness.

bb.23–40   Drop the tone again at b.23, as the restatement reverts to its 'normal' dynamic. In b.31 it is best to treat the crotchet on the third beat together with the four grace notes as a sextuplet group, like the subsequent upbeat group:

At b.36 be sure to take the LH up to the third

on the second beat as at b.4, etc. but here a little more strongly, to 'balance' the RH rest and 'lift' to the high emphasised syncopated RH tied quaver A. 'Lean' well on the RH quaver E flat on the first beat, slurring this off cleanly to the quaver A, and then **lifting** the hand to 'fall' with singing emphasis on the high A. Allow a slight 'vocal' *tenuto* on this note, and be conscious that the next LH crotchet third (F/D) is the third beat (or second **main** beat) of the bar – this ensures that while allowing some freedom in the shaping of the run, you retain the overall rhythmic shape of the bar. Observe that the run has sixteen notes, including the first tied note – at first it will help if you think of it in two groups of eight notes, so that the A (the ninth quaver of the run) will more-or-less coincide with the LH third on the slightly delayed fourth beat of the bar. When the notes are more familiar, the groupings can, of course, be merged more loosely. As always in such 'free' runs, feel that the LH is guiding the RH (and **not** the other way round) so that the LH, while 'giving' a little, is maintaining its **shape** as described for b.4 (see General Introduction under ''Free' runs'). Have the LH octave B flat ready to 'meet' the RH as it arrives in a collected manner on a quiet first beat of b.37. Poise yourself for an instant through the second half of b.39 ready to 'ease' through b.40 into the new section. Lean a little on the inner RH minim C (**listening** as this resolves to the B flat on the second beat of b.40), and also 'leaning' a little on the tied LH upbeat (D) to b.40, matching this with a slight 'hold' on the RH upbeat sixth. Then let this sixth 'fall' smoothly to a quietly singing minim G on the first beat of b.40, as the lower chords move easily on over the quiet resonance of the lower LH G with an onward feeling into the next section.‡

bb.40–91   Poise yourself just for an instant again on the upbeat to b.41, and then lead into b.41 in a warm, light, but rather subdued tone, playing with a hymn-like simplicity. Most players move on the tempo a little here (rightly, I feel, as this passage can sound somewhat dull) with a definite sense of 2-in-the-bar. Indeed, Niecks records that Chopin's pupil Gutmann played this section 'quicker than the rest, and said that Chopin had forgotten to mark the change of movement' (Vol.2, p.264). Shape the melody in long smooth curves, feeling a very slight swell up towards, and down from the A flat on the third beat (or second main beat) of b.43. Execute the broken chord figure in bb.44

and 48 thus:  allowing a tiny give through the second half of these bars

to allow time to spread this chord gracefully, and also to 'point' slightly the tied LH upbeat as you prepare to 'start again' in bb.45 and 49. Lead on from b.49 in a brighter, rather more

‡Here again Jane Stirling's copy has a pencilled phrase mark from the second beat of b.40 'on and over' into b.41.

purposeful tone, making a swell and *diminuendo* as indicated, and then a greater swell from b.53. (It is presumed that the ornamented chord in b.52 should be executed like those in b.44, etc.) As you *diminuendo* from the second half of b.56, quietly 'point' the slurred LH upbeat to b.58, and note the tied inner RH E flat on the first beat of b.58. Support the RH throughout this episode with a smoothly phrased and ongoing LH. Pause with as much anticipatory significance as you can muster on the chords at the end of bb.62, 63 and 64.* Then spread the chord in b.65 in a leisurely, quiet, and again anticipatory tone, **listening** as the sound quietly reverberates within the pedal before letting the *pianissimo* D's ease back into the reprise.

Tail off the run through b.86 in such a way as to lead poisedly into the *pianissimo* final appearance of the principal motif. Give the emphasised dotted minim RH G on the first beat of the penultimate bar sufficient tone to sing over the carefully balanced inner chords through the second and third beats, and then linger a little on the dotted quaver C on the upbeat to the final bar before resolving quietly to the long tonic major chord. Let this final RH chord (the middle G is tied) coincide with the bass G, and take plenty of time to listen to the wide span of quiet resonance as you rise in a long, slow sweep towards the high B natural, then placing the last, repeated B with quiet finality.§

The pedalling needs careful attention. It can be held through the first two beats of b.1 (see the Vienna Urtext and Paderewski Editions), and then each beat could be lightly pedalled through to the end of b.2. Then through bb.3, 5, and 8 the pedal should be changed only on each first and third beat to retain the bass resonance through the first and second half of these bars. In b.4 the bass note could similarly be held in the pedal through the first and second beats, and then changed on the third and fourth beats. Through bb.9-13 the held LH notes and partly syncopated RH line create more complex resonances, and the pedal needs to be changed on each beat – ensuring throughout that the LH conscientiously sustains all minims and tied notes.

Nocturne No. 12 in G major
Op. 37 No. 2 (8+)

In skilled hands the effect of this Nocturne is entrancing, with its swaying barcarolle-like rhythm and liquid, deliciously inflected curls of RH thirds and sixths. But it is not a piece to be lightly undertaken. The necessary smoothness and pliability in the RH is far from easy to achieve, and a performance that sounds effortful, even for an instant, and 'allows the works to show' is a disaster. Setting a tempo is a problem. Some players take it fast so that the music scuds rather than sways, perhaps not merely to show off their facility, but also to enable them to maintain the same tempo for the second theme (bb.28-68 etc.). Others play the first section at a more relaxed tempo, and then, to avoid the second theme sounding sticky, move the tempo on a little from b.28. This, providing the 'moving on' is skilfully managed so that the change is not too marked, is perhaps the best solution, better anyway than that on one recording by an eminent pianist, who sets an unusually slow opening tempo, and then grinds on conscientiously, reducing the second theme to a mud-clogged plod. A tempo of between ♩. = 56-60 is suggested, moving on a notch or so from b.28.

bb.1–4 Practise the LH first, absorbing the physical sensation of the continual easy **6/8** swing as you curve smoothly up to and down from the topmost note on the second main beat of bb.1-4. Then before you start working out the fingering of the RH thirds and sixths, practise the **upper** RH line alone. **Imagine** the first three LH quavers

338

'bringing you in' through the first beat ready to enter with a light 'lean' on the first RH quaver, and then 'tail off' the semiquavers gracefully up towards the crotchet on the first beat of b.2. Imagine the LH quavers leading you on, ready to 'lean' again on the quaver on the second beat of b.2, and then, having tailed off the line again to the first beat of b.3, make an easy 'lift' up to the sixth on the second semiquaver of b.3, and, holding this for a tiny instant as a singer would, shape the semiquavers downwards in easy curves towards the crotchet on the first beat of b.4.*

Then practise this **upper** line with the LH until you are able to shape the melody easily and gracefully within the continuing even swing of the LH quavers. If you really take time to study these four bars, you will understand in a **physical** sense the fundamental motion and shape of the whole of the first section (bb.1-28). You will then be able to implement the various inflections of rhythm and contour without losing the fundamental rhythmic impulse. You will also, having learnt how you want to shape the phrase, be able to fine-tune your fingering of the thirds and sixths to optimum effect. It is a thousand pities that Chopin left no fingering indications for this piece – he would surely have given some marvellously curve-enhancing slides (1-1 or 2-2 from black note to white and so on) which few editors appear to have considered. The fingering throughout must be governed by the shape of the hand. Henle and the Vienna Urtext Edition suggest the same fingerings for bb.1-4 and in b.3 these do not lie happily for a small hand. It is obviously impracticable here to enter into detailed suggestions. But merely to give some idea of the sliding options, I suggest some alternatives below for bb.1-4:

When you finally put 'hands together' as written, practise very slowly at first, shaping the curves of both hands meticulously in time in slow motion at first, and then, as you gradually increase the tempo freeing the rhythm a little to allow for the subtle expressive nuances of the RH. Always adhere to the dynamic shapes indicated by Chopin, i.e. show the lean upon the quaver third on the second main beat of bb.1 and 2, and the *diminuendo* as you rise towards the first beat of bb.2 and 3; and then, within the overall curve of bb.2-3, show the lift up to the second semiquaver of b.3 and the *diminuendo* as you descend towards the first beat of b.4, and so on. Do also **listen** acutely to the varying intervals of the RH – thirds, sixths, fourths, and so on.

bb.4–28   Start your second overall 3-bar phrase on the second beat of b.4, perhaps in a slightly raised dynamic. Then in b.7 note the changed shape of the LH, in which the highest note falls on the third **quaver** pulse of the bar instead of on the second main beat (this change is actually 'prepared' in b.6). It is particularly important to 'peak' this LH curve clearly in bb.7 and 8 etc. when the RH has a quaver rest on the second main beat. This gives an entirely different inflection to the LH, giving a nicely gauged 'lead in' to the RH, with this time an ongoing little **swell** towards b.8 as opposed to the 'tailing off' through bb.1-2, etc. As you swell (not too violently) into b.9, take a little extra time for the much wider leap up to the high sixth on the second semiquaver pulse (the new phrase mark here

*A particularly interesting detail is pencilled into Jane Stirling's score, showing the intended articulation of the

descending semiquavers through b.3.   This accords nicely with the

idea of the 'lift' up to, and miniscule 'hold' on the high sixth.

accentuates the effect of this extra 'lift' suggesting just the hint of a vocal *tenuto* on this high sixth) and then curve down smoothly, allowing time to show the curls and inflections of the alternating intervals. (Play through the underlying harmonies from b.7 so that you thoroughly understand the basic progressions: G major in b.7 → B flat major in b.8 → D flat major in b.9 → E flat minor in b.10, and so on.) 'Go to' a singing tied third on the first beat of b.13, the first sustained sound so far, and show the longer, smoother overall line from here through to b.15.†
Let the LH 'go to' a clear F sharp on the second main beat of b.16, ready for the RH sixths to enter on the offbeat. Then 'point' the chord on the sixth quaver pulse of b.16, feeling this as a 'poising' upbeat to b.17, ready to 'lift' again up to the high sixth in b.17. Take an extra instant to 'point' the change to the minor colour through the last two quaver beats of b.22, and again, to listen to the 'concealed' interrupted cadence at bb.23-4. Then draw out gradually as you listen to the wide-spanned modulating curves and mysterious chromatic slides of the LH as the music subsides towards b.28. (These dark-toned downward chromatics through bb.26-7 look forward to Rachmaninov.)

bb.28–68   The 'join' here is a curious affair, further complicated by the fact that Chopin deleted b.29 in Jane Stirling's copy.

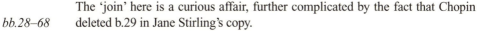

Both Henle and Peters Editions **include** this 'doubtful' bar. In both the Vienna Urtext Edition and the Paderewski Edition it is omitted.

Note: For those using these latter editions there is therefore a discrepancy in the bar numbers from this point onwards i.e. for b.30 read b.29. The Vienna Urtext Edition notes that Chopin deleted b.29 'presumably because it disrupted the 4-bar writing from b.13 onwards' and the deletion apparently confirms that the new melody leads in from the second main beat of b.29 (compare with bb.84-8 and 134-8). However, at least one eminent artist, who **retains** b.29, makes it clear that he is treating bb.29 and 30 as linking bars, and that he is beginning the tune proper in b.31, ushered in by the dominant seventh harmony in b.30. If b.29 is omitted the transition feels somewhat abrupt – and if it is retained it feels like a prolonging hiccough (as if the record is stuck in the groove) so we take our choice. I incline towards omitting b.29. But players must, of course, resolve this ambiguity in their own way.

In any event, allow a little give as you rise in a little *crescendo* through the second half of b.27, to land on a clear chord of E minor on the first beat of b.28. Then if you are retaining b.29

play the ⟨music example⟩ in a smooth, rather subdued 'linking' manner, and 'lead in'

clearly from the second beat of b.29. If omitting b.29 make it clear that you are bringing in the tune on the second beat of b.28. In either case allow the melody to 'swim in' smoothly, quietly yet buoyantly, listening to the descending bass line as the harmony moves smoothly through the dominant seventh to settle briefly in C major at b.31. Then feel the 'lift' as you rise to the

---

†Henle ties the RH dotted crotchet third over to the second main beat of b.13. In the Vienna Urtext and Paderewski Editions this third is played again on the second main beat – perhaps a prettier, more melting effect.

onward leading upbeat quaver to b.32, then letting the line 'fall' in *decrescendo* as indicated towards b.33. Make it clear that a new subphrase starts on the second main beat of bb.33, 37, etc. while maintaining the easy, overall onward melodic flow. This great melody – it has even been called the most beautiful Chopin ever wrote (Huneker, p.146) – is gloriously sunlit and breeze-borne. Let it sail along, shaping the dynamic curves smoothly in a continuing onward 2-in-the-bar motion over the quietly shifting harmonies. Feel the impending temporary change of mood as you 'hold' the D major chord for an instant on the second beat of b.44. Then feel a more urgent, onward impetus as you begin the steady *crescendo* from b.45, supporting the RH with carefully balanced bass notes and chords. 'Peak' your *crescendo* clearly on the first beat of b.51, and then unwind easily through bb.51-2 ready to sail off again from the second beat of b.53.

Again the 'join' comes suddenly at bb.68-9. Draw out somewhat as you heighten

bb.68–140   the *crescendo* through b.68 ready to launch back into the reprise in tempo, this time in a fuller tone. At bb.79-82 shape the longer RH semiquaver curve as before, 'lifting' up to and 'falling' from the high sixth on the second semiquaver pulse of b.80 (and again similarly as the pattern continues an octave lower in the next bar). Ease into b.84 and 'finish off' the LH gracefully up to the quaver F sharp in b.84 ready for the RH to lead quietly but clearly into the melody from the second beat. Be aware that the melody acquires a new colour and timbre in this new, lower register. Following the *crescendo* towards the first beat of b.106, and the *diminuendo* through bb.106-8 re-enter in a whispered *pianissimo* on the second beat of b.108. Take time to arpeggiate gracefully up to the high A

sharp in b.119  and draw out once more towards b.124. Listen to the

steep downward progression of LH quavers through bb.132-3, taking time to 'point' the breathcatching interrupted cadence here. Some players allow the quiet wide-apart resonance of the RH chord and low bass C sharp to hover within the pedal through the pause. Others clear the sound ready to lead in with a more open sounding crotchet B flat on the second beat of b.133. In either case lean well on this B flat, letting it 'fall' expressively to the quaver C sharp as shown, going to a quietly resonant tied dotted minim on the first beat of b.134, ready to drift in with the *pianissimo* postlude from the second beat. Place the last chords with quiet finality.

Pedalling needs to be very light through bb.1-28, etc. – the effect of Chopin's considerably detailed markings will be too heavy on the modern piano. Judicious light touches of pedal are suggested on the first beat of bb.1, 2, etc. with light touches only, or the faintest 'haze' of half-pedalling through the longer sequences (bb.3, 6, etc.).

Nocturne No. 13 in C minor
Op. 48 No. 1 (8+)

This is one of those great works, one of the few from any period, that evolves magisterially from the sound of the first note, and progresses in unassailable and inevitable grandeur

---

*The RH notation shown here, B B D sharp A sharp follows that given in most editions, rather than A sharp B D sharp as in Henle. See Vienna Urtext, Critical Notes.

of design and proportion towards the very last. As Herbert Weinstock has said, 'So big, so varied and so narrative-seeming a piece, would not, in fact, have been appreciably misplaced as a fifth Ballade' (p.257). Niecks (and his must be a lone voice) found that, along with its companion Op.48 No.2, it was not 'of the number which occupy the foremost place among its companions' (Vol.2, p.265). Perhaps he found it too grand for its genre – too big for its boots! It is really a piece demanding the skills of the virtuoso. However, since its stature is such that even if the heights cannot quite be scaled, its study cannot fail to bring rewards, and since beside the other major single works, the Ballades, Scherzos, and so on, it is comparatively short, I have decided to include it under Grade 8+. (Its wide-spanned spread chords (b.25 onwards) and massive octave passages also, of course, hold fewer terrors for the larger-handed student.)

bb.1–4   Bear in mind, in setting your tempo, what has been said above. There is no introduction, no 'easing in'; the inexorable march starts with that first LH octave. Have your tempo 'well in the system' therefore, **before** you start, imagining a slow but swinging stride, spacious and masculine without being heavy. A pulse of around ♩ = 56-60 is suggested. Practise the LH alone, establishing a perfectly rhythmic 'suspended' kind of swing, from the bass octaves up to the chords and down again, visualising a series of connecting arcs, rather than isolated 'plonks'. Then practise the RH, **imagining** the continued tread of the LH below. This is an example of the LH as 'conductor' if ever there was one (see General Introduction under 'The Left Hand' and *'Rubato'*). The long declamatory line of the RH is entirely dependent upon, and governed by this continual tread in the LH, bending a little as if rounding a corner now and then, but only momentarily, and always rhythmically. Articulate the RH exactly as indicated. Place each crotchet in b.1 in a spaced, 'speaking' manner, giving each its exact value and no more. Then let the hand 'fall' with a slight emphasis on the offbeat crotchet G in b.2, going on to feel a further onward leaning emphasis on the tied quaver 'upbeat' to the third beat, ready to shape the remainder of the phrase in a long 'breath' right through to the third beat of b.4. Chopin's fingering 3, 3, 3 for the first three crotchets (not indicated in Henle but see Vienna Urtext and Paderewski Editions) shows us exactly how he wanted these notes to be played (see General Introduction under 'Fingering'). Show the curve up to and down from the G at the end of b.2, and then time the dotted rhythm figures precisely through b.3; the semiquaver will sound jaunty if too short, sloppy if too long. Give the tied G on the first beat of b.4 sufficient tone to 'buoy the line along' into the downward turning semiquaver phrase ending. While punctiliously observing all rests (bb.1-2, 4-5, etc.) do at the same time 'sing over' the rests so that the whole of the first section (bb.1-23), in reality an immense phrase, has a continuing overall onward line, a continuity through the silences. Now play bb.1-4 hands together **in time** in order that you may see how little the tempo needs to be pulled around. This does not suggest rigidity – if you try playing the LH in strict time it is remarkable, provided that you phrase the RH like a vocal line (and indeed it is a good plan to try **playing** the LH while **actually** singing the RH), how much freedom the melody line can enjoy within the steady tread of the LH (see General Introduction under *'Rubato'*). The stretto in b.4 (in some editions including Henle) is problematic – it appears that Chopin deleted it in one copy. Perhaps his original stretto indicated the intended 'onward' sense of the phrase ending **over** the rests towards the next phrase, rather than a feeling of 'stopping', then 'starting again' in b.5. Interpret the *mezza voce* as a weighty kind of quietness, distant perhaps, but not light in the sense of languid. Listen particularly to the placing of the LH crotchets beneath the RH rests or beneath held or tied RH notes (e.g. on the second and third beats of b.2, and the second beat of b.4 etc.). Do observe Chopin's pedal indications, catching the octave in the pedal on each first and third beat so that its sound is held **through** each half bar.

Relatively inexperienced players so often make the mistake of changing the pedal on every crotchet beat.

bb.4–24   As you 'finish off' the melody line of the first phrase in b.4, feel the LH marching steadily on to lead you into the second phrase, perhaps in a rather stronger, more purposeful tone. Listen to the onward push given by the detached LH semiquaver octave in b.6, feeling this as an 'upbeat' to the next beat, being conscious once more of the precise placing of this LH figure beneath the RH tied offbeat quaver. Listen to the *portamento*-like 'fall' to the tied lower quaver D in b.7, and then in b.8 take care to shade off the sound of the tied F sharp carefully into the demisemiquaver 'curl', matching the RH B flat neatly with the LH slurred semiquaver 'upbeat' to the unison G's on the third beat.* Listen to the downward march of the LH from b.8 towards the low octave C on the first beat of b.10 as you 'come in' again with an expressively 'planted' emphasised RH tied crotchet A flat on the second beat of b.9. Then curve expressively up to the B flat at the end of b.9, and up again from the 'doubled' grace note G flat up towards the high semiquaver A flat. The LH will need to bend a little to accommodate the RH here, particularly between the second and third beats of b.10, if you interpret the timing of the grace notes literally. Many players, however, take some licence, starting the grace note figure early (i.e. approximately on the second quaver pulse) so that the semiquaver triplet falls **on** the second beat, and thus becomes a **quaver** triplet. This, however, may be considered expedient rather than correct! The first grace note, the 'doubled' G flat, should ideally be placed just after the

second crotchet beat: (Chopin fingers

the grace notes   ). Then place the 'doubled' F of the broken

chord grace note figure **with** the bass octave D flat on the third beat. From the 'planted' tied crotchet on the second beat of b.9, feel the line is opening out expansively towards the third beat of b.10. There is then a sense of moving on towards another 'planted' crotchet on the second beat of b.11, with a further 'flowering' through the second half of b.11 towards the third beat of b.12. Then feel the increasing urgency of the short sequential figures (b.13

and b.14)   and the subsequent slight

relaxation in b.15. Phrase the melody with increasing ardour from b.17.† Rise to a ringing tied high C on the second beat of b.21,‡ pursue the curving semiquaver line with all possible

---

*A punctuating line appears in b.7 of Jane Stirling's score, indicating that the RH should be lifted after the dotted crotchet E flat, the better to 'point' the upbeat semiquaver F sharp to b.8.

†J.-J. Eigeldinger draws attention in b.19 to Chopin's use of an ornament 'widely used in *bel canto*' (pp.114 and 115). By repeating the previous note, the acciaccatura, placed **on** the beat, enhances the eloquence of the 'fall' to the minim C (see also General Introduction under 'Ornamentation').

‡As in b.7 there is a diagonal line between the first and second beats of b.21. This time the deliberate lift and fall of the RH will predispose an expressive emphasis on the high C.

expressiveness towards b.23, and stride down in a full-throated, declamatory tone towards immensely resonant unison C's on the first beat of b.24. Within this powerful unison sound, draw out the inner RH thirds a little, while at the same time feeling that these are leading you on inexorably into the major section.

bb.25–38   The slower tempo here is more illusory than actual. The chords must move with dream-like smoothness, *sotto voce* at first, while at the same time maintaining the measured tread of the opening section now advancing in a kind of celestial march. Negotiate a seamless 'join' as you move into b.25, establishing the new mood, and tempo change if any, on and from the minim chord on the first beat. Play in perfectly even time, placing the dotted rhythm figures carefully as before, thinking of each semiquaver chord as the upbeat to the next beat, and not as the tail-end of 'its own' beat. Show how the new phrase begins on the second beat of b.26, and then raise the dynamics by a layer as you move into b.29, playing the arpeggiated chords with a harp-like 'spread'. 'Hold' the inner triplet for an instant on the upbeat to b.37, lingering slightly on the dotted quaver D, as you poise yourself to return to *pianissimo* in b.37. Chopin's intermittent 'spreading' of the chords in this passage is problematic, particularly since most players will anyway have to spread most of the LH chords from b.29 onwards. Many pianists take the course of spreading the wide **LH** chords through, for example, bb.29-31, while only continuing the spread through into the RH on the first and fourth beats of b.30 and the first beat of b.31 as Chopin has indicated. Some 'block' the LH chords thus ⎍ while again others tend towards a continuous spread effect. Players

must experiment and find their own best solution, which in the case of those with smaller hands will largely be dictated by expediency. The overall objective must, of course, be steadiness of rhythm, beauty of sound, and continuity and smoothness of the melody line. Many players

execute the dotted quaver chord on the upbeat to b.28 thus:

Then, in view of the long 'lift' up through the spread minim chord on the first beat of b.31, it gives a good effect if you take the top G with the LH.§

bb.38–46   Make a measured *crescendo* from the second beat of b.38, keeping steady at all costs. The tendency is to 'pre-panic' here, and thus reach b.39 having already lost the beat. Once the beat is lost, the battle is lost, and if you then (as all too often happens) indiscriminately start battering the octaves in the effort to keep a grip on the situation, you will only precipitate a speedy collapse. It cannot be too strongly stressed that it is essential to retain the underlying **sense** of the onward marching crotchet pulse – and realising that this whole passage, from b.37 onwards, is a splendid elaboration of bb.29-36, rather than a mere occasion for octave pyrotechnics. This pulse must 'bend' a little here and there as the octaves slightly *accelerando*, or draw out, but always with the sense of being 'brought back into line'

§J. Petrie Dunn gives an elaborate interpretation of this passage in which the **majority** of the LH chords are arpeggiated. However, it appears that Chopin 'allowed' the omission of certain notes e.g. the upper LH notes from the second beat of b.34, through to the end of b.35. (See Eigeldinger p.266).

by the melodic chords on the first or third beats (of bb.39, 40, etc.). It is a good plan to try playing the top line only, thus *etc.* quite slowly at first, and keeping strict time. Follow the little dynamic swell through the semiquavers in b.39, and then *crescendo* up to the third beat of b.40. You will find that the semiquaver triplets automatically fall into a slur pattern *etc.* You will also see that it is essential to **start** each octave 'run' relatively quietly, so that in each instance, from b.40 onwards, there is an upward *crescendo* towards the next chord on each third or first beat, with, of course, a gradual **overall** build-up towards b.46. When you start to practise the passage as written, be sure that you continue to retain the vital sense of the beat, always being sure to give the chords, **particularly** the crotchet on the third beat of b.39 and the minim on the third beat of b.40 their full value. It will also help to practise the octaves in varying rhythms: and *etc.* In b.39 you will have to take an extra instant after the last triplet octave to leap up to the strong crotchet chord on the third beat. Then having taken another extra instant to 'get down' to the F sharp octave after the first chord in b.40, there is a natural slight, *accellerando* towards the minim chord on the third beat. Similarly, allow an extra instant to 'get up' to the quaver chord on the third beat of b.41, and so on. Note the implied slight 'hold' as you 'lift' to the emphasised last chord of b.41, feeling this as an 'upbeat' to the quaver chord on the first beat of b.42 (and similarly at bb.43-4). Be particularly sure to start the long octave run through b.42 (and similarly b.44) relatively quietly, and then to continue to feel the **sense** of the crotchet pulse (and particularly of the 'anchoring' third beat) within the run. 'Draw out' a little from the third beat of b.44 as you make a final *crescendo* towards a mighty chord on the first beat of b.45. Hold this chord for an extra instant before you plunge down to make a powerful *crescendoing* rumble through the low trill taking care to give this trill its full dotted crotchet duration. Allow another extra instant as you leap up again to another powerful chord on the third beat, and then 'brake' firmly as you *crescendo* on towards a yet more grandiose chord on the first beat of b.46. (The bar numbering in Henle is confusing here – the half-bar at the beginning of the third line, marked 42 is the second half of **b.41**; and the twelve semiquavers at the beginning of the last line are marked b.45, whereas they in fact comprise the second half of **b.44**.)

bb.46–48 **Hold** this huge semiquaver chord for an instant on the first beat of b.46 as you poise yourself to launch into the octave cadenza. Play these octaves with improvisatory freedom, starting off relatively slowly, and increasing speed as you descend (while retaining the rhythmic sense of triplets as indicated) and drawing out again towards an immense chord on the first beat of b.47. Take time to leap up again towards the high E flats and again drawing out the first few notes of the descending chromatic scale. Then deliver the RH chords powerfully and rhythmically through the second half of b.47, above the continuing downward run of the LH. 'Lean' on the last RH chord in b.47, feeling this as a powerful upbeat to b.48. This chord is slurred in Henle thus:

 This creates a splendid curve from this upbeat chord up through the

first triplet group of the descending octaves in b.48. Feel the semiquaver octaves E, therefore, as the peak of this slurred curve, from which they cascade down towards the *sforzato* C major chord on the third beat. Hold this chord for an instant, then drop to *piano* immediately as indicated, ready to make an *accellerando* like an onward 'push' into the *doppio movimento*.†

bb.49–77 This final section, a transformation rather than a varied version of the opening section, stirs up hornets' nests of controversy and inevitably inconclusive discussion. It is presumably because the indication *doppio movimento* is in itself so problematic that editors so significantly avoid even mentioning it! Whether Chopin is suggesting the doubling of the speed of the crotchet pulse of the opening, or whether, as Rudolph Ganz asserts, 'the triplets in eighths (quavers) are the same as the sixteenths (semiquavers) of the preceding bar' (Hutcheson, p.226), either interpretation would produce 'an inartistic precipitation' (Huneker, p.147). It would in any event, 'artistic' or not, be virtually impossible to play at such a hectic tempo. As Dr Hutcheson says *'tempo primo ma agitato* would better express the intention' (p.226). And indeed this seems to be the solution adopted by most pianists. Even so, this whole section is far from easy to bring off, and many a boxing contest do we have to endure between eminent performers and their Steinways – the unfortunate melody line lost among pounding, hammering chords, and buffeted into submission amid chaotic cross-rhythm. To avoid this effect it is well to think of the **overall** dynamic as *piano* – *agitato*, after all, implies palpitating anxiety, not the wielding of sledge-hammers or the progress of steam-rollers.

Treat the series of swells and *crescendos* between bb.52 and 64 therefore as small **surges**, which return more or less 'to base'. Only from this point (b.65) should the volume gradually be 'opened out' (and even then slightly 'drawing back' in the first half of bb.66 and 68 before a greater surge up to a higher plateau from the second half of b.68. The LH needs to carry the RH on a buoyant, overall 2-in-the-bar pulse. Practise it alone, therefore, feeling the significance of the bass octaves on the first and third beats of each bar which propel this 2-in-the-bar movement, and making as smooth a curve as possible over each group of six quaver triplets. Then practise the RH thus, really 'leaning' on the melody notes and keeping the chords relatively quiet:

Then when you practise the RH as written, continue to 'lean' on the melody notes, leaving the inner part of the hand free so that you can balance the inner chords sensitively with your melody line. When you put hands together continue to listen acutely so that your melody line (particularly when you *crescendo* and eventually arrive in *forte*), is **never** engulfed by the chords. This, needless to say, requires a great deal of control, as well as being extremely taxing to the 'weak' fingers of the RH.

Start from b.49 in a **real** *pianissimo*, as if the melody is materialising on an uneasy breeze, conveying the breathless anxiety of the *agitato* to the best of your ability. As you play the semiquaver chords in cross-rhythm in b.50 in a 'speaking' just-detached style, be sure to keep the LH triplets steady, feeling that the RH chords are fitting in with the LH, and **not** the other way around. While, needless to say, there are different interpretations of the 'correct' placing of various figures, there appears to be no controversy here about the placing of the dotted rhythm in relation to the triplet on the second beat of b.51. Jan Ekier gives this

†The ascending bass octaves may be taken with both hands through the last three **quaver** beats of b.48, according to an indication in the copy belonging to Camille O'Meara-Dubois.

as the **exception** to his rule that the semiquaver should coincide with the third triplet

quaver  (see the Preface to the Vienna Urtext Edition): here, he states, it

should definitely be played as written (see General Introduction under 'Some Explanations and Amplifications', and see also 'Remarks on Interpretation' in the Vienna Urtext). In

Henle the RH in the second half of b.51 is given whereas

it is usually given and played On the last beat of b.55

and the third and fourth beats of bb.57, 61, etc. the treble quaver is usually placed

thus: although some players play them in cross-rhythm with the LH triplets

(this is, of course, more difficult). On these various points players must feel their way towards their own preferences. In any event, it is a good plan before settling to serious work on this section to re-study the melody line in its original context (bb.1-24) refreshing those melodic emphases and impulses which you will endeavour to translate in this new mood and texture.

From b.64 rise gradually towards an impassioned high C on the second beat of b.69. Keep the rhythm under firm control as you progress through the phrase in semiquavers from the third beat of this bar in a glorious fullness of sound towards an immense chord on the first beat of b.71; but even here leave some reserve of tone to continue towards the huge interrupted cadence (bb.71-2).† 'Space' the upbeat triplet to b.72 in preparation for the impact of the chord on the first beat of b.72, letting the tied minim C ring out with all possible splendour, balanced by a resonant bass octave. Expand the line here with the resonance of an organ, curving up towards the high A at the end of the bar and 'pouring' down, as if in a *portamento*, to a vibrant tied minim B natural in b.73. Give your all to this passage – one of the most splendid that is given to a pianist to play! I believe (though many pianists plainly do not!) that the immense sound here should be maintained as you draw out through the second half of b.73 towards vast unison C's on the first beat of b.74. This instinct to 'carry on' to this point is backed up by the

†Again in the O'Meara-Dubois score there is a welcome simplification for small hands of the dense chord-writing through the first half of b.70.

fact that **this** is the final tonic, and Chopin only indicates the *diminuendo* from the second beat of this bar.‡ Draw out the LH from the second beat of b.74 in a gradual *diminuendo* and *rallentando* towards the bass C on the first beat of b.75, and then tail away the RH line upwards, savouring each inflection in an infinitely expressive curve towards a quietly singing high C. Play the final chords with quiet measured solemnity.

Note: The comments and reproduced annotations on this Nocturne in J.-J. Eigeldinger's *Chopin, Pianist & Teacher* are of paramount interest. And Von Lenz gives a revealing glimpse of Chopin at work with a pupil, illustrating his meticulous sense of phrasing:

> How exacting and finicky Chopin was over the four opening bars – which appear so simple! . . . He was not easy to satisfy with the first bar of the Nocturne: the crotchets G, A flat, should emerge as thematic elements, but were always too loud or too soft for his liking . . . In the second bar the final semiquaver, G, was to glide smoothly into the following C (first beat of the third bar), and Chopin was never satisfied. He told me: 'since it lies within your *capabilities*, you *must* be able to do it.' I finally succeeded, after long efforts: either the G would be too short and the C arrive too soon, or else the reverse. 'It must have an intention', said Chopin. He was no less exacting when it came to the descending C before the quaver rest at the end of the semiquaver group (fourth bar, third beat); the C was either too short or too long. I found a way out by 'combing' this with the thumb, that is by sliding the finger along the key and releasing it only upon reaching the outer edge. This way the end of the phrase at last satisfied him; but that was nothing beside Chopin's own playing in these two passages! . . . He wanted a *question* on the G-C (bars 2-3), a *response* on the C (bar 4).
>
> Eigeldinger, pp.80-81

Nocturne No. 14 in F sharp minor
Op. 48 No. 2 (8)

Eclipsed perhaps by its mighty companion in Op.48, the C minor, the more modest pleasures of this piece tend to remain unsung. Possibly also it is not an altogether successful concert item. In Op.15 No.2 or Op.32 No.2, for example, the contrasting sections seem to evolve from the context of the original thought. Even in Op.15 No.1 the storm at b.25 breaks as if it has been

‡This idea is borne out by the detailed doubling of the bass and inner LH resonances pencilled in the score belonging to Jane Stirling.

impending through the calm of the previous bars. Here, though, the central section appears to be inserted like an obligatory chunk of 'contrast'. Nevertheless there is much of beauty – the long first section is like a protracted vocalise, the melody line flowing on in an unbroken stretch of twenty-six bars. The principal 2-bar descending motif (bb.3-4) with its ascending answer (bb.7-8) occurs again and again with, on the face of it, little variety. But treated in a truly vocal manner, imagining all the time how a singer would wordlessly express the continually curving, swaying phrases and the varying chromatic inflections, the effect is cumulatively very lovely.

bb. 1–7   The melody line (i.e. from b.3) must always be cushioned and buoyed along by a smooth, ongoing but rhythmically very stable LH, at an easy-moving but unhurried crotchet pulse. If you **sing** the melody, imagining these LH triplet figures bearing you lightly on, you will find the tempo that feels 'right' – at a suggested ♩ = 88-96, and with an overall 2-in-the-bar feeling. Practise the LH of bb.3-7 carefully, shaping

each slurred figure ![musical notation] in a smooth, overall curve, feeling the 'lift' from each

bass note up to the third triplet quaver and down to the crotchet. The crotchet must always receive its full value, so that you avoid the possible tendency to 'fall on' into the third beat of each bar, and then into the first beat of the subsequent bar. At the same time these crotchets must have an 'onward' feeling, like continual upbeats to each third and first beat, avoiding any feeling of 'sticking' on the second and fourth beats.

Then practise the RH alone: place the crotchet F sharp quietly but definitely on the first beat of b.3, and imagine a vocal 'lift' as you rise lightly to the high F sharp on the second beat. Curve 'through' this note, and then feel the leisurely 'uncurling' of the line through to the first beat of b.5. Then 'lift' lightly again up to the F sharp on the second beat and imagine 'sliding' chromatically in a *portamento* effect down to the E on the third beat. Play the triplet at the end of b.6 like an ongoing upbeat as you prepare to end the subphrase on the F sharp on the first beat of b.7, which 'overlaps' as the first note of the new subphrase.

Phrasing indications vary in different editions. In Henle the melody begins on the first beat of b.3, whereas in the Vienna Urtext Edition, the Paderewski Edition and Peters, the introduction ends on the first beat of b.3, and the melody proper begins from the second beat. In Henle, however, the opening motif returns on the **second** beat of bb.25, 31, etc, as in other editions. In the Paderewski Edition new phrases begin on the second beat of bb.5, 7, 9, 11, and so on. But as has already been said, the overall melody line flows in an unbroken stream through bb.3-28; and all such punctuations suggested here or provided in various editions must be felt as nuances **within** this overall line. Thus the description above of the ending of the first 4-bar subphrase and the beginning of the next, answering subphrase on the first beat of b.7 is a **suggested nuance**, rather than a point to be laboured. Similarly the second 4-bar subphrase will both end and lead on into the next, on the first beat of b.11. And such nuances will, of course, vary in different interpretations. Then practise the LH while actually **singing** the RH, thoroughly absorbing the sense in which the LH cushions and buoys along the melody.

Now study the two introductory bars. Have your overall pulse in mind before you begin. Then, starting these introductory bars a little slower, let the rising phrase 'grow' towards your tempo proper. Listen to the quiet resonance of the low, held C sharp as the upper line expands into the beginning of the melody in b.3. Balance the sound carefully as you place the 'doubled' RH C sharp carefully on the second beat, and listen also to **its** resonance as the melody in sixths 'grows' in a smooth swell up towards the chord on the third beat of b.2. 'Hold' this partly tied chord for an instant as you poise yourself to lead into b.3 from the upbeat dominant seventh chord. Place the acciaccatura A in a 'speaking' manner, on the first beat of b.3, and immediately establish your easy moving tempo as you 'lift' up to the high F sharp over your ongoing LH. (The D natural in the Henle edition on the fourth beat of b.1 was amended by Chopin to D sharp in teaching copies – see Vienna Urtext and Paderewski Editions – and may thus be taken as an authentic correction.)

bb.7–56 Lead on into b.7 as described, perhaps in a slightly fuller tone, listening to the line of the sustained, more purposeful 'doubled' bass minims through bb.7-8.

Give the RH tied minim on the third beat of b.7 and again b.9 sufficient tone to carry over the barline, feeling each of these notes 'leaning' on into the subsequent bar. Rise in a little swell towards the high B on the third beat of b.10, and lead on into the restatement in the dominant with an increase of expressive warmth. Expand the tone as you rise towards the high F sharp on the third beat of b.18, balancing this high RH line with a resonant-toned LH. 'Fill out' the curve through the second half of b.18, and descend towards the *forte* minim at b.20 in an impassioned, but always smooth line. Then let the minim line move on from b.20 in a sonorous stride, feeling a strong onward impetus towards a splendidly resonant long D sharp on the first beat of b.22. Here you can vary the dynamics with equally expressive effect: either continue the impetus, keeping up the full tone until the *diminuendo* in b.25, or 'draw back', both dynamically and impetus-wise, and continue from the second beat of b.23 in a quieter tone. In either case, 'lift' up to the high G sharp on the second beat of b.25 in a delicate echo effect, and then take an extra instant to 'point' the defining RH turn into the major on the upbeat to b.27. Let the LH subside gently beneath the quietly ringing long G sharp, yet at the same time give the feeling of leading on to 'grow' into the 'reintroductory' bb.29-30, ready to sing on from b.31. Allow a little 'give' at the end of b.28 to make it clear that you are 'beginning again' with the dominant broken chord in b.29. 'Hold' the LH triplet a little through the first beat of b.41 to accommodate the RH 'turn'. Some players may anticipate the normal placement of the second RH quaver C sharp and thereby take less time over the 'turn'. Others (and this, skilfully managed, is prettier) place the C sharp 'correctly' (i.e. in cross-rhythm with the LH triplet group) and therefore have to 'hold' the LH for longer, arranging the notes

approximately thus:  It is essential to maintain

the **sense** of the LH triplet rhythm 'going to' the crotchet on the second beat while allowing the pulse to 'bend' sufficiently for the 'turn' to sound clear and unhurried, with time to 'lift' delicately up to the high C sharp on the second beat, regaining the even tempo through the second half of the bar. Allow the octaves to 'fill out' the sound in a heightened *appassionato* from b.43, and this time drift into a dreamlike *piano* at b.51.

bb.57–101 Niecks records that Chopin told his pupil Gutmann that the *molto più lento* section should be played like a recitative: 'A tyrant commands [the first two chords]', he said, 'and the other asks for mercy.' (Vol.2, p.265). This highly effective imagery tells us exactly how to play it. The tempo settles best at around ♩= 66. If it is taken much slower, this section is liable to 'stick' disastrously (see the Vienna Urtext and Paderewski Editions which give only *più lento* – Chopin erased the *molto* in teaching copies). **Use** the *ritenuto* and *crescendo* through bb.55-6 to prepare as convincing a 'join' as possible. Then play the pair of chords in b.57 in a full-toned, commanding style, swelling **into** the second chord in a smooth slur as indicated. Then 'space' the five-semiquaver figure evenly and expressively, feeling this as an ongoing, upbeat group towards a 'speaking' dotted-rhythm

figure in b.58,  and so on through bb.59-60,

61-2, etc. Each semiquaver figure must be carefully fingered to best advantage so that in every instance you make a smooth upward and overall sweep into and through the subsequent bar as indicated. Doubtless many players have resorted to dividing the semiquavers between the hands. But the effect is not the same as that produced by the 'effort' of negotiating the notes in the RH. Be sure to give the minim A flat on the second beat of bb.58 and 62 its full value so that you don't 'fall into' b.59, and then feel the 'onward lead' of the dotted rhythm upbeat figure as the line of b.60 curves down towards the *piano* chords

at b.61.  Allow an extra instant to leap up from the

last note of bb.61, 63, etc. to a **poised** chord on the subsequent first beat. Again feel the chord on the third beat of b.64 as the upbeat to b.65, and proceed solemnly yet expansively through

bb.65-70, playing the spread chord on the first beat of b.66 thus:

Crescendo towards and into b.70, and feel the onward 'push' on the dotted quaver chord on the upbeat to b.71, and again on the second beat of b.71 as you advance in a *stretto*, momentary **2/4** effect. Then 'rein back' through a resonant dotted crotchet chord on the first beat of b.72, making a *portamento*-like slur down to the semiquaver 'upbeat' to the third beat, and poising yourself on this third beat chord ready to 'start again' from b.73. Take an extra instant to 'point' the harmonic shift at b.75, and again to 'point' the change of direction and register as the LH upbeat group leads down into b.83. *Crescendo* precipitately through b.95 into b.96, timing the suddenly urgent 'telescoped' repetition of the dotted rhythm figure peremptorily as you *crescendo* on towards the *fortissimo* chords at b.97. Keep up the full tone as you cascade downwards in a splendid but **controlled** semiquaver sweep towards the chord on the first beat of b.99. According to the manuscript source this semiquaver arpeggio should

be played ♩ ♩ ♩ ♩ ♩ ♩ ♩ ♩ ♩ ♩ ♩ ♩ ♩ (see Commentary in the Paderewski Edition)

i.e. four semiquavers through the second beat and the remaining nine through the third beat. Take time to 'point' the interrupted cadence (bb.99-100) and **listen** to the resonance of the F sharp minor chord as you ease through b.100 towards the major beginning of the reprise.

Even with the help of the 'tyrant/mercy' imagery, this section is far from easy to hold together. It cannot be too strongly emphasised that rhythm is all-important. Despite, or because of, the recitative-like sense of 'free' declamation, there needs to be a continuous, albeit flexible, sense of the rhythmic **3/4** impulse. The predominant 2-bar figures (bb.57-8, 59-60, etc.) are meaningless unless there is a strong sense of this underlying crotchet pulse. Be sure, therefore, always to give the two chords their precise value in b.57 etc, avoiding the tendency to cut short the **second** chord and thus to **anticipate** the upbeat semiquaver group. The 5-note group then becomes too 'loose', and loses its necessary clear upbeat impulse. Having led convincingly into b.58, be sure, as already said, to **listen through** to the end of the minim in b.58, and so on. It is well worth studying this whole section **away** from the piano, **thinking** or **singing** the music through as you 'conduct' yourself with a steady **3/4** beat.

Leading into b.101 from a clear semiquaver upbeat, take time to shape the spread

bb.101–137

chord gracefully:  'Point' the emphasised tied minim

A sharp on the third beat of b.105, a 'warning' that we are about to take an unexpected turning, and then move onwards in an improvisatory manner as you swell upwards through the fourth beat of b.106. Drop the tone a little at the beginning of b.107, ready to curve upwards yet more expansively through to the fourth beat of b.108, and then keep up your tone as you let the melody pour onwards through b.109 ('lifting' the hand from the first quaver E sharp on the first beat – see General Introduction under 'Articulation'), and on in a downward curve towards b.112. 'Go to' a full-toned tied D on the third beat of b.111, and listen as the melody line 'divides' into b.112. Carry the treble line on down to a resonant minim B, then feel that the **LH** is 'carrying you on' ready to sweep up to a ringing high F sharp on the first beat of b.113. Shade the solo line freely and expressively downwards, taking time to make a *portamento*-like 'fall' to a quiet C sharp on the first beat of b.115.* Some players now move into a rather slower tempo to enhance the dream-like atmosphere as each thought in this eventful coda unfolds and grows into the next. In any event, enter again on the second beat of b.115 in a light-breathed *pianissimo*, and let the line drift on towards a whispering trill through bb.117-18 (letting the first grace note F sharp coincide with the LH C sharp on the first beat of b.117). Listen to the continuing quiet movement of the LH through these two bars and ease into b.119, ready to move on a little, while at the same time **listening** to the quietly changing progressions of the LH beneath the smooth chromatic line of the RH minims. 'Point' the tied minim slightly on the third beat of b.121, and then take time through the second half of b.122 to prepare to ease into b.123. 'Scoop' up gracefully to

*In the copy belonging to Chopin's pupil Camille O'Meara/Dubois Chopin wrote *8va⁻⁻* over the minim F sharp in b.113. The Vienna Urtext suggests the following variant, descending from this high F sharp.

the high octave, playing the lower C sharp on the beat. The third grace note (C sharp) is usually

tied thus:  Move on in an easy *crescendo*, listening to

the downward line of the bass notes from bb.123-6, beneath the warm-toned RH chords and take time again to spread the RH grace note figure expressively (either on, or anticipating the chord on the third beat) as you swell through the second half of b.126 towards a resonant 'lean' on the RH chord on the first beat of b.127. 'Lean' again on the tied octave on the second beat of b.127, listening to this held F sharp resonance, in combination with the pedal point effect of the bass F sharps through these bars as the inner melody line moves quietly towards the first beat of b.129. 'Retake' the RH F sharp with quiet resonance on the second beat of b.129, and take time again to listen as the inner line moves into the major through the end of b.130. Here the music takes on a barcarolle-like sway. Keeping the LH moving quietly on, lean a little on the first note of each trill (i.e. on the grace note B sharp, placing this on the beat – see General Introduction under 'Ornaments'). Tail each trill off with an airy 'lift' up to a light quaver on each fourth beat. Allow a little extra time to lift with gossamer lightness up to the high third on the fourth beat of b.133. Let the long trill billow a little from the second beat of b.135, and then die away as it merges imperceptibly into the upward run, listening at the same time to the descending line of the LH through bb.135-6. Never mind when the run starts (it can be slower, starting soon after the second beat of the bar, or faster according to how late you begin it), providing that it runs smoothly and evenly and tails off gracefully up towards the first beat of the final bar, allowing as much of a 'give' as your ear approves. To begin with, less experienced players could group the notes

approximately thus:

See the editorial suggestion in the Vienna Urtext Edition that this was a typical instruction by Chopin for a 'less skilled pupil'. The scale can start later, and the groups be differently, more loosely merged as confidence increases (see General Introduction under ''Free' Runs'). Disperse the sound to a mere wisp, ending in a tiny pinpoint on the treble and bass crotchets. Close with a gracefully spread chord.

Nocturne No. 15 in F minor
Op. 55 No. 1 (7)

This is a favourite student piece. Its resulting overexposure has perhaps contributed to the disproportionate critical disdain it receives. I always think of it as a 'poor man's' version of Op.48 No.1 in the sense that, on an infinitely slighter scale, it has a similar sense of organic unity, and had it been written some years earlier, one could imagine detecting the outline of the magisterial progress of the great C minor.

bb. 1–8   As in the opening of the C minor the motion of the LH is all-important. The rhythm and shape of both are similar, but here the tread is lighter, less grand, and the tempo more onward moving. Practise the LH through bb.1-8 feeling an easy suspended kind of swing between the bass notes and upper chords, imagining a lightly moving, though not jaunty strolling step at about ♩ = 88-96. It is important at the same time to feel an overall 2-in-the-bar movement, with a continual onward impulse towards each bass note. This is not to say that the chords on the second and fourth beats are less important. On the contrary, it is they which supply the 'upbeat' onward impulse **towards** the 'main' beats, and they need to be placed just as carefully as the bass notes.

When you come to practise the RH, have the pulse 'well in the system' before you start so that you **place** the upbeat crotchet in its rhythmic context, with an implied emphasis, and onward leading 'lean'. At the same time be sure to give this tied upbeat crotchet its full value, **feeling** the first beat of b.1 as you listen to its continuing sound. Then feel that the line is curving up towards the F on the second beat of b.1 in a 'vocal' manner so that the phrase is shaped up to, and curves gracefully downwards from this F. Articulate the dotted rhythm figures delicately in b.2 (rather than beating them out doggedly in the unfortunate manner so often heard), leading on to a quiet but warm-toned tied minim C. Take care to give this note enough tone to sing over the beat but without giving it a 'clonk'! Since this two-bar motif recurs so many times, take time to absorb this shape, so that you can vary the nuance of your vocal curve a little each time. If the four-square

effect of this [music: a)] is pedestrian, the

predictability of an exaggerated [music: b)] is equally tedious.

When you put hands together take the greatest care how you place the bass note on the first beat of b.1. Balance the bass sound carefully beneath the tied note in such a way that this bass note clearly launches off the gentle rhythmic swing from the first note of b.1. Now practise these two bars over and over, in a continuous movement, back from the end of b.2 to the beginning of b.1, until you are thoroughly familiar with the shape and easy rhythmic swing. Feel that you are 'leaning onwards' through the long C through the second beat of b.2, feeling this as a long upbeat as the LH carries on 'walking' back to b.1. Listen not only to the RH line, but also to the bass line, F-G-A flat-E natural-F, and so on, and to the upper line of the inner chords, F-E flat-A flat-G, within the overall 2-in-the-bar movement.

Now practise through to b.8. Let the grace note in b.4 'speak' rather than squashing it in –

approximately [music] 'Go to' a slightly stronger minim C

on the first beat of b.6, and then move on rather more purposefully. Curve up through the D flat at the end of b.6, and on down to a fuller toned minim A flat on the first beat of b.7, and then spread the RH chord warmly on the third beat, as you prepare to carry the melody line smoothly down to the minim F on the first beat of b.8. Allow a tiny give as you end the phrase, allowing time for the acciaccatura A flat to speak (placed on the beat). Make a new start on the C on the

354

third beat of b.8, show the quiet 'lean' on the tied upbeat to the next bar, and then 'cut' back to the beginning and go over these eight bars several times until you feel at ease with the motion and shape of these bars with the confidence, as already said, to vary the nuances subtly each time they occur. Phrasing details vary in different editions but feel the sense of two 2-bar subphrases through bb.1-4 and a longer 4-bar phrase through bb.5-8 all within the sense of an overall sentence from bb.1-8.

The principal motif, it hardly needs to be pointed out, has a tendency to droop, and the piece can all too easily wilt to a standstill. The motion must therefore never be allowed to stick or grow ponderous, and the mood needs to remain lightly melancholy rather than cloying or seriously doleful. When you come to perform the piece, always **feel** the easy rhythm before you start so that you can 'bring in' the melody with a convincingly rhythmic, onward-leaning upbeat, giving this first note perhaps even a little more than its full value.

Note Chopin's pedal indications, being sure to catch the bass note in the pedal on each first and third beat. On the modern piano the pedalling may sound too heavy through the first half of bb.2, 4, etc. and could be pedalled more lightly, or with a half-pedal change on the second beat.

bb.8–45   Listen to the LH as the RH comes briefly to rest on the minim F on the first beat of b.8 and then, as already said, make a new start with the RH C on the third beat.

In b.14 **begin** the trill with the grace note prefix so that the grace note A natural coincides with the LH B flat on the third beat of the bar (in accordance with Chopin's preferred practice – see General Introduction under 'Ornaments'). Feel that the grace note prefix is 'opening out' into a melodious, easy-running rather than showy trill. 'Hold' the LH chord a little on the fourth beat to allow time to 'turn' the five-note trill-ending delicately and expressively, starting this five-note 'turn' just after or, if this is too difficult, **with** the LH chord

on the fourth beat.  These trill-endings occur

three times, here and at bb.30 and 46. Take out each of these bars and practise them in a series so that you are perfectly sure of the difference between them and can then give each one its own expressive inflection (students so often do not bother to do this, and scramble through them in a splodge of notes, vaguely hoping that they will 'come out right'). Do also take the trouble to play these 'little' notes in a just-detached style. Whether or not you lighten the pedal through the end of the bar, the just-detached style 'speaks' quite differently to *legato* (see General Introduction, under 'Articulation') and in addition prevents you from hurrying. Think of an overall phrase line moving down through b.13 (and 30 and 46) with the line 'merging' into the trill in b.14, inflecting in an upward curve through the turn, and then moving on through b.15 to come to rest on the F in b.16. (In b.30 space out the four grace notes even more 'speakingly' – since they run in a straight line and create quite a different effect to the other two endings. In b.46 allow a little longer since not only does this 'turn' have six notes, it is also the third and last before the change of mood at b.48.)

Practise the LH carefully from b.16, showing the momentary change of character. There is an implied slight emphasis on the minim third on the second beat of b.16. Listen to this held third, slurring it smoothly towards the chord on the fourth beat, as the lower line moves down chromatically towards the minim E flat on the first beat of b.17, resuming its 'normal walk'from the third beat. Feel a lightening of the mood and a feeling of moving on as the RH starts afresh here on the third beat of b.16 in a new, 'upturning' and more cheerful vein. Make an easy little swell towards the minim C on the first beat of b.18 as if cresting a little rise, and then another, as you open out the tone towards b.20. Let the LH tone expand in support, balancing the RH with a resonant low bass C on the first beat of b.20. Feel that the RH line continues its curve up to the F on the third beat of b.20 before making a gradual *decrescendo* down again towards b.24. As the RH line gently subsides through bb.22-4 listen to the sustained pedal point effect of the lower LH dominant minims beneath the carefully balanced inner chords, taking care that these 'separate' inner chords don't 'hang on' over the subsequent beats. Listen particularly to the partly tied upbeat chord resolving on to the minim dominant seventh harmony on the second beat of b.24 as you prepare to 'space out' the repeated RH C's in a little *ritenuto* before setting off again with a 'leaning' upbeat C into the next phrase.

It is effective to tail away the sound through b.26 towards the beginning of b.27 so that you start the triplet variant in a delicate *pianissimo*, gradually swelling towards b.29. Feel that the LH is 'guiding' the RH here, while at the same time allowing the triplets to sound free and improvisatory. It is effective to 'hold' the LH chord fractionally on the second beat of b.27 as you start the triplets in a whisper, and then to 'move on' as you *crescendo* towards b.29. Then when the triplet figure recurs at b.43 it can be treated rather differently (see below). Do maintain the **sense** of the rhythmic movement in the LH through these triplet passages, even when 'holding' a little or moving on a little, feeling that the RH triplets are subject to the ongoing LH rhythm (and **not** the other way about). At risk of labouring the point do here again vary the nuances, not only from phrase to phrase, but from day to day, with all the artistry you can summon – in this piece particularly any tendency to 'set' the expressive reflexes spells death to the music. From b.43 then, feel a stronger sense of moving on in a rather fuller tone, and continue the *crescendo* through the seven-quaver figure towards b.45. Once more maintain the **sense** of the LH rhythm, though allowing the hint of a 'hold' on the chord on the second beat of b.44 as you sing out the RH seven-quaver figure, 'going to' a strong 'lean' on the tied minim C as you *crescendo* on into b.45. Space out the

seven quavers thus:  Practise at first without the

acciaccatura and then when you add it, allow time for it to 'speak', within the overall sense of 'going on to' the tied minim C.

bb.45–56   From b.45 many pianists make a *diminuendo* and *rallentando* towards the first beat of b.48 so that they can start the new section with a *subito forte* on the second beat of b.48. Others, and I prefer this effect, continue from b.45 in a full tone with the feeling of moving on and 'growing into' the *più mosso*. In any event, arrive on a clear crotchet chord on the first beat of b.48, whether in *piano* or *forte*. Then make a tiny break ready to make a new start as you launch into the unison triplets on the second beat, shaping each run in an improvisatory, full-voiced curve down towards resonant crotchets on the first beat of bb.49, 51, etc. The secret of keeping control of this passage is to 'apply the brakes' between each triplet run with firmly **rhythmic** chords through bb.49, 51, etc. These runs are surprisingly treacherous. It is essential to work out the fingering carefully (be sure in particular to use the **thumb** in the LH on the **fourth** triplet of each run, as indicated in most editions) and then to practise assiduously until the hands are perfectly coordinated. Practising in different

rhythms, particularly ♩♪♪♩♪♪ will help. In performance create a 'free' effect by

slightly 'braking' the first two or so notes of each run; and then **move** with a free onward impetus towards the crotchets on the first beat of the subsequent bar. Be sure to catch these bass crotchets in the pedal, **listening** to their resonance as you leap up (imagining a wide arc, not two isolated plonks) towards an emphatically stressed minim chord on the second beat (since the 2-in-the-bar feeling is even stronger in this faster tempo, this emphatic minim chord creates a strong syncopated effect).

As you launch into the *più mosso* it is important that you **feel** the pulse of your new tempo, in other words the exact time in which you will play these chords. This in turn will be tempered by the overall tempo at which you can safely negotiate the triplet runs. Many pianists, relieved no doubt to escape from the repetition of the first section and champing to show their paces, hurtle off gratuitously here, rather than letting the *più mosso* appear to grow from the previous *andante*. It is a good plan to practise the whole passage with the metronome. You will see that despite the slight holding back and moving on of the runs, the **overall** pulse of each bar as a whole remains constant. Be sure in particular always to give each 'syncopated' minim chord its full value, **feeling** the held third beat of the bar. Then note the slight *decrescendo* as you play the chord on the last beat of b.49 and on the first beat of b.50 in perfect time, ready to launch into the next run. Note the slight re-*crescendo* through the beginning of b.52, ready to leap down to the shorter run on the third beat. Many players arpeggiate the chord and acciaccatura on the first beat of **b.52**, as indicated on the first beat of **b.56**, but this, I feel, is wrong. The chord in b.52 should sound martial (placing the

acciaccatura on the beat)  whereas the spreading of the chord in b.56

creates a gentler effect to be played thus: in preparation for the

start of the new section in *piano*.

bb.56–72 *Crescendo* a little into the chord on the second beat of b.56 but in a different, more melting manner than at b.52. Then allow a small break in order to clear the sound as you poise yourself to lead into the new section with the two 'speaking'

RH crotchets G. Study the LH carefully from b.57, shaping each

figure smoothly up to a clear crotchet on the second and fourth beats of each bar. In the RH shape each 2-bar phrase carefully in accordance with the indicated dynamic rise and fall. Take equal care to show the smooth line of the inner voice from b.58, carefully balanced so as to enhance, rather than swamp the treble line. When you put hands together feel the slightly *agitato* character of this section from the quiet beginning, almost under the breath, with a gradual overall *crescendo* and sense of moving on towards a grand resonance at b.65. Listen all the time to the LH (this whole passage is controlled by the LH rhythm, still moving in an overall 2-in-the bar) being careful not to 'clip' the crotchets on the second and fourth beats. Be particularly aware of this on the second beat of b.57 and the fourth beat of b.60 etc. where, beneath the held RH minim, there is a tendency to 'fall into' the subsequent third or first beat. Increase the volume steadily through bb.63-4, and then draw out a little through b.65, listening to the splendid overall resonance. As you *diminuendo* gradually (moving on again), be aware of the sound of the two pedal point resonances – the lower D flat and the inner RH B flat, through bb.65-8. The pedal may be held through the whole of b.65 with good effect to retain the bass resonance, and thereafter half-pedalled as you *diminuendo* through the next bar or so. Surge up again through the second half of b.68 towards a declamatory crotchet chord on the first beat of b.69. Most pianists hold the sound of this chord within the pedal at least through the first two or three beats of the downward run, and this must be a matter for individual experiment and taste. Feel that you are sweeping up from the crotchet chord to the high F as if in a wide arc, and then shape the inflections of the run expressively and improvisatorially, in a flowing overall line, feeling the curve 'back' up to the B flat on the second beat of b.70, and then slowing as you prepare to turn into b.71. Take great care through bb.71-2. The inner chords must be played with the **RH** so that the LH can phrase the lower smoothly as indicated. Practise the RH alone, 'leaning' on the melody notes, and playing the inner chords at first in a light *staccato* so that you learn the skill of keeping the upper line smooth, changing fingers as necessary. The fingering usually given is not happy for smaller hands, and I suggest the

following ♩♩♩♩ | ♩ ♩ ♩ ♩ | ♩ ♩ ♩ ♩ | When you put hands together

listen acutely to the upper and lower melody lines and to the shifting inner harmonies as you move in anxious *stretto* through b.71, and then draw out expressively through b.72. Linger expressively for an instant on the A flat on the third beat of b.72 as well as through the pause, as you poise yourself for the return of the opening theme. The pedal needs to be managed with the greatest of care through these two bars (see suggested pedalling:

). i.e. changing the

pedal with each **harmony** (as opposed to each **melody**) note. (This creates an acceptable slight overlapping in the melody line.) Then as you slow at the end of b.72, the pedal can be changed on the last two quaver beats, being sure to **hold** the dotted quaver G to preserve the *legato* as you 'lift' up to the upbeat C.

bb.72–101   Many editions and many pianists tie the semiquaver C over the bar line into b.73 to create the former upbeat effect. This, it appears, is not correct, although it seems more logical. The coda is outstandingly beautiful. Listen once more to the placing of the LH F beneath the tied C on the first beat of b.77, and feel that the RH is moving up in a smooth arc to 'merge' into the triplets as the LH 'walks' on, so that this passage 'grows' naturally from b.76. To this end it is effective to play the final statement of the opening theme from b.73 very quietly and to move into the coda in a distant whisper, holding back a little as you start 'from the top' in b.77, and gradually increasing the tempo and the volume of sound (not too much) as you descend, as if the sound is gradually growing nearer. Listen acutely to the subtle chromatic inflections of the triplets as the RH is 'guided' downwards by the gently accelerating LH. Do not be overawed by the impressive displays of the virtuosi here – you are aiming to create an exquisite rainbow of sound, not a demonstration of your finger technique. Allow a little give through the end of b.80, and the first beat of b.81 as you 'regroup' to continue the descent from the second beat of b.81. Broaden the sound a little as you listen to the melodic intervals of the LH from the second beat of b.83, and draw out through the second half of b.84, 'pointing' the 'doubled' RH notes (the upper and lower C's through the third beat, and the E natural on the fourth beat). Feel this RH E natural as an onward leading upbeat into b.85, supported by the implied emphasis on the tied LH upbeat C to b.85. Let the LH go down to a resonant low F on the first beat of b.85, taking care to **hold** the tied upbeat C. **Listen** to the resonance of this tonic pedal point from here, which is 'retaken' in b.89 to last right through to b.97. Then, and this is one of the best moments from among all the Nocturnes, let the inner LH 'lift' up to a resonant inner G flat giving this note a slight emphasis and *tenuto*, and phrase this inner line downwards with the utmost expressiveness as the RH arpeggios billow up to and down from their summits on the first beat of bb.86 and 88 as indicated. Be sure to **hold** the bass F from the first beat of b.85, playing the inner G flat with the thumb, and sliding it smoothly off onto the F on the third beat (even most small hands can manage this). Imagine how a cellist would shape this line right through to b.89. Reach home momentarily on this first beat of b.89 (note the gently emphasised RH quaver F) and then let the RH triplets ease upwards again in the major, accelerating according to your abilities, over the long tonic tied harmony, and gradually reducing the sound to a tinkly shimmer disappearing towards b.97. Keep control of this RH by shaping each curve up to its little 'peak', the F on the second beat of b.89, the A natural on the fourth beat, the C on the second beat of b.90 and so on. On the third beat of b.89 those with small hands can stress the A natural a little with the **RH** to avoid abandoning the bass note. The pedal can then be partially changed through bb.89-92 according to taste and conditions of piano and acoustics, and then, as the sound ascends and diminishes, left on from the middle of b.92 as indicated. Lift the pedal for an instant at the end of b.97, and then play the concluding chords with measured and resonant solemnity. Listen to the smooth treble line of these chords descending from a full-toned upper D flat on the first beat of b.98, and then swell the tone of the tonic chords through to the last bar, spreading the sound generously through the final chord.

Nocturne No. 16 in E flat major
Op. 55 No. 2 (8+)

Many and wondrously at odds are critical opinions of this piece, whose stock seems to have steadily risen from Chopin's day to our own. Niecks talks of the 'monotony of its unrelieved sentimentality' and 'longs to get out of this oppressive atmosphere' (Vol.2, p.265). Even Herbert Weinstock, nearer to our own time, considers its 'simpler and less accomplished' than the F minor, Op.55 No.1, and that it 'lacks distinction and, in the final sense, character' (p.271). But Lennox Berkeley, with his composer's ear, finds this 'one of the most beautiful and flawless in the whole series – a small masterpiece in which technical skill and inspiration go hand in hand' (Walker, p.180). How right he is – even a glance at the strands of melody and intermittent countermelody interwoven with arcs of elaborately inflected arpeggio figuration, more like a third voice than an accompaniment, is enough to activate the musical tastebuds. If you are about to embark on a study of this piece, compare the printed appearance of the richly convoluted lines of its first two pages with, for example, the clean, simple and consistent patterns of those of Op.48, No.2, and you will gain a healthy respect for the task ahead! As Jim Sampson says 'Right from the opening bars the accompaniment figure generates a dissonant counterpoint with the melody' (p.92-3). Try **singing** the melody of the first few bars slowly and rather loudly against the LH arpeggios. As you listen to the effect of each LH note against the voice line, the ear will be astonished by the extraordinary succession of harmonic implications and dissonant intervals. Here, as in the next Nocturne, Op.62 No.1, and the 'extra' Prelude in C sharp minor, Op.45 Chopin seems to be held in some kind of musing, richly improvisatory state of abstraction.

bb.1–4

Study these opening bars with the greatest care. If you thoroughly absorb the rhythmic and melodic flow of either hand, and the interaction of the lines when you put hands together, you will be set fair to cope with the increasing complexities as the music unfolds. We are faced with an immediate ambiguity – the long melody notes B flat and D in b.1 (harmonised through the second half of the bar with a dominant based arpeggio), have an introductory character, as if leading into the true beginning of the melody, over a tonic harmony on the first beat of b.2. When, however, we turn to b.9, and then to b.35, this opening motif appears in a contracted and varied form, neither in an introductory sense, nor even at the beginning of the phrase. As Lennox Berkeley says 'no analysis can explain the natural growth of the melodic line' (Walker, p.180) and indeed the attempt to do so, or to fuss around trying to work out 'matching' phrase lengths, will hamstring our ability to sense and to transmit this natural growth of the contours of the piece. Set a tempo that gives an easy **12/8** swing. There is bound to be a good deal of give and take, but the overall tempo needs to allow the LH arpeggios to provide a continual sense of movement so that the melody lines never begin to stick, but on the other hand, have time to 'point' the expressive inflections of the upper and inner voices. In other words, a balance has to be struck between sounding hurried or plodding. This can vary considerably according to the rhythmic sense and expressive capacities of the performer, but a basic tempo of between ♩. = 60-69 is suggested. First practise the RH alone. The melody lines throughout must be shaped and expressed in a truly vocal sense. Play the opening B flat in a warm, full tone and imagine a vocal 'fall' down on to the grace note C, as you prepare to let the trill 'grow' from this C (placed **on** the third beat of the bar). Feel that you are 'leaning onwards' through the trill (letting this run easily in a full tone, not as an exhibition of speed) towards the tonic dotted crotchet on the first beat of b.2. Phrase the whole of these four bars in a luxuriously smooth, full tone, exactly as a singer would, showing the curve up to the A flat on the second beat of b.2, and then descending to the B natural as if with a slight *portamento*, and feeling this note as an onward-leaning upbeat towards the tied crotchet C on the first beat of b.3. Carry the line on smoothly through b.3, curving up 'through' the crotchet G on the fourth beat, and lingering fractionally on this note, ready to 'fall' expressively towards a warm-toned dotted minim D on the first beat of b.4. **Listen** to the continuing sound of this D so that you can 'tail off' smoothly to the E flat on the third beat ready to start the new phrase on the upbeat to b.5. Practise the LH equally carefully, making a smooth sweep up to and down from the A flat at the end of b.1, and up again to the F at the end of b.2, and so on. It is just as important to shape the curves of the LH in this vocal manner, paying careful attention to the varying shapes of these curves: i.e. noting that through bb.1-3 each one reaches its 'summit' on the last note of the bar, while the shorter curves in b.4 'peak' on the fifth quaver, then on the eleventh and so on. There are many different possibilities for fingering, of course, and every pianist must find those that suit his or her hand. I prefer the use of the thumb on the topmost note of each curve when possible – this helps to give a natural slight definition to the upward curve – and also the use of 5, 5, to define the new (LH) phrase in the middle of b.2. The suggested fingerings given below for bb.1-4 are, I dare to suggest, nearer to Chopin's practice than those given in most editions, and may be helpful in particular to those with smaller hands.

When you put hands together, listen acutely to the relationship between the lines of the two hands, moving predominantly in contrary motion, continuing to shape the LH curves just as carefully as you did when practising hands separately. Have the LH ready to 'meet' the RH on the grace note C in such a way that you immediately establish the easy quaver movement within the overall **12/8** – also, from this opening moment, show the sense in which the 'counterpoint' of these LH waves of sound cushions and buoys along the rich melodic lines of the RH.

bb.4–12   Listen to the continuing onward movement of the LH as you start the new RH phrase on the upbeat to b.5, cleanly 'bringing in' the inner voice with the emphasised upbeat B flat. Practise the upper and inner RH lines carefully, both separately and together, 'pointing' the smooth downward step of the inner line to the syncopated tied minim A flat in b.5, and the eloquent inner fragment

 beneath the smoothly singing upper notes. Be sure to let

the second finger 'lift' from the inner quaver G here (see General Introduction under 'Articulation'). Then take care to give the upper E flat on the first beat of b.6 sufficient tone to sing through its full value, making it clear that the dotted minim G on the second beat belongs to the **inner** line. Then listen to the inner tied G flat on the upbeat to b.7 with its enharmonic change to F sharp as the inner line moves on into the four quavers in cross-rhythm. Allow the LH to 'give' a little through the end of b.7 to accommodate the eight-semiquaver 'turn' but accomplishing this rhythmically, so that you preserve the onward sense of the LH quavers. Feel, as always in such instances, that the RH is fitting in with the LH and **not** the other way around, as you 'space' the eight just-detached semiquavers gracefully and expressively beneath the continuing sound of the upper dotted

minim A natural.  Allow a slight 'hold'

as you come momentarily to rest on the chord of G on the first beat of b.8; then draw out the LH a little as it carries you back towards the tonic at b.9 while the RH concurrently sweeps upwards from the third beat of b.8 to 'meet' the dotted crotchet version of the opening minim motif on the third beat of b.9. While the upper line pursues its varied version of bb.1-4, listen acutely to the infinitely expressive inner interjections

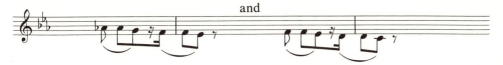

and the longer inner phrase from the 'upbeat' to the fourth beat of b.11.

bb.12–34   'Finish off' the inner phrase cleanly beneath the tied upper E flat on the third beat of b.12, ready to begin anew on the 'doubled' upbeat quaver to b.13. Feel a sense of moving on as you lead into this less complex but rather urgent passage, feeling that you are pressing on (but in a **controlled** manner) as you make a **gradual** crescendo through to the end of b.18. Show the upward sweep of each arpeggio from each resonant bass note. Feel the implied emphasis on the dotted RH minim E flat as you begin a new phrase on the second beat of b.15, and the particular onward 'push' beneath it of the arpeggio beginning on the third beat. Balance the resonance of the LH carefully beneath the 'speaking' repeated A flats as you swell through bb.17-18, drawing out the end of b.18 a little as you 'peak' the *crescendo* through the last beat. Then allow an instant to clear the sound in preparation for a beautiful *subito piano* at b.19. Maintain the sense of onward movement as you ease into this quieter, more tranquil new strain. Expand the tone again as you 'lift' up towards the tied dotted minim G on the third beat of b.22 (shaping the LH once more in a long sweep through b.22) and yet again as you 'lift' towards the high C on the third beat of b.24. *Crescendo* onwards a full toned B flat on the first beat of b.25, and then expand through the second half of the bar as you space out the ten quavers expressively over a resonant LH sweep **rhythmically** drawn out to accommodate the expressive sense of the RH. Linger slightly on the high A flat near the end of the bar so that you can 'fall' eloquently and 'vocally' towards the E flat in b.26. Let the LH carry you on in another smooth, now *diminuendoing* sweep into the next phrase beginning quietly on the upbeat to b.27. Listen acutely once more as the inner voice enters again on the 'upbeat' to the fourth beat of b.30, leading into a marvellously expressive modulatory passage from b.31. Study the treble and inner lines again with great care, making it clear that the inner voice is breaking off and 'coming in again' on the offbeat quaver after the fourth beat of bb.31 and 32. The resonances created here by the held upper and inner notes are extremely complex. Do take care therefore to study these lines slowly and carefully. Note the syncopated placing of the inner minim (E flat) on the third **quaver** pulse of b.31 (and similarly the inner minims in bb.32 and 33). While the grace note figure on the upbeat to b.31, and on these syncopated minims in bb.32 and 33 should, strictly speaking, doubtless be placed **on** the main note (i.e. **on** the fourth crotchet pulse in b.30 and **on** the syncopated minim in bb.32 and 33), there can be no doubt that they sound less rushed and more eloquent when allowed to anticipate the main note. The more slowly you practise bb.31-3 at first, the better you will absorb the sense and interrelation of these two melodic lines. Even in performance most players 'bend' the tempo very considerably through this passage, otherwise this 'speaking' inner line will sound merely flippant.

bb.34–55   Pick up the tempo again a little on the upbeat to b.34, moving on through the second and third beats of this bar as you make a continuous, *crescendoing* chain of trills (feel the movement of the LH 'guiding' the trills here). Then draw out again a little through the last beat as you prepare to play out the further elaborated version of bb.9-12 in a full-throated *fortissimo* from b.35. But beware of banging here, and do not allow the tone to rise beyond a level at which you can control the eloquent shaping of the outer and inner lines paying particular attention to the eloquent articulation of the little flurries of just-detached inner semiquavers from the ninth quaver pulse of bb.35, 36, and 37, and the third quaver of b.38. Hold the *sforzato* chord on the third beat of b.38 for an instant, ready to drop the tone as indicated on the subsequent LH quaver, as you poise yourself to move on through the elaborated version of bb.13-18. Listen to the sweep of the LH through bb.43 and 44, and then take time to 'point' the marvellous harmonic shift as you *diminuendo* and ease onto the G flat major harmony beneath the suspended treble A flat on the first beat of b.45. Take time once more to 'grasp' the emphasised 'upbeat' to the inner downward *forte* cascade from the third beat of b.46. Allow an instant again after the *sforzato* chord on the first beat of b.47 as you prepare to restate the passage from b.13 once more, this time further elaborated, and beginning at the half-bar. Let the little offbeat inner semiquaver figure 'fall' eloquently from the topmost note (A flat in b.48 and B flat in b.50). The Vienna Urtext Edition takes the view that the inner trills at bb.52-5 should begin on the principal note (since they are an elaboration of the inner line from bb.44-6), while the editor of the Paderewski Edition feels that they should begin on the upper note. In the event most pianists will view this as a matter of expediency! The essential is that the chain of trills create as beautiful an effect of shimmering sound as possible. When you start to practise this passage in the RH alone, let the trill run quite slowly and lightly, while 'leaning' on the upper melody notes, so that you get used to the effect of 'leaning' on those 'weaker' outer fingers which play the melody notes while leaving the weightier thumb and forefinger feeling free and light. As you are able to increase the speed of the trill, take care to preserve the sense of freedom in the inner part of the hand, otherwise the trill will grow heavier, the thumb and forefinger will 'jam' and the passage will grind to a halt. When you put hands together feel again that the RH is being 'guided' by the LH as you make a *diminuendo* through b.52, and then gradually *crescendo*, but not overpoweringly, opening out the tone as you finish off the trill up towards the high sixth on the second beat of b.54. Listen to the inner line swelling as indicated as you move on towards the *sforzato* chord on the first beat of b.55.

bb.55–67   Drop the sound again in the LH after the *sforzato* chord as indicated, and as you listen to the overall LH curve beneath the held RH sixth, be conscious at the same time that you are establishing a tonic pedal point which lasts right through to b.63. This coda is pure mystery and magic. Find a new and profoundly contemplative sound as the harmony changes to the minor on the first beat of b.56, and listen again acutely to the LH as you *diminuendo* towards the hushed strange C flat on the first beat of b.57. Continue to feel that the LH is 'guiding' you as you 'arch' smoothly up to the high C flat and on up to the high B flat on the second beat of b.58; and, feeling the sense of the overall curve right through bb.56-9, start 'pearling' the sound downwards in a gradually diminishing haze of sound. Give the upper B flats through bb.59-60 a tiny but penetrating ringing sound, listening particularly to the line of the LH here as you space out the inner groups of five quavers evenly. Take time through b.61 to show how the last quaver of each RH group creates a **descending** line as the **overall** line rises, growing still quieter as you move towards the spread chord on the first beat of b.62. Without an exaggerated pause carry straight on into the phrase of simple chords. Then shade off the arpeggio delicately in contrary motion towards the widely spaced bass and treble dotted crotchets on the first beat of b.64, **listening** to this wide span of quiet sound held in the pedal through the first half of the bar. Playing in time, show the inner LH line as indicated as you *crescendo* towards the dominant seventh on the first beat of b.65, and then end with carefully placed full-toned tonic chords.

Nocturne No. 17 in B major
Op. 62 No. 1 (8+)

Like its companion in spirit, Op.55 No.2, this has had a mixed press. Hardly surprising perhaps, for here Chopin seems to have embarked on some kind of other-worldly voyage, even more abstracted than in the E flat major. Jim Samson talks of a 'carefully guarded private world, distanced from the immediacy of life' (p.94). Who knows how significant were the distressing upheavals of Chopin's last periods at Nohant with Georges Sand, the time of composition of these two last Nocturnes of Op.62. Chopin was not on the face of it a visionary man, yet here he verges on the mystical more closely than either he or many another great composer has, before or since; and a fine performance of this piece is a moving and searching experience for player and listener alike. Little wonder that this profoundly inward-looking, yet at the same time outward-stretching music was meaningless, or even sickening, to generations accustomed to more 'organised' musical procedures. Niecks spoke disparagingly of its 'tender flutings, trills, roulades and syncopations' and found that neither of the pieces of Op.62 interested him 'sufficiently to discuss their merits and demerits' (Vol.2, p.266); while Weinstock says: 'it is a composition to justify Chopin's mostly undeserved reputation for effete or overripe creation. Peculiarly satiated, it is not rescued from unpleasant pallor by its coloratura vocalising, or its famous – and very difficult – chain of trills' and considers that 'the whole is feverish, self-pitying, and less than ingratiating' (p.283). Even today it is seldom played. Perhaps we still find this Chopin hard to take, so far removed from the Chopin of the Salons, or the Polish patriot that we think we know and love.

bb.1–10   Play the wide-spread broken chord in a full tone, spreading the notes evenly and almost deliberately up to the high E, as if to announce that something important is to come. Allow time to **listen** to the reverberation of this harmony before shading the sound down to the dominant seventh in b.2, and allow plenty of time again for the sound to come to rest here. Obviously the timing of these introductory chords is 'free' although you need to have your overall tempo **in mind** as you play them. Then feel your 'real' tempo through the half-bar rest, so that you are poised to enter, straightaway in time, in an easy-moving *andante*. Think of a leisurely but 'moving' stroll, one stride to the crotchet pulse – too slow and these bars, which have a deceptive innocence and simplicity, will sound laboured; too fast and the detail, particularly from bb.12-14, will sound scrambled. A basic tempo of around ♩ = 72-84 is suggested, allowing for a considerable degree of rhythmic give and take through the curving phrases, and varying episodes of the piece. Let the four solo quavers 'usher in' the melody in a sweet-toned *legato* as indicated. Shape the treble line in smooth curves, letting the quavers 'fall' in a little dip from the first quaver B. Then feel the smooth 'lift' up to the crotchet D sharp on the first beat of b.4, curving downwards again through this bar, with another smooth lift up to the three 'speaking' crotchet F sharps in b.5, and so on. Editions vary considerably in the phrasing of this opening – some, as in Henle and the Vienna Urtext Edition, break the phrase in the middle of b.4, while the Paderewski Edition carries the phrase right over from b.3 to the middle of b.8; (the Vienna Urtext also breaks the phrase again in the middle of b.7). In view of Chopin's overlapping phrase endings and beginnings, and the complex relation of the upper and inner lines from b.10 onwards, it is counterproductive to be dogmatic – the important thing is that the interrelating strands of melody flow onwards to b.21 in a continuing stream of evolving sound. If you **sing** the upper line, you will soon discover how to shape it. You will feel the gentle impulse of the first four quavers towards the first beat of b.4 and the further, still gentle impulse towards the last of the three crotchet F sharps on the third beat of b.5, and then a slight unwinding through b.6 ready to 'start again' from b.7. You will also understand far better than by playing it, or by theorising about it, how to 'overlap' the phrases as Chopin ends the first statement of his melody while simultaneously beginning the second with the four-quaver motif at the beginning of b.7. It goes without saying that these impulses, overlappings, etc. are all fine nuances of which we need to be aware (rather than points to be laboured) within the smooth ongoing movement of the whole. Study the inner RH, and the LH just as carefully. Listen to the smooth upward sweep of the LH as it rises to 'meet' the RH on the second beat of b.4 with its quietly 'pointed' 'doubled' notes, B, F sharp, C sharp and F sharp. Listen also to the subtle toying with the B sharp and B natural in the LH through b.5, and take time also to listen acutely to the tied and held inner resonances of what we expect to be cadential chords at bb.6-7, but which in fact lead us on, as we have seen, into the varied restatement of the first phrase. Again in b.10, while we have in one sense a clear perfect cadence, the RH voices are at the same time drawing us on into a new train of thought from b.11 – incorporating nevertheless, inner echoes of the opening motif.

Allow time to spread the crotchet octave gracefully on the first beat of b.4 as you 'lift' towards the D sharp; and to articulate the spread third on the fourth beat of this bar, playing

the acciaccatura unhurriedly thus:  Similarly take time to 'lift'

smoothly through the spread chord on the first beat of b.5, the third beat of b.8, etc. towards a quietly singing upper F sharp (placing the lower note **on** the beat – see General Introduction under 'Ornaments'). The acciaccatura in b.8 is more expressive when allowed slightly to anticipate the beat.

bb.10–19   Practise the two RH voices carefully from b.10, feeling the sense of the onward lead into b.11 as you make a little swell up towards a gentle, syncopating

'lean' on the RH crotchet sixth ![notation] lingering fractionally here ready to

move easily onwards from the 'staggered' LH and RH upbeats. Then show clearly the entry of the new melodic fragment on the quaver D sharp 'upbeat' to the third beat of b.11.

![notation] Follow the inner line just as expressively, feeling the implied

slight emphasis on the syncopated crotchet G sharp on the sixth quaver pulse of b.11, and then curve up to, and on through the expressive fragments from the beginning of b.12.

![notation] Allow the LH and inner voices to 'give' a little

so that you can shape the treble grace note turn expressively up to the dotted crotchet F sharp on the fourth beat of b.12. Then feel a sense of onward movement towards a slight *tenuto* on the octave F sharp on the sixth quaver pulse of b.13. Imagine a slight *portamento* from this high crotchet F sharp down to the F double sharp on the fourth beat and allow time to negotiate the semiquaver intervals gracefully, even sentimentally, as you *diminuendo* down towards the third beat of b.14. As the upper melody comes to rest momentarily on this crotchet F sharp, feel at the same time the onward impulse of the inner and lower parts, ready for the melody to move on from the upbeat to b.15 in a simple, more easy-walking manner. Go up to a clear, singing tied G sharp on the second beat of b.15, and then shape this phrase smoothly down towards the last beat of b.16. 'Retake' the melody line clearly on the first beat of b.17 (some editions 'retake' this phrase on the upbeat, i.e. on the last chord of b.16). From this point, within a simple, rocking, onward-going quaver movement beneath an apparently ingenuous treble melody, we seem to be sliding unnervingly (over a D sharp pedal point which continues through from bb.17-28) as if a mind is 'losing itself', towards the strange interlude from b.21.

(Note the quaver figure through the second half of bb.17 and 19

anticipating the semiquaver motif from the end of b.21.) 'Point' the warning clash of the LH C double sharp and RH E on the sixth quaver pulse of b.18, and then show the implied emphasis on the tied treble upbeat (B) to b.19 – it is from here that this 'slide' becomes more inevitable.

bb.19–36   Curve the line smoothly from this tied B up to the D sharp on the second beat of b.19, and then let the line 'curl' down towards the quaver chord on the first beat of b.21. Some players make a pronounced *diminuendo* **and** *rallentando* towards b.21. I find it infinitely more telling to *diminuendo* and, with only a slight 'give', if any, at the end of b.20, to let the LH go straight on to 'point' quietly the syncopated crotchet A, followed by a similarly 'pointed' treble crotchet A, with virtually no break in the movement. Place both these A's (and particularly the treble) with infinite care, with a soft, faraway, yet penetrating sound, and then shade the treble semiquaver line downwards in a delicate haze of sound over the quietly and smoothly syncopated LH, also listening acutely to the sharp LH minim seventh beneath the tied A, and then to the changing harmonies of the LH minim chords. Always show the tiny implied emphasis on the syncopated crotchets within the quiet resonance of the minim chords. *Diminuendo* to a whisper at b.23, rising again to the slightly emphasised A on the second beat, and allowing the LH to 'bend' a little to accommodate the subtle treble ornamentation. Then play the little dying fragment (bb.25-6) with the greatest delicacy, and, having 'pointed' the syncopated inner crotchet A in b.26 with a fractionally stronger emphasis, burst into the astonishingly *forte* explosion with all the resonance you can muster. The exact spacing of the notes of the run cannot, of course, be laid down, and will vary from performance to performance. Study the shape of the LH, shaping the curve up from the resonant chord on the third beat of the bar towards the F sharp on the fourth beat, and then 'drawing out' towards the powerful D sharp minor chord on the first beat of b.27. Then, realising that the scale is simply F sharp major, (i.e. starting on the fourth note of the scale and 'peaking' on the high E sharp) feel that you are fitting the scale to the shape of the LH, and **not** the other way around. Make the scale as brilliant as possible, feeling a crescendo to the top note which you will hope to reach just before the LH quaver F sharp, and plunging down to a huge toned A sharp on the first beat of b.27. If you preserve the shape of the LH, drawing out through the end of the bar as required, you will find that it is amazing how the RH will obey the impulse of the LH and arrive in one piece on the A sharp. The effect of this passage is indescribable, as if a vast water-chute of Edgar Allan Poe-ish proportions suddenly erupts and then subsides without disturbing the glassy calm of some strange, disembodied expanse of water. Collect yourself as you listen to the reverberations of this D sharp minor chord, **feeling** the main beats of the bar (i.e. avoiding an exaggerated pause) so that you preserve this curious sense of undisturbed continuity as you lead on into b.28. 'Space' this triplet upbeat tellingly up towards a warm-toned tied minim D on the first beat of b.28. **Feel** the beats once more through this hovering attenuation of the opening motif before carrying on into the shortened reprise. Though the melody proceeds much as before from the second half of b.29, neither the playing nor the hearing of it can be unaffected by what has come before. Draw out through b.34 towards the further attenuation as you pause on a resonant dominant seventh harmony on the third beat. 'Walk on' again from b.35, and then allow a little extra time through b.36 as you prepare to ease into the new section.

bb.36–67   Once again some editions phrase the RH chord on the fourth beat of b.36 as the upbeat to b.37. In any event, show the implied onward-leaning emphasis on the LH tied upbeat as you prepare to launch into the immense span of melody which rolls on from here to b.67. Some players may like to bring in this melody quietly, almost mysteriously, while others may launch in with a full tone, giving bb.37-43 a broad swing with a tinge almost of vulgarity. Since there is no dynamic marking, and since Chopin's *sostenuto* can apply in either a quiet or a full tone, there is scope for either view. In any event there is a definite sense of moving on, with an overall feeling of 2-in-the-bar. If you **sing** the melody you will have no difficulty in phrasing it convincingly. Show the continual onward nudge of the implied (or indicated) syncopated emphases in the LH on the crotchets on the second and sixth quaver pulses of b.37, and on the slurred LH quaver upbeat to b.38 and b.39, and so on. (The slur over the crotchet fifths in b.37 and over the crotchet and quaver chords in bb.39, 40, etc. is not a tie. It indicates that special just-detached style of playing such accompanying chords, giving an even, little 'push' on each.)

Show the broad curve of the melody from the third beat of b.39 up to the high F in b.40, and down, as if with a *portamento* to the low minim E flat on the first beat of b.41. Take a little extra time to curve expressively up to and 'through' the high G on the fourth beat of b.43, and to show the implied emphasis on the tied quaver upbeat to b.44, while also listening to the resonance of the inner minim chords, and the lower syncopated emphasised E flat crotchets. Make a little *tenuto* on the minim F through the second beat of b.44, ready to *diminuendo* towards the first beat of b.45, and allow an extra instant to listen to the chromatic upward movement of the upbeat LH quaver to the first beat of b.45. Feel you are starting anew here (though without breaking the overall flow) as you begin a gradual *crescendo*. There is an increasing sense of *agitato* as the LH syncopated chords push onwards in an implied *accellerando*. 'Hold' the ending of the trill slightly as you clear the sound into the *dolcissimo* at the beginning of b.51, and then move on again as you *crescendo* through the enharmonically inflected trill into b.53. Play from b.53 in a warm-voiced *forte*, and 'point' the line of the inner LH, and the bass melodic fragments through bb.53-6. *Diminuendo* gradually from b.57, and shape the bass fragment expressively across the barline (bb.58-9). Slightly mark the 'warning' LH chord on the third beat of b.60, and go on to 'lean' expressively on the appoggiatura-like minim D natural on the first beat of b.61 as Chopin 'stops' the melody here, preparatory to veering into a new, plaintively abstracted passage from the upbeat to b.62. This is a delicate moment. Shape the upward sweep of the LH smoothly through b.61 towards the crotchet on the fourth beat (delicately 'pointing' the LH C flat en route) while **listening** to the resolution of the RH D natural to the crotchet E flat on the offbeat in careful synchronisation with the LH quaver G, before leading on with a *pianissimo* RH quaver upbeat. Similarly shape the LH carefully through each of bb.62-5, as the *pianissimo* treble melody curves waywardly above, finally coming to rest on the spread E flat major chord at b.67.

bb.67–75 The chain of trills and arabesques from b.67 growing, so it seems, from thin air – although it is, of course, a richly decorated reprise of the opening melody – is one of the most ravishing effects Chopin, or any other composer, can ever have conjured. Leave the sound of the spread E flat chord within the pedal, and go straight on to 'lean' into the trill – the pause is **on** and through the trill, not before it. Allow plenty of time therefore to let the sound of the trill billow and swell gently as you prepare to deliver a quietly resonant F sharp with the LH on the first beat of b.68. Of course, to bring off this passage with beautiful effect is a formidable test of artistry and what I should prefer to call keyboard sophistication rather than mere technique. However, if players will only treat the trills as embellishments at the service of the melodic and rhythmic shape of the music rather than as ends in themselves (as relatively inexperienced players invariably do in such circumstances) the passage becomes less formidable than it may at first seem. Above all, let the carefully shaped LH 'guide' you. Practise it thoroughly alone then. 'Lean' well on the long F sharp on the first beat of b.68, giving this note plenty of time, and let the line 'fall' through the two quavers ready to take the crotchet E on the first beat of b.69 with the RH. Initiate your *poco* *più lento* from the beginning of b.69. It is the LH not the RH which will 'find' the right tempo. So allow time to listen to every detail as you make a smooth wide curve up from the low F sharp through the 'doubled' F sharp to the high crotchet E, back down to the low B and up again to the high octave F sharp, then listening to the intervals (octave, fifth and third) moving inward in contrary motion, and so on. Of course, your tempo will 'bend' a certain amount to accommodate the lift of the RH up to the third beat of bb.69 and 70, and through the long run in b.71 and so on, but if your *tempo primo* was about ♩ = 72-80 it is likely to settle at about ♩ = 50-2 here (i.e. approximately a third slower than *tempo primo*). It is clear from the appoggiaturas that Chopin intended the trills to start on the **main** note, (see also Introduction, p.29) and also that the first note of the appoggiatura grace note figure on the third beat of bb.69, 70, etc. should coincide with the relevant LH note.† Obviously the fingering must be a personal matter. My own preferred fingering is

(which is also, in most particulars, given in the Paderewski Edition). It seems less disturbing to the evenness of the trills to retain the 3 2 3 2 fingering from the upbeat quaver (B) and through the first quaver of b.69, while taking the lower E on the first beat of b.69 with the thumb. I also find that the continuous use of the thumbs on the appoggiaturas through the descending chains gives the intended bell-like sound to the main notes – in effect

†J. Petrie Dunn (p.25) gives a clear overall interpretation of this chain of trills (reproduced here with **his** fingerings):

The essential is to aim for the most continuous shimmer of beautiful sound that you can possibly accomplish rather than worrying about the precise placing of every note in a mathematical sense. Everyone's idea of this beautiful effect will vary, and will and should vary from day to day. Take time to spread the LH quaver chords gracefully in b.71, and draw out the long run a little in a *diminuendo*-ing *frisson*, timing it so that the top of the curve, i.e. the highest B, coincides approximately with the last LH quaver G sharp. You can then 'fall' in a liquid *diminuendo* from this high B to another 'bell-like' C sharp on the first beat of b.72. (I suggest

this fingering  as being more Chopinesque

than that given in most editions.) Be sure that the LH maintains its smooth poise beneath this run, rising in a smooth curve up from the bass E on the third beat of b.71, through its high E and down again towards the bass F sharp on the first beat of b.72, as in an overall arc. As always in such instances, feel that the LH, though 'giving' a little to accommodate the run, is 'guiding' the RH, and **not** the other way about (see General Introduction under ''Free' Runs'). If you think of the run in two groups of seven notes and two of eight, the RH will fit with the LH approximately thus:

Draw out the first beat of b.73 a little to allow the grace note turn to begin just **after** the LH octave on the second quaver pulse, and 'curl' these three turns with the utmost delicacy through the second, third and fourth quaver beats. 'Fade out' the trill to a whisper through the second half of b.74 as you prepare for the magical, almost Beethovenian *pianissimo* shift to the dominant seventh of G major in b.75. Allow time to register this transition as you draw out this bar in the finest thread of sound towards and **through** the silent pause.

bb.76–95   Shape the chordal modulatory passage from b.76 in a free improvisatory manner, but within the **sense** of the *tempo primo*. Listen acutely (but without wallowing) to the marvellous complexity and subtlety of the harmonic inflections as you descend through b.76, turn the corner and climb again from the second quaver pulse of b.77 with increasing urgency towards the climactic spread chord on the fourth beat of b.79. Hold this chord for an instant and then let the phrase gradually unwind with a sense of inevitability, towards 'home' on the first beat of b.81. This coda is, of course, an expansion of the strange interlude from bb.21-7, this time suspended over a tonic pedal point. As at b.21, my own preference is for only a very slight 'give' after the tonic chord on the first beat of b.81, so that you go almost straight on to the quietly emphasised LH crotchet F sharp, to establish the smooth on-going syncopated movement. As before, shade the RH line down in a veiled *legatissimo* from the slightly emphasised high dotted quaver, and up again through b.83 towards the high semiquaver D sharp in b.84, 'curling' the intervals en route through the third beat of b.83. Dip smoothly down through the end of b.84, to ascend again in a quieter whisper as if through an additional film of veiling towards a distant *pianissimo* yet penetrating dotted quaver B on the second beat of b.85. Note Chopin's revealing fingering given in Henle and the Vienna Urtext Edition as you descend through b.84, and ascend

in b.85.  This whole passage,

from b.81, is of surpassing, other-wordly beauty. Here indeed Chopin was not within his elegantly clad person in Paris, Nohant, or anywhere else, but in some strange outer space. The only keyboard music to which I can liken it, however removed in time and climate, is Scarlatti's Sonata Kp.208 in which the chromatic wanderings of the treble line are similarly abstruse and mesmeric. From the second 'rise' to the B on the second beat of b.85, the chromatic inflections curl downwards and up again in a haze of increasing incorporeality, each bar bathed in 'a halo of pedal' (to look forward to a favourite direction of Poulenc). Come to rest on the tonic at b.89, and then spin out the increasingly tenuous line in a gradual *calando*, 'pointing' the syncopated inner LH crotchet G sharp in b.90. Play the final bars with simple solemnity, sounding the D sharps like a continuing quiet bell, and drawing out the penultimate bar a little towards the final tonic.

Nocturne No. 18 in E major
Op. 62 No. 2 (8+)

This is an 'easier' work than the previous two numbers, in the sense that it has on the face of it a more formal (as opposed to evolving) type of structure. In addition, it is less abstracted, less rapt, and more immediate. It is nevertheless a difficult piece to bring off successfully – the sections do not evolve with that sense of natural progression which makes for 'easy' interpretation and the 'joins', as we shall see below, must be negotiated with skill and sensitivity. Through the first 32 bars the broad, sustained principal melody (bb.1-8) is varied and developed to beautiful effect in three further 8-bar sections. From b.32 the melody moves into a new phase over a running semiquaver counterpoint, which in turn leads into an *agitato* central section at b.40. The problem here is that if you move on the tempo, as the inner syncopated quaver motion allied to the indication *agitato* suggests, the effect of the chromatic inflections of each voice tend to become submerged amid a general clatter. Since general clatter is not condusive to a sensation of *agitato*, many pianists temper the indicated *forte* and set off at b.40 comparatively quietly and, while giving the illusion of 'moving on', do not in fact do so (and this involves considerable skill).

bb.1–8 Like several of the other Nocturnes, this needs an onward 'walking' tempo, imagining an easy stride to each crotchet pulse, just a little broader, perhaps (but only a little) than that of Op.55 No.1 at about ♩ = 80-92. The laboured 'sticking' tempo adopted by some players in the effort to sound expressive, acts like a tournequet on the pulse-flow. In addition, at too slow a tempo Chopin's exquisitely fluid arabesques and roulades, which grow so felicitously from the melody and its supporting harmonies, sound instead like dutifully stuck-on decorative encrustations. First **sing** the melody and absorb the shape of bb.1-8: the strong, onward leading crotchet upbeat, the curve up to and down from the E on the fourth beat of b.1, the dip down to the first beat of b.3, and the swell up to the minim C on the first beat of b.4. If you negotiate this phrase in one breath, and then take a breath between each subsequent fragment, on the quaver rest in bb.4, 5 and 6, you will soon learn how to express the overall line of these eight bars. When you play the melody, give it a sustained singing tone, being sure to give the longer note on the first beat of bb.1-4 sufficient tone to 'carry through' its full value. Then practise the LH alone, scrupulously shaping the slurred chords in bb.1, 2, 5, etc. When you put hands together, balance the sound of the LH carefully with the RH melody. Notice how the LH buoys along the RH with the implied emphasis on the slurred chord on the second beat of bb.1 and 2 beneath the held melody note (showing particularly the upper thumb-line C sharp-B in b.1) and then feel the 'onward walking' impulse of the bass octaves and upper chords through bb.3-4 etc. Feel the particular importance of the LH on the **third** beat of bb.4, 5 and 6 beneath the RH quaver rest. In b.4 this bass octave on the third beat 'pre-supports' the implied little emphasis on the syncopated RH crotchet C sharp immediately following it; in b.5 the diminished seventh interval with its inner minim resonance similarly underpins the entry of the offbeat RH fragment, and in b.6 the bass D sharp gives a little onward 'push' towards the entry of the RH on the offbeat quaver A sharp. Shape these RH upbeat quavers to b.7 expressively up to the A natural, and then feel the onward movement of this longer fragment towards the warm-toned minim E on the first beat of b.8. Practise these first eight bars over and over until you have absorbed their rhythmic, melodic and harmonic shape, and the natural slight give and take within the overall phrase.

bb.8–32   As you 'finish off' this RH phrase, shading the long E over to the quaver D sharp on the third beat of b.8, feel at the same time the implied emphasis on the LH minim B and slurred G sharp on the second beat, giving an onward impetus into the next phrase. The Vienna Urtext Edition overlaps the ending of the previous phrase and the beginning of the next on this quaver D sharp, an effect I prefer to the usual phrase-change here, as it suggests the onward lift from the lower to the upper D sharp, carrying the line 'up, over and on' into the next phrase. In any event draw out fractionally as you 'lift' and swell up to the dotted quaver D sharp and on into b.9. Allow a fractional 'give' in the LH again to accommodate the delicate, airy *dolce* RH ornamentation in the second half of b.9, and then feel the onward 'push' of the slurred LH octave B sharp on the upbeat to b.11. Expand the tone from the LH octave on the third beat of b.12 through to b.15, listening to the downward march of the LH octaves, and taking time to spread the LH chords generously through the second half of b.14 as you listen to the broad-toned, wide-spanning intervals in the RH. Rise from the quaver C sharp on the fourth beat of b.14 with an expansive swing over the semiquaver rest feeling the semiquaver G sharp as a strong, ongoing upbeat towards a ringing crotchet G sharp on the first beat of b.15. Let the line 'arc' onwards down the interval of a ninth to an emphasised tied crotchet F sharp on the second beat and then ease off the phrase in an expressive *diminuendo*. From b.17 Chopin embarks on a short sequential 'development' of the principal motif of bb.1-2. Beginning quietly, and perhaps a little questioningly through bb.17-18, take a breath on the crotchet rest at the end of b.18 and savour the rich modulatory inflections as the LH marches magnificently downwards in *crescendo* towards a resonant dominant octave on the first beat of b.22. Then draw out the curve of the LH phrase through b.22 as you *crescendo* towards a powerful RH high crotchet G and bass B on the first beat of b.23 (placing the acciaccatura **on** the beat). Bb.23-4 need careful study. Place the LH sixth resonantly on the second beat of b.23 beneath the tied RH G, and then as the RH plunges down to a powerful ornamented quaver G natural on the third beat, balance it with a resonant LH diminished fifth, clearly showing the sense of the 'crossed' lines here. Then, keeping up the full tone, 'flick' the RH semiquavers back up to the detached quaver G, 'braking' this fourth beat for an instant as you **lift** the RH so that it 'falls' naturally onto the slurred semiquaver upbeat A sharp, which in turn 'leans' on towards carrying unison B's on the first beat of b.24. 'Fill out' the sound of the RH *sforzato* minim with a resonant LH sixth on the second beat of b.24 and then *diminuendo* as you ease back into the further elaborated version of the opening melody from b.25. Play the run through the second half of b.25 as if tossing a delicious spray of droplets into the air to fall with the utmost delicacy towards a quiet but warm-toned minim B on the first beat of b.25. This run lies beautifully under the hand, and there is no cause for panic if you treat this bar for exactly what it is, an attenuated version of b.1. Shape the LH exactly as in b.1, but just 'drawing out' the fourth beat a little to accommodate the gentle fall of the RH through the end of the bar. Let the RH 'meet' this LH chord just after 'turning the corner' at the top of the run (see General Introduction under ''Free' Runs').

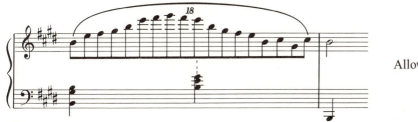

Allow an extra

instant to 'point' the hushed, interrupted cadence (bb.26-7), and then move on as you *crescendo* through bb.29-30, supporting the RH with resonant LH octaves and chords. Draw out once more through the second beat of b.31 to accommodate this more vigorous RH roulade, letting the RH cascade down towards a full-toned trill on the dominant on the third beat. Allow time to 'finish off' cleanly to a quiet tonic on the first beat of b.32.

bb.32–40   Practise the LH carefully from here, shaping each fragment smoothly up to and down from its highest point – up to the A on the fourth beat of bb.32 and 33, and then up to the quaver G on the third beat of b.34. Then listen to the long 'curl' of the LH up from the C sharp on the sixth quaver pulse of b.34, and then down through b.35 beneath the tied inner minim A towards the low E on the first beat of b.36, and so on. Phrase the RH in a quiet, but luxuriantly expressive tone, being sure to give the long melodic chords (e.g. on the first beat of bb.33 and 34) sufficient resonance to sing through their full value. The sense of 'moving on' from b.32 is illusory – occasioned by the transition of the LH into the gently running semiquavers. The overall pulse does not quicken, if anything it eases a little, for this is a quietly moving, musing passage, the LH semiquaver movement expansively meandering rather than 'busy'. When you put hands together, practise from the second half of b.31, allowing a little give at the end of the bar as described, and learning to make a convincing 'join' as the LH eases smoothly into the new semiquaver pattern. Maintain the curves in the LH which you have already practised in solo as you bring in the RH on the upbeat to b.33, letting the upbeat figure 'go to' a warm-toned chord on the first beat of b.33. Then feel the little swell towards and back from the next sustained chord on the first beat of b.34. Then feel the 'lift' from the end of b.34 up to a singing crotchet C sharp on the first beat of b.35. 'Finish off' the slurred RH quaver sixths gracefully through the first beat of b.36 ready to 'carry on anew' in the RH with a smooth offbeat entry. Enter with a quietly resonant RH dotted crotchet E on the sixth quaver pulse, then swell up towards an expressive, singing chord on the first beat of b.37, and feel that you are continuing the swell up to, and through the F sharp on the second beat before curving smoothly down again. Interpret the spread chord on the first beat

of b.38 thus:  placing the B sharp on the beat to coincide with

the LH semiquaver G sharp and with a 'lean' – as in an appoggiatura effect on the F double sharp. (Alternatively, and perhaps more expressively, the F double sharp could be placed before

the chord as suggested for the chord on the first beat of b.76.)

Then feel that the music is gathering momentum as you phrase the alternating LH-RH fragments in an overall *crescendo* towards the third beat of b.39. Allow a slight 'vocal' hold on this semiquaver A and **listen** to the intervals of the downward curving semiquavers so that you are poised to launch into the *agitato* section in a controlled manner rather than 'falling into' it.

bb.40–60   'Hold' the semiquaver E for an instant on the first beat of b.40, to 'establish' the first note of your melody line, thereby fractionally delaying the entry of the inner syncopated thirds. When you practise the RH alone 'bring out' the melody line resonantly while keeping the inner syncopated line extra quiet so that you get used to the sensation of 'leaning' on the melody notes with the 'weaker' fingers, avoiding swamping the line with the continuously syncopated inner quavers played by the 'stronger' fingers. Practise the LH line with equal care, shaping the curves as smoothly as possible and showing the emphasis on the syncopated quavers in bb.44 and 45. Then play the treble and bass lines together **without** the inner syncopated parts so that you thoroughly absorb their separate but interrelating movement. (You will also experience some aural surprises!) When you finally put all the parts together, assiduous slow practice will be required, **listening** acutely to the balance between the upper and lower lines and the onward propelling but never swamping inner syncopated lines. As you increase the tempo, practise the 'join' carefully between bb.39-40 as at bb.31-2. Again, as we have seen, the change at b.40 is one of mood rather than tempo. And also, as already said, take care not to start too loud, or you will steam-roller the sense of *agitato*, and in addition leave yourself no 'room' to *crescendo*. 'Point' the phrasing nuances of the treble line through bb.40-1 and 42-3 while at the same time showing the swell of the overall phrase 'reaching' on up towards the last crotchet of b.41 (B natural), then 'starting again' from b.42 in a higher dynamic, and reaching on up towards the end of b.43. Also 'point' the lower LH fragment from the second beat of b.42 as it overlaps with and echoes

the treble motif. [music notation] Then feel the change to a kind of

'busyness' at b.44 (as opposed to the 'reaching onwards' from bb.40-3) as the LH pattern changes – taking time to show the expressive LH semiquaver fragment through the second half of the bar. Then as you *diminuendo* from the second half of b.45, there is a smooth sliding sensation as if the reiterated semiquaver figures are 'falling away', almost out of control. 'Take hold' of tempo again as you 'point' the mysterious interrupted cadence at bb.46-7, and then gather momentum again through bb.47-8, as at bb.38-9, ready to launch into the restatement of this *agitato* passage in a higher register. In b.48 sweep the LH semiquaver line smoothly upwards into the RH, as indicated by the wide arc of the phrase line. Then from the second half of the bar listen to the strong inward contrary motion movement of the hands towards b.49, taking time to register the astonishing intervals, and poising yourself as you *crescendo* through the LH upbeat trill so that you don't 'fall into' b.49. At the beginning of b.49, in view of the increased inner density of the texture you need to take even greater care to 'establish' a firm treble line than at b.40. *Decrescendo* through bb.54-5 towards a hushed *pianissimo* at b.56. Then once again practise the 'join' carefully as you swell and diminuendo through the semiquaver curve through b.57 in a leisurely *ritenuto*, and ease back towards the reprise at b.58.

bb.60–81   Take an extra instant to 'point' the *pianissimo* LH octave A beneath the held RH F sharp on the first beat of b.60. *Crescendo* purposefully from b.62 towards a radiant-toned chord on the second beat of b.65, taking time to 'spread' the grace note arpeggio expansively upwards towards a ringing dotted quaver G sharp letting the acciaccatura

G sharp coincide with the LH chord.  Carry the full tone

through into b.66, 'holding' the dotted crotchet on the first beat for an extra instant, and then let the quaver line 'dissolve' into b.67. Let the triplets curve in improvisatory arcs through bb.68-9, balanced by steady LH chords and then poise yourself through the second half of b.69 to move smoothly into b.70 as at bb.31-2.* Take time to 'point' the elaboration in this passage, giving it a more lingering, extemporary feeling than at its previous appearance from b.32. Execute the appoggiatura and spread chord on the first beat of

b.76 thus   'leaning' and lingering a little on the appoggiatura B.

Then allow time to listen to the beautiful overall progressions through b.77, and particularly to the inflections of the LH. Linger a little on the syncopated treble quaver C sharp near the end of this bar, and then make a *portamento*-like 'fall' down the interval of a seventh, ready to lean expressively on the appoggiatura-like spread fifth on the first beat of b.78. **Listen** to the Mahlerian resolution of the leading note onto the 'doubled tonic' on the fourth **quaver** pulse of the bar as the semiquavers curve up from the bass E in a carefully shaded *diminuendo* towards the high crotchet G sharp on the first beat of b.79. Play the final sequence with

---

*In the copy belonging to Chopin's pupil Camille O'Meara/Dubois Chopin wrote 8va‾ over the G sharp on the last beat of b.68. The Vienna Urtext suggests the following variant descending from this high G sharp.

thoughtful simplicity. Feel the quiet impulse of the 'speaking' repeated crotchet B's towards the tied crotchet on the first beat of b.80, balancing the spread chord carefully on the second beat beneath this held B and then **listening** to the beautifully drawn-out preparation for the 'fall' of the treble line towards the final tonic. Show the inner resonance of the LH minim E through the second half of b.80, and then listen to the resolution of the inner RH C sharp to the dotted minim B on the second beat of the final bar within the sustained overall tonic harmony.

Nocturne No. 19 in E minor
Op.posth. 72 No. 1 (7)

In his three last Nocturnes, particularly Op.55 No.2 and Op.62 No.1, Chopin was reaching towards strange and distant horizons. Here we are very much on home ground, and this is an excellent piece for relatively inexperienced players. Thought to have been composed between 1828 and 1830 it is the first of the Nocturnes, so far as is known.† But already there are, to quote Jim Samson 'indications of a new approach to melody and ornamentation. The successive ornamental variations of the opening idea are less concerned to dress it with fancy frills than to enhance and intensify its expressive qualities, and to reveal it in constantly changing lights.' (pp.41-2). A flowing RH melody line is supported and buoyed along by a continuously curving triplet accompaniment. It is important to understand that the successful shaping of the expressive RH melody line is entirely dependent on these supporting waves of sound in the LH. This LH must be therefore practised assiduously on its own until its shape and harmonic sense are thoroughly absorbed.

bb.1–5 · There is doubt as to the authenticity of the metronome mark ♩ = 69 given in Henle and the Paderewski Edition. However, this gives a pleasant 'walking' tempo, though a slightly slower pace will suffice providing the LH triplets always maintain a sense of onward movement. As Lennox Berkeley has pointed out, 'the LH triplets are given a greater intensity than usual by the fact that the middle note of the second and fourth triplets continually form an *appoggiatura* to the harmony.' (Walker, p.172). This appoggiatura note (i.e. C through bb.1-4), is also, of course, the topmost note of each 2-beat curve. Practise the shape carefully therefore through bb.1-4, curving up from each bass note, 'through' this appoggiatura note, and down to the next bass note. This creates continuing waves of sound through each bar, giving the sense of an overall 2-in-the-bar movement. Then feel the different shape of the LH through b.5 as it rises to the high B on the third quaver, and then dips right down again ready to lead on through the last beat into b.6. When you practise the RH, let the acciaccatura 'speak' (on the beat) as you 'lift' up towards the opening long G. **Listen** to the sound of this G through its full duration so that you learn how much tone it needs to sing through these three beats. Then feel the two quavers F sharp and E as the **upbeat** to another singing long note D sharp. Similarly feel the dotted rhythm figure as the upbeat to b.4, lingering expressively for an instant on the dotted quaver while at the same time feeling its onward 'lean', ready to 'go to' a warm-toned dotted crotchet B on the first beat of b.4. Then feeling the quaver F as the 'upbeat' to the third beat, 'lift' up to the quaver third on this third beat and let the line 'fall' smoothly towards b.5. Play the crotchet thirds in b.5 in an ultra-smooth, horn-like *legato*, feeling the indicated slight 'push' on the second beat and then 'tailing off' cleanly to the quaver third on the third beat. As you play this 4-bar melody absorb the sense of its overall span falling

†This was edited by Chopin's friend Julius Fontana, and published in 1855, along with Ops. posth.66-73. Numerous textural differences, and variants in directions for tempo and dynamics occur in different editions. As elsewhere (in general) I have used the Henle Edition, but see also the Vienna Urtext and Paderewski Editions.

from the high G in b.2 down to the F sharp in b.5. Then **sing** the RH while playing the LH, listening closely to the effect of the LH 'counterpoint' – so much more than a mere accompaniment – and your ear will immediately understand how the hands interrelate and complement each other. As you **sing**, absorb the expressive sense of the cross-rhythm through the upbeat to b.3, and again as the RH thirds 'fall' through the second half of b.4 (realising that the RH single quaver F sharp in this bar – frequently mis-read as a triplet – is also in cross-rhythm with the LH).

When you put hands together, practise these first bars over and over shaping the melody in this 'vocal' manner, until you have thoroughly absorbed the fundamental shape and motion of the phrase. Listen to the way that the curve of the LH fills out the sound, and maintains the sense of onward movement beneath the long melody notes in bb.2-4. Then show the new shape of the LH through b.5 as already described. Note the pedal indications: the long pedal through b.1 and b.2 and the precise markings through bb.3-5. The predominating pedal indications throughout the piece are for two pedals per bar (see bb.3-4, b.6 onwards, etc.). Students so often make the mistake of pedalling **each** beat, thereby losing the bass sound as well as tending to 'chop up' the overall 2-in-the-bar movement.

bb.5–10 Take care to 'finish off' the RH phrase cleanly to the quaver on the third beat of b.5, and then listen to the rising LH quavers as they 'usher' you into b.6. Practise bb.6-10 as you did bb.1-5. Feel the implied 'lean' on the treble minim B on the second beat of b.6 as the inner RH voice moves up chromatically, and swelling slightly into b.7. Then let the treble D's 'speak' as you *diminuendo* again towards a quietly singing 'lean' on the semibreve C sharp on the first beat of b.8 listening to the chromatic downward step of the inner line here. 'Finish off' the RH phrase clearly on the first beat of b.9, and then imagine a *portamento* curve down to the D sharp so that you move straight on to begin the *crescendo* towards b.10. Now practise through from b.6 to the first beat of b.10. Show the differently shaped wide sweep of the LH through bb.7 and 8, listening to the upbeat E sharp as the LH 'turns the corner' into b.8, and allowing an extra instant through the end of b.8 to negotiate the wide-spanned LH curve down to the bass F sharp and back to 'meet' the RH on the dominant unisons on the first beat of b.9. Then listen to the LH line descending in contrary motion to the RH as you draw out in *crescendo* towards b.10. When you join the two sections (bb.2-5 and 6-10), listen, as you 'finish off' the RH phrase gracefully on the quaver third on the third beat of b.5, to the LH dominant broken chord leading you on into b.6.

bb.10–23 Lead off from b.10 into the amplified version of bb.2-5 in fuller-toned, smooth and confident octaves. At the sight of the short flight of octaves at bb.11-12 inexperienced players are invariably gripped by panic. The rot sets in before the beginning of b.11, when the LH, in sympathetic anticipation of trouble, starts a stampede for the exit at b.12. In fact, of course, the triplet octaves are quite leisurely at the overall easy tempo. If you actually practise the passage with the metronome, the panic will soon disappear, and then when you leave off the metronome, continue to be 'conducted' by the even, easy-moving LH triplets. Take care to place the LH quaver G carefully beneath the tied octave D sharp on the third beat of b.11 so as both to steady yourself and to give a little rhythmic 'springboard' for the upward line of RH octaves. Feel that the triplet octaves, ascending in a smooth little swathe, are 'going to' a singing dotted crotchet octave on the first beat of b.12, and then lean a little on the upper crotchet B on the third beat of this bar so that it sings out over the chromatically descending inner quavers. Feel a light 'lift' from the partly tied quaver third on the second beat of b.13, with at the same time the sense of making a slurred effect up to a singing RH sixth on the third beat. Then allow an instant to clear the sound at the end of the bar for the *piano* change to the minor on the first beat of b.14. Pay particular attention to the shaping of the two RH voices through bb.14-15. Be sure to give the upper dotted minim D sufficient tone to sing through the first three beats of b.14, while at the same time listening just as clearly to the inner line. Take care how you play the inner minim E, and then particularly the F natural as the tied treble upbeat sings

over into b.15, so that the treble line sounds clearly: 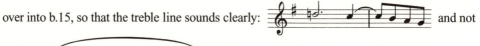 and not

 Most players interpret the trill in b.15 (and at

bb.31, 32, etc.) simply thus: Let the sound 'fall' towards the

middle of b.15 before starting a gradual *crescendo* from b.16, with a sense of onward movement. Listen particularly to the expressive curve of the LH up to the fifth and eleventh quavers of these bars, as you 'space' the RH quavers eloquently against the rhythmic flow of the LH triplets. Move on from b.16 towards a full-toned minim chord on the first beat of b.18, and on again towards the emphasised minim chord on the first beat of b.19, rising to the peak of your *crescendo* on the third beat of this bar. Grade this *crescendo* carefully from b.16 so that you do not get too loud too soon, and also **listen** to the quality of your tone so that you rise to a fine full-toned, never harsh resonance through bb.18-19. The careful balancing of the bass sound is all important in this respect. 'Peaking' your *crescendo* as described, hold this sixth for an instant on the third beat of b.19, and then let the music gradually subside towards b.22, always listening acutely to the inflections of the LH as well as to the two RH voices. Tail the LH off further through b.22 ready to waft in with the minim third on the first beat of b.23 in a dreamy *pianissimo*.

Aspiratamente* could mean 'breathed' or 'aspiringly' (yearning) – either would
bb.23–30   fit! Phrase the RH thirds in a smooth whisper, giving the little *crescendo* through
b.25 a plaintive quality, as you rise smoothly to 'lean' expressively on the chord on the first beat of b.26. Whether or not it is 'correct' to play the acciaccatura thirds **on** the beat, it is prettier (as most players do) to play them just before. Show the appoggiatura effect of the upper third on the first beat of b.26 as it resolves onto the B major harmony on the second beat. Then feel the LH leading you on through the remainder of the bar to re-enter with the amplified RH in a warm, expressive full tone in b.27. Show the upbeat chord to b.28 clearly as a quaver, in cross-rhythm with the LH triplets. Balance the RH carefully through bb.28-9, letting the treble line sing out above the inner sustained third through b.28, and shaping the inner thirds expressively beneath the long A sharp through b.29. Feel through b.29 that you are 'going to' the quietly emphasised chord on the first beat of b.30. Listen here to the inner crotchet E resolving to the D sharp on the second beat of b.30 beneath the upper dotted minim third as the LH triplets curve upwards and then draw out expressively as they descend, while at the same time leading on resolutely towards the *forte* ornamented restatement of the opening melody.

Listen carefully again here to the quality of your tone so that the melody line
bb.31–39   always **sings**, and the LH triplets maintain their expressive curves, giving a
continual onward movement. Be sure that the ornamented fourth beats, the four semiquavers in b.31 and the sextuplets in bb.32 and 33 are 'spaced' expressively, while at the same time giving an upbeat impulse towards the first beat of bb.32, 33 and 34. Take particular care to keep the LH triplets steady beneath these ornamented upbeats. Sympathetic panic can

*Probably not authentic, see Commentary in Paderewski Edition.

easily set in again here with the LH losing its grip and scrabbling to keep up with the RH through these upbeats, so that the player progressively and ever more frantically 'falls into' bb.32, 33, 34, 36 and 38. Make an overall *crescendo* from b.31 to 'peak' through the first beat of b.34. Take an extra instant at the beginning of b.34 to let the acciaccatura D sharp 'speak' as you prepare to 'lift', not snatch, up to the high F sharp. 'Hold' this high F sharp fractionally in a 'vocal' manner on the first beat of b.34 as you listen to the LH rising towards the 'doubled' G on the second beat which gives a supporting resonance to the descending diminished seventh arpeggio. Let this 'fall' in a controlled manner towards a clear crotchet sixth on the third beat. The 'spacing' of the runs in bb.34, 35 and 37 must of course be an individual matter, but less experienced players can at first group

the descending arpeggio in b.34 thus  and the

ascending runs in bb.35 and 37 thus:

Then when you have gained confidence, the groups can be more loosely merged, and varied according to personal taste. Continue to feel that these runs in bb.35 and 37 convey the feeling of an upbeat onward 'lead' into the subsequent bar. The important principle throughout this whole passage is to feel that the **steady** LH is 'guiding' the RH and **not** the other way around. The LH may need to 'give' a little (but just a very little since these are not very 'crowded' runs) through the very end of b.35, and a little more through the end of b.37, but it must do so in a **rhythmic** manner, picking up the tempo at once again at the beginning of the subsequent bar (see General Introduction under '' 'Free' Runs'). In b.35 time the little upward flutter of grace notes to start on the third quaver pulse of the bar and let the repeated triplet quavers 'speak' through the second beat with the feeling of 'going to' the crotchet on the third beat of the bar. Then feel that the upward run is 'growing' from this B on the third beat rather than starting with a bump. Let the trill run easily from the third beat of b.36 again, rather than starting with a bump and start the trill in b.37 on the upper note so that there is no break in the 'chain'. Let the thumb lie lightly on the inner B through the first half of b.37, and similarly on the A sharp (using either the thumb or second finger on this A sharp, and releasing it just before you begin the scale) so that the outer part of the hand is free to carry on the trill. The fingering of the trill through b.37 can be 5 3 5 3 or 4 2 4 2 or you can change from one fingering to another during the course of the trill. If all else fails and the move to the inner RH A sharp on the third beat of b.37 causes a disastrous lurch in the trill, this A sharp could be taken with the LH thumb, taking care that this doesn't sabotage the smooth curve of the LH triplets. Again here try to let the upward run 'grow' out of the trill from the fourth beat of the bar. *Crescendo* towards a ringing octave B on the first beat of b.38, and then as at b.9 feel the *portamento* effect down to the D sharp ready to lead on into b.39.

bb.39–57 As at bb.11-12 let the steady LH 'guide' you through this further amplified restatement. Be careful to let the repeated octaves 'speak' rather than bang at the beginning of b.41, and then listen to the descending inner RH line, A-A-G sharp-G natural as at b.12. Feel a light 'lift' up to the high E on the second beat of b.42 as in b.13, and then allow an instant to listen to the LH moving up from the last quaver of the bar to the 'warning' sound of the diminished seventh harmony on the first beat of b.43. Listen to the new shape of the LH through b.43, while at the same time feeling a sense of moving on in *crescendo* towards the chord on the first beat of b.45, and on again in a full tone towards the tonic major chord on the first beat of b.46. Let the grace notes in b.45 anticipate the chord on the third beat. After the chord on the first beat of b.46 some players draw back in a *diminuendo* to move into b.47 in a whispering tone as at b.23. Others, and I prefer this effect, continue into b.47 in a fairly full tone, then make a *diminuendo* as they ascend through bb.48-50. At b.46 the tonic pedal point is established, to be maintained right through to the end. The continuance of the full tone into b.47 with a subsequent **gradual** *diminuendo*, allows this tonic sound to 'make its point' more surely. But editions vary – Henle and the Paderewski edition have no indication, the Vienna Urtext Edition gives a *pianissimo* at b.47, Peters a *dolce*. In any event lead into b.51 in a distant, sweet-toned *piano* and give the inner RH G sharps a soft bell-like resonance that enhances rather than swamps the languishing 'fall' of the upper voices. Keep the LH moving quietly and evenly as the RH gently subsides towards the tonic at b.54. Give the diminished semibreve chord a quiet 'pressed' sound through b.55, showing its appoggiatura effect, as it resolves yet more quietly onto the tonic third in b.56. Continue to listen to the gradually slowing and diminishing movement of the LH as you 'arc' the RH down to the final low E.

Nocturne No. 20 in C sharp minor (7)*

This interesting piece has a complicated history (see Brown pp.51-3 and the Preface to the Henle Edition, the Vienna Urtext, and the detailed commentary in the Paderewski Edition). Sent by Chopin to his sister from Vienna in 1830, and not entitled a Nocturne by Chopin himself, it quotes (bb.19-20 and 23-4) the opening theme from the last movement of the Concerto in F minor, and also (bb.28-30) a sizeable fragment from his song *Zyczenie* ('Maiden's Wish'), then breaking into a dance-like interlude from bb.31-41. As a further point of interest, one version (No.20a in Henle) has an overall **4/4** rhythm, and the concerto motif is 'tailored' to fit the LH quaver pattern. In another (No.20b in Henle) the overall rhythm is an *alla breve*, and the concerto motif is in its original form (in **3/4**) so that it is in cross-rhythm with the LH quavers:

In this version the song-motif is also in **3/4**, and is similarly in cross-rhythm with the LH.

This piece is not published in the Paderewski Edition's volume of Nocturnes, but is given in their volume of Minor Works. It is often titled as *Lento con gran espressione*. Both the Vienna

Urtext and the Paderewski Editions print only one version – corresponding more or less to the first version in Henle (No.20A). But John Vallier gives the 'cross-rhythm' form in his selection of Chopin pieces in the 'Oxford Keyboard Classics' series. While more experienced players will surely wish to explore the cross-rhythm version, the notes here refer to the first version (No.20a in Henle) since in this form the piece makes a valuable addition to the limited Chopin repertoire available to less experienced players. For all pianists John Vallier's editorial suggestions and comments in 'Oxford Keyboard Classics' are helpful.

This piece has been summarily dismissed by various commentators. Weinstock, for example, considers it 'ungrateful in performance, appearing to be shards glued together without sense of balance or design' (p.317). I feel, on the contrary and perhaps because the 'shards' are so arresting, that the piece has an inexplicable yet compelling unity, as if one is passing through a dreamlike landscape whose contours, however bizarre, seem to evolve with a strange inevitability. This is certainly the effect of, for instance, the persuasive performance recorded by Peter Katin. Bar numbers here refer to the first version (Henle No.20a). In Henle **20b** and also in the Vienna Urtext Edition and the Oxford Keyboard Classics' version, the introductory chords are written out twice instead of being repeated as they are in Henle **20a**. For those using these versions there will therefore be a 2-bar discrepancy in bar numberings from b.3 onwards (i.e. for b.3 read b.5 and so on).

bb.1–10   Play the introductory chords quietly and with solemn expectancy, giving each chord its exact value, **feeling** each quaver rest fully so that each quaver chord gives a new, onward 'upbeat' impetus. At the same time note the RH inner 'syncopated' dotted crotchet, and then the tied inner quaver, implying a rather deliberate, though quiet 'lean' on these quaver chords. Make it clear that the introduction is completed as you arrive on the dominant crotchet chord for the second time, coming **off** in time, and **feeling** the beats through the rest as you poise yourself to lead off into the main theme. Imagine any easy strolling step to the crotchet pulse, but with an overall 2-in-the-bar feeling (see No.20b in Henle). The tempo needs to be flexible but a basic ♩ = 76-84 gives the right feeling of onward but unhurried movement. The introductory chords could be just a little slower (or faster) than this, but not to the extent of destroying their forward intent towards the main theme. Practise the LH alone, shaping each group of four quavers in such a way that they create a continually curving onward movement, up from each bass note to the topmost, third quaver and back to the bass note again.

The melody is one of the most truly vocal that Chopin ever wrote – indeed it cries out for a Callas or a Sutherland! **Sing** it therefore for all you are worth (never mind how horrible you sound) and you will soon feel the impulse and shape of the phrasing. Note that initially there are no dynamic indications – we are only enjoined to play *con gran espressione*. In any event (whether you feel you should enter in a dreaming *pianissimo* or in an incipient *appassionato*), 'bring in' the melody in a pure, clear tone over the smoothly undulating LH quavers. Feel the impulse of the first two minims towards the minim on the first beat of b.4, and then 'shade' this note down to the C sharp on the third beat while at the same time mentally phrasing onwards and upwards towards the C sharp on the first beat of b.5, 'drawn on' by the movement of the LH quavers. You could either start the trill on b.3 on the main note or, following Chopin's practice in other instances from a grace note prefix beginning on the lower note and placed **on** the beat (see b.9) and also Op.32 No.2, b.8; Op.37 No.1, b.8; Op.55 No.1, b.14, etc.). Or you could perhaps start the trill **on** the main note in b.3, and with the lower grace notes in b.11. Feel the little swell through b.5, allowing the hint of a vocal 'hold' on the first note (C sharp) of the triplet on the fourth beat before you 'fall' expressively from this upper note, towards a singing minim A. Feel once more that you are 'phrasing onwards' as you take a breath through the second half of b.6 ready to re-enter with the answering phrase in b.7. Let the lower grace note (C sharp) coincide with the bass note on

the first beat of b.9.  and let the trill billow a little

through the bar, then fade towards the quaver C sharp upbeat to b.10.

bb.10–18   Enter in a fuller tone on the upbeat to b.11, feeling a vocal 'lift' up to the high G sharp on the first beat of b.11. Then allow just a little 'give' through the end of this bar as the trill 'merges' into the grace note suffix, with the feeling of 'going to' the G sharp on the first beat of b.12. *Crescendo* through the second half of b.12, feeling that you are curving right up towards and 'through' the high D, in b.13. 'Space' the triplets in an operatic manner as you 'turn the corner' at the top of the run, ready to descend in a full-throated *appassionato con forza* over a **steady** and resonantly supporting LH. In all the runs in this piece (here, and in bb.50, 55, 56, etc.) it is vital that the LH 'holds the reins' rhythmically so that even when it may have to 'bend', in b.56, it is the LH that is the 'conductor' and **not** the other way about (see General Introduction, under ''Free' Runs'). *Decrescendo*, but not too much, as you descend towards the long A in b.14, giving this note sufficient tone to 'sing on' towards the low D natural on the first beat of b.15. 'Lift' again up to the high D on the third beat and then go to a full-toned trill on the B sharp on the first beat of b.16 (starting **on** the main note here), making a further short *crescendo* through the demisemiquavers to the strong crotchet E on the third beat. Keep up the full tone right through to the low C sharp on the first beat of b.18, **lifting** the hand from the quaver G sharp on the first beat of b.17 so that it 'falls' to make a natural, resonant emphasis on the minim A on the second beat (see General Introduction under 'Articulation'). All through this first section listen carefully to the balance between the hands so that the LH quavers support and complement, but never swamp, the melody, and making sure that the melodic tone, however full-throated, never becomes strident.

bb.18–64   'Shade' the LH off through the end of b.18 ready to enter in a whispering *pianissimo* in b.19. There is a feeling of moving on just a little here, as if in a distant, half-remembered fragment of dance (particularly in the cross-rhythm version), with the pedal point A giving the hint of a musette feeling. Keep the LH quavers very steady though, even if at a slightly faster tempo, fitting in the varying RH note values neatly and smoothly. (In the cross-rhythm version it is none too easy to maintain rhythmic equilibrium. The essential is to maintain this perfectly even LH quaver movement, concentrating on ensuring that each RH crotchet is synchronised with the first quaver of each LH group. Feel that the RH is adjusting its alternating sense of **3/4** and **4/4** to the steady LH pulse and *not* the other way about.) Play bb.21-2 in a more open tone, expanding a little into and through b.22 as you play the dotted rhythm sixths in a precise but rather jaunty style, 'going to' an emphasised minim sixth as indicated before returning to a whisper at b.23. Expand again from b.25, here with the sense of leading on into the *forte* at b.27. The quotation from the song is, as mentioned above, from b.28, and the song itself has a very dancing accompaniment, drawing Chopin's train of thought on perhaps to the dance-like interlude from b.31. Play bb.27-8 in a full-throated but expressive tone, spacing the repeated detached quavers through the second beat of b.28 in a speaking manner with the feeling of 'going to' the emphasised syncopated dotted crotchet D sharp. Then play the answering phrase from b.29 more lingeringly and thoughtfully. The 'join' in b.30 is an awkward corner further complicated by the chaotic range of solutions given in different versions. Henle's No.20A continues the **4/4** movement through b.30, changing to **3/4** in b.31.

Others, including Paderewski give

which makes far better rhythmic sense. (For those using this edition this added bar creates a further one-bar discrepancy in bar numberings.) The Vienna Urtext Edition adopts a similar principle, but prints one **5/4** bar divided into **2/4** and **3/4** sections. The best approach is to follow the **second** example above, making a very slight *rallentando* from the beginning of the **2/4** bar, and then pausing for an extra instant on the dotted crotchets B sharp (on the second beat of the **3/4** bar) ready to launch into the dance movement in the subsequent bar. The alternative, but I think less satisfactory procedure, is to *crescendo* and move on through the first half of b.30 (taken as a **4/4** bar as in the first example), to start straight into the dance movement with the triplet on the third beat. (The Polish pianist Zbigniew Drzewiecki in his recording on the Muza label takes this second alternative.) If you do follow the first example, linger a little on the unison dotted crotchet B sharps as said above, and then play the upbeat semiquavers with a clearer than normal emphasis – with a sort of onward 'kick' to launch you into an immediate brisk **3/4** in b.31. In any event maximise the surprise element at b.31 by making these bars as dance-like as possible (John Vallier suggests *'tempo di Mazurka'*). It is much more effective if you come **off** the crotchet on the third beat of bb.31, 33, etc. and then show an implied emphasis on the dotted crotchet on the second beat of bb.32, 34, etc. so that you have an alternating rhythmic emphasis on the first beat of b.31, the second of b.32, and so on.

The extra notes shown in the Henle and Paderewski Editions in the treble (bb.33-5 and 37-9) are **not** thought to be authentic, since Chopin intended the indicated LH-RH distribution through bb.33-42. Distance the sound mysteriously as you *rallentando* and *diminuendo* from around b.38 and then, placing the low bass G sharp quietly on the first beat of b.42, disperse the sound upwards in a delicate trail. Give the high G sharp a soft but penetrating ring so that the sound 'carries you on' towards the reprise from the upbeat of b.44. You can either break the sound just before entering with the upbeat or, imagining a downward *portamento* effect, carry straight on into the upbeat, an effect which I prefer. In either case, give the upbeat its full value, but with an onward leading 'lean'. Show the more continuous sense of the line this time as you 'lift' and swell up to the high A on the third beat of b.47, and again as you *crescendo* upwards through b.50 to carry on the *appassionato* song in the higher octave (remember to keep the LH steady through b.50 so that your ardour does not get out of hand!). Let the tone billow through the trill in b.54 and subside towards a quiet but warm-toned minim C sharp on the first beat of b.55. Let the run seem to grow from this note above the continuing LH quavers. These runs through bb.55-58 create a strange *frisson* (presaging the mysterious 'water-spout' in Op.62 No.1 b.26). They appear to well up from nowhere, an effect accentuated by the unconcerned, almost disembodied continuance of the LH quavers within a double tonic pedal point. There can be no precise demarcation of the runs into groups. Each run has a different span and character, but returns in each instance to a quiet, bell-like G sharp. Plan therefore that in b.55 you will turn the corner at the top of the run just before the LH D sharp on the fourth beat, as indicated in the score. (Note the semi-detached descending notes in the first and last runs. This precludes rushing downwards, and suggests a little 'give' in the LH at the end of the bar). Then in bb.56, 57 and 58 the top note of the run will more or less coincide with the LH D sharp. The long run in b.56 must, of course, be as fast as possible, and provided that it is curved in a *crescendo* up to and down from the topmost note, and allowing a substantial 'give' in the LH through the end of the bar, it is not too difficult to negotiate. The third and shortest run has a delicate, hesitant quality, and in the last, more delicate still, let the detached notes *rallentando* gracefully towards the major harmony at b.59. The essential is, as already said, that the LH 'guides' the RH. Here, therefore, be sure that you always shape the LH beneath the runs in a curve up to and down from the D sharp on the fourth beat of the bar. The LH will, as already said, need to 'give' a little through the end of b.55 and again, substantially through both the third and fourth beats of b.56. (At the end of b.58 a *rallentando* is in any event indicated.) The essential is that the LH 'leads' in a rhythmic not random manner, regaining the tempo at once in the subsequent bar (see General Introduction under ''Free' Runs'). It is a good plan to play the LH from b.55 while **singing** the RH. Any kind of 'zooming' noise to represent the runs will do, and will give you the idea of the swell up to the top note over the curving LH, being conscious of the placing of the top note of the run in each instance in relation to the LH D sharp. Arrive on a soft yet penetrating RH G sharp on the first beat of b.58 as you ease into the major in the LH. (In other editions, and in Henle 20B, the major E sharp is delayed until the penultimate bar.) Let the quavers *rallentando* gracefully, and then **listen** to the fading sound as the hands diverge in contrary motion up towards tiny pinpoints of sound on the wide-apart unison C sharps. Let the sound fade almost into silence before lifting the hands and the pedal.

Nocturne No. 21 in C minor (6)*

This is a sadly flaccid affair, whose date of composition seems to be in doubt. It was only published in 1938, and at first thought to be an early piece. Other authorities suggest the date 1837, but Jan Ekier (see the Preface to the Vienna Urtext Edition) considers it more likely to have been written in 1847; and it certainly has the weary ring of Chopin's last pieces, when he was too weak to rally his inventive spirit. This shows itself most clearly in the monotony of the LH, so different to the living counterpoint of the LH part in most of the Nocturnes. Nevertheless, for a novice player this is a useful 'learning' piece. It gives good practice in the shaping and phrasing of a melody line in a vocal manner, as well as coping with relatively simple 'free' runs in uneven groupings over an even LH quaver accompaniment. Further, since there are virtually no indications, it provides a good opportunity for the imaginative use of dynamics through the many repetitions of the opening motif.

Note: This piece is not published in the Paderewski Edition's volume of Nocturnes, but is given in their volume of Minor Works.

bb.1–4   Practise the LH alone, making a continual curve up from each bass note to the upper chord on the second and fourth beats and down again,

creating the effect:  Be careful to retain this shape

in the LH when you put hands together. The use of the 5 5 fingering as shown facilitates this shaping, and is by far the best for small hands, certainly through bb.1-16 as it enables the hand to remain in the most advantageous (i.e. 'natural', rather than extended) position.

Set an easy moving crotchet pulse at a suggested approximate ♩ = 76, imagining a comfortable strolling stride to each crotchet beat. The principal melody moves in two 2-bar subphrases, within an overall 4-bar phrase (bb.1-4). Begin in a light, easy tone, and lead in from a clear crotchet upbeat, being sure to give this its full value. Shape the first subphrase in an overall curve up towards the dotted quaver A flat on the second beat of b.2 and down again to the minim C sharp. Carry on smoothly into b.3, and in b.4 shape the run in a delicate curve up towards the A flat, and down again to the minim D on the third beat of the bar. Time the dotted rhythms cleanly but expressively through the first half of bb.1-3, and be sure to allow time for the grace notes to 'speak', placing them **on** the second beat

of bb.2 and 3.

Be sure to have the LH 'ready' to meet the RH on the first beat of b.1, and to establish immediately that even quaver rhythm which will support and guide the RH throughout the piece. The LH will 'give' just a little on the second beat of bb.2 and 3 to accommodate the RH ornaments, and again just a little as the RH 'turns the corner' through the end of the RH run in b.4. Take great care to ensure that the LH quavers remain rhythmic through each semiquaver run. When they 'bend' a little, they must do so rhythmically (see General Introduction under ''Free' Runs'), immediately picking up the tempo in the subsequent bar. Always feel that the RH is 'fitting in' with the LH and **not** the other way around. At the end of each subphrase (through the second half of bb.2, 4, etc.) listen to the LH quavers leading you on beneath the held RH minim towards the next bar. This skill of maintaining a steady LH beneath an ornamented melody line is an extremely important lesson for student players.

bb.5–16   Space the 5-note RH turn elegantly through the first beat of b.8, again taking care to keep the LH quavers steady. Feel that these five notes are 'going to' the dotted quaver on the second beat, holding this note fractionally before 'falling' spaciously towards the crotchet C. Be sure to **lift** the hand from this C as if taking a breath, ready to set off again from a clear upbeat quaver (see General Introduction under 'Articulation'). 'Open out' the line as you swell towards the tied minim on the third beat of b.14, giving this note plenty of tone to sing over the barline. Then feel you are continuing the line right over from this high tied C down the scale to the C crotchet on the fourth beat of b.15 and go on to end the phrase with a graceful arabesque-like curve up to the E flat and down to the crotchet C on the third beat of b.16, again allowing the LH to 'give' a little through the second beat of this bar.

bb.16–44   As you take another 'breath' after the third beat of b.16 listen again to the LH quavers carrying you on towards the next section as they rise through the end of the bar ready for the high RH to lead off from the upbeat and into b.17 in a rather fuller tone. Feel the implied emphasis on the tied crotchet F on the upbeat to b.18 'carrying you on' into b.18. Then you could either play out the high triplets expressively in a full tone through the first half of b.19, or alternatively play these two bars as a whispered echo of bb.17-18. In any event lead into b.21 quietly, and take care to keep the LH steady once more in b.22 as you make an airy little 'lift' up towards the high D flat on the second beat, allowing a slight 'hold' on this note. Then feel the onward impulse towards the high F on the upbeat to b.23, going on to play out the descending quavers in a full tone through b.23. 'Point' the LH quaver C neatly on the first beat of b.24 as you take a quick 'breath' before entering neatly on the offbeat with the quiet little 'answer' in the RH. Bb.25-8 are, of course, an elaborated version of the four previous bars. Endeavour, therefore, to preserve the overall shape and nuances of bb.21-4 as you negotiate the runs and arabesques. Feel an even stronger impetus towards the high upbeat (tied this time) to b.27, making a clear upward 'lift' so that you play it with a natural emphasis. Inexperienced players will probably need to arrange the runs in groups to fit in with the LH quavers. Then when more assurance is gained, the groups can be more loosely merged, and varied at will. The essential is that the LH is always the 'conductor', bending a little, particularly in b.28, but always 'guiding' the RH. The groupings given below for the 'uneven' runs (i.e. those in bb.25, 27, 28, 32 and 44) are, of course, suggestions only.

In b.25 make a little swell up towards the high A flat. In b.27 allow a little vocal 'hold' on the tied high F over a neatly 'pointed' LH B flat on the first beat as you poise yourself to descend and, whatever the hazards of the descent, be sure that you arrive in one piece on the low dotted semiquaver F, perfectly coinciding with the LH G, and feeling this fourth quaver pulse of the bar as a clear 'upbeat' to the third beat. In b.28 feel the curve upwards towards, and through the high D flat and then 'fall' gracefully towards the minim F on the third beat. In b.32 feel a similar, though less 'crowded' curve, rising to the dotted semiquaver C, and lingering fractionally on this note before 'falling' to the minim A flat. At b.33 notice the different timbre as the section from b.17 is restated a fourth lower in the tonic. Draw out a little towards the end of b.43, and place the bass octave quietly but definitely on the first beat of the last bar, ready to tail off the RH run expressively towards the final quietly spread chord.

THE STUDIES

Introduction:

The 24 Studies, Ops.10 and 25, are among the marvels of piano literature. Chopin draws poetry from arpeggios, thirds, octaves and sixths in the same sense as a great choreographer draws poetry from the technical skills of the highly trained dancer. 'Never', as Louis Kentner has said, 'has there been such a perfect fusion of the athletic and aesthetic' (p.151). And this fusion is the more complete in that these pieces are a practical demonstration of Chopin's inborn understanding of the human physique in relation to the keyboard, and in particular of the **natural** individual characteristics of each finger. Immensely demanding as he is on every level, technical and musical, Chopin explores, exploits and enhances in each instance this natural conformation, rather than attempting to impose extraneous and distorting movements on the physical equipment of the player. His achievement is the more remarkable in that he started work upon, and actually composed several of the Op.10 set when he was only nineteen. While his almost complete lack of formal training as a player is no doubt in part responsible for his natural and objective approach to technical problems, it also demonstrates, particularly in the context of the Studies, the complete and 'pre-formed' nature of his extraordinary gifts.

The Studies must be the most discussed, analysed, annotated and 'taught' works in the entire piano repertory, and detailed discussion of those pieces in the virtuoso category would be superfluous here (see Preface). There are, however, several numbers, more than perhaps is generally realised, which are accessible to players of a standard of Grade 8 or so (for rewarding study at least, and even in one or two instances for performance). And as I hope to show below, it is well worth while for players at around this level to take time at least to examine as many as possible, even of the most virtuosic of these pieces (Op.10 Nos 1, 2 and 8; Op.25 Nos 4, 6 and 10, to name but a few). The fact that Chopin's metronome marks are, almost without exception, very fast, indeed so fast as to exceed the capacities of **most** sets of fingers, should not deter the enquiring player (see General Introduction under 'Tempo'). In each study the technical problems are so clearly 'stated' that the slow, intelligent practice of even a few bars will bring immense benefits, not only in a purely technical sense, but also in the understanding of the capacities and resources of the keyboard, and of the relationship between the human physique and the demands of the keyboard.

As Niecks said of both sets of Studies, 'A striking feature . . . is their healthy freshness and vigour' and indeed in a special sense these are among the happiest of all Chopin's works. Happy not in the sense merely of light-hearted, for here, besides several especially high-spirited numbers (Op.10 Nos 5 and 8 and Op.25 Nos 4 and 9 for example), there is, as in most other areas of his work, power and pathos, fury, grandeur, or sheer poetry. But happy in the sense that in each piece he had set himself a task for which he was uniquely suited; the pursuit of (in the main) one idea, unencumbered with the problems of contrasting sections, linking passages and the like. Because his involvement with the 'athletic and aesthetic' was so complete and so immediate, the Studies are, without doubt, among the most intuitive and spontaneous of all his works.

In compiling the commentaries below, I have, as usual, used the Henle Edition. However, for pianists at all stages the Cortot Edition de Travail is an invaluable adjunct. I use the word 'adjunct' advisedly, for his editorial additions, excellent as they often are (despite his unfortunate habit of altering or ignoring Chopin's fingerings without comment) need to be seen in the context of the Urtext.*

---

*Although Cortot was probably unaware of various fingerings and other indications in scores belonging to pupils of Chopin, since some of these have only come to light over latter years.

386

Notes:

Since most of the Studies are concerned with a single musical or technical idea, a large proportion of the discussion of each number is inevitably centred upon this one 'idea'. The text is therefore not divided into bar-numbered sections as is the case throughout most of this book.

In the Studies Henle reverse their usual practise and give **original** fingerings in ordinary print (see their Preface). Vienna Urtext however, continue to give original fingerings in italics. This becomes confusing to say the least, when making comparisons between the two editions. (Vienna Urtext generally give more such 'original' fingerings than Henle, and furthermore these fingerings do not always tally, since they may be drawn from varying sources, such as scores belonging to different pupils of Chopin).

Op. 10 No. 1
Study in C major (VA)

The Bachian inevitability of this magisterial piece has often been remarked upon. While in technical terms it is one of the most formidable of all the Studies, it is also one from which less advanced players can gain a great deal, even from the study of the first few bars. The primary essential is to understand the sense in which the arpeggios of the RH arise from and are governed by the march of the LH octaves. To this end practise in chords from b.1 through to the C major chord at b.9 thus, **with** the pedal, in a reasonably full tone over strongly resonant LH octaves:

You will at once appreciate not only the fundamental 'drive' of the LH, but also the immense resonance that is created by the pedalled sound of the ascending and descending chords over the sustained bass octaves. Listen particularly to the continuing resonance of the tied LH tonic octave through bb.1-2, and to the continuing sound of the tied dominant octave through bb.7-8 as both the harmony and the pedal change at the beginning of b.8. Listen also to the implied slight hold on the emphasised upbeat to b.9 which poises this upbeat, giving an emphatic onward 'lean' ready to launch off again at b.9.

This piece is not, as is so often assumed, an impossible assignment for a small hand. On the contrary, although obviously taxing, it is perfectly possible providing that the hand is really flexible. For this is an exercise in the lateral opening and contracting of the hand rather than an exercise in 'stretching'. Cortot's first exercise demonstrates this

clearly:  Immediately the E

is struck with the fifth finger (those with small hands can imagine an upward slur or *portamento* rising to the E as smoothly as possible, rather than 'snatching' at it), the hand is allowed to 'snap' to a natural closed position. Then, immediately the C is struck with the thumb the hand 'snaps' open again to extend towards the next E, and so on, with this opening and closing 'snap' continued in reverse on the downward journey. Then when you practise the RH as written, rise to the accented E on the second beat in strict time, very slowly at first, allowing the hand to 'come with you' (see General Introduction under 'Some Explanations and Amplifications') to reach the closed position as the thumb prepares to strike the middle C. Allow an instant's relaxation at this closed point before 'snapping' the hand open again to climb, in strict time, to the next accented E on the third beat. This movement calls to mind the famous description of Chopin's hands expanding like the mouth of a serpent about to swallow a rabbit whole (see General Introduction under 'Chopin's Playing'). Even at a fast speed it is this fraction of a second's relaxation as the hand is 'closed' that makes the performance of this piece possible, and without which the strongest hand and arm would collapse within a few bars. Cortot's exercises Nos 10 and 12-15 are particularly helpful towards mastery of this 'snapped' lateral opening and closing of the hand. (His use of the third finger on the second semiquaver of bb.4, 14, etc, as opposed to Chopin's fourth finger indication, may for some hands, give a stronger effect.)

Further, the implied sense of a dynamic rise and fall through each arpeggio allows a continual and **regular** fluctuation in the degree of effort involved: feel that each arpeggio 'grows' from the bass octave, entering with a relatively quiet offbeat semiquaver, and climbing in stages through each accented beat towards the summit on the first beat of the subsequent bar; and then as it returns downwards, feel a degree of relaxation of the hand as the sound decreases, and the hand comes **off** on the first beat of bb.3, 5, etc. In fact this sense of an upward climbing *crescendo* is more illusory than real, caused by the increasing carrying power of the rising notes within the overall resonance of the expanding span of sound rising from the powerful bass octave. Think of the overall rise and descent of each arpeggio as a wide-sprung 'arc', rather than as a pair of diagonal upward and downward pointing lines. On the part of the player it is more of an upward 'lean' than an actual increase and decrease of force, and this is another lesson that can be learned from this piece. Once you have learned the notes of bb.1-8 hands together even at a fairly slow tempo (and this can as well apply to the chord exercise suggested above), try to play the sequences sitting upright like a ramrod without a trace of movement in the torso. Then try again, allowing yourself to lean upward and a little forward in a natural movement towards and back from the topmost note and see how much easier it becomes. The disposition of this rhythmic upward lean together with the ascending arpeggio creates the sense of the *crescendo* without conscious effort on the part of the player. For amateur players in particular, the objective of working thus at these few bars is the understanding of the overall physical and aural coordination (never mind if some of the notes misfire) which can be applied as well to many other situations.

When you begin to **play** the first eight bars (and eventually the whole piece) always **listen** to the resonance of the LH octave line, never losing the sense of the growth and upward thrust of the harmonic 'arc' of each RH arpeggio from this bass octave. At risk of labouring the point, it is, as already said above, the **LH** that motivates and propels the RH arpeggios. In our anxiety to 'get the notes right' and make a brilliant show in the RH, we tend to compound the difficulties by letting the RH struggle along on its own, rather than using the LH resonance and motivating power from which to let the arpeggios grow, like 'bow strokes' as Chopin himself said (Eigeldinger p.68).

There needs to be a sense of approach to, and arrival upon, the dominant at the beginning of b.8. Then allow an extra instant to point the emphasised D sharp as the upbeat to b.9. This upbeat 'lean' gives an essential 'braking' and 'poising' point in the flight of the arpeggios, allowing the RH to 'gather itself' to 'start again' from b.9. Indeed, it is important to feel the strategic significance of the upbeat group at the end of **each** descending arpeggio, otherwise there may be a tendency to fall onwards into each subsequent first beat. Note also, and use, the implied strong 'lean' on the tied LH upbeat to b.46 (and similarly on the LH upbeat to b.47) beneath the momentary rest in the RH; and there is another strong upbeat lead in both hands into b.61. Since the tumultuous arpeggios press on in ceaseless four-octave sweeps (save for a temporary change of pattern at the bb.42-4 and momentary respite at the end of bb.46 and 47) there is, of course, no let-up in terms of athletic endeavour. However, it is worth noting that there are **no** *fortissimos*, and that Chopin has 'catered for' the creation of a powerful resonance as described above, and by the way in which the wide span of sound over each arpeggio is caught and maximised within the pedal. To try and force the sound is therefore both unnecessary and counter-productive. Most players, however, take the chance to drop the tone a little at b.17, and to benefit from the *diminuendo* from bb.36 and 48. There is also the sense of a slight easing of the tumult from the upbeat to b.70, with a more melodic 'lean' on this upbeat, and on each beat of b.70 and again on each beat of b.72.

Op. 10 No. 2
Study in A minor (VA)

The difficulties here are formidable, but once again even the first eight bars or so make an admirable study. When performed in an immaculately clear but predominantly *piano* dynamic as Chopin has indicated (with the *crescendos* always 'returning to base'), the chromatic scales over the sharply 'plucked' minor chords suggest a high-pitched kind of hum, 'quite eerie' as Robert Collet has said (Walker, p.130). This is a far more exciting effect (and more difficult to achieve) than the exhibitionist clatter, like iron-shod hooves on cobblestones, favoured by many a lion of the keyboard.

The first task is to acquire fluency in the continual crossing of fingers three, four and five, a routine skill (as regards the 'middle' fingers, two, three, and four) for players in the harpsichord era. Start practising the semiquaver line alone, **without** the inner chords, using the most obvious fingering (Chopin's own) up and down the scale as in bb.1-2:

Then practise various other combinations of fingering (Cortot suggests no less than six permutations), and when you have mastered the crossing-over effect smoothly, practise the

scales in different rhythms.

Experiment with the position of the hand, closely observing the effects. It will soon become obvious that this is crucial. Try playing the scales, using Chopin's fingering, with the hand straight, i.e. at right angles to the keyboard; then tilt the hand somewhat to the left; then conversely tilt the hand somewhat to the right. You will immediately observe that if the hand is allowed to tilt slightly to the right, **as much as it wants to,** 'hinged' by a flexible wrist (and retaining approximately the same angle for the descent so that the fundamental angle does not change at the top of the scale), the 'crossing-over' process is greatly facilitated, and the fingers therefore run more fluently. You will find that the scale becomes much more difficult if you play it with the hand 'straight', and that it becomes virtually impossible with the hand tilted slightly to the left. If you retain a flexible wrist you will find that the hand itself will find the most advantageous position, continually allowing the tilt to adjust slightly according to the shape of the semiquaver pattern.* Another essential is to keep the hand 'well into' the keyboard so that you do not have to swoop inwards to reach the black notes (see General Introduction under 'Some Explanations and Amplifications').

Then add the inner chords. Cultivate a light 'plucking' action with the thumb and forefinger so that the hand 'flicks' back to its natural 'closed' position, rather than allowing the thumb and forefinger to remain 'hanging back' over their notes (see General Introduction under 'Some Explanations and Amplifications'). Thus as the outer ('weaker') part of the hand proceeds up the scale it brings the lower ('stronger') part of the hand with it. It is essential that the hand remains as far as possible in this advantageous closed position, rather than in the disadvantageous extended position which will result if the thumb and forefinger are allowed to remain over their notes. There are many different possibilities for the fingering of the semiquavers, as various Editions demonstrate, and in setting our eventual fingering, we have to take the overall view – the way in which the individual hand copes best with the complete pattern, i.e. the execution of the semiquaver line in combination with the inner chords. Cortot, for example, alters Chopin's fingering substantially. But Chopin always has a reason for his fingerings, which are especially detailed in this Study. So it is wise (as well as respectful!) to practise his fingerings first. Then adjustments can be made according to the individual hand. (Chopin's fingerings are given in Henle and in the Vienna Urtext and Paderewski Editions.)

Now practise the LH pattern, and feel the impulse of the neatly 'plucked' and perfectly rhythmic quaver notes and chords towards an implied slight emphasis on the chord on the third beat of b.2, and then of the chords through b.3 towards the emphasised partly tied crotchet chord on the second beat of b.4. Similarly, through b.7 feel the impetus towards the *sforzato* octave (clearly emphatic, but not banged) on the second beat of b.8.

When you put hands together, practise very slowly, in immaculate time. Balance the layers of sound carefully, the bass notes and chords, the inner RH thirds or fourths, and the upper line. The tendency is to concentrate all the attention on the upper line so that it has to stagger along on its own! Things proceed immeasurably better if you feel that the RH is subject to the governing impulse of the LH movement, maintaining the impetus towards the third beat of b.2 and the second beat of b.4 and so on, as when you practised the LH alone. As already said, it is important that each little *crescendo* 'returns to base' (see General Introduction under 'Chopin's Playing'). Note that the little *crescendo* 'peaks' in the RH on the **second** beat of bb.2, 6, etc, while the LH 'goes on up' to the chord on the third beat.

Feel the implied emphasis on the slurred LH chord on the second beat of b.17, on the emphasised slurred upbeat to b.18, and then on the slurred octave on the **second** beat of b.18. These emphases create a slightly syncopating, cross-rhythm effect here. Then allow a little 'give' in the RH as it descends from the third beat of b.18 ready to set off again on a new, more sinuous tack from b.19. Then, observing the details of slurs and emphases precisely use the more pronounced and sustained resonances of the LH to support the RH from the third beat of b.24 through to b.35. Given that in a **4/4** bar the first and third beats are the stronger, the second and fourth the weaker, there is a continuing sense of syncopation through this passage – in the emphasised minim octave on the second beat of bb.25, 26 and 29, and the slurred octave or chord on the second beat of bb.27-8 and 30-1, and the upbeat to bb.28-9 and 31-2. Listen particularly to the effect of the clash of the LH augmented fourth with the RH through bb.30-1. Then **listen** to the held resonance of the tied dominant octave through bb.32-5 beneath

---

*Tilting to the right is meant in the sense of a slight horizontal hinging of the wrist, and NOT in the sense of leaning the WEIGHT of the hand towards the fifth finger, which would be worse than counterproductive.

the descending flurries of the RH. Point the tied semiquaver in bb.33 and 34, which gives a little 'upbeat' push to the upward return of the semiquavers towards the second beat of these bars. Poise yourself neatly as you 'turn the corner' through the third beat of b.35, ready to set off again into the reprise in b.36. Point the LH 'syncopated' emphasised minim octaves as the LH marches down through b.45 and b.46 in contrary motion to the RH, again taking care to turn the corner neatly at the top of the RH scale as the LH prepares to come to rest on the tonic, while the RH poises itself to 'fold' downwards in a carefully graded *diminuendo* through bb.47-8. Without making an exaggerated *rallentando,* 'give' a little through the end of b.48, ready to point the major ending with a soft but clear chord.

Op. 10 No. 3
Study in E major (8+)

This is one of the great tunes, not just of Chopin's, but of the world, as popularisers of succeeding generations have recognised. Niecks records that Chopin told his pupil Gutmann that 'he had never in his life written another such beautiful melody; and on one occasion when Gutmann was studying it, the master lifted up his arms with his hands clasped and exclaimed "O my fatherland!" ' (Niecks, Vol.2, p.253). But as many amateur players ruefully discover it is far from easy to do justice to this immense span of melody, stretching from bb.1-21, played by the 'weak' fingers over a murmuring inner semiquaver accompaniment above a quietly insistent syncopated LH pattern. And the central section, uniquely improvisatory among the Studies, and with complex technical demands, is far from easy to hold together. However, it is not a hopeless assignment for a post-Grade 8 player, although there are problems for not-so-flexible small hands.

As Jim Samson shows (pp.63-4), a continual and unbroken line of melody 'leans' onward, from the upbeat quaver B through to the tied crotchet F sharp on the second beat of b.1, which in turn 'leans' onward towards the G sharp on the second beat of b.2, and so on. And this onward leaning and overlapping of phrases and sub-phrases continues up towards a climax at b.17, the peak of an overall melodic 'arc', and sinks down again towards the *pianissimo* close at b.21. This can, as ever, be immediately understood if you **sing** through to this point. Obviously this is a difficult melody to sing since, owing to the continual 'overlap' there are no clear breath points! However, pianists are begged to make the attempt – endeavouring, by continuing to sing while taking a breath (no matter how awful the noise) to keep the sound going continuously. If you do this, singing as expressively as possible in the circumstances, you will know with intuitive certainty how you want to phrase the melody. Younger players will not remember the 'So Deep is the Night' version of this melody, but it is in this sort of context that we have much to learn from the best of the so-called 'popular' singers. They have the instinctive ability to 'sing on' through overlapping phrases and 'breaths' (and to carry on the sense of continuity over rests when they occur).

bb.1–21   Practise the melody line alone. Be sure to give the upbeat quaver its full value while at the same time feeling its onward, upward, *portamento*-like 'lean' towards the quaver E on the first beat of b.1. Then listen particularly to the **sound** of the long tied crotchet on the second beat of b.1 and the second beat of b.2, and so on (always feeling the steady movement of the quaver pulse within the long notes), so that the sound of these long notes 'merges' on into the semiquavers as the melody carries on into bb.2 and 3. It is a good plan to sing along with yourself at first and then, when you play the melody without your vocal support, to continue to imagine the vocal sound of the line. When you play the line on its own it is not possible to decide upon your final fingering. So meanwhile use any fingering that comes naturally and makes a smooth effect, taking the opportunity to experiment with 'finger substitution' (see General Introduction under 'Fingering') as and when the occasion arises. Then practise the inner semiquaver line, listening to the quietly rocking intervals. Next, **sing** the melody as you play this inner line and you will at once sense when a little give and take is required in the inner line.

When you practise the LH alone, keep a steady tempo, listening to the quiet resonance of the 'doubled' note on each main beat, while at the same time feeling the continual onward impulse created by the little 'push' on the emphasised syncopated quavers. Then practise the three voices in different combinations as you would the voices in a contrapuntal piece, the melody line with the bass, then with the inner line, the bass with the inner line, and so on, and finally play the inner and bass lines while **singing** the upper line.

When you put the RH parts together, consider the fingering of the melody line carefully. There are, of course, various possibilities, and allowance will have to be made here and there for small hands. Unfortunately (for this is an instance when his fingering would have been particularly revealing) Chopin has only left fragmentary indications throughout the first 21 bars, though his fingerings are more plentiful through the middle section. I find some (though not all) of Cortot's fingerings quite awkward and often disturbing to the equilibrium of the inner line, and he disregards Chopin's very

characteristic 4-4 shift in b.6.  (This is shown in the

Vienna Urtext Edition but not in Henle.) On the other hand I find his 5-5 shift between bb.1-2

 (and similarly at bb.2-3) gives a better effect than the usual

editorial finger substitution here. And similarly I prefer his

in b.4 to the often given. But these are all matters for the

individual hand. The only guideline is to use finger substitution or 'shifts' as and when, in relation to the idiosyncrasies of your own hand, they enhance the continuity of the melodic line and/or the textural equilibrium of the whole. Practise at first 'leaning' on the notes of the melody line in a full-toned sustained *legato,* while playing the inner semiquaver line in a **light** *staccato* so that you absorb the physical sensation of 'bringing out' the melody with the weaker fingers while keeping the inner part, played with the stronger fingers, relatively light.

When you put hands together continue to listen acutely to the balance between the individual parts so that the melody is carefully poised above the even inner semiquavers, with the syncopated LH line giving a smooth but continually felt onward impulse to the whole. This balance is a subtle one – the melody needs to sing out clearly, but not so much that it is left 'high and dry'. The strands are essentially interdependent, the inner semiquavers creating a soft undertow, and the whole gently propelled along by the LH syncopated rhythmic pattern. As regards the tempo, it appears that Chopin originally contemplated what seems to us a startling *Vivace,* eventually settling at *Lento ma non troppo* (Brown, p.79). Although it is evident that the ♪ = 100 feels slightly fast for most pianists, we must ever beware of the danger of wallowing, and thereby reducing this great melody to a clogging mess of gratuitous slop. This has everything to do with 'moving on' (as opposed to 'bursting') into the middle section from b.21 (see below), and likewise with the management of the return towards the reprise from bb.54-62.† There are numerous implied tiny nuances: for example through the tiny swell in b.2. (and similarly in b.5), a hint, but no more, of a *tenuto* on the **second** i.e.

slurred G sharp  while on the other hand the similar figure in b.3 'goes

on' towards a slight *tenuto* on the C sharp on the second beat. Then from b.5 there is an onward feeling towards the *tenuto* and *ritenuto* through the second beat of b.8. The essential is that the onward movement is resumed following each *tenuto* or 'give': 'elastic' (a favourite term of Elgar) in the sense of returning upon itself, rather than continually stretching. (At the risk of labouring my recurring point, all this can be established with perfect clarity by the simple expedient of **singing** the melody.) By the same token, ensure that the small *crescendos* always 'return to base', so that having begun in a quiet but sustained tone, you do not begin your real climb until b.14. Even here be sure that you **start** b.14 from *piano*, for Chopin has gauged his *crescendo,* stretto and *ritenuto* meticulously here, and if you start too loudly at b.14 you will be banging horribly before you reach b.17. Follow Chopin's indications scrupulously therefore, gradually increasing the tone through the 'spaced out' chords in b.16. This is, of course, a supremely expressive passage, but keep your fervour well this side of hecticness as you rise towards a magnificent fullness of tone on the *fortissimo* chord at b.17. Allow a fair 'hold' here, but without losing too much of the sense of continuity in the inner part, and then **gradually** allow the line to subside and 'unwind', expressively but without sentimentality towards the

pianissimo tonic chord at b.21, playing the grace note figure **on** the beat.

Pianists who so often play the first section too slowly, then hurtle away here as if they are setting off into a new piece altogether. Taking note of the *poco più animato*, in relation to his original tempo marking. Chopin obviously intended the central section to grow out of the first. Allow full value but not too much more, therefore, to the tonic chord on the first beat of b.21, with just enough time for a new 'breath' as you lead on from the second beat in the slightly faster tempo. It is a good plan to study the treble line alone so that you absorb the overall melodic shape of the 2-bar recurring patterns from here

through to b.29. Feel the slight

tenuto effect as you 'lean' lightly on the emphasised semiquaver E on this second beat and then

bb.21–77

---

†Chopin's various attempts to define his intentions in his opening indications for this study are discussed by Thomas Higgins in his article 'Tempo and Character in Chopin' (Musical Quarterly No. 59, 1973).

move on a little, feeling the impulse towards the quaver C sharp at the end of the bar, and 'finishing off' the phrase neatly through the first beat of b.23 before the next 'lean' on the emphasised semiquaver on the second beat as you 'lean' into the restatement, and so on. Then when you add the inner voice, endeavour to preserve the illusion of melodic smoothness in the treble so that this overall melodic shape is enhanced, not sabotaged, by the 'double stopping' effect. When you practise the LH alone, observe the details of articulation in bb.22-3, etc; the five *staccato* semiquavers and then the three slurred semiquavers at the end of b.22 etc, and the three slurred semiquavers at the beginning of b.23 etc. The careful implementation of these details when you put hands together will miraculously check and control any slithering that may tend to occur through the RH voice writing through this passage. Take particular care with the 'finishing off' through the first beat of bb.23, 25, etc, ensuring that the 'staggered' effect is neatly shaped, i.e. the LH 'finishes off' on the third slurred semiquaver and the RH on the fourth. Then allow an extra instant as you leap up in the RH to 'start again' on the second beat of the bar.

Carry on the sequence a tone higher in a rather fuller tone from the second beat of b.25. Then feel a slight drawing out as you *crescendo* through the end of b.29 ready to move on again through b.30, giving the upper thirds a warm and smooth *forte* tone, carefully balanced with the inner RH thirds, with the dotted rhythm figures in the bass line, and with the inner LH syncopated reiterated E's. The greatest care needs to be taken here so that all these four strands are clearly heard both in b.30, and in the *piano* minor at b.31, rather than the blob of loud sounds followed by a blob of quieter sounds that so often passes for an 'echo' effect here. Allow an extra instant to clear the sound at the end of b.30, ready to point the minor C natural on the first beat of b.31. 'Go to' a clear chord on the first beat of b.32 (whether or not you play this chord in the *forte* given in Henle and Paderewski, but not in the Vienna Urtext Edition – Cortot gives a *sforzato*) and allow a fraction of a second for a 'breath' before you launch into the slurred semiquaver sequence. Allow a tiny 'hold' as you poise yourself on the first slurred semiquaver thirds, and then keep control of the rhythm as you ascend through the sequential patterns, by always feeling the syncopating 'lean' on each offbeat couplet. Then apply the 'brakes' firmly, with clearly spaced semi-*staccato* chords ('leaning' a little on

the first of these ) as you lead into b.34. Allow an instant's

'breath' once more following the chord on the first beat of b.38 etc. before you launch into the contrary motion sequence of augmented fourths expanding in a smooth sweep towards the first beat of b.39, and again to b.40. It is the fine balance between allowing time to 'breathe' and preserving the sense of continuity through these fluctuating sequences of passage-work that makes this section difficult to hold together. Then keep careful control of the pulse as you expand more resolutely in contrary motion through bb.40-1, 'drawing out' a little towards the *fortissimo* B major chord on the first beat of b.42. (One would love to know the reaction of Chopin's contemporaries to this astonishing passage.) Allow the slurred dominant seventh to cascade downwards (but controlledly!) through bb.42 and 45, 'braking' firmly with the forceful semi-*staccato* chords through bb.43 and 45, as you *crescendo* towards a powerful B major chord on the first beat of bb.44 and 46. Note the different indications: *con forza* through b.43, and then *con fuoco* as you drive on into b.46, but allowing an extra instant this second time to leap up as if in a controlled arc (rather than snatching wildly) to the slurred sixths on the second semiquaver pulse of b.46. Feel once more a very slight *tenuto* here as you launch in with the *bravura* sixths. This is, of course, a virtuosic passage which will need prolonged and systematic practice. Practising in dotted rhythms will be helpful, and Cortot gives a range of excellent preparatory exercises. In performance the essentials are, not to let your stretto outstrip your capacity, and **never** to lose sight of the underlying 'normal' pulse, despite the syncopating effect of the continually slurred offbeat couplets. Make a controlled *ritenuto* as you *crescendo* towards the B major chord at b.54, and allow an extra instant as you poise yourself and take a breath through the semiquaver rest ready to enter quietly and *legatissimo* once more on the second quaver pulse. As Cortot says, however, 'the interpretation of these eight bars (54-61) should nevertheless retain something of a prolonged quivering, like that of some exalted mood subsiding only by degrees'. Feel the implied offbeat 'lean' on the slurred LH quaver E and RH semiquaver sixth as you re-enter in b.54, as well as the indicated emphasis on the slurred LH and tied treble quaver upbeat to bb.55 and 56. Study this passage carefully 'parts separately' once more, so that the expressive emphases and eloquent LH fragments all 'make their point'. Note particularly the slight emphasis on the treble G sharp on the second quaver pulse of bb.56 and 57, on the treble and inner upbeat quavers to bb.57 and 58, and on the syncopated D sharps and the inner G naturals in bb.58 and 59. Do not, however, allow these points to become laboured or you will destroy the sense of inevitability as you lead back towards the reprise at b.62. In terms of tempo this passage is often felt to be problematic. It need not be so if Chopin's evident overall intentions are understood (see above). The *ritenuto* **into** b.54 prepares the more sober tempo that will lead with a naturally arising slight adjustment through the *smorzando* and *poco rallentando* through bb.60-1 into tempo 1 at b.62. Some pianists play the reprise in a quieter, more musing tone with good effect. This, taking into account the *legatissimo* from b.62, rising to *forte* at b.70 rather than the previous *fortissimo,* was perhaps Chopin's intention. Let the lower semiquavers move on quietly through the first beat of b.73 (noting that there is no *ritenuto* through b.72), and then point the lower semiquaver C natural on the second beat of this bar. Do not grow **too** slow through b.75 or the line will 'stop', but then take time to 'space' the last melodic fragment through the end of the penultimate bars towards the quiet final tonic.

Op. 10 No. 4
Study in C sharp minor (VA)

The effect of this piece in a brilliant *con fuoco* performance approaching Chopin's $\s" = 88$ is nothing short of demonic. The technical demands on the performer are equally demonic – it is even more difficult than it sounds. There is little to be gained except discouragement by attempts at preliminary study by players of less than virtuoso standard. The tightly-knit texture, the lightning change from hand to hand of the fire-cracking semiquaver patterns, the quick-change flexibility required by the sequential patterns at bb.35-6 and 39-45, and the fearsome final '*con più fuoco possibile*' present formidable challenges even to players of the highest rank. I cannot agree with Robert Collet that 'it can sound equally convincing at **considerably** slower speeds' (Walker, p.131). It is a lashing, vicious tour-de-force (another facet indeed of the exquisitely attired dandy of the Paris Salons) and little short of a hurricane force tempo will do. Cortot gives comprehensive suggested practice patterns. Condemned as a student to long hours of fruitless practice of this piece, with little help from eminent professors (except exhortations in effect to play clearer, play faster, play louder, coupled with humbling exhibitions of their own mastery of the apparently impossible), I wish I had known then what I know now: when all the preliminary practice is yielding results, the patterns have been learnt, and the parts are being assembled, be aware that, as the semiquaver patterns succeed each other in either hand, it is the **other** hand which controls the whole.

Thus, from the opening upbeat through to the upbeat to b.5, it is the relentless impulse of the **LH** chords (and then through b.4 the LH **octaves**) which control and propel the overall impetus – the relentlessness of this crotchet beat unaffected by the dynamics. Thus, following the 'bite' of the opening figure, the LH continues like clockwork as it drops immediately to *piano* on the second beat of b.1, *crescendoing* onwards until the RH 'takes over' on the upbeat to b.5, with an implied drop to *piano* again after the first beat of b.5, and so on. This simple change in the focus of attention on the part of the player can galvanise his direction of effort in a miraculous way. There is of course, no substitute for the assiduous preparatory practice of the semiquaver patterns, but as was pointed out in connection with Op.10 No.2, the tendency with relatively inexperienced players is for the semiquavers to 'take the brunt' and attempt to stagger along under their own steam, rather than being seen as subject to the guiding impetus of the chords in the 'other' hand.

Op. 10 No. 5
Study in G flat major (VA)

This is another tour-de-force, but one in which the RH triplet semiquavers lie nicely under the hand. It has a sophisticated kind of exuberance – the brilliance of its semiquavers like shooting lights from a spinning diamond, over a sometimes jaunty, sometimes suave, but always rhythmically persuasive LH. As observed in the General Introduction under 'Fingering', Chopin has not to this day been altogether successful in laying the ghost of the thumb-on-the-black-note taboo! For this, if for no other reason, less experienced players will benefit from some preparatory study of this piece. Most players seem to have an inborn fear of the black notes. Even relatively advanced pianists, obeying a subconscious instinct, I suppose, to give them a wide berth, often retain a tendency to 'fall off' the edge of the keys, i.e. to play as near to the outer edge of the white keys as possible. In this piece, of course, it is necessary to maintain a 'well in' hand position, with the thumb over the black keys so that it is always in position to play. The player is thus obliged to resist this curious urge to pull away from the keyboard, which necessitates frantic inward swoops when the need arises to reach the black notes (see General Introduction, under 'Some Explanations and Amplifications').

Play the chord of G flat major in the RH, i.e. the complete octave chord with the hand squarely on the keyboard (in other words, with the arm and wrist at an angle of 45° to the keyboard, rather than tilted to right or left), and the fingers in a natural, **slightly** curved position (not exaggeratedly 'curled under'). It will be seen that the second, and particularly the third finger will be so far in towards the back of the keyboard that they are nearly touching the open lid. Again, play from the beginning of **b.3** very slowly. If you place the RH over the first three notes (D flat, A flat, D flat) with the hand lying easily over the keys, it will be seen that the second finger, lying over A flat, will be almost touching the lid again. Now play the three notes in the written order (D flat, D flat, A flat, etc.). Once more the second and (the silent) third fingers will be almost touching the lid. Immediately you have played the fifth semiquaver (A flat) with the thumb, allow the hand to 'flick' upwards while holding this A flat with the thumb so that the fifth finger 'falls' silently over the upper A flat, with the hand lying open and relaxed on the surface of the keys and over the A flat octave. The

396

hand is then in position to repeat the pattern through the second half of the bar, and similarly to progress upwards through b.4.

Once it is understood that it is as easy to play the black notes as the white, providing this 'well in' hand position is maintained, much of the fear and awkwardness in reaching the black notes will be removed. But since the black notes stand higher, and are narrower than the white, the other fear, that of slipping off them, is more real. In the interests of accuracy and sure control of tone, it is important that **all** notes, black or white, are struck **centrally** so

that you feel each finger goes to the 'core' of the note: 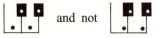 and not

This is doubly important in the case of the black notes in order to minimise the risk of slipping off. To this end, Cortot's Exercise 1 is helpful in familiarising the player with the physical sense of playing with the hand 'well in', and striking to the 'core' of each note.

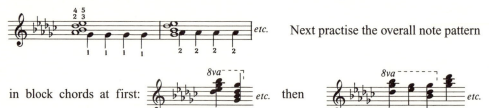

Next practise the overall note pattern

in block chords at first: *etc.* then *etc.*

Now practise the RH sequence of bb.1-4 over and over until the hand is completely familiar with the pattern. When the hand moves downwards from the first chord position in the first

half of the bar: to the next position in the second

half of the bar: it is vital that the hand 'comes with you'

(see General Introduction under 'Some Explanations and Amplifications'). The instant the thumb strikes the D flat on the second main beat of the bar, let the hand 'flick over' using the thumb as a pivot so that the hand is ready in position for the fifth and second finger to play the subsequent G flat and B flat. Then when the thumb strikes the G flat near the end of b.1, let the hand 'flick' downwards so that the fourth finger is ready to play the B flat, and so on. Similarly on the upward journey through b.3, the instant the fifth finger strikes the **fourth** semiquaver of the bar (D flat) 'bring' the thumb up, so that the hand is in the 'closed' position, with the thumb 'in place' ready to play the A flat. Then as the thumb strikes this A flat, 'flick' the hand 'open' so that the fifth finger is ready to play the subsequent high A flat, and so on. Now practise in

various rhythms:

Varying fingerings are given in different editions. I much prefer Chopin's fingering through bb.1-2 to, for example, Cortot's. Chopin's 3 (or 2) 5 1 4 2 4, 1 5 2 3 1 4 enhances the downward shift of the hand, whereas Cortot's 2 5 1 3 2 3 etc. tends to 'hold the hand back' towards the treble. And in b.3 the fingering 1 5 2 5 1 5 etc. may be better for smaller hands than the often given 1 4 2 4 1 5.

Practise the LH thoroughly and perfectly rhythmically. It is vital that the LH chords, immaculately articulated, underpin the RH throughout, with perfect rhythmic poise and stability. While the RH has to be performed with the utmost brilliance, its giddy flights are at all times 'guided' by the rhythmic and harmonic impulse of the LH. And in this piece the balance between the hands has to be particularly finely tuned – sometimes the LH tends to be left to dab around like a forgotten appendage – again in other performances the LH is pounded out as if on a hurdy gurdy. It is important that the sense of the **2/4** pulse is always felt so that the third chord of bb.1, 2, etc. is securely 'placed' as the **second** beat of the bar, rather than left adrift in the middle of the bar. Then feel the last quaver of b.3 (A flat) as the **upbeat** to b.4, and give the dotted crotchet D flat on the first beat of b.4 enough resonance to sound on through its full duration beneath the emphasised inner chord. Then make a clear 'lean' on the crotchet fifth in b.7, balancing this syncopated effect with two firm and steady spread quaver chords in b.8 and so on. The implementation of all these details colours and 'points' the activities of the RH. When you put hands together, however slowly, ensure that the LH is played perfectly rhythmically so that it provides this absolutely stable foundation for the RH. 'Pluck' the notes of the *staccato* chords in such a way that while they are perfectly clear and sharp, they are not so sharp as to sound like mere 'spikes' of sound. The fragments of melodic movement in the

LH, i.e. of the inner thirds in b.1, the lower thirds in b.2, the upper

thirds in b.3, etc. must be clearly heard. Take care when the hands are put together that the last quaver beat of bb.1 and 2 etc, when the LH is silent, is not skimped in the RH, causing the sensation of 'falling into' the next bar.

Allow a nice 'give' as indicated through the broken octaves through the second half of b.8, ready to set off again in b.9. Note the dynamics carefully – the brilliant *forte* in b.1, the echo effect in b.2, and the climb back towards *forte* through bb.3-4.

In b.17 the tone changes to a delicious tinkly nonchalance over a suavely persuasive LH. The descending RH lands on the emphasised tied upbeat to bb.19 and 23 as if with a light 'crouch', ready to change direction and shoot up again from the tied semiquaver in bb.19 and 23. (Take particular care to keep the LH steady between these bars: 18-19 and 22-3.) Then since this is a showpiece par excellence, begin a '**show**' of momentary passion from b.23. Ensure that the RH *staccato* notes are 'picked out' like sparks of light on the second beat of b.23, and the first and second beats of 24-6 as the triplets circle in arcs, *crescendoing* towards b.27. Feel here that you are 'lifting up to', not **snatching** at, the high B flats in bb.27 and 28, then 'picking out' the implied treble fragments: B flat-A flat-G flat-D flat, supported by a resonant 'lean' on the syncopated LH sixth on the second quaver of these bars. From b.23 the more resolute progressions of the LH play an increasingly important role in building up the overall resonance towards b.33 (and again from b.41 towards the beginning of the reprise at b.49). Take care to keep the LH perfectly steady again through bb.29-33, observing the *legato* slurs. Support the RH as it zooms smoothly through the wide arcs through bb.33-6 and 37-40 with carefully balanced resonances in the LH, held within the pedal as indicated. Listen to the horn-like quality of the LH through bb.41-4 and then to the richer harmonic quality from the second quaver of b.45, drawing out the upper LH line with a shade of luxuriance through b.48 as you poise yourself to leap into the reprise from b.49.

Allow time through the end of b.64 as you approach the *pianissimo* spread chord on the first beat of b.65, and then 'holding' the sound of the RH semiquaver E flat for an instant in the air, let the arpeggio fall in the most delicate 'shower', drawing out through b.66 as you poise yourself to leap off quietly, in perfect time, into the coda in b.67. Let the RH sport around over the smoothest possible LH, bound by the tonic pedal-point through bb.67-9 and 71-3.

The most difficult passage of all is the climb from b.79, where panic is wont to set in, even among the bravest of players. The essential is to keep steady. As often as not the rot sets in **before** you start the climb, by failure to 'finish off' cleanly with the quavers on the first beat of the bar, and consequently 'falling into' the first of the accented triplet groups unpreparedly and therefore unrhythmically. Feel you are *crescendoing* through b.78 towards powerful quavers on the first beat of b.79. Then allowing an instant's break to 'gather' yourself and 'poise' the RH, think of the first RH triplet figure as the 'upbeat' to the second beat of the bar, so that the upward climb takes off in earnest from the **second** main beat of the bar.* Then as you climb, keep an absolutely solid sense of the two main beats of the bar. Practising in

rhythms will help: [musical notation] and [musical notation] Arriving again

on **strong** semiquavers on the first beat of b.83, allow time to leap up to the high G flats, and 'drawing out' the first octave fractionally, then give the **sense** of an *accellerando* as the octaves shoot downwards towards powerful unison tonic quavers on the first beat of the penultimate bar.

Op. 10 No. 6
Study in E flat minor (8)

This is a study in concentrated *legato* playing. There are occasional problems for smaller hands, but many of these can be solved by the judicious and unobtrusive taking of inner semiquaver notes by the 'other' hand or by finger substitution as and when necessary. It is, perhaps, a player's, rather than a listener's piece. The inflections of the inner semiquaver line creeping between the sustained lower line and the upper and inner RH melodic lines are almost too subtle for the ear to absorb. The tempo is problematic. The ♩. = 69 gives a rollicking beat hardly in tune with the general mien, nor with Chopin's *Con molto espressione*. Yet, bearing in mind the *Andante* he cannot have meant ♪ = 69, although many players, anxious to give their all, cannot resist lowering the tempo to such a turgid, self-indulgent plod, as if assuming that the metronome mark was indeed meant to be ♪ = 69 – a lugubrious *largo*. If, on the other hand, there is a lighter, continuously onward (though unhurried) movement, the piece has a shadowy quality, dirge-like, but infinitely finely shaded, rising, as Arthur Hedley has said, to an intense lament (p.143). To preserve the Bachian clarity of the complex polyphonic texture, the pedal should be used with extreme discretion, with light touches highlighting and 'pointing' harmonic and expressive effects rather than in a continuous blanketing effect.

bb.1–16   As the inner semiquaver line, to quote Jim Samson, 'winds its chromatically tortuous way through the texture' (p.67), it is in many senses the predominant 'presence' and motivating impulse of the piece. I therefore suggest studying this first so that when you study the upper and lower lines, you can imagine this continuous semiquaver movement above or beneath. Practise in close *legato,* listening acutely to the chromatic inflections within the quietly 'rocking' curves. Notice how, in rising to the E flat at the end of b.1, this doubled E flat becomes the upbeat to the treble B flat in b.2, and also 'brings in' (i.e. is the tied upbeat to) the **inner** RH melodic line. As the semiquaver line moves on through b.2 in the inner LH voice, feel the implied slight emphasis on the tied upbeat to b.3. Then in bb.4 and 5 the **eleventh** semiquaver is 'doubled' and 'remains

---

*It is also important to DROP the tone after the first beat of b.79, so that you have 'room' to crescendo as you climb.

behind' to form a tied quaver upbeat to the inner LH semiquaver line in the subsequent bar, while at the same time the semiquaver line moves on up, to 'double' with the inner RH voice as a tied upbeat to b.5, and with the upper voice on the upbeat to b.6. This complex intermingling of the voices is immediately demonstrated in these few bars, and must be studied with the greatest **aural** attention. Now play, and **listen** to the sustained lower line from bb.1-8, and then put the two lower parts together, noting the 'hollow' effect of the intervals (perfect fifths, augmented fourths and fifths, etc.) which occur on the first beat of each bar (and the second beat of bb.6 and 7) and around which the semiquavers continually weave.

Then practise the upper and inner RH lines separately and together. Feel the consistent 'lift' up to the sustained treble melody note on the first beat of bb.2-6, and when you put the voices together, show the 'entry' of the inner voice on the upbeat to b.2, and once more listen to the 'hollowness' of the intervals (the partly tied fifth on the first beat of bb.2 and 3, the augmented fourth on the first beat of b.4, and so on). When you put all the voices together, practise assiduously without the pedal until you have thoroughly absorbed aurally the sense of everything that is 'going on', and the ways in which the voices interrelate. When you do use the pedal (with the utmost discretion as already cautioned) make it your concern to ensure that the inner line is never submerged or blurred. Be sure to give the opening upbeat its full value while at the same time feeling its 'onward leaning' impulse. And beware, in your concern to 'point' the various details discussed above, that you do not make the unfortunate effect so often heard, of 'stopping' on the upbeat to each bar. Feel, on the contrary, that the upbeats, tied or 'doubled' as the case may be, give an onward leading effect towards the singing long note on the first beat of each subsequent bar. Give the inner LH **and** RH tied upbeat to b.5 a particular (though not 'bumped') importance as it is these 'staggered' combined resonances which create a natural *crescendo* effect towards the *forte* in b.5. Give the emphasised tied E flat on the first beat of b.5 sufficient expressive resonance to last through its full value, and then let the line 'fall' in an expressive *decrescendo* towards the telling augmented fourth on the first beat of b.6. Listen particularly through b.5 to the movement of the semiquaver line through the first half of the bar beneath this treble E flat, and then to the effect of the clash between the LH B flat and RH C flat, 'resolving' to the unison A flats on the sixth quaver pulse. Draw out a little as you *crescendo* gradually without too much of a 'surge', into the restatement at b.9. The treble appoggiatura will be placed **on**

the first beat of b.8:  *etc.* or *etc.*

As you close on the tonic on the first beat of b.16, listen to the LH moving on

bb.16–53 downwards. The *pesante* direction is somewhat surprising, but Chopin undoubtedly means the LH to move on in a more purposeful sense – this onward leading semiquaver line already more 'open', and its curves more wide ranging, as they are to remain throughout the middle section. The RH has its only rest here, like a breathing point, before 'growing' onwards again in a less enclosed, more overtly expressive vein. From this point the semiquaver line is taken predominantly by the RH, and the feeling of continuity must be carefully preserved where the LH takes over temporarily, from the upbeat to and through bb.18 and 20, or takes the occasional note, e.g. the inner G sharp in b.26. Practise the upper melody line through bb.17, 19, and from b.21, together with the inner semiquavers, but without the inner notes of the chords, 'leaning' on the treble notes and playing the semiquavers in a light

staccato (as in Op.10 No.3).

etc. Then similarly,

practise the complete RH, again 'leaning' on the sustained upper notes and playing the inner semiquavers in a light *staccato*. Keep the fifth finger close to the keys so that there is as little break as possible in the treble sound as the F is repeated and you move on up to the G natural and then the A flat.

Then when you put the hands together as written, endeavour to ensure that the treble line sings out, but the inner notes of the chords and the inner semiquavers are perfectly audible and meticulously smooth and balanced, over a smooth, and supportively resonant LH line. This, need it be said, is far from easy to achieve – the RH balance is far more complex than in Op.10 No.3. Make a controlled, again not 'gusty' *crescendo* into b.18, then draw back a little, ready to make another slightly stronger *crescendo* towards the *fp* chord on the first beat of b.21. Hold this chord for an instant to 'point' this magical harmonic shift, and to clear the sound as you move into this sudden, sunlit clarity of E major. These few bars (21-4), like a short break in the surrounding clouds of harmonic and interpretative ambivalence, have an extraordinary beauty, quietly poignant, yet radiantly expressive.

The mood changes again, moving into C sharp minor from b.25. Feel the sense of moving on towards the first beat of b.26, and then a greater and more anguished surge up towards the first beat of b.28. Drop the tone again towards the beginning of b.29 before you begin the *crescendo* and stretto towards the *forte* chord on the first beat of b.32, taking care to avoid too much shrillness in the RH by providing increasingly resonant support with the LH octave line. Draw out the semiquavers a little through the first beat of b.32, ready to drop the tone as the climactic diminished seventh harmony resolves into the dominant seventh harmony through the second half of the bar. Then listen acutely to the shifting harmonic inflections of the RH over the chromatically descending LH octaves as the music gradually subsides towards the tied dominant bass on the first beat of b.39, and draw out a little as you lead back towards the quiet beginning of the reprise at b.41. The emphasised chord of F flat on the first beat of b.47, repeated in bb.48 and 49, is like a quiet, warning call before the sudden 'opening out' towards the chord of A major on the second beat of b.49. Take a little extra time to listen to the *sostenuto* progression back towards the F flat chord in b.50. Then listen acutely as the inner semiquavers continue in gradually subsiding waves within the sound of the held outer tonic unisons, taking an extra instant to place the final resolution to the tonic major.

Op. 10 No. 7
Study in C major (VA)

At Chopin's ♩. = 84 this piece is formidably difficult. Played at a slower speed for less advanced players it still makes a marvellous study in suppleness, and clarity of articulation both in the outer, 'weaker' fingers, and in the continual light (and lightning) changing of thumb and forefinger on the repeated inner notes. Cortot gives a comprehensive selection of preparatory exercises, and rightly draws attention to the necessity of maintaining a flexible wrist which, as he says, should remain slightly lower than the hand. The tendency is for the wrist to rise higher and higher with the hand contracting into a state of spasm, the fingers reduced to rigid claws! Within the apparently simple pattern of the RH throughout the piece, there is a great deal going on. There is in

one sense an inner upper melody: 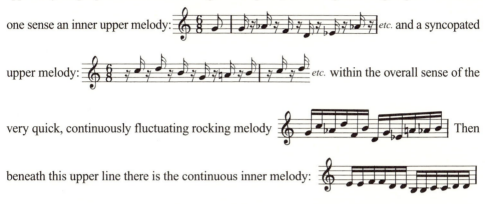 etc. and a syncopated

upper melody: etc. within the overall sense of the

very quick, continuously fluctuating rocking melody Then

beneath this upper line there is the continuous inner melody:

These points need to be 'understood' within the inner ear of the player, rather than laboured – indeed, there is not time to labour them in performance. Then providing there is perfect clarity, the texture will 'look after itself'. The problem, of course, is that the inner repeated notes taken by the 'strong' thumb and forefinger tend to sound heavier than the upper line. Cortot's two exercises under heading No.3 are especially helpful in this context, particularly if the upper semiquaver triplets are played strongly over **lightly** held tied lower quavers.

continuing chromatically

Chopin plainly intended an overall *legato* effect in the upper line, in view of the slur marks over each bar, not the spiky, juddering *staccato* so often to be heard, and the two exercises above will help to this end.

Practise the LH also carefully alone, absorbing the sense of its various emphases and inflections. While in performance the hands must, of course, be carefully balanced so that the LH supports but never swamps the RH, it is, however, once more the LH which throughout guides and acts as 'conductor' to the RH (see General Introduction under 'The Left Hand'). Place the opening detached quaver octave neatly, then feel the quaver rest precisely, **lifting** the hand so that it falls naturally to create a slightly syncopating emphasis on the quaver A flat, giving this note a fractional *tenuto* effect, and then phrase the line smoothly down again towards the detached quaver C on the first beat of b.2. This time, through b.2, listen to the sustained sound of the 'doubled' minim C as you again phrase the line down smoothly from the emphasised A flat. In b.3 show the implied slight emphasis on the tied lower quaver C sharp preparatory to a nice 'lift' up to the high quaver C sharp on the second beat, and then shape the two voices smoothly, as you move back towards the dominant in the second half of b.4. Poise yourself for an instant at the end of b.4 as you prepare to set off again in b.5, listening once more to the effect of the sustained lower C's through bb.5 and 6.

When you put hands together, very slowly at first, scrupulously maintain the shape and punctuation of the LH phrases, and notice how these LH inflections subtly influence those of the RH: there is the suggestion of a slight 'hold' on the third quaver pulse of b.1, then a sense of moving on towards the first beat of b.2. From the third quaver pulse of b.2 there is again a sense of moving on towards the middle of b.3 (here be aware of the filling out of the texture with the double stopping in the LH), and then a slight drawing back towards the end of b.4, and so on. At speed, of course, these are miniscule inflections, but the **awareness** of them makes the difference between a subtly shaded performance or a mere exhibition of dexterity. This piece is often presented in a metallic clatter. In an ideal performance it has, despite its high-speed effect, a delectable *grazioso* quality, the RH like two high voices engaged in blithe chatter, guided by a benign, wiser, lower-toned voice in the LH. Feel the sense of the overall dynamic curves from the opening towards the slight 'expansion' through b.3, as both LH and RH reach the peak of their respective curves and move downwards again towards the end of b.4, ready to 'start again' in b.5. Then feel the sense of lighter 'aeration' as you rise to the higher register in b.8, with a growing radiance of sound as the LH texture momentarily consolidates from the middle of b.11. There is a whole scenario in this piece, humorous and vivid for those of us for whom imagining is part and parcel of musical interpretation (however much some stern musicologists may frown). At b.17 the RH voices recede into a more passive, tinkling movement, as if looking on,

while the LH performs a delicately skipping dance-like figure. Slur the

figure neatly down towards the *staccato* bass notes, and show the pronounced, but not harsh emphasis on the accented crotchets on the second beat of bb.18 and 20. Then in the LH in b.22 run neatly up in a little swell towards the dotted quaver on the second beat of b.22. Poise yourself for an instant on a clear G major chord on the first beat of b.24 so that you 'place' the syncopated *sforzato* chord cleanly on the second quaver pulse of the bar, rather than collapsing into it. Then slur the LH octaves smoothly up to the *staccato* octave on the first beat of b.25, poising yourself again to **place** the *sforzato* chord, and then let the bass upbeat octaves 'go to' a **resonant** *sforzato* tied octave on the first beat of b.26. Listen to this sustained bass sound as the RH chatters upwards through bb.26-8. From b.29 the RH again takes a more passive role as the LH 'arcs' up to a warm-toned F sharp on the second quaver pulse of the bar. Phrase this LH line warmly and expressively as it descends in stages through bb.30-3, poising yourself once more on the dominant through the second half of b.33 (as in b.4) ready to set off into the reprise from b.34. From b.40 the texture of the LH 'thickens' to carry the RH more resolutely up towards b.42. Feel that the LH is 'taking the bit between its teeth' on the second quaver pulse of b.40, progressing purposefully up towards the stressed chord on the first beat of b.42, and emphasising the appoggiatura effect of the inner C sharp resolving to the D on the second beat. Draw out the end of b.42 a little, and poise yourself gracefully through b.43 as the LH rises with airy smoothness on a dominant seventh harmony. Then listen to the lower tonic pedal point as the inner LH and the RH voices proceed in gracious little surges through bb.44-7 (showing the RH curve up toward the **fourth** quaver pulse in bb.44 and 46, and to the **fifth** in bb.45 and 47. See the 'shape' of the hairpins here.). 'Finish off' neatly on the first beat of b.48 before letting the LH 'take off' with cheerful abandon from the second quaver pulse of the bar in a broad downward sweep, and again similarly in b.50.

Land on a firm tonic on the first beat of b.52, and then, showing the RH swell up to and down from the fourth quaver pulse of bb.52 and 53, implement the *sforzato* LH upbeats and tonic fifths firmly (bb.52-3 and 53-4) before whirring through bb.54-6 in a frisson of syncopated dominant and tonic chords. 'Finish off' on a neat tonic on the first beat of b.56 before the final upward flight. This is almost the most difficult moment, and few pianists can reach the top without a fluff or two! Poise yourself for an instant after the detached RH sixth and then, rather than blundering wildly upwards, preserve within yourself the sense of the two main beats in the bar, supporting the RH with a firm spread chord on the first beat of b.57. End with vigorous tonic chords and resonant final unison dotted minims.

Op. 10 No. 8
Study in F major (VA)

This is another formidably virtuosic piece. The RH sports up and down in exuberant arcs over a bouncing jaunty LH; it is no surprise to learn that this was one of the earliest of the Studies – Chopin was still a young blood, as yet uncushioned by the enticements of the Salons of Paris. Once again it is worth the while of less advanced but technically eager players to examine at least the first 14 bars. The patterns of the RH are, in a harmonic sense, simple to learn, based on the tonic through bb.1-3, dominant through bb.4-7, and so on. Since, in the main, these patterns lie easily under the hand, they are admirably suited to the small hand (see though bb.37 onwards). The essential skill to be learned here is that of 'flicking' the fourth finger over the thumb in the descent through bb.1, 3, etc, and conversely the easy movement of the thumb under the fourth finger followed by the quick upward 'flick' of the second finger on the upward

journey. It is helpful at first to practise thus: play the first four notes

and then 'flick' the fourth finger over with a lightning sideways-downward movement of the wrist, aiming the fourth finger towards the A so that it lands lightly and loosely on the surface of the note with a light 'plop' (rather than with sufficient pressure to make the note play). Then **play** the A with the fourth finger, and proceed downwards in the same way, 'flicking' over to the next A. Then, 'turning the corner' into b.2, perform a similar 'flick' going upwards so that the **second** finger lands silently on the F, and so on. Practise the actual **notes** very slowly while concentrating on getting the 'flick' itself as quick as possible. Try as well placing the thumb on the C and 'flicking' over to reach the A with the fourth finger, and then 'flicking' back up to reach the F with the second finger. Pause between each 'flick', concentrating again on getting the movement of the wrist as fast as possible as you 'flick'. If you practise the pattern in chords

thus: *(musical example)* *etc.* it will be seen that the hand takes up the same position as

it plays each 'chord'. It is essential, therefore, that by means of this quick 'flick' the hand is prepared to take up its previous 'position' ready to play each subsequent 'set' of four semiquavers. Since the fluency of this repeating pattern is, from a technical point of view, the main object of this study, it is essential to master this wrist movement, eliminating all unnecessary movements of the arm which would sabotage the free and even flow of notes. Then

practise in this rhythm *(musical example)*. Take care now that the thumb does not get 'left

behind' on the downward journey, but that as soon as it has played its C it 'opens out', also with a quick flick to get into position to play its next C. Similarly on the upward journey through b.2, be sure to release the thumb as soon as it has played the C, ready to move up to the next C and then the next. Now practise in even semiquavers as written. As the pattern becomes more fluent and you can go faster, the wrist movement becomes proportionately smaller, so that the hand and arm move downwards then upwards in a smooth horizontal movement from 'main position' to 'main position' (see the chord patterns above). To achieve perfect continuity and evenness the flexibility of the thumb becomes all important. In a performance by a skilled player, the right arm will be seen to move smoothly up and down the keyboard, with the wrist sufficiently supple to accommodate the changes of direction of the hand. Practise often in the

rhythm above and in other rhythms: ♩♪♪♩ ♩♪♪♩ etc. When you practise the RH as

written, be very conscious of the **shape** of the curves – the downward sweep followed by the upward climb, taking scrupulous care in each instance, at the bottom and top of each arpeggio, that you 'turn the corner' cleanly and with poise, creating a continuous series of glistening 'arcs' of sound. The observation of the accents is essential in a rhythmic sense, but be sure that they are very light **finger** accents, acting as rhythmic and 'geographic' footholds, rather than bumps in the line.

It is the LH, of course, which carries the melodic line and 'spells out' the overall rhythmic pattern and impetus. Practise it, therefore, until its rhythmic and melodic shape is thoroughly absorbed and understood. The sense of an overall two-in-the-bar is essential (see the metronome sign ♩ = 88, and indeed in some editions the alla breve ¢ is given), otherwise the movement, chopped into four-in-the-bar, becomes disastrously plodding. 'Lean' on the long fifth on the first beat of b.1, and then play the quaver on the third and fourth beats in jaunty and rhythmic *staccato,* articulating the acciaccatura with a smart 'flick' and with the feeling of 'going to' the bass octave on the first beat of b.2. Then leap off this bass octave so that the hand falls with a natural onward directed 'lean' on the dotted quaver D, ready to make a nice 'lift' up to a firm A on the third beat of the bar. Similarly feel the lift up to the *sforzato* crotchet on the upbeat to b.5. The better you 'lean' on this note, feeling the sense of a slight *tenuto,* the easier it is to carry out the wide-spanned broken chord effect on the first beat of b.5. Similarly lean well on the *sforzato* upbeat to b.9 to 'carry you on' into the *forte* at b.9. When you put hands together ensure that the LH **leads** so that the RH, as it darts up and down, is fitting in with the LH and **not** the other way around. 'Fill out' the sound with keenly resonant LH chords through bb.9-11, underpin the RH with resolute dominant chords through b.13 and the first half of b.14, and then allow a little 'give' through the end of b.14 as you prepare to lead back into b.15, allowing time to launch off again with a poised LH tonic spread chord. When the LH 'joins in' in contrary motion with the RH from b.37, practise hands together **slowly** in different rhythms to ensure perfect coordination. In performance be conscious of the steadying effect of the deliberately rhythmic LH marching down *marcato* through bb.38 and 40 (and again through bb.47-50). Similarly, note and implement the rhythmic and resonant significance of all LH emphases, and tied and held notes. From b.37 some of the patterns are difficult for a small hand unless it is particularly flexible. For preparatory practice for bb.47-50 see under Op.25 No.12, where the basic pattern is similar in the sense of the need for the lightning 'opening' and 'closing' of the hand. Grade the dynamics up to a glistening implied *forte* at b.55 then *diminuendoing* down to a shimmer at b.57, and 'opening up' the sound again through bb.58-60 as you prepare to launch into the reprise at b.61. Take time to practise **slowly** from b.75, **listening** to the marvellous effect of the RH inflections combining with the resonances of the LH, more sustained and musing here. One wonders, listening to the way many soloists rattle through this passage, whether they have troubled to study it **aurally** – it should surely have this musing effect even at high speed. The final tumultuous burst of unison semiquavers (bb.89-94) is a formidable challenge, and there is no substitute here for assiduous slow study, practising in varied rhythms.

Chopin's fingerings are particularly plentiful in this study. In overall performance the RH has to achieve a fleeting, scudding effect, smoothly articulated, but at the same time glisteningly clear, 'riding' the 'sprung' jaunty rhythm and line of the LH.

Op. 10 No. 9
Study in F minor (8+)

Cortot airily dismisses the technical difficulty for the LH here as 'but a secondary one, more apparent than real – at any rate, for a normal sized hand – and one which will be easily overcome by practising a few well-considered exercises'. He concentrates instead upon the 'declamation [of the RH] which is at times breathless, at others slow and heavy, as if burdened with memories and regret...'. He is right, of course, in stressing the importance of the special *portando* type of articulation required for this 'declamation' (which he calls *portamento* – see the General Introduction for discussion of these terms *portando* and *portamento*) but for most hands the continually fluctuating extensions of the LH are fairly demanding, and unless the hand and wrist are extremely supple, they will stagger to the end in a condition approaching rigor mortis. But for the owners of small hands, particularly those of the hard, bony type so often encountered, this provides (apart from the obvious technical benefits) a beautiful opportunity to discover the degree to which real suppleness and agility can compensate for bemoaned limitation of span. This is also an excellent exercise for the thumb – that member prone to be so 'lazy' in that it likes to hang around inertly as a vague 'extra' finger, instead of cultivating and capitalising upon its independence from the main body of the hand. To aid this independence, practise thus: place the second finger on C, allowing the weight of the hand to 'lean' lightly on this second finger, and 'exercise' the thumb by striking the notes of the scale, D flat-E flat-F-G, etc. as far as a comfortable stretch will allow, in a 'loose' *staccato,* cultivating the maximum easy movement and flexibility of the whole of the thumb shaft (i.e. from the tip to the point at which the bone joins the main body of the hand near the wrist). Then repeat, holding the C with the third finger, then the fourth:

It may be that when the second finger is held down on the C, the thumb will only extend as far as the A flat. But try performing the exercise with a rigidly stiff hand and wrist, and then in a state of the maximum possible looseness across the knuckle area, and it will readily be seen that the more flexible the disposition of the hand, the easier and wider the stretch can be extended. As to the eventual fingering, every hand must settle into its own most comfortable patterns. Chopin's fingerings for the opening LH figure: 5 4 1 4 1 4, 5 4 etc. are given in Henle and the Vienna Urtext. But with a hand of very average female span and proportions, and not possessing Chopin's exceptional span between fifth and fourth fingers, I find, for example, that through bb.1-2 this fingering 5 3 1 4 1 3 (or 4), 5 3 1 4 1 4, 5 3 1 4 1 3, etc, is happier. Obviously the LH has to be thoroughly learnt first, for the LH must 'carry' the RH in continually advancing and receding 'surges' of sound. Ensure that you establish a secure three-quaver rhythm **within** each sextuplet, so that the bass note is always rhythmically and clearly placed, and the implied melodic fragments played with the thumb (A flat-B flat-C-D flat, etc. in complement to the RH quavers, F-G-A flat-B flat) are properly defined. To this end it is a good

plan to practise thus:  etc.

The agitated 'panting' character of the RH is, of course, largely created by the predominant pattern of the principal motif, i.e. of quaver rests on the main beats with consequent **off**beat entries of each melodic fragment. The phrasing patterns are crystal clear if they are **sung**. Take a quick 'panting' breath before starting, and again on the second main beat of b.1 and the first of b.2. Then feel the curve of the longer phrase from the second quaver pulse of b.2, up through the high A flat, pressing on *con forza* through b.3 downwards towards the emphasised long C in b.4. **Hold** the sound through to the end of b.4, releasing it only in order to take a quick 'pant' again on the first beat of b.5, and so on.

Turning to the *portando* style of articulation, it can perhaps be best understood by means of the voice. If you say HAH HAH with a **long** A as in the written representation of a laugh, but 'stylised' as in operatic laughter (as if there were a *staccato* over the second H in each word so that you come **off** the end of one HAH just in time to pronounce the next), you will have the right emphasis and degree of articulation. Then transfer this to the keyboard – as Cortot says, each finger should 'press down into the key thoroughly, as if to imprint itself in the keyboard', and each note must be released as if with a small but strong 'spring' – the releasing of each note accomplished with as clear a definition as the imprinting. The note will thus be longer than a *staccato* but will be released before the next note is depressed. This style of articulation is applicable in many different circumstances, and the sensitive player will instinctively adjust the length of the notes according to the expressive sense of the passage. For example, in the Nocturne Op.9 No.2, in bb.8 and 16 the *portando* indicates a delicately expressive, barely detached articulation which 'speaks' languishingly – whereas here the notes will be more detached, though always longer than *staccato*. I make no apology for labouring this point in view of the number of performers who, unwilling to interpret Chopin's clear intentions, 'go at' this RH either in a 'picky' *staccato* or in a series of 'sloshy' slurs, completely destroying the 'breathless' effect created by the deliberately calculated quaver rests and *portando* quavers.

When you put hands together scrupulously preserve the rhythm and shape of each LH semiquaver sextuplet, listening acutely to ensure that the RH quavers and the LH 'thumb line' are perfectly synchronised, particularly in the instance of the offbeat couplets in bb.1, 5, etc. and feeling the sense in which the music is 'anchored' by the persistent tonic pedal point effect from bb.1-16.

bb.1–16   The sense of straining urgency must be conveyed from the first note, within a tautly controlled rhythmic propulsion. For less advanced players this taut, rhythmic attack, allied with a keen dramatic sense, is far more important than fruitless attempts to reach the very fast ♩. = 96. Show the overall curve of the first phrase, from b.1 through to the end of b.4, making a steep little *crescendoing* 'lift' up to the A flat on the fifth quaver pulse of b.2, and keeping the tone up *con forza* through b.3 down towards the accented dotted minim on the first beat of b.4. Holding this note (as when you sang it – see above) quickly clear the sound at the end of the bar, ready to 'start again' relatively quietly in b.5. This time make a more pronounced *crescendo* and 'lift' up to the C on the fifth quaver pulse of b.6. Then give the semiquavers at the beginning of b.8 a keen 'bite' as you 'go on up' to the strong syncopated minim A flat (this A flat is sometimes given as a tied crotchet). Draw out the remainder of the bar as indicated, keeping the *forte* up in the LH (even making a point of 'marking' the LH A flat and D flat on the fifth and sixth quaver pulses), and then make a tiny break, ready to spring off again in *sotto voce* in b.9. Play this *sotto voce* as if in a furtive whisper, without losing an iota of the sense of wild urgency.

bb.17–28   At b.17 (as the music prepares to 'ease' from the grip of the tonic pedal point) change the tone colour completely with this more *legato*, almost pleading phrase, making a warm-toned *crescendo* towards b.19, when the *forte* quavers snap back angrily as they leap down forcefully towards a resonant *sforzato* crotchet on the first beat of b.20. It is vital to consider thus the contrasting character of each phrase (again something so many virtuoso players fail to do). Cortot in his old recording creates an almost overpowering expressive intensity by his phrase 'characterisation' – the anxious pleading from the upbeat to b.21 'going on to' the emphasised tied G flat on the second main beat of b.22, and pressing on into the feverish (but controlled) stretto and continuing progressive *accelerando* towards b.28, with the gun-shot semiquavers shooting up to a piercing, offbeat high octave D flat.

bb.29–36   The repeated octave figures from b.29 are like wild and terrible nocturnal cries. Take care to 'phase' the LH tremolo effect carefully through the second half of b.28 to prepare for the maximum impact of b.29. **Listen** to the acute discordant effect of the D flats through bb.29 and 30 against the persistent LH dominant pedal point, and allow an instant break in the sound at the end of bb.29, 31, etc, just sufficient to clear the *forte* for the eerie *pianissimo* echo. Feel the sense in which the repeated octaves 'go on through' to the accented crotchet on the second beat of bb.29, 30, 33 and 34, starting with a *forte* a little less loud, and a *pianissimo* even quieter,

thus:

Less experienced players, worried by the group of five quavers in bb.33, 34, etc. can space

them thus at first: It is above all essential to ensure that

the LH semiquavers continue perfectly rhythmically so that the RH group of five fits in with the **LH** and **not** the other way about. As you become familiar with the notes and are able to increase the speed, you will find that you are able to stop self-consciously 'placing' the five quavers, and that, providing the LH pursues its course steadily, they will 'look after themselves' as they drive (or whisper) onwards towards the 'objective', the accented crotchet on the second beat. While the crotchet C on the second beat of bb.31, 32, 35 and 36 is **not** explicitly accented, ensure nevertheless that you similarly 'go towards' it, giving it a clear-carrying tone quality, whether in *forte* or *pianissimo*. Then draw out through b.36, poising yourself through a carefully graded *rallentando*, ready to set off in renewed *agitato* from b.37.

bb.37–66   Feel the increased intensity as the octaves are added from b.45. Then from b.49 grade the long *crescendo*, and from b.51 the stretto, in a gradual climb up towards a ringing octave A flat on the second beat of b.52, dropping the tone a little at the beginning of b.53 to start the final wild *crescendo* and *accelerando* towards b.56.

The ceaseless pounding of the tonic pedal point is an essential element in the cumulative power of this whole reprise. 'Pull back' sharply (momentarily) on the second beat of b.56. It is probably necessary to change or half-change the pedal on, or just after, this second beat to clear the sound ready for the *piano* upbeat to b.57 – but as you do this, be careful to **hold** the RH minim octave D flat until its sound has been 'caught' in the 'new' pedal. Play the repeated RH semiquavers in b.61 like a burst of machine-gun fire, again placing the group

of five 'consciously' at first, if necessary: 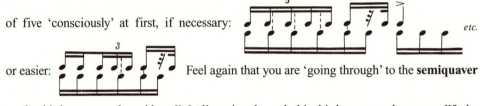 *etc.*

or easier: Feel again that you are 'going through' to the **semiquaver**

on the third **quaver** pulse with a **slight** lingering through this third quaver pulse as you **lift** the hand from the high octave (see General Introduction under 'Articulation'). Then think of the demisemiquaver octave as the 'upbeat' to the emphasised crotchet octave on the second main beat. Draw out as indicated through b.63, performing the *pianissimo* echo in a lingering style through b.64. Then play the high tremolo semiquavers in a disappearing shimmer, 'placing' the final staccato quavers as minute pinpoints of sound. This *pianissimo* shimmer is not too difficult providing you preserve the **sense** of the overall two-in-the-bar rhythm, though without obvious accents.

Chopin's pedalling may be found somewhat heavy on the modern piano. Players may prefer a **shorter** pedal on each main beat than is indicated in the opening bars. Then, through Chopin's longer pedal indications from b.19 onwards, effects of half-pedalling might be used, and similarly from bb.53-6. Here however, by this long pedal indication Chopin underlines the intended 'all in one breath' effect of this climactic upward sweep. (The pedalling of b.56 is mentioned in context.)

Op. 10 No. 10
Study in A flat major (VA)

This is one of the most difficult of all the Studies. A laboured performance is an agony – but in the hands of a true virtuoso as opposed to a mere technical wizard, its 'aural flight', to quote Cortot, is as intoxicating in terms of sheer exquisite sound as anything Chopin wrote. There is

virtually no let up in the  pattern of the RH, which means that the

RH, which is virtually always in the 'extended' octave position, has to be supremely supple and flexible if it is not to seize up before the first page is out. Then the rhythmic sense has to be of the surest to maintain a stable overall pulse at speed, within the continual crossing and counter-crossing of the beat – and these cross-rhythm effects need to be implemented by means of the skilled and subtle varying of the **touch** rather than by lumping accents. Nevertheless, players less formidably equipped have much to gain from studying the first 16 bars or so. Practise the

RH of bb.1-4 at first in chords thus: *etc.* so that the hand knows

exactly where it is going. Then practise the RH with the lightly syncopating slurs as written. The trick is to cultivate a small down-up movement of the forearm, wrist and hand so that the hand falls onto each slurred sixth, and lifts from the single quaver played with the thumb, ready for the arm to move upwards over the keyboard and ready to fall again on the subsequent slurred sixth. This fall creates a natural slight accent on each sixth, with the thumb following more lightly. The fingers must not, of course, drop flaccidly onto the keys, and particular attention must be paid to the sound of the fifth finger, which must be used sufficiently firmly and resiliently (not stiffly) to let the upper note of each sixth stand out sufficiently to shape the implied melody line. Then the thumb, although played relatively lightly, must be sufficiently active to give a tiny 'kick' to the hand as it lifts, thus sending it on upwards towards the subsequent sixth. This effect can be practised in scale

patterns: *[musical notation]* *etc.* *[musical notation]* *etc.* Ensure that the

hand relaxes for an instant during each lift – this is essential, otherwise progressive and crippling tension will accrue. If this principle is properly implemented in **slow** practice, it will be maintained even at high speed, although both the degree and the instant of relaxation will, of course, be infinitesimal. Note the 'hairpins' (bb.1-2, 2-3, etc.) taking care that each little swell 'returns to base' or the overall volume will get louder and louder with each swell, reaching saturation point within a few bars.

With the change of rhythmic pattern from b.5, the thumb must at all costs remain flexible. As each sixth is played (whether accented or not) let the thumb 'move up' and place itself **loosely** over its next note, so that the hand relaxes from its extended 'octave position' for an instant. Thus, as the first sixth is played on the second quaver pulse of b.5, the thumb will 'move up' ready to play the B flat, and so on. Again this effect can be practised up and down

the scale. Practise also in this rhythm: *[musical notation]* *etc.* Let the thumb hang loosely

over 'its next note' as you pause on the sixth, and then strike lightly and loosely, in the sense of an 'upbeat' to the subsequent sixth. This pattern can profitably be practised in varying rhythms. Then from b.9 return to the 'fall and lift' movement of bb.1-4 in reverse. To fall onto the naturally heavier thumb is much easier than the 'fall' onto the sixths in bb.1-4. The all-*staccato* passage from b.13 is wonderful practice. Cultivate a close-to-the-keys action in both hands, with tiny **plucking**, not striking, movements, again with nicely firm and resilient fingers. Try to give equal weight and definition to **each** RH quaver, that is, each single note and each sixth,

avoiding any tendency to this effect: *[musical notation]* *etc.* so that the lower (i.e.

thumb) and upper melody lines are equally consistently drawn. The active plucking of each *staccato* note or sixth creates a continuing rebound or spring which 'sends the hand on' towards the next pluck in a continually self-generating springing movement.

Practise the LH carefully too, 'pointing' the bass notes a little at the beginning of each six-quaver group. These bass notes set the harmony of each half-bar and, together with the 'doubled' note on each second and fourth beat through bb.1-8, serve to define and maintain the stability of the **12/8** pulse, beneath the fluctuating rhythmic cross-currents arising in the RH.

When the hands are put together, it will be found that bb.1-4 are by far the most difficult rhythmically since, as already said, the offbeat slurs have a syncopating effect, as opposed to a mere 'straight' cross-rhythm effect from b.9. However, if the rhythmic emphases are fully absorbed hands separately, they will eventually 'look after themselves' when played together, 'guided' by the consistently outlined **12/8** in the LH. With the turn into E major at b.17, there is the sense of a more full-throated harmonic resonance for the space of four bars, reverting to the slurred couplet pattern at b.21 with yet another subtle nuance of articulation and emphasis. At b.43 the new RH pattern grows from the previous richly inflected *crescendo* through bb.39-42. Let the RH sweep up and down in glistening arcs, the sound 'filled out' by a resonant and carefully balanced LH. Few moments in piano music are as seductive as the delicious inwards 'slide' through b.54 when it is played properly *dolcissimo* (which it seldom is) with just the right amount of 'give' in the tempo to poise the player to set off again in *pianissimo* from b.55.

Op. 10 No. 11
Study in E flat major (VA)

There are few pieces by Chopin, or anyone else, to equal this in terms of radiant, celestial beauty of sound. Again, this is a piece for performance by virtuosi. But also for the **relatively advanced student**, it is not only a valuable technical and musical study – it is also a piece which (at a fairly leisurely tempo) a player of a post Grade 8, or 'advanced' Grade 8 standard could shape sufficiently well to enjoy playing as a whole.

There is some doubt as to whether Chopin intended each arpeggio to be played in one long sweep from bass note to treble, with the bass note falling **on** the beat, **or** with the upper notes of the two hands **coinciding** on the beat and treating the notes of the arpeggios like anticipatory grace notes. Cortot, in his 'practice' edition, unequivocally takes the latter course: 'In order to perform this study with the required expression, it is necessary to suppose it has been written

as follows:' *etc.* However, Jim Samson suggests that here (as

elsewhere) a study by Moscheles 'provided a stimulus for Chopin' (p.69). He goes on to illustrate an extract from the Moscheles model and quotes Moscheles's instructions, which he suggests may be relevant to the interpretation of Chopin's study: the notes 'must all be played as an arpeggio, that is to say they must be played one after the other, from the lowest to the highest'. Besides this Moscheles precedent there are other reasons to consider the 'overall' arpeggio effect; in the light of modern scholarship it is generally accepted that in **most** cases Chopin intended broken-chord, grace note figures and ornaments to be placed on the beat (Cortot's edition was published in 1915); also the 'overall' arpeggio is much more difficult to execute smoothly and evenly, and on this account is perhaps more likely to reflect Chopin's intentions in such a comprehensive and demanding set of studies; and finally the fact that this effect is infinitely more lovely. Cortot and many others adopt a much faster tempo than the given ♩ = 76. But at this quite gentle *Allegretto* it becomes possible (given the implementation of Chopin's pedal marks) to create an almost continuous harped sound as opposed to the 'Brrp Brrp Brrp' 'Cortot' effect. However, this must remain a matter for the individual. Most players appear to hedge their bets by compromising in a happy hotch-potch of effects, tending to adopt the Cortot course in the main, but here and there making a musical point by means of the intermittent 'full spread'.

As Robert Collet says (Walker, p.133), players with relatively small hands can cope perfectly well with the spread chords providing that the wrist and hand (particularly over the knuckle area) are truly flexible. The problem invariably is that the relatively inexperienced player 'leaves the hand behind' in the vicinity of the lower note of the arpeggio, instead of letting the hand 'come with itself'; thus, in the arpeggios in b.1, having played the lower E flat, the LH will tend to remain **extended** as if trying to 'hang on' to this E flat, rather than 'coming with itself' as it plays the B flat and upper G. Similarly in the RH chord on the first beat of b.1, the hand will tend to remain extended towards the lower B flat.

Try, therefore, finding the natural 'closed' position of the hand by letting it hang loosely downwards. Then play the LH spread chord of b.1 letting the hand revert to its natural closed position after it has played the bass note so that it 'comes with itself' as the arm moves up towards the upper G. (See further discussion of this matter in the General Introduction under 'Some Explanations and Amplifications'.) It is then vital that, coming **off** the upper note with a light 'flick', arm and hand continue on momentarily in the same lateral direction (i.e. towards the right) so that the movement is 'followed through', rather than 'stopping dead' on the upper G. (This, of course, is the principle of the tennis stroke, the golf swing, etc.). At speed, inevitably, there is 'time' for only a very small 'follow-through' movement, but unless this principle is observed, the perfect 'harp' effect will not be achieved . For the 'overall' arpeggio effect, practise one chord, say the second chord in b.1, over and over, going from the bass note upwards 'in one thought', as in a harp stroke. 'Direct' the notes in such a way that you 'go up to' the treble note, giving a tiny 'kick' to the RH fifth finger so that this top note stands out with a tiny 'ping'. Go up the arpeggio slowly at first, gradually increasing the speed of the overall movement, and always thinking towards the treble note so that the **LH** thumb maintains its light onward, upward 'flick', rather than stopping with a bump. Then practise b.1 over and over, creating a consistent melody line with the softly 'pinging' little finger. If you decide to adopt the Cortot approach, the technical pattern of the 'follow-through' movement is similar, and since the LH and RH land on their upper note simultaneously, you need to ensure, as Cortot points out, that the upper RH note always predominates over the upper LH note. Whichever course you adopt, the objective is the same, to create an even flow of exquisite harp-like sound.

Ensure that the slurred single quaver upbeat gives a clear onward 'lean' towards the first chord of b.1. Give the *sforzato* chord a warmly 'ringing', not harsh, emphasis, and with the sense of a **slight** *tenuto* on the treble E flat, then dropping to *piano*, and making it clear that this short phrase begins with the **second** chord of b.1. Take care to support the RH with a carefully gauged bass resonance on the first beat of b.1. Then feel a sense of 'moving on' through b.1 towards the wider-spanned chord on the first beat of b.2. Feel the 'lift' up to this high F, allowing a fraction of extra time to span this wide spread chord, then moving on again through b.2 to make a greater 'point' of the yet wider-spread and higher chord on the first beat of b.3. Then show the line of the longer overall phrase from the second chord of b.3 and through bb.3-4. These little *tenutos* and 'movings on' are extremely slight – the last thing anyone wants is the disastrous gusty stops and starts sometimes heard. But this sense of 'spanning' the wide intervals, e.g. on the first beat of b.1, and then 'moving on' towards the 'spanning' of the next, higher and wider interval on the first beat of b.2, engender that slight sense of elasticity as opposed to the far from celestial effect of a metronomic series of upward arpeggiated 'rips'. Note Chopin's pedalling indications through bb.1 and 2. Cortot, on the other hand, recommends changing the pedal on each crotchet beat, presumably finding Chopin's pedalling too 'thick' for the modern piano. This again must be an individual matter, subject also to the qualities of varying pianos and varying acoustics. I prefer the 'haloed' effect of Chopin's pedalling, which, of course, retains the bass note through b.1, but this can be modified by the extent to which the pedal is depressed, or by some degree of **partial** pedal changing. Through bb.3 and 4 the pedal needs to be changed on each chord, which Chopin presumably intended even on pianos of his own time, since he did not 'cancel' the pedal indication placed at the beginning of b.3. (In many editions there is no pedal indication at all here.)

The inner RH line needs to be subtly defined through bb.25, 27, 29-31, etc, together with the inner LH line, and the RH fragments in bb.50 and 51 played with lingering expressiveness over the continuingly harp-like LH chords. Take care that the tone remains predominantly *piano*, with an overall soft radiance and 'sheen' – billowing here and there, but never growing gusty or jagged – the *con forza* at b.24 and the brief *forte* at bb.43 and 48-9 interpreted in a full, warm, not aggressive tone. There are no thunderstorms here, only breezes of subtly varying strengths.

Op. 10 No. 12
Study in C minor (8+)

Like the Polonaise in A major, this is one of those time-honoured war-horses at which every reasonably competent pianist will, at some time or another, take a 'hack'. And 'hacked' it usually is, as if with an axe in the right hand and a chain-saw in the left.

While in Stuttgart in 1831, en route from Vienna to Paris, the news reached Chopin that the Russians had finally crushed a long-running Polish uprising. While the agony of spirit this disaster provoked cannot be doubted ('Father! Mother!', he wrote, 'Where are you? Corpses? ... Poor suffering Mother, have you borne a daughter to see a Russian violate her very bones? ... God, shake the earth, let it swallow up the men of this age ... ' (*Chopin's Letters*, p.150) there appears to be little foundation for the legend that he vented his fury and despair specifically in this piece. Nevertheless, the title 'Revolutionary' will persist, if only because unlike the artificial musical titles acquired by numerous other compositions by Chopin and others, it is justified by the seething and turbulent nature of the music.

While on the face of it this is an exercise for fluency, agility and endurance in the LH, it is as much a study in coordination between the hands, in the 'backing up' of the impassioned declamation of the RH with the tumultuous thrust and surge of the LH. It is a piece which a confident post-Grade 8 player can tackle, if not for performance (and whether or not the tempo can even approach the very fast ♩ = 76), then at least for considerable domestic satisfaction, as well as for the many lessons in technique, coordination, and the harnessing of demanding passage work to dramatic-expressive ends.

There are two predominant patterns in the LH which should be 'taken out' and mastered first of all: a) the descending flight in the LH (bb.1-2, 3-4, etc.) ('doubled' by the RH in bb.5-6); and b) the upward and downward 'zoom' over two octaves or one octave (bb.9-14, etc.). When first studying the descending pattern (bb.1-2) the accents can be well marked and the

passage practised also in various rhythms:

absorbed and is thoroughly 'in the fingers', begin to think of the entire figure 'from the top downwards', so that you feel the first two notes, A flat and G, as the 'upbeat' to the accented F on the second beat, and then the E flat and D as the 'upbeat' to the accented B natural on the third beat, and so on, suggesting this overall shape

within the overall descending line. Thus, while the accent is still present, there is a continual sense of onward movement towards the next crotchet beat, rather than of a 'chopping up' of the bars into four 'crotchet' compartments. Over and above this, at high speed there is a clear feeling of *alla breve*, as given in Henle and also offered as an alternative in the Vienna Urtext Edition. Note the *legatissimo*, and the sweep of the overall LH phrase line through bb.1-2, 3-4, etc, indications of which we perhaps always need to remind ourselves – that while the passage must be brilliantly articulated, Chopin plainly does **not** want a burst of machine-gun fire here, but rather a 'zoom' of powerfully descending sound. Feel a *crescendo* through the short tremolo through the second half of b.2 so that you 'go to' a strong quaver B natural on the first beat of b.3, and leap off this note with a powerful spring so that the hand is 'directioned' upwards again to start the next downward 'zoom'. Practise bb.1-4 over and over until the downward sweep and the upward leap, ready for the **next** downward sweep are fluent, in the sense of a continuing clockwise 'circle', rather than a series of diagonal lines proceeding in jerks. It will be apparent that a **fractional** drawing out must be allowed (through the end of b.2), to prepare the upward leap, and then another extra **instant** to **make** the upward leap. It is then helpful, both musically **and** in order to steady yourself, to draw out **slightly** the first two notes of the next downward sweep, immediately picking up the tempo from the second crotchet beat of the bar. This slight 'holding' through the end of b.2 and the beginning of b.3 is essential to the poising of the 'join' between bb.2 and 3, although in performance it needs to be so slight that it is virtually undetectable, appearing only as part of the natural flow of the passage. Another, and slightly longer instant must be allowed to negotiate the wider leap in b.5 and to poise the 'joining in' of the RH in the unison *con forza* (or often indicated as *con fuoco*) descent through bb.5-7.

Similarly the RH must be practised alone until the 'aim' of the upward leap (bb.2-3, 4-5,

etc.) is perfectly secure. Practise thus at first: ... and then the overall figure ... Never mind if you misfire at first – concentrate on the powerful upward **aim** of the movement, from the semiquaver up to the **strong** minim octave, thinking of the semiquaver as the upbeat to this strong minim, and your 'score' will soon improve. Do realise, however, that an extra fraction of time has to be allowed for the upward leap and sure landing on the chord on the first beat of bb.3 and 5. This tiny extra instant for the 'spanning' of the leap is part and parcel of Chopin's calculated effect, and maximises the impact of each of these high chords.

When you put hands together, launch in with a ringing minim chord on the first beat of b.1, and bring the LH in as if it is 'growing out of' the RH chord. Then synchronise the hands precisely on the last beat of b.2, and again b.4, thinking of the complete

fourth beat  as an overall upbeat figure to bb.3 and 5, taking

particular care that the **last LH** semiquaver is precisely synchronised with the RH upbeat semiquaver octave. It will now be seen that the tiny extra instant that is necessary for the upward leap 'fits in' with the very slight drawing out of the LH through the fourth beat as described above. At the end of b.4 there will, as already described, be a slightly longer 'extra' instant for the wider leap up to, and stronger dynamic impact (*sforzato* – or sometimes marked *fortissimo*) of the higher chord. Leap off this RH quaver chord and LH single B natural on the first beat of b.5 with a powerfully 'directioned' upward spring, ready to hurtle downwards in the immense 'doubled' *con fuoco* sweep. Allow the tone to drop slightly at the beginning of b.7 (without sacrificing an iota of clarity of articulation) and then build up the sound again as if in an accumulating 'rumble' towards b.8, dropping a little again towards the beginning of b.9. Feel a little 'lift' up to and implied accent upon the semiquaver G's on the second quaver pulse of b.7, followed by a little downward *diminuendo*, a slightly greater accent on the B flats on the sixth quaver pulse of b.7, and a 'peaking' accent on the E flats on the second quaver pulse of b.8, thus:

Play these opening bars in a controlled but electric *forte*. If you start in a wild *fortissimo* there will be 'nothing left' at bb.36-46. Following the very slight 'drawing out' over the 'join' of bb.2-3, there will be a slight sense of moving on as the LH descends through bb.3-4, and similarly through bb.5-6 after the 'join' of bb.4-5. These fluctuations are hardly more than **suggestions** – nothing is worse than the sense of stopping and starting in jerks and gusts, caused by an exaggerated pulling around of the tempo.

Now practise the upward and downward 'zooms' through bb.9 and 10, showing the surge and *crescendo* up to and down from the E flat on the third crotchet beat of b.9, and the smaller surge to the E flat on the second and fourth crotchet beat of b.10, etc. It is essential, both rhythmically and for the interpretation of the **controlled** turbulence of this passage, that these 'surges' are always shaped to and from these greater or smaller 'peaks'.

Study the details of the RH here with scrupulous care. Note the overall *crescendo* through the predominant declamatory figure in bb.10-11 and 12-13 (and likewise through the similar RH figure, bb.11-12 and 13-14) and similarly each time this predominant motif recurs; inexperienced players invariably crash in with the octaves C and D, instead of 'directing' the whole figure in an overall upbeat sense towards the ringing minims on the first

beat of b.11: When you put hands together pay careful

attention to the synchronising of the hands, feeling the RH semiquaver octave C and LH semiquaver D as the 'upbeat' to the **fourth** beat of b.10, and the RH semiquaver octave E flat and LH semiquaver G as the upbeat to the first beat of b.11 (**within** the **overall** upbeat sense of the complete figure towards b.11). Then the rhythmic surge of the LH towards the high E flat in b.11 gives a secure rhythmic 'springboard' for the entry of the RH upbeat figure to **b.12**. Be sure to **drop** the tone to *piano* as indicated here (which few players do) with a small *crescendo* towards a warmer-toned minim chord on the first beat of b.12, 'slurred off' to a clear quaver octave G on the third crotchet beat (note the tied inner notes). Then 'go to' an emphatic and urgent semibreve chord on the first beat of b.14. Feel that you are 'leaning into' this *tenuto* chord as if to simulate a *crescendo* **through** b.14 (abetted by an active, ongoing LH) and then leap off the strong quaver chord on the first beat of b.15, as if with a vigorous 'kick' so that the hand 'falls' with natural emphasis on the accented crotchet chord on the second crotchet beat of the bar. Then take care to bring the RH **off** on the third beat, ready to articulate the subsequent upbeat chords with biting precision. Note the slur and

'lift' effect through the first beat of b.16 (see General Introduction

under 'Articulation') within the general impetus towards a powerfully carrying tied chord on the first beat of b.17, and on again towards the accented chord on the first beat of b.18 (taking care to hold on the inner B natural here as you slur this octave E flat off to a clear octave D on the second crotchet beat). Underpin the RH with an athletic LH through bb.15-16 – it is necessary here to feel four definite crotchet beats through these bars so that the LH shoots up and down to a strong thumb and then fifth finger on each topmost or lowest note. Then dropping the LH tone a little **after** the bass G on the first beat of b.17, let the semiquavers ascend in a *crescendoing* 'rumble' up towards the B flat on the second crotchet beat of b.18 before making a *diminuendo* as you descend through the remainder of the bar, ready to 'start again' from the first beat of b.19.

Be sure to note the *piano* start in the RH in b.20, and then the *crescendos* to the *sforzatos* on the first beat of bb.23 and 24. Many players, to good effect, drop the tone somewhat at the beginning of b.25, the better to highlight the intensity of the *crescendo* towards b.27. It is essential here that the syncopated RH chords are balanced by a perfectly rhythmic LH in which, as through bb.15-16, the crotchet beats must be securely defined. This syncopated RH line needs to 'ride' the LH, as if advancing on a powerfully cresting wave which finally 'breaks' in b.27. Reinforce this onward surge with a **controlled** upbeat stretto through the end of b.26, and then sweep the LH up through b.27, curving it up towards the high G, and down again to 'end' cleanly on the bass B flat on the first beat of b.28. (Henle give the more effective version of the LH here

as opposed to 'plain' semiquavers

throughout the bar.) If you adopt this version, 'hold' the dotted semiquaver fractionally to accentuate the 'peak' of the curve.

Be sure to 'finish off' cleanly in both hands on the first beat of b.28, allowing an extra instant as you leap up a tenth to make it clear that the LH is 'starting again' on the second semiquaver of the bar. While the music briefly enters a more conciliatory phase here, this is nevertheless probably the most difficult passage, in a technical sense, in the entire piece. Amazingly, however, confronted with the apparently alarming plague of accidentals and double sharps, students often fail to appreciate that the actual **harmonic** pattern is extremely simple. When it is realised that the LH through b.29 is merely a decorated chord of G sharp minor, and similarly through b.30 a decorated chord of D sharp minor, and so on, the whole passage appears less daunting, at least from the point of view of grasping its overall shape.

Practise thus first: *etc.* and Then

practise in various rhythms: *etc.* Cortot also gives

excellent patterns: and *etc.*

When you put hands together, sing out the RH chords in a strong but warmer-toned *forte* (in contrast to the defiant clarion tone of b.10 onwards) buoyed along by carefully balanced swirls of sound in the LH, each of these swirls 'launched' from a carefully balanced bass note on each first beat and always listening acutely to the chromatic inflections of the LH. Feel the overall *crescendo* from b.33, with the sense that the tone in the RH is 'opening up' towards its previous *appassionato*, ready to burst forth in *fortissimo* at b.37. There is no need to force the tone here though; a vigorously articulated LH 'growing' from a powerful bass note on the first beat of bb.37 and 39 (this note held within the pedal for most if not all of the bar) will create a huge resonance beneath the powerful sweep of the RH chords. Then from b.41 play the *fortissimo* restatement of the introductory bars with all possible vigour and athleticism. Launching once more into the declamatory motif from b.50, invest the RH triplet variants with mounting rhythmic tautness and excitement. Be sure to **lift** the hand to show the semiquaver or demisemiquaver rests in bb.52, 55, 56, etc. (see General Introduction under 'Articulation'). And once again take care not to **begin** each RH figure (on the upbeat to bb.51, 52, 53, etc.) too loudly so that you have 'room' to *crescendo* towards the subsequent first beat.

Implement the mounting intensity and complexity of these RH figures, 'pointing' the last one (through b.62) with an extra 'push' up to the high octave F, and allowing this high F to 'hang' in the air for an instant. Then, with the feeling of taking the bit between the teeth make a mighty swell in the LH through b.64 beneath the stentorian and 'bare' RH chord towards the release of full power at b.65. Once again there is no need to bang – 'lean' with all possible natural **weight** on the RH chords backed up by a vigorous LH, again maximising the resonant power of the the bass notes. After the *sforzato* chord on the first beat of b.69, there is a gradual subsidence of sound and turbulence. Note the immediate *piano* following this *sforzato* but also note the continuing hairpin surges in the LH, reducing the **volume** of each of these in context as you move towards b.73. Then beneath the long quiet resonance of the carefully placed tied RH sixth, listen acutely to the now 'distant' ascending chromatic 'rumble' of the LH. As the RH 'disappears' towards the D on the third crotchet beat of b.75, feel the tiny surges of the LH (up towards the B flat on the second crotchet beat and then 'back' towards the G on the fourth beat, and again to the D on the second **quaver** pulse of b.76) within the overall *diminuendo* and *smorzando*. **Place** the treble C quietly on the first beat of b.77, but in such a way that carries through its full tied duration. Note the 'punctuation' of the inner and lower unison quavers, and then shape the LH run quietly **down** from the top D flat as indicated. Then make a *crescendo* like a quiet dying rumble towards the first beat of b.79. There is inevitably some divergence of opinion about b.81. Modern Urtext editions give a small *crescendo* through the end of b.80 to a *piano* chord on the first beat of b.81, with a *fortissimo* from the first notes of the 'doubled' semiquavers. Older editions tend to anticipate the *fortissimo* 'burst' by *crescendoing* through b.80 towards a *fortissimo* chord on the first beat of b.81. There seems little doubt, though, that with his carefully calculated *poco rallentando* through b.80, Chopin intended the C major chord to be *piano*, thus maximising the shock of the violent *fortissimo* outburst. In any event, take an extra instant to leap upwards, articulate the semiquavers with viciously 'lashing' finger articulation, and end with chords as defiant as possible, maximising the resonance of the final *staccato* crotchet chords with a 'shot' of pedal – a **short**, sharp pedal stroke on each.

It cannot be too strongly emphasised that Chopin's dynamic indications must be closely studied and adhered to. They are calculated to define the overall architectural effect and thereby to generate the maximum excitement. If you thrash through in a deadening *fortissimo* you will wear yourself out besides exhausting the ears and deadening the senses of your unhappy listeners.

If the LH simply cannot stay the course, a helping hand (literally) can be given in extremes.

In bb.11, 13, etc. the RH can take the top three notes

The late Harold Craxton recounted that Cortot sometimes did this, but it is only recommended as a last resort.

Almost uniquely among the Studies, there are no pedal marks (see the General Introduction under 'Pedalling' for the comments of the Editor of the Paderewski edition). This must be an instance where the pedalling required is too complicated to indicate, as it seems impossible that Chopin should have used no pedal at all here (Cortot gives copious and somewhat arbitrary indications) but it needs to be done with extreme discretion and aural sensitivity to the complex chromatic inflections. I suggest a **short** pedal on the opening chord for the approximate duration of the first crotchet beat, then a light pedal on the fourth beat of bb.2 and 4, and another short pedal on the **first** beat of bb.3 and 5. The foot needs to hover over the pedal in order to 'flutter' according to the dictates of the ear and the circumstances of the acoustics, e.g. there might be a light, instant touch through bb.7 and 8 to highlight the little 'surges' here, and a stronger, longer touch to 'hold' the bass sound on the first beat of bb.9-14 and to colour the RH through this passage (with an additional **touch** perhaps on the high E flat on the second main beat of bb.9, 11, etc.). Then a longer pedal stroke can be used to hold the bass again on each **main** beat through bb.15-16, and again through b.25, the first half of b.26 and b.27, but with a separate pedal on the third and fourth **crotchet** beat of b.26. Then, as Joseph Banowetz suggests in his book *Pedalling* (Indiana Press) bb. 29-32 can take a degree of 'flutter' pedalling. But this must all be a matter for experiment, experience and the individual ear. No two pianists will pedal a piece in exactly the same way, least of all this one.

Op. 25 No. 1
Study in A flat major (8+)

This is one of the latest of Chopin's Studies. It was written during his visit to Dresden in 1836, a time of happy optimism when his hopes of eventual marriage to Maria Wodzinska were running high. (Chopin had been friendly with the wealthy Wodzinski family during his schooldays in Warsaw.) Along with the 'Revolutionary', Op.10 No.12, this is the Study at which every pianist of reasonable competence wants to 'have a go'. It goes without saying that a technically perfect performance requires an advanced and sophisticated control of touch and dynamics. Nevertheless, for a sensitive player of less than virtuoso accomplishment, this can still be a worthwhile assignment. I have had quite young students who, given a flexible hand and a keen ear, have given a beautiful account of it, and at the same time learnt a great deal about quality and gradation of sound.

This is one of those happy and rare instances where we have a detailed contemporary description of Chopin's playing. And the fact that the writer was Schumann himself gives this description a unique value. Although the quotation is so well known, I must reproduce it in full here. For one thing, Schumann, presenting such a precise and inevitably poetic idea of how Chopin played this piece, gives us a clear ideal towards which to strive. For another, his words have much wider implications, giving us a picture of Chopin's style in a wider sense, with an imprint as clear as that of a recording. J.-J. Eigeldinger states that, contrary to traditional acceptance, the **first** part of the description as usually quoted (given in the first paragraph below), refers not only to No.1, but to several studies from the Op.25 set (p.144). The cap fits, however, and for better or worse the 'Aeolian Harp' tag will persist.

'Let one imagine that an Aeolian harp had all the scales, and that an artist's hand had mingled them together in all kinds of fantastic decorations, but in such a way that you could always hear a deeper fundamental tone, and a softly singing melody, then you would have something of a picture of his playing.

'It is wrong to suppose that he brought out distinctly every one of the little notes: it was rather a billowing of the chord of A flat, swelled here and there by the pedal; but though the harmonies could be heard in sustained tones, a wonderful melody, and only in the middle section, did a tenor part once stand out more prominently from the chords and the principal theme. When the study has ended you feel as you do after a blissful vision, seen in a dream which, already half-awake, you would fain recall.' (Hedley, p.121).

It immediately strikes the player that the piece would have been far easier if Chopin had allowed the hands to mirror each other – if the broken chords were written in 'straight' contrary motion – so that the hands were simultaneously moving in a continual 'straight' curve back and forth

between the thumb and fifth finger.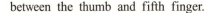

But of course when we try it, we hear how comparatively banal that would sound.

That is what an 'ordinary' study-writer would have done – it takes a Chopin to think

of the undulation **within** the RH broken chord  against the

wider LH curve and thus create the delicious overall aerial,

fluttering texture.

It is well to practise bb.1-2 over and over until the hands are able to synchronise the different shapes of the RH and LH patterns. To this end try first practising and similarly in other rhythmic patterns (see Cortot). The melody line needs, of course, to 'stand out' but at the same time to be part of, and as if growing from, and contributing to the general flow. Obviously while this melody line can sound relatively *legato* through the first three bars, the notes can be held for progressively shorter duration as the span of broken chords grows wider; for example from b.4 onwards, and increasingly through the middle section. (We note also that Chopin has **not** 'doubled' these notes by adding crotchet stems.) The fifth finger needs to remain relatively firm, **softly** firm, one might say, imagining that it is making an imprint in the keyboard as Cortot suggests in a very different context (see Op.10 No.9). Here it will be **softly** imprinted, but with varying degrees of pressure

according to dynamic context. Practise thus: etc. etc, and

etc. getting the **feeling** of this 'imprinting' of the melody notes

while the remainder of the hand remains as loosely flexible as possible.

The usual problem here is caused by the urge to keep the hand 'stretched over the notes' instead of allowing it to 'come with itself' (see under Op.10 No.11 and in General Introduction under 'Some Explanations and Amplifications'). When practising the LH therefore, let the hand move up 'with itself' towards the middle C's through bb.1-2, so that it is in a relatively 'closed' position as it reaches each C, and similarly 'going back with itself' towards each A flat. Through bb.1-3 the **RH** will remain relatively extended since a) it will be trying to 'establish' a simulated *legato* sound in the melody line and b) because the notes do not extend much beyond the octave span. However, in the RH as well, do be conscious from the outset of maintaining maximum suppleness over the knuckle area, avoiding the continual bony, white-knuckled stretch so often encountered. In particular allow the thumb to revert a little to its natural position after playing each lower E flat, rather than remaining stuck out like a dead twig.

Practise these first two bars over and over, slowly at first, listening for perfect co-ordination between the hands, and as you gradually increase the speed, turning your attention to the **overall** flow of sound, over and above the 'individual' articulation of the notes.

Pay great attention to the bass notes which throughout must be carefully balanced to enhance and sustain the varying dynamic resonances. Let the sound 'billow' and fluctuate, listening acutely to the balance between melody and accompaniment as the sound increases and diminishes. Now learn the whole piece, working in short sections (bb.3-4, 5-6, etc. practising

420

and **listening** as described above). Allow a little extra time for the wider span of the 'lift' up to and down from the high B flat on the first beat of b.4 – in effect you will linger very slightly **on** (not **before**) this note, so as to prepare for the downward span to the E flat. This principle applies to all the wide leaps: bb.26-7, 39, etc. 'Go to' the high notes more or less in time, lingering slightly, according to 'geographical' or musical context, **on** the note and not before it, and then 'making up time' through the remainder of the beat. Inexperienced players in general do the opposite – and by lingering **before** the high note, create a series of irritating artificial hesitations.

Less advanced players will not be able to match Chopin's tempo mark (see General Introduction) and indeed, I have heard some platform personalities, in the quest for originality, adopt amazingly slow tempos. This piece does, however, need to 'move'. At much below ♩= 88 there is an increasing tendency for the sounds to 'separate', instead of merging in an overall sonority. The indication, *Allegro sostenuto* is an unusual one. *Sostenuto* is more often appended to a *Lento* or *Andante* indication, with the implication of a certain density and concentration of sound. Here, in this *Allegro* context a continuously spun 'skein' of arpeggiated sound is suggested.

Lead in from a quietly singing upbeat crotchet, taking care to give this its full value if not more, aiming to let this note 'grow' into the series of repeated E flats, giving each of these a quietly 'speaking' quality as they 'sail' above the accompaniment. Feel the overall curve of the line in a slight swell towards and back from the rise to the F on the first beat of b.2. Notice particularly Chopin's pedalling – incorporating the rise to the F in a slight overall 'blur', and changing only on the **second** beat of b.2. Then note the small dynamic curve in b.3 (correctly interpreted in the Vienna Urtext Edition surely, as leading towards, and back from the rise to the **third** beat, instead of to the fourth beat as in Henle), and then feel an easy 'lift' up to the B flat on the first beat of b.4. Make a rather larger swell towards the high C on the first beat of b.6, and imagine the melodic downward leap of a seventh (from the third to the fourth beat of b.7) like a *portamento*. Chopin apparently intends the full tone to be kept up through to the end of b.8, with a *subito piano* at b.9, but many players make a *diminuendo* through the end of b.8. In any event, allow a little 'give' through the end of b.8, making it clear that you are 'starting again' at b.9. Do remember that the tone of the piece is predominantly quiet, and do not therefore attack and prod the high notes through bb.11-12 but rather 'skim' up to them, so that the sound seems to be 'brushed' in passing, as it were, rather than 'articulated'. In most editions (but not in Henle) an implied inner RH line through bb.15-16 is shown in 'doubled' notes†

'Point' this delicately, not too blatantly, within the general flow. Then from b.17 the music takes on a rather more robust, purposeful tone with the entry of the LH tenor line. Let this change remain very subtle though, carefully grading your **overall** *crescendo* (incorporating another drop to *piano* as you ease into C major at b.22, and further numerous longer or shorter hairpins) towards the climactic *appassionata* from the upbeat to b.35. It is vital that the *decrescendo* signs as well as the *crescendos* are observed. Otherwise you will reach a rampaging *fortissimo* far too soon. Indeed, some players, to beautiful effect, go *pianissimo* on the upbeat to b.30 (an effect one feels Chopin may have sometimes used, in the light of his reputation for never playing a piece twice in the same way), starting the final climb only from b.32. Do remember the principle (see above) of 'going to', and lingering very slightly in a

---

†That Chopin intended this effect is clear from autograph sources, and these inner melodic notes are also 'doubled' in the score belonging to Jane Stirling.

vocal manner **upon** the high notes (rather than hesitating **before** them) thus pointing the highest notes of the curves, the D flat on the third beat of b.26, the C on the third beat of b.27, etc. This lingering must, of course, be very slight or it becomes as irritating as the anticipatory hesitation – it is rather a question of identifying and 'pointing' the 'peak' notes of the phrases.

Apply the Cortot example shown above  *etc.* in **both** hands when

working at all instances of wide leaps (from the upbeat to b.26 onwards

etc.   etc.).

Whether or not you play from the upbeat to b.30 in a *pianissimo*, drop the tone a little before the beginning of b.32, ready to make the ascent towards the upbeat to b.35 in a continuous *crescendo*, and with a **controlled** sense of 'moving on'. The consciousness of the regular tolling of the bass dominant pedal point is an immense help towards the rhythmic and dynamic control of this passage. Many pianists drop the tone through b.35 – it appears, on the contrary, that Chopin intends the impassioned volume of sound to carry on through to the *sforzato* unisons on the first beat of b.36 (he would not, after all, be likely to indicate *appassionato* to apply only to the upbeat and first beat or so of b.35).* Take the greatest care through this passage that the tone never grows coarse, aiming instead for a gloriously vibrating resonance, arriving on full-toned, not stabbing, unisons at b.36. Linger an instant on this *sforzato* first beat of b.36, to 'make the point' of the arrival on the tonic unisons, then drop the tone immediately, 'clearing' the sound on the second beat as indicated, to resume the *piano*, perhaps in a quieter yet more dream-like mood than at the opening. Just 'brush' the high F in b.39, then making a beautifully graded *diminuendo* and *smorzando* on through bb.40-3 while 'pointing' the inner thumb-line (B flat-A flat) with the utmost delicacy through bb.42-3. Place the bass A flat with very quiet deliberation on the first beat of bb.44, and then 'feather' the arpeggios in a delicious *frisson* of aerial sound. 'Think' in sweeps from the bottom to the top through the longer arpeggios with the barest suggestion of lingering on the lowest and highest notes (given in large print). Then 'twirl' the short arpeggios from the second beat of b.46, imagining the playing of the breeze on the Aeolian harp as the sound swells and recedes, and tailing the sound away to the barest whisper as you prepare to place the unisons and then the chord on the first and second beats of b.48 with the faintest 'ping'. Think of the bass trill as a low, distant **rustle** rather than a feat of notes to be 'got in', and then spread the notes of the final chord as if feathers are playing over the keys. Cortot advocates placing the grace notes

in anticipation of the penultimate RH chord  *etc.* . However, the

---

*Indeed it appears that an original decrescendo from the second beat of b.35 was later cancelled.

piquant discordancy of placing the D natural on the beat  *etc.*

gives a touch of ironic nonchalance to the ending, as well as according with Chopin's usual intentions in such cases (see the Vienna Urtext Edition and the General Introduction under 'Ornaments').

Chopin's pedal indications are explicit throughout. Take the greatest care to 'hold' all wide-apart bass and/or treble notes for an instant until you **hear** that their sound is 'caught' by the pedal. (This ties in with the ideas expressed above for the negotiation of the wide leaps.) The *una corda* sound is essential to the ethereal *pianissimo* effects towards the end.

Op. 25 No. 2
Study in F minor (8)

This is a lovely piece, both for study and for performance, for a young student with small hands but fluent fingers. It was written in Dresden at the same happy period as Op.25 No.1 in A flat. And again Schumann heard Chopin play it, and luckily for us, recorded his impressions. 'Again one in which his individuality impresses itself unforgettably: so charming, dreamy, and soft that it could be the song of a sleepy child.' (Eigeldinger, p.70). This impression is backed up by Chopin's direction *molto legato*, which in this context, suggests a 'curling', 'pearling' effect that is at the same time exquisitely clear. To achieve this, making it sound like the 'song of a sleepy child' at the tempo of Chopin's metronome mark of $\downharpoonright$ = 112, requires a touch of surpassing flexibility and subtlety of inflection, qualities which were hallmarks of Chopin's own style. But it can still sound beautiful at a considerably lesser tempo. Better this than to generate the fraught *Flight of the Bumblebee* buzz that is so often heard from eager beavers intent on getting it 'up to speed' at all costs. (Although this latter approach may reflect Chopin's original intention, since it appears that the triplets were at first written in semiquavers with the heading *Presto agitato*.)

The ostensible difficulty is that of the synchronising of the differently 'paced' LH and RH triplets, which create a continual cross-rhythm effect. However, provided that the rhythmic and melodic shape of each hand is thoroughly studied alone, and the shapes maintained when the hands are put together, it will be found that the individual flow of the two hands, apparently at cross-purposes, will merge quite happily – any conscious manipulation of the cross-rhythm will be unnecessary and indeed disastrous.

It is well to study the LH first, as it is the crotchets of the LH which propel and **carry** the RH quaver triplets. Be sure to establish a stable overall 2-in-the-bar by placing the first note of each crotchet triplet rhythmically on each **main** beat of the bar (conscious at the same time of both the resonant and the harmonic importance of these notes as the **bass** note of each triplet. At the same time feel the 'lift' up to and down from the **middle** note of each triplet (try **singing** the LH line at a moderate pace) so that the LH proceeds in

a series of curves  *etc.* rather than diagonal jerks. Avoid the tendency to 'snatch' at this 'middle' note when there is an upward leap of a tenth (i.e. up to the second note of bb.1-3 etc.) by this sense of 'lifting' up to and down from it. Work at the first eight bars until the curves are nicely fluent and the rhythm perfectly stable at a moderate pace.

Turning to the RH, work at this in 'conscious' triplets, though without obvious accents, listening acutely to the chromatic 'curls' through the first two beats, feeling the 'lift' up to the G at the end of b.1, and descending 'cleanly' to start the next series of 'curls' on the first beat of b.2. Then feel the 'lift' up to the A flat on the second last quaver of b.2 as you prepare to lead on into the light upward flight through b.3. Carry the curve in a **light** swell up towards the high D flat at the end of b.3, and then shape the descent from this little peak in a gradual 'curling' *decrescendo* through bb.4-6 ready to take off from the beginning of b.7 in a more airy flight up towards and down from the high D flat. Curling downwards again through b.8, go back to b.1 as in a continuous flow, and practise these eight bars over and over until, like the LH, they are perfectly fluent. Before putting the piece hands together, practise the cross-rhythm

effect in various simple figures, e.g.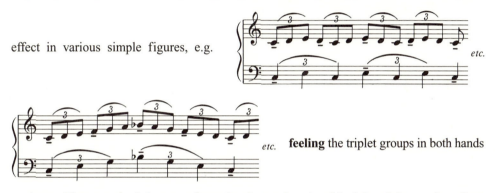

etc. **feeling** the triplet groups in both hands

as shown. Then practise b.1 over and over hands together, 'marking' the triplets again at first, then marking only the two **main** beats, and then forgetting the accents and 'letting it go', gradually increasing the tempo until you can circle on and on, as if on automatic pilot. Remember that the RH is governed by the LH, and it is therefore the RH that is 'fitting' in with the **LH**, and **not** the other way around. Let the consciousness of the even motion of the LH crotchets and the awareness of the constant coincidence of the RH and LH triplets on the two **main** beats of each bar rest lightly in your consciousness, and you will find that the cross-rhythm movement will soon quite happily look after itself. It will be seen that the piece falls into clearcut though continuous sections (bb.1-8, 9-15, 16-19, 20-8 and so on). Learn each section carefully, practising at first in very short 'blocks', two bars at a time, or even bar by bar, absorbing the sense of the harmonic basis of each bar: dominant seventh through b.1, tonic through b.2, diminished seventh through b.3, and so on.

Note that the RH upbeat is a **full** crotchet (i.e. not a 'triplet' crotchet as in the LH), and give this note a soft but definite 'inleading' lean. Then preserve the melodic shapes that you have previously studied hands separately as you play through bb.1-8 at first in a **moderate** tempo. Listen acutely to the intervals created between the

hands:  *etc.* and to the way in which the RH triplets

weave around the basic harmony of each bar. (To this end try playing the harmony of each bar in the LH, and **listening** to the subtle ambivalence of the passing-note/appoggiatura effects as the RH triplets 'circle' around each harmony.)

Allow a little 'give' through the end of b.8 as you poise yourself to set off again from b.9. 'Point' the higher flight up to the upbeat to, and beginning of b.12, and then as you descend through the end of b.15 prepare for a change of tone-colour at b.16. Mark the LH F flats on the second beat of bb.16 and 17 as if with a gentle 'push', not a bump (these LH figures are like a slightly

quizzical query ). Then you could open up the tone a little

as the LH rises to the E natural on the first beat of b.19, but allowing another little 'give' through the end of this bar as you prepare to 'start again' at b.20.

    Feel the more expressive yet resolute turn of the music through the modulatory passage beginning from b.37, rising in a gradual *crescendo* towards a short *forte* at b.43. But let this be a 'soft', not clattering *forte*, 'peaking' the *crescendo* through the third crotchet beat of b.43, and quickly 'withdrawing' the sound towards the *piano* echo through bb.45-6. Feel the quiet 'lift' from the lower to the higher G at the beginning of b.47, then let the line fall gently, ready to 'lift' again even more softly, within a *poco ritenuto*, to the high G in b.48. Then, moving through the tiniest swell as indicated, tail the sound away to a whisper at the end of b.50, but noting the *a tempo* (**in** b.50) so that you run quietly, straight in to the final reprise.

    Note the semi-*staccato* detail through the second half of b.57, letting these triplets 'speak' delicately as the line 'peaks' and falls, with just a little sense of lingering. Rise through b.61 with a sudden streak of *crescendo*, and linger for an instant on the high A flat in b.62 with almost a hint of the histrionic. Then run down the chromatic scale in a continuing full tone, 'lifting' back up to the high D flat on the second crotchet beat of b.63 before letting the sound diminish in a gradual *decrescendo* through to the end. Arrive on a quiet but clearly emphasised F on the first beat of b.66, and allow an extra instant for an airy 'lift' up to the high C.* It is as if the piece 'ends' on the first beat of b.66, with the two downward runs through bb.66 and 67 like a little afterthought, or tiny coda. End with a whispered, but clear spread tied chord, letting the three final C's speak, and waiting through the pause until the sound has almost faded. The

grace notes at the end of b.67 may be interpreted .

    The pedalling needs to be of the lightest. Even Chopin's intermittent pedal indications will sound too heavy on the modern piano if the pedal is fully depressed. His marks can be interpreted as a light 'dusting' of pedal sound to enhance a harmonic point, through bb.11-13 for example, and at the beginning of bb.16-18, and again from the second half of b.18 through to the end of b.19. Otherwise let the foot hover over the pedal just to 'point' a particular nuance, or to 'flutter' here and there (see General Introduction under 'Pedalling') and similarly with the soft pedal.

*In Jane Stirling's copy a diagonal stroke after the RH F on the first beat of b.66 indicates a little break, allowing time for this light 'lift' up to the high C. Fingerings in the previous bar (65) are also marked i.e. the thumb on the third and ninth quaver (B flat and A flat).

Op. 25 No. 3
Study in F major (VA)

To throw this off in all its delicious, abandoned gaiety, changing tack at bb.9, 17, 29, etc. with the easy aplomb of a synthesiser operator is indeed an assignment for a virtuoso. In **performance** the tempo has to approach Chopin's ♩ = 120, otherwise the opening, geared to the demands of bb.9-16, sounds painfully slow. But there is much to be learned here by the competent player in terms of general keyboard know-how, and of the interpretation of the subtleties of notation, quite apart from the sheer fun of the piece. So heavily is the Chopin legend draped in languid pallor that we forget he had a reputation as a wit, and was often in the highest spirits. 'Here' said Schumann 'the concern was more with bravura, but of the most pleasant kind.' (Eigeldinger, p.70).

As will be seen, the LH maintains an almost constant pattern (lightened into a single-line figure only at bb.29-31 and 33-41). Since this LH figure therefore remains the stable factor underpinning the changes of emphasis and figuration in the RH, it is well to study it first. Be

quite clear that the LH is written in two distinct parts: the upper *etc.*

and the lower *etc.* . Practise the upper semiquavers thus at first in a

slurred effect: *etc.* (with thumb and second finger) letting

the thumb 'fall' onto the upper A note and 'lifting' from the second note F, ready to 'fall' again onto the A in a perpetual 'down/up' movement. Then practise the lower quavers also in a slurred

effect. *etc.* Now practise holding down the C with the third finger

and playing the upper A and lower F in an easy *staccato*, like a pendulum moving back and

forth over the 'pivot' of the held third finger: *etc.*

Then practise thus: *etc.* 'lifting' off the lower F with a little 'kick'

in such a way that the hand is 'directioned' upwards ready to 'fall' onto the subsequent sixth (see General Introduction under 'Some Explanations and Amplifications'). The third finger still acts as a pivot, so that the lower line (i.e. the two quavers C and F) also has a slurred effect within the indicated **overall** slurred effect of the whole figure. Then practise the b.1 figure as written, 'lifting' off the lower quaver F with that little kick, and 'directioning' the hand upwards to 'fall' onto the sixth so that you perform a perpetual clockwise semicircular movement from one figure to the next. It will be found that following the impetus of the light 'fall' onto the sixth, the **second** upper semiquaver will 'play' almost of its own accord. Learn the first eight bars thus until they are perfectly fluent at a moderate tempo, always being conscious of the two separate parts – the upper semiquavers and the lower quavers.

Now practise the RH. Again the figures are written in two parts, but the pattern is more complex since a) the upper part consists of an appoggiatura-like semiquaver 'resolving' to a dotted quaver, and b) the inner quavers, proceeding in perpetual broken octave patterns, 'cross' from the lower to the higher F, which lies **above** the two notes of the **actual** upper part. However, the 'fall and lift' principle operates in the same way as in the LH.

Practise at first  *etc.* etc, coming **off** the dotted quaver with just

enough time to 'lift and fall' onto the next semiquaver. The light 'impact' of the 'fall' onto the semiquaver will help to ensure that the implied light emphasis falls on the semiquaver and **not** on the dotted quaver.

Now practise the 'inner' quavers once more with a slurred 'fall and lift' movement: *etc.* When you put the two parts together, the **second** finger

on the RH C acts as a pivot in much the same way as the **third** finger on the C in the **LH** figure. Maintain the easy 'fall-lift' movement, using the same principle of 'directioning' the hand, in this case downwards towards the second beat, upwards towards the third, and so on. Ensure also that the appoggiatura effect is maintained in the upper part

and **not** but holding the dotted

quaver until you release it simultaneously with the second quaver F in the overall lift, preparatory to the 'fall' on the subsequent sixth. Practise the first two figures of b.1 over

and over *etc.* until you achieve a fluent 'fall-lift'

movement as in the LH, again trying, as in the LH, to remain conscious of the two separate parts within the overall slurred effect of each figure.

Now put hands together and practise these first two figures of b.1 until the hands are fluently synchronised in their overall slurred, 'fall-lift' perpetual motion. Then study the first eight bars as outlined above until you can play them fluently at a moderate tempo. Because of the way in which one 'fall-lift' movement leads on to the next, with an instant of relaxation during each 'lift', the piece should not be tiring. Be conscious of this **instant** of relaxation in both hands. At speed, of course, this instant is miniscule, but without it the wrists and hands would seize up within the first page. Feel that the figures are flying lightly upwards through b.4 (and similarly b.8) allowing an extra instant to 'lift' downwards at the end of the bar, ready to start again at b.5. Then make a yet clearer fresh start at b.9. Here the principle of the movement remains exactly the same. Again the impetus of the light 'fall' onto the RH sixth will help the fingers to play the demisemiquaver 'shakes' almost involuntarily, provided that the hand is really supple over the knuckle area. Try this fingering for the demisemiquaver figure (4 2 3 2) and try also 3 2 3 2. Or you could 'rest' the hand by using a combination, i.e. 4 2 3 2 on the sixth on the first and third beats of b.9, and 3 2 3 2 on the fifth on the second beat, and so on. The 'inner' quavers (i.e. the 'doubled' fourth note of each treble demisemiquaver 'shake' –

C, F and C in b.9) 'lift' simultaneously with the high quaver F in the continuing overall slurred effect. Practise slowly hands together ensuring perfect synchronisation with the LH which, as already said, preserves the same pattern as in bb.1-8. Of course, the perfect execution of this passage at tempo requires a trained hand in prime condition, but **practising** it even at a slowish tempo offers a marvellous lesson in co-ordination. Chopin's pedal indications are detailed and explicit (see bb.1-4 etc.). Lift the pedal after each slurred figure, either simultaneously with, or just after the 'lift' of the hands, according to how much of a 'break' you want between each figure. This can, of course, vary from section to section (see below). Then note the pedal indications through bb.3, 4 and 8. In b.3 perhaps the pedal should be changed on **each** beat on the modern piano, as in bb.1-2, etc. But through bb.4 and 8 Chopin clearly wants the effect of a light overall rising 'puff' of dominant, then (in b.8) tonic sound. From b.17 show the more expressive quality with a more *legato* feeling, effected primarily manually, but also with the help of a **longer** pedal stroke through each beat. Point the beautiful melodic

implication in the inner LH   *etc.*   and to a lesser degree

the inner RH part.   *etc.* Then listen to the piquant lower pedal

point effect from b.21, and again from b.25, and draw out grandly from the end of b.27 as you 'home in' towards B major at b.29.

Here once again, from b.29 the technical principles remain fundamentally almost the same – but in this instance 'place' the RH sixths and fifths etc. relatively lightly, then 'go up' to the accented quaver as if with a light 'push', coming **off** with a clean 'kick' of the fifth finger, and allowing the hand to 'rebound', 'directioning' it decisively downwards, or upwards as the case may be, ready to 'place' the next fifth or sixth. Do not make the accent too forceful – that comes later with the *sforzatos* at b.49. But even **at** b.49 think of an exuberant 'kick and rebound' movement with the fifth finger, not an aggressive **prod**. Many a concert performer hacks into these passages (bb.29-36 and 49-56) either in a lather of earnest striving, or as if pursued by the furies, whereas the sheer exuberance of this 'reversed' emphasis, with an effect like high-octane kangaroo jumps, should make an audience want to leap along with the music, and laugh and shout. Separate these two passages with another more expressive span from b.37, *diminuendoing* gradually from b.44, and drawing out markedly once more from the upbeat to b.48, ready to spring off in exultant *forte* at b.49. Note that here the second upper RH note is a **semiquaver** and **not** a dotted quaver, and is therefore **released** as you play the second 'inner' quaver – this enables the fifth finger to give a freer, more vigorous *staccato* 'kick' to this high quaver. Note the detailed indications after b.56: the *sforzato* quavers end here yielding to 'plain' *staccatos* for four beats (in the Vienna Urtext Edition the *sforzatos* end on the **first** beat of b.56); the accents on the second quavers are resumed in *piano* for six beats from the second beat of b.58, and the 'plain' *staccatos* again from the second beat of b.60. Then the *staccatos* are 'phased out' from b.64 (from the **second** beat of b.64 in the Vienna Urtext). There is an intoxicating sense of almost running away as the figures slide downhill in *diminuendo* through bb.59-64. Keep careful control of the crotchet pulse, however, so that the sense of running away remains an **effect** rather a reality! Practise the LH carefully alone through these bars, 'directioning' the hand even more consciously upwards as it 'lifts' from the lower quaver (note the 'new' *staccatos* here) so that it rebounds with a lightning upward leap, ready to 'position' the 'fall' onto the subsequent sixth, seventh or fifth. *Diminuendo* progressively through these bars until you reach 'home' at b.64, and then show the tiny swell towards the first beat of b.65,

428

then fading the sound progressively again through the long held pedal from b.66. Tail the sound away in an upward wisp through b.69 towards a tiny pinpoint F on the first beat of b.70. End with quiet, sober chords. There are various possible fingerings for the difficult

inner trial through b.68

or a continuous  *etc.* If all fails the quavers can be taken

with the LH.

Op. 25 No. 4
Study in A minor (VA)

At Chopin's tempo of ♩ = 160 this is an immensely demanding piece. The concentration has to be undeviatingly beamed upon the accuracy of aim in the LH, and as well as this exacting exercise of concentration, the LH is extremely taxing in a physical sense. But once again there is much to be gained from study of even the first eight bars by players at a standard of Grade 8 or so. At Chopin's tempo the piece has an almost frenetic *agitato* urgency which, it goes without saying, has to be under unshakeable rhythmic control. At a lesser tempo it assumes a much jollier aspect, like a cocksure balletic strut.

I disagree fundamentally with Cortot's advice for the LH: 'strike the quavers with the hand raised as high as possible'. Most players today would advocate exactly the opposite, with an action more akin to plucking. Try the LH of b.1, plucking the quaver A on the first beat, giving it a little kick-off with the fifth finger so that the hand is lifted by the little kick-off or spring in the fifth finger, and 'directioned' upwards towards the sixth, which in turn is plucked, with a little spring or kick-off 'directioning' the hand **downwards** again to pluck the quaver C on the second beat. The hand is thus 'set off' into a state of perpetual movement, the plucking/kicking-off action sending the hand upwards or downwards with a continuing rebound movement towards the next pluck (see General Introduction under 'Some Explanations and Amplifications'). The plucking action is the same for the RH, allowing the hand to rebound after each pluck, and 'directioning' it towards the placing of the next chord. Ensure that the plucking action in **either** hand is always sufficiently solid, whether in *piano* or *forte*, to ensure that the notes sound melodic and not merely 'picky'. This is particularly important in the RH where the syncopated melodic line has to stand out subtly from the general 'chord block'. Be conscious also of the fact that the sound of the **single** bass note on each crotchet beat has to be balanced with the volume of the offbeat **chord**. Since each of these chords has five (or sometimes six) notes, the sound of the **single** bass notes has to balance that of the combined LH and RH offbeat **chords**. Otherwise the rhythm, instead of sounding

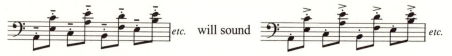

Learn the first eight bars until they are perfectly fluent at a moderate tempo before

moving on. Note the emphasis on the slurred LH upbeat crotchet and be sure to give this note its full value, while at the same time giving it a good in-leading 'lean', to poise you to set off into b.1 in a 'keen' *piano*. Be sure to feel the sense of the overall *alla breve*. This, of course, becomes more apparent and more necessary the faster the tempo. Listen acutely to ensure a consistent bass-note line (subtly pointing the descent to the dominant on the upbeat to b.4 and on the first beat of bb.5 and 6) and a clear syncopated treble melodic line. Shape the little swells up towards and back from the chord on the upbeat to b.4 and similarly, towards and back from the middle of b.7. Allow just a suspicion of 'easing' through the end of b.8 as you prepare to change tack at b.9, immediately regaining tempo at the **beginning** of b.9.

Place the first two quavers of b.9 carefully, in particular perhaps placing this first RH offbeat chord a little extra lightly and in such a way as to highlight the subsequent melodic 'lean' on the slurred emphasised syncopated treble minim A. As you 'slur' this A off smoothly to the G sharp at the end of the bar, maintain the neat and quiet *staccato* in the inner RH chords, taking care to keep these lower voices immaculately clear beneath this smooth treble fragment. Let the treble line sing out as smoothly as possible from b.10, following the dynamic curves and phrase punctuations expressively. If you have hands too small to negotiate the ideal finger changes (and **anyway** when *legato* is impossible for **most** hands – bb.13-14, etc.) cultivate a 'clinging' touch with the fifth finger above the continuing rhythmically plucked inner chords. Arrive on the treble dotted minim E in b.16 in a quiet but carrying tone, so that this note sings through its full duration. Drop to mouse quietness at b.17, and then make a vigorous *crescendo* through b.18, with a (controlled) sense of pressing on into an energetic (but not raucous) *forte* at b.19. Do notice the *legato* treble fragments (bb.19 and 21) and the now definite, even insistent RH offbeat emphases from here, as opposed to the 'even' quality described above. It is well to drop the tone slightly and momentarily at the beginning of b.23, to allow for the long *crescendo* up towards b.27. (Note the *legato* treble from the third RH chord in b.22, through to the first beat of b.27, with another short *legato* phrase **through** b.27.) Slowing as indicated through bb.31-2, give the melody line a lingering, yearning quality (noting that the RH chords here are full crotchets). Tail away the sound through the end of b.32 ready to burst into resolute *forte* from b.33. Note the 'all-crotchet' RH chords again here, but coming **off** on the first beat of b.34 and similarly on the fourth crotchet beat of b.34. Define the quiet chromatic oscillation through bb.35-7, easing a little through the end of b.38 as you prepare to set off again from b.39. Note the heavier syncopated accents from b.41 against which the LH single quavers need to remain consciously and scrupulously rhythmic. They also need to be even more carefully balanced here so that they nicely 'set off' the syncopated effect without disappearing entirely. Observe the dynamic indications meticulously from b.54, shaping the treble curves from bb.55-63 smoothly and with the utmost expressiveness, aided by touches of pedal as indicated. Point the B flat harmony with subtly varied emphasis on the third chord of bb.58-60, and on the upbeat to bb.62 and 63. (The Vienna Urtext Edition and Cortot give a 'doubled' and slurred

bass A on the fourth crotchet beat of b.62.)  The effect of this, in the

context of the given *rallentando*, 'pointing' the quiet clash of the bass A and the treble B flat is

430

exquisite. Then play the spread chord in a lingering harp-like effect, incorporating the RH

grace note D thus:  as suggested in the Vienna

Urtext Edition. Be sure to allow time for the chord to reverberate quietly through its full
duration, **holding** the tied inner RH notes and only the indicated **two** LH notes (F and A)
through b.64 as you 'finish off' the treble line expressively towards the final chord.

The pedal needs to be used with the utmost caution throughout, with only **light** touches
even when Chopin has given indications. It is doubtful, for example, whether he would have
indicated a long pedal from the middle of bb.19 and 21 on a modern piano.

Op. 25 No. 5
Study in E minor (VA)

The subtle piquancy of this piece with its array of finely differentiated details of notation can
only be caught by a master hand, at any rate at Chopin's fleet tempo. Even some of the cleverest
pianists miss the essentially playful lightness of the texture, and succeed only in evoking a
gaggle of bobbing, cackling hens. The fleeting, discordant effect of the continuing inner RH
appoggiatura effect against the treble line and LH chords creates a quizzical, even ironic kind
of quirkiness – and these discordant effects simply need to be suggested, as if brushed in
passing rather than rammed home in a series of sharp stabs. Less advanced players, however,
can only enhance their aural understanding and sensitivity by trying the different sections
themselves, achieving their own tempo in their own time.

The appoggiatura effect of the principal motif is similar to that of the RH in
Op.25 No.3 in reverse – less complicated in terms of voice-crossing etc. but more
difficult to execute because of the continual stretch of a sixth or a seventh. Practise
at first [music] etc. etc, and then [music] etc.

etc, showing the slight 'lean' on the slurred semiquaver so that the rhythm is clearly
[music] etc. and not [music] etc. . Now practise
the RH as written, making sure that you release each upper note (B, E, and G in b.1, and so on)
as well as the lower note (D sharp, F sharp, and A sharp) as you play each dotted quaver.
Imagine that **both** the **upper** note and the **lower** note of each sixth or seventh is slurred towards
the **single** dotted quaver, at the same time lightly 'sketching in' the implied upper melody line,
B, E, G, G, F, etc. Release the thumb from the dotted quaver just in time to allow the hand to
'lift' sufficiently to 'fall' with light natural emphasis on the next appoggiatura, so that the
general effect is as smooth as possible – i.e. with as little a gap as possible between each slurred
figure. (Compare this smoother 'lift-fall' technique with the similar but more bouncy
movement described for Op.25 No.3.) In each instance allow the hand to retract from the
stretch that is necessary for the execution of the sixth or seventh to a position of momentary

relaxation on the dotted quaver. Small hands will need (and others may prefer) to finger some

figures ♪♩. particularly, for example, on the second beat of b.6, the first beat of b.8, the

third beat of b.12, and so on. (But be sure that the same articulation and emphases prevail, whatever the fingering.)

Now practise the LH alone and in **time**, however slowly, so that you feel the chord on each **third** beat as the **upbeat** to the next bar (being sure to come **OFF** through each second beat). 'Harp' the chords with a light upward flick, letting the hand 'come with you' (see General Introduction under 'Some Explanations and Amplifications'). When you put hands together ensure that the LH bass note coincides with the RH **on** the beat, and listen acutely to the intervals created by each appoggiatura and its resolution against the LH harmony. The pedal needs to be used very sparingly, with perhaps the very lightest, shortest touch (if any) on the upbeat and first beat chords. Shape the overall line in a light curve up towards, and down from the upbeat to b.3, and then with a rather more pronounced curve up towards the upbeat to b.7.

Allow the tiniest break at the end of b.8 to make it clear that you are 'starting again' at b.9. The co-ordination from here is far from easy for **any** pianist. Practise the LH carefully alone,

ensuring that you avoid the [musical notation] effect, particularly on the first beat

of bb.9-11 and all through b.13 etc., where there is a leap of a tenth towards the **thumb** on the dotted quaver. When you put hands together endeavour to keep the LH appoggiatura effect **light**, and the overall LH curve smooth through each bar 'against' the **just** non-*legato* effect in the RH. Rise towards a confident *forte* at b.14, letting the upper melody line sing out here and spreading the LH chords with clear but resonant 'rolls' (noting the pedal indications here). Then ease through b.16 to set off at b.17 in an ingratiating *dolce*.

Play from here as prettily (in the true sense) as possible. Use the pedal as indicated through each bar to create the implied more 'harmonious' resonance, permeated by the quiet but penetrating bell-like sound of the syncopated emphasised inner LH minim D's through bb.17-24. Let the RH quavers sound consciously and suavely even from b.21, and then let these slurred quaver figures fly upward and down through bb.25-8 in a smooth G major flurry (holding the G major harmony within the pedal as indicated from b.25, and releasing it on the second beat of b.27). Authorities are agreed that the acciaccaturas from b.29 should be placed **on** the beat. The effect as regards the actual acciaccaturas will therefore be virtually the same (at speed, at any rate) as at the beginning. But the upper line, of course, has to be shaped in as *cantabile* a curve as possible. Using the usually given fingering, slipping off the black

notes with the thumb when possible [musical notation] etc.

this is practicable for **most** hands through most of the passage. But when a *legato* proves impossible, cultivate that warm, clinging touch in the fifth finger (and also when this fifth finger is anyway used consecutively, i.e. between the third beat of b.29 and the first beat of b.30, and again similarly at bb.31-2, etc.) **holding** each treble note as long as is practical and releasing it with just comfortable time to 'place' the next.

Then play from b.37 once more with 'conscious' evenness, this time in both hands. *Crescendo* up through b.41, and sweep 'outwards' to the treble and bass *sforzato staccato* crotchets in a slurred effect as indicated, holding the acciaccatura chords within the pedal.

Many pianists play the third of these acciaccatura/crotchet figures (in b.44) in a rather arch *piano*, though Chopin's intention seems to be that they should all be strong; in other words **not** anticipating the implied *subito piano* of the *più lento* at b.45. The chord figures can be

interpreted thus:  *etc.* However, in many older editions

the LH grace note chord is in **each** instance spread, and many pianists of previous generations

seem to have played the figure thus:

a course also advocated by J. Petrie Dunn.

The glorious melody of this central section is one of the most unblushingly romantic ever written by Chopin, or for that matter, by anyone else. Its *sostenuto* tenor resonance filled out by the 'counterpoint' of the wide-sweeping triplet broken chords anticipates the style of Rachmaninov. Shape the LH in broad melodic curves, cultivating a soft but deep-toned resonance in the inner melody line. Shape the RH in smooth upward and downward sweeps (bb.45-6, 47-8, 49-52, 53-4 etc.). Put hands together very slowly at first so that you can listen to the marvellous effects of the continually 'passing' intervals between the hands, the RH B's against the LH C sharps on the upbeat to and through the first and second beats of b.46, the delicious appoggiatura/resolution effect of the RH quavers A-G sharp over the LH G sharp on the third beat of b.48, and so on. 'Point' the eloquent differences in the LH melody line through the varied restatements with all possible expressive fervour (short of sentimentality!): the dotted crotchet and quaver in bb.53 and 55, etc, the implied slight lingering on the dotted quaver on the upbeat to b.84, and above all, on the upbeat to b.90. Show the inward movement of the 'doubled' RH melodic fragment in contrary motion with the LH octaves through bb.69-71, and rise towards a radiant-toned *forte* at b.73, holding the bass octave within the pedal as indicated through the first two beats of bb.73 and 75 as you 'roll' the spread LH chords resonantly.

Making a little 'give' through the end of b.80, resume the previous tempo smoothly as you ease lightly and silkily into the RH semiquavers. Let the LH line fall to a very quiet, yet 'carrying' tied G sharp on the first beat of b.96, **listening** to the sound of this note as you take the RH sound away to a whisper through b.97, ready to spring off into the light *scherzando* again from b.98. Although by virtue of the fuller, three-voiced RH chords the sound will be denser here, take care that the appoggiatura effect is preserved and that the chords do not become lumpy.

The powerful *crescendo* through bb.122-3 towards the *fortissimo* at b.124 prepares player and listener for the extraordinary ending. B.124 creates a huge volume of sound by virtue of the wide span from top to bottom of the keyboard – held within the pedal through into b.125. Drop the sound to a dark-toned *piano* in the bass octave from the upbeat to b.127, playing the acciaccatura and spread chord quietly in b.128, and slurring off the **inner** LH dotted minim E smoothly to the D sharp in b.129. Then, taking an 'upbeat' breath on the rest at the end of b.129, play the acciaccaturas and chord like a strong, controlled 'slam' (the acciaccaturas 'snapped' on the beat), and making all the tied unison E's ring out on the first beat of b.130 so that they resonate powerfully over the reiterated 'snapping' of the inner parts. Surge into the inner trills from b.134, *crescendoing* powerfully towards and through the **con forza** 'turn' in thirteenths. Draw out the last three notes of this 'turn' towards the final inner G sharp and powerful bass note, letting the arpeggio rise in powerfully reverberating *crescendo*, with the overall major tonic resonance held within the pedal.

Op. 25 No. 6
Study in G sharp minor (VA)

This brilliant Study in thirds, is, as Weinstock says 'fascinating to pianists' (if also dreaded!) but 'fascinates listeners only when a rare technical titan plays it. Either it is technique heightened to sorcery, or it is nothing but notes'. (pp.213-14). In the hands of a player who can create this sorcery the thirds generate a *frisson* that is almost eerie (in rather the same sense as Op.10 No.2) like the outer flurries of a desert sirocco. Those who cannot aspire to such heights had better work at their thirds in more mundane gymnastic form. This said, even a pianist of relatively modest attainment can gain from learning a few sequences of the thirds, e.g. bb.1-6, 7-10, 11-12, and so on, and then, however slowly, learn the skill of tailoring these RH trills and scales in thirds to the rhythmic, melodic and harmonic requirements of the LH. On the evidence of many performances, many a star player would do well to do likewise, and really **listen** to the LH, rather than letting the RH streak around showily under its own steam. For one thing the opening *sotto voce* is seldom observed – the thirds should surely materialise on a breath instead of in a clatter. And the 'turns' in the RH through b.4 eddy in complement to the circling of the LH quavers, with the chromatic scale through bb.5-6 ascending not just for the sake of it, but in contrary-motion counterbalance to the descending line of the LH. Note the way that the LH slurs begin on the fourth and eighth quavers of bb.3 and 4, i.e. on the 'upbeat' to the main *alla breve* beats (the Paderewski Edition gives a **4/4**) creating a series of

overall upward sweeps  Then Cortot gives some elaborate

suggestions for the shape and articulation of the LH through bb.5-6. I suggest however that had he wanted to, Chopin would have indicated such details (see bb.12 and 14) and that what he

therefore requires is, in fact, an **evenly** drawn line

through the long curve of the phrase through bb.5-6. The kind of touch required in these LH chords is discussed in detail under Prelude No.4 in E minor – here the descending melodic line, playing with the thumb and second finger, needs to sing out quietly but clearly beneath the rising RH, with the line 'carrying on down' evenly as the RH thirds 'lift off' from the second crotchet beat of b.6. Allow a fraction of extra time for the LH to 'lift' from the bass G sharp on the first beat of b.5 (and similarly in b.9) to begin the descent in a poised manner on the second quaver of the bar. Again in bb.11 and 13 take great care to poise the descending line of the LH fragments from a clearly placed seventh chord on the second quaver pulse. Note the details of LH articulation through bb.12 and 14, where Chopin **has** made his intentions perfectly plain. Through bb.15-16 pedal exactly as indicated to show the overall F sharp pedal point effect, and then show the little surges up towards and down from the second main beat of b.17 and the fourth crotchet beat of b.18. Make a tiny break to clear the *crescendoed* sound at the end of b.26, ready to let the 'staggered' thirds figures descend in the lightest 'tinkle' from b.27 over the quietly sustained LH, pointing the lightly syncopating emphasis on the minim seventh chord on the second crotchet beat. Chopin evidently intends a *subito forte* at b.31 (not shown in Henle) or perhaps an **almost** *subito forte* with a *crescendoing* 'push' just through the **last** crotchet beat of b.30. Then, holding the sound of the first beat quaver chord (of b.31) within the pedal through to the second beat, let the double 'staggered' thirds descend in a tumultuous cascade of sound, perhaps 'fluttering' or 'vibrating' the pedal as you descend through bb.31-4, as Cortot suggests. Support the *forte* downward streak at b.47 with the resonance of two spread chords held with the pedal as indicated, 'returning' the sound to *sotto voce* at b.49. Note all Chopin's pedal marks while at the same time treating them with some caution on a modern piano. The pedal needs to be **lightly** touched, rather than 'dug into' through, for example, bb.3-4 (see General Introduction under 'Pedalling'). Allow the foot to hover over the pedal ready to give the lightest touch, or 'flutter' effect according to the dictates of the ear in the context of the qualities (or failings!) of the individual piano in relation to the acoustics of room or hall.

Op. 25 No. 7
Study in C sharp minor (8+)

This is a study for the LH only in a superficial sense. With its sorrowful song-like quality, it is often compared to the Nocturnes. In fact the concept is somewhat different. The expressive beauty (and sometimes grandeur) of Chopin's Nocturnes is essentially based upon the pattern of melody and accompaniment, however complex and original in terms of harmonic richness and freedom the resulting 'counterpoint' at times becomes (as, for example, in Op.48 No.1 and above all, Op.55 No.2 and Op.62 No.1). In contrast this two-voiced lament is indeed a **study**, in which the meditative melodies of the LH and RH, each intensely expressive in its own right, in combination achieve a unique density of concentrated melodic counterpoint. As Weinstock says 'One melody begins after the Introduction; the other – its fraternal, but not identical twin – begins in the topmost voice of the RH, in the second measure. The result is complex musical poetry of an exalted and heart-shaking sort.' (p.214). (Astonishingly, Niecks, referring to this melodic duet, pronounces it merely 'very sweet, but perhaps somewhat tiresomely monotonous, as such *tête-à-tête* naturally are to third parties' (Vol.2, p.254).)

It goes without saying that the melody lines have to be studied separately and with the closest scrutiny. Most students of Chopin know that the cello was virtually the only other instrument for which he wrote (see the early Introduction and Polonaise in C and the Grand Duo in E, and the late Sonata in G minor Op.65) and there are a number of instances of cello-like writing in his piano works, the Prelude in B minor Op.28 No.6, and bb.66-81 of the Polonaise in C sharp minor Op.26 No.1 among others. Here, if we imagine how a cellist would shape the eloquent curves of the LH melody, we will immediately understand how to 'draw' these expressive phrases on the keyboard. Indeed, the best possible lesson is learned by asking a good cellist to play the LH line. I have studied the piece with many students, and have yet to find one with courage to extract the full expressive import from the introductory LH phrase. Instead embarrassment takes over, and players seem to want to 'get through it' as unobtrusively as possible en route to the 'proper beginning' at b.1. It is indeed an entrance to challenge the confidence, for from the opening note the phrase has to be played with full commitment to its meaning in terms of the expressive contours. However, this phrase is so uncompromisingly stringlike that if you allow yourself to 'visualise' aurally the almost tangible sound of the 'lift' up to the D sharp and the **greater** 'lift' to the A, **hearing** the sound of the bow drawing across these long notes, and with the subsequent 'curl' upwards to the high B and downwards again towards the entry of the LH melody line proper in b.1, you cannot fail to shape it beautifully.

Have this sound in the 'mind's ear' before starting, therefore, as you place the opening crotchet G sharp carefully, and then feel this 'lift' up to and slight 'lean' upon the dotted crotchet D sharp. Be sure to give this dotted crotchet its full value, listening acutely so that you **hear** how much sound remains at the **end** of this note, and can therefore gauge the tone required for the subsequent quaver C sharp. Then think of these

three notes  as the 'upbeat' figure to the dotted crotchet A, feeling

the greater 'lift' up to this A, and again being sure to give this note its full value. Then shape the semiquavers in an expressive 'curl' up to the B natural with the hint of a *tenuto* on this peak of the overall curve down, before curving again in stages towards b.1. While this introductory recitative needs to sound free, at the same time it must give a sense of the underlying pulse so that there is a clear feeling of 'leading on' and 'in'. The tempo of the beginning proper at b.1 should therefore be securely 'in the system' before you start the recitative. While most pianists seem to start at a rather slower speed, only reaching 'tempo' at b.1, this introductory tempo should at least **relate** to that at b.1. Most pianists also play the piece as a whole at a few notches below Chopin's ♩ = 66. On the other hand, this is a piece that must **move**, not trudge. Laden though it may be, it is not a dirge – it is worth noting that its phrases turn **upwards** as often as **downwards**. Say then that you adopt a basic tempo of about ♩ = 58-60, set the metronome at this mark, and try playing the recitative **with** the metronome. You will find that a remarkable degree of freedom can be conveyed **within** the sense of the overall crotchet pulse (see General Introduction under 'Rubato'). While it would of course be absurd to play this phrase metronomically, occasional use of the metronome nevertheless provides a valuable discipline which can well be applied to the entire piece, enabling us to see **where** and why we need or want to give a little here, move on a little there. In the instance of the introduction, the relatively inexperienced player invariably fails to give full value to the dotted crotchets D sharp and A, thereby both diminishing the effect of the expressive 'lean' on these notes, and undermining the rhythmic sense of the whole phrase.† Shape the *diminuendoing* semiquavers in a gently undulating curve towards the end of the phrase, and as you prepare to 'ease' into b.1, think of the last four semiquavers, and particularly the last **two** (C sharp and D sharp) as the upbeat group to b.1.‡

†Among several interesting pencilled indications in the score belonging to Jane Stirling are pause signs over each of these dotted crotchets.

‡This sense of leading on into b.1 is born out by another indication in Jane Stirling's score: the closure of the introductory phrase line is erased and the line is extended 'on and over' into b.1.

It is vital that through bb.1-2 the basic pulse of the piece is made clear. This is achieved through the conscious establishment of this crotchet pulse **within** the inner RH quaver chords. So keenly (and understandably) is the player's concentration beamed upon the expressive shaping of the LH and RH melody that these inner chords tend to be forgotten, and left to bump along at random, or as if operating under their own volition. In fact they have two principal functions essential to the framework of the piece: they provide a) a quiet and persistent inner rhythmic *ostinato* (it will be seen that they are present in some form almost continuously throughout the piece); and b) a continual harmonic 'ballast' between the two melody lines. In the first role they must always maintain the **sense** of the ever-present crotchet pulse supplying the essential feeling of onward movement (without obvious accents, of course, and giving a little or moving on a little, according to the musical or expressive sense of each phrase). In the second role their sound must be continually 'monitored', so that according to dynamic context, they always balance and enhance, but never swamp the melodic lines. In this sense it is essential that they always maintain their 'accompanying' role, never usurping the treble line. Thus in b.1 for example, the chords must be played *pianissimo* as indicated so that they do not anticipate the **beginning** of the treble melody in b.2, nor undermine the **establishment** of that melody through bb.2-4, and so on. Particularly in b.4 it must be made clear that the double dotted crotchet treble G sharp, held through from the second beat, and the 'single' semiquaver upbeat G sharp to b.5, are the **melody** notes, with the inner chords on the fourth, fifth and sixth quaver pulses of the bar needing to be kept proportionately quiet. To this end, Cortot's exercise

is particularly helpful: 'Lean' on the

melodic notes with the fifth or fourth finger, allowing the remainder of the hand to feel perfectly free so that you can play the inner chords lightly and easily. Having acquired this feeling of 'leaning' on the melody notes and playing the inner chords lightly, play the first RH phrase as written, cultivating the skill of playing the inner chords as smoothly as possible, so that the sound is as nearly continuous, that is, as *legato* as possible. (See under Prelude No.4 in E minor for a more detailed discussion of this technique.)

Now practise the LH through from the last beat of the introduction so that you feel the 'upbeat' sense of these last four semiquavers as they 'ease' but at the same time 'direct' the line towards the singing minim E on the first beat of b.1. Placing the lower acciaccatura E on the beat, let it speak (rather than merely 'squashing it in'), feeling a *portamento* 'lift' effect up to an expressive-toned minim E. As you **listen** to the sound of the long E, imagine the even rhythm of the quietly pulsating RH quavers above, and shape the line as expressively as possible through to the crotchet B sharp on the first beat of b.4. Feel the ♩. ♪ figure at the

end of bb.1 and 2 as the **upbeat** 'going to' to the long note on the first beat of bb.2 and 3 (taking care to give each of these long notes sufficient tone to sing through its full value); and similarly feel the semiquaver figure on the third beat of b.3 as an expressive upbeat curve down towards the B sharp on the first beat of b.4, thus creating the essential sense of continuing onward movement.

Now play the two melody lines together **without** the inner chords, absorbing the aural sense of the independence and at the same time the interrelation of their phrase shapes. Listen acutely also to the sound of the actual intervals ocurring between the hands. When you finally put hands together as written practise these first four bars until you are thoroughly familiar with the movement of, and the balance between the LH and treble lines with the inner chords. As already said, the RH chords need to be kept very quiet through b.1. At the same time the opening treble melody note (i.e. the minim E on the first beat of b.2) must seem to 'grow' from these chords through the preceding bar, giving the effect of **joining in** in equal duet with the LH rather than emerging with a bump, or at the other extreme, creeping in in a half-hearted 'accompanying' effect. Let the two lines sing out with a quiet, sorrowful kind of fervour through bb.2-3, and then make it clear that while the LH phrase ends on the B sharp on the first beat of b.4, the treble phrase ends with the double-dotted G sharp lasting through the second and most of the third beat.

Study this bar very carefully, giving the RH G sharp sufficient tone to sound through its full duration, and then making it clear that the new phrase begins with the upbeat semiquaver to b.5. Meanwhile in the LH be sure to come **off** on the quaver rest on the second beat as indicated and show clearly that you are beginning the new LH phrase in the middle of the bar, feeling the six

semiquavers as an overall upbeat group towards b.5. Show

the more expansive feeling of the wide-spanning LH intervals from b.5, noting here and through as far as b.14 the sense of the shorter phrases in the LH against the longer-breathed treble lines. 'Space' the LH triplets expressively but with an ongoing sense through b.6 beneath the even movement of the RH quavers, and be careful to show that, melodically speaking, the treble line ends its second main phrase with the quavers E and D sharp on the first beat of b.8, with the RH 'withdrawing' temporarily to an accompanying role from the second main beat of the bar as the LH begins its climb towards the varied restatement from b.9 (phrasing details vary here). In the score belonging to his pupil Camille O'Meara-Dubois, Chopin indicated that the LH trill in b.7 (and similarly in bb.37 and 51) should begin on the upper note, i.e. D sharp (see Eigeldinger, p.131, and also the Vienna Urtext Edition). Also in bb.4-5 we have a revealing instance of Chopin's fingering (see the example above). Whether or not you adopt this fingering, it shows exactly how he wanted these notes to 'speak' (see General Introduction under 'Fingering').

Tail the sound away towards the end of b.10 ready for the LH arpeggio to ascend in a whisper through b.11 beneath the long-breathed treble line, and barely touched inner chords. Bring the LH arpeggio up towards, and down from the high D sharp in an ultra smooth curve, allowing the sound of the high D sharp to 'hang' for an instant in a vocal manner. Then bringing the LH up smoothly again from the second beat of b.13, beneath the sustained treble A, let the semiquavers 'curl' through bb.14-17 in a light 'haze', listening acutely to the chromatic inflections beneath the long, held treble notes, and again barely touched inner RH chords. Be sure to 'finish off' the treble line clearly on the second beat of b.17, showing the rest on the third beat as the LH leads on from the upbeat to b.18. From b.18 let the LH sound like romantically distant horn-calls, allowing the sound to 'fall' from the high semiquaver E on the first beat of b.18 (and once more letting this note 'hang' for an instant where the RH is momentarily silent). End the phrase quietly but clearly on the first beat of b.20. Then, 'beginning anew' on the second quaver chord let the RH E major chords 'drift' upwards within the pedal, but in an evenly 'spaced' manner as indicated by the so that the chords still convey a sense of onward movement within their 'drift', towards b.21.

At b.21 there is straightaway a new sense of urgency, but this can be conveyed as an **underlying** unease, rather than by starting to bang, as many players do. There needs, however, to be a slight, though not over-obvious sense of moving on, while at the same time playing the treble and bass phrases, moving in contrary motion curves, with the utmost expressive pathos.

Allow an extra fraction of time to let the RH turn 'speak' through the second beat of b.21, and be sure to take the end of the phrase up to the crotchet G sharp on the second **quaver** pulse of b.22, then 'finishing off' the LH phrase equally carefully, with the little ornament 'going to' a clear quaver B on the second crotchet beat of the bar. Then as the RH retracts momentarily to an accompanying role, let the LH demisemiquavers, starting from a quiet but definite bass F double-sharp, ascend like a rapid water chute (beneath the steady pulse of the RH chords) towards the crotchet F sharp on the first beat of b.23. Rise to no more than a *mezzo piano* or *mezzo forte* at b.23, so that you leave plenty of room for a more powerful upward 'chute' towards b.25, and then for a progressive *crescendo* towards the mighty *fff* at b.27. In b.24 note that while this time the treble and LH phrases end concurrently on the **second** crotchet beat of the bar, the RH again 'lifts' to a **crotchet** which therefore in this instance sings out over the **beginning** of the LH upward run. Later generations of editors have thought up various different fingerings for these runs through bb.22 and 24. The following fingerings are suggested incorporating those marked in copies belonging to pupils of Chopin. I suggest the same basic fingering for each run, with adjustments to fit the

notation at the end of the second run.

Let the LH rise to a clarion dotted

quaver B on the first beat of b.25, and then *crescendo* resolutely through this bar and b.26. The negotiation of bb.26 and 27, terrifying to the relatively inexperienced player, becomes infinitely less daunting once it is realised that the LH runs must fit in with the basic RH pulse, and that this must remain **stable** so that, as it draws out through b.27, it must do so in a rhythmic and not random manner (see General Introduction under 'Rubato'). Usually exactly the opposite happens – the RH chords progressively lose their rhythmic grip as panic looms at the end of b.25, and takes hold through b.26, so that by the end of b.26 the RH rhythm has gone haywire, preparing the way for a general collapse around the middle of b.27. Practise the LH first until you have mastered its general shape, and secured the fingering. Suggested fingerings are again given for b.26, incorporating Chopin's use of the thumb. The fingering for b.27 is straightforward.

Then practise the RH alone, keeping a steady pulse as you imagine the swirl of the LH beneath through bb.26-7. Feel an implied strong 'leaning' emphasis on the **minim** chord (i.e. the melodic treble third on the second beat of b.26) and then **gradually** draw out through b.27 towards the *sforzato* chord on the first beat of b.28. Then put the hands together fairly slowly, keeping the RH going steadily at all costs. After the first **whole** beat of b.26, through which the LH will divide approximately into two groups of seven notes, play the groups of four and six demisemiquavers with some deliberation (see the accents) as you *crescendo* downwards. Then as you launch into b.27, **keep the RH going again** but with a steady and deliberate 'expansion'

*In Jane Stirling's score there is a pencilled 'facilitation' of the LH runs in b.22 and 24. The first ten notes are erased, and the remaining four notes are turned into semiquavers to coincide with the last two RH chords.

of the beat towards the immense chord on the first beat of b.28. Never mind if at first the LH gets left behind and has to skate over the last part of the run in order to 'get to' the bass E flat in time – nor if, alternatively, the LH arrives too soon and has to 'wait for' the RH towards the end of the bar. Gradually you will be able to match the spacing of the LH to the RH chords with increasing confidence, and consequently with increasing freedom. Make guidelines at first, perhaps arriving on the LH E flat above middle C on the second main beat of the bar, and on the C flat on the third beat or in any other combination that feels logical: J. Petrie Dunn for example suggests a grouping of $8 + 8 + 9 + 9 + 12 + 12$. If this bar proves stubbornly difficult to control, it is an idea to practise the RH chords over a 'plain' scale of E flat in the LH (i.e. in the given span, from the low B flat up to the high G and down to the low E flat), so that you grow used to the **feeling** of the free LH run beneath the RH chords. Take care in performance that you do not bang out the RH chords indiscriminately, but that you always show the treble

melody line through bb.26-7. Also take care

to keep some tone in reserve for the final thrust down towards the huge *sforzato* LH bass E flat and RH chord on the first beat of b.28. Allow an extra instant for the sound of this chord to register, then immediately 'close down the bellows' as you play the three inner RH quavers in *piano* **within** the pedalled sound of the chord, but perhaps 'flicking' the pedal a little to disperse some of the sound. Pianists tend to let the dynamics flag, consciously or perhaps unknowingly, through the end of b.27, as if in preparation for a gentler arrival on this *sforzato* chord on the first beat of b.**28**. But the sense of the music, as well as Chopin's detailed indications in b.28 suggest a climactic **arrival** on this chord, with then an immediate 'retraction' to *subito piano*, then *pianissimo*. Allow a fractional break for the sound to clear further before leading on in *pianissimo* from the upbeat to b.29. Be conscious of the magical enharmonic shift towards B major here, while at the same time securely reestablishing tempo 1. Note also that here the **treble** has the main melody line over the reiterating LH figure 'falling' from the dotted quaver D sharp on the upbeat to each bar (feeling the implied soft 'lean' on this D sharp). This section passes in an exquisite haze of sound. Chopin's pedal marks are not 'too much'. Using the soft pedal and playing the downward LH arabesque with the lightest touch, as if feathers are passing over the keys, will create a beautifully 'haloed' overall sound on all but the most strident of pianos. (If a particular piano tone proves unmanageable, the sustaining pedal can be almost imperceptibly 'flicked' to lighten the sound.) Leave room to allow for an even more ethereal *pianissimo* at b.35, taking an extra instant to 'harp' the spread chord unhurriedly up to the high A on the first beat, and holding this sound within the pedal as you tail the LH away downwards in b.36.† Take the two pedals off **slowly** so that the sound evaporates into silence, and be sure **physically** to take a breath here through the pause, resuming with the LH melody from the quietly emphasised upbeat to b.37, as if in weary resignation.

Point the interrupted cadence in b.39, taking care to bring the RH quietly **off** as the LH continues with the onward leading upbeat figure to b.40. Bring the semiquavers up towards the crotchet A on the second beat of b.40 as if in a query, and then take care to give full value to the rest before moving resignedly on again from b.41. There is some doubt as to whether the inner RH G on the second beat of b.38 and the first beat of b.39 is a sharp or a natural, and editions vary; see the Vienna Urtext Edition. The compromise solution adopted by many editions of using G sharp in b.38 and G natural in b.39 is, as Paul Badura Skoda says in the Vienna Urtext,

† Jane Stirling's score shows pencil marks here, tying the RH upbeat chord over into b.35 (as printed between bb.30-31) facilitating a more beautifully phrased accentuation of the treble line here.

'musically acceptable' (and indeed to most of us 'seems right', whether or not only because it is familiar!).

Take time through b.44 to listen to the *pianissimo* semiquavers before making an implied *crescendo* through the upbeat to b.45 towards the resonant first beat of b.45. There is no need to bang this *sforzato* E – feel instead that you are fortifying its singing resonance with the full sound of the C sharp grace notes, held within the pedal.† The implication is that this reprise should be played in a fuller tone than from bb.1 and 9, with more intensity and with a hint of urgency. Note the 'intensifying' touches: the ornament in b.47, and the bass grace note in b.50. Then having practised b.52 in the manner outlined for b.27, let the scale ascend in a smooth 'zoom', grading the *crescendo* up towards a full-toned minim E on the first beat of b.53. Take care not to bang out the RH through b.52, keeping the octaves and chords strong and steady through the second and third beats, but remembering that they are in an accompanying, not melodic role here (as in b.8).

While observing the *decrescendo* in the LH line from this *sforzato* E on the first beat of b.53, it is a mistake, I believe, to drop the tone too much, although many pianists do let the tone fall away quite quickly and markedly. The intensity of the RH chords through bb.55-6, the emphases in the LH from the upbeat to b.56, and the nature of the LH climb from b.57 up to the high B on the second beat of b.58, all suggest that the tone should remain relatively full, only dropping to *pianissimo* at b.60 – but this, of course, is a personal view. In any event, listen to the 'laden' expressive inflections of the RH chords through bb.55-6; point the LH emphasis on the trilled LH upbeat to b.56, then taking the LH line up as if in a wide arc to 'cross' the inner RH on the emphasised G sharp on the second beat of b.56, and down again to a warmly emphasised bass upbeat to b.57. Then **listen** to the sound of the carefully judged tied treble A from the second beat of b.57 over the even chords as the LH climbs towards and descends expressively from the high B on the second beat of b.58. Draw out the top of this curve a little in a vocal manner, though without disrupting the overall equilibrium of the pulse. Play the horn-call figure from b.60 in a yet more distant and nostalgic manner than at bb.18-19. Then 'gather' the tone through b.62 as you draw out a little towards the splendid resonance of the chain of sevenths beginning on the upbeat to b.63. This type of sequential progression, one of Chopin's favourite devices, looking forward to Debussy, is discussed by Gerald Abraham (p.87). Note the *tenuto* on the LH tied C sharp on the first beat of b.63, feeling a similar *tenuto* 'lean' on the tied upbeat to b.64, and on the emphasised dotted quaver upbeat to the low tonic on the first beat of b.65. At the same time listen acutely to the sustained line of the treble and to the shifting inflections of the inner chords as you gradually decrease the tone a little **towards** b.65. It is again a mistake, in my view, to *diminuendo* **too much**, as many players do, through bb.63-4. The richness of the progressions suggests that Chopin intended a fairly full tone to be maintained through to the arrival on the 'final' tonic on the first beat of b.65. It is only **then**, from the second beat of this bar, that he disperses the tone in a *smorzando* as the music lingers around this tonic harmony through bb.65-6 (with, en route, a last, quiet but expressive 'lean' on the dotted quaver on the upbeat to b.66). Be sure to come **off**, though not abruptly, to let the silence 'hang' through the pause in b.65 before ending with quietly resonant chords.

Chopin's pedal marks are, as will be seen, very occasional. This would not mean that he **only** wanted the pedal used when indicated, but rather that he wanted **longer** pedals at certain points, e.g. through the first half of b.11, the whole of b.20, and especially for the hazed effect from b.29. Otherwise the pedal needs to be used with extreme discretion. In the introductory recitative it might be used on the long notes, or not, according to whether the player wishes to

---

†Many players take this E with the RH, an option evidently sanctioned by Chopin himself, by a pencilled mark in the score belonging to Jane Stirling.

make a warm-toned or more 'open string' effect. Then in bb.1 and 2 the pedal could be held through the first two beats, or changed on the second beat if you prefer a more defined effect. In bb.3 and 4 it will be changed on every beat. Normally it needs to be changed whenever there is a change of harmony, and probably also in such instances as between the first and second beats of b.5, where the harmony remains the same, but the melodic line of treble and bass needs to be defined, and similarly between the first and second beats of b.4.† In semiquaver passages, as from b.14, let the foot hover over the pedal ready to apply tiny touches as the ear and circumstances dictate. This is also a piece where the sustaining and soft pedals will frequently be used in combination (bb.15-20, and from the upbeat to b.29, etc.). Then the sustaining pedal is used to enhance (not cover up!) the runs through bb.22-7. Try at first changing the pedal on each **quaver** pulse of the runs through bb.22 and 24 and through bb.26 and 27. Then listen to the effect of changing the pedal only on the **main** beats of these bars, and so on, testing the level of resonance that the ear will accept. No rules can be laid down here, but if you experiment thus with different effects, and also with effects of half-pedalling through these runs, you will build up a reserve of pedalling effects upon which to draw.

Op. 25 No. 8
Study in D flat major (VA)

Like Op.10 No.10, which is also concerned with sixths, this needs to be thrown off with the semblance of perfect ease. But in purely technical terms this is an even more formidably difficult study, and there are few players, even amongst virtuosi of high order, who can play it without signs of labouring! For one thing, **both** hands proceed mainly in double notes, and for another, the RH remains constantly in the 'extended' position necessary for the continuous long phrases of sixths, without the opportunity to 'retract' as in Op.10 No.10. This is extremely taxing to all hands, particularly, of course, to small ones, unless they are absolutely supple across the knuckle area (we have evidence that Chopin's hands were exceptional in this respect). For players less splendidly equipped, the exercises suggested by Cortot in paragraph 3 of his notes on this study are especially helpful for practising sixths in general: particularly

etc. and etc. Feel that you are 'leaning'

lightly on the *legato* quavers played by thumb and second finger, allowing the rest of the hand to remain perfectly supple so that the fourth and fifth fingers can play the *staccato* semiquavers freely and easily. Then reversing the figure, ensure similarly as you 'lean' lightly on the fourth and fifth fingers, that the lower part of the hand remains supple so that the thumb and second finger can play freely. This is comparatively easy, of course, with the first sixth played with the thumb and fourth finger. The real 'stretch' comes with the second sixth played with the second and fifth fingers, when (with most hands) a conscious auto-'instruction' will have to be issued to 'let the hand go' over the knuckle area. The freer the hand, the easier and wider the possible stretch. This is easily demonstrated by the 'white knuckle' test – if the hand is stiffly stretched

†In Jane Stirling's score there are pencilled indications for a long pedal through b.1, another through b.2, a change of pedal on each beat through b.3, and another long pedal through b.5. These indications are apparently not in Chopin's hand, and anyway may be subject to modification on the modern piano. Alternatively, a skilled player may prefer to create a slight 'misting' of pedal through bb.1, 2, 5, etc. as suggested by these indications.

in the $\frac{5}{2}$ position, the inner fingers 3 and 2 will be sticking up like bits of wood, and the knuckles and the bones between knuckle and wrist will show white under the stretched skin. If the hand is relaxed, the fingers 3 and 2 will be 'lying' loosely on the keys, and the bony whiteness will have disappeared, leaving slight dimples over the knuckles, with a resulting feeling of elasticity which allows this whole knuckle area to expand far more comfortably and easily.

The LH needs to be studied with as much care as the RH ensuring that the bass notes are securely placed on the first and second main beats of bb.1 and 2, the first and second main beats **and** the fourth crotchet beat of b.3, and so on, so that the harmony of each 'arc' of double notes is securely registered. Then leaping off each bass note so that the hand is 'directioned' swiftly upwards (see General Introduction under 'Some Explanations and Amplifications') ensure that the slurred overall 5-quaver 'arc' through the **first** half of b.1 and the more undulating shape of the 5-quaver curve through the **second** half are both phrased smoothly and graciously. In the RH similarly shape the undulations as smoothly as possible, showing the little curve up to and down from the fourth crotchet beat of bb.1 and 2, and then the greater curve up to and down from the fourth beat of b.3, with the tiniest give through the end of b.4, ready to 'start again' from b.5. These are, of course, but nuances of shape within the **overall** phrase curve of bb.1-4. Various commentators have remarked, with justification, that this is the most 'Study-like' of the twenty-four. But those players who **are** equipped to perform it should perhaps underline in red Chopin's indications *mezza voce* and *molte legato*. The sound needs to materialise 'on a breath', not with a clatter of hooves. Equally it is vital that all little swells through the first sixteen bars should 'return to base', only starting an overall build-up of sound from b.17.

Op. 25 No. 9
Study in G flat major (8+)

This piece is no doubt stuck forever with the 'Butterfly' title. But as Weinstock says it is one we should forget. It is the shortest of the Studies, occupied entirely with its single motif, which Chopin pursues with almost ruthless economy and certainty of direction. Although it must enter on the lightest touch, the articulation, and rhythmic 'spring' of this motif has a kind of spunk, of kicking up of the heels, rising to defiance at bb.33-4, which has nothing to do with the fluttering and darting of butterflies (charmingly caught by Grieg in No.17 of his Lyric pieces). Although at anything approaching Chopin's ♩ = 112 this is a virtuoso piece, on the other hand it is one that can be played with some satisfaction (even if not in public) at a considerably lesser tempo. It is one of those pieces in which vitality of rhythm and articulation, and above all of spirit, can go a long way to compensate for speed. In any event, there can again be immense technical benefit and gain in terms of keyboard know-how from practising only a few bars.

The RH motif is 'propelled' by the perpetual rhythmic spring of the LH, and it is a good plan to study this LH first. The 'spring and rebound' technique here is similar to that of the LH of Op.25 No.4, and has been discussed in some detail there. There is, however, a subtle difference in a rhythmic sense (apart from the fact that it proceeds at a slower tempo than No.4) in that it is 'carrying' a semiquaver figure in the RH (as opposed to 'matching' quavers in No.4). Because of the 'lean' on the doubled RH quaver on each **main** beat, there is the **rhythmic** need for a slight 'kick' on the **LH** chord on each **offbeat**. This will give each of these chords an 'extra' upbeat impetus towards the bass note on the subsequent main beat, thus ensuring the perpetual-motion 'spring' which, as already said, 'carries' the RH.

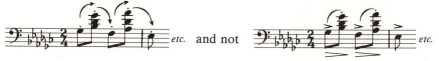

This little 'kick' on each offbeat chord creates an essential balance to the strong **main**-beat / weaker-offbeat pattern of the RH. It is essential to master this perpetual spring between bass note and chord through the first eight bars before proceeding further.

The articulation of the RH is often misunderstood by students (and also in some old editions). It is **not** but the less obvious, more difficult

. (The first, incorrect version would also iron out that subtle

rhythmic relationship between the hands outlined above.)

In the RH it is the 'lean' on the doubled quaver on each main beat which gives the impetus to 'carry the hand on' through the remainder of each semiquaver figure towards the next 'lean' on the subsequent main beat, creating a different, longer-spanned perpetual-motion impetus to that in the LH. If you allow the thumb to 'fall' onto each quaver, the upper third will (with the hand in the 'fall' position) virtually play itself. Then 'lift' the hand from each of the two *staccato* octaves, ready to 'fall' onto the next quaver. The pattern is

thus: This 'fall-lift' action needs to be so mastered

that it goes onto automatic pilot. Practise b.1 over and over therefore, until this overall movement becomes self-generating. The essential is to allow the hand to relax for an instant as the thumb 'falls' on each doubled quaver, and again as the hand 'lifts' from each *staccato* octave. As in the LH, learn the first eight bars thoroughly first. On the first beat of bb.5 and 6 merely reverse the direction of the 'fall' onto the fourth and second fingers. When you put hands together practise very slowly at first, scrupulously maintaining the rhythmic 'integrity' and articulation of each hand. Inability by a small RH to manage the 'ideal'

fingering need not preclude study of this piece. A

simulated *legato* can be achieved by the momentary 'binding' of the inner note (as in scales

in thirds): and indeed this may be less tiring for many hands,

particularly of the average female size. Note Chopin's pedal indications which are absent until b.8. If any pedal is used through bb.1-8 it must be confined to **lightning** quick, and **light** touches on the bass note on each main beat. Allow a little extra time through b.8 to 'harp' the spread chords in the LH and to 'end' clearly on the quaver tonic harmony on the **second** beat of the bar, drawing out the last three RH semiquavers fractionally as you 'gather' yourself to set off again from b.9. Be sure to let each little swell (from b.9 and then b.13) 'return to base' at the end of b.12 and b.16 respectively, so that you set off **quietly** again from b.13 and b.17. Feel the rather more pliant, expressive moment through bb.17-20, though without slackening the rhythmic impetus. Some pianists cannot resist making a *crescendo* through b.20 and blazing down from b.21 in a resounding *forte* so that they 'drive straight on' in a continuing *forte* from b.25. This, although convincing enough at the moment of impact as it were, detracts from the overall architecture of the piece by which the **main** *crescendo* from b.25 is directed towards the climactic bb.33-4. It seems more likely that Chopin intended to maintain the *piano* in a high tinkling effect from b.21, with perhaps a spurt of *crescendo* through the second half of b.24, ready to spring off in *forte* from b.25.

There is no need to bang from b.25. If you let the RH 'have its head' in a dynamic sense, it will ring out with no need to force its tone over the added resonance provided by the sturdily springing (again not banged) LH octaves held within the pedal as indicated. Take care to avoid

the horrible pumping effect often heard:  In other words

continue to give the chord on each second and fourth quaver its upbeat 'kick', and also to pedal

as modern marking would indicate:  *etc.* (see General Introduction

under 'Pedalling'). Grade the *crescendo* carefully so that you only reach full throttle at b.33, and listen acutely to the balance between the hands – the RH ascent from b.29 will sound increasingly shrill and strangulated unless it is well supported by the resonance of the LH. Note the slurred LH upbeat to b.33, which gives a calculated 'push' **into** b.33. Here 'open up' the tone in a full flood of impassioned sound, **listening** to the marvellous persistent appoggiatura effect in the RH octaves against the LH chords on the second and fourth quaver of each bar. (In the reissue of his old recordings, Cortot inexplicably appears virtually to ignore the *crescendo* from b.29, and plays the *appassionata* passage in a prissy, almost unpedalled *mezzo forte*.)

Although many players make a *diminuendo* towards b.37, it seems clear by the RH accents leading on through b.36 that Chopin intended to maintain the *fortissimo* through to a powerful *sforzato* bass G flat and RH chord on the first beat of b.37. Draw out as indicated, therefore, through b.36, 'directing' the RH accented quavers strongly downwards through the second beat, and 'using' the implied emphasis on the partly tied upbeat semiquaver to 'prepare' for the sound of the RH crotchet octave on the first beat of b.37, over a resonant bass quaver. Allow an extra instant for this unison sound to register before 'pointing' the LH tied D flat on the second quaver, ready to 'set off again' in a *subito piano*, in **tempo** from the second beat of the bar. (Some older editions, including Cortot's, place the *sforzato*, apparently wrongly, **on** this tied D flat, rather than on the bass G flat.) Following this impassioned declamation from bb.33-7, it is effective to play on from b.37 in a rather nonchalent, 'throw away' manner, **listening** from here to the alternating LH dominant-tonic-dominant-tonic harmony, over the bass pedal point effect. (Cortot suggests, apparently without evidence – but with a nice effect – **holding** the LH tied D flat right through to b.41.) Leap up to carry on from the second beat of b.41 in the lightest possible tinkling echo.

Arrive on a neat quiet chord on the first beat of b.45, allowing an extra instant here to 'place' the bass quaver G flat as the RH curves up smoothly into the new slurred figures. Then being sure to catch and hold this bass G flat within the pedal as indicated, pick up the tempo to create the smoothest possible, featherweight aerial curves in the treble, 'suspended' over the lightly 'pinged' LH *staccato* tonic chords or octaves, taking the sound down to a mere breath towards b.49. On the modern piano it seems more effective to raise the sustaining pedal after the first quaver of b.49, as most players do. (On the other hand, many play from b.45 with no pedal.) In any event, play the LH octaves from b.49 in pinpoint clear *staccato*, within, or without the pedal, with no *rallentando*, allowing just a tiny 'give' through the last quaver of the penultimate bar, in the sense of an upbeat to a tiny, perfectly neat final chord.

Op. 25 No. 10
Study in B minor (VA)

Even with the most favourable physical predisposition in terms of handspan, strength and suppleness of wrist and general coordination of movement, there can be no denying that prolonged octave playing is tiring for most players. To negotiate the dense double-octave *con fuoco* sections here and arrive at the end in one piece is indeed a feat of resilience and endurance. And since it is a matter seldom discussed in books on piano playing, nor indeed by most teachers, it is worth mentioning here that octaves are particularly tiring for most women players. Apart from the obvious factors of hand span and wrist strength, there appears to be a certain difference in the 'set' of the average male and female hand in that the 'dome' within the palm is more pronounced, with a more defined and dense muscular rim in the male. This enables the male hand to bestride the octave span in an easy grasp, while the female hand tends to flatten and splay over the knuckle area. (There are exceptions, of course, in that some female hands are more 'male' and vice versa, but the truth of these generalisations can be observed by the ease with which the average male hand will grasp and undo the most obstinate jar lid!)

All this said, the practice of a few bars of this piece is an excellent exercise, even for relatively inexperienced players, in that it demonstrates an essential principle of octave playing: that of the **impetus** carrying on and over from one strategic rhythmic point to the next. Thus in a triplet or sextuplet rhythm, as here, the impetus created by a greater 'effort' on the **first** octave of each group: 𝄢 [rhythmic notation] or [rhythmic notation] will 'carry' the remaining octaves in the group (with a much reduced 'effort' on each of these) towards the next effort/impetus, on the first octave of the next group, and so on, thus creating a perpetual 'impetus/recovery' movement. (Inexperienced players generally attempt to hammer each octave with a similar degree of effort which, apart from inducing muscular seizure within a few bars, is entirely counterproductive in terms of speed.) The first six bars of this piece give an excellent demonstration of this principle. Through bb.1 and 2 a greater 'effort' will be made on the first and second main beats (i.e. on the first and third crotchet beats). Through bb.3 and 4 the 'effort' will be made on the syncopated third quaver of each triplet group, through b.5 again on the first and second **main** beats, and through b.6 on each **crotchet** beat. I use the word 'effort' to describe a greater movement, i.e. the **raising** of wrist and/or arm from which the greater 'fall' onto the octave in question will provide the impetus which will allow the hand and arm to 'coast' through the subsequent octaves towards the next greater 'effort'. This 'effort' is thus seen to be different in kind from a mere 'prodding' **accent**, which would not necessarily supply the vital 'impetus'. Since the implication here of the long phrase-slurs is that the octaves are to be played as *legato* as possible, the movement must be kept as close to the keys as possible, i.e. emphatically **not** as in a 'high-hitting' *martellato*. But at the same time, the movement has to incorporate the anticipatory 'raising' necessary for the creation of each rhythmic **impetus**. Smaller hands will not be able to manage the usually suggested fingering. It is far better to use a consistent-toned $\frac{5}{1}\ \frac{5}{1}$ than to be wasting time and energy on squirming around to 'reach' the octaves with fourth or third finger (see General Introduction under 'Fingering'). This is also an instance where the absence of any pedal indications cannot be assumed to mean the total absence of pedal. (See Eigeldinger, p.130. He quotes the Paderewski Edition which suggests that 'these passages in which Chopin has not marked the pedalling are generally explained by the fact that the pedalling required is very simple, and is therefore self-evident; or, on the contrary, that it is so subtle as to be too complicated, if not impossible, to indicate'; and suggests that this is one of the latter instances.) The experienced player will instinctively use touches and 'skims' of pedal which will iron out the 'gaps' occasioned by the strategic preparation for the 'impetus points'. These rhythmic points will also be 'helped' by the momentary touch of resonance provided by a **quick** pedal stroke on the **main** beats (i.e. first and third crotchet beats) of bb.1-2, on the offbeat accented octaves through bb.3-4, and particularly to enhance the denser resonances on the main beats of b.5, and on **each** crotchet beat of b.6, and so on.

In performance the heavings and eruptings of the currents and cross-currents are of maelstromic force – what Chopin's contemporaries made of it all we can only wonder. It is important to gauge the volume of sound so that you start **relatively** quietly, with an overall build-up of sound from b.1 to b.28, and again from b.100 to the end. If you launch in with hammer blows you will undermine the essential architecture of the sound, quite apart from the fact that few, if any, players could stay the course at full throttle. And few eruptions in piano music are as electrifying as the climb from a low growl to a shout between bb.1-5. Here, at b.5, be sure that you use to the full the added resonance provided by the inner minims, then crotchets, holding these in each instance for as great a proportion of their full value as is possible. Then, taking advantage of the momentary respite on the emphatic crotchet chord on the last beat of b.6, it is advisable to drop the tone a little, ready for the next climb from b.11 towards the *fortissimo* from b.13. Note the **slurred** effect of the inner minims on the first beat of bb.7-10 towards the crotchets on the second main beat. Be sure to leave some tone in reserve for the wild climb from b.25, 'peaking' on the high D's to descend with fullest force onto the *fff* chord on the second main beat of b.27, ready for the final spurt towards a violent 'stop' on the second crotchet beat of b.28.

Following this jolt and subsequent hiatus, nothing could seem more lovely than the effect of the quiet unison fragment 'melting' into the expressive pliancy of the long breathed octave melody of the middle section, over the warm-toned, subtly punctuated LH, and with, here and there, the delectable emergence of strands of inner counterpoint. From the upbeat to b.90 the warning inner quavers materialise in a scarcely breathed *sotto voce*, 'circling' with increasing menace, ready for a precipitous *crescendo* and *accelerando* back to tempo 1.

Op. 25 No. 11
Study in A minor (VA)

Considered by many commentators to be the finest of all the Studies, this is certainly one of the most titanic in a technical sense as well as in terms of sheer physical endurance. It is dominated and motivated by an all-pervading LH theme, above which the RH sweeps ceaselessly over the keyboard in brilliant semiquavers. The LH 'carries' these RH semiquavers in the same sense as in Op.10 No.8. But here the magisterial LH theme has a march-like pomp, and the RH semiquavers, richly decorated in a harmonic and melodic sense, are tumultuous, not sportive – the concept, in other words, is infinitely grander. As Jim Samson says 'the RH 'accompaniment' combines harmonic and melodic functions in a uniquely formulated and strongly characterised pattern, sweeping across the registers to create a dramatic and powerful counterpoint to the main theme.' (p.72).

It is one of the few studies, along with Op.10 No.4 and Op.25 No.8, which less advanced players had best leave alone. To those who aspire to play it, or at least to study it, it is worth stressing the necessity to study the LH with the utmost attention. It is essential to **use** its rhythmic impetus and special emphases to underpin, propel and **carry** the RH. It is especially important to **use** the resonance of the bass notes (on the first beat of bb.5, 7, 9-13, etc.), 'catching' these surely in the pedal as indicated, so that their sound **lasts** through the half-bar or bar (the duration of sound of these pedal indications may need modifying on the modern piano). This is not, of course, to suggest that the RH be relegated to a cypher-like tinkling – every note of this brilliant 'counterpoint' must glitter like shooting multicoloured lights from a ceaselessly spinning meteor. There is, of course no substitute for assiduous practise in the RH, and once more Cortot's practise patterns are recommended. First of all though, take time to absorb thoroughly the

harmonic and 'geographic' shapes by practising in double notes

and from b.9 etc.

The introductory bars need to be delivered with all possible gravity and sense of portent – rather than (as is too often the case) as a cursory kind of pre-appendage, as the player flexes his muscles ready for the 'off' at b.5.

It is essential from the outset to feel the overall 2-in-a-bar pulse. It is also vital to 'grade' the overall volume of sound, and to start *forte* and **not** *fortissimo*, otherwise, quite apart from exhausting yourself, you will have no 'room' for the later *fortissimo*, and for the last dynamic 'push' towards the final chords. Players need to take advantage of every possible respite, not only for the sake of their own physiques, but also for the ears of the listener. Chopin has indicated a *diminuendo* from bb.7, 15, etc. i.e. from the halfway point of each downward cascade; then there is an implied **gradual** build-up of sound again from the middle of b.8 etc. so that you crest the dynamic 'hill' with a ringing chord on the second main beat of b.12, ready to launch into the next downward cascade from b.13; and again at the end of b.22 as you scale the summit of the longer overall upward climb from b.16. (In their anxiety to 'get on', players

448

often fail to take full advantage of the chance to 'take a breath' through the rest at the end of b.12, and similarly to 'use' the sense of preparing to 'round the corner' at the end of b.22, allowing in both instances an instant to 'gather themselves' ready to launch downwards again from b.13 and b.23.) It is also important to 'point' all the indicated emphases in the LH: the *marcato* dotted rhythm figure in b.9 and again in b.19, this time accented, and the emphasised slurred upbeat to bb.10, 11, 18, etc. Indeed, all through bb.9-12 and 19-22 the RH has to allow time for the LH to 'make its points', and again particularly at bb.17 and 18, where the LH has to have an extra fraction of time to 'reach' the chord on the second main beat (**both** of these are spread in many editions). All these figures, the dotted rhythm figures in bb.9 and 19, the triplets in bb.10, 11, 12, 17 and 18, etc. must give the feeling of 'going to' the chord or note on the

second **main** beat of the bar:  *etc.*

Assuming an implied *diminuendo* through bb.33 and 34 (as through bb.7 and 8, etc.) there is the feel of a respite, in a dynamic sense, from b.35, where the RH passage-work becomes less tumultuous and more 'filigree', with an implied *subito forte* at b.41 where, of course, the RH must emphatically 'take over' the march theme. Then most players play more reflectively from b.45, with a *più piano* echo effect from b.47, and another *subito forte* at b.49. Here, through bb.49-52, the LH has to be particularly defined and resolute leading into a carillon of richly modulating RH semiquavers through bb.53-4 (**listen** to the effect of the broken intervals here, diminished fifth, major seventh, diminished fourth, major sixth, etc.) over resonantly 'harped' LH chords. Then **use** the resonance of the held pedal point to help build up the sound through b.59 towards the mighty dual outburst from b.61, arriving on a lashing *sforzato* chord on the second main beat of bb.62 and 64. Then make sure the *piano* figures are perfectly timed through b.65. These have an almost 'throw-away' quality, which at the same time conveys an expectant onward impetus into the furious but **gradual** build-up from b.66. Then draw out fractionally through the last beat of b.68 as you poise yourself to surge into the reprise.

Through bb.83-4 the LH needs to ring out with stentorian resonance, with a steep *diminuendo* through the end of b.84, ready for the final overall build-up from the *piano* at b.85. Once again **use** the huge bass sound of the theme picked out in the accented semiquavers through bb.89-90. Many players adopt the variant of the B on the fourth crotchet beat of b.89

(given in the Vienna Urtext and Paderewski editions).

Cortot, giving both versions, prefers the continuous A since, in his view, it 'conforms better to the orchestral meaning of the Coda'. This must remain a matter of choice, as the alternative view, that the B 'conforms better to the principal theme', is equally, perhaps more valid. Allow the slight *diminuendo* from the end of b.90 so as to 'point' the effect of the frenetic descent of the *marcato staccato* quavers through b.92 (be sure to let the LH 'lead' here) towards the thunderous final chords.

After the Herculean efforts of the previous ninety bars, it is a tall order to 'gather oneself' and negotiate the long unison scale. It is half the battle to start the scale **on** a clear beat. Having thrust through bb.93-4 towards an immense tonic chord on the first beat of b.95, come **off** this chord with a rhythmic **swing** so that you land on the unison first notes of the scale as if on the

second crotchet beat, ready to 'zoom' upwards to 'arrive' on the final ringing high crotchets exactly on the first beat of the last bar. **Feel** the third and fourth crotchet beats within the upward 'zoom' so that even if you have to 'stretch' them a little, you still feel this sense of 'arriving' at the summit on the first beat.

There are various ways of coping with the RH fingering for this 'arrival':

a) 1 2 3 1 2 3 4 / 3   b) 1 2 3 1 2 3 4 / 1   c) 1 2 3 1 2 3 4 / $\frac{5}{1}$ etc.

The essential is to focus the attention on the **objectives**, i.e. the top A's, and to 'go to' these from a strong upbeat note G sharp. If you use fingering a), come **off** the G sharp so as to be able better to **define** the A, rather than 'sliding off' the G sharp on to the A. Similarly, if you use fingering b), come fractionally **off** the G sharp, and if you use c), again come **off** so that the hand can 'fall' onto a powerful octave. Holding the sound of the semibreve chord in the pedal through the whole scale, change the pedal rapidly to give a swift short stroke **on** the final A's. Apart from the fact that this defines the **sound** of the A, it also, by the 'sympathetic' movement of the foot, helps to 'poise' the progress from the 'upbeat' to the final note.

Op. 25 No. 12
Study in C minor (VA)

With the magisterial Bachian progress of its chorale-like 'ground' beneath an unchanging pattern of sweeping arpeggios, this last Study, as various commentators have remarked, completes a circle back to the style of the first. Although both hands are equally involved, the technical demands here are less than in Op.10 No.1 because the arpeggios are shorter, and also the necessary extension and contraction of the hands span only an octave rather than a tenth or more. But since the melody line of the 'ground' is carried **within** the arpeggio by the RH thumb, the resonances are in a sense more complicated. Although the technical demands here are also less titanic than those of Op.25 No.11, this is nevertheless a weighty undertaking in terms of physical endurance – the respite from the full span of the surging arpeggios occurring only at bb.7-8, 30, 45-6, 53-4, 65-6 and through the three final bars. But this piece provides a splendid opportunity to acquire the vital skill of expanding and contracting the hand in a series of quick 'snaps' – one which many pianists find so difficult. (We know that Chopin's hands were exceptionally supple in this respect: see discussion of the technique under Op.10 No.1.) Just as importantly, it offers a splendid adventure in terms of the projection of powerful resonance.

It is well to study the mechanics of the necessary physical movement through one arpeggio only at first. And for this purpose it is best in the RH to take the model of b.2, since this pattern lies most comfortably under the hand, whereas the pattern of b.1 is one of the most awkward (the 5-1 finger change taking place on the black note, and in addition the second finger has difficulty in 'finding' the white note G with each shift of the 'black note' octave position). The b.1 pattern is the best, however, for the **L.H.**

Practise at first thus:    and

> **slowly,** and changing fingers **silently** on the

5-1 and 1-5 with a lateral 'shut-open', 'snap' movement (see Op.10 No.1.). Bring the RH thumb up immediately after the fifth finger has struck the D so that it is ready to 'replace' the fifth finger with the hand then shooting 'open' again so that the fifth finger is 'ready' in place to play the next D, and so on (reversing the movement as you descend). Then add the A flat and practise

in a dotted rhythm as in  still changing fingers

silently. Practise this at first at a **slow** beat, say ♪ = 50. If you keep a rock steady quaver beat, but 'snapping' the hand 'open' immediately you have changed fingers 5-1, the second finger will obviously have to 'wait' until it is time for it to play the semiquaver A flat. This is an essential part of the preparation for the overall movement, since in performance it allows a vital split second of relaxation as you 'change feet' on this repeated note. Keeping the slow beat, therefore, concentrate on acquiring a **lightning**-quick, silent finger change, and then, shooting the second finger into place, let the 'open' hand lie relaxed over the keys until it is time for the second finger to play. Then, if you think of the A flat as an 'upbeat' 'going to' the emphasised fifth finger, it will be found that the second finger will virtually 'play itself' as it 'directs' towards the fifth finger (or in descent, towards the thumb) on the subsequent D. Practise this movement

similarly in the LH,  Practise this RH and LH movement

slowly, in time, playing the arpeggio over and over in a continuous movement, and gradually increasing the speed of the crotchet pulse until you can play it in a moderate tempo with an easy swing. Then practise b.2 **slowly** hands together (if you prefer a more concordant sound,

combine the RH with a different LH harmony  for example).

It is a good plan at this point to practise bb.1-7 in chords thus:

and then ... *etc.* so that the sense of the

harmonies, and then the upward and downward 'direction' of the hands are thoroughly absorbed. Now practise the whole of bb.1-7 **as written,** 'changing feet' neatly on the repeated notes, hands separately at first, then hands together and then practise in varying rhythms:

Next, the 'bringing out' of the melody line has to be studied. First practise in chords 'leaning' the weight of the hand towards the thumb. Then practise

thus: and making an overall slurred effect so that you

'lean' on the thumb, playing the upper fifth or broken fifth relatively lightly, and 'lifting' the hand from the fifth (or second semiquaver) so that the hand 'falls' naturally towards another resonant 'lean' on the thumb. Now practise in 'half' arpeggios from the top note:

And then practise *etc.*

bb.1-7 as written, over and over, slowly at first, and gradually increasing the speed until you can play fluently at a moderate tempo. It is vital that the body as a whole is involved in the upward and downward sweeps across the keyboard exactly as in Op.10 No.1 – try the 'ramrod' test outlined under the notes for that Study. (Stiff, dry performances of this piece can often be transformed simply by understanding the need to allow the torso to 'go with' the movement of the hands and arms.) As also in Op.10 No.1, the arpeggios need to 'grow' from each melody note, rather than merely to intervene between one 'plonk' with the thumb and the next. Nothing is more awful than the kind of performance with a mere 'accent' on bass and treble. On the contrary, each note must be a fully alive **part** of each sweep, but 'directed' towards each objective, i.e. the highest and lowest note on each arpeggio. Feel the RH thumb note and LH bass note as a powerful resonance from which each arpeggio 'grows', and the highest note as the crest of each 'wave' of sound. The movement ideally then becomes self-generating – the impetus from the emphasised low note 'directs' the hand upwards and similarly the sense of 'rounding the corner' on the top note 'directs' the hands downwards again.

The relatively inexperienced player will almost invariably feel, and give, the sensation of 'falling into' each bar, caused by the 'skimping' of the last two semiquavers of the previous bar. This is obviated by **consciously** treating these two notes as the 'upbeat' to the subsequent

emphasised first beat, and practising temporarily

In performance beware, as so often in such a piece, of starting at full throttle. Lead off, therefore, in a **controlled** *forte* resonance, 'directing' the first six bars towards, and through the 'peak' of the 'thumb' melody (the F on the first beat of b.3) and onwards in such a way that you land on the tonic unisons on the first beat of b.7 with a sense of 'arrival'. Then let the sound 'ease away' from the second crotchet beat of this bar sensitively pointing the 'doubled' descending treble offbeat line, and poise yourself momentarily through the end of b.8 ready to 'start again' from b.9. Raise the dynamic level slightly at b.13, the peak of this second 6-bar 'melodic' period, ready to arrive on the tonic major at b.15 in the new, extended arpeggio pattern. Feel that you are still cresting the wave as you turn the corner on the top offbeat note of the long arpeggios – but without the sense of objective felt in bb.1-6, etc. so that the arpeggio is immediately 'directed' downwards again towards the offbeat emphasised fragment. These fragments are differently marked in various editions:

In any event, whichever option you adopt, a fraction of extra time must be allowed for these emphases to 'make their points', particularly the syncopated effect as you land on the doubled note on the second crotchet beat of bb.16, 18, etc. Give each 'extended' arpeggio (i.e. through bb.15, 17, etc.) a powerful resonance, then feel that you are 'gathering yourself' from the emphasised second crotchet beat of bb.16 and 18, ready for the next grand sweep. It is then possible to lower the tone a little through bb.21-2 as you return to the 'normal' pattern, ready to launch off in *forte* again from b.23. Most players then drop the tone considerably at b.31, ready to make a gradual climb towards the powerful *fortissimo* appoggiatura effect at b.43 'resolving' to the dominant at b.44; and then dropping the tone in a *subito piano* at b.45, and building up again towards b.47. Listen here to the lower dominant pedal point resonance through bb.43-4, transferred to the **RH** from b.45, and maintained through to the end of b.46 against the chromatically rising bass. Draw out a little through the last beat of b.46 ready to drive off into the reprise from b.47. Many players again start more quietly from b.55, controlling the immensely long *crescendo* rigorously so that there is tone in reserve for the last arpeggio through bb.79-80, and for the final colossal thrust of sound from b.81. Arrive with immense power on the unisons on the first beat of the last bar so that you feel that the impact allows the weight to rebound, to make a 'throw', 'on and upwards' towards the final chord.

With proper use of the pedal there is never any need to force the sound. The combined resonance of each melody note and bass note needs to be **completely** caught in the pedal. This sounds too obvious to state, but it often is **not** caught to the optimum extent, i.e. not changed at precisely the optimum instant, resulting in incomplete 'catching' of these first beat resonances and consequent thinness of sound, with the player having to work twice as hard 'manually', as it were, to make up for the missed pedalled sound. The first note of each arpeggio has to be held for just an extra fraction of a second to give time for the pedal to be changed and the sound 're-caught'. This can be practised in slow motion, **exaggerating** the hold on the first note, and operating to a count of five crotchets

through each arpeggio:

Listen to the strong resonance that is caught on the held first note, and **naturally** built up through the rise and fall of the arpeggio within the pedalled sound. Then at bb.16, 18, etc. Chopin has indicated the separate pedals which assist in the definition of the extra emphases. (There is a case here for also giving the 'syncopated' second beat a separate pedal, as Cortot does.) Through the final bars from b.81 there is again no need to force the sound. Within the long pedal held over to and through the last chord, the huge bass notes, pounding like cannon balls, create a massive, self-generating swell of sound within the overall welter of *crescendoing* semiquavers, with comparatively little effort on the part of the player.

TROIS NOUVELLES ETUDES

These three pieces were written in 1839 as a contribution to a piano Method by Fétis (an eminent musician, scholar and critic of the time) and Moscheles. Different editions place them in varying order, but in both Henle and the Vienna Urtext Edition they are given: F minor, A flat, and D flat. Assuming familiarity with cross-rhythms, neither the F minor or the A flat is demanding in a technical sense, although a nice fluency is needed through the continuously arpeggiated LH in the F minor. But each of these pieces is a subtle and penetrating musical exposition of the expressive potential of cross-rhythm, as well as a study in the shaping of long-breathed phrases. The D flat Study, an equally enchanting, more whimsical piece, is much more difficult, with its dual-voiced RH proceeding in continuous *legato* in the upper line and *staccato* in the lower. Tucked away as they usually are at the end of Op.25, and indeed often not included in editions of the Studies, they seldom seem to be performed. Perhaps this is because, paradoxically for studies written to order as it were for a Piano Method, they are pieces of a specially inward kind of expressiveness, ideal territory therefore for the domestic player.

No. 1 in F minor (8)

The kinship between this piece and the F minor study Op.25 No.2 has been noted by many commentators. Besides the continuous cross-rhythm movement of both pieces, there are resemblances in the sinuous, often chromatically 'curling' character of the RH melody and the broken chord movement in the LH and indeed in the general spirit of the two studies. In Op.25 No.2, however, the LH is more melodic, so that the hands perform more of a duet – whereas here the LH moves in a regular arpeggiated pattern, thus ensuring a more definedly **harmonic** role in support of the RH melody. The tendency is to play this piece far too slowly. There is certainly a feeling of melancholy, but it is a light, 'skimming' kind of sadness. If it is too slow the music becomes turgid, choking itself on the inherent richness of its harmonic inflections. A tempo of around ♩ = 80-90 is suggested, with of course plenty of room for give and take, and for allowing the phrases to 'breathe'.

It is well first of all to study and thoroughly learn the LH, since the smooth expressive shaping of the long RH phrases is dependent upon perfect fluency in the LH. The arpeggiated quavers need to move in continuous waves. These LH waves, gracefully curved but not flaccid, provide a ceaseless 'cushioning' onward movement, which is nevertheless flexible and subtly responsive to the dynamic rise and fall of the RH line, and to the fluctuating sense of 'moving on' and 'easing' (see General Introduction under *Rubato*). Feel that the quavers are moving in continuous arcs from the bass note to the crest of each wave, and back again to the next bass note, thus defining the two-in-the-bar rhythm. The sound of each bass note must be carefully judged – not in the sense of an **accent**, but **listened** to as a **resonance** that pervades and 'sets' the harmony of each bar. Take time to find your preferred fingering: whether and when it suits the individual hand to use thumb or second finger on each top note. Through bb.5-14 it will

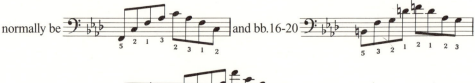

normally be ⟨music⟩ and bb.16-20 ⟨music⟩

and through bb.21-2 ⟨music⟩ and so on. But in certain bars

(e.g. b.15) 5 2 1 2 1 2 1 2 might be preferred (for a small hand) to the often given 5 3 2 1 2 1 2 3, and in b.39 try 5 1 3 2 1 2 3 1 rather than 5 **2** 1 3 2 3 1 2 etc.

Now study the RH melody line, shaping its curves in long phrases like a vocalise. Practise at first in a fairly slow tempo, keeping a **regular** 2-in-the-bar pulse. Shape the continuously curving phrases as a singer would, and see how much of a sense of freedom you can achieve **within** this regular pulse. Feel the rises and dips within the overall curve and slight dynamic rise of the introductory phrase. If you **sing** this phrase you will immediately feel how it is shaped in two 1-bar phrases and one longer 2-bar phrase:

making a small overall curve through each short phrase and a greater curve through the longer 2-bar phrase up towards, and through the A flats and coming to rest on the tonic in b.5. These subphrases are suggested in many editions but must be understood as nuances **within** the overall upward curve of the whole phrase.

Imagine the LH tonic arpeggio moving in steady, even curves through bb.5-8, and then enter in perfect time on the offbeat in b.9. Once again (and throughout the piece) if you **sing** the phrases you will aurally understand the 'landscape' of the curves, and the subdivisions within each long overall phrase. (Do this rather **slowly**, since with its wide spanning dips and rises (bb.10, 11, etc.) it is a difficult melody to sing.) Henle and the Vienna Urtext Edition indicate the original very long phrases, extending through bb.9-21, 22-9, and 30 right through to b.65. In the Paderewski edition and in Peters, subphrases are marked (e.g. beginning on the second crotchet of bb.9, 13, 15, 17, 19, etc.). These should not, however, be felt as **breaks** in the *legato*, but as **delineations** of the smaller curves within the long overall curve. It is extremely important to work out your fingerings and to **stick** to them when you put hands together. So often, fingerings carefully studied hands separately get 'lost' when the hands are put together. The occasional original fingerings for the RH which survive never fail to 'describe' the shape and expressive implication of the phrases.* One instance is particularly interesting. As a student I learnt this piece from an edition with 'sensible' editorial fingerings. Returning to it much later, when I had learnt a little more about fingering (much of it from the study of Chopin's own practice), I found myself using the thumb on the three consecutive notes between

bb.40-1, 42-3, and 46-7 *etc.* evidently feeling

instinctively that these notes needed this special 'pointing' (see General Introduction under 'Fingering'). Querying my unconscious use of this highly 'unconventional' fingering, it was gratifying to find that this was indeed Chopin's intended fingering to 'point' a slightly *marcato* effect through this 3-note motif.

When you put hands together, have your overall 2-in-the-bar pulse well 'in the system' before you start (however slow it may be at first). 'Feel' the silent first beat so that the opening phrase can 'drift' in (but **in time**) on the offbeat, and you can immediately establish the **sense** of your basic pulse from the second beat of the bar, though without obvious accents. You may wish to play this introductory phrase fairly freely, starting perhaps somewhat slower than your

*These are taken from the score belonging to Chopin's pupil Camille O'Meara/Dubois, and are shown more liberally in the Vienna Urtext Edition than in Henle.

intended overall tempo, and gradually 'moving on' until you reach and set your basic tempo in the LH at b.5. Nevertheless, from the outset there must still be a sense of the eventual 2-in-the-bar pulse as you shape the broad curve, as outlined above, up towards the end of b.4, to 'close' on a clear crotchet F on the first beat of b.5. Have the LH ready to 'meet' the RH on the first beat of b.5, to establish the tempo in soft, perfectly regular waves as described above. Point the bass note a little on the first beat of b.9, allowing a little 'give' through the first half of the bar so that the RH can make a soft but clear entry on the offbeat, as if growing out of the LH arpeggios. Practise through to b.21 over and over until the coordination between the hands is quite fluent, gradually increasing the pulse until you arrive at a tempo that moves in a comfortable *andantino* without a trace of stickiness. Listen carefully to the balance between the hands as you make a gradual *crescendo* towards the end of b.18, and then a gradual *diminuendo* as the melody moves upwards towards the end of the phrase. The LH has constantly to be sensitive to the demands of the melody, its resonance filling out and supporting but never swamping the RH, and with the pedalling perfectly synchronised so that the bass note is always 'caught' and held within the pedal through each bar. (It is often difficult to wean students away from the 'choppy' effect of changing the pedal on each **half** bar – see General Introduction under 'Pedalling'.) Listen particularly to the line of the bass notes, moving from the tonic (bb.5-9) in an overall curve towards the dominant at b.17 and back to the tonic at b.21. Allow the tempo to ease a little as you continue the upward *diminuendo* through the end of b.20, picking it up again in the LH as the RH ends the phrase on a quiet tonic crotchet on the first beat of b.21.

Be sure to come **off** in the RH in b.21, imagining what a large breath a singer would need to take between these long phrases. Although of course the sound is held within the pedal, this 'coming off' ensures the right sense of the new entry in b.22 (see General Introduction under 'Articulation'). The gentle rocking of the RH here (bb.22-4) has a quiet, tolling quality – listen also to the hinted descending inner LH melodic fragment through the **second** beat of bb.21-3 – F, E flat, D flat. Then after the little swell through bb.24-6, let the sound tail away again from b.27 towards b.29 (as through bb.18-21). Feel the wide RH intervals from the first to the second crotchets of bb.33-6 etc. as vocal 'lifts', not 'snatches', and do not make the *crescendo* too heavy from b.32, being sure to *decrescendo* again through bb.35-7. From b.37 the feeling becomes more *agitato*, with a more intense chromatic snaking through bb.37-40. Take care again not to 'snatch', but to 'lift' up to the RH C flat on the second crotchet of b.38. The repeated thumb fingering referred to above gives the sense of a strong upbeat impulse into b.41, and again into bb.43 and 47. Feel a strong but **controlled** sense of onward movement from b.41 when the *forte* gets under way, taking care also to keep the dynamics under careful control, since the overall *crescendo* still has a long way to go, right through to b.52. Listen carefully to the balance as the volume of tone rises so that the RH line is well supported and filled out, rather than being left to struggle along on its own. It is perhaps a good plan to drop the tone just a little after the first crotchet of b.49, ready to make the final *crescendo* and *stringendo* up towards the end of b.52. This also 'points' the establishment of the long tonic pedal point which lasts through from bb.49-60. Make a final *portamento*-like 'lift' up to the A flat at the end of b.52, making a slight vocal 'hold' on this note (at the same time feeling its 'on and over' upbeat 'lean') before starting the gradual 'unwinding' from b.53 (with an implied return to tempo after the previous *stringendo*). In Henle and the Vienna Urtext Edition there is a *diminuendo* through the first half of b.53 with a swell from the second half of the bar and through b.54, with a further *diminuendo* from b.55. However, the Vienna Urtext considers that this is possibly a slip on Chopin's part, and indeed, an overall gradual *diminuendo* from b.53 as in the Paderewski Edition (tailing away upwards to b.57) seems more satisfactory. In any event, **hold** and **listen** to the quiet, long F through b.57, as you prepare to ease into the 'tolling' figure in a hazy *pianissimo*, making a slight swell as if on a breeze, towards and back from the middle of b.60.

Allow a little 'give' through the middle of b.62 so that the LH can lift **off** without abruptness. Let the RH move on to 'speak' through b.63 with quiet resignation, rather than merely fizzling out as it so often does. Feel that the melody line leads on through the end of b.63 to the minim D flat and on through to the F in b.65 in this final cadence. Then give the low tonic chords a horn-like quality, playing these with a sense of quiet finality, and letting the sound fade almost into silence through the pause.

No. 2 in A flat major (7)

Technically simpler than the F minor, this is in some senses more musically searching in that its infinitely subtle harmonic and expressive inflections arise **within** the RH chords, often in the inner voices (rather than as in the F minor within a single melodic line). The chordal-cum-melodic RH triplets are complemented rather than accompanied by the LH quavers, from which melodic fragments from time to time emerge, e.g. through bb.9-11 and 13, and in a long span from the second beat of b.16. Like the F minor, this piece is often played too slowly, and with even more unfortunate results. The overall movement, with its chordal RH writing, is more 'stationary' so that if the tempo is too slow the performance becomes disastrously plodding. Once again the movement needs to have a 'skimming' effect, not in the sense of superficiality, but in order to allow the harmonic and melodic inflections and implications to be finely shaded, rather than baldly **stated.** There is therefore a fairly wide margin for choice of a basic tempo. The essential is that the piece **moves**, and in a sense the more skilled the player, the slower the possible tempo at which this sense of movement can be conveyed. But there are limits – there is one recording which grinds along most dismally at a tempo of around ♩ = 54. Bearing in mind the indicated *allegretto*, a crotchet pulse of around ♩ = 69-76 is suggested. Henle gives no dynamic indications except for a *decrescendo* sign in the penultimate bar. The Vienna Urtext Edition gives a *piano* in b.1, a suggested *crescendo* from b.25 and a *forte* at b.29, a *decrescendo* through bb.39-40 and 43, a *pianissimo* from b.56 and, as in Henle, a *decrescendo* in the penultimate bar. The indications in the Paderewski Edition are similar, with several additional editorial 'hairpins'.

Once again, it is perhaps best to study the LH first, which is a great deal more complex than it at first appears, in terms of articulation, the 'pointing' of 'doubled' notes, melodic fragments, etc. Obviously it is not possible to play the widely spaced quavers *legato* (bb.2, 3, etc.), while on the other hand the more melodic fragments should be smoothly phrased. The wide apart

quavers (e.g. through bb.2-3) need to be treated as if marked

and given an even, just-detached touch which gives a 'suspended' quality to the line as opposed

to the effect of slurred 'pairs'. 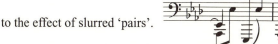 'Point' the opening, doubled

A flat, and the tied doubled E flat on the second beat of b.1, ensuring that this note is held through into b.2 by changing fingers as indicated (5-2 **or** 5-3), and then playing the quavers in the just-detached 'suspended' style through bb.2-3. Shape the ascending quavers more 'melodically' through b.4, returning to the pattern of bb.1-3 from b.5. From b.9 the line becomes more melodic. As you shape the curve expressively, in a vocal manner up to and down from the high C in bb.9 and 10, **listen** to the held doubled second quaver which acts as a kind of resonant anchor on the dominant – changing fingers again, 1-5 (or 1-4 or 1-3), on the E flat in b.9. Alternatively bring the fifth finger up to the second E flat in b.9 so that the fingering is 5 5 1 2 (see the application of this principle in the LH of the Prelude in D flat, Op.28 No.15). Then feel the last quaver of b.10 as the upbeat to b.11, and go on to shape the melodic fragments expressively again through bb.11 and 13, reverting to the 'suspended' kind of articulation through b.12 and again from b.14 through to the middle of b.16. (Note the fingering for the A flat and G in b.11 (1, 1), and give the acciaccatura time to 'speak' on the second beat of b.13.) Do feel the vocal quality of these LH curves throughout this piece, up towards and down from the uppermost note (on the second beat of bb.11, 13 and 18, the first beat of b.20, the last **quaver** of b.23, and again on the first beat of bb.26, 28, and so on).

'Finish off' the LH phrase cleanly, up to the second quaver E flat in b.16, then making it clear that you are leading on into a new phase with the two descending quavers through the second beat of the bar. From here be careful to finger the upper notes of each curve for maximum smoothness, e.g. through bb.17-20 try:

The 5-1 and 1-5 finger

changes may seem like a counsel of perfection, but apart from the fact that this was a frequent practice of Chopin, it gives a slight 'pointing' to these notes, creating a subtle rhythmic anchor on the upbeat to b.19, and the second beat of b.20. The curve through

bb.23-4 could be fingered  and through bb.25-26

and so on.

Turning to the RH, the treble line of the chords can in places be played *legato*, i.e. momentarily on the second beat of b.1 and the first beat of b.2, and through the second beat of b.4. But this is a piece eminently suitable for those

with **relatively** small hands, for whom even a *legato* in b.1 is awkward. Far more important than squirming about trying to play a treble *legato* is to cultivate the skill of playing repeated notes or chords in a barely detached 'clinging' style, discussed in detail under Prelude in E minor, No.4 Op.28. Here, however, there is the added problem of the gentle 'bringing out' of the treble line, and sometimes of lower fragments: e.g. through b.17, and bb.20-1, etc; and of always being acutely aware of the movement of inner and lower voices. To this end it is a good plan to

practise thus: 'leaning' lightly on each crotchet and holding it as long as possible, only releasing it just in time to play the next crotchet (and practising b.17 etc. similarly 'leaning' on the lower notes with the thumb).

Practise the whole piece in short sections (i.e. bb.1-4, 5-8, etc.) listening acutely to the conjoint or staggered movement of the voices, i.e. in b.1 all three voices move downwards

and in b.2 the treble voice first moves down a tone over the 'stationary' lower

voices, and then the lower voice moves down beneath the 'stationary' upper voices, and so on.

Study these subtle movements very slowly so that you

thoroughly 'understand' them in an aural sense. Then play through from bb.1-16 and 17 to the end, creating a smooth 'on-and-on' flow through these immensely long phrases. Allow the dynamics to fall and rise in natural, very gentle curves as the line dips through bb.1-2, rises again in a nicely 'rounded' swell towards and through b.5, dips again through b.6, and so on.

When you start to put hands together work slowly again in short sections at first before practising through the long phrases. Point the opening doubled A flat as already mentioned so that the RH has a quiet but definite 'springboard' from which to 'cast off'. The RH needs to 'swim' smoothly and quietly, as if suspended over the LH quavers, the LH at one and the same time supporting, directing and punctuating the movement of the RH. Allow the tone to rise a little through bb.3-4, 'drawing out' the movement a little through the end of b.4, with at the same time the sense of expanding as you carry on and over into b.5, where the overall curve peaks and turns downwards again from the second beat. Then curve up gently again towards the high G in b.8, 'easing' a little through the end of the bar ready for the LH to take its more prominent melodic role from b.9. **Listen, listen, listen** to the movement of the RH voices, to the changing patterns of the LH in relation to the melodic line and harmonic progressions of the RH. 'Finish off' the first overall phrase quietly and clearly to the second quaver of b.16 in the LH, and to the second triplet quaver in the RH. Then feel the third RH triplet, i.e. the first of the repeated octave A flats, as the 'upbeat' to the second beat of the bar, as you prepare to lead off into the modulatory middle section, giving a clear onward upbeat lead in the LH from the second beat of the bar. There is a suggestion of moving on here. Phrase the LH with warm expressiveness, listening acutely also to the movement of the lower RH voices through bb.17 and 20-1, and to the treble voice from the upbeat to b.18 and again through b.22. Feel each LH melodic sentence (through bb.17-20 and 21-4 etc.) as a subphrase within the overall movement (allowing a little 'give' at the end of bb.20 and 24, ready to 'start again' in bb.21 and 25). It is well to drop the tone from the end of b.24 so that you start the gradual climb from b.25 quietly. Grade the implied overall *crescendo* very carefully from here so that you 'peak' on the second beat of b.33. Listen *en route* to the resonance of the inner RH dotted crotchet on the first beat of bb.25-8 over the widely striding LH curves, as you move in a gradual *crescendo* towards b.29. Then 'drop back' slightly through bb.30-1, ready for a strong expansion of tone through b.32 towards a luxuriant (but not overblown) fullness through bb.33-4. I suggest dropping the tone just a little again through bb.35-6 to allow for another but slightly lesser swell towards the second beat of b.39.

A degree of carefully managed fluctuation of tempo is implied through bb.25-41. There is a feeling of 'pressing on' as you *crescendo* from b.25, and then a very slight drawing out as this 'foothill' *crescendo* peaks through b.29, and a slight easing off through bb.30-1 along with the easing of the tone. Then there is a sense of moving on through b.32 as the tone expands fervently towards b.33, with a drawing out through bb.33 and 34, and a feeling of moving on again from b.37 towards b.39. Then 'unwind' through b.40, layering the tone downwards, and taking plenty of time through the second half of the bar as you prepare to ease into b.41.

You could play the reprise in an even gentler, more dreamlike *piano* than in the opening. Let the LH 'leave off' as if in mid-thought at the end of b.55 as the RH continues in a murmur, quietly pointing the inner movement to the tonic on the fifth quaver of b.56, and making the quietest possible interjection with the slurred LH quavers in b.57. Tailing the RH away to the quietest whisper, think of the LH trill as just a flutter beneath the 'subsiding' RH movement, drawing out the last three RH triplet chords towards a gentle 'lean' on the dominant seventh chord, resolving to a very quiet but clear tonic. Place the prefix to the

trill on the beat  (see General

Introduction under 'Ornaments'). Invariably in such instances inexperienced players panic and allow the trill to 'take over' (see General Introduction again). Feel that this LH 'flutter' is being guided by the RH chords, and **not** the other way around.

Although Chopin gave no indications, it is unthinkable that he did not expect this piece to be pedalled. This is another area in which the music is more complex than it at first appears. Much depends on the tempo. At a faster tempo a pedal on each crotchet beat is acceptable, but at a slower tempo the movement among the RH voices, sometimes triplet by triplet, needs to be more defined, i.e. often with 'extra' pedals for LH quavers or even sometimes for individual RH triplets. The expert pedaller will 'flutter' the pedal according to the dictates of his experienced ear, taking into account the resonance of different pianos and acoustics. This is expecting too much of less experienced players who, according to their deftness of ear and foot had best pedal lightly (i.e. not depressing the pedal too far – see General Introduction under 'Pedalling') on each crotchet beat with perhaps an occasional longer pedal to retain the bass sound through those bars in which the RH harmonies remain 'static' e.g. bb.19, 23, and so on.

No. 3 in D flat major (8+)

As already said, this graceful piece, charmingly expressive in a light-spirited way, is much more difficult than the previous two. Even without the *legato staccato* effect, the RH proceeding almost entirely in continuous 'double stopping' would be far from easy. As it is, to maintain throughout a *legato* in the treble and *staccato* in the lower line requires technical control of a high order. And the *allegretto* needs to 'move', with the treble sailing smoothly over the lightly jogging inner *staccato* quavers, like the motion of a nicely sprung gig, drawn by a light-footed pony. The tempo must depend upon the skill of the player – the further it falls below about ♩ = 120, the more it is in danger of sounding like a cart drawn by a stocky cob, although on the other hand, at too fast a tempo it loses its gracious charm and begins merely to scurry. Happily, Chopin gave detailed pedal indications, and admittedly his intended inner *staccato* is often 'contained' within the pedal (see the first two beats of bb.3 and 5, the **whole** of bb.4, 6 and 8, etc.). But it is the *staccato* articulation which gives this light jogging feeling to the movement of the line, even within this pedalled sound. If both voices were played more or less *legato*, the effect would be more 'sloshy', whereas Chopin has made his intentions perfectly clear (see General Introduction under 'Articulation'). As Weinstock says with reference to this *legato/staccato* problem, 'Without performing this difficult feat – difficult, at least, in a nicely conceived *allegretto* – a pianist can still make a considerable musical effect with the piece, but the perfect carrying out of Chopin's intention heightens that effect by many degrees. Its apparently continuous melodic line calls forth a light shimmer of harmonic shiftings that lays a lovely glow of colour over the whole Etude'. (p.311).

First of all play through the RH in short sections (bb.3-6, 7-10, and so on) in double notes, noting the fingering of the treble line, and altering it when necessary to suit the individual hand. For many hands for example, the **third** finger will be happier on the E flat on the fourth quaver of b.6. Now practise the treble line alone, **using** those fingers you have worked out. As in Nos.1 and 2, the melody moves in immensely long phrases – 'almost continuously' as Weinstock points out. The melody is like a vocalise, as is that of No.1. **Sing** it and you will learn exactly how to shape the rises and dips in the line. Feel a slight expansion through b.6 as the line curves up, over, and on into b.7, resuming the easy movement in b.7, from where the phrase expands again on towards and through the long tied D flat in b.14, and so on.

Now practise the inner line in a quiet, neatly rhythmic 'plucked' *staccato*, fingering the quavers mainly 1 2 1 2 1 2 etc, except, for example, through b.6 when 1 2 1 1 1 2 will probably suit most hands.

Now practise the LH alone. Chopin made no indications for articulation through bb.3-15 and 33-41. I cannot agree with Weinstock that this is a Waltz in disguise. The LH is **not** Waltz-like – it is the 'spaced-out' style, in combination with the inner *staccato* quavers which creates this special light jogging movement referred to above. This suggests a lightly detached (rather than *staccato*) articulation of the LH, as if you lightly implant each note or chord, coming off with a little spring directed upward or downward towards the next implant. This creates a continuously lightly sprung movement which nicely carries the upper voices. Practise bb.3-15 thus, perfectly rhythmically, and then show the implied 'lean' on the slurred upbeat crotchet to bb.16 and 17. Point the tied minim on the second beat of b.24, being sure to hold this through into b.25, and then listen to the smooth resonance of the dominant unisons through bb.25-9. Note the *staccatos* through bb.43-7, suggesting a quiet, neatly 'pointed' whimsicality here. Practise bb.61-3 assiduously. The LH 'aim' needs to be very sure, since this passage in combination with the RH ninths is far from easy to negotiate. Place the acciaccaturas on the beat, then using the idea of the slurs to make an easy 'scoop', rather than a 'snatch' from each acciaccatura up to the crotchet. Depart here for once from the virtuous precept 'practise without pedal'. The resonance of each dominant acciaccatura caught within the pedal gives confidence to the ear, thereby reducing the urge to 'snatch' up to the crotchet.

Now practise the LH in combination with the inner quavers, and then with the treble line (**without** the inner quavers). Do this while keeping a steady, very even crotchet pulse (perhaps even with the help of the metronome) so that you absorb the steady **physical** sense of the lightly 'springing' crotchet pulse. It will be seen that exaggerated *rubato* is out of place here – just a little give here and there, i.e. between bb.6-7 and through the end of b.32, and with rather more sense of freedom from b.42. Similarly practise the two RH voices **without** the bass, taking the *staccato* quaver line **with the LH** so that you can demonstrate to yourself an 'ideal' realisation of the *legato* line over immaculate staccato. Then straightaway play the voices in the RH as written, again without the bass, aspiring to maintain the poise you achieved with two hands. In bb.50-1, those with small hands could take the inner RH E flats and D natural with the LH (spreading the resulting tenth on the third beat of b.50, and the first of b.51 is a preferable alternative to 'breaking' the long treble F). And through bb.61-3 the RH ninth must be broken if necessary. When eventually you put the two RH voices together with the LH, practise very slowly at first with lynx-like aural attention to every detail.

Feel the crotchet beats of the silent first bar so that the first quaver is perfectly timed, giving the sense of a clear upbeat lead into b.1. Play these introductory quavers like gently 'pointed' little steps, 'easing' just a little so that the G flat and A flat give a neatly poised upbeat lead, with the feeling that the quavers are 'going on' continuously into b.3 beneath the entry of the treble melody (rather than 'stopping and restarting'). Give the opening treble melodic crotchet F a quietly singing quality, and then let the tone 'fall' gently towards the middle of b.4, rising gradually towards the third beat of b.6, and so on. The grace notes are difficult to incorporate pleasingly. According to Chopin's practice they should be placed on the beat as shown in the

Vienna Urtext Edition: But it is a very clever player who can

achieve this smoothly. Most will have to settle for more of a triplet effect **on** the beat, **or** for playing the grace notes **before** the beat. Better to incorporate the ornaments **smoothly** within the melodic line in the most expedient manner possible, than to end up with a series of jerks and spasms through bb.4-5, etc. Take the 'corner' gracefully through b.6 as already described, then let the line 'fall' gently again and rise gradually from the middle of b.8.

Use the spread LH upbeat to b.14 to give a little 'push' towards b.14, giving the tied treble D flat plenty of tone to sing through to b.15. Then feel the implied upbeat 'lean' on the tied D flat on the third beat of b.15, reinforced by the 'lean' on the slurred LH crotchet C. Build up the tone a little here, again using the resonance of the spread LH upbeat to b.18, as you open up the tone towards a warm *mezzo piano* or *mezzo forte* at b.18, the climax of this first half of the piece. Keep up the tone through b.18 and the beginning of b.19, and then gradually *decrescendo* towards b.24,but showing the implied 'lean' on the tied treble upbeat to bb.20, 22 and 23. Then through bb.24-9 **listen** to the resonances of the LH tied and held notes and dominant pedal point effect from b.25 beneath the quietly 'rocking' RH, 'pointing' the dotted rhythm upbeat figure eloquently towards the minim on the first beat of b.28.

Arrive on the treble A flat on the first beat of b.29 with the sense of 'finishing off' the previous section, while at the same time leading on from the second beat as the line rises chromatically towards b.33. Although there is a feeling of moving on here, this rising RH line will lose coherence unless you maintain the **sense** of the even crotchet pulse through the 'lean' on the tied treble upbeat to b.31, the syncopated upward melodic movement through b.31, and the implied 'easing', as you prepare to lead off again from b.33.

Make a **controlled** *crescendo* from b.39, 'using' the resonance of the bass notes, and in particular of the strong 'lean' on the slurred bass octave on the upbeat to b.42, to give a 'push' into the climax of the *crescendo* in b.42. 'Open out' the sound here, holding the bass resonance within the pedal as indicated as you draw out a little as the RH makes a controlled leap (rather than a snatch) towards an implied slight 'vocal' *tenuto* on the high tenth. Then do not immediately drop the tone, only **gradually** *diminuendoing* through the 'peal' of alternating fifths and fourths through bb.43-4 (again being careful to hold the pedal through b.43 to the second beat of b.44 as indicated), and then making a steeper *diminuendo* from the upbeat to b.45. There is a sense of moving on from here through bb.45-7. Then, returning to the smooth effect in the LH from the upbeat to b.48, there is an implied slight swell into the long tied F in b.50, carrying on in a warmly expressive tone through bb.51-3, returning to the quiet 'rocking' effect at b.54.

Then as you rise in an implied *crescendo* from b.61, keep steady control of the crotchet pulse, **using** the pedalled resonance of the bass acciaccaturas to create an 'anchoring', continuous dominant pedal point effect. The treble needs to ring out here, avoiding shrillness by careful balancing with the LH resonances. 'Arriving' on a strong first beat of b.63, keep up the ringing tone, pedalling carefully so that you hold the bass sound through the first and second beats of this bar, then repedalling so that you **hold** the bass dominant upbeat to b.64, through to the first beat of b.66 as indicated. Then releasing the pedal, observe Chopin's indications precisely, since he does **not** do as one expects, that is end in a gentle upward trail of sound. Make a pronounced *diminuendo* through b.66, therefore, as indicated, 'pointing' the dotted minim on the first beat of bb.67 and 68, and then, as the detached quavers rise, turn the corner in a continuing *diminuendo* through b.68. Then march downward from the end of b.69 in a purposeful *crescendo* of resonantly 'plucked' quavers, ending without a *rallentando* with emphatic, full-toned chords.†

†Chopin's devil-may-care fingering of this descent with a continuous thumb tells us exactly what he wants here!

(See footnote in Vienna Urtext Edition. This fingering has recently been authenticated.)

THE SCHERZOS

The Scherzos differ from the Ballades in an important sense. They are 'formal': in other words, they are constructed in clearly defined sections involving statement, episode and restatement, roughly A B A (and by definition considerable areas of repetition), as opposed to the evolving, highly personal, and in each case individual structures of the Ballades. It follows that they are, in an interpretative sense, easier to play. In a sense too they are easier or at least more straightforward technically. Although they all require a high degree of virtuosity, that virtuosity is more overt, at least in Ops 20, 31 and 54, as opposed to the more 'integrated' virtuosity of the Ballades. In this sense they are perhaps therefore more accessible, at any rate for purposes of study, or at least exploration, by capable but 'subvirtuoso' players. This applies particularly to Ops 20 and 31, and for this reason they are treated in more detail than other works in the 'Very Advanced' (VA) category.

As in the case of the Ballades, Alan Rawsthorn provides an excellent introduction in his examination of the individual Scherzos (Walker, p.62 onwards), as does Jan Ekier in the Introduction to the Vienna Urtext Edition of the Scherzos. In appropriating the title Scherzo, Chopin likewise appropriated and ennobled the genre. The word scherzo means 'joke', and in the Baroque era the title was given to light, if not necessarily joke-like pieces, usually in **2/4** time. There is little in Chopin's expanded structures that can be related either to the Baroque type, to the symphonic or sonata scherzo of Beethoven, deriving as it did from the classical minuet form, nor yet to the lightweight examples by any of his contemporaries. The only obvious feature relating to the symphonic model is the dance-like **3/4** time common to all four works. Professor Ekier also points out that all four are built upon 4-bar phrases. The outer sections of Ops 20, 31 and 39 are dramatically contrasted with more contemplative central episodes. The character of Op.54 is rather different, and more obviously in tune with the humorous origins of the Scherzo.

Scherzo No. 1 in B minor
Op. 20 (VA)

It is thought that this was written in Vienna or Stuttgart in 1830-31. Chopin was possibly licking his wounds in disappointment at the indifference of the Viennese public, in contrast to the success of his first visit two years earlier. It is also suggested that it was written in a fit of patriotic fervour following news of a Polish uprising (as is similarly popularly supposed in the case of the 'Revolutionary' Study). Whether or not either circumstance is relevant, this is a work of white-hot ferment and jagged emotion, an effect heightened by the violence of contrast between the wild outer sections and the stillness of the middle, in which Chopin makes one of his rare references to a folk tune, a serene Christmas lullaby.

The momentum is fierce, and a diamond-sharp technical attack and considerable stamina are required. On the other hand, there is a great deal of repetition – too much, most would agree. Following the introductory chords, the first statement (bb.9-68) is, if the repeat is observed, played no less than six times, and the second statement (bb.69-124) three times. There are less actual notes to be learnt, therefore, than a work of 625 bars would suggest. This scherzo can succeed at several notches below the ♩. = 120. As so often, rhythmic verve, keen fiery-spirited attack and a clean finger technique are more important than reaching the 'correct' metronome mark.

bb.1–25
As Arthur Hedley says, 'The work opens with an epoch-making challenge, a cry, followed by a zig-zag theme which surges upwards like a flame' (p.169).

It is essential to have the pulse well 'in the system' before starting, so that you **feel** the 1-in-the-bar pulse running through the tied introductory chords. Deliver the high first chord with as ringing a 'cry' as can be mustered, **feeling** that beat through bb.2-4, and then be conscious of creating a **different** though equally powerful resonance as you plunge down to the low *sforzato* chord at p.5. Be conscious too of **poising** yourself through this second chord so that you bring the hands **off** at the optimum moment (i.e. preferably on the first beat of b.8 but holding the sound of the chord within the pedal to the **end** of the bar), ready to leap into b.9 with a sharp 'crack' on the *sforzato* diminished seventh. The rhythmic precision of the LH is vital to the stability of bb.9-24. Practise it alone, therefore, in precise time. Enter with this sharp crack on the first beat of b.9, performing a clean-fingered slurred flick down to the low B, in such a way as to drop the sound immediately to *piano* as indicated. Then follow on with a quiet but keen, slurred-third figure on the first beat of b.10. Get the feeling of letting the hand fall onto the first beat of b.9, lifting and 'directioning' it upwards to fall on the first beat of b.10, then lifting and 'directioning' it back downwards to fall again on the first beat of b.11, and so on – so that you achieve a rhythmically continuing 'fall and lift' pattern through bb.9-13 (see General Introduction under 'Directioning the Hand').

Next practise the RH alone. **Imagine** the LH *sforzato* on the first beat of b.9, and then bring in the RH in precise time, quietly but again keenly. Feel the first three quavers in the sense of an upbeat group towards the first beat of b.10, and then make a clean-fingered *crescendo* up to the *sforzato* quaver B on the first beat of b.11. Then put hands together and practise this figure over and over in a continuous movement through to the middle of b.11 and back to the middle of b.9 until the notes and the rhythmic patterns are thorough absorbed. Now carry on in the same way to the first beat of b.13, rising in a slightly higher dynamic towards b.13.

Then practise the staccato LH through bb.14-16 in a taut-rhythmed swing with a feeling of onward propulsion towards a strong *sforzato* sixth on the first beat of b.16. When you practise the RH here, feel the first four quavers as an upbeat group towards b.14, coming in relatively quietly so that you make a steep *crescendo* towards a stinging *staccato sforzato* crotchet B on the first beat of b.16. The RH can be practised

at first  and in various rhythms:

Then when the hands are put together, feel that the RH is subject to the rhythmic impetus of the LH and **not** the other way around.

Now practise bb.9-16 over and over, gradually increasing speed until these bars are fluent at a fairly fast tempo. It is essential that the LH drops to *piano* as described after the *sforzato* on the first beat of bb.9 and 11, so that the RH can 'take over' to *crescendo* up to a whiplash quaver B on the first beat of b.11 and to a slightly stronger D on the first beat of b.13. Then be sure that

466

the RH is not late on the second beat of b.13, or the LH will correspondingly be late on the first beat of b.14, and the rhythmic momentum, on towards the objective on the first beat of b.16, will be sabotaged. It is vital to spend time mastering this all-important eight bar pattern before going on.

Take care to poise yourself as you leap off the first beat of b.16, ready to 'crack' in again in precise time on the first beat of b.17. Rise to a higher dynamic level from b.22, taking an extra instant to **leap** (rather than lurch blindly) up to a higher and yet stronger *staccato* crotchet on the first beat of b.24. Arrive on this note with this strong impact, but without a sense of stopping – in other words, with the sense of 'on and over' towards a strongly placed RH F sharp and LH dominant seventh on the first beat of b.25.

In his Instructive Edition Cortot advocates playing the RH of b.25 thus

bb.25–67  (as printed at b.33) and also detaching the

upper **LH** crotchet F sharp, and many pianists do indeed phrase it thus. This is certainly effective, and helps to control the transition from b.24 to b.25 – however, Chopin makes his intention clear. Played as he wrote it, a 'consciously' strong inner LH minim G on the second beat will provide a necessary rhythmic and resonant anchor. Whip out the downward spiralling RH quavers with fingers of sprung steel 'braked' by sharply rhythmic LH *staccato* crotchets through bb.27-8, and by vigorous inner diminished fifths and thirds over a well marked lower dominant pedal point through bb.29-33. Leap on downwards with equal attack from a strong second beat of b.33, taking care to articulate the RH with ever greater sharpness through the potentially 'muddy' register (bb.35-6) even if you *diminuendo* here, as many players do, ready to *crescendo* again from b.37. Switchback up, down and up again through bb.37-42, underpinning the RH with a strongly resonant LH. The LH semi-*staccato* crotchets in b.40 need to be strongly projected towards the sustained *sforzato* minim diminished fifth on the first beat of b.41. Arrive on strong quavers on the first beat of b.43, leaping off in such a way as to land forcefully on the first *fortissimo staccato* chord, but leaving enough tone in reserve to 'go on' with tremendous propulsion towards a yet stronger chord on the first beat of b.44. Come **off** this chord with a strong rhythmic 'push', immediately 'braking' so that you allow an instant to 'rein in' the dynamics, ready to slur the octave G down to the A sharp in an almost unctuous tone, in *ritenuto* towards the long tied octave B. Be sure to give this octave B a quiet, but sufficiently carrying tone to last through its full duration, with the RH 'following on' in an imitative slurred effect in b.46. Implement the indicated dynamics with keen imagination here and, as this 4-bar pattern is reiterated, notch up the level of intensity as implied, leading on in *forte* from b.48, and making an urgent 'lean' on the tied RH upbeat chord to b.50. This declamatory dialogue, from b.44 through to the double bar is far from a mere respite between bouts of frenzied action. It is a pause for breath indeed, but implicit with intense overtones of alternating anxiety, defiance, fear, compliance – as may occur to the individual imagination. It can sound highly charged or remarkably dull – it is all up to the player. The tempo can pick up momentarily

at bb.52-5 with the agitated crotchet figures ⌐

Then broaden the tempo again from b.56 as indicated, leaping up towards quietly resonant, 'speaking' unison tied E's on the first beat of b.58, and gradually 'disperse' the tone, and agitation away, towards the tied dominant seventh at b.65, taking care to 'catch' the upbeat acciaccaturas in the pedal before b.62. If returning to b.9, be sure to **feel** the beat through the long dominant seventh ready to 'bite in' again at b.9.

bb.67–276   If going on, resolve to the tonic precisely on the first beat of b.67, coming **off** on the second beat and **feeling** the silent first beat of b.68, ready to lead off again exactly on the first beat of b.69. The LH attack here, although in a furtive *sotto voce*, must be just as 'keen' as in b.9, leading off similarly with a smart downward 'flick'. Let the RH take over to 'go to' a quiet but clear emphasised crotchet on the first beat of b.70, with the LH then 'going to' another neat 'bite' on the first beat of b.71, and the RH 'lifting' (with a feeling of 'allowing the air in') towards a quiet 'ring' on the high *staccato* quaver F sharp on the first beat of b.72. Listen to the momentary silence poising yourself to start again precisely on the first beat of b.73.

Throughout these ten bars (69-78) keep steady by feeling the pendulum-like swing created by the lightly-emphasised first beats alternating between the hands. Then from b.79 feel the continual light emphasis on the LH seventh on each first beat, while also slightly 'pointing' the tied RH quaver upbeat to bb.80-6. Then from b.85 continue to point the LH thumb on each first beat as you prepare to climb in gradual *crescendo*, taking care from b.86 to 'clear' the RH at the end of each bar. Let the LH 'take hold' more decisively from b.94. The LH slurred figure needs to be executed with a sharp and very clean 'flick' from here, with the RH 'following on' confidently on the second beat of each bar with another strong overall 'flick' of the slurred quavers. As you reach *fortissimo* at b.101, the RH intensifies its own 'bite' on each second beat

so that the rhythmic effect in each bar is a powerful | ♪ ♪ | . It goes without saying

that it is vital to the overall resonance of this passage that the LH chord on each first beat is securely caught and held in the pedal throughout the bar. This will also help to **control** the *sempre più animato* (i.e. *accelerando*) by reinforcing the secure sense of the first beat accentuation.

Arrive on an immensely powerful *sforzato* chord on the first beat of b.109, springing **off** precisely on the second beat ready to tear into the tumultuous descent from b.110 with

maximum impact. It is relatively easy here to implement the powerful | ♪ ♪ |

effect with alternating thumbs. Surge into the cross-rhythm effect at b.117 with a forceful rhythmic swing, maintaining the dynamic drive, though perhaps allowing a slight *rallentando* but **not** a *diminuendo* through b.124 as you prepare to leap off again from b.125. Allow also a fractional break at the very end of b.124 ready to 'bite' into the reprise with the LH *sforzato* diminished seventh on the first beat of b.125. A high degree of control is needed here to negotiate this transition from bb.124-5 with the required instant dropping of the tone after the LH *sforzato* in b.125.

bb.276–388   At bb.279-80 and 281-2 the chromatic variant potently intensifies the impassioned declamatory effect. From b.298 phase the *calando* assuagingly towards the change of key, with the suggestion of a pause on the dominant unisons in b.304.†

---

†Against this is the testimony recorded by Bronislaw von Pozniak (a pupil of Chopin's pupil Mikuli), that 'before the middle section, and also before the coda, Chopin would feverishly intensify [this] passage, making a *crescendo* and *stringendo*. This would be relaxed only on the very last chord preceding the middle section [b.304]; but this intensification would continue before the coda, so that the piece finished with tremendous impetus.' (Eigeldinger, p.84).

The melody of the central section is, as has already been said, based on a lullaby-like Christmas carol 'Sleep Little Jesus'. This knowledge – together with Chopin's instructions *sotto voce e ben legato*, tells us exactly how to play it. To achieve the gently hovering stillness of this melody, however, particularly in the context of the surrounding tumult, requires considerable technical and **self**-control. Those with small hands need to cultivate a smooth, 'horizontal' connecting movement between the RH lower and upper notes, very slightly 'pointing' the lower (thumb) line, but not at the expense of the aural **sense** of the continuing span of the intervals of a tenth, ninth, etc. It is important to realise that the melody

line is  and **not** as it is often mistakenly

interpreted ... Similarly the LH needs to be

shaped with the greatest care and smoothness as you **listen** in each bar to the overall shape of each curve. Indeed, the serenity of the whole is largely dependent on the smooth, even, 'cushioning' motion of the LH. There is so often an unfortunate sense of 'stopping' on each crotchet third beat. Instead, these crotchets, while being given in every instance their full value and conveying a sense of 'completion' of each bar, need at the same time to give an onward upbeat feeling towards the next bar. (The other possible and equally unfortunate effect is, conversely of seeming to 'fall onwards' into each bar by failing to give these crotchets their full value.) Make an overall slight swell with a sense of onward movement as the inner melody line rises towards the first beat of b.308. Then feel a slight drawing back through the remainder of b.308, ready to being another little swell again from b.309 through to the end of b.310. Point the tied upbeat to b.310 a little, and then feel a slight expansion up towards the high G sharp on the third beat of b.310, with a corresponding 'subsiding' through bb.311-12. Linger a little on the emphasised upbeat to b.313, ready to 'start again' from b.313. Point the tied upbeat to b.318 rather more than at bb.309-10 in preparation for the slight *ritenuto* from b.318. Linger just a little again on the emphasised slurred chord on the upbeat to b.320, 'finishing off' the phrase quietly and clearly in the RH on the first beat of b.320. Listen to the LH leading on here as you prepare to begin anew in the RH in a new, warmer tone from the upbeat to b.321.* Play from here with the utmost expressiveness (but avoiding any tendency to grow mawkish) gradually heightening the 'temperature' as you *crescendo* ready to expand into the *con anima*. Fill out the sound with a discreetly resonant inner RH line, and place the grace note ornaments from b.322 **on** the beat in accordance with Chopin's custom (see General Introduction under 'Ornaments'): e.g. approximately

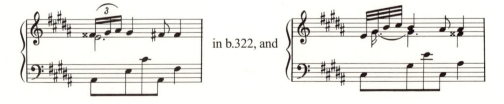

in b.322, and

in b.324. In the Vienna Urtext Edition Jan Ekier suggests that in b.329 the acciaccatura could

---

*In many editions the RH crotchet upbeat to b.321 is emphasised and tied.

anticipate the spread diminished fifth, although personally I prefer it taken 'all in', i.e.

Move on towards a warmly resonant climax at bb.327-8,

and then `scale down the volume gradually from the upbeat to b.329. 'Go to' a quiet but clear tied C sharp on the first beat of b.333, giving this note sufficient tone to sound through to b.336 over the quietly 'pointed' inner line. Draw out through bb.335-6, placing the inner crotchet E quietly on the third beat of b.336 in such a way as to give a gentle upbeat 'lean' towards the restatement from b.337. Point the premonitory change in the LH from b.374, and gradually fade the music into an almost unbreathing stillness from b.382. Time the ending of b.384 in such a manner as to maximise the impact of the ear-splitting shriek in b.385. The effect of this chord held in the pedal, as Chopin indicates, while the *pianissimo* rocking figure carries on in *ritenuto*, is intensely dramatic. The second chord is more difficult to manage aurally. Henle gives no pedal indications here. The Vienna Urtext Edition, on the other hand, gives a through pedal over bb.387-8, as in bb.385-6. While it seems unlikely that Chopin meant these bars to be 'naked' of pedal, it is difficult on the modern piano to enable the *pianissimo* RH to sound effectively within the pedalled context of the low chord. This problem can be solved by very careful half-pedalling, i.e. possibly by lifting the pedal a **little** on the second beat of b.387, and again a **little** on the first beat, or each beat, of b.388.

bb.388–625 Allow the sound of the last note of b.388 to hang momentarily in the air as you gather yourself to leap into the attack with renewed fury at b.389. By his *molto con fuoco*, his omission of the 'usual' immediate *piano*, and the extra 'bite' as the **RH** enters, creating a cross-rhythm accent, Chopin clearly suggests a heightened impact of attack here. (At the final appearance of this principal motif at b.505 Chopin drops the tone to piano again after the *sforzato* on the first beat.) Having made the *rallentando* from b.558 through to b.561, whip back to tempo sharply from the sudden *forte* at b.562, driving on in a fierce *accelerando* towards the powerful tonic octave on the first beat of b.569. This octave at one and the same time ends the previous sentence, and poises the launch into the coda. While the RH quavers need to be hurtled out with maximum brilliance, the LH resonance, properly used, carries much of the load. Take care not to start too loud, and leave 'room' for the overall *crescendo* towards b.594. Deliver the bass octaves, therefore, in a determined but not deafening, and **gradually** increasing *forte*, being sure to catch their full resonance in the pedal, and then give the rhythm a vigorous 'push' by giving the chord on each second beat a similar

strength so that the effect is 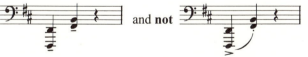 and **not**

Shape the inherent curve within the RH quavers by the sense of 'going up to' the high quaver on each second beat with a lashing fifth finger (complementing the second beat 'push' in the LH), and dipping down again towards the appoggiatura-like first quaver of the subsequent bar. Reinforce this second beat with extra LH 'punch' as indicated from b.573. Deliver the LH chords with clarion vigour from b.581 beneath the glittering clatter of the high RH quavers, increasing in force towards **almost** maximum volume on the first beat of b.585, and then

†The arpeggiation sign is not given in Vienna Urtext.

underpin the downward chute of the RH dominant seventh arpeggios with pounding crotchet octaves through bb.586-8. Catch an instant's breath at the end of b.588, ready to articulate the viciously buzzing RH chromatic quavers over fiercely 'nagging' LH quaver couplets through bb.589-92. 'Go to' a powerful bass crotchet octave on the first beat of b.593; taken with the LH. Hold this sound with the pedal, as you leap off this octave to 'join' the RH in a swingeing chord on the first beat of b.594. **Hold** this for its full value, and then drop the tone slightly so that you start the sequence of repeated chords at a slightly lower dynamic, enabling the chords to charge ahead with increasing ferocity towards b.601. Leap off this RH tonic chord on the first beat of b.601 in such a way as to allow the RH to fall with natural emphasis onto the third on the second beat, thus creating a natural 'kick-off' for the downward hurtle. 'Rattle out' the RH quavers with all possible brilliance, impelled and controlled by rigorously rhythmic, springing LH crotchets. Spring off the *sforzato* quaver chord on the first beat of b.609, snatching an instant's breath ready for a controlled start to the upward chromatic scale in a slightly lower dynamic. This scale is far less alarming than it may seem, providing that it is approached **rhythmically** – i.e. that the first four quavers are felt as an upbeat group, and the subsequent first beats are clearly felt, as indicated, notching up the dynamic level on each first beat. 'Save' enough tone to finish on ringing high B's (try Chopin's fingering 3,3 for the last two RH notes, or alternatively the very strong 3,1), press on with forceful and strongly rhythmic crotchet chords, and help the resonance of the final chords with a hugely powerful LH.

Scherzo No. 2 in B flat minor
Op. 31 (VA)

Note: In recent years, for obvious logical reasons, the key has sometimes been given as D flat major.

Although this is one of the most assaulted and battered of Chopin's longer works, it remains one at which every relatively advanced student must and will take a tilt, and at the same time one which, in a fine performance, will never lose its power to fire the spirit. As Arthur Hedley has said, 'It is a work that has everything to strike the imagination and charm the ear – suggestions of impending drama; a whispered motive, an expectant pause, the answer in ringing chords; and then one of those soaring melodies of which Chopin had the secret' (p.170). It is a vastly more complex work than Op.20, both in structure and in the variety and the inspired juxtaposition and development of its multiple elements.

While it is, of course, a virtuoso piece, it is more accessible than most of Chopin's major single works, many of which, such as the Ballades, the Fantasy or the Barcarolle, offer little but discouragement after the first page or so to the enthusiastic but subvirtuoso player. Here, because the music is so clearly sectionalised, and also relatively open-textured, the advanced amateur can at least struggle with it with some degree of reward and satisfaction.

The pulse is a rapid 1-in-the-bar. There is no metronome mark, and this is a work which needs considerable rhythmic freedom. However, the immense contrasts of material and figuration which predispose this rhythmic freedom at the same time necessitate a clear **relation** of pulse through the varying sections. All too often, for example, following a brisk gallop through the first main section, a snail takes the stage at b.265. This section is not, as Cortot points out in his Edition, an episode in the sense of that forming the central section of Op.20. 'On the contrary', he continues in his inimitable language, 'it seems to prolong the same ardour, the same quiverings, and, despite a less feverish rhythm, palpitates with a similar emotion.'

bb.1–46 So ground into our consciousness are the opening bars that we may forget to notice that for sheer gut-gripping drama, this is one of the most sensational openings in piano music. And for Chopin himself the drama could evidently never be enough – his pupil von Lenz records that: 'Right from the first bar there was a problem: the repeated triplet group ... so innocent seeming, could never be played to Chopin's satisfaction, "It must be a question," taught Chopin; and it was never played questioningly enough, never soft enough, never round enough (*tombé*), as he said, never sufficiently weighted (*important*).* "It must be a house of the dead", he once said. [... In his lessons] I saw Chopin dwell at length on this bar and again at each of its reappearances. "That's the key to the whole piece," he would say. Yet the triplet group is generally snatched or swallowed.' (Eigeldinger, pp.84-5). On the other hand, on account of its very familiarity, too many players want to 'do something' with the opening (i.e. bb.1-46). Ernest Hutcheson records (p.232) that Paderewski took the opening almost metronomically. And this, I believe, is right – the tauter the pulse, the starker the drama.

Referring to von Lenz's description of Chopin's preoccupation with the opening figure – this is certainly something over which the student player agonises. The essential is to describe a 'down-up' movement of hand and arm, that is, to make a quiet but definite 'lean' on the opening minim B flats, and then a clean-fingered upward-slurred 'arc' towards the crotchet F's, coming **off** on the second beat of b.2 ready to let the hand fall to make a second similar upward arc. The F's are frequently, if not usually, played *staccato*. This is undoubtedly easier, but it is not what Chopin wrote. If they are given their precise crotchet value, the effect is subtly but distinctly more mysterious. These bars (1-3) are enormously facilitated if (with the 1-in-the-bar pulse well 'in the system' **before** starting) you consciously direct the upward-slurred triplets to arrive on the F's **precisely** on the first beat of the subsequent bar. (A skilled performer will perhaps lengthen the second figure very slightly – an effect sought by Chopin, it is said.)

Then be sure to **feel** the first beat of b.4. In fact, the experienced player instinctively poises himself on this beat ready to burst in with the *fortissimo* response on the first beat of b.5. Give these B flat unisons as powerful a ring as possible (being sure to catch their full resonance in the pedal) and feel you are rising in a powerful arc, not a lurch, to descend on the high chord with maximum impact precisely on the first beat of b.6. Start b.8 in a very slightly lower dynamic, so that you can 'go through' in perfect time in an implied dynamic 'push' towards the B flat minor chord on the first beat of b.9. Do time the dotted rhythm properly in b.8 – many players do not. If the quaver is too short it sounds merely jaunty – if too long, it becomes ponderous, as well as throwing out the rhythm. Arrive on a ringing chord on the first beat of b.9, springing off it in such a way that the hands are 'directioned' downwards (see General Introduction, under 'Directioning the Hand') and switch instantly back to *pianissimo* so that the subsequent upward arcs are perfectly timed and poised. The next *fortissimo* sequence (bb.13-17) has a mellower (though no less powerful or vigorous) tone than bb.5-9. Following the chord on the first beat of b.17, let the F major chords pound downwards with a **controlled** sense of pressing on towards an immensely powerful bass octave on the first beat of b.20. **Hold** this octave through into b.22, jerking off it with as rude a thrust as possible **precisely** on the second beat. You may find that you can produce a better resonance by taking the upper note of both these octaves with the RH. The **holding** is important: striking the octave and letting the hand (or hands) come off and hang around will **not** produce the same rude jerk. Then **feel** the three silent first beats of bb.23-5, poising yourself to enter in immaculate rhythm again on the upbeat

---

*To elaborate on the enigmatic word '*tombé*': Lenz, writing in German used the word '*gewölbt*' meaning in French '*voûté*', in English 'arched'.

to b.26 The varied counterblast (bb.30-33) may be declaimed with even greater power, and again in tautly sprung rhythm, but still saving some extra power for the final *fortissimo* of the sequence, with its immense keyboard span from the low bass (b.37) to the high treble. **Use** the power of the bass octaves here, held within the pedal, rather than merely thrashing the treble. Pound downwards again through bb.42-3, maximising the effect of the 'landing' on the long appoggiatura-like E naturals in b.44.

Jerking the *sforzato* octave off again on the second beat of b.46, **feel** the first *bb.46–64* beat again of bb.47 and 48 through the rests as you poise yourself to 'spread-eagle' to the extremities of the keyboard on the first beat of b.49, and then to shoot downwards with the RH in a powerful slurred arc (holding the huge bass and treble resonance within the pedal right through to b.52 as indicated). The conventional RH fingering for

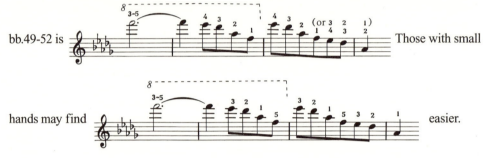

bb.49-52 is ... Those with small

hands may find ... easier.

It is essential to the equilibrium of this RH arc that it is buttressed by a powerful bass resonance on the first beat of b.49, and then by strongly slurred LH figures, giving each of these a clear upbeat 'push' towards the first beat of bb.50 and 51. Feel a sense of **lightening** as the RH descends so that you arrive on the A flat on the first beat of b.52 with a clear but not lumpy crotchet.

Following these mighty downward sweeps as they do, the quiet interludes (bb.53-6 and 61-4) are extraordinarily difficult to control. The essentials are to maintain a secure sense of the first beats, and to give each hand equal importance. (Too often the LH, particularly through bb.54 and 56, is left to 'look after itself', with consequent undermining of rhythmic equilibrium.) Supporting the RH with a quiet, carefully placed LH octave on the first beat of b.53, run up the scale in a neat, clear *diminuendo*. Then, as the RH 'finishes' on a neat quaver B double flat, let the LH 'take over' with a little 'push' on the first beat of b.54, and take the greatest care to place these LH chords in another neat, clear *diminuendo* ready for the RH to 'take over' again with a tiny 'push' on the first beat of b.55. There is thus a clear sense of the main pulse alternating between RH and LH through these four bars. Take a fraction of extra time through the end of b.56 to prepare for another poised 'spread-eagle' on the first beat of b.57. Then through b.61 as from b.53, feel a **tiny** 'push' (here in a still quieter dynamic) with a little upward *diminuendo* in the RH through the bar, and similarly in the LH through b.62. Then through bb.63 and 64 gauge the *ritenuto* rhythmically (here the previously suggested little 'push' on each first beat is **indicated**) in preparation for a confident 'launch' into the *con anima*.

As the LH scale descends in quiet *ritenuto* through b.64, have the RH 'ready' *bb.65–264* to enter, taking the greatest care that hands are perfectly synchronised on the first beat of b.65. As the RH leads off with a quiet but clear and decisive tied augmented fourth, the LH 'finishes' cleanly on the 'doubled' D flat, and then immediately moves on to establish its onward-impelling, quietly undulating quaver rhythm from the second quaver of the bar. This is one of the most ecstatic melodies ever conceived by

Chopin, or by any other writer for the keyboard. (Von Lenz records that Chopin characteristically exhorted: 'You should think of... Italian Song, not of French Vaudeville' (Eigeldinger, p.85).) But this melody is unthinkable without its counterpart, no mere accompaniment but a counterpoint of radiant, free flowing quavers, of marvellous buoyancy yet subtlety of inflection. Von Lenz says that Chopin was as exacting over the playing of the LH as of the melody. And indeed, the LH needs to be practised assiduously. The RH depends entirely upon this buoying LH flow, so it is of no use to put hands together until at least the shape of the LH is thoroughly absorbed. There is an enriching rhythmic ambiguity within its contours. When the quavers are shaped, as they need to be, in a curve up to and down from the topmost notes in each bar, a pattern of **two** groups of **three** quavers is suggested – whereas, of course, the rhythmic pattern is **three** groups of **two** quavers. The doubled bass note needs to be clearly established (and caught within the pedal) on each first beat, so that it not only 'sets' the harmony of each bar, but also provides a continual implied lower voice right through this passage, occasionally assuming greater prominence (bb.80-3 and 97-9).

When practising the RH alone, **imagine** the flow of the LH quavers beneath. Feel the impulse of the treble line from b.65 towards a lift up to, and 'lean' on the emphasised tied G flat on the first beat of b.68. Then allow the tone to dip a little through b.70, 'lifting' again to the B flat on the first beat of b.71, with a sense of moving on through the repeated B flats towards the first beat of b.73, and moving on again towards the next 'lean' on the emphasised A flat on the first beat of b.76, and so on. Listen acutely to the movement of both voices – to the **sound** of the inner note as much when it is stationary (e.g. through bb.65-6, 69-70, 73-4, etc.) as when it is moving. And students who should know better so often fail both to **hold** the treble tied note through bb.68-9 and 76-7, and to trouble to place the inner note on the first beat of bb.69 and 77 in such a way that it enhances, rather than kills the sound of the held treble note. When the hands are put together, go very slowly at first so that you can **listen** to the inflections of the voices in relation to each other. There are continuously shifting layers of voices: four voices, occasionally five from bb.65-80 (counting the 'doubled' bass quaver as a voice), three from b.81, four, then five from b.100. It is a passage in which Chopin's dynamic markings seldom are, and indeed really cannot be too studiously observed, since the music must flow in complete freedom, giving a little here, moving on a little there (varying subtly through the two restatements from bb.197 and 648) but always subject to the impulses of the onward buoying one-in-the-bar pulse. There is a concentrated richness in the dual melody lines from b.65; then from b.81 the line takes off in a free-soaring solo, subsiding a little from b.90 and then taking off again from b.97 in gradually increasing strength and purpose in an overall *crescendo* towards b.117. From around b.109 feel that you are 'opening out' over the long dominant pedal point (of D flat) towards the *fortissimo* at b.117. Arriving on a clarion D flat chord on the first beat of this bar, and securing this resonance within the pedal, lead on with strongly propelled LH upbeat quavers, 'going to' a resonant crotchet D flat on the first beat of b.118. It is essential that the RH is fully 'ready' to take over with a purposeful quaver arpeggio, 'going to' a strong sixth on the first beat of b.119.

Similarly have the LH 'ready' to underpin the RH sixth with a powerful bass A flat, and then to lead on again with strong upbeat quavers into b.120, and so on. There is thus a tremendous continuing rhythmic swing towards each first beat as the hands move in wide interconnecting and continuing arcs through to b.126. Always be sure to catch the bass resonance in the pedal on the first beat of bb.117, 119, 121, etc. as indicated, **holding** the resonance through each 2-bar span. Sustained by the full D flat resonance held within the pedal through from b.125, let the solo arpeggio sweep up to the A flat at the end of b.126 and

474

down to the bass octave in b.129 in huge-spanned arcs, then leaping up again to ringing unisons in b.130 as if in another great arc. The downward sweep can be divided between

the hands, as Cortot suggests

This may help those with small hands. It also, when properly controlled, effectively implements the inherent cross-rhythm implication of this wide broken chord sweep to good effect. Then **use** the 2-bar rest to collect yourself to start again from the upbeat to b.134.

Make the most of the variants in bb.148 and 172, 'spacing out' the five-chord, and then the four-chord group through each of these bars with a sense of impassioned deliberation. Beginning the prefix to the trills in bb.179-80 **on** the beat, create a fearsome *crescendo* rumble, carefully gauged to erupt with maximum impact (feeling the 2-note suffix as an upbeat) onto the 'spread-eagle' in b.181. Note also the 'filling out' through bb.233-4. Arriving with full strength again on the high unisons at b.262, hold the pedal this time through the 2-bar rest (compare Chopin's pedal indications with bb.130-32), lifting the pedal at the end of b.264, just in time to clear the resonance for the new A major sound.

bb.264–309   Since in various editions different inflections are given to the opening motif of the A major section, the version given in both Henle, Paderewski and the Vienna Urtext Edition (which clarifies an area which frequently puzzles the player) is given below:

The intended shape of the motif is infinitely clearer in these versions than in the previous usual versions, in which the inner C sharp (bb.265-6) is uniformly tied at each statement. Also the layout of the chords between the staves in these editions facilitates understanding of the movement of the voices, making it clear that the first chord (b.265), 'goes to' an implied slight emphasis on the tied chord in b.266. Then at b.285 there is an indicated emphasis applying to the inner C sharp which this time **is** tied and therefore then sings on between the outer RH unisons until it in turn moves on from the second beat of b.287. As already said, the change of tempo must not be too drastic here. Apart from the necessity of at least **relating** to the previous tempo, this sequence, by virtue of the static nature of the progressions, is prone to drag disastrously, with a consequently obvious 'whipping up' at bb.277 and 302. This passage is also all too often treated perfunctorily. When it is played with a sense of movement and with acute attention to the smooth and expressive movement of the two upper voices, it can glow with a quiet, almost *religioso* radiance. Lead off in a sustained *sotto voce* tone, and with your tempo well in mind so that you **establish** it as you place the chord on the first beat of b.266 with, as already said, a slight implied emphasis. Take care to **feel** the first beat of b.267 so that the movement of the inner RH voice is not anticipated and then, **listening** to the continuing sound of the tied harmony, shape the inner voice in an expressive curve through bb.267-8, ready to 'start again' from b.269. 'Finish off as if with a quiet horn-call from the upbeat to b.275, and listen to the quiet resonance of the (present) tonic through bb.275-6. Then, allowing a split second's break, lead off in b.277 with a quiet clear-toned dotted minim C sharp. Through this little passage (bb.277-81; and bb.302-6) the LH counters the *scherzando*, puckish manner of the RH with ingratiating suavity, and the two hands must be shaped with equal care. Slur the LH upbeat chord neatly towards the chord on the first beat of b.278, and then shape the little LH phrase from the upbeat to b.279 with the utmost smoothness. Allow a little 'give' as you prepare to finish off the RH phrase on the first beat of b.281, and then diffuse the broken chord upwards in a delicate haze of sound held within the pedal. The pedalling here presents a certain problem. In the Vienna Urtext Edition Jan Ekier suggests allowing the grace

notes to anticipate b.281  Or you can place the LH

chord **on** the beat, and let the RH 'wait' on the C sharp for an instant, pedalling as indicated:

Alternatively you can make a pretty effect by

placing the LH and RH C sharps **on** the beat, and then 'diffusing' the upper LH notes quietly

upwards 'among' the sound of the RH notes thus:

Whichever option you adopt, retain the **sense** of the one-in-the-bar pulse, so that the broken chord ascends within a rhythmic framework rather than at random (see General Introduction under 'Free Runs'). Let the broken chord figure disappear into the air with the tiniest 'ping' on the topmost C sharp in b.284, then resume the serious tone in b.285. In this restatement of bb.265-76, Chopin expands the second phrase with an extra and most expressive curve through b.293. **Feel** the rest through b.298, and then give the tied C sharp just enough of a *pianissimo* ring to last through to the beginning of b.301. Then play the little *slentando* curve with gentle whimsicality to lead back to the higher registered version of the *scherzando* passage. Do be clear about the difference between bb.281-4 and 306-9, **listening** this time to the tied treble G sharp from b.306 through its full duration, and taking particular care with the placing of the bass G sharp in b.307 before easing upwards in a free yet rhythmic haze from the fourth quaver of b.307.

Having 'finished off' once more on the high crotchet on the first beat of b.309,
bb.309–333 make it clear that you are starting something quite new with the two solo crotchets G sharp and F sharp, allowing a considerable 'give', but at the same time conveying a clear sense of leading quietly forward towards a gently singing tied dotted minim E. These two crotchets are of the greatest importance, moving as if with a clear introductory gesture into the new section. If the melody from b.65 is one of Chopin's most ecstatic, this, from b.310 is one of his most charming and confidential – in its first guise, that is. Simple enough on the surface, it is far from easy to play. The texture is highly intricate with its marvellous richness of shading and inflection, like a multi-voiced conversation. Study the voices separately, and then in various combinations, as if working on a true contrapuntal piece. When you put the two RH voices together, pay careful attention to the notation of the treble line, **holding** the tied dotted minim from bb.310 and 314 over the first beat of bb.311 and 315, etc. and conversely taking the crotchet C sharp **off** on the second beat of b.312, and so on. The inner voice, on the other hand, is like an almost continuous quiet running commentary beneath the clear treble sentences. The management of these two RH voices requires considerable poise. The inner voice has to 'curl' neatly and smoothly, always 'going to' the quietly emphasised inner tied dotted minim, giving this note sufficient resonance to sing over the subsequent first beat without swamping the sound of the treble tied crotchet.

In the LH the dotted minims must proceed in an evenly singing line beneath the quietly undulating inner crotchet line. Place the lower C sharp quietly but firmly on the first beat of b.310, and then feel the 'lift' up to the inner crotchet on each second beat, going on to make a slight implied emphasis on the tied inner upbeat to each bar. Listen acutely when all the voices are put together, endeavouring to follow each line in relation to the others to achieve this delightful interacting conversational effect. Begin in a quietly persuasive *piano* with a gentle, waltz-like motion, opening out the tone a little as you rise to a higher register from b.317. Then as you begin to 'close down' the tone a little again from about b.325, there is an implied little 'give' through this bar, moving on again from b.326 with another little 'give' through bb.332-3 as you ease towards b.334. At b.326 the LH voices change places. Listen to and quietly 'point' the dotted minims, now in the inner line, and then carry the tied notes harmoniously through b.332 up to the D sharp on the first beat of b.333.

bb.333–460 Allow just an instant to listen to the sustained dominant seventh harmony as you arrive quietly on the first beat of b.333 before leading on with light stepping treble crotchets into the *leggiero*, waltz-like passage from b.334. Study the detailing of the LH assiduously, for it is the LH which leads, controls and directs the deliciously vaulting arabesques of the RH. Shape the bass line smoothly down through bb.334-6, feeling that you are 'going on down' to an implied slight emphasis on the slurred dotted minim B in b.337. Then bb.338-40 are more jaunty as you spring off the bass note to make a little 'lean' on the slurred third on each second beat. Then feel a quiet emphasis on the tied minim third on the second beat of b.340 as the LH crotchets prepare to 'gather' the music ready to 'start again' in b.342. Play the RH quavers with light-fingered grace, feeling the shape of the curves as they rise and dip like a bird in flight. When the hands are put together, the RH seems infinitely easier when it is allowed to **depend** upon the supporting LH than when it is left to struggle along 'on its own'. There is a definite feeling of 'moving on' from b.334 (though once again not so much as to lose 'connection' with the previous passage). And then from b.350 the music takes the bit between its teeth with the feeling of 'moving on' with sterner purpose. Continue to 'direct' the

music with the LH (a strong-intentioned  in bb.352 and 356 acts as a

controlling 'brake') and sweep the RH down towards a huge bass *sforzato* E on the first beat of b.358. Then, holding the bass sound within the pedal as indicated (right through to b.364), keep the pulse on a firm rein as the RH leaps upwards again from the second beat. Administer a powerful boost with a vigorously spread *sforzato* chord on the first beat of b.360, and then be sure to feel the shape of the continuing upward sweep towards the third beat of b.360 before hurtling down again towards a powerfully resonant bass E in b.364. Then **use** the rest through b.365 to collect yourself for the second statement of the A major episode, this time in a rich-toned *forte*. At b.395 Chopin elaborates on the 'extra' bar with expressively turned quavers. (The fact that these are given as grace notes suggests a certain freedom of execution.)

bb.460–516 From b.468, following the up and downward sweep as at bb.358-64, Chopin forges onward with a powerful modulating passage leading to an *agitato* working out of the previous C sharp minor passage. Sound a note of urgency with the bass octave D in b.468, and sweep up and down the arpeggio in a continuingly powerful tone. Then **holding** the bass slurred D through bb.474-5 as if **pushing** the sound towards a vigorous octave C sharp in b.476, declaim the LH octaves in commanding fashion as the RH devours the keyboard in broad sweeps. Follow the LH phrase indications precisely, carrying the first fragment through to a strong minim octave on the first beat of b.478, and continuing on as if in a wide arc through the pounding, descending C sharp octaves. Then shaping the next four-octave fragment through to the C sharp on the first beat of b.482, leap down decisively, making it clear that you are starting a new fragment with the F double sharp on the second beat, and so on. Draw out fractionally as you 'home in' towards the *sforzato* G minor chord on the first beat of b.492. Allow an extra instant for this chord to make its impact, and then leap in to the *agitato* version of the C sharp theme in brisk tempo. Players often make the mistake of launching in here far too loudly. The *agitato* is far better conveyed within a relatively quiet tone range, with a controlled sense of pressing on towards a steep *crescendo* from b.512. Ensure that the inner quaver figure always 'goes to' a definitely emphasised tied dotted minim on the first beat of bb.493, 495, etc,

then play the descending treble crotchet figure  from the second beat in a clear slurred effect. Listen too, to the line of the bass notes, **using** these emphasised first beats and the implied slight emphasis on each slurred second beat to urge the music along with a **controlled** sense of onward movement. It is effective to drop the tone a little at bb.507-8, allowing a **slight** give in the tempo, picking up again from b.509 ready for the surge towards b.516.

bb.516–544   Allow an instant for the interrupted cadence to make its impact as you arrive on the *fortissimo* chord on the first beat of b.516, holding its sound within the pedal as indicated, and immediately whipping back into tempo with the LH upbeat to b.517 as you prepare to hurtle down through bb.517-19. The connecting passage from b.520 leading to b.544 generates a frenetic rhythmic tension, which must be both promoted and controlled by a rigorously rhythmic LH. Articulate the treble scale with razor sharpness, 'going to' a clear C natural on the first beat of b.521, with the LH ready to 'take over' in taut rhythmed chords to 'prepare' for the descending RH scale through b.522. Then lead on purposefully with the LH octaves through b.523 towards the next downward hurtle, and so on. Drop the tone a little at the **beginning** of b.528, ready to make a carefully gauged *crescendo*, with a rigorously controlled sense of pressing on towards b.544. The sense in which the LH 'brakes' yet leads on through bb.531 and 535 is particularly important to stability. Then the high RH quavers, gathering brilliance from b.536, are propelled onwards by the powerfully slurred LH chords from the upbeat to bb.537 and 538, and then 'braked' by the hammering repeated octaves from the upbeat to b.539. 'Go to' an immense chord on the first beat of b.540 ready to crowd downwards in **controlled** cross-rhythm *stretto* effect. Let the RH and LH 'fall' alternately with an implied emphasis on each slurred figure so that you create a vigorous momentary sense of **2/4**, arriving with emphatic resonance on the bass F on the third beat of b.543. Then spring off this bass note, allowing an extra instant to leap upwards in both hands ready to launch into the *con fuoco*.

bb.544–585   The power-driven rhythm of this tumultuous passage bounds and rebounds like sprung steel. It is effective as well as helpful, if not essential to the player's poise, to 'hold' the rhythm a little from the second beat of b.544 through to the first beat of b.546, then 'whipping it up' progressively from the second beat of b.546. In his recording, Rubinstein, that master of rhythmic suspense, balances this 'holding' and 'whipping up' with tight-rope accuracy. Once again the LH is all important with its pounding bass octave line, and the implied 'secondary' emphasis on the slurred octave on each second beat. The arpeggiated effect from b.553 is a long-standing headache for pianists, since at tempo it is almost impossible either to 'get the chord in' in arpeggiated form, or to give it sufficient strength. As Jan Ekier suggests in the Vienna Urtext Edition, it is much easier as well as giving a more decisive effect to play the chords in 'block' form. However, he does not take into account the many players, particularly female, who cannot manage the stretch in bb.554, 556, etc. Perhaps the best solution for those who cannot stretch the tenths (and perhaps even for those who can) is to arpeggiate each LH tenth **against** a block chord in the RH. Similarly, the LH octaves on the first beat of bb.553, 555, etc. could be broken. By this 'breaking' of the LH an extra instant is gained in reaching the octave or chord, at the expense, perhaps, of slight loss of driving power. Whatever your solution to the problem, this passage has to be played out at full throttle and on a taut rhythmic rein. Many players begin to wilt at around b.563, if not before. But while there is some natural thinning of the sound with the loss of the RH octaves from b.563, the rhythmic and dynamic urgency should be maintained (stamina permitting) until the *diminuendo* indication in b.567. Then grade this *diminuendo* carefully so that from the *calando* the unison motif can disappear on a dying mutter (**feeling** the rests through bb.576-7 and 580-1) towards b.582. Then **feel** the rests again through bb.583-4, ready to embark on the recapitulation with renewed vigour, entering once more in the most mysterious possible *sotto* *voce* on the upbeat to b.585. Note that here the triplet figures 'go to' a significantly mysterious **long** F through bb.586-7 and 594-5.

From b.697 begin to notch up the rhythmic and dynamic tension keenly through
bb.585–781   the extension of the previous material over the extended dominant pedal point.

Then driving on through bb.709-15 allow an instant at the end of b.715 to take the bit even more strongly between the teeth ready to hurtle down through bb.716-19 and 720-23 with ever increasing momentum, controlled once more by the persistent LH figures. In particular show the incisive bite of the LH crotchets entering on the offbeat in bb.718 and 722, then applying a controlling touch of 'brake' with a strong 'lean' on the slurred minim chord through the first two beats of bb.719 and 723. Poise yourself again at the end of b.723 to 'get set' to launch into that extraordinary sprint through bb.724-32. The secret here is the understanding of and proper implementing of the slurs. Feel a slight emphasis on each RH **second** beat, then make a vigorous overall 'flick' up to a **strong** crotchet third on the subsequent first beat, and **spring** off this in such a way as to 'direction' the hand downwards to 'start again' on each second beat. The hand and arm thus operate in a self-regenerating series of arcs. The LH slurred octaves abet the RH by giving a continual strong, slurred upbeat 'push', and this 'staggered' slurred effect creates an electric propulsive momentum. Be sure to drop the tone considerably after the chord on the first beat of b.724, thereby maximising the effect of the onrushing *crescendo* towards b.732. The pedal indications are somewhat confusing here. The most effective way to pedal this passage is as indicated from b.727, i.e. changing the pedal on the second beat so that you catch **each** entire slurred sweep in **each** pedal. I feel it is best to start this pedalling pattern earlier, i.e. in b.726 as in the Cortot and Paderewski editions, or even in b.724. Take an extra instant to place the landing on a mighty *sforzato* chord on the first beat of b.732. Then leaping downwards with a strong rhythmic spring, 'send' the triplet figure up towards the crotchet on the first beat of bb.733-5 with a vigorous upbeat 'flick' – almost a 'push', and with a **controlled** sense of pressing on. Holding the powerful unison A flats within the pedal from the first beat of b.736, leap up to land emphatically on the high tied dotted minim chord in b.737. Be sure to **feel** the held first beat of b.738, and then start from the second beat in a rather lower dynamic so that you can 'go through' the crotchet chords in a *crescendoing* salvo towards b.740, showing the inner RH and upper LH movement within the pounding reiterated outer notes.

In the Vienna Urtext Edition Jan Ekier suggests holding the A flats within the pedal from b.744 right through to b.755, thereby implementing a powerful dominant (of D flat) pedal point effect through this passage. This certainly creates a wonderful clangour. Less bold-hearted players may prefer a more cautious half-pedalled effect – holding the full pedal through to the end to b.747, and half changing the pedal on the first beat of b.748, and thereafter as the ear dictates, so that a residue of the A flat resonance is retained through to b.755. In any event, drop the tone a little through bb.746-7 and then 'take the bit between the teeth' once more as you notch up the dynamics, tempo and rhythmic tension towards bb.755-6. Note Chopin's

indications  etc. which show exactly how this passage should be

played, in a pounding, almost slurred effect. 'Brake' fractionally as you reach the dominant in b.755, giving this chord an extra 'bite', with a change of pedal, as you collect yourself to tear down through bb.756-9, supporting and controlling the RH with a rigorously rhythmic and stabbingly articulated LH. Note, however, the *legato* LH phrasing from the second beat of b.758. This gives a steadying 'push' towards a strong 'lean' on the stentorian chord on the first beat of b.759. This chord has the effect of a momentary slamming on of the brakes, ready to tear down again from b.760. Arrive on a clear D flat chord on the first beat of b.764, and then feel that the two LH crotchets G and A flat are 'pulling' you on towards the RH slurred octave on the first beat of b.765, with the LH then 'goading on' the RH through bb.765-6 and 767-8. Drop the tone a little at the end of b.769. Then shoot through the *staccato* chords in a *crescendoing* volley towards the first beat of b.772, pressing on again from b.773 as if the single crotchet chords and the final dotted minim chords are a continuation of the spurt from b.770. End with maximum power, holding the D flat sound in the pedal from b.776 as indicated, and taking an extra instant to leap outwards from the acciaccatura chords towards perfectly 'plumbed' final dotted minims. **Listen** to this huge spanning sound, through an approximate bar-long pause ready to come **off** with a vigorous 'clunk' on the first beat of an imaginary b.782.

Scherzo No. 3 in C sharp minor
Op. 39 (VA)

This is the most profound and emotionally charged of the four Scherzos. It is also the most concentrated and integrated in construction. Alan Rawsthorn refers to its Beethovenian characteristics (Walker p.69). And while Beethoven and Chopin were hardly musical soul-mates its outer sections have a spare, granitic force and rhythmic thrust that are more reminiscent of Beethoven than perhaps anything else that Chopin wrote. It is dedicated to Adolph Gutman who, it appears, was not only a favourite pupil, but enjoyed a special understanding with Chopin – somewhat surprisingly, since it appears that Gutman 'never took account of his teacher's tastes, slashing and thumping the piano unconcernedly' (Eigeldinger, p.166). Another more dutiful pupil, von Lenz, records acidly that Gutman was 'strong enough to punch a hole in a table' (Walker, p.68). Whether or not this 'amiable accomplishment' prompted the dedication of this particularly powerful work we cannot know.

I cannot agree with Ernest Hutcheson that this is 'easier than the other Scherzos' (p.233), nor with James Friskin and Irwin Freundlich that the octave passages 'are not exceptionally tiring or difficult' (p.108). Played '*con fuoco*' as they should be, these passages continuing through a long span, bb.25-151, **are** taxing, especially for the majority of women players. In an interpretative sense this is also an exceptionally demanding assignment. There are dark forces at work here, in contrast to the open-spirited radiance of Op.31. The work was conceived in Majorca early in 1839, and finished in the happier surroundings of Nohant later that year. In the mysterious stirrings of the opening, erupting into the driving *risoluto* section, which in turn alternates with the chorale-like major motif with its celestial decorations, it is not too fanciful to imagine the contrasting forces of good and evil, and the reflection of those troubled times at Valdemosa.

Much has been written on the subject, or rather the questions posed by the opening bars. It is this passage, along with the enigmatic, near atonal Finale of the B flat minor Sonata, which provoked Alan Walker's view of Chopin as a 'displaced person' of musical history (see General Introduction under 'A Short Profile'). Casting off in ambiguous tonality and cryptic cross-rhythm effect, Chopin generates a suspense so brilliantly calculated that it seems more knife-edged the more one studies the passage. The dynamic indications are in themselves ambiguous. Most editions give a *forte* on the upbeat to bb.7, 15, etc, and most players start in *piano*, as indicated, building up through the two upward-turning, questioning fragments towards a more

emphatic statement through bb.5-6, with ringing, or even crashing rejoinders in the high repeated chords. There is, however, no certainty about a *forte* on the upbeat to bb.7 and 15.*
And while the conventional approach creates a fine enough dramatic effect, Sviataslav Richter's reading on record in my view greatly heightens the atmospheric tension. Playing the opening fragment as indicated in *piano*, he builds up a **little** towards bb.5-6 but maintains the hovering sense of suppressed unease, and then plays the repeated chords like a distant, restraining call. Repeating the overall effect on a rather higher dynamic level through bb.9-16, he then delivers the truncated fragment tersely (bb.17-18), arriving with a good 'punch' on the repeated chords ready to drive off from b.21 not wildly, but in a martial *risoluto*, which gathers momentum with relentless propulsion. It is vital to the dramatic effect of controlled tension that the tone is dropped to an ominously gliding *piano* at b.35, to explode in a short violent burst of *crescendo* from b.39 towards b.41. Then, having dropped the tone again at b.51, the LH needs to begin at b.57 in a tiny, spiked *staccato*, pressing on implacably beneath the quietly sustained RH from b.59, and building up the rhythmic and dynamic tension inexorably but **gradually** towards an imperious *fortissimo* from b.99. Then the effect of the long overall gradual subsidence towards the *meno mosso* at b.155 needs to be equally carefully gauged.

From b.152 the reiterated dominant emerges with quiet affirmation leading in *rallentando* into the simple major melody. The hymn-like quality of this motif has often been remarked, transfigured by Chopin's inspired decoration into the highest realms of pianism. Once again Richter's treatment of this sequence is magical. Most pianists, when they have 'finished' each chorale fragment, take extra time to 'heave' upwards and prepare for the downward run of quavers, thereby dividing melody and decoration into separate compartments. Richter, on the other hand, seems to make a very slight *rallentando* as he progresses in smooth and stately *crescendo* towards the chord on the first beat of bb.159, 167, etc, and then manages to 'get up' in almost perfect time so that the descending quavers seem to sprout in a delicate shower directly from the mouth, as it were, of the previous chord. This effect is clearly implied by the phrasing in Vienna Urtext

whereas the phrasing in many editions, including Cortot and Paderewski, is

This lengthy passage (from bb.155-319) is often mauled around in the interests of 'trying to do something with it'. Whereas it only needs to be allowed to speak for itself in its quiet but magisterial calm. This, however, is a tall order in terms of technical and musical control. From b.243 a series of gloriously inflected, spinning arpeggiated quavers evolves from resonant low

*See Henle and Vienna Urtext.

bass notes, finally skimming down a long scale from b.280 to resume the chorale briefly again at b.287.

The *sostenuto*, then *sotto voce* linking passage from b.320, again a sequence of marvellous subtle and shifting interpretive implications, leads back through a powerful *stretto* to a shortened restatement of bb.25-154.

It is a peerless moment when halfway through the return of the chorale section (in E major), Chopin turns into the minor from b.494, slowing the tempo and paring down the texture of the chorale motif into one, two, then three voices. As Arthur Hedley says (p.171) it is another great moment when, from b.542, the chorale motif rises and expands over the long bass dominant pedal point. The LH quavers carry the RH on a gradually swelling and increasingly buoyant flow of quavers, surging upwards from b.558, forcing the tempo onwards through a taut double octave *stretto* into the ferocious coda. Chopin tears into the keyboard in a welter of *con fuoco* quavers goaded on with stabbing quaver figures in the LH, and with fiercely prodding octaves from b.581. The tautly sprung rhythm of the LH is all important here, in propelling and at the same time controlling the wildly scurrying RH quavers. Through a fearsome passage of skyrocketing unison quavers, Chopin hurtles into a final *stretto* fusillade of double octaves in contrary motion to end in a blaze of major chords in triple *fortissimo*.

Scherzo No. 4 in E major
Op. 54 (VA)

This is by far the least familiar of the four Scherzos. One reason perhaps for the rarity of its appearances on recital programmes is its inordinate length (967 bars!). But there are other less obvious reasons. It is in a particular sense rather unique among Chopin's works. As Alan Rawsthorn has pointed out (Walker, p.71) it has the character of a caprice, and 'caprice' is not a word we associate with Chopin, although in life he was, as has been remarked in the General Introduction, a man of accomplished and sometimes biting wit. The temper is almost entirely sunny with little of Chopin's 'popular' characteristics of passion or melancholy, nor of dramatic rhythmic and dynamic contrasts or, as Jim Samson says 'of the tension generated by those internal ambiguities which ruffle the surface of so much of his music' (p.171). The dynamic level is predominantly quiet, and through the inspired ramblings (for such they are) there is little sense of architecture, in terms of construction, or of building and diffusing of climax. In short, the work as a whole seems not altogether of the Chopin that we like to think we know and love. The recurring *staccato* chord figure (bb.17-25) has the skittishness of the young Mendelssohn, and there are momentary strong flavours of Schumann (particularly from b.130) with whose music Chopin had little sympathy. Yet Chopin's hand is utterly sure, his passage-work at its most mercurial and iridescent, and the central section has that quality of abstracted yet concentrated musing characteristic of much of his later work. It is a 'difficult' work in many senses. On account of its great length and meandering nature, it is inevitably hard to hold together. And in a wider sense its performance poses a problem of a special kind; that of 'putting over' a work of large dimensions that is almost consistently on a very intimate scale. Also, at the fleet tempo that the music assumes, the passage-work requires virtuosity of a restrained and highly refined order. This is marvellous music, but of a domestic rather than public kind, save in the hands of an artist of rare perception and imagination.

The opening is quietly smiling, with its smoothly breathed opening unisons, teasing hold through bb.5-8 and its little 'shove' on the first beat of b.9 into a little anticipatory *scherzando* skip through bb.10-12. From the second 'hold' through bb.13-16 Chopin skitters off into the

'Mendelssohnian' figure, hopping lightly up to and down from the high chord in b.20 with pinpoint *staccato* chords. These alternating phrases of gliding *legato* and air-borne *staccato* are wonderfully light-spirited and even humorous, without a trace, as Alan Rawsthorn says, of 'that fatal quality of archness which frequently besets the German romantic composer when he sets about being capricious' (Walker, p.71). And the little spurts of *leggiero* quavers in bb.66-72, etc, are equally entrancing, expanding later into a brilliant éclat of descending unison quavers from bb.122-9. The confidential intervening *legato* passages bb.59-65, 73-81, etc. convey fleeting shades of expression by the simplest yet most subtle means: the hint of warning in the B sharps in b.76, the Schumannesque upturning question (bb.96-7), the distant, horn-like alert (bb.139-40), the suddenly 'important' *forte* (bb.141-5), and the strange little disappearing slither down from the held A's (bb.210-13).

From b.217 a more extended passage of flowing quavers interlaces with a 16-bar melodic sequence transferring from RH to LH, and incorporating a meltingly expressive LH phrase from b.225 beneath scintillating scales of chromatically inflected quavers. A restatement of this passage, one tone higher leads into a deliciously ingratiating passage in cross-rhythm effect from b.249, interposed with little shooting arpeggios (bb.254-6 and 262-4). Returning to the opening motifs from b.273 there is a sudden spurt of urgency from b.353 'piling up' in *accelerando* and *crescendo* towards a burst of fierce *stretto* chords from b.377. Breaking off with a vigorous wrench on the first beat of b.382, Chopin prepares the way through a quietly sustained solo line into his central section, whose musing mood, as has already been said, is characteristic of much of his later work: the two Nocturnes Op.55 No.2 and Op.62 No.1, Prelude Op.45, and the Barcarolle among others. In fact, the movement generated by the LH moving in softly rounded arcs is in itself rather Barcarolle-like. And this suggests the tempo: *più lento* but always moving. This section can, with some justification, be considered long and meandering. But in the hands of an artist who has discovered its rapt quality and who can maintain this sense of movement, it seems not a moment too long. The melody moves in serene curves, quietly buoyed along by the LH, whose own little curves reach a gentle impetus-creating 'peak' on each dotted crotchet (bb.394, 396, etc.). The melody moves into a deeper, alto tone at bb.427 and then fills out with a second voice from b.433. The little downward-sliding scales (bb.423-4, etc.) are reminiscent of the chromatic windings of the coda of the Nocturne in B major, Op.62 No.1. The marvellous subtle 'pointings' and touches of variation throughout the section within a dynamic range no higher than *mezzo piano* repay the closest study. From bb.497-9 the melody 'dies' and a slightly troubled LH, climbing on diminished seventh arpeggios in *diminuendo*, leads back towards a quiet resumption at b.513. Then towards the end of the section, as Jim Samson points out (p.173) the LH assumes increasing importance as the RH subsides into a more harmonic role. And from b.553 Chopin initiates a long build-up towards the return of the Scherzo movement over a dominant pedal point, rising to a dynamic peak on a dominant ninth chord at b.577. From here, over the continuing dominant pedal point, the RH takes off in an impetuous flurry of quavers, *crescendoing* in an insistent buzzing from b.593 towards a *forte* version of Tempo 1 at b.601. This reprise leads into a scintillating and volatile coda. After a final lingering glance at the 'Mendelssohnian' figure through bb.914-25 there is a marvellous build-up of resonance in *accelerando* over a tonic pedal-point. This leads into a thrilling fusillade of downward rocketing unison octaves, and the piece rushes towards its final chords through an upward streaking tonic scale.

THE BALLADES

It is in these four works, together with the Fantaisie, the Polonaise-Fantaisie and the Barcarolle, that Chopin most convincingly explores and establishes his personal interpretation of the 'larger' forms. In the Sonatas, the Scherzos, and in a different sense, the larger Polonaises, he is placing his own very definable stamp on frameworks, or at least the **idea** of frameworks that were already current. Coining the title 'Ballade', Chopin moves onto his own patch, absolving himself 'from the necessity of conforming in any way to the "laws" governing the original forms', as Arthur Hedley has said (p.173). Detailed discussion of Chopin's formal procedures is outside the scope of this book. Suffice to say that, at least in the first, third and fourth Ballades, Chopin pursues his own kind of **evolving** structure rather than the 'conventional' concept based on contrasting, more segmented elements. The introductory paragraphs to Alan Rawsthorn's discussion of the Ballades (Walker, p.42 onwards) are particularly recommended. There is no doubt, as he says, that there are undertones in the music of that 'narrative' element inherent in the title. But efforts to pin down these associations are both fruitless and trivialising – that was not the way Chopin worked. In the Vienna Urtext Edition of the Ballades there is also an excellent Introduction by the Editor, Jan Ekier. One tangible common thread runs through the four works: their **6/4** or **6/8** pulse. Commenting on the 'dance-like' characteristics, Professor Ekier says 'We do not know whether Chopin deliberately incorporated this dance element, or whether he used it intuitively, sensing that the ballades' origins lie in the dance'.

From the point of view of the performer all four works are large assignments, both in the technical and interpretive sense. While the third, Op.47, is the lightest in technical demands, its very lightness of spirit, as is so often the case, requires a high degree of keyboard sophistication. But as has been urged in the General Introduction, 'difficult' music is not, or should not be, the sole property of the virtuosi. In the Ballades in particular, there is plenty of music that can at least be examined, and thereby more rewardingly understood by the less advanced.

Ballade No. 1 in G minor
Op. 23 (VA)

This is perhaps the best loved of the four Ballades. It combines sweetness and dark-toned tragic power in a compelling dramatic unity. Chopin's mastery of the short introduction has frequently been noted: in the first movement of Op.35, the last movement of Op.58, and in numerous other instances. Upon this supreme example many thousands of words have been expended. Our attention is seized by the commanding opening tied minims, and the upward sweep of the unison quavers is uniquely and magisterially portentous. Then, as Alan Rawsthorn says (Walker, p.46) 'it seems to lose its confident swing, and to take on a kind of pathos', ending in bb.6-7 'on an almost agonising question', from which the principal motif from b.8 seems to unfold as inevitably as day follows night. This motif, always entering on an emphasised offbeat, has, again as Alan Rawsthorn comments, 'a very persuasive and almost confidential quality', with at the same time undertones and hints of anxiety, of turbulence to come. Following the 'written out' pause on the tied RH B flat that ends the Introduction, the bass D on the second beat of b.8 needs to be most carefully placed, so that the overall 2-in-the-bar pulse is confidently initiated from the middle of this bar. The predominating first subject motif (bb.8-10) invites an infinite variety of nuance, and no two pianists will play bb.8-21 alike. Launched by this bass D the quaver figure enters with a hint of hastening as it 'curls' through to the dotted minim G on the first beat of b.9. Then the hand lifts to 'fall' with a slight emphasis, and the suggestion of a *tenuto* on the high D, to be slurred off to a clear C. There is then the sense of a tiny intake of breath, ready to enter again on the offbeat, 'going down to' the E natural on the second beat of b.11 with quite a different expressive 'answering' inflection; and through the next two-bar figure a sense of expansion as the line lifts to the high G in b.13, and so on. The 'doubling' of the first three quavers of each figure occasions the most subtle implication of nuance, the emphasis on each minim indicating a sustaining 'lean' rather than an accent. Less advanced players examining these opening bars often muddle the rhythmic shapes. Within the overall 2-in-the-bar pulse it is important to maintain the sense of the **6-crotchet pulse** so that within each RH quaver figure there are clearly **three 2-quaver** groups, **not** two 3-quaver groups. It is again important to **feel** the quaver rest on the second main beat of bb.10, 12, etc. making sure that the subsequent quaver figure is clearly understood as an offbeat group of **six**, and **not** a vague 5-quaver group, and then to be clear about the different effect in b.14, when the quaver figure **does** enter on the beat. The greatest care must always be taken to ensure that the inner RH and LH accompanying crotchets are always placed in a quiet **even**, just-detached

style 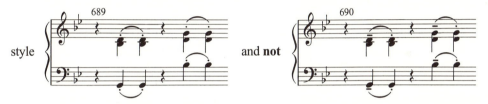 and **not**

When properly placed and balanced they create a continual offbeat *ostinato* which stabilises and anchors the expressive phrases in both a rhythmic and harmonic sense. From b.22 there is a sense of moving on with the now more active LH offbeat figure propelling the rhythm forwards. Then while there must be some expansion through the second half of b.33 to accommodate the expressive nuances of the treble run, the sense of the rhythm, guided by the LH chords must, at the same time, maintain its onward direction. Through the transitional passage from b.36 the placing and proper valuation of the bass notes on the main beats needs to be scrupulously maintained (particularly in the more *agitato* emphatic syncopated version from b.40) so that the slurred RH figures on the second and fourth crotchet beats do not begin to sound like the **main** beats. The LH is particularly important throughout this work in both a rhythmic and resonant sense. For example, through the *sempre più mosso* from b.45 it is the LH which 'controls' the acceleration as well as underpinning the switchbacking RH arpeggios, and the bass resonances play a vital part in the gradual 'dying down' from bb.56-7 towards the emergence of the second subject melody at the upbeat to b.68. This second subject melody, growing as it does from the preceding rocking LH F major figure of fourths and fifths, has a rare sweetness, nostalgic but never cloying. In view of the occasional cross-rhythm implications within the quietly swinging **6/4** rhythm, less experienced players can again easily muddle the rhythm here, (e.g. through bb.73-4 etc. where the RH assumes a momentary **3/2** line over the LH **6/4**). Similarly, through the feathery *pianissimo* passages from b.82 (recalling the opening motif, as Alan Rawsthorn has pointed out) the more securely the basic pulse is felt, the more delicately the subtle oscillation between the triplet and 'plain' quaver values can be demonstrated. Following a short appearance of the opening motif in A minor beginning at b.94, a dramatic and tautly strung transition leads to the triumphal return of the second main melody, now in *fortissimo*. (Chopin does not so much develop this theme as utterly transform it. Its final appearance from b.166 is rhapsodic, accompanied by waves of LH quavers.) Here, from b.106 the *fortissimo* RH chords and octaves are buoyed along by LH harmonies moving in expansive arcs, to create a magisterial resonance rising to an immense triple *fff* at b.124.* A wild flurry of *agitato* quavers leads on into a waltz-figure of reckless gaiety from b.138 'sprung' by a leaping LH rhythm.

From b.208 Chopin tears into the immense coda, a *presto con fuoco* of impassioned brilliance. Many a performance on the verge of shipwreck from this point would regain course if the RH were **controlled** by a stable LH rhythm rather than left to strangle itself on its own momentum. The three-, then four-octave scales (bb.251-2 and 255-6) are the terror of pianists. How the nineteenth-century ear reacted to the flailing discordance of the contrary motion octaves from b.258 'colliding' to descend in violent unison, we can only imagine. To us today it seems the only possible final thrust to a work which leaves hardly a shade of human emotion untouched.

Ballade No. 2 in F major
Op. 38 (VA)

On the face of it this is the odd man out among the four Ballades, since its sections, and by the same token, its changes of temper are clearly separated, with the opening melody recurring as a connecting thread. Even if it were no more than a connecting link however, the predominating motif of this melody is so persuasive that it cannot help pervading the whole work. In fact it is much more than this – its development, from b.82, forms a central block in the overall construction and in the building of the onrush towards both the second *presto con fuoco* (b.140) and the coda (b.168). Strenuous and inconclusive efforts have been made to 'programme' this work and to link it to a specific poem of Chopin's compatriot Mickiewicz (and Schumann does record that Chopin told him he had been 'inspired' by the poems of Mickiewicz). I have often wondered, however, whether the *andante* melody is folk-based. There are just a few instances of Chopin using a folk-tune, and this melody has a telling simplicity akin to that of the central melody of the Scherzo in B minor, Op.20, based on a Polish Christmas carol.

There can be few amateur pianists who have not swum happily into the opening section, only to find that their efforts fail woefully to match the sounds in the mind's ear. Needless to say, such apparent simplicity is far from easy to recreate, and the problem with most players is that they cannot leave the music alone. It is recorded that Chopin played these bars with almost no nuance (Eigeldinger, pp.65-6) and, we can imagine, with an exquisite softness and delicacy within a hypnotic rhythmic flow. As Alan Rawsthorn says, 'We are never quite sure precisely where the phrases are going to begin and end' (Walker, p.51). Indeed, the phrases do not so much end as arrive at points from which they 'renew' themselves, i.e. on the second main beat of bb.5, 9, 13, etc. And the opening is at its most beautiful when the unisons materialise, rather than begin, establishing the rhythm by suggestion rather than by 'pointing', and in such a way that the melody can in its turn 'materialise' from these unisons.† Beneath the smooth undulations of the treble melody line, we need to listen acutely to the movement of the inner and lower voices, to the 'hollow' sound of the predominating fifths and fourths in the LH, to the occasionally emerging lower or inner melodic fragments (bb.6-9, 18-20, 24-6) and particularly

---

*The upward octave scales from b.119 are much less fearsome than they may seem, provided that they are understood to be governed by the STEADY rhythm of the LH – rather than, as so often happens, scrabbling upwards at the mercy of a 'sympathetically' panicking LH.

†In this connection J.-J. Eigeldinger points out an interesting example of Chopin's pedalling indications: the long pedal is retained from the first note through to the second beat of the second complete bar, allowing the F major harmony to 'materialise' within the continuous sound of the unisons, and only changing with the emergence of the inner B flat on the second main beat of the bar.

to the lower line from the second beat of b.37. The whole is wafted along by the quietly swaying LH and inner RH rhythmic *ostinato* ♩ ♪♩ ♪ with occasional implied slight emphases in the treble line, e.g. on the tied second main beat of bb.9, 17, 37, etc, and with the little swell up to the first beat of b.20, falling again like a tiny sigh to a scarcely breathed *pianissimo*. The timing of the fading out of the repeated A's towards the pause, and the 'direction' of the pause towards the initial crash of the *presto con fuoco* is a matter of fine judgement; or rather, of allowing the intuitive inner clock to take charge. This is a prime case for the 'breath test' (see General Introduction under 'Pauses').

Many a young hopeful hurtles in at b.46 in a bravely attempted grand slam, only to founder in b.47, recover in b.48, founder again in b.49, and so on. The difficulty of these bars is considerably eased if we will only follow Chopin's indications. Entering with full power at either end of the keyboard, we need to let the LH octaves take much of the burden through b.46, 'going up' to a firm crotchet octave C on the second beat while letting the brilliant RH semiquavers *decrescendo* through the bar. Then start relatively quietly in both hands at the beginning of b.47, *crescendoing* upwards again and **lifting** the RH at the end of the bar ready to launch off again at the beginning of b.48. Then while the RH semiquavers descend with all possible brilliance through bb.50-53, feel again that the LH is taking much of the burden as it rises in *crescendo* towards the middle of b.51, and again towards a powerfully resonant tied octave on the second beat of b.52. Then through b.53 there is a sense of 'gathering' forces ready to burst forth again from b.54.

It is important to drop the tone at b.62 to leave room to *crescendo* towards the impassioned descent from the climactic high chord on the second beat of b.68. And from b.62 it is, of course, the **RH** chords that control the zooming scales in the LH, and again through the gradual subsidence from b.70. Following a return to the opening motif from b.82, breaking off hesitantly at b.87, Chopin embarks on a concentrated and eloquent development of the melody, by turn poignantly expressive and passionately declamatory, and driving in *accelerando* from b.132 back into the *presto con fuoco*. This time a powerfully resonant LH motif based on the opening melody imposes itself from b.156 beneath a continuing double *tremolo* figure in the RH, to lead with thunderous trills into the coda. This furiously *agitato* coda is formidably difficult, and once again the LH is all important, providing essential rhythmic stability and 'braking' power to the stuttering machine-gun fire of the 'double-stopped' RH. Observation of Chopin's frequently ignored phrasing punctuation is half the battle: the LH leaps off the quaver octave on each main beat so that it falls with a natural emphasis on each slurred quaver couplet. The RH slurs coincide with the LH so that the **first** offbeat semiquaver is like an upbeat to the

slurred **second** quaver beat.  The awareness of

this pattern makes the RH much easier to control, demonstrating that the RH and LH are working in concert from a rhythmic point of view. Otherwise, as often happens, the RH proceeds in overall juddering, 5-note (or 11-note) blocks, apparently locked in mortal combat with the LH. The coda drives on through a frenetic ascending passage from b.184 (again both propelled and controlled by the LH) through a brief reference to the *presto con fuoco* passage towards a violent 'stop' on a spread *sforzato* chord at b.196. Then Chopin ends in a softly echoing fragment of the opening melody.

Ballade No. 3 in A flat major
Op. 47 (VA)

This is the lightest in spirit of the four Ballades, which is by no means to imply triviality, nor slighter value. As Arthur Hedley says, 'The music flows with an ease which conceals the art whereby the artistic result is achieved' (p.175). As already said, it is also the lightest in technical demands, at least in terms of technical **stamina**, as opposed to technical **finesse.**

The opening theme is by turn winning, gracious and urbane. The first eight bars converse in alternating voices – the first treble phrase, half statement, half question (bb.1-2) is answered by a warm-toned tenor voice through bb.3-4. The treble motif of bb.1-2 is transferred to the bass (bb.4-5), and answered conclusively by the RH voices in the tonic (bb.7-8). Alan Rawsthorn (Walker, p.54) notes that the 2-note figure at the end of the first

2-bar phrase [music notation] is a constantly recurring motif throughout the work, in a

melodic, harmonic, or sometimes purely rhythmic sense. Indeed, as many commentators have shown, it is through Chopin's brilliantly conceived interweaving and combining of the motifs of the opening and the second main theme that this work appears to evolve with such seemingly spontaneous unity. Following the 'exposition' of the first eight bars, there is a protracted prancing and light-hearted skirmishing over and around this persistent quaver/crotchet fragment, breaking into and out of a titillatingly disjointed dance-like figure (bb.17-20 and 21-4). From b.25 a skittering, mock-purposeful, alternating chord motif and contrary-motion arpeggio figure, leads through a restatement of the opening motif and its brief 'working' in low-slung sequential counterpoint towards the second main theme. This wafts in on the dominant of F major from a high tied chord (bb.50-52) in the rocking rhythm stemming from the familiar quaver/crotchet motif. This theme proper, starting from the upbeat to b.54, has a delectably debonair kind of bounce which, the more you consider it, the more laughter-provoking, or at least smile-inducing, it becomes – not such a frequent occurrence in Chopin's music. To quote Alan Rawsthorn again, 'The theme is given a charmingly lurching effect by having the chords on the offbeats, and single notes on the strong ones. It is a device which not every composer can bring off successfully. Brahms has tried it in an Intermezzo in E minor (Op.116 No.5), and the result resembles imperfectly cooked porridge', adding acidly that Brahms **marked** it '*Grazioso*'! (Walker, p.55). Moving towards F minor from b.63, this second theme takes the bit between its teeth and moves into a more serious phase, rising to an impassioned *fortissimo* at b.81. A sequence of falling, semiquaver arabesques introduces a short waltz-like episode of whirling semiquavers from b.124. Then a short rhapsodic section from b.136 dwelling on the

already familiar falling quaver figure [music notation] leads into a return of

the rocking second main theme in D flat. 'Crossing' into C sharp minor at b.157, Chopin launches into a much-discussed development, which in its consummative effect is almost like a giant coda. One wonders how belittlers of Chopin can fail to succumb to such a display of compositional virtuosity. First Chopin pursues the second (F minor) part of the second main theme (see b.65 onwards) in the RH in *mezzo voce* over an eerily snaking LH semiquaver counterpoint. Then from b.165 he transfers the melody to the LH beneath a high dominant pedal point in flying RH broken octaves, progressing in powerful *crescendo* towards a tumultuous *fortissimo* version from b.173. None of this is inordinately difficult providing that the RH is allowed to 'lead' from b.157, and the LH from b.165; and then that the clangourous

RH 'broken' version of the melody from b.173 is underpinned by a powerful LH resonance. Following the angry syncopated stabbings and bass grumblings from b.183 Chopin unveils his master stroke – the combination of the motif from the second main theme (bb.185-9) with the motif from the first main theme (bb.189-93), at first in *sotto voce,* egged on by buzzing LH semiquavers. Making a long *crescendo* from b.203, and gathering steep impetus from b.209, Chopin blazes into a radiant *fortissimo* statement of the first theme from b.213. Then notching up the harmonic tension in a taut *stretto*, he defuses this dynamic splendour in a shower of switchbacking semiquavers, ending in a straightforward final burst of chords.

Ballade No. 4 in F minor
Op. 52 (VA)

In terms of expressive compass and in the complexity yet unity of its design, this 'magnificent narration' (Weinstock, p.264) is unquestionably the greatest of the four Ballades. Indeed, many consider it the greatest of Chopin's entire works. It is at one and the same time a 'triumph of architecture', as Jim Samson says, and a 'synthesis of many aspects of [Chopin's] art, ranging from the most popular to the most severe, from the elegance and grace of the waltz to the rigour and logic of strict counterpoint' (p.187). This truth accounts for its capacity to appeal at all levels. Thus the musical child who cannot fail to be enslaved by the evocative melancholy of its principal melody will equally, in later life, marvel at the inspired logic of means and design by which Chopin arrives at such exalted intensity of expression. It is the most demanding of the Ballades on both an interpretive and technical level. But the technical demands are of an 'integrated' rather than overtly virtuosic kind, in that the expressive and technical are essentially interrelated as part and parcel of the grand design.

The introductory bars have an all-knowing yet beatific sadness. This is one of the most beautiful ideas in the piano literature – the texture is exquisitely limpid, with the LH alternately materialising in fragments of counterpoint, and receding in accompaniment beneath the quietly swaying RH quaver octaves and inner semiquavers. This introduction, ending on a dominant question in b.7, does not so much set the scene as draw us on into the narrative.

The principal theme is 'led in', as Alan Rawsthorn points out, by the 'hesitant three notes' (Walker, p.56)  and enters properly only with the last two quavers of b.8. This theme, only four bars long, is more of a motif than a melody, with its fragments and pervading the whole work as they continually recur in numerous guises and phases of development. Every commentator calls this theme 'haunting' – and indeed there is no other word to describe its will-o'-the-wisp quality, hesitant yet at the same time a little eager. Keyboard swooners who maul it about should be shot – the melody needs to be supported and gently propelled by a beautifully rhythmic LH which Chopin has shaped in such a way as to allow the melody to speak with the most subtle expressiveness within the steady **6/8** pulse. Its unfolding from b.13 onwards in subtly contrived harmonic variants and 'pointings' is not a moment too prolonged, when from the end of b.37 the emerging LH fragment leads us downwards towards the strange passage in G flat which passes in a mysterious and nuanceless flatness of scarcely-breathed LH octaves and static RH chords. The little swell through b.45 is like a weary sigh preparing to take up the second motif of the main theme again in *mezzo voce* from b.46, at first hesitantly, and then in combination with the first motif to be developed and expanded in gloriously rich-textured fashion, rising from b.58 in a long and increasingly impassioned *crescendo* towards b.71.

From b.72 Chopin launches into a joyously agitated flurry of semiquavers which ease out from the end of b.78 towards the quietly rocking second main theme, which is introduced through a series of subtle rhythmic and harmonic 'pointers' through bb.80-83 to begin at b.84. Alan Rawsthorn writes, without exaggeration, 'the beauty of this theme is of a kind no other composer has realised, and although this exquisite tenderness is to be found elsewhere in Chopin's work . . . it seems here to have reached its apotheosis' (Walker, p.57). A rhapsodic improvisatory passage leads on from b.100. Evolving through strongly stated fragments of the principal theme, Chopin eases miraculously but at the same time with seeming inevitability into a reappearance of the introductory theme at b.129 in a quietly breathed A major. Following a drift into an exquisitely abstracted arpeggiation in 'free' *dolcissimo* double quavers (b.134), this musing mood continues through a long breathed two- and three-voiced contrapuntal exploration of the principal motifs. From b.152 the music gathers momentum in another gloriously rhapsodic development, initially of the first theme, and then from b.169, of the second. The music 'accumulates' with an intensely persuasive power in a rising flood of impassioned grandeur towards b.191. Pealing arpeggios lead into thrilling salvos of detached chords, ending in a tremendous thrust into C major, the dominant at b.202. There follows, as Alan Rawsthorn says, 'eight bars of the most breathless suspense in all music – five chords which prepare the way for the coda. Both time and emotion seem to cease' (Walker, p.58). The suspense of the long-held dominant chord (bb.207-10) is released in yet another magnificent coda. Chopin devours the keyboard in one of his most dazzling, perhaps **the** most dazzling display of rigorously bridled virtuosity, with a hard-edged clarity and brilliance which few players can achieve.

THE SONATAS

Sonata in C minor
Op. 4
Allegro maestoso (VA)
Menuetto – Allegretto (8)
Larghetto (7)
Finale – Presto (VA)

It is not surprising that this unlovely work seldom, if ever, finds its way into recital programmes, and it will in effect be passed over here. Signs of the early, let alone the mature Chopin are virtually undetectable, and it would be a musician of astonishing perspicacity who on hearing it 'blind' for the first or even the tenth time could spot the composer. Written in 1828, it was dedicated to Jozef Elsner, Chopin's revered teacher, and as Jim Samson says 'it bears all the marks of a highly gifted student's laboured attempts to impress his teacher with an ambitious "learned" work' (pp.38-9).

Note: This work is not published by Henle, but is available in many other editions, including Paderewski.

The first movement is built on a single-line quaver figure and a fragment of this

is worked to saturation point and beyond, much of the

treatment of an earnest contrapuntal nature.

In the minuet movement a single-line figure is again treated contrapuntally. The movement is tightly built, making a bow in the direction of Beethoven with its stern *sforzatos*, and so unlike Chopin as to be almost amusing.

In the slow movement, the most likely moment for better things, Chopin again fails to reveal his identity. The player is left adrift in an amorphous **5/4** rhythm, of which it is difficult to make any rhythmic, melodic or expressive shape.

The very long final movement is truly awful. A martial theme of minims and crotchets is overlaid with unremitting *con fuoco* quaver flourishes and busily worked sequential passages, as exhausting to the listener as to the stamina of the player.

Sonata in B flat minor
Op. 35

It is ironic that there should have been so much critical debate over the merits of a work built around that musical inspiration which has become central to European ceremonial tradition, the Marche Funèbre. Even Schumann, usually Chopin's champion, spoke of its movements as 'four of Chopin's most unruly children under one roof'. The March itself was written in 1837 (the circumstances appear to be unknown) and Chopin wrote the other three movements two years later, during his first summer spell at George Sand's country home, Nohant. But, as Arthur Hedley has said 'It was the March which furnished Chopin with the seed from which the first movement and the Scherzo sprang and stimulated him to embody

492

within the framework on the Sonata the emotions which the vision of death aroused in him' and 'the Finale . . . has no existence apart from the preceding movements' (pp.157-8). The Sonata as a whole is, of course, a work of blinding originality. In each movement Chopin seems possessed by some overriding inner compulsion, of which nevertheless he is in total command.

It goes without saying that performance of such a vast-scaled work, as ambitious and indeed problematic in its interpretive as in its technical demands, can only be attempted by pianists of the first rank.

Grave – Doppio movimento (VA)

With the impact of the first octave of the *Grave*, as magisterially portentous an opening as any in piano music, from which we are pitched towards the rampant *agitato* of the *Doppio movimento*, a rigorous control of rhythm and dynamics must be exercised. The least faltering of this control, and the driving rhythmic tension of the movement will be dissipated. Again, an *agitato* does not pound, but rather seethes and erupts. It follows that the dynamics must be kept on a tight rein, starting in a breathless *piano* after the *sforzato* octave on the first beat of b.5, marking the *forte* jolts decisively at bb.17 and 19, and making a **controlled** climb from b.25 towards the *fortissimo* at b.37.

The gun-shot octave on the first beat of b.5, and the surging 4-bar preparation initiate a whiplashing rhythmic tension. The first subject motif is an extraordinary one for a first movement – one might rather expect to find it in a Finale. Its seething momentum dominates the movement, straining at the bit from b.9, jerking ominously in the bass through the first half of the development, and erupting into the treble towards a climactic outburst of colossal sonority from b.137. The beatific second subject from b.41 should not be allowed to meander as it so often is, but needs to be carried in a broad melodic sweep so that the underlying impulse is maintained. A tumultuous development of this melody in a long overall climb from b.57 leads into a new figure in insistent *agitato* repeated chords, with an upward/downward plunge (bb.91-3) of a discordant stridency that ambushes the ear even today. Omitted from the recapitulation, the first subject motif makes a brief appearance in the bass near the end, goading the RH chords in a furiously impelled final *stretto*.

Scherzo (VA)

The Beethovenian character of the Scherzo has often been remarked. If for Chopin, in this context, Scherzo retained its meaning of 'joke', the joke is a grim and hectoring one. If, on the other hand, this is a Scherzo in the Haydn-Beethoven sense, then Chopin has transformed it into an onslaught, rather than a dance, of demonic ferocity. With its juddering repeated octaves and wildly leaping chords, it is extremely taxing to play, and once again this onward-hurtling violence has to be under rigorous rhythmic and dynamic control. It is essential not to start too loud, so that the RH repeated octaves and rising LH figures through bb.1-2, 3-4, etc. can make their eruptive dynamic surges as indicated. Similarly, following the swipe of the *sforzato* unison octave on the first beat of bb.37, 41, etc, the scale needs to start from a virtual *piano* so that it can shoot upwards in a screeching *crescendo*. And as in the first movement, the music must surge, not pound relentlessly, taking every opportunity to vary the tone, and dropping to a real *pianissimo* at bb.17 and 59.

Following a tumultuous sequence of leaping chords in a swingeing cross-rhythm effect through bb.73-6 which drives the first section towards a violent 'stop', the gentle rocking of the *Più Lento* is exquisite balm. This softly contoured melody is one of Chopin's loveliest ideas, with the nudging inner LH melodic 'hint' E flat-D flat through bb.81-7 quietly materialising in a falling fragment from the second beat of b.88. And from the double bar (bb.144-5) a cello-like LH quaver line emerges in duet with a sustained melodic and harmonic RH. At bb.178 and 180 quiet LH trills, rather like the low portentous trills of Schubert, warn of the inevitable return (sidestepped the first time by the repeat of this section) through a steep *crescendo* and *accelerando* towards Tempo 1. The brief return to the first melody of the *Più Lento* is, as Weinstock has said, an inspired 'bridge to the mournful pomps to come' (p.240).

Marche Funèbre (7) (O)

No amount of familiarity can undermine the majestic dolour of the great March. So does it assail us time and time again, and so must it be overlaid with associations for all of us, that it seems ludicrous, if not impertinent, to discuss it in terms of crotchets and quavers, sharps and flats. However, since there can be no pianist of even modest aspiration who does not at some time take a tilt at it, a few pointers will be given. It cannot be too strongly urged that this music is at its most potent when played absolutely 'straight'. Chopin's dramatics are meticulously calculated and need no help from us in the form of exaggerated *rubato* or fancy expressive touches.

bb.1–14   Inexperienced players so often find it difficult to do the simple thing, i.e. to feel rhythm in a **physical** sense. Thus, when confronted with a march or a dance, the last, rather than the first thing they will do is to relate the music to a physical **step**. Then when they are persuaded to do this, and preferably actually to **step** to the music, they are astonished and delighted by the improvement in their playing resulting from relating the music to the relevant **actual** physical movement. Thus it is not too obvious to point out that a march, whether swinging and buoyant or slow and 'dead', as here, has a regular pendulum-like stride. There can be few people who have not watched a filmed official funeral from some corner of the globe, and who cannot instantly feel this slow dead tread of a funeral march. Through the first 18 bars the bleak, hollow-sounding chords of the LH must provide this quietly thudding tread. It is vital that the dotted rhythms of the RH are accurately timed and not allowed to degenerate into sloppy triplets. On the other hand, double dotting weakens the rhythm, and gives an unseemly 'jiggy' effect (see General Introduction under 'Dotted Rhythms'). Set your tempo as slow as you dare, at around a suggested ♩ = 44, remembering that the slower the beat the greater the demands upon the rhythmic stability of the player. Enter in a quiet yet definite, sepulchral tone, and feel the impulse of each treble repeated-note figure through bb.1 and 2 towards the minim on each third beat.

 Make sure in each instance (and similarly in bb.4 and 6)

that these minims are given sufficient tone to sing through the second half of the bar, so that the

melody sounds clearly 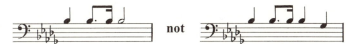 not

Also there is often a tendency for the chord on the fourth beat of the bar to be placed carelessly beneath these minims, resulting in a tendency to 'fall into' bb.2, 3, etc. The LH and inner RH lines must continue in quiet but implaccable support of the melody line. You could raise the dynamic level very slightly, as you move into the higher register at b.5; and then feel the implied 'leaning' emphasis upon, and *decrescendo* from the chord on the first beat of bb.7 and 8, with

494

a similar but more forceful effect in bb.11 and 12.* The grace notes should fall **on** the second

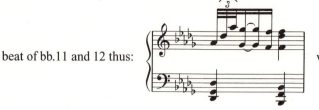

beat of bb.11 and 12 thus: without sabotaging the rhythm

of the LH chords.

bb.15–30   Feel that you are 'taking hold' of the emphasised upbeat to b.15 ready to notch up the dynamic level from b.15, as if marching columns are rounding a corner into closer earshot, rising to a powerful, ringing minim chord on the first beat of b.16. With the abandonment of the *ostinato* tread in the LH from b.15, particular care has to be taken to keep the crotchet pulse steady. Be sure therefore that the dotted rhythm sequences tread 'uphill' through b.15, and 'downhill' in the LH through b.16 in implacable rhythm, ready to start the next 'climb' from the upbeat to b.17. Allow an extra instant however, from the upbeat to b.16, feeling the sense of an upward 'heave' towards, and sense of arrival upon, the big chord on the first beat of b.16 (though still reserving tone for the amplified dynamics at bb.23-4). Feel the strong 'lean' on the LH slurred crotchet upbeat to b.19, and then, playing the first LH grace notes **on** the beat (see General Introduction under 'Ornaments') create a powerful drum-roll effect through the LH trills beneath **rock**-steady RH chords. Then letting the sound 'distance' momentarily through bb.21-2, burst into a fierce *fortissimo* on the upbeat to b.23, but still not so loud as to leave no room to *crescendo* up towards the climactic chord on the first beat of b.24.

bb.30–85   Taper the sound away through bb.29-30, but without altering the tread, and then feel the sense in which the LH slurred octaves lead on, with no more than a little 'give', into b.31. If only players will leave this middle section alone, they cannot fail to create the distant, 'flat' and unearthly sound that Chopin clearly intended, between the granite-cast and entirely earthbound pomp of the march sections. Chopin's only directions here are *pianissimo* from b.31, a *crescendo* from b.40 (very gradual and not too great), and a reversion to *pianissimo* after a 'hairpin' swell through b.46. Create a thin clear line in the treble over quaver arcs that are so even as to achieve that magic amalgam of stillness within motion, or motion within stillness. Some pianists move this middle section on. If this is done very little and almost imperceptibly it is acceptable. But in my view an unchanging pulse from start to finish of the movement, in other words the concept of the beatification of, and the return to, the pulse of the earthbound march is infinitely more telling. This is born out by Von Lenz's description of Chopin's playing of this Trio: 'Never . . . did his subdued expression . . . strike me as contradicting the character of the March'. He found this experience 'indescribable. Only Rubini [a renowned tenor of the day] could sing like that.' (Eigeldinger, p.86). At the end of the second repeated section anything more than a hint of a *rallentando* is superfluous. Chopin's rest on the fourth beat of b.54 (second-time bar) 'allows' for the player to prepare the resumption of the bleak tread in b.55.

Finale – Presto (VA)

Chopin's own description of the Finale as 'the LH and RH gossiping in unison after the march' is typically laconic and self-deprecatory. Perhaps he intended an effect as mundane as this.

---

*Some editions (including Paderewski) give equal quavers in the RH through the first beat of bb.7 and 8 (by analogy with bb.11 and 12), as opposed to the dotted rhythm in Henle. See the commentary in Paderewski.

Perhaps, with his sphinx-like reserve, this comment hides a far more personal, macabre or extra-mundane notion. In any event, many thousands of words have been expended in the effort to 'explain' a movement which, as Alan Walker says 'is without precedent in the entire history of the keyboard'. It is futuristically athematic from beginning to end – no wonder Mendelssohn disliked it – and its continuous swirls of stark sounding octaves reminded Anton Rubinstein of 'night winds sweeping over churchyard graves' (p.247). Alan Walker goes on to say 'the music lies a long way behind the notes; few pianists get there' (p.248). It is formidably difficult, and needs to go very fast, and the more minimal the use of the pedal, the clearer the shape of the continual flux of tiny surges within the overall *sotto voce e legato*, the more skeletal the texture, and the more spectral the effect. A performance stands or falls not by whether it is good or bad, but by its relation (either as a summation or, equally valid, as a question mark) to what has gone before, and ultimately by its ability or failure to chill the spine. This said, it is a fascinating study for the less advanced student of Chopin to trace in slower motion the extraordinary processes that the ear only glimpses as an **effect** at high speed.

Sonata in B minor
Op. 58

This Sonata was written in 1844, five years after Op.35, during Chopin's last great creative flush, the period of the Barcarolle, the Berceuse, the Polonaise-Fantaisie and the remarkable late Nocturnes Op.55 No.2 and Op.62 No.1. It is just as imposing as Op.35, but very different.

Op.35 is by definition intensely romantic, viewed in the sense of the 'programmatic' relation of the whole to the kernel, the Funeral March. Op.58 by contrast appears more self-contained, absolute, and more classical. For the performer it is, as a whole, at least as formidable an assignment as Op.35, and if anything, more of a technical Parnassus, certainly as regards the Finale.

Allegro maestoso (VA)
The first movement is, as Peter Gould says, 'packed with material' (some say burdened) 'sufficient for twenty-five Sonatas by a composer twenty-five years previously' (Walker, p.161). It follows that cohesion is all important, and as Alan Walker points out in the same book (p.254) this is essentially achieved by the gauging of a 'long-range **basic** tempo', the 'pulse behind the pulse . . . against which the performance may brake and accelerate, according to immediate, spontaneous needs'. This, of course, is the cornerstone of all successful performance, but here particularly so – spelling the alternative between chaos and, in the hands of a performer who can sense, gauge and implement that vital force, a closely reasoned interpretation that is unassailable.

The virile, declamatory opening motif (bb.1-4), as 'developable' as a first subject by Beethoven, dominates the whole movement, and Alan Walker has cogently expounded upon the relation of the numerous offshoots of this motif, as well as of the second subject theme, to the 'parent' (pp.251-4). The transitional matter leading towards the second subject is tumultuously rich. From b.23 a two-voiced phrase sings out canonically over abstracting trails of rising chromatic semiquavers; and from b.33 an energetically worked syncopated figure is combined with active semiquaver passage-work over a long dominant pedal point (of D major), dissolving from b.39 towards the second subject. The D major second subject melody is one of Chopin's most rhapsodic, and it is vital that it is not allowed to wallow – in other words, that the quiet nocturne-like accompaniment maintains the sense of movement. This melody seems to have a limitless ability to evolve, as it does, gathering and dispersing momentum through a period of 50 bars, up until the double bar.

The tightly knit contrapuntal workings through the first section of the development need to be meticulously delineated within a sure rhythmic framework. (At bb.115-16, as the LH 'prepares' the entry of the second melodic idea of the second subject (b.57) we have the momentarily disorientating sensation of being about to surge into the opening of the Schumann Fantasie Op.17.) As in the first movement of Op.35, Chopin's elaborate development leads into the recapitulation with the tonic major entry of the second subject melody at b.149.

Scherzo – Molto vivace (VA)

Nothing could be further from the lacerating tumult of the Scherzo of Op.35 than the busy but light-spirited outer section of this movement. It is much less taxing, but nevertheless, at the desirable bustling speed, it requires a high degree of fluency and agility. The punctuating LH fragments provide vital rhythmic anchorage for the scamperings of the RH. Entering as they usually do on the upbeat, the implied 'lean' on these slurred and/or partially tied LH upbeats needs to be carefully placed. In the burst of unison writing that ends each outer section, there is a momentary, slightly eerie sense of flashback to the Finale of Op.35. Jim Samson (p.136) points to the Brahmsian flavour of the middle section, with its gently swaying motion. The quiet, concentrated resonances of the upper RH voices and the inner melodic lines over the long sustained lower LH harmonies, pedal points and occasional bass fragments, are highly complex in an aural sense. The quiet and rather ominous trombone-like ring of the repeated RH octaves (bb.93-4 and 101-2) over the gruff bass octave line is, in particular, strikingly Brahmsian. Amid the teeming invention and technical vitality of the first two movements, this whole passage has a beautiful solemnity – quietly glowing rather than sombre – which few pianists are able (or perhaps take the trouble) to find.

Largo (7) (O)

Note: For those using the Paderewski Edition there will be a one-bar discrepancy in bar numberings (i.e. for b.1 read b.2, and so on). This arises because Paderewski counts the first bar (an incomplete bar) and Henle does not (see General Introduction under 'Bar Numberings').

Providing that (as with the mid-section of the Funeral March) players will only leave it alone, the slow movement can cast a rare spell. It is true, as has often been remarked, that a large part of this spell lies in the ineluctable rightness of its place in the Sonata as a whole – so much for Chopin's alleged inability to orchestrate the grand plan. But it is, at the same time, a superb study in rhythmic poise and sustained sonorities for the musically mature player at about Grade 7.

Tempo is something of a problem – as ever, there is no one 'right' tempo – but it is a long movement, and there has to be at all times a sense of continuing motion, which, however, needs to have considerable flexibility. The fact that the melody line in both the outer and middle sections is of a somewhat static kind (i.e. moves within a narrow span) and the accompaniment in the outer section is in a 'fixed' rhythm, makes it all the more essential that this continual sense of movement is maintained. Jim Samson talks of the 'stately measured tread, whose dotted rhythm acts as a form of steady, gentle propulsion, lending to the melody something of the classical poise of a late Beethoven or late Schubert slow movement' (p.136). In fact, the motion as well as the spirit of the outer sections is remarkably akin to that of the slow movement of the great Schubert Sonata in B flat. The tempo is that of a leisurely walking pace, with a slow kind of 'suspended' swing. My suggestion of a crotchet pulse of around ♩ = 50 is a strictly personal one, since the sense of a 'leisurely walking pace' varies enormously in relation to individual metabolism.

bb.1–4 With this crotchet pulse well in the system, and **feeling** the silent first beat securely, declaim the introductory unison sequence in ringing tones, and in deliberate rhythm. Think of the demisemiquavers always as the 'upbeat' to each double dotted quaver (see General Introduction under 'Dotted Rhythms') and feel that you are 'going towards' and *crescendoing* **into** the unison dotted minim E's on the second beat of b.2. **Listen** to this unison sound through its full value so that you can place the chord quietly on the first beat of b.3, thus enhancing rather than killing the remaining sound of the tied upper E. Then 'diffuse' the phrase in a quiet, *religioso* tone up towards a warm-toned dominant 7th chord on the first beat of b.4.

'Finish off' the phrase carefully to the tonic chord on the third beat of b.4 so that you can make a clear 'fresh start' into the melody from the upbeat to b.5, taking care that this upbeat is strictly solo, i.e. that the pedal is changed after the tonic chord. It is a mistake to mess around with the tempo here, and far more effective to end the phrase in time so that the tempo is 'set', ready for the melody to lead off convincingly from this upbeat to b.5. These introductory bars are of great moment, and it behoves **any** player to study their effect with the utmost concentration.

bb.4–18 It is well to study the LH first since it is this unchanging LH rhythm that 'carries' the RH melody through bb.4-18. For players whose rhythmic sense is

none too sure, it is a good plan to practise this at first  *etc.*

so that the sense of the basic crotchet pulse becomes well rooted 'in the system'. Then practise as written, but counting in **quavers** at first, to help ensure that the semiquaver is always perfectly timed (neither 'tripletised' nor double dotted). Once more, always feel the semiquaver as 'going to' the subsequent quaver in the nature of an upbeat (see again the General Introduction). Imagine also that the LH is moving in continuous 'arcs' from bass notes to upper chords and down again, rather than in sharp-lined diagonals, with the hand 'lifting' not jerking off the low detached quaver, and then playing the repeated chords in a close-to-the-keys, just-detached style. (The marking of the upper notes of these repeated chords may be misunderstood – they are **not** tied – see a similar instance in the RH chords in the Coda of the Waltz in A minor Op.34 No.2.)

Then practise the RH **imagining** the LH proceeding steadily beneath. The *cantabile* line has a kind of cool eloquence that is naturally expressive: in other words it will shape itself without the need for meaningful effects or exaggerated dynamics. Let the upbeat lead quietly but very definitely, with the sense of an onward upward 'lean' towards a singing minim D sharp on the first beat of b.4, ensuring that this note has sufficient tone to sing through its full value. You will have no difficulty in timing this long note if you really **feel** the LH moving beneath. Time the dotted rhythms carefully through bb.4-5, etc. as in the LH. and take care to shape the triplet 'turn' evenly in b.5. Phrasing details vary in different editions. The essential is to create a long-breathed overall eight-bar line from the upbeat to b.4 through to the end of b.11, but with an implied gentle feeling of 'renewal' on the upbeat to b.8 as indicated by the two 4-bar phrases in the Paderewski Edition. (Henle has the more fussy effect of a new phrase from the semiquaver 'upbeat' to the third beat of b.5, with this phrase then carrying on over to the end of b.11.) Allow a degree of freedom as you expand up towards and down from the fourth beat of b.10, imagining a slight 'give' in the LH to accommodate this expressive and full-toned 'vocal' RH curve. Then listen acutely to the diminishing sound of your carefully graded minims through b.11, ready to 'begin again' with the *piano* phrase from b.12. Feel the vocal 'lift' from the lower to the higher tied G sharp here, and again similarly in b.14.

If, when you put hands together you are ever conscious of the continuing rhythmic movement of the LH, there will be no difficulty in synchronising the RH 'upbeat' semiquavers with those in the LH. It is remarkable how much of a sense of freedom the RH can enjoy within the framework of this gentle, steady tread in the LH. There needs to be just a little 'give' through the third beat of b.7, ready to point the upbeat to b.8, and as already said, a sense of expansion through the second half of b.10, with perhaps another tiny 'give' at the end of b.11, ready to move on into a rather lighter dynamic from b.12. Allow an extra instant too at the end of b.15 to clear the sound for a quietly breathed *pianissimo* from b.16, **listening** from here to the added soft resonance of the quietly oscillating inner RH line F sharp-G sharp.

If the offbeat cross-rhythm effect in bb.5, 9 etc. proves difficult, it can be practised thus

at first:  *etc.* In b.13 where the LH harmony

spans a tenth it is better to take the upper LH F sharp with the LH than to spread these chords.

bb.18–27 Arriving on the quiet dominant seventh chord (of E major) on the first beat of b.18, ensure that the tied treble D sharp sings on over the quietly 'harped' chord on the third beat. Then with a sense of slightly moving on, shape the RH solo fragments in a 'speaking' recitative-like manner, with quietly resonant 'answers' in the lower register, feeling a slight emphasis on the minim chord on the second beat of bb.19 and 21, being sure to **feel** the held third beat. Then feel a further sense of moving on from the second beat of b.22, with a light 'lean' on the slurred RH crotchet on the second beat of b.22 (and similarly b.23) with another implied 'lean' on the trilled chords on the upbeat to bb.23 and 24. 'Go to' a warm-toned treble G sharp on the first beat of b.24, ensuring that the melody line here is clearly G sharp-G sharp, and not G sharp-B-D sharp-G sharp. Feel a sense of expansion through bb.24-5 towards the tonic chord on the first beat of b.26, **listening** to the resonance of the treble semibreve B as the LH sextuplets (thinking in groups of 3+3) emerge in the LH, curling gently as they fall from the high C sharp, preparing the way into the new section in the subdominant.

bb.27–59 Allow a fair amount of 'give' through the second half of b.27 as you poise yourself to establish the new motion from b.28. There is a clear sense of 'easing onward' here, into an overall 2-in-the-bar movement.

Through bb.28-30 listen to the rapt duet between the inner LH voice and the treble. Shape the LH curve with all possible eloquence beneath the quietly-breathed, almost stationary line of the treble, listening also to the nudging inner RH resonances, the doubled dotted crotchets G sharp, and doubled crotchets E and B in b.28 (and so on in each bar) within the easy overall sextuplet flow. Then, from the middle of b.30 support the RH with carefully balanced LH chords. (Note that the RH sextuplets are in cross-rhythm with the LH quavers in bb.29, 45, etc. Similarly the quaver chords in bb.36, 38, etc, and the RH upbeat quavers to bb.41, 42, etc. are 'plain' quavers, **not** sextuplet quavers.) It goes without saying that the balancing of these beautiful and subtle resonances requires a sensitive and experienced ear and a fine technical control. Niecks (Vol.2, p.228) rightly says this is 'more of a reverie than a composition' although he paints an unfortunate picture of Chopin with 'dilated eyes and rapture in his look' – a notion sickeningly foreign to the mien of the almost paranoically reserved Chopin! Draw the minim line smoothly down through bb.32-4 in a softly pealing tone, and then carry the sextuplets up in a light sweep towards the quietly questioning chords in b.36. In these upward sweeps (bb.35-6, 37-8, etc.) there is a hint of the much extended improvisatory swathes in the Introduction to the Polonaise-Fantaisie written two years later. The subsequent bars have an exquisite murmurous stillness, 'waiting' through bb.39-43 to resume the quiet song from b.44.

In b.58 (b.59 in the Paderewski edition) most editions give this eloquent

bb.58–97

LH variant   (not given in

Henle – though remarked in the Critical Commentary), then from b.60 Chopin expands into a modulatory musing upon the material of this mid-section. Listen to the line of the bass octaves moving in a gradual swell towards a warm-toned *forte* at b.66 as the sextuplets billow, filling out without swamping the sound of the upper melody line. From b.75 Chopin works back towards E major at b.78 by infinitely subtle chromatic snaking. Listen particularly to the held resonance of the upbeat quavers to b.75; to the doubled sixth quaver of b.75 and then to the exquisite enharmonic shift to the beginning of b.76; and to the quiet eloquence of the just-detached falling inner sextuplet quavers through the first half of b.77. Then take time through the second half of b.77, spreading the wide LH interval generously on the third beat as you prepare to ease back towards b.78. From b.86 diffuse the sound in a diminishing trail as the sextuplets curve upwards, then down through b.87 in a wide arc, and upwards again within a haze of pedal towards the crotchet D sharp on the first beat of b.89. Then listen acutely again as Chopin disperses the harmonies in a breath-holding modulatory chain back towards the home dominant on the first beat of b.97. This sequence has a spatial quality of stillness worthy of late Beethoven. (The enharmonic change at the end of b.95 is **silent**.)

bb.97–119 Be sure to give full value to the minim chord on the first beat of b.97, then take a 'breath' on the third beat, ready to lead back to the varied version of the opening section from the upbeat to b.98. The triplet accompaniment suggests a more dream-like feeling here, but in the same tempo as from b.4. For the timing of the RH

semiquavers with the LH triplet, see the General Introduction under 'The ♩♪ Question'.

Allow the LH to 'give' a little through the last beat of b.101 to accommodate the RH run, played with a silvery softness, and feel the last LH quaver clearly as the upbeat to b.102 as indicated by the slur. The RH could 'meet' this upbeat quaver around, or approximately between the eleventh and twelfth notes of the run (i.e. the E or F sharp) then easing up in a little vocal curve up to the high A sharp, ready to fall gracefully to a quietly singing D sharp on the first

beat of b.102

(see General Introduction

under 'Free' Runs'). Be sure to allow time for the treble ornament to 'speak' in b.103, timing

it approximately thus:

etc. Listen again to the marvellous

modulatory progressions *decrescendoing* through bb.110-11 towards the coda. From here shape the LH sextuplets in a murmuring but clear *pianissimo* beneath the softly breathed treble line and quietly sustained inner chords. There is a Mahlerian attenuation of sound here as the line tapers upwards towards the sustained E in b.117 while the bass sextuplets search for the final tonic. In b.114 allow an extra instant again to let the elaborated

turn 'speak':

Finale-Presto non tanto (VA)

With their habitual sang-froid, most musical commentators omit to mention that a fine performance of the Finale offers one of the most electrifying experiences available to a recital audience. The cresting momentum of its principal motif, particularly, when on later appearances it is goaded along by heaving bass semiquavers, is like some wild Valkyrian ride to the open seas. And each lunge of the abrasive, epigramatic second subject figure (bb.52-4, 56-8, etc.) provokes an answering spume of headlong semiquavers. There is scarcely an instant's let-up in the course of the nearly 300 bars, and it follows that for the player it is a gargantuan assignment – one upon which, as Weinstock says 'countless pianists have suffered shipwreck' (p.275).

Here, as so often, Chopin's introduction is masterly. He slices into the keyboard with upward swingeing octaves *crescendoing* towards a pause on the dominant. The main theme enters in *piano agitato* – indications which, together with the *presto* **non tanto**, pianists ignore at their peril: if the later semiquavers cause a jamming on of the brakes, the 'remorseless surge which should span the whole movement' (Walker, p.164) will be undermined. The quieter the beginning, from b.9, with a suppressed 'hunting' momentum, the more effective the **gradual** dynamic climb through the first span, ready for the second theme in the tonic major to leap straight in *fortissimo* at b.52. This is a marvellously constructed sequence. The 'abrasive' figure thrusts through to the chord on the first beat of b.54, and the LH leaps on to 'carry' the RH downward semiquaver chute through to the first beat of b.56, with both hands 'pouncing' onto the second main beat to repeat the sequence a third higher. It is the audacious continuity of this passage that is so galvanising – but which many pianists do not quite have the courage to carry through. From b.76, the semiquavers take off in a climbing sequence of stunning élan, tumbling downwards again with reckless force from b.90 to surge back into the main theme from b.100. Here Chopin compounds the rhythmic propulsion by setting the theme against quadruplet quavers, and then from b.207 against the 'heaving' semiquavers. The head of steam thus generated escapes, as it must, through a coda of unrivalled brilliance. After eight bars of hectically switchbacking arpeggios (bb.254-61), the music spirals upwards in a chromatic semiquaver sequence in implied cross-rhythm with the tautly coiled rhythm of the LH quavers – one of the most exciting passages in the repertoire. The final descent from b.274, equally thrilling, drives into the final sledgehammer chords. Again, as so often, we marvel at the virility and dramatic power that emanates from the Chopin of the Paris salons, who was so concerned with the cut of his dove-grey trousers and the elegance of his wallpaper.

THE IMPROMPTUS

The three Impromptus, written neither as a set, nor belonging to a large genre, inhabit something of a no-man's land – especially since they are generally considered to be a somewhat lightweight, rather than a 'significant' part of Chopin's oeuvre. It appears, however, that Chopin had a predilection for Nos 1 and 3 – in particular for No.3 (Eigeldinger, p.70); and in many respects Nos 2 and 3, which have elements of the futuristic wanderings both of the late Nocturnes (Op.55 No.2 and Op.62 No.1 in particular) and of the single Prelude, Op.45, are more significant than they are given credit for. Nos 2 and 3 also are a great deal more difficult, in both a technical and musical sense, than they may seem when **listened** to, and neither is easy to hold together. They have therefore been listed under Very Advanced. No.1 is traditionally a 'nice' piece for a young student. It is certainly less demanding, but even so there are inner inflections and subtleties of expression and emphasis to which mere dexterity cannot do justice, and it has therefore been listed under Grade 8+.

Impromptu No. 1 in A flat major
Op. 29 (8+)

Nieck's description, flowery as it seems in our more prosaic age, nicely catches the spirit of this piece: 'The first section, with its triplets, bubbles forth and sparkles like a fountain on which the sunbeams that steal through the interstices of the overhanging foliage are playing.' (Vol.2, p.259). Henle gives an *alla breve*, and there is definitely the sense of an overall 2-in-the-bar. However, since most editions, including the Vienna Urtext Edition, give a **4/4** time signature, the commentaries below are 'counted' in **4/4**. Most players adopt (or aspire to) a tempo of about $\downarrow$ = 144, with a certain amount of give and take (e.g. a sense of moving on through b.3, a little 'give' at the end of b.4, another sense of moving on from b.15 and easing through b.18, and so on). Much slower, and it loses this sunbeam quality – much faster, and the constantly shifting inflections of both LH and RH tend to disappear into a general mêlée.

    The circling flight of the RH depends on a perfectly stable LH. Since the LH is in some senses more difficult than the RH, and certainly more complex in its harmonic inflections and subtle tiny emphases, I suggest, as so often, that the LH is studied first.

          As Jan Ekier suggests in the Vienna Urtext Edition, it is likely that the *legato*
bb.1–4   applies as much to the LH as to the RH, with the implication of a *legato* 'pointing' of the fourth, sixth, tenth, and twelfth quavers of bb.1-2 etc. – a technique which he calls 'harmonic *legato*', and other writers sometimes refer to as 'finger pedalling'.

 This, as he also says, 'requires great

dexterity, precision and lightness' so that the effect is fleetingly 'implied' rather than 'stated', without causing any bumps or hiccoughs in the light-footed triplet flow. Practise bb.1-4 until the LH is perfectly fluent, shaping each triplet in a light curve **within** the overall flow. Many hands, of course, will not be able to reach the interval of a tenth on the first and third beats of bb.1-2 etc. But this is not an obstacle to the **illusion** of smoothness if you shape each triplet group as an arc, and think of a light, easy 'lift', rather than a snatch up to and down from the thumb on the middle note. These thumb-notes create the hint of another offbeat inner subsidiary melody line C-C-D flat-D flat/C-C-D flat-D flat/E-flat-E natural-F-F, etc.

etc. A good way to practise this figure is by

holding down the inner E flat with the third finger through bb.1 and 2, and similarly the A flat and

B flat (with the second finger) through b.3, etc. *etc.*

Feel the inner held finger as a pivot as you practise the necessary easy lateral movement of the wrist, enabling you to reach the tenth in an easy lift. When all the details are mastered and you achieve a fairly fleet tempo, the LH assumes the character of a rather open kind of hum, like a lively spinning- or mill wheel. Now practise the RH through bb.1-2 over and over until it is quite fluent. Feel that each little phrase is opening out through the bar, with a light lift up to the C on the second beat, and another to the highest note, the F. Do not arrive with an obvious 'plonk' on the crotchet E flat on the fourth beat, but rather feel that the curve is falling from its highest point, the F, to a lightly singing E flat, and then imagine taking a **tiny** breath, ready to 'start again' in b.2. Since this is the germinal (and continually recurring) motif of the outer sections of the piece, take plenty of time to absorb its 'landscape' so that you can shape it with a seemingly spontaneous grace and fluency. Open up the dynamics a little more in b.3 as you curve up to the high C on the second beat, and then 'curl' easily down through b.4 ready to set off again, in b.5.

When you put hands together, scrupulously preserve the shape and detailing that you have absorbed when studying hands separately. The RH crotchet on the fourth beat of bb.1 and 2 not only ends each 1-bar melodic phrase, but at the same time acts as an onward-leaning link towards the next phrase, while the LH leads on, in the sense of an upbeat, towards the subsequent bar. Although there is certainly the sense of a infinitesimal 'give' at the end of bb.1 and 2, as you imagine that tiny 'breath' the exaggerated *rubato* affected by some players between bb.1 and 2, and 2 and 3 stops the flow of the music before it has got going, chopping bb.1-4 into three separate boxes instead of feeling an **overall** 4-bar cycle. There is then the sense of moving on a little through b.3, easing a trifle through the second half of b.4 as you poise yourself to set off again from b.5 (the held LH dominant from the third beat of b.4 provides a little 'brake' here). There are no overall dynamic indications (despite the numerous 'hairpins') until the *forte* at b.23, but the piece should surely start softly, as if entering on a light breeze, with the kind of smooth clarity of articulation which is 'soft-edged' rather than brilliant. The ornament on the first beat of bb.1, 2, 3, etc. is preferably played **on** the beat (see General Introduction under 'Ornaments') although pianists of the older school tend to play it before the beat. I find it easier to incorporate it smoothly into the melodic line when it is placed on the beat – but as always the important thing is that it is clearly, smoothly and 'vocally' shaped, rather than merely 'stapled' on to the beginning of each little phrase.

bb.5–18 Expand the tone a little more as the RH flies up towards the high G in b.7, *diminuendo*ing smoothly down again towards the dominant on the third beat of b.8. Then feel the little chromatic scale fragment, as an upbeat group 'going on' into b.9, making a little *crescendo* up to an implied soft melodic 'lean' on the tied G flat on the second beat, and on to a 'lift' up to, and further 'lean' on the tied upbeat to b.10. At the same time give the LH 'doubled' triplet B flat the sense of an onward upbeat lead into b.9, and continue quietly to 'point' the line of these doubled crotchet notes through the subsequent bars as the RH 'falls' from the high upbeat to b.10 towards another light 'lean' on the tied upbeat to b.11, the second beat of b.11, and so on. Show the little surge up towards and down from the end of b.13. Then bring the tone up a little to the second beat of b.15, where the RH doubled notes join in with those in the LH, and make a smooth *decrescendo* down to the first beat of b.16, bringing the tone up again on the second beat of b.16, and so on, as indicated. As the doubled RH and LH lines make these little falls through bb.15-17, there is the lovely sensation of sliding downhill in a **controlled** slight *accelerando*. Take care to collect yourself momentarily at the end of b.17 so that you don't 'fall forwards' into b.18, and allow a little give at the end of b.18 (which is like a little linking fragment) ready to set off again in b.19.

bb.19–34   Allow the tone to expand freely from b.21, the first real *crescendo*, and then let the line of emphasised offbeat quavers peal downwards through bb.23-4, keeping control of the rhythm with the help of the emphasised bass notes on the first and third beats. Then, collecting yourself through the slight *ritenuto* in the second half of b.24, 'disperse' the sound in a *diminuendoing* frisson as you *accelerando* from b.25, again controlling the rhythm with the help of the doubled bass notes from the second beat of b.27. It is far from easy to keep track of the chromatic vacillations of RH and LH through bb.27-8, and through the tiny offbeat emphases through bb.29-30. The RH is particularly difficult to control. The fingering 2 1 4, 2 1 5 may be found easier, particularly by small hands, than the 2 1 4, 2 1 4 usually given (and by Chopin also). Practising

it thus   [musical notation]   and   [musical notation]   will help. Continue to be

conscious of the stabilising rhythmic influence of the doubled LH crotchets through these bars, though without bumping them out too obviously. Let the sound disappear as on a puff of air up to *pianissimo* but clear quavers on the third beat of b.30, 'holding' the silence as if in a momentary 'hover', and then landing with a quiet 'lean' on the slurred dominant seventh chord on the upbeat to b.31. The reiterated figure through bb.31-2 is also tricky. I find the

fingering   much easier than the 3 4 3, or

3 5 3 sometimes given. Practise at first   [musical notation]   feeling the triplet as an

upbeat 'going to' a light 'lean' on the upper E flat. Then when you add the inner line (having also practised this separately) the execution of the figure as a whole will be greatly facilitated (indeed, for most hands it will be unavoidable) if, on each second and fourth beat you **release** the thumb on the inner crotchet G as you play the third treble triplet quaver, or even earlier. Providing that you give this G a tiny emphasis (which it any way requires, to 'show' the two-part figuration here), this early release will be hardly detectable to the ear. Feel the sense of an onward 'push' through the last beat of b.32, then allow a tiny break at the end of the bar ready to 'plant' the *forte* tonic harmony on the first beat of b.23. Support the RH octave with a resonant spread LH chord, shoot down the scale with a flourish, and then feel that the two emphasised crotchets are 'going on' through the second half of b.34 to usher in the F minor melody of the middle section.

bb.35–47 Some players take this middle section at a pronouncedly slower tempo – mistakenly I feel, for two reasons: a) this strong 'lead in' implies a continuation of movement, which, even if slightly slower, must at least **relate** to the previous tempo; and b) this section, by the nature of its predominant minim tread (conveying the clear sense of a 2-in-the-bar swing) and crotchet accompaniment, can easily degenerate into a dragging plod. Let the RH enter in b.35 in full-throated *sostenuto* minims, as if 'taking over' from the previous upbeat crotchets and shape the melody line in a broad sweep up towards the minim C on the first beat of b.38. Note the important phrasing details: the 'break' in b.38, then the onward urging effect of the emphasised minim B natural, and similarly of the D flat on the third beat of b.40. Then carry on the phrase in an overall sweep from this D flat, feeling that the dotted crotchet and quaver in b.42 are leading on in an upbeat sense into the varied restatement from b.43.*

Practise the LH carefully alone, **feeling** the silent first beat of b.35 (and then of bb.37, 39, 41, etc.) so that you 'come in' rhythmically on the second beat. The *staccato* bass notes suggest the way that the hand should **spring** from the bass up to the chord on each third and first beat, creating a strongly rhythmic swing upon which the RH melody can ride. When you put hands together lead off confidently with your resonant RH minim C, bringing in the LH in such a way that this strong rhythmic swing will immediately establish itself securely when the hands 'join' on the third beat of the bar. Allow a little 'give' through the second half of b.42 ready to 'start again' (though without breaking the phrase curve) from b.43. There must be some elasticity in the pulse to accommodate the ornament through the second half of b.45, and a wider 'stretching' through the second half of b.48. In b.45 it is best to imagine the semibreve as a tied minim so that the repeated grace notes 'slide in' **after** the third beat (as suggested in the Vienna

Urtext Edition).  *etc.* Feel that the whole ornament

is, with a gentle impulse, 'going to' the minim C on the first beat of b.46. Then, starting the new phrase clearly with a warm 'lean' on the D natural on the third beat of the bar, allow a slight 'hold' on this note to let the sound clear a little ready for the lingering *subito piano* in b.47.

bb.48–66 Imagine again that the G on the third beat of b.48 is tied so that, in the *piano* context here, the ornament 'drifts' quietly in. Then, as already said, allowing a considerable 'give' in the pulse, let the high B natural coincide approximately with the bass G, and with a **suggestion** of a 'vocal' *tenuto* on this B flat, let the remaining

*Characteristic fingerings are marked in Jane Stirling's score:

notes 'fall' in a little flurry towards a quietly singing long tied C on the first beat

of b.49 (see General

Introduction under ''Free' Runs'). You could gradually pick up the tempo in the LH through bb.49-50, or play the LH more contemplatively through these bars, picking up the tempo from b.51. In any event, **listen** to the upper **and** to the minim line within the quiet progression of the LH beneath the held RH C, and give a definite onward lead with the RH quaver upbeat to b.51 as you prepare to move on in a warm-toned *forte*, making a *subito piano* echo effect in b.53. Then sing out the RH warmly as the voices 'divide' from the third beat of b.55, **holding** the resonance of the bass notes within the pedal through each bar as indicated, and spreading the RH broken chord generously on the first beat of b.58. The intended placing and nuance of this spread chord on the first beat of b.58 and then b.74 can be open to different interpretations (see General Introduction under 'Free Runs'). The essential is that it is spread easefully and sonorously, in a *piano* context, at b.58, and more full-throatedly at b.74.

It will be seen that each 8-bar section (bb.59-65, 66-75 and 75-82) is a varied version of bb.51-8. The run through b.61 can be divided approximately into groups of three, three, three and four notes (see General Introduction again). 'Lift' up to the high C with feather lightness, again as in b.48 allowing the hint of a hold on this top note. Then feel that you are moving on, 'led' by a steady but on-going LH towards b.62. Support the chain of RH trills with generous-toned spread chords in the LH, making sure that the full resonance of each LH chord is caught within the pedal. Play the prefix to the first trill **on** the beat (see General Introduction under 'Ornamentation'), with the main notes of the second and third trills starting on the beat thus:

Make a powerful *crescendo* towards b.64, being sure to lift the hand from a ringing crotchet C on the first beat of b.64 so that it 'falls' with strong emphasis on the D flat on the third beat – thus creating the effect of punctuating, but at the same time carrying on the melody line so that the *crescendo* 'peaks' on this D flat, sustained by a strong LH, with the resonance of the spread F minor chord held within the pedal through the bar.

bb.66–82   Keep up the full tone through to the end of this phrase, and then allow an extra instant through the third beat of b.66 as you prepare to drop the sound to a *mezzo voce* from the upbeat to b.67.* Let the triplets 'feather' in a little flurry up towards

*Sweep down to the lower D flat on the first beat of b.65 with a strong thumb (Chopin's fingering)

a quietly singing dotted minim A flat on the first beat of b.70. Through b.71 the run could be shaped in approximate groups of three, four, four and four, or three, three, four and five.

Lean well on a resonant minim sixth on the third beat of b.72, and then let the descending 'double-stopped' figure in triplets ring out fervently towards the spread chord in b.74. The RH passage through b.77 alarms many players. Providing that the LH is allowed to 'guide' the RH, it is very much less difficult than it appears. But what generally happens is that the LH panics in 'sympathy' with the RH, guaranteeing a mutual scrabble towards a nervous F minor chord on the first beat of b.78. Practise **slowly,** controlled by a rigorously steady LH, and maintaining a clear sense of the RH triplet rhythm within the crotchet pulse, and **using** the doubled triplet quavers, D natural and G, as little footholds as you ascend. While the LH admittedly must convey the sense of 'moving on' towards b.78, it must resolutely maintain the **sense** of the crotchet pulse. Indeed, throughout this middle section, although considerable elasticity of tempo is required, it is essential that the LH provides a continuing **sense** of the pulse (see General Introduction under *'Rubato'*).

The ♪ ̇ in b.78 is in effect the same as the ♫ ̇ in b.62. Draw out the first four notes of the run in b.81 as you 'lift' to the high C, and then let the remaining notes cascade downwards 'pointing' the last note, D flat, a little as you lead into a resonant chain of trills pedalled as indicated. Then allow a tiny give at the end of b.82, playing the suffix to the last trill quietly in the sense of the 'upbeat' to b.83, ready to set off blithely into the reprise. The fingering for the run in b.81, shown below, taken from the scores of two of his pupils, is a typical example of Chopin's principle of maintaining the hand in a compact and balanced position (see General Introduction under 'Fingering').

'Finish off' the reiterated figure (bb.113-14 and 116-17) to a quiet airy spread
bb.83–127   chord on the first beat of bb.115 and 119. Give this chord a short pedal as
indicated, making a clear break to show the quaver rest, and then play the chord sequences in a quietly breathed, smooth and rather solemn (or mock solemn) *sotto voce*, after the style of the *religioso* passage in the two Nocturnes in G minor, Op.15 No.3 and Op.37 No.1. Let the sound 'vanish' from the chord on the first beat of b.121, then play the diminishing chord sequences (bb.122-3, and 124-5) as if the 'thought' of the whole piece is disappearing into distant thin air, ending with scarcely breathed, but even tonic chords.

Impromptus Nos 2 and 3

As said above, both of these works contain considerable technical difficulties, and both are hard to hold together. Mere virtuosity is not enough. A sensitive ear is needed, a feeling for tone colour, and an appreciation of changes in mood and fluctuations of tempo. For performance both are, in my view, best left to the experienced artist. But it seems a pity that the relatively advanced domestic pianist should altogether miss all of the wonderful music that is here. For this reason both works are discussed below in greater detail than most of the music in the Very Advanced category.

No. 2 in F sharp major
Op. 36 (VA)

This is a work which has received, and continues to receive, a mixed press. With its strangely strung together sections, it is like a great brooding improvisation, in contrast with the relatively 'neat' ABA construction of Nos 1 and 3. The arrival of the march-like theme at b.39 is an extraordinary moment, and the sudden eruption of the flying demisemiquavers from b.82 scarcely less so. Huneker suggests that there is 'something sphinx-like' in its pose (p.134), and he and other commentators have suggested the possibility of an underlying programme. While this notion is in a general sense alien to Chopin's musical ethic, there is no doubt that this is a work which sets the imagination racing. There is an anticipation of strange events to come in the ambulatory LH 'ground' which persists through the first 30 bars, and these expectations are not disappointed. The transitions between the varying sections are effected through 'joins' that seem almost consciously awkward, particularly in the case of the tortuous (and much discussed) slide from D major to F major between bb.58 and 61. It is this stringing together of sections that are almost violently contrasted in climate that creates the impact – and the impact, like that of a disjointed, highly coloured dream-sequence, cannot be denied, whether or not it pleases some formalists. Chopin himself referred to this piece in a letter to his friend Fontana (10 October 1839) amidst instructions about new lodgings and new items for his wardrobe – 'An Impromptu which perhaps is poor; I don't know yet, it's too new. But I hope it's good; not like — — — (here various punning names) or a pig's or some other animal's, because by my reckoning it ought to bring me in at least 800 francs.' (Opienski, *Chopin's Letters*).

bb.1–30   The LH crotchet ground moves in even, 6-bar cycles of 'walking' crotchets through bb.1-30. It seems to be quietly circling or prowling as it rises from the bass tonic and progresses through repetitive little fragments, with rather the flavour of a half-tune, towards a half-close on the dominant in b.6, ready to start the next 'cycle' in b.7. Many and various are the tempos adopted by different players, and also of the tempos of each section in relation to the individual Tempo 1. Although Chopin marked no tempo changes, there is a general and probably inevitable tendency to play slower from b.30, slower again from b.39, and slower still from b.82. In any event, it is a mistake, I believe, to play the opening section too slowly, or it loses its 'walking' movement, and begins to drag. (The fact that Chopin wavered between a **4/4** and an *alla breve* suggests that he wanted the sense of movement that a ¢ conveys). Some editions, including Henle, give a **4/4**. Others a ¢. For the sake of clarity I have, as in Impromptu No. 1, adopted **4/4**. Cortot in his reissued recording adopts a nicely moving tempo of about ♩= 116. And despite his customary fluctuations (not to mention arms, rather than fists, full of wrong notes from bb.47-58), his overall speed remains satisfyingly closer to his Tempo 1 than that of most players.

In view of the extended octave passage from b.47, those with very small hands are unlikely to be embarking upon this piece, but if necessary, it is better, as Jan Ekier suggests in the Vienna Urtext Edition, to take the upper D sharp (in bb.1, 2, etc.) with the RH, rather than to 'break' the ninth. Cultivate a gliding smoothness, as if walking in a dream. Place the opening bass octave with a quiet resonance, and then feel the 'lift' up to the D sharp on the second crotchet beat of b.1 so that you create the sense of a broad arc with the notes then 'falling' by step from the high D sharp, ready for another, smaller 'lift' from the A sharp on the first beat of b.2, and then with a gradual 'terracing' downwards, towards b.4. Arrive as if a little quizically on the upper minim G sharp in b.4, to continue evenly, but 'speakingly' through the two-bar 'tag' bb.5-6, as the lower line walks calmly on. Listen acutely, as you establish this ground (bb.1-6), to the constantly shifting intervals between the two voices. Then allow a little give through the end of b.6, ready to 'start again' as the RH joins in b.7. I say 'joins in' advisedly, for the RH enters as a third voice, albeit a quietly predominant one, rather than as a solo riding over a subordinate accompaniment. Be sure to preserve the shape of the LH as the RH phrase curves up to the C sharp on the third beat of b.8, and 'terraces' smoothly down again towards b.10.

Listen acutely again to the intervals between the hands through bb.14-16, the RH B sharp against the LH D double sharp in b.14, and again, as you shape the eloquent little offbeat RH fragments expressively, to the sharp momentary clash of the RH D sharp with the LH E in bb.15 and 16, and so on. Through the runs of bb.17 and 29 it is essential that the LH guides any necessary slight drawing out of the pulse (see General Introduction under ''Free' Runs'). The prevalent sense of the 'lift' in the LH up to the second crotchet beat, approximately corresponding to the octave lift from the lower to the high RH A sharp in b.17 (and similarly in b.29) is important to the overall shape here. Thus the pulse will be allowed to do most of its drawing out around the **second** crotchet beat as the RH 'lifts' up to the higher octave with the barest hint of a 'vocal' *tenuto* on the high A. Through the remainder of b.17 the pulse then moves on gradually towards the resumption of Tempo 1 in b.18. In b.29 the case is rather different in that the pulse through the second half of the bar must prepare for any degree of alteration of tempo from b.30 drawing out to a greater or lesser degree through the last beat of the bar. In b.17 the RH obviously matches the LH in groups of five notes to the crotchet. In b.29 I prefer this approximate grouping

to that given by J. Petrie Dunn (6+6+6+5 – see p.58).

bb.30–61   Once again it is, in my view, a mistake to play too slowly from here. The dominant-based chord sequences are like beckoning horn-calls, drawing player and listener on towards the D major march from b.39. At too slow a tempo these figures become ponderous and overtly portentious rather than expectant. Feel the sense of 'carrying on through' the end of b.29 towards fairly resonant crotchets on the first beat of b.30 and, holding the sound of this 'wide-apart fifth' with the pedal, leap up to place the tied dominant seventh chord with a little 'lean' as indicated, and in such a way that you immediately establish your renewed (or new) tempo. And be sure to **feel** the tied third beat of bb.30, 31, etc, maintaining a secure sense of the crotchet pulse as you **listen** to the smooth melodic movement of the treble and inner LH voices within the dominant-based chord sequences. Draw out markedly through b.38 to 'crouch' mysteriously through the pause on the dotted quaver chord on the fourth beat, then feeling the semiquaver octave as the upbeat to the new rhythm as you prepare to launch into the march tempo. (Few players, of however limited an imagination, can fail to evoke a shiver at this moment of 'casting off' into D major.) Initiate the 'tread' in a mysterious and distant *pianissimo* that is at the same time compellingly rhythmic. For this is an implacable, iron-shod march, with the 'rigid' *ostinato*, as Jim Samson says, 'anticipating such later glories as the Trio of the A flat major Polonaise' (p.97). Let the LH mark this tread in a relentlessly accurate dotted rhythm beneath, at first, quietly resonant RH chords. Shape the long *crescendo* with deadly aim, listening acutely to the balance between the hands so that you arrive with stentorian resonance at b.51, still leaving a little reserve of tone in order to 'peak' the *crescendo* at bb.54-5. Always feel the LH semiquaver as the **upbeat** to the subsequent dotted quaver so that the semiquavers always have the sense of 'going to' the dotted quavers.

Phase the *descrescendo* carefully from b.55, taking care to keep the LH rhythm steady beneath the RH 5-quaver group through the second half of b.57, and then drawing out as indicated through b.58 (pedalling each crotchet beat as indicated here) towards the problematic bb.59-60. Have a clear sense of where you are going (i.e. to F major) as you **listen** to the movement of both RH voices through bb.59-60, using the sustained sound of the LH B's as a pivot as you ease towards the six-four F major chord in b.61.

bb.61–82   The tempo of this section is problematic, particularly in terms of the negotiation of the next 'join' into b.82. Some players, regaining an approximate Tempo 1 from b.61, make a pronounced *rallentando* and *diminuendo* through bb.79-81 and, ignoring Chopin's *forte*, 'drift' into b.82 in an ethereal *pianissimo* in a considerably slower crotchet pulse. While this allows a convincing and effective join, Chopin appears, on the other hand, to intend a gradual **overall** *crescendo* from the *pianissimo* at b.61 towards the *forte* at b.82 (see the *crescendos*, bb.67-8, and 72-4). One solution is to play the whole section rather slower than in Tempo 1, merging from b.60 into b.61 in a dreamy *pianissimo*, and maintaining the slower tempo as you build up the resonance in a finely graded overall *crescendo*. You will then be approaching *forte* as you arrive at b.79, swelling the sound luxuriantly as the music hangs around the dominant (a foretaste of Rachmaninov here) and drawing out a little through b.81 ready to 'take off' in b.82. In any event create the smoothest possible line from b.61, over the softly-wafted (rather than 'notey') triplet outline of the original LH ground.†

bb.82–110   Few players would want to attempt a tempo of much more than $\bullet$ = 88 here on a modern piano – the *forte-leggiero* effect would have been easier both for the fingers and for the ear on the earlier instruments. It is important to realise that the flight of RH demisemiquavers is governed by the rhythmic impulse and harmonic and melodic progressions of the LH. Study the LH meticulously, therefore, so that its shape is thoroughly absorbed: the line of the doubled lower notes through each bar, the syncopating 'lean' on the dotted crotchet on the sixth quaver of bb.82 and 83, and similarly on the dotted crotchet fifth in b.84, and so on. The rhythmic impulse of each of these bars towards this 'lean' on the sixth quaver pulse balances the RH curve as it descends from its peak on the third crotchet of the bar (the pulse here becomes more of **4/4** than a ¢). Aim for the kind of articulation in the RH that creates a brilliant but shining smooth 'zoom', up to and down from the peak on the third beat of each bar. Ensure that the *crescendo* through the first half of bb.82 and 83 'returns to base', through the second half of the bar, with a longer *crescendo* from b.84, *diminuendoing* from the middle of b.86. It is effective to 'start again' in *pianissimo* from b.88, as marked by Chopin in the copy belonging to his pupil, Camille O'Meara-Dubois. The difficult bars (94-7) are much facilitated if the RH allows itself to be guided by the articulation of the LH and the naturally arising, slightly syncopating leans on slurred figures, etc. Let the sound trail away upwards from b.98, *diminuendoing* to a barely touched final high arabesque through the end of b.100, and 'lifting' the sound into thin air from the high quaver C sharp on the first beat of b.101. Then the returning chord sequences could be played in a more 'distant' *pianissimo* than previously, ending with a full and commanding but not coarse-toned octave and chord.

†In the copy belonging to Jane Stirling there are various pedal indications through this section: the pedal is cancelled on the third beat of b.61 with a similar marking in b.67, and a pedal change is marked on the third beat of b.73. This, in the light of the printed indications in bb.1, 7, etc, could be taken to suggest the idea of a pedal change on first and third beats **in general** through bb.1-29 and bb.61-81, allowing for more detailed pedalling when the harmonic movement is more defined (e.g. through bb.10-12, 15-18, 69-72, 77-81, etc.).

No. 3 in G flat major (VA)

This is an extremely deceptive piece. Lacking the obvious relatively virtuosic features of No.2, it seems at first sight to be comparatively easy in a technical sense. But there are concealed difficulties. The LH through bb.3-5 is far from easy to coordinate smoothly with the closely detailed inflections of the RH, and this coordination is, of course, doubly difficult from b.11, when the 'double-stopped' variant in the RH in itself demands technical artistry of a high order. The tone of the piece is also elusive and ambiguous, often straying into those areas of refined, other-wordly abstraction characteristic of Chopin's later work. Much, of course, depends upon the tempo. It appears that Chopin changed his original indication *Tempo Giusto*, to *Allegro Vivace* and finally *Vivace* (see the Vienna Urtext and Paderewski editions, and the Critical Commentaries in these editions and in Henle). In this context *Vivace* seems to imply a smoothly fluent kind of fleetness – not so fast as to endanger the *legato* of the long phrase-lines, nor to lose the subtle shading of the RH in combination with the airy lightness of the LH. Many players anxious no doubt to reveal these delights, adopt such a sober tempo that the feeling becomes at best ruminative, and at worst turgid, rather than *vivace*. Once again Cortot, at a tempo of about ♩. = 126-30, seems to find the right kind of easy fluency, like a light-spirited, subtly inflected conversation, with plenty of give and take, allowing room to breathe, and for light-touched punctuation and variety of emphasis. This tempo, however, is one which few players will care to emulate.

bb.1–10   Apart from the *crescendo* through bb.1-2, there are no dynamic indications of any kind until the further *crescendo* at b.17. The introductory solo quavers, however, should surely enter 'on a breath', curving up in a graceful arc, and allowing a little 'give' through the end of b.2 ready to launch into the principal motif in b.3. Let the LH join in with a carefully placed bass crotchet on the first beat of b.3, as the RH leads off in smooth curves, as if engaged in urbane chat, supported by the lightly and smoothly sprung, more 'bobbing' curves of the LH quavers. This LH, as already said, is far from easy, and will need to be practised carefully alone, and then **slowly** in combination with the RH so that the relationship between the hands is thoroughly understood in an aural sense (particularly in such niceties as the passing discordant effects through the fourth beat of b.4, and the second and third beats of b.6, and so on). As the melody line enters a new phase at b.7, 'point' the tied dotted crotchet G flat a little with a nice melodic 'lean' on the first beat, and then feel that the RH quavers are curving onwards towards another 'lean' on the B flat on the first beat of b.8 and so on. Listen acutely to the inner and lower held resonances as the voices divide through b.7. Listen again to the harmonic inflections of the LH through bb.8-9, beneath the rising RH line, feeling that each LH quaver group is 'going to' the quietly resonant chord on the subsequent second or fourth beats. Allow a nice 'give' through the second half of b.9 as you trail the treble quavers upwards in a detached, 'speaking' manner as indicated, and then gather yourself through b.10 ready to 'start again' in b.11.

bb.11–48   To avoid a bumpy ride from here, the fingering will have to be carefully worked out for the individual hand, with eventually a **light** skim of pedal to help smoothness. Make full use too of the punctuating 'leans' in the treble line on the dotted crotchet on the first beat of b.12 and the tied quaver upbeat to bb.13, 14, etc. Draw out a little again as you rise in *crescendo* through the second half of b.17, this time in melodically chiming sixths. Allow the treble voice to 'take a breath' in the quaver rest near the end of b.18, ready to lead on from the quaver upbeat to b.19 in a new, more reflective tone, letting the RH trail downwards dreamily through b.19 in a 'halo' of pedal. Allow another little 'give' at the end of b.20 to clear the sound for an exquisite *pianissimo* in b.21. Spreading the RH chord generously on the first beat of bb.23-5, **listen** to the effect of the held inner RH G and LH A through these bars within the quiet play of the treble and LH quavers. At b.32 a more sober train of thought obtrudes and takes over. Curve the LH line of bb.33 and 34 expressively down through the first three beats, and up again to the E flat on the fourth beat beneath the more sustained RH, and play the chord fragments through bb.35-6, 39-40, etc. in a quiet, smooth, '*religioso*' style rather as in the chord sequence near the end of Impromptu No.1. Note Chopin's consecutive use of the thumb through the inner RH chromatically descending fragments through bb.37 and 38 (see General Introduction under 'Fingering'). Lifting with a feather-light leap up to the high octave at the end of b.38, let the sound hang in the air for an instant through the pause. Then feel the airy whimsicality of the upward flights of the detached treble quavers through bb.41, 43 and 45.

bb.48–105   As the RH 'finishes off' cleanly at the beginning of b.48, let the LH 'take over' and lead on, in the sense of a long, overall upbeat group, into the new melody from b.49. There is an inevitable slight broadening of the tempo through this middle section as the music moves into an *alla breve* (or **4/4**). However, I believe that this should not be too pronounced – this is one of Chopin's most ardently romantic melodies, and ardour does not plod. In addition, this melody needs to grow, as if 'flowering' from the first section, rather than being slotted in as a 'new' separate section. Let the melody 'cast off' in a smooth warmly expressive descending line, supported and 'urged on' by carefully balanced offbeat RH triplets. Articulate the curving quavers eloquently through b.51, and 'finish off' the 4-bar melodic phrase cleanly on the dominant (of E flat minor) on the third beat of b.52, ready to lead off again from the upbeat to b.53. Allow time to savour the delicate fragments of treble counterpoint through b.53 and b.54, and then, as you carry this second 4-bar phrase down to the dotted quaver on the third beat of b.56, make it clear that you are 'leading on' from the semiquaver B flat, treating the 🎵 as an upbeat group to b.57. Let the repeated crotchet G flats sing out with warm resonance through b.57, allowing a little extra time for the 5-note turn to 'speak' expressively as it curves up to the B flat, feeling this dotted quaver B flat (and similarly the C flat in b.59) as the 'crest' of this 2-bar melodic curve. Keep the melody moving as you span the wide melodic sweep from b.61 down to the B flat on the third beat of b.64 ready to lead on with increasing fervour from the upbeat to b.65, to reach a glorious fullness of sound from b.69, allowing time to listen to the marvellous inflections through b.70. Let the sound gradually subside from b.71, feeling the quiet tolling quality of the repeated crotchet B flat on the second beat of bb.72-4. Listen also to the inflections of the RH offbeat triplets 'against' these LH crotchets, in particular 'pointing' the upper F flat a little in b.74. This soft emphasis on the second crotchet B flat in each of these bars creates the effect of a 'lean' carrying the phrase on into the subsequent bar, again in the nature of a long overall upbeat group. Feel a 'lift' from the second B flat in b.74 like an upward *portamento* to the C flat, then drawing out the triplets through b.75, and 'pointing' the strange resonance of the sustained RH interjection, as you gather yourself to set off again into the reprise from b.75.

Tail the sound away on a breath towards the wide-distanced D flats on the first beat of b.103, and then end in full-throated chords, spreading the final chord with a grand resonance.

Fantaisie-Impromptu
Op.Posth. 66 (8+)

This much-played piece was published after Chopin's death by his friend Fontana. It was written in 1835, before the first of the Impromptus, Op.29, and it is presumed that Fontana added the 'Fantaisie' to the title. It is not known why Chopin did not publish it during his lifetime. Since it is treated dismissively by most commentators on numerous counts (weak construction, repetitiveness, effeteness and lack of direction in the middle section, general frivolity, and so on) it has been widely assumed that Chopin suppressed it because he also thought poorly of it. Arthur Hedley on the other hand, suggests that Chopin was embarrassed by its resemblance to a recently published Impromptu by Moscheles (pp.155-6). Whatever the reason for its suppression by Chopin, no amount of high-toned critical opinion has dimmed, nor will dim, its perennial popularity – there can be few Chopin lovers who did not thrill at an early age to the rush of its effervescent semiquavers. Indeed, writing as long ago as 1900, Huneker remarks that 'it is the joy of the Piano Student, who turns its Presto into a slow, blurred mess of badly related rhythms, and its slower movement into a long-drawn sentimental agony' (p.135). He nicely sums up the problems of the piece. However, while nothing is more awful than a blunderbuss attack on the cross-rhythms by rhythmless players, it is, on the other hand, a lovely show-piece (and an excellent 'learning' piece as well) for a young student with nimble fingers and a keen sense of rhythm.

Both Henle and the Vienna Urtext Edition give two versions of the piece in their volume of Impromptus. Henle prints a version based on an autograph discovered by the late Arthur Rubinstein, and then gives the Fontana version. Vienna Urtext's first version is similarly based on the Rubinstein autograph. Then in an Appendix they print a version based on contemporary copies, referred to by Jan Ekier, the editor, as a 'cleaned up version which matches the sources and dispenses with Fontana's modifications'. Among many interesting divergences are the differently inflected (and more difficult) LH in Rubinstein's autograph version (bb.13-24), the extra LH resonance through bb.35-7, and different indications of phrasing in the middle section. However, the comments below refer to the Fontana version, since this is the 'traditional' and familiar version given in most editions (including Henle again in their Chopin 'Album'. Major divergencies will be mentioned in context and, for the sake of simplicity, the versions are referred to as R (Rubinstein) and F (Fontana).

bb.1–8
F gives a metronome mark of ♩ = 84, which is apparently not original. While this tempo may be on the ambitious side for the student player, this is a piece which does need to move. At much below about ♩ = 76 the 'works' begin to show, i.e. the cross-rhythms start to grind along like two separate machines turning at different speeds instead of fusing together in an exciting overall rhythmic effect.

Strike the opening *sforzato* octave with a full-toned resonance, with your tempo already well 'in the system', so that you **feel** the two-in-the-bar pulse as you **listen** to the sustained unison sound through bb.1-2. Following this opening *sforzato*, many editions give a *forte* on the quaver octave on the first beat of b.3, and then a *decrescendo* towards a *piano* entry of the RH at b.5, and this works well in practice. R, on the other hand, gives a *forte* on the opening octave, with a hairpin *decrescendo*, and an *fz piano* on the first beat of b.3. In any event, while giving the opening tied octave its full value, feel at the same time a strong onward 'lean', feeling this resonating dominant unison like a long upbeat towards the first beat of b.3. Then, having **felt** the two-in-the-bar pulse through bb.1-2, **establish** it securely from the first beat of b.3 as you *decrescendo* in a tonic 'shimmer' towards the first beat of b.5. It is essential to realise that it is the LH which 'sets', impels and controls the rhythm right through the outer (and indeed also the middle) sections; and to understand that the brilliant RH tracery is dependent on the secure LH foundation, and **not** the other way around. It is suggested, therefore, that the LH is studied thoroughly first by itself through bb.5-8 until it is perfectly fluent. Feel the quavers in even threes within the overall sextuplets so that you progress in smooth 'arcs' from bass note to top note within each half-bar group. (These groups of three, i.e. the bass and top notes, are accented in R.) It is extremely important in both a rhythmic and harmonic sense that the bass 'line' C sharp-E/ C sharp-E/ D sharp-F sharp/ G sharp-G sharp/ etc. is always clear and perfectly rhythmic.

When you practise the RH, be very sure always to **feel** the beat on the semiquaver rest at the beginning of bb.5-7 so that you enter in perfect time and without a bump on the offbeat. (You could **play** the LH quaver on each first beat at first.) Then feel the rhythmic impulse towards the D sharp on the second main beat and, rising towards the high G sharp, come **off** with a little 'flick' that sends the hand back to start again in b.6, and so on. (R gives a hairpin *crescendo* through to the end of each of bb.5 and 6.) Feel a swell through the first half of b.7 towards the high B on the second main beat of the bar, and a *decrescendo* down again from this point, ready to 'start again' in b.9.

When you put hands together be sure to point the LH quaver a little on the first beat of bb.5-7 so that you give a little springboard for the offbeat entry of the RH. Then feel you are 'going to' the next little rhythmic 'foothold' i.e. on the second main beat of b.5, and then on to the next on the first beat of b.6, and so on. The join between bb.7-8 is a danger point. The LH has to be perfectly confident in its leap down to a clear dominant G sharp on the first beat of b.8 (allowing just a fraction of extra time to span this wide interval) so that it can support the long downward run of the RH. If the LH misses the G sharp, the RH inevitably collapses and there is a general scrabble through b.8 towards home at b.9. Allow the tiniest 'give' at the end of b.8 as you 'point' the tied RH upbeat (this is accented in R), poising yourself to set off again from b.9. It is suggested that these four bars are practised over and over without stopping (i.e. 'going on' through b.9 and then back to b.6) until you attain sufficient fluency and speed to achieve the rhythmic 'fusion' mentioned above. Practise slowly at first thinking in a crotchet pulse. Then as you are able to increase speed, switch over to an overall feeling of two-in-the-bar. Those who are 'thrown' by the offbeat RH entry can practise

at first:

Assuming a *decrescendo* through bb.3-4, the RH should ideally enter 'on a breath' in b.5. The little *crescendo* through bb.5 and 6 as given in R promotes the *agitato* effect, dropping to a 'breath' again at the beginning of b.6, and again at b.7. R accents the first RH semiquaver in b.7, implying a rather fuller tone as you begin the *crescendo* here. Aim overall for a 'shooting star' brilliance of the RH semiquavers, that is, the kind of articulation that is both brilliant and smooth.

Point the little 'signpost' towards the dominant minor, the A sharps in the first *bb.9-24* half of b.10, *crescendo* rather more purposefully through b.11 and then cascade almost recklessly downwards through b.12 ready to launch into the thumb melody from b.13. (This is the effect suggested by the RH accents on each crotchet beat in R, rather than the daintier *diminuendo* in F.) The emphases from b.13 vary in the different versions. In F the thumb line is **accented** in a *forte* dynamic

 with a drop to *piano* at b.17 with the

accentuations transferred to the offbeat top notes.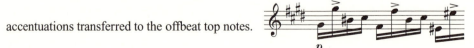

Then there is a *crescendo* from the second half of b.18 towards *forte* in the second half of b.19, and a *decrescendo* dropping to *pianissimo* at b.23. R on the other hand, defines the thumb

melody line by 'doubling' the semiquavers  right through

from bb.13-24, pressing on in a *sempre più animato* from b.17, with a *poco ritenuto* through b.24. In the version in the Vienna Urtext Edition Appendix there is no marking of this thumb-line melody. Whichever option you choose, launch into b.13 with full-throated (but controlled!) abandon and, having dropped to *piano* in b.17, rise to a *forte* peak on the second main beat of b.19, feeling a sense of moving on as you *decrescendo* from b.20. Take an extra instant at the end of b.22, to poise yourself to drop to a ravishing *subito piano* in b.23, and then allowing some 'give' through b.24 as you 'gather yourself' to start again from b.25. As mentioned above, in R the LH from bb.13-24 is differently notated:

instead of

Beginning a gradual *crescendo* from the second half of b.29, take care to keep
bb.24–41 the LH steady, and to ensure that the LH gives a sufficiently resonant and 'controlling' support to the RH, otherwise the rising semiquavers will 'strangle'

themselves. The slight 'pointing' of the LH quaver on the first beat of b.31 when the RH once again 'enters' on the offbeat, and a steady and confident leap down to the B sharp on the second main beat of b.32, will have the effect of a touch on the brake, thereby avoiding the tendency to run away through this passage. Take care too to control the dynamic rise so that you reach fullest tone at b.35 and not before. The differences between F and R in bb.35-42 are shown below.

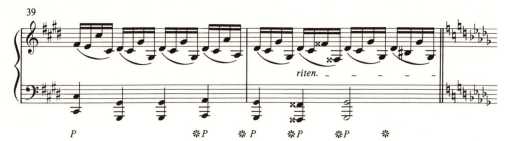

There is no doubt that the syncopating effect of the powerful sustained LH chords in R reinforces the *con forza* scale with more immediate and dramatic impact. On the other hand, others might prefer the stark 'arrival' on the bass unison G sharps on the first beat of b.37 as in F. Then through bb.37-9 the tumultuous descent has perhaps more bite in R with the RH appoggiatura effect resolving to unisons, than the more harmonious resolution in F. Whichever version you choose, arrive on a resolute short six-four chord on the first beat of b.35, allowing time to leap up so that you can **poise** the RH to launch into the long descending scale with maximum bite and brilliance, supported by a powerfully resonant LH chord, whether placed as in F or R. In either version feel that you are, if anything, *crescendoing* as you descend, arriving (in F) on the most powerful possible unison quavers on the first beat of b.37. Then holding the G sharps within the pedal as indicated, leap up as if in a wide arc (rather than 'snatching') and underpin the cascading RH semiquavers with powerful octaves to create a torrent of tonic sound as you descend.* Having 'arrived at the bottom' in b.39, players tend mistakenly to flag as they move through bb.39-40. Carry on through these two bars and on into b.41, drawing out a little in luxuriant fullness of tone as Chopin clearly intended (in R the *fortissimo* in b.41 makes this intention even more obvious) only making a *diminuendo* through b.42.

bb.41–82   Following on from the above, a clear rhythmic momentum must be maintained through the triplet quaver arpeggios of bb.41-2 towards the middle section. It is this triplet-sextuplet movement which carries the melody of the **middle** section, as it carries the RH semiquavers in the **outer** section, thereby providing a connecting rhythmic impulse through the entire piece. Thus the tempo of the middle section, although slower, must still **relate** to the tempo of the outer section, as if the RH is about to show a different **aspect** of the overall train of the thought that is carried on by the LH quavers. The degree of 'drawing out' that must take place through bb.41-2 is therefore crucial – it must seem as if a fairly strong 'brake' is being applied, maintaining the sense of the overall two-in-the-bar pulse towards a continuation in a lower (but not too much lower) gear from b.43. In R the *sostenuto* and

*Practise this descent at first in chords – together WITH the LH octaves:

Then practise in dotted rhythms:

complementary *con anima*, both straddling the barline between bb.42-3, admirably pre-empts the unhappy tendency to wilt progressively from b.43 into that 'long drawn sentimental agony' referred to above.*

Let the RH melody 'take off' therefore in a lightly singing, soft and expressive but not sickly tone from b.43, supported by quietly billowing LH quavers which never 'forget' their rhythmic impulse in threes within the sextuplet groups. Shape the melody in an overall vocal curve up towards the minim A flat on the second main beat of b.44 (this note is emphasised in R; note also the long phrase-line) and down again through b.45, with a slight lingering on the dotted quaver F on the fourth beat as you prepare to 'fall' to the A flat on the first beat of b.46. Then, making a warm-toned 'lean' on the tied minim B flat, feel this note as an 'on-and-over' bridge into b.47, leading on into the second half of this songful, overall eight-bar melody.

'Turn' the grace notes expressively in b.49, starting the turn on, or just after, the fifth LH quaver, and allowing just a tiny 'give' through the second LH triplet group as you 'go towards' a slight 'lean' on the dotted crotchet F. **Listen**, as in the first section, to the line of the bass quavers, and fill out the RH melody by subtly 'pointing' the implied LH inner line from the

high A flat in b.44  and similarly

the implied offbeat upper LH line through b.48. (The *ritenuto* and *a tempo* in bb.50-51 are absent in R.) The differences in the two versions in dynamics and the notation of the run in b.60 are shown below.

However you may decide to time this run in b.60 it is essential that while the LH may draw out a little through the end of the bar, particularly in the R version, it must do so **rhythmically**, and maintaining the forward impulse with the feeling that the RH is fitting in with the LH and **not**

---

*Again in this middle section the two versions vary in a number significant harmonic and melodic details.

the other way around. The simplest approximate spacing is

or

(See General Introduction under ''Free' Runs'.) Ensure also that the RH 'goes to' a clear minim on the first beat of b.61 (in a simulated 'slur' down from the previous high A flat), picking up the tempo immediately in the LH in b.61.

Allow a fractional 'hold' through the second LH triplet of b.62 as you bring the RH off (see General Introduction under 'Articulation') ready to 'point' the *subito piano* on the second main beat as you prepare to lead back into the restatement. (This *subito piano* is absent in R.) As you approach the end of the section tail the sound away though as you *ritenuto* through b.82, ready to set off again from b.83.

bb.83–138 Press on in an exultant full tone from b.119. Once again the LH is different in F and R. In F, the more difficult version here, the LH switches to 'straight' quavers against the offbeat RH emphases. Keep the LH rock-steady, but with a clear curve up to and down from the second quaver of each group. This creates the hint of an

upper LH 'line'  whereby this

slightly emphasised upper note provides a syncopating rhythmic 'anchor' throughout the

passage. It helps to practise thus:

(In R the LH continues in the pattern from

b.119 and there are various differences in the RH notation between bb.123-6.) Feel a sense of moving on from b.125, as you tail the sound away towards b.129 ready for the LH to enter with a distant, *pianissimo* horn-like bass fifth. Then shape the LH melody line in a soft velvet-toned curve up towards the emphasised semibreve G sharp in b.132, then gradually subsiding to a whisper as the line falls towards b.136. The awkward lower LH E sharp in b.135 may have to be taken with the LH, but even then is difficult to manage unobtrusively. In R this note is (mercifully!) replaced by a G sharp. Tail the sound away as you slow through b.136, and spread the final chords evenly on a *pianissimo* breath. In R the final tonic is not spread.

THE RONDOS

Of Chopin's four Rondos, three were written before he left Warsaw, that is, before the age of 20. The fourth, Op.16, was apparently also begun in Warsaw and finished later after he had settled in Paris. Scholars tend to treat these essays dismissively. However, while no one could suggest that they contain great music, much of the material has that open, fresh air quality characteristic of the best of Chopin's early music, and there are patches of fun to be had even in Op.1, and a great deal more in Ops 5 and (Posth.) 73. As Jim Samson has pointed out, the instrumental rondo of Chopin's day was influenced by the manner of the *opera buffa*, and it is surely in this spirit that these pieces should be enjoyed. As has been urged in the General Introduction, we should not forget that despite his precocious talent, Chopin was a young man of the most normal, or even particularly high spirits, addicted to caricature, mimicry and high jinks of all kinds. And although real humour seems rather rare in his music, there are occasional hints of parody in some of his early pieces (as has been noted in the case of the Polonaise in B flat, Op.71 No.2, and the Polonaise in G flat), and certainly of sheer artless exuberance, as for example in some of the very early Mazurkas and in the three Ecossaises. It is when Chopin is encumbered with the demands of a fixed formal framework (such as the large set-piece bravura rondo fashionable at the time, as opposed to the other large forms which even in the case of the Sonata he was able to 'interpret' in his own fashion) that he grows tedious – grinding from Section A to Section B and so on through lengthy sequences of modulating passage-work. And it is in the E flat Rondo, Op.16, that the grinding of this 'dutiful' passage-work has taken over to the extent that it appears to have become an end in itself.

Each piece is built around a principal theme of a dance-like nature, and in each the technical demands are considerable (in the case of Ops 16 and 73, formidable). In any case, the kind of virtuosic 'padding' that is endemic to this type of keyboard showpiece needs to be thrown off with the highest virtuosity. Their appeal is therefore necessarily limited either to the serious student of Chopin's style, or to the enterprising virtuoso in search of the occasional programme novelty. All four are in the virtuoso category, and only brief notes are therefore given below, although it must be urged that Op.5, and certainly Op.73 in its second two-piano version, are worthy of more than the very infrequent airings they in fact receive.

Note: The four Rondos (including both the solo and two-piano version of Op.73) are published in the Paderewski Edition Volume XII. The notes below are based on this edition of these works. At the time of writing (1997) these works have not been published in the Henle or Vienna Urtext Editions. But Ops 1, 5 and 16 are published by Peters in Volume 2 of their Complete Works, and they also publish Op.73 in the two-piano version.

Rondo in C minor
Op. 1 (VA)

This was written in 1825 when Chopin was 15, probably somewhat later than the Polonaise in G sharp minor, which nevertheless is the more successful both as a composition and also in the sense in which Chopin 'adorns' the keyboard. This is the shortest of the Rondos, and also the lightest in terms of technical demands. In another sense, though, it is this lightness and transparency that makes the passage-work particularly demanding. The principal motif (bb.5-12) with its awkward quick turns in bb.5-7 etc, has an exuberant bumpiness, like a jerky wooden-legged dance. Chopin cannot have meant to be serious here, and the introductory bars should surely be played tongue-in-cheek, like a stilt-walk leading in to the bumpy ride from b.5. The tempo needs at least to approach the ♩ = 108, with rhythmically spaced LH quaver chords from b.5 maintaining a springing but steady controlling 'brake' on the capers of the RH. And the ensuing increasingly high-pitched passage-work following on from b.29 through to b.65 needs to be kept clean and light-toned (even when approaching *forte*) rather than tending to grow Beethovenian.

The slower and more suave second theme from b.65, in E major, is still dance-like, with also an operatic flavour, and here again the LH needs to control the RH ornaments and little roulades within a neatly spaced quaver 'step'. At b.81 Chopin sidesteps into one of his occasional episodes of almost Mendelssohnian solemnity, followed from b.100 by passages of ostentatious flourishes (bb.100-101, 104-5, etc.) alternating with sequences of smooth-spinning semiquavers (bb.102-3, 106-7, etc.).

The third and central theme in A flat from b.130 returns to Tempo 1, with a constantly repeated dotted rhythm melodic figure 'urged on' by a billowing LH accompaniment of sextuplet semiquavers. (This tempo seems inordinately fast here.) Reaching a *forte* at b.147 this motif is then gradually 'dispersed' over a long dominant pedal point (of the home key) towards high *pianissimo* octaves (bb.155-7) which set the scene for the return of the principal theme. From b.213 Chopin embarks on a new, somewhat mundane theme in D flat, rather akin to the 'Mendelssohnian' episode from b.81, but here buoyed along by arcing semiquaver scale-work, which in turn gives way to some mellifluous, rather Lisztian arpeggiations from b.243. Following the return of the second theme from b.275, a neat insertion (from bb.307-17) of the dominant pedal point passage heard at bb.147-58, brings us to the final appearance of the principal theme from b.318. Instead of launching into the grandiose coda that he appears to be about to announce from b.350, Chopin leads quaintly, if rather lamely towards the final chords with a quiet little drum-beat motif (springing from nowhere) through bb.354-5.

Rondo à la Mazur
Op. 5 (VA)

Seldom has Chopin worn his heart more plainly on his sleeve than here. The opening unison motif, with its quietly insistent affirmation of the Lydian sharpened fourth (the B naturals in bb.1 and 3) could as well form the introduction to one of his later Mazurkas; and the persistent rhythmic and harmonic figures of the two principal themes (bb.5-8 etc. and 93-6 etc.) have an irresistible and catchy freshness, and are equally typical. Were it only half as long, and not encumbered with the 'obligatory' bravura passage-work (although as Jim Samson says, this is to some degree 'contained'), it would stand as a wholly delightful Polish pot-pourri. While the piece as a whole is highly exacting, less advanced players may well like to investigate the thematic material of the main sections.

Considerable problems of tempo arise. One feels the need for a somewhat faster tempo than the given $\downarrow$ = 132. However, the detail and expressive intent of the first main theme, in its harmonised form from b.4 (and certainly of the second from b.93) can lose its inherent slight rhythmic 'jolt', and grow too streamlined if the tempo is **too** fast. On the other hand, the fleeter and, by the same token the lighter-spirited the passage-work from bb.123, 328 and 432, the less tedious does it appear. There is therefore the need for considerable flexibility, as indeed in the case of the Mazurka proper. The first section (bb.1-36) is built upon the motif of the four introductory bars. This unison introduction needs to 'emerge' in a low-breathed *sotto voce*, articulated in a 'slidingly' smooth, even furtive, style that is at the same time immaculately clear and rhythmic. Follow the phrase marks meticulously, arriving at b.5 in such a way that the treble statement of the theme grows on naturally from the slurred

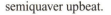

semiquaver upbeat.  Then this theme can 'dance' as jauntily

as possible over a rather bouncy, immaculately rhythmic LH. The articulation and phrase indications, which are very precise, are essential to this jaunty character. Note particularly the implied emphasis on the dotted crotchet B natural on the second beat of bb.5, 9, etc, and the dashing triplet slide up to these B naturals in bb.13 and 15. There is a nice insouciance, too, to the tied crotchet and 'tailing off' semiquaver figures through bb.35 and 36.

There is a sense of moving on from b.37, while at the same time capitalising on the operatic absurdity of the *scherzando* figures from this point. This operatic sense continues through the *lusingando* figures from b.53 which evokes all kinds of stagey by-play. Then from the *risvegliato* (awakened, animated) from b.73 the tempo can be gradually sharpened to whip through bb.81-8 with glittering triplets before subsiding with mock mysteriousness through bb.90-92 towards the second principal theme at b.93. This is a charming figure with its expressive RH motif, *tranquillamente e cantabile* and perhaps a little plaintive, over a continuing dancing,

mazurka rhythm 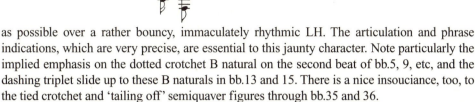 in the inner LH voice,

supported by sustained lower drones in fifths or sixths. Time needs to be allowed to 'point' the facetiously mournful 'slide' into the first beat of b.113, allowing a lingering *rallentando* through bb.114-16, with a return to tempo at b.117 and once more a 'whipping-up' from b.123. Take particular care through bb.123-6 to maintain the 'dancing' rhythm in the LH, so that the descending 5-quaver figures can be confidently 'spaced' over **stable** LH crotchets. The passage-work from b.127 looks forward to the similarly 'vaulting' passage in the B flat minor Scherzo (bb.334 etc.). The sustained LH minim on the second beat provides a nice 'anchor' in both a rhythmic and resonant sense, through bb.127-35. And again the implied emphasis on the minim bass octave or treble chord on the second beat of bb.136, 138, etc. creates a controlling rhythmic 'brake' through bb.136-43.

Once again the transference of the principal motif to the LH at b.151 is typical of Chopin's mazurka writing. It is best to keep the passage-work light in tone and spirit from b.159, but allowing time to listen to the 3-voice counterpoint from b.167. And similarly, sprightliness rather than earnest endeavour is the best policy from b.241 as Chopin dutifully develops his 'operatic' motifs, and again from b.365, with brilliant rather than pounding LH octaves from b.377.

Following the final restatement of the principal theme, Chopin takes off in a showy coda from b.432, with an implied whipping up of the tempo from b.449, towards a final fusillade of brilliant unison quavers from b.457.

Rondo in E flat major
Op. 16 (VA)

As indicated above, there is little to love about this grandiose concoction. It is in that open and unaffected fecundity that the charm of Ops 5 and 73 resides, and by the time Op.16 was completed when Chopin was settled in Paris, that first fine careless rapture was well and truly past. The principal themes, from bb.52 and 112, as well as the subsidiary ideas have little of the appeal of those of Ops 5 and 73, and even of Op.1. By definition, therefore, the relentless passage-work, Beethovenian in its thoroughness, is no more than meaningless glitter which, with all the virtuosity in the world, can only engender 'a plethora of bustle, indicating action without plan' (Weinstock, p.202). Apart from bb.380-93, where there is a brief bout of operatic humour, the interest of the piece lies in the first part of the Introduction. The opening motif (bb.1-4) is remarkably Schumannesque, although Chopin's regard for Schumann's music (as for that of most of his contemporaries) was hardly generous. The *agitato* outburst from b.13 is also striking, although more Lisztian than Chopinesque in its 'heaving' style of impassioned declamation. From the second section of this protracted Introduction, however (*più mosso*, b.23), grandiosity is the order of the day.

Rondo in C major
Op. posth. 73
Solo version (VA)
2-piano version (VA)

Musical scholars, almost to a man, remain sternly resistant to the blandishments of this piece, although Humphrey Searle at least finds it 'charming' (Walker, p.218). But this is 'fun' music – it chortles, bubbles, protests ostentatiously now and then, and spills over with joie de vivre – and he who is impervious to the absurd skittishness of the principal theme (b.25 etc.) and to the delicious unctuousness of the A minor tunes at bb.73 (in the 2-piano version) and 103, has a heart of granite. Once we have left behind the Introduction with its portentous semiquaver flourishes, and rather beautiful but inappropriately solemn *religioso* 'answer', the atmosphere is pure palm-court. Once again we are reminded that Chopin, in his youth at least, was anything but a languid drip, and perhaps this introductory solemnity is a joke.

The piece was originally written for solo piano in 1828, but Chopin arranged it for two pianos very shortly afterwards. Evidently he was pleased with it, as he wrote to his friend Titus Woyciechowski: 'I re-arranged that C Major Rondo . . . for two pianos, and tried it over with Ernemann at Buchholtz's. It goes quite well. We are thinking of playing it sometime at the Club.' (Hedley, *Correspondence*, 9 September 1828). This two-piano version was published in 1855, and the solo version (of which the autograph is reproduced in the Paderewski Edition) only in 1954. The 2-piano version is infinitely more beguiling. It is the opportunity for extra touches of counterpoint afforded by the second pair of hands which so delectably fills out the harmonic texture. And while in the solo version the showy passages tend to pound and grind, the two instruments, paradoxically, sound more open in texture, as well as gaining a substantial extra fillip and brilliance. Above all, the solo version has no melody at bb.73 and 261 (i.e. the triplets have only a simple 'oom-pah-pah-pah' accompaniment) and it is in this unctuous melody with its sycophantic triplet counterpoint that Chopin reaches his high point of calculated *schmaltz*. Here (if not in the other Rondos) he knew exactly what he was doing, and did it to perfection, and why this is not the pet party-piece of any 2-piano duo I cannot imagine. In either version the piece is far from easy, and earnestness is the enemy. Humour, lightness of touch (in terms of spirit) are all-important, together with the ability to ingratiate as well as to glitter, and to allow the rhythm to dance.

THE VARIATIONS

Like the popular rondo, sets of variations on a well-known air (perhaps operatic or National, and often improvised) were essential musical set-pieces in the salons of Chopin's day. Obviously the variation idea gave carte-blanche to the pianist to indulge his idiosyncrasies, and to show off his virtuosity to the best advantage. Neither the *Variations on a German Air*, nor the *Souvenir de Paganini* are excessively demanding, apart from the treacherous flurry of broken elevenths in 'Souvenir', b.70. However, although as is always the way with variations of a relatively superficial nature, they need to be carried off with considerable keyboard sophistication.

Note: The *Variations on a German National Air*, the *Variations Brillante* Op.12, the *Souvenir de Paganini*, and the *Variation from the Hexameron* are published in the Paderewski Edition Volume XIII (Concert Allegro and Variations). **The notes below are based on this edition of these works.** At the time of writing (1997) these works have not been published in the Vienna Urtext Edition, and the Henle Edition has published only the *Variations on a German National Air* and the *Variations Brillantes* Op.12 in their volume of Klavierstücke. These two are also published by Peters in Volume 3 of their Complete Works.

Variations on a German National Air (often known as *The Swiss Boy*) (8+)

It is thought that this set of variations on an Austrian folk song was written about 1824, when Chopin was 14, and he is reputed to have tossed it off in a few quarter-hours. The theme and its accompaniment are simple, and much of the writing does not merely sound like Schubert, it also, under the hands, **feels** like Schubert. Since the style is thus so strikingly un-Chopinesque, the piece is unlikely to be of great interest to players. However, while the Variations are modestly conceived and limited in adventure, the writing is assured and graceful, and the whole, in tune with the simplicity of the theme, has a gentle, musical-box charm.*

The introduction (bb.1-14) consists of a series of flourishes strung together with gracious formality. As always, such flights of flowery passage-work need the support of a carefully balanced and **rhythmic** LH. Thus the LH octave and then the spread chord in bb.1 and 3 need to be placed purposefully and rhythmically to provide a firm springboard for the showy gestures of the RH. Then the chord sequences through bb.2 and 4 must be articulated in a neat, straightforward style, and the RH scale flourishes from b.5 underpinned by steady, logically progressing chord sequences in the L.H

The theme needs to be played with warm but clear-toned simplicity, letting the repeated just-detached crotchets 'speak' through b.15 over a nicely poised, even-toned quaver accompaniment, in an easy, overall 2-in-the-bar movement.

In Variation 1 the pleasing curve and burble of the RH triplets needs to be supported by scrupulously 'spaced' and very rhythmic LH crotchets through bb.27-30. Then care must be taken to keep steady through b.32 with the help of a quiet 'lean' on the treble A on each main beat, and with neat rhythmic support from the LH, (and similarly in b.34). In this easy-running movement the semiquaver in the treble in bb.32 and 34, and in the LH in b.35 will coincide with the third quaver of the relevant

triplet group: 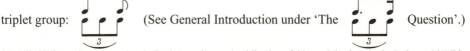 (See General Introduction under 'The Question'.)

*Detailed information concerning the background to, and publication of this work is given in the Paderewski Edition. Bar numberings are taken from this edition (see above in Introduction to the Variations).

Variation 2 has an almost Beethovenian vigour. The dynamic contrasts need to be projected with vitality, but (bearing in mind the *Scherzando* heading) without becoming too hectoring.

In Variation 3 it is essential, but not altogether easy to maintain the poise and calm of the theme in the RH above the smooth running but active LH semiquavers.

Variation 4, written mainly in four voices, is rather self-consciously dark-toned, as if the sombre mood has been dutifully 'turned on' for the obligatory minor Variation.

The final variation is a sprightly waltz-time, evolving into a more suave variant of the second section of the theme from b.97, and the whole is rounded off with the customary burst of virtuosic clatter.

The metronome marks throughout these Variations are somewhat erratic, apart from the ♩ = 100 for the theme. They differ substantially from those in Henle.

Souvenir de Paganini (8+)

Like so many musicians of his generation, Chopin was dazzled by the musical wizardry and personality of Paganini, whom he first heard in Warsaw in 1829. This is a set of Variations on a Venetian Air, 'Carnaval de Venise', and it is thought that Chopin may have heard Paganini playing his own set of Variations (Op.10) on this melody. The Variations run continuously over an unchanging LH tonic-dominant accompaniment in gently rocking barcarolle-like rhythm. Comparisons are inevitably drawn with the *Berceuse*, and indeed this is in effect like a poor man's version of that later marvel. But not such a very poor relation. Admittedly, it is less than half as ambitious a concept in every sense – the *Berceuse* is, after all, a product of Chopin's high summer of creativity. But, when sensitively played it can exercise a gentle charm which lingers persuasively in the mind's ear, and, like the *Berceuse*, it is one of those pieces which needs to be played superlatively well or not at all. It was first published in 1881, and is currently available in the Paderewski Edition Volume XIII. It is also included in the *Oxford Keyboard Classics* 'Chopin'. As John Vallier, editor of this Oxford album, says, 'this piece is of particular interest to Chopin lovers in showing how Chopin, at the age of 19, 'was exploring new ground in his search for an entirely new approach to piano playing'.

This is, to quote Humphrey Searle, 'a real Gondoliera' (Walker, p.221) and the tempo needs to be relaxed yet sufficiently moving to maintain a continuing softly rocking impulse. An overall tempo around ♩. = 54-60 is suggested, but allowing for considerable give and take. It is vital in a piece of this type, with an elaborately ornamented song-line over an evenly moving LH, to realise that it is the **LH** which 'carries' the melody and must, therefore, always maintain the sense of even onward movement. When the LH quavers need to 'give' a little to let the melody breathe, and to accommodate the quiet roulades and arabesques (and compensatorily to move on a little) they must do so in an evenly graded, not random manner, so that the fundamental rhythmic impulse is never allowed to 'die' (see General Introduction under 'Rubato'). This LH looks so simple, and yet it takes considerable expertise to be able to maintain this even flow, forming continual 'arches' of quavers which are rhythmically stable yet at the same time responsive to the whims of the RH – in exactly the same way as the opera conductor is responsive to the slightly varying inflections of a singer, say, on a Monday or a Wednesday.

With your basic tempo well 'in the system', play the opening chords in a carrying tone, placing the acciaccaturas resonantly on the beat in bb.2 and 3. The spacing of these chords (in terms of the register) creates a particular reverberation – rather cavernous or 'hollow'. **Listen** to this sound, especially through b.3, so that the melodic upbeat is perfectly placed in both a tonal and rhythmic sense as you poise yourself to 'cast off' in b.4. Shape the RH song in simple and graceful curves through bb.4-19, always listening acutely to the relation between the hands, and ensuring that the LH describes its softly rounded 'arch' through each bar (as much through bb.5, 7, etc. when the RH is 'taking a breath' as when it is actually singing). And, gently buoyed along by these LH curves, phrase over the rests as a singer would, rather than thinking in little 2-bar 'boxes'.

Arriving on the last note of the theme in b.19, allow the LH to draw out just a very little through this bar as you prepare to lead on into b.20, and then endeavour to avoid any turbulence in the LH as the RH sets out on its progressively elaborate decoration of the melody. Execute

the grace notes in bb.20 and 24 thus: ( *etc.* etc.) and similarly place all

grace notes and acciaccaturas on the beat (bb.31, 75 and 85). Always feel the shape of such bars as 22, 28, 32, etc. in a little curve, as if with a little swaying movement up towards and back from the highest note on the second main beat of the bar. In bb.26, 29, etc. feel that the line of the descending scale is falling from the highest note in a little *decrescendo*. Then as you 'sway' up towards and down from the second beat of b.32, be sure to articulate the RH double stopped figure exactly as indicated, **lifting** the hand gently from the sixth on the third quaver beat and again from the third on the second **main** beat and so on (see General Introduction under 'Articulation'). Articulate the RH throughout with a clear but limpid touch, allowing the sound to advance and recede in gentle swells, and making imaginative use of the soft pedal. There are no heavy breakers rolling in here, and even in the *forte* at b.36, keep the sound airy, leaning a little on the trill on each main beat, and 'dispersing' the sound upward towards each high quaver as indicated. The trills could either start on the main

note, using five notes [musical notation] or on the upper note, then using six

notes or four.

Let all the little *staccato* scales descend or ascend (bb.38, 47, etc.) with the utmost delicacy, and create little cascades, like tiny droplets of water, with the descending triplets (bb.42, 58, etc.). Allow a little extra time to make a light, slurred, *portamento*-like 'lift', rather than a snatch, up to the high notes in b.44, and again to show the details of articulation through b.46. Take care that the ascending sixths through b.50 do not get heavy – it is far more graceful to make an airy *decrescendo* as you ascend. Listen to the quiet chime of the sustained inner fourths through bb.52-3 and 56-7. The most vigorous moment is at b.60, when the RH needs to emerge and return like a gleaming water chute, supported by the unchanging movement of the LH – a foretaste of the remarkable effect in the B major Nocturne Op.62 No.1. The descending semiquavers at intervals of elevenths through b.70 are horribly difficult, and most players, certainly those with small to average sized hands, will have to allow a substantial 'give' here. The more tinkly and *dolcissimo* the tone, the more natural (rather than merely expedient) this 'give' will sound.

It is helpful to think of this passage, and to practise it as if in slurred couplets from each high

note downwards [musical notation] Then when you put hands together

'blend' this implied cross-rhythm effect delicately with the movement of the LH quavers.

Quietly 'point' the appearance of the subdominant at b.80, beneath the delicately articulated 'fall' of the RH scale. The forte at b.84 may be taken with a pinch of salt. A rise towards a warm

528

mezzo piano at b.85 would be more in keeping, maintaining this warm tone through the sixths through bb.86-7, and then letting the tone fall away to a whisper through bb.88-9, and ending with a very quiet 'harped' tonic chord.

Variation in E major from the 'Hexameron' (on Bellini's *March of the Puritans*) (7)*

This was Chopin's contribution to a set of Variations on the March from Bellini's opera *The Puritans*, commissioned for a charity concert in 1837. The other contributors were Thalberg, Pixis, Herz, Czerny, and Liszt who, in characteristic fashion, appears to have masterminded the operation, and wrote the Introduction, connecting passages and a Finale. Although the title was *Grande Variations de Bravoure*, Chopin not untypically went his own way, and produced this far from bravura fragment. It is an arresting and powerfully atmospheric piece – Chopin on a grand scale within a mere nineteen bars – and as such is of particular interest to less advanced players, and will therefore be discussed in particular detail. It is published in the Paderewski Edition Volume XIII.

Set a tempo that is measured, yet 'moves'. Since the melodic motif is so static, centred around the mediant (see bb.1-4), the LH triplets need to convey the sense of a steady swing, albeit in a low gear, with a suggested tempo of around ♩ = 50-56. The first task is to practise the LH until it is perfectly fluent, cultivating an even, smooth curve up towards and down from the highest chord in each bar. As will be seen, the shape of the curve varies in each bar. There is an undulation within the overall upward curve in both b.1 and b.2, which in b.1 reaches its peak on the sixth quaver triplet; whereas in b.2 this overall curve 'peaks' on the eighth triplet; then in b.3 where there are two upward sweeps, feel that you are 'returning' towards the bass octave on the third beat, and on the first beat of b.4 in a shallow 'arc', rather than snatching downwards in a sharp diagonal. These shapes need to be studied until they are thoroughly absorbed 'into the system', so that when you put hands together you will be able to 'use' them to best advantage to complement the melody line.

Having learnt the LH, it is a good plan to play it as you **sing** the RH, so that you get the feel of the way that the melody line 'rides' the LH triplet arcs.

When you put hands together have your tempo (i.e. the swing of the LH triplets) well 'in the system' so that you are ready to enter *sotto voce*, but in a steady and confident rhythm. Let the melody enter 'on a breath' (imagining how a singer would shape the phrase) and 'space' the repeated G sharps, as if each is pronouncing a word, **towards** an expressive soft 'lean' on the tied crotchet on the first beat of b.2, and on again towards the long G sharp on the third beat of b.2. Then, even if it were necessary to take a breath at the end of the bar, the singer would give the illusion of continuing the phrase **over** that breath, so that the G sharp would seem to sound on towards b.3. The phrase would thus move in a long span through bb.1-4 – whereas an unthinking pianist might chop the phrase into two distinct halves. The secret of this feeling of continuity lies both in giving the minim G sharp sufficient singing tone to last through its span, and to **listening** to its continuing sound, as if with an onward 'lean' towards b.3. Your ear can then tell you exactly how to 'carry on' the G sharp sound from the first beat of b.3. It is as if you are 'speaking on' into b.3, with a new word but still within the same sentence. Listen acutely to the intervals of the LH (fourths, fifths, etc.) and to the rising chromatic inflections at the end of b.1, giving these last two triplets the feeling of an upbeat

movement towards b.2 Feel this onward upbeat movement again and particularly as the chromatically descending octaves 'draw on' the sound of the treble minim G sharp towards b.3.

As you finish the first overall phrase in b.4, **listening** again to the RH minim G sharp through its full duration, allow a little 'give' as you shape the LH smoothly downwards from the high sixth on the second beat of the bar. Then feel a definite onward lean as you lead on with the RH crotchet B natural and the chromatically descending LH octaves from the upbeat to b.5, perhaps playing the second statement in a rather fuller tone. Listen carefully to the **different** shaping of the LH, quietly 'pointing' the implication of the D naturals in b.6, and the return to the D sharp in b.7, and shaping the expressive inner fragments clearly from the emphasised tied C sharp on the third beat of bb.7 and 8.

The LH could make a controlled swell through b.9 ready to lead purposefully into the *fortissimo* at b.10 with the bass slurred upbeat octaves. Balance the sound carefully from b.10, allowing the treble melody to sing out strongly over the inner RH chords, supported by powerfully resonant but not swamping bass octaves. Less experienced players will need to study and **listen** to this RH 'balance'. The problem is, of course, that the 'weaker' fifth finger has to sustain the melody line above the inner chords played by the 'stronger' fingers.

Try at first playing thus 'leaning' with as strong

a tone as possible on the melody notes, and playing the chords very lightly. Then

practise thus again 'leaning' strongly on the

melody notes, and playing the inner chords in a **light** *staccato*. Then, when you play the passage as written, feel that the inner harmony is 'filling out', without swamping the melody line, the whole sustained by a resonant bass octave line.

Arriving on a powerful chord on the first beat of b.13, disperse the sound progressively through the bar (*raddolcendo* means becoming sweeter, softer, calmer). Listen particularly to the downward chromatic movement of the LH to the octave F sharp here, conscious of the enharmonic change of the long treble B sharp to C natural, and then allow time to listen to the inner RH detail as you prepare to lead back into the tonic reprise in b.14 in a softly breathed

pianissimo (playing the inner *acciaccatura* expressively on the beat).

Tail the sound away progressively through b.17, and take time as you 'finish off' the LH up to the crotchet fourth on the second beat of the last bar, to **listen** to the fading sound of the final RH minim octave. (This ending has been added by the editors to replace the original bridge-passage supplied by Liszt to lead on to the next variation.)

The thorny problem of the timing of the triplet/semiquaver figures recurs here (see General Introduction under 'The ♩ Question'). Here the problem is compounded (or eased, according to your viewpoint) by the fact of the original rhythm of the march theme, which is, of course, ♩. ♩ . While I personally have no doubt that

I prefer the ♩ effect, as opposed to ♩ this must remain a choice for the individual, as always in this matter, and the question is well discussed in the Paderewski Edition. There can, however, be no doubt that at bb.10-12 the figure in **double**-dotted rhythm should be played as printed.

Variations Brillantes Op. 12
(on a theme from Herald's *Ludovic*) (VA)

This is an undisguised pot-boiler. Chopin, by his very nature, was almost incapable of producing work that is not pianistic in the widest sense, that is, in terms both of the qualities of the keyboard, and by the same token, of the physique of the player in relation to the keyboard. Taking this as read, there is little else to recommend this offering, save for the occasional virtuoso with time on his hands.

There is a conventional introduction of flourishes and pseudo-expressive fragments. The melody is played out (bb.32-58) and worked through in three Variations, with a final 'rounding up' in a *Scherzando vivace*. There are fleeting glimpses of genuinely Chopinesque passage-work, several flashes of wit, and here and there an interesting Schumannesque touch, as occasionally noted elsewhere, such as in Op.16. Otherwise all is pretty gesture, and the type of superficial glitter tailored to the salon tastes of the day.

MISCELLANEOUS WORKS

Andante Spianato (8)
and
Grande Polonaise Brillante
Op. 22 (VA)

These two items make strange bedfellows. The *Andante Spianato* is a solo piece written in 1834, while the Grande Polonaise, which has an orchestral accompaniment, dates from 1830-1. They were published together in 1836 with the *Andante* serving as a prelude to the Polonaise. This work is not published by Henle, but appears in the Paderewski Edition (Volume XV, Works for Piano and Orchestra), and is also published by Peters.

The *Andante* is a flowing piece in Chopin's most elegantly languorous style – more nocturne-like, in the perceived sense, than most of the Nocturnes themselves. The indication *spianato*, which has nothing to do with spinning, as one might suppose, means even, level, from the word *spiana* – a carpenter's plane, denoting therefore an ultra-smooth, gliding style of playing. The metronome mark of ♩ = 69 is distinctly fleet, and the piece can take a tempo several notches below this, provided that a continual sense of movement is maintained. The LH is all-important in this respect, and it is as well to study it first since the poise of the RH melody is entirely dependent upon the fluency of the gentle waves of LH semiquavers. The delicate elaboration in the restatements of the principal melody (bb.17, 41, 43 and 49 etc.) is by no means easy to negotiate gracefully. A notable feature is the prevalence of the tonic pedal point effect throughout the basic 8-bar melodic phrases: bb.5-12 continuing through bb.13-20, and similarly right through bb.37-66.

bb.1–19   The understanding of the actual **shape** of the LH arpeggios, demonstrated in the opening bars and maintained throughout the piece, is essential to the gentle overall momentum. Practise slowly, shaping the semiquavers carefully up towards and 'through' the high D on the third quaver pulse, and down again in a smooth rounded curve, and then feel the last two quavers as the upbeat to the subsequent bar as if phrased thus:

This, need it be said, must be accomplished with the utmost smoothness, with no sense of a break before the 'upbeat' semiquavers – just as an **idea** of giving these last two quavers an upbeat **sense** to help create the feeling of continuous onward movement. And the curve needs to move in an overall sweep, avoiding an accent on the second beat of the bar so that there is in effect almost a feeling of 1-in-the-bar. It is best to master thoroughly this arpeggio shape in the tonic, gradually increasing the tempo to approach that of your eventual easy-moving *Andante* before moving on. Endeavour to shape each curve in a beautifully rounded undulation, ironing out any tendency to make a 'corner' at the top or bottom of the curve. Cultivate a touch of feathery quality, swelling gently towards, and back from, the first beat of b.3.

The melody is one of Chopin's most vocal. Once you have learnt the notes, practise it, therefore, by **singing** it. It then becomes apparent that the opening span (bb.5-12) moves in one long-breathed phrase, with a forward impulse towards, and a little swell towards and back from the long high tied E on the first beat of b.8. This long note is both the climax of the **overall** phrase, and the onward leaning bridge to its second half. Feel the 'fall' from the quietly singing opening dotted crotchet B like a soft vocal *portamento*. Feel a very light swell through b.7 as

532

you prepare to create a warm and sufficiently carrying tone on the high E to last through its full value. Feel also that this note is 'leaning' onwards into another soft 'fall' to the crotchet D on the second beat of b.9, with another little curve up to the quietly syncopated crotchet C coinciding with the eighth LH semiquaver of b.11. Allow a little freedom, in other words an extra fraction of time for the placing of this C like a gentle 'lean', and then finish off the phrase with a quiet 'sliding' fall to the G in b.12, placing the grace notes **on** the beat so that the G itself coincides approximately with the second LH semiquaver.

When you put hands together, draw the sound back a little through the end of b.4 ready to float the opening B in, in a quiet musing tone on the first beat of b.5. In this kind of melodic piece, in which the melody flows mainly in longer notes over a 'wavy' semiquaver accompaniment, it is essential (at risk of labouring the point) to remain conscious of the rhythm and shape of the accompaniment. This is hard for the relatively inexperienced player to encompass. But once this is understood (in a personal, **physical** rather than merely an 'instructional' sense) it becomes apparent that the LH is indeed the 'conductor', and the RH to a wonderful extent does 'look after itself' (see the General Introduction under 'Left Hand', and in particular, the commentary on the Nocturne in D flat, Op.27 No.2).

The last two bars of the first overall phrase will be accommodated approximately:

Note the pedal indications, the long pedal through bb.1-5, and then one pedal per bar through bb.6-11, and so on. Take care to 'catch' the bass note as you change the pedal on each first beat (of bb.6-12 etc.) so that you retain its quiet resonance through each bar. Be sure to take the RH **off** through the second half of b.12, ready to 'start again', perhaps in a quieter, even more musing tone from b.13. The LH must 'give' a little through the third **quaver** pulse of b.17 to allow time for the ornamental arpeggio to make a soft but clear *glissando*-like fall to a light quaver D on the second beat, with the LH picking up the tempo again through the second half of the bar. This little arpeggio falls easily into a pattern of three and then four notes, to 'fit in' with the last two semiquavers of the LH group (see the General Introduction under '"Free' Runs').

bb.19–36 Take a little extra time to point the 'speaking' syncopated treble quavers through the second half of b.19, with the feeling that you are approaching the end of the phrase in b.20 with a slightly greater (though very quiet) sense of 'arrival' than at b.12. Then 'point' the last two LH upbeat semi-quavers as you prepare to move into E minor, feeling the change of airstream with the hint of underlying, though still quiet, turbulence, as the waves of sound in the LH grow a little more urgent. After the swell towards the first beat of b.24, drop the tone to *piano* as indicated in Peters. At the peak of the next swell, feel the sense in which the phrases overlap, i.e. the crotchet C on the second beat of b.28 not only ends the previous phrase (bb.25-8) but at the same time leads on into the next.* Then let the alternating fragments (bb.29-33 marked *piano* then *forte* in Peters) speak with all possible eloquence, while always keeping a sense of 'moving on' as you rise towards an ardent-toned *forte* at b.33. Carry the LH upwards in a broad sweep beneath the long, singing, tied D sharp, letting the RH semiquavers enter 'on the crest of the wave', on the upbeat to b.35 and only commencing the *diminuendo* and *rallentando* **after** the first beat of b.35, letting the semiquavers subside in a halo of sound down

---

*This effect is made clear in the Paderewski Edition.

to the fifth quaver pulse of b.36. Then allow time to point the RH broken octave (D natural) upbeat to b.37, changing fingers 5-1 on the last semiquaver so as to make a smooth 'lift' up towards the dotted crotchet B to begin the elaborated restatement.

bb.37–66   At the second ('doubled') main beat of b.45 an inner voice enters beneath the main melodic motif, rather in the style of the coda of the Nocturne in D flat, Op.27 No.2. The semiquavers of the inner voice need to be delicately articulated in a 'speaking', just detached (bb.45, 46, etc.) then smooth style (b.47, etc.) as indicated, beneath the continuingly smooth singing treble line. There must be a fractional drawing out through the end of b.47 with an implied slight swell towards the wide-spanned chord on the first beat of b.48 (placing the acciaccatura **on** the beat). The run in b.49 can be grouped thus:  or thus:

The sound can be quite strongly built up from

b.50 (**using** the resonance of the continuing bass tonic pedal point and of the singing long notes of the RH duet) rising to a full toned *forte* on the first beat of b.52. Then leaping off this treble diminished seventh, let the sixths cascade downwards in a free and voluptuous *forte* in *ritenuto* towards the first beat of b.53. Arriving on a clear tonic on this first beat of b.53, allow an instant to clear the sound, as the RH 'lifts' to ease into the codetta in a dreamy *leggierissimo*, feeling that the semiquavers are falling in a drift of little droplets from the high E. Pedal as indicated, delicately 'pointing' the inner RH dominant pedal point effect and the hinted inner melodic fragment through bb.55-6, and then start the next downward sequence from b.57 in an even more distant *pianissimo*.† Let the sound drift away to the tiniest whisper at bb.65-6.

bb.66–114   A tiny slowing through the very end of b.66 is necessary (but not too much, just the impression of a gentle breaking off of thought to allow 'room' for a new idea), with a little break after the last LH semiquaver, ready to lead off into the central section in a light-toned smooth flowing **3/4**. This has a gentle folk-like feeling. In fact a lightly-moving mazurka rhythm is suggested by the syncopating effect of the repeated melodic 'tag' bb.68-9, 70-2 etc. At the same time there is a quiet *religioso* tinge – but not too solemn, and it must not be allowed to drag – it needs an overall feeling of 1-in-the-bar, and a tempo of about ♩. = 44 is suggested. The music moves in 3-bar periods, variously subdivided. Note the punctuation of the subphrases precisely – the first 4-beat fragment with a 'lean' on the minim chord on the first beat of b.67, and the slightly syncopating 'lean' on the first quaver of the repeated motif from the second beat of bb.68 and 69. Listen also to the movement of the other voices: the **different**, i.e. overall phrasing of the lower LH line, and the held resonance of the inner LH tied G from the first beat of b.67 and the doubled D through b.69. Feel you are taking a breath at the end of b.69 as you prepare to repeat the phrase from b.70. Then, taking a more significant break at the end of b.72, you could play the higher registered motif in a more open, rather stronger tone, showing the brighter mood of the up-turning fragments (bb.74 and 75) and synchronising the

---

†There are doubts as to the placing of the accents through bb.55-6, i.e. as to whether these emphases should in fact fall on the notes FOLLOWING the pedal point Ds, (and which form the hinted inner line), rather than on the Ds themselves.

This inner melodic fragment is shown in doubled notes in some editions, but not in Paderewski. See the Commentary in Paderewski.

movement of the inner LH line carefully with the other voices (the part-writing is surprisingly tricky here). Listen particularly carefully to the movement of the voices as Chopin passes through E minor and returns towards the elaborated restatement, with a little 'lean' and 'hold' on the dominant harmony of C major on the second and third beats of b.78. Ensure that the ornamenting double triplet figures are clear and unhurried through the first beat of bb.83 and 87. Once again this passage, indeed, the whole of this section, is deceptive. It looks so simple, and can either sound charmingly artless, or if the part-playing is ill-managed, clumsy and plodding. The 'join' between the end of this section and the repetition of the 'codetta' passage is awkward – indeed, the repetition of this codetta passage seems no more than a recapitulatory gesture to fill out the proportions of the *Andante* as a 'complete' piece in its role as a scene setter for the Polonaise. This 'join' needs careful papering over, with a little 'lean' on the chord on the second beat of b.95, and a careful slowing through the pauses on each beat of b.96. Then **listen** to the quiet sound of the last quaver A as you prepare to trickle the sound downwards again from the high treble in b.97. The motif from the central section is brought back to form a bridge to the Polonaise with a pause on the last chord, now the dominant of C minor, ready to leap off into the *molto allegro*.

The Polonaise itself is a hectically virtuosic caper – it forms, as Jim Samson has said, a 'fitting coda' both to Chopin's early showy (as opposed to the later heroic) realisation of the polonaise idea, and also to his attempts to involve himself with the orchestra in any significant sense. In this instance there is some humour to be had in 'spotting' the orchestra, reduced as it is to the role of a desperate suppliant pursuing a megalomaniac monologist. It is more effective when (with the little adaptation that is necessary) it is performed as a solo item. And, fearsomely difficult as it is, mere mastery of the notes is not enough. It is the kind of piece which is a bore unless galvanised by the rhythmic élan and high-octane, almost manic technical wizardry of a Horowitz, as the reissue of his old recording triumphantly demonstrates. It appears that Chopin played it only once in public – when he was 25 – and it is the music of a young man on a springtide of confidence in his capacity to please and impress, both in a compositional and virtuosic sense. The principal theme is all gestures and fashionable strutting, the central C minor motif more expressive and yielding. Overall Chopin is 'discovered' as Niecks says 'posturing, dealing in phrases, and coquetting with sentimental affectations' (Vol.2, p.244). But he does so with heady exuberance and fecundity which we in this sober musical age might do well to allow ourselves to applaud.

Bolero
Op. 19 (VA)

Tarantelle
Op. 43 (VA)

A large body of Chopin's work is concerned with the dance. The polonaise and mazurka rhythms were anyway in his bones, and then, by the time he was musically conscious, the ballrooms of Europe had succumbed to the sway of the waltz. Apart from the tiny Ecossaises, whose regional links are somewhat tenuous, the *Bolero* and the *Tarantelle* were his sole ventures into more exotic musical climes. Both these capers, for such they are, need to be carried off with a touch of virtuosity, and the *Tarantelle* in particular takes a fair stretch of rhythmic and technical stamina.

The *Bolero* was written in 1833. There is something inescapably amusing about Chopin, by this time well ensconced in his elegant Parisian habitat, venturing into the unlikely field of

Spanish music. The direction of his genius was far from that of a Debussy or a Ravel. As Niecks says, his talents were concentrated in 'the strength of his subjectivism in the first place, and his nationalism in the second' (Vol.2, p.221). After a stentorian call to attention with three *fortissimo* unison octaves, there is a busy 30-bar flourish in glancing **3/8** semiquavers. The most 'Spanish' part of the piece (albeit Bizet-Spanish) is in the ensuing *Più lento – con anima*, which should surely be acted out more than a little tongue-in-cheek. The rhythm of the main body of the piece, the *Allegro vivace* in **3/4** from b.88, is, as has often been remarked, that of an (emasculated) polonaise beneath a picky RH dotted rhythm motif (of which we have had more than enough long before the last of its umpteen appearances). On arrival at the *risoluto* at b.136 we throw a quick double-take, when we seem momentarily to have veered into the A major Polonaise. Much of the passage-work through this section has the character of Chopin's early pre-1830 work, and indeed, Niecks suggests that the piece was written some years before it was published (Vol.2, p.221). The 4-bar *risoluto* motif is reinserted at b.250 to hasten a somewhat unconvincing ending.

The *Tarantelle* is a clever piece, but who, on hearing it or even studying it, would guess it to be Chopin's? It was evidently paid for in advance by the publisher, and appears to have been regarded by Chopin as a chore he was eager to be done with. He wrote to Fontana, 'I don't want to lose 500 francs', and goes on, 'It's a bore for you to copy the beastly thing, but I do hope it will be a long time before I write anything worse.' And he refers to it in a later letter as 'that wretched *Tarantelle*'. However he was evidently anxious to 'get it right' since he tells Fontana to check the rhythm with that of a Rossini *Tarantelle*. 'I do not know whether it is written in **6/8** or **12/8**. People write it both ways; but I should like it the way Rossini has it.' (*Chopin's Letters*, p.227). It is, like any *Tarantelle*, a *moto perpetuo* of ever-mounting momentum, with only a second here and there for a quick snatch of breath. It can sound highly effective, and even charming, when played as a **dance** rather than as a stampede. The stampede approach may indeed dazzle the audience. But the more dance-like approach allows 'room', not only in the rhythmic sense, but also to 'point' the changes of texture and subtle inflections (bb.48-50, 51-5, 90-3, etc.). Above all it is the continual switching of dynamics, the *subito pianos* and *fortes* that keep the ear 'alive', as opposed to deadening it with unremitting clatter. We could, for example, fall to a breathless *piano* at bb.24, 40, 52, and so on, and start the long final build-up from b.228 from a **true** *pianissimo*.

Allegro de Concert
Op. 46 (VA)

This is an item of the greatest interest to students of Chopin. Scholars assume that it was intended as the first movement of a projected third Piano Concerto. There is no doubt that Chopin planned a third Concerto (his father wrote to him in 1835 'You don't mention whether you have finished your third Concerto'). There can also be no doubt that this was conceived as a work or movement with orchestra. If it was indeed part of the projected Concerto, Chopin appears to have been working on it well before 1835 although it was not published until 1841. Thus it is likely that much of the material derives from an earlier date, buttressed by inflections of later style if not of actual subject matter. Maurice Brown says 'The music was taken up again in the spring of 1841, after a promise to Friederike Müller, later Mme Streicher [a favourite pupil, and one of Chopin's few professional students] to compose a concert piece for her. The "Allegro de Concert" is thus a pastiche of early work in which the original *soli* and *tutti* passages are still distinguishable.' (p.77). Niecks quotes an interesting review by Ebenezer Prout of a performance of the work by Pachmann in 1888 (Vol.2, pp.224-5).

There can be no mistaking the opening section of 86 bars as an orchestral *tutti*, comparable in its rather plain style to those of the two Concertos. The preparation for the solo entry from b.77 is arresting, as is the entry itself on the high sustained F natural in b.87, leading through a short and highly expressive improvisatory flourish into the first solo theme. This has a musing Nocturne-like character, becoming increasingly rhapsodic from b.95. The solo takes off from b.105 into some brilliant passage-work (with a sudden *scherzando*-like motif, thrown in in passing (bb.115-16) and recalling the Study in F Op.10 No.8) leading to a second song-like passage in the dominant at b.124 based on the second subject of the *tutti* (see from b.41). The treatment of this melody, on the face of it quite simple, is once again musing and strikingly beautiful, with a powerful underlying intensity. As Peter Gould has pointed out (Walker, pp.156-7), the shooting run in b.134 is similar to that in the Nocturne in B major Op.62 No.1 (b.26), and indeed this is only one instance in which the concentration and intensity of the writing resemble that piece. Leading on from a high 'pedal point' trill at b.136, the decoration once again grows rhapsodic, increasing in dramatic tension until the solo takes off again in a further bravura flight from b.150. The passage-work in this piece has a curious hybridity. While resembling the bravura style of some of his early work in the sense of 'virtuosity for its own sake', it has on the other hand a condensed, almost driven intensity, demonic in effect as well as in physical difficulty. Following a further 'tutti' from b.182, the theme from b.124 returns in a further decorated form in the tonic minor (b.200). From b.216 this theme (now returned to the tonic proper) erupts in stupendous *fortissimo*. Cutting off from the dominant of E in b.224, Chopin launches into the final bravura section, shooting upwards in a mercurial triple scale in triplet semiquavers, and descending in a complex sequential four-part chain of quavers into a light spirited passage in the style of the A flat Impromptu. This final lap evolves, or rather escalates onwards with hair-raising brilliance and quixotic complexity, and the piece ends with a bombastic *tutti* section.

The scope and sheer difficulty of this work speaks volumes for the gifts of Mlle Müller. A curiosity this may be, but in Chopin's day it would have been perfectly acceptable to adapt and perform a concerto, or other piece with instrumental backing, as a solo. And today, when we seem to be emerging from a long period of prudish standards towards a more tolerant acceptance of the more ad hoc musical habits of previous eras, this piece is worthy of more than an occasional hearing. It contains fascinating music, which in the hands of a player of technical wizardry and keen dramatic sense, can have a powerful impact.

Fantaisie in F minor
Op. 49 (VA)

This is generally considered, along with the F minor Ballade and the Barcarolle, to be one of the greatest, and by some, the greatest of Chopin's longer works. And it is a work of magnificent originality and expressive power. Chopin handles his material with absolute mastery, conveying a heady sense of freedom, and at the same time an intense concentration, grandeur and inevitability of design. In particular his highly personal manner of accumulating and dispersing resonances (as opposed merely to building and dismantling climaxes) is demonstrated to the highest degree in this work. For the player it is a large undertaking. From a technical point of view there is nothing showy – the technical demands are inseparable from the musical, and as such are more, rather than less searching. The least sensation of mechanical effort, or of the intrusion of technical show is wholly destructive to the musical flow. It is true, of course, that in any piece, from the tiniest miniature to the largest-scale sonata, we have to take the overall view, seeing the components in relation to the whole. Here this is more than ever vital – and more complex – since there is no obvious climactic point, rather a continual onpouring sequence of events. The music evolves on different planes, amassing and diffusing in a manner that puts extreme pressure on the equilibrium of the performer. So often, for example, players hurtle off at b.43, instead of allowing the music to grow in an overall 'piling on' of sound and intensity towards the onrush from b.64 into the main theme from b.68. And from b.68 a strong and stable sense of a 2-in-the-bar pulse has to be established in the LH to 'anchor' the syncopated anxiety of the RH line. Again, from b.85 the RH has to be underpinned by strongly **rhythmic** LH chords instead of, as so often happens, being left to screech around on its own fallible momentum. All this said, it is at the same time a work from which the less advanced player, examining the music at his own pace, can gain valuable and rewarding insights into Chopin's style at its very finest. The opening sequences have an evocative quality which colours the whole work, although they never in fact recur. From the way in which many pianists 'interpret' these first 34 bars, one could imagine that they have failed to notice the heading *Marcia, Grave*. Chopin thus makes his intentions plain enough, and they are supported by von Lenz's comment that 'in the march-like Introduction, Chopin played the enharmonic modulation in b.17 strictly in time, which only enhanced its effect' (Eigeldinger, p.70). The implication clearly is that he played the **whole** section in strict rhythm (since he [even] played the modulatory transition in time), and this must, in the light of the *Marcia* heading, be the right approach.

The effect of the sepulchral march step (bb.1-2, 5-6, etc.) with its consolatory answering figures (bb.3-4 and 7-10, etc.) is dependent on a **continuing** quiet tread. And we can imagine the effect Chopin would have made: austere yet infinitely finely shaded, mysterious and subtly portentous. After the sudden steep *crescendo* towards *fortissimo* at b.19, the tone drops quickly again to lead off from b.21 in a new, more long-breathed version of the march idea, which in itself acquires a subtly ironic, more dance-like motion. Stern chords from b.37 draw the opening section towards its close, ending on a 'disappearing' fragment of the 'stepping' figure through bb.41-2, which at the same time leads on to merge into the improvisatory triplets from b.43. This is one of Chopin's most sensational effects. From the low bass tonic on the first beat of b.43, he quietly builds the layers of sonority towards a 'hold' in b.44, repeating the sequence in a higher register and augmenting dynamic towards b.46. These waiting 'holds' create an extraordinary, echoing and uneasy shiver of expectancy. Then Chopin piles on the layers of sonority in a rising, accelerating *stretto* effect towards an abrupt 'stop' through three clarion-toned unison octaves on the dominant of E flat minor (bb.52-3). 'Starting again' from b.54 he expands the climb, reinforcing the RH with a powerful LH octave line from b.60. Rising in an immense *crescendo* towards b.64, a tumultuous scale hurtles down through bb.64-7 to surge straight into the principal theme of the work. This, as Alan Rawsthorn says, is 'a dark and tempestuous theme, deriving a kind of desperate energy from its syncopations' (Walker, p.61). This agitated syncopated melody, swept along by rolling and surging triplets in the LH, breaks into breathless fragments in quaver thirds from b.73, which in turn evolve into a jubilant two-voiced melody in quavers from b.77 against the continually onward buoying LH triplets. From b.85 a tempestuous passage in RH triplets goaded on by insistent LH arpeggiated chords leads into a new, fiercely impassioned melodic fragment from b.93. As already said, these 'goading' LH chords need to be tautly rhythmic, or chaos will ensue from b.85. Driving on through passages of ever increasing dramatic tension and intensity, incorporating a taut-nerved quick-march episode at b.127, there follows an agitated working-out of the triplet material of b.43 onwards, leading into a restatement of the principal theme, now in C minor from b.155. Chopin then calms the storm with a version of the improvisatory passage of bb.43-68, which he uses this time to disperse rhythmic tension and sonority in a long *diminuendo* towards b.198, slowing to a *pianissimo* pause on the dominant of the B major *lento* section. The melody here is in Chopin's *religioso* vein, with a solemn yet radiant serenity which is short lived, and we are soon catapulted back into a recapitulation from b.235. From b.316 there is a *fortissimo* downward chute of parallel chromatic sixths punctuated by stabbing crotchets at intervals of diminished fifths and augmented fourths, arriving on a six-four chord of A flat (the key in which Chopin ends) for a brief reminiscence of the *lento sostenuto* motif. From b.321 a short improvisation upon this motif, a decoration of the A flat chord, leads on and prepares for the ending, a billowing and then *diminuendo*-ing arpeggiation of this affirmative A flat harmony.

Berceuse
Op. 57 (VA)

Along with the *Barcarolle*, this is the only one of Chopin's works with a descriptive title, in this case a defined imaginative 'programme'. The image of Chopin as a fond baby-dandler is hardly one that springs to mind. Nevertheless, from the reminiscences of various contemporaries, as well as affectionate references to children in his own letters, it appears that Chopin was readily charmed by the children of his friends, and Jim Samson suggests that this piece may have been inspired by his happy relationship with the baby daughter of his friend, the singer Pauline Viardot, who had stayed at Nohant in 1843, the year before he wrote the Berceuse (p.96). Whatever its sources, this is one of his most sublime concepts. Comparisons are inevitably drawn between this piece, written in the full flowering of Chopin's late maturity, and the comparatively simple *Souvenir de Paganini*, written fourteen years earlier. They are indeed similarly conceived, but are, not surprisingly, light years apart in terms of accomplishment. And there is a comparable difference in terms of the demands on the performer. While the *Souvenir* is within the capacities of the comparatively inexperienced player, the *Berceuse* requires technical control and musicianship of a sophisticated and refined order.

An unchanging LH moving in continuing smoothly moulded curves provides a continuous 'ground' for a quietly evolving cornucopia of exquisitely drawn variations on the simple melodic phrase of bb.3-6. The shaping of the LH is crucial. The curve rises towards the second main beat and then 'settles' on the dominant crotchet on the fourth quaver pulse of the bar. This 'stopping' on the crotchet is not an emphasis, but conveys a sense of completion, while at the same time 'leaning' onwards towards the subsequent bass note initiating the next upward curve. It is an interesting exercise to try playing the first few lines with an accompaniment running in

continuous quavers:  We quickly perceive

the importance of the crotchet, both as a rhythmic 'anchor' and at the same time a bridge 'drawing on' the rhythm from bar to bar. Having established the shape of the curve, the art is to maintain it so that the increasingly elaborate roulades and arabesques of the RH are safely suspended over this gentle but sure rocking movement. The whole piece passes in a halo of mesmeric sound, slightly veiled yet with a celestial clarity. The melody needs to materialise rather than enter on the first beat of b.3, and similarly, the inner voice to 'materialise' on the upbeat to b.7. There is an exquisite piquancy in the passing ninths through bb.9-12. The treble slurred acciaccatura figures are placed **on** the beat through bb.15-18. The sound remains on a *piano dolce* level throughout, with a sense of only the lightest possible rise and fall of the breath.

The Cortot edition gives useful patterns for practice, particularly in the case of the sixth variation (bb.27-30), which is difficult for a small hand, indeed well-nigh impossible unless the wrist and knuckle area is really supple. The greatest care has to be taken to keep the LH tempo constant when the RH breaks into different rhythms, particularly after b.34, when the figuration reverts from semiquaver triplets to 'plain' semiquavers in b.35, then back to triplets from the upbeat to, and second quaver of b.36, into demisemiquavers from b.37, and triplet demisemiquavers from b.39. And hot-blooded young virtuosi may need to be reminded that Chopin gives no indication that a storm is brewing from b.37. These demisemiquaver passages are infinitely more effective in an etheral *pianissimo*. If a little licence with the tempo is necessary or desirable in b.44, it needs to be accomplished in such a way that the **sense** of overall rhythm is maintained (see General Introduction under 'Rubato'). The trills here have a delicious, quietly gurgling quality, setting off the upward flicking arpeggios like spurts of thistledown. From this high point the ornamentation is diffused as the triplet demisemiquavers gradually 'deflate' downwards through bb.45-6, and a more serious contemplative note is struck with the return to 'plain' semiquavers and the *sostenuto* indication from b.47. And this mood is deepened by that stroke of genius, the luminously echoing C flats from b.55 in preparation for the movement towards the final cadence through the subdominant at bb.59-60, and the beautifully protracted downward drift of the melodic motif over the pure tonic sound.

Barcarolle
Op. 60 (VA)

Arthur Hedley called this 'the finest Nocturne of all', and goes on to sum it up thus: 'It represents the climax of Chopin's lyricism, his final outpouring of melody, a synthesis of his piano style, and a summary of his achievement as a harmonist' (p.155). And it is all of these things, radiant, luxuriant and affirmative, reflecting no hint of the slow fuse that was burning within the domestic life of Chopin and George Sand (see the General Introduction). To choose the 'greatest' among the major works of such a composer as Chopin is both presumptuous and frivolous. But if forced to choose one single work of Chopin en route for the proverbial desert island, many devotees would surely pick the Barcarolle. It was completed during the summer of 1846, Chopin's last at Nohant, and its meridional quality is both significant and poignant in view of the rapid decline of Chopin's health and strength that was to follow the final break with George Sand. The remaining major works, the Polonaise-Fantaisie and the Sonata for Piano and Cello show Chopin moving into a new, more experimental and exploratory phase, that final 'stretching out towards the future' which he had neither the time nor the creative energy to pursue.

While a large body of Chopin's work is directly based upon, or at least associated with dance-rhythms, the Barcarolle and the Berceuse are the only pieces with actual descriptive titles (see the General Introduction) and both are among his most exalted imaginative achievements. Like all Chopin's major works, the performance of the Barcarolle is a large undertaking. Because, in a harmonic sense, it is so densely concentrated, the actual learning of the notes is a considerable task. Many a student, deceived by the apparent lack of virtuosic display, has discovered this and ruefully abandoned the struggle within the first page or two. The technical demands are entirely contained, in the sense that they are inseparable from, the musical processes. There is not an inch of 'room' for any extraneous flights of virtuosity, and not a single note that does not contribute to the overall aural glow cast by this magical music. The idea of the Barcarolle (boating song) romantically associated with the songs of the Venetian Gondoliers, has been adopted by many composers – Mendelssohn, Fauré and

Offenbach among others. The usual rhythm is a **6/8** or even **9/8**. Chopin's **12/8** is fundamental to his long-breathed lines, enabling him, as Weinstock has observed, 'to present the melodic overlay in a longer, more flowing line' (p.277).

Chopin's wizardry in the matter of the short introduction is nowhere more apparent than in the three opening bars, in themselves a searching study in the grading and 'layering' of resonances. A keen harmonic and rhythmic tension is initiated by the opening, on a dominant ninth harmony, as the upper notes of the chord fall with a syncopating 'lean' on the second beat over the carrying resonance of the bass dominant octave. Chopin then dissolves this tension through a series of concentrated, shifting harmonies over the dominant pedal-point while at the same time this passage draws us in towards the main movement with marvellous prescience. The timing of the mid-thought ending in b.3, the 2-beat rest and the quiet materialisation of the barcarolle movement in the LH is perfectly gauged by Chopin, with no need for the 'helpful' manipulation found necessary by many players. The sense of the slightly emphasised 'offbeat' entry already noted on the second beat of b.1 is extremely important. There is an implied slight 'lean' on the second beat as the melody enters in b.6 (observe the *decrescendo* **from** this opening third). Then each 2-bar period begins with the 're-entry' of the RH on the second beat of bb.8 and 10, and the sequence of sixth 'falls' from the emphasised dotted crotchet sixth on the second beat of b.14. Again, the second beat of b.11 is emphasised, and there is an implied emphasis on the partly tied 'upbeat' to the second beat of bb.20 and 21, and so on. The opening principal motif (bb.6-7) is explored with increasing richness and diversity, the RH ornamentation always buoyed along by the barcarolle flow in the LH. The RH song proceeds in two or more melodic voices in a continual, onward-pouring flow, and the coalescing of the 'vocal' needs of the RH with the continuing lapping movement in the LH demands techno-musical skills of the highest order. The shaping of the falling spray of delicately articulated semiquaver sixths from the emphasised dotted crotchet on the second beat of b.14, and the smoother, shorter 'falls' from the second and fourth beats of b.15 are exquisitely teasing to the player seeking an ever finer shading and limpidity of sound. A 'waiting' bar (b.16) subtly prepares for a shift into B major leading back through increasing richness and concentration of arabesques, double trills and intensity of sound towards an elaborated restatement of the main melodic motif in a triumphal (but not overblown) fullness of tone from b.24. The arrival in *forte* at b.32, and the phased upward *diminuendo* over the sonority of the pedalled bass dominant is an especially rich effect.

Another 'waiting' bar (b.34) prepares for the link to the second main section in A major from b.39. This link in solo quavers 'gathers' the new tempo in quietly skimming solo quavers, pointing in veiled and scarcely breathed inflections towards the infinitely subtle but unmistakable change of mood at b.39. Within the *sotto voce* theme is a new sense of urgency in the onward moving LH quaver/crotchet motion, and in the emergence in b.40 in the inner RH voice of the new 'turning' accompanying figure beneath the long treble A. This melodic section is less difficult than the first. Nevertheless, the blend of the three voices needs to be very finely poised. The obvious danger is that the treble melody will be swamped. On the other hand, it must not be allowed to 'struggle along on its own', deprived of the subtly 'urging on' effect of the movement of the lower voices. The whole needs to 'swim along' in a delectable amalgam of voices and rhythm, each melodic phrase ending in a lightly 'breezed' upward arpeggio (bb.43, 47, etc.). The dynamic momentum is gradually heightened in an ever intensifying range of sonorities and tone colour. At b.62 Chopin defuses this intensity of sound, launching into an easy-going melodic passage with, as Lennox Berkeley says, something of the flavour of a popular song (Walker, p.186). A long linking passage from b.72 leads us back towards the recapitulation. At b.78 Chopin digresses into a nocturne-like cadenza over a dominant pedal point, whose decorated RH line gathers momentum through bb.82-3 to pour itself into the magnificently reinforced version of the opening melody, and, from b.93 a jubilantly impassioned recapitulation in the tonic of the melody of b.62.

The coda, from b.103, is a marvel of intensifying, then gradually subsiding sonority over a long tonic pedal. A final simple, quiet melodic passage in the LH from b.113 is decorated by wandering treble demisemiquavers, which unexpectedly descend through b.115 in a powerfully *crescendo*ing chute towards a low bass tonic, to end this sumptuous work, as Lennox Berkeley calls it, in powerfully affirmative unison octaves.

Funeral March in C minor
Op. Posth. 72 No. 2 (7)*

Whether this piece was written for a particular occasion is not known. Its date of composition is variously given as 1827 or 1829 – in any event before Chopin left Poland for good. The piece is given in two versions in the Paderewski Edition's volume of 'Minor Works': the first and 'plainer' version published by Fontana as Op.72 No.2 (along with Nocturne in E minor Op.72 No.1, and the three Écossaises Op.72 No.3); and the second rather more elaborate version published in the Oxford Edition in 1932.

While there is a strong touch of Mendelssohn, as Huneker has said, there are also pointers towards the great funeral march written ten years later. These are more evident in the second version given in the Paderewski Edition, particularly in the rising motif in dotted rhythm (bb.25-6). This second version shortens the outer sections by omitting the restatement of bb.11-18, fills out some of the chords with octaves, drum-rolls and various inner inflections (bb.14-15 etc.) and adds a 7-bar coda (considered to be spurious by the editors of the Paderewski Edition). The notes below are based on the second version. Unfortunately even the first version is fairly dependent on octaves, otherwise this would have made a useful addition to Chopin's none-too-plentiful repertoire for novice players.

bb.1–10   The given tempo of ♩= 84 is fairly brisk for a funeral march, in other words, not as slow and portentous as the usual 'State Funeral' tread (which indeed the musical content would hardly justify).* Practise at first **without** the tremolo drum-roll, so that the rhythm of the introductory motif (bb.1-2) is securely set. The tremolo could be added in semiquavers at first, showing the pulse with a tiny accent on the

second beat   Then practise the tremolo in sextuplets and finally if

possible in demisemiquavers. The important thing for the less experienced player to realise is that the tremolo is a 'rumble' **effect**, not a specific number of notes to be 'got in'. The essential is to keep the rhythm of the two bars rock-steady, making as effective a rumble as possible, but accepting that the tremolo is subject to the overall rhythm and **not** the other way around. Come clean **off** on the fourth beat of b.2, and then play the opening motif of the march proper (bb.3-4) in a clear straightforward style, in perfectly regular rhythm. Play the acciaccatura on the beat in b.4 (see the General Introduction under 'Ornaments'). 'Join in' with a clear LH line from b.5, down to the dotted quaver on the first beat of b.6, and then let the dotted rhythm figures 'lead on' in rigorous time towards b.7. Apart from the opening *pianissimo*, there are few dynamics in this version of the march, and it is suggested that the more plentiful indications are 'transferred' from the first version: i.e. giving a *piano* through bb.3-4 (but with a slight swell towards and

---

*Nevertheless a considerably slower tempo may, with justification be adopted.

542

back from the chord on the first beat of b.4); a *crescendo* from the second half of b.5 through to *mezzo forte* at b.7; a further *crescendo* through b.9, with a *decrescendo* to *piano* from the upbeat to b.11, and so on. The Trio will then be predominantly *piano*, with a slight swell towards and back from the fourth beat of b.21, a *crescendo* to *forte* through b.33, and a *decrescendo* back to *piano* through b.42.

It is essential that all dotted rhythms are precisely timed, always feeling the semiquaver as the 'upbeat' to the subsequent dotted quaver (see the General Introduction under 'Dotted Rhythms'). This is particularly important in the case of a sequence of dotted rhythms e.g. through b.6. If they are double-dotted, the rhythm loses its 'solidity', if 'tripletised' the effect is sloppy. Allow an extra instant to spread the chord generously on the upbeat to b.10, feeling a slight implied upbeat 'lean' and *tenuto* effect, rather than 'skimping' this beat. End the phrase cleanly on the third beat of b.10, allowing a tiny break so that you make it clear that you are leading on with a new phrase with the unison dotted rhythm upbeat to b.11.

bb.11–18   Playing this phrase *piano* as suggested above, listen to the movement of the lower LH and inner RH voices through b.11, to the resonance of the held inner B natural and lower LH dominant through b.12, and similarly to the movement of the inner voices through bb.15-16. Ensure also that the treble dotted crotchet F sings over the fourth beat of b.14 with the quaver F sharp shown clearly as the upbeat to b.15. The ornament in b.12 can be interpreted and the bass roll in b.17 anticipating the fourth beat thus:

bb.19–75   The Trio has an almost jaunty, dance-like lilt. Be sure once more to come cleanly **off** on the fourth beat of b.18 so that you can 'take off' in this new sunnier tone.

Practise the LH carefully alone to achieve a perfectly poised quiet rhythmic swing between bass notes and upper chords. In the RH ensure that the minims sing out over the inner chords, which need to be comparatively lightly **touched**, and **not**, as usually happens in such instances, allowed to 'hang on' over the subsequent beat. Practise at first 'leaning' extra strongly on the minim, and playing the inner chords in a very light *staccato*. When you put hands together, listen acutely to the balance between the hands, ensuring above all that the treble melody sounds

Take care that the two semiquaver C's are given time to 'speak' in b.20, thinking of them as the 'upbeat' to the third beat of the bar. As the RH finishes the 4-bar phrase on the minim C in b.22, listen to the line of the LH leading on with the upbeat quavers into b.23. Listen carefully also to the treble line through bb.25-6, ensuring that it curves smoothly and graciously up towards a quietly singing minim B flat on the first beat of b.26, and 'finishing off' the phrase cleanly and quietly on the crotchet A flat on the third beat. Allow a tiny break after the chord on the third beat of b.34 (as in b.10) so that you can lead on clearly with the upbeat to b.35. Feel that this unison upbeat figure is 'going to' strongly singing tied minim F's on the first beat of b.35. **Listen** to the held resonance of these tied notes as you play the inner RH and LH chords relatively quietly on the second and third beats, and then feel that the unison dotted rhythm figure is again leading on in an upbeat sense. There is an implied melodic 'lean' on these tied minims (see the emphases on the equivalent notes in the Fontana version). Ensure therefore that they sing out resolutely. Then listen also to the tied lower resonances from the third beat of bb.39 and 40, taking care to preserve a smooth line through all the voices here. End the phrase cleanly on the minim G in b.41. Allow a tiny break after the second beat and then lead on with the unison quaver figure, making a gradual *decrescendo* as you descend. Make a little 'give' through the end of b.42 allowing an extra instant to leap up in the RH as you poise yourself for the restatement from b.43. As you 'finish off' clearly on the third beat of b.50, be sure to allow a full crotchet rest as you prepare to resume the march tread in b.51. Through the coda ensure that each dotted rhythm upbeat figure 'goes to' a singing dotted minim, playing the inner RH and LH chords in bb.69-73 with quiet precision as you gradually fade the sound away towards a *pianissimo* final bass note beneath the held RH chord.

Three Écossaises
Op. Posth. 72 No. 3

It is thought that Chopin wrote a number of Écossaises in his early years, and these three, dating from 1826,* were published by Fontana in 1855. The links with Scotland appear to be tenuous, and the title is a generic one for a type of country dance, in the same sense as 'contredanse' (see under Contredanse in G flat major). Although critical opinion can spare few kindly words for these pieces, their popularity persists. And why not, since, to quote Jim Samson these are pieces written 'as an easy spin-off from more serious work' in the same sense as the dances of Mozart and Schubert (p.122). The pity is that Chopin must have written or improvised so many pieces of this kind that have been lost (see also some of the early Mazurkas, Nos 50, 51, etc.). None of these pieces can be called easy, and ideally all need to be thrown off with the kind of rhythmic élan which goes hand in hand with a considerable degree of keyboard know-how. Of the three, the first needs the greatest brilliance. The second, evidently in Huneker's day as 'highly popular in girls' boarding schools' (p.177) as it is today, is rather easier. In the third the double-voiced RH figures require a certain knack and agility, as do the upward shooting semiquaver figures through bb.15-16. But joie de vivre is more important than speed, and all three can take a tempo some few notches below the given ♩ = 108, providing that the rhythm is vital, springing and poised, and the articulation diamond bright.

No. 1 in D major (8)

Note: For those using the Paderewski Edition there will be a discrepancy in bar-numberings from b.9 and b.17, since in this edition both first- **and** second-time bars are counted: i.e. for b.9 read b.10 and so on (see General Introduction under 'Bar Numberings').

As said above, this is the most brilliant of the three, and poor is the spirit who cannot want to leap and dance to a virtuoso performance of it.

bb. 1–8   It is a good plan to study the LH first, since it is the poise and spring of the LH quavers which both impels and controls the leaping 'snapped' figure of the RH. The LH pattern suggests a brightly detached or *staccato* style that creates a 'spring', that is even rather than 'lame', i.e. so that each quaver has virtually equal emphasis:

not   Then in bb.3 and 4 there is the

---

*or certainly before Chopin left Poland for good in 1830.

sense of 'going to' a slightly firmer, longer chord on the second main beat; and in b.7 feel the implied little 'push' on the partly tied chord, feeling this as the 'upbeat' to the chord on the second main beat.

In the RH 'lean' into the movement with a fully timed yet onward-pointing quaver (see General Introduction under 'Upbeats'). The RH demisemiquaver/quaver figures need to be played with a neat 'flick', treating the semiquaver as a *staccato*

Practise this very slowly, springing **off** the semiquaver A on

the first beat of b.1 in such a way that the hand is 'directed' upwards to 'land' on the high slurred demisemiquaver B, 'flicking' this note neatly to the A and springing off again in a downward direction towards the demisemiquaver G, and so on. This smartly 'directed' spring is all important, rather than allowing the hand to 'hang about' as it comes **off** each semiquaver (see General Introduction under 'Directioning the Hand'). It is helpful to practise this in an ultra-slow tempo, but delivering the actual 'flick' and upward or downward spring very quickly, in such a way that you land **silently** for an instant on each demisemiquaver before 'flicking' it

towards the subsequent semiquaver.

When you put hands together practise again ultra slowly at first, only gradually increasing the tempo, and always feeling that the **LH** quavers are both controlling and propelling the leaping RH. Gradually increase the tempo, aiming eventually for a brilliant and jaunty kind of insouciance. Launch off in a bright *mezzo-forte* as indicated, and slightly 'point' the extra 'lift' up to the high demisemiquaver E in b.2. Then feel a slight sense of moving on towards the first beat of b.4, with a tiny 'give' after the **second** beat as you gather yourself to 'start again' in b.5. As you reach *forte* on the second beat of b.6, 'point' the 'lift' up to the high E a little more obviously, with the suggestion of a tiny 'vocal' *tenuto* before you skip giddily down the scale.

'Finish off' neatly on the quaver chord on the second main beat of b.8, and if
bb.8–24   repeating, allow an extra instant through the second half of the bar to poise
yourself to 'launch off again in b.1. 'Finish off' similarly in the second-time bar, come **off** in both hands, and then feel a poising kind of 'lean' almost like a little pounce on the RH quaver upbeat to b.9. You could go up to an emphatically emphasised dotted quaver A on the first beat of b.9, and play bb.9-10 with a bit of a swagger, strutting through the more sustained dotted rhythm in bb.11-12, then reeling off the semiquaver sextuplets with spinning brilliance from b.13. Alternatively (or varying the style for the repeat) you could go up to a melting toned 'lean' on the A on the first beat of b.9, and play bb.9-10 with a dainty hesitancy, holding back the pulse a little, then playing bb.11-12 rather suavely, 'melting' into the sextuplets and gathering speed through bb.14-15 to run up the scale, coming off the high quaver D with a little 'flip' on the second beat of b.16. However you decide to present this second half, ensure that the LH quavers remains rhythmic, 'giving' a little here, moving on a little there, as they guide the caperings of the RH. Allow a little extra time as you end this section through the second-time bar. Coming **off** the high D, draw out the second half of the bar a little as you 'gather yourself' to set off again from the upbeat to b.17.

No. 2 in G major (7)

Note: For those using the Paderewski Edition there will be a discrepancy in bar-numberings from b.9, since in this edition both first- **and** second-time bars are counted: i.e. for b.9 read b.10 and so on (see General Introduction under 'Bar Numberings').

bb.1–8 Here again it is well to study the LH first. The rhythmic implications of the LH notation are rather different to those of No.1. The 'doubling' of the quavers on the first and second beats of bb.1-2 and 5-6 indicates a greater resonance of these notes with the implication of a slurred effect over each LH couplet in sympathy with the overall slur over the RH figures. The whole creates a jolly kind of churning effect. Through bb.3-4 feel that you are making a wide curve up to the high third on the second beat of b.3, and down again to 'finish' neatly on the quaver third on the second beat of b.4 (and similarly in bb.7-8).

With the pulse well in the system, be sure that the RH upbeat notes are given their proper, 'full' semiquaver value, and **not** played as two-thirds of a triplet. Let these semiquavers give a clear, onward lead towards a little 'lean' (without lingering) on the first note of b.1. 'Twirl' the triplet smartly, 'going up to' a bright quaver B, coming **off** this note with a little 'kick' as if in a *staccato* so that the hand falls to make another natural emphasis on the first note of the subsequent triplet. This 'lean' and *staccato* effect, in which the hand and arm perform a series of down-up movements, creates a natural self-generating rhythmic continuity from one overall slurred figure to the next. Then from the second half of b.2 shape the semiquavers in a wide curve up towards and down from the E on the fourth quaver pulse of b.3, 'giving' just a little through the very end of b.4 as you prepare to 'start again' from b.5. When you put hands together ensure that the hands are always perfectly coordinated, with the feeling, as in No.1 that the LH is both propelling and guiding the RH. Take particular care to keep the LH steady through the curve through bb.3-4, showing the 'staggered' peaks of the curves in b.3, i.e. on the second main beat in the LH and the fourth **quaver** in the RH. The wide arpeggio in the second half of b.2 is difficult for a small hand. Those of us not blessed with Chopin's supple stretch

between the fourth and fifth fingers may prefer to the given 1 2 4 5.

A very small hand might even try (somewhat unconventional, but it

'falls' quite neatly, particularly when following on from the usual fingering for the triplet

twirl of 1 3 2 5:)

bb.8–16 'Finish off' neatly in both hands on the second beat of b.8, then allow a little break so that the RH quaver gives a clear and strong upbeat lead into b.9 (or similarly with the two semiquavers if going back to b.1). Launch into b.9 with vigorous RH chords over energetic LH semiquavers. This LH will need careful practice. The tendency is for the third and fourth, and seventh and eighth semiquavers to 'telescope' so that there is a sense of continually 'falling onwards' into each main beat.

546

Thinking of these semiquavers as the 'upbeat' to each main beat helps to avoid this. In practice those with small hands will need to come **off** each second and sixth semiquaver (i.e. the high B and C sharp in b.9) which in effect assists this upbeat effect of the subsequent two

semiquavers. *etc.* (This is, in fact, the phrasing given in the

Paderewski Edition.) From b.9 feel that the **RH** chords are both controlling and leading the LH semiquavers on towards b.12. Play these three bars with the utmost vigour, feeling that you are 'going to' a strong chord on the first beat of b.12, giving this RH chord and LH quaver C sharp a slight 'hold'. Then allow a little 'give' as you shape the LH semiquavers down through the remainder of the bar (in the sense of an overall upbeat group) ready to 'churn off' again from b.13.

No. 3 in D flat major (8)

Here the RH pattern through bb.1-8 creates another 'churning' effect similar to bb.1-2 etc. in No.2. Although being in two parts it is more difficult, it requires the same type of 'down-up' movement described under No.2.

bb.1–8 Through bb.1-8 the LH moves in a plain tonic-dominant pattern. Practise this first until it is perfectly fluent, creating a fairly energetic, perfectly regular swing between bass notes and upper chords, articulated in a springy detached style. As in No.1, avoid the **sense** of a slurred effect from bass note to chord. Think rather of giving each **chord** the feeling of an upbeat little 'kick' down towards the bass note on each main beat. The 'directioned' spring is essential (see the comments for the RH in No.1), so that you direct the spring from each bass note up towards each chord, and similarly direct the spring from each chord down towards the subsequent bass note. When you practise the RH, launch off from a strong, detached quaver upbeat, and let the hand 'fall' with a little emphasis onto the first beat of b.1. 'Twirl' the triplet energetically (using the second finger on the lower RH quaver F as a firm 'anchor' for the hand), and then 'lift' the hand from the semiquaver B flat ready to 'fall' with a similar emphasis on the second main beat, and so on. Practise the lower part also separately, and

in perfect time so that the quaver beat is perfectly steady. *etc.*

When you put hands together ensure that the quaver pulse remains rock steady – the tendency is for the second and fourth quaver beats to be 'clipped', with the consequent sense of continually 'falling onwards' into the subsequent main beat. To avoid this, be sure to differentiate consistently and consciously between the RH **triplet** semiquavers and 'plain' semiquavers, helped by the realisation that the RH is subject to the steady **LH** quaver rhythm, and **not** the other way about. Practise bb.1-4 over and over until the rhythm begins to feel as if it is on automatic pilot, and you can begin to make an exhilarating whirling or churning effect. 'Go to' a **clear** RH quaver sixth on the second main beat of b.4, and then be sure to bring the RH **off** on the rest, letting the LH upbeat quaver chord help poise you to 'start again' in b.5.

bb.8–32 'Hold' the LH chord on the fourth quaver pulse of b.8 for an instant as you prepare to leap up in the RH. Also feel the hint of a *tenuto* on the high quaver on the first beat of b.9, and then feel you are moving on as the scale dips down to b.11 and rises again, drawing out fractionally at the end of b.12 as you prepare to poise yourself again on the high C in b.13. Interpret the trills in b.9 as

You could launch into the scale at b.9 in a strutting *forte*, as in the rather similar situation in b.9 of No.1, or start the scale from a more melting quaver C, or again interchange these effects as the scale recurs in bb.13, 25 and 29. The RH passage through bb.15-16 is awkward. In b.15 it helps to think of the fourth semiquaver (the high F) as the 'upbeat' to the E flat on the second beat of the bar, and similarly the high B flat as the upbeat to the A flat on the first beat of b.16,

imagining the phrasing thus   Feel that

you are 'going to' a strong quaver sixth on the second beat of b.16, starting relatively quietly therefore in b.15 so that you can *crescendo* positively towards this 'objective' on the second beat of b.16. Above all keep the LH steady here (feeling that this is also *crescendoing* towards the 'objective'), so that the RH can rely on the rhythmic control supplied by the steady LH quavers. As you leap off this chord on the second beat of b.16, allow an extra instant to gather yourself ready to launch off again from a strong quaver upbeat to b.17.

MISCELLANEOUS WORKS WITHOUT OPUS NUMBERS

Souvenir de Paganini (See under Variations).

Lento con Gran Espressione (See Nocturne No.20, listed under Grade 7).

Cantabile in B flat major (4-5)*

This charming little piece (written in 1834) is like a miniature nocturne – the sort of thing Chopin would perhaps have offered as an 'Album Leaf' for a friend. It is another welcome addition to the repertoire for novice players and is published in the Paderewski Edition (Minor Works). While comparatively simple it is also genuinely Chopinesque in its fine melodic shadings and inflections of harmony. Chopin evidently took some pains over it, since the indications for dynamics etc, are original.

bb.1–4   Set an easy **6/8** swing that is relaxed, and yet gives a continual sense of onward movement at about ♩. = 116-26. The motion, and also the texture and general layout, in abridged form, are rather like that of the familiar Nocturne in E flat Op.9 No.2. Practise the LH alone first through bb.1-4 until you have achieved a secure easy-moving fluency. Give the bass notes a slight prominence so that there is a clear bass line which 'sets' the harmony through each main beat, and listen acutely to the even spacing of the two rising chords through the remainder of each beat. This is not an 'oom-pah-pah' accompaniment – the LH needs to move in even curves from the bass note up to the chord on the third quaver pulse and back to the bass notes in continually onward-moving 'arcs'. The *staccato* over the bass notes denotes not a sharp 'prod', but the kind of clearly detached slight prominence, with a 'lift' which will send the hand up towards the chords. When you add pedal, ensure that each bass note is given just sufficient length to allow it to be 'caught' by the pedal. Shape the RH in gracious expressive curves. Let the opening repeated D's 'speak', feeling the slight 'lean' on the crotchet on the second beat of b.1, shape the line smoothly through to the dotted quaver on the second beat of b.2, and then 'lift' up to the high B flat in a vocal manner.* Let these three upbeat semiquavers 'go to' a warm 'lean' on the dotted quaver G on the first beat of b.3. Similarly 'lean' on the tied quaver on the second beat, and then shape the wide curve smoothly towards a warm-toned *tenuto* tied C on the first beat of b.4.

When you put hands together listen carefully to the balance between the hands so that the RH sings out in a clear *dolce* tone over the LH which, quiet though it needs to be, at the same time gives carefully judged harmonic and 'onward-buoying' rhythmic support. Allow just a little 'give' in the LH through the second half of b.2 to allow the RH to 'lift' easily to the high B flat, and again through the second half of b.3 to allow 'room' for the curving RH semiquavers to expand a little. Arriving on the *tenuto* RH C and quietly resonant bass F on the first beat of b.4, take an extra instant for the LH to leap up to the high sixth, and then listen to the smoothly descending inner line as the LH moves on, ready to 'start again' from b.5. Take care to synchronise the hands sensitively on the last quaver of the bar so that the RH gives a clear upbeat lead into b.5.

---

*The finger-change 3-1 on the B flat in b.2 is editorial, implying a legato up-and-over lift into the next phrase. An **ACTUAL** lift of the hand from the lower B flat up to the high upbeat semiquavers would point the intended punctuation more 'speakingly' here, within the sense of the overall four-bar phrase. (See General Introduction under 'Phrasing' and 'Articulation', where the discussion of punctuation within the overall phrase is particularly relevant to this piece).

bb.5–13 Noting the little *crescendo* into b.5, perhaps this phrase could be played in a slightly fuller tone. Listen acutely to the inflections of the LH through b.6 and to the effect of the sharpened RH G, and then allow a tiny break after the first quaver of b.7 (**within** the pedalled sound) to let the RH leap up easily to the high G. Then feel a sense of moving on a little towards a singing B flat on the first beat of b.8. Let the LH give a little again as it leads downwards in *decrescendo* through the second half of b.8, to clear the sound for the *pianissimo* at b.9. Play this phrase in a gentle, whispered *pianissimo*, yet leaving 'room' for an even more quietly breathed *diminuendo* from b.11. Take time through b.12 to listen to the 'spaced' LH quaver chords (see General Introduction under 'Articulation') beneath the quietly sustained RH dotted crotchets. Then, **feeling** the rests on the main beats, tail away the sound of the just-detached quaver couplets through b.13 like departing steps, down to an infinitesimal, yet definite, final bass B flat.

Contredanse in G flat major (6)*

This is a charming little piece, although who would guess on hearing, or even on closely examining the principal and recurring motif (bb.1-4) that it was by Chopin? Contredanse merely means a 'country dance', of a simple and cheerful kind, rather than a dance of specific rhythm or steps. Aristocrats through the ages have indulged in games of rustic make-believe, and such dances, English in origin, became popular in the Courts of Europe from the seventeenth century. This one was written in 1827 for Titus Woyciechowski, Chopin's intimate friend and lifelong correspondent. It is published in the Paderewski Edition (Minor Works). The dynamic indications and various details of phrasing are editorial.

bb.1–8 Set an easy 2-in-the-bar swing with a nice spring, almost like a kind of smooth bounce, to the rhythm at a suggested ♩. = 63-9. Be sure to **feel** the first two silent beats so that you enter with clear, perfectly timed upbeat quavers giving a confident lead-in ready to establish a secure pulse from a clear treble and bass crotchet on the first beat of b.1. Feel a sense of onward movement as you swell lightly towards an implied 'lean' on the tied treble D flat on the second beat of b.2. Ensure that this note sings through into b.3 over the quiet and steady inner RH and LH chords, and then *decrescendo* smoothly down to finish the phrase on the dotted crotchet on the second beat of b.4. Then make it clear that you are 'starting again' with the RH upbeat group, the semiquaver and quaver sixth. Novice players will need to practise the RH carefully. Work out the most advantageous fingering for a clear treble line, and then practise the treble line alone, **using** your preferred fingering. (I suggest that from the second beat of b.2

the fingering  is more conducive to

smoothness, certainly for small hands, than the given fingering. Or, for a more punctuated

effect: The ornament in

550

b.1 etc. is placed **on** the beat.  Then add the inner RH voice,

playing this in a **light**, barely touched *staccato* at first, so that the hand grows accustomed to the feeling of 'leaning' on the melody notes while keeping the inner notes relatively light. When you put hands together, listen acutely to ensure that the melody always sings out clearly while being buoyed along with carefully balanced chords.

bb.8–16 Finishing off the second phrase cleanly on the quaver chord on the second beat of b.8, allow a tiny break to make it clear that the upbeat quavers F and G flat are leading off into a new episode. Play this melody in a more expansive tone, curving freely up towards and down from the high B flat in b.11. Support the melody with a carefully shaped LH, curving each three-quaver figure in a smooth sweep up from the bass note towards a clear crotchet on the second beat of each bar, giving a continual sense of buoyant onward movement. Then as you expand the tone from b.13, feel similarly that the LH figures are 'going to' the crotchet chord on the second beat of bb.13 and 14. From b.13 phrase the RH in a broad curve, almost with a tinge of vulgarity, up to the chord on the first beat of b.15, allowing a hint of a 'vocal' hold here, and then let the line 'subside' gradually through bb.15-16. Take plenty of time through b.16 as you spread the LH grace notes up to the quaver F and then show the complementary LH line through this bar. Feel an implied slight emphasis and 'hold' on the slurred LH dotted crotchet upbeat C as you poise yourself to set off again, shaping the line of this LH upbeat fragment clearly down to the crotchet G flat on the first beat of b.17.

bb.17–56 Allow a little more of a break after the quaver chord on the second beat of b.24 to clear the sound for the *dolce* upbeat to the Trio. This section could be played in a more ethereal style, perhaps in a very slightly slower, or at any rate, more flexible tempo. Shape the wide-spanning intervals of the RH in smooth, airy curves, feeling the impulse towards the emphasised crotchet on the first beat of bb.26 and 28, supported by smoothly curved LH figures, similar to, but rather more gently moving than those through bb.9-12. Allow 'room' for a tiny give in the RH as you finish the first phrase in b.28, and start the next clearly on the second beat, treating the three quavers as an upbeat group. Through b.29 it is better to take the inner LH line with the RH thumb than to break the LH chords – in fact, by so doing, the necessary clearer 'break' as you leap up to the high upbeat quaver C flat helps to clarify the melodic shape here. Allow an extra instant here to listen to the intervals between

the treble and inner LH voices  seventh, augmented fourth

and seventh. Then, leaping as if in an easy 'arc' (rather than snatching) up to the high C flat, allow a slight 'vocal' hold on this note. As you shape the treble downwards through b.30 and up again as you swell through b.31, **listen** as the LH line 'joins in' in complementary sixths from the third quaver pulse of b.30, moving into the inner RH line through b.31. *Decrescendo* gently through b.32, allowing a little give as you finish off the section gracefully on the second beat. Then make a tiny break again as you prepare to set off blithely once more from the upbeat to b.33. The pedalling through the principal sections (bb.1-8 etc.) needs to be kept very light, just a touch of pedal through each half bar. Then from b.9 the pedal could be retained **through** each bar, with more frequent pedal changes again through bb.15-16. Again the pedal could be held **through** b.30 to retain the resonance of the bass F flat.

Feuille d'Album (4-5) (O)*

This pleasant piece was written in 1843 for Countess Anna Cheriemetieff whose younger sister, Elizavieta was a pupil of Chopin. The span of the opening melodic phrase (bb.1-2) with its 'wide-walking' LH accompaniment (rather in the manner of the F minor Nocturne Op.55 No.1) suggests quite an 'important' piece. It is, however, only twenty bars long, and constructed in a neat A B A pattern. With its predominantly chordal pattern it is not altogether suitable for small hands.

bb. 1–8   A tempo of around ♩ = 80-88 is suggested. The LH needs to move with that easy, pendulum-like or 'walking' swing (as in Op.55 No.1), so that the RH is always 'cushioned' by this onward moving LH impulse. Practise the LH thoroughly alone therefore, until it is perfectly fluent at this walking pace, listening particularly to the steady line of the bass notes.

   *Be sure to give the RH upbeat crotchet its full value, with at the same time a definite onward and upward 'lean' towards a singing minim F sharp on the first beat of b.1. Ensure that this F sharp has enough tone to sing through its full value, placing the inner crotchet fourth relatively

lightly so that the melody line sounds clearly 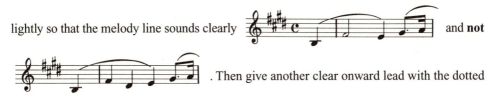 and **not**

. Then give another clear onward lead with the dotted

rhythm figure on the upbeat to b.2, while at the same time maintaining the sense of the overall curve of the phrase from the opening upbeat up towards the crotchet E on the fourth beat of b.2. Be sure to **lift** the hand from the quaver A sharp on the first beat of b.2 (and similarly after the quaver C on the second beat – see General Introduction under 'Articulation'), and then think of the semiquaver B as the 'upbeat' to the ornamented second beat of the bar. Place the ornament

on the beat   allowing a fraction of extra time to let this

little figure 'speak'. When you put hands together be sure to maintain the onward-walking swing you achieved in the LH alone. Feel a slight sense of expanding expressively as you make the little swell up to the high E on the fourth beat of the bar, 'holding' this note for an instant, and then allow a tiny break as you prepare to move on with the more matter-of-fact answering phrase (bb.3-4). Let the repeated melodic F sharps 'speak' through b.3 as you listen to the smooth descent of the LH crotchet fragment. 'Finish off' the sentence in neat time to the third

*Note the phrase-patterns through bb.1-4: the first two sub-phrases as indicated, but WITHIN the first overall sentence

And then by implication a further sub-phrase through to the third beat of b.4, with another from the upbeat to b.5, leading 'on and over' into the restatement.

beat of b.4, and then take a little extra time to allow the RH acciaccatura and spread chord to 'speak' expressively on the fourth beat while at the same time giving a good onward lead into

restatement from b.5. Place the acciaccatura before the beat thus:

Allow a longer hold and more pronounced break at the end of b.6 (see the pause over the bar line) to clear the sound for the *pianissimo* answer in b.7.

bb.9–20   Feel that you are taking a good breath at the end of b.8 ready to lead into b.9 in a new, fuller and perhaps brighter tone. Feel you are 'going towards' a melodic 'lean' on the dotted crotchet E on the third beat of b.9, taking care once more to place the inner RH chord relatively quietly, and once again placing the grace note figure expansively **on** this third beat. Take care to keep steady through b.10, allowing the dotted rhythm to 'walk' upwards with an easy stride. As you arrive on the chord on the fourth beat listen to this dominant seventh harmony with the sense of 'leaning onwards' as you prepare to move into b.11 in a still fuller tone. Then draw out expressively as you *diminuendo* through b.12, again poising yourself on the dominant seventh on the fourth beat, ready to move quietly back into the reprise from b.13.

Fugue in A minor (7)

This seems a curiosity indeed – a complete two-voice fugue with a purposeful 6-bar subject and countersubject, partial entries of the subject in *stretto* and determinedly modulating episodes. As with the Contredanse in G flat, who would guess it was Chopin's – yet remembering his devotion to Bach, perhaps we should not be too surprised. It was written in 1841-2, and is published in the Paderewski Edition (Minor Works).

bb.1–15   Despite its minor colour, the subject is far from lugubrious, and needs to move in an easy 'walking' swing. Thinking of one pace to the crotchet, a tempo of around ♩ = 108 is suggested, with an overall feeling of 2-in-the-bar. The opening

figure of the subject is like a firm statement of intent, which is

then commented upon through bb.2-6, leading on with a clear sense of onward movement towards the next statement from the upbeat to b.7. Play this opening figure with clean definition therefore, in a confident *mezzo piano* leading in from a clear onward-leaning upbeat quaver 'going to' a firm dotted crotchet on the first beat of b.1. Phrase this statement as a little entity in itself within the overall flow of the subject, taking care to time the dotted crotchet and quaver precisely as you 'go to' a clear crotchet G sharp on the second main beat. Come **off** precisely on the fourth beat, ready to shape each little phrase in a neat curve through b.2 and b.3, and then from b.4 feel that you are leading on towards the clear entry of the answer in the RH from the upbeat to b.7. Show the 'matching' effect of the rising fourth as the countersubject enters in b.7, and then let the LH 'go down' confidently to the D sharp on the first beat of b.8 and to the G sharp on the first beat of b.9. While it feels more convincing to begin the trill on the note, others may feel that since this is a fugue, it should begin on the upper note. Pursue the contrary motion movement between subject and countersubject smoothly but purposefully through bb.10-12, and **listen** again to the intervals through the contrary motion figures through the short episode from b.13. Show the implied emphasis on the LH tied quaver A in b.15, and more emphatically on the tied LH upbeat to b.16 ready for the firm RH entry of the subject (taking particular care to ensure clear lines when the voices almost, but do not quite cross here.)

bb.16–69   Following the partial entry of the answer in the LH (bb.22-4) follow the upward curve of the episode from b.25 rather energetically as the crotchet/quaver, and quaver figures alternate between the hands.

 Then listen to the snaking

chromatic LH movement through b.29 ready for the partial RH entry of the answer on the upbeat to b.30. Make sure that the LH entry of the subject in D minor is clear on the upbeat to b.39. In bb.48-50 the wide-spanning curves in either hand are quite awkward and will need especial practice hands separately.

Long trills, as at bb.57-9 and 61-5 are death-traps for the relatively inexperienced player, with the tendency for the trill to 'take over' and grind to a halt, thus causing the 'other' hand to collapse. Ensure that the rhythm and shape of the LH are not sabotaged by the RH trill through bb.57-9, and similarly in reverse through bb.61-5 (see General Introduction under 'Ornaments'). Through bb.61-3 show the implied emphasis on the tied RH notes, **feeling** the pulse on the held second main beat of b.61, and the first beat of b.62 etc. so that these notes are given their full value – these strong offbeat 'footholds' are vital to the vigour of this RH passage. The RH trill could be 'stopped' on the main note (E) on the fourth quaver of b.59, and similarly the LH trill on the last quaver of b.65. Let b.65 move purposefully towards an emphatic statement of the opening motif in contrary motion in b.66. Allow a tiny break after the seventh quaver of b.67 so that you can 'direct' the LH upbeat quaver clearly down to the dotted crotchet D sharp on the first beat of b.68, and then draw out a little as you proceed towards firm final tonic unisons.

Largo in E flat major (6)*

There is little to be said about this very un-Chopinesque item of unknown date.* It has the character of a rather stolid march, and this is the only way to play it, with that Mendelssohnian solemnity occasionally assumed by Chopin. Weinstock makes the amusing suggestion that 'Chopin may have been pondering a new National Anthem, so closely does it resemble that usually square and self-satisfied musical hybrid.' (pp.311-12). This is published in the Paderewski Edition (Minor Works).

(Mazurkas, Waltzes etc. without Opus numbers appear in the Graded List, and in the Commentaries under the relevant headings).

*(now ascribed to 1847).

OTHER WORKS

Piano and orchestra

This series is concerned only with the solo piano repertoire, and the concertos are therefore outside its scope. However, since Chopin wrote so little for other instrumental combinations, and nothing in which the piano was not involved, a word may be said about the chamber music, the songs, and those works in which the orchestra plays so minimal a part that they can almost be, and indeed often were, performed as solos. (And as Jim Samson remarks, orchestral standards were often so poor that 'composer-pianists often **preferred** to play their concertos as solos' (p.222, note 5, and p.44)). These latter are the *Variations on 'Là ci Darem la Mano'* from Mozart's *Don Giovanni* Op.2, the *Fantasia on Polish Airs*, Op.13, and the *Krakowiak Rondo*, Op.14 (the *Polonaise in E flat*, Op.22 has already been mentioned along with its introductory solo piece, the *Andante Spianato*). These three items are discussed in some detail both by Gerald Abraham (pp.10-12 and 16-24) and Humphrey Searle (Walker, pp.212-16). All three, whatever the formal intent suggested by their titles, are in effect musical pot-pourris. This was music designed to please instantly while at the same time allowing the composer-performer to display his virtuosity, and with it the stamp of his own musical character and idiosyncracies. However well such music may or may not come off today on the concert platform, there is much to delight the ear, particularly in the *'Là ci Darem' Variations*. This is the music of a young man delighting in his mastery of the keyboard, and in his ability to please. But also, as Gerald Abraham writes of the *Fantasia* and the *Krakowiak Rondo*, these pieces 'are full of the lights and shadows of coming events', and 'the filigree ornamentation of the quieter passages already suggests the Chopin of the later Nocturnes' (p.16).

Note: Ops.2, 13 and 14 are published in the Paderewski Edition (Vol.XV, Works for Piano and Orchestra), and by Peters. The bar numberings quoted below refer to the Paderewski Edition.

The *'Là ci Darem' Variations* can fairly be said to have launched Chopin into the wider European cultural scene. They called forth the famous 'Hats off, gentlemen, a genius!' from the percipient and ever-generous Schumann. And on Chopin's first visit to Vienna in 1829 the influential publisher Haslinger not only bought the score, but arranged an important concert to show off the new piece. Chopin wrote to his parents: 'In the Imperial and Royal Opera House I made my entry into the world! . . . As soon as I appeared on the stage the bravos began; after each Variation the applause was so loud that I couldn't hear the orchestra's *tutti*' (*Chopin's Letters*, pp.52-3). The success was not surprising. These Variations were the perfect showcase for Chopin: his command and understanding of the keyboard were already there under his hands, as it were, in terms of the trappings of his style, if not the content. And the Viennese – always ready for new, if quickly forgotten sensations – must have been entranced by this fresh, finely drawn, elegant yet exotic style, accustomed as they were to what Chopin called the 'piano pounding' of the current crop of 'mainstream' virtuosi.

This is a work on a large scale. Through the improvisatory introduction there are passages of entrancing pianism, and what a spell they must have cast under Chopin's young hands in 1829. Some of the writing is extraordinarily Schumannesque, such as that from b.45, and again from b.51. Entering as it does upon the tail of an improvisatory musing on its first motif over a dominant pedal-point (following b.63), the theme proper takes on an almost comic aspect. There follows a series of conventionally brilliant Variations. But such is their assurance that interest never flags (the manner in which the orchestra 'clumps' in to link each Variation has once again a comic tinge). The *Adagio* Variation has, presumably with intent, a *Don Giovanni*-like ring of doom, and the writing, at the very least, compels attention. In discussing various late works of Chopin I have several times drawn attention to foretastes of Rachmaninov, but who can fail to think of Rachmaninov at this very early date in the 'vacillation' around the chord of G flat major in b.11 of the *Adagio* Variation, and again through the pounding descending figures through bb.53, 56, etc. of the Alla Polacca. But the style of the Polacca as a whole is typical of Chopin's early 'Polish' pieces – the 'salon' touches of national rhythm and colour, which in his self-imposed exile were to evolve in a personal and far more profound style.

In the second section of the Fantasia Op.13, a set of variations on a folk-tune in **6/8**, some of the writing is very much in the style of the Studies: from b.81 for example; and in particular from b.114 the arpeggio patterns over a long pedal point. (Chopin was near, at any rate, to beginning work on some of the Studies at this time.*) The next section is based on a theme by Kurpinski, a popular Polish composer of an older generation. The Chopin of the Nocturnes has certainly almost arrived in the *Lento quasi Adagio* from b.155. From b.216 in the subsequent *molto più mosso* there is again a foretaste of the Studies when the piano accompanies the woodwind in a truncated version of the pattern of Op.25 No.12. The piece ends with a high-flying Kujawiak, normally the slower movement of the Mazurka genre, here whipped up to a spirited ♩. = 66.

The *Krakowiak* is a quick dance in **2/4** with frequent accents on the second or fourth quaver beats, or both. But Op.14 opens with a 2-part introduction in **3/4**, an *Andantino quasi Allegretto* in which the piano has a quiet unison motif two octaves apart over subdued sustained chords in the orchestra – a most haunting effect, and one which Chopin himself admitted to be 'original – more so than I look in my felt greatcoat.' (*Selected Correspondence*, p.19). The rondo theme itself is announced by twenty bars of 'important' solo flourishes, initiating an immense span of ceaseless activity for the pianist interspersed by brief ritornello-type interjections from the orchestra. Again there are many interesting points in the piano-writing, and once again, as in the *Fantasia*, we are skirting the territory of the Studies – the passage following the first orchestral interjection is so nearly Op.10 No.1 (from b.71). And later, after the appearance and development of the *scherzando* second theme, there is a brief burst of RH chord and LH semiquaver writing from b.272, a passage strikingly similar to the preparation for the coda of Op.10 No.4, before we touch again upon Op.25 No.12 and Op.10 No.1. The virtuosity of this piece is, as Jim Samson says, more 'focused' than in Ops 2 and 13 (p.50). This does not mean less difficult. In fact the technical demands are unremitting, and in a sense more concentrated here, though perhaps as concert items these three pieces proceed in a diminishing order of effectiveness.

Grande Polonaise in E flat

Op. 22 (See with *Andante Spianato*, also Op. 22, listed under Grade 8).

*Ops.13 and 14 were written in 1829 and 1828 respectively (before Chopin left Poland), although not published until 1834, a year after the Op.10 Studies.

CHAMBER MUSIC

The *Polonaise-Fantaisie* Op.61 and the Sonata for 'cello and piano Op.65 were Chopin's last major works, written during 1845-7. Like the *Polonaise-Fantaisie*, the Cello Sonata is a 'difficult' work, in that its appeal is not immediate. But the difficulties are of different kinds. The *Polonaise-Fantaisie* is elusive in the sense that it is hard at first to find one's way among its sometimes abstruse wanderings – in short, it seems on first acquaintance too 'loose'. Conversely, the problem of the Sonata is that in the case of its outer movements it is too packed – almost **compacted** – for the ear to take in at a first, or even a second and third hearing. Crudely put, the first movement in particular seems at first too much of an earful. This must account, at least in part, for its relatively rare appearances in recital programmes, and we can sympathise with Niecks, who found that the 'first and last movements are immense wildernesses, with here and there only a small flower' (Vol.2, p.229).

Tantalising is a mild word for the thoughts provoked by these two works, on the direction in which Chopin seemed poised to extend, at a period of his life which we would today consider his young maturity. On the one hand is the improvisatory 'stretching out' to the future of the *Polonaise-Fantaisie*. On the other the launching into a new instrumental medium with a fully fledged, large-scale Sonata. Another possible reason for the comparative neglect of this work as a concert item suggested by Peter Gould is that string players have difficulties coping with Chopin's writing. He says, 'While *rubato* is frequently misunderstood by pianists, the peculiar needs in this respect in Chopin's music are frequently incomprehensible to instrumentalists whose relatively small repertoire is based on major works by Bach, Beethoven and Brahms. And there are many passages in this [the first] movement which suffer from the inability of string players to gauge the relaxation and tensions implicit in the constantly shifting emphases of Chopin's harmonic and melodic writing' (Walker, p.166). This is a fascinating, if unprovable hypothesis, in which there is perhaps a ring of truth.

It appears that Chopin had enormous problems with the Sonata, and Jim Samson gives some details of sketches and drafts that were left (pp.137-8). Chopin wrote to his family, 'Sometimes I am satisfied with my Violoncello Sonata, sometimes not. I throw it in a corner, then take it up again.' (*Chopin's Letters*, p.311). The first movement alone would repay months and years of study. It is magnificent music, and no one can suggest that this is anything but splendidly integrated writing – better, indeed, on the level of the mechanics of duo writing, Jim Samson suggests, than other more popular works in the cello and piano repertoire. Interestingly, when the cello takes over the second subject melody (bb.65 and 180) the string sound is strikingly Elgarian. The Scherzo is positively Brahmsian in its dimensions and texture, tangibly so in some of the piano writing, and the cello has an extended say in the long-breathed melodic span of the central section. The Largo is a simple dialogue between cello and piano. A mere 27 bars long, there is an elegiac quality in its quiet understated beauty of line. I have heard it played as a recital encore, when it exerted an atmosphere of mesmeric calm over an excited audience. The Finale is an exciting movement in which, however, the balance has to be carefully gauged. The texture of the piano writing is often dense, and at the necessary lively tempo can all but annihilate the string line.

There are also two pieces for cello and piano. The first, the *Introduction and Grande Polonaise*, Op.3, written during a visit to the Radziwill family's estate in 1829, is the more attractive. Although Chopin wrote: 'there is nothing in it but tinsel; a salon piece for ladies', there is some effective writing for both instruments in the *lento* introductory section. Chopin's letter goes on, amusingly: 'You see, I wanted Princess Wanda to learn something. She is young, seventeen, and God knows how pleasant it was to guide her little fingers on the keys'! (Harasowski: *Chopin, his life and music*). In the *Polonaise*, the cello and piano share out statements of the principal theme in jaunty fashion, with the piano then providing neat but conventional back-up for the cello in the more lyrical second theme.

The second piece, the *Grand Duo* on themes from Meyerbeer's *Robert the Devil*, was written in 1832 in collaboration with his friend, the cellist Franchomme, for whom he wrote the Cello and Piano Sonata, Op.65. The best that can be said about this truly awful piece is that it is relieved by some patches of gratuitous hilarity – the moment when, after an introductory build-up of hugely grandiose proportion, the 'rumpty-tum' theme is finally trundled in, is worthy of inclusion in a Hoffnung musical extravaganza. And humour, which cannot have been intentional, does redeem the succeeding bouts of boxing and hide and seek as the themes lurch around between the instruments.

Critical opinion has been too unkind, I believe, to the Trio, Op.8. 'Serious' writing it may not be in the sense of balanced use and distribution of the strings and piano. But there are happy musical effects, and an air of ease in the writing far removed from the rigours of the Sonata, Op.4, that earnest student endeavour with which it tends to be bracketed. The last movement is the least happy. Neither of its principal themes, both of a 'salon-folk' type, is of sufficient charm to weather their many repetitions. But the first movement has charm in plenty. The heading 'Allegro con fuoco' is perhaps too pretentious. After the *risoluto* opening statement, the music bowls along with an easy grace that is at times almost Dvořákian (in particular in short touches at bb.28, 31 and in a longer span from b.53). And the piano writing, at whatever expense to the strings, is unfailingly grateful.

The Scherzo, *con moto, ma non troppo*, retains a hint of the minuet – particularly in its prim little phrase endings (bb.4 and 23-4). And here the instruments are more happily integrated. Curiously, in the Trio (bb.5-12) there is another pre-echo of Dvořák in the little dotted rhythm motif in the piano part.

If the opening of the *Adagio* is somewhat portentous in relation to what follows, this is a mellifluously expressive movement once it gets under way from b.5. The string and piano sound from b.43 is beautiful by any standards, and there is an exquisite moment at bb.53-4 when the violin's A flat is suspended over the bar line over the G flat augmented harmony. Then as the ornamentation of the piano line subsides, there is a radiant hush over bb.56-63. Whatever else, this is no mere student exercise, and Chopin's musical ideas emerge clear and alive.

THE SONGS

Nineteen songs by Chopin are given in the Paderewski edition, with separate English translations. According to Jim Samson Chopin 'composed, and often improvised, songs to Polish texts throughout his life, but made little effort to preserve them for posterity.' (p.101) These nineteen that survive were written at varying dates, from around 1829 (before Chopin left Poland), until 1847, two years before his death. Seventeen of these were published by Fontana as Op.74 after Chopin's death, and the remaining two, *Czary* ('Witchcraft') and *Dumka* in 1910. All are set to Polish texts, and several are of powerfully patriotic colour. The accompaniments are perhaps disappointing for pianists. They are neither 'pianistic' in the sense that one might expect, nor 'integrated' in the manner of the German Lied. In other words, they are for the most part ballad type accompaniments. The songs are discussed in some detail by Jim Samson (pp.100-103) and by Bernard Jacobson, who gives translations of each song (Walker p.187-211). (Lizst transcribed six of them for piano solo.) Chopin himself arranged the second song of the group *Wiosna* ('Spring') for piano solo, and also used a motif from the first *Zyczenie* ('The Wish') in the posthumous Nocturne in C sharp minor. This is a charming song with a Mazurka-like accompaniment. Another with a dance-like movement is the frolicking *Moja Pieszczotka* ('My Darling'). Several are of considerable dramatic power, particularly *Leci Liście* ('Leaves are Falling'), a lament for the woes of Poland. *Melodia* or 'Elegy' is perhaps the most moving of all, and the grieving declamatory *Nie ma Czego Trzeba* ('Faded and vanished'), the most haunting. The best of the songs are, as Bernard Jacobson says, 'far too good for the neglect they have fallen into. These two songs at least can hold up their heads in the best company there is in the repertoire' (Walker, p.211). Language is no doubt part of the problem, and in translation the difficulties of matching words to musical sense evidently loom particularly large.

PERSONS MENTIONED IN THE TEXT

Alfred Cortot (1877-1962)
An eminent French pianist who made a special study of Chopin. His *Editions de Travails* of many of the works of Chopin, particularly of the Studies, are frequently quoted here. His recordings, many of which have recently been re-issued, are of outstanding interest to pianists.

Princess Marcelina Czartoryska (1817-94)
The most gifted of Chopin's aristocratic pupils, and a devoted friend. Along with Chopin's sister and George Sand's daughter Solange, she was with Chopin when he died. She was an outstanding pianist, whose style was said to be closest to that of Chopin himself.

Eugène Delacroix (1798-1863)
An eminent Romantic painter. He was a devoted admirer of Chopin both personally and musically. He became one of Chopin's most favoured friends outside his close Polish circle.

Camille Dubois (née O'Meara) (1830-1907)
One of Chopin's favourite pupils; a fine pianist, and through her annotated scores, a valuable source of Chopin's performing indications.

Józef Elsner (1769-1854)
As with his piano playing, Chopin had only one teacher of composition, Jozef Elsner, who was a prolific composer, conductor at the National Theatre in Warsaw, and Principal of the Conservatoire of Music there. He gave Chopin a thorough grounding in musical theory and counterpoint, but had the wisdom to allow him to develop in his own direction.

Julian Fontana (1810-1869)
Fontana was a friend and fellow student of Chopin in Warsaw. He followed Chopin to Paris where he was closely associated with him, acting as a general amanuensis, copyist and, it must be said, dog's body. In 1842 he left Paris to live in America, but returned after Chopin's death to edit and posthumously publish various of Chopin's works under the Opus Numbers 66-74. The fact that Fontana's and Chopin's handwriting were very similar has created considerable problems for later editors in identifying Fontana's editorial additions.

Auguste Franchomme (1808-1884)
A distinguished French cellist who, like Delacroix, became one of Chopin's closest non-Polish friends. He was the dedicatee of the Piano and Cello Sonata Op.65, and also collaborated with Chopin on the Grand Duo for Piano and Cello on themes from Meyerbeer's *Robert le Diable*.

Emile Gaillard (1821-1902)
A Parisian banker, friend and pupil of Chopin, and dedicatee of the Mazurka in A minor (No.53 in Henle).

Adolph Gutmann (1819-1882)
A favoured pupil of Chopin – surprisingly so since his style of playing was apparently brash and noisy. See under Scherzo in C sharp minor Op.39.

Sir Charles Hallé (1819-1895)
A German pianist, conductor and composer who settled in England and was the founder of the Hallé orchestra. He was a friend and keen admirer of Chopin.

Ferdinand Hiller (1811-1885)
An eminent German pianist and composer. He was a great friend of Chopin during his early years in Paris, and the dedicatee of the Three Nocturnes of Op.15.

Frédéric Kalkbrenner (1785-1849)
One of the finest pianists of his generation, whom Chopin greatly admired. Soon after Chopin arrived in Paris he considered taking lessons from Kalkbrenner, but wisely cried off when he realised that Kalkbrenner required him to 'enrol' for three years.

Jan Kleczyński (1837-1895)
A Polish pianist and teacher, Kleczyński was not a pupil of Chopin, but studied with Princess Czartoryska, Camille Dubois and Georges Mathias, all of whom were devoted exponents of Chopin's principles of playing and teaching. Kleczyński was apparently a remarkable teacher, and appears to have relayed the Chopin tradition in a particularly detailed manner. He has left valuable accounts of Chopin's teaching practices, which were warmly endorsed by the above pupils of Chopin.

Wilhelm von Lenz (1809-1883)
A diplomat and enthusiastic amateur pianist. He was a pupil of both Liszt and Chopin, and has left detailed and intimate impressions of Chopin as pianist, teacher and personality.

Antoine-François Marmontel (1816-1898)
Pianist and teacher at the Paris Conservatoire. He was not a pupil of Chopin, but has left valuable and informed accounts of Chopin's playing.

Georges Mathias (1826-1910)
One of Chopin's professional pupils. He was a fine pianist, and taught for many years at the Paris Conservatoire. He is considered to be one of the most faithful exponents of the Chopin 'tradition'.

Karol Mikuli (1821-1897)
Another of Chopin's professional pupils, and like Mathias, a dedicated upholder of the principles of Chopin's playing and teaching. His edition of Chopin's works, published in 1880, claimed to be 'based for the most part on the composer's own indications'.

Ignaz Moscheles (1794-1870)
An eminent pianist and composer, one of the few among his contemporaries for whom Chopin expressed genuine regard. Chopin's 'extra' Three Etudes (commonly called Posthumous) were written for the *Méthode des Méthodes*, compiled by Moscheles and the French scholar Fétis.

Frederick Niecks (1845-1924)
An eminent German scholar who settled in Scotland and became Professor of Music at Edinburgh University. He wrote major biographies of Chopin and Schumann. His work on Chopin is indispensable not only for his immense and thoroughly sifted fund of information (in view of the myths that already surrounded Chopin's memory by the end of the nineteenth century) but also for his numerous personal contacts with those who knew and heard Chopin.

Delfina Potocka (1807-1877)

A beautiful Polish Countess, prominent in French society, and dedicatee of the F minor Concerto. She was also a fine player. There have been inconclusive suggestions of a love affair with Chopin, fuelled by the sudden 'discovery' in 1945 of letters of uncharacteristic content, purportedly addressed to her by Chopin. Whatever the truth, such was Chopin's regard for her that he requested that she should come to sing to him as he lay dying.

George Sand (1804-1876)

The pen-name of Aurore Dupin, later Mme Dudevant. Celebrated for her voluminous literary output, her advanced social views, countless love affairs and her penchant for male attire. She and Chopin became lovers in 1838, and she initiated the fateful Majorcan trip in the winter of 1838-9. Thereafter they remained closely involved with each other until 1847.

Jane Stirling (1804-1859)

A Scottish pupil of Chopin. She was undoubtedly in love with Chopin, and to his annoyance, fussed over him devotedly but excessively during his visit to Britain in the year before his death. She also helped him with immense financial generosity during his last illness. She was not one of his most gifted pupils, but her annotated scores have, like those of other pupils, provided much valuable information.

Friederike Streicher (née Müller) (1816-1895)

One of Chopin's finest pupils who has left valuable accounts of her lessons with Chopin. (See Niecks Vol. 2, Appendix 3.)

Adalbert Żywny (1756-1842)

Chopin's first music teacher, and his only piano teacher. He was a native of Bohemia, and was primarily a violinist. He imbued Chopin with a love of Bach and the Viennese classics, and Chopin retained an affectionate and loyal regard for him throughout his life.

APPENDIX

These two extracts are taken from Kleczyński's *Frederick Chopin; An Interpretation of his Works* (Felix Mackar, Paris, 1880. See under 'Suggestions for Further Reading'.).

Extract 1: (p.74)
'[His] style is based chiefly on simplicity, and rejects all artificiality as well as exaggerated changes in tempo. [This] is a prime condition for the interpretation of Chopin generally; . . . the richness and variety of his arabesques might convey a hint of precocity and affectation if the execution is not as simple as the theme . . . Hence for example, his many arabesques are not just adornment and commonplace elegance, but transparent mosaics through which we glimpse the main theme with enhanced delight. The pianist must not forget this. These pieces, these clusters of notes, appear when the motif returns afresh, and this many times. Simple and plain at first, it later becomes richer at every appearance. It is necessary then to treat the motif with the same light and shade, whatever its pattern may be . . .'

Kleczyński goes on to cite the Nocturne in F sharp major Op.15 No.2, in which the opening motif is cloaked in ornamentation and arabesques of ever increasing elaboration; and the middle section of the Impromptu in E flat Op.29 in which the theme from b.51 is likewise adorned.

'Neither must these passages [i.e. the arabesques, roulades, etc.] be moderated, but on the contrary accelerated towards the finale. A *rallentando* . . . would give them too much importance, an implication of special, independent ideas, while they are only fragments of the phrase with which they must merge and disappear, the same way as a small stream is lost in a large river; or also, they are the interludes which, delivered swiftly, have more effect than if one dwelt on them. Here are some examples of these pieces of music which must be played slowly at first, and accelerated at the end:

    a) The Nocturne in E flat (Op.9 No.2) compositions [i.e. bars] 16 and 24.
    b) The *larghetto* of the Concerto in F minor, compositions 26, 28, 30, 40, 75 and 77.
Interludes which must be played quickly and very softly:
    a) The Nocturne in A flat (Op.32 No.2) compositions 14 and 22.
    b) The Nocturne in F (Op.15 No.1) composition 20 (and the same when the motif returns).
    c) The Nocturne in G minor (Op.37 No.1) composition 36.

'Chopin differed in the way he interpreted arabesques and interludes from the current fashion of his time, which was to emphasise them, as in the closing measures of musical compositions of the Italian school. He was absolutely right. In the spoken word, we do not use the same tone of voice for the main argument and incidental expressions: the latter are not accentuated, and correctly so. The whole theory of the style which Chopin taught his pupils rested on this analogy between music and language, on the necessity to separate different phrases, to punctuate and variegate the strength of the voice and the rate of delivery.'

Extract 2: (p.78)
'[So] we are going to give some of the main precepts of punctuation and musical reading and delivery.

'If a musical phrase is composed of approximately eight measures, the end of the eighth will denote the end of the theme; which, in the spoken or written language, we would indicate with a full stop, and with a pause and lowering of the voice.

'The secondary divisions of the foregoing phrase of eight measures, at every second or fourth measure, demand a shorter pause of the voice, which in a word is a comma or a semicolon. These pauses are very important; without them music would become a succession of disconnected sounds, an incomprehensible chaos, as language would be without paying attention to punctuation or varying the tone of voice. A small example will suffice. Let us take the well-known waltz in A flat [Op.69 No.1] written like this:

'The musical idea is divided into periods of two measures; and so the final note of every second measure must be its shortest and weakest, and it should be executed like this:

[Note the small hairpins, accents, etc. showing exactly how the phrases should be shaped.]

'One can imagine the ludicrous effect that would be caused by an execution similar to the one I have illustrated in [the next] example.

'From these general rules Chopin reached a conclusion to which he attached great importance, 'ne pas jouer par trop petites phrases'; that is to say, don't hold up the tempo . . . on unimportant parts of the theme, and don't prolong the theme too much by holding up the tempo, as this tries the attention of the audience listening to the interpretation . . . In addition, Chopin used to point out, quite rightly, that every long note is also a strong note, but if held for less duration it needs less strength, exactly as occurs with the long and short syllables in rhymed verse. The highest note of a melody, or a discordant note, is also the strongest. We give as an example a part of the *canto* of the Scherzo in B flat minor. We have indicated the punctuation, as well as the strong and weak notes.'

BIBLIOGRAPHY

Abraham, Gerald, *Chopin's Musical Style* (Oxford University Press, 1939)

Beckett, Walter, *The Master Musicians: Liszt* (J.M. Dent, 1968)

Brown, Maurice J.E., *Chopin, An Index of his Works* (MacMillan, 1972)

Chopin's Letters, edited by Henryk Opieński and E.L. Voynich (Harmsworth, 1932)

Chopin Studies, edited by Jim Samson (Cambridge University Press, 1988)

Chopin Studies 2, edited by John Rink and Jim Samson (Cambridge University Press, 1994)

Dunn, John Petrie, *Ornamentation in the Works of Frederick Chopin* (Novello, 1921)

Eigeldinger, J.-J., *Chopin, Pianist and Teacher as seen by his pupils* (Cambridge University Press, 1986)

Frédéric Chopin. Profiles of the Man and his Music, edited by Alan Walker (Barrie & Jenkins, 1979)

Friskin, James, and Irwin Freundlich, *Music for the Piano* (Dover, 1973)

Harasowski, Adam, *The Skein of Legends around Chopin* (MacLellan, 1967)

Harasowski, Adam, *Frederic Chopin: His Life and Music* (unpublished)

Hedley, Arthur, *The Master Musicians: Chopin* (J.M. Dent, 1949)

Higgins, Thomas, 'Tempo and Character in Chopin', *The Musical Quarterly* no.59 (1973)

Higgins, Thomas, 'Chopin's Practices', *The Piano Quarterly* no.113 (1981)

Huneker, James, *Chopin, The Man and his Music* (Dover, 1975)

Hutcheson, Ernest, *The Literature of the Piano* (Hutchinson, 1975)

Kallberg, Jeffrey, 'Hearing Poland: Chopin and Nationalism', Nineteenth Century Piano Music, ed. Larry Todd (New York, Schirmer Books, 1990).

Kentner, Louis, *Yehudi Menuhin Music Guides: Piano* (Macdonald, 1976)

Kiorpes, George A, 'Arpeggiation in Chopin – Interpreting the Ornament Notations', *The Piano Quarterly* no.113 (1981)

Kleczyński, Jean, *Frederick Chopin: An Interpretation of his Works* (Felix Mackar, Paris, 1880; reprinted Palma de Mallorca, 1970)

Marek, George, and Maria Gordon-Smith, *Chopin* (Weidenfeld & Nicolson, 1978)

Niecks, Frederick, *The Life of Chopin* (London, 1888)

Samson, Jim, *The Music of Chopin* (Routledge & Kegan Paul, 1985)

Samson, Jim, *The Master Musicians: Chopin* (Oxford University Press, 1996)

Schonberg. H.C., *The Great Pianists* (Gollancz, 1978)

Selected Correspondence of Frederyk Chopin, edited by Arthur Hedley (Heinemann, 1962)

Taylor, Kendall, *Principles of Piano Technique and Interpretation* (Novello, 1981)

The Cambridge Companion to Chopin, edited by Jim Samson (Cambridge University Press, 1992)

Weinstock, Herbert, *Chopin, the Man and his Music* (Alfred A. Knopf, 1959)

Zamoyski, Adam, *Chopin* (Granada, 1981)

INDEX OF CHOPIN'S WORKS

Works with Opus Numbers
For Solo Piano

Works for Solo Piano
Without Opus Numbers

Cantabile, B flat major: **548-9**

Contredanse, G flat major: 543, **549-50,** 552

Feuille d'Album, E major: **551-2**

Fugue, A minor: **552-3**

Largo, in E flat: **553**

Souvenir de Paganini: see below under Variations

Mazurkas: (numbered as in the Henle Edition)

No.50, G major: 119, 124, **205-6,** 207, 211, 212, 543
No.51, B flat major: 119, 205, **206-7,** 211, 543
No.52, A minor ('Notre Temps'): 124, **207-9**
No.53, A minor ('Émile Gaillard'): 124, 189, **209-11**
No.54, D major: 124, 211, **211-12**
No.55, B flat major: 211, **212**
No.56, C major: 211, **213**
No.57, A flat major: 211, **214-15**

Appendix: 124
No.1, A flat major: 211, **215**
No.2, D major: 211, **215**
No.3, A major/minor: 211, **215**

Nocturnes: (numbered as in the Henle Edition)

No.20, *Lento con gran espressione,* C sharp minor: 299, **378-82**
No.21, C minor: 299, **382-4**

Polonaises: (numbered as in the Henle Edition)

No.11, G minor: 257, 291, **291-2,** 293
No.12, B flat major: 291, **292-3**
No.13, A flat major: 291, **293-5**
No.14, G sharp minor: 7, 291, **295-6,** 298, 521
No.15, B flat minor: 291, **296-7**
No.16, G flat major: 291, **298,** 521

Prelude, A flat: **117-8**

Trois Nouvelles Etudes: 454

No.1, F minor: 20, 41, 454, **454-7,** 457
No.2, A flat major: **457-60**
No.3, D flat major: 20, **460-63**

Works for Piano and Orchestra

Chamber Music

Songs